1 oo

D0050700

ALSO BY J. ANTHONY LUKAS

Common Ground:
A Turbulent Decade in the Lives of Three American Families

Nightmare:
The Underside of the Nixon Years

Don't Shoot—We Are Your Children!

The Barnyard Epithet and Other Obscenities:
Notes on the Chicago Conspiracy Trial

BIG

A Murder in

a Small Western Town

Sets Off a Struggle for the Soul of America

TROUBLE

J. ANTHONY LUKAS

SIMON & SCHUSTER

SIMON & SCHUSTER
Rockefeller Center
1230 Avenue of the Americas
New York, NY 10020

Copyright © 1997 by J. Anthony Lukas
All rights reserved,
including the right of reproduction
in whole or in part in any form.
SIMON & SCHUSTER and colophon are
registered trademarks of Simon & Schuster Inc.
Designed by Edith Fowler
Map by Jeff Ward
Picture section by Meryl Levavi
Manufactured in the United States of America

10   9   8   7   6   5   4   3   2   1

Library of Congress Cataloging-in-Publication Data

Lukas, J. Anthony, 1933–1997.
   Big trouble : a murder in a small western town
sets off a struggle for the soul of America /
J. Anthony Lukas.
      p.   cm.
   Includes bibliographical references (p.   ) and
index.
   1. Steunenberg, Frank, 1861–1905—
Assassination.   2. Idaho—Politics and
government.   3. Caldwell (Idaho)—
History.   4. United States—Politics and
government—1901–1909.   5. United States—
Social conditions—1865–1918.   6. Social conflict
—United States—History—20th century.
I. Title.
F746.L84   1997
979.6'031'092—dc21
[B]   97-21359   CIP
ISBN 0-684-80858-7

The photograph on both the cover and the title page
shows miners detained without charge in the 1899
"bullpen"—an indignity that the state contended
led the Western Federation of Miners to kill Frank
Steunenberg six years later. (#8-X25, Barnard-
Stockbridge Collection, University of Idaho Library,
Moscow, Idaho).

To Christopher William Lukas
my brother, my friend

Since the trouble largely originates in hostile organizations of men known as labor unions, I should suggest a law making the formation of such unions or kindred societies a crime. Surely history furnishes argument sufficiently in favor of such a course.

GENERAL HENRY CLAY MERRIAM, 1899

•

Mr. Hawley says they have made trouble and you ought to get rid of them, and a good way to begin is to hang the secretary-treasurer. That is the way to begin to get rid of the Western Federation of Miners, because they have made trouble. Yes, they have made trouble, thank God, and more power to them. Nothing good in this world ever came excepting through trouble and tribulation and toil.

CLARENCE DARROW, closing argument, 1907

•

The Modern Sleuth sees the need and listens to the call. He organizes a system, a business. He establishes bureaus of information, puts men in the factories to report disaffection and to stir up trouble, if none is brewing.

ROBIN DUNBAR, *The Detective Business,* 1909

•

When a detective dies, he goes so low that he has to climb a ladder to get into Hell —and he is not a welcome guest there. When his Satanic Majesty sees him coming, he says to his imps, "Go get a big bucket of pitch and a lot of sulphur, give them to that fellow and put him outside. Let him start a Hell of his own. We don't want him in here, starting trouble."

BIG BILL HAYWOOD, 1911

Contents

CANADA

Spokane
• Coeur d'Alene
Wallace

Lewiston

Snake River

ROCKY MOUNTAINS

MONTANA

Missouri   River

• Helena

Caldwell
• Boise
Nampa

IDAHO

Snake   River

• Pocatello

WYOMING

North Platte River

Green River •

Rawlins •

Laramie •

Cheyenne

Salt Lake City •

Green River

Colorado   River

Denver •

Cripple
Creek

NEVADA

UTAH

Telluride •

Arkansas   River

COLORADO

River

Colorado

ARIZONA

NEW
MEXICO

CALIFORNIA

0   100   200   300
Scale of Miles

© 1997 Jeffrey L. Ward

Author's Note

I'm writing in Suite 306 of the Idanha, once Idaho's grand hotel, now a creaking relic of its former splendor, operated by the Heaven on Earth Inns Corporation, a subsidiary of Maharishi Mahesh Yogi's Transcendental Meditation Program. For all its shabby gentility and the odors of South Indian cooking seeping down the corridors, I love this old hotel—precisely because it has witnessed so much of the history that has long preoccupied me.

I've been coming to the Idanha for seven years now, two or three times each year, to piece together the events surrounding the assassination of Idaho's former governor, Frank Steunenberg, in December 1905. From my home in New York, I'd been drawn to this venerable hostelry—and to this strange saga nearly a continent, and a century, away—after finishing another seven-year effort, on *Common Ground,* a book about three Boston families caught up in the school desegregation wars. When I embarked on the Boston project, I thought I'd be grappling with the great American dilemma of race, but I kept stumbling over the twin issue of class. The more I delved into Boston's crisis, the more I found the conundrums of race and class inextricably intertwined. Since the federal district judge who ordered Boston's school desegregation was prevented by Supreme Court precedent from including the suburbs in a metropolitan plan, his order embraced largely the poor and working class of all races, while exempting most of Greater Boston's more privileged citizens —a critical problem, I thought.

Casting about for my next book subject, I kept returning to the matter of class. It wouldn't be easy, I knew, to pick this thread from a social fabric so professedly egalitarian that as late as 1991 one survey showed that 93 percent of all Americans regarded themselves as members in good standing of the great middle class. But Americans at the turn of the century didn't know it would turn out this way. Indeed, there was a widespread perception then that collisions between labor and capital were reaching a critical intensity that might plunge the nation into ruinous class war.

It would be interesting, I thought, to examine that moment in our national experience when we came closest to such warfare. After months of reading, I began to focus on the years 1899–1907 in the Rocky Mountain states, and eventually on the roots and consequences of the assassination of an ex-governor of Idaho, Frank Steunenberg.

As I read the yellowing documents at the Idaho State Historical Society, I realized the story would carry me across a broad swath of turn-of-the-century America: into the mining wars of Colorado and Idaho's Coeur d'Alene region; to the history of the Twenty-fourth Infantry Regiment, one of the army's four black units at the time; to the mounting resentment of the monopolistic power of American railroads and other great corporate trusts; to the countervailing fears stirred by the Socialist and anarchist movements that were then gaining ground, in particular among the Eastern and Southern European immigrants of our large cities; to Theodore Roosevelt's vigorous efforts to stave off an approaching social apocalypse; to the formalistic jurisprudence of Oliver Wendell Holmes, John Marshall Harlan, and their colleagues on the Supreme Court.

But Americans did not live by law, politics, and ideology alone. I soon concluded that one couldn't understand what happened here nearly 100 years ago without understanding more about what kind of a society Idaho—and America—had been at the opening of the twentieth century. Accordingly, I have briefly examined the cult of the American private detective; the rise of the American reporter; the heyday of the theatrical road company; the development of modern psychology; the growth of the conservation movement; the allure of new hotels and Pullman cars; the competitive fervor of sports; the vogue of fraternal societies like the Odd Fellows and Elks.

Thus, the book is both a narrative of a sensational murder case and a social tapestry of the land in which that case unfolded. I hope that in telling this big story I've helped illuminate the class question at a time when the gap between our richest and poorest citizens grows ever wider.

J.A.L.
Idanha Hotel
Boise, Idaho
December 1996

1

THE MAGIC CITY

IT BEGAN to snow just before dawn, chalky flakes tumbling through the hush of the sleeping town, quilting the pastures, tracing fence rails and porch posts along the dusky lanes. In the livery stables that lined Indian Creek, dray horses and fancy pacers, shifting in their stalls, nickered into the pale light. A chill north wind muttered down Kimball Avenue, rattling the windows of feed stores and dry goods emporia, still festooned for the holidays with boughs of holly, chains of popcorn and cranberries. Off to the east, behind the whitening knob of Squaw Butte, rose the wail of the Union Pacific's morning train from Boise, due into the Caldwell depot at 6:35 with its load of drowsy ranch hands and bowler-hatted drummers.

Sounding up the slope of Dearborn Street into Caldwell's jaunty new subdivision of Washington Heights, the whistle brought an unwelcome summons to the former governor of Idaho, Frank Steunenberg, as he lay abed that final Saturday of 1905. The governor—as he was still known, five years out of office—had spent a bad night, thrashing for hours in sleepless foreboding. Now while the snow piled up beneath his cottonwoods, he burrowed deeper under the bedclothes.

One of his favorite boyhood songs had evoked just such a moment: "Oh, it's nice to get up in the morning, when the sun begins to shine / At four, or five, or six o'clock in the good old summertime / But when the snow is a-snowing and it's murky overhead / Oh, it's nice to get up in the morning, but it's nicer to lie in bed!" The Steunenbergs, though, were sturdy Hollanders imbued with a Protestant work ethic, and it offended the governor's temperament to idle away even a weekend morning. So he hauled himself out of bed and put on his favorite six-dollar shirt with its flowered design. When it had shrunk so much he couldn't fasten the collar, his sister Jo, in her motherly fashion, had cut a chunk out of the tail to expand the chest. She was still looking for matching material to repair the back, but the governor liked the cheerful old shirt so well he donned it that morning anyway, short tail and all. Then he went down to the kitchen and built a coal fire in the great iron stove.

When his wife, Belle, joined him, she remarked that he seemed ill at ease.

"The good and evil spirits were calling me all night long," said the governor, who sat for a time with his face buried in his hands.

"Please do not resist the good spirits, Papa," his wife admonished. A devout Seventh-Day Adventist, Belle persuaded her husband, who generally eschewed such rituals, to kneel on the kitchen floor and join her in reading several passages from Scripture. Then they sang Annie Hawks's fervent hymn:

> *I need thee, O, I need thee!*
> *Every hour I need Thee;*
> *O, bless me now, My Saviour!*
> *I come to Thee.*

When their devotionals were done, Frank set out across the barnyard—joined by his white English bulldog, Jumbo—to milk his cows and feed his chickens, goats, and hogs.

The family's eccentric gray-and-white edifice, a hybrid of Queen Anne and American Colonial styles, bristled with gables, porches, columns, and chimneys. It was barely seven-eighths of a mile from Caldwell's center, but the governor, with one young hand to help him, maintained a working farm on the two and a half acres, replete with barn, windmill, well, pasture, livestock pens, and apple and pear trees mixed among the sheltering cotton-woods.

After feeding his stock, he turned toward the house for breakfast with Belle and the children—Julian, nineteen, on Christmas vacation from the Adventists' Walla Walla College in Washington State; Frances, thirteen; Frank Junior, five; and eight-month-old Edna, an orphan the Steunenbergs had adopted that year—as well as Will Keppel, Belle's brother, who was staying with them for a time while working at the family bank. Their hired girl, Rose Flora, served up the austere breakfast prescribed by Adventists: wheat cereal, stewed fruit, perhaps an unbuttered slice of oatmeal bread (the sect believed that butter—like eggs, bacon, other meats, coffee, and tea—stimulated the "animal passions").

Had the governor allowed his melancholy to infect the breakfast table that morning, it would have been out of character. With his children—on whom he doted—he generally affected a puckish humor, spiced with sly doggerel, such as the verse he'd composed a year earlier for his daughter: "Frances had a little watch / She swallowed it one day / Her mother gave her castor oil / To help her pass the time away."

After breakfast came a phone call from his younger brother Albert—universally known as A.K.—the most entrepreneurial of the six Steunenberg brothers and cashier of the Caldwell Banking and Trust Company, of which Frank was president. An important matter awaited the governor's attention, A.K. said: Edward J. Dockery, a Boise lawyer, a former Democratic state chairman, and now a business associate of the Steunenbergs, would be arriving in Caldwell later that day and expected to meet them at the bank. No,

Frank said, he wasn't in the right frame of mind for such a meeting. He asked A.K. to tell Dockery he'd see him in Boise next week.

In days to come, the governor's disinclination to do business that day was much remarked. Some said it was the weather, which by late morning had turned nasty, four inches of snow driven by blustery winds drifting along the roadways, temperatures plummeting toward zero. But Frank Steunenberg was still young (forty-four years old), husky (six foot two, 235 pounds), and healthy (an avid hiker and camper who scorned the big eastern cities, with their creature comforts, their smoke, noise, and dirt)—in short, not a man likely to be intimidated by a little Idaho snowstorm.

Others said his reclusiveness that day was merely a bow toward Belle's Sabbath, which lasted from sundown Friday to sundown Saturday. Although Frank was by no means an Adventist, some believed that he was gradually accommodating himself to his wife's recent conversion. Others who knew him well insisted he was profoundly skeptical of Belle's piety and would never have canceled a meeting on religious grounds. He might well have been weary. For only the day before he'd returned from a strenuous trip—by train, buggy, and horseback—to his sheep ranch near Bliss, a hundred miles to the southeast. With his business associate, James H. "Harry" Lowell, he'd also inspected an irrigation project along the Wood River. A. K. Steunenberg—his brother's confidant—believed there was a quite different explanation for Frank's behavior that day. Later he told reporters the governor must have received a warning late in the week, which would account for his "unusual" manner. On Friday afternoon at the bank, he'd walked the floor with a "meditative and troubled expression" on his face.

Whatever the reason, Frank clearly didn't wish to engage with the world that snowy Saturday. Toward noon, a young man called at the house, introducing himself as Theodore Bird of Boise, representing the New York Life Insurance Company. He'd come down from the state capital, he said, to renew the governor's $4,500 life insurance policy, which expired at year's end, barely thirty-six hours away. With some reluctance—and only because the deadline was so close—Frank agreed to meet Bird at the bank in late afternoon.

Most of the day, as wind-driven snow hissed at the windowpanes, the governor read and wrote in his study. At four o'clock he put on his overcoat, a slouch hat and galoshes, but no necktie: he was known throughout the state for his stubborn refusal to throttle himself with those slippery eastern doohickeys. Some said the habit began in the governor's youth when he was too indigent to afford a tie. In any case, for the rest of his life he'd button the shirt around his neck, leaving the uncovered brass collar button to glint like a gold coin at his throat.

People loved to speculate on this eccentricity. "His friends have exhausted all their persuasive powers on him," said the Populist James Sovereign. "Newspapers have raked him fore and aft with editorial batteries, theatrical companies have held him up to laughter and ridicule, he has become the basis of standing jokes in bar-room gossip and sewing circles, orators have plead [sic] with him, doctors have prescribed for him and politicians have lied for him, but all of no avail." Indeed, a fashionable Washington, D.C., hotel had once refused to serve him because he wore no tie, an exclusion that he bore with "magnanimous mien." A bemused Wall Streeter remembered him, on one of his excursions East, as "a rugged giant who wore a bearskin coat flapping over a collarless shirt."

Some Idahoans thought he carried sartorial informality a bit too far. On the day he was nominated for governor, he was said to have appeared at the Democratic convention lacking not only a necktie but a collar, with trousers so short they showed off his "cheap socks" and a sack coat so skimpy "as not to exclude from view the seat of his pants."

As usual, the governor didn't spend much time that morning stewing about his appearance. Bundled a bit awkwardly against the storm, he set off down Cleveland Boulevard toward the business district of his thriving little country town. Each time he strode that spacious avenue, he wondered at the transformation wrought on this wasteland in scarcely two decades. When first he'd set foot there in 1887, fresh from the black loam of his native Iowa, he'd been dismayed by the barren reach of alkali desert. Writing to his father, he called it "the worst land that can be found.... It is full of potash and the sun draws it out in a white crust on top. It is 'death' on shoe leather and where it drys and mixes with the dust and a 'dust wind' starts up, the best thing you can do is to close your eyes, stand still and take it."

It was that choking, biting dust, the "white desolate glare" broken only by sagebrush and greasewood, that had dismayed Caldwell's founders, Bob and Adell Strahorn, making them feel at times as if it were "a place deserted by God himself, and not intended for man to meddle with." When Bob Strahorn was a newspaper correspondent covering Indian wars along the Powder River, he'd joined so lustily in the cavalry's battle cries that he permanently damaged his vocal cords. Bringing that same zeal to his new job as publicist for the Union Pacific Railroad, he clothed raw data—as his wife put it—"in an attractive garb that it might coquette with restless spirits in the East who were waiting for an enchantress to lure them to the great mysterious West." Over the next few years, Strahorn produced a gaggle of guidebooks championing Western settlement—and generating passenger revenue and freight tonnage—without disclosing that they emanated from the railroad. His *Resources and Attractions of Idaho Territory*—published in 1881 by Idaho's legislature but secretly underwritten by the railroad—bubbled with braggadocio: "the healthiest climate in America, if not in the world...the richest ores known in the history of mining... the peer of any mining region in the universe...luxuriant crops, emerald or golden, trees blossom- and perfume-laden, or bending to earth with their lavish fruitage."

He didn't hesitate to promise glittering rewards, as in his flat assertion that cattle raising in Idaho was "a sure and short road to fortune." Only rarely did he suffer twinges of conscience for misleading wide-eyed eastern settlers: "I could not but feel that, for a time at least, many of them would be grievously disappointed in what we could already visualize and enthusiastically paint as a potential land of plenty."

In 1883, the lanky Strahorn, with his aquiline nose and lofty airs, graduated from publicity to the lucrative role of town building along the railroad's sprawling rights-of-way. As general manager of the Idaho and Oregon Land Improvement Company—an independent enterprise in which both railroad officials and local nabobs enjoyed juicy financial interests—he colonized land along the Oregon Short Line, a Union Pacific subsidiary, so named because, by skirting San Francisco, it provided a shortcut from Omaha to Portland, linking the parent road directly to the rich resources of the burgeoning Northwest. In this capacity, Strahorn had a major voice in determining where the tracks would go. Infant communities throughout the West desperately sought access to the railroad, for it often spelled the difference between bleak isolation and bustling prosperity.

In 1883, Boise was waging a fierce campaign for a rail connection. All that spring, the territorial capital seethed with rumors about where the Short Line would ford the Boise River on its way west, a crossing that speculators were sure would mark the site of Idaho's future metropolis. One June morning, the Strahorns set forth by buckboard from Boise, ostensibly to visit a northern mining camp. But once out of sight, they abruptly swung west, and after some thirty miles Bob drove the first stake, intoning in mock frontier lingo, "Dar whar we stake de horse, dar whar we find de home."*

When Boiseans discovered what had happened, they railed at Strahorn's betrayal. A mob hung him in effigy and vowed that, if ever they laid hands on him, they'd hang him in earnest. Strahorn had sufficient grounds for his decision: the stubborn conviction of the Union Pacific's chief locating engineer, a stolid Dutchman named Jacob Blickensderfer, who stoutly opposed the notion of dropping six hundred feet from grade just to embrace Boise in an awkward "ox-bow" bend. The *Idaho Daily Statesman,* voice of the capital city, attributed Strahorn's actions to sheer greed: "an ambitious young man [whose] syndicate is investing in desert lands for a town-site," it called him. The officers of Strahorn's company did stand to realize handsome—and legitimate—profits from the sale of town sites in Caldwell, Hailey, Mountain Home, and Payette, not to mention from the building of highways, bridges, telegraph lines, hotels, and irrigation works up and down the Short Line.

But since the officers were notified in advance of others about the exact route the road would take, they had ample opportunity to make illegitimate profits as well. One reason Boiseans so bitterly resented Strahorn was that

---

* Will Visscher, a Western entertainer, used to say in his dialect lecture: "Dar whar de hen scratch, / Dar whar you find de wurm / Providen' no previous hen / Ha' scratched dar afore."

he'd bilked them out of a bunch of money. While the new town site was still a closely held secret, he'd quietly bought the Haskell ranch north of the Boise River, then made sure that news of his purchase leaked out. Convinced they'd now smoked out the town site, Boiseans snapped up thousands of acres around the ranch, inhabited only by jackrabbits and golden-mantled ground squirrels. Some speculators were permitted to buy up much of the ranch itself —at a nifty profit for Strahorn. Only then did he reveal that he'd acquired the town's real location—miles away on the river's south bank.

In its dyspeptic campaign, the *Statesman* called Strahorn's new town Sagebrush City. Others derisively dubbed it Alkali Flats. But Adell Strahorn had already named it Caldwell after Alexander Caldwell, the former U.S. senator from Kansas. With Andrew Mellon, the Pittsburgh banker and industrialist, Caldwell had put up most of the capital for Strahorn's improvement company and, in return, the patriarchal figure with his flowing white beard had been named its president.

If "the senator" provided substantial resources, he did not lend the enterprise much luster. While others had fought at Manassas and Antietam, Caldwell had made a fortune during the Civil War transporting military supplies by ox-drawn wagons—not unlike J. P. Morgan and John D. Rockefeller, who'd procured substitutes to serve in the army for them, or Andrew Carnegie, Philip D. Armour, and Jay Gould, who "preferred the emoluments of the market place to the miseries (or glories) of the battlefield." After the war, Caldwell was elected to the Senate. Rivals argued that he'd secured the post through bribery—by no means unusual in an era when senators were elected by state legislatures, not renowned for their immunity to commercial influence. Another candidate in the same race kept a suite of rooms, known variously as the Soup House and the Bread Riot, where legislators were plied with "eatables," "refreshments," and other, more lubricious, inducements. Alexander Caldwell, backed by the Kansas Pacific Railway and other formidable interests in his hometown of Leavenworth, countered with thick bundles of cash: up to $15,000 per legislator's vote, a substantial sum in those days. When a senatorial committee found against him in 1872, Caldwell attributed his discomfiture to "a mean spirit of revenge" but promptly resigned.

Boise's partisans held that the disgraced senator was precisely the man to lend his name to the odious little tank town that had filched its railroad. When a construction crew finally brought the tracks through Caldwell in September 1883, the *Statesman* noted, a bit hyperbolically, that the place had "eleven saloons and one pump." And it was pleased to report that two guests at the reception offered there for railroad officials had their horses stolen outside the hall. "The entire population of the city started in pursuit of the thieves," the paper chortled, "but at last accounts had not caught up with them."

If Caldwell had been born a colonial dependency—founded by an eastern con man, named for a Leavenworth grafter, bankrolled with Kansas and Pennsylvania money to serve the interests of the Union Pacific Railroad—it gradually achieved a resonant sense of its own identity: bold to the point of pushy, fiercely competitive, out for the main chance. Settlers who found their way to Caldwell in the 1880s and 1890s, drawn by the grandiose promises of promoters like Strahorn, were animated by a faith that the West would somehow liberate them from the economic servitude that prevailed by then in much of industrial America.

Some explorers had warned against false expectations. Captain James L. Fisk, who led a government expedition to the Idaho Territory in 1863, admonished prospective emigrants: "Have a good reason for loosing from the old anchorage before going in search of a better. Do not start on such a journey with the idea that it is going to be simply a fine play-spell, and that when you get through you will tumble into some gulch and come forthwith laden with your fortune in gold. Success in any new field of civilization and labor can only be reached through hardship, privation, endurance, and great industry."

But later propagandists—often, like Strahorn, in the pay of railroads and land companies—managed to persuade ambitious young Easterners that places like the Idaho Territory were free of the old class divisions, the encrusted privileges long associated with Europe and now with much of the New World. In boomtowns like Caldwell—so the message went—everybody started on the same footing, and because the agricultural, timber, and mining resources were prodigious, the prospects for enriching oneself were limitless. The bold of heart would leave the past behind; the future opened wide before them.

From the start, Caldwell shot for the stars. On December 9, 1883—when the town was just a clump of canvas tents and frame shacks along a dusty track, the only boardinghouse a converted railway car—the first issue of the *Caldwell Tribune* boasted of "the great city that she will become, a fact that even the Boise City Board of Trade map cannot hide—the center of commerce, the center of education, the pivot about which the great social fabric of Western Idaho will revolve." Such conviction was no more unshakable than many other booster prophecies across the land, represented by the 1890s promoter who wrote of Chicago, "the place was pregnant with certainty." But though such transformation struck some as an unlikely feat of prestidigitation, the newspaper began calling its tiny village the Magic City.

When a rival journal in Hailey, 120 miles to the east, pointed out derisively that the word *Caldwell* had appeared 187 times in one *Tribune* issue, the paper's editor, W. J. "Uncle Bill" Cuddy, shot back: "It will be found 187,000 times before we get through. That is what we are for and that is what we are doing."* When the *Boise Republican* questioned the "Caldwell boom," the *Tribune* offered "to cut off a chunk and send it up to show you what metropolitan life and vigor is." Like other booster papers across the West, the weekly *Tribune* was a major instrument for town building, even if—or precisely because—it "sometimes represented things that had not yet gone through the formality of taking place." Western newspapers, like western railroads, often ran well ahead of settlement—a process that, in many bleak locales, was still waiting to happen.

Boiseans worried that Caldwell might snatch the state capital away, as it had the railroad. Don't worry, the *Tribune* reassured them, "we prefer business to corruption." Business was surely Caldwell's métier. Its merchants called themselves "rustlers," proud of their "vim, vigor and vitriol" and of the "close and sharp" competition that had made Caldwell "synonimous [*sic*] with the word enterprise."

The town would thrive on the sheer exuberance of late-nineteenth-century American capitalism. In their rampant boosterism, its promoters appealed to the naked self-interest of potential settlers. In that respect, it was no different from thousands of other towns across the West. "The spirit of the times, which we called the spirit of progress," wrote the Kansas editor William Allen White, "was a greedy endeavor to coax more people into the West, to bring more money into the West. It was shot through with an unrighteous design for spoils, a great, ugly riproaring civilization spun out of the glittering fabric of credit. Everyone who owned a white shirt was getting his share of some new, shiny, tainted money in those days."

But somehow Caldwell seemed a bit more brazen, more unashamedly greedy than many western communities. "Caldwell is a straight business proposition," the *Tribune* calculated in 1893. "It is a cold-blooded, money-making consideration. You don't want to come here solely for your health and religion. . . . Your health will improve in Caldwell with the swelling of your assets, and salvation comes easier with prosperity."

Indeed Frank Steunenberg and his five brothers, all of whom migrated there shortly after the town's founding, had prospered mightily in Caldwell these past years—in sheep ranching, banking, retailing, newspapers, and real estate. Now, as the governor slogged through ankle-deep snow in the gathering dusk, he could pick out palpable symbols of that prosperity along this grand new thoroughfare, named Cleveland Boulevard after the nation's twenty-second—and twenty-fourth—president.

On the first corner was the turreted home of the governor's old friend John C. Rice. A big lantern-jawed man just turned forty, Rice was Caldwell's

---

* It was the ubiquitous Robert Strahorn who'd sought out Cuddy, then a cub reporter on the *Omaha Bee*, and installed him as editor of the fledgling *Tribune* to provide a vigorous voice for the struggling town (Strahorn, *Ninety Years*, 341).

most successful lawyer, practicing in an office over Steunenberg's bank. But increasingly he was off in Boise arguing before the state courts, as he was that very day, representing that city's *Evening Capital News* in a bitter lawsuit against James H. Brady, chairman of the Republican state committee, over control of the feisty newspaper.

A former mayor of Caldwell, and now—with his law partner, J. M. Thompson—its city attorney, Rice had long been one of the governor's closest business associates: an organizer of the Steunenberg bank and still a board member, he served as an adviser on the governor's multifarious commercial enterprises.

People said Rice had built his elegant Queen Anne mansion—so similiar to those rising in comfortable neighborhoods of San Francisco and Chicago—to satisfy the luxurious tastes of his wife, Maude. If so, it had filled the bill, providing no fewer than four porches and an airy sewing room in a turret. The Rices could use the space. With four children already, Maude was pregnant again. In anticipation, she was expanding her household staff, advertising for a "competent girl to do general housework."

The Rice and Steunenberg mansions, looming in the southeast corner of town, were outposts of gentility in what was still a parvenu neighborhood. When the governor moved there in 1893, so rural were its surroundings that he was said to be occupying his "country seat." But Steunenberg had built there precisely to promote that relatively undeveloped quadrant of the community, for the Steunenberg brothers were trying to market lots in their own adjacent Steunenberg-Hand addition. They stood to benefit as well from new construction in the addition, and elsewhere in town, as they were officers of Caldwell's Independent Lumber and Manufacturing Company, headed by their colleague Harry Lowell, who also served as manager of the newly formed real estate department at the Steunenberg bank. Lowell and the Steunenbergs reaped thousands of dollars from exclusive sales rights on the remaining lots of the Caldwell Land Company, once run by Bob Strahorn.

There were those in town—"mossbacks," they defiantly called themselves—who thought that "airy, lightweight newcomers" like Lowell were too big for their bumptious britches. Newcomers, in turn, pictured the mossbacks as "rubbing their eyes which had become bleared by their long Van Winkle repose." Caldwell's relentless booming invoked a civic unity that never quite existed. For years, the mossback faction—men like tavern keeper Chris Fahy; the town's first butcher, Mike Roberts; and hardware dealer W. H. Redway, who hauled the first wagonload of nails into Caldwell—chafed at the brass of "johnny-come-latelies" like Lowell, haberdasher J. F. Herr, and lumber, sash, and door man and all-round "go-getter" Harry Crookham.

For the most part, Caldwell's first families—among them the Reverend William Judson Boone, a Presbyterian minister now heading Caldwell's fledgling College of Idaho; John T. Morrison, the former governor; William

Isaacs, a sheep rancher; the druggist Henry Blatchley and his wife, Carrie, the town's social arbiter, widely known as Queen Carrie—all lived north of Indian Creek and the railroad, in the town's best residential neighborhood.

But as Caldwell boomed in the new century—more than doubling its population, from 997 to 2,200, in the first five years—it expanded south and east. The scale of Cleveland Boulevard—some eighty feet in breadth—suggested that it would soon be one of the town's most prestigious addresses. It was already lined for two miles with Western Colonial or bungalow-style houses—rustic, rangy dwellings with graceful porch posts, bits of colored glass in their door panels, dormer windows (when a man made some money in Caldwell, he got himself a dormer), and spacious verandas, perfect for whiling away long summer evenings amid the thrum of cicadas.

Scarcely a neighbor was in sight that afternoon of the governor's walk, save for packs of neighborhood boys pelting one another with snowballs, a practice the town fathers were trying to discourage. A few days earlier, little Ella Lowe had been smacked in the face with a hard-packed ball that had smashed her glasses and driven shards into one eye, which doctors said she would surely lose.

Plunging on through the storm, the governor tried to keep his footing on the icy boardwalks that lined the city's major thoroughfares. Cement sidewalks were still rare in Caldwell; ten feet of the new underfooting, among the first in town, had just been laid along Main Street in front of Hartkopf's Tin Shop, paid for by surly Sam Hartkopf himself. Few merchants could yet afford that extravagance, so they relied on the icy boardwalks, which popped and crackled under a man's weight.

But no walkway could protect the townspeople from Caldwell's immutable realities: dust and mud. In summer, the powdery dust rose in choking billows under iron-rimmed wagon wheels and the hooves of sheep on their way from feeding lot to range. The municipal sprinkler wagon, pulled by a plodding team, with its driver dozing under his yellow umbrella, dutifully made its rounds, laying down a fine spray of water on each baking street twice a day; but the caked soil seemed to suck up the moisture as soon as the cart rounded the next corner. A growing faction in town pressed for macadam surfacing of all principal thoroughfares, but the city fathers shied from the expense, preferring to experiment with sand from Indian Creek.

The first few automobiles—"buzz carts" or "devil wagons," as they were known—had made their appearance in Caldwell, among them the big black beauty of Ralph Cowden, cashier of the First National Bank, and the sporty roadster belonging to Walter Sebree of the power company. But both the town and the county roads were so bad it took a prominent judge rushing to his courtroom almost three hours to drive the twenty-nine miles from Boise to Caldwell. In winter and spring, the gumbo engulfed wheels and hooves and boots alike, spattering skirts and waistcoats along even the finest boulevards.

If the town still had to reckon with dust and mud, at least it had beaten back the damned desert. Nothing had contributed more to Caldwell's startling prosperity than reclamation of the parched wasteland through a host of irrigation projects. As early as 1864, individual settlers had channeled Indian Creek's waters onto their land. The town's network of roadside "ditches" got under way in earnest in the 1880s. Later, water was drawn from the Boise River into larger systems of reservoirs and canals, dug the hard way with hand plows, scrapers, and shovels. Frank and A. K. Steunenberg, often led by Harry Lowell, invested in many of these projects; recently they'd participated in a more massive scheme to reclaim 250,000 acres in the Twin Falls area, 130 miles to the southeast.

The week before, under the heading "Musings on Our Material Progress," a *Tribune* correspondent had extolled the lush cultivation along Caldwell's own Sebree Canal. "One is favorably impressed," he wrote, "with the belief that this country is fast improving in all lines of farming industry when he rides along this canal, as compared with what it was a few years ago. In the haying season, it is no uncommon thing to see from three to eight hay derricks going at once.... All we desire is for the Government canals to start, and we will truly be living in 'God's own country.' "

The earth was volcanic ash, dry as sawdust but immensely rich. As water seeped into the parched cinders, it turned the landscape from ghostly white to vivid green. Alfalfa, timothy, clover, sugar beets, apples, peaches, and pears all flourished in the fertile new soil. In 1890 alone, Caldwell had planted more than four thousand trees. Seemingly overnight, sagebrush and greasewood gave way to cottonwoods and box elders, Lombardy poplars and catalpas, black willows and elms. Nobody was more thrilled by this transformation than Frank Steunenberg, who had ached for the luxuriant foliage of his Iowa youth.

On a train trip East in 1904, gazing through the windows at the dense woodlands of southern Indiana, Steunenberg wrote home, "The great forests are a never ending joy and comfort and I never tire of looking at the graceful trees, now right at the car window, now covering an adjacent hillside and again gracing a distant ridge with glory and grandeur.... Oh, the happy days of my boyhood amid the trees. There was not a tree within a mile of our home I had not climbed.... The first time I saw the grand old trees of my native Iowa, after some years' stay in Idaho, I was seized with a strange feeling, and a big lump arose in my throat. And today as I look at the trees from the car windows, solemn and somber in their winter stillness, I hear happy voices from out of their solitude and feel them beckoning, 'Come, come and be at peace.' " Indeed, in conversation with Charles E. Arney, another Idaho politician who'd emigrated from Iowa, he spoke of "returning to Iowa sometime, and buying a great old country home, where quiet and comfort and peace would prevail." When Cleveland Boulevard was laid out, Frank and others had made sure it was lined with a double column of American elms. In summer it was a swaying bower of green, but even bare of leaves and crusted in snow, the pendulous elms made him feel at home.

Most of those who'd taken a chance on this burgeoning neighborhood cut lesser figures in town than Rice and Steunenberg, but they were eager young strivers with boots firmly planted on the ladders of mobility. In brash new towns like Caldwell, saloonkeepers were men to reckon with, and Cleveland Boulevard could boast the homes of three: Dan Brown, a husky man with a bushy black beard, who ran the Caldwell Club, a murky cavern redolent of stables, tobacco juice, and stale beer; Perry Groves, co-owner of the Palace saloon, a slightly more upscale establishment, which advertised itself as "headquarters for stockmen and farmers" and touted its "fine line of wines, liquors and cigars . . . [and a] first class lunch counter" (serving fresh oysters, hot tamales, and fish and game in season); and Rasmus Christenson, who ran the Board of Trade saloon, offering "clubrooms and pool tables," and doubled as agent for Kellogg's Old Bourbon, which, with Squirrel and McBryan, was one of the West's most popular brands.

Among other prominent merchants who'd built handsome residences on the boulevard were Jack Harrington, the real estate and insurance man; J. G. Gartin, proprietor of Fashion Livery; and Harry Jones, who ran a furniture store–cum–undertaking establishment. "All those things which go to the furnishing and beautifying of a home," Jones advertised, "[with] a room especially fitted up for the reception and care of bodies."

At Kimball Avenue—the town's major north-south thoroughfare—the governor turned right to cross the deep channel of Indian Creek on a narrow footbridge. Frozen now in sheets of black ice, in spring it would run with angry brown swells, aswarm with ice cakes and driftwood; then, in summer, it would turn semiclear over a white, sandy bottom. The far bank was dominated by the paddocks and barns of Pete Engel's Corral Feed and Livery Stable ("First Class Rigs for Commercial Men"), one of seven livery operations that clustered along the creek.

Livery was the town's principal industry. In those stables the itinerant drummer rented a horse and rig to make his forays into the farm country; there the farmer left his team and wagon when he came to town to stock up on provisions. Fancy buggies, ladies' landaus, and arabesque sleighs were available for more frivolous occasions. The stables harbored every sort of horse-drawn vehicle, from the hotel's hacks and the funeral hearse to the lawyer's carriage and the town water cart.

But livery also formed the muscle and sinew of the town's economy. By century's turn, Caldwell was one of Idaho's major market towns and transshipment depots, two million pounds of wool alone passing through the community each year. "All roads lead to Caldwell" was one slogan of its incessant boosterism. Bob Strahorn's critics had been right: the iron horse had made Caldwell. Henceforth, when people for miles around said, "I'm going to the railroad," they meant they were going to Caldwell. Even when a spur reached Boise in 1887, Caldwell and neighboring Nampa remained the region's quintessential railroad towns, where rolling stock thumped and shuddered on the sidings and a thick coating of coal dust settled on the wash fluttering like sooty banners along the rights-of-way.

Yet those gleaming rails penetrated only so far into the hinterland. To carry wool from the ranches of Owyhee County and ore from the Jordan Valley mining camps to the railhead—or candles, gunpowder, bacon, flour, or salt in the other direction—meant turning to the flesh-and-blood horse. Raw materials and finished goods alike were hauled in enormous wagons, pulled by teams of ten, twelve, even sixteen horses, driven by a "freighter" who, astride the wheel horse, controlled the team through a jerk line to the lead horse's bridle. Caldwell's freighters were boisterous, hard-drinking men who doubled as horse breakers, taming the Owyhee mustangs popular as cavalry mounts. Legends like Jack Mumford, Clyde Davis, and Hank Ballard could turn one of their twelve-horse rigs around at a downtown intersection, churning up clouds of dust and drawing raucous approbation from the men who drifted out of the saloons, whiskey glasses in hand, to assess the performance.

The freighters were figures of adulation to Caldwell youths of all classes. Herbert van Wyngarden, Frank Steunenberg's nephew, lived by their principal route through town. One day when he was twelve, he set his family's cane-backed dining room chairs outside in five pairs, as if they were a ten-horse team, then harangued them in the freighters' rough-hewn cadences. Herbert got paddled twice: once for subjecting good furniture to the elements, again for using that kind of language.

The boys of the town were fascinated, too, by the livery stables, strenuously male environments where stable hands, hostlers, hired men, hack drivers, grizzled pensioners, and the town's earthier politicians sprawled in the shade, smoking clay pipes, playing checkers or cards, and trading tall tales. It was in these dim grottoes that Caldwell's lads learned how to "spit, swear, and swagger" and picked up what passed for the facts of life.

Servicing Caldwell's massive freighting industry required not only livery stables and corrals but blacksmith shops—the town had five—harness, saddlery, and feed stores, warehouses, rooming houses, Chinese laundries, restaurants, saloons, dance halls, and bawdy houses. The largest horse market in those parts was Charles H. Turner's Horse and Mule Company on Tenth Street. And for years Caldwell's most tangible symbol was the weather vane in the shape of a great Percheron horse installed high atop Dan Campbell's livery stable, visible for miles in all directions.

It often seemed as though the needs of horse and horsemen came before those of the town. The municipal landscaper, a Mr. Schuman, had done his best to sow bluegrass and plant rose bushes along the city's roadways—local expressions of a national drive for roadside beautification—but of late he'd warned that "thoughtless draymen," who permitted their horses to trample the greensward, were complicating his task. The bouquet of fresh manure hovered over Caldwell like the morning fogs that clung to the mud-slick roadways. Crossing the footbridge, the governor noted once again how Engel had built out over Indian Creek, so the stable boys could simply kick the piles of dung into the water—a common habit up and down the stream.

It had occurred to some Cassandras that such practices might have something to do with the typhoid epidemic raging through Caldwell. Among those taken to their beds were John Rice's six-year-old daughter, Martha; Ralph Scatterday, a young attorney; Frank Smith, the osteopath; M. I. Church, the probate judge; and the governor's own niece, Grace van Wyngarden, a student at the University of Idaho. Three days before Christmas, W. H. Howard's two-year-old son had died after his temperature soared to 104. Despite relays of ice packs the child had seemed "literally to burn up from fever." Doctors weren't sure whether this was some virulent new form of typhoid or a more dread malady.

In a recent letter to the *Caldwell News*, a correspondent calling himself "I. M. Sane" had inveighed against the unsanitary conditions that had contributed to "the awful scourge" of typhoid and to the diphtheria epidemics that periodically beset the town. The "filthy streets and alleys," as well as "many unsightly and decaying weeds," he wrote, continued to "spread their sad havoc, carrying disease and death" and demanding speedy action—here perhaps a note of sarcasm crept in—by the city's "zealous and progressive town council." Later the *News* warned: "The practice of throwing the carcasses of dogs, chickens etc. into Indian Creek should be stopped at once."

There was a wild side to Caldwell all right, reminding folks that the genteel manners of the emerging bourgeoisie were still a fragile veneer imposed on the natural order of things. Clouds of giant mosquitoes, armies of ferocious red ants, and periodic plagues of grasshoppers (folks still talked of the "great grasshopper scourge" of 1868) could make summer hell, as they had when Caldwell was called Bug Town. Horned toads, kangaroo rats, and diamondback rattlers prowled the prairie. On winter mornings, you could still find a five-foot bull snake coiled and hissing by the kitchen stove. Bull snakes weren't poisonous, but unless you'd grown up with them around the house, they could unnerve you a bit. After Frank Steunenberg had killed four of the reptiles, his wife "bundled up" and left for a time. " 'The independent life of a farmer' that we hear mentioned frequently still has a few drawbacks," Frank wrote the family in Iowa.

Coyotes bayed all night on Canyon Hill and scavenged for garbage in people's backyards. The state recruited men to hunt coyotes and wolves, supplying each of them with two boxes of ammunition and two bottles of strychnine. As recently as February 1904, Billy Snodgrass, proprietor of the City Barbershop, had shot a coyote on Main Street.

To a young lawyer recently arrived from the East, Caldwell in those years seemed "the most primitive sort of cow town." But it was no Wild West show. The wildest animals in town were two pet bear cubs that the saloonkeeper Dan Brown kept chained to a telephone pole behind his Caldwell Club. As Adell Strahorn noted, "an agricultural town has not the vim, rush and whoop of a mining town." Nor did it have the gratuitous gunplay of the classic cow town: few men got killed on Main Street anymore. The last was a Missourian named Charlie Bays, who'd spent a day in 1901 drinking nonstop in several saloons. His binge ended when he pushed the Kincaid brothers in the mud, then pulled a pigsticker on them. W. J. B. Kirkpatrick, the town marshal, hit Bays on the arm with a cane made from the heavy end of a billiard cue, and when that didn't stop him, the marshal hit him again, this time over the head. Bays fell dead. Opinion in town was sharply divided as to who was at fault. Nobody wasted time mourning for a scoundrel like Bays, but merchants feared that violent death in the heart of town could only discourage further settlement. Ultimately, the marshal was tried for manslaughter—and acquitted.

If you looked for trouble you could still find some at the west end of Main Street—a neighborhood people called Tough Town—where bordellos like Fanny Boyd's "boarding house for young women" stood scrawny cheek by scraggly jowl with the most notorious saloons. For fear of these "gilded hells" and "scarlet resorts," the "better class of people" prohibited their young folk from straying into Tough Town.

Picking his way through the manure that pocked the new-fallen snow, the governor moved on down Kimball Avenue into the town's compact but thriving business district, still aglow with Christmas baubles. "Caldwell is the place to go," went one promotional ditty, "For bargains great and small, / In clothing, groceries and such / In implements and all." The frosty air filling his lungs, the governor hurried past John A. Baker's feed store, C. C. Smith's harness shop, L. W. Botkin's Caldwell Pharmacy, and C. E. Barnes's grocery, which that holiday season was offering fresh oysters, candied orange peel and raisins, and "everything for that Christmas pudding."

Reaching Main Street, the governor could spy on the opposite corner the familiar brick print shop of the *Tribune,* his first undertaking in Caldwell, indeed his first love. At age sixteen in 1877, he'd left school in Knoxville, Iowa, to serve his printing apprenticeship at the *Knoxville Journal,* where he remained four years. Later, he became a compositor on the *Des Moines Register,* where he'd gained a certain panache as the most prolific typesetter in the frantic weeks following President Garfield's assassination. After two years out for study at the Iowa Agricultural College at Ames—"I cannot say that I love it," he wrote home, pleading "send me a [news]paper once in a while"—he returned to his chosen craft, serving as publisher of the *Knoxville Express* until late 1886.

It was then that Frank Steunenberg, still only twenty-five, received an urgent summons from A.K., who'd wandered west as a tramp printer, working for a time in South Dakota and Wyoming, then settling earlier that year in the infant Caldwell. A.K. had spent his first night in town wrapped in a blanket under the Main Street bandstand, but before long he was one of Caldwell's young men on the go. In December, he bought the moribund *Caldwell Tribune* from its second editor, George P. Wheeler, moving it into new quarters above the Odd Fellows Lodge, of which A.K. was a charter member. But to get the paper back on a sound footing A.K. needed his older brother's help, so Frank resigned his post at the *Express* and sat up three days and two nights on the hard wooden seats of a clangorous Union Pacific "emigrant car."

By the time Frank arrived on January 9, A.K. had already published his first issue with a bold salutatory. Customarily, he'd written, an editor launched his newspaper by proclaiming that he was "there for the sole purpose of scattering literary light o'er the benighted multitudes, and that he will be . . . a fountain of truth and wisdom for those seeking light and knowledge." Not for A.K. such hollow pieties. "We are here for the money," he wrote, ". . . because this country is going to go boom and we want to boom with it. We shall endeavor to make the *Tribune* a live local paper, and solicit your patronage."

Live it was: four pages of waggish gossip and sly wit rolling off the old flatbed press every Saturday afternoon. At first, A.K. and Frank focused their irreverence on an acute municipal concern: the dire shortage of women. In those early years, a scant half-dozen unmarried girls cast sidelong glances at forty-five randy bachelors (among them A.K.—though not Frank, who in 1885 had married his first cousin, Eveline Belle Keppel of Keokuk, Iowa). It was a grave disparity, producing some famous brawls and grudges. For a time, a Caldwell Social Club held periodic dances in town to bring lonely men and eligible women together, but soon they petered out for lack of "respectable ladies." Only recently, the *Tribune* had warned "men of Caldwell who are in the habit of visiting back doors of married ladies' houses as late as 11 o'clock at night . . . that they had better stay away as it might cause some one to get hurt."

So the Steunenbergs—Frank and A.K. had now been joined at the paper by their younger brother Charles (better known as Pete)—launched a column called "The Marriage Bureau." Listing the town's bachelors, they invited young ladies to write "any name which may tickle their fancy." Soon love-starved females—more likely, news-starved Steunenbergs—filled the weekly column.

One addressed Mike Devers: "Mr. M. DeVers—Noble Sir. I am an aesthetic widow, good looking, wealthy, affable, loving and of sweet, retiring disposition. All I want is one to love, and must be a Frenchman, as your name clearly shows you to be. . . . My former husband was a German; he died drinking beer. May you never meet a like fate is the wish of, Your Friend, Mrs. A.C. Gilloohey." Another wrote Orville Baker: "What's in a name? It's a man I want, and am perfectly willing to look over any minor issues. Do you mean biz? If so, say so and we'll hitch. I'm a gushing girl of 35 very short summers; your age is immaterial.... Yours for Business. Gushing Ann."

Soon the column reported meetings of the Bachelors' Club, replete with a president who wielded a yard of stale bologna in lieu of a gavel, a Committee on Suspicious Characters (which recommended against admission of grocer Barnes on evidence that he was married), and matrimonial threats from a terrorist band called the Female Night Caps. The *Tribune* awarded prizes for the handsomest woman in town, which for several years running went to a dazzling hairdresser named Delia Gilgan. Dr. Bill Maxey was the town's fashion plate, frequently decked out in white spats and a soft felt hat, but the "most dashing gentleman" award went to Colonel J. O. O'Connell, whom A.K. puckishly termed "an Irishman of uncertain habits."

Animating the column was the conceit that Caldwell's bachelors were in flight from packs of rapacious women bent on matrimony. In fact, most men in town were downright desperate for female companionship. Sure enough, the roster of bachelors dwindled relentlessly and when A.K. himself took a wife in 1891, the club was disbanded amid "wails of anguish." It was promptly replaced by the Happy Fathers' Association.

Single or married, the men who ran Caldwell then were remarkably young, most in their twenties and early thirties. By 1891, Caldwell boasted the only athletic club in the state, with its own handsome building, where forty members, "young and full of blood," disported themselves with robust vigor. "They leaped into life like the boys they still were," A.K.'s daughter, Bess, recalled. "They were exuberant, ambitious, intoxicated by the heady experience of a chance to build from scratch. They worked and struggled, sang and laughed, politicked and clowned, and played outrageous practical jokes upon one another." It was a young man's town, a town rich with possibility, lush with expectation, where the future beckoned as it does to youth.

Increasingly, the raunchy proclivities of footloose blades collided with the more conventional aspirations of Caldwell's young burghers—a tension often found within the same man's breast. Ultimately, marriage, children, and financial exigencies inspired creeping respectability. When a renowned saloon known as "the dive" threatened to become too "unruly and boisterous," the *Tribune* warned that unless the proprietor "quickly shows a disposition to be more civil, another committee will wait on him." A few days before the governor had set out on his walk, 267 residents prayed the city council to pass an ordinance closing the saloons on Sunday, and the council promptly instructed the city attorney, John Rice, to draft such legislation.

The Sunday-closing campaign was part of a wider reform movement, aimed at shucking Caldwell's air of boyish rascality and assuming a high-minded mien more appropriate to its growing stature in the state. The impetus came, in part, from the town's active temperance societies. Of late, Canyon County had been a hotbed of prohibitionist sentiment. The president of the

Idaho State Women's Christian Temperance Union was Caldwell's own Ellen D. Crawford. The governor's wife and his sister Lizzie were charter members of Caldwell's chapter, which held receptions at the Steunenberg residence. All this left the governor little choice but to embrace the teetotaler's standard. The Presbyterian Church—now pastored by the Reverend David A. Clemens but still influenced by the stern, authoritarian William Judson Boone—waged a zealous crusade for "moral reform." Boone himself, concluding that admonition alone wouldn't beat back the forces of evil, poured his formidable energies into politics. In 1900, he ran for governor as a Prohibitionist—more to give his cause statewide credibility than anything else. In 1905, he'd joined Caldwell's Citizens Ticket and won a seat on the seven-man city council, where—with Mayor Roscoe Madden, a realtor—he was pledged to close saloons on Sunday, abolish gambling, and suppress the town's gaggle of prostitutes, whom the *Tribune* called "wayward tidbits and old cats."

Like many other Idaho communities of that era, Caldwell was sharply divided between a "saloon" crowd and a "church" faction. The saloon crowd —heavily male—favored an "open town," open to the time-honored pastimes of such places. The real foot soldiers in the church movement were the town's formidable women, many of them members of both the WCTU and the Presbyterian Church. Caldwell's middle-class women were a strong-willed lot, if only by dint of surviving the harsh rigors of the place. In the 1890s, a magazine called the *Idaho Woman* was published in Caldwell and mailed throughout the state; it was edited by a man, Rees H. Davis (who'd bought the *Tribune* from the Steunenbergs some years before), but heavily supported by the three Gilgan sisters—Anna, Delia, and Martha—who ran millinery and hairdressing shops on Main Street.

This clutch of activist women had a keen sense of political possibilities. In the 1896 election, Idaho voted two to one to become the fourth state—after Wyoming, Colorado, and Utah—to grant women the vote. The next year, Caldwell became the first Idaho community to put a woman in elective office, that of alderwoman. This drew a huzzah from the *Idaho Woman:* "There will hereafter be no question respecting the ability and intention of Caldwell women to engage intelligently and actively in political affairs."

Boone's rallying cry against the evils of whores and whiskey encountered an eager response among the town's womenfolk. Men were less receptive to the didactics of the preacher with his swooping nose and great balding brow. As a group, they were not much for church attendance: surveying the faithful in the Presbyterian Church one day, a visitor remarked that there would "not be enough men in heaven to carry the bass." Not surprisingly, many of the freighters, barkeeps, and ranch hands groused that "Boone is killing the town." Rees Davis at the *Tribune* was profoundly skeptical of all these moral crusades. "The plain fact of the matter," he wrote, "is that there are no serious evils in Caldwell to be reformed, except such as God Almighty planted in the human breast."

It was the WCTU that, in March 1900, founded the Caldwell Free Reading Room, a nascent public library. If they closed the town's saloons, the women reasoned, they were obliged to provide some other place where men could be assured of "light, warmth and welcome." Originally quartered in the rear of S. N. Moe's jewelry store, the room was supported by a series of "ice cream socials," then by monthly subscriptions from Caldwell's businessmen. By 1906, the room housed seven hundred books and subscribed to five magazines. One Caldwell youth who made heavy use of the Reading Room was a former *Tribune* printer's devil named Lawrence Henry Gipson, who in 1904 was awarded Idaho's first Rhodes scholarship to Oxford University and who would go on to receive a Pulitzer Prize for his magisterial study of Great Britain before the American Revolution.

In that era, when feminine cultivation was seen as the redemptive antidote to the unruly masculine world, Caldwell's women never flagged in their relentless quest for high culture. As early as 1901, Grace Darling Morrison—soon to be the state's first lady—led the town's women in a study of the "History and Appreciation of Art." These same women formed the Forward Society, which promoted lectures and concerts, and the Village Improvement Society, dedicated to broad-gauged moral uplift.

A regular reader since college—particularly in history and political economy—the governor was a loyal client of the Reading Room. At times, though, he wondered whether his thinking apparatus wasn't rusting for lack of use. "You have probably thought many times what I found to engage my gigantic intellect out here in the western solitude," he'd written his family in Iowa, "but if you could see gentle 'Blizzard' [the family milk cow], you would have no more anxiety that my mind might decay through inactivity. It takes all the eloquence of a Demousthenes [*sic*], the strategy of a Napoleon, the wisdom of a Solomon, the patriotism of a Washington, the craftiness of a Tecumseh, the strength of Samson, and the humility of a Sister of Charity, to draw the lacteal fluid from her udder."

At the corner of Kimball and Main, the governor turned west up Main Street, past the Railroad Chop House, which boasted the best plank steaks in town; Frank Wood's bakery, its distinctive sign, a loaf of bread, shapeless under a puffy frosting of snow; W. H. Redway Hardware, where a few days before Christmas the governor had spent $2.50 on a dazzling red sled for his son; Swain Beatty's barbershop, bath rooms, and cigar store, crowded today as every Saturday with ranch hands getting their monthly trims and leaving off their laundry; and Ah Kim's Chinese restaurant, one of Caldwell's four Asian eateries.

"We have been asked by a number of strangers if there is a white restaurant in town," the *Tribune* had recently noted. "To all such, we must reply, we don't know, but Charley Kim is half white and well done." The color of the hands that stirred the soup was an old concern among Caldwell's citizens. In 1884, the Pacific Hotel advertised "none but white cooks em-

ployed." Gradually, miners, ranchers, and railroad men came to relish Ah
Kim's, Lee Chung's, and Sing Lee's chop sueys and egg foo yungs; children
bought firecrackers from the pigtailed fellow who ran a laundry on Main
Street; and the town's housewives bought their vegetables from the wizened
China Jim, who rattled through the streets in his wagon chanting "green
onion, radish, lettuce, turnip." But they weren't pleased with eighty-eight-
year-old Guy Lee, said to be running an opium den. Nor were they entirely
comfortable with the influx of Chinese to the lower end of town, many of
them ex–railroad workers now digging Canyon County's irrigation ditches.

Few of the Cantonese immigrants had ever felt much at home in Caldwell either. These "coolies" had been brought in by the thousands to lay track
on the Union Pacific, and when those jobs ran out, they dispersed to the
mining camps. By 1870, the Idaho Territory had the largest concentration of
Chinese in the trans-Mississippi West outside California: 4,274, or 28 percent
of its population of 14,999. Appropriately enough, for a people who'd come in
search of the "Golden Mountain," some five hundred of them worked gold-
mining claims along the Snake River Canyon southeast of Caldwell. Tolerated by the earliest pioneers, they were not welcomed by white miners
determined to defend their turf. Indeed, all along the Pacific Coast and
through much of the Rocky Mountain West, Chinese immigrants encountered fierce resistance from laboring men, who saw them as threats to their
livelihood.

Soon this opposition took its toll. By 1900, the Chinese foothold in Idaho
had shrunk to 1,467. In 1904, when a lone Chinese man disembarked from a
stagecoach in Twin Falls, 180 miles down the Snake River from Caldwell, a
citizens' committee gave the "venturesome Celestial" the best meal the town
afforded, then took him to the ferry and told him to "hit the breeze" for
Shoshone. "The idea that Chinamen are a factor in civilization," noted the
Twin Falls News, "is not entertained here."

Nor was it entertained in Caldwell. In 1886, the Anti-Chinese League
resolved that, since the Chinese were "unsocial in their habits, treacherous in
their instincts, and barbarous in their nature," it would "prevent the further
influx of Chinese" and would seek to "rid ourselves of those who are already
in our midst." By 1890, the last Chinese had been expelled from town.

By the new century's first decade—with their numbers, and thus their
perceived threat, considerably diminished—they filtered back but once again
met resistance. Several Chinese restaurant men were driven from the area—
sometimes by municipal authorities, sometimes by young toughs who played
"football" with the restaurants' fancy crockery. In nearby Emmett, the town
marshal ordered Charlie Tong to leave town after he was accused of "famili-
arities with little girls." That same evening another "Chinaman" was severely
beaten.

When the governor and John Rice announced plans in 1903 to launch a
Caldwell beet sugar factory, the *Tribune* warned that this would encourage the

employment of Chinese and Japanese. "Will they endure to see the white man brought into direct competition with the raw fish-eating Orientals?...Did not Caldwell rise in her majesty a dozen years ago and expel from her noble precincts the radish raising Chinaman?"

Caldwell wasn't exactly partial to Jews, Negroes, Italians, Indians, or Basques either. The one Jewish merchant—clothier Isidor Mayer—was something of a curiosity. One Halloween, he found his shop door blocked by a huge boulder, which took four men an hour to dislodge.

Always ready for a little foolery himself, Frank Steunenberg once gave a dinner party served by a Negro who was positively obsequious to the governor and his guests: "Yassuh, boss" and "Sho nuff, boss" and all that. Only at dinner's end did the servant reveal himself as Sam Clay, a senior clerk at the Caldwell Trust and an old family friend, who had used handfuls of ash from the iron stove to make himself up in blackface. They all had a big laugh that evening.

No Negroes lived in town (in 1900, a scant 293 could be found in the entire state). Some of Caldwell's young folk had never seen one, save for McKanlam's Colored Vaudeville troupe, which played once a year at Isham's Opera House. Occasionally, a couple of black prizefighters, known as "thugs," came down from Boise to do battle for the delectation of the Pastime Club. Two of the best riders in Caldwell's renowned Fourth of July parade were ranch hands named Nigger Bill and Indian Jake. People said the colored boy could ride anything that wore hair, but that didn't mean they wanted him at their supper table.

Basque herders had begun to emigrate to Canyon County's sheep country but from the start were vigorously resisted by ranchers already working that range. Terming the swarthy newcomers "filthy, treacherous and meddlesome," the *Tribune* warned that "unless something is done [they] will make life impossible for the white man."

The governor's first errand that snowy afternoon was to Al Isham's office in the Opera House Block for the physical examination he needed to renew his life insurance. One of Caldwell's most indefatigable entrepreneurs, Dr. Albert Franklin Isham had emigrated from his native Vermont to Idaho in 1883 to serve as the Oregon Short Line's assistant surgeon. The next year, he resigned the post to settle in Caldwell and devote himself to a thriving private practice and a new pharmacy and soda fountain on Main Street. Caldwell's doctors often doubled as pharmacists, filling their own prescriptions, rolling their own pills. Later Isham launched a creamery to supply the town with fresh milk and butter, bought the Pacific Hotel, and built a new brick building to house his drugstore and medical office, rental business suites, and the Caldwell opera house.

Like a thousand other "opera houses" in towns across the land, Isham's had never played host to a real opera, and wasn't likely to. In nineteenth-

century America, the word *theater* still had a disreputable ring, so managers
routinely called their houses something else—usually "opera house" but
occasionally "museum," "auditorium," or "academy of music"—to reassure
virtuous ladies and high-minded gentlemen that attendance wouldn't blight
their prospects for salvation.

Caldwell's opera house was a modest theater, with rows of benches
toward the back, lines of kitchen chairs, and a few proper theater seats
(thirty-five cents if reserved in advance), with boxes draped in velour flanking
the stage. Before long it was a regular stop for vaudevillians, blackface minstrel shows, itinerant culture on the Chautauqua lecture circuit, as well as
traveling theatrical companies. Audiences were too small to attract New York
road companies, but the house got regional troupes out of Chicago or Denver,
sometimes traveling by wagon. It was attractive to some companies because it
helped round out their schedules between Salt Lake City and Portland.
Graduation services and political rallies filled the rest of the bill.

The governor attended the theater every chance he got. A passionate fan
of the dramatic arts, he preferred "those entertainments that pictured the
lighter side of life." Nobody could laugh more heartily than he, great guffaws
rumbling out of that substantial belly.

The opera house's impresario, at age forty-seven, was a striking figure
with a handlebar mustache, dark hair slicked with pomade, and piercing eyes.
A bit of a dandy, Isham managed to appear onstage in a formal cutaway at
every program, if only to announce coming attractions, and his appearances
grew more elaborate as he ran for—and became—mayor. Though he had a
wife, Lida, and two daughters at home in his handsome Main Street residence, he was a notorious ladies' man who carried on a long surreptitious
affair with Laura Patton, a Caldwell schoolteacher. He was also a skilled
physician, regularly attending the Steunenberg family. That afternoon, finding the governor in good health, he certified as much to the New York Life
Insurance Company.

From the doctor's office, the governor crossed the street to his bank, the
Caldwell Banking and Trust Company. That crossroads—Seventh and Main
—was the heart of Caldwell's business district and its most prestigious inter-
section. To the north, at the end of Seventh Avenue, loomed the Union
Pacific–Oregon Short Line depot; to the south, the site of the new Italian
Renaissance city hall, for which ground was soon to be broken. The four
corners in between boasted the Saratoga Hotel, the Caldwell Banking and
Trust Company, the First National Bank, and the Odd Fellows Building.

In the middle of Seventh Avenue, north of Main, stood the bandstand on
which the eighteen-piece Caldwell Cornet Band—the ultimate expression of
community pride in turn-of-the-century America—under the baton of its
"musicologist," Professor A. T. Gordon, performed each Friday evening from
April through November. With snow banked up on all sides, the bandstand
didn't look inviting that night. But the governor relished soft summer eve-

nings when the whole town turned out, tapping their feet to the rat-a-tat-tat of the snare drums, singing along with those grand old patriotic airs. The setting sun glinted off the brass tuba, casting shimmers of golden light along Main Street; gray heads nodded over their knitting in camp chairs set against the bank's wall; sheep men, drowsy with beer, gawked from the windows of the Palace saloon.

The architectural vista at Seventh and Main inspired lofty comparisons. As plans for the new city hall were unveiled, the *Tribune* rhapsodized: "The scene that will present itself to a person as he steps off the train will be the most beautiful in the city." Aside from the hotel and the bank, "the two most handsome" buildings in town, "the city hall in the distance will remind [one] ... of Trinity Hall, Boston."

The governor had good reason to be proud of the bank he and his brother had erected only the previous year at a cost of $20,000. Seeking something truly distinctive, the Steunenbergs had turned to Idaho's preeminent architects, J. E. Tourtellotte and Company of Boise, who produced a structure quite unlike anything in town—a graceful building, perhaps a bit eccentric, but right up-to-date in the "commercial style" of the fashionable Boston architect H. H. Richardson. Boston was clearly in the minds of Caldwell's young citizens, just as the trees of Iowa had stuck in the governor's head.

Two stories high, the bank's red-brick facade was broken by rows of great white arches framing the windows. On the Main Street side, a stairway led down to Hart Norman's popular O.K. Barbershop, while a Romanesque doorway opened on a marble stairway leading up to the bank proper. The high-ceilinged main banking room presented a row of ornate brass tellers' cages across the rear wall and desks for junior officers up front; to the left and up a steep stairway was the Steunenberg brothers' three-room executive suite. Clerks filled the first room. As befitted a former governor, Frank occupied the spacious corner office, bathed in light from five arched windows. A.K., the bank's cashier and himself a former mayor of Caldwell, worked in a smaller adjacent room, overlooking Seventh Avenue. Office space in the rear was rented out to John Rice and the Rocky Mountain Bell Telephone Company. All the offices, and the connecting hallway, were lined with polished oak wainscoting, lending those chambers a sobriety distinctive in that raw townscape.

Theodore Bird, the agent the governor had agreed to meet in his office that afternoon, represented the nation's largest insurance company. New York Life had been active in Idaho for four decades, paying its first death claim there in 1865. Given the perils of western life, insurance was a popular commodity (nearly a third of those on whom New York Life paid death claims in nineteenth-century Idaho died violently, many by gunshot). The company—then in a spirited struggle with its major competitors, Mutual and Equitable—pressed its branch offices to recruit and hold clients. In 1895, it had established an elite rank of agents called Nylics, after the company's initials, who were awarded five escalating Nylic ranks in recognition of the business they brought in. Nylics were entitled to wear the appropriate badge on their watch chains. At company conventions, cheerleaders sang the "Nylic Song":

> *Nylic, Nylic, lic, lic, lic.*
> *When you write 'em, make 'em stick.*
> *Do we write 'em? Well I guess.*
> *Nylic! Nylic! Yes! Yes! Yes!*

Theodore Bird had displayed the requisite Nylic zeal in pursuing the governor's policy renewal. Barely forty-eight hours later, revelations of an immoderate pursuit of profit among these "protectors of widows and orphans" would drive New York Life's president, John A. McCall, from office. The insurance scandals—revelations of political slush funds, retainers paid to U.S. senators, huge sums to corrupt the press, a company-sponsored bordello called the House of Mirth—had already forced resignations by the chief executives at Equitable and Mutual.

But little of this was known to Bird and Steunenberg as they transacted their business. Handing over Dr. Isham's hour-old certificate and his new premium, the governor received a freshly endorsed policy, which he carefully folded into his coat pocket.

After the insurance man had left, the governor spoke briefly with his brother and with Sam Clay. If Frank then kicked his feet up on the big oak partner's desk—on which he liked to whittle with a favorite pen knife—and gazed out the wide windows at the ever-falling snow, he could have reflected on the solvency of his multiple enterprises. The Steunenbergs had realized a tidy profit from the sale of the *Tribune* to Rees Davis in 1893. "If we've enlarged our supply of the world's goods, we think we have earned them," they wrote in their last issue. "We bought the *Tribune* as a business proposition, have run it as a business proposition, and part with it on the same grounds." That rang with the brothers' steely realism, but one suspects it was something of a pose as well. They must have loved the newspaper game, since they couldn't stay out of it, at various times over the next decade owning part or all of the *Caldwell Record* and its successor, the *Caldwell News*.

But never again were they full-time newspapermen. By April 1894, Frank —with several Caldwell partners—was panning for gold in the hills north of Boise. "Mr. Steunenberg has great faith in the ultimate success of his venture," the *Tribune* reported, "and his host of Caldwell friends sincerely hope that inside of a year he will have acquired a few millions." He never hit the mining jackpot, but on the day of his walk, he held interests in gold and silver mines worth $1,800.

In 1894 as well, A.K., with John Rice, James Ballantyne, and others, founded the Commercial Bank. A decade later, when Frank was brought in as president, it became the Caldwell Banking and Trust Company. Spurred by

A.K.'s zeal, the brothers established other banks in St. Anthony, Paris, and Glenns Ferry, Idaho, and in Wallowa and Vale, Oregon, which eventually yielded the governor banking stock worth $12,000. Meanwhile, the brothers had moved into real estate with a land speculator, Colonel Charles A. Hand, laying out the "Steunenberg-Hand addition" in southeast Caldwell. With other parcels in town, the governor now had some $11,000 worth of prime building lots. Not to mention his four-hundred-acre sheep ranch near Bliss and other land in the Twin Falls area, now worth $16,000 but soon destined to quadruple in value owing to the irrigation project there. Then there were the 10,500 merino sheep Frank owned with Charles S. Coon, his share worth some $7,000; thirty-three shares in the Barber Lumber Company, $3,000; and his house and personal property, $3,600.

Altogether, the governor was worth more than $55,000—equivalent to almost a million in 1997 dollars—not bad for a forty-four-year-old who had come west eighteen years before with only the few hundred dollars he'd sunk in the *Tribune* and who had earned only $3,000 a year during his four years as governor. A few years back, the *Tribune* had said he was "getting rich."

And he wasn't through by any means. "We are here for the money," A.K. had proclaimed years before, and, indeed, money seemed these days to be the governor's preoccupation. Several weeks earlier, he'd written an Idaho industrialist a letter brimming with fresh prospects for profit:

> My business ventures are all looking well—some of them a trifle slow—but safe. What mining deals I am in are all being conducted in the other fellow's money—I am at such hand every day, either with the sheep, at the ranch or in the timber, and I have within the last month looked up a number of new things, and have two that are good viz, one, an irrigation deal of 12,000 acres in Eastern Idaho; some one of the roads building west will have to come through it.... I have also investigated the timber belt of Eastern Oregon on the lower Grande Ronde and entire Wallowa rivers. It is the best lumbering chance I have ever seen.... If I find time this winter I will try to float a deal on both these propositions.

Yet prosperity hadn't brought the governor peace of mind. The sepia photographs and other memorabilia of his gubernatorial years that covered his office walls never failed to stir a sense of loss, even bereavement. His years in public office had begun, as did many such careers in the West, with the very process of state making. In 1889, his neighbors chose him as one of nine delegates to represent Ada County (Canyon County wasn't carved out of Ada until 1892) in the convention called to write the Idaho constitution. Thus emboldened, he won a seat the next year in the first state legislature, served two terms on Caldwell's city council and a stint as Canyon County auditor. By August 1894, as his gold-mining operation failed to pan out, the *Tribune* reported that Steunenberg was getting serious about politics and henceforth would "engage actively" in it, and as a Democrat, too, although his father and brothers were all Republicans—another sign of his stubborn independence. Soon he seized the critical position of secretary to the Democratic State Committee and from there made a nimble leap into the governor's office.

Frank couldn't escape the feeling that high office had been snatched away from him unjustly, that he'd been blamed unfairly for mishandling labor unrest in the state's northern panhandle. In 1900, recognizing that his gubernatorial days were over, he'd made a bold bid for a U.S. Senate seat, only to be humiliated by his "arch enemy," the former Republican senator Fred T. Dubois. Sensing a power vacuum among the Democrats, the shrewd Dubois simply walked in, took over, and ensured his return to the Senate on the Democratic ticket. In 1902, Steunie—as the Dubois faction contemptuously called him—tried to regain control of the party, hoping to install his sidekick Frank Martin as governor, then capture Dubois's Senate seat for himself. Instead, he was soundly thrashed again.

By now Dubois had a firm grip on the state's Democratic machinery, keeping Steunenberg at bay. Moreover, the continued flood of conservative Midwestern emigrants, particularly from the governor's native Iowa, had helped transform Idaho into a largely Republican state, erecting additional barriers to his ambitions. For all these reasons, Steunenberg took a couple of years off from politics in 1903–04.

But the old itch kept demanding to be scratched. With Fred Dubois's term in the Senate running out in March 1907, Steunenberg dreamed of paying his old rival back. "There was strong talk of running him again," recorded his sister Jo. His frequent trips around the state, to visit his sheep ranches, banks, and irrigation projects, were convenient excuses to get back in touch with his supporters. Only that past summer, he and his son Julian had made a six-week trip by buckboard and pony to the Salmon City area in central Idaho, ostensibly to do some salmon and trout fishing but trolling in other waters as well. He was a natural campaigner; even his critics conceded that he was "a great, open-minded fellow, hearty and cordial in his actions and manner of speech." For months, he'd been spending three or four days a week in Boise, now a burgeoning city of 18,000,* or elsewhere in the state, talking with merchants, bankers, farmers, and sheep ranchers, returning to Caldwell and his family only on weekends.

On election day that fall, he and Sam Clay had been talking politics when Frank exclaimed, "Oh, I love it! It's a great game and I would rather play it than to do anything." He surely did miss politics. People kept telling him he could win. After New Year's, there'd be some tough judgments to make.

As the governor left his office around five o'clock, he paused for a moment in the blowing snow to cast a proprietary glance at the family's latest venture: the half-sunk foundation of a matching office building, to be called the Steunenberg Block, which would soon rise beside the bank. Excavation

---

* By 1905, Idaho's population had barely reached the 200,000 mark.

had begun three months before and, though construction had been suspended for the winter, the two-story brick structure was scheduled for completion by summer. Three broad-shouldered emporia would elbow one another at street level, with offices on the floor above. And the name Steunenberg would be carved in a rectangular parapet above the second-story windows. The governor could be pardoned if he relished the notion of future generations seeing his name there chiseled in stone, impervious to wind, storm, or the passage of time.

The Steunenberg Block was one of a host of downtown projects that had already broken ground or were in an advanced stage of planning. The acquisitive town sizzled with rumors about the latest ventures, fresh real estate purchases, mysterious strangers from back East said to be buying land on the sly, snapping up buildable lots before they were gone. "Get hold of all the town lots you can," a Caldwell businessman confided to a reporter down from Boise, "buy them with as little payment as possible, then put on a long face and hold out to the end."

By 1905, Caldwell was enjoying a classic boom. Within five years, it had added electric power (the generators didn't come on until dusk and shut off at midnight), two telephone companies (many merchants subscribed to both companies, proudly advertising "both phones"), a municipal waterworks, Idaho's first public park, new county fairgrounds, a flour mill, a creamery, a new hotel, several dozen stores, and start of construction on a new city hall "suitable to the wealth and dignity of this city." One week that fall, seven private homes were under construction in various parts of town.

The Oregon Short Line was so overburdened with freight and traffic in and out of Caldwell that some businessmen thought of chipping in and hiring a man "to help the boys at the depot." That didn't mean the Short Line and its parent, the Union Pacific, were beloved institutions in Caldwell. Indeed, all along those tracks, the "railrogues" were Idahoans' favorite objects of derision. Folks could remember not so many years before when Populist orators spoke from a wagon near the Odd Fellows Hall in the light of a great bonfire made of railroad ties from "the great monopoly Union Pacific." Now the *Evening Capital News* of Boise could carp: "The Oregon Short Line Railway seems to be short in more ways than one, short in engines, short in cars, short in service, short in light for its cars and short in efficient officials."

Merchants, farmers, and mine operators alike seethed at the freight rates, which they considered extortionate—as well as at the railroads' practice of heavy rebates to the biggest shippers, like Standard Oil and Armour, which only drove rates up for smaller customers. These widespread abuses had stoked explosive resentment across the country, which Frank Norris, the California muckraker, captured in his 1901 polemic, *The Octopus*, depicting the iron horse as "the galloping monster, the terror of steel and steam, with its single eye, Cyclopean...flinging the echo of its thunder over the reaches of the valley, leaving blood and destruction in its path; the Leviathan, with tentacles of steel clutching into the soil, the soulless Force, the iron-hearted Power, the Monster, the Colossus, the Octopus."

Judge Frank J. Smith of the Seventh Judicial District, which included Caldwell, feared that the railroads' clout could only stir deep unrest in Canyon County. "Conditions in Idaho," he warned in a press interview, "are bad enough to make anarchists of nearly everybody." The root of the problem, he thought, was blatant favoritism in railroad taxation. "The railroads [in Idaho] are assessed at the rate of $9,500 a mile. In Montana they are assessed at $16,000 a mile." Some Idaho trackage, he thought, was easily worth $25,000 a mile. On the other hand, the judge remarked, when the tax assessor visits the lowly shack of the homesteader, he "notes the sewing machine, the lone cow, a pig, half a dozen chickens and levies an assessment on each for their true value. No wonder the people have anarchistic tendencies."

Quick to feel the depth of public anger, Wisconsin's Progressive senator, Robert La Follette, had launched a well-publicized investigation of railroad income. In Washington, President Roosevelt made railroad rate regulation his top priority: that very month he demanded legislation that would at last give the Interstate Commerce Commission authority to prevent the railroads from imposing "unjust or unreasonable rates."

As the governor crossed Seventh Avenue, he approached the pale cream facade of the Saratoga Hotel, Caldwell's principal hostelry, the fulcrum of its social life. One of divers hotels across the land—as well as a Chicago bordello and a Dodge City saloon—named after the swanky New York racing resort, it was further evidence of Caldwell's homage to eastern models. A dandy little hotel for a town this size, it belonged to a rival banker, Howard Sebree, president of the First National Bank, who'd entrusted the management to his son Ralph. The Sebrees had spared no expense to create an establishment "first class in all its appointments and fully up to the requirements of the place for many years." For $2.50 a night, each of its fifty rooms supplied hot and cold running water, steam heat, and electric light, courtesy of the Sebrees' own Caldwell Power Company. They had spent upwards of $40,000 on construction and furnishings.

Built in the French château style popular at the moment, the Saratoga had a mansard roof with a line of dormer windows, corner turrets, a Palladian window, and bay windows flanking the canopied Main Street entrance. From that arched doorway, a broad corridor led to a rotunda, where tables provided blackjack, faro, and roulette to meet the needs not just of hotel guests and local gamblers but of the big spenders who came through town on stagecoaches bound for California. Farther back was a comfortable bar, the favorite watering hole for the town's more prosperous merchants; a spacious dining room that, gourmands down from Boise were pleased to report, set "a very good table"; and an adjacent ballroom, where, on St. Patrick's Day, 1904, one hundred invited couples had waltzed and reeled into the wee hours to celebrate the hotel's grand opening.

The governor was a man of fixed habits: every Saturday he was in Caldwell, he crossed the Saratoga's threshold just before six to pick a *Tribune* from the stack of papers on the gift shop counter. Press time was 5:00 p.m. Saturday—and the first bundle always went to the Saratoga—so these copies were barely an hour old. There they were now, the ink still wet on the grainy paper, smudging slightly under the pressure of his thumb. How he loved that smell. It swept him back nearly three decades to his days as an apprentice at the Knoxville *Express,* where one of his tasks had been to carry the papers from the press to waiting delivery wagons. The aroma of wet ink and pulpy newsprint had lingered in his nostrils ever since, the sweet fragrance of fresh news.

Sinking into a creaking leather chair in the Saratoga bar room, hard by a fire in the brick hearth, Caldwell's first citizen may have ordered a cup of the hotel's mulled cider—strictly nonalcoholic—to ward off the blizzard's chill. Then, with a palpable flush of satisfaction, he spread the good old *Tribune* on his knee and began his practiced perusal.

Under "Commissioners' Proceedings," he would have noticed with deep satisfaction that the Canyon County Board of Commissioners had that week opened sealed bids for $62,605.20 in bonds to fund the new courthouse, a project for which the governor had strenuously campaigned the autumn before. After years of palaver, the county would finally have a real temple of justice, a bright, clean place in which the district judge and the probate judge could dispense due process.

Another page 1 item announced the imminent arrival of yet another fraternal organization to go with the town's Elks, Odd Fellows, Masons, and Knights of Pythias lodges, the sturdy foci of its social life. "An Eagle Aerie will be instituted in Caldwell on the evening of January 10," it said. The Aeries of Pocatello, Weiser, Nampa, Boise, and Mountain Home would attend. And the paper brought welcome news: the Reverend William Judson Boone had married the children of two of the governor's oldest friends. John J. Plowhead, a promising attorney and the son of his former banking partner Jacob Plowhead, had quietly wed Ella Horn, the daughter of the town's veteran newsdealer Jake Horn.

On page 3, the governor surely skipped chapter 9 of "The Wife's Secret, or a Bitter Reckoning," by Charlotte M. Braeme, a novel the *Tribune* was running in weekly installments. But if his eye strayed to an adjacent column of aphorisms, he might have smiled at a few of the pallid pleasantries: " 'Many a man,' says one of the lady journalists, 'has fallen in love with a dimple.' Yes, and discovered later that it was only a wrinkle."

On page 4, the *Tribune* published a self-serving colloquy:

"Where are you going to, my pretty maid?"
"I'm going a shopping, sir," she said.
"And who gets all your valued trade?"
"The store that advertises, sir," she said.

Finally, toward the back of the paper was a column of "personals," long the most popular of the *Tribune's* features. The governor noticed that his brother Pete got a mention that week: "Mr. and Mrs. Ettenger of New Plymouth were among those who spent Christmas in Caldwell. They were the guests of Mr. and Mrs. C. B. Steunenberg." There was news of the younger set: "Miss Dolly Dement entertained about 20 of her High School classmates Tuesday evening. The young people spent a most enjoyable evening." And dispatches from the world of agriculture: "A splendid milk cow and 50 February lambs for sale by V. D. Hannah."

In a quarter hour, the governor skimmed the cream off the week's news. Just then, he heard the whistle at the Caldwell Steam Laundry, which blew four times daily—at 8:00 a.m., noon, 1:00 p.m., and 6:00 p.m.—to mark off the town's working day for those who didn't carry a watch. It was time to head home; the rest of the paper would have to wait until supper was done. Folding the *Tribune* into a neat square, he stuffed it in his overcoat pocket. In the lobby, he exchanged a few words with Mike Devers, manager of the Caldwell Clothing Store across the street and a charter member of the Bachelors' Club, who'd stopped by for a drink or two at the crowded bar; he waved to Alex Ballantyne, who, with his brother Hiram, ran a mining supplies company just down the block. Then, sniffing the wood smoke curling from his neighbors' chimneys, Frank Steunenberg set off through the darkening evening toward his own glowing hearth.

Caldwell was known as a "Saturday night town," with stores staying open late for the benefit of ranchers and sheepmen who came in to pick up supplies, then make a round of the saloons, perhaps ending up at a dance hall or bordello in Tough Town (where one madam offered a weekend special for hands who wanted to sleep into Sunday). The storm discouraged pedestrians that night; yet, with New Year's Eve impending, shoppers scurried under the new carbide street lamps, returning Christmas gifts or laying in delicacies for the approaching revels. At the hitching posts along Main Street, teams in harness and gleaming saddle horses stomped and steamed in the blowing snow.

Store windows were decked with illuminated balls, red and green crepe paper, and heaps of pine boughs. Every shop made its unique appeal to holiday appetites. Baker and Ford, a fancy grocery, offered crocks of hot sauerkraut, roasted oysters, and mincemeat. The Steunenberg household spent fully twenty-five dollars each month at Baker and Ford, for the governor was a renowned trencherman. Food was plentiful and cheap in Caldwell: with creamery butter thirty cents a pound, breakfast bacon sixteen cents a pound, honey ten cents a pound, it was hard for Frank to stop eating. In a typically self-deprecating letter, he wrote his parents in 1890: "I only weigh 212 pounds —a falling off of one-half (1/2 pound) during the year. If this rate continues it will only take 424 years to reduce me to nothing.... Still I confess, I would rather pine away to nothingness at the rate of one-half lb. per year than to be guaranteed perpetual existence with a gain of one-half pound per year; for instance, at the age of 5,000 years I would weigh 2712 pounds, which you all will agree would be somewhat of a burden even in 'Sunny Idaho.' "

It wasn't so much his size that made people cock an eye at the governor; it was the way the weight was distributed, much of it packed around his stubby neck and sloping shoulders, then again just above his belt. A long swatch of auburn hair was invariably plastered flat across his right forehead. The cumulative picture of awkward dishevelment gave many people the feeling there was something "a little bit different" about Frank. One amiable commentator said he was "a fit subject for a portrait by Rembrandt." Another thought he had "the face of a Roman Senator," but not the heroic features of Marcus Antonius, more the slightly cockeyed visage of Popilius Lena. A friend fondly remarked, "He didn't have so many peculiarities, but those he did have, he hugged very close to him."

Farther down the block, Eddie Adam, the mustachioed newsdealer in his bowler hat, who'd recently had a large abscess on his cheek lanced, was back at his old stand offering periodicals, "peerless root beer," ice cream sodas, cigars, and exotic tobaccos ("Better smoke on earth than in hell," he advertised). Tom Little, the cranky Irishman who ran the town's largest dry goods store, displayed silks and linens and Hart, Schaffner, and Marx tweeds. Isham's Opera House Pharmacy tempted passersby with French bouillon and oyster cocktails.

It had been a profitable season for the town's merchants. The day after Christmas, the *Statesman*'s Caldwell correspondent reported: "Never before in the history of Caldwell have the holiday sales of the several stores at this place been greater. Never before have there been more presents sent away to friends both east and west. Never were there fewer poor. This all evidences that the people of this section are prosperous and look forward toward the future with a most hopeful outlook."

The reporter's comforting assertion about the dwindling poor, accurate enough in its broad strokes, disguised more than it clarified. The poor were still there in ample numbers, though difficult to track to any locality, for Caldwell hadn't yet fragmented into socially or economically homogeneous districts. The only section in which the working class had begun to predominate was the "Golden Gate" strip along the Boise River, designated as the yards for the new San Francisco, Idaho, and Montana Railroad. But the working poor often lived side by side with substantial citizens: Walter Sebree, proprietor of the Caldwell Power Company, and George Chaple, manager of the Independent Telephone Company, for example, built substantial homes right down the street from several boardinghouses chockablock with Italian quarry workers and Greek railroad laborers.

There were no enterprises in town large enough to attract a working-class settlement. The county's biggest employers were its ambitious irrigation schemes, which recruited hundreds of Asians and southern Europeans to dig and maintain the "ditches." Carpenters, masons, roofers, and the like—at a premium in Caldwell's construction boom—also worked all over town. None of the town's individual firms—livery stables, flour mills, lumber companies, plow and tractor dealers, the brickyard, creamery, bottling works, or even the two telephone companies—employed more than a dozen or so workers apiece.

Nonetheless, Caldwell had a tradition of labor organizing. In 1888, the Knights of Labor had founded a Caldwell branch—Local Assembly 1118— embracing a curious amalgam of agricultural workers, day laborers, skilled craftsmen, even a few small merchants. For the Knights drew their principal distinction not between labor and capital but between producers and parasites. Only the latter—a category that lumped lawyers, bankers, gamblers, and saloonkeepers—were rigidly excluded. In 1894, Caldwell's Knights nearly put their own candidate in the state legislature. But ground down by friction with craft unions, the Knights of Labor atrophied both nationally and locally. By the turn of the century, Assembly 1118 had dwindled away.

Then, early in 1903, Caldwell's blacksmiths organized to exact what advantage they could from the relentless demand for their services. Led by Al Butts and Tom Ward, two renowned wielders of hammers and tongs, they seemed destined to become Caldwell's first independent craft union. Something intervened. For three weeks later, the smiths voted to cast their lot instead with the American Labor Union, a Chicago-based federation that, professing its faith in Socialism, had set out to wrest working-class allegiance from Samuel Gompers's sober American Federation of Labor. Though the blacksmiths retained leadership of the Caldwell branch, with Butts as president and Ward as treasurer, other officers represented a wide spectrum: Loren Tompkins, a carpenter; Frank Hardy, operator of the Exchange saloon (whose occupation would have excluded him from the Knights); and Herb Van Housen, proprietor of the Pioneer Barn. According to the *Tribune,* the branch's first fifty-five members were drawn from "nearly all the trades of the city." Interest in the new organization was intense; by month's end, its membership neared a hundred.

The *Tribune* welcomed the new union to town, with deep misgivings about its Socialist principles. Caldwell's merchants were even more distrustful of the larger unions muscling up in metropolitan centers to do battle with corporate trusts. Indeed, the town looked with suspicion on all "combinations"—as such agglomerations of economic power were known—whether assembled by labor or by capital.

What true destitution persisted in Caldwell was widely scattered: itinerant farmworkers, out-of-work ranch hands, out-of-luck miners who drifted through Caldwell, pitching tents or building shacks on vacant lots along the railroad right-of-way, even on undeveloped stretches of up-and-coming Cleveland Boulevard. Furnished rooms were so "desperately scarce" in town that the *Tribune* offered to run ads for them free of charge.

In that winter of 1905, few of Caldwell's citizens dwelled much on endemic poverty (any more than most Americans had heeded Robert Hunter's bold assertion in his book *Poverty*, published the year before, that fully ten million persons lived in poverty in a nation of eighty million). So vigorous was the town's economy, so busy its construction crews, so roseate its prospects, it was easy for its citizens to forget the squalor of the "money shuffle," which in many cases had sent them trekking west in the first place. As the new year began, the deposits in Caldwell's three banks together totaled nearly $1.5 million. An editorial in the *Tribune* had assumed the voice of an imaginary man who'd left Caldwell to prospect for wealth in California and was now back for a look at his old town. "Ought to have staid here with the other boys, and I would now be with them on millionaire row," he moaned. "Wealth just seems to grow here in Caldwell. Beats the world. Everybody getting rich."

The community's general air of well-being was reflected in the bustling jollity of Caldwell's holiday festivities, formally ushered in on Saturday, December 23, with Christmas exercises at three downtown churches. The most impressive were those at the Presbyterian Church, the house of worship that attracted many of Caldwell's leading citizens. Belle Steunenberg had stood proudly among its founders, a teacher in its Sunday School, a doyenne of the congregation, a community leader "jeweled with Christian graces," until her inexplicable defection to Caldwell's tiny eight-member Adventist Church when it was inaugurated a year before—an act of such breathtaking betrayal it had left a strong residue of resentment in the front pews.

To assuage some of the bitterness among Belle's former congregation, the governor still attended an occasional Presbyterian service, though without much enthusiasm. He once confessed to a friend that "his church attendance, he feared, was prompted more by anticipation of an intellectual treat than spiritual improvements." He had to concede that the Presbyterians knew how to put on a show. That Saturday, the adult choir's "Joy to the World" had been followed by songs from the youngest congregants, including a solo by the governor's niece, Grace van Wyngarden, still pale from her bout of typhoid; a "Rock of Ages" pantomime by Mrs. Stone's class, the young ladies dressed as the heavenly host, all in gold and silver, with wings sprouting from their shoulders; and finally the smallest child of all, Gladys Gordon, singing a "rock-a-bye" with the aplomb of a prima donna and "a clear, sweet voice which sounded to the roof."

Then a portly member, dressed as Santa Claus, pulled up in a sleigh and, taking his traditional position in the choir loft, delivered a gay, bantering speech. "Have all you children been good this year?" he asked to squeals of affirmation. Descending to the foyer, Santa opened his sack, tossing out green net bags tied up with crimson yarn, each containing candy, nuts, and a bright golden orange. All this in the glow of an admirable balsam—which the congregation's men had cut in the crisp air of the Owyhee Mountains—now dressed out in cardboard angels and colored balls and illuminated this year, for the first time, by genuine electric lights.

At noon on Christmas Day, the governor and Belle had attended the traditional family dinner at A.K.'s house. The hustling young entrepreneur and his family occupied an imposing Colonial Revival mansion, its great front portico supported by three Tuscan columns, approached by a new cement sidewalk on North Kimball Avenue, where the city's "quality" clustered in the lee of the Presbyterian Church.

Although Frank, A.K., and their wives certainly ranked among Caldwell's first families, they were less self-assured than they appeared. In a town that had long cherished the notion of unrestrained opportunity, the uncomfortable specter of social class reared its head. When James Munro, a clerk in the Steunenberg bank, married Estella Cupp, the eldest daughter of the town's most prominent real estate broker, the *Tribune* called them "popular young society people"—a frank recognition that a "smart set" was coalescing in this nominally egalitarian community. A Young Man's Dancing Club invited these socially active young people to occasional soirees at Armory Hall.

Some of Caldwell's new elite never quite felt they belonged. During a prolonged stay in the nation's capital, Frank Steunenberg shied away from the fashionable dinner parties to which he was invited. "Why," he told a friend more eager than he to see how the smart set lived, "to accept one of these invitations means the wearing of an evening costume and what a pretty figure I would cut!"

A. K. Steunenberg had a thick sheaf of credentials. But consider his reaction as a guest of Bob and Adell Strahorn, the most worldly members of Caldwell's inner circle, at their summer home in northern Idaho. "You can imagine my consternation when I 'butted' into a regular dress suit card party," A.K. wrote his wife. "I was the only one who did not wear a white front and a claw hammer. And to make matters worse they played a game called 500 I think that I had never played before. Being like a fish out of water anyhow that did not tend to give me any reassurance.... I sailed in and got through without making any very bad breaks or spilling my coffee. The ladies were perfectly lovely and seemed to try and relieve my embarrassment and I guess the men did too.... The main theme of conversation at the card party was the help problem ... not being able to procure help of any kind."

None of these insecurities could be detected that Christmas afternoon as a gracious A.K. welcomed the boisterous clan beneath his portico. No fewer than thirty Steunenbergs gathered around the heavily laden table, headed by the seventy-two-year-old patriarch, Bernardus, a shoemaker by trade, a Mexican War veteran who'd come west from Iowa to join his children earlier that year. Seven of his ten offspring were there that afternoon: five sons—Frank; A.K.; Pete, the most raffish of the brothers, a part-time printer who sometimes dealt cards down at the Saratoga; Will and John, lifelong bachelors and partners in a shoe store ("Fitters of Feet," they called themselves) just behind the Saratoga—and two daughters—Elizabeth ("Lizzie"), married to Gerrit van Wyngarden, a Caldwell contractor who'd built both Frank's house and the new Caldwell Banking and Trust building, and Josephine ("Jo"), at thirty-four still unmarried, who made a home for John, Will, and Bernardus at her commodious house on Belmont Street, while finding time to repair Frank's shirts as well. The "plump" and "jolly" A.K. played Santa at his own festivities, distributing elaborately wrapped gifts to all the children.

The "social event of the season" took place that night, a gala masquerade ball at Armory Hall, next door to the Saratoga, attended by several hundred townspeople decked out in garish masks and costumes. Tailors in town did a booming business in rented evening wear of all kinds.

But the most celebrated holiday event that year was a progressive dinner called A Trip around the World, a benefit sponsored by the ladies of the Reading Room, representing many of the world's cultures through their distinctive food, drink, art, and language. The first such extravaganza ever held in Caldwell, it had an air of urbane sophistication that drew many of the town's leading citizens. Livery stables donated carriages to shuttle the gentry from house to house at half-hour intervals. It began at the home of J. G. Cowden, a preacher, with hot mulled punch and gingerbread cookies in a Boston setting; then on to Africa to examine the "pickaninnies" and taste stuffed dates at the residence of William C. Stalker, the town's leading dentist and ardent Prohibitionist; Holland at the home of realtor William Cupp, just recovering from a vicious kick by a horse at Campbell's livery stable; Japan, replete with a "magic fish pond," at attorney William Stone's; and finally La Belle France at the Blatchleys', where "Professor" Gipson—the Rhodes scholar's father—explained the oil paintings on the walls in French "to the amusement, if not the edification, of those present."

The town mounted professional exhibitions as well. On December 27, Isham's Opera House was packed for the Great McEwan, a hypnotist and prestidigitator who'd built a regional reputation with his recondite feats ("You'll laugh, you'll scream, you'll shriek at the antics of the hypnotic subjects"). The Methodist Church presented the Lilliputian Sisters, midgets named Lucy and Sara Adams, with an "amusing, elevating and refining" program of duets, dialogues, and posings. And, of course, there were countless private entertainments. One night, twenty-five young people gave a skating party at Scovel's Pond—a few show-offs competing for attention by carving fancy figures in the ice, while most couples were content to glide arm in arm in great lazy circles under the shimmering stars.

The night before the governor's walk had witnessed the season's grandest dinner party, cohosted by Caldwell's social arbiter, Queen Carrie Blatchley; William Judson Boone; and their spouses for a group of refined young couples, including two attorneys, an insurance agent, a pastor, and the manager of a lumber company. "Very pleasant," Boone recorded in his diary. "Fine time."

Indeed, to Boone, his guests, and many others, that winter in Caldwell seemed a fine time and place to be alive. Despite its early dependency, there lingered in town a fragile sense of autonomy—the notion that its citizens controlled their own destiny—which had animated so many American communities in decades past but which had widely atrophied of late. Perhaps because Idaho was the last of the forty-eight states to be entered by whites—it was settled almost as an afterthought by pioneers who'd pressed through to the Pacific Coast, then doubled back—the heady feel of self-determination hung on there longer than it did elsewhere. And with it came a certain egalitarianism, an impression—quixotic perhaps—that no man in town stood too far above another, that no path was permanently closed off to anyone who kept his shoulders in his work, his faith in Almighty God.

On that snowy night of the governor's walk, Caldwell looked for all the world like the quintessential nineteenth-century American community, sufficient unto itself, proof against an uncaring world. But there were ample warnings that this Currier and Ives print was no longer quite true to life. Many in town had felt the first whiff of anxiety that America's social landscape was changing, that corrupt forces were abroad in the land, relentlessly impinging on the autonomy Caldwell had taken for granted. Among these perceived threats were Chinese, Italian, Greek, and other swarthy immigrants; the railroads, resented for inflating freight rates and otherwise gouging customers; corporate trusts, concentrating ever-greater economic power in their hands; labor unions, meeting employers' challenges with conglomeration of their own; the relentless encroachments of class distinction. Even the impulse to purge the town of drink, gambling, and loose women seems to have grown, in part, from a forlorn hope that a newly purified community could better stave off external threats. But nothing stemmed the mounting uneasiness that Caldwell's citizens weren't fully in control of their own lives, that malign forces threatened their well-being.

Such perhaps were some of the bleak thoughts that had troubled the governor's sleep the night before. Now his mood may have lifted a bit as he negotiated the icy boardwalk along Main Street and swung back onto Kimball again, crossing Indian Creek, then retracing his steps up the wide, dim boulevard. As he followed the frozen plume of his breath, his boots crunching eight inches of freshly fallen snow, some of his fears may have been swept away, at least for the moment, by the dazzling whiteness of his beloved town. He could look forward to a hearty supper warming on the big iron stove, then a long winter's evening in the bosom of his family.

Entering Sixteenth Avenue, he could see the lamplight burning behind the columns of his front porch, the warm glow filtering through the lace curtains of his living room, where, minutes before, Belle and their two youngest children had knelt at their evening prayers. He reached down and pulled the wooden slide that opened the gate leading to his side door. As he turned to close it, an explosion split the evening calm, demolishing the gate, the eight-inch-thick gatepost, and the nearby fencing, splintering yards of boardwalk, scooping a shallow oval hole in the frozen ground, and hurling the governor ten feet into his yard.

At first, Belle thought the potbelly stove had exploded. But thirteen-year-old Frances, who was especially close to her father, had been eagerly glancing out the window, impatient for his arrival. Having seen the flash by the gate and watched Frank fall, she was at his side in a few seconds, joined almost immediately by Belle. For one terrible moment, mother and daughter stared in blank incomprehension at the governor, sprawled on his back, naked from the waist down, blood seeping from his mangled legs, staining the snow an ugly pink.

Across the street, the door to a modest one-story house burst open and C. F. Wayne, a nurseryman, rushed into his yard.

"Has anything happened?" he yelled.

"Come here, quick!" shouted Belle.

Wayne sprinted toward the side gate, through which he'd passed barely fifteen minutes before. He and his family had lived in Caldwell for three years, but he scarcely knew the Steunenbergs, having bought his property in the fall and moved in only on December 10. He'd glimpsed Frank Steunenberg from afar, though they'd never met face-to-face. But the boy who usually did the Steunenbergs' farm chores was away for the holidays and Wayne had agreed to handle them in his absence. That evening he'd milked the cows and fed the goats and chickens, finishing about six. After stopping off for a few words with Belle, he'd gone out through the side gate and home to his own dinner. He was taking off his overshoes when the blast tumbled chairs and shook dishes from the table. His wife thought it was an earthquake.

Now Wayne joined Belle at her husband's side. "Is this Mr. Steunenberg?" he asked. But the governor made no reply.

"How did this happen?" Wayne asked.

"Send for Mama," said the governor, although his wife was standing right there. Then he stirred and mumbled, "Who shot me?" Then, "Take me inside. I'm freezing."

Wayne tried to lift him, but not only was he too heavy for one man to carry, his lower body was so broken, his limbs "mere shreds of flesh," that the nurseryman dared not move him. To one townsman who saw the governor's heavy frame a few minutes later, it looked "as if mice had chewed his clothes," so riddled were they by fragments from the explosion. His favorite shirt, the one with the cheerful flowered pattern, now had a dozen holes in front to match its missing tail. For days thereafter, passersby were picking "little bits" of the governor out of the debris.

Most of the damage had been done to his right side, which had been turned toward the gate as he sought to close it. His left shoe and overshoe and his left glove were still "good as new," while not a shred of the right shoe or glove was ever found.

The governor grew impatient. "Why don't you take me in the house?" he demanded.

Wayne said he'd go for help. After admonishing Frances to telephone family friends, he raced out to Cleveland Boulevard, where he tried to rouse John Rice, but the lawyer's wife said he hadn't yet returned from arguing his big case in Boise. He tried two more neighbors before finding Bill Lesley, a richly mustachioed construction worker who lived a block southeast on Cleveland and had been shingling houses that year along the boulevard. Before Wayne and Lesley could get to the governor's house, Julian Steunenberg and Will Keppel came running. A sturdy youth with a shock of blond hair, strikingly like his father in face and figure, Julian had been particularly close to the governor. He and Will had been strolling two blocks behind him when they felt the explosion, then dashed with pounding hearts to Frank's side, where they were quickly joined by Gerrit van Wyngarden, the governor's brother-in-law, who lived two blocks west on Dearborn. Together the trio tried to lift the grievously wounded man, but as they did the flesh on his legs simply gave way. Finally, someone got a blanket, into which they placed the governor, managing to carry him that way into the house and lay him on a bed in his daughter's downstairs bedroom.

From all over Caldwell, townspeople streamed through the icy night toward the governor's house. Frances's first frantic phone call had reached Ralph Oakes, a family friend and co-owner, with his brothers Adrian and Charles, of the Oakes Brothers dry goods store on Main Street. Ralph believed the governor's boiler had exploded and passed the word.

When the bell at the Arthur Street firehouse began to toll, the town's able-bodied men followed a well-established routine. Anyone on Caldwell's streets with a team of horses raced to the firehouse—a shed tacked onto a shack called City Hall—where they hooked up the two hose carts, each with six hundred feet of hose, and the hook and ladder. (In this dollar-driven town, their haste wasn't entirely altruistic: the first wagon to reach the fire with a hose cart earned $2.50, the second $1.50.) Others grabbed axes and ladders. Even when they discovered that there was no fire at the Steunenbergs', folks kept coming. Eventually nearly five hundred persons—fully a fourth of the town—were gathered on Dearborn Street across from the governor's.

The Reverend Mr. Boone and his wife had been entertaining their closest friends, the Blatchleys, when they heard a "terrific" noise. They thought something had fallen on the roof.

Cy Decker, the bellboy at the Saratoga Hotel, was buying a sweet bun at Frank Wood's bakery, where they said a gasoline engine at the governor's house must have exploded.

A. B. "Shorty" Martin, who operated the Caldwell Steam Laundry, was eating supper at home. It was so cold he'd left the fire on under the boiler at the laundry; now he assumed it'd blown up. But reaching the laundry, he found the building intact. When the town's barber, Swain Beatty, an Iowa State boxing champion, ran up to tell him the trouble was over at the governor's house, they raced together across an apple orchard toward Dearborn Street. "Lord, it was cold," Martin remembered.

At A. K. Steunenberg's house, Josephine had come for supper. Everyone was sitting down to dinner when the chandelier rattled. At Sam Clay's house, the "dishes danced" on his table. Nearby, Pete Steunenberg thought the tank on his roof must have exploded. He called central. When the telephone girl said he was wanted at the governor's right away, he began to run.

Will Steunenberg had just eaten supper and was back at his store arranging a display of boots when the concussion spilled them on the floor. A minute later, Ralph Oakes rushed in to say there'd been an explosion at Frank's house. Will asked him to telephone for doctors and a team of horses, then took off up Dearborn Street. It was like trying to scramble across an ice floe in a nightmare. "The ground was so slippery it was very hard to run," he said later, describing how he'd slid a foot back for every two feet gained.

When he reached the house, his brother had already been moved inside. Belle was lighting kerosene lamps to replace the electric ones, for the neighborhood's electric power had been knocked out by the blast. Windows on the north and west sides of the house had been shattered, as had those in other houses for blocks around. Shards of glass littered the floors. A large clock had toppled from its shelf, striking five-year-old Frank Junior, who'd been lying on the leather couch below.

"Frank has shot himself somehow," Belle told Will, in a curious conclusion. "Hurry in there."

When Will entered the front bedroom, it was "horrible": the governor writhing on the bed, his right arm hanging by a few shreds, his right leg mangled, both legs broken at the ankles. He kept asking to have his legs rubbed.

Struggling to raise himself on his one good elbow, he said, "I'm a dead man."

Falling back, he asked twice to be turned on his side. When those around him complied, he said, "Turn me over on my belly." But he couldn't get comfortable. "Lift me up," he implored. "Lift me higher." They raised him to a sitting position.

Three of the town's doctors—John Gue, W. E. Waldrop, and John A. Myer—had arrived. There was nothing they could do.

Cradling his brother in his arms, Will asked him twice whether he'd seen anyone in the street before the explosion. The governor didn't answer, staring up at him with wide, stunned eyes. Although he spoke clearly enough, he couldn't seem to hear the questions, leading his family to assume that his eardrums had been broken by the bomb's concussive force.

Just past 7:10 p.m., he gasped three or four times, like a man trying to catch his breath, and muttered something unintelligible. As Will leaned closer, trying to hear those last syllables, the governor sank back and died.

Later, several newspapers and magazines reported that the dying governor had looked up at his wife and said, "What's the matter, Mother? What does it mean?"

Frank Steunenberg never uttered those words. But the questions were real enough, reflecting a thirst in the press and the public alike to know just what had happened that snowy evening in Caldwell. What sinister forces were lurking out there in the dark, waiting to strike down the best among them?

2

THE SWEATBOX

"FRANK DIED in my arms," Will wrote a sister in Iowa, "and I hope the fellow that killed him will also die in my arms, only in a different manner."

Dour and stern, with dark eyes glowering at the world above a fiercely bristling mustache, Will took after his Dutch forefathers. He had his crotchets: he grew indignant when anyone called him a cobbler, which suggested that all he did was patch up people's old shoes. He was a "shoemaker," a craftsman in leather, he insisted. The leader of the obdurate, implacable branch of the family, he brooded grimly over Frank's death. "Life has seemed to me like a never ending nightmare since this has happened," he wrote. "I feel just as though I didn't want to stay here anymore."

Pete Steunenberg was a more worldly man. Dealing cards at the Saratoga, he'd seen all sorts of people across the green felt tables and had learned to play life as it lay. An avid fly fisherman, he knew how to stalk his prey. A thoroughgoing pragmatist, he caught the stench of death as soon as he entered his brother's house that night, and he knew he could do nothing useful there. Even before Frank breathed his last, Pete turned and raced toward town, determined to gather some men and cut off the murderer's avenues of escape.

Tearing down the boulevard, he encountered Jasper P. "Jap" Nichols, the Canyon County sheriff, Undersheriff Frank Payne, and deputies Charles Paynter and Frank Breshears, coming fast in the other direction.

"Where you going?" huffed Pete.

"The gov's been blown up," said the sheriff.

"You can't do anything up there," Pete snapped, his dark eyes blazing. "The man who blew him up isn't sitting there waiting for you. Let's get busy in town."

At the wooden courthouse on Belmont Street, they assembled a posse. One of the first men they turned to was Dan Campbell, the livery stable operator, a former two-term sheriff and widely known "law and order" man. Within an hour, sheriff and former sheriff had deployed a hundred newly deputized men in a rough cordon around the town. Calls went out to neighboring communities—Nampa, Emmett, Wilder, Meridian—asking for volunteers to join the dragnet. John A. Baker, the feed store proprietor who doubled as town marshal, and constables W. B. Banks, John Henshaw, R. E. Bowman, and William Ames were assigned to stand guard at major roads and bridges out of town, on the watch for anyone behaving in a peculiar fashion. Others manned the railroad depot. The rest were stationed in woods and fields on Caldwell's outskirts, where they stopped ranchers and construction workers trudging homeward toward their suppers. One party followed the footprints of a man who'd been seen running from Steunenberg's place after the explosion and was said to have hightailed it down the railroad tracks. They set bloodhounds on the trail, but the drifting snow had erased all scent.

The explosion had been heard at Parma, sixteen miles west, but not in Boise, which was almost twice that distance. It took a phone call, shortly after 7:00 p.m., to alert Frank Gooding, Idaho's new Republican governor, at his home on fashionable Warm Springs Avenue; he rushed to the *Statesman* building seeking further information, then telephoned Sheriff Nichols for a briefing. About nine, the governor asked the Oregon Short Line for a special train to take him and his party to Caldwell.

At 9:43, an engine, passenger coach, and baggage car left the Boise depot, bearing some of the capital's leading figures, among them Governor Gooding; William E. Borah, a Boise attorney and prominent Idaho Republican; Frank Steunenberg's former lieutenant governor, Joseph H. Hutchinson; Frank Martin, the former attorney general; Sheriff David H. Moseley of Ada County (which encompassed Boise); and Sheriff Harvey K. Brown of Baker County, Oregon, who happened to be in Boise that night. Remaining space on the train—platforms, steps, even roofs—was jammed with other volunteers. Brandishing squirrel rifles, broom handles, and baseball bats, they bellowed their defiance into the dark. Everybody could tell they were on their way, since someone had tied down the train's whistle; its mournful tones could be heard for miles around, howling through the arctic night.

The trip from Boise to Caldwell normally took the best part of an hour; the "special" made it in forty minutes. The tracks were clear: at the governor's orders, all other trains moving through Canyon County that night were stopped and searched. Dismounting at the depot, the Boise dignitaries found the little square between the First National bank and the Odd Fellows Building thronged with townspeople eager for some target on which to vent their rage. Governor Gooding addressed them briefly, promising vigorous pursuit of the assassin, then convened "a council of war" attended by his advisers, some of the town's worthies, and A. K. Steunenberg, representing the family, in the chambers of Frank J. Smith, the district judge. For more than two hours they reviewed the enemies Steunenberg might have had, how he'd spent his last day, the most promising avenues for the investigation, and who would lead it. It was nearly 1:00 a.m. when they adjourned.

Meanwhile a dozen of the town's most substantial merchants met at the

Saratoga Hotel to organize a Citizens Committee, among them George Froman, a real estate man who'd been a government scout during the Indian
wars, later a deputy warden of the state penitentiary, and then Caldwell's
town marshal; Mike Devers of Bachelors' Club fame; Ralph Sebree, the
Saratoga's manager; Walter Sebree, proprietor of the Caldwell Power Company and manager of Caldwell's baseball team; Charles Oakes, like his brother
Ralph a close friend of the Steunenberg family; and Tom Little, the hardware
man and strutting martinet who until recently had been captain of the town's
National Guard company. This conclave pledged to find the perpetrator of
the outrage that had blighted their community's reputation.

The state, Governor Gooding told them, would put up $5,000 as a
reward for information leading to the bomber's capture. Soon the mine owners of Shoshone County in northern Idaho—where the late governor had
fought his most bitter struggle—added another $10,000. Canyon County,
whose seat was Caldwell, chipped in $1,000, hoping to authorize $5,000 as
soon as the county commissioners met. The Steunenbergs' Caldwell Banking
and Trust Company would put up $2,500 and other Caldwell businessmen
promised $2,500 more to make an even $25,000.

Although officers scoured the grounds around Steunenberg's house by
lantern light, it was not until the next morning that the governor's party
could assess the explosion's force. Drifting like specters through the mist,
investigators found pieces of iron, brass, copper, and gun wadding blown for
hundreds of yards in all directions. Iron scraps were pried from tree trunks
and clapboards. A fragment of Frank Steunenberg's hat brim was discovered
two hundred yards from the gateway.

On a nearby lawn, Sheriff Angus Sutherland of Shoshone County found
a dead yellowhammer, a bird with brilliant yellow and blue feathers, perfect
in every particular but blown from the skies by the blast. The sheriff took the
bird home to mount it on his mantelpiece. Considering its beauty and the
circumstances of its death, he wouldn't take fifty dollars for it.

One of the principal searchers was Joe Hutchinson, Steunenberg's lieutenant governor, a balding man with full lips and dreamy eyes. As he told
friends, his mood those dark hours had been a mix of grief for his dead friend,
rage at the assassin, and exasperation at the petty politics of the Republican
administration. A Democrat, he hadn't been invited to ride Gooding's special
train from Boise; he'd simply clambered aboard. Squeezed into a corner of
one carriage, the engineer with the pugnacious air of a prizefighter felt
"frozen out" by the governor's people. In Caldwell, he wasn't asked to join
Gooding's deliberations. So, "while Gooding and others were toasting their
cold feet by a warm fire, and pledging their lives and fortunes and sacred
honor to ferret out the murderers," he wrote a friend, "I went out myself to
examine the premises."

At first light, he scrutinized the area. A former mine owner and explosives expert, he knew what to look for. Sniffing a distinctive odor on Frank Steunenberg's hat brim, he announced that the principal ingredient of the bomb that had killed the governor was nitroglycerin, perhaps as dynamite.

Shortly, the investigators made another significant discovery. Scouring the roiled earth by the gate, they found a length of waxed silk fish line, one end of which was burned, and a part of a trigger mechanism to which the fish line had evidently been attached. Hutchinson concluded that the bomb itself had lain beside the north gatepost, which now had ceased to exist. The gate swung outward from the south post, which had been to the governor's right as he passed through. The north gatepost, with its deadly package, was to his left. Since the force of the explosion had been to his right leg and arm, Hutchinson reckoned the governor had been turning to close the gate when the bomb went off. But why hadn't it gone off when he opened the gate? Hutchinson concluded the assassin must have been hidden nearby, waiting until the governor was inside the gate before he pulled on the fish line, activating the trigger.

That Sunday morning, as Caldwell's most respectable citizens streamed out of services at the town's five churches, at which prayers were offered for Frank Steunenberg's soul, the streets were still gay with holiday decorations. Placards announced that four days hence William Judson Boone would give a lecture and demonstration of his famed "x-ray" machine, through which "you can see your bones."

But today the tiny community was thronged with detectives, Boise police officers, Caldwell constables, and newsmen, not to mention hundreds of country folk, drawn from farms, ranches, and villages for miles around by news of the night's events. Strange men with six-shooters at their belts were everywhere in town, "big, husky devils," Shorty Martin recalled.

Overnight, the dragnet had tightened around the town. Five "suspicious characters" had been detained. Now the search continued, as the authorities, augmented by the special deputies, scoured the community, picking up anyone who failed to give an adequate account of himself and his presence in Caldwell. Crockett Bales, who had the bad luck to arrive from Colby, Kansas, that week with his wife and children, bent on settling in Caldwell, was stopped by half a dozen detectives in those first hours and asked what he was doing in town.

So intense was this scrutiny that it struck some observers as excessive. A reporter for the *Capital News* found the investigation in "chaos," with "rumors fly[ing] thick and fast, but when run down they usually amount to nothing." A "multitude of officers, too many it would seem," were on the scene, several "working on private clues of their own."

It wasn't a complex search. The current boom notwithstanding, Caldwell was still a small town. No stranger could linger even a few hours without several townspeople's knowing what he looked like, where and what he drank, and with whom he consorted. As each suspect was apprehended, he was brought before a group known as "the sweatbox committee," which met at the courthouse. Sometimes the newspapers reported that a suspect was put "in the sweatbox," a term that proved so inflammatory the *Statesman* felt compelled to offer a clarification. Many readers, the paper explained, had assumed that the term was used literally, that it was "a place of torture... heated to an unbearable degree and the suspect thrust in it and kept there until he divulged what he knew." Indeed, the original sweatbox, developed during the Civil War, was an interrogation cell heated by a fire of old bones and rubber, which produced such heat and odor that the prisoner would confess to almost anything to get out. For years, it was a "third degree" technique, practiced by many police departments. But the *Statesman* stoutly denied that such duress was employed in Caldwell these days. "The 'box,'" it said, "is any pleasant room, like the office of the chief of police or sheriff, and the 'sweating' is merely a process of close questioning."

By 1905, "sweatbox" no longer meant an overheated cell; "sweating" could, indeed, take place in an ordinary room. But neither the room nor the interrogation was necessarily "pleasant." The sweatbox committee—Sheriff Nichols, Sheriff Moseley, and Andy Johnson, a Boise special officer, augmented at times by Dan Campbell, George Froman, even Judge Smith himself—had ample experience in persuading a suspect to talk.

One of the first strangers to go before the committee was Theodore Bird, the New York Life agent who'd been the last man to talk at any length with the governor. Since he'd been seen as well outside the Steunenberg house that morning, he was an obvious suspect. But a call to Homer Bostwick, director of the company's Idaho branch office in Boise, clarified Bird's role, and he was released shortly after midnight.

To many in town, the insurance agent was too ordinary a creature to have committed such a terrible act. "Only a fiend, soulless, white-livered, fresh from hell, could have planned the crime," wrote a friend of the governor's. Most vulnerable during the manhunt were those who looked alien, especially those with dark skin, a southern European or Asian cast to their face, or a low brow, generally taken at this time to suggest low intelligence or character. Within hours of the explosion, several "aliens" became prime targets of the investigation.

One was an "impertinent little fellow" named Montford, variously identified as an Englishman and a Welshman. Said to be "an anarchist of the Red Mouth variety," he was working on the Canyon Canal and had been sleeping in Campbell's livery barn the past week or so. He claimed he'd been at the Calvert Hotel's supper table when the explosion occurred, but shortly thereafter he'd gone to the livery barn, rolled up his bedding, and taken it to the powerhouse next to the depot, apparently in preparation for leaving town that night. Under "sweating," Montford expressed his unmeasured hatred for the government, saying he "thanked God he was not a citizen of this country." Swearing roundly, he said there were more criminals in America than in any other country, to which Judge Smith replied that "most of the criminals in America were foreigners." The *Capital News* reported that Montford had an "ugly face, unkempt hair and shaggy eyebrows" and "looked capable of committing the offense."

Another suspect picked up that night was said to be a Russian miner, although he claimed to be a German from Pennsylvania. Informants said he'd visited Caldwell periodically for three years, staying about a month each time. While in town, he frequented the Caldwell Club, Dan Brown's murky saloon on Main Street, where he always seemed well supplied with money. What particularly aroused people's curiosity was that for the first time in anyone's memory the fellow had refused to take a drink all day Saturday, even when a "treat" was proposed. Finally—and this would seem to be the clincher—he'd left the bar about 5:00 p.m. and not reappeared until after the explosion.

That the miner was believed to be Russian only deepened the authorities' suspicions. For the policemen and sheriffs' deputies widely shared the opinion of the *Baker City Herald,* from just across the state line in Oregon, which wrote two days after the assassination that it was "hardly possible that an organization consisting of the greater part of Americans could or would sanction such a crime." Such tactics, it said, were more characteristic of "the Russians or the Mafia."

Not surprisingly, then, suspicion soon focused on Mr. and Mrs. Dumonda Mono, believed to be members of a "foreign anarchist organization." Officers were curious about letters the pair had received from a New York explosives manufacturer. When one policeman tried to question her, Mrs. Mono slammed the door on his foot, and police had to get a warrant for the pair's arrest. Mrs. Mono was very dark and, according to the *Statesman,* "dresses very much like a gypsy." She spoke in "broken English." Her husband, who was described as having a "dark complexion, low brow, narrow, deep-set eyes" and being "of very sullen disposition," professed not to speak English at all and was apparently unemployed. His wife supported him by peddling women's hosiery and skirts.

Another warning about the Monos came from Mrs. Swain Beatty, the wife of Caldwell's barber and justice of the peace. Mrs. Beatty alerted her husband after Mrs. Mono knocked on the door of her fine house at the top of Main Street, seeking to display her goods. Herself a former "modiste," Mrs. Beatty grew suspicious when the woman "jammed everything together and rolled it up just like anyone does with a lot of dirty clothes to be sent to a laundry." In watching Mrs. Mono display her wares, Mrs. Beatty "got the impression that she did not appear so anxious to sell them as other peddlers of her ilk usually appear. I could not help but surmise that her occupation as a peddler is a blind, merely performed to show a reason for her presence here. I cannot get from my mind the impression that this woman and her husband are engaged in some kind of crooked business." But after much "sweating," the Monos turned out to be innocent Austrians. They were allowed to entrain for Boise, where Andy Johnson, the special officer, promptly rearrested them for peddling without a license. Only when a thorough search of their belongings failed to reveal anything suspicious were they permitted to go on their way.

So disposed were the authorities to attribute the governor's assassination to an alien conspiracy, that they were prey to the wildest alarums and excursions. Witness the flutter over a letter received by Boise's police chief: "Sir: Da man dat killa dat ex-governor dat ___ ___ ___ Steunenberg. He out of state time you getta this letter. Dis ex gov—he no more senda gooda men to da Bull penna. He gotta him good and plenty. Viva. Viva! Guiseppi Baratti." On the letter was a picture of a black hand, the sign of a cross, and the legend "In Hoc Signo Vinces" ("By this sign you will conquer").

If Idahoans seemed too eager to pin the rap on a wild-eyed Mediterranean, that was perhaps understandable. For the years on either side of the century's turn had witnessed more than a few assassinations attributed to European anarchists: those of Czar Alexander II of Russia in 1881, President Sadi Carnot of France in 1894, the Spanish premier, Antonio Cánovas del Castillo, in 1897, Empress Elizabeth of Austria in 1898, and King Humbert I of Italy in 1900.

There was nothing inherently violent in anarchism, the belief that government should be replaced by voluntary agreements between individuals and small groups. Early anarchists such as William Godwin and Pierre-Joseph Proudhon envisioned a social equilibrium maintained by the natural harmony of benevolent beings. In practice, anarchists so deeply distrusted electoral politics that they often saw no recourse for dislodging entrenched regimes short of terrorism.

Anarchism gained an American foothold in 1882 when Johann Most emigrated from Germany to New York, transplanting there his sardonic journal, *Die Freiheit*. A fiery orator and mordant wit, Most could rouse an audience to rage or dissolve it in bitter laughter. In scathing pamphlets— *The God Pestilence* and *The Social Monster*—he set the pace for anarchist rhetoric, soon founding the anarchist wing of the International Working People's Association, which would gain some five thousand members and even more sympathizers, many of them German and Bohemian immigrants. A major center of IWPA activity was Chicago, where, before the decade was over, eight anarchists were convicted of murder after a bomb was thrown into the ranks of police dispersing a workers' rally in Haymarket Square. Four defendants were hanged, a fifth defendant committed suicide, and for a generation of Americans, Haymarket was a symbol of the chaos lurking beneath the era's gilded crust.

Fears of political assassination mounted in early 1898, on the eve of the Spanish-American War, when threats on President McKinley's life abruptly multiplied. Letters signed "The Devil" and "Your Enemy Blood for Blood" expressed anger that the president had failed to declare war on Spain or otherwise aid the Cuban insurrection. One signed "A True American" threatened to blow up the White House. The next summer the Secret Service was alarmed by a flurry of credible warnings about plots to kill the president, many of them said to involve Italians. For more than a decade, the nation had been titillated by reports of the violence wreaked by Italian immigrants, then among the least assimilated of immigrants. Indeed, by 1900, the old German-Bohemian-Scandinavian backbone of the anarchist movement had been largely supplanted by Italians, Russians, and Jews.

Newspaper accounts often failed to distinguish between the depredations of Italian anarchists and those of the Mafia, or the Black Hand Society, as it was sometimes called. In one Pennsylvania community dubbed Helltown, detectives discovered what they called a "school for assassination," in which young Sicilians allegedly practiced with daggers and stilettos on dressmakers' mannequins. After the 1891 killing of David Hennessy, a New Orleans police chief who'd set out to break the Mafia, the *Baltimore News* editorialized, "The disposition to assassinate in revenge for a fancied wrong is a marked trait in the character of this impulsive and inexorable race." Eleven Sicilians were promptly lynched by New Orleans mobs.

But it was the shooting of King Humbert in the summer of 1900 by Gaetano Bresci, a silk weaver formerly of Paterson, New Jersey, that induced special anxiety about an Italian cabal. A day later, an eager Secret Service agent urged a tightening of presidential security, citing a memorandum from his agency's files, written in 1898 by a government agent named E. Moretti, who'd infiltrated a cell of Italian anarchists in Paterson. Moretti had warned that the Paterson cabal was planning to exterminate the rulers of the Western world, in the following order: the empress of Austria, the king of Italy, the czar of Russia, the Prince of Wales or the queen of England, the president of the United States, and the emperor of Germany.

The memo stunned Mark Hanna, McKinley's adviser. For the first two rulers on Moretti's list—the empress of Austria and the king of Italy—were already dead, and in April the Prince of Wales had narrowly escaped an assassin's bullet in the Brussels railway station. Could the president's turn be far behind? A few days later, the White House received a letter postmarked New York, August 2, which named the Paterson anarchist assigned to each mission. Bresci had indeed drawn King Humbert, it said; the president's assassin was one Arturo Giovanetti, already in Washington waiting his opportunity to strike.

The confluence of these reports caused the Treasury Department to beef up its protection of the president, adding an operative named George E. Foster, a stout fellow who wore a derby tipped over his brow, where it shadowed a tiny bow tie. Nobody who glimpsed him in the president's entourage was ever in any doubt about the nature of his work.

He and two other Secret Service men were with the president at the International Exposition in Buffalo a year later when a man drilled McKinley with two shots that shortly proved fatal. The assassin, Leon Czolgosz, was neither an Italian nor a member of any known anarchist cabal. But the first-generation Polish American believed that all rulers were enemies of the people and was strongly drawn to anarchists like Emma Goldman, though she resisted his clumsy efforts to enlist in her entourage. After his arrest, Czolgosz said he'd shot the president because he "didn't believe one man should have so much service and another man should have none."

Even as security was tightened around McKinley's successor, Vice President Theodore Roosevelt, disconcerting incidents persisted. The end of 1905 and start of 1906 was an especially nervous time at the White House. The most celebrated incident occurred on January 4, 1906—five days after Steunenberg's assassination—when Mrs. Minor Morris, the fifty-year-old sister of an Ohio congressman and wife of a prominent physician, demanded to see the president concerning her husband's dismissal from the Army Medical Museum. An aide referred her to Secretary of War William Howard Taft. When Mrs. Morris refused to move, Secret Service men seized her roughly, ripping her organdy dress as they trundled her off to the House of Detention. Mrs. Morris—whom a White House memorandum described as "a woman of generous build"—kicked at the officers, tried to bite them, and screamed, "Do you know who I am? I am an authoress and a high-born lady!" (She carried a poem of her own composition entitled "Insomnia.") The episode stirred a tempest on Capitol Hill, where one legislator suggested that when the president stood in the presence of an American mother he stood in the presence of his superior. But most Americans agreed that a chief executive must be protected from such intruders.

Turn-of-the-century anxiety about political assassins was heightened by mounting concern over the devastating new weapons at their disposal. For much of recorded history, the world's workhorse explosive had been "black powder," or gunpowder, developed by the Chinese between the tenth and twelfth centuries. All that changed in 1846 when an Italian chemist named Ascanio Sobrero developed a new "blasting oil" called nitroglycerin. Sobrero demonstrated that a blotter soaked with a few drops of the oil and smacked with a hammer would rattle windows for blocks around. In 1863, at his Stockholm factory, Alfred Nobel had begun manufacturing nitroglycerin.

But this powerful substance proved extremely volatile. In 1864 the Nobel factory blew up, killing five people, including Alfred's youngest brother. Similar uncontrolled explosions followed in Germany, Panama, New York, San Francisco, and Sydney. Nobel searched for a less volatile medium in which the nitro could be embedded and, in 1867, settled on a siliceous earth called kieselguhr, which rendered the oil safe from all but the most severe blow or heat. When nitroglycerin and kieselguhr were mixed, then packed in a batonlike cylinder, the result was dynamite, marketed at the turn of the century under such brand names as Giant Powder, Vulcan Powder, Neptune Powder, and Hercules Powder, all suggesting a primal force stolen from the gods.

Relatively inert, dynamite could be transported, stored, cut with a knife, and handled without fear of accidental explosion. Conversely, inducing explosion was an easy matter: a match, a fuse, and a blasting cap embedded in the dynamite produced twenty times the explosive effect of black powder. Moreover, it was astonishingly cheap: $1.75 a pound at the start. Almost overnight, it enabled mines to be dug deeper and quicker, rock quarried, harbors widened, roads straightened, farmland cleared and irrigated.

It proved as valuable in destruction as it did in construction, and soon a "cult of dynamite" grew up in Western societies. Just as gunpowder had helped the bourgeoisie topple feudalism, so dynamite was seen as offering the working class a potent weapon against capitalism; it would equalize the disparity of force in modern society, permitting the worker to hold his own against the might of the state or corporate hired guns. "One man armed with a dynamite bomb is equal to one regiment of militia," declared the *Alarm*, an anarchist journal in Chicago. The *Nemesis* of Baltimore asserted: "Dynamite is the emancipator! In the hand of the enslaved it cries aloud: 'Justice or—annihilation.'"

In July 1885, Johann Most published a ten-cent booklet entitled "Revolutionary War Science: A Little Handbook of Instruction in the Use and Preparation of Nitroglycerine, Dynamite, Gun-Cotton, Fulminating Mercury, Bombs, Fuses, Poisons, Etc., Etc." Revolutionaries were urged to keep some dynamite, "the proletariat's artillery," at hand at all times, just as the anarchist professor in Joseph Conrad's *The Secret Agent* carries a dynamite bomb in his pocket as he walks the streets of London.

The use of dynamite for political assassination was associated in the public mind with Russia, where it had claimed its first notable victim, Czar Alexander II, in 1881. More recently, a dynamite bomb had killed the interior minister, Viascheslav Plehve, in July 1904 and another Grand Duke Sergei Aleksandrovich in February 1905. Dynamite had been widely used as a weapon of industrial warfare in this country, notably at Haymarket in 1886, where it killed seven policemen and an equal number of civilians. It had been employed in several unsuccessful assassination attempts—especially in mining territory, where men were used to handling it—but so far as can be determined, the killing of Frank Steunenberg was the first successful use of dynamite in the assassination of an American individual.

Idaho in those days was filled with rootless men—ranch hands, sheepherders, miners; the unemployed, footloose, and vagrant of all stripes. In Boise, the police were devoting much of their time to ridding the city of "so-called undesirable citizens, those who drift in here and stay as long as they can without working, living off women of the alley, through tin-horn gambling and very often by watching drunken men and robbing them of their money." In Caldwell, where rental housing was at a premium, such drifters often threw up tents on vacant lots and cooked their meals around campfires. Normally, their presence attracted scant attention, but now they were automatic suspects.

The tidal flux of these drifters prompted Sheriff Moseley of Ada County to advocate an unusual step. No man, woman, or child, he suggested, should be permitted to leave Caldwell until the authorities were confident they had Steunenberg's assassin in custody. That such a quarantine would work a hardship on the community's honest citizens was undisputed, the sheriff conceded, but the importance of the case justified extreme measures.

Although a dragnet had been thrown around the town after the explosion, those in charge knew they couldn't keep it in place indefinitely. Instead, they made certain that the guest registers at Caldwell's hotels and rooming houses were scrutinized, and anyone not known to them was detained.

One stranger who immediately drew their attention had shown up at Caldwell's Pacific Hotel a half hour after the explosion and asked for a "two-bit" (twenty-five-cent) bed. Told every one was taken, he left. But shortly he returned and said he'd take a fifty-cent bed. Asked to register, he first declined, then told the clerk to write down "John Smith," saying that was "near enough." Earlier, he'd stayed at the Calvert Hotel under the name McIntosh. When the dragnet picked him up for questioning Sunday morning, he claimed to be a sheepherder named Doyle. Later he was identified as a drifter named Larry Herron. Although he was eventually released, McIntosh/Smith/Doyle/Herron fascinated detectives for weeks to come, if only because of his multiple identities.

A report from a Boise attorney named Silas W. Moody set off another search. Moody said two men who'd sat behind him on a train to Caldwell two days before the assassination were discussing Governor Steunenberg. One condemned Steunenberg in emphatic terms. When the other disagreed, an argument broke out. With that, a short, heavyset man in a brown mackinaw coat who'd been seated several rows away hurried over and whispered a few words to the men. One of the men said, "All right, I won't," and henceforth they conversed only in whispers. This was regarded as a "strong clue." Officers were in hot pursuit of the trio.

Surely the most alluring of all those under suspicion was a "mysterious woman" dressed in black, wrapped in a long fur coat, her face covered by a veil, who got off a train just after dawn several days after the assassination and asked where the jail was. She walked along Main Street and "disappeared" into the early morning mists.

Then there was the "respectable" Caldwell man whom detectives kept under night-and-day surveillance, a man who had "never known the feeling of fear" and whose name couldn't be printed "because too many would be horrified with surprise when it became known." A private detective from Boise—probably Eugene Johnson of the Boise Secret Service and Merchants'

Patrol—told reporters of this man, who had lived only "a short distance" from Steunenberg's house and had "worked into the confidence of the Steunenberg family."

This fits the description of C. F. Wayne, the nurseryman who lived across Dearborn Street from Steunenberg. Wayne had been interrogated following the assassination, and some detectives remained convinced he was involved in the plot. He brought fresh suspicion on himself when, under questioning, he objected strenuously to the description of himself as a "hired man." He was no hired man, he insisted, but had done the governor's chores as a favor. One detective agency sent a Denver operative racing to Wayne's hometown—Glenwood Springs, Colorado—to inquire among his friends and neighbors. The "op" proved resourceful, hiring a horse and sleigh to take "Miss G.," a former lady friend of Wayne's, dashing through the new-fallen snow while he plied her with questions. However, whatever he found out must have been innocent enough, for soon Wayne was dropped from the roster of suspects.

Finally, there was another man who'd been in Caldwell off and on since September; on December 13 he'd booked himself back into the Saratoga, signing the register as "Thomas Hogan" of Denver. Clean-shaven, dressed in a dark three-piece suit and a bowler hat, evidently "well supplied with money," he was vague about what had brought him to town. Sometimes he claimed to be an itinerant sheep dealer who'd already bought some thirty-five thousand head for shipment to a customer in Nebraska; on other occasions he seemed more interested in buying Caldwell real estate, and he boasted to one guest that he was a part-time gambler who'd gone into one game of late with only seventy-five cents and emerged several hours later with three hundred dollars. He slept late in the forenoon—a mark against him in a hardworking town like Caldwell—and ate only two meals a day: breakfast at noon, dinner at six.

If he sounded mildly eccentric, there was nothing overtly suspicious about the ruddy-faced, mild-mannered Hogan. Most of the time he lounged around the hotel's bar room, playing cards with the regulars and "making himself a good fellow." Cy Decker, the bellboy, thought he was "a nice little man" with hands "as soft and white as a woman's." Clinton Wood, the desk clerk, had talked with him some during the holidays. Wood was a relaxed sort of fellow who'd lean over the counter to chat with the traveling men hanging around the lobby those cold winter mornings. Wood noticed that Hogan seemed nervous during Christmas week; he said he usually spent the holidays with his sister in Spokane and wished he could be there that year.

Late Saturday afternoon, Hogan had been in the Saratoga's card room kibitzing a game of solo whist between several farmers. He left for a while, but barely three minutes after the bomb went off he was back again. As the dust settled out at the governor's place, Hogan offered the bartender, Ray Inman, a steady finger as he tied the bow on a New Year's package of candy. Half an hour after the explosion, he was in the hotel dining room taking his supper. Generally Hogan had a hearty appetite, but that night the waitress noticed that he ate very little.

When Clinton Wood's turn at the front desk ended at midnight, he asked Hogan whether he'd like to go up to the governor's house and survey the damage. Sure, said the traveling man. Neither seemed to know the way, so they had to ask directions. Scuffling through the gathering drifts, they talked about Steunenberg. Wood said he'd always heard him spoken of as a very good man. Hogan said he'd seen him only a few times, but had been told that when the governor got out of office he'd had a "big wad" of money, given him by northern Idaho mine owners. When they finally reached the governor's house, the crowds were so large they couldn't see much, so they went back to the hotel.

By then the Saratoga's bar and lobby were thronged with agitated men debating the bombing, each, it seemed to Wood, advancing a theory on what had happened and who'd done it. Abruptly, Hogan approached one knot of townspeople gathered around the brick fireplace and plucked at the sleeve of Fred E. Fisk, a Parma hardware merchant and prominent Republican who served as chairman of the county commissioners.

"Do you know where I can buy a good bunch of wethers?" he asked with cool composure. (Wethers are castrated rams, good wool-bearing sheep that are easier to control than the fully equipped originals.)

The chairman was taken aback. In the light of the evening's events, the question seemed incongruous, the manner in which the stranger had asked it just a bit too offhand to be believable. Clinton Wood also noticed that Hogan was the "only one present that did not seem concerned" and that he took "no part in the conversation that was so general among citizens and traveling men about the lobby." People started asking whether this fellow wasn't going out of his way to seem uninterested in the only event that most people in town were talking about that night.

On Sunday morning, George Froman, the ex-marshal and stalwart of the Citizens Committee, credited with having tracked down forty fugitives in his day, was walking past the Saratoga Hotel with his friend Pete Steunenberg, who was snuffling from a severe cold he'd picked up during his strenuous activities in the icy night. Froman had been one of the first people Hogan approached when he came to town that past fall. As a realtor, Froman assumed the newcomer was "on the square" when he said he was looking for sheep and some good grazing land on which to raise them. When Hogan told Froman he was a Mason, the realtor had invited him to the annual installation and banquet at Caldwell's Mount Maria Lodge no. 39. But when Froman tried to discuss Masonic matters, the traveling man was so ignorant of the basic rituals that Froman grew suspicious and withdrew the invitation. Deciding the stranger was "stringing him along" and might be in town to rob a bank,

Froman watched him carefully. But Hogan did nothing overt, except coaxing others into conversations in which the governor's name often figured.

Pausing now before a cloudy window of the hotel lobby, Froman pointed toward an easy chair where Hogan—who'd slept until 11:00 a.m.—was sitting reading the Sunday *Statesman*, whose page 1 streamer shouted: "Ex-Governor Steunenberg Falls Victim to Dynamiters."

"There's the man we should be watching," he told Pete Steunenberg. "I'm convinced that he either did the job or knows who did. He's been hanging around here for months doing nothing. He has plenty of money, but he doesn't have any business here. And a coupla times he asked about Frank."

Later that morning, Pete passed the information on to Joe Hutchinson, the aggrieved former lieutenant governor. Meanwhile, Alex Ballantyne recalled that he'd seen Hogan leaving the Saratoga just before six, a few minutes before the governor began his walk home. S. W. Dee, the hardware man, expressed dark suspicions about Hogan to his friend Henry Griffiths, a lawyer, who in turn passed them on to Sheriff Brown of Baker County, Oregon. Brown took a look at Hogan through the hotel window and thought he recognized him as a miner he'd known in the Cracker Creek section of eastern Oregon. When he confronted Hogan with this suspicion, Hogan stoutly denied he'd ever been there. When Brown said some people in town suspected that Hogan was involved with the assassination, he blithely volunteered to see Sheriff Nichols, claiming, "I can soon clear my skirts of suspicion." Nichols, busy with his investigation, told Hogan he'd send for him later.

On that morning after the explosion, Hogan was still acting like a man who had nothing to fear. In the Saratoga bar he encountered Pat O'Connor, a Short Line section hand and Irish tenor who sometimes favored his fellow drinkers with a Celtic ballad or two. Hogan and the gregarious railroad man —sometimes joined by Frank Steunenberg's senior clerk, Sam Clay—had often whiled away those long winter nights playing solo whist. Clay thought Hogan "a nice chap." Now, though he'd already been up to the governor's house with the desk clerk, Hogan asked O'Connor if he'd like to take another look. This time they were halted at Cleveland Boulevard. So dense had been the throng of curiosity seekers and souvenir hunters surrounding the Steunenberg residence all night and morning—picking up fence splinters, digging metal scraps from tree trunks, and otherwise interfering with potential evidence—that armed deputies had been stationed on all sides to keep the public away.* As Hogan and O'Connor stood on the corner, straining for a look at the governor's house, Hogan said that it was "a terrible thing," that "an American would not do it," and—now playing into the town's own firmly settled conviction—that "it must have been done by a Russian or an Italian."

---

* Ralph V. Sebree, manager of the Saratoga Hotel, was one of the souvenir hunters. He picked up a splinter six inches by three inches and placed it in an envelope, in which it remains today at the Idaho State Historical Society, a relic not unlike those collected by early Christians and purporting to be from Christ's cross.

O'Connor nodded, adding that every stranger in Caldwell would be required to "give an account of himself"—a remark that left Hogan solemnly pondering his situation.

While Hogan was sightseeing, Joe Hutchinson took advantage of his absence to follow up on Pete Steunenberg's tip. About 11:00 a.m., Hutchinson talked with several of the Saratoga's employees, who provided some new information about the traveling man.

One was a Japanese chamber man known as Charlie Jap, who looked after Hogan's room at the hotel. Charlie spoke only broken English, but through an interpreter he told Hutchinson that before he came to town he'd worked on the railroad, where he became familiar with explosives. While cleaning the carpet in front of Hogan's bed one day, he'd noticed a "white substance" similar to gun cotton used for blasting on the railroad. He and the hotel's Japanese porter took some of the particles out to the Caldwell Power Company and wanted to test it there—apparently because they thought the electricians might help them identify the powder—but the man in charge ordered them away. On the way back to the hotel they touched the material with a match, at which it ignited just as the railroad powder did.

Cy Decker, the hotel's bellboy, had noticed that Hogan once said something in a low tone to Wesley Ashton, a miner, and then passed on as if he didn't know the man, his face as bland and expressionless as a sugar wafer.

The other employee with whom Hutchinson spoke that morning was Lizzie Vorberg, a waitress in the Saratoga's dining room, who'd struck up a friendship with the mysterious visitor. The daughter of a German brewer from Hailey, twenty-seven-year-old Lizzie and her sister, Theresa, twenty-one, had been working at the Saratoga for several months. Although some reporters portrayed Lizzie as a languid seductress, a photograph obtained by the *Denver Post* showed a sturdy young woman with a Teutonic jaw and firm mouth, only her lively eyes suggesting that she might be playful. In any case, Lizzie quickly caught Hogan's eye. She found him a "perfect gentleman, a good conversationalist with a fund of good stories and anecdotes, in fact, a man whose company she greatly enjoyed." They started taking evening strolls together along the town's snowy lanes and soon were together much of the time she wasn't on duty. Hogan had a rifle at the hotel and on occasion would invite Lizzie to go target shooting with him on the town's outskirts. Some people in Caldwell suspected the relationship had gone further than that and, according to at least one published account, they did have a brief sexual dalliance. While Hogan was "usually genial and good-natured," a few days before the assassination he grew "gloomy and morose" and said to Miss Vorberg: "You think me a good fellow, but I am not. Some time you may learn what a villain and scoundrel I really am and despise me for all time." The girl thought his despondent manner was due to an attack of "melancholia."

When Hogan entered the dining room after the explosion, Lizzie recalled, his face was white and his hands trembled. When she approached to take his order, he didn't look up and smile as usual, and as he ate he kept his eyes on the tablecloth. Suddenly, with an "icy chill" in her heart, she knew that he was the assassin, that she ought to run to the lobby and denounce him, but somehow that night she couldn't.

According to several accounts, it was Lizzie who the next day first suggested to Joe Hutchinson that he ought to search Hogan's room. In any case, she got him the key to Room 19, the next to the last on the hotel's second floor, affording a good look across Seventh Avenue into the governor's office at the bank. While Lizzie's sister, Theresa, stood guard at the top of the stairs, the former lieutenant governor—accompanied by George Froman, Sheriff Nichols, Walter Sebree, and Mike Devers—gained admittance. What they found was enough to prompt further doubts about Hogan. Towels had been draped over the inside doorknobs of two doors leading into the room, so as to block anyone from looking through the keyholes. In the chamber pot were traces of plaster of paris, which investigators believed had been used to hold elements of the bomb together. And on the carpet, they found traces of the powder Charlie Jap had described. As the officers removed it from the room, the *Statesman* reported, Charlie cried, "Don't touchee; blow'ee all to hell!"

By midafternoon Sunday, the "sweatbox committee" had ample reason to question Hogan. But when Sheriff Nichols summoned him to Judge Smith's office, he made a convincing witness in his own behalf. "I understand I'm under suspicion," he said, "and I would like to clear myself." Wearing a neat suit, a derby hat, and well-polished shoes, he remained confident and relaxed, a light smile playing over his chubby face. Hogan said he worked in Denver as a contract employee of the Mutual Life Insurance Company but had come to Caldwell on private business, looking around for real estate.

The committee didn't believe him. Although Sheriff Moseley of Ada County regarded Hogan as "one of the coolest men I ever met," he said later, "he can't meet your eye. When he meets your glance his eyes do not waver exactly, but slide away, smoothly, easily, and almost imperceptibly." Some committee members were for placing him under arrest at once, but George Froman persuaded them to wait, predicting that Hogan would try to "grab a rattler," as the hoboes said—that is, board a passing freight train to get out of town. So they assigned Sheriff Brown of Baker County to keep him under close surveillance. Hogan was told that he was on "parole," that he was not to leave the hotel. But they hoped he'd try—and thus lead them to his confederates.

Soon after Hogan's return to the Saratoga, Harry L. Crane, the *Statesman*'s city editor on assignment in Caldwell, saw him in the lobby looking "perfectly cool and collected." He asked if Hogan was concerned at being named a suspect.

"I can't blame the officers for hauling me up for a quizzing bee," he said with the same calm he'd displayed during the interrogation. "It's probably their duty, but it's rather humiliating. They didn't seem to take stock in all my story, probably because I didn't have the goods to prove all the facts, but I guess they'll be satisfied when I show them the evidence."

Was he working for the Mutual Life Insurance Company while in Caldwell? the reporter asked.

"No-o-o, not exactly," Hogan replied, pausing to bite off the end of a fresh cigar. "In fact, I haven't been working for the insurance people for about seven months."

"What has been your business in this part of the country then?" Crane asked.

"Well, not much of anything. I've been looking for investments in real estate a little," he said.

Then he smiled broadly, as if greatly amused at some thought that had just struck him, and said: "That was a great joke, wasn't it? My being pulled up as a suspected murderer. I can imagine what kind of roasts my friends will hand me when I get back to Denver, if the story ever gets out."

As the law closed in on Hogan, the whist players in the Saratoga's lounge didn't regard him as a suspect. "The boys liked him," recalled Ralph Scatterday, one of the regulars. "He was a little round-faced, red-faced fellow, a whole-souled Mick."

That evening was New Year's Eve. Normally there would have been abandoned revels at the Saratoga and down the street at the Exchange, the Palace, and the Board of Trade saloons. But Caldwell wasn't in a mood for celebrating that night; it'd had enough pyrotechnics for one weekend. The governor, the various sheriffs, and the Citizens Committee met behind closed doors at the Steunenbergs' bank. In those last minutes of the old year, it is unclear whether the committee made a formal decision to arrest the suspect. George Froman still urged them to hold off, but others were in a hurry to clap the man in jail, notably the Boise plainclothesman Andy Johnson, who was eager to collect the handsome reward, as well as to gain credit for solving the case and possibly earn promotion from plainclothes special officer to full-fledged city detective.

The new year dawned cold and clear. At the Canyon County Probate Court, the first business of 1906 was an appearance by Johnson, who presented a complaint charging Hogan with murder in the first degree. Judge M. I. Church, recently recovered from typhoid fever, was on the bench. He issued a warrant and, toward four that afternoon, Nichols and a deputy strode into the Saratoga bar, where Hogan was having a drink—for the first time since his arrival in Caldwell he'd been drinking heavily—and arrested him. Putting up no resistance, he let the sheriff escort him to the office of the county prosecutor, Owen M. Van Duyn, in the courthouse. There Van Duyn advised Hogan of the charge against him.

At five, the officers took him to the Caldwell depot, intending to board a train for Boise, where they'd resolved to consign Hogan to the state penitentiary. The governor, Joe Hutchinson, and others from the capital feared a lynching, a murder, or an escape if Hogan was left in the Canyon County jail, which the *Denver Times* called "a primitive little affair." But Sheriff Nichols and other Caldwell nabobs were aghast at the notion of transferring Hogan to the capital, which would announce to the world that the town's lawmen couldn't be trusted with such an important desperado. Ultimately, Caldwell won out, and Hogan was installed in the brick jail, hard by the courthouse.

Soon after the jailhouse door slammed on the accused, a husky man with soulful eyes, a walrus mustache, and an air of bristling self-confidence stepped off the 4:00 p.m. train from Spokane, Washington. Captain Wilson S. Swain was northwestern manager of the Thiel Detective Service, an agency with headquarters in Chicago and branch offices in fourteen cities. Swain brought with him to Caldwell a reputation for aggressive, if sometimes foolhardy, law enforcement. Born in Princeton, Illinois, of Scotch-Irish descent, he'd drifted west in the 1870s, trying his hand at mining in Central City, Colorado, then in 1883 joining the Denver police, where he rose to become the department's second-ranking uniformed officer, a captain with the title Chief of Detectives.

But Swain had a spastic trigger finger. As early as June 14, 1885, on duty downtown, he came on a "rumpus" outside the *Rocky Mountain News* building. When one brawler turned and fled, Swain fired a shot down a crowded sidewalk toward the fugitive. In a chiding account entitled "The Ready Revolver," the *News* said: "those who were standing around congratulated themselves on [their] narrow escape from the policeman's bullet."

Months later, Swain was back in the news, this time caught in a more weighty imbroglio. On February 26, 1886, Swain was standing outside a Larimer Street restaurant when he heard a shot near Joe Solomon's pawnshop. Rushing down the pavement with his .45 drawn, bellowing for bystanders to get out of the way, the captain took refuge behind a pawnshop mannequin draped in a secondhand overcoat, while he got a closer look at the curious figure who'd lurched from Solomon's doorway. Tall and gaunt under his broad-brimmed sombrero, the stranger was trying to force a .45-caliber cartridge into a .44 revolver—a gun he'd just taken from the pawnshop, prompting the clerk to fire the warning shot that had attracted Swain's attention. But, according to most eyewitnesses, the putative desperado—whose name was John Fitzgerald—wasn't threatening anyone. The only expression on Fitzgerald's face was perplexity, as to why he couldn't get the cartridge in the chamber.

Nonetheless, after a split second's pause behind the sidewalk dummy, Swain fired point-blank into Fitzgerald's groin, inflicting a wound from which the gunman died hours later. Bystanders later testified that Swain had said nothing before he shot, but after Fitzgerald had fallen, the captain exclaimed: "You'll draw on me, will you, you son of a bitch?"

Before he expired, Fitzgerald told police that he hadn't intended to kill anyone else, that he had wanted the gun to kill himself. Indeed, acquaintances of the dead man later told reporters that Fitzgerald was a day laborer inclined to melancholy when he drank but "a harmless kind of fellow." And on one thing they agreed: if he'd shot anyone, it would have likely been himself. In any case, the pistol with which Fitzgerald had been fumbling proved to be unloaded.

A bystander was so outraged by the "wanton and unnecessary" shooting that he brought murder charges against Swain. The captain's friends rallied round him. The coroner quickly determined that Swain had shot "without felonious intent." After two days of testimony, a judge dismissed the charges. But a letter to the editor of the *Denver Tribune-Republican* said the paper would have no difficulty finding upstanding citizens whom Swain had "drawn his ready gun [on] for the most trivial matters, or he has lied about most shamelessly." The letter was signed simply "Justice."

Though Swain had been legally exonerated, his reputation was sullied, particularly among Denver's Irish, who contended that he deserved at least a manslaughter conviction in the killing of their countryman. Their protests grew so insistent that on March 15 Swain resigned. "I'm not particularly stuck on the police business, anyway," he said. "I've been exonerated by a trial before a Justice of the Peace. Now I have several good openings in business offered to me, and as I can get a living very well in a private capacity, I think that it is the best thing for me to do. Then the chronic kickers at policemen or any person in a public position can enjoy themselves as much as they please."

But "the police business" was too much of a habit to kick so quickly. Like others in such circumstances, Swain joined a detective agency and now, at age forty-eight, was a twenty-year veteran of Gus Thiel's outfit. After six years in Spokane, he enjoyed close relations with the Idaho mine owners, for whom Thiel had long worked. Because most of Idaho's mines were concentrated in the north, adjacent to Washington State, the agency's operations on behalf of the mine owners—principally infiltrating undercover operatives into the mines and smelters to report on the union—were supervised out of the Spokane office, with Swain in charge.

Indeed, for several years after the turn of the century, Swain had pulled off something of a coup, achieving a tenuous primacy in the Coeur d'Alene mining region. He devised a complex code for the blacklisting of union workers: a man with an *X* after his name was a union member; one regarded as a "dangerous agitator" had *XX* after his name, while a "dangerous unemployed" worker was designated by *XXX*. Swain's single most notable achievement was the placing of a superagent, Edward L. Zimmerman—also known as Operative 58A or Operative Z—deep within the miners union. Zimmerman's reports kept the mine owners, notably those at the huge Bunker Hill and Sullivan Company, informed of everything the miners were up to. More important still, Zimmerman—under Swain's detailed instructions—managed to get himself elected financial secretary of the union, a position that gave him full access to the union's records and an opportunity to subvert the union from within—which he effectively did.

As a result of these exploits, Swain enjoyed a high standing with the owners. So close were these ties that the moment he heard of Frank Steunenberg's assassination and calculated its connection to northern Idaho's persistent mining unrest, he wired Governor Gooding to say that he, Sheriff Angus Sutherland of Shoshone County, and several Thiel "operatives" were on their way. Then he and his entourage hopped a train for Caldwell, by the only rail line then connecting Spokane and southwest Idaho—a circuitous arc through Pasco, Washington, and Pendleton, Oregon—which put them into Caldwell late that New Year's afternoon, after a trip of some twenty hours. On arrival, Swain told Gooding that he was there at the mine owners' behest—which probably exaggerated a bit the formality of his assignment.

Gooding had dealt with Thiel before and knew Captain Swain as an experienced, if at times bombastic, detective; moreover, he didn't wish to offend the mine owners, whose man Swain certainly was. As night fell that Monday, the governor announced that Swain would take full charge of the bombing case.

That the state should entrust this important investigation to a private detective agency, operating on behalf of employers with a direct interest in the case, was scarcely unusual at the time. For one thing, Idaho's law enforcement apparatus was meager indeed. As late as 1892, the state's attorney general had no staff whatever, answering his own correspondence in longhand. In 1906, the only publicly supported investigators at his disposal were the sheriffs and constables of the several counties and villages, whose expertise was, to put it mildly, rudimentary. A few eastern states—Massachusetts, Connecticut, and Pennsylvania—had recently founded state police forces with their own detective bureaus, but such entities were as yet unknown in the West. Nor could the state call on the federal government, which still had no national investigative body except the Secret Service, whose duties were restricted by statute to the protection of the president and the war against counterfeiters (the Bureau of Investigation, forerunner of the FBI, was three years from formation). U.S. marshals, those legendary frontier lawmen, won their reputation principally in the U.S. territories, not yet admitted as states, where all laws were by definition federal. In the states, marshals and their deputies concentrated on protecting the U.S. mails, government property, and Indians on authorized reservations, while serving warrants and subpoenas for federal courts. Empowered to make arrests, they were discouraged from conducting their own investigations.

Moreover, the notion of law enforcement as a private function had deep Anglo-Saxon roots. In the seventeenth century, the English evinced distaste for a state-controlled police force—both because it would require new taxes and because it smacked of authoritarian rule. "The Police of Foreigners," wrote London's waspish magistrate Sir John Fielding (1721–80), "is chiefly employed, and at an immense Expense, to enquire into and discover the common and indifferent Transactions of innocent Inhabitants and of harmless Travellers. . . . This policy may be useful in arbitrary Governments, but here it would be contemptible."

It was the French national police, founded by the apostate priest Joseph Fouché, that encapsulated the anxieties of freedom-loving Englishmen. With formidable powers to inquire into the lives of private citizens and operate a vast network of spies, it merited the mot of Yves Guyot: "The citizen is free to do whatever he likes, but under police supervision." After several hideous murders in London in 1811, one British commentator remarked: "They have an admirable police at Paris, but they pay for it dear enough. I had rather half a dozen people's throats should be cut in Ratliffe Highway every three or four years than be subject to domiciling visits, spies and all the rest of Fouché's contrivances."

Nobody shaped the Anglo-Saxon view of the Continental detective more than Eugène-François Vidocq, the ex-forger who during 1812–27 headed the Sûreté, the criminal investigation division of the French national police. In 1832, he founded the Bureau de Renseignements, the world's first private detective agency. His ghostwritten memoirs—in which he appeared both unscrupulous and omniscient—horrified British readers. For years, the very word *police* was an alien graft on Britain's body politic. A parliamentary committee in 1822 believed it was "difficult to reconcile an effective system of police with that perfect freedom of action and exemption from interference which are the greatest privileges and blessings of society."

Britons preferred their own pattern, in which detection was "the province of the injured party, his surviving friends or anyone else who likes to take the trouble." The few professionals involved were a parochial patchwork of justices of the peace, parish constables, and nightly watches. But that fragile shield was buttressed by rewards and incentives to encourage private citizens, mercenaries, even criminals themselves, to rid society of miscreants. A "Tyburn ticket," named after the site of London's gallows, exempted from parish and ward duties any citizen who claimed credit for convicting a felon. Criminals won pardons for turning in their accomplices. Even constables received a portion of the fines from those they apprehended.

Such bounty hunters were known as "thief-takers," a term that took on the stench of disrepute. Because they earned their "blood money" not on arrest but on conviction, there was ample incentive to perjury. In 1816, four thief-takers whose false evidence had sent an innocent man to his death were placed in London's pillory and pelted with oyster shells, one fatally.

The most renowned thief-taker was Jonathan Wild (1683–1725), in whom the roles of detective and malefactor were intricately mixed. He specialized in recovering stolen goods, an occupation that put a premium on maintaining intimate relations with the criminal classes. In fact, he was less the scourge of those classes—"The Thief-Taker General of Great Britain and Ireland," as he titled himself—than the Master Criminal of the realm. His "Lost Property Office," which returned stolen goods for a fee, was a fencing operation for his gang's loot; more often than not, the criminals he "brought to justice" were members of rival gangs trespassing on his turf. Wild was the model for Peachum in John Gay's *Beggar's Opera*, who declares: "A Lawyer is an honest employment, so is mine. Like me too he acts in a double capacity, both against Rogues and for 'em; for 'tis but fitting that we should protect and encourage Cheats, since we live by 'em."

Even those who administered the system bemoaned it. "However lamentable it is to think that Magistrates were compelled to have recourse to such expedients," magistrate Patrick Colquhoun wrote in 1797, "...there is no alternative on many occasions but to employ a thief to catch a thief." By the time the term *detective* came into common usage in England in the early nineteenth century, its connotations were diabolical. "To detect" derives from the Latin verb "to take the roof off," thus, by extension, "to uncover what is hidden." As legend had it, the devil offered loyal henchmen the voyeur's pleasure of peering into all the houses of a town by removing their roofs. Hence, detectives were the devil's disciples.

Eventually, the home secretary, Sir Robert Peel, recognized the need for a professional constabulary. In 1829 he obtained parliamentary approval for a uniformed London metropolitan police, soon known as Scotland Yard, or, to its detractors, "Peel's bloody gang." The plainclothes investigators of its detective department became the model for the police detectives of Victorian novels: upright, methodical members of the middle class like Dickens's Inspector Bucket and Wilkie Collins's Sergeant Cuff. But feeble public confidence in these stalwarts was further eroded by a string of unsolved murders, culminating in the hysteria of 1888 over police bungling of the manhunt for Jack the Ripper, the slayer of East End prostitutes. In popular fiction of the era, the police detective was a stolid bureaucrat, unequal to his task, while his role was usurped by the gifted amateur, an embodiment of the Englishman's treasured notion that law enforcement was best entrusted to private interests.

The private detective as exquisite gentleman is exemplified by Conan Doyle's Sherlock Holmes. His deductive techniques reflect the scientific rationalism of his age ("Dear me, Watson, is it possible that you have not penetrated the fact that the case hangs upon the missing dumb-bell?"), his manner the chivalrous refinement of late Victorian noblesse oblige ("You owe a very humble apology to that noble lad, your son, who has carried himself in this matter as I should be proud to see my own son do, should I ever chance to have one"). And he mirrors the bluff complacency of his time (if evil was only a temporary ripple on the sea of life, then once Moriarty had been disposed of, Holmes could retire into "some more placid line in life," leaving the war on crime to Inspector Lestrade).

For even temporary panics, like that over Jack the Ripper, didn't persuade most Britons that their world was essentially malign. Americans, with their nagging anxiety about urban unrest and their Jeffersonian abhorrence of cities, were more likely to despair about the forces of anarchy threatening to dissolve the very social order.

The colonists were as suspicious as the mother country of anything resembling a state spy system. For decades, they, too, relied on patchwork alliances of watchmen and constables, augmented by high-minded private bodies like the Society for the Suppression of Vice and Encouragement of Religion, which took from Edmund Burke its motto: "When bad men combine, the good must associate." In rural areas, constabulary powers were often vested in "anti–horse thief associations," while respectable citizens banded together as "slickers," "stranglers," or "vigilance committees" to restore "civilized values" to roiled communities.

Only in the mid–nineteenth century, with the growth of industrial cities —and the specters of proletarian mob, vicious hooligan, and degenerate wastrel—did fears of social disorder overwhelm distrust of the omnipotent state. Boston's police created the first municipal detective bureau in 1846, New York following in 1857, Philadelphia in 1859. But scandals revealed that many of America's public detectives, like Britain's thief-takers before them, were little more than "bagmen," collecting payoffs from amiable felons and arresting those who failed to render tribute—in short, scarcely eradicating crime on behalf of the common weal, as mythology had it, but regulating malefaction in their own interest and in that of their political employers.

Thus it was scarcely surprising when "municipal" crime detection was largely returned to overtly private hands. The first American private detectives were former municipal constables, like New York's Gil Hayes, who in 1845 opened an "independent" office to retrieve stolen property for a fee. By the 1850s six private agencies had sprung up across the country; by 1884 fourteen flourished in Chicago alone—among them the nation's largest, the Pinkerton National Detective Agency, founded in 1850 by an immigrant Scot named Allan Pinkerton.

Raised in Glasgow's Gorbals, the noisome slum known for its brothels, grog shops, and lurking footpads, Pinkerton was no stranger to working-class grievances. As a youth, he dabbled in Chartism, a movement whose adherents demanded better living conditions, universal suffrage, and annual parliaments. After a skirmish with the King's Forty-second Foot, the young barrel maker's name appeared in the royal warrants for arrest. Smuggled aboard a ship in the Clyde, Pinkerton and his bride set sail for Nova Scotia and from there went on to Chicago, which they reached in early 1842.

Resuming the cooper's trade in Dundee, forty miles to the northwest, he found himself in a hotbed of "wildcat," or bogus, money. While cutting wood for barrel staves, he chanced on counterfeiters whose arrest he quickly contrived. Merchants retained him to track down others, and as his reputation spread he became successively deputy sheriff, Chicago's first municipal detective, and an agent of the U.S. mails. In 1850, Pinkerton and a Chicago attorney opened the North-Western Police Agency, operating in Illinois, Indiana, Wisconsin, and Michigan. When the attorney departed, the agency became Pinkerton and Company.

At first, it specialized in providing police—"cinder dicks"—for half a dozen railroads. One contract was a $10,000 annual retainer to protect the Illinois Central from felons within and without. Frequently, while collaborating on security matters, Pinkerton and the railroad's vice president, George Brinton McClellan, consulted the Central's lawyer, a gaunt Springfield attorney named Abraham Lincoln.

If not for Pinkerton, Lincoln might never have taken the presidential oath. While investigating threats against another railroad, the detective uncovered a conspiracy to kill Lincoln as he passed through Maryland during his procession to Washington. Pinkerton foiled the plot by arranging for the president to transit Baltimore swathed in an invalid's shawl. Pinkerton's men cut telegraph wires and detained reporters until the president reached Washington. The detective proclaimed Lincoln's survival with the message: "Plums arrived with Nuts this morning." Lincoln was "Plums," Pinkerton "Nuts."

When the Civil War began, McClellan, recently named a Union general commanding midwestern militias, asked Pinkerton to head his intelligence branch. This he did, under the nom de guerre Major E. J. Allen. Soon some of his best operatives were providing information from behind enemy lines. Pinkerton made his own foray into rebel territory, masquerading as a gentleman from Georgia and returning with important intelligence.

In November 1861, McClellan was named general in chief of all Union forces and Pinkerton went with him. McClellan proved an exquisitely prudent commander, unwilling to commit troops to battle without odds overwhelmingly in his favor. Accordingly, Pinkerton's estimates wildly inflated enemy troop strength. In this, he seems to have followed his general's lead; in one memo to McClellan, Pinkerton notes that his numbers were, as they'd agreed, "made large." One analyst of these events concludes that McClellan "did not just believe he was badly outnumbered"; the more he repeated the inflated figures the more they became "a solemn truth." Pinkerton, whose loyalty to McClellan bordered on sycophancy, "yielded his judgment to that of his erratic chief." Late in 1862, when McClellan did not order troops to pursue Lee's men after Antietam, an exasperated Lincoln relieved him of command. Pinkerton resigned his intelligence portfolio and served out the war as a claims investigator.

Lafayette C. Baker, another government detective serving as the War Department's special provost marshal, said on his own exit from the military in 1867 that a detective bureau was "contrary to the spirit of... Republican institutions in time of peace." Not everyone agreed. To a shrewd entrepreneur like Allan Pinkerton, peace only multiplied his opportunities.

For war had bred a new lawlessness—an era of Ku Kluxers, lynch mobs, White Caps, night riders, and outlaws. Saber-brandishing cavalrymen and swashbuckling raiders who'd left bloody trails through Kansas and Missouri now balked at the prospect of enforced tranquillity. Many had been soldiers in name only, using the uniform as a cover for banditry; some with a price on their heads could ill afford to surrender their weapons. War's end spawned a host of new banditti—the Youngers, the Daltons, the Renos, the James boys —who patrolled the Middle Border in those years, robbing trains and banks.

To Pinkerton, the battle against such disorder was no less a war than the struggle with the Confederacy. "I shall not give up the fight with these parties until the bitter end and the last die is cast whatever that may prove to be," he wrote. "It must be war to the knife and knife to the hilt." Such was Pinkerton's pursuit of the Reno brothers—Frank, John, Simeon, and William—who terrorized Indiana, Illinois, and Missouri in 1865–66. First, their headquarters in Jackson County, Indiana, were thoroughly penetrated by operatives posing as a saloonkeeper, a gambler, and a railroad switchman. When these agents confirmed that the Renos controlled the county courts, Pinkerton resolved to kidnap John, the gang's leader, and take him where he *could* be tried. One evening an undercover man lured Reno down to the depot; then Pinkerton himself, with six sheriff's deputies, rode in on a "special," snatched Reno off the platform, and carried him into Missouri, where he was convicted of robbing a county treasury. "It was kidnapping," Pinkerton conceded, "but the ends justified the means."

The detectives' "extradition" may have encouraged the growth of outright vigilantism in Indiana. Pinkerton admired the night riders who ran rampant there, believing them the only means of stopping the outlaws. When detectives arrested the other three Reno brothers, jailing them in New Albany, Indiana, a masked posse—from the Southern Indiana Vigilance Committee—hung them from the rafters. Some thought the Pinkertons instigated this lynching out of fear that juries would acquit the Renos.

Eight years later, the Pinkertons organized their own force of retribution. Chasing Frank and Jesse James and their allies the Youngers had proved costly: three agents shot dead. Pinkerton vowed revenge: "My blood was spilt and they must repay, there is no use talking, they must die." In January 1875, hearing the James boys were visiting their mother at her farmhouse in Clay County, Missouri, Pinkertons surrounded the house and threw an explosive through a window that tore an arm off the Jameses' mother and killed an eight-year-old half brother. But the James boys themselves weren't there.

The press, which had earlier celebrated the Pinkertons, now vilified them. "Everyone condemns the barbarous method used by the detectives," chided the *New York Times*. The double humiliation of failing to apprehend the James boys and reaping a raft of bad publicity left its imprint on Allan Pinkerton, setting the stage for ill-advised ventures to come.

Even as they walked the border of illegality themselves, the Pinkertons sought recognition as a modern business operation. The Civil War had been a bonanza for the agency, providing $40,000 in profits, with which it now broadened its reach, becoming the Pinkerton National Detective Agency. In 1866, it opened a New York office, soon manned by Allan's younger son, Robert, who ran the company's eastern and southern regions from there. The founder's other son, William, remained in Chicago, there to oversee midwestern and western operations.

Allan's wartime exploits lent panache to his civilian enterprise. Every office in the company now displayed a framed enlargement of Mathew Brady's photograph of Lincoln, Major General John McClernand, and Pinkerton before a tent at Antietam. It was the most powerful advertisement any company could muster. Pinkerton was an early maestro of the promotional arts. On the facade of his Chicago headquarters hung the company's motto, "We Never Sleep," stripped under a huge, unblinking black-and-white eye— the Pinkertons' trademark and the source of the expression *private eye*. The notion of the hardworking, never-sleeping detective was one that Allan Pinkerton sought to implant, both in his agency and in the public at large.

Distressed by the low esteem in which his life's work was held, he proclaimed the detective's career "a high and honorable calling." The detective, he said, is "an officer of justice and must himself be pure and above reproach." When he realized just how irremediably the term *detective* had been soiled, he began calling his field men "operatives" instead.

After suffering a paralytic stroke in 1869, he withdrew from daily operations, relying more heavily on his sons and his longtime general superintendent, George H. Bangs. Increasingly, he devoted his energies to redressing the sullied reputation of detectives in general, Pinkertons in particular. At the opening of his undated "General Principles and Rules," he set down a principle so sweeping it fairly takes the breath away: "Only such business will be undertaken as is strictly legitimate and right, and then only for the purpose of furthering the ends of justice and bringing Criminals to punishment." To sanitize the sleazy portrait presented in penny dreadfuls, dime novels, and the *Police Gazette*, Pinkerton, over the next decade, published no fewer than eighteen memoirs of detective life, among them *The Expressman and the Detectives*, *The Model Town and the Detectives*, *The Detectives and the Somnambulist*. Seven ghostwriters were kept busy churning out this material. Their language tended toward the highfalutin—a good night's sleep was "the refreshing companionship of Morpheus," a Negro caller "my sable visitor." But the books portrayed detective work as plodding, methodical, and free of taint from the underworld. Pinkerton pictured his operative as a twentieth-century scientist, applying the most advanced techniques of deductive inquiry (though Pinkerton himself was an ardent believer in phrenology, the pseudo-science of skull reading. He once objected to a suitor his daughter wanted to marry because the man's head was too small).

"My officers are not accidents," Pinkerton wrote, "but chosen salaried associates who have therefore no motive either for dalliance with crime or favoritism to criminals." No special training or background save plain common sense was required of the operatives, who sprang from a wide variety of callings: bookkeeper, grocer, and wine merchant. Pinkerton conceded that "it frequently becomes necessary for the Detective, when brought in contact with Criminals, to pretend to be a Criminal; in other words, for the time being to assume the Garb of Crime." But once the ends of justice were met, the Pinkerton operative was expected to "return, of course, unblemished by the fiery ordeal through which he has passed." As one contemporary sympathetic to the Pinkertons put it, the detective "must touch pitch and not be defiled, handle fire and not be scorched, bathe in filth and yet remain clean." It was a tall order.

Pinkerton conceded to Bangs, "There are but few detectives that are honest and reliable." For the record, he required of his gumshoes the rigor of a Spartan, the austerity of an apostle. A Pinkerton rule book warned: "The character of the operative must be above reproach, and only those of strict moral principles and good habits will be permitted to enter the service."

Pinkerton prohibited the "habitual use of intoxicating beverages," except under extreme circumstances in "the detection of crime." Drink was a persistent problem in the highest reaches of the company. Allan's older son, William, was an inveterate bon vivant who often drank to excess, so Allan kept him under his thumb at headquarters. When Bangs was found "drunk as a lord, reeling and staggering" down a Philadelphia street at nine in the morning, Pinkerton wrote him: "Oh! Shame, Shame! That any of my officers should get so debased as to drink whiskey to steady his nerves. The Agency is disgraced by such doings."

Pinkerton, writes one of his biographers, was "a rigid martinet, persnickety, obstinate, irascible, egocentric, self-willed and dictatorial, brooking no opposition even in the most trivial of matters." He was also a bit of a prig. After finding his twenty-one-year-old daughter, Pussy, on a couch with a suitor, he flew into such a rage that she left home for months. A strict code of behavior for operatives warned that "profane and obscene language" would not be tolerated. Operatives were not to borrow money from, or lend money to, other operatives. Gambling was prohibited in the Detective Room, as was discussion of political and religious matters. "Soiled linen" was not to be scattered about. The agency spied on its operatives to make sure they abided by such regulations.

When they succumbed, the Principal—as Pinkerton was known—fell into bleak depressions alternating with towering rages. "My God! George," he wrote Bangs of an embezzlement in the New York office, "do you realize that I am in misery, misery from this whole concern?"

Bent on shedding its shady past and putting on a sober professional face, the Pinkerton agency, by the last decades of the nineteenth century, was becoming a mirror image of the great corporations that were its clients. "We work," Pinkerton proclaimed, "along the same lines that a business man builds up a great business." His determination to turn the careless youths he hired into disciplined paragons of Christian virtue paralleled efforts by John Henry Patterson, founder of the National Cash Register Company, to transform the footloose drummers of the nineteenth century into sober disciples of modern sales techniques. In requiring their employees to conform to such rigorous standards, Pinkerton and Patterson helped rationalize American business as it entered the twentieth century.

Pinkerton's blunt identification with the business community intensified as labor strife spread toward century's end. In 1878, a year after a rail strike paralyzed the nation and set off violent clashes with the military in several cities, Pinkerton wrote, "These trade unions of every name and nature are but a relic of the old despotic days. The necessities for their creation, if they ever existed, have passed away.... In just the proportion that all classes of workingmen refused to be cowed and embittered by these pernicious societies, in just that proportion do they rise above the previous conditions, and reach a nobler and happier condition of life." As if anticipating how such sentiments would be received among workers, Pinkerton insisted he'd "earned the right to say plain things" to laborers. "I have been a poor lad in Scotland buffeted and badgered by boorish masters." But America had redeemed him and should have redeemed everyone else.

Increasingly, the agency, through its Pinkerton Protective Patrol, provided "watchmen" for strikebound plants, mines, and railroads. A uniformed unit, decked out in blue flannel and slouch hats with gold cord and tassel, the patrol drilled with military discipline and weaponry. Robert Pinkerton, the founder's favorite son, pressed relentlessly for its expansion. When Allan died in 1884, the balance of power shifted to Robert in New York and, with it, a much larger role for the Protective Patrol. Having begun as a railroad police force, the Pinkertons were now becoming a protector of industry. Over two decades, the agency intervened in some seventy strikes, often with violent consequences.

No collision rivaled that which took place in July 1892 at the Carnegie steelworks in Homestead, Pennsylvania. A labor dispute led the company to close the plant, the strikers to seize it, then the company to hire three hundred Pinkerton "watchmen" to take it back. When the watchmen glided down the Monongahela River on two barges, they confronted thousands of strikers and their supporters on the bank. A rifle and artillery battle ensued, leaving seven strikers and three Pinkertons dead and dozens injured. Many detectives were savagely beaten by the populace after they surrendered. These events led to congressional investigations, generally upholding the propriety of the Pinkertons' actions, though a House minority report warned that public laws should not be enforced by "private individuals in the employ of private persons or corporations." With corrective action left to the states, twenty-four—among them Idaho—prohibited armed mercenaries from crossing their boundaries. Even before most states acted, the Pinkerton agency drew its own conclusions: that supplying men in labor disputes was "extremely dangerous and undesirable." Henceforth, Robert's watchmen were shunted off to guard racetracks, jockey clubs, and bookmakers, while the agency's intervention in labor disputes became largely covert, a matter of infiltrating spies into the workforce.

As Robert Pinkerton had pursued his hazardous watchman strategy, William hewed to his father's emphasis on "detection." Still a high liver, the elder son shouldered his way through Chicago's saloons and nightclubs, one hand clasping a jar of amber whiskey, the other outstretched to clap gamblers and gentleman burglars on the back. With gruff affection, Chicago's demimonde called him the Eye, referring both to his company's slogan and to William's encyclopedic knowledge of the underworld. After Homestead, the balance of power shifted once again, back to Chicago—to William and his detectives. Henceforth, the agency concentrated on the war against professional criminals, targeting hobo burglars (called yeggs), bank robbers, and jewel thiefs.

The turn of the century was a boom time for the Pinkertons. In 1899 alone the agency hired fifty-eight new detectives, the next year another sixty-five. Between 1895 and 1907, it opened twelve new offices, bringing its national network to twenty. By then, detectives had carved out a place for themselves in American society quite unlike that in any other Western nation. As the Socialist writer Robert Hunter pointed out, in most civilized lands the state had "gradually drawn to itself the powers of repression, of coercion, and of aggression." Only in the United States was it "still possible for rich and powerful individuals or for corporations to employ their own bands of armed men ... [or] their own private police." Through detective agencies, corporate America could employ "thugs, thieves, incendiaries, dynamiters, perjurers, jury-fixers, manufacturers of evidence, strikebreakers and murderers."

When the twentieth century opened, most American detectives were as scorned as their British counterparts, and for the same reasons. In 1906—as Captain Swain took on the Steunenberg case—Thomas Beet, a prominent British detective visiting the States, said 90 percent of American private detective agencies were "rotten to the core, and simply exist and thrive upon a foundation of dishonesty, deceit, conspiracy and treachery."

Samuel Gompers, president of the American Federation of Labor, noted somewhat later that "never has the private detective been used to such an extent, or with such unscrupulousness," as during the first decade of the twentieth century. "They have been not only private soldiers, hired by capital to commit violence, and spies in the ranks of labor: they have been and are being used in the capacity of *agents provocateurs*—that is, in disguise, as union men, to provoke ill-advised action, or even violence, among workingmen."

But if detective work produced handsome profits for the Pinkertons, all that honey drew a swarm of hungry competitors. By 1904, New York City

boasted seventy-five agencies, Chicago and Philadelphia some thirty each.
Arthur Train, a New York lawyer, warned that detectives were everywhere:
"The insignificant old Irish woman who stumbles against you in the department store is possibly watching with her cloudy but eagle eye for shoplifters.
The tired-looking man on the streetcar may, in fact, be a professional 'spotter.'
The stout youth with the pince nez who is examining the wedding presents is
perhaps a central office man.... There are detectives among the chamber-
maids and bellhops in the hotels, and also among the guests; there are detectives on the passenger lists and in the cardrooms of the Atlantic liners; the
colored porter on the private car, the butler at your friend's house, the chorus
girl on Broadway ... may all be drawing pay in the interest of someone else."

Although Train's prose sometimes swells toward hyperbole, it captures
the fin-de-siècle craze for the detective. So pervasive was this cult that a
confidence man swindled ten to two hundred dollars from gullible New
Yorkers by "appointing" them private detectives and presenting them with
elaborately scrolled commissions. Ultimately, he was arrested by a New York
City detective.

The sheer ubiquity of the detective testifies to a massive erosion of trust.
The growth of industrial empires and mass markets, combined with the
decline of the family farm and bucolic village, contributed to the decay
of mutual confidence. The organic web of personal association no longer
encouraged good-faith dealings between employer and employee, banker and
farmer, merchant and customer; these lacunae were filled, in part, by the paid
informer and industrial agent. The national obsession with the detective also
acknowledges the stark terror stirred in many Americans by the rise of the
cities, with their alien swarms and evil resorts. Just as they dreaded the
irrational chaos set loose in such quarters, so they fastened on the detective, a
symbol of scientific optimism and cool reason, whose function was to keep
that terror at bay.

The most intensively surveilled sector of late-nineteenth-century America was the railroads, then flinging their silver tracks across the continent. As
the burgeoning transportation of goods and passengers across state lines
outran the shelter of traditional law enforcement, the trains and their contents—as well as bridges, tracks, and terminals—were increasingly at the
mercy of hijackers, hooligans, resentful farmers, and angry homesteaders. But
an even greater threat came from railroad employees who, with astonishing
regularity, appropriated fares and freight for their own accounts.

The surveillance of railroad employees inevitably involved detective
agencies in the very activity that for centuries had repelled Anglo-Saxons on
both sides of the Atlantic: spying. Not surprisingly, both the agencies and
their clients preferred the term *testing*. Those who engaged in it were called
"testers" or "spotters." But, to many American workers and much of the
public, they were nothing more nor less than spies.

For years, the Thiel agency marshaled the largest force of railroad spotters. Gus Thiel had been one of Pinkerton's most valued operatives as an agent during the Civil War, then in the Chicago office. Disgruntled over some now-forgotten slight, in 1873 he formed his own firm, based first in St. Louis and later in Chicago—a personal betrayal Allan Pinkerton never forgave. Before long, Thiel gained a major foothold in the West.

So identified was Thiel with spying on railroad employees that in 1889 a disgruntled railroad man, writing as Martin P. Wheeler, penned a diatribe called "Judas Exposed; or the Spotter Nuisance," lampooning Thiel's agency as "Zeal's Railway Inspection Service." Zeal did most of his recruiting in "the saloons and low resorts of St. Louis," where he had no difficulty finding agents with the "faculty for sneaking, lying and dissembling even to [their] most intimate friends and relatives."

Distasteful as it was to most Americans, spying was inherent in the detective's role. As Arthur Train noted, "the largest part of the work for which detectives are employed is not in the detection of crime and criminals, but in simply watching people, following them and reporting as accurately as possible their movements . . . a willingness to act as a spy and to brave the dangers of being found out." Robin Dunbar, another early student of American detectives, put it even more bluntly. "A spy's business is to deceive his victim, to gain his confidence, to learn his secrets and plans and then to betray him. A sleuth's life is a lie. He is both Judas and Ananias."

By the late nineteenth century, detectives pervaded American, as well as British, popular literature. The progenitor of American detective fiction was Edgar Allan Poe, whose works reveal the uncanny chord between detective and villain. The theme of the double is made explicit in "The Murders in the Rue Morgue," in which the sailor and the orangutan are "like warring halves of a single personality," while the detective, Dupin, subsumes both identities, using "the genius to detect and restrain the brute in himself." At Reichenbach Falls, Sherlock Holmes holds his sworn enemy and mirror image, Professor Moriarty, in deadly embrace. "There is a sense," writes the critic David Lehman, "in which every sleuth is every culprit's double." This theme reverberated in the new craze for psychology. Freud's psychoanalyst played the "detective" to the patient's "criminal." The patient erected defenses against the analyst's inquiry, but if the patient stayed the course, the detective-analyst would help him to self-knowledge.

In fiction and memoir alike, center stage was increasingly occupied by the bipolar Great Detective: infallible, implacable, omniscient, if often devious, unscrupulous, even perfidious. One compelling memoir was *Knots Untied* (1871), in which George S. McWatters, once a private detective, a Socialist by disposition and literary man by aspiration, struggled to reconcile the detective's dubious techniques with his "noble" ends. The American detective, McWatters conceded, was "the outgrowth of a diseased and corrupted state of things, and is consequently morally diseased himself." But he also regarded the detective system as the one redeeming feature of a corrupt society. "It is, at least, the silent, secret and effective Avenger of the outraged majesty of the law when everything else fails."

Whatever the character of detectives, Americans attributed to them special powers bordering on the magical. "Detectives the world over are alike in the focusing power of the eye," one admirer wrote in 1908. "They may shuffle or be alert little Irish laddies, or be tired out and smutty, but they all of them possess a seeing eye, that eats holes into the makeup of the passerby."

The myth of the Great Detective—as deceiver, betrayer, avenger, and redeemer—found its ultimate vehicle in the American dime novel. Earlier pulp fiction, which targeted adults, dealt principally with the Old West: stirring tales of brave settlers and nick-of-time cavalry. But as these clichés lost their novelty in the 1870s, dime novels focused on the new urban frontier, dramatized in the gritty struggles of detectives and criminals. And increasingly they were aimed at boys of the lower and middling classes.

The first dime novel detective was Harlan Page Halsey's Old Sleuth. Modeled after Allan Pinkerton, the Old Sleuth admitted: "I cannot stop the great tide of evil that sweeps onward, but here and there I can snatch some poor innocent victim from the black whirling current." In the New York Detective Library (1882–98), the Old Cap Collier Library (1883–1910), the Nick Carter Library (1891–1915), and the Secret Service Weekly (1899–1915), the middle class transmitted its fear of disorder in the cities to impressionable readers.

In *Mephisto: or the Razzle Dazzle Detective* (1899), Halsey captured the cold dread at the diabolical schemes afoot in urban America: "During the last 50 years many mysterious assassinations have occurred in the great city of New York, and these mysterious murders have rarely been traced. . . . One thing is certain—at all times, in all great cities, terrible dramas are in progress." If such sanguinary hokum rings comical to us, we must remember how threatening the new industrial cities, with their swarms of immigrants, were to the Protestant majority who formed the principal audience for these cautionary tales.

Moreover, like the British, Anglo-Saxon Americans had a strong preference for amateurs in crime detection. Just as they romanticized the self-made entrepreneur in industry, so they belittled the need for professional credentials in law enforcement. Anyone could be a detective. "There are a very large number of persons who go into the detective business for the same reason that others enter the ministry—they can't make a living at anything else," wrote Train. The dime novel sleuths were invariably men who'd begun as something else: reporter, athlete, blacksmith, sailor, preacher, even tramp or orphan boy.

A prolific producer in this genre was Thomas C. Harbaugh, who, under the name Captain Howard Holmes, ground out dozens of books like *Velvet Foot, the Indian Detective, Lucifer Lynx, the Wonder Detective, Little Lon, the Street Singer Detective, Father Ferret, the Frisco Shadow, Plush Velvet, the Prince of Spotters, Detective Zach, the Broadway Spotter, Gideon Grip, the Secret Shadower, Jason Clew, the Silk-Handed Ferret, Phil Fox, the Genteel Spotter,* and *Captain Coldgrip, or the New York Spotter.*

One of his most daunting detectives was Kent Keen, the Crook-Crusher, also known as "the dread Crook-Crusher," "the tireless Crook-Crusher," "Keen, the Keenest," "the Grand Master in the craft," "the dead-game detective," "the pink o' perfection, an' the friend of the poor and needy, but at the same time the eternal enemy of the guilty."

Kent Keen opens with a bumpkin from Spokane debarking in New York and asking a wharf hand how to get to police headquarters. "I am here on a little manhunt," he confides.

"Then you don't want to see the police," says the wharf hand. "I can do better than that for you. I can take you to Kent Keen, the best man-taker in this city. Old friend of mine, you know. What he can't do in that business isn't worth talking about."

For more than two centuries, that had been the refrain of Anglo-Saxon manhunts, fictive and real alike: You don't want the police. I can do better than that for you.

While the swashbuckling Captain Swain and his operatives tightened their dragnet around the dynamiters, for a few hours on Tuesday morning Idaho's leaders paused to honor the bombers' victim. Belle would have preferred a small private service, but, as the governor's sister Jo recorded, "the public demand that they be admitted." With most other activities suspended, Caldwell's schools, public offices, and businesses were shuttered tight. Flags flew at half-mast. Patriotic bunting, wound with black crepe, draped storefronts and lampposts.

At 9:30 a.m., Harry Jones's hearse, drawn by a pair of coal-black mares, took the governor's body to the First Christian Church on Cleveland Boulevard at Kimball—chosen because it was the largest church in town—where it lay in state. Jones had sent to Portland, Oregon, for a $250 carved mahogany casket with silver trim large enough to accommodate the strapping governor (Pete Steunenberg's wife, Nina, thought the casket was "like Frank, plain yet strong and substantial looking"). To the surprise of many, the casket remained open, for the explosion had somehow left the dead man's face utterly unmarked. "Frank looked so nice," Jo reported. "He had a sweet, peaceful expression as tho he were sleeping." In a sixteen-dollar suit supplied by the undertaker, he lay in the nave beneath the three great stained-glass windows as his friends and neighbors filed past, many of them unable to hold back tears.

The widow had passed a terrible couple of days. The night of the assassination, Belle had been so distraught some in her circle thought she might go mad. But gradually she'd quieted under the influence of "opiates" the doctors prescribed and round-the-clock attendance by her sister-in-law Lizzie van Wyngarden and her close friend Ora Oakes. Notes of sympathy, covered dishes heaped with food, and other tokens of commiseration piled up on the family's doorstep. That Belle was unable to receive people personally, that she had been utterly devastated by finding Frank's shattered body leaking life into the snow, everybody in town could well understand.

But long before the explosion, Belle Steunenberg had been regarded in Caldwell and Boise as something of an eccentric. Once her husband had called her "a bright and kindly helpmate," but she hadn't improved with age. Her conversion to Adventism had puzzled many in town, who regarded this new sect as theologically—and socially—inferior to the Presbyterian faith she'd abandoned. Belle's regular attendance at services conducted by Elder A. C. Bird for the eight charter members of Caldwell's new Adventist Church strained relations with her former coreligionists, who now regarded her as a rigid—even hysterical—zealot. A Pinkerton detective would soon describe her as "somewhat of a religious fanatic."

Those same tensions were evident at home. For Belle, always a bit severe behind her rimless spectacles, had now adopted the bleak asceticism of Ellen G. White, a founding prophet of Adventism, who likened each person's "vital force" to a bank account. God deposits in all his creatures a limited ration of that force, which is depleted by every subsequent withdrawal. Since each sexual act uses up an irreplenishable quantity, those who intemperately exhaust their account face premature decline and early death. Of late, Belle—whom one woman described as "a pleasant-faced, portly woman, short in stature, and of those general characteristics that are ordinarily called 'motherly' "—had largely suspended conjugal relations with her husband, advising him, when the urge came upon him, to take a cold shower or walk around the block. The governor's brothers and sisters plainly resented their sister-in-law's single-minded dedication to her unorthodox sect. Some thought she was suffering from neurasthenia, the catchall ailment of the day. Relations were particularly strained between Belle and Carrie, A.K.'s wife, who thought Belle had "gone off the deep end."

And some of her children were in open rebellion. A strict disciplinarian, Belle frowned on casual dress, forbade the use of nicknames, and squelched their favorite amusements, all in the name of keeping them "pure." Adventists regarded checkers, chess, and backgammon, not to mention dancing, as unpardonable frivolities. Frank Junior recalled her as a "very opinionated" person, who set out with "crusading zeal" to convert the rest of the family (which she failed to do). She often warned them that the end of the world was near. Earlier that year, in chiding Julian for having "fooled along in a way that was perfectly disgusting in a boy of sense" both at Caldwell High School and at Walla Walla College, the governor admonished his son for his adolescent insubordination. "If you had not then lost confidence in your mother," he wrote, "your sense of respect for her was dormant, to say the least." Julian deeply resented being sent off to what he called a "missionary college," identified with his mother's sect.

The family feared that Frank's death would only exacerbate these tensions. Indeed, Belle had insisted that the funeral sermon be delivered by Elder Snyder, the president of Walla Walla College. But otherwise she had proved surprisingly flexible. With a resigned sigh, she left funeral arrangements in the capable hands of Frank's close friend Harry Lowell. Moreover, she went out of her way to conciliate other members of the family with remembrances of Frank that would have special meaning for them. A.K., once his coeditor at the *Tribune*, got one of the governor's printer's rules. His brother George, a military instructor at the University of Idaho, received the old fiddle on which the governor loved to saw of an evening. Pete got a coin that was in his pocket the night he was killed and a collar and cuff case. Delia Brobst, the oldest sister, who'd raised them all after their mother's death in 1876, got the family Bible Frank carried in his satchel. Will got the governor's fine rifle with his name on its stock. Sister Jo got the flowered shirt he had on the day he was killed, the very one with a piece out of its tail she'd been wanting to mend. ("That shirt is a sight now," she wrote her family in Iowa, "right side and sleeve is riddled to tatters and looks as tho it had seen years of war.")

Now, shortly before eleven, Belle entered the lead carriage, accompanied by her brother John and her children Julian and Frances, for the ride down Cleveland Boulevard. They had all "sombered" their clothing but avoided black, a color Frank detested. The trip was only three minutes, but it was so cold that heated bricks and soapstones were placed at their feet. The rest of the family followed in four other carriages, except for Bernardus, who was too overcome by grief to attend the services. ("Is that so?" was all the family patriarch had said when they told him of his son's death, but he took it hard. "Poor old Daddy," wrote Will, "it nearly broke his heart.")

A.K. barely made it to the funeral. "I am all 'broke up,' and can't pull myself together as yet," he wrote a friend a few days later. "[Frank and I] were almost inseparable from childhood's hour. We went swimming and nutting together and worked during the summer vacation side by side on the local brick yard or for some farmer. We learned the printer's trade in the same office and have been associated together in everything since we arrived at man's estate.... With all his great intellectual powers, he was always just a boy to me—the same one that worked and played with me in years gone by.... To lose him would be sorry, but to have him blown all to pieces seems to be more than I can bear."

As the family set out, the dignitaries formed a procession in front of the Saratoga Hotel for the four-block march to the church. Two by two in order of rank came Governor Gooding; the former governors Frank W. Hunt and John T. Morrison; William Borah; Edgar Wilson, a former congressman; Chief Justice Charles O. Stockslager of the Idaho Supreme Court and Justices James F. Ailshie and I. N. Sullivan; Judge James H. Beatty of the United States District Court; and hundreds of Caldwell's citizens. With the seating severely limited, dozens stood against the walls, and hundreds more huddled in the snow outside, hoping to catch some of the service through the doors, which, despite the cold, were left ajar.

Whatever the outward appearance of solidarity in the face of political terrorism, the serried ranks of dignitaries harbored some deep personal resentments. At the depot that morning, as the train pulled in from Boise, E. J. Dockery, Frank Steunenberg's close friend and business associate, turned to Joe Hutchinson, who'd once been critical of the dead governor's policies, and boomed: "You have redeemed yourself in a great measure, Hutchinson, for your past sympathy with the dynamiting outfit." The ex-miner gritted his teeth and, in deference to the solemnity of the occasion, let the jibe pass.

After an invocation by William Judson Boone, a quartet of Frank Steunenberg's closest friends—John Rice, Ralph Oakes, Sam Clay, and Clark Stiles—sang "I Have Found a Friend." Some people had worried about Elder Snyder's sermon, fearing they would get a lot of Adventist quirkiness, perhaps even hear a slight to the town's Presbyterian orthodoxy. But the elder quickly defused these apprehensions, paying generous tribute to a man who had resisted not only his wife's spiritual blandishments but perhaps even the evangelical fervor of the elder himself. Recalling a meal they'd shared when the governor visited his son in Walla Walla, Snyder said, "I never formed but one opinion of ex-Governor Frank Steunenberg, and that opinion was never changed. I believe that he is one of God's noblemen. I did not at that time dream that I should soon be summoned to officiate in the funeral rites for this man. His death is the source of great sorrow to me, but I have this consolation: I know from what he said during and after that last meal with me that his hope was in God. We can be assured that he is still a nobleman—now a nobleman in God's kingdom."

Boone, long his neighbor, spoke on behalf of the community:

> During his eighteen years in this town, he held the good will of all citizens. He was a kind man; he had a good word for everyone and a smile for all he met. In these respects he never changed; he was always the same. He was especially interested in the development of the town and the surrounding country. In every public improvement he had a hand. In all public matters his advice was sought and heeded. When it came to dividing territories into counties and making county seats, a frequent expression often heard was: "Well, what does Frank say about it?" On investigation it was usually learned that Frank had little to say but was already working on the particular subject under discussion. This was characteristic of the man. He said little, but thought and did much.

Then it was Borah's turn. It was no surprise that Borah should have been chosen to deliver the principal oration. Not only was he a close friend and legal adviser of the late governor's, he was one of the state's most renowned trial attorneys, a tall, commanding, strikingly handsome figure, widely regarded as the leading candidate for the next opening in the U.S. Senate. Moreover, he had a well-deserved reputation for golden-throated eloquence.

As he strode to the pulpit, the audience in the church subsided into hushed attention.

"Idaho consecrates her soil today with all that is mortal of her first martyr," Borah began.

> In contrition and anguish our young state lingers for a time beside his open grave, not alone that honor may be given to the dead, but that the citizenship and courage of the living may catch the parting inspiration of his steadfast soul. Those who count the cost when duty calls will never know his worth. But those who in this world of self-interest and expediency hear amid it all duty's commanding voice and hasten at all hazards to obey, will realize that Idaho puts beneath the sod today her most illustrious son.
>
> Frank Steunenberg was of the rarest type of manhood. Open, sincere, modest and unassuming—he was in his purposes and plans as inflexible as honor itself. Rugged in body, resolute in mind, almost massive in the strength of his convictions—he was of the granite hewn.

Oakes, Rice, Clay, and Stiles concluded the ceremony with a close-harmony rendition of "I Need Thee Every Hour," the hymn the governor had sung that last morning after wrestling all night with the "good and evil spirits."

From the church, a dark procession of fifty carriages crawled up the long gravel road on the snowy face of Canyon Hill, where the governor's body was lowered into the frozen earth. He wasn't buried in the family plot, which at that time held only his first son, Felix, dead in 1894 at the age of six. The day before his assassination, as he and Harry Lowell had returned from their trip, Frank Steunenberg had gazed out the train window at the old town graveyard on Canyon Hill and remarked how "dreary and desolate" it was, overgrown with sagebrush, graves piled with boulders to keep the coyotes and other varmints from digging there. So Lowell selected a new part of the burial ground, free from the dense sagebrush and chaparral thickets, more open to light and air, overlooking the valleys of the Boise and the Snake.

Even as Idaho's leaders gathered on that icy hillside, investigators were building the case against their principal suspect. That morning Sheriff Nichols marched Hogan across the frozen yard from the jail, with two officers in front, two more in back, for his arraignment in the cramped courtroom with sky-blue walls at the Canyon County courthouse.

Harry Crane of the *Statesman,* who only the day before had found Hogan composed and inoffensive, abruptly detected a more malign creature, whose "cruel gray eyes" fixed on Judge Church as Andy Johnson read the charges. In an era accustomed to reading character in physical attributes, Crane now concluded: "The face of the man suggests cruelty, cunning and contempt for everything that appeals to ordinary persons, the eyes being of that shifting character that suggests an evil nature." The next day the *Statesman* called Hogan "a devil incarnate."

The judge said he would set a date for the preliminary hearing as soon as Hogan obtained counsel. "If this is published in the papers," Hogan said, "one lawyer, maybe two, will start for here at once." How long would it take them? asked the judge. "About a day and a half from Spokane," said the prisoner. The officers marched their man back to jail, but not before he gave the courtroom a last "contemptuous" glance.

Shortly after the hearing, Swain, Sheriff Nichols, and Andy Johnson called on Hogan in his cell. With his consent, they searched him thoroughly for the first time and, secreted in his shoes, found keys to his trunk, a suitcase, and a valise. In his room, they'd already found a baggage check for the trunk, which Hogan had apparently left at the depot.

The trunk was removed to the sheriff's office, where it was opened in the presence of Governor Gooding and Captain Swain. It was found to contain clothing (a blue cheviot coat, a panama hat, two striped flannel nightshirts, a pair of balbriggan drawers); two pairs of rubber-soled shoes, one pair still wet and muddy; a stack of calling cards for "Thomas Hogan, Silverton, Colorado, Agent Mutual Life Insurance Company"; a fishing rod with tackle; a Winchester shotgun, sawed off so it could be hung around the neck and concealed under a coat; and a cloth mask. In the valise they found a fishing reel with the line missing; a pair of field glasses; an electric flashlight; a set of brass knuckles; a loaded Colt automatic with a shoulder holster; twenty-one shells; a fuse; a pair of wire nippers of the kind miners used to set caps in gunpowder; a sack of plaster of paris; four packages of chemicals, several of which were found to contain explosives; and a leather postal card containing New Year's greetings addressed to Charles Moyer, president of the Western Federation of Miners, the Denver-based organization that represented all gold, silver, lead, and copper miners west of the Mississippi. "It was one of the nasty kind," wrote one newspaper, "the mailing of which is prohibited, and Hogan, discovering that it could not be transmitted, had evidently put it back in his pocket."

After completing this inventory, the investigators went to the Steunenberg house, where they picked up tracks in the snow—which had stopped falling shortly after the explosion—leading from the side gate through the lot, speckled with apple trees and sagebrush, that separated the residence from Cleveland Boulevard. Although the tracks were quite old by then, a few were in good condition. When the wet shoes found in Hogan's trunk were fitted to these tracks, they—and particularly a set of nails in the soles—matched perfectly.

At nine that evening, Captain Swain summoned several reporters to his room at the Saratoga. With a note of triumph in his voice, he proclaimed: "You may announce to the world that we have conclusive evidence that the bomb used in the assassination of Governor Steunenberg was manufactured in Room 19 of the Saratoga Hotel and that the details of the plans were probably formulated there." To Crane, he confided that the evidence against Hogan was now "overwhelming."

Although Swain and his associates were convinced they had their man, they didn't rest for a minute. So steeped were they in the conspiratorial notions of the day that they couldn't conceive that Hogan had acted on his own. "There is now no doubt," the captain told the *Capital News,* "that Governor Steunenberg's death was the result of a conspiracy that was most carefully planned, and which the conspirators were months in bringing to a conclusion." Sheriff Nichols also doubted that Hogan had acted alone. He spent fruitless hours trying to identify two men with whom Hogan had allegedly been drinking at an unnamed saloon shortly before the bomb went off.

In the search for confederates, suspicions quickly settled on two mysterious figures who'd holed up for a while at the Commercial Hotel in Nampa, the gritty railroad town fifteen miles east of Caldwell. On the day before the assassination, they'd abruptly boarded a train toward Caldwell. On Sunday, in the initial dragnet for drifters and other suspicious chracters, they were arrested at Weiser, a tank town fifty miles to the north.

The first, Frank Campbell, had a reddish-brown Vandyke beard on his thin, fine-featured face and wore a slouch hat. His hands were strangely white and without calluses, indicating to detectives that he was not accustomed to hard work. The second man, ultimately identified as Fred Wahn, had a dark mustache and a bold red scar running from his left ear to his mouth, which in the popular press quickly lent him the moniker Scar Face.

After questioning in Weiser, they were released for lack of evidence but rearrested a day later in Council, another town on the railroad sixty miles farther north. Returned to Caldwell that evening, they were "sweated" for hours by relays of detectives who seemed convinced they'd both been miners in the Coeur d'Alenes in 1899, which reinforced the conviction that they were Hogan's accomplices. For days, neither man would give a straight answer. The press and the public grew intrigued by reports out of Denver that Scar Face was actually a man named Slim wanted at Cripple Creek, Colorado, for murdering a woman in a house of ill fame. But the excitement evaporated when it was learned that Colorado already had Slim in custody. Ultimately, Campbell and Wahn turned out to be nothing more exotic than workers on the Pacific and Idaho Northern who'd gone off on a drunken spree and, once they fell under suspicion, strung out the mystery, perhaps to embarrass the authorities, perhaps just for laughs. They were both released.

But soon the detectives turned up another potential accomplice of Hogan's: a "sullen, disagreeable, taciturn man," a bit portly, with a heavy mustache, wearing a broad-brimmed derby pulled low over the "small, piercing and very dark eyes of a shifty character." In Caldwell on Monday he attracted attention by his bold swagger and "his manner of watching the officers." His demeanor was that of an "outcast—one who hated the law and regards an officer as his natural enemy." Arrested on his return to Nampa that evening, he said, "My name is John Doe and that is all you can get out of me." To every subsequent inquiry he grumbled, "That's for you to find out."

Captain Swain regarded "Doe" as an important piece of the puzzle. "He is just the character of man that smart criminals would use to send to the vicinity of such a crime . . . not for the purpose of taking an active part, but to be used as a 'stall' to direct suspicion away from the guilty parties while they make their escape." But the connection could never be demonstrated and he, too, was released.

Finally, the Thiel detectives picked up the trail of the most intriguing accomplice of all. While examining hotel registers in Caldwell and Nampa, Operatives Carter and Stewart discovered that Hogan had checked into hotels in both towns those past few months with a man named J. Simmons. From his description, the detectives suspected that Simmons was actually L. J. "Jack" Simpkins, a former organizer for the Western Federation of Miners in northern Idaho and, since 1902, a member of its executive board. Sure enough, when they produced a photograph of Simpkins—a stooped, heavyset man in his early forties with a tawny mustache, crooked nose, and squinty left eye—several hotel employees and others said that was indeed the man they'd seen. Among those who made positive identifications were B. F. Dennison, the proprietor, and Mrs. J. P. Smith, the waitress, at the City Restaurant, where Hogan was known to have taken many of his meals while in Caldwell. Moreover, Sheriff Sutherland examined the signature in one hotel register and claimed to recognize Simpkins's handwriting.

The detectives talked to Guy McGee, a student at the College of Idaho, who lived a few miles out of town and every morning walked down the railroad tracks to school. On several occasions in November, he'd noticed two men on the tracks looking toward Steunenberg's house. He identified one of the men as Hogan and said the other looked "something like" Jack Simpkins. But Simmons, or Simpkins, was nowhere to be found. If he'd been in Caldwell for the assassination, as many suspected, he'd taken it on the lam and was surely miles from there by now.

Meanwhile, the detectives returned to their prime conspirator, but now they knew a bit more about him. Sheriff Edward Bell of Teller County, Colorado—who'd sped to Caldwell with Samuel D. Crump, the attorney of the Colorado Mine Owners Association—took one look at the prisoner in the county jail and identified him as Harry Orchard, a miner who'd worked in the Cripple Creek–Altman region. This identification was confirmed by Sheriff Brown of Baker County, Oregon, who'd thought Hogan reminded him of Orchard but was now sure of it.

Another piece of the puzzle fell into place the same day with the arrival of a telegram from Spokane, Washington, paid by the law firm of Robertson, Miller and Rosenhaupt. The message said simply: "To T. Hogan, care sheriff, Caldwell, Idaho: Attorney Fred Miller will start for Caldwell in the morning. [signed] M." Since Hogan had sent no messages since his arrest, Fred Miller must have been acting on his own initiative or in response to some client's wishes. The firm had close ties to the mining unions and had represented Idaho miners charged with serious crimes in 1899.

Wednesday morning, deputies escorted the prisoner to the sheriff's office, where Swain, Nichols, and Johnson put him through his most rigorous interrogation yet, recorded by Gilbert Shelby, Judge Smith's court reporter.

"What is your right name?" Swain asked. "Thomas Hogan?"

"No, sir."

"What is it?"

"Harry Orchard."

Well, they thought, that sagebrush was cleared away. Now they could get on with the rest of it. "Let me ask you this," Swain bored in, "what explanation have you to make of your conduct and actions in this town? What has been your business?"

"I have not been doing anything," Orchard insisted. "I have been looking for a place. I have been thinking of locating in this part of the country, I have just been loafing here." He paused, then went on: "I have a private disease. I have been waiting here to kind of get rid of it." Then, almost as an afterthought, he put in: "I was going to get a little place here, so that I would have a home here or somewhere."

Reviewing his personal history, Swain got Orchard to admit that he'd been in the Coeur d'Alenes in 1899, that he was familiar with various Colorado mining towns where trouble had broken out in recent years, and that he knew the leaders of the Western Federation of Miners, though he stoutly denied that he'd been in touch with them lately.

Andy Johnson took over the questioning.

"Can you state about any explosives on the floor and in the room, and what the chamber [pot] was used for or anything?"

A shrug of the shoulders. "I don't think that I ever used the chamber while I was there."

Swain cut in. "What did you do in that room besides sleeping there?"

"I wasn't doing anything," Orchard shot back.

"What did you make in the room?"

"I don't know as I made anything except some dice, I made once, or I tried to make some."

"What did you make them of?"

"Plaster paris," said Orchard. "I was going to load them with shot. That is the way for making them. . . ."

"You were making loaded dice?"

"Yes, sir."

"What do you do with all this artillery there, these guns?" Swain wanted to know.

"I always carry a six-shooter and a shotgun."

"You are a kind of sporty fellow in the hunting business," Swain said, unable to resist some broad sarcasm. "You have a fishing rod and gun.... What about the knuckles?"

"I carry them," Orchard deadpanned. "I had them in San Francisco when I was there."

"What were you doing with the flashlight?"

"I had that for curiosity," Orchard said blandly. "It is handy when you go to a room. It is handy for that when there is no light. I have got nothing there but what is all right."

As for possible accomplices, Orchard conceded under close questioning that he knew Jack Simpkins. They'd been hunting together that fall upstate, where they'd bagged some deer and other game. Then Simpkins came down to Caldwell with him but left well before the governor was killed.

"Do you know what became of Jack?" Swain put in.

"No, sir," said Harry Orchard.

Now they were getting nowhere. As they gathered up their papers, Andy Johnson turned one last time to the prisoner.

"You can't tell us where those dice are?" he asked. "That would be a protection for you."

Harry Orchard gazed back with just a trace of insolence. "These dice I did not finish up," he said, "and I quit that. I don't remember whether I threw them away or left them in my pocket. I only made a couple."

With that, they took him back to jail. Orchard occupied one of four holding cells in the single-story brick building, which dated to 1884. In the front was a largish room called the "kitchen," with a stove and cooking utensils, where the prisoners were allowed to prepare their own meals and where they spent most of their waking hours. Behind it, the small cells looked out through barred windows on the barren yard behind the courthouse. The prosecution readily conceded some weeks later that the Caldwell facility was "crowded," "not a comfortable jail," and "probably unsanitary." From time to time, the jailers still put the more recalcitrant prisoners in balls and chains and leg irons. Since the assassination, an officer had stood in front of the jailhouse.

From the moment Orchard was arrested on Monday, rumors had circulated in town that a mob was going to break into the jail and string him from the nearest tree. Sheriff Nichols was convinced the attack could come at any moment. His deputies had heard it, too. When he asked them to stand extra guard duty outside the jail, they begged off. One had a poker game. The other had to take care of his children because his wife was at his mother-in-law's. So Nichols asked Dan Campbell, the liveryman and ex-sheriff, to send a messenger to Ed Morgan, a former Texas Ranger who lived on the edge of town. For several days, with his Winchester repeating rifle across his knees, Morgan sat outside the jail. On several occasions groups of sullen-looking men came by, exchanged words with Ed, then moved on.

The Steunenberg brothers passed some cautionary words, too. Pete told his associates around the Saratoga's gambling tables. Will and John confided in customers at the shoe store. They didn't want the man lynched. They wanted him tried and executed. The family didn't think Orchard had acted alone. Before punishment was meted out, the Steunenberg brothers wanted to make sure they had the whole rotten gang who'd killed Frank.

Indeed, more than a few people wondered whether Orchard hadn't been just a little too easy to catch. One Boise businessman who came down to Caldwell on the governor's train the night of the murder later told the *Capital News*: "Hogan impressed me as being a smart Irishman who hungered for notoriety.... He seemed to be courting recognition and I thought at the time that he was maneuvering to have suspicion directed towards him ... while the real criminal got away." The family shared some of these doubts. Pete Steunenberg thought that Orchard was guilty but that, as he wrote a friend, the man was "a hired assassin and did his part for money, a business proposition as far as he was concerned." The moving force of this conspiracy still wasn't in custody. Sister Jo was even more suspicious. If Orchard had placed the bomb, why did he just sit around the hotel waiting to get caught? Why hadn't he tried to get away? "The fellow seemed to invite suspicion intentionally," she wrote home to Iowa. "He wasn't very smooth if he didn't." Was he a decoy? she wondered. If Orchard was lynched, they'd never know why somebody would want to kill "great, magnificent Frank."

3

IMPS OF DARKNESS

FLOUNDERING THROUGH snowdrifts toward his brother's deathbed, Will Steunenberg had thought, It's the Coeur d'Alenes! Within hours of Steunenberg's death, Governor Frank Gooding reached the same conclusion. "The foul deed," he wired Senator Fred T. Dubois in Washington, "can be traced directly to the lawless forces which for years dominated the Coeur d'Alenes." The next day, the *Statesman* elaborated the notion. "A great many minds," the paper said, "turn to the troubles in the Coeur d'Alenes and to the 'inner circle' which was said to rule by blood and which has often been described as an organization that never ceased to pursue those marked as victims. These believe the governor has fallen a victim to that campaign against the dynamiters in the north which made his name known from one end of the country to the other and which won him a high place in the estimation of all law-loving citizens."

The simultaneous convergence of so many persons on the "troubles" in the Coeur d'Alenes reflected the strange power of those remote episodes to haunt twentieth-century Idaho politics. For decades to come, the very phrase *Coeur d'Alenes* evoked a stirring morality play whose lessons depended entirely on where one took one's stand: behind the afflicted mine owners or with the aggrieved miners.

Idaho has been called a "residual state," since it comprises territory left over after Oregon, Washington, Montana, and Wyoming took their pick of available land. Thus its curious shape—a bare forty miles wide at the Canadian border but three hundred miles broad at its base, and in between a nearly impenetrable swatch of snow-capped mountains, pine forests, rapid rivers, and jagged canyons. North and south were separated not only by formidable geographical barriers but by divergent climates, populations, and economies. In its natural state, the south was a great sagebrush desert, though capable, when irrigated, of supporting a lush agriculture; the northern panhandle, blessed with normal rainfall and a history of geological upheavals, produced impressive stands of timber and immensely valuable mineral deposits.

The riches buried beneath the panhandle's ragged peaks and sculpted valleys can be traced to events 1.2 billion years ago. At that geologic moment, blistering hot springs erupted from cracks in the ocean floor west of present-day Spokane, spewing clouds of metal sulfides, which eventually settled on the ocean floor to form sedimentary rock rich with minerals. Later—some seventy million years ago—faults along what is now the Coeur d'Alene river valley began to shift, opening fractures in the older rock, permitting water-borne metallic particles to flow into these openings and form mineral veins plunging ten thousand feet beneath the valley floor.

These riches remained hidden from man until the close of the nineteenth century. Then, in August 1883, Andrew Prichard and his grizzled partner, Bill Keeler, strode to the bar of a Spokane Falls saloon, their buckskin pouches bulging with four pounds of gold nuggets and flakes. Two hundred men abandoned their whiskey glasses and poker hands to surge around the pair, pressing for details of their find on a small tributary to the North Fork of the Coeur d'Alene River.* That euphoric night marked the start of the great Coeur d'Alene gold rush.

When the Northern Pacific Railway issued a circular booming Prichard's discovery, the rush became a stampede, nearly eight thousand miners thundering toward the Coeur d'Alene district—barely ten miles wide and thirty miles long, sandwiched between the state of Washington to the west and Montana to the east. Staking out claims along Eagle and Beaver Creeks, the lucky few found that a pan of gravel scooped from those streams could bring as much as a hundred dollars. "Spokane boomed," a lawyer of that era recalled. "Bars were crowded. In neighboring districts business counters stood deserted. Plows rusted in their furrows. Herds shifted for themselves. Wagons came rumbling over rough mountain roads. Dusty horsemen lashed their mounts in from the cattle country. Every stagecoach brought in its quota. Every Northern Pacific train discharged a small army of men."

When spring sun and warm chinook winds filtered through the pine and larch forest, melting the snows that drifted up to twenty feet in the canyons, it became clear that most of the good "diggins" had already been snapped up. In early 1884, swarms of resentful prospectors trudged across the divide to sample the swift creeks emptying into the South Fork. There they found not gold but a black substance called galena, or sulfide of lead, often mixed with zinc and silver. At first, miners fixated on gold ignored such base ores, but a few, like John Carton and Alameda Seymour, recognized the value of lead and silver deposits. Their claim on Canyon Creek—which became the Tiger mine—was filed in May. Succeeding years brought a host of other mines—the Poorman, Helena-Frisco, Black Bear, Gem, Granite, Custer, Polaris, Bunker Hill and Sullivan—strung in a great V along the South

---

* The name *Coeur d'Alene*, which means "heart of an awl," or "awl-hearted," was apparently bestowed by early French trappers on a northern Idaho Indian tribe—perhaps because the tribesmen proved such tough bargainers. The name was applied first to the tribe, then to a lake, a river, the mountains it drained, and finally to the entire mining district straddling those mountains (Smalley, "Great Coeur d'Alene Stampede," 4).

Fork and Canyon Creek, converging in the mercantile settlement of Wallace.

The men who descended into these lode mines found an enterprise altogether different from the surface mining they'd known. Of the lustrous metal they'd once scooped from California's streams, a military governor had said: "No capital is required to obtain this gold, as the laboring man wants nothing but his pack and shovel and tin pan with which to dig and wash the gravel." But the gnarled veins of galena locked in recalcitrant rock along the South Fork couldn't be exploited without capital, technology, and expertise. Shafts or tunnels had to be sunk in the ground; these mines also required tracks, hoists, explosives, concentrators to pulverize and wash the crude ore for smelting, and, of course, plenty of paid labor. Such operations were beyond the means of the small operators who'd prospected for western gold. Into this vacuum moved heavily capitalized corporations, often based in the East, with stockholders like Andrew Mellon and John D. Rockefeller, functioning in the West through salaried managers whose responsibility was to the bottom line of the corporate ledgers. A few "miners"—the label still applied to all who sought mineral deposits—became fabulously wealthy from these undertakings. For most, the vision of untold riches proved a bitter deception. As the *San Diego Union* put it: "The great attendant expenses of such mines convert the individual into a factor in the corporation and de- grades [*sic*] the sturdy miner into a drudge in the drift, toiling at so much per day, while his bosses—his owners in fact—reap the great profit of his endeavor."

That endeavor was desperately hard. "View their work!" wrote Eliot Lord of Nevada's Comstock mine, rich in silver and lead. "Descending from the surface in shaft-cages, they enter narrow galleries where the air is scarce respirable. By the dim light of their lanterns a dingy rock surface, braced by rotting props, is visible. The stenches of decaying vegetable matter, hot foul water and human excretions intensify the effects of the heat. The men throw off their clothes. . . . Only a light breech-cloth covers their hips, and thick soled shoes protect their feet from the scorching rocks and steaming rills of water."

All this flew in the face of Caldwell's buoyant faith that the West gave every man a fresh start, each an equal chance to enrich himself in a glorious free-for-all, an "open season on natural resources." If refugees from "the dark satanic mills" of Europe and the eastern seaboard had hoped to slip the bonds of nineteenth-century industrialism in the West's wide spaces, western mining replicated the very worst of the industrial system beneath the Rock- ies' sparkling spine. If the westering experience was expected to produce the Jeffersonian ideal of a self-sufficient yeomanry, each sturdy citizen rooted in his own land, church, and family, the silver-lead mines of the Coeur d'Alenes —like those in Silver City and Leadville—produced the polar opposite: a wage-earning proletariat at the mercy of absentee mine owners and their managers, helpless in gut-wrenching cycles of boom and bust, never sinking roots in permanent community, destined to drift from one ramshackle mining camp to another in a futile quest for their lost dream of western autonomy.

To contest this alien system, hard-rock miners in Nevada and California began by the 1860s to organize workingmen's associations or unions, initially little more than mutual-aid societies that adopted the grips and passwords of fraternal lodges. Unions reached the Coeur d'Alenes much later, triggered by wage reductions and inadequate food in company boardinghouses. In 1887, workers at the Bunker Hill and Sullivan mine formed the Wardner Miners Union, which was followed by similar units at Gem, Burke, and Mullan.

By 1891, as confrontation loomed, each side mobilized for action. On New Year's Day, the four unions agreed to coordinate activities through a central executive committee of the Miners Union of the Coeur d'Alenes. Seven weeks later, thirteen mine owners—from the giant Bunker Hill and Sullivan Company to the tiny Stemwinder—founded the Mine Owners Protective Association of the Coeur d'Alenes, known as the Mine Owners Association (MOA), a loose league often split on other issues but frequently united on resisting labor's demands. For months the two sides skirmished, gauging each other's strength and intentions.

By year's end, the MOA took the offensive, the ostensible cause a decision by the Northern Pacific and Union Pacific railways to raise by two dollars per ton their rates for ores shipped to Omaha and Denver smelters. Contending that the increase would imperil their profits, mine owners said they'd rather halt production than operate at such slim margins. When the railroads refused to budge, the MOA shut down all mines under its control as of January 16, 1892, throwing two thousand miners out of work.

Freight rates were by no means the only spur to the owners' bold stroke, for when the railroads restored the old rates on March 15, the mines remained shut. Pincered between a decline in lead and silver prices and the union's fierce resistance to a wage cut, the mine owners seized on the freight dispute as the occasion to reduce wages for unskilled car men and shovelers, known colloquially as "muckers." Many muckers had been miners until displaced by the new compressed air drills, for one man with an air drill could do the work of five hand drillers. The owners cut the muckers' "unreasonable and unjust" wage from $3.50 for a ten-hour day seven days a week—the same as for skilled miners—to $3.00. When the unionized miners struck, the owners locked them out, making clear they were determined to break the union. "We'll never hire another union man," said Alfred M. Esler, the manager of the Helena-Frisco mine and a MOA leader.

As it became clear that they were in for a long struggle, both sides looked out of state for help. The union appealed to the West's most powerful labor organization, the Butte (Montana) Miners Union, which assessed each of its members five dollars a month to supply their colleagues in the Coeur d'Alenes with thirty thousand dollars a month, provisions, and organizers.

In turn, the owners imported nonunion workers—recent immigrants from Scandinavia, Poland, and Austria recruited in Michigan and, later, miners from California and Colorado. Although union miners greeted these scabs with abuse, a force of fifty-three armed guards, employed by the MOA, assured their passage into the Coeur d'Alene valley. By June, eight hundred nonunion workers had arrived, allowing seven of the district's principal mines to resume operations.

In early July, two events—both involving the Pinkertons—ignited the tinder of grievance that had been accumulating in the Coeur d'Alenes. The first was the July 6 clash between union workers and Pinkerton guards at the Carnegie steelworks in Homestead, Pennsylvania—an example of labor's "direct action" and thus a prod to the "fighting element" in the Gem Miners Union. The second event was the discovery by the Gem union that one of its most trusted members was an undercover Pinkerton.

In September 1891, as tensions had built in the Coeur d'Alenes, the mine owners had asked the Pinkerton agency to send an operative to infiltrate the union. The Pinkertons sent Charles Angelo Siringo, a resourceful detective who'd been operating undercover out of Denver for five years. The agency thought highly of this forty-four-year-old "cowboy detective," the son of an Italian father and an Irish mother from southeast Texas. As a young man he'd run a combination cigar store, ice cream parlor, and oyster bar in Caldwell, Kansas, when a blind phrenologist ran his fingers through Charlie's hair and declared, "This is a fine head for a newspaper editor, stock-raiser, or detective." Charlie chose the last of the three. Though barely five foot eight and 130 pounds, Siringo specialized in physically demanding assignments on the range. "He is as tough as a pine knot," William Pinkerton observed, "and I never knew a man of his size who can endure as much hardship as he does."

After receiving instructions from John A. Finch, the mine owners' secretary, Siringo—under the name C. Leon Allison—went to work as a mucker in Finch's Gem mine, hanging around the saloons, making himself "a 'good fellow' among 'the boys.' " He so won the miners' confidence he was elected the union's recording secretary, which gave him access to its books and records. Soon he arranged for his shift boss to fire him, so he'd have more time to observe union leaders like George A. Pettibone, financial secretary of the Miners Union of the Coeur d'Alenes, whom he described as "a rabid anarchist." Every day he mailed a handwritten report to the nearest Pinkerton office, in St. Paul, Minnesota, which typed and relayed it to Finch. These dispatches kept the owners a step ahead of the miners all year.

The miners were constantly on the lookout for detectives; indeed, a Thiel operative had been run out of Gem just weeks before Siringo arrived. Aware he could be denounced at any time, Siringo never left his boardinghouse without a Colt .45 in a holster beneath his left arm and a pearl-handled bowie knife strapped under his trouser leg. Early in July, he recognized a man named Black Jack Griffin he'd known in Nevada, and evidently Black Jack recognized him, for one night at a union meeting he was all but accused of being a detective. With lively badinage, Siringo managed for the moment to deflect these suspicions.

A few nights later—on Saturday, July 9—Gem's single street, running along the creek bed between high canyon walls, surged with angry union members brandishing rifles. Managers of the Helena-Frisco mine posted Thiel guards around the concentrator where ores were processed, but two nonunion workers who slipped into town for a drink were badly beaten. With no time to send reports via St. Paul, Siringo sought out John Finch, at home in Wallace, warning him to expect big trouble in a matter of days.

Back in Gem on July 11, Siringo learned that armed union men were outside laying for him. Deciding it was time "to emigrate," he hid under the floor, then crawled beneath the boardwalk of the main street. Through cracks in the walkway he could see union men searching for him, but he found a path to the rear, escaping to Finch's Gem mine.

Seething at the spy's escape, the union men vented their rage. At 5:00 a.m., firing broke out between unionists in the hills above the Helena-Frisco mine and nonunion men behind the "scab forts" at the mill. About nine, a charge of dynamite came hurtling down the penstock, a sluice carrying water to the mill complex, and the four-story old mill, not then in use, blew up, killing one nonunion worker. At that, some sixty scabs in the mill complex marched out under a white flag and were held prisoner in the union hall. At the nearby Gem mine—where Siringo had taken refuge—the gunfire killed a Thiel guard, a nonunion worker, and three union men. Ultimately, seventy nonunion men there surrendered, too, joining their colleagues at the union hall. Once again the elusive Siringo escaped into high timber.

Following the victories at the Gem and Helena-Frisco, the union quickly gained the upper hand throughout the mining district. Some four hundred armed union men rode flatcars down the valley to Wardner, where they seized the concentrators at the Last Chance, Sierra Nevada, and Bunker Hill and Sullivan mines, warning managers to dismiss nonunion labor or see their valuable machinery blown sky-high. Whether dynamite was ever set there remains in doubt, but management complied. Trains hauled the scabs out of state, to the jeers of onlookers. By nightfall, miners milled through Wallace, celebrating what seemed an unequivocal victory.

It was not to be. Barely forty-eight hours later, Norman B. Willey, the Republican governor, proclaimed Shoshone County in "a state of insurrection and rebellion," declared martial law, and ordered six companies of Idaho's National Guard into the county. Simultaneously, he asked President Benjamin Harrison for federal troops. The president complied; within days, a combined force of fifteen hundred state and federal troops was encamped in the district's principal towns and mining camps, under the joint command of Colonel William P. Carlin of the Fourth Infantry and General James F. Curtis, inspector general of Idaho's National Guard. The Fourth Infantry escorted

250 scabs back from Washington, and under military protection the mines reopened with nonunion labor. Stunned at their reversal of fortune, union workers were said to be "crestfallen and sullen."

Beginning on July 15, the troops arrested some six hundred men—not only union miners but merchants and saloonkeepers who sympathized with them—placing them in wooden warehouses surrounded by fourteen-foot stockade fences—enclosures that came to be known as "bullpens." For two months, they languished there without hearings or formal charges. By September, most were released on their own recognizance, while state or federal charges were brought against dozens of union "leaders," with Siringo the principal witness against them all.

Ultimately, thirteen unionists were convicted of contempt of court; four others—George Pettibone among them—were found guilty of criminal conspiracy. But in March 1893, the United States Supreme Court overturned the conspiracy charges, holding that the crimes were not against the United States but against Idaho. Since the Court's decision cast doubt on the contempt charges, a federal judge released the two men still serving contempt sentences.

Yet the defendants' brief imprisonment at the Ada County jail in Boise had one lasting result. In jailhouse talks, James H. Hawley, a lawyer defending the miners, argued that the only way to shore up their perilous condition was to join with the powerful Butte union and other miners' organizations in a union able to confront the mine owners. The Coeur d'Alene events triggered similar conclusions elsewhere. Soon after their release, five Idaho prisoners went to Butte, where they joined thirty-seven delegates from Montana, South Dakota, Colorado, and Utah to found "a grand federation of underground workers throughout the western states" called the Western Federation of Miners.

William Hard, a street-savvy Chicago reporter, understood the WFM better than most of his contemporaries. Later he wrote:

> The Western Federation of Miners gets its tone from adventurous native-born Americans suddenly thrown from the position of frontiersmen into the position of workingmen.... There are farmers who preferred prospecting to plowing. There are city men who burst the bars of their cages to breathe the open air of the West. These adventurous characters, going out into a new country and plunging into the virgin, everlasting hills, where it would seem that at last all men would stand on the same footing, have suddenly discovered that amid these primitive surroundings the modern industrial system is...found at its worst.

As edited by A. K. and Frank Steunenberg, the *Caldwell Tribune*'s commentary on the Coeur d'Alene events tilted ever so slightly toward labor. One could, for example, detect skepticism about the use of state militia to support the mine owners in this carefully written editorial note in late August 1892: "This is a great year for strikes and militia. The citizen soldiery were called out in Idaho to suppress a miners' strike, in Pennsylvania to protect the iron barons, in Tennessee to protect the convict labor contracts and in New York to protect the New York Central railroad. Evidently something is wrong somewhere in this great land of the brave and the free." As a Democrat, Frank Steunenberg might have assailed the Republican governor for his pro-owner bias. As a former union typographer in Iowa, he might have rallied to the support of embattled labor. He did neither. Most of the *Tribune's* reporting and commentary on the events of 1892 was exquisitely cautious.

As the 1896 campaign began, few Idahoans envisioned the mild-mannered country editor from the sheep-and-vegetable district of Caldwell as a powerful campaigner, much less their next governor. But the region's politics were in convulsion, roiled by the grievances of western farmers and ranchers against eastern monied interests, or what one hard-pressed yeoman called "the plutocrats, the aristocrats, and all the other rats." This struggle focused on the currency, pitting creditors seeking to preserve the value of money owed by hewing to the gold standard against debtors seeking relief through the inflationary minting of silver coin, with sixteen ounces of silver equal in value to one ounce of gold. In that year's presidential race, the gold standard was championed by Republican William C. McKinley out of small-town Ohio, while the banner of silver was brandished by the Democratic-Populist Lochinvar off the Nebraska plains, William Jennings Bryan. At that July's Democratic convention, the thirty-six-year-old Bryan had mesmerized delegates with a rhetorical flourish: "You shall not press down upon the brow of labor this crown of thorns. You shall not crucify mankind upon a cross of gold." Matching their chief's fervor, the Democratic press excoriated "goldbugs" as being as "seductive as the vampire, as poisonous as the serpent, as destructive as the tiger."

In turn, many goldbugs saw in Bryan's candidacy echoes of the Jacobin rising during the French Revolution. "Marat, Marat, Marat has won!" someone shouted when news of Bryan's nomination reached the office of the *Emporia* (Kansas) *Gazette*. Another newsman depicted the Great Commoner's supporters as "anarchists, howlers, tramps, highwaymen, burglars, crazy men, wild-eyed men, men with unkempt and matted hair, men with long beards matted together with filth from their noses... men whose feet stank" and whose smelly armpits "would have knocked down a brazen bull." The leisure class made plans to decamp. "Many of my friends are saving their money for the purchase of suitable residences in Paris," the future secretary of state, John Hay, wrote Mrs. Charlton Paull that September. Then, in a mordant reference to the site of the inexorable guillotine, he asked, "Shall we next meet on the Place de la République?"

Thomas Beer, an acute observer of turn-of-the-century America, recalled his own adolescence in that year: "Something furious stirred the air around heads of children on sea beaches. Ladies were gasping, with hands on corsets, about rebellion and the horrible things John or Mason had told them about Mr. Bryan.... Behind the plunging orator in his private car was this wave of queer names and uncomprehended identities: Altgeld, the anarchist, Debs, the socialist, Populists and Silver Republicans.... It was slightly awful to be a child in the summer of 1896."

The currency debate produced palaver from people who knew nothing about monetary policy. Theodore Roosevelt's nine-year-old son, Ted, spoke on the veranda at Sagamore Hill to an audience of hired men and maids, using a loaf of bread and a heap of coins to demonstrate "the fallacy of free silver." In patrician law offices and Irish saloons alike, men sported white or gold chrysanthemums in their lapels to proclaim their monetary preferences. Strange threats were chalked on the coaches of express trains hurtling through the night, themselves potent symbols of the dizzying pace of social change.

The battle front didn't always run along class lines. In western states like Idaho, Colorado, and Nevada, some of the white metal's most ardent advocates were owners and managers of silver mines, who saw in free coinage at the sixteen-to-one ratio the best way to prop up the fluctuating price of ore. Even Caldwell's staunchly Republican merchants weren't immune to the new panacea. A Free Coinage saloon opened on Main Street and smokers savored a locally manufactured "16 to 1" cigar.

So caught up in the silver craze were Idahoans of all social classes that it made a hash of the state's political configuration. Mainstream Republicans stuck by McKinley, with encouragement from party panjandrums back East: Republican delegates from northern Idaho traveled to their Boise convention aboard a private railroad car supplied by the Republican "boss" Mark Hanna of Ohio, replete with wine, cigars, a phonograph, and records of McKinley's speeches played for their "edification." Others sounded a different note. The *Lewiston Tribune* sent the Idaho delegation off to the national convention in St. Louis with a trumpet blast: "Idaho not only needs a new deal, but a new deck, a new shuffle and a new cut." An Idaho faction led by Senator Fred Dubois joined other insurgents who stalked from the convention to form the Silver Republicans.

More important was the mounting influence of the Populists, who voiced agrarian and labor demands for railroad regulation, workman's compensation, and exclusion of foreign immigrants, as well as for silver coinage. In 1892, the Populists and Democrats had together delivered Idaho's electoral vote to the Populist candidate for president, James B. Weaver. In 1896, the Populists envisioned a more sweeping alliance, at state and national levels, with the Democrats—themselves split by the defection of goldbugs loyal to President Grover Cleveland.

In mid-August, two silver parties descended on Boise for simultaneous conventions, mainstream Democrats at the Sonna Opera House, Populists four blocks away at the Columbia Theater. As Democrats convened in the "Opry," they were flanked on one side by a placard proclaiming "No Crown of Thorns," on the other by "No Cross of Gold." When Steunenberg, one of five gubernatorial candidates, endorsed "fusion" with the Populists—an electoral alliance in which the two parties would back a common slate for state and national offices—the delegates whooped and stomped.

As in twenty-seven other states where these parties joined forces for state races, it was one thing to accept fusion in principle, quite another to allocate offices on the joint ticket. For three days in the stifling August heat, while tempers chafed and ambitions rankled, frazzled negotiators shuttled between the Sonna and the Columbia. At noon Thursday, fusion seemed out of reach. Then, at 4:00 p.m., the Democrats slapped a final offer on the table, giving the Populists one hour to take it or leave it. After intense debate in the fetid Columbia, the Populists accepted the division of spoils, in which they would contest the two principal national offices, U.S. senator and congressman, along with the state posts of lieutenant governor, auditor, and secretary of state, while the Democrats laid claim to governor, attorney general, Supreme Court justice, and treasurer.

It remained only for Idaho's two "great unwashed" parties—now known as the Popocrats—to put names by those offices. The gubernatorial contest had narrowed to a choice between Steunenberg and a gregarious Boise grocer named Phil A. Regan, both relatively untried Democrats. Some Steunenberg supporters seized on his youth and midwestern birthplace to liken him to Bryan: he'd been born a scant eighteen months before, and 180 miles southeast of, the Great Commoner. He was firmly in the silver camp and progressive on social and economic issues. "My environments have all led me to feel that I am a brother of the working man," he once said, "and because I have temporarily ceased to earn my living by toil and sweat only intensifies my adhesion to the cause of the honest laborer." When a friend quoted a Robert Burns verse, "Man's inhumanity to man makes countless thousands mourn," Steunenberg said, "That line ought to be printed at the top of all the note paper used by the inordinately rich." But his affinity with Bryan stopped there. Steunenberg lacked the Commoner's evangelical zeal. Barely adequate as a stump speaker—his secretary said he was "averse to speaking from the public rostrum"—he never displayed Bryan's power to wring from strong men both cheers and tears.

Nonetheless, his campaign was shrewdly managed. On the first ballot, he captured fifty-one votes to Regan's forty-four. On the second roll call, he got within a vote of an absolute majority and Bannock County put him over the top. "Cheer upon cheer rent the air," the *Statesman* reported, "half the delegates being on their feet and yelling like wild men." But the goldbug paper signaled that the general election would be no walkover: the Republicans would do anything to thwart "this monstrous combination which is aiming its poisoned arrows at the heart of our fair state." The Democratic *Blackfoot News* saw it differently. "From every misty mountain top in Idaho," it said, "the roosters greet the rays of the rising sun with: 'Steunenberg's the winner!'"

With the support of Democrats, Populists, Silver Republicans, and organized labor—and only token opposition from McKinley Republicans—Steunenberg went on to defeat David H. Budlong by the largest margin ever received by an Idaho governor, 22,096 to 6,441. Bryan swept Idaho four to one, though he lost the nation by a margin of seven to six.

Steunenberg's landslide victory seemed to presage big changes for Idaho, but they did not come to pass. Though only a single state legislator had been elected in opposition to him, the alliance that had put Steunenberg in office soon broke down in the face of renewed tensions in the Coeur d'Alenes.

Since 1892, Idaho's panhandle had remained a troubled region. The union had continued its campaign to intimidate nonunion miners, giving them drumhead trials at the union hall, then driving them up the valley and over the snow-capped Bitterroot mountains into Montana with only the clothes on their backs and no food to sustain them. Then on July 3, 1894, came a particularly gruesome incident, forty masked men executing John Kneebone, who'd testified against union miners at their trial after the 1892 outbreak. Nobody was ever convicted of this crime, but it helped trigger a new confrontation between the union and the mine owners, causing President Cleveland to station two companies of federal troops in the district for a couple of months that year.

At the urging of the Bunker Hill and Sullivan Company, Governor William J. McConnell had agreed to form two National Guard companies composed of the company's nonunion employees and outfitted by the state with two hundred carbines. Widely perceived as Bunker Hill's private army, these troops would give the company a decisive advantage if it came to another test of armed might.

By 1896, the Populists had consolidated their political grip on the Coeur d'Alenes. Aggressively taking up the cause of northern Idaho's embattled miners, they turned Shoshone County into a Populist stronghold. Though their opponents derided them as "dynopops," an amalgam of "dynamiters" and "populists," the miners embraced them wholeheartedly. In 1894 they captured nearly all—and in 1896 all—county offices.

Now, with Steunenberg as governor, the Populists and the miners union were more determined than ever to wrest economic power from the mine owners as well. After all, the MOA victory in 1892 had been achieved precisely by the decisive intervention of the mine owners' allies in the White House and the statehouse. Politics had made all the difference. At last, the miners thought, the shoe was on the other foot. With a friend in the governor's office, they now fully expected state government to reinforce, rather than frustrate, their demands.

On April 17, 1897, the Populist commissioners of Shoshone County wrote Steunenberg, asking him to disband the two National Guard units, which they held to be "a source of discord and uneasiness to all citizens." At first the governor seemed inclined to comply. But the mining companies warned that such action would fatally undermine even the tenuous sense of security in the mining district. Then, two days before Christmas in 1897, Frederick D. Whitney, a nonunion foreman of the Helena-Frisco mine, was taken from his bed by a band of masked and armed men, marched through the streets of Gem, and fatally shot. In the wake of that atrocity, Steunenberg concluded that the National Guard units must remain at Wardner.

He tried to regain some Populist support with the nomination of James R. Sovereign, once grand knight of the Knights of Labor, to the newly formed State Board of Arbitration, but it was too late. The electoral alliance that had put Steunenberg in office in 1896 was shattered. In 1898, the Populists split, then reunited, but, led by "the genuine longhaired, dyed-in-the-wool, fire-eating, greenback inflation element," declined to fuse with the Steunenberg Democrats. The Democrats and Silver Republicans again backed Steunenberg, who triumphed by a much narrower margin than he had two years before.

Along Canyon Creek, the mine owners largely accommodated themselves to the political strength of the Populists and the union, hiring union workers and paying all underground workers the "union wage" of $3.50 a day. But one company—Bunker Hill and Sullivan—remained adamant. Since 1893, when the state legislature outlawed yellow-dog contracts—requiring individuals to promise not to join a union as a condition of employment—the company had violated that law by flatly refusing to hire known union men. Only Bunker Hill and the neighboring Last Chance—which depended on Bunker Hill for compressed air to run its drills—remained nonunionized and only they paid skilled miners $3.00 and unskilled muckers $2.50. As the region's most determined enemy of union labor, Bunker Hill became the union's prime target.

The claim to Bunker Hill's deposits had been staked out in 1885 by a carpenter named Noah Kellogg, but like many original locators, he lacked the resources to develop his rich property, and in 1887 he sold it to a Portland, Oregon, entrepreneur, Simeon G. Reed. An art connoisseur, skilled trout fisherman, and horse breeder—who named his prize stallion Coeur d'Alene —Reed had difficulty with Bunker Hill's low-grade ores, which required intensive processing before smelting. The expense associated with such ores made the company especially conscious of labor costs and thus resentful of the miners union.

In early 1892—just in time for that year's labor crisis—Reed sold the mine to a San Francisco–based syndicate fronted by a mining engineer, John Hays Hammond. In his autobiography, Hammond describes with relish his role in bringing a boxcar of nonunion miners into Wardner. At Tekoa, Washington, he mounted the engine, crying to the engineer: "We've got to beat the union miners from Wallace! Let her go!" They arrived just in time to man the barricades at the mill.

If Bunker Hill's antiunion stance was grounded in business considerations, it took on a more ideological cast under Frederick Worthen Bradley, who assumed the managerial reins in 1893, becoming president in 1897. Bradley had attracted Hammond's attention by extracting healthy profits from low-grade ores at California's Spanish mine. But in Idaho, his concern for the bottom line was reinforced by his anxiety about Populist control of the county and near panic about the increasing stranglehold of union and for-eign-born workers on the mining industry. Convinced that the company's labor problem was rooted in the intransigence of Irish-born miners, he was determined by early 1894 to weed out the eighty-three "Irish" among his 332 miners and replace them with "Americans." To that end, he encouraged the founding of a local branch of the anti-Catholic American Protective Association, drawn from the town's Protestant merchants and artisans. Brad-ley looked to the 120-man APA not only as a source of anti-Catholic agitation but as a league of the "best citizens" and a "secret society for the preservation of law and order." Before long the APA warned that it would lynch anyone who interfered with the company's business.

The strength of the town's nativist movement became evident in early 1897, when a schoolteacher named Lila Johnson read an essay at a Washing-ton's Birthday celebration sponsored by the Junior Order of United American Mechanics. America, she warned, had become "the dumping ground for the human refuse from the slums of other countries." Given the influx of "the pauper and criminal classes," was it any wonder that "the menacing murmurs of industrial discontent, that for thirty years have been rumbling from shore to shore, all over our fair land, have swelled to a roar"? Charlie Burrus, editor of the *Wardner Citizen*, took umbrage at Johnson's remarks. "When a horsey woman, who is the picture of all that is vulgarly sensuous, takes the stage to vilify people not fortunate enough to be born in the United States," Burrus wrote, "she stirs up a hornet's nest.... What a picture for a goddess of liberty, warning all not native born to avoid polluting her skirts with the touch of their hands." His piece stirred such anger in town that more than a hundred people—many members of the Order of United American Mechanics—escorted Burrus to the depot and requested that he "proceed in the direction of Wallace, which he did without delay." When Burrus sued the "committee" that had driven him from town, its members were revealed as the same merchants and mechanics who filled the ranks of the pro–Bunker Hill APA. Eventually, a magistrate elected with Populist votes fined them sixty dollars apiece for their role in the episode.

With the APA consolidating its hold on Wardner and the National Guard and their carbines to back it up, and with Pinkerton and Thiel detec-tives infiltrating the union, Bunker Hill could be forgiven for feeling compla-cent. By July 1896, Bradley wrote his acting superior: "It may be too soon to crow, but I believe that we have such a control of the labor situation that it cannot be wrested from us."

In 1898, however, the War Department put out the call for state militias to fight in the Spanish-American War. Idaho's National Guard sent all the men it had under arms: two battalions of four companies each, totaling 32 officers and 468 men. Of the 104 men sent from Shoshone County, 80 were Bunker Hill employees. Not only did their departure weaken the company's lines of defense, it created a labor shortage that benefited the union.

As the nineteenth century drew to a close, Bunker Hill was a thriving enterprise. In 1893, when Bradley assumed its management, the corporation had been deeply in debt and had never paid a dividend. In the years since, it had moved into the black, paying over $600,000 in dividends. By April 1899, the miners union concluded that the time had come to confront Bunker Hill head-on, in hopes of compelling union recognition and union wages. Early that month, Ed Boyce, president of the Western Federation of Miners, then based in Butte, met with leaders of the Wardner union. On April 18, notices sprouted in the mining camp warning anyone not yet a union member to join immediately. On April 23, a workers' delegation called on Bunker Hill's acting manager, Frederick Burbidge, to present its demands. Burbidge put into effect a plan aimed at driving a wedge between the union members (roughly 100 men) and the rest of the company's workforce (about 350). He promptly granted a wage increase—to the "old scale" of $3.50 a day for miners, $3.00 for muckers—thus, it was hoped, satisfying the nonunion faction. But he refused the request for union recognition. Albert Burch, the superintendent, said the company would "shut down and remain closed for twenty years" before it would recognize the union. Union men should report to the office, where they'd be paid and dismissed. On his own initiative that day, Burch fired seventeen men he believed to be union members.

Three days later, some 150 unionists, many of them armed, turned workers away from the mine with dire threats, while another group seized the tramway carrying ore from mine to mill, effectively halting Bunker Hill's operations. Fearing for his life—with some justification—Fred Burbidge fled to Fairfield, Washington, where he wired Steunenberg in Boise, reporting the situation and adding: "County authorities unable to cope with mob, and we appeal to you for protection for ourselves and our men." Steunenberg promised to investigate but reminded Burbidge of the new state law providing for arbitration of labor disputes. "Nothing to arbitrate," Burbidge fired back. "I again renew my request for protection." Steunenberg telegraphed James D. Young, the county's Populist sheriff, asking for a report, to which Young replied: "Am on the ground. All is quiet. No armed mob. Matters are orderly."

Early on April 29, Burbidge heard from undercover detectives that more efforts would be made to intimidate his nonunion workers. He promptly alerted Steunenberg, who warned Young to stay on top of the situation.

The threat that bright spring morning came not from Wardner's embattled union but from the entrenched unionists along Canyon Creek. Up the narrow canyon in the cramped mining camp of Burke, the Northern Pacific's "down train" was about to make its seven-mile morning run to Wallace, when the engineer, Levi W. Hutton, and the conductor, George Olmstead, noted 250 miners in their "digging clothes," some wearing masks and others armed with rifles, climbing aboard the two passenger cars and eight boxcars. Hutton and Olmstead later claimed innocence in the matter, though authorities accused them of "moral cowardice and truculent subserviency." According to Hutton, two masked men with Winchesters jumped into his cab and told him, "Pull out for Wallace, and be damned quick about it!" A mile down the track, in the mining camp of Mace, a hundred more miners got on. The masked men ordered another stop at the powder house of the Helena-Frisco mine, where workers loaded eighty wooden boxes, each containing fifty pounds of dynamite. At Gem, another 150 to 200 miners armed with rifles joined their colleagues on the train, along with three freight cars to accommodate the newcomers.

When the train completed its scheduled run at Wallace, the station platform seethed with 200 more miners, who'd walked seven miles from Mullan, retrieving weapons cached in a manure pile along the way. The authorities later pointed to this as proof of how carefully the operation had been planned, allegedly at mining camp meetings the night before (the men of Mullan—representing the largest local union in the state—defiantly refused to wear disguises). Now the masked men in the cab ordered Hutton to head for Wardner, twelve miles west. "We can't go to Wardner," he said he told his captors, explaining that the Northern Pacific track didn't go there and they'd have to ask permission to run on the "foreign track" of the Oregon Railway and Navigation Company. Even with running orders it wasn't safe: "This engine weighs about 115 tons and we'll go through the bridges. Besides, there are trains on the O.R. & N. and we're liable to have a collision and kill fifty men."

A railway agent named Lambert refused permission to run on his tracks, but the masked men were adamant. So the rogue train pushed through the transfer switch, ringing its bell and sounding its whistle, which Hutton had rigged with a chime made by a Wallace plumber, giving it a distinctive tone. As an additional precaution, Hutton ordered the brakeman, Thomas Chester, to act as flagman, waving his red banner to warn any oncoming train of their unscheduled run. Since there were many curves on this stretch—requiring the flagman to intercept any train that might be out of sight round the turn—the train crawled along, reaching Kellogg just before noon. A mile from its destination, several hundred men from the Bunker Hill and Last Chance mines managed to squeeze aboard. As the train pulled into the Kellogg depot, which served as the railhead for Wardner's mines and mills, nearly a thousand men were jammed onto the nine freight and ore cars, one passenger coach, and two engines (one front and one rear). Some two hundred had covered their faces with masks made from pillowcases, buckskin, or American flags; these same men were armed with Winchesters, shotguns, and baseball bats.

The train was "literally black with men," recalled a Spokane newsman. "The engine itself was covered all over with armed men and everywhere a man could gain a place to sit or stand or hold on to, he was there." Each miner on the train wore a strip of white muslin in his buttonhole or a white cloth tied around his right arm.

Disembarking at Kellogg, many men sought "liquid courage" at three saloons across the street. Fearing they would become more reckless, Sheriff Young, who'd ridden down from Wallace on the rogue train, ordered the saloons closed. Meanwhile, other miners had unloaded the dynamite they'd taken from the Frisco magazine, piling it in a five-foot pyramid in the street. The sheriff, who enjoyed heavy support from the miners, climbed atop the dynamite and shouted: "In the name of the sheriff of Shoshone County and the people of the State of Idaho, I command you to disperse." Nobody moved. Conner Malott of the Spokane *Spokesman-Review*—a paper sympathetic to the mine owners—asked Young what he intended to do. "What can I do?" asked the sheriff, armed only with a .38 Colt revolver. "I've ordered them to disperse and they won't disperse." Later he testified that for an individual "to do anything with a mob of that kind was almost equal to facing death." Steunenberg disbelieved these protestations; he was probably right in suspecting some degree of collusion between Young and the rioters.

Shortly thereafter, a man who appeared to have some authority among the unionists shouted: "Wardner to the front!" "Burke!" "Mullan!" Masked and armed men—an eyewitness counted 150—formed ranks two abreast in front of the depot and marched down the tracks, while the remaining 850 miners, the "unwashed" majority, who apparently didn't know what was going on, milled about the depot in a holiday mood, swigging from bottles and singing ditties like "There'll Be a Hot Time in the Old Town Tonight." After a few hundred feet, the advance party turned toward the Bunker Hill concentrator, one of the world's largest, which had cost the company some $250,000.

About a half mile from the concentrator, this forward party halted, deploying skirmishers to advance on the building with "military precision," while preventing bystanders from getting too close. Riflemen fired toward the concentrator. For a time, they seemed to be firing at their own advance men. A twenty-eight-year-old union man named Jack Smythe, who'd been part of a scouting party advancing up the foothills south of the concentrator, was shot and killed—apparently in error—by his own colleagues. The advance guard took several prisoners, one a nonunion worker named James Cheyne, who was shot in the hip by the union men and died a few days later. Another prisoner, R. R. Rogers, a Bunker Hill Company stenographer, was slightly wounded by a bullet—or perhaps merely barbed wire—that grazed his upper lip.

In midmorning, Fred Burbidge had telephoned the mine superintendent at the concentrator to warn the nonunion men to "make for their own safety." When the attackers realized the concentrator was unmanned, they sent word to the main party still gathered by the train, to bring forward its lethal cargo. Even then, it isn't clear whether these seven to eight hundred men knew what was about to happen. In 1892, a smaller group of unionists had come to Wardner, persuaded Bunker Hill executives that dynamite was in place beneath the mine's concentrators, then used that leverage to get rid of the scabs. Many who boarded the train seven years later may have expected a repeat of that famous bluff.

Others had a bolder scheme in mind, placing sixty boxes of dynamite at three locations beneath the concentrator. At 2:35, they lit the fuses. In a few seconds three consecutive blasts reduced the concentrator to splintered wood and billows of dust. The Bunker Hill office containing all its records, the company boardinghouse, and several smaller buildings were also destroyed by explosion or fire. By 2:50, the raiding party and most of the others who'd arrived in Kellogg at noon were back on the train—now dubbed the Dynamite Express—which hastily retreated. From Kellogg to Wallace, ranchers and laboring people lined the tracks and, according to one eyewitness, "cheered the [union] men lustily as they passed."

In bed that day at Boise's St. Alphonsus Hospital, Frank Steunenberg had a severe case of the grippe and was able to attend to state business only with difficulty. But he sat bolt upright when, just before noon, he received a wire from a third party deeply offended by violations of railroad protocol. "The armed force at Coeur d'Alene mines took possession of a Northern Pacific engine and are using our tracks," wired Adam L. Mohler, the president of the Oregon Railway, from his Portland headquarters. "Will you protect us against use and damage of our property?" The news didn't improve the governor's state of mind or body, and he took out his mounting irritation on Sheriff Young, whom he telegraphed: "Representations are made that you are not able to cope with those who threaten disturbance.... Up to this time I have relied upon your power and ability to protect property and preserve order. Wire me the situation and any contemplated or actual violence, as reports seem to call for prompt and vigorous action by the State."

The next word wasn't from the sheriff but from Adam Mohler in Portland again, this time in a near frenzy about potential damage to his railroad: "Conditions at Wardner could not be worse. Rioters have set fire to Bunker Hill mill.... Rioters have cut wires, have appropriated Northern Pacific trains, and have interrupted all business.... I can not urge too strongly that you exhaust every means to bring this matter to successful termination and that not one moment's time be lost."

The news from Wardner struck Boise "like a thunder clap out of a clear sky," for the governor and his aides had thought the Coeur d'Alene crisis was passing. The sense of emergency was so intense that at midafternoon, against his doctors' advice, the governor dressed and hurried down to his office, where he convened a meeting of his "war cabinet," a small group of ranking officials who advised him on such matters. As they gathered, Steunenberg

placed calls to Sheriff Young; the county attorney, Henry F. Samuels; and
private citizens in Shoshone County. When none returned his call, the impatient governor managed to confirm the substance of Mohler's telegram with a
Wallace telephone operator.

On those grounds—the views of a railroad executive three hundred
miles from the events and a telephone operator who hadn't left her switchboard—the governor and his advisers opted for military intervention. But
with all five hundred men of the Idaho National Guard currently on duty in
the Philippines, Steunenberg had no troops at his own disposal. So he
promptly wired President William McKinley, asking him to "call forth the
military forces of the United States to suppress insurrection in Shoshone
County."

It was an anxious time for the twenty-fifth president of the United
States. A relentlessly political man, given to fretting about his standing in the
republic, McKinley "walked among men a bronze statue," wrote William
Allen White, "for thirty years determinedly looking for his pedestal." Now a
rebellion in the Philippines that had to be put down with volunteer troops
eager to go home; Democratic cries of "Imperialism!"; a bitter Senate battle
over the peace treaty with Spain all bedeviled plump and dapper William
McKinley in that final spring of the nineteenth century.

But what troubled McKinley most was the infirmity of his wife, Ida,
suffering from severe epileptic seizures accompanied by bouts of hysterical
depression. That spring her condition was exacerbated by the strain of a
murder trial that drew attention to scandalous doings in her family. A brother
of Ida's, a Lothario with a long trail of conquests behind him, had persuaded
an attractive seamstress named Anna George to leave her husband and two
children to live with him, then had abruptly jilted her for a merry widow.
Approaching the widow's home one day, he was killed by a volley of gunshots,
and Mrs. George was charged with his murder. In April, with the trial drawing to an end, the president took his wife to New York for a weekend of
shopping. As they checked into their seven-room suite at the Manhattan
Hotel, overlooking Forty-second Street, they learned that Mrs. George had
been acquitted. To Ida's horror, a theatrical company was offering the seamstress five hundred dollars for a week's engagement, a prospect that threatened to expose Ida's—and the president's—family to further ridicule. As
New Yorkers clamored to entertain the president and his wife that evening,
McKinley retired to his suite and apologized for himself and his wife: "I must
have rest. I came here for a brief season of quiet, and not to see the sights.
Some other time perhaps."

The next day, he sought to calm Ida with a four-hour cruise up the
Hudson River on a navy tug. The only matter of state that seemed to arrest
his attention was the rebellion on Luzon, where U.S. advances had prompted
the Filipino rebels to sue for peace. It was on the McKinleys' return to their

hotel that the president received Frank Steunenberg's telegram, relayed from the White House. He does not seem to have hesitated—or even deliberated much—about his response to the governor's appeal for troops.

Although Americans had long believed that a standing army in peacetime was "dangerous to the liberties of the people," there was ample precedent for military action to put down domestic disorders: as early as 1794, George Washington had sent troops to quell the Whiskey Rebellion in Pennsylvania; Lincoln dispatched Union regiments to control the 1863 draft riots in New York; during the "great strike" of 1877, President Rutherford Hayes had sent troops to Baltimore, Pittsburgh, and other cities; Cleveland had used soldiers to break the Pullman strike of 1894. It was an era of labor unrest—between 1881 and 1905 capital and labor collided in thirty-seven thousand strikes—but also a time when presidents and governors rarely hesitated to use military force to contain such disputes. From 1877 to 1903, federal or state troops intervened in more than five hundred such confrontations, invariably on the employers' side. Moreover, there was considerable support for such intervention from the business community, a constituency that invariably drew a ready response from William McKinley.

Within twenty-four hours of the Wardner explosion, telegrams began arriving—it had the feel of an orchestrated campaign—from Bunker Hill stockholders, among them the company's treasurer, William S. Crocker of San Francisco, and the Chicago banker James L. Houghteling. The only sign of presidential caution was McKinley's request that Attorney General John W. Griggs review the legal form of the governor's appeal, a hurdle it quickly passed. Preoccupied with his wife's condition and with bulletins from the Philippines, McKinley had, by the evening of the twenty-ninth, delegated the matter to the War Department, where Assistant Secretary George D. Meiklejohn stood in for the amiable but erratic secretary, Russell A. Alger, then in Michigan preparing to announce his candidacy for the U.S. Senate.

It was the able adjutant general, Henry C. Corbin, who chose the operation's commander, chiefly on geographical grounds. Brigadier General Henry Clay Merriam, Corbin told the president, was "the nearest to the scene of trouble, Denver being from sixteen to eighteen hours away." On April 30, Corbin wired Merriam, informing him of the situation and passing along "the president's direction" and the acting secretary's orders that he "repair at once to the capital of that State and after conference with the authorities . . . to the seat of action, calling to your aid such troops as may be most convenient."

To his bitter disappointment, in that year of stirring strife in Santiago and Manila, Merriam was a desk-bound officer, commanding two of the army's administrative departments: the Department of Colorado (headquartered at Denver's Fort Logan and embracing Arizona, Utah, Colorado, New Mexico, and Wyoming) and the Department of the Missouri (which included Iowa, Nebraska, Missouri, Kansas, Arkansas, the Indian Territory, and the Territory of Oklahoma, directed from Omaha's old Federal Building). Given his dual command—resulting from a wartime shortage of command-worthy generals—the sixty-one-year-old Merriam spent a lot of time shuttling between his two headquarters. On April 30, he returned from Omaha to Denver to find Corbin's telegram. Hungry for action, Merriam wasted no time. Hastily assembling his field kit, he and a young aide-de-camp boarded a 6:30 p.m. train, due into Boise at 2:30 a.m. on May 2.*

Steunenberg had felt well enough the day before to return to Boise's Branstetter House, where his wife had arrived from Caldwell to care for him. But when he learned of the general's arrival time, it struck him as terribly late to begin consultations. Thus, he and two advisers—Attorney General Samuel H. Hays and Adjutant General John L. Weaver—resolved to intercept Merriam at Glenns Ferry, seventy-five miles southwest of Boise, and accompany him to the capital so they could make essential decisions before retiring for the night.

About 12:30 a.m., the general and the governor, with their aides, met in the smoking room of the general's sleeper as the train rattled toward Boise. Merriam asked whether troops were still required; the governor reported that Wardner was calmer, but troops were needed to restore full law and order there. From the train, Merriam wired commanders of infantry companies in Spokane and Vancouver, Washington, and cavalry troops in Boise and Walla Walla to entrain for Wardner.

Once the council of war adjourned, the general retired to his berth. The governor—whose flu had taken a turn for the worse—huddled in his greatcoat until the train reached Boise at 2:45 a.m.; worn out by his exertions, he returned to his bed at the Branstetter House. Shortly after dawn, Merriam called on James H. Beatty, the federal judge, and Frank C. Ramsey, Idaho's U.S. marshal, then met with a *Statesman* reporter. Though the general was in civilian clothes, the reporter thought he looked "a soldier even without the gold lace." Stroking his iron-gray mustache, Merriam regretted he could disclose none of his plans. "Nothing would please those high-handed murderers in North Idaho more than to know my plans," he said as he left for another conference with the governor.

At some point in the meeting, Merriam called for six more infantry companies to set out for Mullan, bringing the total number of troops now converging on the district to over five hundred. Further talk with Steunenberg before catching the train north gave him "the impression that [the governor] was in doubt whether to declare martial law." Cabling Corbin, Merriam said that he'd order troops to "control outlets from mining camps" and that "if not disapproved I will direct [them] to scrutinize travel outward and detain suspected passengers. This is martial law but no other course likely to secure rioters."

---

* Along with Washington, Oregon, and the Territory of Alaska, Idaho belonged to the Department of the Columbia, but Merriam's orders now allowed him to operate there.

Reaching Walla Walla the next day, he learned that the president had approved his action. This may have suggested that the gloves were coming off so far as the president and the adjutant general were concerned—that henceforth they'd use bare knuckles. That impression was underlined by a telegram from Steunenberg that he had indeed declared martial law in the Coeur d'Alenes.

Accompanying the general and his aide, John B. Bennett, to Spokane were Attorney General Hays and Marshal Ramsey. Farther back in the train were some sixty-five troopers belonging to Troop F of the Fourth Cavalry (but none of their horses, regarded as inappropriate to the region's rough terrain). As Merriam and his party left Spokane the next morning and crossed into the Coeur d'Alenes shortly before noon, they learned that Troop A of the same regiment had passed that way by train the day before, the first unit to reach Wardner.

In the general's mind, however, the dismounted cavalry only supplemented the force on which he counted to restore order: the Twenty-fourth Infantry Regiment. By that spring, the Twenty-fourth had been scattered at isolated garrisons all over the Northwest. Now, in a flurry of telegrams, Merriam drew most of the regiment together under his command, summoning Companies A and G from Fort Douglas, Utah; Company B from Vancouver Barracks, Washington; Companies C and F from Fort Russell, Wyoming; Company D from Fort Harrison, Montana; Company K from Fort Assiniboine, Montana; Company M from Fort New Spokane, Washington.

In military terms, the choice was sound, for the Twenty-fourth was widely regarded as one of the best outfits among the seventeen thousand troops left in the continental United States. But there were other considerations, for it was one of the army's four "colored" regiments, black troops led by white officers. Merriam may have summoned "colored" troops precisely because the unruly miners were white—mostly Irish, Cornish, Italian, and Scandinavian—ensuring that his men wouldn't bond with the "rioters." Fraternization between white troops and white rioters had occurred during the 1877 rail strike. For that reason, in years since, the army had sometimes called on black troops to restore domestic order.

Or maybe it was simpler than that. With his military career nearing an end, perhaps Merriam was revisiting his rousing youth, invoking the heady idealism that had made him a soldier in the first place.

When Confederate guns opened fire on Fort Sumter in April 1861, Henry Clay Merriam was completing his first year at Maine's Waterville College, preparing to practice law in Houlton, a town on the Canadian border where his father was a middling farmer. But, as he recalled later, "the atmosphere which pervaded the home, the school, the colleges and the churches" was so drenched with abolitionist fervor that many of Waterville's stalwarts quit their studies. "In our childhoods," he remembered, "we heard our fathers, with trembling voices read the stormy debates of Congress.... When Senator Toombs made the monstrous boast that he would call the roll of his slaves on Bunker Hill, it was too much even for the sluggish Puritan blood of New England."

In July 1862, after Lincoln's appeal for 300,000 volunteers to defend the Union, Merriam left college to enlist in the Twentieth Maine Infantry, setting out to recruit Company H in the state's farming and fishing country. Elected the company's captain, he and his men—among them his younger brother, Lewis—boarded a steamer that landed them at Alexandria, Virginia, on September 6. As part of General Daniel Butterfield's Light Brigade, they slogged toward Antietam in brutal heat. At nightfall on September 16, Merriam led his farmboys and fishermen to a ridge east of town, where they stood in reserve during the next day's carnage, though Merriam did enough on that terrible battlefield to be cited for "gallant and meritorious service." The regiment saw more action at Shepardstown Ford and then fought at bloody Fredericksburg, stacking corpses before them as shields against the frightful Confederate fire.

The Twentieth Maine became one of the Union's most celebrated regiments, distinguishing itself at Gettysburg, The Wilderness, and Bethesda Church. But Merriam wasn't with it. On January 7, 1863—after certification by the Army of the Potomac as "a brave and efficient officer in battle and a gentleman in camp"—he resigned his commission to take up new duties with a black regiment then forming in New Orleans.

The notion of blacks serving as Union soldiers had been opposed by many Northerners—indeed, by Abraham Lincoln himself—early in the war. Only radicals regarded the war as a struggle over slavery and saw its principal goal as emancipation. Conscious of Northerners' reservations, preferring where possible to conciliate rather than enrage the South, determined not to push the border states into the Confederacy's arms, Lincoln framed the war as a limited conflict to preserve the Union. Moreover, many Notherners had grave doubts about the Negro's courage, arguing, "Niggers won't fight." As late as August 1862, when an Indiana delegation offered two colored regiments, Lincoln said he'd "employ all colored men as laborers, but wouldn't promise to make soldiers of them."

This position eroded under pressure from radical legislators and bold experimentation by a few Union commanders seeking any advantage against a determined foe. Long before Lincoln proclaimed it national policy, officers in widely scattered campaigns, often derided as "niggadier generals," armed and trained black freedmen and fugitives—as the First Kansas Colored Volunteers, the Louisiana Native Guards, and the First South Carolina Colored Volunteers—then tested their mettle in limited engagements with the enemy.

Their promising performances, along with pressure from blacks like Frederick Douglass, pushed Lincoln to issue the Emancipation Proclamation on January 1, 1863. But in that document the president said only that emancipated blacks would be "received into the armed service of the United States to garrison forts, positions, stations, and other places and to man vessels of all sorts," which would have kept ex-slaves in defensive roles.

One powerful advocate of enlisting black troops as the full equals of whites was Lincoln's vice president, Hannibal Hamlin of Maine. Hamlin had been influenced by his sons, Charles and Cyrus, and the son of his friend John Appleton, Maine's chief justice—all three of whom, as Union officers, ardently supported black enlistment. Several times in late 1862, the vice president had vainly pressed Lincoln on this matter. Once the president took his equivocal stance on black troops in the Emancipation Proclamation, the stage was set for another attempt to push him off the fence. One night in mid-January, Captain Cyrus Hamlin appeared at his father's rooms with ten other young officers—most from Maine, among them probably Henry Clay Merriam—who so believed in arming freedmen they were willing to surrender their current positions to command Negro units. Would the vice president use his influence to that end?

At 9:00 a.m., the vice president and the uniformed officers presented themselves at the White House. So moved was Lincoln by their commitment to this cause that he wrote Secretary of War Edwin M. Stanton asking him to organize a new Negro brigade officered by the men the vice president would introduce. Hamlin's initiative merged with an effort, now stalled by official misgivings, to form a colored brigade led by Daniel Ullmann, commander of the Seventy-eighth New York Volunteers. Once Stanton saw Lincoln's note, all caution fled. On January 13, Ullmann was appointed brigadier general and ordered to raise a brigade of "Louisiana volunteer infantry," recruited among colored freedmen there, with white officers from the Northeast.

Seeking 250 officers, the war secretary turned to three states with powerful abolitionist traditions. Governor Abner Coburn of Maine nominated officers for two regiments, New York's governor two, and the governor of Massachusetts one. The criteria were like those for officers in a Massachusetts black regiment: "young men of military experience, of firm Anti-slavery principles, ambitious, superior to the vulgar contempt of colour, and having faith in the capacity of coloured men for military service"—in short, "the finest, sharpest men" available. The officers required a principled selflessness, for according to William James—whose brother had volunteered—"in this new negro-soldier venture, loneliness was certain, ridicule inevitable, failure possible." As it turned out, Maine men commanded three regiments. Governor Coburn proposed Henry Clay Merriam for the rank of lieutenant colonel, but—in the first of many such rebuffs—he achieved only a captaincy, commanding Company F in Cyrus Hamlin's Third Regiment.

These idealistic officers reached New Orleans early in April. During its first weeks in Louisiana, the Third Regiment recruited troops, scarcely a difficult task, for "hordes of darkies of every age" followed the flag wherever it appeared, "the symbol of peace, plenty and 'Massa Linkum.' " That spring, Merriam's company fought in several engagements along the Mississippi, including the battle of Port Hudson, where the Native Guards distinguished themselves in a doomed but gallant charge.

It was the conjunction of this attack and, eight weeks later, the gallantry of the Fifty-fourth Massachusetts that tipped the balance of public opinion. In particular, the charge of the Fifty-fourth's black ranks against merciless gunfire from Fort Wagner—which killed their commander, Colonel Robert Gould Shaw, and killed or wounded 247 of his men—left little doubt about black courage.

In May 1864, Merriam was made lieutenant colonel and given command of the Seventy-third Infantry Corps d'Afrique, probably the nation's oldest black regiment, as it had been mustered in three months before the Emancipation Proclamation.

As 1865 began, Merriam and his regiment found themselves in Morganza, Louisiana, on a bend in the Mississippi northwest of Baton Rouge. It was "wet and disagreeable" that winter along the great river, which laid relentless siege to the regiment's campground. Merriam sought vainly to stem its advance with a suction pump, while keeping himself and his kit as presentable as possible, with the help of his black manservant, Sam. On January 24, he "arose late—weather very cold—river and mud very high. Camp half occupied by the river . . . [which] seems to contest my title to the ground on which we are quartered."

Merriam, who'd made Phi Beta Kappa at Waterville, passed the time in his rain-soaked tent reading an article about Chief Justice Roger B. Taney in the *Atlantic Monthly*, a slim folio of Dante, and two volumes of Tennyson's poetry, a gift from the regimental chaplain. The colonel was something of a poet himself, many of his verses dedicated to Lucy Getchell back in Waterville: "I remember, when spring with soft whisper was cheering / The timid young buds into bloom / In the wake of the wild winter's gloom. / A scene to my heart that is ever endearing / No matter what beauties these eyes / May behold under soft southern skies."

Life with the Seventy-third Regiment was anything but soft. One night, Captain Guest of Company H was testing the guard posts when he was shot by a Negro sentinel. Merriam carried Guest's body to his tent. "It was warm," he wrote in his diary, "I half thought I felt pulsation, but no, the femoral artery had been severed in the left thigh high up, and no ligature—he must have died in a few moments. It is doubly bitter to loose [*sic*] so good an officer." But, he concluded, "no one seems to be to blame. I have released with praise the poor fellow who shot the captain. . . . He manifested a laudable degree of discipline and coolness."

General Ullmann—whom a colleague described as "a polished speaker, a gentleman of high culture, a fair lawyer, but not a general"—behaved badly.

One night he returned from town "so drunk that two men had to hold him on his horse." His staff, brought in by carriage, was "worse off." Such doings Merriam thought "most disgraceful."

Clearly smitten with Lucy back in Waterville, the twenty-eight-year-old officer with the guardsman's mustache wasn't immune to the attractions of Louisiana women, notably two "creole friends" named Anna White and Eliza Dubois, whom he took to the Varieties in New Orleans on February 15. "I find Anna a very pleasant little companion," he reported in his diary. Returning by steamer to his regiment, Merriam encountered a Mrs. McCauley, whom he found "very pretty and very interesting company."

Soon Merriam's regiment was ordered into the war's last major battle— an assault on Mobile, Alabama. With the rest of the First Division, Merriam's troops slogged some 250 miles through "horrible swamps," along "indescribably bad roads" in southern Louisiana. Mounted on his horse, Arab, he watched his troops' performance with great pride: "It surpasses anything I ever saw—nine days hard marching on half rations and not a man too sick as to fall out of ranks, while the ambulances of other rgts. have been full." He compared his stoic men to the white soldiers he saw "wallowing in the mud." He'd never seen men "so much discouraged and so unreasonably helpless"; instead of assisting the mired wagon trains, "they only cursed and complained, some of them crying, others offering five dollars for a 'hard tack.'" The "uniform good spirits of the colored troops" he assigned less to them than to the "superior efficiency of their [white] officers."

On April 2, Merriam's troops laid siege to Fort Blakely at Mobile. Seven days later, he requested permission to attack. Under shot and shell, he led his men over the battlements, his regiment the first to place its flag on the parapet. For "gallantry," Merriam won the Medal of Honor. Most of his men displayed similar courage. He spotted only one black soldier "skulking" in the rear. "I drew my revolver and shot him," Merriam reported. The neck wound wasn't fatal, but now "he has a mark of which he will be ashamed all his life."

On April 17, Merriam and his men learned that their heroics at Fort Blakely had been superfluous. Hours before they'd stormed those ramparts, Lee had surrendered at Appomattox. "Now," Merriam wrote, "we can look for speedy peace."

Mustered out in late 1865, he returned to Maine a hero, married Lucy, and resumed legal studies at the college. He paid for this instruction—he was proud to say—with his earnings at sawmills and farms; he wasn't among the favored few admitted to West Point because of their parents' connections. For his prewar work, the college had granted him a B.A. in absentia; now he added a masters degree. But civilian life seemed insipid. The military drew him because "beyond all other professions, it has been the stepping stone to honor and fame." An ancestor had fought at Concord and Lexington. Hungry for such laurels, Merriam sought a regular army commission. It would require a reduction in rank, since his lieutenant colonelcy had been in the volunteers, but that was no impediment to youth's fervor. In July 1866, Merriam became a major with the Thirty-eighth Infantry, another black regiment.

During the Civil War, 179,000 black soldiers had seen action, of whom 36,847 were killed and perhaps the same number wounded or missing. By July 1865—before the Union army began demobilization—123,156 Negro soldiers made up 12 percent of the million Union soldiers under arms, organized in 120 infantry, 22 artillery, and 7 cavalry regiments. Despite their exploits, unreconstructed Southerners and Northern Democrats now pressed to abolish the black regiments. In July 1866, Congress struck a compromise, reducing the 149 black units to 6—4 of infantry (the Thirty-eighth, Thirty-ninth, Fortieth, and Forty-first) and 2 of cavalry (the Ninth and Tenth).

The East didn't want them; nor did the Midwest, and certainly not the South. Henceforth, black regiments were assigned exclusively to the West's dusty ranges, where they weren't likely to encounter influential citizens. Between 1870 and 1900, only one black unit was ever stationed, even temporarily, east of the Mississippi: a troop of the Ninth Cavalry spent part of 1891 at Fort Myer, Virginia, as a reward for helping rescue the white Seventh Cavalry ambushed by Sitting Bull's Sioux the previous December. But its presence aroused such protest among Virginia whites that the company was sent back West. Nor was the experiment tried soon again. For years, black cavalrymen battled the Sioux, Cheyennes, and Apaches, while black infantry units pulled garrison duty at desolate posts from Montana to New Mexico.*

Merriam's first command with the Thirty-eighth Infantry was at Fort Bayard, New Mexico, from which he harassed the Apaches. In 1869, when Congress reduced the army from forty-five to twenty-five regiments, it cut the black infantry regiments once again, the Thirty-eighth and Forty-first merging to form the Twenty-fourth Infantry, the Thirty-ninth and Fortieth to compose the Twenty-fifth Infantry. In 1869, Merriam became a lieutenant colonel in the Twenty-fourth, for eight years commanding a succession of dreary forts in southern Texas.

Near Fort Concho, on April 24, 1870, Merriam suffered a terrible loss. He, his wife, and two-year-old Mamie, with a party of servants and soldiers, were camped on the great Staked Plains near the headwaters of the Rio Concho. About midnight, a storm triggered a flood of "unprecedented volume and force." Hail "rattled down like a discharge of artillery," injuring Merriam's wife and daughter. Once the storm subsided, Merriam put them in a horse-drawn ambulance and headed for higher elevation. The group nearly reached safety when a fresh torrent swept the ambulance "with its precious

---

* In fairness to the military, it should be said that relatively few white soldiers served east of the Mississippi either; it was the West, plagued with Indian raids and border incursions, that required the bulk of active-duty troops (Fletcher, *Black Soldier*, 22).

contents" into the river. Lucy and Mamie, two servants, and two soldiers drowned. As Lucy was washed downstream, she was said to have cried, "My darling husband, goodbye!"

Merriam's own moorings were nearly swept away too. "The gentle vine and tenderest bud," he wrote, "which clung so sweetly about my life, softening every care, and sweetening every pleasure, [was] ruthlessly torn away without a moment's notice, and so cruelly that my very soul shudders at the picture." Until Merriam remarried in 1874, he buried himself in his border duties.

These responsibilities escalated during the Mexican Revolution of 1876, when Nueva Laredo—just across the border—was taken and retaken by contending forces. When American citizens were arrested and their lives threatened, Merriam obtained their release through negotiation, backed by military intimidation. When Mexicans shelled Laredo, Merriam unhesitatingly—and without authorization—returned their fire.

But as the years went by, firefights with Mexicans across the Rio Grande and pursuits of Indians along the Platte gave way to garrison and administrative duties, Merriam's career stalling like a mule train in heavy mud. For two decades, he shuttled across the West to commands in Idaho, Washington, Wyoming, South Dakota, and Colorado. According to one commentator, he was devoted to two things. One was drill. "Night and morning, morning and night, discipline is uppermost in the mind of this man, who is a soldier himself, and who will have all others around him soldiers." His regiment was regarded by some as the army's most disciplined unit; "as a drill instructor," wrote one journalist, "General Merriam has no equal." He wrote treatises on drill and infantry tactics for the *Army and Navy Register,* among them a manual on "pitching camp."

The other object of his devotion was the Merriam Infantry Pack, a knapsack he developed after studying packs carried by European armies. The result was a sturdy backpack, weighing thirty-two pounds when filled with the standard kit. The *Journal of the United States Infantry Association* called it "the best knapsack yet invented."

Increasingly, another obsession seized him: a fierce quest for promotion. He worried incessantly about who was passing him in rank. When a recommendation for unpaid promotion was lost at division headquarters, he complained to his diary: "So are the laurels of subordinates trifled with by their superiors!" Concluding that his promotion had been delayed because of his service with black troops, he asked, "in the absence of any necessity to the contrary, to serve in a white regiment." Starting in 1876, with assignment to the Second U.S. Infantry, his regiments were white, but that didn't speed his climb.

Not until 1885, at age forty-eight, did he make full colonel, commanding the Seventh Infantry Regiment at Fort Laramie, then at Fort Logan. His status anxiety, however, was not entirely eased. By 1896, he stood second on the colonel's seniority list for promotion to brigadier general. Despite campaigns of letters to the White House and Congress and the dispatch of his brother to lobby for him, he was passed over eight times.

Merriam thought he knew who was doing him in: a military physician named Robert Maitland O'Reilly, whom he described as "the only enemy I have in Washington." The colonel and the doctor had conceived a mutual distaste in 1891 when Merriam commanded Fort Logan and O'Reilly served as post surgeon. A soldier's complaint that O'Reilly had required him to perform onerous duties while a patient in the post hospital had gradually escalated into a feud that brought Merriam a rebuke from the acting war secretary. The colonel got his revenge: when O'Reilly asked leave to Denver for one day, a privilege routinely accorded other officers, Merriam refused.

Merriam had chosen the wrong subordinate with whom to trifle. For O'Reilly wasn't only a skilled physician but a cultivated man and graceful courtier who'd served as White House physician to Grover Cleveland. He often went duck hunting with the president on Chesapeake Bay and surely had ample opportunity to block his antagonist's promotion. There is no evidence that he did so, but there was no blinking the fact that, a full decade after Merriam had made colonel, no further advancement had come his way. In April 1895, Merriam wired President Cleveland: "I learn from Buffalo and elsewhere Doctor O'Reilly has threatened to prevent my promotion. Please investigate any such attempt." The War Department reviewed its files but found no record of any such effort by O'Reilly.

There were other factors militating against the choleric colonel. His prickliness antagonized the War Department and Congress. In 1891, his brother passed on a warning from a Maine senator that "you were hurting your own interests by being so aggressive in the use of words and in speaking of things that you were not familiar with." He had a disconcerting habit of criticizing his superiors, then, when called to account, blaming reporters for misquoting him.

Colonel Aldebert Ames, Merriam's commander in the Twentieth Maine, detected another problem. In 1895, he wrote General Joshua L. Chamberlain, the regiment's second commander and now the retired president of Bowdoin College: "I understand Merriam's offense is that he is not a West Pointer. I am one and I protest against such injustice to him and to West Point. The time to show his inferiority was from 1861 to 1865—not now in 1895." Chamberlain warned the president that by overlooking volunteers from modest backgrounds, Cleveland might contribute to a feeling that "there is a 'class distinction' here." Yet the lack of a West Point commission didn't hinder Merriam's comrades. By 1901, of twenty regular army generals, only four had attended West Point, the rest earning their commissions through active service. Whatever the grounds for his suspicions, Merriam didn't obtain the yellow sash until Cleveland—and O'Reilly—left office. Only in June 1897 did McKinley elevate him to brigadier general.

As the United States and Spain reached the brink of war, Merriam sensed his last opportunity to achieve "honor and fame." In April he wrote the major general commanding the army, Nelson Appleton Miles, begging "not to be overlooked in case of mobilization." Instead, three days later, he was appointed commander of the Department of California, including the entire Pacific Coast and the Hawaiian Islands, with headquarters at San Francisco. His heaviest responsibility—unglamorous but vital—was to ensure that arms and supplies moved swiftly through the port of San Francisco and other West Coast ports on their way to General Wesley Merritt's eleven thousand troops in the Philippines.

The blow was softened a bit when Merriam, with several other brigadier generals, was named a major general in the wartime volunteer army, but Merriam wasn't assuaged. The general he'd replaced in San Francisco had gotten the job he craved, leading the expeditionary force against Cuba. Major General William Rufus Shafter—with whom Merriam had served in the Twenty-fourth—was, at sixty-three, a gouty 330-pound blimp, a sort of "comic cartoon of a sedentary general," hardly suited to active command in the tropics. It was said that one reason Shafter got this starring role was that, like Secretary of War Alger, he hailed from Michigan, and Alger liked him. But then the *Nation* noted that the generals in the Spanish-American War were mostly selected "upon the principle which governs kissing."

All through the Cuban and Philippine campaigns, as he shuffled papers in San Francisco, Merriam brooded at the injustice of it all. As hostilities drew to an end, he got another sign of his low standing; along with some other wartime generals, in February 1899 he was relieved of his volunteer rank of major general (though he remained a brigadier general in the regulars). Like a man possessed, he campaigned for the permanent rank of major general. In March he wrote Corbin: "I am led to believe that my discharge from my volunteer rank may have been influenced by the fact that I have failed to secure assignment to foreign service, either in the Spanish or Philippine Wars.... It has *not been my fault* that I have not gone abroad and it is not pleasant to be punished for it."

How anguished he was by these snubs was reflected in his reaction when bypassed once again: "It would have caused me much less pain had President McKinley shot me rather than passed over me in this manner. My professional position is dearer to me than my life."

One wonders whether his ordeal was made heavier still because his son Henry McPherson Merriam—one of five children his second wife bore him—was even then fighting in the Philippines. In February 1899, young Henry wrote his father of a battle at Santa Ana: "You could hear nothing but the zip zip of the Mausers, as they went past, and every ten or fifteen seconds the roar from the guns of the First Washington as they sent volley after volley into the enemy. As I went for my horse I said to myself, 'Now is your time, Henry, Do or Die.' . . . I send in this letter a piece of an insurgent uniform that I cut from one of their killed."

That letter and that scrap of cotton could hardly have failed to remind the general, restless in his dusty chamber on the wharves, of a glorious afternoon in Mobile, thirty-five years before, when he'd led his black men up the battlements, thinking to himself something very like "Now is your time, Henry, Do or Die."

Nor could it have escaped Merriam's notice that, while he languished at home, the black regiment he'd helped to shape had distinguished itself in the Cuban fighting. Indeed, few regiments had emerged from the Spanish-American War crowned with such proud laurels as the Twenty-fourth Infantry.

For blacks who served in the military between the close of the Civil War and the turn of the century, the glamorous assignment lay with the Ninth and Tenth Cavalry Regiments, who, with spurs jingling and sabers rattling, pursued the Sioux and the Apaches across the plains, riding into something like immortality as "the Buffalo Soldiers." There was nothing glamorous, though, about the life of black infantrymen during those years. Invariably stationed at dusty forts in wastelands like the Staked Plains of Texas, the Dakota badlands, or the Wyoming highlands, they performed humdrum, though often arduous, duties: clearing sagebrush and chaparral, building roads and bridges, hunting horse and cattle thieves, and occasionally pursuing bands of Indians across the plains, until the Buffalo Soldiers arrived to take the credit.

Not surprisingly, members of the Twenty-fourth resented their work details and their postings. While the cavalry was "chalking up glory," they were "housekeepers." From the Twenty-fourth and the other black regiments, their families, and their friends came requests for better postings—to a northern state or the environs of a large city.

From 1870 to 1896, the War Department held firm to its policy of isolating the black regiments. The only relief the Twenty-fourth got from its early assignments in the Staked Plains and along the Rio Grande was several expeditions scouting for Indians. In July 1875, for example, Colonel Shafter, then the regiment's commander, assembled such a force from two companies of the Twenty-fourth, one of the Twenty-fifth, nine troops of the Tenth Cavalry, and a company of Indian scouts. This "little army," almost exclusively black, set out from Fort Concho bound for the Brazos River with sixty-five six-mule wagons, a seven-hundred-mule pack train, and its own beef herd. The blue-clad column marched thirty miles a day through an ocean of waving grass. Huge buffalo herds lumbered on its flanks, while antelope turned to gaze as the soldiers passed. After great hardship, the expedition returned to Fort Concho on Christmas Eve. Along the way it had drawn the region's first map, raided Indian villages, and captured hundreds of ponies and several squaws.

No regiment had been penned into the Southwest quite so relentlessly as the Twenty-fourth. In 1880, after eleven consecutive years in Texas, it was divided, some companies remaining in Texas while others were transferred to the Indian Territory, where they took charge of reservations holding the Kiowas and Cheyennes. In 1888, the regiment moved to Fort Bayard in the New Mexico Territory and Forts Huachuca, San Carlos, Thomas, and Bowie in the Arizona Territory. Most of these posts were regarded as "hellholes," especially Fort Thomas and Fort San Carlos, where the summers were "intensely disagreeable," with a sky like hammered brass, clouds of fierce black flies, and a climate so hot and dry it cracked human skin.

By 1895, after the Twenty-fourth had spent a quarter century in such odious surroundings, pressures mounted to give it some relief. That January, Representative George W. Murray, a black congressman from South Carolina, warned the secretary of war that "depression and demoralization results [*sic*] from service too long in the wilderness" and urged that the Twenty-fourth be assigned to a northern station "near a large city." The lieutenant general commanding the army, J. M. Schofield, partially concurred. When no action had been taken a year later, Colonel J. Ford Kent, the Twenty-fourth's commander, urged the adjutant general to give his regiment "a good station," noting that "a natural feeling prevails that it is on account of their color that the regiment is debarred from the better locations."

Ultimately, the War Department capitulated, but with a presidential election approaching in 1896, it placed the Twenty-fourth where it could do the least political harm: Fort Douglas, on a hill east of Salt Lake City. Having achieved statehood only that January, Utah was small, without clout in Washington, and dominated by Mormons, whose polygamy aroused little sympathy elsewhere in the land. In short, if Salt Lake's citizens weren't pleased with the move, they couldn't make much of a fuss.

The response was mixed. On October 10, the *Salt Lake Herald* wished "Glory and Honor to the Sixteenth Infantry," the white regiment that had occupied Fort Douglas and was now headed for Idaho and Washington. But it added: "Welcome to the Twenty-fourth Infantry." The *Salt Lake Tribune*—which a black editor called "the greatest Negro-hating sheet in the West"—saw it differently, noting, "While the colored man is just as good as the white man ... there is no occasion on earth to try to force a change in conditions which will involve a strong revulsion in the minds of the main business part of the city.... When our theaters are running, the best people of the city, in crowds, have to take street cars to go home at night. They do not want to be brought in direct contact with drunken colored soldiers." If such facts were laid before the war secretary, the *Tribune* said, he might "send the colored men to some other station ... where they would not be a source of apprehension and discomfort." Senator Frank J. Cannon of Utah did meet with Secretary of War Daniel S. Lamont to ask that the Twenty-fourth be sent elsewhere, but the secretary declined to change the order.

Back in Salt Lake, anxieties grew on September 10 when there disembarked at the depot "about 100 colored women and a number of dark sports who follow the regiment from post to post." Some of the women were undoubtedly wives (fifty soldiers were married, their wives serving as servants or laundresses to white officers); others were probably girlfriends, camp followers, or prostitutes. The "dark sports" were probably gamblers, whiskey salesmen, pimps, and other vendors who catered to military men.

On September 15, and again on October 22, came the regiment's blue-clad companies, greeted at the depot by most of the city's tiny black community (no more than six hundred). As the soldiers marched behind their high-stepping band through the Temple District, white spectators looked on with curiosity and apprehension. When the flag passed, held by a black sergeant, some whites removed their hats and cheered. For the troops themselves, their passage down the city's boulevards lined with marble halls must have been eye-opening. One reporter found them "gratified at having been transferred from Texas to the promised land."

Colonel Kent went out of his way to minimize friction between the regiment and Salt Lake's residents. Admonishing his men to be on their best behavior, he said arms were not to be carried in the city. The soldiers weren't permitted to take part-time work. In interviews, the colonel tried to ease citizens' fears about five hundred black troopers in their midst, deploring "an erroneous impression [which] was in circulation, putting the boys in a bad light. I do not say this from conceit, but you will find our regiment better behaved and disciplined than most of the white soldiers."

Another influence was Allen Allensworth, the regiment's chaplain. Born a slave in Kentucky and later a disciple of Booker T. Washington, Allensworth sought to "improve and uplift" his race, "to change public opinion by meeting its demands." In the *Broad Ax,* a black-owned newspaper in town, he argued that blacks needed to "improve [their] social status" and to "draw the line between the refined and the unrefined." Allensworth toured the South, seeking "especially desirable recruits" for the Twenty-fourth. On one trip, he found "seven brickmasons, four shoemakers, two blacksmiths, four printers, eight tailors," and a host of others. Several graduates of Booker T. Washington's Tuskegee Institute and other black colleges were said to be awaiting places in the regiment.

Allensworth asked the city's vice mongers to shun the new black clientele. The *Broad Ax* said of him that he "desires to inform the good people of our beautiful city that he would be more than pleased if all the saloons, gambling houses and immoral houses would absolutely refuse to entertain the negro soldiers, for he believes that there are a thousand white men who are willing to go to hell with the black man, but there are a very few who care to go to heaven with him."

The chaplain's plea didn't keep soldiers from the city's grog shops, bordellos, or other venues of mischief. In mid-November, H. B. Ballantyne and W. P. Gunn were the first members of the regiment to appear in police court, both fined for public drunkenness, while Gunn also got a fine for "packing a machete." On balance, though, over the next eighteen months, the "dusky lads" proved well-behaved. Like other black regiments, the Twenty-fourth had unusually low alcoholism and desertion rates (for seven years toward century's end, it had the lowest desertion rate in the army, an important indicator of discipline and morale). Its members were "neat, orderly, and obedient, [and] seldom brought before courts martial."

One object of the soldiers' energies was the regimental band, called by some the army's best, which played for dances, led marches through the city, and gave public concerts. The regiment also produced two crack baseball teams, the Browns and the Colored Monarchs, which whipped military and civilian teams alike. Enlisted men belonged to secret organizations like Noah's Ark Lodge and the Society of Prognosticators or to more public associations such as the Christian Endeavor Society—where Nella Allensworth, the chaplain's daughter, held forth one day on "Confidence"—and the Frederick Douglass Memorial Literary Society, which sponsored debates. One topic was, "Resolved, that there is no future for the negro in the United States," which was decided in the affirmative.

That was scarcely surprising in the last decade of the nineteenth century, as midcentury abolitionism gave way to a crabbed materialism that had little patience with "the Negro problem." The Supreme Court had led the way in this revisionism. In 1883, it overturned the Civil Rights Act of 1875, which had prohibited racial discrimination in public accommodations. When Mississippi and South Carolina ratified constitutions that disenfranchised blacks, the Court sanctioned such restricted suffrage. In *Plessy v. Ferguson* (1896), it supported segregation on public carriers, stamping its approval on the "separate but equal" doctrine. During the century's last years, southern states enacted Jim Crow laws that took back the rights blacks had won during Reconstruction. Between 1885 and 1900, the United States chalked up twenty-five hundred lynchings, mostly of blacks. A week after the sinking of the *Maine*—in which twenty-two black sailors died—a black postmaster in South Carolina was assaulted by a white mob that torched the post office, killed him and his infant son, and gravely wounded his wife and other children.

But if prospects for the American Negro looked bleak indeed that spring of 1898, the Spanish-American War created fresh opportunities for blacks. In an army limited to twenty-eight thousand, much of which had sunk into drowsy decrepitude during three decades of peace, the four black regiments operating in the West were the only American forces boasting recent military action, albeit against Mexicans, Indians, and horse thieves. The white officers of the black regiments never doubted that their troops would do their duty against Spain. "Had they not seen them," asked one such officer, "in Indian campaigns, march and fight, go hungry and thirsty, and as scouts and guides, carry their lives in their hands across weird, silent wastes of curling grass and chaparral, through gloomy, resounding canyons, and over wild crags and mountain tops, as if they did not know what fear was?"

Moreover, the new war's battlegrounds—Cuba, Puerto Rico, and the Philippines—were tropical, and it was widely believed that black men were better suited than whites to fighting in the wet heat of those exotic lands. Indeed, most American blacks (and some southern-born American whites) were thought to be immune to malaria and yellow fever. In May 1898, Congress authorized the War Department to raise an additional volunteer force of up to ten thousand men "possessing immunity from diseases incident to tropical climates." Eventually, the department raised ten so-called immune regiments, six white and four black, intended for garrison duty in the tropics. But the notion of an absolute immunity extending to every member of a black regiment considerably overstated the case. Blacks, both in Africa and in the southern United States, sometimes got yellow fever, but those who lived in areas where the disease was endemic usually got a very mild form as children, acquiring an immunity for life. Those who contracted it as adults—often mulattoes or blacks raised in the northern or border states—usually got a much less severe form than whites and their death rate from the disease was much lower than for whites.

All four regular black regiments saw extensive action against Spain. Ten days before Congress declared war in mid-April 1898, the *Salt Lake Tribune* found that "both officers and men [of the Twenty-fourth] seemed to be rubbing up a trifle on Spanish, for they accosted one another with 'buenos noches,' 'compadre' and 'adios.' "

On April 17, a *Tribune* reporter found a black soldier preparing to depart for Cuba, "his kit spread out on the floor of the veranda in front of his barracks. It contained besides the usual camp equipment, a cracked blue mug with a gilt label, 'From One Who Loves You,' running diagonally across its face. An inscription on the photograph gave Mobile, Ala., as the place where it was taken, and as the soldier rolled up his belongings he hummed: 'Down Mobile, down Mobile, How I love 'at pretty yellow gal, Down Mobile.' "

On April 20, nearly twenty thousand whites lined the city's streets to bid the Twenty-fourth good-bye. The same "Negro-hating" *Tribune* that eighteen months before had protested the black soldiers' assignment to Salt Lake City now celebrated them with patriotic pride: "It was with a magnificent outburst of patriotism, as spontaneous as it was all pervading, that the citizens of Salt Lake bade godspeed to the departing Twenty-fourth infantry yesterday.... Such an ovation no body of men in Utah ever received as that given the colored Twenty-fourth." Governor Heber M. Wells had "voiced truly the sentiment of Utah" when he turned to Colonel Kent and said of the departing troops, "I am proud of them." Colonel Kent responded, "You may well be proud, Governor, of such a people."

That doubts still lurked in some breasts about how the Twenty-fourth would perform in a modern war is suggested by Allen Allensworth's parting admonition—the same words that had stiffened the Philistines' backs as they marched against the Israelites—"Quit yourselves like men and fight!"

The regiment left for Camp Thomas, Georgia, where it trained until April 30, when it was directed to Tampa, Florida, the staging point for the Cuban expedition. With the Twenty-fifth, it pitched camp on Tampa Heights. Soon four thousand black troops, with twelve thousand white ones, were massed around the city.

From the start, the black infantry encountered hostility from Tampa's white press and residents. While the *Morning Tribune* found the black cavalry "splendid horsemen" who showed off "to great advantage," it said the Twenty-fourth and Twenty-fifth Infantry had "made themselves very offensive to the people of the city." A white officer with the Tenth Cavalry later ruminated on Tampa's racial climate: "The people of the South did not seem to realize what military training does for a negro. They knew the negro as a slave, as a menial servant, and as a vagrant, criminal, and pauper, but they did not seem to know him as a soldier, they could not believe that he had any fight in him." In a letter to a friend, a black infantryman described his regiment's reception in Tampa: "Prejudice reigns supreme here against the colored troops. Every little thing that is done here is chronicled as Negro brazeniness [*sic*], outlawry, etc."

Unaccustomed to the South, the black troops, many of whom had been recruited in the North, were astonished at what black civilians put up with: not so much segregation itself as the blunt lack of civility—"We don't sell to damned niggers!"—that enforced it. The "black boys in blue" insisted upon being "treated as men." The Twenty-fourth was particularly outraged when whites on the road between Tampa and Fort McPherson, Georgia, objected to blacks guarding light-complexioned Spaniards.

All this came to a head on June 6, when white Ohio volunteers "decided to have some fun" with a two-year-old Negro boy. One held the child, his head down, at arm's length, while the others practiced their marksmanship by seeing how close they could come without hitting the boy. Their sport complete, they returned the child to his mother. Black troops retaliated by charging through the streets, shooting in all directions, smashing up saloons that refused them service, and breaking into white brothels. While white officers reclined on the broad veranda of the Tampa Bay Hotel, "order" was restored by the white Second Georgia Volunteers; twenty-seven black soldiers and three white volunteers were treated for serious injuries.

Three days later, the Twenty-fourth boarded the steamship *City of Washington*. Blacks and whites were segregated on board, with blacks getting the least desirable quarters. One Negro described his berth as "under the water line, in the dirtiest, closest, most sickening place imaginable." Reaching the harbor of Santiago de Cuba on June 20, the ship stood off the battlements of Morro Castle for five days until the troops, driven wild by the stench and heat, were loaded into navy whaleboats and deposited ashore.

The army's expedition against Santiago—Cuba's second largest city, located on the island's southeastern tip—had been ill-conceived from the beginning. It got under way in Cuba's hottest, rainiest season, the worst possible time to launch an operation. The original justification for the hurriedly improvised campaign was to support the U.S. naval blockade of the port of Santiago, where a squadron of Spanish armored cruisers had been trapped. Once Admiral Dewey's Asiatic squadron had outdueled a Spanish flotilla at Manila Bay, the Philippines, in early May, a nation mesmerized by these heroics demanded nothing less at Santiago. As the navy saw it, the army's mission was to seize the fortresses guarding the harbor's mouth, permitting minesweepers to clear the way for U.S. warships.

General Shafter didn't see it that way. Determined that the army should carry the day, he pressed a different strategy, confident he could take Santiago by land. His instrument was the Fifth Army Corps, the seventeen-thousand-man expeditionary force that had embarked amid terrible confusion at Tampa in early June and now came ashore with equal tumult at Daiquiri and Siboney. The corps was built on three divisions—two of infantry, commanded by Brigadier Generals J. Ford Kent (recently promoted from colonel) and Henry W. Lawton, and one of dismounted cavalry, eventually headed by Brigadier General S. S. Sumner. According to the plan, Lawton's seven thousand infantrymen would seize the Spanish garrison at El Caney on the north. Thus secure against a flanking attack, Kent's infantry and Sumner's cavalry—another eight thousand troops—would strike east, overrunning Spanish blockhouses along the barren ridges, seizing the high ground east and north of Santiago, pinning the garrison against the bay.

Nothing went as planned. Beforehand Lawton had exclaimed: "Well, this will be better than chasing Apaches!" But, with the five hundred Spanish defenders at El Caney putting up gritty resistance, Lawton couldn't turn south, as intended, and support the major assault. The other divisions, funneling through a narrow trail surrounded by bush, came under devastating fire from Spaniards on the heights.

Richard Harding Davis, reporting for the *New York Herald* and *Scribner's,* captured the feel of that place. A few days before, gazing across the valley between the rain forest and the heights, Davis thought the scene "so quiet and sunny and well kept [it] reminded one of a New England orchard." But then, yellow trenches appeared on the hillside, and now those rifle pits were spitting fire, turning the willow-green valley into a killing ground that became known as the "bloody angle." The troops huddled "in the high grass that was so high that it stopped the wind, and so hot that it almost choked and suffocated those who lay in it. The enemy saw the advance and began firing with pitiless accuracy into the jammed and crowded trail and along the whole border of the woods.... Our men were ordered not to return the fire but to lie still and wait for further orders.... Many saw nothing but the bushes under which they lay, and the high grass which seemed to burn when they pressed against it."

For three hours—in the absence of orders from Shafter, suffering from malaria three miles to the rear—the men of Kent's and Lawton's divisions lurked in the grass, listening to the "hot, spitting song" of the Cuban bullets, absorbing appalling casualties. They couldn't stay there; they had to attack or retreat. About 1:00 p.m., at General Sumner's urging, Shafter's aide-de-camp authorized the two divisions to advance against the terrible fusillade. "Yes!" the novelist Stephen Crane exulted from the jungle's rim, "they were going up the hill, up the hill! It was the best moment in anybody's life!" For many, it was their last moment. "It is a marvel that any living thing thereabouts was not either killed or wounded," recalled a surgeon. The British military attaché gaped in admiration. "By Gawd," he exclaimed, "it's plucky!"

To the right, the black troopers of the Ninth and Tenth Cavalry charged up Kettle Hill, named for an iron pot at the summit used in sugar refining. Davis noted the Negroes, but what caught his attention was a colonel in a snappy blue uniform custom-made at Brooks Brothers, with a blue-and-white polka-dotted bandanna flying from his sombrero: Theodore Roosevelt, astride his chestnut stallion, Texas, leading his First Volunteer Cavalry, the Rough Riders, over the crest. Roosevelt and Davis had known each other for a decade. Privately, Roosevelt thought Davis "an everlasting cad," but he'd shrewdly cultivated him and it was no surprise that to Davis the colonel was the most vivid force on the battlefield. "Mounted high on horseback, and charging the rifle-pits at a gallop and quite alone," he wrote, "[Roosevelt] made you feel that you would like to cheer." Cheer he did, in his highly colored articles, and this celebrity put Roosevelt on every lip. It was, someone said, "a charge which began in the jungle and ended in the White House."

Kettle Hill fell that afternoon to Sumner's dismounted cavalry: the black regulars of the Ninth and Tenth Cavalry; the white troopers of the First, Third, and Sixth; and one regiment of volunteers, the Rough Riders. The larger hill behind it and to the left, the storied San Juan Hill, was assigned to Kent's infantry. Unwisely, he'd ordered his only volunteer regiment, the inexperienced Seventy-first New York, to lead the advance. Officered by languid Manhattan socialites, these white troops panicked in the "terrible fire" from the heights and refused to move. So Kent turned to men he knew. He'd led the Twenty-fourth until barely a month before, when, having been named to head the First Division, he turned its command over to Lieutenant Colonel Emerson H. Liscum. Now he addressed his successor: "Liscum, take the first trail to the left, cross the ford, pass all troops you find in position [the Seventy-first New York], go into line and fight anything you see." Mindful of what had just happened with the New Yorkers, Liscum replied: "General, my boys will not disgrace the flag."

John R. Conn, a private in Company H, recalled Kent's telling the troops that "he was depending on his boys of the Twenty-fourth to make history, and that the fate of his record and possibly of the nation depended" on them. The troops threw down all their extra baggage and blanket rolls. Each man, in his blue flannel shirt, wool trousers, and broad-brimmed hat, a toothbrush invariably stuck like a bright feather in the band, carried nothing but his canteen, his rifle, and two hundred rounds of ammunition. Private Conn advanced with Allen Allensworth's words ringing in his ears: "Quit yourselves like men and fight!"

Liscum brandished his sword toward the sunny hillside five hundred yards ahead and shouted: "Deploy as skirmishers, forward, march!" Bugler William Brent blew "to the charge." The Twenty-fourth was on the extreme left of the battle line, the white soldiers of the Ninth, Thirteenth, Sixth, and Sixteenth to their right. At the order, the black soldiers surged through the slippery grass, "as though they were wading waist high in water," while a squall of small-arms fire beat from above. Before he got a hundred feet, Colonel Liscum was shot through the shoulder. Henceforth, the regiment was led by Captain James J. Brereton, who displayed "marked coolness" as he pushed through the grass brandishing a pistol and shouting, "Follow me," his company obeying orders "as if on drill." Private Conn thought the men charged "like a pack of demons." Before long, the black men stood on the summit, waving their hats in the air.

Four regiments of white infantry shared the credit for taking San Juan Hill. But the nearly universal assignment of that honor to Roosevelt's Rough Riders—due, in part, to Richard Harding Davis's conflation of the fights at Kettle and San Juan Hills—was plainly an error. True, well after the infantry were on the hillside, Roosevelt led some of the Rough Riders and other dismounted cavalry puffing over from Kettle Hill. But, as between Roosevelt's men and Liscum's men, San Juan Hill itself should be entered in the Twenty-fourth's column. The wife of Lieutenant Colonel John Milton Thompson, later the Twenty-fourth's white commander, wrote in her diary that the "Colored 24th real hero of San Juan Hill, not T. Roosevelt and the Rough Riders." The Spaniards and Cubans who felt the regiment's attacks didn't underestimate the blacks, whom they called admiringly "Smoked Yankees."

The regiment paid a substantial price for the glory it achieved that day: two white officers and ten black enlisted men dead, six officers and sixty-seven enlisted men wounded. After the "garlics," as the Americans called the Spaniards, were driven off the hill, the Twenty-fourth took part in the "desultory firing" that rattled on through the night. Over the next two weeks, it manned trenches on the ridge, but on July 15, with the surrender of Santiago imminent, it pulled back from those positions.

Filthy from the mire in which they'd worked and slept for weeks, damp from the incessant rain, the men of the Twenty-fourth had reason to expect some recuperation. But as they came off the hill, Kent ordered them to report to the Fifth Army Corps's rear base at Siboney, where some six hundred soldiers suffered from yellow fever. They set off on a fourteen-mile night march, toiling through quagmires and reaching Siboney at 3:30 a.m.

There, Major A. C. Markley, the regiment's new commander, found "such misery as I had never before seen," hundreds of desperately sick men floundering in acres of mud and their own detritus on the narrow strip of rocky ground between the cliffs and the sea. When the major commanding the army medical bureau begged for help, it took Markley only minutes to put the Twenty-fourth at the bureau's disposal. According to one account, the Twenty-fourth was actually the ninth regiment "asked" to assist in caring for the victims of the yellow fever epidemic, the other eight having refused. One wonders whether the alleged "immunity" of the black soldiers was invoked to persuade them to take the risk.

The most urgent need was for sixty-five "nurses" in the "pest camp," where the army isolated yellow fever cases. Another seventy men were required as nurses, cooks, and burial parties for the hospital proper, a row of open tents facing the beach. Markley asked the regiment for volunteers. "This was the crucial test of the mettle of the men," he recalled. The response was overwhelming. Soon all positions were filled.

By the end of July, yellow fever had overrun all the hospitals. Siboney was one huge pest camp, hundreds of patients vomiting black blood, suffering convulsions and coma, often dying from the disease. Surgeons and nurses had it; officers and men of the Twenty-fourth had it. Of the sixty-five black soldiers assigned to the original pest camp, most now had the disease, their places quickly filled with other volunteers from the Twenty-fourth. By August, of the 456 enlisted men who'd made the night march to Siboney, only twenty-four had escaped "the saffron scourge" altogether. When the final roll was called, one of the regiment's officers and thirty of its enlisted men had died of it.

These figures, to be sure, raise questions about partial black immunity to yellow fever (though it may be that those who died or fell seriously ill were mulattoes whose immunity was diluted or men recruited outside the Deep South, the only region where the disease had recently been endemic). But the figures also underlined the Twenty-fourth's selflessness. General Kent said the men's "matchless heroism" at Siboney was "nobler and grander" than their gallantry on San Juan Hill.

On August 26—nearly two months after that famous victory—only nine officers and 198 enlisted men were well enough to march behind a depleted regimental band as they started home. On September 2, they reached Camp Wikoff on Montauk Point, at Long Island's eastern tip. This remote spot was chosen so that men suffering from yellow fever, malaria, and typhoid could be effectively quarantined in a detention camp, then given some rest and recuperation. On September 23, the regiment's survivors boarded trains for their new posts: six companies went back to Fort Douglas, four companies proceeded to Fort Russell, Wyoming.

In those first weeks back in the States, the men of the Twenty-fourth, like their colleagues-in-arms, were widely regarded as heroes. Few Americans knew the regiment's role at San Juan Hill, but in the first flush of victory, most

Americans generously accorded all veterans of that engagement—black and white—extravagant credit for their feat. And because it surprised so many people, the black performance drew special praise. The Twenty-fourth, in particular, was hailed as "the most famous regiment of African blood since Hannibal slaughtered 70,000 Romans at the Battle of Lake Trasamene." Lieutenant John J. Pershing—whose nickname, Black Jack, stemmed from service with the Tenth Cavalry—spoke for most white officers who led black troops in the Santiago campaign when he said: "We officers of the Tenth Cavalry could have taken our black heroes in our arms. They had again fought their way into our affections, as they here had fought their way into the hearts of the American people." In Congress, Representative John F. Fitzgerald—Jack Kennedy's grandfather—expressed his pride in "the dare devil work of the black-skinned men who, with gleaming eyeballs and shining teeth, rushed to the assistance of the Rough Riders." The Tenth Cavalry marched down Washington's Pennsylvania Avenue, took President McKinley's salute, then was feted at a reception hosted by an officer's wife. All across the country, at parades and rallies, others honored the blacks as "splendid heroes." The army recognized their achievements with five Medals of Honor.

Theodore Roosevelt's views were more equivocal. In *Scribner's* he wrote, "No troops could have behaved better than the colored soldiers"; but he added that, under strain, black infantrymen "began to get a little uneasy and to drift to the rear.... I jumped up, and walking a few yards to the rear, drew my revolver, halted the retreating soldiers, and called out to them that I appreciated the gallantry with which they had fought and would be sorry to hurt them, but I should shoot the first man, who on any pretence whatever, went to the rear." When Robert J. Fleming, a white lieutenant who'd served in Cuba with the Tenth Cavalry, wrote Roosevelt objecting to this account, Roosevelt—by then governor of New York—elaborated more forcefully in a private letter. A panic in elements of the Twenty-fourth Infantry and Ninth Cavalry he now traced to "the superstition and fear of the darkey, natural in those but one generation removed from slavery and but a few generations removed from the wildest savagery." These private remarks seem closer to Roosevelt's true feelings than the version he'd published.

Had they known his private views, many blacks might have been deeply offended. As it was, a few took umbrage at the *Scribner's* article. But most black Americans—particularly those who'd fought at his side—continued to regard Roosevelt as a friend of the race. On New York City's West Side, a partly black neighborhood on an elevation between Fifty-ninth and Sixty-second Streets became known as San Juan Hill. Meanwhile, a legend developed that blacks had "rescued" the Rough Riders in Cuba, a notion that contained a germ of truth: in a June 24 skirmish at Las Guasimas, sixteen Rough Riders were killed and more might have lost their lives had the Tenth Cavalry not ridden to their support. Later the tale was elaborated to bracket Roosevelt himself with individual black soldiers. When Jefferson Morris returned from

Cuba, for example, his family understood that he'd "saved Roosevelt's life on San Juan Hill," and when his grandson was born in 1919, the child was named Theodore Roosevelt Halsey in honor of that event. More than a few blacks bore Roosevelt's name for much the same reason.

Although the events on San Juan and Kettle Hills remained a matter of surpassing pride to black Americans for years to come, the particular blacks who'd charged those heights found their status as heroes short-lived. For many Americans, the returning soldiers were still "damned niggers."

The black Ninth Cavalry went West aboard the same train as the white First Cavalry. George W. Prioleau, the Ninth's black chaplain, recalled: "While the cheers and the 'God Bless You's were still ringing in our ears, and before the warm handshakes had become cold, we arrived in Kansas City, the gateway to America's Hell." Both regiments, Prioleau noted, had fought at San Juan Heights. "[Both] were victorious, and returned home with victory perched upon this country's banner." And yet at the Kansas City depot, "these black boys, heroes of our country, were not allowed to stand at the counters of restaurants and eat a sandwich and drink a cup of coffee, while the white soldiers were welcomed and invited to sit down at the tables and eat free of cost. You call this American 'prejudice'? I call it American 'hatred,' conceived only in hellish minds."

Whatever snubs the Twenty-fourth received on its trip back to Utah remain unrecorded. When the train passed through Chicago, a captain made sure his men got coffee by paying for it himself, running up a bill of $17.65. A new man who watched these proceedings reported: "No finer looking body of men ever wore uniforms than those brave fellows, trained on the plains and in the mountains, hard as ironwood, lithe as panthers, and as modest and quiet as they are worthy." But when the newsman asked to interview a "fine-looking young fellow," the soldier replied: "I do not talk to reporters any more. They make me say 'ovah yon' and 'ain't gwine.' We don't talk that way, but it always comes out that way in the paper." This self-confidence was likely the product of the troops' Cuban feats, demonstrating their manhood once and for all, most importantly to themselves.

The train reached Salt Lake on September 30. The next day, sleet and snow couldn't chill the welcome celebration. Thousands of white people lined the route as the Twenty-fourth, in battle dress, marched four abreast to the strains of "Onward, Christian Soldiers." Banners proclaimed: "Heroes alike in Battle and Pestilence. You are most welcome" and "Out of the Cuban jungle you brought immortal fame."

Within weeks, relations between the black troops and white residents cooled markedly. As the *Broad Ax* noted, many enterprises that had welcomed the regiment home weren't so enlightened in their business practices. "The Vienna Cafe had the name Twenty-fourth Regiment painted all over their windows," the paper noted, "which we thought was very bad taste upon the part of its owners, for they will not permit a respectable negro to frequent their establishment." Nor would most of the city's other restaurants or its quality retailers.

At one time the Twenty-fourth had accepted such restrictions with a resignation born of slavery, but after their Cuban heroics the men had higher expectations of their due as American citizens. During and after the war, the regiment had received many young recruits, more impatient and less disciplined than the veterans they'd replaced. Finally, their anger may have been stirred by several gruesome racial incidents: a black newspaper burned and nine Negroes killed in North Carolina in late 1898; the slaughter of six black citizens in Georgia the next March; and, in April, the burning at stake of another Georgian.

One incident closer to home stirred indignation in the Twenty-fourth: the exclusion from an otherwise all-white jury of a former corporal in the regiment, J. Gordon MacPherson. When MacPherson was accepted by both sides, the eleven white jurors objected to serving on a jury, and thus being forced to associate intimately, with a black man. Ultimately, the judge removed MacPherson. The former corporal, among the first men to reach the crest of San Juan Hill, felt his humiliation keenly. "I'm an American citizen," he said, "I fought for the country and went through yellow fever in Cuba in the service of this country. I wonder how many of those who have treated me this way have done as much for the country."

During the winter and spring of 1898–99, members of the regiment—so rarely in trouble before the war—were convicted of many infractions, military and civil. In military courts, they were variously disciplined for offensive language to a noncommissioned officer, scandalous conduct in the presence of ladies, assault upon another soldier, theft, and desertion. A number of men were sent to the army's disciplinary barracks at Alcatraz and eventually received dishonorable discharges. Meanwhile, in Salt Lake's police court, others were convicted of stealing a suit, being drunk and disorderly on a streetcar, extorting money, striking a woman, and using indecent language.

The anger that mounted in the Twenty-fourth was probably heightened by the regiment's dispersal to bases throughout the Northwest. Thus, by May 4, 1899, as General Merriam and his old regiment converged on the Coeur d'Alenes, both nursed powerful grievances that may have affected their behavior in months to come.

Reaching the Kellogg depot at noon on May 4, Merriam was delighted to find a contingent of the Twenty-fourth—Company M from Fort New Spokane—already on hand. Also on the platform was Governor Steunenberg's newly appointed "personal representative" in the Coeur d'Alenes, Bartlett Sinclair, the state auditor.

There were those who wondered why, if Steunenberg was too ill to go to the Coeur d'Alenes himself, he hadn't sent his lieutenant governor, Joseph Hutchinson, who had the advantage of being a mining engineer. But Hutchinson and Steunenberg weren't in tune on labor policy. "I have broken bread with [miners], drunk with them, prospected with them—yes I have belonged to their organizations," Hutchinson later explained. "Therefore, the Governor selected the right man to do the work he wanted."

Steunenberg had turned first to Charles J. Bassett, his commissioner of immigration and labor, who declined, perhaps because his wife was recovering from meningitis. Only then did he give the nod to Bartlett Sinclair. The son of a Confederate officer, Sinclair had been born in South Carolina in 1864, while his father was at war. Not long after Appomattox, the Sinclairs opted for the winning side; moving to New Jersey, Bartlett studied law at Columbia University, then practiced in Manhattan before migrating to Texas and thence to Idaho in 1890. For nearly a decade he lived at Bonner's Ferry, at Idaho's northern tip, where he practiced law until elected state auditor as a Silver Republican in 1898. A lively orator and vivid writer, Sinclair soon formed a close friendship with the governor, cemented on long walks through the Boise hills.

In dispatching him to the Coeur d'Alenes, Steunenberg had given Sinclair a verbal grant of authority to take all means necessary to "suppress that riot and punish the scoundrels guilty of the crimes." Arriving in Spokane on April 30, he stayed the night at the Spokane Hotel, the red-brick gathering place of northern Idaho politicians and mine and timber magnates. That evening he met in his room with the leadership of the Bunker Hill and Sullivan Company, the "four B's," as they were known—Fred Bradley, its president; Fred Burbidge, its manager; Albert Burch, its superintendent; and Charles W. Beale, a former district attorney of Shoshone County and now a Bunker Hill attorney—as well as with Joe McDonald, the manager of the Helena-Frisco mine. Late that evening, he telegraphed the governor: "Burbidge fears death upon return to Wardner till troops are there. Beale confirms his fears. Your course universally approved here."

Whether the governor's course was approved by all the district's mine owners isn't clear. But certainly it was by Bunker Hill and Sullivan, the company that had fought the union most tenaciously and that, in turn, had been singled out for the most violent retaliation. Although Steunenberg would later insist, "There will be no subserviency to any private interests," the governor's representatives and General Merriam worked hand in glove with Bunker Hill people throughout the crisis. In particular, they relied on three company lawyers: Charles Beale; Curtis H. Lindley, a suave San Francisco attorney who'd long handled the company's important legal matters; and Myron Folsom, a younger man brought in at Lindley's request.

The next day, May 1, Sinclair went on to Wardner, where he supervised the first round of arrests by state deputies, supported by Captain Joseph B. Batchelor and Company M of the Twenty-fourth Infantry. Over the next few days, the deputies and the black soldiers rounded up 128 men in Wardner and Kellogg suspected of having been aboard the rogue train on the twenty-ninth or of otherwise supporting the union. "Oh, how the colored soldier boys did enjoy it!" chortled the pro–Bunker Hill *Wardner News.*

On May 4, Sinclair organized a more ambitious venture up Canyon Creek, into the very heart of union territory: the mining camp of Burke, where the Dynamite Express had been hijacked on April 29. When Merriam reached the Kellogg depot at noon on May 4, four state deputies, accompanied by Major Charles Morton and Troop A of the Fourth Cavalry, were about to depart for Burke. In a hurried platform conference, Sinclair warned there might be resistance, the Burke miners having a reputation as "a fearless, devilish lot [who] loved nothing better than a fight." For safety's sake, Merriam ordered the Fourth Cavalry's Troop F to join the operation. Since officers suspected that Burke's miners might place dynamite on the tracks, a lone engine preceded the train, which "fairly crept along." No explosives were encountered.

To Sinclair it was clear that the people of Canyon Creek had "a criminal history." Specifically, "the entire community" of Burke "had been engaged in the crime" of April 29, so "the entire community, or the male portion of it, ought to be arrested." If that struck some as hyperbole, a white cavalry officer who came to know Burke well reported that spring:

> It is difficult for one who has not been on the ground to understand to what an extent "unionism" was carried [here]. It pervaded the entire population, everybody was subject to it. Storekeepers, saloonkeepers, barbers, proprietors of restaurants, even the Houses of Prostitution.... The wages paid in Canyon Creek were $3.50 per day. The work was dangerous, unhealthy and the mines very wet. With the Unionists, however, the burning question was not wages. It was "The Union." This was everything to them, wages, politics, religion. The subject had been discussed and brooded over so long that they were fanatics on the subject.... [But] leaving the Union entirely out of the question, the miners are not generally bad citizens. Scattered in a thousand cities and towns, they would not be classed as criminals.

When the army's special train reached Burke that afternoon, the four deputies and two hundred blue-clad troopers spilled into the extraordinary town. Wedged between the canyon's steep walls, Burke's single street ran parallel to the creek and the railroad tracks, a row of low-roofed miners' huts and tiny stores on either side. With Company F working one side and Company A the other, the soldiers "took the dragnet down the canyon." Conner Malott of the Spokane *Spokesman-Review,* who witnessed the events, wrote: "It was one of the most remarkable arrests ever made in any country. The captors recognized neither class nor occupation." They searched every house, and if nobody answered their thumps, they broke down the door. As Sinclair had ordered, they arrested every male: miners, bartenders, a doctor, a preacher, even the postmaster and school superintendent.

Miners were seized as they came off their shifts, cooks and waiters arrested in the kitchens, diners at their supper tables. George Cornell, a dealer in secondhand clothes, was eating at the Tiger-Poorman boarding-house with a fireman and an engineer from the Northern Pacific when an officer burst in and ordered them into a boxcar. All of Burke's saloons—ultimately, all those along Canyon Creek—were closed indefinitely. "Men who've had any experience in the affairs of the world," Sinclair explained, "know that crimes of this character are frequently hatched in saloons." For desperate criminals, the men of Burke went quietly; the only gunshot was aimed at a "vicious watch dog."

The deputies and the soldiers loaded a total of 243 men into four boxcars. When the train arrived in Wardner about 10:00 p.m., the entire male population of Burke was herded into an old barn, a two-story frame structure 120 feet long by 40 feet wide and filled with hay, where prisoners from Kellogg and Wardner were already detained. This structure came to be known as "the old bullpen," the name used for such enclosures in 1892 and 1894. In early May it was still very cold in those altitudes, and Sinclair later conceded that the men held in the barn, most of them snatched from their homes and work-places without so much as a blanket, suffered some from the weather.

On May 6, similar raids at Gem and Mullan arrested 350 men, swelling the prisoners' ranks to more than seven hundred (and soon to 1,000, the number aboard the Dynamite Express). As the barn could no longer accom-modate all the inmates, the overflow was held in boxcars parked near the Kellogg depot. On May 9, carpenters assisted by reluctant prisoners set to work with raw pine boards building the new bullpen on a hill overlooking the depot. A hollow rectangle of one-story buildings enclosed an exercise yard. The only entrance pierced the west side, flanked by the kitchen and hospital, with bunkhouses on the other three legs, each with rows of cots separated by a narrow passageway. The building sealed off its own perimeter, but for extra security it was surrounded by a six-foot barbed wire fence patrolled by Winchester-toting soldiers, while a twenty-foot tower afforded other soldiers a view of the entire complex. Most prisoners were moved into the new facility. But conditions remained primitive. Three inmates died there. After prisoners were discovered digging an escape tunnel, the entire population was put on a bread-and-water diet for eight days and forced to drill seven hours a day in the summer heat.

Though Merriam visited the bullpen, he wasn't accessible to the in-mates. When a prisoner pressed the point, a soldier told him, "It's no use for you common people trying to see the General. You couldn't hand him a red apple on a long fish pole."

The most prominent prisoners were held in a nearby "guardhouse." There, on May 6, were installed two of the three Shoshone County commis-sioners—William R. Stimson, a Gem watchmaker, and William Boyle, an "easygoing" prospector—as well as Sheriff Young. In a telegram to Steunen-berg, Sinclair had labeled the county government "a perfect farce," utterly ineffectual because utterly captive to the union. Accused of aiding and abetting the miners, the Populist commissioners were confined for days in the tiny guardhouse with only a scattering of hay on which to sleep. Each man, the Spokane *Spokesman-Review* reported, was "assigned to a melancholy corner, with instructions to think his thoughts in silence.... A dusky soldier stands at the doorway to see that [none] of them does any talking." Now and again, black soldiers, disciplined for being drunk on duty, were thrown in with them. To ensure that the commissioners and the sheriff didn't have it too easy, Sinclair ordered that they do "their full share of dishwashing and other menial work."

Asked why only two commissioners had been arrested and the third, Moses S. Simmons, allowed to remain at large, Sinclair explained: "With [Boyle and Stimson] in the bullpen, a quorum of the board would be impossible, and that organization would be prevented from ... incit[ing] the people of the county to overt acts." Ultimately, all three commissioners and Sheriff Young were removed from office on July 11 by order of the district court, which found that they'd neglected their official duties, both by failing to arrest the men who'd blown up Bunker Hill's concentrator as well as by committing such peccadilloes as issuing liquor licenses without requiring sufficient bonds.

As the new sheriff, Sinclair installed the county coroner, Hugh France, one of two non-Populists elected in 1898 and a pugnacious hard-liner. When he perceived an effort by union members to regain control of the situation, he urged that union leaders be locked up in the bullpen for a long while. "The disease," he prescribed, "needs radical treatment."

The simile was appropriate, for France was Bunker Hill's staff physician. There was a pattern here. The new regime's principal patronage—the fat contract for supplying food and drink to the bullpen's prisoners—had gone to Tony Tubbs, the former manager of Bunker Hill's boardinghouse, destroyed on April 29. Likewise, most of the thirty men Sinclair hired as special "state deputies" were either employees and former employees of the Bunker Hill Company or contractors for it. Among the most prominent was a saloonkeeper named W. C. "Convict" Murphy, who'd served time for horse stealing and cattle rustling. When Convict Murphy broke down people's doors, he was sometimes asked for a search warrant or other authority, at which he would draw a pair of six-shooters and say, "These are my warrants." ("State deputy" was a new job designation. At a congressional hearing, one congressman asked what they were deputies of. "They were Deputy Sinclairs," quipped another. But what was Sinclair? Nobody had ever heard of a governor's "personal representative." A congressman suggested that he was "sort of a Pooh Bah.")

It was all very well to shuffle jobs in county government, but where were the ringleaders of the April 29 bombing? The day he arrived in Wardner, Merriam had telegraphed General Corbin in Washington: "Indications are most leaders of mob have escaped, going east or west into Montana and Washington; others hidden in the mountains. Sheriff at Thompson Falls,

Montana, reports many arriving on foot over mountain trails." In May, snow still lay deep atop those mountains, slowing the exodus and making the fugitives vulnerable to interception.

With Sinclair and Steunenberg pressing for vigorous efforts to capture these men, Merriam authorized a bold strike into Montana. As its leader he chose Captain Henry G. Lyon, a West Point graduate and seasoned veteran of riot duty who'd been seriously wounded on San Juan Hill. Now recovered and commanding Company D of the Twenty-fourth Infantry, he was told his company's official status was "United States troops, in the field, changing station"—a palpable subterfuge. If asked, he was to insist that his troops were merely accompanying four Idaho deputies, that they would "make no arrests or assist in making arrests," that they were there only for "moral effect."

In fact, his detachment of sixty-five black soldiers entrained for Missoula, where they arrested a reported "ringleader" named Eric Anderson. Leaving that evening, they captured another suspect—Frank Turner, a deputy sheriff under the deposed Sheriff Young—hiding in a carload of lumber on a freight train. At Thompson Falls, the deputies and soldiers made three more arrests.

Merriam assured Lyon that the governor of Montana had promised to arrest escaping "rioters." But Montana officials didn't cooperate with Lyon; in some cases he encountered "indifference or treachery"; on May 9, he got word of an effort to free his prisoners through habeas corpus. Finally, on May 10—in response to pressure from Idaho authorities—he received a telegram from Governor Robert B. Smith, saying Montana would "not interpose any objection to removing prisoners to Idaho without requisition papers. This is your authority." Leaving Missoula, he turned ten prisoners over to the military at Wardner. Unfortunately for Lyon and Merriam, one man arrested was a Montana citizen with no connection to the Wardner events.

The legal deficiencies of the Montana raid went still deeper. Even if, technically, the arrests in Montana were made by the Idaho deputies, not the Twenty-fourth Regiment, a deputy of one state had no authority to arrest citizens in another state unless clothed with authority by officials of that state. Moreover, it was by no means clear that Governor Smith of Montana could waive formal extradition proceedings, and it seems doubtful that the paper on which he waived them was proper authority for removing the men from his state. Altogether, Lyon's raid seemed "a gross violation of the law," as later charged by congressional Democrats. Sinclair showed little patience with such quibbles. He told a congressional committee: "I did not sit down and study the Constitution while those men were escaping over the hills."

While Captain Lyon chased fugitives, Idaho's attorney general, Sam Hays, tended to the legal-political issues. Before leaving Boise, the combative Hays had asked Frank Steunenberg, "What do you say, if there is a good chance to clean up the whole situation, shall we do it, or shall we be satisfied with quieting things down as they are now?" According to Hays, Steunenberg said, "Well, Sam, I don't exactly see how you can do anything, but if the chance comes, clean it up entirely."

Shortly after his arrival on May 4, Hays had asked Frederick Bradley, president of the Bunker Hill and Sullivan Company, to gather the district's mine owners. On the evening of May 7, he met with them in the Spokane offices of John A. Finch and Amasa B. Campbell, proprietors of the Gem mines. Present, in addition to Finch, Campbell, Bradley, and his manager, Fred Burbidge, were owners or managers from most of the other mines. Hays asked them to declare publicly that they wouldn't hire any miner who belonged to the WFM or its affiliate, the Miners Union of the Coeur d'Alenes. To his surprise, they resisted. By then some owners and managers—notably Bunker Hill's Burbidge—so feared for their safety they shrank from accepting responsibility for a policy that might bring retaliation.

Well, Hays asked, would they simply dismiss "every man that took part in the riots"?

After a moment of silence, one owner said, "That isn't possible. We own mines elsewhere and there would be trouble in those places, and besides you can't do anything about it."

"All right," Hays snapped, they'd employed "criminals" who'd endangered life and property. If they wouldn't undo this intolerable situation, the state would. "So long as martial law is maintained in this district, the state will supervise the men that you employ in your mines."

Hays recalled later that some of the mine owners—among them, the Bunker Hill and Sullivan Company—were "glad to have the State take this position." Others had trepidations, especially the owners of Canyon Creek mines where unionism was an accepted condition of doing business. Later Finch testified: "We, the mine owners, rather felt that the state authorities were severe in demanding that the men should take out a permit." Finch's partner, Amasa Campbell, shrewdly asked Hays to "give us notice to that effect in writing." With written instructions, they could insist they were simply obeying constituted authority.

The day after the Spokane meeting, Hays told the *Statesman* of Governor Steunenberg's exasperation with half-suppressed insurrections. This time must be different. "We have taken the monster by the throat and we are going to choke the life out of it," he said. "No halfway measures have or will be adopted. It is a plain case of the state or the union winning, and we do not propose that the state shall be defeated."

Among the Bunker Hill officials attending the May 7 meeting was Curtis Lindley, the company's principal attorney in San Francisco, site of its corporate headquarters. Now Hays asked Lindley to draft the proclamation, and according to several accounts, the final product was Lindley's handiwork. "To the Mine Owners of Shoshone County," it began, "Certain organizations or combinations existing in Shoshone county have shown themselves to be criminal in purpose.... You are therefore notified that the employment of men belonging to said or other criminal organizations during the continuance of martial law must cease. In case this direction is not observed, your mines will be closed." All miners seeking work were required to obtain from Sheriff Hugh France a permit signifying that they were law-abiding citizens. Without such a permit, nobody could work in the district's mines.

Hays mailed the document to Sinclair in Wardner. On May 9, Sinclair took it to Merriam and asked whether the general would signify his approval. Merriam suggested one addition: a procedure by which "an innocent member of an innocent union" could obtain a permit—by denying participation in the April 29 "riots" and denying or renouncing membership in any society that had "incited, encouraged or approved of said riots." (The order never named the Western Federation of Miners or the Miners Union of the Coeur d'Alenes, but those were clearly the societies it had in mind.) Eager for the general's backing, Sinclair promptly accepted the revision. So, at the bottom, under "By order of the Governor and Commander in Chief" and just below Sinclair's own signature, the general penned: "Examined and approved, H. C. Merriam, Brigadier-General, United States Army." Without much deliberation, Merriam had thrown the full weight of the federal government behind efforts to break the miners union—a blatant violation of the state's prohibition against yellow-dog contracts.

The general later insisted that his signature merely signified his awareness of an action taken entirely on the initiative of "the duly constituted State authorities." He did his best to disassociate himself from the proclamation's main thrust: that the WFM was a criminal organization that must be outlawed. Merriam's protestations were undercut by publication of remarks he'd made to Wardner merchants on May 5, four days before the proclamation appeared as a poster tacked up on trees and fences throughout the Coeur d'Alenes. "I have only abhorrence for such conditions as exist here," he'd told the businessmen, "and I should rather live under the tyranny of the Russian monarchy than to live in terror of the mob such as rules in the Coeur d'Alenes. I have tried in vain to discover what motives may prompt men to such deeds of crime.... Since I cannot discover the reasons, I am forced to believe that the only way to quell these disturbances is by the aid of martial law—a one man power where gun shall be met with gun and dynamite with dynamite." And he added: "Since the trouble largely originates in hostile organizations of men known as labor unions, I should suggest a law making the formation of such unions or kindred societies a crime."

When this remark, so close in tone to the proclamation, stirred the predictable response, Merriam insisted—as he had in the past—that the reporter had misquoted him. "I have never pronounced those unions criminal organizations," he said, but nobody took his denial seriously.

The new regime was acutely sensitive to press criticism. Some of the boldest attacks on the bullpen and its keepers came from Wilbur H. Stewart, the delicate-looking editor of the weekly *Mullan Mirror*. As he was making up his editorial page one day that spring, Bartlett Sinclair appeared at his print shop door, accompanied by a major and several black soldiers with unsheathed bayonets. "I find that you have been publishing a seditious newspaper, inciting riot and insurrection," said Sinclair, "and we have concluded that publication of your paper must cease." Stewart was taken to the bullpen, where he was assigned to empty the garbage bins and the privy cisterns. But his imprisonment didn't halt the *Mirror*'s publication. Stewart's young wife, Maggie, published it every week, and when Sinclair sent the cavalry to impound her type, she had the *Mirror* printed by a sympathetic publisher. Eventually, her husband was released with Sinclair's pointed "suggestion" that he hew to the "law and order" line. Stewart preferred to sell his paper, which he did to one P. L. Orcutt, a backer of the status quo.

Although the *Mirror* was the only paper against which this kind of pressure was brought, the authorities took other steps to control press coverage. General Merriam's aide, Lieutenant Bennett, was appointed military censor with authority to review all reports filed at the local telegraph office.

By then, Bartlett Sinclair had begun to release some of the bullpen's inmates. The proceedings were most irregular, a kind of kangaroo court, sometimes presided over by Sinclair himself, at other times by Fred Burbidge or Curtis Lindley. Soldiers would escort a prisoner from the bullpen to the courtyard of a Wardner stable, where the presiding officer would question him about his affiliations and political preferences, then decide whether or not to release him. Since no prisoners had as yet been charged with anything and since none were accompanied by attorneys, the decision was entirely subjective, dependent on the officer's whim. "Absurd technicalities," the attorney general explained, "will not be allowed to stand in the path of justice."

Steunenberg's medical condition had improved sufficiently for him to examine the Coeur d'Alene situation at first hand. Arriving in Spokane May 12, he met that evening at the Hotel Spokane for further discussion of the permit system with eleven of the district's leading mine owners, among them Bradley of Bunker Hill and Sullivan, Finch and Campbell of the Gem, S. S. Glidden of the Tiger-Poorman, and Charles Sweeny of the Empire State. So cozy were Steunenberg's relations with the mine owners that he spent four nights as a guest at Sweeny's home. To a *Statesman* reporter, Steunenberg said he was determined to "totally eradicate from this community a class of criminals who have for years been committing murders and other crimes in open violation of the law." There was "no war upon organized labor as such," he said, but Coeur d'Alene labor organizations weren't like unions elsewhere. "They have been, and are now, controlled by desperate men" who'd imposed a "reign of terror" on the district.

He went on the next day to Wallace, where he conferred with Merriam on a timetable for troop withdrawals. The Twenty-fourth Infantry was scheduled to go to the Philippines in mid-June, and four of its companies left the valley in mid-May, replaced by troops of the white First Cavalry. Moreover, Merriam was restless, eager to go home to Denver—a move the War Department finally permitted on May 25.

But the general couldn't escape the gathering storm. As news of the proclamation and the bullpen filtered out of the Coeur d'Alenes, unions and other labor sympathizers raised hell. On May 14, New York's Central Federation Labor Union protested "General Merriam's unwarranted use of military power to browbeat the striking miners." Its statement was followed by a similar resolution from the Western Labor Union charging that miners "have been thrown into a corral like so many cattle for the slaughter and have been denied the right of counsel and the actual necessaries of life" and protesting, in particular, the proclamation denying work to members of the miners union.

Public charges of such an incendiary nature prompted second thoughts at the White House. On May 26, George B. Cortelyou, McKinley's acting secretary, sent word to Secretary of War Russell A. Alger that "it was the President's understanding that no orders whatsoever have been issued by General Merriam as to who shall work or not work, and that he has only been supporting the State authority in preserving the peace." Adjutant General Corbin passed that message on to Merriam, concluding with the chilling phrase, "President wishes a statement of facts at once."

With lofty equanimity, Merriam said the state required the permits but "troops are taking no part in this unless keeping the peace does so. Every mine owner I have seen strongly approves." Returning to Denver, he found a telegram from Alger ordering him to tell Major Allen Smith of the First Cavalry, left in command at Wardner, "that he is to use the United States troops to aid the state authorities simply to suppress rioting and to maintain peace and order." These, said Alger, "were your original instructions. The army must have nothing whatever to do with enforcing rules for the government of miners or miners' unions."

In this transparent effort to shield himself from the outrage building over the Coeur d'Alenes, Alger clearly misstated the record. The "original instructions," wired by Corbin to Merriam on April 30, were merely to go to Boise, confer with Steunenberg, then proceed to the Coeur d'Alenes and take charge of the troops assembling there. In a prickly letter, Merriam asked Corbin to supply him "with the paper to which reference is made." No document was forthcoming. Nonetheless, the general noted, "the Secretary's telegram containing the hurtful intimation was given out at the War Department for publication, and was published very generally throughout the country." The general, who carried a full set of grievances, now added others toward the War Department and the White House.

With pressure building in Washington to end military occupation of the Coeur d'Alenes, the kangaroo court released the bullpen's inmates in ever-larger numbers. Its population, nearly 1,000 at the start of May, had declined to 450 by May 12 and to barely 150 by July. Ultimately, thirteen men were tried in federal district court on a minor charge—interfering with the United States mails—based on evidence that the mail carried by the hijacked train had been delayed for twenty-four hours. Ten defendants were convicted and sentenced to twenty to twenty-two months in San Quentin.

But convictions on a technical charge scarcely satisfied those behind the prosecution. Steunenberg, Bartlett Sinclair, and Chester Lindley insisted that murder charges be brought against some April 29 "rioters." By midsummer, a state grand jury had indicted nine men for murder, arson, conspiracy, or some combination of the three. Most were ordinary unionists. James Hawley, who'd represented the miners in 1893 and now joined the prosecutors, said later that the state's purpose was "not so much to impose punishment on those who had been connected with the crimes committed," since "the men whose guilt could have easily been proven were comparatively unknown members of the union and their conviction would do little good." The prosecutors wanted to begin with a case against someone of "high standing" to demonstrate that "the law could reach anyone," that immunity to prosecution no longer prevailed on Canyon Creek.

The choice ultimately fell on Paul Corcoran, the thirty-four-year-old financial secretary of the Burke Miners Union. The state had no evidence that Corcoran had wielded the rifle that killed Jim Cheyne or had even been within eyeshot of the crime, though it did produce witnesses who'd seen him riding atop a boxcar of the Dynamite Express. It argued that all those who'd planned the Wardner depredations had a common responsibility for every act carried out by any one of them.

The father of three and a highly respected member of the Burke community, Corcoran went on trial in Wallace on July 10. The prosecution team was headed by J. H. Forney, a Moscow, Idaho, attorney who'd represented Bunker Hill and Sullivan in at least one civil case and enjoyed close ties to its leading officers. The way for his appointment as special prosecutor and acting county attorney had been cleared by the forced resignation of Henry F. Samuels, the Populist county prosecutor since 1898. Forney's salary and that of the entire prosecutorial team—as well as the cost of other Coeur d'Alene prosecutions—were paid for by a grant of $32,000 from the Coeur d'Alene mine owners, of which Bunker Hill and Sullivan anted up $7,500.

The decisive stroke came from Forney's and Hawley's co-counsel, William E. Borah, who at risk to life and limb reenacted Corcoran's putative ride atop the boxcar from Burke to Wardner, grasping a rifle in one hand as the train traveled at thirty miles per hour. When three witnesses testified to Borah's ride, whatever doubts the jury may have harbored evaporated. On July 27, Corcoran got seventeen years at hard labor—an object lesson in the dangers of aggressive unionism in the Steunenberg era.

That left eight more men charged with murder and/or arson (though hundreds of uncharged men remained in the bullpen). Before they could be brought to trial, the eight escaped. On August 25, Sergeant of the Guard Lewis J. Crawford led them in twos or threes past the guard posts, explaining, "These men are going to the hospital." By the time Captain Frank A. Edwards, the bullpen commandant, realized what was going on, all had vanished into the Coeur d'Alene night, never to be heard from again. Crawford—who'd joined the army as a bugler at age twelve and served it well for seventeen years—was arrested the next day in Missoula, Montana, with several hundred dollars in cash, money with which he'd been bribed to contrive the escape. Ultimately, he was court-martialed and sentenced to thirteen years of hard labor at Alcatraz. Crawford was a heavy drinker, gambler, and frequenter of bordellos, but his military record was a good one. At least one newspaper suggested that, like the biblical goat banished to the wilderness, he'd been compelled to carry more responsibility than he deserved for the bullpen debacle. Though the white sergeant bore much of the official opprobrium, the full weight of Canyon Creek's rage fell on the Twenty-fourth Infantry, who'd served as the bullpen's principal guards.

If the War Department had sought to avoid fraternization between troops and miners by relying on black troops, the strategy worked. Animosity between miners and the men of the Twenty-fourth clearly aggravated the situation. The Scandinavian, Italian, Irish, Cornish, and American-born miners of the Coeur d'Alenes would have resented their incarceration had it been white troops who herded them into the bullpen. That the face behind the bayonet was often black left the miners enraged. Though the mining camps of Canyon Creek embraced a broad range of European immigrants, they drew the line at Chinese and Negroes. No Chinese washermen were permitted on the creek, the miners' wives doing all the laundry. The deep resentment of blacks may have harked back, in part, to the brief use of the Twenty-fifth Infantry during the intervention of 1892. Not only did the miners share the turn-of-the-century American view of "niggers" as second-class citizens, they regarded them as pawns of the mine owners.

These feelings surfaced frequently during the investigations that followed the crisis of 1899. Levi Miller, a fifty-five-year-old Civil War veteran and night watchman at the Tiger-Poorman mine, told of a black guard prodding him toward the urinal and shouting, "Get along lively there, get along lively!"

"Look here, my friend," the Burke miner remembered saying, "be a little lenient with an old man. Thirty-four years ago I was down South helping to free such people as you.... I've got an honorable discharge from the United States service—something which you, perhaps, may never get."

To that, Miller testified, the soldier said, "I don't give a God Damn what you have got. Dis gun wants to smoke, anyhow," as he threw a cartridge into his rifle.

"Shoot, you black son of a bitch," Miller replied, "I'm old enough to die."

Frederick Martin, a Burke miner, recalled that when he and other bull-pen prisoners tried to exercise in the courtyard, soldiers of the Twenty-fourth's Company M shouted, "Get back there, you white sons of bitches." And on one occasion, a black sergeant pulled his revolver, held it to a miner's nose, and said, "I want you to understand that we are the bosses."

William Powers, a Mullan miner, was tossed into the bullpen but released because he'd served as a Mullan constable. Later, Powers echoed a theme frequently heard along Canyon Creek: that after tormenting white prisoners in the bullpen, the black soldiers went downtown at night to sleep with the miners' wives. "The women weren't used to nigger soldiers, or niggers of any kind, and they were afraid of them." He recalled "many complaints of negro soldiers...calling at the houses and trying to get in." One Gem woman whose husband was in the bullpen had been sitting in her bedroom when a black soldier tapped on the window. She asked him what he wanted. "I want to spend some money with you," he said. She ordered him away.

Later, Bill Haywood of the Western Federation of Miners said that, while his brothers were languishing in the bullpen, "the black soldiers were at home insulting, outraging, ravishing their wives, mothers, sisters and sweethearts."

On July 17, the miners union sent the White House seventeen sworn affidavits from citizens along Canyon Creek, containing a litany of complaints about the Twenty-fourth. Frank Monty of Gem said he'd been arrested by black troops and thrown into a boxcar. As he tried to talk to a friend outside, a black sergeant shouted at him, "God damn you, I will fix you when I get you in the bullpen. I will make you wish you were in hell, you son of a bitch!" Bartholomew Creedon said he saw a Negro soldier stab an aged man with his bayonet because he wasn't moving fast enough. Creedon claimed he later heard a white officer of Company M tell his black troops, "Show no mercy to those sons of bitches," to which the soldiers echoed, "No more mercy to those sons of bitches than we would have to rattlesnakes."

The rage many unionists felt toward the Twenty-fourth was driven to an extreme by certain segments of the labor press. The *Railway Conductor*, normally a voice of moderation, wrote of the black soldiers: "Fit representatives, indeed, are such hyenas to uphold the law. The reign of terror these imps of darkness have instituted...will leave a blot upon the page of our nation's history that has no parallel." The *Courier*, published in the mining community of Pueblo, Colorado, denounced the "whole rapscallion horde of thieving, lecherous, drunken soldiers," from whose "hideous advances" no woman was safe, a regiment led by "white men who sank lower in the depths of depravity, than were the black beasts under them." Of their commander, it hoped that "a Filipino bullet will bore his cowardly heart and send his soul reeking with sin sliding into hell." Looking past Merriam to those it held finally responsible, it said: "McKinley and Steunenberg are equal partners in the odium which attaches to the unparalleled outrage of locking up men in a filthy prison.... The Governor of Idaho and the President of the United States deliberately entered into a foul conspiracy to violate the Constitution and for their treachery they should be impeached."

Facing an election the next year, McKinley had grown increasingly sensitive to the Coeur d'Alene furor. In response to angry letters, the War Department sent out a statement noting that "the presence of troops in Shoshone County, Idaho, is due to the request of the Governor of [that] State. ... The constitution and laws of the United States required the President to comply with this requisition, and any application for relief should be made to the Governor of Idaho." On September 28, the new secretary of war, Elihu Root, wrote Steunenberg seeking once more to disassociate the McKinley administration and the army from the governor's troubles. Asking whether the insurrection "has not now been suppressed," he said he was "much disinclined" to have U.S. troops retain custody of citizens "who have remained so long without being tried."

In a response that read like a negotiated document, Steunenberg urged the administration to keep troops in the Coeur d'Alenes but assured Root they'd no longer guard the bullpen and gave the president the disclaimer he'd sought: "The State of Idaho is responsible for all that has been done in Shoshone County, relative to [the] call for troops, the arrest, detention and care of prisoners, the regulations under which the mines can and have been operated."*

Although this admission was widely publicized, the growing anger at the governor reflected in part the earlier perception of him as a friend of labor. Little had been expected of the reactionary McKinley, the "pusillanimous tin soldier" Merriam, or the "sub-human" black soldiers. But Steunenberg was seen as a turncoat, a friend who'd betrayed his onetime supporters. Samuel Gompers noted that Steunenberg had been an honorary member of the Typographical Union, then pointed out that there'd seldom been a noble cause that hadn't given birth to a traitor.† "Our revolutionary war for independence had its Benedict Arnold," he said. That organized labor should have a Steunenberg "may be cause for chagrin but not for dismay."

With the 1900 presidential race heating up, the furor became politicized. In December 1899, Congressman John Lentz, a partisan Ohio Democrat, took the House floor to demand an investigation of charges that Merriam had imprisoned hundreds of United States citizens "under the most brutal and tyrannical conditions" and had otherwise violated the rights of Idahoans. The House assigned the task to its Committee on Military Affairs, which convened in Washington early in the New Year to hear testimony from miners

---

* When Root later met Steunenberg in Washington, he declared that the governor was "one of the strong men of the country" (Connolly, "Moyer-Haywood Case," part 2, 21).
† Pete Steunenberg, in an interview with Irving Stone, thought his brother had been a full-fledged member of some typographical union in Des Moines but didn't pay his dues very long.

who'd been held in the bullpen as well as Merriam, Sinclair, Steunenberg, and many others.

Although the investigation ostensibly focused on Merriam and his troops, Steunenberg drew the most combative questioning. While Merriam spent four days at the witness table, the governor got an eight-day grilling. Representative Lentz went after him with controlled fury. "You do go breaking into the houses of innocent men and women, through soldiers, do you not?" he asked at one point.

"I refuse to reply to such a question as that," said the governor. "It's an insult."

The governor gave as good as he got. A lawyer for the minority said: "So, in other words, you are authorized by a mere statute of the legislature to deprive a county of a republican form of government indefinitely?"

"The inhabitants themselves deprive themselves of a republican form of government by insurrection and rebellion," Steunenberg shot back.

He never dodged the blame. "I assume responsibility," he said, "for every arrest that was made in Shoshone County, whether by General Merriam or by anybody else." Nor did he invent an elaborate rationale. "I acted according to my ... conscience and desire to bring order out of chaos."

Ultimately, the sixteen-man committee divided along party lines. Nine Republicans concluded that (1) "the military power of the United States exerted in Shoshone County was in strict accordance with their instructions and with the law," (2) "the governor of Idaho, in his efforts to enforce the laws of the State, is to be commended for his courage and fearlessness," and (3) "the colored troops who stood watch over the prison at Wardner had stormed the hill at San Juan, and their manly bearing, courtesy, and dignity tell of the true soldier." The seven Democrats saw it differently, holding that "neither law nor order, nor justice, nor equity, nor decency nor humanity would tolerate the despotic system which perpetrated upon thousands of men, women and children the brutality of the bull pen and the blacklisting system" and calling for it to "be confessed with shame and humiliation that our Chief Executive and our army officials have become so callous to the rights and liberties of labor that these things could have been perpetrated in the year of our Lord 1899 and 1900."

During those lonely months in Washington, Steunenberg was aware of the rage building against him. He heard it in testimony before the committee, from Democratic congressmen, in press commentary—and face-to-face. In mid-March 1900, walking through the Capitol, he encountered F. B. Schermerhorn, a friend from the Iowa Agricultural College. Inviting Schermerhorn back to the Raleigh Hotel, Steunenberg remarked, in melancholy tones, that this might be the last time they'd meet. With that, he produced a well-thumbed stack of a dozen letters, badly written in what looked like disguised handwriting. Most had been mailed from Colorado; five seemed to be from the same person; all threatened Steunenberg's life. "He knew that he was a marked man," Schermerhorn recalled, "and that it was only a question of time as to when the Federation would get him."

Over the years, there'd been other messages—his clerk, Sam Clay, thought as many as fifty—warning the governor that his time was short. Occasionally, too, there'd been a troubling incident. In February 1901, five "would-be toughs" blew into Caldwell and stirred up quite a ruckus. Roistering through the town's saloons, they claimed to be Coeur d'Alene miners who'd served time in the bullpen and said they'd come to Caldwell to dynamite "the collarless governor." The sheriff didn't take them seriously. Two were convicted for selling goods without a license, then all five were escorted to the edge of town and told to "keep going." People wondered what they'd really been up to.

When Belle Steunenberg broke her silence about the governor's assassination, she confirmed that during the 1899 crisis "Mr. Steunenberg was greatly worried, and one evening after he'd made his final stand, he told me he thought it would cost him his life." His friends urged him to carry a .45 revolver, but he refused, saying, "If those fellows want to do anything, they'll get me in the back, anyway." But as the years went by and no overt move was made to kill him, his fears began to wane. In recent years, she said, "he never believed his life was in danger, and I had practically forgotten the ordeal through which he'd passed, as I believe he had."

4

THE GREAT DETECTIVE

"I HAVE SPLIT more rails than Abraham Lincoln ever did, but I have not received as much publicity for it," the Honorable Charles O. Stockslager, chief justice of the Idaho Supreme Court, once groused. An Indiana farm boy turned country lawyer, Stockslager practiced law in Kansas, proving as deft with writ and plea as once he'd been with ax and saw.

Rising within Kansas's Democratic Party, he served as Cherokee County prosecutor. Then, in 1887, President Grover Cleveland handed him a juicy hunk of political pork, running the U.S. Land Office in Hailey, Idaho. Henceforth, his advance was rapid: in 1890 he won a district court seat, in 1900 a six-year term on the Idaho Supreme Court; soon, he was named chief justice. By 1905, with his high-court term about to expire, he took aim at the Democratic nomination for governor and all through early winter assembled potent support within his party. Insiders gave him an even chance of unseating Gooding if nominated.

Charley Stockslager, a newspaper once noted, was "not a pretty man." Twenty years before, on a hunting trip to the Wood River, a companion had accidentally shot out his left eye. Spurning a patch, the judge presented to the world a squint-eyed visage above a bulky body appropriate to his nickname, Stocky. Nor did he dress with much care, perpetually turned out in the same scruffy black coat, generally worn with trousers and vest of contrasting colors. He liked his liquor: one lawyer recalled sipping from the judicial water pitcher on Stockslager's bench, which turned out to contain "almost straight gin." But such peccadilloes notwithstanding, he was a popular man, at fifty-eight a vigorous campaigner, the "best handshaker" in the state.

Now he and Frank Gooding each scrambled to exploit the "calamitous" events in Caldwell. If the governor had stolen a march by ordering a special train the night of the assassination, the chief justice wasn't far behind. The next day—New Year's Eve—he and his colleague Justice I. N. Sullivan, off the bench a prosperous grain and alfalfa rancher, boarded the first westbound train from the capital. By midmorning, with his well-honed penchant for intrigue, Stockslager had plunged deep into Caldwell's investigative thicket.

•

Though Idaho officials of all political stripes had deplored the bombing and extolled the dead governor—"a plain, square-jawed, clear-eyed, big-shouldered and big-hearted man," the *Boise Clipper* called him—those expressions did little to disguise the fierce political infighting that Steunenberg's assassination set off in the intense little world of Idaho politics. In early January, J. M. Woodburn, a Boise physician, wrote his friend Senator Fred Dubois in Washington about the political repercussions on the Dubois wing of Idaho's Democrats, known as the "dynamite wing" because it had opposed Steunenberg's tough tactics toward the WFM.

"Anent the catastrophe at Caldwell," Woodburn wrote, "your friends of our party as well as many Republicans are resenting in unmistakable manners the silly and boorish slobbering, if I may use the word, over the unfortunate ending of Steunenberg.... This 'gush' is born of a desire to impress the public with their apparent earnestness in behalf of law and order rather than any heartfelt serious sympathy, either of the manner of the taking off of the ex-Governor or toward the bereaved family.... [It] is commencing to act as a boomerang already."

A prime example of the shenanigans under way, Woodburn told Dubois, was the "intention[al] suppression" of Dubois's "message of condolence" to Mrs. Steunenberg. On January 1, Dubois had telegraphed Belle Steunenberg in Caldwell, saying, "Mrs. Dubois joins me in sincere sympathy to you and your family in your great bereavement," but somehow the missive had never made it into the Idaho press. Woodburn ridiculed Governor Gooding's suggestion that it had been "lost." According to the Boise physician, the senator's friends believed that the burying of Dubois's telegram was an effort "to cast aspersions upon you personally and thus to, in an indirect manner, assist creating a feeling against the 'dynamite wing of the party.'" It was "the limit of Gooding's littleness and defies description.... They are simply hanging themselves and our plain duty is to allow them sufficient rope whereupon to perform the last rite to their puny little souls."

Gooding, a mainstream Republican, had scarcely been a great friend of the Silver Democrat Steunenberg, but he was exploiting the assassination for all it was worth, telling visiting newsmen that the dead man was "one of the squarest, straightest men I have ever met." In mid-January, Charles H. Jackson, a Boise attorney and Democratic state chairman, wrote Dubois: "I hear generally that there is to be a determined effort made to throw the blame for the Steunenberg murder on the Democratic party and on you.... Gooding will go strong on 'Law and Order.'"

But Dubois and his supporters saw at least as much opportunity as peril in these events. D. K. Larimer was an editor of the anti-Mormon *Salt Lake Herald*, which supported Dubois as one of the West's fiercest critics of Mormonism. He crowed to Dubois: "This Steunenberg business is playing into our hands, for Gooding, if renominated, will not get a labor union vote in the state." He went on to warn: "I don't believe it would be good policy for our side to make a campaign issue of Gooding's course toward the Miners' Union officials, for that would be playing with fire; but our side will get all the benefit of the union labor resentment toward Gooding, without having to identify itself with the dynamiters."

The Democrats sought to strip off Gooding's pose as defender of Idaho's stalwart burghers against the forces of anarchy. Joe Hutchinson, still seething over his exclusion from the Caldwell meeting on assassination night, wrote Dubois: "Some man must be named for Governor that can stop this Law & Order and Holier than Thou Art! talk and make Gooding talk on his record."

Charley Stockslager wanted that job, and toward that end he would do almost anything. Despite his august position at the apex of the state's judiciary, he felt largely uninhibited by legal or ethical constraints, for at the turn of the century, codes of judicial conduct were scarcely contemplated. (Although the American Bar Association adopted its first ethical guidelines for lawyers in 1908, it waited until 1924 to proclaim its first Canons of Judicial Ethics.) Through the nineteenth century and into the twentieth, most judgeships were openly political offices, heatedly contested in partisan elections. In the former western territories, judges were accustomed to being full participants in the political hurly-burly. Though some graduates of prestigious eastern law schools would have raised their eyebrows at a judge's personal intervention in a case that could well come before him, few Idaho lawyers of that day suffered such scruples.

Only hours after his arrival in Caldwell, Stockslager placed a call from the Saratoga Hotel to the Pinkerton National Detective Agency in Denver, asking to speak with James McParland, the manager of Pinkerton operations west of the Mississippi. The Pinkerton agency in those days had three divisions: the eastern, headed by John Cornish in New York; the middle, run by E. S. Gaylor from Chicago; and the western, run by McParland in Denver.

The chief justice and the detective had known each other for two decades, ever since Stockslager was the Cherokee County prosecutor and McParland a young sleuth working out of Pinkerton's Chicago office. In 1886, McParland obtained a key confession that broke open a sensational arson and fraud case in the county seat of Columbus, laying the groundwork for one of Stockslager's early prosecutorial triumphs. As both men rose in their respective professions, they remained in touch. Now, sensing that the assassination was bound to figure prominently in the approaching election, Stockslager was determined not to cede the law-and-order label to the Republican incumbent. With McParland as principal investigator, the chief justice might influence, if not actually control, the course of the inquiry.

When McParland came on the phone that afternoon, Stockslager asked him to catch the first train north. McParland demurred. "I'm not operating," he said, meaning he was no longer working in the field as a common operative. Moreover, the detective said, this wasn't the way to obtain his services.

Although he ran the agency's western division, Pinkerton protocol required that such requests go to the general superintendent in charge of the appropriate division within the region—in this case, James Nevins in Portland, Oregon, who supervised Pinkerton's northwestern operations. (The Pinkertons took these divisions very seriously: when operatives from one division "invaded" the territory of another, they paid the invaded division a "commission" on all fees collected for such work.) Moreover, McParland said the request must come from the state's chief executive, the very man Stockslager was maneuvering to outflank, Frank Gooding.

The next afternoon—New Year's Day—Stockslager drafted a telegram to Nevins asking for McParland's services. The governor initially went along and Stockslager wired McParland to prepare for departure when he received Nevins's authorization.

But before Gooding could get a wire off to Spokane, it was preempted by a telegram from Captain Swain, the Thiel man there, announcing that he and his operatives were on their way and claiming that he was acting on behalf of the Coeur d'Alene mine owners. This put the governor in a bind: the mine owners were a powerful constituency he could ill afford to offend by rebuffing their detective. Moreover, Canyon County's commissioners preferred to deal with Swain, since they assumed the mine owners would pick up his bill. So when Swain reached Caldwell on January 1, the governor put him in charge of the investigation—keeping the Pinkerton initiative on hold for the time being.

Undeterred, Stockslager continued to press for retaining the Pinkertons, if only as partners with Thiel. The competitive Swain couldn't have welcomed this notion, but eventually he acquiesced. On January 4—even as Swain was inducing Harry Orchard to admit his real name—the captain's assistant in Spokane telephoned across town to the Pinkerton superintendent there, Edwin R. Taber, to say that one of Swain's clients wanted the Pinkertons to join Thiel in the case.

This left Taber in a quandary, unsure who was asking for them and under what terms. Without time to consult his superiors, Taber sent his deputy, Gustavus J. Hasson, to Idaho to get some answers.

When Hasson reached Caldwell a few days later, he found it teeming with law enforcement officers. "The city swarms with detectives, both amateur and professional," the *Capital News* reported on January 6, "and the air is kept charged with sensational rumors of what the officers have discovered." The *Statesman* found wildcat rumors "as thick as fleas on a yellow dog." Still other detectives, drawn by the mounting reward, jostled for a piece of the pie. Within forty-eight hours of the governor's death, F. F. Lischke, a former Pinkerton man now a municipal detective in Portland, Oregon, offered his services to Bill Borah. "From past experience with the dynamiters and general knowledge of detective work," he wrote, "deem that I am perhaps better qualified to do the work than anyone that could be secured." With so many gumshoes already on the scene, Lischke's services weren't required.

Gus Hasson found Swain living at the Saratoga Hotel, his headquarters installed in Judge Smith's chambers and nine of his operatives scurrying around the town. As the Pinkertons' longtime deputy superintendent in Spokane, Hasson had gone head-to-head with Swain before and didn't have much use for him. Now, in his reports to Taber, he expressed ill-disguised contempt for Swain's men, so clumsily transparent they were already known to half the town. (Dashiell Hammett, later a Pinkerton operative in Spokane, wrote: "I know a detective who once attempted to disguise himself thoroughly. The first policeman he met took him into custody.")

Soon Hasson's own casually assumed cover as a Portland attorney was blown. When accosted by a *Capital News* reporter, he exclaimed: "How did you know I was connected with the case?" The reporter said he'd "surmised" it. Shrugging off the setback, Hasson henceforth operated openly as McParland's advance man.

From Caldwell, Harry Crane of the *Statesman* reported "some misunderstandings" between Thiel and Pinkerton men. Moreover, Swain's ponderous manner nettled Caldwell's law-and-order men. Swain himself complained about "less harmonious cooperation than is desirable": a scrap of metal that had fallen from the governor's side and was retrieved by a Caldwell constable hadn't been turned over to the captain.

Sheriff Nichols—an angular young man in a white Stetson, with a small, pursed mouth and a twitchy temperament—rankled at the swagger with which Swain and his "so-called detectives" had assumed command in Caldwell. Judge Frank Smith, who had to share his chambers with the man, told people that "Old Swain" had butted into the investigation with "a gang of the dirtiest low-lived sons of bitches" he'd ever seen congregated in one place.

Since Orchard's arrest on January 1, the Thiel operatives had produced sheaves of paper, which Swain relayed to Governor Gooding. Some of their work proved useful; much did not.

On January 3, employing a time-honored detective's device, Swain had H. Baxter, an operative from Portland, thrown into jail with Orchard, hoping Baxter could wheedle something out of the suspect. There were already eight other prisoners besides Orchard sharing the jail's four holding cells and its cramped "kitchen," among them a gambler charged with shooting a fellow cardplayer; two men accused of holding up a Japanese restaurant; "Indian Jake," one of Canyon County's renowned horsemen, charged with stealing two horses in Payette; and two other suspects in the Steunenberg assassination—the mysterious figure with soft white hands and the "shifty" character with dark piercing eyes. For two full days, Swain's undercover agent tried in vain to talk with Orchard, who was undoubtedly on guard against such a ploy. Only toward the end of the second day did Baxter maneuver Orchard into a corner for what he called a "more or less conversation." They talked about the "sporting women" at Della Dolman's bordello in Nampa's red-light district. Orchard and the homicidal gambler were on such good terms with Nampa's prostitutes that Baxter thought they must have been pimps there. As they talked, Baxter gave Orchard the WFM high sign, but Orchard—who'd recognized Baxter as a detective almost immediately—refused to give the countersign. Baxter turned up so little he was pulled out of jail on January 5.

Swain wouldn't give up. Days later, the *Statesman* reported that "a very mysterious person" had signed into the Saratoga, using a red pencil, as "John Doe"; soon Sheriff Nichols told the paper: "That man is one of the Thiel detectives and wants to be arrested on suspicion so as to be placed in jail with Orchard for the purpose of spying on the prisoner. It was tried once before and I bit on it but I don't take the same bait twice.... No more suspects will be put in Orchard's cell."

Meanwhile, Thiel detectives followed other trails, many of them cold. Captain Swain had the hotel's cesspool examined, in the vain hope that Orchard had flushed incriminating evidence down his toilet. Operative W. T. Simmons spent days "roping in"—buying drinks for and otherwise getting friendly with—Jack Goodwin, a blacksmith at the Canyon County Machine and Blacksmith Shop originally regarded as a prime suspect; the exasperated detective was "not able to induce him to drink very much." Operative A. S. Peterson, who assiduously visited Caldwell's saloons, reported the presence of "several strangers and suspicious people." One of his criteria seemed to be "vicious talk" about Steunenberg, and one man who talked that way was Arthur Brown, a barkeep at the Board of Trade saloon. "This man Brown is continually talking unionism," Peterson reported, "[and] is very vicious against all those who oppose the same." Operative J. C. Stewart stalked the Monos, the dark-complected foreigners believed for a time to be Italian anarchists. Outside Steunenberg's house, Operative C. Harry Williams found a ball of wire that the manager of the electric plant identified as one his men had discarded that fall. Operative W. W. Carter called on Harry Jones, the undertaker, in hopes he might have found something significant on Steunenberg's body, but except for a few copper scraps from the bomb, Jones had nothing to offer. G. M. Taylor and T. H. McDermot shuttled back and forth to Boise carrying metal and powder for examination by the state chemist. J. M. Manes investigated two suspicious characters who'd run into the Calvert boardinghouse minutes after the bomb exploded, but he never identified either. Manes spent time at several Caldwell sporting houses, billing the investigation $6.40 for his disportation.

Gus Hasson, for the time being the lone Pinkerton in Caldwell, found himself crossing tracks with the Thiel operatives. When James J. Sullivan, a Denver lawyer believed to be acting on Orchard's behalf, arrived in Caldwell on January 6, Hasson and two Thiel men—Stewart and Manes—fell all over one another trying to keep him under surveillance both in Caldwell and on a side trip to Baker City, Oregon.

A reporter for the *Capital News* watched Manes watching Sullivan:

> The detective is short of stature, and as the attorney was walking at a rather fast gait, had to fall into what might be termed a "dog trot." Seeing that he was fast overtaking his quarry the sleuth walked very slowly and crossed the street when he reached a point opposite the Antlers hotel. Upon reaching the corner by Judge Currey's office the sleuth, observing that his man had turned and, evidently not knowing that the court house was in the next block, did a double-quick stunt for the next corner south where he craned his neck in vain to observe his prey. Failing to see the attorney, the "rubber-shoed" man took a position near by to await the return of Sullivan.

The attorney, said the reporter, "takes their vigilance as a huge joke and says he would prefer that they put real men on his tail as the blundering awkwardness of their sleuthing is painful to behold." On the train to Baker City, Hasson plopped down in the seat facing Sullivan and simply refused to move until Sullivan got off. When Sullivan checked into the Geiser Hotel, so did the Pinkerton man.

Hasson tried to find out what the Thiel men were up to, but Swain bluntly refused to share information, which infuriated Hasson. He was damned if the Pinkertons would share their own gleanings with a swaggering braggart like Swain and his squad of inept operatives. When Hasson's reports reached the company's principals—William A. Pinkerton in New York and Robert A. Pinkerton in Chicago—they endorsed his proposals: if invited by the governor, the Pinkertons would take the case. But they would insist on complete independence from other investigators. Under no circumstances would they report to, or share information with, Swain and his men. And certainly the Pinkertons must be on "equal footing" with the Thiel agency.

The Pinkertons particularly resented Swain's penchant for talking to the press, advancing his theories of the case, and claiming all credit. "Some detectives work largely on theory," Gus Hasson told the *Statesman*. "My agency does not work on theories. We work on facts, making our chain of evidence by connecting one fact with another."

By January 7, the fierce competition between the two detective agencies was clearly hampering the investigation. Deputy Sheriff Floyd R. Thompson of Cripple Creek, Colorado, who'd sped to Caldwell with his boss, assessed this chaos for the *Capital News*. "Detectives," he said, "are like all other professional men, in that there is more or less jealousy existing among them, and each organization is apt to work on different theories so that there is a great deal of confusion.... Had there been an organization at the start, with one directing head and all others working on tasks assigned to them, in my opinion much more would have been accomplished."

The melancholy saga of the Boise special officer Andy Johnson was a case in point. Proud of his early achievements—it was he who swore out the warrant for Orchard and helped Sheriff Nichols make the arrest—Johnson felt entitled to the $25,000 reward, as well as to a greater role in the investigation. When he failed to get either, he quit the Boise police, setting up in town as a private detective. But his career only went downhill from there. He loudly threatened to sue Governor Gooding for the reward and to sell prosecution documents to the highest bidder. Drinking heavily, he got into a public brawl one night with another private detective, Larry Maloney of the Nampa Merchants' Patrol, firing two shots at Maloney before his antagonist administered a severe beating, leaving him "bruised and cut in a fearful manner." When Johnson tried to sell material to the defense, one of the defense lawyers called him "the most unmitigated liar in Ada County."

Under telegraphic prodding from his Pinkerton supervisors, Gus Hasson moved on January 5 to cinch his deal with the State of Idaho. That afternoon —accompanied by the Pinkertons' principal advocate at the capital, Justice Stockslager—he sat down with the governor. Stockslager and Gooding, their rivalry notwithstanding, finally agreed to call on the Pinkertons.

But with the Thiel people already at work, the Pinkertons' bargaining position was weak. Thiel was charging only six dollars per operative per day, a full two dollars below the Pinkerton rate. "In order to meet competition from the Swain people," Hasson violated a long-standing agency rule against reducing its established fee and drew up a contract in which the state agreed to pay the agency eight dollars a day for each operative employed during the first thirty days but only six dollars after that (a concession for which Hasson would later draw a sharp rebuke from his superiors).

With these preliminaries out of the way, Gooding formally requested William Pinkerton to order McParland in from Denver. On January 7, Pinkerton complied. McParland was elated. Before leaving for Boise, he wrote James Nevins, the superintendent in Portland, suggesting that the case could have important consequences for the agency—by weaning the mine owners away from Thiel. "This is one of the most important operations ever undertaken in the Portland District," he wrote, "and if through our offices we are successful, it will mean a great deal to the Spokane office so far as the mine operators are concerned.... I am highly pleased to note we have been employed on this case, although I am afraid that if Swain is still retained in this matter he will be a stumbling block in our path. I will have to take this up with Governor Gooding and Judge Stockslager upon my arrival in Boise."

Gooding wanted McParland in Boise "immediately." The detective took his time getting there, perhaps so as to send Gooding a message: that a detective of his eminence was not to be summoned like a butler. Finally, he took the 7:00 a.m. train on Tuesday, January 9, scheduled to arrive at 3:00 p.m. Wednesday. Mechanical troubles delayed the train three hours. Waiting on the platform of Boise's spacious new Union Pacific depot on Front Street, stamping their feet and blowing into their hands on that bitterly cold night, were Gus Hasson and Idaho's chief justice—an impressive reception committee for a mere detective.

Stockslager accompanied the two Pinkerton men part of the way to Boise's best hotel, the Idanha, promising to meet McParland after dinner for a full-dress conference with the governor. Eager to ingratiate himself, the governor made sure that the detective was assigned one of the hotel's best suites, number 35, a spacious bedchamber and adjoining parlor looking out onto Tenth Street.

Hasson, who'd come up from Caldwell to meet his chief, had been spelled there by a rising young Pinkerton star, S. Chris Thiele (no relation to the rival detective agency) of the Seattle office. Over dinner in the hotel dining room, Hasson briefed McParland on his preliminary negotiations with the state and the competition from the Thiel people. After dinner, a pack of Boise newspapermen intercepted McParland as he crossed the ornate lobby. He proved—in one reporter's words—"quite uncommunicative." The only subject on which he seemed willing to expatiate was the martyred Steunenberg. "I was quite well acquainted with the ex-governor," he said. "I knew him before he was elected to office, I knew him while he was governor and I have met him a number of times since. He was a very good man." As for what McParland was doing in town, he would say only, "I expect to stay in Boise a day or two."

At seven that evening, as arranged, McParland met the chief justice and the governor in the hotel office and the three men then adjourned to the detective's room for their first discussion of the case. Gooding began with a gaffe, telling McParland he hoped the Pinkertons would work "in conjunction" with the Thiel agency. McParland flatly refused. The state could hire the Thiel people or anybody it wanted, but if the Pinkertons signed on, the governor mustn't show their reports to anyone except Judge Stockslager or the attorneys who'd try Steunenberg's murderers. Nor did the Pinkertons wish to see the Thiel reports. "We will work independent," McParland proclaimed, "or not at all."

The chief justice interjected: "Governor, I told you that you might as well try to remove Plymouth Rock as to change the established rules of the Pinkertons. Their plans are right. Look at the information you have got from the fine reports of Mr. Hasson who has only got on the ground as it were."

According to McParland's report, the governor, "a strong willed man," pondered the matter for several minutes, then told the detective: "I accept your proposition. You are right. As the judge has told me and Mr. Hasson's reports show, you don't work on the same lines as Swain, but you must stay with us for a week or so till we get things started right."

The governor apologized for Swain's continued presence on the case. The captain's claim to be working for the mine owners, Gooding conceded, had put a temporary hold on plans to call in the Pinkertons—a delay he now professed to regret. But the governor insisted he hadn't employed Swain, wasn't responsible for him, didn't know for sure who'd employed him.

Privately, McParland suspected that Swain had "got on the ground in his usual way without first being employed by anybody." If so, the wily captain had bluffed the governor into accepting his presence as a fait accompli. But McParland was less interested in rehearsing the past than in ensuring that Swain would no longer interfere in Pinkerton operations.

"Swain wanted to be present at this conference," the governor confided. "I had agreed to that and he is now downstairs to be called up. I thought when I talked with you that you would not object. I can see where you are right. You ask no favors and don't give any." Gooding sent word to Swain—probably through the chief justice, who now left the meeting—that he wouldn't be needed that night. One can imagine the impatience with which the captain had paced the lobby. Undoubtedly tipped to McParland's arrival date, Swain had checked into the Idanha that afternoon, hours before his rival's grand entrance. He'd been waiting ever since. Dozens of people had seen him cooling his heels like an errand boy; now the governor had sent him packing. It was a snub that left Swain seething with rage.

In Suite 35, Frank Gooding and James McParland, facing each other in easy chairs before a guttering fire, reviewed the case in detail for the next five hours. Once the two men reached matters of substance they found themselves in close accord.

McParland had been in Idaho barely three hours—his advance man, Gus Hasson, barely five days—but already the Pinkerton manager had reached some firm conclusions: that Orchard had planted the bomb that killed the governor; that he'd been assisted by at least one accomplice, Jack Simpkins; that Orchard and his colleague(s) had acted on behalf of the Western Federation of Miners' "inner circle," which in turn sought revenge for the governor's stance during the Coeur d'Alene miners' unrest of 1899.

He told the Pinkerton brothers in a report composed the next day:

> I am satisfied that there were other people in this plot besides Orchard and feel almost sure that Orchard was the tool of the others. Some of them may be in Caldwell yet. The evidence shows that Orchard in company with Simpkins, under the alias of Simmons, visited Caldwell in the early part of September and remained there for some time, and that Orchard returned in November and again in December.... From my conversation with the Governor, I am led to believe that the state has sufficient evidence to warrant them holding Orchard and with what is being gathered now, I think we will be able to convict the man.

The speed with which McParland had reached these conclusions— before speaking with Orchard or, indeed, with anyone except the governor, the chief justice, and Hasson—suggests that he brought such notions largely intact from Denver; he'd had thirty-six hours on the train to ponder the situation and apply lessons drawn from his career as an operative specializing in labor unrest.

When that first meeting with the governor broke up well past midnight, Gus Hasson hurried back to McParland's suite for a recapitulation of the evening's events. The Pinkertons had good reason to congratulate themselves —not only on an investigation well launched, a prime suspect imprisoned, and an accomplice identified but on outwitting a principal competitor for one of the most important contracts of this, or any other, year. A visible emblem of their victory was a letter the governor now gave Gus Hasson to take with him on his return to Caldwell. Dated January 11 and addressed to Sheriff Nichols and A. K. Steunenberg, it introduced the bearer as someone who had been "detailed on the Steunenberg case." Then it proclaimed that "the Pinkerton association has been employed on the case, and will work under the supervision of Inspector McParland. . . . Any assistance that can be given Mr. Hassen [*sic*], or the operatives under his supervision, should be cheerfully rendered and will be fully appreciated by me." The letter left no doubt as to which of the competing agencies had prevailed.

It had been a bad night indeed for the Thiel agency and its captain. Still fuming about his treatment at the Idanha, Swain managed to put on a cheerful face the next day when he encountered Harry Crane, the saturnine *Statesman* correspondent, in Caldwell. With a broad smile and a knowing wink, Swain admonished the reporter, "Tell your readers that everything is working lovely for us, just as fine or finer than we expected."

But Swain knew he was in deep trouble. Beyond the challenge posed by McParland's arrival, the captain realized that his contingent had aroused the resentment of the sheriff and the district judge. The county commissioners were growing restive at the bills Swain and his operatives—now grown to twelve—kept submitting. At ten dollars per day for Swain's services, six dollars per day for each operative, two to three dollars per day for each man's subsistence, and with the cost of train fares, phone calls, and incidentals in the surveillance of Caldwell's saloons and sporting houses, the Thiels were costing the county $150 per day, nearly $2,000 already. Days before, the commissioners had favored Swain precisely because they thought the mine owners would cover his bills. As Swain's unpaid bills piled up, they felt misused.

On Friday, January 12, the commissioners called Swain in and posed him some hard questions: just who did employ him, who was supposed to pay his bills, how many operatives did he have at Caldwell, why did he need so many, and how were the Pinkertons, with fewer operatives, able to compete so effectively? When they'd heard him out, the commissioners allocated $1,000 to get rid of Swain and his men. Sending the check to the governor, they suggested he use it to pay half the Thiel bill, for which Swain should sign a receipt acknowledging "payment in full." Otherwise, they said, Swain shouldn't get a penny—since, strictly speaking, nobody had employed him.

On receiving the commissioners' letter the next day, Gooding raged at the Thiels, convinced they'd deceived him, too, about who would pay their bills. He regarded their charges as excessive. "I can now see why you could not work with a crowd of bunco men," he told McParland. "I have sent for Swain and will order him to discontinue all his men."

McParland must have had difficulty stifling a chortle. For, as he wrote the Pinkerton brothers that evening, "I have done what I could to overthrow Swain, never letting an opportunity pass." Indeed, from the moment McParland arrived on the scene, he'd set out to destroy his rival's reputation.

The two detectives detested each other. It was a luxury most men in the "gumshoe game" couldn't indulge. Since no detective knew what client might engage him next, alliances shifted; a detective ranged against you one month might turn up on your side the next. But the enmity between Swain and McParland went back a long way—to the mid-1880s, when both were young detectives in Denver, Swain working for the city's police department, McParland opening the Pinkerton office there. Then, when Swain scored his coup by inserting the Thiel "super operative" Edward L. Zimmerman as financial secretary of the Wardner Miners Union, it made the mine owners forget about McParland's similar achievement in 1892 with Charles Siringo. For McParland, that was unforgivable presumption. The healthy juices of competition had long since curdled into something more malign; by now, the two had abandoned the last traces of professional courtesy.

Sometimes McParland attacked head-on. Once, driven to distraction by Swain's claims to still be running the investigation, McParland wrote the governor, "It looks to me as though this man is crazy." He never lost an opportunity to remind Gooding that Swain had committed a "cold-blooded murder" on Denver's Larimer Street twenty years before. More often he worked surreptitiously, passing stories he knew would be repeated, impugning Swain's investigative skills, ridiculing his minions, suggesting the captain was in league with the WFM.

He'd taken care of Swain all right, he told his superiors, "but done it in such a way that I am not suspected." That was to say, the governor would never see that McParland had torpedoed his rival. But Swain, nobody's fool, would know who'd done him in and henceforth, McParland boasted, "he will steer clear of me."

By plucking this choice case out of Thiel's hands, the Pinkertons settled several scores simultaneously. At one level, the struggle had been a bitter personal match between McParland and Swain. At another level, it was a competition by the two agencies for a critical market. It was also a joust between Governor Gooding and Chief Justice Stockslager to position themselves as law-and-order candidates in the coming campaign. Finally, it posed a choice between two groups of mine owners—the Idaho wing, concentrated in the Coeur d'Alenes, and the Colorado owners in Cripple Creek and Telluride. While the two detective agencies had long been active in both states, Thiel had the upper hand in northern Idaho, the Pinkertons in Colorado. With McParland's ascendancy, the Colorado mine owners had gained control of the far-reaching investigation of Frank Steunenberg's assassination.

But if McParland thought he'd seen the last of Swain, he was wrong. Though Gooding had proclaimed his intention to "discontinue" Swain's men, he relented the next day. The captain got this reprieve by offering to produce the man the state most wanted, Jack Simpkins, Orchard's alleged accomplice in Caldwell. Swain told the governor "he could lay his hands on Simpkins at any moment." Having maneuvered Swain to the brink, McParland could be magnanimous. He assured the governor that the Pinkertons were interested not in credit but in results. "I advised him," he recorded, "to notify Swain that he would furnish him with an application for the extradition of Simpkins from the state of Washington, and to have Simpkins arrested at once."

Swain's information about Simpkins's whereabouts came from Thiel operatives who'd sighted him at the depot in his home city of Spokane as early as January 4. An operative reported Simpkins still in Spokane the next week. Even before the governor's go-ahead, Swain had assigned the Simpkins investigation to C. Harry Williams, a deputy sheriff of Shoshone County, who doubled as a Thiel operative. Williams had worked in Caldwell since January 7, but his usual base was the mining town of Mullan, Idaho—some forty miles east of Spokane—and he knew Simpkins by sight.

Williams's assignment took him on a baffling trek through the frozen northland. At first, he seemed to be hot on Simpkins's trail. Railroad workers at Tekoa, Washington, recognized Simpkins's picture as that of a man who'd passed that way days earlier, boarding a train for Chatcolet, Idaho, fifty miles to the southeast. Williams pursued but could find no trace of him there. Returning to Spokane, he learned that his quarry had been in the city that very morning. For days he kept Simpkins's house under surveillance, only to learn that Simpkins had left once more for his timber claim at the headwaters of Idaho's St. Joseph River. Pushing up that frozen waterway, the operative encountered snows so deep that he paused to buy snowshoes. Eventually he lost Simpkins's trail again. Williams concluded that his man had taken refuge at a friend's home at Wolf Lodge, on the ice-bound shores of Lake Coeur d'Alene. Armed with a warrant, he reached Wolf Lodge hours after Simpkins had left. Slogging back to Spokane, he discovered that two nights before, under cover of darkness, a wagon had spirited Mrs. Simpkins out of town— not to be seen again.

Simpkins's escape from Spokane and Operative Williams's miscarried pursuit were serious blows to the Thiel agency. On January 30—three days after Williams conceded temporary defeat—Swain fired off a letter to Gooding, trying to put the best face on the unhappy situation. Concluding that a Wallace editor had warned Simpkins that detectives were after him, the captain ended with characteristic bravado: "It is only a question of a short time until Simpkins can be apprehended."

The governor was unimpressed. Already Gooding had shut down most of Thiel's operation. In mid-January, nine of its agents were pulled out of Idaho. On January 27, Deputy Williams was cashiered as well. That left just one Thiel operative working on the Steunenberg case. Unlike the detectives who descended on Caldwell after the murder, making only the most perfunctory efforts to disguise what they were up to, Operative 53 had long worked undercover inside the WFM. For a time, he was secretary of the miners union at Wardner. Of late, he'd worked inside the miners union at Goldfield, Nevada. He was trusted by many union members in mining camps throughout the Northwest. In early January, Swain put out a call for him, praising him as "one of the best men in our employ"; the operative reached Caldwell on January 11 and was promptly assigned to Silver City, a mining town fifty-five miles to the south where William D. Haywood, the WFM secretary-treasurer, had served his union apprenticeship ten years before.

In his first report, filed January 13, Operative 53 said that R. J. Hanlon, financial secretary of the Silver City Miners' Union, complained that Haywood and Charles H. Moyer, the president of the WFM, were "trying very hard to get the Silver City Union mixed up in the [Steunenberg] affair." Hanlon said the two union officials had telegraphed him the day before to hire John F. Nugent, a Silver City lawyer and old friend of Haywood's, to defend Harry Orchard. An ex-miner who'd turned to the law after he was seriously injured in a mining accident, Nugent was serving as prosecutor of Owyhee County, where union sympathizers were in the saddle, but Nugent —perhaps seeing a conflict of interest—declined to take the Orchard case. Hanlon and other union members talked of a split between Idaho's "hotheaded" unionists to the north and more conservative Silver City miners, who were reluctant to become embroiled in "this mess."

The *Owyhee Nugget*, a Silver City newspaper friendly to the union, reported that the Steunenberg assassination was "a serious affair in which [the miners] will do well to play 'hands off.'" Many Silver City miners, the paper said, remembered Haywood from his days there and regarded him as "very impetuous" but "an honest man in his personal dealings, industrious, and wonderfully devoted to [his] wife."

As snow blanketed the mining camp, the operative found it "a hard matter" to get union men to talk about the case. "When some of them get a little intoxicated," he reported, however, "they begin to talk a little." Over several weeks, he spent more than fifty dollars buying drinks for cold, thirsty miners. Eventually, several told him that the WFM had recently voted to "clean up" the union's enemies, among them Steunenberg, and that four or five men had been appointed to get those "damn sons of bitches," which they'd do if it took a hundred years.

On February 7, Operative 53 received a letter from Swain asking him to obtain an exchange of letters between Haywood and Hanlon discussing the hiring of Nugent and other measures to protect the WFM. The operative replied: "It is a hard proposition to get [the letters] and operative will have to work very slowly and carefully.... Everything is under lock and key." The next week, the operative broke into the locked room and got his hands on the Haywood-Hanlon correspondence, but before he could send it to Boise, his cover was blown. On February 18, the Thiel agency got word that Silver City miners were "wise to operator there." Operative Baldwin in Boise called him and told him to hire a rig and drive the thirty miles to Murphy. Fearing what would happen if he was stopped and the letters found on him, Operative 53 buried them behind his boardinghouse. Then he and his wife drove to Murphy. Several days later, another operative dug up the letters and brought them to Boise.

The Silver City episode was a bit of derring-do that in other circumstances might have redounded to Captain Swain's credit. But it was too late. Publicly, Swain kept up a good front, telling reporters on February 22: "We have been in this case for more than six weeks, and we are still in it. We will show these fellows [the Pinkertons] when the time comes that we are in it, too." Over the next few months, he passed random intelligence to the governor—evidently to ingratiate himself with Gooding in hopes of future contracts or to cast a bad light on his archrival, McParland. But in his cups at a hotel bar he grumbled to a reporter, "I got elbowed out of the case."

In weeks to come, the search for Simpkins went on. Fresh reports placed him in British Columbia, Denver, Utah, and Oregon. One frustrated detective thought that he and his colleagues were victims of "a clever plan" devised by the assassins, "that a number of men have been employed who resemble Simpkins to go about the country assuming his name and identity." How could a man with a crooked nose, a squinty eye, and a five-thousand-dollar bounty on his head disappear off the face of the earth?

Days went by without an official statement on the investigation. The detectives were keeping mum. All through that dreary midwinter, Idaho's newspapers hinted that something significant was about to happen. As early as January 21, the *Statesman* reported that "the trails being followed are growing warmer and warmer." Three days later, it quoted an unidentified detective as saying, "There are great things happening which we dare not let the public know about."

For the Great Detective, great things took meticulous preparation. In strictest secrecy—from press and public, even from most of his own colleagues—he elaborately prepared the ground. Within hours of his arrival in Boise, he pressed the governor to get Harry Orchard out of the Caldwell jail and into the state penitentiary at Boise, advancing three reasons for the move: (1) the jail was "insecure," and Orchard's "friends" would eventually contrive his escape; (2) since Orchard was "the key to the conspiracy" and could finger his co-conspirators, they wouldn't risk his talking; if they failed to get him out, they'd use poison or dynamite to kill him; (3) Orchard's transfer to the pen, where he could be isolated on murderer's row, was essential to McParland's plan to obtain his confession.

The governor promised to do what he could but soon encountered obstacles. One was Jap Nichols, the Canyon County sheriff. No sooner was Swain out of his hair than along came McParland. Already Nichols—who enjoyed a following in Canyon County's Republican Party—was proclaiming that, whatever pressure came from the Pinkertons or the state, Orchard would stay in Caldwell. He was supported by Judge Frank Smith of Caldwell's district court, designated to preside at Orchard's trial, who insisted there was no authority justifying removal of the prisoner from Canyon County.

The governor didn't feel comfortable muscling the sheriff or the judge. On January 12, Gooding tossed the task into McParland's lap. The governor would fetch Smith to McParland's hotel room that evening, then arrange to be called away and leave the job to the detective. If McParland could persuade the judge to effect the transfer, he should also extract a promise that Smith wouldn't grant Orchard a writ of habeas corpus, an order requiring authorities to produce a prisoner before a judge and explain the rationale for his detention.

Shortly after eight that evening, the boyish, open-faced Smith was ushered into McParland's suite at the Idanha. After a brief three-way exchange indicated that the judge was standing firm, the governor excused himself. When Smith and McParland were alone, the judge cast a look at the insignia in the detective's lapel—an elk's head and antlers against the face of a clock set at eleven over the letters *BPOE*—and said with a fraternal smile: "I see that you are an Elk."

"So is the governor," McParland said, "but I never allow myself to so far forget my obligation to the Order [as] to use it in any way to forward my plans in any case."

It was a brief exchange but piquant nonetheless. For judge, detective, and governor shared an allegiance as potent as any in the sparsely settled reaches of the West. Most of the new Middle Border and Rocky Mountain towns had yet to produce that rich humus of church, charity, fellowship, guild, and society which in the East yielded the thick cords of community. In their stead, a clump of synthetic fraternal organizations—Elks, Moose, Odd Fellows, Knights of Pythias, Woodmen, Foresters, and Red Men, not to mention the Independent Order of Gophers, the Prudent Patricians of Pompeii, or the Concatenated Order of Hoo-Hoo—sprang up to meet the same needs. At century's turn, some five million Americans belonged to seventy thousand local lodges of nearly three hundred separate fraternal orders, many of which thrived as mutual insurance societies. The rawest western communities—a few saloons, some livery stables, feed barns, and Cantonese restaurants—

could boast an Odd Fellows or Knights of Pythias lodge. But none of these organizations had quite the repute of the Elks.

The Elks were born in 1867 when a young Englishman named Charles Vivian, just off the boat from Liverpool, banged through the swinging doors of John Ireland's Star Chop House on New York's waterfront and—with a few renditions of "Who Stole the Monkey?" and "Jimmy Riddle, Who Played the Fiddle?"—launched his music hall career. The song-and-dance man owed his success, in no small part, to a game he introduced to the tavern.

Called the Cork Trick, it began when a dupe was brought to a table full of genial men and invited to join "the Jolly Cork Society." Each member put a cork on the table. The Imperial Cork (Vivian) explained that, when he counted three, the last man to raise his cork bought the next round of drinks. At the sound of three, the dupe instantly brandished his cork above his head. It took a bit of explaining to show him that, though he was first, he was last as well, for none of the others had so much as raised their corks off the table. Grousing under his breath, the new Cork paid up and promptly began plotting revenge on the next sucker.

Before long, the Cork Trick was the rage of New York's theatrical world and Vivian found himself presiding over an ever-growing organization. But there was a hitch: blue laws kept the city's theaters and taverns closed on Sunday, thus cheating bibulous show business folk of the one day on which they were free to disport themselves. To evade this regulation, the Jolly Corks found a new meeting place on Delancey Street and formed an appropriately high-sounding body to lease it, the Benevolent and Protective Order of Elks.

At the start, Elks came almost exclusively from "the theatrical, minstrel, musical, equestrian and literary professions," but gradually the doors were opened to doctors, businessmen, even clergymen. And since theater people were incessantly on tour, they carried the order with them across the land. If the Elks began as a way for New York actors to drink on Sunday, it rapidly became a socially acceptable excuse for men of all pursuits to make merry whenever they felt like it. (The Ancient Arabic Order of the Nobles of the Mystic Shrine—better known as the Shriners—had its inception at another New York tavern, the Knickerbocker Cottage, at about the same time, and once more at the behest of an actor. Perhaps it took a theatrical imagination to conceive these fanciful bodies.)

The Elks' most rapid growth came at the turn of the century: in 1896 the "herd" numbered 32,025; by 1901 it had grown to 99,827—an explosion that stemmed, in part, from significant changes in Elkdom as the century drew to a close.

From the start, like other fraternal organizations, the Elks had reveled in secret grips, passwords, badges, blindfolds, aprons, banners, plumed hats, flowing capes, and ceremonial swords—in short, all the regalia so at odds with the democratic credo of the nation, though undoubtedly slaking a suppressed American thirst for rank and ritual. Such folderol notwithstanding, the Elks had long reflected a certain openness and a tolerance for diversity characteristic of theater people. Immigrants from all corners of Europe were welcomed as members. But in 1890, as a tide of nationalism rose in the land, members were required for the first time to be American citizens. Six years later, the Grand Lodge resolved that "the Altar drapery shall be the flag of the United States, upon which the Bible shall rest, surmounted by the Antlers." With the outbreak of the Spanish-American War in 1898, Grand Exalted Ruler Meade D. Detweiler warned all lodges that the Elks were "emphatically and exclusively an American Order," responding to "the great American ideas which gave it birth."

This patriotic fervor, and its grounding in ritual and heraldry, helped spread Elkdom, for, as one Grand Exalted Ruler explained, "it put the visible stamp of patriotism upon every lodge and associated the banner of our country, the Bible and our Order's emblem in an immortal trinity." By the turn of the century, in thousands of communities across the country's midsection, membership in the Elks was a badge of belonging, of being not just an American but a loyal, reverent, and dutiful American. George Hurstwood, the suave manager at Hannah and Hogg's saloon in Theodore Dreiser's *Sister Carrie*, is a big wheel in the Elks, and George Babbitt, the quintessence of bourgeois values in Sinclair Lewis's novel, is fond of fingering the order's elk-tooth emblem.

There were always those who regarded Elkhood less as a badge of arrival than as a means to advancement. By 1883, the Elk hierarchy recognized the sin of "commercialism" and took measures to prevent members from exploiting the order for business purposes. A regulation provided: "No brother shall use his certificate of membership, nor expose any emblem of the Order, as a sign in his business transactions." There was no prohibition against one Elk's dealing with another. And more than a few brothers read the rule as saying something like this: Being an Elk will benefit you in your business transactions, but for goodness sake, do it discreetly.

That, in any case, was the way Judge Smith and McParland seem to have viewed it. For, after noting the prohibition, the detective and the judge proceeded to act as though they and the governor were bound by some special fraternal bond, some special congruity of interest. For a few minutes, McParland and Smith relished their common distaste for Captain Swain and his operatives. The judge reported that the people of Caldwell, the sheriff, even the reporters were sick of those "sons of bitches."

Having quickly established a sturdy bridge of rapport, the two men moved on to the issue at hand. By the time they parted at 12:45 a.m., they'd broken the logjam, Smith promising to use his influence with the sheriff to have him transfer the prisoner to Boise, while further agreeing not to issue a writ of habeas corpus unless directed to do so by the state supreme court.

When McParland reported his successful mission to the governor the next morning, Gooding dispatched him to the supreme court to make sure the justices would go along. There he took the matter up with Stockslager, the very man who'd broken trail for McParland in Idaho and remained the detective's closest ally in the state. In turn, Stockslager summoned his close friend Associate Justice Sullivan. After a few moments' consideration, the two justices—a majority on the three-man bench—assured McParland it was "perfectly legal" to bring Orchard to the pen. Moreover, they solemnly promised to sustain Judge Smith in denying the prisoner a writ of habeas corpus.

But the trio of Elks knew they would have tougher going with Sheriff Nichols, who'd been growing ever more indignant at the notion that the prisoner should be removed from his jurisdiction. A small-town merchant with little self-confidence, Jap Nichols was ever on the lookout for a snub or outright humiliation. If Steunenberg's assassination had given him an investigation he considered worthy of his talents, it had also brought to town more experienced lawmen, bent on elbowing him out of the spotlight.

For days, Nichols groused in Caldwell's saloons: he was under bond in the case, responsible to the bondsmen for the prisoner in his custody; nobody could relieve him of that trust; he was damned if he'd violate it for this band of interlopers. Then on January 11, he went public, telling Crane of the *Statesman,* "I want it distinctly understood that this man Orchard is under my charge and I propose to hang on to him until he is discharged as innocent or found guilty and sentenced. He will not be taken to Boise or to Milwaukee or anywhere else until his trial is over. He is going to stay right where he is." Nichols went on to spill out his accumulated bile at those who'd usurped his authority: "There has been too much butting in by outside officers.... The prisoner's removal would be a reflection upon the ability of myself and my men.... You may state in your paper that Orchard stays right here until the case against him is decided, and state it strong enough so that it will be understood by everybody." The next day, he indignantly told the *Capital News* there was no truth to reports that the militia would soon be called to Caldwell to preserve order—reports that were no doubt a byproduct of rumors about a raid on the county jail. "We have the peace of this community well in hand," he declared.

His messages got through. Late on January 16, Governor Gooding brought Nichols to McParland's suite and together the governor and the detective gave the sheriff a good working over. After an hour, McParland could report, "I think that we'll succeed in getting the prisoner transferred in a very short time."

Indeed, on the eighteenth, citing "grave, serious, unusual and extraordinary circumstances," Nichols formally petitioned the governor to remove the prisoner from Caldwell's jail. And the next afternoon Nichols and his deputy Frank Breshears bundled Harry Orchard aboard the afternoon train to Boise. To ensure maximum security and minimum publicity, the prisoner never entered either depot but embarked and debarked on the tracks several hundred yards from those stations. At the Boise end, he was delivered to the penitentiary's warden, Eugene L. Whitney, who placed Orchard in a cell on death row, adjacent to two convicted murderers who were awaiting execution. At McParland's explicit orders, relays of guards watched Orchard night and day but spoke not a single word to him.

When questioned about the gap between Wednesday's resistance and Thursday's acquiescence, Sheriff Nichols gave reporters a curious apologia: "I was firm in the belief that nothing could change my mind when I made this statement, but the matter was put to me in an entirely different light...one that I deemed reasonable."

Which of McParland's arguments, if any, finally convinced the sheriff we don't know. Perhaps it was a January 17 letter from James H. Hawley, the seasoned Boise attorney who that very day was engaged to represent the state in the case and wrote Nichols: "I don't believe your jail or the jail of any county is at present a secure place and you would be justified in...temporarily place [sic] Hogan in the Pen....I don't believe any responsibility would rest on you for any bad results."

Or it may be that Nichols was never persuaded, merely overwhelmed by the three Elks and their allies. Several days later, newspapers reported that the sheriff had "collapsed under the great strain" of his responsibilities in the Steunenberg murder case and was recovering at home. Although he recovered sufficiently to resume his position several weeks later, his reputation had been thoroughly compromised.

McParland's two weeks of maneuvering began to pay off. At 2:15 p.m. on Monday, January 22, the detective boarded the streetcar outside the Idanha Hotel and rode to the end of the line, at the eastern edge of town. There he was met by Warden Whitney, attended by two trusties, who drove him in a rig to the penitentiary, which stood at the foot of a sandstone mesa east of the city called Table Rock. Whitney escorted McParland to his office, introduced him to Harry Orchard, then left the two men alone.

Taking their seats on hard wooden chairs, the detective and the prisoner studied each other for a long moment. Orchard saw a corpulent man of sixty-two, rather squat-looking at five foot eight, his legs slightly bowed, his right hand grasping a bone-handled blackthorn walking stick; a broad-brimmed hat pulled well down over his forehead, covering all but a few thin strands of silver hair; a silk cravat fixed with a jeweled stickpin; a tweed suit and vest that did little to disguise their bearer's ample girth, across which draped a thick gold watch chain; a drooping gray mustache brushing his heavy jowls; and behind gold-rimmed spectacles with extrathick lenses, a pair of shrewd blue-gray eyes, sizing up the prisoner.

What McParland saw was a stocky (five foot eight, 180-pound) man half his own age, his youth reinforced by close-cropped reddish-brown hair and a clean-shaven chin. But if nothing else about Harry Orchard seemed remarkable, his face struck the detective as "about as determined a countenance as I have ever seen on a human being, with the most cold, cruel eyes I remember having seen."

McParland led off with a carefully prepared statement of some twenty-five minutes, in which he argued the case for cooperation with the prosecutors. If Orchard dealt honestly with the state, admitted his role in the crime, and gave evidence about his co-conspirators, the detective suggested, he might reasonably expect a certain leniency in his sentence.

"I don't know what you're getting at," Orchard replied. "I have committed no crime. I have heard and read over forty times just such talk as you have made, and there are instances where such talk has only made innocent men confess to crimes that they never committed and to implicate others who were also innocent. Talk about acting square with the state! I never heard tell of a man that did but what he afterwards paid the penalty!" Moreover, his lawyer, Fred Miller, had instructed him to say nothing.

Expecting such resistance, McParland was prepared with a telling response. It wasn't always true, he said, that men who turned state's evidence paid the full penalty. Did Orchard know of the prosecutions of the Molly Maguires in the Pennsylvania coalfields some thirty years before, in which several important Mollies who became state witnesses were spared the death sentences imposed on the others?

Oh yes, Orchard knew about the Molly Maguires.

Had he ever seen a photograph of James McParland, the Pinkerton detective who assembled the most damaging evidence against them?

No, Orchard said, he hadn't.

Well, the detective said with calculated flourish, I am that McParland.

The Molly Maguire saga was one of the nineteenth century's favorite detective stories, a tale familiar to every habitué of the barbershops and hotel lobbies where the *Police Gazette* and its ilk were consumed so voraciously. Allan Pinkerton himself, never shy about trumpeting his agency's achievements, rushed out *The Molly Maguires and the Detectives* (1877), a muddy amalgam of documented fact and fictive elaboration, produced on tight deadline by a ghostwriter. Sir Arthur Conan Doyle spun a richer tale in *The Valley of Fear,* one of the few stories he ever set largely in the United States. Sir Arthur had run into William Pinkerton on an ocean voyage, heard the Mollies story one night in the liner's smoky lounge, and was haunted ever after by what he called that "singular and terrible narrative." In telling his own grim version, Doyle contrived an encounter between the legendary Holmes and the formidable McParlan: "He leaned against the mantelpiece and sucked at the cigar which Holmes had handed him. 'I've heard of you, Mr. Holmes, I never guessed that I should meet you.'" For the world's most popular spinner of detective fiction, it was unprecedented homage to a flesh-and-blood detective.

Not surprisingly, as the story's protagonist James McParland became, for a time, not only America's most renowned detective but a genuine celebrity. As the years went by, though, fewer people remembered the detective's exploits. By 1906, his reputation had begun to fade around the edges, like one of the sepia prints in the Sunday supplements where McParland's youthful triumphs had once been such a staple.

In Drumahee, County Armagh, where his family scratched a living from the rocky soil, the name was rendered McParlan or McParlen. They were Catholics in the heavily Protestant province of Ulster, an unhappy minority status that had been known to engender self-hatred, even renunciation of one's ethnic or religious roots. Quitting school at an early age, Jamie joined his parents in the fields. At nineteen, off to seek employment in England, he saved railroad fare by walking the first twenty-one miles to catch a steamer across the Irish Sea. Settling in Gateshead, amid the bleak welter of coal mines and foundries on the banks of the river Tyne, he worked for three years at the Tyne Chemical Works. For a while, he toured with a traveling circus, serving as roustabout, gambling shill, and barker. Returning to Ireland in 1866, he became a stock clerk in a Belfast linen warehouse.

But all that shuttling across the Irish Sea was simply marking time. For a young Irishman eager to make his mark in the world, the real drawing card was America, just emerging from its bloody civil strife and bursting with entrepreneurial energy. In June 1867, McParlan took ship at Liverpool aboard the Inman Line's *The City of London,* landing in New York City in the clammy heat of midsummer.

His first job was at McDonald and Boas, a grocery at Ninth Avenue and Thirty-sixth Street. Six weeks later he took a position with a country dry goods store in Medina, New York, on the Erie Barge Canal. But on arrival he learned that the proprietor hadn't paid what he owed his last clerk, so once more McParlan moved on, this time by Great Lakes steamer to Chicago.

That first winter in the burgeoning western metropolis, the slim red-headed Irishman turned his hand to a bit of everything: driving a meat wagon, a road contractor's cart, and a private coach; chopping wood; sailing as a deckhand on a lake steamer. Then, in July 1868, he signed on with the Merchants' Police Agency, the "watch" division of W. S. Beaubien and Co., one of the city's first detective bureaus. According to McParlan, he "travelled a beat" for Beaubien, suggesting he was little more than a night watchman.

Eager to make some real money, he turned to the lucrative liquor trade. After several months behind the counter of Dodge and Brothers Liquors, in 1869 he opened a combined package store and saloon at Twelfth and Centre Streets. Business was strong in the hard-drinking town when, on October 8–9, 1871, the Great Fire took his premises and everything he owned. The next April, McParlan returned to the detective business, this time with Pinkerton's.

He began on the agency's lowest rung, as a spotter on the city's trolleys, watching conductors suspected of pocketing fares. But he caught the attention of Allan Pinkerton himself, for before eighteen months had passed the Principal handed him one of the most dangerous—and rewarding—jobs in the agency's history.

The Molly Maguires came along just when the Pinkerton agency needed them most: during the depression of 1873. By August 1872, the Pinkertons faced a critical cash shortage. "We are in great want of money," Allan Pinkerton wrote Captain Fitzgerald, his Chicago superintendent. "On every hand I am in debt, yet I cannot get any person to help me, but everyone whom I owe a shilling to are calling me on it." The agency borrowed heavily, but by the following spring its financial straits, aggravated by Pinkerton's losses in the stock market, had only deepened. On May 18, Pinkerton conceded to George Bangs, his general superintendent, "Many a time I am perfectly bewildered what to do," but then he came up with a suggestion: "Go to Franklin Gowan [*sic*].... Suggest some things to Mr. Gowan about one thing and another which would be feasible and I have no doubt he will give us work."

Franklin B. Gowen, president of the Philadelphia and Reading Railroad, was a logical resource for Pinkerton to tap in bad times. He was already a client of the agency. In January 1870, after receiving a letter from a passenger charging that he had been cheated by one of the Reading's conductors, Gowen hired Pinkerton operatives to sniff out fare pocketing and other irregularities by the railroad's employees. Soon the Reading required more urgent Pinkerton assistance to protect its coal properties. Beatings of mine supervisors, derailings of cars, and the burning of a coal tipple prompted the dispatch of several Pinkerton operatives to the mining district around Glen Carbon. It was from there, in early October 1873, that the agency received a report that led Benjamin Franklin, the Pinkerton superintendent in Philadelphia, to write Gowen, "The operatives report the rumored existence at Glen Carbon of an organization known as the 'Molly Maguires,' a band of roughs joined together for the purpose of instituting revenge against any one of whom they may take a dislike."

This was scarcely the first sighting of a group by that name. Forty-odd years before, a secret society called the Molly Maguires had operated in north central Ireland, threatening, beating, sometimes killing English landlords and their agents. If there was ever a woman named Molly Maguire, who she was remains a matter of scholarly dispute. In Ireland, the bravos who adopted the name disguised themselves by dressing in women's clothing and smearing their faces with burnt cork. The name resurfaced in Pennsylvania in 1860–63, during agitation by Irish coal miners against the Civil War draft. Several men who tried to enforce conscription paid with their lives. Over the next decade, unconfirmed reports of Molly depredations cropped up every few years.

Now the financial straits of the Pinkerton agency and the corporate imperatives of the Reading produced a convergence of interests. In mid-October—barely three weeks after a bank collapse plunged Wall Street into ruinous panic—Allan Pinkerton journeyed to Philadelphia for a meeting with Franklin Gowen.

A protean figure, deftly juggling a motley set of personae, Gowen had been, by turns, a beguiling Irish politician, an eloquent Fourth of July orator, a shrewd district attorney, a resourceful chief attorney for the railroad, and, since 1869, the vastly ambitious ruler of the Reading empire. In barely four years as chief executive, Gowen had not only achieved a virtual monopoly over transportation to and from northeastern Pennsylvania's lower anthracite region but quietly acquired more than a hundred thousand acres of its prime coal lands, giving the railroad a big hand in production as well.

Of late, Gowen had turned a baleful eye on labor, determined to break the power of the Workingmen's Benevolent Association, an early union that had led the miners in the strikes of 1868, 1869, and 1871. The WBA was run by Lancashire men adamantly opposed to violence. But the Reading's canny president saw an opportunity to paint the union with the Molly brush, which he did in testimony before a state investigating committee—remarks that owe their rhetorical flavor to Marc Antony. "I do not charge this Workingmen's Benevolent Association with it," he said, "but I say there is an association which votes in secret, at night, that men's lives shall be taken, and that they shall be shot before their wives, murdered in cold blood, for daring to work against the order. . . . I do not blame this association, but I blame another association for doing it; and it happens that the only men who are shot are the men who dare disobey the mandates of the Workingmen's Benevolent Association."

When Gowen met with Allan Pinkerton in the company's sumptuous Fourth Street offices, the detective knew of the president's determination to tarnish, if not break, the union (in coming months, at Gowen's request, four other operatives were assigned to spy on the union itself). But nominally the company was concerned that day only with halting Molly Maguire "terrorism."

To that end, in the great Anglo-Saxon tradition, Gowen shunned the public constabulary. "Municipal detectives, employed by the police authorities of cities, who operate only for rewards, are the last persons to whom you could trust an enterprise such as this," he said later. Instead, Gowen and Pinkerton resolved to send a superagent into the coal region to infiltrate the Mollies and gather evidence to prosecute their leaders.

Infiltration had long been one of Allan Pinkerton's crime-fighting techniques, but this assignment required a special breed of operative. Since the Mollies were believed to be Irish Catholics, the agent must be one himself. Since they worked in the mines, he must be strong enough to bear heavy manual labor. He should be a gregarious sort, who could drink and roughhouse. And since the Mollies were regarded as ruthless killers, he should be unmarried, so if it came to that, he wouldn't leave behind a widow and a brood of helpless babes. In short, he had to be "enough of an Irishman to pass as a Mollie and enough of an 'American' to keep faith with Pinkerton and civilization."

As he surveyed his Chicago operatives, Pinkerton's eye fell on twenty-nine-year-old Jamie McParlan, still pulling a tenderfoot's duty on the trolleys. Summoning him to headquarters on October 8, the Principal asked whether he was familiar with the Mollies. When McParlan said he was, Pinkerton sent him home to put down everything he knew. For two days, in his cramped rooming house, McParlan labored over his report. Submitted on October 10, the eight pages of spidery script reflected painstaking hours with quill and ink, if an uncertain grasp of spelling and syntax.

McParlan began in the mid–eighteenth century when English and Scottish "land jobbers" imposed onerous rents on Ireland's Catholic peasantry. The enraged tenants responded by organizing the first of many secret societies, the Hearts of Steel, to wreak revenge on the landlords, who, in turn, formed their own organ of vengeance, the Orangemen. The pattern of centuries was established: mutual terror, unleashed first by one side, then the other. Contemplating the profusion of Catholic societies—with names like White Boys, Threshers, and Ribbonmen—McParlan remarked that "few or none of the educiated or Repectable Catholics ever belonged to thes last named Societies it was principally composed of the poor and Ignorant classes... constant Broils and Evils & even high handed Murder was going on bet. the Orangemen and their Antagnists homes sacked Churches Burned."

When famine ravaged Ireland in 1846–47, peasants in the north and west, "resolv[ing] not to starve so long as there was any food stowed away in the public Markets or warehouses," organized "under the name of Molly Mc-Guire." Their object was "to take from those who had abundance & give to the poor who were then dying by Hundreth with hunger.... The leader or Molly as she was called went to the Storekeeper provided he knew he was pretty well off & demanded of him the Amount Levyed on him in the shape of meal flour & general Groceries."

In the United States, the Mollies settled in mining districts, where they "organized in a more formidable force than ever but Instead of performing the simple Acts of taking from the rich & giving to the poor the commenced hostilities something after the fashion of the Kuklux Klann of the Southern states of this Country but as the had no negroes to kill the commenced by shooting down Lanlords Agents Bailiffs or any offending neighbor.... High-handed murder prevailed everywhere through the country where this Society existed... being the name Ribbonmen or Molly McGuire was now considered treason this Society assumed a new name which was called the Ancient Order of Hibernians."

At the end, McParlan penned an apology to Pinkerton: "I presume by the time you have got this read you will get tired as most of it or infact all of it may not be very Interesting to you nevertheless it is a brief sketch of Irish Societyism."

It was an imperfect sketch, stronger on northern Irish societies than on southern, exaggerating parallels with the Klan. Nonetheless, the Principal was impressed. Within days, he dispatched McParlan to Philadelphia for a briefing by Superintendent Franklin. On October 27, the new operative, bearing the pseudonym James McKenna, set off for the coalfields. Dressed as a tramp—in Pinkerton's version, "with his head covered by an old dilapidated slouch hat, plenty of space for his cutty pipe in its narrow, faded band; a greyish coat of coarse material, ragged shirt, frayed cuffs, frayed vest"—he would have attracted little attention in the second-class coach.

As his train labored up the Schuylkill valley into the anthracite region, McKenna peered out at "this gloomy land of black crag and tangled forest," lit by "the red glow of the furnaces," that Conan Doyle, in *The Valley of Fear*, called the "most desolate corner of the United States." The train trip gave McKenna several hours to ruminate, perhaps even to confront misgivings about his mission. For now he was a spy—or, blunter yet, an informer. Though much turn-of-the-century "detective work" was little more than informing, McParlan was being asked to betray not only his temporary companions but his countrymen and coreligionists, with whom he shared a bond of blood, soil, and myth. Because Irish insurrections had long been riddled by informers in the pay of the English, that role took on a special opprobrium for Irish emigrants. No figure in all of Celtic history was so despised.

If the Mollies discovered McParlan's treachery, his penalty would be almost certain death. Twelve dollars a week was modest pay for such a risk. Just how the man who called himself James McKenna rationalized his role, we cannot be sure. Perhaps, as a Catholic Ulsterman, he felt some secret rage at the religion that stigmatized him. His reports suggest he may have believed himself to be acting as a kind of purgative, cleansing his people and his religion of an activity both alien and impure. Pinkerton wrote that McParlan would have to "degrade [himself] that others might be saved." The "savage" nature of the Mollies, on the other hand, allowed McParlan to go beyond civilized techniques—to treachery and perhaps provocation of violence—in extirpating them.

On arrival in Port Clinton, he began a systematic forage through Schuylkill County's inns, taverns, and unlicensed shebeens, seeking places where the Ancient Order of Hibernians might gather and, in turn, harbor nests of Mollies, or Sleepers, as they were often known in those parts. One of his first calls was at the Sheridan House in Pottsville, administered by a hulking publican named Patrick Dormer. Embracing a hotel, saloon, bowling alley, and card room, it was a popular gathering place for Irish miners and was said to be a secret Molly lair. According to Pinkerton, it was also noted for its "drunken brawls and midnight orgies." Once inside, Jamie McKenna assumed the theatrical role of the Wild Irish Lad, buying rounds of drinks for the "bhoys," dancing a jig, bellowing—in fluent Gaelic—a Donegal ballad about the Mollies' assassination of a malevolent land agent, brawling with a man he accused of cheating at cards. Once McKenna had conned Dormer with his blarney, he whispered that he wasn't really a bum at all but a crook "on the lam" from a murder in Buffalo, New York, supporting himself now by passing counterfeit money ("shoving the queer").

If there were plenty of boys to beguile at Pottsville, McKenna learned that to plumb the Mollies' mystery he needed to cross Broad Mountain into their stronghold around Shenandoah and Mahanoy City. January 3, 1874, found him at McDermot's saloon in Mahanoy City, which he characterized to Superintendent Franklin as "a God-forsaken place—the most miserable so far visited." The "city" was actually a single street snaking down the narrow valley, one side solidly Irish, the other Welsh, English, and German. Mutual suspicion was particularly intense between the Irish and the Welsh, who had been experienced miners in the Old Country and were generally preferred by Pennsylvania's mine operators.

On January 30, McKenna reached Shenandoah, his base for the rest of his stay in the coalfields. Pat Dormer had introduced him to Michael "Muff" Lawler, the Hibernians' Shenandoah "bodymaster"—master of the member-ship—and so pleased was the tavern keeper with the newcomer that he invited him to move into the family quarters above the public house. McKenna assured his superiors that he had at last found "the stuff," "the thorough-breds," the genuine Mollies. Soon he met Ed Lawler, Muff's nephew, who "seems to be much feared by everyone—is reported to have shot and maimed some 4 or 5 men, although he is only 21 years old.... He said he would as soon shoot some of the bhoys as he would a dog."

Muff Lawler trained his own breed of fighting gamecocks ("muffs"), which he pitted against other men's birds in his basement arena. Cockfights were just one of the amusements with which the Shenandoah boys whiled away their time: drinking bad whiskey at licensed or unlicensed drinking places, wagering on dogfights, foot races, even barroom brawls, parading the streets bawling ballads and brandishing revolvers, dancing the night away at "Molly Maguire balls" to raise funds for indicted colleagues, poaching fowl, or skirmishing with other secret societies, notably with a gang of Welsh miners called the Modocs or a rival Irish society known as the Iron Clads.

For months, Muff had promised to admit the newcomer to the Hiber-nians. On April 14, he kept his word. In a room over the saloon, with four other miners looking on, McKenna knelt to be sworn into the Shenandoah lodge. The ceremony was innocuous enough. He swore, among other things, to "be true and steadfast to the brethren of this society, dedicated to St. Patrick, the holy patron of Ireland, in all things lawful" and to "propagate friendship and brotherly love." McKenna paid his three-dollar initiation fee and his thirty-five-cent monthly dues, receiving, in turn, the passwords, sig-nals, and countersignals by which to recognize fellow Hibernians—which, in Schuylkill County, he was convinced meant Mollies.

By now, McKenna believed the Mollies were controlled by an inner

circle of bodymasters and county officers (frequently tavern keepers with a
hand in politics). Whenever a grievance was lodged against a mine manager,
English shopkeeper, or Welsh miner who'd offered offense, it was the bodymaster who decided whether the target was to be beaten or murdered, then
selected the men to do the job. Sometimes a warning—known as a coffin
notice—was nailed to a man's door, warning him to get out of town or face
death. One journalist received the following: "Mr. Editore wie will give ye 24
hurse to go to the divil out of this ye son of a Bitch. . . . We ain't done shooting
yet." When a Welshman was ordered out of town, he asked where the notice
had come from. "From Hell" was the terse reply.

The stress of this investigation, a few weeks' labor in the mines, nights
carousing with the boys, and a cold caught during a night meeting combined
to undermine the detective's sturdy constitution. Soon he looked "thin and
cadaverous." Losing most of his hair, he donned a bushy blond wig, prompting some Mollies to call him "the man with the big head."

Meanwhile, tension built between the mine operators and the WBA. As
1874 drew to a close, the operators—now tightly organized by Franklin
Gowen in a "pool" controlling production and prices—had rarely been in a
stronger position to impose long-sought pay cuts, if not actually to break the
union. Indeed, the operators' wage proposals called for cuts of 10 to 20
percent, with further reductions of 1 percent for each three cents that coal fell
below $2.50 a ton. These cuts were nonnegotiable; the miners could take them
or leave them. It looked as if Gowen was determined to precipitate a strike in
which to crush the union once and for all.

At the beginning of 1875, three of Pennsylvania's four anthracite coalfields—the Lehigh field to the north and the two so-called southern fields—
were largely shut down by a work stoppage that, as it dragged on, came to be
known as the Long Strike. By spring, storekeepers began restricting, or actually cutting off, credit for mining families (the taverns, often run by Molly
proprietors, kept dispensing the grog "on tick," debits chalked on the wall
behind the bar). Many families in the mining "patches" were near starvation.
In May, the owners began reopening the mines unilaterally, promising protection for "blackleg" miners willing to work. The men flooded back. In mid-
June, the strike ended. The WBA disbanded.

It was a humiliating defeat, memories of which lingered on in song and
legend. With the union dead, the miners found other channels for their sour
rage. The WBA and the Ancient Order of Hibernians had drawn from the
same pool of Irish miners (McParlan estimated that the AOH had about 450
members in Schuylkill County, of whom 400 belonged to the WBA). By July
6, McParlan reported a surge of fresh support for the Mollies. "Men, who last
winter would not notice a Molly Maguire are now glad to take them by the
hand and make much of them. If the bosses exercise tyranny over the men
they appear to look to the association for help."

In midsummer, the anger in these men spilled into faction fights and tavern brawls. One evening, at Charlie Hayes's saloon, Hayes and some others beat up a Welshman who'd tried to clobber a miner named Kelley. "Hayes said he [Kelley] had been around to whip a man named Buffy who had made the assertion that he had helped to dip an Irishman in Blood at Wales." In September, Muff Lawler, deposed as bodymaster in a factional dispute, was waylaid by Shenandoah Mollies and beaten for failing to kill Gomer Jones, a Welshman accused of killing an Irish miner.

If many ingredients went into these confrontations—private squabbles, workplace quarrels, ethnic resentments, class grievances—through them all ran a common thread: a preoccupation with injustice, a conviction that, as one Molly said, "it did not seem as if an Irishman could get any law in Mahanoy City." Judges, lawyers, and policemen were overwhelmingly Welsh, German, or English, while the Mollies came disproportionately from Donegal and Mayo, Ireland's wildest and harshest counties. When the coalfield Irish sought to remedy their grievances through the courts, they often met delays, obfuscation, or doors slammed in their faces. No longer looking to these institutions for justice, they turned instead to the Mollies, where they'd come to expect a prompt settling of scores. Before the summer was over, six men—all Welsh or German—paid with their lives.

On June 28, three Shenandoah Mollies shot at, badly wounded, but failed to kill William "Bully Bill" Thomas, a Welsh roughneck and former prizefighter thought to be involved in efforts to kill a Molly named Dan Dougherty. A week later, after a tumultuous Independence Day celebration in Tamaqua, two other Mollies shot and killed Benjamin Yost, a German who was one of the town's two police officers, as he extinguished a street lamp near his house. The night of August 14 was particularly wild in the streets of Girardville, with roughnecks roaming the streets brandishing revolvers. After an assault in one of the town's saloons, Squire Thomas Gwyther, a Welshman who served as justice of the peace, was about to serve a warrant on the alleged perpetrator when he was shot and killed. That same night, four miles northeast in the hamlet of Grover's Grove, Gomer James, the Welshman the Mollies suspected of killing an Irish miner in 1873, was gunned down while tending bar at a fire company picnic. Two weeks later, on September 1, Thomas Sanger, a Cornish pit boss, and William Uren, his bodyguard, died in gunfire from five Mollies near Heaton's colliery. Two days later, John P. Jones, a pit boss at Summit Hill, was shot dead at the Lansford depot.

McKenna was never present at these murders, but he found himself implicated in assassination. For by now he was a trusted Molly, secretary of the Shenandoah lodge, at times filling in for the absent bodymaster. As such, he couldn't avoid advance knowledge of murder.

Several times he managed to sidetrack the assassins until the target could be warned or until word could be passed to a fellow Pinkerton, Robert J. Linden, an assistant superintendent brought into the case in May 1875. Nominally, Linden served as a captain in the Reading Railroad's own Coal and Iron Police. But he also headed up a secret "flying squadron" composed of seven Pinkertons and seven coal and iron policemen, who were to stay in close touch with McParlan. On his advance warnings, they tried to be present when a crime was committed so as to gather the eyewitness accounts and physical evidence necessary for convictions.

It was this procedure that later gave rise to suspicions that McKenna was an agent provocateur who encouraged Mollies to commit crimes, then arranged for Linden to witness them. This is difficult to prove. But it is worth noting that the Mollies' Shenandoah division didn't gain its reputation for homicide until McKenna became its secretary. Moreover, there is good reason to wonder whether McKenna did all he might to warn the intended victims and whether he and Linden hadn't, on more than one occasion, let a murder plot ripen in order to obtain evidence the agency needed for convictions.

Allan Pinkerton now cast off all restraints and pursued the Mollies with undiluted zeal. For the society's rampage in the summer of 1875 followed by months the botched Pinkerton raid on the house of Jesse and Frank James's mother in Clay County, Missouri. Condemned by the press, frustrated by his inability to catch the James boys, who'd killed three of his agents, Pinkerton was in no mood to trifle with the Mollies.

By the summer of 1875, his frame of mind was echoed by many of the county's English, Welsh, and Germans. One woman had a man arrested, claiming he meant to kill her. As they'd passed each other, he'd wriggled his fingers at his ears and mumbled, "Billy-willy-wincumboom"—hardly a Molly warning. The establishment press clamored for a vigilance committee to take "direct action" against the secret society. "One good, wholesome hanging, gently but firmly administered, will cure a great deal of bad blood, and save a great many lives in this community," said the *Miners' Journal*, which, despite its name, spoke for the operators. The *Tamaqua Courier* called for action "sure, swift and terrible."

This was the climate in which Allan Pinkerton wrote George Bangs on August 29, 1875: "The M.M.'s are a species of Thugs. You have probably read of them in India. Their religion taught them to murder. . . . The only way then to pursue that I can see is, to treat them in the same manner as the Renos were treated in Seymour, Indiana. After they were done away with, the people improved wonderfully and now Seymour is quite a town. Let Linden get up a vigilance committee. It will not do to get many men, but let him get those who are prepared to take fearful revenge on the M.M.'s. I think it would open the eyes of all the people and then the M.M.'s would meet with their just deserts."

Three months later, an attack took place that seems to reflect the strategy outlined in Pinkerton's memo. Before dawn on December 10, men wearing masks and oilskin coats broke into a two-family house in Wiggans Patch, a mining community near Mahanoy City. Among those asleep in the house were three Mollies whom McKenna had identified as participants in the killing of Sanger and Uren three months earlier. Two escaped, but the intruders roped the third man, Charles O'Donnell, dragged him from his bed, pumped some twenty-five bullets into him, then set the corpse on fire. They also killed—probably inadvertently—Charles's pregnant sister, Ellen McAllister, whose brother-in-law, James McAllister, had been accused by McParlan of being one of the Sanger-Uren gunmen; now she became the first female victim of the coalfields violence.

The circumstances suggested a vigilante raid. Evidently McKenna thought so, because the next day he protested to his agency: "What had a woman to do in this case? Did the Sleepers in their worst time shoot women? If I was not here the vigilant committee would not know who was guilty. And when I find them shooting women in their thirst for blood, I hereby tender my resignation." Though willing to accept another posting, he was disgusted with this one. "Now innocent men of both parties will suffer and I am sure the Sleepers will not spare the women so long as the vigilants has shown the example."

Franklin managed to talk McKenna out of resignation, but other pressures threatened to bring about the same result. "The Mollies are now confident that there is a traitor in their midst," the detective reported the day after the killings. At first, many Mollies suspected the discredited Muff Lawler but gradually fingers began pointing at McKenna. After three years inside the Mollies, he'd learned all he was going to learn about the society. The time had come to quit the Valley of Fear.

For several weeks more, McKenna managed to brazen it out. Heatedly denying that he was a detective, he confronted his accusers one by one. Among them was a priest opposed to the Mollies but aghast when he learned in clerical circles that a fellow Irish Catholic had turned informer on his compatriots. The Church was generally hostile to the Mollies, often warning them of excommunication, in part because their oath-bound secrecy violated bans on joining clandestine societies.

Finally, relying on his popularity among the rank and file, McKenna demanded that he be tried before a county convention. Reaching Shenandoah on the appointed day, he realized that the boys were gathering all right, but not for a convention; a dozen were down at the depot with tomahawks and sledgehammers, waiting to kill him. After a dash by sleigh across the frozen countryside, with an armed Molly in close pursuit, McKenna left the coalfields for good on March 7, 1876.

His written reports and the accumulated lore of his two and a half years inside the Mollies were instantly put at the disposal of the prosecutors, now joined—if not actually led—by Franklin Gowen, who for a time managed to combine the duties of railroad president with those of special counsel to the Schuylkill district attorney. (Such mixing of public and private functions wasn't unusual at the time; when three Mollies were tried for killing the mining boss John P. Jones, the prosecution was led by Charles Albright, a retired Union army general and counsel for the Lehigh and Wilkes-Barre Railroad, Jones's employer. The Lehigh paid the trial costs, as the Reading did in other cases.)

Gowen wanted more than McParlan's paperwork; he wanted the detective as his star witness. This, however, would violate a condition of McParlan's employment. As in most other agency operations, the client stipulated in advance that the operative wouldn't be called to testify, both because that would destroy his capacity to work undercover in other matters and because it could lead to retribution. Gowen argued that in several cases prepared by McParlan's undercover work, there were no eyewitnesses. Thus his testimony about the assassins' admissions to him could be critical.

McParlan resisted. Gowen weighed in with another argument: that McParlan alone could clarify the role of the Catholic Church in uncovering him, by testifying that the priest who blew the whistle had intensely disapproved of the Mollies. Otherwise, the cases could bog down in polemics by Catholics and anti-Catholics. For McParlan, an observant Catholic, that argument may have counted heavily, as, certainly, did the urgings of Allan Pinkerton. In making his decision, he had the advice of two brothers, Charles and Edward McParlan. Pinkerton records show that the agency paid each of them fifteen dollars per week from December 9, 1876, to March 21, 1877. What had brought them to Pennsylvania isn't clear, but by this time they were evidently helping protect and support their brother through this difficult period.

Ultimately, James McParlan agreed to take the witness stand. On May 6, flanked by Linden and two bodyguards, he entered the courtroom in Pottsville's Schuylkill County courthouse to testify against James Carroll, James Boyle, Hugh McGehan, Thomas Duffy, and James Roarity for the killing of the Tamaqua policeman, Benjamin Yost. In four days on the stand, under Gowen's questioning, he provided an insider's tale of the machinations leading to Yost's death. He drew a vivid portrait of the Mollies' inner circle, its rituals and procedures for wreaking vengeance. When a juror died of pneumonia, the judge declared a mistrial; but Gowen's orchestration and McParlan's revelations made such a deep impression on the public that they set a pattern for the trials that unrolled over succeeding years.

Defense attorneys in trial after trial—McParlan testified in nine of the twenty-three Molly trials—tried to impugn the detective, suggesting that he'd encouraged the Mollies to commit their crimes. "He was their leader, their guide, and their general," argued Martin L'Velle. "He was the man who had the cash to supply the whiskey and fire the brain of these poor susceptible, youthful enthusiasts." (When L'Velle brandished McParlan's expense accounts to show that he'd treated his colleagues to as many as sixty-seven shots of whiskey on a single day, the detective shot back, "The kind of criminals I had to deal with were a whiskey drinking crowd.") The defense attorneys played on Americans' repugnance for a tattletale. "You all dislike a spy," L'Velle told one jury. "This man who will take you to his bosom, gain your confidence and stealthily work upon your affection, your favor or your esteem, and then like a viper turn upon you and betray you, ought to be condemned by every honorable and right-thinking person."

The juries didn't buy it. Ultimately, twenty Mollies were convicted and sentenced to death. On June 21, 1877—Black Thursday in Irish American circles—ten men were hung on a single day: six on a rude gallows erected in the yard of the red-brick Schuylkill County jail in Pottsville, four more in the corridor of the Carbon County jail in Mauch Chunk, forty miles to the east. It was a deliberate demonstration of the state's power to exact the ultimate penalty, a day of awful retribution remembered for generations in the coal patches of Pennsylvania, in mining camps, and in Irish American communities across the land. Over the next two years, ten more Mollies went to the gallows.

Of the twenty deaths, McParlan could be directly credited with nine, including those of a broad swath of the society's leadership. Indirectly, McParlan's testimony paved the way for executing the other eleven men and sentencing another twenty-six to terms in county jails, as well as putting a price on the heads of nine or ten fugitives. "There is not a place on the habitable globe where these men can find refuge and in which they will not be tracked down," Gowen warned. "Pinkerton's Agency may sometimes permit a man to believe that he is free who does not know that he may be traveling 5,000 miles in the company of those whose vigilance never slumbers and whose eyes are never closed in sleep." Indeed, the Pinkertons brought one Molly back from Canada and another from Illinois to face trial.

It was the twenty executions, the affecting stories of Molly after Molly walking to the gallows in the pale light of dawn, often holding a single rose sent by a wife or a girlfriend, that stirred people's morbid curiosity. One wonders how such men's deaths affected the detective who sent them there. After all, these were men with whom McParlan had lived for two and a half years, working in the mines, singing ballads, swapping yarns, and getting drunk. Did he feel even the slightest pang of regret at his betrayal of their confidences or at their gruesome ends in white hoods, strangling in the hangman's noose? If he did, nowhere in his reports or letters, then or later, is it recorded.

For years after the trials ended, McParlan basked in the admiration of politicians, the press, and the public. "If there ever was a man to whom the people of the county should erect a monument, it is James McParlan," proclaimed Gowen. On another occasion, he called the detective "the blood red wine marked 100," an encomium derived from a theater piece of the time. Inside his own agency, McParlan was, by all odds, the star performer. When Superintendent Franklin, seeking a pay raise, invoked his own role in the

Mollies caper, an angry Allan Pinkerton shot back: "The praise, honor and glory of breaking up the MM's belongs to McParlan." Not long thereafter, he sacked Franklin, replacing him with Robert Linden.

So intense was Pinkerton's approbation of McParlan's work that, when the young detective remained ill, the Principal invited him to recuperate at The Larches, his 254-acre estate south of Chicago. A Scottish laird's manor transplanted to the Illinois prairie, The Larches took its name from thousands of those graceful trees that Pinkerton imported from his native Scotland. It was in their dappled shade that James McParlan—perhaps accompanied by his brothers Edward and Charles—regained his health. After some months, he paid a prolonged visit to his family in Ireland. In 1878, he rejoined the Pinkertons in Chicago.

About 1879, James McParlan became James McParland. We don't know why. Perhaps the name was spelled that way so often he simply gave in to the more common rendering. Perhaps he found the new spelling more euphonious. Or perhaps—and this seems the most likely—he thought it sounded more American. For the headstrong working-class immigrant was gradually adopting the protective coloration of the diligent, tractable American middle class. When the agency evaluated him in October 1880, that evolution was well under way, if scarcely complete:

> *General Deportment and Appearance:* Genteel Irishman.
> *Classes of Society Can be Readily Adapted to, whether higher or laboring class, sporting men or thieves:* Both.
> *Ability for Making Investigations:* Good.
> *Knowledge of Criminals:* Not Good.
> *Whether Moderate in Expense or Inclined to be Extravagant:* Medium.
> *Impulsive or Cautious:* Impulsive.
> *Determined or Timid:* Determined.
> *Secretive or Talkative:* Talkative.
> *Self-reliance:* Good.
> *Failings to be Guarded Against:* Operating too fast.

Under "remarks," the evaluator noted that the operative engaged in "excessive drinking," a habit that could hardly have endeared him to the abstemious Principal.

A picture emerges of a brash, self-confident thirty-six-year-old dressed in the latest fashions, a bit of a dandy who enjoyed his nights in the city's cafés and saloons, a little boastful in the Detective Room about his achievements, impatient with Pinkerton bureaucracy, not eager to spend much time studying the agency's mug books and other records, a loner inclined to forge ahead on a case a bit more quickly than his deliberate superiors preferred, but a dogged, determined, relentless operative if allowed to call the shots. Once, in response to a reporter's question, he said, "There's no romance in the life of a detective. It's just work; hard, hard work. That's all."

McParland's trail is harder to follow in the 1880s, though he remained a specialist in labor unrest. The national rail strike of 1877 had opened an era of domestic disorder. As the Knights of Labor and other unions became more aggressive, with strikes, marches, and clashes with armed militias proliferating, embattled employers frequently put out a call for the Pinkertons.

In March 1886, the Knights of Labor struck Jay Gould's Southwestern Railway System. No plutocrat aroused such loathing among workingmen as the "giant fiend" Gould. All along his system—through Texas, Missouri, Kansas, and Nebraska—strikers disabled engines, blocked or wrecked trains. A principal trouble spot was Parsons, Kansas, where Gould's system maintained a roundhouse and shops. When the railroad tried to move trains out of the Parsons yards, Knights and their supporters blocked all traffic. On March 30, they derailed an approaching passenger train, injuring a mail agent. Declaring martial law, the governor said the Knights had "acted like madmen" in Parsons. Four hundred National Guardsmen occupied the town, taking up positions in the yards, at bridges, and at intersections.

Meanwhile, detectives recruited by Thomas Furlong, Gould's chief special agent, moved silently into Parsons. Among them was James McParland, whose undercover skills were at a premium. There is no evidence that McParland infiltrated the Knights of Labor itself, but he quickly found his way about town.

Among those he cultivated was Jacob McLaughlin, who operated the Grand Central, a notorious hotel not far from the rail yards. For years, its staff had preyed on visitors—notably Texas cattlemen who, having driven their herds up the Chisholm Trail to Abilene, returned through Parsons with bulging pockets. The hotel provided everything the footloose cowboy or railway man might require: liquor, drugs, gambling, and prostitutes. But once a man had savored these delights, he was likely to find his pockets picked, his horse stolen. If a guest proved recalcitrant, he was chloroformed, butchered, then buried in the basement or thrown in the Neosho River.

Well before the strike began, the Grand Central had come under siege from a reform element determined to clean up the town's drinking and gambling dens. In February 1885, the *Parsons Eclipse* could report: "Empty is the police court, the bums are thirsty." Not everyone in town was pleased with the bluestockings. A group calling itself the Stuffed Pelican Club puckishly proposed that Parsons be enclosed with "a tight board fence not less than ten feet high" to keep out bad characters.

In June 1885, Jake McLaughlin was convicted of selling liquor and fined fifteen hundred dollars. Two weeks later, an associate named Wash Bercaw was assessed a hundred dollars. When they declined to pay their penalties, they were sent to the county jail, where among their fellow prisoners was a horse thief named Frank P. Myers. During their incarceration—while prostitutes caught in the dragnet warbled the bawdy ballad "Whoop 'Em Up, Liza Jane"—Myers learned much about what went on at the Grand Central. Later, after McLaughlin and Bercaw were released pending appeal, Myers sought to trade this information to the authorities for a reduction in his own sentence. On August 5, Myers vanished from jail; the next day his body was found floating in the Neosho. In April 1886—just as troopers brought the strike under control—McLaughlin and Bercaw were charged with Myers's murder.

The courthouse gang soon became aware that a Pinkerton named McParland was working wonders on McLaughlin's behalf. The brothers Frank and George Davis, prosecution witnesses at the preliminary hearing, abruptly changed their tune. They hadn't watched McLaughlin and Bercaw drag Myers from the jail after all. Indeed, they admitted that E. C. Ward, McLaughlin's lawyer, had paid them two hundred dollars to revoke their original testimony—which they said had been a lie anyway. Once the Davises reneged, the judge reluctantly dismissed the charges against McLaughlin and Bercaw, proclaiming, "I never saw such unblushing and shameful perjury as has been flaunted in my face during the past few days." The Davis boys went to prison for perjury. Ward was disbarred. Meanwhile, Jake McLaughlin strolled the streets of Parsons, a smirk on his face, while the man many blamed for the perjured testimony—James McParland—slipped out of town as quietly as he'd appeared.

Two decades later, when McParland popped up on the Steunenberg case, this matter was resurrected. A meeting in Parsons, chaired by the treasurer of the city's Socialist local, denounced the "infamous" detective. Where money was to be made, it said, "he will do anything, no matter how low or vile, to accomplish his purpose.... There is not today, in the United States outside prison walls, a more conscienceless and desperate criminal than McParland." What lay behind these accusations is difficult to say. If the resolution originated with the town's Socialist local, there are grounds for skepticism, at least about the rhetorical overkill. But some of Parsons's leading citizens—judges, lawyers, and merchants—vouched for the essential facts of the case.

Since the Pinkertons rarely worked for the defense in a criminal case, it is hard to imagine how McParland found himself allied with a scoundrel like McLaughlin. But if the story is accurate, one can only speculate that the Grand Central's impresario may have been one of McParland's informants, perhaps even an undercover operative, during the labor unrest. McParland may have felt obliged to use every means at his disposal—including subornation to perjury—to secure his associate's freedom.

As his agency's most celebrated operative, McParland drew major cases all over the country. In Columbus, Kansas, he uncovered an elaborate conspiracy to dynamite Cherokee County's records vault to prevent detection of fraudulent mortgages. Later, he helped convict Oliver Curtis Perry, the so-called gentleman-desperado, a dapper young man with the nerves of a trapeze artist who committed sensational train robberies on the New York Central. McParland also helped apprehend the slick brigand who lifted $320,000 in gold from a smelting company near San Francisco—the largest theft of bullion in U.S. history.

But McParland's first major advance in the agency's hierarchy grew less from these achievements than from his old gift for infiltration.

Allan Pinkerton had long resisted hasty expansion of what was, at heart, a family enterprise. Preoccupied with maintaining his firm's reputation for rectitude, he feared that a venture beyond its traditional bastions of New York, Chicago, and Philadelphia would strain its capacity for supervision. In a profession so vulnerable to temptation, an unsupervised outpost invited corruption, if not outright thievery. But when Allan Pinkerton died in 1884, his sons succumbed to the lure of growth. By then, the exploitation of mineral and timber resources in the western territories offered lush pickings for criminals—and ample work for detectives. The Pinkertons found it difficult to exploit such opportunities from their westernmost outpost in Chicago. Then, in 1885, their bitter rival, Gus Thiel, dispatched one of his veteran operatives, John F. Farley, to open an office in Denver, the closest thing to a metropolis between Chicago and San Francisco. Goaded by this gambit, the Pinkertons put their fourth office in Denver in mid-1886 and placed at its head a trusted associate, the assistant superintendent in Chicago, Charles O. Eames.

Before long, reports reached the principals that something had gone badly awry at their newest office. Eames was reported to be siphoning profits directly into his own pockets and those of his most trusted subordinates. William A. Pinkerton decided to put an operative in the Denver office to find out what was going on. Who better than that virtuoso of undercover work James McParland?

In the spring of 1887, McParland was named assistant superintendent in Denver, a position that gave him ample opportunity to scrutinize his boss's activities. In a matter of weeks, he discovered that Eames was charging clients for work never performed. One technique involved assigning multiple cases to one operative, then billing each client the full six-dollar daily rate plus expenses. Moreover, Eames was apparently running, off the agency books, his own merchants' protective service, from which he took all the profits. To ensure that these machinations went undetected, he'd enlisted as co-conspirators both the bureau's bookkeeper and its "lady stenographer."

Virtually everyone in the Denver office played some role in these schemes, above all, two strong-arm types named Doc Williams and Pat Barry. According to Charles Siringo—the same "cowboy detective" who'd later infiltrate the miners union in the Coeur d'Alenes and the only Denver operative not handpicked by Eames—Williams (who'd once served time in an eastern penitentiary for blowing safes) and Barry were openly robbing the merchants they ostensibly protected. They kept their loot in trunks they maintained in the Detective Room, where they boasted of their latest thefts.

Siringo saw them beat a merchant they accused of a crime Barry had committed. When Siringo reported this incident to the superintendent, Eames tried to have him discharged and Barry and Williams swore corporeal revenge. Siringo wasn't a man you could easily push around, but he recognized trouble when he saw it; he wrote a friend that he feared for his life every time he entered the office and that he never went there without his "best friend," his Colt .45.

In the summer of 1887, McParland made his report; Eames and his entire staff—save Charlie Siringo—were dismissed; and Pinkerton named McParland Denver superintendent. Two years later, he was elevated to assistant general superintendent, in charge of all Pinkerton operations west of the Mississippi.

Before long, McParland played a pivotal role in unraveling one of fin-de-siècle America's most sensational murder cases. In April 1891, Mrs. Josephine Barnaby, a prominent Providence, Rhode Island, dowager known to appreciate "a good naughty story," a couple of drinks, and the company of attractive men, died on a visit to Denver after drinking some "fine old whiskey," laced with arsenic, sent by an anonymous admirer. The Denver district attorney called it "the first murder by mail, probably in the world, certainly in the United States." Suspicion focused on Mrs. Barnaby's physician, Thomas Thatcher-Graves, who, in conversation with an undercover Pinkerton in Providence, admitted having sent the lethal whiskey to Mrs. Barnaby, though he denied lacing it with arsenic. But how to get the crafty doctor from Providence to Denver, where he could be tried for the crime? McParland found the answer. He drafted a telegram—ostensibly from the district attorney—informing the doctor he was needed urgently in Denver to testify before a grand jury considering the indictment of another man. Delighted to see someone else charged with the crime, Thatcher-Graves went to Denver, only to be arrested, tried, and convicted. The following year he committed suicide in his cell.

During the century's waning years, McParland contracted for the services of a notorious gunman named Tom Horn, who once said, "Killing is my specialty. I look at it as a business proposition, and I think I have a corner on the market." In 1899, the Pinkertons sent Horn to work for Wyoming cattlemen. Charlie Siringo, who was closely associated with McParland during those years, later reported that Horn had a contract with the cattlemen to murder suspected cattle rustlers: "It was understood that whenever a corpse was found with a stone under its head for a pillow, Horn was to be paid $600 and no questions asked." According to Siringo, Horn killed seventeen people while employed by the Pinkertons. Among them was a fourteen-year-old boy named Willie Nickell, a victim whose murder Wyoming authorities could not countenance. For that crime, he was tried and hanged in Cheyenne in November 1903. Later, Robert and William Pinkerton exchanged regrets that Horn's death had come while he was in their service, and McParland said he might have saved Horn's life had the gunman kept his mouth shut. Evidently, Horn knew too much about the murderous campaign waged by Wyoming's cattlemen, and it was the cattle interests who decreed that he must die.

In 1903, McParland was named full-fledged manager of Pinkerton's western division. From his office in Denver's Opera House Block, he supervised some ninety operatives and other part-time or casual informants between Laredo and Seattle. As in Shenandoah and Chicago, his principal expertise —and interest—remained the radical labor movement, which had gained influence over recent decades. Denver was a convenient outpost for such surveillance since it had recently become the headquarters of the Western Federation of Miners, which many regarded as the most militant labor organization in the land.

As he aged, the Great Detective grew crustier. Dashiell Hammett is said to have patterned his boss, "the Old Man," in his *Continental Op* series after McParland. It seems doubtful that Hammett ever worked directly for McParland. But the western manager was something of a legend in the agency by then, and his character would certainly have been the stuff of gossip in the Detective Room. In any case, Hammett seems to have him right in *Red Harvest:* "The Old Man... was also known as Pontius Pilate, because he smiled pleasantly when he sent us out to be crucified on suicidal jobs. He was a gentle, polite, elderly person with no more warmth in him than a hangman's rope. The Agency wits said he could spit icicles in July."

McParland had put on a lot of weight in the past decades. The muscular frame, called "wiry" in his Molly Maguire days and later "stocky," was now distinctly portly. He suffered from rheumatism severe enough to put him in bed for days at a time. He still drank heavily—a Socialist correspondent described his "awful hankering for 'red licker'"—but his wife, Mary, did her best to control his consumption. They were childless; Katie, McParland's daughter by his first marriage, had died of diphtheria in 1890 at the age of eight. Some suggested her death had taken the last real joy from McParland's life. In March 1906, a beloved nephew who to some degree had replaced Katie in his affections was killed when passenger trains collided near Florence, Colorado. The previous winter, while McParland waited in a blizzard for a trolley, one of his heels had become frostbitten and eventually had to be amputated; now he got about with the help of a gold-headed cane his admirers had given him. But to all outward appearances the McParlands still enjoyed a good life. They lived quite comfortably on his salary of forty-five dollars a week, occupying a comfortable bungalow on Denver's Columbine Street, guarded by the detective's pet bulldogs.

He and Mary were devout Catholics. The detective was a staunch supporter of the Denver diocese in secular matters as well, notably in the uproar that followed Bishop Nicholas C. Matz's harsh condemnation of the Western Federation of Miners for its flirtation with Socialism. Citing Pope Leo XIII's *Rerum novarum* as his authority, Matz had called Socialism "a system of confiscating private property" in violation of God's commandment "Thou shalt not steal." It was nothing more than a "wild and reckless and revolutionary appeal to the slums of humanity" and could not be embraced by any true son of the Church. The WFM struck back, contending that workers had no obligation to provide the bishop with "an easy living while he is proving to be their enemy," and suggested that they should not contribute to the bishop's plans for a "magnificent cathedral in Denver where he can with more splendor condemn the working class." Matz was McParland's kind of prelate, a profoundly conservative two-fisted fighter against evil; and in a city where 44 percent of churchgoers were Catholics, Matz had clout. He denounced libraries as "sinks of corruption" that "place within reach of the masses the infidel teachings of Voltaire and the sensational dime novels," and he railed against Sunday excursions that took Denver's working-class Catholics too far from their devotionals (indeed, when he sensed that his admonitions were not being heeded, he nearly doubled the length of the early Sunday Mass, making it all but impossible for the faithful to perform their Sabbath duties and still breathe some fresh country air).

McParland and Matz, in concert on so many issues both spiritual and temporal, met frequently to confer on the Socialist menace in Colorado. The detective contributed substantially to the bishop's building fund for the Cathedral of the Immaculate Conception and, when it was completed, he and Mary attended Mass there every Sunday.

But McParland was by no means fully accepted in Denver's Catholic community. Many of his coreligionists remembered all too well how he'd ingratiated himself with the Hibernians of Schuylkill County, then testified against his fellow Irish Catholics, sending nine to their deaths. To many Catholics, McParland was a traitor.

These resentments were evident in the course of his bitterly contested election to the Knights of Columbus, the preeminent Catholic fraternal organization. At the turn of the century, the Knights had no presence as yet in Denver. In the spring of 1900, an emissary of the Kansas City Knights visited Denver to establish an affiliate there. By tradition, the visitor called first on the bishop, but this time he went to McParland, presumably because the devout detective was an excellent channel to the bishop. McParland, in turn, obtained from Matz the names of other Catholics considered to be desirable members of a Denver council. The charter application was quickly granted and in November a Kansas City team arrived to form Denver Council 539.

But on the night the council was established and fifty-nine charter members—"the cream of Catholic manhood"—were initiated, McParland was away on Pinkerton business, which compelled him to stand for election at a subsequent meeting as would any new candidate. When his nomination came to a vote, the ballot box held just twelve white balls and twenty-nine black balls, with another twenty-four members not voting, ostensibly because the pollers had run out of black balls.

The stunning rebuff by Catholics of his own diocese must have been painful indeed to the proud detective. Shortly thereafter, he sought admission as a charter member of San Francisco's new Council 615 and it was there, in that far-off city by the bay where he was but little known, that James McParland finally gained Knighthood on January 19, 1902.

Once Harry Orchard realized just who his portly visitor was, he sat a little straighter in his chair, fixing the detective with an attentive eye. Quick to exploit the opening, McParland returned to his lesson of the moment: the happy fate of the Mollies who'd turned state's evidence, notably one Daniel Kelly, alias Manus Cull, alias "Kelly the Bum."

Kelly had served three years in prison for biting the nose off a man in Wilkes-Barre. At one time, there were no fewer than nine warrants out for his arrest, some for assault and battery, some for burglary, others for highway robbery. It was Captain Linden who, in late 1876, found him serving a ten-year term for highway robbery in the Pottsville jail, where he told a cellmate that he'd "squeal on Jesus Christ himself if I got out of here." Kelly promptly produced a wide-ranging confession providing evidence against an entirely new set of Mollies, in a murder case fully eight years old.

On October 17, 1868, after a night of drinking and plotting at Tom Donahue's saloon, six Molly Maguires had hidden by a watering trough on the road from Centralia to Mt. Carmel, Pennsylvania. Shortly after dawn, Alexander W. Rea, a mining superintendent, came along in his buggy. The six jumped out and demanded his money. He had only sixty dollars on him, but down on his knees, he offered his gold watch, then promised them a check for forty thousand dollars if they'd spare his life. They shot him dead. Kelly put the last bullet in his head, remarking, "Dead dogs wag no tails." Several suspects were arrested, but their trials ended in acquittals and for eight years that was where the matter stood.

Now Kelly admitted his own part in the murder and named his co-conspirators. Eventually, three Columbia County Mollies were executed for the crime. Although several witnesses testified that Daniel Kelly was a notorious crook, the state let him off scot-free. And—according to McParland—the people of Columbia County were so grateful they paid him a thousand dollars so that he might leave the county ahead of those Irishmen who would do him harm.

Orchard paid such close attention to the story of Kelly the Bum that the detective was certain his point was getting across. But still the prisoner offered nothing. His lawyer, he said, had instructed him to keep quiet about the case at hand and he did not, therefore, have anything to say.

Nonetheless, sensing that Orchard was intrigued by the Molly Maguires saga, McParland went on. He'd interceded for the men who'd turned state's evidence in the Mollies cases, "not because they were innocent, but because they'd allowed themselves to become the tools of the men of the inner circle of the Molly Maguires, who were more guilty than they who actually committed the crimes and were free and living in luxury." The "poor devils" then were in the same fix as Orchard was now.*

As for his lawyer's instructions, "in the case of the Molly Maguires, the attorneys for the tools had advised them as his lawyer had advised him, that is, not to speak, knowing that if they did it would endanger the lives of the inner circle, who in reality were the clients of the attorneys.... It is the duty of the lawyers to buoy up the spirits of the tools in this case as it was in the former case, until they have been executed, when their life blood would be spilled and their lives sealed."

Eventually, Orchard opened up a bit, complaining that it wasn't right to put him on murderer's row even before he was tried. His cell was cramped, he said, and he needed exercise.

McParland explained that Orchard was in the pen to "protect him from his friends, as he was a menace to those whose orders he had obeyed until such time that they killed him or that the state convicted and hanged him."

As for the night and day guards, they were a death watch on the man in the next cell, a convicted murderer named Fred Bond, sentenced to hang for shooting and hatcheting the husband of a Boise woman with whom he'd had an affair. The state would put Bond out of his misery all too soon, McParland pointedly confided. They were "fattening him up for the occasion." At that little scrap of gallows humor, Orchard laughed heartily.

And if the guards seemed to watch him more than they did the condemned man, said McParland, that was because Orchard was "such a great criminal that the guard was hypnotized." Again Orchard chuckled. Seemingly pleased by McParland's attempts at levity, he asked whether the detective would visit him again. McParland dodged a definitive response, though he promised to use his influence to see that Orchard got some exercise.

At 5:30 p.m., after three hours of conversation, McParland left the penitentiary, and that evening he gave the governor such a detailed briefing on his meeting with Orchard that the pair didn't adjourn until a half hour past midnight.

Pleased by their first encounter, McParland had planned to call on Orchard again two days later, on Wednesday, January 24. But on second thought he decided it wouldn't hurt for the prisoner to "reflect" a little longer on what he'd said. After getting the warden's assurance that Orchard would be

---

* Evidently, Orchard had followed the Molly cases closely, for he asked McParland why he hadn't taken custody of Thomas Hurley, the man accused of killing Gomer Jones in 1875. (Arrested years later in Gunnison County, Colorado, Hurley had committed suicide in the county jail.) The detective put this inquiry to good use. Hurley, he told Orchard, was simply the tool of Jack Kehoe, the Molly kingpin, "just as you are the tool of Moyer, Haywood, Simpkins and others.... What did I want with convicting and hanging a poor tool like Hurley? In this case you stand just as Hurley did, a poor, unfortunate tool, and that being the case, to tell you the truth, I hate to see you hung and those that are more guilty escape" (Pinkerton Reports, Idaho State Historical Society, January 25, 1906; Broehl, *Molly*, 229–30, 317–18, 332).

permitted a bath, a shave, and a little exercise, he asked the warden to meet him at the end of the car line early Thursday afternoon.

The second meeting between the detective and the accused assassin lasted some three and a half hours. According to his reports, McParland began by asking whether Orchard had thought about their conversation, particularly about the treatment of state's witnesses. Orchard said he'd thought of little else, but he didn't quite understand why the detective seemed to have such an interest in him.

Oh, McParland said, in one respect he had no interest in him whatsoever, no more than he would have in any other "wilful murderer." On the other hand, as an advocate of law and order, he had an interest not only in the welfare of Idaho but in every state that was affected by the blight of the Western Federation of Miners. And knowing full well that Orchard was simply the tool of the federation's "inner circle"—something Orchard himself surely knew—he couldn't help having a certain sympathy for the prisoner.

As he had from his first day on the case, McParland applied the Molly Maguire model to the Steunenberg assassination. If the Mollies had been directed by a tight little inner circle of county delegates and bodymasters, so the Western Federation was run by an inner circle of its principal officers. Likewise, if the rank-and-file Mollies were mere tools of the inner circle, so McParland regarded those who did the WFM's bidding as pawns of its leadership.

Clearly, McParland said, Orchard was a man of intelligence and reasoning power, as indicated by the shape of his forehead. He could therefore do much good in the world, as well as the evil he'd done by associating with "a crowd of socialists, anarchists and murderers." He could still use that intelligence if his feet were put on the right path.

Orchard asked if they were speaking confidentially. McParland assured him they were.

"That being the case," said the prisoner, "let us suppose a case for the sake of argument. I will now say to you I am guilty of the crime as charged. I have committed the crime." He paused. In the silence, both men seemed aware that they had reached a critical point in their feeling-out process.

"Now you understand this is not a confession," Orchard put in, "but for the purpose of getting information that I want, or rather for argument's sake." McParland readily assented.

"Now, you are the detective; you come to me for a confession; you have already stated to me that you have absolute proof of my guilt. Such being the case, why do you come to me and talk to me as you have done? I committed the crime, you know it and claim to have proof of the facts."

McParland reminded the prisoner that, on the first day they'd spoken, he hadn't asked whether Orchard set the bomb that killed the governor. The state had "proof positive" of that. But since Orchard was the tool of the

WFM inner circle, hanging him would give the state little satisfaction. If he'd confess, the state would "no doubt take care of him." But if he confessed, he must tell the whole truth and not cover up for any conspirator.

Orchard paused, fixing the detective with a hard look. "Suppose," he asked, "several parties had guilty knowledge of a murder that was committed and were not present at the murder, what good would it be for the murderer to make a confession?"

All right, said McParland, he'd explain it. "Now, Smith, Brown, Jones and yourself conspire to murder Johnson. Johnson lives away at a distance. Smith, Brown and Jones, being men in authority, detail you to go and commit the murder, furnish you with the means to commit the murder, advise you how to do it, furnish you with the means to travel and support yourself while engaged in this matter, and when you arrive at the place where Johnson resides, you discover that you will have to have help. Therefore you take into your confidence Bob White and Bill Black.

"After making proper arrangements Johnson is murdered. Bob White and Bill Black make their escape and you are arrested. Sufficient evidence has been gotten to convict you and hang you according to law, although you might not have wielded the dagger, pulled the trigger or exploded the bomb that killed Johnson."

Absent other evidence, McParland went on, the state would "simply try all three of you, convict you and hang you together, but if you confessed it would be quite different as your testimony would reach the very foundation and the head of these cut-throats known as the Inner Circle of the Western Federation of Miners. This being the case, the State would gladly accept your assistance as a State witness and see that you are properly taken care of afterwards." (In his report, McParland hastened to add that he hadn't promised Orchard immunity from prosecution, or even from the death penalty, though surely he came very close.)

"I think, Mr. McParland, I now understand the proposition that you take," said Orchard. "But supposing that I turned State's evidence, that my evidence convicts the leaders, as you have explained, the State takes care of me by eventually giving me my liberty, then I would be taken back to Colorado and tried for some of the crimes they claim I have committed there and it would be out of the power of the State of Idaho to resist."

McParland explained that, if he testified truthfully, "we would get the leaders and that was all that the State of Colorado or the State of Idaho wished." He assured Orchard that he wouldn't be prosecuted in Colorado.

But Orchard objected: "The people of the State would never be satisfied to allow me to go unpunished. The Governor has got to hearken to public sentiment, and I know full well that that sentiment means that I'd be executed."

No, McParland countered, if he told the truth, public sentiment would be reversed, and instead of looking upon him as a notorious murderer, people would see him as a "savior."

According to McParland, Orchard exclaimed: "My God, if I could only place confidence in you. I want to talk. I ought to place confidence in you. Your talk is right. I know every word you have said is true. You cannot live one hundred years longer. You certainly have not got to build a reputation as a detective, and I am satisfied that all you have said is for my good.

"I don't now look upon you as a snide detective, the same as the damned sons-of-bitches that they threw into the cell with me at Caldwell. If it were not that their actions were so contemptible I would have pitied them. They are the kind of men that swear men's lives away. I know that you would not take the witness stand and testify as to one word that has passed between you and I here, nor would you add a word to what I have said. I have that much confidence in you."

The detectives placed in Orchard's cell at Caldwell were Thiel men, operatives of McParland's archenemy, Captain Swain. It suited McParland's purpose to have Orchard disparage his rivals. Moreover, the encomium to McParland placed in Orchard's mouth was just the way the legendary detective wished to be perceived—as the senior statesman nonpareil of his profession. Orchard may indeed have made the statements as reported, but they seem a trifle too convenient.

However he expressed it, though, there can be little doubt that Orchard had developed considerable trust in—even dependence on—the ingratiating detective. As their second meeting ended toward 6:00 p.m., he exacted a promise that McParland would return the next day.

Return he did, on Friday and Saturday; then, accompanied by his personal stenographer, Wellington B. Hopkins, on Sunday, Monday, and Wednesday. Hour after hour, Hopkins took the confession in shorthand. By Thursday, February 1, the Great Detective held in his hands sixty-four pages of foolscap, comprising the most extraordinary confession in the history of American criminal justice. For not only did Harry Orchard confess to setting the bomb that killed Frank Steunenberg, he accepted responsibility for killing seventeen other men—two supervisors in a mine explosion, thirteen men in the bombing of a railroad depot, a detective gunned down on a Denver street, and an innocent passerby who picked up a booby-trapped purse intended for somebody else—and attempting to assassinate the governor of Colorado, two Colorado Supreme Court justices, an adjutant general of Colorado, and Frederick Worthen Bradley, president of the Bunker Hill and Sullivan Mining and Concentrating Company, all on behalf of the inner circle of the Western Federation of Miners, particularly Charles H. Moyer, the federation's president; William D. Haywood, its secretary-treasurer; and George A. Pettibone, the former Coeur d'Alene miner who had been imprisoned for a time after the hostilities of 1892 but was now an honorary member of the organization and a close adviser. Finally, Orchard identified two other men, in addition to Jack Simpkins, who'd been his accomplices during various phases of these years: Steve Adams and Vincent St. John, both miners and longtime members of the WFM.

Orchard recounted all this mayhem in a curiously understated, matter-of-fact manner: "I was just going around and taking chances once in a while," he said on one occasion. But his confession was so utterly damning to him and his associates that McParland had to ask him whether he thought McParland or anyone else had used force or coercion to obtain the statement or had made any promises of immunity. To both questions, Orchard said no.

Then why, McParland asked, would anyone incriminate himself and his confederates in this fashion? Orchard's response—in the official text of the confession—bears the imprint not only of McParland's Molly Maguire theories but of his notions, already outlined to Orchard, about parallel WFM skullduggeries.

"I awoke," said the accused man, "as it were, from a dream, and realized that I'd been made a tool of, aided and assisted by members of the Executive Board of the Western Federation of Miners, and once they had led me to commit the first crime I had to continue to do their bidding or otherwise be assassinated myself, and therefore, not caring what would become of me, knowing that I did not deserve any consideration, but on account of the crimes that I assisted in, I resolved, as far as in my power, to break up this murderous organization and to protect the community from further assassinations and outrages from this gang. That is all I have got to say on this matter."

At the bottom of the last page, James McParland appended the following note: "Orchard broke down and cried several times while making the above statements, but seemed very much relieved after he got through."

5

BIG BILL

STEAM FIZZED from the brakes of the great black locomotive easing to its berth in Denver's Union Station on April 21, 1904, nearly two years before Frank Steunenberg's assassination. Even before the train stopped moving, a bugler leaped to the platform and blew assembly. Olive-clad troopers of the Colorado National Guard, carbines and six-shooters at the ready, formed a single rank facing out toward knots of trainmen and other onlookers. Into the corridor between train and soldiers moved a ten-man escort surrounding its prisoner: Charles Moyer, president of the Western Federation of Miners, who'd been arrested when martial law was imposed during labor unrest in the mining town of Telluride.

A bustle of stenographers from the WFM offices pressed forward and one of them seized Moyer's hand. He smiled but kept walking, hurried on by the soldiers behind. At this moment, a burly man in a dark three-piece suit and broad-brimmed black Stetson advanced on the party, as if to shake the prisoner's hand as well. He was quickly intercepted by an officer, Captain Bulkeley Wells of Troop A, First Squadron Cavalry, who shouldered his way between the two men. "You cannot speak to Mr. Moyer at this time," Wells told Bill Haywood, the Western Federation's secretary-treasurer.

Turning his head and recognizing the officer he knew all too well, Haywood said nothing but struck Captain Wells in the face with a half-opened hand. When a sergeant rushed to intervene, Haywood swung at him, too, but missed. In an instant, Haywood was surrounded by a dozen troopers, flailing at him with the butts of their carbines and pistols. Trapping him in a narrow space between two cars, one soldier took him by the throat. Another leveled his carbine at Haywood's bloodied forehead.

"Pull it, you son of a bitch, pull it," rasped Haywood.

At that, Sherman M. Bell, Colorado's adjutant general, knocked the barrel aside. "Stand back, stand back," he said. "You are a military prisoner, Mr. Haywood. Stand over there by Mr. Moyer."

"I'm not a prisoner," thundered Haywood. "You damned bastards have no right to arrest me. There's no martial law here."

A trooper, placing his gloved hand over Haywood's mouth, shoved him into the protective square formed by the escort. On a sharp command, the soldiers locked cartridges into the chambers of their Krag-Jorgenson rifles. Then, with the guidon of Troop A snapping at the column's head, they marched their two prisoners a block to the Oxford Hotel, a modest hostelry popular among commercial travelers.

There the prisoners were separated, the stoic, slightly built Moyer ordered to stand near the elevator, while Haywood was marched into a recess where the hotel proprietor had his office. A trooper shoved a chair at him and ordered him to sit down.

"I will not sit down," shouted Haywood. "I will talk to Moyer and you can't stop me."

A tall soldier seized him by his thick neck and forced him into the chair. With an oath, Haywood sprang to his feet, his face "like a scarred mountain," his deep-chested voice bellowing at those about him. In an instant, the troopers were at him again: Walter Kinley, one of the husky gunmen hired by the mine owners, knocked him partly down a flight of stairs leading to the basement, while others struck him repeatedly in the face with the barrels of their revolvers. Some bystanders believed he might have been killed had Adjutant General Bell not called a halt to the melee.

Hands to his temples, Haywood collapsed into a chair, the blood from multiple head wounds staining his shirt and tie. So heavy was the bleeding that officers dragged a nearby cuspidor up to receive the flow. Eventually, police doctors needed seven stitches to close the cuts. Showing them to a colleague some years later, Haywood growled: "I hope to live long enough to repay the bastards for the blows on my head."

Meanwhile, a squad of troops fixed bayonets to hold off a restive crowd of workers milling in the street before the hotel, which newsmen quickly dubbed "Fort Oxford." Inside, military and civil officials squabbled over custody of Haywood. Ultimately, the question went all the way to James H. Peabody, the fastidious Canon City banker and vestryman of the Episcopal Church then serving as the governor of Colorado. At day's end, Peabody ordered Sherman Bell to hand Haywood over to the sheriff of Denver with the understanding that he would then be surrendered to the sheriff of San Miguel County, where Haywood and Moyer were charged with desecration of the American flag.

Moyer had been arrested twenty-five days earlier, ostensibly for his role in printing and distributing a Western Federation poster of the flag with slogans inscribed in bold black ink on each of the thirteen stripes ("Martial Law Declared in Colorado! Habeas Corpus Suspended in Colorado! Free Press Throttled in Colorado!" etc.). He'd been jailed in the tough mining town of Telluride, two hundred miles to the southwest, until a habeas corpus petition required his appearance before the state supreme court in Denver. When Haywood heard there was a Telluride warrant out for him on the same charge, he cleverly stage-managed a mock detention in his hometown,

ensuring that he could not be removed to Telluride. Persuading his friend
Jake Wolf to bring the charge, he arranged for a sympathetic justice of the
peace to place him in the mildest form of protective custody; attended night
and day by an amiable constable, he ostensibly sought to raise three hundred
dollars' bond pending an indefinitely postponed trial. That morning of April
21, 1904, he was still in Denver's gentle grasp, though without the constable,
when he and the stenographers went to the depot to greet his less fortunate
colleague.

The rage and blood spilled that day marked but the latest stage in
years of collision between Governor Peabody's militantly business-oriented
administration, staunchly backed by Colorado's mine owners and other industrialists, and the Western Federation of Miners, led by Moyer and Haywood in an increasingly confrontational posture. Of the two WFM officials, it
was Haywood who supplied the volcanic anger and penchant for violence.
Indeed, by that spring William D. "Big Bill" Haywood probably ranked with
Eugene V. Debs—the lanky labor organizer from Indiana who now headed
the Socialist Party of America—as the most feared radicals in the land.

When the city of Denver resolved to honor Colorado's pioneers by
erecting a monument at the entrance to its Civic Center Park, it awarded the
commission to the American-born sculptor Frederick MacMonnies. From his
studio in Giverny, France, MacMonnies proposed to place atop the granite
slab an Indian brave in flaring warbonnet reining in a rampant cayuse and
surveying the territory he once had ruled but now had surrendered to the
pioneers. When the sculptor presented this scheme to the monument's sponsors, the city quickly chose up sides. The chief editorial writer of the *Denver
Post* proclaimed the proposed sculpture a "work of gracefulness and charm,"
but others mounted strenuous protests, among them Bill Haywood.

Instead of MacMonnies's bronze-skinned warrior, Haywood wrote the
Rocky Mountain News, the place of honor ought more appropriately go to a
Pony Express rider, "his mount a Morgan-Spanish half-breed, [with] full
saddle and mail pouches, the rider a typical Western pioneer, about 25 years
of age, six feet, 175 pounds, his horse on a full gallop, under steady rein. The
rider, leaning slightly forward, easing up on his saddle, is glancing back over
his shoulder—you can imagine at a gathering cloud of dust in the distance—
his countenance bespeaking danger to himself, to his horse and his mail, but
in every lineament is calm judgment, steady nerve, the personification of
magnificent western manhood."

There can be little doubt where Haywood found the model for all this
magnificence. His father had been a pioneer, setting out from Columbus,
Ohio, in the 1860s, making first for Iowa, then for Salt Lake City. Along the
way, he served as a Pony Express rider, bearing—as his son observed—
"precious burdens of commerce and love" (though, if he was truly 175 pounds,
as his son suggests, he would have violated the company's limit of 125 pounds

for its riders). Only in the last months of his life did he take a turn at silver mining in the Oquirrh Mountains southwest of Salt Lake City, while his wife, Henrietta, and two children remained at home in the city. Bill Haywood scarcely knew his father, who died of pneumonia when Bill was three. But he felt the loss no less acutely. Visiting the cemetery for the first time, the youngster flung himself onto the fresh grave, digging as deep as his small arms would reach.

Because there was so little experience from which to construct a portrait of the elder Haywood, his son was free to imagine him as he would: the lone rider unfettered by the artificial restraints of the East, unafraid of man or beast. That was scarcely an accurate picture of the Pony Express, which, like any other outfit distributing the mail, had to meet rigid schedules and, thus, carefully supervise its fleet of riders. The myth of individualism had been imposed on it by propagandists wishing to inflate the image of frontier independence.

Young Bill's identification with the mythic father only grew with the years until, by the time he was eleven, he abandoned his middle name and took his father's—becoming, in fact, William Dudley Haywood Jr. He was adopting more than a new middle name; he was staking out another, more potent identity.

In Haywood's relentlessly romantic imagination, the pioneer West was a unique, even precious moment in human experience. Once, as he testified about his father's days as a Pony Express rider, an attorney interjected, "In this western country?" and Haywood snapped back, "This is the only place where that ever took place—ever occurred—so it must have been."

Not only did he identify with the cowboy and the pioneer ("Get me a Stetson hat," he told his friend Ralph Chaplin. "I have to have my Stetson."), he felt kinship with the outlaw as well. "I'm a two-gun man from the West, you know," he was fond of telling audiences, as he hauled a Socialist Party card from one pant pocket, an Industrial Workers of the World card from the other.

In fact, Bill Haywood's earliest years were a good deal tamer than such bravado suggested. The Salt Lake City into which he was born on February 4, 1869, was a disciplined, immaculate community of broad boulevards and shining temples. From the snow-capped mountains ringing the city, water ran down neat irrigation ditches to freshen the gardens in which its best houses were set. Founded in 1847 as Zion, the capital of the Church of Jesus Christ of Latter Day Saints, Salt Lake drew its orderly ethos from the stern authoritarianism of the Mormon elders. Moreover, unlike the roughneck lumber camps and mining patches of the West, Salt Lake had been settled by full-fledged families, in which women were a "civilizing influence."

But two months after Bill's birth came a watershed moment for the Mormon realm and the nation at large. On May 10, the Union Pacific drove its golden spike at Promontory, just across the Great Salt Lake, completing the first rail link between the Atlantic and the Pacific. Within a few months, the transcontinental railroad set off a boom, which altered the city's face, ringing Temple Square with the grim detritus of capitalism: factories, warehouses, dry goods establishments, rooming houses, and saloons. But, most important, it encouraged the exploitation of Utah's mineral resources, an activity that Brigham Young had long sought to deflect. Mining, he feared, would divert his saints from the kingdom's immediate needs to the quest for quick wealth. Now revenue from minerals mined in Utah ballooned from barely $190,000 in 1869 to $1.5 million a year later and $10 million in 1882.

One of those lured west by Utah's glittering ores was a miner named William Carruthers, whom Henrietta Martha Haywood married four years after her first husband's death. High in one of the Oquirrhs' remote canyons were silver deposits so rich they inspired early prospectors to register their claims under euphoric labels like Miner's Delight and Wild Delirium. When a lode of horn silver was found on Silverado Hill on August 23, 1870, the boomtown that sprang up on the canyon slopes was named Ophir after King Solomon's fabulous mines.

"One of the wildest mining camps of the West," Bill Haywood would later proudly call it, and indeed Ophir's narrow main street offered a storied clump of saloons, dance halls, brothels, and gambling dens. The place quickly spawned legends, like the memorable poker game played out by miners Frank Payton and Digger Mike. Though neither man had anything to speak of in his hand, they bluffed and counterbluffed until the table was piled with $12,000 worth of gold dust, coin, and currency. Ultimately, Payton topped Digger's pair of treys with his own couple of fours. Several days later, his body was found in a nearby ravine, his skull staved in, the money gone.

One day, on his way to school, Haywood saw Manny Mills and Slippery Dick exchange gunfire and Manny drop dead in ankle-deep mud. Another night a disgruntled customer bombed one of Ophir's hotels. "These scenes of blood and violence happened when I was seven years old," Haywood wrote. "I accepted it all as a natural part of life." Indeed, he seemed to relish it; for the rest of his life, he boasted of these sanguinary adventures.

But the bloodiest encounter of his youth came at his own careless hands. At age nine, he was whittling the stock of a slingshot when his knife slipped and punctured his right eye, blinding it for life. Other children mocked him with epithets like Squint Eye and Deadeye Dick. Henceforth, in posing for photographs he always turned his head to offer the unimpaired left profile. But he never had a glass eye installed in place of that dead eye with its milky glaze. Did he somehow enjoy the lopsided, even sinister cast it gave his face?

Another incident in his ninth year formed his character even more than the loss of his eye did. When Ophir's school closed one term for lack of a teacher, he joined his stepfather in the Russian mine—an early start on decades of wage labor. Returning to school the following year, he lasted but nine months before quitting for good. By then, the family was back in Salt

Lake City, where the mining boom had triggered a ruinous inflation. To help keep the family afloat, Haywood worked successively as a farm laborer, retail clerk, usher at the Salt Lake Theater, messenger boy, fruit vendor, bellboy at both the Continental Hotel and the Walker House.

But he was marking time. From early childhood, Haywood felt destined to follow his father and stepfather into the mines. So in 1884 he left for Humboldt County, Nevada, where Carruthers had been named superintendent of a twelve-man workforce at the Ohio Mine and Milling Company. A brutal, primitive operation, the Ohio mine was little more than a few holes gouged from Eagle Canyon's hardpan. In quavering candlelight, the miners pounded their eight-pound sledges on steel drill bits, riddling the granite face with two-foot-deep holes; these were then packed with gunpowder or dynamite. The explosion spattered the tunnel with rock chips and precious ores, which the miners shoveled into carts. In a ten-hour day, a dozen men might blast their way through only five feet of defiant rock.

Unlike Ophir, Eagle Canyon boasted no brothels or gambling halls. There was little to occupy a young man's off time, so he spent most of his nights lounging around the company barracks playing chess or cards by candlelight and listening to tales told by the older men. One gnarled Irishman, a veteran of Knights of Labor organizing in the 1880s, exercised a particular fascination for the young miner. At first, Haywood didn't know what to make of Pat Reynolds's blather about class struggle and capitalist exploitation. Then the May 1886 bombing in Chicago's Haymarket Square and the subsequent trial and execution of the rioters' "ringleaders" stirred his imagination—as it did that of many more across the land. Haywood was particularly struck by August Spies's last words as he stepped onto the gallows: "There will come a time when our silence will be more powerful than the voices you are strangling today." Haunted by that formulation, Haywood told Reynolds he wanted to join the Knights of Labor. Looking back several decades later, Haywood saw the Haymarket case as a turning point in his life.

But class oppression was by no means the only thing on Bill Haywood's mind. Women certainly were. As early as 1885, a Winnemucca newspaper had appealed for a dozen marriageable girls for the men working the Ohio mine. The notice brought no takers. By 1887, the men were finding their own companions at housewarmings, fairs, and dances in the burgeoning settlements along the Quinn River Valley.

Just turning eighteen, Haywood was a fixture at many of these events. One New Year's Day, he was pitted against a local athlete, Charles Wallace, in a much-ballyhooed mile race. Haywood won, taking home the hundred-dollar purse, badly needed since by then the Ohio mine had closed and he was eking out a meager living as the custodian of the padlocked premises.

In April 1887, the Winnemucca *Silver State* listed Haywood and Miss Nevada Minor among the guests at a housewarming on Assemblyman Charles O'Connell's ranch. Nevada Jane Minor was the daughter of well-connected Willow Creek ranchers, William and Philoma Minor. William had come to Carson City, the capital of Nevada, in 1871 to clerk for his brother James, then Nevada's secretary of state. When James lost office in 1879, William and Philoma pulled up stakes and moved to the Quinn River Valley, where they raised thousands of cattle and nine children.

Nevada was their firstborn. As a teenager, she was spindly and sickly, suffering from a brand of rheumatoid arthritis that the doctors believed had its start with spinal injuries she suffered when thrown from a horse at age three. Her only good photograph, taken some years later, depicts a drab, even homely woman with penetrating eyes. A friend called her "thoroughly western in manner and appearance," whatever that means. Nonetheless, something—perhaps her very vulnerability—attracted Bill; they kept company for more than three years. Then, in 1889, while Haywood was working in the Brooklyn mine in Bingham Canyon, Utah, Nevada became pregnant. That October, under pressure from her family, they were married in Pocatello, Idaho. Two days later, a son was born prematurely. He lived just a week.

It was an unnerving start to the marriage, but at twenty-one Bill and Nevada were ready for new challenges. With mining work hard to come by, Haywood signed on as a ranch hand. Nevada's brother Tom, a richly mustachioed broncobuster and rodeo performer, was already working for Thad Hoppin, a Quinn River Valley rancher. For barely a year, Haywood rode beside him. Given the sentimental portrait Haywood carried of his cowboy father ("calm judgment, steady nerve, the personification of magnificent western manhood"), it must have been a chastening year. He quickly found that the life of a cowboy in the century's last decade bore precious little resemblance to the myth cultivated by pulp magazines, dime novels, and Wild West shows. Later, in his autobiography (ghostwritten and not entirely reliable), he'd draw a parallel between the two crafts he'd followed in his youth: "The cowboys and miners of the West led dreary and lonesome lives. They had drifted westward from points of civilization, losing contact with social life. Young and vigorous, they were bursting with enthusiasm which occasionally broke out in wild drinking sprees and shooting scrapes. They were deprived of the friendship of women, as the country was not yet settled, and when they visited the small towns on the railroad they gave bent to their exuberant feelings."

Disheartened by the numbing routine of the range, Haywood tried his hand briefly at surveying, threshing, and horsebreaking. Then came an opportunity to pursue an enterprise at the very heart of the westering experience: homesteading. It was a chance to turn his back on wage labor—whether in the mine or on the range—and to work land soon to be his own. The homestead laws provided that, on tracts designated for entry, any American citizen could stake out 160 acres, then have five years to build a house and till the land, after which it would belong to him.

The tract now opened was the old Fort McDermit on the Quinn River,

by the Oregon border. He knew the six-hundred-acre reservation well because William Minor, his father-in-law, had recently been designated its
custodian. Now the senior Minor, his son Jim, and Haywood all marked out
the boundaries of their homesteads. Haywood built a one-room house with a
lean-to kitchen, insulated with burlap, then whitewashed. Soon he was joined
in the new house by his wife and infant daughter, Vernie, whom Haywood
had delivered one morning in November 1890, when his mother-in-law and a
midwife both fainted during the child's birth.

"Life began to take on a new aspect," he would write later. "Every tap
of work I did, building fences, digging ditches, was all for ourselves." But
improvements to his homestead required lumber, tools, seed, and fertilizer.
To earn the wherewithal, Haywood worked stints at several nearby mines.
Then, in 1893, work dried up. That spring, a financial panic, starting with a
ruinous collapse on Wall Street, had sent a tidal wave of repercussions crashing through the land. In the worst economic crisis the country had yet
experienced, mines, factories, railroads, and retail establishments went belly-
up, disgorging thousands of unemployed men and women into skid rows and
"hobo jungles." Battalions of the jobless tramped the highways or rode boxcars, vainly seeking work that no longer existed.

Bill Haywood and Jim Minor set off for Delamar, Idaho, to work in the
silver mines, but the camp was aswarm with unemployed men as desperate as
they were. Returning to Nevada, Haywood was dealt a still more devastating
setback. The United States government had assigned both his homestead and
his father-in-law's to an Indian reservation. Without a dollar's compensation
for all the toil he'd put into his land, the government had taken his 160 acres,
the house he'd built, the fences he'd run. At age twenty-four, he was starting
all over again. "It seemed as if a black curtain had been pulled down on the
future," Haywood would write. "There was no ray of hope."

His tiny hoard of savings was exhausted. Real work—not to mention the
"magnificent western manhood" he attributed to his father—seemed beyond
reach. For a time, he rode along with a contingent of Coxey's Army, the band
of unemployed men heading for Washington under "General" Jacob S. Coxey,
a maverick merchant from Massillon, Ohio. Haywood picked up a couple of
days' wages prodding cattle on a stinking freight bound for Chicago. It was
more than he could take; he dropped off at Winnemucca, more depressed, he
said later, than he'd ever been in his life.

Then came the railroad strike of 1894, the largest concerted labor action
in the nation's history, orchestrated by Eugene V. Debs's American Railway
Union. In several states, governors called out the militia to get the trains
rolling again, but many of these part-time soldiers refused to move against
their fellow workingmen. In Chicago, however, federal regulars sent in by
President Grover Cleveland broke the ARU's strike at the Pullman car shops.
When Debs was jailed for contempt of court, railroad men and others expressed indignation.

For Haywood, the strike was intoxicating. If the Haymarket trial seven years before had provided his first glimmer of class consciousness, then the anguish of 1893 and the strike that followed suggested that class solidarity could be the way out of the darkness. The discovery was like "a great rift of light."

In October 1895, Haywood went to work at the Blaine mine in Silver City, Idaho, fifty-five miles south of Caldwell. The following June, he brought Nevada Jane and Vernie out to join him in a little rented cabin. Two events the following year reinforced Haywood's faith in working-class solidarity. When he mangled a hand underground in June 1896, his fellow workers presented him with a purse of silver to support his family until he could go back to work. To Haywood, it was a dramatic confirmation of his growing conviction that the workers could rely only on themselves.

Two months later, his right arm still in a sling, Haywood was among several hundred miners who filled the Silver City courthouse to hear a speech by Edward Boyce, an Irish-born miner and former Populist legislator from northern Idaho newly elected as president of the Western Federation of Miners. We do not know just what Boyce may have said that evening, but we do know it was so persuasive that Haywood came back two nights later, on August 10, to hear him again. This time, Haywood and more than a hundred other miners signed membership cards in the new Silver City Miners' Union, Local 66 of the WFM. Before long, the new local embraced virtually all of the thousand miners in the camp.

But Ed Boyce's influence on Haywood far transcended those first brief encounters. Over the next few years—as Haywood advanced to become financial secretary and president of the Silver City local, then in May 1900 a member of the WFM executive board—Boyce would serve as Haywood's mentor and model, his standard of what a union leader ought to be.

Boyce proved a vivid exemplar for his younger colleague with a restless, energetic style of leadership. Under its first five presidents, the WFM had shuffled papers hither and yon, but little real communication took place between the widely dispersed locals. Now the thirty-four-year-old Boyce set off on an exhausting tour of the mining West—from Montana to the Arizona Territory—speaking in drafty union halls, assessing grassroots leaders, swapping views with the rank and file, organizing new locals. Meanwhile, he put his bold stamp on WFM policy by declaring independence from the eastern labor movement. Ironically, it was Boyce who, in July 1896, had sought to reinforce the federation's clout by bringing it into Samuel Gompers's American Federation of Labor. But almost immediately the relationship went sour.

Gompers and Boyce went together like warm beer and vinegar. A stumpy Jewish immigrant from the London ghetto, Sam Gompers was shaped by the world of his father, who rolled rich cheroots and aromatic panatelas in cigar-making lofts on New York's Lower East Side. When young Sam, in turn, became a cigar maker, he relished the tradition of the "reader," one of the workers' own number who was designated to read from current periodicals, newspapers, and books while the others wrapped their fragrant leaves. They gladly paid the reader in cigars at the end of the day, so he would suffer no loss of income. For the rollers were educated men, their craft an ancient skill, their union like that of the medieval guilds, designed as much to protect their hard-won turf from less-skilled workers as to wrest concessions from their employers.

Not surprisingly, then, the AFL, which Gompers founded in 1886, was sometimes regarded as a league of petit-bourgeois tradesmen seeking to protect their status from challenges by the industrialized masses. To black freedmen in the former Confederate states, Chinese coolies laying tracks across the prairies, Welshmen drilling for lead in Colorado, Polish stokers in Ohio steel mills, or Finnish lumbermen in the high timber of the Northwest, Gompers and his lieutenants, with their silk hats and waistcoats, their lifelong habit of philosophical disputation over glasses of steaming tea, often looked like a band of privileged elitists.

But if Gompers had a "fatal attraction to the powerful" and did not fully comprehend the emerging proletariat of the West, he had an intuitive feel for labor's ambiguous place in America. However intense their specific grievances, Gompers believed that most American workers still accepted capitalism, sought to rise within it, even loved it. His instincts told him that American workers would never accept Socialism. In 1903 he told the Socialists: "I have kept close watch upon your doctrines for thirty years.... I am entirely at variance with your philosophy.... Economically, you are unsound; socially, you are wrong; industrially, you are an impossibility."

A thoroughgoing pragmatist, Gompers followed the dictum of his mentor, Ferdinand Laurrell, the former leader of the United Cigarmakers: "Study your union card, Sam, and if the idea doesn't square with that, it ain't true." He kept his eye on short-term goals, notably higher pay, a shorter workweek, and better working conditions. Eschewing grand programs of economic or political reform, he advocated a stripped-down activity known as "business unionism," or "pure-and-simple unionism."

Ed Boyce's brand of "industrial unionism" grew from a different constituency embedded in different social conditions. Boyce's miners were, for the most part, relatively uneducated men without highly marketable skills, who were often confronted with mine owners and state governments ready to put down labor unrest with strikebreakers, vigilantes, and militias. Such workers saw no advantage to huddling within their traditional crafts; they sought to mobilize all workers across a given industry to confront employers—and governments—with their aggregate clout. With little stake in the status quo, they invested their faith in sweeping political programs to remedy the grim conditions in which they worked and lived.

The events that hammered a wedge between Boyce's WFM and Gompers's AFL began in September 1896 in Leadville, Colorado, one of the world's great sources of lead ore. When the Cloud City Miners Union there sought restoration of the fifty cents a day cut from their wages during the depression of 1893, the mine owners balked and the union struck. The mines imported strikebreakers; the union turned some back and fought with others until, on September 21, union militants blew up an oil tank and a wooden mine structure. Four members of the union were killed and twenty-seven unionists, Ed Boyce among them, were jailed. A British journalist, visiting in October, found a grim standoff: "No surrender; no compromise; no pity. The owners mean to starve the miners to death; the miners mean to blow the owners to atoms." Ultimately, many miners deserted the union and returned to work. Later, Boyce would write of the "dreary days" he spent in Leadville during the strike.

In some desperation, he went, hat in hand, to the AFL convention in Cincinnati that December. The AFL executive committee laconically suggested that its affiliated unions give the WFM "moral and financial support," but that halfhearted endorsement produced scarcely enough to cover canvassing costs. On the way home, Boyce stopped off in Terre Haute, Indiana, to visit with Eugene V. Debs, who had his own bitter memories of Gompers's unwillingness to support the American Railway Union. Warmed by the fire of their grievances, the two men found common ground.

In February, with the Leadville situation continuing to deteriorate, Boyce wrote Gompers appealing for direct AFL assistance. Either the letter failed to reach its destination or it was misplaced; in any case, no help was forthcoming. As Boyce smoldered, rumors reached Gompers that the mining federation was planning not only to leave the AFL but to organize a regional federation of labor in the western states.

On March 9, an out-of-sorts Gompers wrote Boyce a letter: "I do not wish to assume that the rumors are correct, but would say that even if it is harbored in the mind of any one, it is most injust, improper, and destructive. ... On every hand we see concentration of wealth in corporations, combinations, and trusts; the wealth possessors do not allow themselves to be divided on sectional lines when their interests are at stake.... There is nothing in this world which so gladdens the gaze of the enemy in battle as to divide the forces with which it is to contend."

By return mail, Boyce denied that there were plans afoot for the WFM to withdraw from the AFL. Then he hinted that that was precisely what he had in mind:

> I presume you did not get my letter or I would have received an answer. However, I will say that is of little consequence. There is an easier way of winning the battles of labor, much easier than sitting down in idleness until the capitalist starves us to death in idleness and hunger.... Do not think me egotistical when I say that I think the laboring men of the West are one hundred years ahead of their brothers in the East.... I never was so much surprised in my life as I was at the [Cincinnati] convention, when I sat and listened to the delegates

from the East talking about conservative action when four million idle men and women are tramps upon the highways.... I am not a trades unionist; I am fully convinced that their day of usefulness is past; and furthermore, since last election there is little sympathy existing between the laboringmen of the West and their Eastern brothers.

On March 26, Gompers attempted to dampen the western insurrection. "Dear Sir and Brother," he began in the convention of interunion correspondence—although he was beginning to wonder whether Boyce was a brother.

I do not wish to discuss the proposition that "the men of the East are one hundred years behind their Western brothers."... Let me assure you that the trade unionists whom you met at Cincinnati are not at all backward or too conservative, they simply desire as a result of their experience and knowledge to couple practical action with their enthusiasm....

As for your suggestion that the resort must be the sword, I prefer not to discuss. I only want to call your attention to the fact, however, that force may have changed forms of government but never attained real liberty.

I ask you in the name of the great interests committed to your care, the great influence you wield with your fellow-workers of the Western Federation of Miners that you use that great power to unite and solidify the forces of labor in our country.

Its elliptical phrasing and formalities notwithstanding—or perhaps precisely because of them—this message seems to have gotten Boyce's goat. He replied in blunt terms, calculated to break off the correspondence.

"After mature deliberation," Boyce wrote, "I am fully convinced that no two men in the labor movement differ so widely in opinion as the President of the A. F. of L. and the writer.... The trades-union movement has been in operation in our country for a number of years, and through all these years the laboring masses are becoming more dependent. In view of these conditions, do you not think it is time to do something different than to meet in annual convention and fool away time in adopting resolutions, indorsing labels and boycotts?"

Then, returning to the original focus of the correspondence, he concluded: "I can assure you that, no matter what action the Western Miners take with reference to the A. F. of L., it will not be hasty, not calculated to injure the labor movement, but now, as ever, I am strongly in favor of a Western organization."

Indeed, at its Salt Lake City convention in May 1897, the WFM withdrew from the AFL. But the convention's most memorable event was Boyce's presidential address. He'd never been known as a spellbinding orator, but this time he struck an arresting note:

I deem it important to direct your attention to Article 2 of the Constitutional Amendments of the United States—"the right of the people to keep and bear arms shall not be infringed." This you should comply with immediately. Every union should have a rifle club. I strongly advise you to provide every member with the latest improved rifle, which can be obtained from the factory at a nominal price. I entreat you to take action on this important question, so that in two years we can hear the inspiring music of the martial tread of 25,000 armed men in the ranks of labor.

Gompers thought Boyce "either a traitor or clearly insane" for talking like this. Boyce later explained that he was responding to the high-handed manner of Colorado's armed militiamen in Leadville and meant only to assert that "miners or any other body of men had as much right under the constitution to have rifle clubs as anybody or aristocrats." In fact, though Boyce's speech would be used as ammunition against the WFM for years to come, none of the federation's locals was known to have founded a rifle club.

Boyce did redeem his promise of a regional and democratic union. In May 1898, delegates from Colorado, Idaho, and Montana convened in Salt Lake City to form the Western Labor Union, dominated by the WFM and dedicated to the proposition that a labor movement limited to skilled craftsmen could not survive. "Such rights as tradesmen now enjoy," its manifesto declared, "will be extended to the common laborer." An AFL man observing the scene wrote Gompers that the new organization was "only the Western Federation of Miners under another name.... Boyce's influence with the miners is unquestionably strong. The majority believe him sincerely."

In his new role, Boyce spoke stridently. "There can be no harmony between organized capitalists and organized labor," he proclaimed. "Our present wage system is slavery in its worst form. The corporations and trusts have monopolized the necessities of society and the means of life.... Let the rallying cry be: Labor, the producer of all wealth, is entitled to all he creates, the overthrow of the whole profit-making system, the extinction of monopolies, equality for all and the land for the people."

If such proclamations reflected Boyce's deepening doubts about the possibility of social justice in a capitalist system, not all miners shared that pessimism. Indeed, Boyce's coruscating rage at the mine owners and their allies did nothing to ingratiate him with the Butte Miners Union no. 1 of the Western Federation, its "Gibraltar," and by far the largest, richest, and most powerful mining local in the West.

The mounting radicalism of the Western Federation could be traced in part to the transiency of western mining camps—places like Leadville, Cripple Creek, and Wardner—hastily assembled, hastily torn apart, temporary expedients for the digging of ore and the coining of money but never communities that inspired much allegiance or much hope for the future. By the turn of the century, on the other hand, Butte was already a populous, if ugly, industrial city of 30,470—"a scaled-down Pittsburgh," "a black and yellow jungle of smelters, roasting ovens, cranes and stacks which breathed out yellow, acrid smoke"—in which workers and bosses alike sought to "settle in" and thus to look for safety, stability, and survival. Moreover, the armies of labor and capital, elsewhere mercilessly pitted against each other, were bridged in Butte by common ethnicity. In 1900, fully 8,026—or 26 percent—of the city's inhabitants were either Irish-born or the children of Irish-born parents. This was no coincidence, for Marcus Daly, the city's preeminent citizen, the monarch of a mining empire built on the rich Anaconda copper mine, had himself been born in Ireland and—in the words of one priest—"did not care for any man but an Irishman and...did not give a job to anyone else." Managers and workers alike belonged to the Ancient Order of Hibernians (here, as distinct from Pennsylvania, essentially an Irish nationalist organization), the Robert Emmett Literary Association, and the Irish Volunteers. Not surprisingly, the Butte Miners Union, though born in a strike of 1878, never again launched a work stoppage—much less a violent action—against the city's mining companies.

When the Butte local took umbrage at Boyce's "rifle club" speech in 1897, Boyce thought he knew why. "The language was too strong to suit Daily [sic]," he wrote in his diary. In turn, he expressed ill-disguised contempt for the "company men" of the Butte union; he wanted to send "such imps...to the perdition of labor's damnation."

This tension culminated in Boyce's decision that spring of 1901 to move the WFM's headquarters from Butte to Denver. The Butte local was livid, but, quite apart from Boyce's struggle with the Montanans, the move made sense. Butte was isolated, off the main trail of western commerce; Denver was rapidly becoming a crossroads town, especially for banking, insurance, mortgages, and investments in the vast region between the Missouri River and the Pacific. By century's turn, it was a city of 140,000. More important, as William Allen White wrote, it was "the clearing-house for everything West of the plains. Money, Indian blankets, scenery, mining stocks, statesmen and news from the desert and the mountains, from the coast and from the cow country in the southwest are dumped into the hopper in Denver. Whatever the Powers there find fit to go East goes; other things are lost."

For several months, the Western Federation operated out of George Pettibone's crowded household-appliance store at 1613 Court Place, which sold clocks, silverware, carpet sweepers, lamps, rugs, and Bibles on the installment plan. A gregarious, sharp-tongued former Coeur d'Alene miner who'd served time for his role in the events of 1892, Pettibone had been a drummer for the American Wringer Company, selling electrical appliances throughout the West, and owned a saloon called the Bucket of Blood in a Montana mining camp. But he remained close to the WFM and advised its leaders. His store would remain virtually an extension of federation headquarters, while the rooming house above the store was a popular lodging place for WFM members as they drifted in and out of Denver.

But before long, Boyce found spacious quarters for the federation in Suite 625 of the Mining Exchange Building at Fifteenth and Arapahoe Streets. A seven-story structure, home to many of the state's most prominent mining companies, the exchange was topped by the statue of an old-time gold prospector, symbol of a more romantic, and a happier, time in the mining industry.

Boyce made another decision that spring. Having worked closely with Haywood on the WFM executive board, Boyce now asked him to take the position of secretary-treasurer, replacing a Butte Irishman, James Maher, who was resigning. One evening in late May, after ten hours drilling ore in a long Silver City crosscut, Bill shut the air off his machine drill. He'd never work below ground again.

After attending a "unity" convention that gave birth to the new Socialist Party of America in Indianapolis at the end of July, Boyce and Haywood both joined the party's Denver local, then invited Gene Debs to address the WFM convention in Denver that fall. After the speech, Boyce went home to read a book, but Haywood, newly elected as secretary-treasurer, and Thomas J. Hagerty, a Catholic priest turned left-wing Socialist, knocked on Debs's door in a small family hotel, two quarts of whiskey tucked under their arms. The Great Socialist was in his pajamas, exhausted from speechifying, but he blithely welcomed his nocturnal visitors. All through the night, the three roared and drank and swapped outrageous stories, the tall, gangly Debs sitting with legs crossed on the bed, a glass of whiskey in one hand, a pipe in the other; Hagerty pacing the carpet; Haywood sprawled in an armchair nearby.

Perhaps because he couldn't blow off steam with this kind of gregarious carousing—though he'd been known, in the privacy of his attic, to take an ax to the furniture—the austere Boyce grew increasingly sour, often complaining of his followers' obtuseness. Though he'd always been thin, the flesh seemed to melt off now, leaving him almost emaciated. That June, writing in the *Miners' Magazine*, the Western Federation journal, he warned that progress would come only "when intelligence masters ignorance, but that will not occur in our day, for there are too many workingmen ready to bow at the shrine of wealth and beg for the crumbs that fall from the masters' table."

Within days of his writing these words, Boyce's life was transformed by a lot more than crumbs from the groaning board of western mineral wealth. On May 14, 1901, he'd been married to a Wardner schoolteacher named Eleanor Day. Watching his pennies carefully, he refused to pay for the wedding certificate because he thought the priest was asking too much. But desperately in love with his "honey dew"—for years he'd inscribed a flowery red *E* in his diary on every day he spent with her—Boyce could record only a terse entry for that day: "Wedding—absolute loss of memory." A month later, a northern Idaho claim called the Hercules—"grub-staked" by Eleanor's salary and worked by her father and brother—struck the richest silver-lead vein yet discovered in the Coeur d'Alenes. As WFM president, Boyce had managed on $155 a month; now he and his wife received $2,500 in monthly dividends from the Hercules. In August, the Boyces left for a six-week honeymoon in Ireland, putting Bill Haywood, the union's second in command, in charge of the Denver headquarters.

Back in Denver that autumn, the Boyces moved in with the Haywoods for a time. The two men worked well together. "When there were matters of importance to discuss," Haywood recalled, "we would sit down at his desk or mine and go over every angle of the situation carefully. When we had arrived at a mutual understanding he would say, as a rule, 'Well, we are agreed.'" Boyce needed that sort of support, for that fall the WFM had reached a perilous juncture: a bitter strike in the twin towns of Rossland, British Columbia, and Northport, Washington, was foundering, and the federation, with barely three hundred dollars left in its bank account, was deeply riven by factionalism. Boyce himself was weary of too many nights alone in dismal hotel rooms, too many miles of dusty road, too many searches of his luggage by nosy Pinkerton men. On January 23, 1902, alone in yet another of those anonymous rooms, Boyce inscribed in his diary: "Oh! I wonder will the fool working men, especially the miners, rise in their might and have revenge on their oppressors and not suffer iniquities forever. Life as president of the WFM is not worth living.... Foes everywhere and no money or men with sufficient determination to banish them."

Six months later—in June 1902—Boyce refused to accept reelection as the WFM's president and retired from office. On June 13, he wrote in his diary, "This is the first day's rest I had in six years and I enjoy it immensely." In the *Miners' Magazine,* Boyce assured his former constituents: "I have not retired from the field of battle while the cohorts of legalized robbers are assaulting our ranks." In his farewell address to the WFM convention, he strenuously renewed his commitment to Socialism: "There are only two classes of people in the world: One is composed of the men and women who produce all; the other is composed of men and women who produce nothing, but live in luxury upon the wealth produced by others.... The most important action which you can take at this convention is to advise the members of your organization to adopt the principles of socialism without equivocation, for the time has arrived when we must sever our affiliations with those political parties who have legislated us into our present state of industrial bondage."

These lofty pronunciamentos notwithstanding, Boyce had finished with union organizing and Socialism for good. Though he attended the next two WFM conventions, most of his time was devoted to building a handsome house for himself and Eleanor in a comfortable neighborhood of Portland, Oregon, buying tailored clothes, going to the theater, eating in fancy restaurants. When he chanced on a union procession through Portland's streets— marching in sympathy with a transit workers' strike—he was pleased to see that the march was "well conducted and the marchers presented a nice appearance."

Looking for something to occupy his time on a permanent basis, he and Eleanor eyed the gabled, vine-clad Portland Hotel, one of the West's grandest hostelries, where they had stayed for a time while their house was being built.

A syndicate purchasing the 326-room hotel invited the Days to participate, and before long Boyce was named manager. Gradually he adopted the protective coloration of his new social class. Once, on a trip to Chicago, he took a letter of credit to the Continental Bank and that evening recorded—in bemused astonishment—"Got along very nice with the bank officials."

Some federation colleagues would label Boyce an opportunist and a social climber. Haywood, in particular, asserted that "money had destroyed his vision," leaving him "musty and vegetating in his prosperity." But such judgments are a bit too easy. At home and abroad, the Irish have always displayed a gift for soaring rhetoric. But, as one shrewd student of the Irish American experience has written, "Mostly the Irish wanted to be middle-class and respectable. Behind the flaming intransigence of the Irish nationalist (or for that matter behind the thundering of Populist and Socialist) there were nine times out of ten an ambitious Horatio Alger figure." Years before, during some of his fiercest confrontations with the mine owners, Boyce liked to say that "the only ideal life for a man is to possess a comfortable home, loving wife and happy children." In the end, Ed Boyce proved much like his old antagonists, the Irish miners of Butte: avid more for the warm bricks of hearth, church, tavern, and sodality than for the chill theorems of the revolutionist.

Not Haywood. In a seven-year apprenticeship with Boyce, he had learned his master's flinty, obdurate side rather than Boyce's more gemütlich qualities. Perhaps for just that reason, Haywood now was teamed with Charles Moyer—a more cautious, less flamboyant member of the executive committee—who, on Boyce's recommendation, was elected president by the 1902 convention.

Moyer had grown up on a farm near Ames, Iowa, the town where several decades later Frank Steunenberg got his two years of college education. His mother died in childbirth before she was forty, and her daughter Mary Alice, age fourteen, became the family housekeeper, caring for her six siblings, right down to one-year-old Charlie, while their father managed the 170-acre farm.

Charlie grew up with a "dare-devil disposition." After barely four years of formal education, he left home at age sixteen, putting in a memorable year as a cowboy in Wyoming, where he became a skilled horseman and "crack shot." Like Bill Haywood, Moyer patterned himself on the western cowboy. In 1885, he drove cattle to market in Chicago and stayed on in the booming city by the lake. Still wearing his Stetson and chaps, Moyer hung out in saloons and pool halls, sometimes shooting balls into the pockets with his revolver, explaining to indignant proprietors, "Oh, that's the way we play pool in the West."

Shortly before Christmas 1885, police on Chicago's West Side arrested the twenty-year-old Moyer and his friend John Keating on suspicion of committing several stickups and break-ins. Keating turned coat, implicating Moyer in a number of crimes. Because these constituted his first offense, he drew only a year at the Illinois penitentiary at Joliet. Moyer felt the stigma of his imprisonment acutely and in later years heatedly denied he'd ever done prison time, but the records on that point are unequivocal.

After his release in January 1887, he served as a night clerk at Chicago's Sherman House hotel, then drifted west to South Dakota, where he worked for the Castle Creek Mining Company. Later that year, on a visit to Iowa, he married Bertha Lena Hauser, returning with her to the Black Hills of South Dakota and eventually finding work as a smelter and miner. Joining the young WFM, he rose rapidly through its ranks, becoming president of the Deadwood local in 1897, president of Lead Local no. 2, then district representative on the union's executive board, and finally president in 1902.

Perhaps as a reaction to the wildness of his youth, Moyer proved a cautious, plodding executive, who whenever possible advocated negotiation and arbitration of the union's differences with the mine owners. Soon bad feelings developed between him and the more volatile Haywood.

As Moyer and Haywood launched their partnership, they confronted a different industrial climate from that which had faced Ed Boyce. The mine owners and other capitalists of Colorado had heeded the talk of Socialism at the WFM conventions in 1901 and 1902. Convinced that the federation was now bent on creating in Colorado a Socialist bastion from which neighboring states could be subverted, business leaders determined to beat back the unionists at all costs. In the state elections of 1902, the Republican Party abandoned its recent "fusionist" tactics and sought to restore a defiantly conservative government directly responsive to the political agenda of business and industry.

Its chief instrument was to be the dapper Canon City banker James H. Peabody, who made no secret of his faith in the application of business principles to public affairs. Indeed, he believed that government was like "any other great corporation and its executive officers should be asked to conduct its affairs along similar lines. The people are like stockholders in the corporation and their profit and loss is contingent largely upon the success or failure of the officers charged with the management of the affairs of the corporation."

In November 1902, Peabody was overwhelmingly elected as Colorado's governor. Before long, he drew powerful support from a new statewide organization, the Citizens' Alliance of Colorado, whose thirty thousand members included many corporate, mercantile, and professional men. Its president, James C. Craig, put his fellow Coloradans on notice that the alliance "ardently supported the governor of the State in his patriotic efforts to maintain law, protect property rights and prevent the brutal persecution of workingmen by other workingmen or their leaders, who ignore and trample on all rights except they be those of a union man." The covenant between state government and big business was explicit from the start: Governor Peabody helped establish a Citizens' Alliance branch in his own Canon City.

Ironically enough, on the very day that Peabody was elected, Colorado voters, by the resounding margin of 72,980 to 26,266, approved a constitutional amendment permitting enactment of a law restricting the workday in certain hazardous occupations, like mining and smelting, to eight hours.

The Democratic, Populist, and Republican platforms had all endorsed the amendment—a way of eliminating from the campaign a deeply divisive issue that had bedeviled Colorado politics for a decade. For years, the WFM had argued that working long hours underground was unhealthy and that the gases generated in smelting ore also damaged workers' health. Thus, when the Cripple Creek strike of 1894 was settled, the agreement provided, among other things, that eight hours should constitute a day's work in that camp's gold mines. The WFM then launched a campaign to push a law through the Colorado legislature that would limit all underground work in the state's mines to eight hours. When Republican legislators argued that such legislation would be unconstitutional, the lower house asked the state supreme court for an advisory opinion. The court replied that the legislature couldn't "single out the mining, manufacturing and smelting industries of the State and impose upon them restrictions with reference to the hours of their employees from which other employers of labor are exempt." Such legislation, it held, would be "manifestly in violation of the constitutional inhibition against class legislation." The bill was promptly tabled.

But a year later, Utah's legislature became the first in the nation to pass an eight-hour law, which in 1897 was deemed constitutional by the United States Supreme Court. Legislators friendly to the WFM promptly introduced in Colorado the verbatim text of the Utah law, adding only a penalty clause. But in 1899, the Colorado Supreme Court rapped the legislature on the knuckles for its "defiance" of the advisory judgment. That the Colorado law was closely patterned after the Utah legislation and sanctioned by the U.S. Supreme Court was beside the point, the Colorado justices held. "This act," they said, "is an unwarrantable interference with, and infringes, the right of both the employer and employee in making contracts relating to a purely private business, in which no possible injury to the public can result."

Given the court's insistence that the law was unconstitutional, the only avenue left open to its proponents was an amendment to the Colorado constitution. Under heavy pressure from an aroused populace, all three political parties supported such a measure. The legislature passed the amendment, and on November 4, 1902, more than 72 percent of those voting adopted it.

But the state's mining and smelting industry only redoubled its efforts to block the measure. John C. Osgood, board chairman of the Colorado Fuel and Iron Company, called the health issue a "subterfuge" to disguise the amendment's true goal: socialistic leveling. "It is a gross injustice to the miners themselves to put all of them on the same level," he said. "Some are more rapid workers and can do much faster work than others. I know of many miners who are educating their sons to take better stations in life than their fathers enjoyed. These men are willing to work overtime, if necessary, to secure money for this purpose."

When skeptics wondered whether this was truly the source of the owners' opposition, a bulletin issued by the employers conceded that they were also worried that an eight-hour standard would add to the costs of production. When the critics suggested that these relatively modest increases might come out of the company's dividends, the owners replied: "Dividends are as the breath of life to growing industries. Every investor demands a fair return for his money; if he does not get it he will withdraw and invest elsewhere."

So, notwithstanding the Republican Party's endorsement of the amendment at election time, once in office Governor Peabody rapidly backed away from it, warning against "radical and far reaching legislation, fundamental changes in our laws, with resultant doubt, uncertainty, litigation and chaos."

Not surprisingly, given the tenacity of its opponents, the bill failed to secure passage in the 1903 session. When, a year later, it managed to get through the Senate, the state's attorney general, Nathan C. Miller, promptly declared it unconstitutional because corporations themselves could not be made criminally liable. Officers of the corporations and their agents could be held responsible, but they had been omitted from the bill's penalty clause. Friends of labor promptly charged that this defect in the law's drafting was the work of legislators beholden to the mining corporations, that it had been implanted as a Trojan horse to render it ineffectual once more. Governor Peabody was importuned to summon a special session of the legislature to remedy the defect, but he declined. Writing to John Osgood, who had helped frustrate the legislation, Peabody indicated that his stance on the eight-hour law was designed to "preserve the commercial and industrial enterprises of Colorado from assault and annihilation." Summing up these months of futility, the muckraker Ray Stannard Baker wrote: "Rarely has there been in this country a more brazen, conscienceless defeat of the will of the people."

This blunt refusal to enact eight-hour legislation was a major factor behind the strikes that beset Colorado during Peabody's administration. Haywood, who felt passionately on the issue, used it with great skill. A labor reporter recalled his incendiary appearances before working-class audiences: "He had tremendous magnetism. Huge frame, one blazing eye, voice filling the hall. When he shouted, 'Eight hours of work, eight hours of play, eight hours of sleep—*eight dollars a day!*' that last line came like a clap of thunder."

Elizabeth Gurley Flynn, later a labor organizer and herself no mean speaker, likened Haywood's oratory to "sledge hammer blows, simple and direct." She credited him with teaching her "how to speak to workers...to use short words and short sentences, to repeat the same thought in different words if I saw that the audience did not understand." Ralph Chaplin, long Haywood's best friend, said, "Speaking was his special gift. Only Debs was his equal. Few who ever heard Bill's great voice could ever forget it."

But what mesmerized working-class audiences wasn't just a resonant voice or plainspoken eloquence but his sheer physical presence. Reporters confronting Haywood for the first time often described him as a giant. One called him "a powerfully built man...big head and a square jaw...with the physical strength of an ox"; another said he was "tall, tremendous, broad in chest and shoulders, erect and displaying physical powers which dwarfed [other men]." A Chicago social worker called him "a great towering hulk of a man." But when he was examined by prison authorities, his height proved quite ordinary, five eleven and a quarter; his weight, in 1906, was a considerable though scarcely gargantuan 236 pounds. Yet there was something in the heft of those meaty shoulders, in the fierce blaze of that single eye, that made him seem to loom over mere mortals.

Under Big Bill's forceful leadership, the WFM moved to augment its already considerable bargaining power. The first years of the twentieth century had been good ones for the federation. Between 1900 and 1902, it had chartered more new locals (fifty-five) and recruited more new members (ten thousand) than it had at any time in its history. By 1903, it could boast between thirty-two thousand (the figure given by its enemies) and forty thousand (the number cited by its officers) members in some two hundred chapters scattered across a half dozen states—with the heaviest concentration in Colorado, Nevada, Idaho, and Arizona—and parts of Canada. (On each membership card appeared the slogan "Labor produces all wealth. Wealth belongs to the producer thereof.") Now the federation projected organizing campaigns in several western states where it had little or no presence: Missouri, Arkansas, Kansas, Minnesota, Michigan, and Wisconsin. It was even considering extending its jurisdiction into Mexico. Still predominantly a union of English-speaking laborers, it was beginning to recruit Italian, Greek, Finnish, and Slavic workers and to translate its ritual into their languages. Given the substantial danger of injury in the mines, the federation devoted special attention to the establishment of union hospitals, as well as to development of health, unemployment, and death benefits. Finally, with Haywood's characteristic zeal, it set out to establish an industrywide federation in line with Ed Boyce's notion of "industrial unionism."

The ores dug by the WFM's miners were reduced to metal by the nonunionized mill and smelter workers of Colorado, who were grossly underpaid and overworked. Smelting activity in Colorado and throughout the West had, since 1899, been dominated by the American Smelting and Refining Company, known to its critics as the smelter trust. ASARCO proved relentlessly hostile to organized labor's efforts to improve the wages and working conditions of smelter men. While union miners worked eight hours to earn $3.50, the men tending the smelter furnaces were at their labors twelve hours, seven days a week, earning as little as $1.80. In the smelters, subject to the ruinous effects of lead poisoning, the men tied damp rags over their noses and mouths in a vain effort to keep out the lethal dust. Once out in the fresh air, many were so impoverished they and their families had to live in tents through the icy Colorado winters.

Haywood and Moyer sent WFM organizers into the state's reduction mills and smelters. In July 1903—weeks after the state legislature adjourned without passing the eight-hour law—members of Mill and Smeltermen's Union no. 93 voted to strike ASARCO's two Denver-area smelters, the Globe and the Grant. Using imported strikebreakers, the company reopened the Grant by September. But the Globe, which the company considered out-moded, was allowed to "freeze" so badly it was never fired up again. For years thereafter, the 352-foot Grant smokestack towered over Globeville—annexed by Denver in 1903—where it was laughingly known as "Bill Haywood's Mon-ument."

But the most bitter mill workers' strike came in Colorado City, a "forlorn little industrial town of tents, tin houses, huts and hovels" at the foot of Pikes Peak and just down the road from Colorado Springs, the lush residential community, sometimes called Newport in the Rockies, where many mining company managers had built luxurious homes. There the employers had responded to the WFM's organizing campaign by hiring Pinkerton detectives to smoke out the unionists, who were promptly fired. At first they were discharged in dribs and drabs, but in February 1903, the Standard mill fired twenty-three suspected union members on one day, bringing their total to forty-one. The Colorado City Mill and Smeltermen's Union no. 125—a con-stituent union of the WFM—countered with a strike against the Standard, Telluride, and Portland mills. When tensions between union and nonunion workers grew, the governor sent in six companies of the Colorado National Guard, which protected corporate property, broke up picket lines, searched the homes of union men, and escorted nonunion men (or strikebreakers, as the union called them) to and from work.

Under heavy public pressure, the governor called a meeting in his office to resolve the matter. After thirteen hours of negotiation, Haywood and Moyer reached agreement with representatives of the Telluride and Portland mills and the picket lines around those mills were withdrawn. But Charles M. MacNeill, vice president of the United States Reduction and Refining Com-pany, which owned the Standard mill, walked out of the talks, refusing to negotiate with men who were not his employees. The spruce little MacNeill struck Haywood as the kind of employer "who had never in his life spoken to a workingman except to give orders." Personally—viscerally—offended, Haywood blamed "this wretched little autocrat" for all that followed.

What followed was one of the epic labor struggles in American history: the battle of Cripple Creek. If industrial unionism had any meaning, it was in just such a situation, when the Colorado City mill workers desperately needed help from the Western Federation's miners to get on their feet. The Cripple Creek mining district, forty miles to the north, produced the gold ore that was reduced in Colorado City. Many of Cripple Creek's miners were reluctant to strike, asking why they should go out just to help a bunch of mill men in Colorado City. But at the urging of the federation's leadership (notably Haywood), the gold miners of Cripple Creek struck on March 17, cutting off the supply of ore to the scabs at the Standard mill.

As his stocks dwindled over the next two weeks, MacNeill signaled that he was ready to deal. Charles Moyer—who apparently never had much stomach for the strike—took a surprisingly conciliatory position, evidently the focus of his first major difference with Bill Haywood. Waiving many of the WFM demands, he gave the Standard until May 18 to reemploy its fired union workers. News of the settlement was greeted in Cripple Creek with the ringing of bells, the blowing of mine whistles, and the crash of giant firecrackers, but the fragile agreement soon foundered on MacNeill's stubborn refusal to reinstate all the fired workers. With Haywood's distrust of Moyer's compromise now vindicated, the union secretary pressed ahead with the strike. On August 10, 1903, some 3,500 Cripple Creek miners went out again, virtually closing down the camp's mining industry, not to mention all of the Colorado City reduction plants.

Five days into the strike, Haywood spoke at a union picnic in Cripple Creek's Pinnacle Park. Hugely enjoying himself, Haywood bantered with representatives of the Mine Owners Association, the Citizens' Alliance, and the Pinkerton agency whom he recognized in the crowd. "The mine owners have said they would finish the El Paso tunnel themselves," he taunted. "I know there are many of you here who will lend them your cast-off overalls." This drew a derisive hoot from his audience, who knew all too well the rigors of underground work. But when he urged them to stand with the WFM until the strike was won, they cheered and stamped their feet, reflecting an impression in union ranks that it was only a matter of weeks before MacNeill and his allies would capitulate before the united might of the federation.

This confidence was rooted in the conviction that the federation solidly controlled the Cripple Creek district, a spatter of small towns and hamlets clinging to a "rough, gaunt and broken" spur of the Rockies eighty-five miles southwest of Denver. Ever since 1894—when the union had triumphed in the first Cripple Creek strike with decisive support from the Populist governor, David "Bloody Bridles" Waite—the federation had consolidated its hold on both the district and Teller County, in which it was located. By 1903, Sheriff H. M. Robertson, his undersheriff, and the coroner were federation members. In Cripple Creek—and the communities of Victor, Independence, Goldfield, and Anaconda—the WFM had installed its own men as aldermen, town marshals, police magistrates, jailers, and police. So firmly entrenched was the union in these towns that juries couldn't be found that would convict a union man of any serious offense.

With this kind of backing, the WFM had been able to drive out many nonunion miners. In the fall of 1901, for example, a notice had been posted all over Cripple Creek warning that, after September 15, "anyone working in and around the mines, mills or power plants of the Cripple Creek district, who can not show a card of membership in good standing of some local union of the Western Federation of Miners, will be considered a scab and an enemy to us, himself and the community at large, and will be treated as such." Three days later, another notice warned: "The 15th of September is near at hand; that time of grace has expired. You have had two pay days in which to decide whether you are for us or against us—there is no middle ground." None of the mines was entirely unionized and no mass deportations took place, but there were many cases in which nonunion men were quietly advised to "hit the trail" and "keep on going." Most of them did.

But Bill Haywood's confidence, and that of his lieutenants, hadn't taken into account the growing strength of the Citizens' Alliance, particularly when backed by the state militia. Within days of the strike's inception, alliance members visited the town's shopkeepers, warning them it would be most unwise to extend further credit to strikers. Soon thereafter, most merchants announced that they would sell goods for cash only. The WFM countered by establishing its own cooperative stores in Cripple Creek, Victor, Anaconda, and Goldfield, supplying them with boxcars of food purchased in Denver. Nonetheless, the enormous clout of the alliance was plain for all to see.

The Cripple Creek mines began to reopen with hundreds of scabs hauled in from Minnesota and Missouri. Violence flared between the newcomers and the union, culminating in an assault on a nonunion worker at the Golden Cycle mine. Thomas M. Stewart, fifty, who'd been building a fence around the mine, was severely beaten, then shot in the shoulder by five masked men who denounced him as a scab. About the same time, others assaulted a justice of the peace said to favor the mine owners and torched a shaft house of the Sunset-Eclipse mine.

The mine owners took advantage of these incidents—unionists contended that the owners fabricated some and exaggerated others—to call for state troops. Sheriff Robertson, no doubt influenced by his federation membership, insisted he had the situation in hand. So the owners appealed to Governor Peabody, complaining of a "reign of terror" in Cripple Creek that required troops "for the preservation of property, peace and good order."

Peabody seemed willing to send the National Guard but contended that the state couldn't afford to maintain it in Cripple Creek for any period. On September 3, the Cripple Creek mine owners agreed that if the governor sent the necessary guard units they'd provide the funds to maintain them, at least for the time being. The troops, as well as those who provided food and other supplies, would be paid in certificates of indebtedness against the state— in effect, bearer bonds—carrying 4 percent interest and payable in four years. These certificates would be cashed by the Mine Owners Association and held until the state legislature ordered them paid. If the legislature paid them off at their maturity, the mine owners would have loaned the state the money for four years. If the legislature failed to honor the commitment,

I

Frank Steunenberg, ex-governor of Idaho, bank president, and sheep-raiser, pictured here—as always, without a tie—shortly before his assassination. After four years in the state house from 1896 to 1899, he left office under a cloud because of his suppression of labor unrest in the Coeur d'Alene mining district.

The Caldwell Cornet Band, led by the famed "musicologist" Professor A. T. Gordon, posed here in late 1905, a few months before Steunenberg's assassination. They stand at the town's most prestigious intersection, Seventh and Main, looking toward the Oregon Short Line depot. On the left is Frank Steunenberg's Caldwell Banking and Trust Company; on the right, the Saratoga Hotel.

The staff of the Caldwell Tribune *in 1890, four years after the Steunenberg brothers bought it. The three journalistic Steunenbergs— A.K., Frank, and Charles ("Pete")—sit left to right in the front row. Frank was then twenty-nine.*

3

4

Seven members of Caldwell's Bachelors' Club gathered on New Year's Day 1889. A. K. Steunenberg, Frank's still unmarried brother, is seated at left in the front row. On the right is haberdasher Mike Devers, whom the Tribune *reported was ardently pursued by the "aesthetic widow," Mrs. A. C. Gilloohey.*

A. K. Steunenberg, the most entrepreneurial of the six Steunenberg brothers, cashier at the family bank, pictured here not long before Frank's assassination. Married by now, he lived in a Colonial Revival mansion in Caldwell's best neighborhood.

5

Eveline Belle Steunenberg, Frank's wife, had been a founder of Caldwell's Presbyterian Church and a leading member of its congregation, "jewelled with Christian virtues," when she switched over to the town's tiny Seventh-Day Adventist Church.

6

Five of the six Steunenberg brothers gathered one day not long before Steunenberg's death for this photograph; bottom to top and left to right: Frank, A.K., John, Charles ("Pete"), and Will. Charles dealt cards down at the Saratoga. John and Will made, repaired, and sold shoes, calling themselves "fitters of feet."

Frank Steunenberg's house, a mix of Queen Anne and American Colonial styles, several days after the assassin's bomb obliterated the gate, the left gatepost, and much of the fence. The windows, broken by the explosion, had been repaired by the time this photograph was taken.

9

James McParland of Pinkerton's National Detective Agency, whom Clarence Darrow once called "the greatest detective in the West," was averse to photographers, and his bodyguards broke the cameras of several who pursued him. But he clearly posed for this rare picture by Boise's Horace Myers during the Haywood trial.

McParland's rival, Wilson S. Swain, was northwestern manager of the Thiel Detective Service, based in Spokane. He claimed to have been dispatched to Boise by the northern Idaho mine owners after Steunenberg's death. McParland ultimately prevailed in the bitter contest between the two detectives and their agencies.

10

Thomas Hogan, aka Harry Orchard, Steunenberg's confessed assassin, as he looked shortly after his arrest in Caldwell on January 1, 1906. Wearing a three-piece suit and a bowler hat, posing as an itinerant sheep dealer, Hogan had been living for several weeks in Room 19 of the Saratoga Hotel.

11

Steve Adams, who authorities contended was an accomplice of Orchard's in some of his bloodiest crimes, became the focus of a fierce struggle between the prosecution and defense. Adams had spent fifteen years knocking about the West, dressing beef, sawing lumber, and mining lead and silver, before allegedly becoming a union assassin.

12

PINKERTON'S NATIONAL DETECTIVE AGENCY.

FOUNDED BY ALLAN PINKERTON 1850.

ROB'T A. PINKERTON, NEW YORK.
WM. A. PINKERTON, CHICAGO.
PRINCIPALS.

GEO. D BANGS,
GENERAL MANAGER
New York.

ALLAN PINKERTON,
ASS'T GENERAL MANAGER,
New York

—OFFICES.—

EASTERN DIVISION.
JOHN CORNISH, MANAGER,
New York.

NEW YORK	57 Broadway.
BOSTON	30 Court Street.
MONTREAL	Merchants Bank Building.
BUFFALO	Fidelity Building.
PHILADELPHIA	441 Chestnut Street.
PITTSBURGH	Second National Bank Building.
CLEVELAND	Garfield Building.

ATTORNEYS.
GUTHRIE, CRAVATH & HENDERSON,
New York.

REPRESENTING
THE AMERICAN BANKERS' ASSOCIATION.

MIDDLE DIVISION.
E. S. GAYLOR, MANAGER,
Chicago.

CHICAGO	201 Fifth Avenue.
ST. PAUL	Manhattan Building.
MINNEAPOLIS	Metropolitan Life Ins. Co. Bldg
KANSAS CITY	622 Main Street.
ST. LOUIS	Wainwright Building.
CINCINNATI	Mercantile Library Building.

WESTERN DIVISION.
JAS. McPARLAND, MANAGER,
Denver.

DENVER	Opera House Bloc
OMAHA	New York Life Buildin
PORTLAND, ORE.	Marquam Bloc
SEATTLE	Alaska Buildir
SPOKANE	Rockery Buildir
LOS ANGELES	Wilcox Buildir
SAN FRANCISCO	James Flood Bl

SPOKANE,
ROOKERY BUILDING.

G. J. HASSON, S.

$2,000.00 REWARD

Governor Frank R. Gooding, of the State of Idaho, will pay a reward of Two Thousand Dollars for the arrest, or information leading to the arrest of

L. J. SIMPKINS, alias J. SIMMONS

Simpkins, alias Simmons, is charged with the murder of Ex-Governor Frank J Steunenberg, of Idaho, at Caldwell, Idaho, on the evening of December 30th, 1905, and a warrant has been issued for his arrest.

DESCRIPTION:

Name	L. J. Simpkins.
Alias	J. Simmons.
Age	40 years.
Height	5 ft. 8 1-2 or 9 in.
Weight	180 pounds.
Build	Heavy, thick chested, slightly stoop shouldered.
Eyes	Blue, with decided cast, shifty glance, very peculiar look.
Nose	Large, slightly crooked.
Teeth	Large, prominent upper front teeth.
Hair	Dark.
Mustache	Heavy, dark and tawny.
Beard	Dark and heavy; may be smooth faced.
Complexion	Medium.

L. J. SIMPKINS

L. J. SIMPKINS

When last seen wore dark gray coat; gray trousers of cheap appearance; black fedora hat with high crown and large brim; long black overcoat; white lay down collar; medium colored four-in-hand tie.

Is member of the Executive Committee of the Western Federation of Miners.

If located, arrest and notify any of the above listed offices by telegraph or telephone.

Pinkerton's National Detective Agency,

306 Rookery Building, Spokane, Washington.

Day Phone Main 234.   Night Phone Main 6647.

Or

G. J. HASSON, Superintendent.

Spokane. Wash., April 5, 1906.

L. J. Simpkins, who as "J. Simmons" had accompanied Orchard to Caldwell but left town 13
before the assassination, remained a mysterious figure. The state of Idaho and several detective agencies conducted a massive manhunt for Simpkins, but he was never found. Some skeptics believed that he was actually a Pinkerton agent provocateur.

When Frank Steunenberg appealed for federal troops in April 1899 to put down labor unrest in the Coeur d'Alene mining district, the War Department chose Brigadier General Henry Clay Merriam to lead the expedition. His actions there opened him to charges that he'd used U.S. military power to "browbeat" and "repress" the aggrieved miners.

Merriam counted on the Twenty-fourth Infantry, one of the army's four "colored" regiments, to restore order. The Twenty-fourth was widely regarded as one of the best outfits among those left in the continental United States during the Spanish-American War, but Merriam may have summoned "colored" troops precisely because the unruly miners were white, ensuring that his men wouldn't bond with the "rioters."

Frank Steunenberg was swept into office as Idaho's governor in 1896, when William Jennings Bryan was the Democratic-Populist candidate for president. The young lady at right carried this banner in a Boise parade during the Bryan-Steunenberg campaign calling for "Free Silver"—the inflationary minting of silver coins.

16

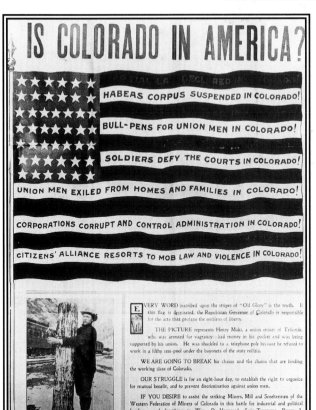

Western enthusiasm for Bryan's crusade faded after William McKinley's victory. In Colorado, Governor James H. Peabody's administration, aided by the mine owners, wrested control of the mining district from the union and deported many dissidents. This poster, designed by Bill Haywood, expressed the miners' outrage.

17

The investigation of Steunenberg's murder was undertaken by Idaho's new Republican governor, Frank R. Gooding. A stout man with a sunburned face whose opponents derided him as "an uncouth sheep-herder," he proved a formidable opponent for labor.

F. R. GOODING.
Idaho

18

As U.S. attorney for Idaho, Fremont Wood had prosecuted some of the Coeur d'Alene miners in 1892, but he had such a reputation as a fair-minded judge that his assignment to handle the Haywood trial was welcomed by all sides.

19

*This photograph of Charles H. Moyer, William D. Haywood, and George A.
Pettibone—the three principal defendants in the trials growing out of Steunenberg's
murder—was taken on the lawn outside the Ada County jail, where they'd been held
for sixteen months awaiting trial. Haywood stands in his characteristic pose, with his
blind and cloudy right eye turned away from the camera.*

Boasting the squarest jaw in American politics, William E. Borah was the darling of Idaho's Republican voters, and especially of his many female admirers. Elected U.S. senator by Idaho's legislature in February 1907, he helped prosecute Haywood and endured his own trial on charges of timber fraud before taking up his seat in Washington.

James H. Hawley, chief special prosecutor in the Haywood case, was the dean of Idaho's bar. With little of the eastern advocates' polish and erudition, Hawley would slouch in a chair with his boots on the tabletop, chewing on a toothpick, while taking ample liberties with grammar and syntax.

Clarence S. Darrow of Chicago, Haywood's counsel, had not yet achieved the national renown as a defender of the unpopular and the dispossessed that he would achieve with the "monkey trial" of 1925. Pictured here a few years before the Haywood trial, Darrow was a formidable courtroom performer, rivaling Borah in his oratorical skills.

23

Edmund F. Richardson, Darrow's colleague in the Haywood defense, was one of the most celebrated criminal lawyers in the Rocky Mountain states, and his Denver firm had long been on retainer to the Western Federation of Miners. Tall, lean, and saturnine, he was a proud and prickly man who deeply resented Darrow's celebrity.

24

The core of the prosecution team was, left to right, Borah; Owen M. Van Duyn, county attorney of Canyon County (top); William A. Stone, representing the Steunenberg family and other Caldwell interests; and Hawley.

The core of the defense team was, left to right, Edgar Wilson, Leon O. Whitsell, John F. Nugent, Fred Miller, Darrow, and Richardson.

(Place of the famous Moyer-Haywood-Pettibone Trial).

The Ada County courthouse, where the Haywood trial was conducted, is shown here on a postcard sold as a souvenir of the trial. The inset is a scene of Judge Fremont Wood's courtroom.

The Haywood jury, left to right: (seated) Samuel D. Gilman, J. A. Robertson, George Powell, Thomas B. Gess (foreman), Daniel Clark; (standing) Levi Smith, O. V. Sebern, A. P. Burns, Samuel F. Russell, H. F. Messecar, Finley McBean, and Lee Schrivener.

A courtroom scene during the Haywood trial. Clarence Darrow (standing) questions a witness. The trio at right are, left to right, Nugent, Haywood, and Richardson.

Another courtroom scene during the trial. The participants are (1) Harry Orchard on the witness stand; (2) John Murphy, WFM staff attorney; (3) with the white beard, William H. Miner, Haywood's father-in-law; (4) Henrietta Haywood, Haywood's youngest daughter; (5) with the large flowered hat, Vernie Haywood, Haywood's oldest daughter; (6) Mary Carruthers, Haywood's half sister; (7) Leon Whitsell; (8) Peter Breen; (9) Darrow; (10) Mrs. Etta Carruthers, Haywood's mother; (11) Haywood; (12) Nugent; (13) partially hidden, Richardson; (14) Harry Crane, Statesman; (15) Martin Egan, AP; (16) William Kennedy, AP.

When Orchard took the witness stand on June 4, he'd been transformed from the unshaven, ill-kempt, shifty-eyed felon of sixteen months before. One reporter thought he "might be a Sunday school superintendent."

31

32

Harry Orchard (3) being transported from the state penitentiary to court by (1) Warden Eugene L. Whitney; (2) Rudie Barthell, gunslinger partner of Bob Meldrum; (4) Daniel W. Ackley, guard at the penitentiary; (5) Edgar Hawley, son of James Hawley; (6) Charles Siringo.

The Idanha, Boise's grand hotel, was headquarters for the trial community. Governor Gooding, James McParland, a clutch of other Pinkertons, and much of the press corps lived, ate, drank, and traded the latest trial gossip there.

Charles A. Siringo, the Pinkertons' "Cowboy Detective," served as McParland's bodyguard during the Haywood trial. In this picture, he is shown with his trademark black Stetson, his Colt .45, and his carved walking stick, which concealed a twenty-inch throwing knife. The inscription on the original reads "To Harry Orchard, Compliments of Yours Truly Chas. A. Siringo."

Calvin Cobb, the editor-publisher of the Idaho Daily Statesman, *lived in a green bungalow with one of the city's first private tennis courts. He is shown here some years before the trial with his wife, Fannie, and their children, Margaret and Lyon.*

Calvin Cobb at the time of the trial. Boise's preeminent newspaperman and a confidant of Roosevelt's, he shuttled back and forth between Boise and Washington, bearing messages and warnings between the president and the governor.

President Roosevelt and Gifford Pinchot, the chief forester of the United States, chat on the deck of a Mississippi steamer boat in October 1907. Pinchot came west that year to sell his conservation policies to Idahoans, but found himself in an uncomfortable position when Roosevelt's ally Borah was indicted for timber fraud.

37

Hugo Münsterberg, a protégé of William James and his successor as director of the Harvard Psychology Laboratory. At age forty-four, Münsterberg was, after James, America's best-known psychologist. He'd come to Boise at the summons of S.S. McClure of McClure's Magazine to study Harry Orchard.

38

Ethel Barrymore made a one night stand in Boise on June 24, 1907, playing Madame Trentoni in Clyde Fitch's Captain Jinks of the Horse Marines. *After lunching with Calvin Cobb, the dazzling young actress visited the courtroom, where she upstaged Clarence Darrow as he opened the defense case. Falling under her spell, Charlie Siringo escorted her out to the penitentiary to meet Harry Orchard, who reminded her of "a respectable grocer."*

Walter Johnson is shown here in the uniform of the Kids of Weiser, seventy-five miles northwest of Boise, for whom he pitched in 1906–1907. Darrow and the trial's press corps flocked to his games. Soon the feats of this sensational young pitcher attracted major league attention, and before the trial was over, he'd been snatched up by the Washington Senators.

Two months after the Haywood trial ended, William Borah won acquittal in Boise's feder-
al court on charges of timber fraud. Boise's Columbian Band played "Hail to the Chief" as
Borah stood on the steel canopy above the hotel entrance and acknowledged the cheers of his
supporters clogging the street below.

the mine owners would have paid for the troops out of their companies' treasuries. Whether the guardsmen were bought outright or merely rented, the arrangement left them—in the words of the *Army and Navy Journal*—"in the relation of hired men to the mine operators and morally suspended their function of state military guardians of the public peace." Concluded the *Journal,* scarcely a radical organ: "It was a rank perversion of the whole theory and purpose of the National Guard and more likely to incite disorder than prevent it."

The troops began arriving in Cripple Creek on September 4, reaching a force of a thousand by month's end. According to one Socialist correspondent, they were largely "bar-room bums from Denver, hangers on in the gambling houses, with a sprinkling of immature high school and college youngsters." They were commanded by Sherman M. Bell, who, in addition to managing important Cripple Creek mining interests, served as the state's adjutant general, a post he took up only after the mine owners agreed to supplement his $1,800 annual salary so as to bring it up to $5,000.

Of all the players in Colorado's melodrama, Bell was the most grandiloquent. Once a Rough Rider in Theodore Roosevelt's famous regiment—the president called him "the gamest man in a game regiment"—he had maintained close ties with his old colonel. In Roosevelt's 1900 campaign for the vice presidency, Bell led a detachment of Rough Riders providing security. When a mob of angry miners attacked the candidate in Victor, Colorado, that September, Bell was given much of the credit for beating back the assault. His eyes blazing, he waded into the mob with such zeal that Roosevelt shouted, "Sherman, I am still Colonel. Get back!" Roosevelt is said to have remarked later, "My chief fear on that distressing occasion was that Bell would begin killing people."

If his campaigns against the federation sometimes took the guise of a holy war, Sherman Bell readily attributed its direction to the sacred trinity of "Me, God, and Governor Peabody." Whatever his military skills—and they were often called into question—Bell had a knack for vivid expression. When asked how he planned to proceed against the WFM, he said, "I came to do up this damned anarchistic federation." Or again: "My orders were to 'wipe 'em off the face of the earth.'" Or again: "Kill 'em—when one of 'em pokes his head up, slug it—shoot 'em down—exterminate 'em." Or about his military principles: "Military necessity recognizes no laws, either civil or social." Those who read such statements in the public prints or saw photographs of the general in his custom-made uniform of gold, lace, cords, and tassels (said to have cost a thousand dollars), his left hand tucked into his tunic, might have been inclined to dismiss him as a smallish man with Napoleonic delusions, a "modern d'Artagnan" given to "flamboyant garrulity and gasconading swagger," but some who'd looked into Sherm Bell's cold blue eyes had described them as brimming with "menace" and suggestive of "deadly and inexorable force."

As soon as the guardsmen arrived, they began rounding up union miners and their sympathizers—among them a county commissioner, a justice of the peace, and the staff of a pro-union newspaper, the *Victor Record*—incarcerating them without charge in Goldfield's old wooden jail. When the union filed habeas corpus petitions for four local leaders, Sherman Bell brushed them aside with a mordant quip: "Habeas corpus be damned, we'll give 'em post mortems!"

One of the most telling lines of the Colorado struggle, that phrase was often linked with another curt dismissal of legal technicalities, spoken by Major Thomas McClelland, the judge advocate of Colorado's guard: "To hell with the Constitution; we are not following the Constitution!"* Given the attitude toward America's basic document reflected in such remarks, is it any wonder that Haywood came to have so little respect for what he called "capitalist-made laws"? Some years later, he would say, "I despise the law and I am not a law-abiding citizen. And more than that, no Socialist can be a law-abiding citizen."

When the four miners' cases came up for a hearing, Sherman Bell ordered the petitioners escorted to court by a full company of infantry with fixed bayonets, while other troops ringed the courthouse and sharpshooters loomed on neighboring rooftops. After Justice W. P. Seeds ordered the miners released from custody, General John Chase stood to tell the court: "Acting under the orders of the commander-in-chief [Governor Peabody], I must at this time decline to obey the order of the court." The court adjourned and the prisoners returned to jail, but late that evening the governor shrank from a confrontation with the judiciary and ordered them released.

By mid-fall, the conflict had spread from Cripple Creek and Colorado City to Telluride and Idaho Springs, with twenty thousand coal and metal miners on strike across the state. So extensive were these work stoppages, so fierce the emotions, so violent the tactics on all sides, that the press took to calling the converging battles between 1902 and 1904 the "Colorado Labor Wars." In retrospect, that rubric seems accurate enough. Rarely in American history have labor and capital faced off in such a prolonged, bitter, and bloody confrontation. If the United States has ever approached outright class war, it was probably in Colorado during the first years of this century.

In Telluride, an important gold and silver mining center two hundred miles southwest of Denver, the battle against the union was led by Bulkeley Wells, manager of the Smuggler-Union, the district's largest and richest gold mine. Born to a wealthy Boston family, Wells had spent several years in Colorado as a boy but returned to Boston for his education. After graduating from Harvard—where he was a track star and club man—he married Grace

---

* It is interesting to compare this remark with one made in 1886 by George Emery, a prominent member of Chicago's Citizens Association, with regard to the Haymarket defendants: "Law! I care nothing for law! They shall be hung whether it is lawful or not!" (Avrich, *Haymarket*, 283).

Livermore, the daughter of Colonel Thomas Livermore, a Boston attorney who had made a fortune in mining investments (among them the Calumet and Hecla Copper Company in Michigan and Telluride's Smuggler-Union).

Just as Bostonians had played a major role in financing and directing the China trade, so now they were heavy investors in western mining. If most Massachusetts attorneys and bankers were content to clip their coupons in the comforting shadow of Beacon Hill, Bulkeley Wells hungered for the genuine western experience. After brief jobs in eastern manufacturing and railroading, in 1896 he went to Colorado Springs as Colorado representative —as well as vice president and managing director—of Livermore's New England Exploration Company of Boston. In his leisure time, "Buck" was a popular figure among Colorado's spirited young married set. Darkly handsome with a full head of lustrous hair, large brown eyes, and an aquiline nose, he was a superb tournament polo player and an active member of the Rocky Mountain Harvard Club, the Denver Club, and the Denver Country Club.

Then on November 19, 1902—during a WFM strike against the Smuggler-Union—the mine's manager, a "forceful, aggressive, no-nonsense" Englishman named Arthur L. Collins, was playing cards with several friends by his own fireside when someone stepped onto his porch and blew him away with a single shotgun blast. Given the way he died, the mine's directors did not have an easy time finding a replacement until Buck Wells, the company's secretary, volunteered to take his place. So in December 1902 this "damned, pretty, young red-cheeked Eastern dude from Harvard"—as one skeptic called him—left his polo ponies, his clubs, his socially prominent wife, and his four children behind and went far into "the hills" to run Telluride's most embattled mine.

Friends feared for him, but Wells seemed to thrive on the notion that his life was in danger. He let it be known that he had with him at home—the same management residence in nearby Pandora where Collins had been shot —a few friends who were "handy with rifles" and "chain lightning on the draw." When the mill men of Telluride went on strike in September 1903 seeking an eight-hour day, local businessmen asked the governor to send the National Guard. The governor balked, complaining as he had in Cripple Creek that the state lacked the funds, so Wells mobilized the bankers and mine owners of Telluride to pay the troops' salaries and upkeep just as the Cripple Creek mine owners had. That winter, Wells went a step further, recruiting among the mine owners, managers, bankers, and merchants of Telluride his own Troop A, First Squadron Cavalry of Colorado's National Guard; early in 1904 the governor commissioned him its captain and put him in charge of the Telluride guardsmen.

Through that year, the dashing young cavalry officer, in his splendid blue-and-gold uniform, was in the forefront of the fight against the union, carrying out dozens of arrests and several major deportations of Telluride unionists. When the governor withdrew the guard, Wells—now just the dashing young mine manager—assembled the Telluride Citizens' Alliance, rounded up sixty more union men and sympathizers, imprisoned them in a vacant store overnight, then ran them out of town.

Wells also made heavy use of an ad hoc gathering of enforcers and gunmen who'd flocked to the Colorado mining country as the shooting began. Foremost among them were a legendary gunslinger named Robert D. Meldrum and his sidekick, Rudie Barthell.

Barthell looked like "a college freshman, having a smooth yellow face, a big nose and a swagger." Meldrum was widely known as Hair Trigger Bob for his habit of shooting men—armed and unarmed—on the smallest provocation. The wooden grips on his .44 Colt revolver bore fourteen notches, each representing a man he'd taken down. A cocky little fellow—barely five foot six and 140 pounds, with icy gray eyes glaring above a flamboyant mustache—he was especially truculent when drunk, which was often. He suffered no penalties for his gunplay since most of it had been performed in the employ of law enforcement agencies or corporate clients. Formerly the town marshal of Dixon, Wyoming, a community notorious for its six-shooter free-for-alls, he'd worked of late for Colorado mine owners. Indeed, notches thirteen and fourteen were added to his gun during the Telluride skirmishing. He'd also teamed for a time with the notorious gunman, and sometime Pinkerton, Tom Horn. Meldrum was thus a classic example of that romantic but often misunderstood figure exemplified by the protagonist of Owen Wister's *The Virginian*, the seemingly free-spirited gunfighter who, in his lethal defense of property rights, played such a large role in imposing a new industrial and corporate order on the rambunctious West.

When the National Guard was called back again that spring, Wells donned his uniform once more, took Meldrum and Barthell with him as orderlies, and continued his arrests and deportations under martial law. So successful was this chameleonlike performance that eventually, when Governor Peabody grew tired of Sherman Bell's histrionics, he named Bulkeley Wells to succeed Bell as adjutant general.

That winter the mood had grown uglier still in Cripple Creek. On November 12 and 16, spikes were pulled from tracks along the Florence and Cripple Creek Railroad in an apparent attempt to wreck a train carrying strikebreakers to nonunion mines. On November 21, a superintendent and a shift boss descending in a cage into the shaft of the Vindicator mine were killed by an explosion. Two months later, another cage was drawn into the wheel in the shaft of the Independence mine, horribly mangling all but one of sixteen men in the cage. In all three of these incidents, employers and union workers blamed one another.

But these episodes were dwarfed by what happened the next spring at the Independence depot, a dank and gloomy spot "peculiarly suited to the perpetration of crime and deeds of darkness." At 2:15 a.m. on June 6, 1904, twenty-seven nonunion workers from the night shift at the Findley mine were waiting for a Florence and Cripple Creek train to take them home. As the whistle of the approaching engine was heard, a tremendous explosion wrecked the station, killing thirteen of the strikebreakers immediately, grievously injuring another six. So powerful was the blast that arms, legs, and other body parts were scattered for several hundred yards around the station. Investigators determined that the explosion had been caused by 150–200 pounds of dynamite placed beneath the station platform and set off by somebody at the end of a wire attached to a chair rung about a hundred yards away.

Since the victims were strikebreakers, initial suspicions focused on the WFM. That afternoon, the mine managers of Cripple Creek convened at the Military Club in the Victor armory and decided the time had come for "drastic measures." A committee of the owners sought out Sheriff Robertson, invited him back to the club rooms, and demanded his resignation. He refused, whereupon guns were produced and a coiled rope was dangled before him. He was told that unless he resigned, the mob outside the building would be admitted and he would be taken out and hanged. At that, he signed the paper surrendering his office. The owners promptly named as his successor Edward Bell, the county assessor and a member of the Mine Owners Association, who then dismissed the union undersheriff and replaced him with L. F. Parsons, secretary of the Cripple Creek Citizens' Alliance, by then a substantial group with five hundred members. At the same time, he appointed a hundred new deputies from the ranks of nonunion miners and superintendents.

Meanwhile, a crowd of several thousand persons had assembled on a vacant lot in downtown Victor, between the union hall and the union store. In midafternoon, Clarence C. Hamlin, a "hard-driving" mine owner and the secretary of the Mine Owners Association, clambered on an empty wagon and, much excited, told his listeners: "The badge of the Western Federation of Miners is a badge of murder. Everyone who is responsible for the outrage at Independence should be driven from the district."

Several men in the crowd began wrestling over a pistol and soon an ugly riot, "a bedlam of cries and oaths," was under way. Twenty or more shots were fired. When the firing ceased, seven men were sprawled on the ground seriously injured, two of them fatally. Some fifty union men in the vicinity quickly took refuge in the union hall. The newly appointed sheriff demanded that the men disperse, but they refused, saying the hall was their "home." At that, the guardsmen outside opened fire, pouring volley upon volley into the building, their powerful rifles puncturing the brick walls "like paper." Some men in the hall returned the fire. But after four unionists were wounded, the miners waved a white flag from an upstairs window and were placed under arrest. By nightfall, two hundred men had been taken into custody and imprisoned in hastily improvised bullpens in Victor, Independence, and Goldfield. Meanwhile, mobs of nonunion men—with prominent Citizens' Alliance men in the lead—surged through the streets of Victor, Goldfield, and Cripple Creek, wrecking union halls and stores and pouring coal over stocks of flour, sugar, and meat. On the blackboard in the Victor hall someone scrawled this prophetic message: "For being a union man, deportation or death will be your fate—Citizens' Alliance."

Indeed, that night ushered in an open season on union members. Whoever was responsible for the Independence depot atrocity—and each side accused the other—the mine owners and the Citizens' Alliance, backed by Sherman Bell's hastily reinforced troops, took advantage of the situation to reverse the balance of power in Cripple Creek once and for all. On June 14, the alliance issued a statement, saying, "The sources of strife in the Cripple Creek District have been the Western Federation of Miners and the Trades Assembly [a grouping of other trade unions].... There is no room in Teller County for these two organizations and their existence will no longer be tolerated."

Over the next few days, many of the union members or their sympathizers who held public offices in the district were deposed as Sheriff Robertson had been, and their places filled by men chosen by the Citizens' Alliance and the Mine Owners Association. A new coroner's jury concluded that the Independence depot violence was "the result of a conspiracy entered into by certain members of the Western Federation of Miners." It indicted forty WFM men—including Haywood and Moyer—for various crimes connected with the Vindicator mine and Independence depot explosions, as well as with the Victor riot. Deputies went up to Denver to arrest Haywood, but he hid out for several days in the home of his friend Colonel John St. John Irby, the scion of a distinguished Virginia family who'd served for a time as a *Denver Post* reporter and was now private secretary to Mayor Robert Speer. Later Haywood went back to the office carrying a Colt .38 revolver in his hip pocket. When he finally went to trial—on the old charge of defiling the American flag on the WFM poster—he displayed a variety of consumer products on which the flag was displayed for advertising purposes: cigar boxes, tomato cans, even the business card of the Pinkerton National Detective Agency. The case was dismissed.

Meanwhile, seven reliable men—the former mayor of Victor, a postmaster, a judge, and several merchants—were named to a commission empowered to decide the fate of union men in the district. They met secretly in the rear room of the Mine Owners Association. Forty-two men were held for criminal trials; many others were deported. On June 7, twenty-eight union men were forcibly loaded on a train to Denver. Another special train, bearing seventy-nine men, left Victor on June 10, heading east. Late the following day, the train stopped a half mile from the Kansas border. Guard officers ordered the men to dismount, walk into Kansas, and never return. To underline the warning, guardsmen fired a volley over the unionists' heads. When Kansas officials blocked their way, they walked back to Holly, Colorado, and most—

with funds wired by the WFM—dispersed to Denver, Pueblo, or Colorado Springs.

Over the next few months, the Cripple Creek commission "tried" 1,569 union men. More than 230—including a former state attorney general, a former judge, the county attorney, and the county clerk—were deported, most of them deposited at the Kansas and New Mexico borders. One group was warned, "If you ever return it will be the bullet or the rope." Asked how the deportees were selected, Sherman Bell said, "They are men against whom crimes can not be specified, but their presence is regarded as dangerous to law and order." But later he summed it up more pithily: "I don't want these men in Colorado."

By the close of 1904, the Western Federation of Miners had all but ceased to exist in the Cripple Creek district. The union never formally called off the strike—launched ten months before with such grandiose promises— but for all practical purposes it had died with the victims of the Independence depot. Thirty-three men had paid with their lives, hundreds more had been driven out of the district. Many sought work in new Nevada gold and silver camps. Others, concluding that union membership was a ticket to nowhere, dropped out of the federation and applied for work permits distributed by the MOA, certifying that they'd repudiated the union. Much the same condition applied in Telluride and Idaho Springs: the WFM was no longer a force to reckon with in Colorado.

Not surprisingly, as their boldest plans foundered in that terrible year, Haywood and, to a lesser extent, Moyer sought to strengthen their hand for the death struggle with the owners. Having quit the AFL eight years before, they couldn't readily approach Sam Gompers. Even if Gompers had been prepared for reconciliation, the AFL was committed to the National Civic Federation philosophy of class collaboration, anathema to the WFM leader-ship. The Socialist Party—the national headquarters in Chicago and the Denver local alike—had done precious little to assist the WFM during the Cripple Creek strike, seeming to regard the struggle as nothing more than a "border feud." Socialist leaders in Colorado warned their followers not to organize protests against the mine owners' tactics but simply to "pursue relentlessly the policy of stating and re-stating the facts of the actual situa-tion, realizing that no accusation is so strong as a temperate, manly statement of the truth."

The Western Labor Union—which had changed its name to the Ameri-can Labor Union in 1902—proved more supportive. Initially it was nothing but the WFM writ large, but gradually, in Denver at least, it recruited a broad range of the urban workforce: the powerful Butchers Protective Union, along with the grocery clerks, laundry workers, cooks, waiters, and hack drivers.

But the WFM needed more help than that. Both within and outside the federation, support grew for another, more ambitious effort to form a broad coalition of unions dedicated to industrial unionism. At the federation's Salt Lake City convention in May 1904, the delegates asked the executive board to take "such action as might be necessary" toward "the amalgamation of the entire wage-working class into one general organization."

Accordingly, a secret conference convened in Chicago on January 2, 1905, to discuss formation of such an organization. Haywood, Moyer, and John M. O'Neill, editor of the *Miners' Magazine,* the monthly journal of the WFM, were the federation's delegates; in recognition of the federation's dominant role at the conference, Haywood was elected its chairman. William E. Trautmann, the editor of the *Brauer Zeitung,* represented the United Brewery Workers, and C. O. Sherman the United Metal Workers; the American Labor Union, the United Brotherhood of Railway Employees, the Bakers Union, and the American Federation of Musicians also sent spokesmen. The Socialist parties weren't officially there, but prominent members of both groups attended as individuals. From Gene Debs's Socialist Party came the labor organizer Mary Harris "Mother" Jones and A. M. Simons, editor of the *International Socialist Review;* from Daniel DeLeon's Socialist Labor Party, there was Frank Bohn, its national organizer.

In three days of intensive meetings, the conferees adopted a manifesto sharply condemning the splintering of the labor movement into craft unions that "far from representing differences in skill or interests among the laborers are imposed by the employers that workers may be pitted against one another." Such distinctions, it said, "foster the idea of harmony of interests between employing exploiter and employed slave." Instead, it called for "one great industrial union embracing all industries ... founded on the class struggle, and ... conducted in harmony with the recognition of the irrepressible conflict between the capitalist class and the working class." All twenty-six conferees signed the manifesto, as did a "Wm. J. Pinkerton," whose name signified a wry recognition that the head of the agency's Chicago office undoubtedly had an operative present.

The manifesto, in turn, summoned a larger "industrial congress" to meet in Chicago that summer. Haywood was again named chairman. On a stifling day in late June, he took the podium over a saloon on North Clark Street to welcome two hundred delegates—representing forty-three organizations of widely divergent political and social philosophies—with one of his most effective speeches: "This is the Continental Congress of the working class. We're here to confederate the workers of this country into a working class movement that shall have for its purpose the emancipation of the working class from the slave bondage of capitalism ... to put the working class in possession of the economic power, the means of life, in control of the machinery of production and distribution, without regard to capitalist masters."

Haywood was less comfortable with the philosophical underpinnings of the new organization, the Industrial Workers of the World, which borrowed heavily from the French, especially Georges Sorel's "revolutionary syndicalism." That he left to William Trautmann and Father Tom Hagerty, Haywood's old drinking partner, both of whom had been influenced by European syndicalist ideas.

A powerful speaker, with a resonant voice and mesmerizing stage presence, Haywood was never highly regarded as a thinker. Talking one-on-one with working-class men and women, he could often be compelling. His definition of the IWW's brand of unionism was short and pungent: "Socialism with its working clothes on." His goal for the organization: "What I want to see is an uplifting of the fellow that is down in the gutter ... realizing that society can be no better than its most miserable." But more sophisticated social critics found him simply bewildering. Mabel Dodge Luhan, the renowned hostess of New York's left, recalled an evening when he was asked to explain the difference between anarchism, socialism, and industrial unionism. As Haywood stumbled, the Harvard-educated journalist Walter Lippmann tried to lead him step-by-step but, as Luhan recalled, "Haywood, so impassioned a speaker, out in the rain before a thousand strikers, talked as though he was wading blindfolded in sand. He couldn't get it into words."

"I've never read Marx's *Capital*," Haywood would say, "but I have the marks of capital all over me." When asked to define the ideal society, he said: "It will be utopian. There will be a wonderful dining room where you will enjoy the best food that can be purchased; your digestion will be aided by sweet music which will be wafted to your ears by an unexcelled orchestra. There will be a gymnasium and a great swimming pool and private bathrooms of marble. One floor of this plant will be devoted to masterpieces of art and you will have a collection even superior to that displayed in the Metropolitan Museum of Art in New York." Hutchins Hapgood once noted that, far from being an intellectual, Haywood was "essentially a poet," who spoke "for the poetry of work." On one occasion, Haywood told a lecture audience: "Socialism is so plain, so clear, so simple that when a person becomes intellectual he doesn't understand socialism."

One theme that persisted in Haywood's public utterances was the ideal of western independence. But that notion became harder and harder to maintain. In September 1905, Haywood's brother-in-law and former sidekick on the range, Tom Minor, came to Denver while traveling the rodeo circuit, accompanied by his nine-year-old son, George. By then, Tom was recognized as one of the best riders on the circuit; weeks before he'd been narrowly edged out of the Cheyenne championship. The Minors stayed with Bill and Nevada, and while reminiscing about his hard days as a ranch hand, Bill conceived the notion of the Bronco Busters and Range Riders Union, to be affiliated with the WFM. It was a curious idea, especially for a romantic who cultivated the legend of his self-sufficient father. Had there ever been a group more thoroughly individualistic, less likely to accept the regimen of a labor union, than the storied loners of the range?

On September 9, Haywood tagged along with Minor to a banquet at the

Adams Hotel thrown by John M. Kuykendall, founder of the Denver Omnibus and Cab Company, whose passionate support of rodeos had earned him the sobriquet "cowboy magnate of the West." In attendance were some fifty cowboys who were performing at that week's Denver rodeo, among them such legendary broncobusters as Harry Brennan and Ross Dollarhide. Champagne flowed freely; spirits were high—until Haywood mounted a chair for what the *Denver Republican* described as a "lugubrious oration to the cowboys on the terribleness of their lot on the wide and burning prairies of the West. They were not getting what they earned and they were making the cattle barons rich and so forth."

They heard him out, but when Haywood tried to collect pledges for the new union, the broncobusters were not receptive. "They had just been paid off and they had just had the greatest feast the hotel could get together and the corks had been popping pretty lively," said the *Republican*. "They were no down-trodden slaves, they were richer than Rockefeller and almost as big as Roosevelt. A demand was made to know why Haywood had been permitted to appear as the Egyptian skeleton at the feast." Haywood beat a hasty retreat.

In his autobiography, Haywood gives a different version of this incident, insisting that a Bronco Busters and Range Riders Union was indeed organized shortly after the Adams Hotel fiasco, with Harry Brennan elected president and Tom Minor secretary. Wages for performing in rodeos were fixed at fifty dollars a day, he says, and for ranch and range riding fifty dollars a month. The union seal was a cowboy on a bucking bronco branded on the hip "B.B.R.R." The detail is persuasive. Moreover, the *Republican* was notoriously hostile to Haywood and the WFM, so it might not have bothered to report this delayed but successful outcome. Finally, a letter from Haywood to a union colleague early in 1906 seems to confirm that a union had indeed been formed but that it soon became moribund; it was revived in 1910 under different auspices.

For Haywood, with his considerable psychic investment in the free spirit of his cowboy father, it must have been hard to concede that such independence hadn't survived on the range, perhaps had never existed at all. This erosion of his father's autonomy—real and imagined—echoed the most haunting of IWW anthems:

> *Your fathers' golden sunsets led*
> *To virgin prairies wide and clear—*
> *Do you not know the West is dead?*
>
> *Now dismal cities rise instead*
> *And freedom is not there nor here—*
> *What path is left for you to tread?*
>
> *Your fathers' world, for which they bled,*
> *Is fenced and settled far and near—*
> *Do you not know the West is dead?*

If Haywood ultimately confronted the counterfeit heart of the western myth, he somehow managed to pass it down intact to his followers. As late as 1939, one of his most faithful disciples, Elizabeth Gurley Flynn, transmitted the legend without an ounce of skepticism: "Haywood's life in the west reads like an adventure story. He was a cowboy, he 'homesteaded.' . . . He was in gold rushes, and knew the Indian tribes. . . . He bore many saber marks on his body of battles with militiamen."

Now and again, Big Bill almost lived up to the myth—notably when he had a few drinks under his belt or when he'd been insulted, or both. Consider election day, 1902, when he was on the ballot as a Socialist candidate for the state senate. Haywood, Moyer, and Dan MacDonald, president of the American Labor Union, had been touring polling places that evening when they noticed the rear door of the Coliseum saloon ajar. All taverns had been ordered closed for the election, but the Coliseum belonged to the liquor dealers McPhillips and Coyle, special favorites of the police and fire board, so liquor was freely dispensed across its wide mahogany bar all day.

Whistles wetted, the union men encountered several "special deputy sheriffs"—politically connected buckos assigned to keep order at the polls— who'd also been knocking back a few whiskeys.

"Pretty badges," sneered Moyer, referring to the red insignia on the lapels of the deputies-for-a-day.

"Don't you like 'em?" asked J. W. Bramer, the combative nephew of a police captain.

"Indeed I do," Moyer shot back. "I'd like to have one for my dog."

With that, Bramer knocked Moyer down with a fist to the jaw. Turning on the other two men, he used his revolver as a bludgeon to fell MacDonald, then delivered a "terrific blow" to Haywood's head. Falling to his knees, Haywood yanked his .38 Colt from a hip pocket and shot Bramer three times. Plainly aiming for the deputy's heart, Haywood was unsteady and all the shots ended up in the deputy's left arm, permanently crippling him. Originally charged with assault to kill, Haywood was released when the police conceded he'd been acting in self-defense.

Most of Bill Haywood's life was mired in more prosaic phenomena, among them the fading of his wife's youthful beauty in the face of chronic illness. At first, her condition fluctuated widely. Sometimes, seeming to mend, she managed to hobble around the house and even took short walks in the woods. But when the arthritis flared up, her swollen joints ached so much she couldn't dress herself. In 1892, Haywood had taken her to Kyle Springs, near Unionville, Nevada, in hopes that the mineralized waters of the spa would ease her discomfort. Every morning, he rolled her in a blanket and carried her to the springs, where he buried her up to her neck in "oozy warm mud," then to the "plunge" and back to their camp. When Haywood put her on a shopkeeper's scale, she weighed only eighty-eight pounds—down a full twenty-five pounds from her normal weight. Concluding that the regimen had been too severe, the Haywoods trekked home to try snake oil, sage baths, and other Indian remedies. After the difficult birth of their second child, Henrietta, in June 1897, Nevada never truly regained her health. For some time to come, Bill was solicitous, even loving, carrying Neva, as he called her, in his brawny grip wherever they went.

Their emotional—and physical—estrangement began in 1903 when Nevada, once active in the Methodist Church, converted to the Church of Christian Science. Haywood was aghast to find her following the strictures of its journal, *Science and Health,* and submitting to treatments, sometimes over the telephone, from women he regarded as charlatans. To Haywood, an avowed atheist since adolescence, "it was all nonsense, based on that profane compilation of fables called the Bible" and "the vagaries of a fanatical and ignorant old woman," Mary Baker Eddy.

While Nevada Jane's sanctimony offended Haywood's skepticism, she was angered by his long absences from home, his seeming absorption in the WFM, which often kept him at the office late in the evenings and over many weekends. "I thought the world of that man," she later told a friend, "but nothing meant as much to him as the labor movement. For it, he gave up his God, his country, his wife and two children—everything!"

For several years, Haywood had indeed spent many evenings hunched over his books in the WFM's "splendid" quarters at the Mining Exchange Building. But in July 1904 federation officers were compelled to give up that four-room suite they liked so well. The mining companies and engineering firms that occupied most of the building were so at odds with the federation by then that, backed by the Citizens' Alliance, they pressured the landlord not to renew the WFM's lease. That summer the federation moved a block down Fifteenth Street into less grand but somewhat roomier quarters in the Pioneer Building.

The new headquarters was surrounded by a welter of murky saloons and all-night cafés where Haywood was a frequent patron. Until those first years in Denver, he said, "liquor and I had been almost strangers. Now I found it to be a sympathetic mistress that would lull me out of an ever-present, ever-growing misery. After a day's work at the office, I would start home, stop in a saloon, maybe two, on the way, to get a drink of whisky to dull my mind against the thought of the superstition that was fastening my family in its meshes."

He sought other forms of solace: in the dance halls, "club rooms," and bordellos that flourished along Market Street, the spine of Denver's red-light district. Market was a notorious thoroughfare that the Denver newsman Gene Fowler described as "bounded on the north by stumbling virtue, on the south by wrecked hopes, on the east by the miserably gray dawn of shame and on the west by the sunset of dissipation." In 1904, Denver's Democratic mayor, Robert W. Speer, struck a deal with the city's purveyors of liquor, gambling, and prostitution, notably with the boss of Denver's underworld, Ed Chase. Nurtured by a municipal detective named Billy Green, the red-light district produced so many Democratic votes on election day that it was known as Green Country. For his part, Green turned an indulgent eye on the district's courtesans and their "macs" (Denver slang for pimps, after the French *maquereaux*). "No effort will be made to make a puritanical town out of a growing Western city," Speer said in his inaugural speech. "You must take people as you find them."

Bill Haywood would have applauded that sentiment, for he was a regular patron of such storied Green Country institutions as Lillian Powers's parlor house, called the Cupola, and Jennie Rogers's House of Faces and Mirrors, a three-story mansion with a mirrored parlor and a facade embossed with phallic symbols. But Haywood's sexual adventurism wasn't sated by exotic whores. Behind his hard-boiled front, he was something of a voluptuary, neatly captured by a future patroness as "a large, soft, overripe Buddha with one eye and the smile of an Eminent Man, ... with two or three maidens reclining at his feet." Another friend recalled "how women of all classes did love him!" Unfortunately, he seemed powerfully drawn to women from his immediate circle. One of his conquests was apparently the wife of George Pettibone, the former miner who ran a household appliance store downtown but remained a trusted adviser and confidant of Haywood and Moyer's. He lived a few hundred feet from Haywood, just across Evans Street.

According to a Pinkerton report, in the summer of 1905—while Moyer was on an extended health leave in California—Haywood went on "a big drunk" so prolonged and unrestrained that he needed to be secluded somewhere for a period of concentrated sobering. For some reason, Pettibone's home was the site. "It was while Haywood was sobering up at Pettibone's that Pettibone discovered that Haywood and Mrs. Pettibone were acting in a rather suspicious manner," reads the Pinkerton report. "Pettibone caught them together and then for a long time would not talk to Haywood." However, this was not the first time that Haywood and Mrs. Pettibone had improper relations with each other and that too was known to Pettibone. It appears that Mrs. Pettibone, a tall, dark-haired woman with lively eyes, used to visit Mrs. Haywood of an evening. "Haywood would go home with her, but would stay out an hour or two. Mrs. Haywood became suspicious, so she sent her little girl ... to shadow them and the little girl reported they went up into a rooming house and remained there for awhile and then Mrs. Pettibone went home and Haywood returned home." It was evidently to this cuckolding that a former WFM official referred when he told the *Portland Oregonian*, "Pettibone swore that he would kill Haywood on sight and got ready to do it for something that is often justified by the public."

Word of Haywood's infidelities was spreading, very likely passed along by McParland's operatives in their effort to discredit the WFM leader within his own circles. David C. Coates, the Populist former lieutenant governor of Colorado, grumbled privately about Haywood's "drunken orgies and immoral life."

But if Bill's affair with Mrs. Pettibone was risky, it wasn't as flagrant as the one he carried on with his own sister-in-law, Myra Winnifred "Winnie" Minor. During the years the Haywoods lived in Nevada, the close-knit Minor family had often cared for Nevada Jane while her husband was at work or off trying to find a job, much of the burden falling on Winnie, the youngest of the Minors' five daughters. She was twelve years younger than Nevada Jane, or just twenty, when the Haywoods moved to Denver in 1901. Evidently Winnie went with them or joined them shortly after they arrived, for soon she was sharing their three-story wooden house on Evans Street. Presumably she'd come to care for her sister, by then confined to bed or wheelchair, and to take on much of the housework. But as early as February 28, 1902, she was addressing envelopes in the Western Federation's new headquarters side by side with Ed Boyce's wife, Eleanor. Within a year, she joined the federation's staff full-time at seventy-five dollars a month, serving in its quartet of stenographers and gradually taking on larger responsibilities until she was working directly, and in close quarters, with her brother-in-law. A petite brunette with upturned nose and playful eyes, Winnie was fun to be with. Before long she and Bill were sleeping together, usually at one of the shabby rooming houses—the Acorn House, the Royal, the Mountain View House, or the Granite—that clustered along Fifteenth Street hard by the Western Federation's offices.

As 1905 drew to a close, Winnie Minor was perhaps Bill Haywood's closest confidante, at home, in the office, and abed. Not surprisingly then, in the days after Steunenberg's murder, he turned once again to Winnie. Hungry for firsthand information on events in Caldwell, Haywood dispatched his twenty-four-year-old stenographer and lover north to Idaho.

On January 4, trainmen and detectives at the Caldwell depot noted the aforementioned "woman in black" alight from the train. Wrapped in a long fur coat and wearing a veil, she asked the way to the jail. Then she walked down Main Street and "disappeared" into the morning mists.

In fact, Caldwell's swarm of detectives soon picked up her trail, just as they did the spoor of James J. Sullivan, the Denver lawyer who arrived at about the same time. Sullivan was a partner in the firm of Sullivan and Cohen, whose offices were directly across the hallway from those of the firm of Richardson and Hawkins, which represented the WFM. Detectives believed that Sullivan often handled business for the larger firm, which might explain his presence in Idaho. He was also said to be a close friend of George Pettibone's. Pinkerton and Thiel detectives made a public spectacle of following him in Caldwell and Baker City, Oregon. Finally, however, a veteran Thiel operative got to speak with a very cool, collected Sullivan, who insisted that Orchard was not the assassin, confided that several years earlier Frank

Steunenberg had "ruined a girl" up in Baker City, and suggested that might be the motive for the murder.

Gus Hasson of the Pinkertons and J. C. Stewart and J. M. Manes of Thiel were more discreet in their surveillance of the "woman in black." Eventually, rumors circulated among reporters and detectives hanging around the Saratoga Hotel lobby. The mystery woman was said to be Haywood's stenographer, who claimed to be accompanying the widow of Charles Kennison, the president of the union's Cripple Creek lodge, to his funeral in Baker City. The *Capital News* called her "Bertha," perhaps because she was traveling under that pseudonym. Some said she'd talked with Orchard in jail (she hadn't). Others said she kept a secret rendezvous with Sullivan at the Nampa depot, where she picked up a message from Orchard and carried it back to Haywood in Denver. To Sheriff Edward Bell of Cripple Creek her very presence was deeply suspicious: "It is my opinion that if Bertha had been held up and her baggage examined, some interesting evidence bearing on the case would have been discovered. It is hardly natural that this woman would make this trip, at this time, under these circumstances, unless she was sent for the one purpose of giving and getting some information that couldn't be trusted to the mails." Her baggage wasn't searched, but some of the detectives, who shadowed her back to Caldwell and bought her forty cents' worth of fruit and magazines, reported that Winnie could be coaxed into conversation, that under their attentions she'd revealed more than she'd intended.

6

VIPER, COPPERHEAD, AND RATTLER

WITHIN WEEKS of Steunenberg's assassination, relays of Thiel and Pinkerton operatives had begun surveillance of the Western Federation of Miners headquarters in the Pioneer Building at Fifteenth and Larimer Streets, in Denver's dreariest quarter. Appropriately enough for an organization dedicated to combating the evils of capitalism, it found itself in a neighborhood that knew all too well the volatile cycles of boom and bust.

Once Larimer Street had been the grandest thoroughfare between Chicago's Michigan Avenue and San Francisco's Market Street. William Thayer, in his *Marvels of the New West*, went still further, comparing it favorably to New York's fabled Broadway. On Larimer Street, said Thayer, "eastern solidity, tact and forethought" were seasoned with "western dash" to yield "a bustling, thriving, inspiring scene."

The 1880s were its golden—or perhaps one should say its silver—age. As Colorado's silver boom flooded Denver, "the great braggart city," with disposable cash, its most palpable manifestations reared their ornate facades along Larimer Street. First came the gray limestone Tabor Block, built in 1880 by the silver magnate Horace A. W. Tabor and soon home to such prestigious tenants as the Colorado Telephone Company and the First National Bank of Denver. That same year rose the Windsor, a grand hotel of epic proportions (three hundred rooms, three restaurants, and a library), where the city's smart set mustered for philosophical disquisitions, symphonic concerts, and masquerade balls, finishing off their evenings with a nightcap or two in its renowned bar, where three thousand silver dollars glittered in the floor. In 1884, across the street from the Windsor, came the Barclay Block, the city's largest office building, best known for its basement baths—Turkish, Russian, Roman, and "electric"—where Denver's bankers and judges, gamblers and grifters gathered in togas to take the waters and close their deals. Nearby were two of the city's best restaurants: Charpiot's (nicknamed the Delmonico of the West), with its parquet floors and oil murals, its extensive wine cellar and Parisian cuisine, and later Richard Pinhorn's Manhattan, which served chunky sirloins and potatoes O'Brien to a well-heeled and well-dressed clientele ("Gentlemen without their coats will sit at the counter"). And gathered all about were lavish drinking and gambling halls such as Murphy's Exchange saloon (known as the Slaughterhouse, for all the murders that took place there), the Chicken Coop, and Ed's Arcade, the last boasting a monumental mahogany bar, a row of oversize chandeliers glinting in the mirrored walls, and a vault in which the underworld king Ed Chase kept an extra $25,000 to accommodate high rollers eager to raise the stakes at his green-felt tables.

But flush times on Larimer Street ended with the panic of 1893—the very crisis that had worked such a change in Bill Haywood's outlook on the world. As markets for Colorado silver sharply contracted, prices for the commodity, so critical to the state's economy, plunged catastrophically. With 435 mines and 377 related businesses shut down, some forty-five thousand Coloradans were out of work by July.

The Queen City of the Plains, as Denver's boosters liked to call it, would eventually recover its prosperity, but Larimer Street had fallen too far too fast ever to recoup its losses. Over the next decade, whatever remained of its vaunted reputation relentlessly seeped away until, by the winter of 1906, it was the city's skid row. Holding on gamely at the corner of Eighteenth Street, the Windsor Hotel was little more than a flophouse where out-of-work ranch hands and out-of-luck miners bided their time waiting for something to turn up. Restaurants that once proffered Veuve Cliquot and oysters Rockefeller now served up watery beer and a free lunch. A surfeit of fifty-five saloons lined the street, an ethnic hodgepodge of Flaherty Brothers, Nicoletti Brothers, Gross and Printz, Moessmer and Skarre, Ashe and O'Connell, Putney and Hill. Many of them fronted for other rooms upstairs, reached through back entrances marked "Ladies." Con artists and bunco men proliferated, peddling tiger marrow, electric underwear, he-turtle extract, even the Sixteenth Street viaduct. One audacious con man, the redoubtable Dr. Gun Wa —actually an Irishman named W. H. Hale—had been run out of town by police for claiming that sexual organs could be restored with his moldy herbs, though two other swindlers, Doc Baggs and Soapy Smith, still fleeced a sucker or two every day. Of Denver's sixteen pawnbrokers, thirteen were on Larimer, seven huddling on the 1600 block alone.

Once a man had hocked his watch, his belt, and his shoes, he slipped gradually over the edge, joining that legion of vagrants and hoboes who roamed this melancholy district. Several times a week the police backed a wagon up to a sleazy saloon called the Aurora and hauled a dozen of the destitute off to jail. When a man hit bottom, the Mission of the Living Waters did its best to retrieve his lost soul from this stew pot of human frailty.

The army of rootless men drifting along Larimer Street offered ideal cover for the Thiel and Pinkerton operatives watching the federation. Sprawled on a stoop, with a four-day growth of stubble on his chin and a bottle of cheap wine in his lap, an undercover detective blended smoothly into the landscape.

Thiel agents were the first to report on their surveillance. By January 18,

Operatives F.P. and C.G. claimed "a clear view" of WFM headquarters on the second floor of the Pioneer Building, including the union's spacious reception room—where unemployed miners could be seen lounging on battered divans —Bill Haywood's big corner office, which connected to Moyer's, and other offices extending back along Fifteenth Street. The detectives' principal mission was to watch for Jack Simpkins, the WFM stalwart believed to have been Harry Orchard's principal accomplice. But they observed all visitors to the federation, noting that "union men generally stop at the Larimer rooming house or the Granite rooming house...just across from the offices of the federation." They kept a special eye on Haywood, trailing him after work to favorite haunts like Gahan's saloon, across from City Hall, run by Councilman Bill Gahan of the Seventh Ward, and the Watrous Bar and Café on Curtis Street, where the night cook was one of Haywood's closest friends.

One evening, a former Denver policeman told the Pinkertons that Haywood and Moyer had entered the café and had "sat in the lower booth for over two hours talking in a low whisper." (It isn't difficult to imagine who the informant was. The café was run by Mart A. Watrous, a former Denver detective, while holding forth behind the bar was his brother George, also a city detective, who had lost his post in 1890 when a grand jury labeled him and four others "licensed bandits.")

The operatives didn't have far to go to survey another of Haywood's watering holes. The Pioneer Building, which the union shared with an eclectic mix of lawyers, dentists, real estate agents, and accountants, leased much of its street level to a single establishment, the Gassell and Hurwitz saloon. Michael Gassell and Benjamin Hurwitz dispensed Tivoli-Union beer on draft and some passable Kentucky whiskeys across their massive bar, under a large stuffed deer and two mounted stag heads. Among those who liked to knock back a whiskey or two among all the dark mahogany and polished brass of the G and H were Bill Haywood and his compatriots from the federation. Partly it was the sheer convenience of the bar, just two stories below the union's offices, and partly it was a political affinity. For Ben Hurwitz was an avowed Socialist, albeit a member of Daniel DeLeon's Socialist Labor Party, the doctrinaire Marxist wing of the movement, founded in 1877. Haywood belonged to Gene Debs's more flexible Socialist Party of America, but the distinctions between the parties had, for the moment, receded with the formation of the IWW. Moreover, Ben Hurwitz was soon to become a determined unionist, founding the Denver Saloonkeepers Union no. 1 and spearheading its long-running dispute with Denver breweries that demanded that independent taverns sell their beer exclusively.

Sometimes through surveillance, sometimes through informants, the detectives kept themselves closely apprised of Haywood's nocturnal habits. He was known to spend twenty-five dollars a night during those weeks, a heavy outlay indeed for a man in his position. He loved to dig into a juicy beefsteak or a grilled chop slathered with mustard, followed by homemade apple pie topped with whipped cream. By his own confession, he was drinking heavily in these years; a "boozer," some called him.

Gooding ordered the Pinkerton surveillance of Haywood and Moyer at a meeting with McParland on January 20—a full week before Orchard implicated the union leaders in his confession. Gooding was reflecting McParland's conviction—evident in his January 10 report—that Orchard was merely a tool of a wider WFM conspiracy. Pinkerton surveillance began on January 21. On January 27, following the first two days of Orchard's confession, George Pettibone became a third target for surveillance.

The operatives did not always take great pains to disguise their surveillance. Late in January, Haywood noticed a red-haired man loitering outside the office. When Haywood and Moyer boarded a streetcar, the red-haired man waited until the last moment, then leaped on, too. When the two union men got off to take in a cattle show at the stockyards, their tail alighted. Returning to the office, they looked out the window and, sure enough, there was the red-haired man leaning against a building. Weeks later, Haywood's wife said Bill had told her "his footsteps were dogged," because "those fellows in Idaho would try to implicate him."

One day, a "fat fellow" calling himself Hynes began hanging around the WFM office, notably the room where the *Miners' Magazine* was edited. He came into Haywood's office and asked for the monthly financial report. What in the world, Haywood wondered, could this man want with a financial report? When the stranger left, Haywood had him followed, and he went straight to the Pinkerton offices in the Opera House Block. At Haywood's suggestion, the *Miners' Magazine* ran a photograph of the operative in its next issue. He sent a complimentary copy to McParland—"as a valentine," he said.

Another Pinkerton agent, identified in the agency's records only as "Denver Operative No. 36"—but very likely a quartz miner named George W. Riddell, who had long worked under that number within the WFM—contributed five dollars to what he called a Western Federation fund for the defense of Harry Orchard. This gave him an excuse for a visit to the Larimer Street offices.

By late January, McParland had become obsessed by the notion that all three of his Denver targets were about to flee. At first the detective gave orders that any of the trio who tried to leave town should be arrested, but then he thought better of it. An arrest of one might prompt the others to flee, perhaps successfully. Haywood had boasted on several occasions that if the authorities ever seriously went after him he would make for Philadelphia, where a badge manufacturer named Callahan would sneak him aboard a ship bound for some foreign port. On January 30, McParland revoked the arrest order. The operatives should simply follow anyone leaving the city, keeping McParland posted on their whereabouts.

By the first week of February, however, surveillance of Haywood and his compatriots had grown increasingly difficult. As McParland wrote the governor on February 4, the federation's leaders had grown "very suspicious, it being almost impossible to shadow them." Therefore, he said, "it was determined that we relieve their suspicion to a certain extent."

The very next day, a small item appeared in the *Statesman* under the headline "Clews in Steunenberg Assassination Case." It noted that, after weeks of official silence, it was now possible to get some notion of the detectives' theory. Indeed, an unidentified detective had told the paper flatly that Harry Orchard had "two accomplices in the commission of the deed. These were in Caldwell on the day of the murder." One was probably Simpkins, the article said. The detectives "feel they have cases against these two and are expecting to land them."

It was the most authoritative-sounding emanation from the detectives in many a week. And with good reason. McParland had arranged for the story to be leaked to William Balderston, the *Statesman*'s editor, and had specifically asked him to give the item out to the Associated Press "as a piece of news that he had received confidentially." The wire service would ensure that the story was carried far and wide, lulling McParland's targets to sleep. "As Pettibone, Moyer and Haywood are well aware that Simpkins was not in Caldwell and that no person assisted Orchard in this matter," the detective told the governor, "they will be thrown off the track and will rest secure for the time being."

Meanwhile, with Harry Orchard's confession now in hand, McParland opened discussions that week with Governor Gooding and James Hawley, the newly appointed chief prosecutor in the case, about how to get Haywood, Moyer, and Pettibone from Colorado to Idaho, so they could be tried for Steunenberg's murder. McParland and the Idaho officials knew extradition of the men would be virtually impossible. The preconditions for extradition are spelled out in Article 4, Section 2, of the United States Constitution: "A person charged in any State with treason, felony, or other crime, who shall flee from justice, and be found in another State, shall, on demand of the executive authority of the State from which he fled, be delivered up, to be removed to the State having jurisdiction of the crime." After a February 2 meeting on the question, McParland reported: "Owing to the fact that neither of these three parties has been in Idaho during this conspiracy, we cannot say that they are fugitives from justice, and we may have considerable trouble in extraditing them. However, we are perfecting plans by which we hope to get them into Idaho in a legal manner, where there is little doubt but that we can convict them."

One wonders whether McParland's mind drifted back to the "murder by mail" of Josephine Barnaby in 1891 and the deception he had practiced to induce the killer, Thomas Thatcher-Graves—no more a fugitive than the union men—to enter Colorado voluntarily. This time, though, he didn't fool with such tricks, opting for a bolder course.

The plan that McParland, Hawley, and Gooding developed over the next week was double-tiered. On the formal level, the State of Idaho would proceed as if it were engaged in a routine extradition, touching all the legal stations of the cross: criminal complaints and warrants of arrest issued in Canyon County; requisitions for extradition signed by Governor Gooding; approval of those requisitions by Governor Jesse F. McDonald of Colorado; finally, warrants of arrest signed by McDonald.

Simultaneously, McParland would devise a scheme for arresting the three men and transporting them to Idaho so swiftly and surreptitiously that no lawyers acting on their behalf could bring a legal challenge in time to stop it. In effect, McParland would mount one of those quasiofficial kidnappings that the Pinkertons had used so effectively during their bitter wars with the midwestern outlaw bands. The forceful removal of John Reno from Jackson County, Indiana, to stand trial in Missouri was the best-known instance; "it was kidnapping," Allan Pinkerton conceded, "but the ends justified the means." Yet the Reno case was by no means exceptional. Indeed, in those days before the founding of the FBI, railroads and other corporations involved in interstate commerce found the Pinkertons particularly useful because they alone seemed willing and able to provide interstate law enforcement to match those far-flung enterprises. Through the late nineteenth century and into the twentieth, if you needed to get a suspect from one state to stand trial in another, your best bet was the Pinkertons.

The crux of McParland's plan was to strike over a weekend, when the courts weren't in session and lawyers were out of their offices or perhaps even out of town, the whole machinery of the law all but closed down. If the labor men could be seized on a Saturday night and placed on a special train early the next morning, they'd be in Boise by the time the legal mills began grinding on Monday morning.

That didn't mean that a determined lawyer couldn't reach a judge at home on a weekend, submit a habeas corpus petition, and get a court order to produce the three men (according to the *Denver Post,* at least two of Denver's sitting judges would have been almost certain to grant such a petition). But an attorney would have to move quickly, and still there'd be the problem of intercepting the men and their captors in order to serve the writ. If McParland's plan went off according to schedule, that would be well-nigh impossible.

McParland's plan had one other important element. Harry Orchard's confession was strong stuff, but standing alone, the detective knew, it wouldn't convict Haywood, Moyer, and Pettibone. The prosecutors required corroboration from other witnesses. Luckily, there were several candidates. In addition to Jack Simpkins, still at large, there were the two other accomplices from the ranks of the WFM that Orchard had named: Steve Adams and Vincent St. John. If at all possible, McParland wanted to take one or both of them into custody at the same time as he brought in the Denver leadership.

In McParland's meetings with Gooding and Hawley that first week of February, it was agreed that the governor himself would approach officials of the Union Pacific in Salt Lake City to arrange for the "special train" that would whisk the arrested men out of Colorado. The Union Pacific and the Pinkertons had a long history of mutually profitable collaboration. For many years, undercover Pinkerton operatives had watched the railroad's conductors and crew for evidence that they were pocketing fares or stealing supplies (McParland's trusted aide, Charlie Siringo, had served a stint as a spy on the railroad's Wyoming trackage, an assignment he privately detested). Later, the agency had put "an army of operatives" into the field to pursue the Wild Bunch, which had been holding up Union Pacific trains. McParland expected no trouble from the UP.

Meanwhile, the detective would open negotiations with Colorado authorities to ensure their cooperation. His two decades of service in Denver had put him on cordial terms with the state's leading figures in government and industry. The year before, he'd noted his approval of James Peabody's unorthodox methods of dealing with the WFM and had boasted that the former governor was "a good friend of the agency," although "few are willing to admit that all he did was in accordance with the Constitution of the United States."

McParland's first approach was to Luther J. Goddard, an associate justice of the Colorado Supreme Court, a rough-hewn character with a bushy beard, known for his pronounced sympathy with the mine owners during the state's labor wars. But McParland began with him for another reason altogether: according to Harry Orchard, Goddard was one of the two justices on Colorado's high court targeted for assassination by the WFM. There was nothing like finding your name on such a list, McParland reckoned, to open your mind to corrective measures.

The detective was content to hold that card for later. In his February 9 letter, it would suffice to emphasize the vast ramifications of what he was about to disclose.

"In making my investigation," he wrote Goddard, "I have unearthed the bloodiest crowd of anarchists that ever existed, I think, in the civilized world, not even excepting Russia." Then he underlined the magnitude of his discovery by invoking his own chef d'oeuvre: "The outrages committed by the Molly Maguires in Pennsylvania were simply child's play when compared with the acts of these bloodthirsty assassins; and I think it was through an act of Devine [*sic*] Providence that I have been enabled to get at the bottom of this conspiracy." He did not dabble in understatement: "This matter is of more importance to the State of Colorado, and all the western states where the blight of the Western Federation of Miners has taken root, than all the cases that you might try on the Supreme Court bench of Colorado in a year, or in fact, during your lifetime." Nor did he lack presumption: "I will be in

Denver on Monday, the 12th, and will be ready to take this matter up with you at nine o'clock a.m. in my office."

The mission that McParland had in mind for Goddard was ambitious indeed: he saw the justice as the man best equipped to persuade Colorado's ruling circles to line up behind the detective's operation and to support the subsequent investigation and trial, with both funds and personnel. In effect, he was prepared to argue a simple businesslike proposition. Idaho would be doing Colorado the ultimate favor: trying, and hopefully executing, the three most feared labor leaders in the state. How much, he was prepared to ask bluntly, was such a result worth to Colorado's leadership?

The time had now come to enlist the cooperation of a few county officials. Formally, responsibility for investigating the Steunenberg murder and prosecuting its perpetrators still fell on the shoulders of the authorities of the county in which the crime had been committed—Canyon County, of which Caldwell was the county seat. There was ample popular support in the county for such a vigorous prosecution. Within three weeks of the killing, Caldwell's city council had adopted a resolution urging that "every effort shall be exerted to establish the identity of all of those who have dared to conceive and carry out the deed so dastardly and deep in sin and to procure that just retribution which in the wisdom of the law has been provided."

In practice, since this was much too important—and expensive—a case for the county to handle on its own, the state had largely taken over. Indeed, since Orchard's transfer to the state penitentiary in Boise on January 18, Caldwell's leading citizens had been deliberately kept in the dark about what was transpiring behind those cream sandstone walls. Certainly McParland had no intention now of bringing the Caldwell people into the little circle of cognoscenti. But to give his operation the camouflage of routine extradition, it would be necessary for Owen Van Duyn, the county attorney, and M. I. Church, the probate judge, to play out their prescribed roles. Van Duyn would have to file formal complaints against the three federation leaders, and on that basis Church would have to issue warrants for their arrest.

On February 8, Governor Gooding summoned Van Duyn to the state-house for a cursory briefing on Orchard's confession. At thirty-one the state's youngest prosecutor, Van Duyn was a graduate of the University of Oregon, had read law at a firm in Eugene, and in 1900 had moved to Nampa, where he served one year as city attorney. Since his election as Canyon County attorney in 1904, he'd won over 70 percent of the criminal cases he'd prosecuted. A curious-looking fellow, with slicked-down hair, watery eyes, and a prissy mouth—all of this perched unsteadily atop a dandy's high starched collar—he was pliant and irresolute. To McParland's relief, when Van Duyn heard what the detective had been up to he was "simply dazed, but did not seem to take any offense that this fact had been concealed from him up to the present time." With that, Hawley took over, instructing Van Duyn in exacting detail as to how the complaints and warrants should be drawn up and how to explain what he was doing to Judge Church, Sheriff Nichols, and Nichols's deputies.

Hawley commanded exquisite discretion. "It will be well in swearing to these complaints to have the Probate Judge cautioned to say nothing about them, and to make no record showing what has been done, that is, any public record. He should be specifically cautioned in regard to secrecy, and to not say a word about it to anybody, under any circumstances."

In swearing out the complaints, "it would really be best to do it yourself," Hawley wrote, "although the Sheriff is, I think, perfectly reliable. The only trouble about the Sheriff is that he may make a confidant of some of his Deputies, and there is one of his deputies whom the Detectives believe is not to be trusted in this affair." Hawley was referring to Undersheriff Frank Payne, whom McParland and Hasson, among others, fiercely distrusted, believing him to have once been a WFM member. Worst of all, according to McParland, he exercised an almost hypnotic control over Nichols. Although Hawley himself did not share these suspicions, he admonished Van Duyn that "this man should under no circumstances be permitted to know anything about our business."

Even more important in giving the extraditions a legal varnish were Hawley's instructions about the form of complaint Van Duyn was to issue against Haywood, Pettibone, and Moyer: "While some of these parties were not actually present at the time the crime was committed, still, under our law they were constructively here, because our statute makes an accessory before the fact a principal, and he must be tried in the same manner as [if] he was a principal, and must be charged like the principal in the information or indictment. It is necessary in the affidavit and the request that the party should be treated as having been a principal in the crime, and having departed from the jurisdiction about the time of its commission."

Hawley was referring to a provision in Idaho law: "The distinction between an accessory before the fact and a principal and between principals in the first and second degree, in cases of felony, is abrogated; and all persons concerned in the commission of a felony, whether they directly commit the act constituting the offense or aid and abet in its commission, though not present, shall hereafter be prosecuted, tried, and punished as principals, and no other facts need be alleged in any indictment against such an accessory than are required in an indictment against his principal."

Van Duyn followed Hawley's instructions to the letter. All three complaints, and their supporting affidavits, were identical, except for the suspects' names. In the affidavit on Moyer, for example, the county attorney said he had "been informed by prominent and reliable citizens of the county of Ada, state of Idaho, that the said Charles H. Moyer was in the state of Idaho on the date of the murder of said Frank Steunenberg" and that "affiant is reliably informed that said Charles H. Moyer left the county of Canyon and the state of Idaho on or about Jan. 1, 1906," and therefore that "said Charles H. Moyer is a fugitive from justice of the state of Idaho."

James Hawley knew Idaho's criminal law as well as any man in the state. But these were curious instructions to give a young subordinate. Was he, in effect, asking Van Duyn to perjure himself in both the complaints and the affidavits? It was one thing to find that Idaho law called for accessories to be tried as principals, quite another to state as a matter of fact that Haywood, Moyer, and Pettibone had been present in Idaho on the day Steunenberg was killed. Moreover, it was questionable at best whether Idaho's criminal statutes had any direct bearing on the law of extradition that any judge would have to apply.

The obstacle, Hawley warned, was the very same instrument that had so bedeviled Colorado's leading circles—habeas corpus—known as the Great Writ or the Freedom Writ because of its centrality to the American system of checks and balances. Lincoln's suspension of habeas corpus in 1861, and the tumult it aroused in Congress, the courts, and the press, was the exception that proved the rule: Americans treasured, above all others, their right to appeal against the arbitrary exercise of executive power. By act of Congress in 1867 and ratification of the Fourteenth Amendment in 1868, this protection was extended from the federal realm to all persons held by state authority in violation of federal law. Though it took some time for the Supreme Court to build a body of law authorizing the application of habeas corpus to a variety of state actions, by 1906 its relevance to an alleged "official kidnapping" such as was planned in the Haywood-Moyer-Pettibone case was not in much doubt.

Quite correctly, Hawley warned the governor and McParland that if a writ of habeas corpus was issued and the three men were brought before a court anywhere along their route before they entered Idaho, any competent judge would order them released. At all cost, then, the operation must be shielded from those potent writs.

Preparing to leave for Denver, McParland hurriedly smoothed his plan's rough edges. As always, his first priority was secrecy. Once he explained to a sympathetic reporter how, as the number of people who knew about an operation grew arithmetically, the chances of a leak expanded geometrically; making a mark like a figure 1, he said, "If I tell you"—and here he made a parallel mark—"that is eleven. And if you tell your wife"—here he made another parallel mark—"that is a hundred and eleven."

He was particularly concerned about the messages that, in days to come, would need to hurtle back and forth between Boise, Denver, Chicago, and New York. Since all urgent messages went by telegraph and could easily be read by employees at both the sending and the receiving stations, not to mention by messengers, desk clerks, and bellboys, the detectives of that era routinely put confidential matters in code. The most common Pinkerton code gave clients and associates names that ended in "wood," while targets and suspects had names ending in "stone." For this operation, however, McParland drew his code from the animal kingdom, a variant offering greater scope and dramatic license. Indeed, as he sat at his desk in the Idanha Hotel that icy February afternoon, he seems to have taken a certain relish in assigning attributes to the key players in the game.

His Pinkerton associates became the noblest, bravest, or sturdiest of birds. William A. Pinkerton was "Eagle"; Robert A. Pinkerton, "Hawk"; George H. Bangs, the general manager, "Oriole"; H. Frank Cary, the Denver superintendent, "Robin"; John C. Fraser, the San Francisco superintendent and assistant manager of the western division, "Blackbird"; the faithful Gus Hasson, still shuttling between Caldwell and Boise, "Lark." And for himself McParland reserved the wisest bird of all, the "Owl." The Pinkerton agency itself was dubbed—with stark simplicity—"Justice."

The governors of Idaho and Colorado—arguably the two indispensable figures in the operation—were accorded the utmost respect. Idaho's Gooding became the king of beasts, although curiously McParland spelled his code name "Lyon." And Colorado's McDonald was granted the one title that, as a loyal member of the Benevolent and Protective Order, McParland was bound to revere above all others: "Elk."

In a similiar vein, James Hawley, second only to Gooding in Boise, became "Tiger," while Sheriff Nichols of Caldwell was "Cougar"; Judge Goddard of the Colorado Supreme Court, "Bear"; and Sheriff Alexander Nisbet of Denver, "Buck."

In contrast, the three principal targets of the operation and their associates in the Western Federation were named for the most sinister of reptiles. Bill Haywood was "Viper"; Charles Moyer, "Copperhead"; George Pettibone, "Rattler"; J. C. Williams, the vice president of the federation, "Constrictor"; M. W. Moor, a WFM board member, "Cobra."

When McParland exhausted his fund of villainous snakes, he invoked other malign members of the animal and insect kingdoms. The three putative accomplices in Orchard's reign of terror—Jack Simpkins, Steve Adams, and Vincent St. John—became "Scorpion," "Fox," and "Coyote." James Kirwan, a member of the executive board, was "Yellowjacket"; Sherman Parker, another WFM official, "Hyena"; and so forth.

And the man who had set the whole operation in motion, the figure who, if he was to be believed, had burrowed deep within the federation for years, then had suddenly surfaced to threaten it with exposure and perhaps extinction—Harry Orchard—was named for that devious marsupial known for feigning sleep or death, the "Possum."

Another code substituted southern and midwestern cities for the Rocky Mountain communities in which the operation would unroll. Thus, Denver became "Canton"; Boise, "Wheeling"; Spokane, "Baltimore"; Caldwell, "Pekin"; Leadville, "Atlanta"; and so forth.

•

Finally, on Saturday, February 10, with most of the planning complete—and with McParland's "timid" but meticulous stenographer, Wellington B. Hopkins, manning the Pinkerton outpost at the Idanha—the detective caught the night train for Denver. A fire on board delayed the train—hardly a propitious omen for an operation that depended on the Union Pacific's vaunted efficiency—forcing a twenty-four-hour postponement of the Goddard meeting. But at 9:00 a.m. on February 13—a scant four days before the operation was scheduled to get under way—the justice met with McParland at the Opera House Block to hear what was on the detective's mind. Although scarcely close friends, the two men felt a certain rapport from their respective roles in Colorado's labor wars of 1902–04. Though hidden from public view, McParland had been one of the principal actors in that drama, a trusted strategist and adviser to the mine owners and their allies in state government. And though Goddard's black robes required him to maintain a public face of neutrality in such matters, there could be little question of his support for the mine owners'—and the governor's—stand against the mounting demands for an eight-hour day and other reforms.

Moreover, the justice and the detective had another area of affinity, one that McParland didn't hesitate to invoke. Like so many other of Idaho's judges, lawyers, and sheriffs, Justice Goddard belonged to the Benevolent and Protective Order. As the two Elks sat down that morning across McParland's desk, the detective summoned his criminal clerk to read Orchard's confession out loud. "To say that Judge Goddard was dumbfounded," he reported later, "would be using a mild expression."

Not surprisingly, the revelation that most intrigued the justice was Orchard's admission that he had set a bomb at Goddard's own front gate late the previous year, a device that had somehow failed to explode and was presumably still buried by his footpath. After the justice and the detective shared a light lunch, Goddard hurried to his home at 2658 Humboldt Street and, sure enough, at the bottom of his gate found the screw to which Orchard said he had attached the bomb's trip wire. When the judge returned to the Pinkerton office that afternoon, McParland proclaimed that they must retrieve the bomb the very next day. Not only would its recovery ensure against the long chance of a delayed explosion, it would provide a critical corroboration of Orchard's story and a vivid demonstration of the need for full cooperation from Colorado's ruling circles.

To extract the bomb, McParland had selected Bulkeley Wells, his trusted colleague from the Colorado mining wars, since April 1905 serving as the state's adjutant general, a position that put him in command of the Colorado National Guard. In his capacity as a mine operator, Wells had been a Pinkerton client since 1894. McParland regarded him as his single most important ally in Colorado, the one man who could be counted on to stand by him to the last bullet. On top of his other talents, Wells was a mining engineer by profession, an expert on explosives.

At eleven the next morning, while two assistant superintendents from McParland's office, E. E. Prettyman and J. N. Londoner, kept pedestrians at a safe remove at both ends of the block, Wells set to work. Dressed in the padded suit he usually wore in the mines, the adjutant general knelt on the frozen ground by Justice Goddard's gate and, with a large jackknife, pried out the bomb buried just six inches below the surface. The device proved to be constructed much like the one that had killed Steunenberg: a box containing ten pounds of dynamite and perhaps a hundred percussion caps, beneath a vial of sulfuric acid. Opening the gate would have tugged the trip line, pulling at a pin embedded in the cork stopper of the vial, uncorking the bottle, and igniting the dynamite. Instead, Wells and McParland determined, the acid had eaten the head off the top of the pin, so that when the gate opened, the line pulled off the pin, leaving the bottle sealed.

Even before the bomb was recovered, Justice Goddard provided emphatic support for McParland's unorthodox extradition plans (though he confided to the governor and the chief justice his grave doubts that the detective could pull off the audacious plot). Firmly sharing Hawley's fears that almost any judge would release the three men if they came before him on a habeas corpus petition, he urged that they be arrested and spirited out of Colorado as quickly as possible. Certainly, they should not be allowed to "roam around" while the searches for Steve Adams and other accomplices dragged on.

Like Justice Stockslager, his counterpart in Idaho, Goddard betrayed no reservations about the propriety of a supreme court justice's playing such a partisan role in a legal proceeding that could one day come before his court. From the start, he gave every sign of having fully enlisted in the Pinkertons' operation, assuring McParland that the detective had a very good case against the three men, one that would surely get them hanged in Idaho, and adding significantly, "I will see that they are gotten there." Looking forward to their prosecution, the justice offered to provide John M. Waldron, perhaps Colorado's leading trial attorney, as a deputy to James Hawley, the Idaho special prosecutor.

Shortly before noon on Thursday, February 15, two of the other key players in McParland's game reached Denver on separate trains. The first was James Mills, the deputy warden of the Idaho state penitentiary, serving as Governor Gooding's personal representative, in part because he had long experience with extradition proceedings and the transporting of prisoners to and from other prisons. Mills, whose face was not known to the WFM, took a taxi from Union Station to the St. James Hotel, where he registered under his own name. In his briefcase, he carried the requisitions for extradition signed by Gooding and addressed to Governor McDonald of Colorado. With nothing to do for the time being, Mills took in a picture show.

On a later train came James Hawley, whom WFM agents might easily have recognized. So the Denver superintendent, H. Frank Cary, picked Hawley up in a closed carriage and whisked him to the Savoy Hotel, where the manager had agreed to waive registration formalities. Cary sternly advised the lawyer that during his stay he should eat all his meals in his room and keep off the streets unless absolutely necessary.

The principal occasion for which he would need to venture forth was the long-awaited meeting with Governor McDonald, at which the fate of McParland's operation would be decided. It was a small but potent group that received Hawley and McParland at ten the next morning in the governor's office: McDonald; Chief Justice William H. Gabbert of the Colorado Supreme Court; Justice Goddard; and James Williams, an attorney representing the extensive interests of two of Colorado's principal capitalists—David H. Moffat, president of the First National Bank of Denver, a major Cripple Creek mine owner and sometime railroad man, and William G. Evans, head of the Denver Tramway Company. Moffat and Evans constituted not only the pinnacle of the corporate community but the leadership of the Republican Party, which now largely lodged with them and the mining tycoon Simon Guggenheim. On guard at the governor's door was none other than General Bulkeley Wells in his dazzling full-dress uniform.

McParland opened the meeting by summarizing Orchard's confession and explaining the plans for "extradition." Governor McDonald agreed that Haywood, Pettibone, and Moyer should be arrested and spirited to Idaho as quickly as possible.

A lengthier discussion ensued over how to give the Pinkerton operation at least the appearance of legality. On the table lay Idaho's requisition papers, based on Owen Van Duyn's sworn complaint, approved by Judge Smith, signed by Governor Gooding. According to time-honored procedures in Colorado and most other states, the requisitions would normally have gone to the state attorney general for review. But McParland warned that Attorney General Nathan C. Miller was "a drunkard" and "liable to talk"; he was simply "not to be depended upon." Worse yet, his assistant, Irving B. Melville, besides being "not removed very far from an anarchist," was a friend of Moyer and Haywood's and had once belonged to the WFM. On these grounds alone, McParland explained, "it would be death to the case" to refer the papers to the attorney general.

But all agreed that, by signing them without referral to the attorney general, the governor would only exacerbate the reaction of the press and the public to his "playing, as it were, the part of a kidnapper." McParland wondered whether the governor could take the "roasting" that would undoubtedly come from the *Rocky Mountain News* and *Denver Times*, both owned by Senator Thomas M. Patterson, a Democrat and an acerbic critic of the McDonald administration.

For a moment, silence descended on the office. All eyes turned to McDonald as he ruffled through Governor Gooding's requisition papers, as well as the unsigned executive orders for extradition. In less sensitive extradition cases, it was the governor's custom to hold a hearing in his office at which lawyers for the defendants could challenge the requisition. But there was no legal requirement for such a hearing and, in this case, McDonald never contemplated one. He knew full well that the requisition papers and Owen Van Duyn's underlying affidavit were in error, that the three union men hadn't been in Idaho on the night of the murder. But the U.S. Constitution provides that "full faith and credit shall be given in each State to the records and judicial proceedings of every other State." The governor could have— indeed, should have—inquired more fully into the truth of the papers before him, but he was under no legal requirement to do so.

After a tantalizing pause, the governor said of the extradition orders: "I will sign them, and the record will not go into the Secretary of State's office until some time next week, and I hope that the prisoners will then be safely in Idaho."

The meeting turned its attention to the particularities of getting the three men into Idaho. Gooding had already arranged for the special train with W. H. Bancroft, the general manager of the Oregon Short Line in Salt Lake City, who in turn had cleared it through Adam L. Mohler, vice president for all Union Pacific lines east of Green River, Wyoming, the very railroad official who'd first alerted Frank Steunenberg to the explosion at the Bunker Hill concentrator in April 1899. So far as can be determined, the railroad donated the special to the operation, its contribution to the restoration of law and order in the Rocky Mountain West and an expense it could easily afford in that palmy year in which it nearly doubled its dividend to an unheard-of 10 percent. Bancroft and Mohler agreed, moreover, to give the train an unusual priority over virtually every other train in the railroad's traffic system. McParland would refine the matter with Union Pacific officials in Denver, but now the detective wanted a clear understanding of who would command the train.

He ached to take on the job himself; the train's race for the Idaho border was the sort of audacious stroke he'd always fancied. But Hawley, Gabbert, and Goddard were all against it: since McParland would be an essential figure in the prosecution, it would be ruinous if he came a cropper with the law as a result of the tainted "extradition." Neither he nor his agency could be linked publicly to the arrest or to the special train (McParland had been so careful to keep his distance, he'd refused to look at the requisition papers or even to carry them to the governor's office, assigning that task to an assistant).

If neither he nor one of his operatives could command the train, McParland wanted "not only a man of intelligence but a man of nerve" in that role. He turned to Bulkeley Wells. Whatever happened en route, he was confident Wells could handle it. "If worse comes to worst," he said, "Gen. Wells can run an engine just as well as any locomotive engineer in the country."

When McParland advanced the name, McDonald seemed uncomfortable. After a long pause, though, he turned to Wells and said, "You are at liberty to go if you want to."

The detective had hoped for something stronger. Couldn't the governor simply order Wells to take command of the train? The governor was plainly unwilling to issue any order bearing on the removal of the prisoners from Colorado. Indeed, beyond signing the requisitions, he wanted nothing to do with the special train. After another pause, he reluctantly split the difference, telling Wells in carefully enunciated terms, "I hereby *authorize* you to take charge of that train and see that these prisoners are landed in Boise City."

The meeting had dragged on for five hours. The next step was to brief Denver's sheriff, Alexander Nisbet, on his role in the operation. With barely twenty-four hours to go, it was late indeed for the detective to be giving the sheriff his marching orders, but McParland had waited until the last minute so as to minimize the chances of a leak from the sheriff's office.

McParland and Nisbet had come to know each other well during the detective's long stay in Denver; they'd worked together so often that their relationship had taken on some personal warmth ("I have no better friend," McParland assured Governor Gooding). McParland knew, however, that these arrests were "a very particular matter" that might give Nisbet pause, as they had the governor. Earlier that week, he'd asked Judge Goddard for help "in such a way that the Sheriff would not refuse to obey my orders." Now such help was forthcoming in the person of James Williams, the mining attorney, who picked the sheriff up at his office and brought him to the Pinkerton offices in the Opera House Block. On the way, he prepared Nisbet for his assignment. Bearing the authority of Messrs. Moffat and Evans, Williams emphasized his clients' support for the operation and assured the sheriff that, however unorthodox these arrests might be, he could count on the business community—and the Republican Party—to stand by him.

Thus, when Williams, Hawley, Wells, and McParland met with the sheriff in the detective's office at 3:30 that Friday, Nisbet was accommodating. "I am at your service," he told McParland, "now you go on and detail just what you want done."

As usual, the detective was ready with a meticulously prepared plan. The sheriff was to hire three carriages, each to be driven by a deputy and each to carry three more sheriffs' deputies and one Pinkerton operative (whose sole responsibility would be to ensure that the sheriff's men arrested the right person). That would make no fewer than five lawmen to guard each of the three targets. To head the teams, Nisbet should select three of his most trusted deputies. McParland cautioned that they must be men he could absolutely count on, for—as he wrote later—any one of them could easily make $20,000 by tipping off the Western Federation in advance.

The Pinkerton operatives who'd been shadowing the three federation men for days would follow them to their homes on Saturday night, keeping watch all through the night to make sure they stayed put. Toward seven, a carriage would proceed to the home of each suspect, presumably sleeping late on that cold Sabbath morning. Each team would take their man quickly into custody, then rush to the Union Pacific's Fortieth Street terminal, where the special train would be ready to depart the moment all three were aboard. Two Pinkerton operatives would stand watch at the station to see that everything went according to schedule.

Having accepted his mission in all particulars, Nisbet promptly formed his arrest teams: one headed by Undersheriff Tom Baird to pick up Haywood; another under Deputy Sheriff Leonard De Lue to apprehend Moyer; the third, headed by Glen Duffield, the warden of the city jail, to arrest Pettibone.

Mindful of the lawyers' warnings against public identification with the operation, McParland had to derive what satisfaction he could from pulling strings behind the scenes. At noon on Saturday, he took up his vigil in Room 217 of the Opera House Block. From there he remained in close touch, by messenger and telephone, with Prettyman and Londoner, the assistant superintendents, and with Captain John T. Howard of the Pinkerton Protective Patrol, who, in turn, carefully supervised the operatives shadowing the suspects.

In the late afternoon, McParland received a phone call from an operative who'd been searching for Steve Adams in the mining districts of western Colorado. Adams, the operative informed him, was holed up in Haines, Oregon, under his own name.

McParland fired off an urgent telegram to Boise ordering Chris Thiele, one of the Pinkerton men still in Boise, to proceed immediately to Haines and there to arrest "Fox." In a hasty note to Gooding, McParland expressed his relief: "This is the best news I have received yet. We will arrest Adams at the same time that we arrest the parties here.... [Then I] suppose that I must come up to Idaho right away in order to break Adams down." Using a popular metaphor for subjecting someone to a rigorous routine, he promised to "put Adams through the same course of sprouts that we put Orchard through."

Ever alert to contingencies, McParland had ordered the teams to hold themselves in readiness all Saturday and through the wee hours of Sunday in case they were needed sooner than anticipated. As the hours dragged by, Superintendent Cary of the Pinkertons plied the deputies with "cigars and refreshments" and a "midnight lunch" to keep them in good humor and ready for action at a moment's notice.

It was a shrewd precaution. For at about eight o'clock on Saturday evening, the Pinkerton man shadowing Moyer observed "Copperhead" leave the office with a gripsack in hand and catch a hansom cab to Union Station, where he boarded the Burlington Railroad's Deadwood Sleeper. The train was bound for South Dakota's Black Hills, where Moyer had once been a member of the Lead City Miners Union, the WFM's second-oldest local, now agitating to reduce the workday of Black Hills lead miners from ten to eight hours. Though the train wouldn't leave until 1:30 Sunday morning, it wasn't unusual for passengers to seek out their berths earlier so they could get a good night's sleep.

When the Pinkerton shadow discerned Moyer's destination, he telephoned McParland, who concluded that Copperhead was about to escape to the northland—and perhaps into Canada. At the detective's insistence, Sheriff Nisbet ordered Moyer's immediate arrest. It would be an awkward maneuver to keep secret, for Saturday evening was a busy time at the Union depot, with throngs of passengers arriving from nearby towns for a night in the big city, while others were on their way home. Nonetheless, De Lue and his team managed to make the "snatch" quietly enough at about 8:45 p.m., with only the conductor as witness. According to McParland, Moyer was carrying $520.75 in cash, a .44 automatic revolver, and a hundred rounds of ammunition (which he claimed he always carried when "on the road"), but he put up no resistance and the agents spirited their man from the station to the gray stone county jail on West Fourteenth Avenue and Kalamath Street, known to Denver's underworld as "Hotel Kalamath."

Once Moyer was in custody, the other two men had to be rounded up quickly. Since Copperhead had been seized in public, McParland feared it was only a matter of time before word of his arrest leaked out, prompting flight or protective measures by Haywood and Pettibone. So the other two teams were dispatched as well, nearly a dozen hours ahead of schedule.

In Haywood's case, the change of plans proved embarrassing. Earlier that evening, Haywood had telephoned his wife from the union office and told her he was going to spend the night at a Turkish bath. Knowing his noctural habits all too well, Nevada Jane would likely not have believed him. She would have been right. Instead, when Bill and his sister-in-law, stenographer, and lover, Winnie Minor, left the Western Federation offices, they crossed the busy thoroughfare to 1228 Fifteenth Street and entered the Granite rooming house.

In months to come, the Pinkertons would contend that the Granite was no ordinary rooming house. One document, for the agency's internal use, called it a "house of assignation." Some months later, in a newspaper interview, McParland said Haywood was arrested "in a well-known house of ill-repute." (When the *Los Angeles Times* picked up that notion, the Socialist weekly *Appeal to Reason* rose in its majesty to condemn the very idea: "The lying scoundrel who wrote that would defame his own mother, and the villainous concern that would publish such an infamous slander would assault a sister of charity. There is not a word of truth in this leprous calumny. It came straight from the putrid heart of the scab *Times,* the foul scavenger that feeds on carrion and is covered all over with its own excrescence.")

Precisely what went on behind the four-story granite facade and cast-iron pillars of the Granite we cannot be sure, but it wasn't a bordello and probably not even a house of assignation, which, strictly speaking, caters principally to prostitutes and their customers. Instead, the Granite was most likely a rooming house open to legitimate travelers as well as to the "soiled doves" who plied their trade on the pavement outside. The 1906 Denver city directory lists it as "furnished rooms," although a year later it was more grandiloquently styled the Granite Hotel. Surely the landlord, Charlie Phillips, was familiar with Bill Haywood, for the Thiel operatives who'd kept watch on the WFM headquarters earlier that year reported that the Granite was one of two rooming houses where members of the WFM's executive board often put up when they were in town for the union's semiannual meetings. In the crisis weeks following the explosion at the Independence depot, many union members from Cripple Creek took refuge from the police dragnet at the Granite. On occasion, the union's leaders held informal meetings there when they didn't want to be overheard by the office workers.

In any case, it was to the Granite that a Pinkerton shadow tracked "Viper" early that evening and it was there, about 9:30 p.m., that Undersheriff Tom Baird, assisted by Leonard De Lue and Glen Duffield, took him into custody. McParland couldn't suppress a note of pious satisfaction as he told his superiors, "We arrested Haywood in this rooming house; he was stark naked and in bed with a woman notwithstanding the fact that he has a wife and child living here in Denver. The deputy sheriffs secured a huge revolver that he had lying on the dressing case in the room where he was arrested." Haywood, who was said to be spending $25 a night, had just $5.85 in his pocket.

The officers showed no particular interest in Winnie (they don't seem to have connected her with the "woman in black"). They evidently released her on the spot, with a warning to keep her mouth shut about the arrest. Presumably the officers knew that Winnie had every reason to keep her affair with her brother-in-law secret, and indeed there is no evidence that she ever talked about her part in that night's theatrics. Nothing was heard from her, or about her, until ten weeks later, in the midst of the WFM annual convention, when she suddenly married Charles H. McKinnon, a delegate who was secretary of the Goldfield (Nevada) Miners Union.

Haywood's version—in his autobiography—understandably makes no mention of Winnie either, indicating only that he was arrested in "a rooming house near the office." He recalls being awakened by a knock on the door at 11:30 (he is almost certainly off by two hours). "I want to see you, Bill," said a deputy whom Haywood knew. "I want you to come with me." When Haywood asked why, the deputy said, "I can't tell you now, but you must come." Despite the .44 Colt revolver on the bureau, Haywood put up no resistance —though, curiously, given his evening's disportation, he insisted vehemently that his invalid wife be informed of his arrest and advised to summon her father from McDermitt, Nevada. Undersheriff Baird declined to do as asked (although eventually a sheriff's deputy did pass along Haywood's message)

For the moment, Baird simply ordered Haywood to get dressed, then hustled him outside, into the carriage, and off to join Moyer in jail.

That left only George Pettibone at large. Either the Pinkerton operative shadowing Pettibone had lost him temporarily as he left his household appliance store on Court Place or he was in such a public spot he couldn't be apprehended without a commotion—one Socialist paper later reported that he'd been at a barbershop—for "Rattler" wasn't taken into custody until after midnight, when he returned to his home at 1225 Evans Street, catty-corner from Haywood's house. Mrs. Pettibone was still at the theater with a friend. Glen Duffield's team surrounded the residence, then hustled the shopkeeper into the carriage and drove him at breakneck speed to the fortresslike jail.

By 1:00 a.m. the three class warriors were installed in separate cells in the jail's secluded west wing, then laughingly known as "bankers row" because it had recently harbored Leonard Imboden and James J. Hill, two bankers charged, in a celebrated case, with embezzling $1.6 million from two savings banks. McParland had no time to savor this juxtaposition: he was impatient to get the rest of the operation under way. The longer the trio remained in jail, the greater the danger that news of the arrests would leak, prompting the men's associates to seek their release—through a writ or by more direct means. When he reached the jail, Haywood had asked an officer to report his arrest to Edmund F. Richardson, a partner in the Denver firm of Richardson and Hawkins, which was on retainer to represent the Western Federation. De Lue later informed Haywood that Richardson had been notified, though he was not.

By 11:00 p.m., some family member had evidently grown anxious, for at that hour, Horace W. Hawkins, Richardson's partner, called the jail to ask if Moyer and Haywood were there. Acting on explicit instructions from McParland to cover that contingency, jailer Duffield flatly denied that he was holding either man. The *Rocky Mountain News* later indignantly charged that several jail employees, as well as other state and county officials, "reiterated this falsehood" all through Saturday night. (Seeking to justify this prevarication, officials later invoked a jail regulation that forbade a prisoner to communicate with anyone after 6:00 p.m.)

Such dissembling did not relieve tension among the sheriff's men. A number of reporters, having heard rumors that something was afoot, assembled at the jail and began asking inconvenient questions. Alarmed that his whole operation was about to blow, McParland called the Union Pacific, urging that the special train's 6:00 a.m. departure be moved forward to 2:00 a.m. But railroad officials demurred, explaining that the train wasn't even "made up" yet. There was no way to accelerate its timetable. Some of the cars hadn't reached the Fortieth Street yards. The train would leave no later than six, they said, but no sooner either. The only concession McParland could wring from the railroad was to switch the departure point from the Fortieth

Street station to Union Station, on the city's north side, saving perhaps half an hour.

Nonetheless, "Owl" wanted his captives out of jail *now*. Once deadlines for the late newspaper editions had passed at about 3:00 a.m.—and the clutch of reporters had drifted homeward or to other nocturnal pursuits—Haywood, Moyer, and Pettibone were taken to the warden's office, where they met for the first time that morning. Then they were spirited out a back door and into carriages that clattered through darkened streets to the Oxford Hotel, the 180-room commercial hotel in which Haywood had been so badly beaten by the Colorado National Guard two years before. There they were hurried down vacant corridors to three adjacent rooms, where they were at last permitted to snatch what sleep they could, while deputy sheriffs and Pinkerton operatives kept watch in the hallway outside. About 5:40 a.m., these guardians shook their prisoners awake and took them into the dim hallway, where, according to the *Miners' Magazine*, their hands were cuffed, their legs shackled, and their arms pinioned to their sides. Then they were escorted through the echoing halls of the largely deserted Union Station to the special train. At 5:50, the prisoners were put aboard, delivered into the custody of Governor Gooding's emissary, James Mills of the Idaho state penitentiary. Though Mills had official custody of the prisoners, it was Bulkeley Wells who held the keys to their handcuffs and leg irons for the rest of the trip.

An hour later, a jubilant McParland dashed off a telegram to William Pinkerton in Chicago, announcing: "Special left for Wheeling with viper, copperhead, hyena at 6 a.m." So excited was the detective that he'd confused "hyena" (Sherman Parker) with "rattler" (George Pettibone).

The special consisted of a steam engine and three chair cars—a "combination" car with seating for twenty-four up front and a rear baggage compartment; the Pullman car Aderno, a twelve-section drawing-room car that could be made up into berths at night; and a "special," or "private," car belonging to the superintendent of the Union Pacific's Colorado division, Ernest Stenger, and in this instance intended as headquarters for the chief dispatcher of each division, who, at McParland's request and Omaha's orders, would ride aboard the train to ensure its precedence over other traffic. (The special might have achieved greater speed with still fewer cars, but at least three cars were necessary to provide the train with sufficient braking power.)

The spartan combination car, which on some branch lines served as segregated quarters for smokers or for Negroes, now provided accommodation for crew members not busy on the engine—the conductor and two brakemen—as well as storage space for luggage and spare parts.

The private car was a perquisite that, by century's turn, proclaimed the traveler's status. At first, those who could afford it settled for nothing less than a train of their own. In 1889, the William Seward Webbs traveled coast to coast in a four-car train, the twelve passengers served by a maid, two cooks, two nurses for the children, and eight porters; beyond Kansas City, a Pinkerton detective was engaged to protect the family against highwaymen and other western perils.

But privileged travelers gradually began settling for the rigors of a private car. The first individually owned one, the City of Worcester, was built in 1876 to take a merchant named Jerome Marble and a party of eighteen on a three-month western safari. Soon every titan of industry had a private car. In 1882, William K. Vanderbilt built a seventy-four-foot giant painted a bilious yellow. Leland Stanford and his wife had his and hers cars. Angus MacLeod built the most luxurious car of all—the stunning Alexander, with an Empire ceiling, leaded glass, costly hangings, and wood carvings. But most private cars belonged to railroad officials. On the Union Pacific, this proliferation grew so scandalous that "every employee above a flagman seemed to have his own car." Superintendent Stenger's car wouldn't have rivaled Vanderbilt's or MacLeod's. But it undoubtedly had a comfortable living room, outfitted with wicker chairs and couches grouped to face the rear observation deck; office space, where the chief dispatcher could ply his trade; a kitchen and dining room, not employed on this trip; and two bedrooms, where the official escorts took turns taking catnaps.

The prisoners rode in the Pullman. (This itself was a touch of irony. After federal troops broke the Pullman strike in 1894, Eugene Debs had vowed never to ride in a Pullman car again, as had many of his Socialist followers. The very name was linked with the most repressive aspect of American capitalism.) In charge of the train, and its precious cargo, was Bulkeley Wells, whose dashing figure personified the union of forces—the mine owners and the McDonald administration—behind this mission. Assisting him were five armed men: James Mills and four guards, two of them deputy sheriffs from Alexander Nisbet's staff and two provided by Wells. The deputies—Albert C. Watson and J. B. Fisher—were seasoned lawmen and crack shots chosen by McParland himself on the basis of long association with Sheriff Nisbet and his men (each received a hundred dollars for his labors). Wells, in turn, had selected two men on whom he'd relied during Colorado's labor wars: D. W. Strickland, a captain in the Colorado National Guard who'd served on Governor McDonald's staff, and Bob Meldrum, now Wells's orderly-cum-bodyguard. Once again, as at Telluride, Meldrum was putting his gunslinger skills at the disposal of the West's new corporate order. As he swung aboard the train, Haywood, Moyer, and Pettibone recognized Hair Trigger Bob as their old adversary, a desperado ready at any moment to put a bullet through them.

Haywood had plenty of opportunity to study Meldrum. Each of the prisoners, still in handcuffs, was watched closely at all times (even when he went to the toilet, it being feared that the fugitive might succeed in squeezing out the toilet window). Although guard assignments shifted, Meldrum seemed to keep his pale eyes on Haywood. "I never saw a human face that looked so much like a hyena," Haywood recalled. "His eyes were deep set and close together. His upper lip was drawn back, showing teeth like fangs."

According to Bulkeley Wells, Haywood took his arrest rather harder than the others, as if he would "grumble with the fates." Moyer and Pettibone accepted their position more "philosophically," Wells reported. Their hand-cuffs notwithstanding, they spent much of the time playing cards. Haywood declined to join them. Deputy Warden Mills remembered it differently: Haywood and Pettibone coolly playing cards, while Moyer sat sullenly off to the side. The *Portland Oregonian,* citing no source, reported that Moyer had been "impassive as an Indian."

The guards, who jawed noisily among themselves, had little to say to their captives. An hour into the trip, Wells finally gave the prisoners the essentials of their predicament: Under arrest on unspecified charges, they were on a special train headed for Boise—period. Mills regaled them with his exploits in arresting desperate fugitives. "We listened for want of better entertainment," quipped Haywood.

Relations between this set of prisoners and guards wouldn't have been cordial under any circumstances, but they were bound to curdle in the close quarters of the Pullman car. For McParland had specified that once all nine men were aboard, the doors to the Pullman car should be locked at both ends and remain secured for virtually the entire trip.

Even the Union Pacific's own dispatcher and regulation crew—engineer, fireman, conductor, and two brakemen—were denied entry. McParland didn't entirely trust the crew, who were, after all, union men themselves. The most prestigious brotherhoods—engineers, firemen, trainmen, and conductors—were scarcely radical. The engineers, in particular, regarded themselves as aristocrats of the road (for years they wore top hats and cravats befitting that exalted status). Determined to protect the privileges of craft, they often identified more with management than with labor. Quitting the Brotherhood of Locomotive Firemen to form the more confrontational American Railway Union in 1893, Eugene Debs had denounced the traditional brotherhoods as organizations of "caste" and "class." On Labor Day, 1905, Haywood himself had reviled the engineers as scabs. Shortly after Steunenberg's assassination, in fact, the Pocatello division of the Order of Railway Conductors had de-plored "this most heinous crime on one of Idaho's most devoted citizens" and pledged its "best efforts in ferreting out and bringing to speedy justice the party or parties responsible for throwing our great state into mourning." Presumably such brotherhoods would have been chary of any alliance with the fire-eating WFM. But McParland took no chances with union men on this trip. He wanted them all kept as far away from the prisoners as possible.

This was only one of an elaborate set of precautions McParland took to prevent the prisoners' associates from halting the train and rescuing the trio.

First was a carefully plotted route. A complex web of possible rail lines stretched off to Denver's south, north, and west, but the choice boiled down to two major alternatives. One struck north along Union Pacific track to the Wyoming border, due west into Idaho, then through Pocatello and northwest to Boise. The other proceeded south from Denver along the Denver and Rio Grande and Colorado Midland lines, then swung west through Pueblo and Grand Junction, Colorado, then north again through Utah into Idaho. Much longer and more mountainous than the northern route, the southern path had only one real advantage: that it would be so unexpected. But it had one flatly disqualifying feature: much of its route through Colorado was mining country, with thousands of miners' shacks huddled along the rights-of-way. Alerted by WFM headquarters, miners might blockade the tracks, seize the train, and rescue their leaders.

McParland had already done what he could to persuade potential pursuers that they'd taken the southern route. At 5:00 a.m., a trusted messenger had been instructed to pick up food and drink for the journey at the Watrous Café on Curtis Street. The messenger was to drink a cup of coffee in the kitchen and then say to Haywood's close friend the night cook, "My God, I must hurry up, I must take these provisions to Burnham." Burnham was the first station south on the Denver and Rio Grande and Colorado Midland lines. The cook would have Sunday off—a holiday that McParland himself had surreptitiously arranged with the café's owner. Once word of the arrests was out, the cook would presumably report the messenger's words to Haywood's associates and they'd search along the southern route, while the special sped northward. "This may work, and it may not," McParland reported, "but it is the best I can do."

McParland had to proceed on the assumption that his ploy wouldn't work, that the hunt would be on for the special all along the northern route. Both the chief dispatcher traveling with the train and the engineer were elaborately briefed. Under no circumstances were they to stop at any station along the way, and certainly not for anyone who tried to flag them down or bar their passage. All messages to the train would go straight to the dispatcher in the special car, and he was to ignore all instructions from any authority save McParland. Most important, the detective emphasized, they should pay no attention "to any writ [of habeas corpus] that any sheriff might present on the way." It was most unusual for a chief dispatcher to ride aboard any train; his very presence would signal to railroaders all along the route that this train had clout.

Finally, the faster the train made the trip, the less time for anyone to intercept it. On open track, the engineer was to run with his throttle all the way out; through stations and yards, as fast as the traffic would bear.

So, while much of Denver slept late that raw Sunday morning, the special knifed through the city's northern outskirts, then out along the bank of the ice-covered South Platte River. Belching coal smoke, reeking of hot metal and valve oil, it highballed for the Wyoming border behind the traditional twelve-point stag's antlers attached to the locomotive's headlights. To the west, catching the first light of the morning sun, were the glistening summits of the Rockies—Mounts Audubon and Ypsilon, Longs and Twin Sisters Peaks—to the east, the short-grass prairie, broken here and there by a rocky butte or the sandy bed of a dry stream. The coal-black special racketed by tin-roofed depots and weathered platforms of the Denver Pacific Railroad in towns like Brighton, Fort Lupton, and Platteville. Occasionally a rancher out early to check his stock or a farm boy with a pail of crystallized milk may have raised his head and cast a quizzical glance at the strange truncated train ripping along at this curious hour, registered on no timetable. But nobody seemed to give it much thought.

Bill Haywood recalled that they were traveling at "terrific speed." Judging from the distances covered, they didn't average much more than fifty miles per hour, although now and then they may have hit peak speeds of up to eighty. (Three months later, when another special, carrying E. H. Harriman, the railroad's chairman, made its historic coast-to-coast run in seventy-one hours, it averaged 53.1 miles per hour over 824 miles of Union Pacific trackage.)

Reaching Ethel Hill, just over the Wyoming border, at about 9:00 a.m., they stopped on a lonely siding where a fresh crew and engine from the Wyoming division replaced their counterparts from the Colorado division (newly adopted work rules required a crew change every hundred miles). The chief dispatcher handed his portfolio over to the Wyoming division's Sullivan S. Morris.

The special would change engines—and crews—at least eight times during the trip. Not only did friction bearings—raw metal on metal—tend to overheat and fireboxes to fill up with ash, causing a loss of steam, but different terrains required different engines. The closest thing to an all-purpose engine was the classic American, designated a 4-4-0 for its four-wheeled front bogie, its four driving wheels, and its lack of wheels on the trailing tender. But flat-out runs across desert or plain called for high-horsepower 4-4-2 Atlantics (known to their admiring crews as Bull Runners) or the more powerful 4-6-2 Pacifics, which could reach speeds as high as seventy-five to eighty miles per hour; and massive mountains required the brawny 4-8-4 Northerns or, on truly precipitous slopes, the 4-8-8-4 Big Boys, with their sixteen driver wheels. To get the most out of the equipment—and for safety's sake—each engine had to be manned by crews who knew the terrain. It would only slow a train to have the engine operated by a man not thoroughly familiar with the track. On the Denver-Boise run, engine and crew changes normally took place at rail yards in Cheyenne, Laramie, and Rawlins, Wyoming, and Montpelier, Pocatello, Glenn's Ferry, and Nampa, Idaho. But on this trip, McParland insisted that these exchanges be accomplished not in the bustling yards, where they were bound to be observed by rail workers and passersby, but on remote sidings well out of public view.

Even a truncated train like the special needed to take on water every twenty-five miles, coal every fifty miles. Each fresh engine came fully watered and fueled, but on a trip of some eight hundred miles, the special couldn't avoid stopping at least twenty-four times for coal or water, though the transactions usually took less than five minutes. McParland demanded that they take place at coal chutes and water tanks in windswept, desolate locations like Cooper Lake, Red Butte, Point of Rocks, and Bitter Creek.

To ensure that the special wasn't impeded in its dash for Boise, the railroad's Omaha headquarters had decreed that the train should have priority over every other Union Pacific train but one. The exception was the daily Overland Limited, the road's premier express, dubbed "the fastest train on the best track in the West" and operated between San Francisco and Chicago.

The chief dispatcher of each division the train traversed was entrusted with maintaining this priority. His principal responsibility was to ensure that the tracks were cleared before the special, both of trains coming in the opposite direction and of slower trains running ahead. Major stretches of the Denver-Boise route were still single-track, meaning that any train heading east would have to be forewarned, so that it could move onto a siding and let the westbound special past. The chief dispatcher would write his instructions out in longhand, usually in cipher for security reasons, then pass them to a station via an "order hoop," the pole with a "butterfly net" at the end in which messages could be delivered without stopping the train. The depot agent would telegraph ahead to another station, which, in turn, would pass the message by order hoop to the oncoming train. Avoiding a disastrous collision or a frustrating traffic jam took intense attention to detail. Given the intricate pattern of obligatory stops for water and coal and for crew and engine changes, the chief dispatcher's task must have felt less like an eight-hundred-mile dash than an elaborate game of chess.

As the newly manned special raced across Porter Creek into Cheyenne's outskirts, the guards in the Pullman checked their weapons and peered around the window blinds. In his planning for the operation, McParland had recognized that its middle stage—a long east-to-west traverse of Wyoming— would be the most perilous. On the opening run through Colorado, as well as in the closing sprint across Idaho, the special would enjoy a degree of gubernatorial protection. Bulkeley Wells, representing Governor McDonald, and James Mills, speaking for Governor Gooding, might fend off a nosy sheriff (though their authority would hardly impress a determined band of miners). But the train would have no such imprimatur in Wyoming, whose Republican governor, B. B. Brooks, was enough of a maverick that none of the operation's architects had approached him. With no political umbrella, some Wyoming sheriff, if ordered to do so by a state court, might insist on exercising his authority.

Moreover, Cheyenne, the capital city through which the special was about to pass, was home to Wyoming's United States marshal. Of all the authorities in whom the Western Federation might have invested its hopes, the marshal in Cheyenne seemed the most likely candidate, not because he was known to have personal sympathy for the WFM's cause but because he was the appropriate instrument for enforcing the writ of a federal court and because he was regarded as at least minimally professional. Indeed, McParland feared that if a full-fledged U.S. marshal armed with a writ ever got aboard the train, even Bulkeley Wells might not be able to resist his commands.

A prosperous sheep rancher and thoroughly political man, the marshal at Cheyenne, Frank A. Hadsell, was no gunslinger. If it took one of that breed to stop the train, the nominee would probably have been Hadsell's chief "field deputy," a legendary gunman named Joe LeFors. Just turned forty, at the height of his powers, he combined "ice-cold daring, skill of the highest order with weapons, and a doggedness bordering on obsession." LeFors had no truck with the Western Federation; he had generally maintained good relations with the Pinkertons, collaborating with them in tracking Wyoming outlaws; and he was not likely to be offended by McParland's bending of the law. But a professional lawman as tough and relentless as they came, he might feel bound to serve a writ of the federal court. Of all those who could block the train's path, Joe LeFors was the man McParland had most reason to fear.

The Cheyenne yards were a busy place with a major terminal, a roundhouse, repair shops, and a cluster of twenty-four-hour cafés, barbershops, and saloons catering to railroad men. Normally, trains crawled through the yards so as not to hit a moving piece of equipment or a wandering trainman with a drink too many under his belt.

To make sure the marshal never got aboard, McParland specified that the special should run through the yards at thirty miles per hour, too fast for anyone to grab a railing and clamber up the steps. But just in case somebody tried, the six guards covered every angle of approach (though Wells later conceded they probably wouldn't have shot a U.S. marshal). In any event, no one tested their resolve. By 10:00 a.m., the special had cleared Cheyenne and was rolling across the frozen Crow River, hell-bent for Laramie.

Wyoming presented other perils. In these bleak highlands, winters were fierce. Avalanches thundered down canyon walls, sometimes trapping a train for days, even weeks, on end. Blizzards battered the mountain passes and high moors, often piling up fifteen feet of snow. Veteran trainmen told of finding sheepherders frozen to death by their flocks or so badly frostbitten they lost feet or hands to some sawbones's knife.

From the start, McParland had warned that the long traverse of Wyoming must be accomplished in daylight. So long as the sun shone, a shrewd engineer had a chance of distinguishing between a genuine emergency that could compel the train to stop and a bogus one serving only as a pretext to seize the special and its confidential cargo. At night, however, "any person with a red lantern could flag our train," McParland warned, and "cause us lots of trouble." Now, with the peril of Cheyenne behind them, and seven hours of precious daylight remaining, the special pushed on toward the Idaho border —some 350 miles away.

Rugged territory loomed ahead: the snow-capped Medicine Bow Mountains crowding in from the southwest, butting heads with the Laramie range, which swerved down from the northeast. Snaking between narrow ridges topped by blue-green stands of lodgepole pine, the train swaggered into the foothills, panting up the rock-strewn grades, careening into the next whitened valley, slamming through the curves, as the engineer fought to keep its screeching flanges on the rails. The precipitous landscape would have made compelling sightseeing had the guards not drawn the blinds over the Pullman's windows to prevent anyone along the route from glimpsing the prisoners.

Thirty miles west of Cheyenne, the tracks climbed the steepest slope in the entire Union Pacific system—the notorious Sherman Hill. When General Grenville M. Dodge discovered this route while seeking to escape an Indian attack, the summit towered a vertiginous 8,247 feet above sea level, but by 1906 the railroad had carved nearly two hundred feet off the mountain to reduce the strain on its equipment and improve the comfort of passengers, who frequently suffered nosebleeds at the summit. Even then, the maximum westbound grade was still a fearsome 1.91 percent (a rise of 1.91 feet per 100 feet of track). It was not unusual to see two huge Big Boy engines puffing and snorting as they hauled a heavy freight up the three-mile Sherman slope. With only three cars to pull, McParland's special made do with one engine.

Somewhere west of Laramie, the guards—who hadn't eaten since four that morning—began thinking about lunch. Though McParland had assured his superiors that "the menu will not be elaborate," when it had come time to order the grub from the Watrous Café he'd erred in the direction of generosity. Laid out on a table in the rear of the Pullman car was $44.95 worth of groceries, a big spread by the standards of most Colorado cookhouses or campfires: twenty turkey sandwiches, twenty chicken sandwiches, twenty beef sandwiches, and twenty ham sandwiches, six cans of sardines, a quart of dill pickles, five bottles of olives, a bottle of mustard, three jars of raspberry jam, a basket of apples, three dozen hard-boiled eggs, a loaf of rye bread, a loaf of white bread, a couple of pounds of Swiss cheese, a hundred cigars, three dozen quarts of Budweiser beer, and a quart of Old Crow bourbon. Beer and bourbon were a bit chancy on a sensitive mission; but, everything considered, McParland thought they were worth the risk. He was confident that General Wells would see that "nobody will get any more of the beer than they are entitled to."

The prisoners were permitted to choose what they wanted from the table but, with their hands still in cuffs, found it "rather awkward" to maneuver hard-boiled eggs and sour pickles into their mouths. That afternoon, when Bulkeley Wells broke out the Old Crow, he gave each of the prisoners a tin cup of bourbon. Finally, all parties lit up the cigars McParland had thoughtfully provided. With the windows firmly shut against the cold—and to ensure against a desperate escape or attack—the car soon began to fill up with cigar smoke. Mixed with coal fumes from the cast iron potbelly stove in the aisle, the cigars made it hard to breathe. But a slug of bourbon and a mouthful of panatela helped a man pass the tedious hours.

About 2:15 p.m., the special sped through Rawlins, the seat of Carbon County, set on a high, treeless desert. Folks said the wind blew longer and harder in Rawlins than in any other place in the West: one day it stopped and everybody in town fell down. The tracks ran along Front Street, a narrow thoroughfare lined with saloons, restaurants, gambling joints, and whorehouses whose doors stayed open day and night. Bands of railroad workers coming on or off shifts provided a steady clientele. Among the motley crew along Front Street that afternoon was one man with a special interest in the passing train.

McParland had arranged for an informant in Rawlins to phone him as soon as the train passed the depot there. Like his operatives, McParland had gone without sleep all Saturday night, manning his outpost in the Opera House Block, from which he directed operations with a blizzard of hand-delivered messages and muffled phone calls. On Sunday, he remained in the office, waiting for word—good or bad—from the train. When Main 534 rang at 3:00 p.m., the informant told him the special had come through Rawlins three-quarters of an hour before. The train was making astonishing time, McParland telegraphed his superiors, indeed the trip was "the most remarkable run on record," considering the mountainous terrain and other potential obstacles.

Late that afternoon, in a message to Gooding, McParland permitted himself to gloat. "When I received this telephone message," he wrote, "I rested easy, as I then realized which you will readily see that every plan that I had layed from my arrival on Jan. 10th up to date had carried without a hitch, and that every promise that I had made to you about being able to control the authorities here in Colorado had been carried out."

All that day and evening, the telegraph wires crackled from Boise to Denver and back again, confirming that the operation was working better than anyone had expected.

"Thiele wires arrested Fox [Adams] placed him in jail Baker City.... Pigeon [Mrs. Adams] located. No trace Scorpion [Simpkins]."

"Lyon [Gooding] congratulates you [McParland], says splendid work."

"Tell Lyon that Owl [McParland] leaves for Wheeling [Boise] tomorrow morning."

"Owl can't leave for Wheeling until Thursday morning."

At Wamsutter, sixty-five miles west of Rawlins, the special crossed the Continental Divide. The high plateau on which the train now ran was a bleak tundra of dust-gray short grass, flecked here and there by yellow rabbitbrush and scampering herds of small antelope. When a morose and ill Robert Louis Stevenson traversed this landscape along these very tracks in August 1879, he saw "not a tree, not a patch of sward, not one shapely or commanding mountain form; sagebrush, eternal sagebrush; over all the same weariful and gloomy colouring, grays warming into brown, grays darkening toward black."

Among Union Pacific trainmen, this desolate stretch of trackage was legendary for train robberies and hijackings pulled off by the Hole-in-the-Wall Bunch, Butch Cassidy and Harry Longbauch (sometimes known as "the Sundance Kid"), and other, less celebrated desperadoes. In 1878, "Big Nose" George Parrot and Dutch Charlie Burris, with two accomplices, had tried to derail the westbound Union Pacific passenger train here by removing spikes that held the rails, but a section boss detected the tampering and warned the oncoming engineer.

Near dusk the train reached Green River in Wyoming's southwest corner. Slicing through a cut in the sage-covered hills, leaning into the curves as it followed the water's serpentine path, it ran through the willows and cotton-woods at the foot of sandstone cliffs. On a siding outside this seat of Sweetwater County—once Butch Cassidy's headquarters for raids on Union Pacific trains—the special exchanged engines and crews belonging to the Union Pacific's Wyoming division for those of the Oregon Short Line. A Pocatello man named Igo replaced Sullivan Morris as the dispatcher in charge.

With daylight just about gone, the special still had 120 miles to cover before the Idaho border. Its throttle full out, its firebox glowing with a fierce orange flame, it ran across barren prairie and low chalk hills, making for the relative sanctuary of that invisible frontier. Years before, Stevenson had noted that his train "was the one piece of life in all the deadly land; it was the one action, the one spectacle fit to be observed in this paralysis of man and nature."

After an evening meal of sandwiches and hard-boiled eggs, washed down by a Budweiser or two, the prisoners—who'd had barely two hours' sleep the night before—went to bed in berths at one end of the Pullman. All of them "seemed to sleep well," Bulkeley Wells reported, while their guards kept a jittery watch. By now, the union men would have had twelve hours to organize their rescue mission, and the few remaining miles of Wyoming would be their last best chance.* But the feared "red lantern" never showed on the track ahead. Around 9:00 p.m., at a town appropriately called Border, hemmed in by grotesquely humped mountains, the special crossed into Idaho.

---

* If news of the kidnapping leaked out, as apparently it did, it was probably at Denver's Union Station, where the three labor leaders had to be walked across the large waiting room and then along a platform, where a few passengers and more than a few railroad workers might have spotted them.

The long beam of its headlight probing the wilderness, the special sped northwest. About 2:00 a.m., it pulled into Pocatello, Idaho's second-largest city, known as a labor town, just the sort of place a rescue attempt might be mounted. Even at that time of night, the extensive yards, with machine and boiler shops spread over six hundred acres, crawled with unionized railroad men—many of them Greek, Italian, and Japanese—part of its workforce of a thousand. Once again, the special ripped past at thirty miles per hour, defying anyone to jump aboard.

Before long, the train had put the city behind; under full steam again, it pushed on toward Boise. But if Bulkeley Wells and James Mills permitted themselves a sigh of relief, it was a trifle premature. About 3:00 a.m., the guards spotted a whorl of sparks from the Pullman's undercarriage; it had developed a hotbox, a housing overheated by excessive friction. The special stopped once so the crew could cool the box, but it only heated up again. A half hour later, the train had to pull onto a siding while the crew replaced a recalcitrant bearing. The guards spent a nervous three-quarters of an hour fingering their weapons, jumping at every strange sound and shadow. But nobody appeared.

As the sun rose that morning of Monday, February 19, it found the train halfway across Idaho, shuddering along the ice-encrusted banks of the Snake River. Now and then the special passed deserted depots in tiny settlements like Shoshone, Gooding, Bliss, and Mountain Home, but most of its path ran through bleak snow-covered desert, "warty with sagebrush, . . . forbidding as an ocean turned to sand." By 8:30 it reached the junction just short of Nampa, where Bulkeley Wells ordered the doors to the Pullman car opened long enough to admit the Canyon County sheriff, Jasper Nichols, and the county attorney, Owen Van Duyn, who joined the prisoners and their captors for the last stage of the journey. The gambit fooled nobody; the press soon found out where the pair had boarded. But it offered, at least symbolically, the fiction that Caldwell's own authorities had brought home the bacon.

Switching onto the spur near Nampa, the special headed into the home-stretch, reaching Boise at 9:15 a.m. It had made the trip from Denver in 27¼ hours, the fastest time on record between the two cities, a full nine hours faster than the train that had brought McParland to Boise just six weeks before. Brooding out the window at the city's ramshackle outskirts, Bill Haywood thought: "I am in the enemy's country."

Huddled under leaden skies on the platform was a clump of state offi-cials, reporters, and curious citizens alerted by the morning *Statesman,* which had carried a breathless account of the arrests, based largely on wire-service dispatches from Denver. Once the guards had disembarked and taken up positions on the platform, the prisoners, still in handcuffs, filed from the Pullman and took seats in two carriages from the state penitentiary that stood at the platform. First from the train was Pettibone, wearing a light overcoat and a stiff black hat, his face drawn and tense as he puffed on the last of

McParland's cigars. Joining Pettibone in the first carriage was Moyer, putting on a better face than his colleague and greeting several acquaintances and reporters. Last came Haywood, who made the deepest impression on the *Capital News* reporter covering the men's arrival. "The expression on his face was set," he wrote, "showing him to be a man of great determination and nerve, and if he felt any uneasiness over the situation he was in he did not express it in his countenance." As Haywood took his place in the second carriage, General Wells, Deputy Warden Mills, Nichols, and Van Duyn filled in the empty seats, the coachmen cracked their whips, and the carriages trotted off toward the pen, where the prisoners were placed in adjacent cells (numbers 9, 11, and 13) on death row.

Putting unconvicted prisoners on death row was an old McParland technique. With Orchard it had paid rich dividends, and the detective may have hoped one of the WFM leaders would crack under the strain. But ever cheerful and irreverent as his cell door clanked shut, Pettibone sang out a contemporary catchphrase: "There's luck in odd numbers, said Barney McGraw!"

The men emerging from the train—captives and captors alike—had been in a speeding time capsule for nearly thirty hours, unaware of the furor that had erupted in Denver and Boise over their irregular journey.

McParland's security measures notwithstanding, the events hadn't stayed secret very long. Even before the special left Denver, sketchy accounts of the arrests had found their way into late editions of Sunday's *Denver Post* and *Denver Republican*, where they had to compete for space with exhaustive coverage of the White House wedding of President Roosevelt's daughter, Alice. Ironically enough, the *Post* and the *Republican* were the two papers closest to the McDonald administration. Worse yet, from the detective's point of view, the *Republican* reported that the arrests were based on Harry Orchard's confession—the first time the confession had been mentioned in public. McParland worried that this revelation would tip off the WFM as to how much he knew and thereby give it time to cover some of its tracks. For this and other leaks in the *Republican*, he angrily blamed Governor McDonald's private secretary, Sam Wood, who had once worked for the *Republican* and still had ties there.

As for McDonald himself, he had fled Denver shortly after signing the requisition, making sure that he was nowhere near the site of the "extraditions." From Colorado Springs, the day after the three men were seized, the governor told the *Portland Oregonian* that he had "no knowledge of a plan to spirit the men out of town." Moreover, he expressed "surprise" that a special train had conveyed them to Boise. Asked if any member of the Colorado National Guard went with the men, he said, "Not to my knowledge." If General Wells was on the train—which the governor insisted he knew nothing about—he was there "as a private citizen."

By Monday morning, papers all across the country had time to put together fuller accounts of these events, accompanied by editorial commentary. As expected, Senator Patterson's *Rocky Mountain News* weighed in with stern criticism of the operation, concluding: "The manner in which the arrests were effected was repugnant to the spirit of the laws and constitution of the state, and the *News* feels that the officials responsible for the proceedings merit the severest censure."

John M. O'Neill, the editor of the *Miners' Magazine* and a member of the WFM's executive committee, said: "Moyer, Haywood and Pettibone were taken to Idaho illegally and the authorities there will have to return them. They are now being held illegally. All three men are residents of Denver and not Idaho. They are not fugitives from justice and therefore requisition papers could not be legally issued for their extradition."

John H. Murphy, general counsel to the Western Federation, though confined to his sickbed with tuberculosis, put it most bluntly of all: "The case is clearly kidnapping, and the local officers, detectives and some others whom I will not mention conspired together to kidnap them. They were not even allowed a chance to test the validity of the extradition papers, nor were they allowed in any manner to notify their attorneys. Why, they could not even tell their wives of their arrest before they were hustled out of the city to a place where it is extremely doubtful whether they will get a fair trial."

This sort of thing drove James McParland to distraction. Here he'd just pulled off the second biggest coup of his crime-fighting career and people were selectively leaking his carefully hoarded secrets, trying as best they could to destroy his case and blacken his name. "You see there are leakages all around," he wrote Governor Gooding on Tuesday, "and I have given a little something to the press in order to assure the public."

"A little something" didn't do it justice. The public relations blitz of the next few days began with a most unusual event: a press release over the name of the usually taciturn detective. And that statement led off with an assertion —indeed, a flat prediction—that would bedevil McParland for months to come: "The officers of the Western Federation of Miners, and those of the executive board, who are implicated in the secret designs of their leaders, will never leave Idaho alive."

The text went on:

> Although they will not leave Idaho, I have information and proof of their connection with a dozen atrocious murders in Colorado that would hang them if they did. I worked single-handed in the Molly Maguire case, and single-handed in this, and I know the ins and outs of both gangs. And let me tell you that the most fiendish work carried on by the Maguires was but child's play compared to the plots hatched by the officers of the Western Federation of Miners and carried into effect by their tools. I felt it was my duty, as a citizen of Colorado, to outroot this gang, and as such I undertook the work.

There followed a formulation that must have been a balm to his spirit, sweet recompense to a sixty-two-year-old man once a hero to many Americans but now out of the spotlight: "These fellows thought that it was so long ago that I had broken up the Molly Maguires that I must now be in my dotage. They weren't afraid of me. But there is a weak spot in every wall, especially such a wall as that upon which the Western Federation was founded, and that weak spot I found. It will cost Moyer, Haywood and Pettibone, and as many more their lives."

The press release was only the start. McParland seems to have met privately with every reporter who asked to see him, and perhaps some who did not. The campaign paid rich dividends, notably with the friendly *Republican*, where a gullible newsman concluded that McParland had literally duplicated the undercover feats of his Molly Maguire investigation: "He went into the Idaho and Colorado fields himself, worked as he had done in the anthracite mines of Pennsylvania, ingratiated himself with the conspirators, heard their secrets, found out the leaders and is now ready to proceed against the assassins." (But even this credulous reporter noted that McParland was "dumb as the proverbial oyster when questioned about details.") Others proved just as gullible. The *St. Louis Post-Dispatch* ran a drawing of "McParlan [*sic*] as he appeared when he went to work among the Idaho miners," wearing a pea jacket and wool hat, carrying a lunch pail, and trailing a long white beard.

Whether McParland made such claims we do not know, but he didn't minimize his achievements. "We have unearthed a conspiracy that will make the blood run cold," he told the *Republican*. "This is not a war against organized labor, but it is a war against organized anarchy and dynamite. It is a war against the most damnable and fiendish crimes that ever degraded humanity, and it is a war against as heartless a band of criminals as the authorities of any state or any civilized country have ever had to deal with, and I need not except Russia."

Certainly he dissembled a bit. Asked about reports that Harry Orchard had given a full confession, McParland was determined to discredit this troublesome story for the time being. So he told the *Milwaukee News* and other papers: "There have been statements made by various persons, but I know of none made by Orchard and as I have been the only man at work on the case I think I would have known of it had there been one."

As for why the men were hustled out of state in such an unorthodox manner, he obfuscated to the *Denver Times:* "I believed that if taken on the regular train from Denver to Boise the train would have been blown up or would have met with some accident and the lives of all the innocent passengers jeopardized. For that reason I refused to permit them to be taken away on the regular train. If anything had happened to that train I would have blamed myself."

The aging detective was indulging himself now in idle bluster (enough to bring a stern reminder from the prosecutors in Boise to "put on the lid and keep it on"). But some of these sentiments were undoubtedly heartfelt. The Socialist and IWW press had ridiculed McParland of late, suggesting that he was over the hill; the Socialist Party executive committee even referred to him as "the decrepit McParland." Thus his favorite refrain, repeated over and over in these months: "They thought I was an old man and in my dotage, but I surprised them."

The Western Federation had, indeed, been caught by surprise. The next move was theirs. The official escort on the train had feared they would pull into Boise only to find a WFM lawyer waiting on the platform brandishing a writ of habeas corpus.

None was there. John Murphy had been too ill to leave his bed. But at 6:10 on Sunday evening—just twelve hours after his clients had been dragooned from town—Edmund F. Richardson, perhaps the most celebrated criminal lawyer in the Rocky Mountain states, boarded the night train for Boise. A farmer's son from the Berkshire hills of Massachusetts, he'd studied law at night while working for a tailoring business, begun his practice in San Francisco, and in 1895 formed a firm in Denver with Horace Hawkins and Thomas Patterson, a partnership that Patterson left in 1904, three years after he entered the U.S. Senate. Tall, lean, and saturnine, with soulful dark eyes, a shiny bald dome, and a dark-red mustache, Ed Richardson, at age forty-three, was an enthusiastic hiker, camper, and hunter. He was proud of his magnificent physique, which he kept in fighting trim by spurning Denver's streetcars and striding back and forth to work.

But he knew that trial lawyers had, at times, to be thespians as well. Once, defending a damage suit brought by a nurse who had fallen from a stepladder while trying to pull down a window blind, Richardson climbed the offending ladder and proclaimed: "Gentlemen of the jury, I am old and bilious, and I weigh 195 pounds and sometimes I get dizzy. I have walked up that stepladder before your very eyes; and I swear that I could dance the can-can on the top of that stepladder with ease and grace." Impeccably tailored and groomed—unlike most western lawyers, he still favored the old-fashioned wing collar—he could be a shade pompous, even bombastic, and deeply jealous of his prerogatives. But nobody doubted his dedication to the cause of labor in general and to the WFM in particular. He'd represented the union over the best part of a decade, for an annual retainer of $10,000, with additional payment for specific services.

First thing Tuesday morning, Richardson appeared in Idaho's Supreme Court to ask the three justices for a writ of habeas corpus. In his brief —evidently composed on the train—Richardson argued that, in bringing Haywood, Moyer, and Pettibone to Boise, "the governors of the state of Colorado and of the state of Idaho alike were actuated by the improper motive of secretly and clandestinely arresting the bodies of these petitioners and removing them from the state of Colorado, with the express avowed intention of avoiding the issuance or service of any writ of habeas corpus which would test their right as to such removal." To justify this bogus extradition, he said, the governors had conspired to allege facts they knew to be untrue, namely "that these men were present and actually committed, by their own hand, the crime of murder upon the body of Governor Steunenberg." Thus the prisoners had been removed from Colorado "under the semblance of the forms of law, preserving the shadow, but destroying the substance."

Warming to his task, Richardson urged the two governors to "perform the duties of their gubernatorial offices in the broad light of day, with the sun of heaven shining freely and fully upon them. Let not the dark evil hours of the footpad be their chosen time for action. Let them remember that the high offices to which they have been called make of them the servants of a sovereign people, not the masters.

"The history of the entire transaction," the defense lawyer said, "reads like one of the raids of Dick Turpin or of Robin Hood. It was gentlemanly in the extreme, but it was dastardly in its execution."

As expected, the defense stressed the constitutional requirement that only a person "who shall flee from justice" can be extradited to the state "from which he fled." Haywood, Moyer, and Pettibone were not extraditable, Richardson argued, because they were not fugitives in the constitutional sense. The county attorney's complaints and affidavits notwithstanding, the three men hadn't been in Idaho at the time Frank Steunenberg was assassinated. Moyer hadn't been in Idaho since October 28, 1905, when he visited the Silver City local; Haywood since July 17, 1901; and Pettibone for at least ten years.

Hammering home that point, Richardson leaned heavily on *Hyatt v. New York,* a 1903 case involving efforts by Tennessee to extradite a man from New York despite the fact that he had not been in Tennessee at the time the alleged crime was committed. In that case, the United States Supreme Court held emphatically that "the person who is sought must be one that has fled from the demanding State" and went on to make sport of official efforts to evade that requirement: "It is difficult to see how a person can be said to have fled from the State in which he is charged to have committed some act amounting to a crime against that State, when in fact he was not within the State at the time the act is said to have been commited. How can a person flee from a place that he was not in?"

To some it may have seemed a compelling argument, but in the Boise court on March 10, the prosecution responded by asking the justices to strike out a ten-page section of the defense brief dealing with the methods by which the defendants had been brought to Idaho. Such allegations were simply irrelevent to the current proceeding, they said, for "even granting that Moyer, Haywood and Pettibone were kidnapped from the state of Colorado, forcibly and illegally brought to this jurisdiction," said James Hawley, "the fact is they are here. It makes no difference how the prisoners were brought here. They are here. That is the point."

Hawley was joined in his argument to the Supreme Court by William E. Borah, who—with the formal indictment of Haywood, Moyer, Pettibone, and Orchard by a Canyon County grand jury on March 7—had just agreed to join the prosecution team. From the start, Hawley had sought the assistance of his sometime rival, sometime colleague, a brilliant courtroom attorney and hands down Idaho's most accomplished orator.

Borah had hesitated on several grounds. First, he was busy mounting his assault on Fred Dubois's Senate seat, which would be up for grabs a year hence, and concerned about antagonizing such an important constituency as labor. But he was also plagued by doubts about Idaho's case against Haywood, Moyer, and Pettibone. So dubious was he about the state's evidence, he argued that Idaho should try Orchard and let Colorado try the WFM leaders. Indeed, he may have felt so uncomfortable with the extradition/kidnapping of the three labor leaders that he preferred to enter the case after that dirty deed was done. Then, too, there was a long history of bad feeling between Borah and Gooding, bitter factional rivals within Idaho's Republican Party. "When is Borah coming into the case?" the governor asked Pete Steunenberg in February. When Pete relayed the message, Borah barked: "I'll get in just as soon as the Governor clears the way for me to get in, and he knows it!" On the other hand, as lawyer for the late governor and a close friend, he felt himself under a powerful obligation to the Steunenberg family. Frank Steunenberg had treated him like a son, always calling him William. As early as January 5, 1906—six days after his brother's assassination—A. K. Steunenberg had written Borah, "When it becomes necessary we of course want you in this case." McParland assured Borah that the Pinkertons would produce ample witnesses and evidence to convict the labor leaders. Once the three men were sitting in the penitentiary in Boise, Borah felt he could no longer drag his feet. On March 7, he agreed to serve, nominally as an "assistant county attorney from Canyon County"—in fact as Hawley's associate counsel—for a fee of $5,000, one quarter of Hawley's retainer.

On different occasions, sometimes even on the same occasion, Hawley and Borah presented two disparate arguments for their position. The first was one of outraged innocence: "What do you mean 'kidnapping'? What we did was perfectly legal extradition!" The other was one of cool realpolitik: "Suppose we did kidnap them? What are you going to do about it?" Their own correspondence reveals that they had no faith whatsoever in the first proposition, but if others—the public at least, if not the court—would buy it, then so much the better. They could, in any case, always wheel out the second, which, unseemly though it was in public relations terms, they knew to be the legal state of affairs.

Before the Idaho Supreme Court, Borah tried out proposition number two. The state might "concede that all these allegations which the defendants' attorneys have brought up"—that the trio had been brought to Idaho forcibly and illegally—"were true," but that was of no relevance now that the defendants were in Idaho. Borah's formulation drew a telegram from the nation's ranking muckraker, Lincoln Steffens, in Washington: "Newspapers report you as saying you got Moyer and Haywood out of Colorado illegally. Please wire me collect the grounds upon which you hold them now." Borah wired back assuring Steffens that his remark had been purely "for the sake of argument," to illustrate that at this stage such questions were beside the point.

Idaho Democrats, though tempted to exploit Borah's admission as well, were nervous that they might be painting themselves into a corner with the dynamiters. On March 11, C. H. Jackson, the Democratic state chairman, wrote Charles E. Arney, Senator Dubois's assistant: "It seems to me a big howl will go up from the labor organizations, if the U.S. Constitution is powerless to prevent two Governors of States conspiring to kidnap a citizen of another state, by means of secrecy, forcible and secret arrest, special trains, etc. Since the [state court] argument there has been some change of public opinion here."

But Jackson cautioned that Democrats should "not raise the question first—we would at once raise a popular howl of joining with the dynamiters, but if we had the expression of labor organizations, we could at least say that we understand the crime, and desired the punishment of the guilty, but the laws of the land regarding individual liberty must not be violated, however commendable the end sought. There is no doubt Gooding will try to get political credit out of the crime and we ought to have some advantage from it."

On March 12, the Idaho Supreme Court handed down its ruling. Quashing the writs, it remanded the prisoners for trial. In a lengthy opinion written by Justice James F. Ailshie, with Justices Stockslager and Sullivan concurring, it barely addressed the petitioners' contention that they had been kidnapped. For that, said the justices, was simply beyond the court's jurisdiction.

Once the prisoners crossed the line into Idaho, ruled the court, they had lost their right to challenge the legality of their extradition. "The question as to whether or not a citizen is a fugitive from justice is one that can only be available to him so long as he is beyond the jurisdiction of the state against whose laws he has transgressed." So long as the three men were in Colorado, the validity of their arrest and dispatch aboard the special could have been challenged in a Colorado court, wrote Ailshie, but once they reached Idaho, the warrants issued by Governor McDonald had accomplished their purpose and could not be contested—certainly not in Idaho.

The justices agreed that if any crime had been committed in "abducting, apprehending, or arresting the accused," those responsible could be "held to answer in the proper jurisdiction," presumably Colorado. But Colorado was hardly likely to bring kidnapping charges against—among others—its own adjutant general and Captain Strickland of the National Guard.

By the time Idaho's high court ruled in early March, the "kidnapping" of the three labor leaders had become a cause célèbre on the American left. Week after week, the saga of the special train—which critics soon dubbed "the Pirate Special"—utterly engrossed the nation's labor and Socialist press, culminating in a remarkable manifesto from Eugene Debs. "Arouse, Ye Slaves!" read the headline in red ink stripped across the front page of the March 10 *Appeal to Reason*, the Socialist weekly. Responding to McParland's bold prediction that the prisoners would "never leave Idaho alive," Debs penned the Socialists' incendiary answer:

> Well, by the gods, if they don't, the governors of Idaho and Colorado and the masters from Wall Street, New York, to the Rocky Mountains had better prepare to follow them.... Nearly twenty years ago the capitalist tyrants put some innocent men to death for standing up for labor. They are now going to try it again. Let them dare! There have been twenty years of revolutionary education, agitation, and organization since the Haymarket tragedy, and if an attempt is made to repeat it, there will be a revolution and I will do all in my power to precipitate it.... If they attempt to murder Moyer, Haywood and Pettibone and their brothers, a million revolutionists will meet them with guns.

According to the radical historian Louis Adamic, this wasn't empty rhetoric. "Debs," he wrote, "wanted to organize an army in the manner of John Brown (whom he admired above all other characters in American history) and march to Idaho and free Haywood, Moyer and Pettibone by force." Debs's levelheaded wife evidently talked him out of the harebrained scheme. But Montana Socialists were so convinced that Debs meant to carry out his threat, they offered to meet him at the Idaho border with ten thousand men on horseback, armed with Winchesters and two hundred rounds of ammunition, to rescue the trio.*

On March 31, *Appeal to Reason* published an issue entirely devoted to the Haywood-Moyer-Pettibone case, a so-called Rescue Edition, for which it claimed a phenomenal circulation of four million. For this issue, George H. Shoaf, a correspondent dispatched to Boise, had obtained brief messages from each of the jailed men. Haywood produced the obligatory defiance of the martyr: "If it requires my life's blood to give impetus to the cause of Socialism, I am ready and willing that it be shed."

Even after the Idaho Supreme Court ruled against them, the defense attorneys didn't lose hope of a legal victory. For there was reason to doubt

---

* In a letter to his attorney general, Theodore Roosevelt cited another threat along the same lines, by the president of the American Flint Glass Workers Union: "If the capitalistic class... persists in its attempt to send Haywood and Moyer to the gallows, I, for one, am in favor of loading ourselves with dynamite, proceeding to Boise City, and blowing that jail to smithereens" (Roosevelt to William Moody, March 26, 1906).

that Justice Stockslager and his two colleagues had been utterly dispassionate. After all, the chief justice himself had been deeply enmeshed in the Steunenberg murder investigation from its inception, had been James McParland's first powerful ally in Idaho, and had remained in close touch with the detective. Moreover, only a few weeks before, he and his bench mate Sullivan had privately assured McParland that they would not free Harry Orchard on a habeas corpus petition. Stockslager might well have recused himself from the case on several grounds of conflict of interest. But preparing to challenge Gooding for the governor's office that November, he was no doubt eager to give a public demonstration of his resistance to the dynamiters.

Suspecting this, the defense attorneys also submitted habeas corpus petitions to Boise's federal bench, in the person of Judge James H. Beatty. But Beatty owed his seat principally to northern Idaho mining interests. A former chief judge of Idaho's territorial supreme court, he'd been named the state's federal judge in 1890 through the efforts of Simeon Reed, then proprietor of the Bunker Hill and Sullivan mine, who desperately needed judicial help in a critical case involving his title to the mine. A thoroughly political man with high ambitions, the seventy-year-old Beatty was that anomaly among the hard-drinking early settlers, a strict teetotaler, who had earned himself the sobriquet Aunt Nancy.

When oral arguments began before Beatty on March 19, Borah changed his tune a bit, arguing in vivid, forceful oratory that the extraditions were perfectly legal since the complaints and affidavits drawn up by Owen Van Duyn were, in fact, altogether accurate:

> If [the prisoners] are deemed co-conspirators, they must, under the law of Idaho, be charged as principals in that murder. The instrument through which they are charged with having committed the crime was here in Idaho, was in Caldwell on the night of the crime—actually committed the crime. If these men, as it is charged, sent Harry Orchard to Caldwell to kill Frank Steunenberg, they are today just as guilty of that crime as if they had stood corporeally present within two feet of Harry Orchard when he exploded the bomb which caused the death of former Governor Frank Steunenberg.
>
> Suppose they had sent Frank Steunenberg an infernal machine through the mails, which, when he opened it, had exploded and killed him? Would they not have been guilty as principals? What is the difference between sending an infernal machine through the mails to kill their marked victim and sending an infernal wretch to do the same work?

Borah was right about the charge. The indictment of Haywood, Moyer, Pettibone, and Simpkins, handed down by a Canyon County grand jury on March 7, 1906, charged all four (and Orchard) equally with "the crime of murder," in that they did, "in the said City of Caldwell," then and there "unlawfully, wilfully, deliberately, premeditatedly, feloniously and of their and each of their malice aforethought, in and upon one Frank Steunenberg make an assault" by setting off a bomb that killed him.

That didn't mean that for extradition purposes the men were considered to be legally present in Idaho. Indeed, in *Hyatt* the U.S. Supreme Court had been unequivocal in its insistence on "corporeal" presence. What one judge scornfully referred to as "a constructive presence in a state and a constructive flight from a constructive presence" wouldn't pass muster. That was the heart of the defense argument.

Yet, once again, that argument proved immaterial. For the following day, Judge Beatty sustained the prosecution's contention that it was "sham and irrelevent" how the defendants' bodies came to be in Idaho. Quashing the writs, he remanded the prisoners to Sheriff Nichols for trial on charges of murder.

The defense promptly went to the U.S. Supreme Court, where its case was merged with an appeal already taken from the decision of the Idaho Supreme Court, in a single case known as *Pettibone v. Nichols.* The stage was set for an epic struggle before the nation's highest tribunal.

The prospects for victory there were scarcely promising. In that first decade of the new century, the Supreme Court, presided over by Chief Justice Melville W. Fuller, was not a particularly distinguished judicial body. President Theodore Roosevelt, increasingly at odds with the Court, accused it of assuming "functions which properly belong to the legislative bodies" and labeled one recent decision "a very slovenly piece of work."

As early as 1895, two of its landmark decisions—*Pollock v. Farmers Loan and Trust Co.,* which invalidated the federal income tax, and *In re Debs,* which upheld a federal court injunction to break the Pullman strike—left the impression that the Fuller Court was hostile to the aspirations of labor and the poor alike. A decade later, this reputation was reinforced by the notorious *Lochner v. New York,* which invalidated a state law placing a sixty-hour ceiling on the workweek of bakery employees, because it violated liberty of contract. Moreover, the Court asserted that private contracts were outside the scope of the law and thus the state couldn't interfere with them. Like no other case before or after, *Lochner* stirred public outrage at the Court's rigidity, preparing a fertile field in which the seeds of Progressive dissent could flourish. Other decisions—*Adair v. United States* (1908), which invalidated legislation protecting union activity, and *Ex parte Young* (1908), blocking enforcement of laws governing railroad rates—put the Court increasingly at odds with the Progressive era. Henceforth, critics writing within that tradition accused the Fuller Court of using the constitutional ideal of "liberty" to camouflage its defense of narrow class interests.

The prevailing judicial doctrine of the time has been termed "formalism," which one commentator calls "less a habit of mind than a habit of style, less a way of thinking than a way of disguising thought." Opinions were frequently "bombastic, diffuse, labored, drearily logical, crammed with unnecessary citations." Underlying the formalistic style was the cherished notion that judges did not make law but merely discovered it in precedent or in the fount of all wisdom, the Constitution.

The cult of the Constitution can be read in the exaltation by Henry R. Estabrook, a New York attorney: "Our great and sacred Constitution, serene and inviolable, stretches its beneficent powers over our land . . . like the outstretched arm of God himself. . . . O Marvelous Constitution! Magic Parchment! Transforming Word! Maker, Monitor, Guardian of Mankind!"

Roosevelt's successor, Republican William Howard Taft, had no ideological quarrel with the Court, but shortly after entering the White House in 1909, he confided to a friend: "The condition of the Supreme Court is pitiable . . . and yet those old fools hold on with a tenacity that is most discouraging. Really the Chief Justice is almost senile; [John Marshall] Harlan does no work; [David J.] Brewer is so deaf that he cannot hear and has got beyond the point of commonest accuracy in writing his opinions; Brewer and Harlan sleep almost all through the argument. I don't know what can be done."

Melville Fuller had been a moderately successful Chicago lawyer with no stature at the national bar when President Cleveland named him Chief Justice in 1888. One newspaper called him "the most obscure man ever appointed Chief Justice." During twenty-two years in office, he wrote few opinions of major importance, contenting himself with the roles of moderator and traffic cop.

By default, the intellectual leadership of the Court fell to two justices— David J. Brewer and Rufus W. Peckham—who reflected the business-oriented conservatism that held sway in Washington for decades before the century's turn. Of the two, Brewer was the stronger personality and his worldview the more bleakly reactionary. As such, he drew Theodore Roosevelt's private but "profound" contempt.

Brewer and Peckham favored "a self-regulating, competitive market economy presided over by a neutral, impartial and decentralized 'night watchman' state." If pressures were building for government to shuck some of its vaunted neutrality in order to avoid social chaos, Brewer at least was having none of it. In a speech to the New York State Bar in 1893—six months after the Pinkerton shootout with strikers at Homestead, Pennsylvania—he asserted that "it is the unvarying law, that the wealth of a community will be in the hands of a few," warned of "the red flag of socialism, inviting a redistribution of property," and cautioned that, unchecked, "the wide unrest that fills the land . . . will culminate in revolution." Time and again, it was Brewer or Peckham who wrote the major decisions of that era, generally assembling a majority from the other Cleveland-Harrison-McKinley appointees (among them Fuller, Edward D. White, and Joseph McKenna).

The bench's two mavericks were outsize men, as different from each other as they were from their less vivid colleagues: Oliver Wendell Holmes and John Marshall Harlan.

Already a towering figure in American law when Roosevelt put him on the Court in 1902, Holmes would later be described by Benjamin Cardozo as "probably the greatest legal intellect in the history of the English-speaking judiciary." But in doctrinal terms, he was not quite the commodity most people had expected. When some Wall Streeters opposed his nomination because of his prolabor rulings on Massachusetts's high bench, Holmes wrote a friend, "Some at least of the money powers think me dangerous, wherein they are wrong." Roosevelt, who had anticipated stalwart support from the new justice, found reason to rue the appointment when Holmes dissented in the critical antitrust case *Northern Securities v. United States* (1903). "I could carve out of a banana a judge with more backbone than that," the president is reported to have exclaimed on hearing of Holmes's position.

If Holmes was more receptive to the freshets of Progressivism than most of his colleagues were, he cringed at its fundamental economic principles. "Economics bored him," says one of his more perceptive biographers, "and utopian economics bored him absolutely." He could be scornful of the majority's obeisance to liberty of contract, as in a quip from his *Lochner* dissent: "The Fourteenth Amendment does not enact Mr. Herbert Spencer's Social Statics." He disdained some members of that laissez-faire majority. When a law clerk once asked what Peckham was like "intellectually," Holmes replied, "I never thought of him in that connection. His major premise was 'God damn it!'"

But he was just as skeptical of those who expected the state to remedy every ill of mankind. "Legislation can't cure things" was one of his central tenets. Ruminating on the "revolt against pain," he told Harvard's graduates in 1895: "From societies for the prevention of cruelty to animals up to socialism, we express in numberless ways the notion that suffering is a wrong which can be and ought to be prevented, and a whole literature of sympathy has sprung into being which points out in story and in verse how hard it is to be wounded in the battle of life, how terrible, how unjust it is that any one should fail." He never quite transcended his Olympian upbringing, once complaining to Francis Biddle about the difficulty of finding a designer for a piece of jewelry because "the best designers were working for the multitude who bought paste at the five and tens." He chanted, as if it were some grumpy mantra, "The crowd has substantially all there is."

The same hauteur was evident in his characterization of his senior colleague John Marshall Harlan of Kentucky as "the last of the tobacco-spitting judges." Regarding him as more demagogue than thinker, and a bit of a windbag at that, Holmes referred to him in debate as "my lion-hearted friend" but once likened Harlan's mental processes to "a great vise, the two jaws of which cannot be closed closer than two inches of each other."

Surely Harlan's verbose pronunciamentos grated on his colleagues. At seventy-three, he was the Court's oldest justice, its "great gnarled oak," its "gray eagle." Justice Brewer once remarked, with some levity, that Harlan "goes to bed every night with one hand on the Constitution and the other on the Bible, and so sleeps the sweet sleep of justice and righteousness." Implacable self-confidence and religious fundamentalism combined to produce a stubborn conviction that, in a colleague's words, often made "differences between himself and others ... impossible of reconciliation."

Temperamentally independent, he was led by no man. A former slaveholder who had seen the light, he was now a visionary on matters of race. Moved by the plight of freed blacks, he broadly construed the federal government's power to protect constitutional rights under the Reconstruction Amendments. He is best known for his powerful dissent from the separate but equal doctrine of *Plessy v. Ferguson* (1896): "Our Constitution is color-blind, and neither knows nor tolerates classes among citizens." Moreover, on a Court generally deaf to issues of procedural due process, Harlan was one of the few justices inclined at times to protect individuals whose rights were abridged in state criminal procedures (though generally not through habeas corpus). His dissents in *Hurtado v. California* (1884) and *Twining v. New Jersey* (1908) reflect his belief that the Bill of Rights ought to apply to the states through the due process clause of the Fourteenth Amendment.

Yet when his personal sympathies were not engaged, Harlan could be as dry and inflexible as anyone in the conservative majority. Like most of his colleagues, he could be rigidly formalistic, blankly refusing to look behind the forms of the law to assess their real results. Consider his comment in a case involving a Chinese woman deported from the United States after a hearing held in English, of which she understood not a single word: "If the appellant's want of knowledge of the English language put her at some disadvantage," wrote Harlan, "that was her misfortune, and constitutes no reason ... for the intervention of the court by *habeas corpus.*"

It was no surprise, then, when Harlan found no reason to free Haywood, Pettibone, and Moyer. Another factor, however, may have contributed to his decision. James Hawley, who argued the state's side of the case before the Court, later confided to James McParland that, while in Washington for those oral arguments in October 1906, he had "a long talk" with Justice Harlan, whom he had known for some years. Hawley told McParland that "he did not attempt to prejudice the Justice in favor of the State of Idaho" but nonetheless "told him some facts" that Hawley thought would have "a good effect." One can only speculate what those "facts" might have been: very likely details from Harry Orchard's confession of mayhem and murder that had not yet been made public. After hearing what Hawley had to tell him, Harlan, in turn, indicated that the Court would rule promptly on the matter. It was a perilous confession for Hawley to make, even to the secretive detective. For if the attorney and the justice discussed the pending case at all, it would have been a clear violation of judicial procedure, which prohibits such ex parte contact, that is, contact between the justices and one party to a case without the other party being present. The horror at ex parte contacts that prevails today was perhaps not quite so fierce in 1906. But had the Harlan-Hawley meeting been revealed at the time, the defense surely would have used it to challenge the Court's decision.

In any case, on December 3, 1906, Harlan spoke for a seven-judge majority—made up of "the Chief"; the other great dissenter, Holmes; the Court's wheelhorses, Brewer and Peckham; the scholarly but "jovial monk," White; and the Court's newest justice, wizened, solemn William R. Day—in rejecting Pettibone's appeal.* Harlan's lengthy opinion did not closely scrutinize the trio's arrest or "extradition" from Colorado, except to say: "We do not perceive that anything done there, however hastily or inconsiderately done, can be adjudged to be in violation of the Constitution or laws of the United States."

That did not mean the Court was satisfied that there had been no improprieties in the methods used to bring the men to Idaho. Indeed, it went out of its way to say it "had not overlooked the allegation that the governor and other officers of Idaho well knew at the time the requisition was made upon the governor of Colorado that Pettibone was not in Idaho on December 30, 1905, nor at any time near that date, and had the purpose in all they did to evade the constitutional and statutory provisions relating to fugitives from justice."

The Court suggested that Governor McDonald might well have gone further to investigate the allegation and establish that the prisoners were truly fugitives from justice within the meaning of the Constitution. But, Harlan noted, the requisition papers before McDonald stated unequivocally that the three men, charged with murder in Idaho, were fugitives from justice. "The governor of Colorado was entitled to accept such papers, coming as they did from the governor of another state, as prima facie sufficient for a warrant of arrest."

The blunt refusal to look behind the assertions in Van Duyn's affidavits was a critical link in the Court's reasoning. On this point, Harlan relied on the authority of none other than John Marshall Harlan, namely his own opinion in the 1885 case *Ex parte Reggel,* which dealt with the sufficiency of requisition papers sent by the governor of Pennsylvania to the governor of Utah seeking the return of a "fugitive" con man, Louis Reggel. Although there were doubts that Reggel was truly a fugitive, Harlan had written then that Reggel "should not be discharged merely because, in the judgment of the court, the evidence as to his being a fugitive from justice was not as full as might properly have been required, or because it was so meager as perhaps to admit of a conclusion different from that reached by him [Utah's governor]."

But in that case, Reggel had properly brought his habeas corpus action in Utah, the asylum state. If the judge there was not required to look behind

---

* For purposes of appeal, the three cases had been consolidated. Any ruling on Pettibone applied as well to Haywood and Moyer.

such assertions, so much less was the judge in a demanding state like Idaho. Once again, as the two lower courts had found, the critical question was one of timing. "It is true, as contended by the petitioner, that if he was not a fugitive from justice, within the meaning of the Constitution, no warrant for his arrest could have been properly or legally issued by the governor of Colorado," wrote Harlan in *Pettibone*. "It is equally true that, even after the issuing of such a warrant, before his deportation from Colorado, it was competent for a court, Federal or state, sitting in that state, to inquire whether he was, in fact, a fugitive from justice, and if found not to be, to discharge him from the custody of the Idaho agent."

But now—as the defendants had heard twice before—it was simply too late. "That he had no reasonable opportunity to present these facts before being taken from Colorado constitutes no legal reason why he should be discharged from the custody of the Idaho authorities. No obligation was imposed by the Constitution or the laws of the United States upon the agent of Idaho to so time the arrest of the petitioner, and so conduct his deportation from Colorado, as to afford him a convenient opportunity, before some judicial tribunal sitting in Colorado, to test the question whether he was a fugitive from justice."

Indeed, as Harlan wrote—dipping his pen in the very inkwell that Chief Justice Taney had used in crafting the infamous Dred Scott opinion—the central question came down to this: "As the petitioner is within the jurisdiction of Idaho, and is held by its authorities for trial, are the particular methods by which he was brought within her limits at all material in the proceeding by *habeas corpus?*"

In appoaching this nub, the Court leaned on two of its earlier cases, *Ker v. Illinois* and *Mahon v. Justice*, in which plaintiffs had been kidnapped by private parties and brought to trial in Illinois and Kentucky, respectively. In both cases, the Court ruled that, once a defendant is brought into a state's custody and charged with a crime against its laws, the state may try him without inquiring into the methods used to bring him into the state, even when those methods amounted to outright kidnapping. Or, as the Court put it now, "a party is not excused from answering to the state whose laws he has violated because violence has been done him in bringing him within the state."

Toward the end of his opinion, Harlan hinted again that the Court did not mean entirely to sanction what the governors of Idaho and Colorado had done. But "if, as suggested, the application of these principles may be attended by mischievous consequences, involving the personal safety of individuals within the limits of the respective states," Harlan advised, "the remedy is with the lawmaking department of the government. Congress has long been informed by the judicial decisions as to the state of the law upon this general subject." But no such congressional action would be of any help to the three prisoners, who had now to stand trial in Idaho.

The opinion was as arid and formalistic as any the Court issued in those years. Yes, the justices seemed to be saying, it was very likely that the plaintiffs had been kidnapped and illegally transported across state lines on the basis of falsified documents based on perjured affidavits knowingly sworn to by high governmental officials and other officers of the law—but all this was simply beside the point. The forms of the law put the prisoners beyond the reach of habeas corpus. Though it was unfortunate, nothing could be done about it.

Against the seven-man majority—one seat was vacant—stood a single justice, a most unlikely dissenter. Joseph McKenna was a former federal judge and four-term congressman from California. On the House Ways and Means Committee, he'd become an ally of its chairman, William McKinley. When McKinley advanced to the White House in 1897, he asked his former colleague to become attorney general, with the understanding that he'd get the next vacancy on the Supreme Court, which came months later with the retirement of Stephen J. Field. McKenna was the weakest nominee to the high bench in some time: a patrician, an avid golfer, a faithful Republican and staunch supporter of high tariffs, sound money, laissez-faire, and the railroads, notably the Southern Pacific Railroad, headed by his close friend Senator Leland Stanford.

Small and birdlike, with delicate features, a close-cropped white beard, and darting brown eyes, McKenna carried himself stiffly erect. When he first ran for Congress, a friendly columnist portrayed him as "sprucely attired, natty in bearing, graceful in gesture, terse and dainty in language, earnest in look, musical in voice." Others assessed him less kindly: "a small man in every way and a cunning trimmer," said one critic.

Nothing in his early years on the Court did much to change this view of him. Ill at ease among his more learned colleagues, unsure of his constitutional ground, cautious to the point of timidity, he anchored his opinions in great clumps of uncritical citations and precedents.

As he gained his footing, he felt his way toward some measure of independence—often picking pointless little fights with the erudite Holmes, of whom he appeared to be jealously resentful. On occasion, though, he was capable of a spirited show of conscience. A devout Catholic, McKenna accepted the doctrine of natural law, the notion that the most fundamental human rights sprang not from man-made statutes but from the divine will of God. Since the state had not made these rights, it could not take them away. Moreover, he was something of a libertarian—though that term was not yet in wide use—eager to protect individual, and corporate, freedoms at all cost. By 1906, McKenna was risking more principled stands, generally when he could ground his positions in natural law.

The Idaho case presented just such an opportunity. For to McKenna, his colleagues' bland stamp of approval on the abduction of Haywood, Moyer, and Pettibone violated the spirit of the Constitution and a higher law as well. He wondered how his fellow justices, sworn to uphold the Constitution, could defend the following propositions: "that the officers of one state may falsely represent that a person was personally present in the state and committed a crime there, and had fled from its justice, may arrest such person and take him from another state, the officers of the latter knowing of the false accusation, and conniving in and abiding its purpose, thereby depriving him of an opportunity to appeal to the courts, and that such person cannot invoke the rights guaranteed to him by the Constitution and statutes of the United States in the state to which he is taken."

As for *Ker* and *Mahon,* he noted that there was one major distinction between them and the present case. In both of the cited cases, the kidnappers were private persons; this time, they were the states themselves, acting through their officers. "No individual or individuals," McKenna remarked, "could have accomplished what the power of the two states accomplished; ... could have commanded the resources of jails, armed guards, and special trains; could have successfully timed all acts to prevent inquiry and judicial interference.

"Kidnapping is a crime, pure and simple," he proclaimed. "All of the officers of the law are supposed to be on guard against it. All of the officers of the law may be invoked against it. But how is it when the law becomes the kidnapper? When the officers of the law, using its forms, and exerting its power, become abductors?"

At stake in this case, McKenna argued, was nothing less than "the right to be free from molestation ... the right of personal liberty in its most complete sense. ... It is to be hoped that our criminal jurisprudence will not need for its efficient administration the destruction of either the right or the means to enforce it. The decision in the case at bar, as I view it, brings us perilously near both results."

But all of McKenna's heartfelt eloquence was to no avail. After ten months of judicial process, the case of the three kidnapped labor leaders was remanded to the courts of Canyon County, Idaho, for trial.

7

THE GREAT DEFENDER

BEFORE FRANK STEUNENBERG was blown up at his garden gate, the most infamous murder in Idaho history was the Diamondfield Jack case, arising from the shooting, in early 1896, of two young sheepherders trespassing on a cattle range in the state's rugged southwest corner. The case became celebrated in part because of its picturesque leading figures: Diamondfield Jack Davis, a gunslinger retained by the Sparks-Harrell cattle outfit, and his sometime companion Diamond Tooth Lil, an itinerant dance-hall girl, prostitute, and madam, who had a one-third-carat diamond embedded in a gold front tooth. But what held the attention of the press and the public were the powerful interests ranged on either side. For this was one of the last great confrontations in the sheep and cattle wars that had raged across the West for a decade.

Cattle operations like Sparks-Harrell needed huge tracts of rangeland on which to graze their herds, generally in small groups; feeding off the juiciest greenery, the cattle left the roots to flourish again the following spring. Sheep traveled in herds of several thousand, sweeping across the range like a firestorm, devouring grasses and other foliage down to the roots, leaving nothing for cattle to feed on. It is difficult to exaggerate the rage cattlemen felt toward sheepmen and their voracious creatures, variously called "desert maggots" and "hoofed locusts." The sheepmen returned the compliment. The war between these two factions had claimed hundreds of lives over the years, leaving untold bitterness in its wake.

By 1896, the sheepmen had definitively breached the so-called deadline along the ridge separating Goose and Deep Creeks, pushing their herds into the bunchgrass that stretched west to the Salmon Falls River. As one of the Sparks-Harrell enforcers, Diamondfield Jack had warned on several occasions, "I'll kill the next sheepherder who crosses that ridge." Not surprisingly, he was the principal suspect when a sheriff's party found the bodies of John Wilson and Daniel Cummings lying in a sheep wagon along Deep Creek, each killed by a single well-placed gunshot.

Sparks-Harrell retained James H. Hawley as its lead lawyer in the defense of Diamondfield Jack, while the Sheep Men's Association employed Bill

Borah and O. W. Powers of Salt Lake City as special prosecutors. The legal struggle dragged on for nearly seven years—through Jack's conviction by a jury, a death sentence, countless appeals to higher courts, and several stays of execution. Year after year, Jim Hawley fought doggedly on his client's behalf —once offering his own neck in exchange for his client's—until, in July 1901, he won a commutation of the death sentence to life imprisonment and ultimately, in December 1902, a full pardon.

In an age when lawyers' collisions were often prime entertainment, the legal duels between Jim Hawley and Bill Borah—Idaho's most renowned attorneys—drew substantial crowds to county courthouses. A year before the Diamondfield Jack case got under way, Hawley and Borah had opposed each other in a celebrated lawsuit brought by three heirs of Milton Kelly, a pioneer attorney and publisher, against a fourth, his daughter Mrs. Joseph Perrault, seeking to set aside Kelly's deed of some hot springs to her.

Shortly after the Kelly trial began, Borah took strong exception to Hawley's questioning of a witness, styling it "pettifoggery." Hawley's famous temper flared up and "a warm crossfire of words" ensued. When both men ignored the judge's admonitions to take their seats, he thundered, "The sheriff will seat the gentlemen." At last they sat.

Though these weren't the first hot words they'd exchanged, Hawley and Borah never allowed their clients' embitterment to permanently sour their own relationship. On several occasions, they'd found themselves on the same side of a major case—notably at the trials growing out of the Coeur d'Alene labor unrest of 1899. Although Borah's precarious ride atop the train to prove his point in the Corcoran case remained the most flamboyant feat in Idaho lawyering, he had no difficulty in acknowledging Hawley—his elder by nineteen years—as dean of Idaho's bar.

Indeed, no Idaho lawyer could match the length and breadth of Hawley's courtroom experience. Like Frank Steunenberg a native of Iowa, Hawley had emigrated at age fifteen to California and thence to northern Idaho, attracted by a gold discovery there. After reading law with a local attorney, he was elected to the territorial legislature as a Democrat in 1870, then became U.S. attorney for the territory and mayor of Boise. By 1890, when he opened a law office in Boise, he was the state's leading defense attorney. There were so few resident lawyers in Idaho's early days that between the years 1881 and 1890 Hawley appeared in nearly 10 percent of all recorded cases. So many matters had he tried on both sides of the courtroom that Borah once remarked of him, "Jim Hawley has defended more men, and got them acquitted, and prosecuted more men and got them convicted, than any lawyer in America." Even *Appeal to Reason* called him "the ablest criminal lawyer in the West."

The very model of an old-time western lawyer, he had little of the eastern advocates' polish and erudition. Loose-jointed, careless in dress and grooming, he liked to slouch in a chair, chewing on a toothpick, his boots on the tabletop. When aroused, this old lion of the law could roar and snarl. He wasn't suave, but few lawyers could move an Idaho jury as Hawley could.

His specialty was murder, a category of crime that produced plenty of legal retainers in Idaho. Since 1890 no longer on the state's payroll as a prosecutor, he'd often returned as a special prosecutor in particularly weighty cases. Now, at the age of sixty-one, Jim Hawley was trying the most spectacular—and consequential—murder case of his career. He was grimly determined to see it through to a conviction.

If Hawley represented his rough-hewn pioneer generation, Borah personified the emerging corporate order of the New West. No lawyer in the state enjoyed as big—and profitable—a corporate practice as Borah; his annual salary by 1906 as a partner in the Boise firm of Borah and Blake was said to be $30,000, equivalent to $540,000 today—making him perhaps the highest-earning professional in the state.

He'd come a long way from Fairfield, Illinois, where he was born at the close of the Civil War. His father was a farmer, stock raiser, and Presbyterian elder, a stern, puritanical, humorless man. From an early age, young Borah blazed his own path, displaying a talent for oratory and running away briefly with a theatrical troupe, with whom he played Marc Antony. By 1885 he'd joined a sister in Lyons, Kansas, and enrolled at the University of Kansas. For a year and a half, he made excellent grades and was pledged to Beta Theta Phi, which passed over his friend William Allen White as "too damned fresh."

White described the collegiate Borah as "thick-necked" and "starry-eyed," a "serious man with no 'side,' no quips and jibes, an honest, hard-working, substantial, serious student who smiled easily but rarely laughed." But in March of his second year, he came down with tuberculosis and left the university for good. Reading law in the office of his brother-in-law, Ansel Lasley, he passed the bar in 1897 and became Lasley's partner. Two years later, he was Lyons's city attorney.

According to legend—repeated by his biographers—Borah got restless in Lyons; following the West's siren call, he took a train as far as his money would carry him and got off in Boise. In fact, Borah had quickly overcome schoolboy inhibitions, become quite a ladies' man, and, in mid-1890, got one Lyons belle pregnant. Her family gave him no choice but to leave town. On the train, he met a gambler who recommended Boise as "a likely town" for a young lawyer, and Borah landed there at a propitious moment—a few months after Idaho joined the union.

Borah neither drank nor used tobacco, but he pursued women voraciously, soon gaining a reputation as Boise's "town bull." He took rooms on Idaho Street, at the edge of the city's red-light district, and his first office was in the district. Legend has it that he frequented two of the better houses, Hattie Carlton's and Dora Bowman's.

Nonetheless, Borah found time for the practice of law and rose rapidly in the ranks of Idaho attorneys, becoming a favorite of the state's mine operators, timber barons, and sheep and cattle kings. Meanwhile, his oratorical skills drew the attention of Republican politicians, who recruited him for campaign duty. In 1891, he lost a first run for Boise city attorney by a scant three votes.

As a part-time secretary to the Republican governor, William J. McConnell, Borah was thrown into contact with McConnell's daughter Mary, who also worked as her father's secretary. A blue-eyed blond active in Boise society, Mamie, as she was known, was Idaho's prize catch. Borah won her and they were married in April 1895, moving to a handsome white gingerbread house designed by John E. Tourtellotte, the architect later responsible for the Steunenberg bank in Caldwell. Borah lined the bright front room with bookcases, assembling one of the state's finest private libraries, where he liked to sit of an evening with a volume of history or economics. But this nesting didn't halt his philandering, which continued through his Boise years and later in Washington.*

By 1896, Borah was an early leader of the Silver Republicans, bolting the GOP to support the Bryan ticket nationally and Frank Steunenberg's silver coalition in Idaho. It was then that Borah and Steunenberg formed a close personal relationship, which lasted until the governor's untimely death.

Most of Idaho's politicians had gone mad for silver in 1896, but the old guard of Idaho's Republican Party—notably Hosea B. Eastman and Joseph Perrault—never forgave Borah's defection. By autumn 1902, he'd returned to the Grand Old Party, becoming a leading candidate for the U.S. Senate. One evening, as a Borah parade assembled in Boise, Perrault—whose family Borah had represented in the bitter courtroom fight with Jim Hawley seven years earlier—spotted his nemesis in the street. From the veranda of the Overland Hotel, he shouted, "I heard you denounce McKinley from this porch in 1898."

Wheeling around, Borah yelled, "What the ———— business is it of yours? I want you to stop denouncing me on the street!"

"I will denounce you any place," said Perrault. "Because it's true!"

With that, Borah raised his cane, reached onto the porch, and cracked Perrault twice on the head, adding, "You would have denounced McKinley, too, if you weren't drawing wages from him."

"You're a liar!" Perrault shot back.

"You're a thief!" said Borah, taking off his coat. "You can't come out in the road?" Perrault was ready to fight, but friends of both men intervened.

---

* Borah had a long affair in Washington with the president's married daughter, Alice Roosevelt Longworth. Getting wind of it, reporters dubbed her—in private—Aurora Borah Alice. When she bore a child in 1924, the inside word in the capital was that Borah was the father. According to one account, Alice wanted to call the girl Deborah, but her husband, Nicholas Longworth, indignantly refused. "With all the gossip going around," he reportedly objected, "why would you want to name her De-Borah?" The child was raised in the Longworth home and eventually married a writer named Alex M. Sturm (Felsenthal, *Princess Alice*, 155–60).

The old guard's fierce opposition notwithstanding, Borah loomed as the leading candidate for the Senate seat. His most vigorous—and significant—support came from Calvin Cobb, publisher of the *Statesman*, who'd once denounced him strenuously for his defection but who'd long since welcomed him back to the fold. For several years, Cobb helped build Borah's Senate candidacy. Later, he would remind the senator that his was the "hand that rocked your political cradle."

By January 7, 1903, when the Republican caucus met in the capital to nominate a senator, Borah seemed to have the spot locked up. On the first ballot, he received eighteen votes to sixteen for Weldon B. Heyburn, a spokesman for the old guard, and seventeen for two lesser candidates. The *Capital News* proclaimed the following day, "W. E. Borah Will Win Tonight." But before the caucus convened, supporters of the other three candidates combined to deprive Borah of his prize. To that end, six or seven legislators were paid $750 per head for their votes, and by evening Heyburn had the nomination, twenty-eight to twenty-two.

This last-minute reversal haunted Borah for the next four years, prompting him to devise a way of beating the old guard at its own game. Since his strength was in the grass roots and his weakness in the legislature, he would have preferred the popular election of senators—but that took a constitutional amendment. So he called for the next best thing: nomination by the state convention instead of by the legislature. As he stumped the state inveighing against the evils of "King Caucus," he garnered wide support. Herein lies the paradox of Borah's politics: though he was the most successful corporation lawyer in the state, with intimate ties to the mining and timber magnates, the fierce opposition of the Republican old guard and their manipulation of the party caucus to bar his way to the Senate compelled Borah to advocate more "democratic" means of electing senators, a position that—with his natural tolerance and generosity—gradually pulled him into the Progressive camp. But whether taking Progressive stands at home or isolationist stands abroad, what characterized Borah most was his lone-wolf style, an almost obsessive independence from bosses, parties, or political organizations (he served a brief stint as Republican state chairman and hated the job). Increasingly he became a freelance moralist, jousting with evil as Don Quixote did with windmills.

Even a loner like Borah had to make some political accommodations. In 1904, he and Frank Gooding, though they never got along either personally or politically, struck a deal: he'd support Gooding for the governorship that year and Gooding would back him for the Senate two years later. But at the Republican convention in August 1906, Gooding tried to welch on the deal, hoping to put the Republican state chairman, James H. Brady—or even Judge James H. Beatty of the federal bench—in the job instead.

After two days of "battle ax and tomahawk," Borah rallied his forces, beat back the challenge, and received the convention's nomination for senator (which would almost certainly be ratified by the legislature when it met in January 1907). Brady took defeat graciously, acknowledging that "no man is bigger than his party." But Beatty fulminated: "A few demogogues want to control the party. A dozen men meet and undertake to tell who the officers of the state shall be." Borah had earned the judge's undying enmity.

By the summer of 1906, with the great prize he'd pursued so long finally within his grasp, Borah gave off a new sense of self-confidence. Whether arguing to a jury or holding forth in the Idanha lobby, he cut a dashing figure with his massive head crowned by a mass of thick brown hair, heavy eyebrows that almost met above his nose, a powerful, square, clean-shaven chin, and a pair of keen blue eyes that conveyed a "remarkable vitality." Dressed in a long coat, tight-fitting ranch trousers, a waistcoat, and a string tie, with a wide-brimmed slouch hat cocked on his head, he walked Boise's boulevards with a lively step that somebody compared to "the walk of a man going for the doctor." But that summer, it was the stride of a vigorous young politician at the height of his powers, on his way to the U.S. Senate—and, some thought, beyond.

From the start, Borah and Hawley had been coolly realistic about Harry Orchard's confession. It was an excellent starting point but surely not sufficient. Idaho law—echoed in many other states—was explicit in its distrust of a conspirator's uncorroborated confession. Lawyers had often observed the falling-out of thieves, encouraged by prosecutors' efforts to pit one malefactor against another. Thus, Section 5464 of Idaho's penal code provided that "a conviction cannot be had on the testimony of an accomplice, unless he is corroborated by other evidence, which in itself, and without the aid of the testimony of the accomplice, tends to connect the defendant with the commission of the offense." It was a doctrine as old as the Bible which, in Deuteronomy 19.15, holds, "One witness is not enough to convict."

By early 1906, the prosecution had concluded that only two men could provide the needed corroboration: Jack Simpkins and Steve Adams. Despite efforts by the Thiel and Pinkerton agencies—and a $1,000 reward offered by the State of Idaho—no detective had turned up a solid trace of Simpkins. Wild rumors circulated: Simpkins was dead, killed by the WFM to ensure he never informed on his co-conspirators; Simpkins had found sanctuary in Australia or Singapore; Simpkins was a Pinkerton plant, an agent provocateur sent by McParland to trigger the Steunenberg assassination as a means to exterminate the WFM's leaders.

With Simpkins unavailable, the prosecutors eventually pinned their hopes for corroboration on Steve Adams. A thirty-nine-year-old itinerant miner and all-purpose roustabout, Adams was described by one reporter as "a shambling, careless figure with a marked face, a wide mouth, a cunning eye with curious drooping eyelids, and a complexion blotched by liquor and exposure." He wasn't entirely trusted by the federation's inner circle because he got drunk after every job. A reporter who spent a couple of days with him found him "very agreeable company," of "a happy, rollicking disposition." Like many cowboys, he was a bit bowlegged. His mussed hair had an orange tint that earned him the nickname Reddy. His family, Adams once proudly recalled, were "all Southerners," whose "word was as good as their notes." Raised on a Missouri farm, he'd left home at age twenty-two and knocked about the Great Plains and Rocky Mountains for fifteen years: farming in Nebraska, dressing beef in the Kansas City packinghouses, sawing lumber in a Spokane mill, mining lead in Missouri and silver in Idaho, ending up, during the fierce labor wars, in Colorado, where he joined the WFM and encountered Harry Orchard. Along the way he became an avid fan of baseball and a dedicated aficionado of prizefighting, having memorized the boxers' records "like the school boy knows his ABC's." When Orchard made his detailed confession to James McParland in mid-January, he implicated Adams in some of the WFM's bloodiest felonies.

By 1906, Adams had settled down with his wife, Annie—a strikingly attractive widow he'd married in Telluride—and her two young sons by her previous marriage on a ranch near Haines, Oregon, that belonged to her uncle, a prosperous farmer and former Kentucky horse breeder named James S. Lillard. At sundown on February 19—as Haywood, Moyer, and Pettibone were aboard the special hurtling toward Boise—Chris Thiele of the Pinkertons, accompanied by Sheriff Harvey Brown of Baker County and Colonel James A. Panting, a special deputy sheriff, came trotting up to the Lillard ranch in a buggy and took Adams into custody.

Held overnight in the county jail at Baker City, he refused to come out of his cell the next morning until he was given his right "as an American citizen" to see a lawyer—and he specified his uncle's attorney, C. A. Moore. (Lillard himself was out of state on a prolonged visit to Texas.) Evidently the officers had already summoned Moore, conferred with him in the jail office, and either intimidated him or won him over. For just as Adams asked for him, Moore appeared at the cell's door. Sheriff Brown hurried client and lawyer along, saying it was time to leave for the Baker City depot, where the party was due to entrain for Boise. Moore accompanied them to the station.

On the platform was the gray-bearded Orlando "Rube" Robbins, a legendary peace officer, now the "traveling guard" of Idaho's penitentiary and Governor Gooding's representative for this extradition. Robbins had carried Gooding's requisition papers to Salem, Oregon, where Governor George E. Chamberlain issued a fugitive warrant for Adams's arrest. Now Adams asked Moore to examine the sheaf of papers. The two of them walked down the platform a few feet, where the attorney said that he could challenge the extradition but that "it would do us no good."

If that was truly Moore's legal opinion, he was wrong. There was no evidence whatsoever that Adams had been in Caldwell—or, for that matter, in Idaho—at the time of Steunenberg's assassination. He was no more a fugitive from Idaho justice than was Haywood, Moyer, or Pettibone. Had Moore gone before an Oregon court with a habeas corpus petition, he would probably have prevailed. Given the methods of their Denver counterparts, Thiele and Brown probably wouldn't have waited for Moore to draw up such a petition. That may be what Moore meant when he told Adams he "might as well go" with the Idaho officers.

At this moment, Sheriff Brown chimed in with his own advice to his fellow Oregonian: "Go down there and do what these fellows want you to, and you will come out all right. I am on the inside, and I know what I'm talking about." Seeing no way out, Adams got on the train to Boise, which arrived there only hours after the special got in from Denver. At the pen, the warden, Eugene L. Whitney, put Adams in the cell with Orchard.

McParland, still in Denver, would later explode at this decision. The detective had wanted Adams totally isolated, as Orchard had been in the days before his confession. "This is a very unfortunate state of affairs," he grumbled on his return to Boise on February 23. "I am now sorry that, notwithstanding the legal advice I received in Denver, I did not come to Boise on the special train with the prisoners. I would then have been in Boise when Adams arrived." But the arrangement didn't work out badly for the prosecution. So thoroughly had Orchard been indoctrinated by McParland and his associates, he promptly assured Adams that neither the detectives nor the State of Idaho were after him. Their prime targets were the WFM leadership. If Orchard and Adams helped convict Haywood, Moyer, and Pettibone, then the governor, the state's lawyers, and McParland would "stand by us and see that no harm comes to us." Orchard kept talking in this same vein for the next four days.

Another message came to Adams through Fred Bond, the convicted murderer who was awaiting execution on the pen's death row. Bond had recently seen Governor Gooding on his clemency plea and the governor had told him "that if [Adams] did not tell what he knew, and what they knew he ought to know, they had evidence that would hang him so damned high salt peter would not save him."

Finally, on February 26, McParland—newly arrived from Denver— came to the penitentiary to visit his anxious prisoner. Adams was escorted to the office, where Warden Whitney introduced him to the soft-spoken detective, who reinforced much of what Orchard had already told him. "It is your duty to your family, your fellow man and your God to corroborate Harry Orchard's confession against the officials of the federation," said McParland. "If you don't, you will be taken back to Cripple Creek and mobbed or hung by the people there, and then where would your wife and your poor little children be? If you do this [confess], you will never be prosecuted and you will come out all right, and be way ahead. The Governor and the officials of this state are all right. They will stand by you."

Adams would later insist that he'd refused McParland's first overture, saying he wanted to await his attorney's return from Colorado, where Moore had gone to clarify what charges Adams would face if he returned there. Adams was placed in solitary confinement for a day, then brought before the detective once more. "You see," he recalled McParland's telling him, "your lawyer hasn't showed up yet; and the Federation hasn't sent you any lawyers either. They'd be glad if you were hung. Certainly, if you were turned loose, you'd be a dead man in no time—killed by one of those Federation men. You better go ahead, make a statement and save yourself."

With that, Adams capitulated, agreeing to make a statement. McParland summoned his stenographer, Wellington B. Hopkins, who took it down in two sittings. McParland later reported that Adams was intensely nervous, with "big beads of sweat" breaking out on his face and hands. "As I had been made aware by Operative No. 9 [Chris Thiele] that Adams smoked continuously, I had provided myself with a pocket full of cigars," the detective said. "I never saw cigars disappear so fast in my life ... as during my conversations with Adams."

McParland and Adams would later differ sharply over how the statement was compiled. The detective insisted that Adams's confession of his misdeeds poured out of him, much as Orchard's had earlier—with the difference that Adams had a terrible memory for dates, times, and other details and McParland had to prompt him repeatedly on such matters. Adams claimed that McParland supplied much more than that, referring constantly to papers he pulled from his pocket (Orchard's confession, no doubt) and guiding the whole recitation. Days later, the detective brought the typewritten statement, not in questions and answers, as Adams had given it, but in narrative form. Adams—who'd been treated better since giving the statement—glanced over it and signed it.

Put in narrative form by James Hawley, Adams's statement seemed to corroborate at least some of Orchard's confession. Although Adams said he was never in Caldwell with Orchard, he conceded that he'd discussed "the Steunenberg matter" with WFM leaders. In the summer of 1904, after the explosion at the Independence depot, he'd met with Haywood and Pettibone in the back room of Pettibone's store in Denver. The two men said they wanted to "get" Steunenberg, and they asked him to go to Idaho to consult Jack Simpkins. When he agreed to go, they gave him two hundred dollars for expenses. Adams said he went to the Coeur d'Alenes and met with Simpkins in Wallace on July 4. Simpkins agreed to go south with him on the Steunenberg job but said he needed more money from the federation. The money did not arrive and eventually Orchard took over the lapsed assignment.

Adams admitted taking part with Orchard in similar attempts to kill James Peabody, the former governor of Colorado, and Justices Goddard and Gabbert of the Colorado Supreme Court. He conceded direct participation in two successful WFM assassinations: the 1902 shotgun killing of Arthur Collins, manager of the Smuggler-Union mine in Telluride, in which Adams said he'd pulled the trigger, and the murder of Lyte Gregory, a former Denver policeman working as a private detective, on a Denver street in May 1904, in which Adams said that he and Orchard tracked Gregory from Cleary's saloon, where the detective had been drinking, but that Orchard committed the actual murder with a sawed-off shotgun.

But, most important, the statement had Adams confessing that it was he and Orchard who'd set the explosives under the platform of the Independence depot, strung the wires to a chair, and then, as the train approached, pulled on the chair rung, setting off the massive explosion that killed thirteen nonunion miners and injured six. This was the most devastating of the violent acts laid to the Western Federation, and if Orchard and Adams could tie the Independence explosion to Bill Haywood, the effect on the jury could be devastating as well.

McParland hoped to keep Adams's confession secret as long as possible so as not to alert the defense attorneys that the prosecution had its eagerly sought corroboration. But on his return from Colorado on March 2, C. A. Moore visited his client in the penitentiary and Adams told him he had made the statement to McParland. Fearing that word would quickly leak out, the prosecution issued a terse statement to the Boise press, announcing that Adams had made a "full confession" and, in so doing, had fully corroborated Orchard's confession.

But just as McParland had sought further confirmation of Orchard's confession by digging up the bomb intended for Justice Goddard, so he now sought to buttress Adams's confession with physical evidence from closer to home. One of the most curious stories in the confession was the tale of Pettibone Dope, Greek Fire, or Hellfire, as it was variously known. According to the confession, George Pettibone manufactured a particularly potent explosive concocted of stick phosphorus, bisulfide of carbon, alcohol, benzine, and spirits of turpentine. This substance was said to be one of the most powerful incendiary agents known to man, so powerful that the fire it started could not be extinguished by water.

According to Adams's statement, Pettibone and Moyer had approached him in September of 1903, just as the Cripple Creek strike was beginning. At a meeting in the back room of Pettibone's store, they asked him to carry out a mission to interrupt the flow of scabs the mine owners were importing from the Coeur d'Alene mines to Cripple Creek. Pettibone and Moyer provided him with a grip containing a tin can that held two quart bottles and three pint bottles of Pettibone Dope. Moyer bought him a ticket to Pocatello, where he was to watch every train as it came through and to throw a bottle or two in a window if he saw a car loaded with scabs.

Arriving in Pocatello, he said, he made inquiries about the scabs and learned that they did not travel in a single car but were scattered through all the passenger cars, so that he could not attack the scabs without injuring, or perhaps killing, innocent passengers. Moreover, it seemed that by that time the scabs had been sent over another route. In any case, Adams abandoned the scheme. But, even inside the grip, the "dope" was giving off an offensive odor, so Adams allegedly found an open trench by an old sawmill some distance east of Pocatello. Placing the bottles in the trench, he covered them with earth and ashes, then threw the grip back into the vacant building. He returned to Denver, telling Moyer and Pettibone he couldn't carry out his mission.

Such, in any case, was the story McParland attributed to Steve Adams, and such was the story he sought to confirm by traveling to Pocatello and finding the bottles of Hellfire. His expedition there at the end of March was unusual because, unlike most Pinkerton operations, it was highly publicized; indeed, it seems to have been designed principally with public relations in mind. For, as McParland explained in his report to the agency, "we will not be able to use this matter in the trials of Moyer, Haywood and Pettibone . . . and as the trades and labor assemblies and other unions have been passing resolutions condemning the action of Governor Gooding of Idaho and Governor McDonald of Colorado in the matter of extraditing these men, we wished to show to the public the class of men the labor organizations were trying to represent as good citizens."

Perhaps for this very reason, Governor Gooding decided to accompany the group, which, at his direction, included not only McParland, Warden Whitney, Operative Thiele, and Rube Robbins, the traveling guard, but also two friendly reporters—Harry L. Crane of the *Statesman* and Thomas H. Hunter of the *Denver Post*.

They left Boise on the 4:00 a.m. train, on which Adams showed "the delight of a boy," removing his shoes and wriggling his toes on the plush seats. They alighted at Pocatello, in a driving rainstorm, at 12:30 p.m. While the governor, McParland, and the two reporters took refuge in a leisurely lunch at the Pacific Hotel, Adams, guarded by Thiele and Robbins, went looking for the old mill. After hours of scuffing along the railroad tracks, Adams pointed out a building he thought had the right configuration, although it had been covered with corrugated iron by its new owner, the Weeter Lumber Company, which used it as a stable. Empty now, it was a "rendezvous for tramps and hoboes." Procuring a key from the foreman, the party gained entry and Adams pointed out the spot where he thought the Hellfire was buried.

Returning later in the afternoon with the rest of the party and some prominent local citizens selected by the governor, they began digging through the floor of a stall layered with hay and manure. Adams, Thiele, and Whitney —aided by Mr. Weeter and his foreman—did the brunt of the work, though even the governor took his turn with a spade. Shortly after 5:00 p.m., they uncovered a glass stopper that, from its odor, Adams thought belonged to one of the bottles he'd buried. They also found a rusted and burned ten-pound lard bucket, its bottom covered with a blackened residue, which Adams identified as the one that had contained the bottles. But of the bottles themselves, they found no trace.

The next day, the Pocatello police chief, C. F. Smith, recalled an incident several years before in which two brothers, Thomas and George McConkey, had uncovered a mass of melted glass while digging out timbers in the old mill. When the McConkeys were summoned, they led Chris Thiele to the spot and recovered the glass, which Thiele promptly proclaimed to be the missing bottles. By then, the rest of the party was on its way back to Boise, so the Pinkerton detective followed with the ball of fused glass in a large brown grip. Thiele also brought with him the register of the Tupper House, a Pocatello rooming house where Adams claimed to have stayed in September 1903. On examination, it proved to contain the name J. Ward, the pseudonym under which Adams said he'd registered.

Although the evidence gathered on the mission was equivocal, McParland chose to regard the trip as a resounding success. To his agency, even before the "bottles" were found, he said that finding the stopper and tin can added up to one of his "biggest hits," comparable to finding the bomb that was placed at Judge Goddard's gate. As prearranged with William Balderston, the editor, the *Statesman* gave splashy front-page play to Harry Crane's coverage of the expedition, replete with McParland's own account of Adams's confession of the Hellfire episode.

By the end of March 1906, then, the Pinkertons and the prosecutors seemed to be sitting pretty, with Harry Orchard's confession and Steve Adams's corroboration firmly in hand. The next move plainly belonged to the defense.

On that bleak February morning when first they learned of their leaders' "extradition," the miners were unsure who would mount their defense. The WFM's longtime general counsel, John H. Murphy, was sick in bed. A former master mechanic with the Union Pacific Railroad at Ogden, he'd studied law after being blacklisted for his involvement in Debs's American Railway Union. Murphy had been instrumental in the passage of Utah's pathbreaking law limiting a miner's workday to eight hours and henceforth became known in labor circles as Eight-Hour Murphy. A beloved figure in the organization— one Socialist correspondent wrote that his name was "a synonym for all that is good and pure and noble in this life"—he was scarcely a high-profile trial attorney and, even had he been healthy, he seemed an unlikely choice as lead lawyer in the case. As he was known to be dying of tuberculosis, eyes turned elsewhere.

In the first hours after the arrests, the WFM looked to Edmund F. Richardson and Horace W. Hawkins, whose Denver law firm had done most of the union's litigation in recent years. It was Hawkins who telephoned the Denver jail, trying to find the three men. And when someone was needed to

race to Boise to file a habeas corpus petition in the Idaho courts, it was
Edmund Richardson who caught the night train for Boise.

But, with McParland boasting that the prisoners would "never leave
Idaho alive," some in labor's camp felt they needed higher-powered representation. On February 21, James A. Kirwan, a member of the WFM executive
committee, who'd arrived in Denver February 20 to fill in for Haywood,
declared, "We will secure the best legal talent obtainable in the country."
Later, the unionists would squabble over who first suggested Clarence Darrow. Kirwan recalled that he and John M. O'Neill, editor of the *Miners'
Magazine,* had gathered at John Murphy's sickbed and that Murphy proposed
Darrow, the Chicago trial attorney who'd recently represented striking coal
miners before a presidential commission. Kirwan wired Chicago asking William Trautmann, secretary-treasurer of the IWW, to see if Darrow would take
the assignment. IWW officers remembered it differently—that it was Alfred
S. Edwards, editor of the *Industrial Worker,* who brought up Darrow's name in a
meeting with Trautmann. Then they wired the WFM in Denver asking
permission to approach the celebrated attorney.

In any case, on or about February 21, Trautmann met with Darrow in
Chicago and told him that the IWW and the rest of organized labor were
determined to give the arrested men the best legal defense possible. Would he
take the job? Darrow was intrigued and ready to take the next step. Early on
February 26, Darrow arrived by train in Denver, where he met with Kirwan;
J. C. Williams, the federation's vice president; and Edmund Richardson, who'd
returned from Boise the day before. The *Rocky Mountain News* reported the
next day that, "upon invitation of Mr. Richardson," Darrow had agreed to
"assist" in the defense, with the title of "associate counsel." Later, that terminology would be heatedly contested.

Speaking with reporters before he left town, Darrow said, "It looks very
much like another case of the oppression of the weak by the strong." In short,
it was a case made to order for Clarence Darrow, attorney for the downtrodden and dispossessed.

The Fourth of July in Farmington began with a fanfare from the town's
brass band, resplendent in gold and white, rumbling down Main Street in a
wagon pulled by a four-horse team. Later, in a shady grove by the river,
there'd be fried chicken, iced lemonade, a baseball match, fireworks, a recitation from the Declaration of Independence—and always a lawyer over from
the county seat to deliver the patriotic oration.

The boy would see the lawyer's horse and buggy at the hotel in the
morning, and think "how nice they were, and how much money a lawyer
must make." When the visitor got up to speak, the boy noticed his "nice
clothes—a good deal nicer than those of the farmers and other people who
came to hear him talk—and his boots looked shiny, as if they had just been
greased." He talked very loud, "and seemed to be mad about something,

especially when he spoke of the war and the 'Bridish,' and he waved his hands and arms a great deal." On he went in the midday sun, about "how free we were, all on account of the Declaration of Independence, and the flag, and the G.A.R., and because our people were such great fighters," and how they must be "ready to fight and to die" for that flag. The farmers clapped their hands and said the lawyer was "a mighty smart man" and "could talk louder than anyone we had ever heard." The boy thought "what a great man he was, and how [he himself] should like to be a lawyer."

Farmington—in Clarence Darrow's autobiographical novel of the same name—is a hybrid of Farmdale, Ohio, where Darrow was born in 1857, and Kinsman, a hamlet two miles east, where he grew to manhood. The authorial voice in this artful work, published a year before Frank Steunenberg's assassination, is that of a "man-child," a cross between the ingenuous jabber of a small-town lad just beginning to poke around his territory and the world-weary rasp of a big-city lawyer who has seen enough of life to convince him it is all a lot of bunk.

Accordingly, we view the country lawyer through twin lenses: his handsome horse and buggy, his fine clothes and shiny shoes, through the credulous eyes of ten-year-old Clarence; his bluster and rant, his pettifoggery and bloviation through the jaded scrutiny of the forty-eight-year-old Darrow who, by 1904, had soured on the rhetoric, the ethics, the very rationale of his profession. The irony of Darrow's midlife predicament lay in the contrast between, on the one hand, his thriving law practice, his distinguished friends, and the esteem in which he was increasingly held by the press and public and, on the other, the acute distaste he felt for the life of a lawyer, the craving for a higher, more aesthetic vocation, the inner doubts bordering on self-contempt at the compromises he felt compelled to make.

Farmington has often been misread as a picaresque idyll, an ode to the pastoral virtues of America's heartland in dappled days gone by. At times it takes on that guise, as Darrow limns the joys of the old swimming hole and of ballgames on languorous summer evenings, in prose "rich and noble in its music." But lurking behind these gentle rhythms is a darker vision of a cramped, sterile, and mean-spirited town: "cunning soulless farmers," the "arrogance and pride" of its gentry, the school that teaches "clumsy, stupid lies" to "young savages, always grasping for the best, ever fighting and scheming to get the advantage," the smug parishioners of the large white church "who had no doubt that they were different from the horses and cattle, and would live in some future world that these others animals could never reach." Indeed, *Farmington* prefigures the "revolt from the village" in American letters, a genre soon to flourish in the rich soil of Sherwood Anderson's Winesburg, Ohio, and Sinclair Lewis's Gopher Prairie, Minnesota. (Asked what book in all literature he'd like to have written, Darrow chose *Babbitt*, Lewis's excoriation of small-town parochialism.)

The dismal strain that snakes through *Farmington* echoes the less than loving home in which Darrow, his four brothers, and two sisters came of age. "I cannot recall that my mother ever gave me a kiss or a caress," he recalled. "I have no feeling of a time when either my father or my mother took me, or any other member of our family, in their arms." His father, Amirus, a cabinetmaker and undertaker who cherished the books he kept piled around him, passed on to Clarence a "quenchless thirst for learning," but his relentless reminder that "John Stuart Mill began studying Greek when he was only three" evoked resentment from a son compelled to quit his play to conjugate a dead language. Amirus had once studied theology with a view to becoming a Unitarian minister, but he'd lost his faith. Now the "village infidel," the only respectable man in town who didn't attend the Presbyterian church on the hill, he bequeathed his son a nonconforming spirit, a skeptical mind, and freelance politics that at times, in Clarence, drifted toward cynicism.

Amirus was a quirkily learned man, more at home in a dusty volume of Voltaire, Paine, or Jefferson than in the affairs of this world, where he often seemed lost. Clarence evoked his father in a passage from *Farmington* that speaks of one who all his life has been "getting ready to begin to do something worth the while . . . waiting for the Summer and waiting for the Fall . . . waiting and dawdling and dreaming until the day is almost spent and the twilight is close at hand."

Eventually, he says, he came "to understand the tragedy of [his father's] obscure and hidden life, and the long and bitter contest he had waged within the narrow shadow of the stubborn little town." By the age of sixteen, Clarence began to escape Kinsman's smothering confines, enrolling at Allegheny College, a Methodist institution in nearby Meadville, Pennsylvania, where his atheist father had once studied for the ministry. But after just a year, the financial panic of 1873 compelled him to go home and help the family through bad times. For a meager thirty dollars a month plus room and board, he served three years as a teacher in the district school at Vernon, seven miles south of Kinsman.

From his woolgathering father, Clarence acquired his own "bias against diligence." When asked later what had turned him toward the law, Darrow would respond disarmingly, "hard labor," going on to explain that as a young man he spent a morning stacking hay on a farm, which left him exhausted. "I haven't done a day of hard work since." Those country lawyers at Kinsman's Fourth of July had impressed him as glamorous figures. Darrow would concede that "young men are ambitious to get into the law game largely because it is a showy profession." He had already demonstrated a penchant for the melodramatic in his performances at debates held every Friday night in the winter at the academy on the hill, where he invariably prevailed by arguing with wicked zest the negative—and usually unpopular—proposition. It was those laurels that persuaded his family that he should pursue a profession that exploited his talent for argumentation. In the autumn of 1877, Darrow enrolled in the University of Michigan's law department, then the largest of those new fangled institutions, American law schools.

Until the Civil War, most American lawyers had trained by clerking in private law offices or had educated themselves by reading the great legal authorities—Blackstone's *Commentaries,* Chitty's *Pleadings,* and Greenleaf's *Evidence.* But as the profession expanded beyond the traditional gentry into the middle class, the students themselves demanded a less exclusionary brand of legal education. Moreover, the introduction of the typewriter in 1874 made the traditional law clerk, with his quill pen, expendable. By 1870, there were thirty-one law schools in the land—of which Michigan was not only the largest but one of the best.

Not inclined to academic rigor, Darrow left Michigan at the end of a year, getting the rest of his legal education in a clerkship at a Youngstown, Ohio, law office. He acknowledged his modest mastery of torts and replevin in describing his Ohio bar examination: the committee of lawyers chosen to examine applicants "were all good fellows and wanted to help us through." All twelve candidates passed the desultory oral quiz. A few weeks past his twenty-first birthday, Darrow was a lawyer.

He completed his coming of age by marrying Jessie Ohl, the daughter of the family that owned the local gristmill. The couple toyed with striking out for the West, as many bolder spirits had done. Darrow even rented an office in McPherson, Kansas, but ultimately settled in Andover, a farming town twelve miles north of Kinsman, where they leased a flat above a shoe store, turning a bedroom into Darrow's law office. Gradually, Darrow built a tidy little practice out of boundary disputes, fraudulent livestock sales, and, now and then, an actual criminal complaint—generally for watering milk or selling hard cider, which was regarded as illegal liquor. But it wasn't the practice Darrow had envisioned. He felt constrained by the parochial ideas of Andover's farmers ("if farmers can be said to have ideas," he scoffed later). So, shortly after the birth of their son, Paul, in December 1883, the Darrows moved to Ashtabula, a rail junction and port on the shores of Lake Erie, the largest community (population five thousand) in Ohio's northeastern corner.

Not long after his arrival, he was elected city solicitor, thanks to the sponsorship of a prominent judge. The job paid seventy-five dollars a month and left him plenty of time to take on private clients. If the cases he litigated were rarely momentous, Ashtabula provided Darrow with a more spacious arena in which to display his talents. Such "country lawsuits," he later recalled, were "filled with color and life and wits ... like a great tournament, as described by Walter Scott. The combatants on both sides were always seeking the weakest spots in the enemy's armor, and doing their utmost to unhorse him or to draw blood." Life in Ashtabula was more cosmopolitan than in dusty country towns like Andover and Kinsman. One of Darrow's literary idols, William Dean Howells, had grown up there and Howells's brother Joseph still edited the *Ashtabula Sentinel*. Darrow found some "congenial companions" around the courthouse with whom he whiled away the evenings playing poker—after baseball, now his favorite pastime. With "a little something to drink" in one hand and a stack of chips before him, he "could forget the rest of the world until the last white bone had been tossed into the yawning jackpot." A Grover Cleveland Democrat and a spirited but unsuccessful candidate for state senator and prosecuting attorney, he was a regular orator at party conventions and civic rituals.

As early as his Ashtabula days, Darrow displayed an embryonic social conscience. Years later, he recalled the "most important case" he tried during his nine years of Ohio practice, *Jewell vs. Brockway*. A prosperous young man, a notorious drunk, had ordered a twenty-five-dollar harness on credit but had failed to pay for it. In turn, he'd passed it on to a local boy who'd attended him during an illness. Now the creditor sought to repossess the harness. Outraged that an innocent party should suffer for a rich drunk's default, Darrow took up the boy's case and—for a scant five dollars—fought it all the way to the Ohio Supreme Court, where, after seven years of litigation, he finally prevailed.

If Darrow was edging toward some larger meaning in his practice, it was scarcely visible even as late as 1887. At age thirty, he remained a rather ordinary small-town lawyer with mediocre education, modest achievements, meager ambition, and comparable promise. Progressives saw what happened over the next years as the gradual revelation of a grander purpose in Darrow's life. They attributed it to his reading of Henry George's *Progress and Poverty*, which argued for a single tax on the "unearned increment" of landlords' profit, and John Peter Altgeld's *Our Penal Machinery and Its Victims*, which urged a focus on the causes of crime rather than on its punishment; to Darrow's arrival in Chicago in the immediate aftermath of the Haymarket massacre; and to his exposure there to radical thought.

Darrow denied that any such beneficent force—any Purpose—was at work in his life or, for that matter, in the universe. He was an ardent admirer of Herbert Spencer, the British philosopher who applied Darwinian principles to theology, economics, and politics, everywhere imposing the stern discipline of evolution. This mechanistic thinking was in the air at century's end, cropping up in such divergent figures as Hegel, Marx, Henry and Brooks Adams, William Graham Sumner, and later Sigmund Freud. Quickly it spread into the popular culture. Spencer popularized Darwin—or, rather, popularized a perversion of Darwinism into a social rather than a biological doctrine; then Spencer in turn was translated into the vernacular by Eugene Fitch Ware, a Kansas lawyer and poet (under the pseudonym Ironquill), a favorite in the Darrow household. Ironquill expressed Spencer's principles this way:

Life is a game of whist. From unseen sources
The cards are shuffled and the hands are dealt;
Blind are our efforts to control the forces
That, though unseen, are no less strongly felt.

If, as Darrow believed, men were not free agents, then how could they be held morally responsible for their acts? To Henley's famous passage from *Invictus,* "I am the master of my fate; I am the captain of my soul," Darrow would respond mockingly, "The captain of his soul! Why, he isn't even a deckhand on a raft." The only thing he ever saw that seemed to have free will, Darrow once wrote, was an electric pump. "Every time we wanted it to go, it stopped."*

If one takes literally Darrow's explanation for his move to Chicago, he surely did not control his fate. In 1887, he was about to deepen his commitment to Ashtabula by buying a house there for $3,500 when the owner reneged, expressing doubt that Darrow would ever earn that much. In anger, Darrow said he didn't want the damn house anyway because—grasping for a reason—he and his family were leaving town.

On March 5, 1887, the *Ashtabula Standard* announced that Darrow, "a young man of far more than ordinary ability," would "shake the dust of Ashtabula from his feet and take up his abode in the wickedest city in the United States." In Chicago, Darrow was caught up in an astonishing whirlwind of farmer-labor Populism, urban Socialism, municipal reform, and intellectual activity that made it at the close of the century not just a magnet for ardent young people throughout the Midwest but *"the* big city of America."

For a generation of midwestern writers, the train trip from the rural hinterland to Chicago—and particularly their first glimpse of the glowering metropolis—was one of life's defining moments. Carrying with them the baggage of nineteenth-century Romanticism, which perceived cities as dark excrescences on the fair pastoral landscape, these fugitives from village and prairie were invariably appalled by the scene unfolding outside their railway car. Hamlin Garland would "never forget the feeling of dismay with which . . . I perceived from the car window a huge smoke-cloud which embraced the whole eastern horizon, for this, I was told, was the soaring banner of the great and gloomy inland metropolis." Waldo Frank lamented, "Chimneys stand over the world and belch blackness upon it. There is no sky now."

These expressions of horror were perhaps a response less to the concrete-and-brick city itself than to the sheer velocity with which this remote trading post had erupted into a voracious metropolis. In 1840, it had been a village of log huts around Fort Dearborn holding scarcely five thousand

---

* Throughout his career, Darrow vacillated between opposing notions of the prime cause: the environment and heredity. He never firmly resolved which was the more important (Livingston, *Clarence Darrow,* 108).

residents; by 1890, it was a city of 165 square miles with one million residents, increasing by some fifty thousand each year, transforming pastures seemingly overnight into swarming tenements. To poetic temperaments, this was America's destiny hurrying toward them. If their first reaction was dread, it was soon matched by awe.

To Frank Norris, "The Great Gray City, brooking no rival, imposed its dominion upon a reach of country larger than many a kingdom of the Old World.... Here, mid-most in the land, beat the Heart of the Nation, whence inevitably must come its immeasurable power, its infinite, infinite, inexhaustible vitality." Chicago elicited from its poets and novelists a language so unrestrained it threatened to break the bounds of the page. Consider Theodore Dreiser's panegyric at the beginning of *The Titan:* "This singing flame of a city, this all-America, this poet in chaps and buckskin, this rude, raw Titan, this Burns of a city! By its shimmering lake it lay, a kind of shreds and patches, a maundering yokel with an epic in its mouth, a hobo among cities, with the grip of Caesar in its mind, the dramatic force of Euripides in its soul."

Such geysers of language were prompted as well by the thrilling notion that these voyagers to Chicago had reached a critical juncture, at which the individualistic, agrarian America of the nineteenth century was giving way to the industrial, urban America of the twentieth. If Norris and Dreiser, Garland and Frank evoked the joys and terrors of such a moment, Clarence Darrow was, in some respects, the quintessential figure of this passage, learning to hold in exquisite tension the country man and city man in himself.

It took time to find his footing on the slippery granite blocks that paved Chicago's business district. Overcome by loneliness, he'd sometimes stand at Madison and State Streets, the city's busiest corner, searching the sea of strangers for a familiar face. "As well might I have hunted in the depths of the Brazilian forest." Taking desk space in somebody else's law office, he made less than three hundred dollars in his first year.

Chicago teemed with lawyers hungry for cases. "Every thin-brained student is, with the utmost candor, advised to 'turn his face toward the setting sun' as the West is the only field where a lack of intellect is profitable," one journal observed. Desperate for self-advertisement, Darrow fell back on one of his few proven skills, public argumentation. Already a fervent disciple of Henry George, he joined the Single Tax Club, where his "sounding metrical phrases" in debate gained him invitations to speak for the Democrats in the 1888 city campaign. After DeWitt C. Cregier was elected mayor, he offered Darrow the post of special assessment attorney for "the fabulous sum" of three thousand dollars a year. Three months later, Darrow was promoted to assistant corporation counsel, and ten months after that, when the corporation counsel resigned because of ill health, Darrow became acting head of the city's law department. For a lawyer barely three years out of Ashtabula (he called it Asstabula now), it had been an astonishing ascent: at age thirty-three, Darrow was one of Chicago's most visible officeholders.

He owed this rapid advance less to his own lawyerly achievements than to his alliance with John Altgeld, the Chicago superior court judge who wrote the scorching indictment of American criminal law that had so impressed Darrow in Ashtabula. With its emphasis on the role of heredity and environment in forming criminals, this book crystallized Darrow's view that most malefactors—formed by nature "red in tooth and claw"—weren't responsible for their acts. Not surprisingly, Altgeld had been among the first public men Darrow sought out in Chicago. Each quickly recognized in the other that combination of sardonic idealism and open-faced guile that would bind them for years to come. Now this exchange of mutual self-interest paid off. For DeWitt Cregier and his bipartisan "anti-machine ticket" largely fronted for Altgeld, who held a grudge against the incumbent mayor, John A. Roche. With a five-thousand-dollar stake from his own real estate interests, Altgeld put Cregier in office, then, among other things, extracted Darrow's appointment.*

Altgeld was a polarizing figure. Some regarded him as a liberal-Populist hero who compassionately sustained Abraham Lincoln's legacy in Illinois. To others, the German immigrant, with his wiry beard covering a harelip, was a manipulative politician and cynical demagogue. There is a bit of truth in both caricatures.

As corporation counsel, Darrow cleared building permits for the gleaming White City of the 1893 World's Columbian Exposition, the fair that brought visitors from far and wide to Chicago (his brother Hubert managed the Fenten Ladies Band at the fair). Meanwhile, he lobbied the state legislature to put Altgeld in the U.S. Senate. Though Altgeld didn't make it, he was suitably grateful. When Mayor Cregier left office, Altgeld had another slot prepared for Darrow: general attorney for the Chicago and Northwestern Railway.

The move was a curious one for a young Democrat already identified with some of Chicago's most "radical" elements. "It was hard," he wrote later, "for me to take the side of the railroad company against one who had been injured in their service or against a passenger." But general counsel for a major railroad was a position of great prestige and large salary, neither of which were unwelcome to Darrow. Moreover, it was an unusual opportunity to continue his self-education. His years with the city had given him an insider's feel for municipal government; now the railroad post would give him an initiate's view of a mighty institution that many of his allies perceived as the enemy.

He took the job, but not without soul-searching. In December 1891, he wrote his friend Henry Demarest Lloyd, complimenting him on a stirring address that, he said, "made me feel that I am a hypocrite and a slave and

---

* In the available source materials, this episode remains a bit murky. The preponderance of evidence suggests that Darrow's appointment was a quid pro quo for Altgeld's support; elsewhere, Cregier indicates that he'd heard Darrow's speech on Henry George and so admired it that he wanted its author in his administration.

added to my resolution to make my term of servitude short." His own "desire
for office and money," Darrow conceded, made it increasingly difficult to take
an independent stand. Unwilling to give up his job altogether, he decided on a
middle path: to exercise the option in his Chicago and Northwestern contract
allowing him to practice privately on the side. In early 1894, he formed a firm
with three well-connected former judges—a Republican, a Democrat, and a
Mugwump—who took rooms in the Rookery Building downtown, perhaps
the most luxurious office space in the city.

Despite the pressure for conformity—or perhaps precisely because of it
—Darrow took some of his most radical steps during his three years with the
railroad. The first was to sign on as unofficial manager of Altgeld's 1892
campaign for governor, helping to assemble the tenuous coalition that backed
this most unconventional candidate. Building on a solid base among Democratic voters, Altgeld picked up votes from Populists, Single Taxers, and
Socialists; labor unions; reform groups like the Municipal Voters' League; and
German American voters. Together they elected Altgeld the first Democratic
governor of Illinois since the Civil War.

When the victor went off to Springfield, Darrow was content to stay
behind, tending to his responsibilities at the railroad and to his law firm while
serving as the governor's Chicago agent. In that role, Darrow played an
important part in the agitation for pardon of the three surviving Haymarket
defendants (four had been hanged, and one committed suicide, in 1887)—an
issue that had deeply interested him since his arrival in Chicago six years
before. Many of those in the Amnesty Association, including Darrow himself,
had thought the governor-elect might make his first official act the pardon of
Samuel Fielden, Oscar Neebe, and Michael Schwab. When he failed to act by
March 1893, Darrow confronted the governor to demand the pardon. Altgeld
told him: "Go tell your friends that when I am ready I will act. I don't know
how I will act, but I will do what I think is right."

When Altgeld finally signed the pardons three months later, an aide
warned him, "The storm will break now." Oh yes, said Altgeld, "I was prepared for that." But nobody was quite prepared for the sheer ferocity of the
assault on the man H. L. Mencken sardonically called the nation's "reigning
hobgoblin." The conventional wisdom of the day, Mencken reported, was that
"Altgeld was a shameless advocate of rapine and assassination, an enemy alike
to the Constitution and the Ten Commandments—in short, a bloody and
insatiable anarchist." The *Chicago Tribune* regularly referred to him as "Viper
Altgeld."

Refusing to fold under this barrage, Altgeld pressed his bold legislative
program—from court reform and indeterminate sentencing to competitive
bidding by state agencies and the state's first inheritance tax—while seeking
to wrest control of the Democratic Party from Grover Cleveland and his
Bourbon allies. Altgeld, running for reelection, and Darrow, nominated for

Congress, led the Illinois delegation at the Chicago convention that nominated William Jennings Bryan. But so frightening was "the boy orator of the Platte" to many sobersided Americans, and so formidable the forces ranged against him, that he took not only the national ticket but Altgeld and Darrow down with him. Altgeld charged—and Darrow apparently believed—that widespread fraud and bribery had cost them the election. In defeat, Darrow reciprocated Altgeld's support in his first Chicago years by bringing his mentor into his own law office as senior partner. It was the last time Darrow would agree to put someone else's name above his own on the office door.

When Altgeld died in 1902, Darrow delivered an extraordinary tribute, calling him "the most devoted lover, the most abject slave, the fondest, wildest, dreamiest victim that ever gave his life to liberty's immortal cause." Altgeld was Darrow's only hero, the last man to whom he gave unstinting allegiance. Perhaps, as one commentator has suggested, Altgeld was the fully competent father figure Darrow had always craved. In any case, with this notable exception, Darrow insisted on charting his own bold but erratic course.

An early signal that here was no conventional young attorney up from the country came in 1893 when he and two seasoned Chicago lawyers, Stephen S. Gregory and James S. Harlan, took the extraordinary step of intervening in the case of Eugene Prendergast, lately convicted of assassinating Chicago's mayor, Carter Harrison, and sentenced to death. None of the three lawyers had been associated with the case at trial. But each had followed it closely and felt an injustice was being perpetrated. Under Illinois law no defendant adjudged insane could be executed—and the three lawyers believed that the young assassin was plainly deranged. Without Prendergast's active cooperation or payment, they challenged his sanity at a special hearing.

The effort failed and Prendergast went to the gallows, but the case launched Darrow's obsessive lifelong crusade against the death penalty. For this son of Kinsman's undertaker, death held a special morbid terror. As a child, he shied from the dark corner of his father's shop where the coffins were piled, and he never entered the building after dark. In *Farmington*, he wrote of seeing a grinning young soldier off to the Civil War, then months later attending his funeral and realizing with "deep dread" that they were putting the boy in the ground. Repeatedly in Darrow's writing, "the grim spectre Death" makes its appearance, prompting "despair and grief," "shudder and horror." Later, as he fought to save clients from the gallows, friends saw him struggling to hold this terror at bay. When he succeeded it was nothing less than a "triumph over death." But what if he were to fail?

"No one can find life tolerable without dope," he wrote. "The Catholics are right, the Christian Scientists are right, the Methodists are right, the drunkards are right, the dope fiends of all kinds are right, but for some of us the dope must be good and strong and shot into the arm." In Darrow's terminology, dope meant any substance or faith that allowed one to get through the night. Everyone had his own bogeyman that could only be banished by dope. For Darrow, evidently, it was death.

Before long, Darrow broadened his opposition to the death penalty to embrace punishment of all kinds. This didn't mean that he wouldn't recommend the confinement or restraint of people who were dangerous to themselves or to others, but he would do so because they were sick, not because they had evil hearts. He was temperamentally averse to prosecution. Once a group of his friends collected four hundred dollars in nickels and dimes to engage Darrow to seek punishment of a Polish policeman who had shot two Italian workers because they refused to move off their own stoop. But Darrow never followed through, later explaining that "his role was that of defender, not prosecutor."

The boldest—and in many respects the most admirable—break Darrow ever made with orthodoxy was his decision in 1894 to represent Eugene Debs and his American Railway Union in the cases growing out of the boycott of the Pullman Palace Car Company. One of the industrial virtuosos of his age, George Pullman had made the railroad cars that bore his name virtually indispensable features of late-century rail travel. Self-satisfied and quick to anger, he was by no means the most retrograde of America's tycoons. Next to his massive factory on Chicago's outskirts, he'd built a neat but antiseptic model village, providing his workers better-than-average housing but smothering them in paternalism. As one worker put it, "We are born in a Pullman house, fed from the Pullman shop, taught in the Pullman school, catechized in the Pullman church, and when we die we shall be buried in the Pullman cemetery and go to the Pullman hell."

The severe recession of 1893–94 so eroded the company's profits that Pullman felt compelled to reduce wages 25 percent. When a delegation of workers complained that he had made no corresponding cut in the model village rents—already higher than for comparable houses in Chicago—Pullman loftily declined to talk with them. In May, the Pullman workers went out on strike. At this point, Debs's ARU—but not the more conservative railroad brotherhoods—swung into action, instructing ARU switchmen to refuse to switch Pullman cars onto trains; if the switchmen were discharged or disciplined, all ARU members would walk out. Many railroads promptly defied the boycott, insisting that their contracts with Pullman were sacred.

The boycott began on June 26, 1894. Within four days, 125,000 men on twenty-nine railroads had quit work rather than handle Pullman cars. The railroads responded by engineering the rather incredible appointment of Edwin Walker, general counsel of the Chicago, Milwaukee and St. Paul Railway, as special federal attorney to deal with the strike. Governor Altgeld refused to intervene in the strike, furnishing another link in the chain that tied his public image to radicalism. So Walker got a sweeping order in federal court barring union leaders from any act to encourage the boycott. When

Debs and other ARU leaders defied the writ, President Cleveland ordered federal troops and deputy federal marshals into Chicago, ostensibly to maintain order but in fact to keep the trains, with Pullmans attached, moving.

As the boycott crumbled under these hammer blows, a federal grand jury in Chicago delivered what was intended to be the final stroke: an indictment of Debs and three colleagues for conspiracy to obstruct a mail train on the Rock Island Railroad. On July 16, the four men were arrested. Though released on bail, they were clearly in acute need of vigorous representation.

Unionists approached Darrow and Stephen Gregory, whose fight to save Prendergast's life had gained wide attention. Gregory quickly accepted. Darrow hesitated. The union had no money to pay fees; he could ill afford the time. But he was on the union's side in this, and when he saw men much poorer than he giving up their jobs for a cause, he could find "no sufficient cause, except my selfish interest, for refusing." Darrow may also have regarded the case as a kind of penance for his railroad work, which had benefited capitalism.

But to represent Debs in a battle with the nation's railroads would require Darrow's resignation at the Chicago and Northwestern. Marvin Hughitt, the railroad's president, was an open-minded man who respected Darrow's differing perspective. Moreover, the politically connected young attorney was a valuable conduit to Chicago's progressive forces. Hughitt asked only that, after the ARU case was concluded, Darrow work part-time for the railroad at half the retainer he'd been receiving. Darrow happily accepted, and that arrangement continued for years.

Darrow fought on Debs's behalf for nearly a year, first in a brilliantly orchestrated assault on the very notion of criminal conspiracy in which he may well have been robbed of a victory by the U.S. attorney's decision to drop the prosecution after a juror's illness; then in a rear-guard action against a contempt of court charge for violating the injunction, on which Debs was convicted and sentenced to six months in jail. Darrow—who now regarded himself as a Populist—admired Debs, calling him "the bravest man I ever knew" and doubting that "a kindlier, gentler, more generous man" ever lived. When Debs assumed leadership of the newly formed Socialist Party of America, Darrow toyed with following him. Surely his association with Debs had radicalized him. In November 1895, he warned that America's land and resources were becoming ever more concentrated in the hands of "a favored few" and that the country was drifting toward a rude awakening. "If it shall come in the lightning and tornado of civil war, the same as forty years ago," he argued, "when you then look over the ruin and desolation, remember the long years in which the storm was rising, and do not blame the thunderbolt." He wrote Henry Demarest Lloyd: "I believe the Socialists are the best Radicals. We have and I always have and always will support and defend them." He regarded the Socialist vision of a cooperative commonwealth as "logical and profound" but never joined the party (the closest he came was when, with Jack London and Upton Sinclair, he helped organize the Intercollegiate Socialist Society—later the League for Industrial Democracy—designed to "awaken an interest in Socialism among the educated men and women of the country").

Over the years he offered several explanations for declining to enlist in the party: "I had too little faith in men to want to place myself entirely in the hands of the mass. And I never could convince myself that any theory of Socialism so far elaborated was consistent with individual liberty." It was too "dictatorial," he said. "If I belonged to the Socialist party, I would be tried for heresy." Philosophical anarchism, as taught by Kropotkin and Tolstoy, appealed to him more, but it was "a far-off dream that had no relation to life."

Darrow could never be convinced that any party or institution was completely good or completely evil. This feeling, he wrote, "prevented me from obeying orders or being a bitter partisan on any question. Instinctively I lean toward the integrity of the individual unit, and am impatient with any interference with personal freedom." In part, this was the unreconstructed "country man" in him. Even as he returned to his private practice in the Rookery Building, rapidly becoming one of the shrewdest denizens of the city's dense legal thicket, Darrow somehow retained the dogged individualism of the rural Midwest. Like his father the village agnostic, like so many other dissenters in Ohio's Western Reserve, he stubbornly refused to adapt his quirky values to the demands of a bureaucratic society. By heritage and temperament, he remained an ornery misfit.

When it came to human relationships, he could be just as maverick. Though he remained loyal to some of his law partners, he broke with many others. He turned over friends, too, and before long his marriage was under severe strain. The homebreaker wasn't a specific woman; "if there was a seducer in the case," wrote one of his biographers, "it was Chicago, whose vitality and brazenness stole away Clarence's evenings and his weekends."

Writing of this period, one of the city's chroniclers has said, "Chicago by now was the most dramatic and tumultuous, laughing and pleasure-seeking city of the land." Beer gardens served up foamy lager, steak houses grilled the famed Chicago beef; at dusky clubs on South State Street, where newly arrived Southern blacks had settled, one could hear the early strains of ragtime; in the notorious New Levee district there was gambling and drinking, dancing and prostitution at the Bucket of Blood, the Silver Dollar, and the Everleigh House. The nation's first skyscraper—the ten-story Montauk Block—had been built there in 1882, and in the years that followed, Louis Sullivan and Frank Lloyd Wright kept the city at the cutting edge of urban design. Journalists like Eugene Field, Finley Peter Dunne, and the young Theodore Dreiser enlivened its press. Few cities could match its literary lineup of Hamlin Garland, Frank Norris, Floyd Dell, Robert Herrick, and Wallace Rice.

Politically, Chicago sizzled. Ever since the Haymarket massacre, the city

had been an effervescent cauldron of social change. "Single taxers, ideologues, lecturers in back halls, eloquent infidels, short haired women with
ideas of education, long haired men with programs of reform, careerists of all
sorts ... dreamers in broad rimmed hats, low collars and flowing ties, radical
Democrats in fedora hats, string ties and blue shirts, gat-toothed men and
buck-toothed men" bawled and squawked, beefed and remonstrated through
the midwestern nights.

Darrow loved the mesmerizing talk at the Sunset Club, founded "to
foster good fellowship and tolerant discussion among business and professional men of all classes." Men of "pronounced anarchistic and socialistic
views" dined with "their more conservative brethren," producing what the
Chicago Herald called "a wonderfully humanizing effect." Convening at six
every other Thursday night for dinner followed by a short speech and lively
discussion, it adjourned "at an hour that permits the members to return home
in time for family prayers."

But Darrow didn't go home early, and sometimes he didn't go home at
all. As the years went by he found ever less to draw him back to Jessie and
young Paul in their modest brick house at 4219 Vincennes Avenue. Jessie was
an amiable young woman who kept the household running without making
great demands on him. But her own interests hadn't grown much since their
Kinsman days. As Darrow was pulled ever further into the city's political and
literary ferment, Jessie drew back, perhaps resenting his involvement in politics and the arts, hoping he'd confine himself to the impressive-sounding
railroad job and to the conventional social obligations it implied.

Finally, in 1897, they amicably agreed to divorce. Since both feared that
his career would suffer if she alleged the standard infidelity or desertion,
Jessie volunteered to let Clarence institute the proceedings. He agreed to pay
her at least $150 a month for the rest of her life and give her title to the house
that symbolized the bourgeois shackles he now wished to shed. Later Darrow
would quip, "I'm in favor of divorce, because it prevents murder." In this he
was apparently referring to his clients, for his feelings toward Jessie remained
warm, even tender. He could never be happy, he wrote her, unless he knew
that she and Paul were happy.

Shortly after the divorce, Darrow moved into the newly completed
Langdon Co-operative Living Club in a crowded tenement district on the
Near West Side, where he shared rooms with a twenty-five-year-old lawyer
named Francis S. Wilson, a cousin of Jessie's. The Langdon, at the corner of
Desplaines and Bunker Streets, was an apartment building patterned after the
model tenements for workingmen and their families in London. While residents had their own quarters, they often gathered for dinner in the common
dining room, then adjourned to the common drawing room for lectures by
visiting scientists and labor leaders or amateur productions of Shaw and
Ibsen.

Since Darrow and Wilson were among the cooperative's more affluent members, they could afford to combine two three-room apartments into a sprawling suite. They furnished it with pieces left over from Darrow's marriage, bright red carpets and curtains, a pair of andirons representing two cats whose glass eyes glowed in the firelight. Darrow's books were piled on every flat surface. The effect was bohemian, which was just what the two bachelors had in mind. Frank Wilson was jovial and gregarious, Darrow eager to widen his horizons, so they entertained often and well. Writers, painters, left-wing politicians, and social workers gathered of an evening for strong drink and wild talk.

The Langdon was located not far from Hull House, the settlement founded in 1889 by Jane Addams and Ellen Gates Starr. A friend of the founders, Darrow was often invited to the settlement—which one visitor called "the salon of democracy"—to lecture or simply for a meal and hours of talk about prospects for social reform.

On occasion, the high-minded women who ran Hull House had reason to be disappointed in Darrow, whose lofty altruism concealed a coolly pragmatic, even cynical aspect. After the triple defeat of Bryan, Altgeld, and himself in 1896, he had returned to a relatively conventional general practice, selling his services to every corporation that cared to buy.

In the mid-1890s, he represented Commonwealth Edison as it sought to override a mayoral veto of legislation granting it an exclusive franchise for electric services to Chicago. This struck some of Darrow's friends as peculiar, since he'd long advocated public ownership of utilities and particularly since there was good reason to believe the corporation had provided bribes—or "boodle"—to the city council in exchange for the franchise. No sooner was the veto overridden than the electric company sold its franchise to another party at an exorbitant profit.

When Ellen Gates Starr of Hull House wrote Darrow, chiding him for his role in the case, Darrow responded in a self-revealing seven-page letter. Acknowledging that many "of my good friends feel hurt (almost personally) in reference to the matter of which you wrote," Darrow conceded that the law had, indeed, been "passed for boodle, like every ordinance granting valuable privileges in this city."

He made no effort to defend such practices or his services to such a corporation. "I am practically a thief," he wrote, "I am taking money that I did not earn, which comes to me from men who did not earn, but who get it, because they have the chance to get it. I take it without performing any useful service to the world, and I take a thousand times as much as my services are worth even assuming they were useful and honest."

Regrettably, Darrow said, he had long since concluded that "the ideal life was well nigh unlivable." He believed that "society is organized injustice, that business is legal fraud, that a land owner is a pirate, who takes money from the poor for standing on the ground [that] should be free to all."

Darrow had thus resolved "to get what I could out of the system and use it to destroy the system. I came [to Chicago] without friends or money. Society provides no fund out of which such people can live while preaching heresy. It compels us to get our living out of society as it is." Accordingly, he'd served his clients, "almost every one of whom are criminals, judged by the higher law in which I firmly believe. I have taken their ill gotten gains and have tried to use it to prevent suffering.... I have defended the poor and weak, have done it without pay, will do it again. I cannot defend them without bread, I cannot get this except from those who have it, and by giving some measure of conformity to what is."

And he concluded with a heartfelt appeal to his friend: "I don't want you to think I did this or anything for the money because I like money, for I do not, I did it as I mean to do all things because I thought it best, because I believe that the only way any person or deed can be judged is by the purpose and the full results."

Evidently this extraordinary confession had its intended effect, for Darrow remained on good terms with Starr and other Hull House workers such as Gertrude Barnum, Helen Todd, Amanda Johnson, and Alice Hamilton, wellborn young women putting their high ideals to the test in the tenement district.

Some of them lived at the Langdon and, like many artists and social activists who congregated there, believed in free love, much in vogue in such circles. It seems clear that Darrow, newly liberated from a claustrophobic marriage, indulged himself with more than a few of these young women. Gertrude Barnum—who had dropped out of the University of Wisconsin in 1891 to join Hull House—was widely believed to be in love with Darrow. When questioned about the relationship later, he would say only that "he could never get excited about large women."

But Barnum and others recalled magical evenings in his Langdon flat, where Darrow was "the center of attraction," reading from Nietzsche, Tolstoy, and Voltaire as his guests sprawled on the Oriental rug before him. Tears rolled down his cheeks when he read Robert Burns's poetry or bellowed the powerful chants of Walt Whitman. He didn't know much about classical music, but he joined in rousing renditions of "The Road to Mandalay."

When he turned forty on April 18, 1897, his friends threw him a party at the Langdon, featuring games, songs, and other foolery. They made Darrow sing a tune he frequently hummed when weary: "The bear went over the mountain / To see what he could see." In the wee hours of the morning, Darrow sobbed, "It's the best party I ever was to."

To Gertrude Barnum, Darrow was the knight errant of the labor movement. "When the weak and friendless masses clamor for the sweat of his very soul in their behalf, Clarence Darrow will appear again and yet again, with flaming sword, their Great Defender," she would write later.

Not everyone at the Langdon was so taken by the middle-aged labor lawyer. One skeptic was Rosa M. Perdue, a student at the University of

Wisconsin, on a field trip in Chicago for research on Hull House. In a report to her supervisor, Richard T. Ely, the pioneering economist, she wrote of the Langdon's denizens: "A more interesting group of peculiar people could not be brought together. Their points of agreement are first, weariness with life as lived by normal society and a desire to live a strained abnirmal [*sic*] life.... Both male and female members of the club smoked and used profane language as they discussed politics and political leaders; lauded extreme socialism and anarchy, and cheered anarchists." The unchallenged leader of the club, Perdue reported, was the man they aptly called "the Household God." So abject was their adoration, "if the sun would but shine on Clarence Darrow, the other members were content to abide in the shadow."

Darrow's celebrity in Socialist-labor circles grew in early 1898, when he took on a case growing out of a bitter strike at the Paine Lumber Company of Oshkosh, Wisconsin, the nation's largest producer of doors and sashes. The defendants were Thomas I. Kidd, general secretary of the Amalgamated Woodworkers International Union, and two "picket captains," George Zentner and Michael Troiber. They were accused of a criminal conspiracy to damage the company, headed by George M. Paine.

Perhaps Darrow was drawn to the case because his father had been a woodworker, perhaps because he'd known and respected Tom Kidd for years, or perhaps because he saw it as a fresh opportunity to attack the notion of criminal conspiracy. "Conspiracy is the child of the Star Chamber Court of England," he told the Kidd jury, "and it has come down to us, like most bad things and many good ones, from the remote past, without much modification. Whenever a king wanted to get rid of somebody, whenever a political disturber was in someone's way, then they brought a charge of conspiracy.... It was not only a conspiracy to try to kill the king, but it was a conspiracy to talk about killing him, and it was a conspiracy even for several to imagine the death of the king."

George Paine's worst mistake was taking the witness stand and subjecting himself to Darrow's withering cross-examination. He was particularly vulnerable to Darrow's inquiries because, for some years, he'd been reducing his labor costs by replacing male laborers with women and children—a practice eschewed of late by most responsible employers. Darrow made short work of him.

But what seems to have won the day was Darrow's skillful diversion of courtroom attention from the charges against Kidd and his colleagues. "This is really not a criminal case," he began. "It is but an episode in the great battle for human liberty." If there was a conspiracy "dark and damnable," it was not undertaken by his clients but by the Paines and the prosecution, who were using the law "for the purpose of hounding innocent men to their death or to a prison pen." Just as Darrow had scant respect for technical expertise in the law—the closely reasoned argument, the well-honed brief, the scholarly citation of precedent—so he expressed utter lack of interest in Kidd's formal guilt or innocence, which he suggested was irrelevent to the issue:

> Gentlemen, I do not appeal for him. That cause is too narrow for me, much as I love him, and long as I have worked by his side. I appeal to you, gentlemen, not for Thomas I. Kidd, but I appeal to you for the long line—the long, long line reaching back through the ages, and forward to the years to come —the long line of despoiled and downtrodden people of the earth. I appeal to you for those men who rise in the morning before daylight comes, and who go home at night when the light has faded from the sky and give their life, their strength, their toil, to make others rich and great. I appeal to you in the name of those women who are offering up their lives, their strength and their woman-hood on the altar of this modern god of gold; and I appeal to you, gentlemen, in the name of those little children, the living and the unborn, who will look at your names and bless them for the verdict you will render in their aid.

This appeal to the "larger" issue would become a staple of Darrow's courtroom oratory. To his admirers, it was a God-given talent for providing "a broad backdrop of history"; to his critics, "a device for excusing anything and everything."

Another technique in the Kidd case would become central to the classic Darrow defense. With formidable powers of empathy, he would spin a narra-tive of the defendant's life so utterly believable that he placed the jury in the man's shoes. His appeal, with its "strong leaven of sentimentality," was more to the jurors' hearts than to their heads. To defuse evidence against Kidd— that he'd used a funeral oration to incite violence—Darrow asked the jurors to consider how they would have spoken over the grave of a sixteen-year-old boy who'd worked for the Paines for forty cents a day, then become the strike's first victim. "Place yourselves there, gentlemen, not in this courtroom, not under calm deliberation, but place yourselves, as a leader in this great strug-gle, and in the presence of a comrade who had died in this strife, pronouncing a few plain, simple words, above his grave.... Would not you have done as Kidd said he would do?"

It took the jury fifty minutes on November 8, 1898, to return a verdict of not guilty—the first of Darrow's great triumphs.

Darrow had charged the Amalgamated Woodworkers only $250 for his defense, with the condition that he be permitted to publish his address to the jury as a pamphlet. Distributed by the publisher Charles H. Kerr, the pam-phlet achieved a huge circulation and wide acclaim. William Dean Howells said it was "as interesting as a novel."

Nothing could have pleased Darrow more, for increasingly he regarded himself less as a lawyer than as a literary man on the model of Howells and Dreiser. As early as 1899, he had staked out a position in the naturalistic school, of which Howells, Dreiser, Tolstoy, Zola, and Flaubert were leading practitioners. "The world has grown tired of preachers and sermons," he wrote. "Today it asks for facts. It has grown tired of fairies and angels, and asks for flesh and blood. It looks on life as it exists, both its beauty and its horror, its joy and its sorrow; it wishes to see it all; not the prince and the millionaire alone, but the laborer and the beggar, the master and the slave." He drew a direct parallel between romantic writers whom privileged young ladies read in hammocks on summer afternoons and the corporate lawyers who represented the bloated rich and the giant trusts. Romantic artists, he concluded, "could no more afford to serve the poor than a modern lawyer to defend the weak."

Darrow found a market for some grittily realistic portraits of the Chicago he knew. On July 1, 1900, William Randolph Hearst opened his midwestern outpost, the *Chicago Evening American,* ostensibly to build regional support for William Jennings Bryan, actually to prepare the way for his own presidential candidacy four years hence. Hearst had asked Darrow to incorporate the paper for him; the lawyer also defended the *American* in a suit for injuries to a pedestrian from falling masonry dislodged by the newspaper's gargantuan sign, containing three thousand electric bulbs, which hung over State Street (when Darrow lost, the victim collected $8,000). Some years later, Darrow would second Hearst's nomination for president, proclaiming "the eyes of the common man are turned on William Randolph Hearst."

In 1902, Hearst opened the pages of his flamboyant tabloid to a series by his attorney called "Easy Lessons in the Law." He never paid Darrow for these stories, but the fledgling writer was delighted to see his work displayed for a mass audience.

In these pieces, Darrow vividly portrayed ordinary Chicagoans victimized by the rigid formalism of contemporary jurisprudence. He dwelt particularly on two legal doctrines—"risks assumed by servant" and "fellow-servants"—illustrating how justice had been warped by commercial life. According to a contemporary legal guide, "risks assumed by servant" meant that "the servant assumes all risks that he ought to know are incident to the discharge of his duties," and "fellow servants" meant that "if the master has exercised due care in selecting and retaining servants, he has done his duty. If, nevertheless, injury results to one servant by the wrongful act or omission of another servant, the master is not liable."

In muscular prose, Darrow captured the feel of turn-of-the-century workplaces—railroads, machine shops, construction sites, coal mines. If the stories lampooned the warped values of business in the Gilded Age, they also indicted the ethics of the legal profession.

Consider the pathetic tale of James Clark, a structural ironworker, whose life expectancy in that job was but ten years. "Had he known this," Darrow writes sardonically, "he might have chosen to be a banker or a lawyer instead." One day, when he was suffering a touch of indigestion that made him dizzy, he went to work on the steel skeleton of a building, twelve floors above the ground. Perched on a girder, he lost his balance and fell. Darrow noted that

Clark might not have fallen so far if his employer had put in floors as the framework rose, a practice contractors had been compelled to follow in other cities. As it was, nothing impeded his fall. Unlikely though it may seem, he survived and, grievously injured, sued the contractor for compensation. But the judge found for the defendant on the grounds of assumed risk.

As a coda, Darrow writes: "That evening the Judge went home and, taking from his library Lecky's History of European Morals, he read how in Pagan Rome the Emperor Trajan had passed an edict compelling a net to be strung underneath the acrobats who were performing in the circus. This was before Christianity and commercialism were born."

Later, Darrow used the same ironic voice in his novel *An Eye for an Eye*. This grim story is told a friend by Jim Jackson on the eve of his execution. An orphan educated through the sixth grade, he peddled vegetables on Chicago's streets. His marriage went bad and he and his wife resolved to divorce, but the Catholic priest advised against it and a lawyer wanted too much money to handle the matter. The couple's debts piled up. "I went one day to see a lawyer, but he didn't tell me anything that done me any good and I had to pay him ten dollars. . . . Lawyers get their money awful easy, don't they?"

One night, after a politician had stood him to some drinks, Jackson impulsively bought a steak for dinner. But his wife, uneasy at his extravagance, grew angry. He accused her of overcooking the steak. Ultimately, he took a poker to her head, then fled but was apprehended and sentenced to death. At this recital's end, Jim admonishes his friend to tell his son "not to be poor. . . . I don't believe I ever would have done it if I hadn't been so poor."

Though *An Eye for an Eye* isn't in the same class with other early realistic novels like Stephen Crane's *Maggie* and Dreiser's *Sister Carrie*, it is the most eloquent expression of Darrow's leitmotif that "the so-called sins of men [are] not crimes, but weaknesses inherent in their being and beyond their power to prevent or overcome." Darrow the novelist poses for the comfortable reader some uncomfortable questions, just as Darrow the courtroom lawyer posed them for juries: Had you been born as this man was, reared as he was, suffered what he did, would you have behaved any differently? Aren't all men capable of crime if pushed into a position where they cannot do otherwise? Is, therefore, the answer to punish—much less execute—the Jim Jacksons of this world or to reform the society that compels them to murder?

The part of Darrow that still believed in the efficacy of reform set its sights, in 1902, on the legislative seat from Chicago's Seventeenth District, the heart of the West Side tenement area known as the Ghetto because more Hebrew, Italian, and Greek were spoken there than English. Rosa Perdue, the Wisconsin student so fascinated and repelled by Darrow, accompanied him and his aide, Amanda Johnson, on their campaigning. In a three-piece suit and bowler hat, fists jammed deep in his pockets, he spoke on the Ghetto's street corners, advocating the initiative and the referendum and public ownership of utilities. Darrow's speeches, Perdue reported, were "most inflammatory, urging the masses to take by force 'the stolen goods of the Capitalist.'" One day, as he was escorted home by the district's "lowest men and boys," Johnson rejoiced that the "demonstrations were like a miniature French revolution."

Darrow, wrote Perdue, "glories in rousing the passions of those too ignorant to know that he is using them as tools by the use of which to gratify a selfish ambition. He expects to be Governor of Illinois and even aspires to the Presidency.... I consider him a dangerous man to be intrusted with power."

Of the one hundred windows in the Langdon residence, a reporter noticed that fall, there were campaign photos of Darrow in all but one. Could the lone dissenter have been Rosa Perdue? If so, she was overwhelmed by voters who liked the man.

Darrow's four years of "power" in Springfield scarcely revealed him as a danger to the republic. Much legislation he supported as an independent reform candidate—for example, a bill to restrict the courts' power to issue injunctions in labor disputes—was defeated. Ultimately he concluded that "no independent man who fights for what he thinks is right can succeed in legislation. He can kill bad bills by a vigorous fight and publicity, but he can get nothing passed." He didn't thrive in public office; his métier was as a freelance advocate, in which capacity he consorted with malodorous ward politicians like "Hinky-Dink" Kenna and "Bathhouse John" Coughlin. Although Populists, Altgeld Democrats, and the transit workers union tried in early 1903 to persuade him to run for mayor against the powerful three-term incumbent, Carter Harrison II, Darrow declined.

That winter of 1902–03, Darrow couldn't resist a starring role in a national drama, the bitter strike by Pennsylvania's anthracite miners. In May 1902, some 147,000 members of John Mitchell's United Mine Workers walked out, demanding a wage increase, an eight-hour day, and union recognition. The mine operators refused to recognize or bargain collectively with the UMW. "There cannot be two masters in the management of business," said George F. Baer, who presided magisterially over the Reading Railroad and its extensive coal-mining interests. "God in his Infinite Wisdom has put the control of business into the hands of Christian gentlemen."

As winter approached, the nation faced an acute shortage of the hard coal used to fire basic industries, run locomotives, and heat homes. Under pressure to head off misery and civil disorder, President Roosevelt maneuvered the parties into accepting arbitration by a commission he'd appoint. The operators assembled a team of twenty-three attorneys to represent them in the proceedings. Mitchell asked Darrow, the reformer Henry Demarest Lloyd, and three mining district lawyers to present the union's case. With little time to prepare, Darrow threw himself into the work with fierce energy. When Hamlin Garland encountered Darrow, Lloyd, and Mitchell in Washington, "they all looked worn." Darrow was "haggard."

In mid-November, the seven-man commission opened hearings, first in

Scranton's superior court chamber, later at Philadelphia's federal courthouse. Sensing that this time the facts were on his side, Darrow reversed his strategy. Instead of shunning specifics and enlarging the context, he strenuously resisted the operators' efforts to talk about union violence, focusing instead on the miners' scandalously low wages (averaging $250 a year) and their grim working conditions.

The union case presented 241 witnesses, of whom the most affecting were several small "breaker boys." (That fall, Darrow wrote of Johnny McCaffery, who at age ten—after his father was killed in the mine—went to work as a breaker boy, snatching slate "from the madly rushing black flood" as he straddled the coal chute. For forty years, he did the same dirty job. Nothing dramatic happened, for "there is nothing dramatic in a life of endless toil.")

In his eight-hour closing argument that February, Darrow called the strike "one of the important contests that have marked the progress of human liberty since the world began—one force pointing one way, another force the other." The operators, he told the commission, "are fighting for slavery, while we are fighting for freedom. They are fighting for the rule of man over man, for despotism, for darkness, for the past. We are striving to build up man."

A month later, Darrow's inspired advocacy paid off as the commission awarded union members back pay, substantial pay increases, and a nine-hour day. Lloyd called the result "a notable victory" for the union. Samuel Gompers termed it the most significant moment in American labor history.

Returning to Chicago early in 1903, after four months of brutally hard work, Darrow was ready to enjoy his celebrity status. For several years he'd been something of a boulevardier, with literary panache to match his radical glamour. One newspaper remarked on his "downright ugliness," but the novelist and social reformer Brand Whitlock termed it "a sort of beautiful ugliness," calling Darrow's smile "as winning as a woman's." George Bernard Shaw, whom Darrow met that year, detected something wild in him. "With that cheekbone," he said, "he wants only a few feathers and a streak of ochre to be a perfect Mohican." When Hamlin Garland encountered Darrow at a party, he was amused "to see how this big, battle-scarred labor leader enjoyed the attentions of a group of pretty women who kept him busy answering impertinent questions. To them he was an object of curiosity. They knew something of his stormy past and delighted in uncovering it. His dark face and wrinkled brow (over which a long lock of hair fell) shone with mocking good humor. He likes these women, and yet, I fear, covertly despised them."

Garland was on to something. Like his models Nietzsche and Schopenhauer, Darrow doubted women's capacity for rationality in public and had reservations about granting them the suffrage. He argued that the American woman had "been less affected by the progress of civilization than man." But if he didn't much respect women in their generality, he was powerfully drawn to them in the particular.

He'd been fascinated by Katherine Leckie, an early feminist and a supporter of labor who was a star reporter on Hearst's *American*. She was also quite a beauty, "the Irish type, with light brown hair, blue eyes and a magnificent figure." For a time they were inseparable; then, for no apparent reason, the relationship ended.

On the loose again, Darrow went one night to read his essay on Omar Khayyám at the White City Club, whose roster included many of the city's best-known writers and artists. As he acknowledged his final round of applause, Darrow sighted his friend John R. Gregg, the inventor of a popular shorthand system, across the room with his wife and a smartly dressed auburn-haired woman. Darrow insisted that she dine with him. Declining, she turned out the lights so everyone would go home, but he held her hand until she agreed. Twelve years younger than Darrow, Ruby Hammerstrom was an aspiring journalist who for some time had written under the pseudonym Ruby Stanleigh (a name she'd plucked from the *Fireside Companion*). She didn't have Katherine Leckie's startling looks, but she had a "blazing wit," and before long she and Clarence were sharing long dinners at Mami Gali's, a favorite of the city's literati.

On July 16, 1903, they were married in a ceremony at the Greggs' apartment presided over by Judge Edward F. Dunne, soon to be Chicago's mayor. Frank Wilson, Darrow's roommate and partner, and Ruby's brother Fred were the witnesses and only guests at the champagne breakfast, after which the whole party adjourned to the Engle Street station, where the newlyweds left for a three-month honeymoon in Europe.

Darrow was already a cosmopolite: in 1895 he'd spent two months in London, Stratford-on-Avon, Paris, Geneva, and Venice, churning out vivid travel pieces for the *Chicago Chronicle*. The European scene seemed to ignite Darrow's creative fires. At Swiss chalets and French bistros, he scribbled away at the manuscript soon to be titled *Farmington*. By the time he and his bride returned, the book was ready for his publisher and Darrow was ready to pick up the frazzled threads of his law practice.

The practice had languished from the distractions of recent years, aggravated by the resignation of two partners. In April 1903—three months before the marriage—Darrow had brought his remaining partner, Frank Wilson, into a new partnership with Edgar Lee Masters, an accomplished legal technician and poet of promise. The strains that soon developed were rooted less in differences between the two men than in their eerie similarities. Both detested the practice of law, saw it as a means of making money, and yearned for the day when they could kiss it good-bye and devote themselves body and soul to literature.

The two lawyers had known each other since 1897, when Masters helped Darrow become attorney for the receiver of a bankrupt building-and-loan association. When the time came to settle their fees, Masters recalled, Darrow "turned on me like an aroused cobra" and promptly "grabbed the larger share of the money, though I had done most of the work." Despite this friction, Masters said Darrow "flirted" with him, hoping to make him a partner. Darrow had "charm" and "plausibility," but he had "gray, greedy eyes, and sudden angers." Masters's wife, Helen, disliked Darrow intensely; his father-in-law thought him "an atheist and an anarchist... an immoral fellow." So Masters declined. Not until 1903, when Darrow renewed his offer and offered Masters a "fair percentage" of the partnership's earnings, did he accept.

"Inside every lawyer is the wreck of a poet," Darrow liked to say, loosely appropriating a mot from one of his naturalist models, Gustave Flaubert.* If enough wrecks could be wheeled into place, he thought, what a law firm he could have! So about the same time he approached Masters, Darrow offered a partnership to Brand Whitlock, a burgeoning novelist. "We need a good man who can do all kinds of work," he wrote. "Literary men and dreamers are not generally the ones who can. Still, I think so much of you that I wish you could." Whitlock, then embroiled in Toledo politics, reluctantly declined. When Whitlock sent him his new novel, *The Turn of the Balance,* a few years later, Darrow called it "a great book" and added, "You can see your finish as a lawyer, and I hope that you will not long need to be bothered with your profession."

In the summer of 1903, the new firm of Darrow, Masters and Wilson moved into freshly decorated quarters on the twelfth floor of the Ashland Block, where some of the city's elite law firms clustered. Masters took his bust of Thomas Jefferson into a corner sanctum where he forbade all to intrude, Frank Wilson occupied another small office, while Darrow, as senior partner, installed himself in a large suite with a private entrance. The walls were done in ivory with black woodwork, there were green velvet carpets, and behind a seven-and-a-half-foot desk of Flemish oak he presided in a genuine judge's chair that rocked and swiveled in all directions.

About this time, Darrow revealed a hitherto-unrecognized taste for physical comfort and—apparently under Ruby's influence—for outright luxury. He'd always believed in "personal gratification," proudly proclaiming, "I am a hedonist and have contempt for anyone who isn't. That's why I can't stomach preachers." But if once he'd occupied relatively modest digs, now he and Ruby took a spacious apartment on Sheridan Road on Chicago's North Side. At Ruby's insistence, he began to dress with more care, in silk shirts, black satin ties (made to order at a special midwidth by Marshall Field's), and hats done to his specifications by the Knox Company back East.

To support this style, Darrow began playing the stock market. He was an

---

* Then there was the somewhat more acute perception of the Spanish philosopher Miguel de Unamuno (1864–1936): "Every peasant has a lawyer inside of him, just as every lawyer, no matter how urbane he may be, carries a peasant within himself."

imprudent investor, losing money on speculation in railroad stock, a stake in a Mexican mine that shortly closed, and, worst of all, a foolhardy banking venture orchestrated by a former circuit court judge.

For a time, the three partners got along well enough. Masters had to concede that Darrow possessed "amiable qualities": his "drawl and his sleepy ways, his humorous turns of speech, his twisted ironies made him a pleasant man to be with," Masters said. "He seemed an old-fashioned soul, easy and lounging and full of generosities." They divided roles: Darrow the quintessential "outside man" who brought in the clients and performed heroic feats in the courtroom, Masters the classic "back office man," a meticulous drafter of briefs and careful manager of process. The firm was prospering, each partner earning between $25,000 and $35,000 a year. Masters—who had regarded the partnership with Darrow principally as a guarantee of substantial income—thought "there was a chance now to be at ease on the score of money, and to have some opportunity for poetry."

Unfortunately for them both, Darrow harbored much the same hopes. "The one thing I want most of all to be is a writer," he confided to Frank Wilson. Increasingly he begrudged the time he had to devote to routine legal matters, particularly corporation law, which still occupied half his practice. "My life has been misspent in musty courtrooms," he wrote a friend, "with hair-splitting lawyers and ponderous judges quibbling over nothing." Whenever possible, Darrow left such responsibilities behind—for more dramatic but less lucrative cases, for lecture tours ("speaking for the liquor interests," Masters charged), to work on his articles or books. Not surprisingly, Masters deeply resented these lapses.

The seeds of his resentment were sown only weeks after the partnership was formed. In May 1903, Darrow began representing striking workers at Chicago's Kellogg Switchboard Company. A series of injunctions against picketing, followed by the jailing of workers for contempt of court, culminated on July 16, 1903—the very day Darrow chose to get married—in the worst rioting the city had witnessed since the Pullman strike. When the couple left that afternoon on their three-month European jaunt, Masters was compelled to step into the demanding case.

On another occasion, citing an out-of-town emergency, Darrow called Masters in to deliver the closing argument in a personal-injury suit against a railroad. The emergency turned out to be a debate in Cincinnati on the question "Is Man a Machine?" Adding insult to injury, when Masters got a split jury Darrow told him, "I suppose if I had been there we would have won all of them."

A more weighty dispute broke out over a lawyer Darrow proposed bringing into the firm. Chicago's city council had passed an ordinance requiring free transfers between the various streetcar lines. When the notorious Union Transit Company refused to comply, the city brought six hundred suits against it, asking a two-hundred-dollar fine for each violation. When the first suit came to trial on April 14, 1902, it took the six-man jury only three minutes to return an acquittal. A second suit ended the same way. It did not take the public prosecutors long to indict seven Union Transit "fixers" for bribing the jurors and the constables who guarded them. Despite Darrow's best efforts as attorney for three of the fixers, all seven were convicted (though several were later freed on appeal). Among those on whom the conviction stuck was a young lawyer named Cyrus Simon.

Shortly after Masters joined the firm, Darrow sought to bring Simon in as well as a full partner. Masters strenuously objected. According to Masters's own account, the dispute focused less on substance than on appearance. Darrow wanted to put Simon in the firm's name, on the stationery, on the door—a characteristic thumbing of his nose at Chicago's legal establishment. Frank Wilson supported his ex-roommate. Masters, who cared more for others' opinions, adamantly opposed advertising their association with the jury briber, who, not incidentally, was Jewish. Jews were firmly barred from many of Chicago's patrician law firms, and the very act of admitting one was unorthodox. Ultimately, the partners compromised by making Simon a junior partner but leaving his name off the stationery and the door. For a time, Simon functioned effectively as a claims agent—a collector of overdue bills —for the firm's clients (lawyers of that era generally performed this dirty work in exchange for half of what they collected). William Pinkerton knew him as "a smart little fellow." Then he was found to be pocketing the proceeds from settlements without reporting them to his partners. Most members of the firm wanted him prosecuted for fraud, but Darrow let him resign with no publicity.

To some of Darrow's friends and associates, the Simon case was a troubling reminder of the Commonwealth Edison case five years before. If he could look the other way as the electric company bribed city officials to gain and then sell at huge profit a valuable city franchise, if he could recruit a known briber like Cyrus Simon for his firm, what else might Darrow be capable of? To a colleague anxious about such matters, Darrow once remarked: "Do not the rich and powerful bribe juries, intimidate and coerce judges as well as juries? Do they shrink from any weapon? Why this theatrical indignation against alleged or actual jury tampering in behalf of 'lawless' strikers or other unfortunate victims of ruthless capitalism?" Some years later, a distraught friend noted that Darrow's defense of bribery "justifies the belief that he thinks such a course right."

Darrow's principal allegiance had never been to the law itself. "Through you I came to know the cant and hypocrisy and iniquity of our [legal] system," Brand Whitlock wrote him. "It was you who taught me not to worship the law as a fetish." In a minor case a prosecutor accused Darrow of cheating the law of a dangerous criminal. "The law?" Darrow shouted. "To hell with the law! My business is to save this defendant from the law!"

But Masters was not the only colleague who found Darrow growing intensely cynical. Hamlin Garland, the novelist and critic, went to dinner at the Darrows' apartment in 1907.

> I found him quite as grave and even more bitter than his writing indicates. He talks with much of the same acrid humor. He read to us some short stories called The Law's Delay, which were intolerably gloomy and savage, but powerful.... His uncompromising honesty of purpose and his aggressive cynicism makes him repellent to many—hence he is to me a lonely figure.... His writing is too monotonous in tone, too bitter in quality, too pessimistic of outlook to succeed.... I feel power but not high purpose in his program. We began our careers on common ground, but he has gone on—or off—into a dark and tangled forest land. He may turn out to be right, but at present he appears to me as a destructive force merely!

Darrow's inner space was, indeed, increasingly dark and tangled. "On the whole," he wrote in *Farmington,* "I believe that life is not worth living." His view of his fellow Americans was increasingly bleak, even contemptuous. To a close friend, Mary Field, he wrote a few years later:

> I am up here making a couple of speeches & as lonesome as hell. Little Jay towns & Jay people who never heard of Nietzsche or any one else excepting Jesus. What is the use? ... I can even forget this dull town & the stupid faces of stupid men & women & boys & girls who roam the streets making a noise— Men & women & boys & girls who are here because the only feeling in the world that can make you forget for a little time is the sex feeling.... The strange thing is that all the D—n fools are in earnest and think it means something and ... they have built churches to fool themselves about God and immortality and states to fool themselves about the importance of it all. And they run for office so their names can be on the tongues of fools & write books and paint pictures so fools will talk about them and they glote [*sic*] in their fame or notoriety & delude themselves with the thought that they are something & will live when the world is cold.

What redeemed Darrow from such cynicism was the frequent outcropping of sardonic humor, often addressed to himself. "I may be an idiot," he told a Senate committee, "but I am not a cheerful idiot."

Whatever Darrow was becoming, Masters, too, bore some responsibility for the deteriorating relations between them. Though Darrow never deigned to mention Masters in his memoirs, Ruby observed that Masters "could be most agreeable, sociable, witty, with an intoxicating, boyish laugh, all of which he shut off instantaneously if anyone not wanted crossed his path," when he would show "what a rotter [he] was...a cad, coward; cruel-hearted, supremely selfish, obsessed with his faith in himself as a genius entitled to anything and everything that he could squeeze out of persons and life in general."

Masters would write later that Darrow's admirers "will try to get a bust for him and make him an heir of fame; but what he did in life, his dishonesty and his treachery and his selfish grabbing and living will seep up from the grass of any pedestal and fill the circumambient air with feculence." Indeed, the very notion of a Darrow bust on public exhibition put Masters in a lather. Eventually, he would ladle all that venom into a poem called "On a Bust," which went, in part:

> *A giant as we hoped, in truth, a dwarf;*
> *A barrel of slop that shines on Lethe's wharf,*
> *Which seemed at first a vessel with sweet wine*
> *For thirsty lips. So down the swift decline*
> *You went through sloven spirit, craven heart*
> *And cynic indolence. And here the art*
> *Of molding clay has caught you for the nonce*
> *And made your shame our shame—your head in bronze!*

But he wasn't finished with the portrait. Perhaps Masters came to recognize how much he and his partner had in common, how much he had learned, even borrowed, from Darrow: critics have noted that the device of graveyard epitaphs that worked so brilliantly in *Spoon River Anthology* owed more than a bit to the "Burying Ground" section of *Farmington*. Or perhaps it was merely the passage of time that softened the earlier vituperation. In any case, six years after "On a Bust" came "Clarence Darrow," which ended with deep empathy for his old antagonist:

> *This is Darrow,*
> *Inadequately scrawled, with his young, old heart,*
> *And his drawl, and his infinite paradox*
> *And his sadness, and kindness,*
> *And his artist sense that drives him to shape his life*
> *To something harmonious, even against the schemes of God.*

Neither poem does justice to the flesh-and-blood Darrow, but read side by side they capture the ambivalence of a nineteenth-century country lawyer in the twentieth-century city. A dinner guest at the Sheridan Avenue apartment would have felt himself in the presence of a thoroughly urban—and urbane—man. The Darrows, at Ruby's insistence, entertained in the continental style—iced caviar as an appetizer, after-dinner coffee in delicate demitasse cups, fine liqueurs in crystal glasses—using the Sheffield steel cutlery with ivory handles that they had bought on their honeymoon in England. The lawyer's desk was piled high with drafts for his next book, typescripts of articles for the *Goose-Quill*, *Rubric*, *Pilgrim*, and *International Quarterly*. If the guest was lucky, Darrow might read to the assemblage from his own work in progress or from Tolstoy, Darwin, Nietzsche, or Schopenhauer.

But even as he flourished in the saloons and salons of Chicago, he cultivated—in court at least—the style of the country lawyer he'd first encountered on Kinsman's Fourth of July. When arguing a case he wore old tweed suits, bagging at the knees; in warm weather he quickly discarded the jacket to reveal midnight-blue or fireman-red galluses of an antique style, a clumsily tied necktie dangling at midchest. At the defense table, he slumped deep down in his chair, noodling on a crossword puzzle or probing, with evident discomfort, a bunion on one foot. When he rose to question the witness, a thumb hooked under one gallus strap, or sometimes both thumbs in the armholes of his waistcoat, his was the slouching, shambling manner of the rural midwesterner. It was his massive farmer's shoulders, sometimes shrugging, sometimes sagging, always "eloquent and incredibly insulting," that best expressed his moods. When he spoke it was in a gravelly drawl, softened by the gentle burr of the border states, which suggested the talk on sagging front porches through long summer evenings. If the total effect was invariably described as Lincolnesque, the model wasn't Lincoln as president but Lincoln as small-town lawyer, ambling and amiable, his face deeply creased around cavernous greenish-gray eyes, an unruly lock of dark hair falling over the right flank of his craggy brow. It was this bundle of mannerisms—which, as one shrewd critic has noted, comes close to the "all-American personality"— that throughout his peripatetic career permitted Darrow to transcend the alien, somehow seeming "down home" to juries in Los Angeles and Detroit and Dayton, Tennessee. But increasingly there were those who caught a whiff of the bogus, sensing behind this artfully constructed rustic the guile, cunning, and cynicism of a big-city fixer.

In March 1906, Darrow went into the WFM case with his eyes open, recognizing from the start that he was up against formidable opponents in the Pinkerton detective agency and the Colorado and Idaho mine owners. In early March, he wrote John Mitchell of the United Mine Workers, whom he'd come to know well during the coal strike two years before: "This is a matter I would rather avoid if I could on account of the hard fight and the serious odds. However I do not see how I can get out of it. I presume they are trying to railroad these fellows because they want to get rid of them." Moreover, Darrow was worried that Gompers's AFL, which had long been at odds with the WFM, might refuse to aid Haywood and his colleagues. Would organized labor, he asked Mitchell, support the defendants "as far as possible"? "Public sentiment," he reminded him, "is very necessary in a great case of this kind." But money was an issue, too: "A successful fight cannot be made so far from home without considerable resources."

In the matter of money, Mitchell's answer was optimistic. "I have no doubt that organized labor is going to subscribe a very large fund for the defense," he wrote. "So far, two of our Districts have subscribed $5,500." As to public sentiment, he was less reassuring. "The Western Federation of Miners has no standing in the American labor movement. The action of its leaders in attaching [*sic*] the leaders of other trade unions has alienated, to a very large degree, public sentiment from them." Mitchell believed the men to be innocent of Steunenberg's murder but warned that "the prosecution will make every effort to pack the jury and, no doubt, the mine owners will subscribe all the funds necessary to accomplish this end."

In May 1906, Darrow was still worried about money. On May 9, the labor organizer Mary Harris Jones, better known as Mother Jones, wrote Terence Powderly, former leader of the Knights of Labor, "I saw Darrow yesterday, he tells me he thinks it will be a long drawn out trial, & it will need a great deal of finance to carry it on, & we must have it." She reported that the defense attorney had recently received "much encouragement and every guarantee of assistance" from Bolton Hall, founder of the American Longshoremen's Union.

Darrow later testified that he was paid $35,000 for the Haywood case; Edgar Masters recalled the figure as $50,000, though only $15,000 of that came into the firm's coffers (which may be how Darrow arrived at $35,000). Whichever figure is accurate, it was a good fee for that era, far greater than the $10,000 for which Darrow had labored long and hard in the coal arbitration.

He spent the late spring and summer assembling his forces. Knowing that he confronted a formidable array of detectives under McParland, he began putting together his own detective force. Although the Pinkertons and other detectives worked almost exclusively for corporate managements or state governments, many agencies accepted assignments from labor unions. McParland believed that, in the early summer of 1906, the Thiel agency turned with its considerable information to the defense. Repeatedly in late 1906 and early 1907, he complained that Thiel detectives were watching his every move just as closely as the Pinkertons were watching Darrow.* Meanwhile, Darrow seems to have turned to another agency—Mooney and Boland of Chicago—for further investigative work. One of the largest and most prominent Chicago agencies, Mooney and Boland evidently assigned a score of detectives to work under Darrow's direction. Finally, Darrow fell back on a couple of men whom past experience had shown he could rely on for highly sensitive and confidential work. Chief among these was a lawyer and detective named George E. Dickson, who for some years had functioned as president of the Workmen's Legal Security Company in Chicago.

Dickson came up with a plan for extracting prosecution secrets from Borah. May Awkwright Hutton, a defense sympathizer in the Coeur d'Alenes (and the wife of Levi W. Hutton, the engineer of the Dynamite Express), had told him Borah was "very suceptible to the charms of young women and that a fairly attractive young woman who is a good stenographer could be used to great advantage etc. She must not do anything to compromise herself, but at

---

* Although McParland wasn't given to airy fantasies, his intense dislike for Wilson Swain, who had competed so strenuously for the Steunenberg job, and a certain inherent paranoia may have bred this particular story. There is no hard evidence to support the notion that Swain and his detectives were working for Darrow.

the same time must not be exactly like a lump of ice. In other words must string him along for a month or two during which time she will be able to get his innermost thoughts and plans. Mrs. H. says that Borah does not know it but that he has been worked in this way before." To Bill Haywood, who not only slept with his stenographer but shared some of his most tightly held secrets with her, this must have seemed an excellent plan. Whether the defense ever carried it out we don't know.

Much of the clandestine work that summer focused on Steve Adams, who Darrow early recognized could be the key to the case. Darrow and Richardson weren't allowed into the penitentiary to see Adams—or Orchard —so they passed messages through the Adams family, notably his wife, Annie; his brother Joe; and friends like Mary Ann Mahoney, a Telluride nurse and close friend of Annie's. Steve seemed curiously phlegmatic among all this coming and going. He liked to stroll out to the gallows in the prison court-yard, climb on the platform, and stretch out in the summer sunshine. One day he chipped a splinter for Annie to mail to her father, a collector of macabre souvenirs.

In the second week of August, Joe Adams arrived in Boise from his home in Meeker, Colorado, and had two or three talks with his brother at the penitentiary. "He is working in the interest of the other side," a troubled Jim Hawley confided to an associate on August 13. Another defense effort to "turn" Adams was reportedly made by a mysterious "woman from Chicago." Detecting "a number of mysterious matters" in the activities of the defense team, Hawley said he had put "several men on watch." Two weeks later, the leadership of the defense converged on Boise for a summit conference. From Chicago came Darrow and George Dickson; from Denver, Edmund Richard-son; from Spokane, Fred Miller.

The gathering was quickly detected by the prosecution's agents. Word of the conclave reached Idaho's governor on August 23, and the governor wrote McParland in Denver in some alarm, wondering what had caused it. The detective hadn't had any time off since arriving in Boise in mid-January. At age sixty-two, he was deeply fatigued. So as summer's heat descended on the region, he'd taken his wife to Chicago for a vacation of more than three weeks, returning to Denver on August 15. Now Gooding urged his principal detective to return to Boise as quickly as possible. That same day, Hawley wrote Owen Van Duyn in Caldwell, "Some movement is on foot, but what it is I can not just fathom."

Responding to the governor's letter on August 26, McParland regretted that "a pressure of business" would prevent him from reaching Boise before the end of the next week. He agreed that the unusual gathering of defense attorneys "certainly has some significance" and said he had "tried to work out why this visit was made," coming up with two hypotheses. Since the defense attorneys surely suspected now that their clients were not leveling with them, the visit "may have been to try to get the prisoners either individually or collectively to make a true statement to their counsel so that they may be informed in advance what the State may be able to prove." Alternatively, since it was well known by then that serious strains had developed between Moyer, on the one hand, and Haywood and Pettibone, on the other, the defense might be seeking a "reconciliation" between the parties.

The depth of the prosecutorial concern about the gathering of defense personnel was reflected in a second letter, on August 27, from McParland to Hawley. In his letter to the governor, McParland hadn't even mentioned Steve Adams. Now, with another twenty-four hours to ponder the matter, McParland began to focus on Adams. Noting his brother Joe's visits, the detective said it would have been useful if Hawley had arranged to talk with Joe and "find out from him what really was the object of his visit and what Joe had to say." Regretting again that he could not reach Boise for another ten days or so, McParland trusted that Hawley and Borah would "have things in very fair shape on my arrival."

That trust was sadly misplaced. Whatever business held him in Denver during the waning days of August and sent him to Kansas City the first week of September seems to have distracted McParland from his own intuition that it was the Steve Adams front that needed shoring up.

For the moment, Darrow was well ahead of the resourceful Pinkerton. Twice that summer he'd traveled to Oregon to meet with Annie Adams's uncle James Lillard, on one occasion accompanied by his colleague John Nugent, Haywood's old friend, on the other by Edmund Richardson. According to an account that came to Darrow's biographer from his widow, Lillard was suspicious at the start, but ultimately Darrow seems to have established rapport with him. Lillard was apparently a bit eccentric, described by one reporter as "a typical character of the West." After several meetings, the attorney convinced him that he should attempt to persuade Adams to repudiate his confession.

How did Darrow do it? In part, no doubt, with his considerable charm. Perhaps with arguments that the prosecution was behaving improperly, even illegally, in holding Adams without charging him with a specific crime. Perhaps with threats. But some evidence points to another possibility.

Early on, McParland had feared a defense effort to bribe his star corroborative witness. In April 1906, he drew Hawley's attention to an operative's report saying that Lillard had talked of putting up bond for his nephew's release. "We can take no chance of allowing him [Adams] out on bond," the detective warned. "There is too much money on the other side for us to take any chances on a matter of this kind." Later, on at least two occasions, McParland—who was generally well informed on Darrow's activities—expressed a considered judgment that Darrow had bribed that "damn scoundrel" Lillard. In April 1907, he wrote a deputy sheriff that he was convinced Lillard had been promised "thirty pieces of silver like Judas of old" if Adams recanted his confession. Although he wasn't sure how much the uncle had been paid, McParland was "pretty well satisfied he had received a monetary consideration."

Some years later, McParland wrote Frank Gooding that he had good reason to believe that Darrow had paid Lillard $75,000, of which $25,000 had specifically been promised to Adams if he'd repudiate his confession, with Lillard to keep the other $50,000.

> It is not drawing very much on our imagination when we say that the visits of Mr. Darrow with his associate counsel was [*sic*] to win over Lillard to assist them. Lillard at that time was trying to defend himself against the attacks of Uncle Sam in the matter of some 14,000 acres of land that the United States Government claimed that he had got unlawfully; besides Lillard at that time was about bankrupt.... [Later] Adams raised hell, demanded of his lawyers and old man Lillard the $25,000.00 that was promised him if he denied his confession, and also claimed that Lillard held that money; that this $25,000.00 was a part of $75,000.00 that Lillard was promised if he held Adams up to the mark, whereby he would stick to denying his confession until he was acquitted. Now I did not hear this myself, but it was simply a rumor and I think the rumor was true.... From rumors that I have heard since the close of these trials, it looks as though old man Lillard got the $75,000.00 and used it and left Stevie, as he called him, to hold the bag, as I was told that Lillard got out of all his trouble and was well off, and it took money to do it.

Accusing Darrow of bribery would have been a convenient excuse for McParland's own failings in the Adams matter. That might explain the 1907 letter. But by 1912, passions had cooled considerably; the detective had ample opportunity to reflect on these events and to cross-check his recollections with others. His second letter, while far from conclusive, lends credence to the notion of bribery. Some newspapermen clearly believed it. The *Denver Republican*, voice of the Colorado mine owners, flatly alleged: "Adams, through his relatives, was bought off."

Already in mid-1906, people close to Darrow were hearing strange reports about the tactics their friend was using in Idaho. Colonel Charles Erskine Scott Wood, a close friend from Portland, Oregon, heard stories about the "crooked methods" by which Darrow was both concocting and eliminating evidence in Idaho. "Little by little, through injudicious people on the inside, it has leaked out in braggadocio that the defense was manufactured," Wood wrote another friend.

W. W. Catlin, an old friend of Darrow's from the Sunset Club, wrote Wood in the summer of 1907: "I agree with all you say as to Darrow.... As a writer he has done much that is fine and strong, and by that let us remember him. For his petty and almost contemptible weakness we need not care— except as a personal disappointment to ourselves. He is a strange mixure of craft and courage, generosity and penuriousness, consideration and despotism, honesty and deviousness; and yet he has a big brain and a kind heart, at base."

John Nugent would later call the Chicago lawyer Old Necessity. Asked why, he'd say, "Because necessity knows no law."

In any case, in early September 1906, Lillard went to Boise, ostensibly to attend the National Irrigation Congress, but he checked into the Hampton rooming house, a modest brick building on Main Street a block west of the Idanha, where members of the defense team often stayed. On September 3, he was permitted to have dinner with his nephew at the penitentiary, and, according to Lillard's account, it was at that meeting that Adams told him that he was being held against his will and instructed him to engage new counsel (replacing C. A. Moore, who had been all too cooperative with the authorities) and take legal steps to get him out of prison.

On the matter of counsel, Darrow executed another deft maneuver. Recognizing that it would not look proper if any of Haywood's counsel directly represented Lillard or Adams in this matter, Darrow turned to one of the state's most prestigious lawyers, John T. Morrison, the Caldwell attorney who'd been governor in 1903 and 1904. Early in 1905, he'd returned to Caldwell to practice law, while also serving as president of the new Boise State Bank. A staunch Republican, Morrison was nonetheless a longtime—and sometimes bitter—factional rival of Governor Gooding's and had lately had a falling-out with Borah. Morrison had deep roots in Frank Steunenberg's Caldwell. A friend of the assassinated governor; a former law partner of Steunenberg's close friend John Rice and, as late as mid-1906, of William A. Stone, the Caldwell attorney who was still a member in good standing of the prosecution team; an early member of Caldwell's Presbyterian Church; a former professor of English and history at William Judson Boone's College of Idaho in Caldwell; and, with his wife, Grace, a patron of music, literature, and art in town, Morrison could not have been more thoroughly respectable or more intricately tied to the circle of the late governor. "Aside from admiring him for his estimable qualities in public life," Morrison had told the *Caldwell Tribune* after the assassination, "I esteemed him as a friend and neighbor." Thus, many persons close to the prosecution in both Caldwell and Boise were stunned by Morrison's willingness to represent a man so deeply connected to, if not legally implicated in, the murder of his old friend and neighbor. He would pay heavily for this decision, suffering social and professional ostracism from many of his former friends and colleagues (though a high-ranking official of Theodore Roosevelt's Justice Department would call him the "one strong man" he encountered in Boise, "fearless, independent and outspoken").

On the morning of September 7, 1906—four days after Lillard and Adams had dinner at the penitentiary—Adams's wife, Annie, who was held in a sort of protective detention with her husband at the pen, managed to deliver an envelope to John Morrison at his Boise law office. Her baby, Adolphus, had diaper rash. Annie told Warden Whitney that her friend the nurse had recommended a certain salve for her baby's bottom. She asked permission to go to a drugstore and, on the way, carried out a handwritten statement by her husband that read: "This is to certify that the statement that I signed was made up by James McParland, detective, and Harry Orchard, alias Tom Hogan. I signed it because I was threatened by Governor Gooding, saying I would be hung if I did not corroborate Orchard's story against the officers of the Federation Union of Miners [*sic*]. Witness: Annie Adams."

That same morning, Morrison went to court and on Lillard's behalf filed a habeas corpus petition for Adams's release. McParland was still in Denver when this bombshell exploded, but learning of it by phone that evening, he rapidly improvised his response. George Stidger, the Denver district attorney —on McParland's instructions—conferred with Sheriff Nisbet. The sheriff summoned Undersheriff Thomas W. Baird, who gave Stidger an affidavit linking Adams to the killing of Lyte Gregory, a Denver detective, on May 5, 1904. Grant L. Hudson, a justice of the peace, promptly issued a warrant for Adams's arrest and Governor McDonald just as promptly signed a requisition for Adams's extradition on the murder charge. By phone, Nisbet informed the Ada County sheriff, David Moseley, of these events. Meanwhile, at McParland's behest, he wired the prosecuting attorney of Ada County, Charles F. Koelsch, that a charge of murder had been lodged against Adams: "A warrant in my hands. Swear out fugitive warrant and hold Adams. Requisition papers are being prepared and agent will start not later than Monday."

In Boise, Hawley and Borah were instructed to make no efforts to block Morrison's petition. There was little the prosecutors could have done at their end; McParland had already assured that Morrison, Darrow, and Steve Adams would have a nasty surprise coming.

Shortly before 2:00 p.m. on September 8, Warden Whitney and two penitentiary guards escorted Adams into Judge George H. Stewart's court. Adams, who appeared in "excellent spirits," and his wife, Annie—who one reporter admiringly said "could pass as a handsome woman"—sat side by side on a bench, whispering to each other, sometimes laughing out loud. The hearing went smoothly and quickly. Darrow reminded the court that, whatever the reason for Adams's original incarceration, no charge had ever been placed against him, and he now wanted his liberty. Deputy Attorney General Edwin Snow, appearing for the state, said, "We have no strings on Mr. Adams and raise no objection to granting him his liberty."

"There seems to be no contention in this case at all," said Judge Stewart. "The state seems to have no charge against the man. I direct that an order be made releasing him from detention in the state penitentiary and from the custody of the warden of that institution. Court is adjourned."

Annie's face was "radiant with the thought that her husband was a free man." They exchanged beatific smiles and embraced. Adams began shaking hands with a beaming James Lillard and his attorneys when, feeling a tap on his shoulder, he turned to confront Ada County's chief deputy sheriff, C. C. "Jerry" Siggins.

"I have a warrant for your arrest, Adams," said the deputy. "Will you step into the judge's office for a minute?"

The smile faded from Adams's face. Lillard scowled darkly at the deputy. Annie Adams pressed forward toward her husband, exclaiming in alarm, "Are you going to play any more tricks on my husband? Are you going to steal him again?"

"Well," murmured her husband, "I knew something was coming."

John Nugent, who was assisting Morrison, huddled briefly with Siggins and Adams, then conferred with Lillard and the other attorneys, explaining the new state of affairs. With an air of sour resignation, they all retired to the judge's chambers, where Adams was formally served with the Colorado writ on the basis of Nisbet's telegram. Then, in the custody of Sheriff Moseley, Adams was taken before a justice of the peace. His arraignment was set for September 10, by which time an agent from Colorado was expected to arrive with the requisition papers. In the meantime, Adams was installed in a cell at the Ada County jail.

McParland, guarded by Charlie Siringo, arrived in Boise the next evening. Reporting that night to his agency after a three-hour conference with Governor Gooding, McParland speculated on what had happened in his absence: "It appears that Adams was made to believe that he could not be convicted for any of the murders he committed in Colorado." The defense team, he felt, wanted to get Adams "into Colorado, without regard as to whether he could be convicted there or no, so that he could not appear as a witness against Moyer, Haywood and Pettibone in Idaho."

Over the next few hours, the Great Detective orchestrated a brilliant riposte. While Darrow and his colleagues were encouraged to believe that Adams was headed for Colorado, McParland had in fact summoned Sheriff Angus Sutherland of Shoshone County, who was on his way to Boise to take Adams back with him to northern Idaho to face charges for the 1904 murders of Fred Tyler and a Frenchman named Ed Boule, alleged timber-claim jumpers.

On Sunday, September 9, McParland held another long strategy session with the governor and Hawley. They agreed that McParland should try to see Adams as quickly as possible to assess his state of mind and try to bring him back into the prosecution camp. Fearing that Sheriff Moseley of Ada County, who'd never been sympathetic to the prosecutors, would refuse any such request, McParland suggested that it come directly from the governor. But Moseley rebuffed even the governor, saying that nobody but Adams's lawyers could see the prisoner. "The actions of the sheriff were not unexpected by either Mr. Hawley or myself," wrote McParland, "as both of us had come to the conclusion that Sheriff Moseley was a traitor." One Socialist journalist referred to Moseley—who doubled as a real estate agent and had the good salesman's ingratiating air—as "the gentleman sheriff."

That Sunday afternoon, Clarence Darrow paid an unusual call on Borah. Apparently Darrow had gotten wind of the charges in northern Idaho, for he said Adams had deceived him by not telling he'd committed those two murders. Had he known about them, he would never have made the move to get Adams out of the pen. If Adams was convicted of the Boule and Tyler murders, Darrow would always feel that he'd been the cause. At this point, to Borah's astonishment, Darrow broke into tears. Quickly regaining control of himself, he implored Borah to make sure that Sheriff Sutherland didn't leave immediately as Darrow was "going down the road for a day" and wanted to be in Boise before Adams was taken away.

McParland and Hawley concluded that Darrow was buying time to spring his own trap on the prosecution. Darrow knew the only feasible rail route from Boise to northern Idaho made a big swing through Oregon and Washington before turning east toward Wallace. Once Adams was outside the state again, his captors could be served with a habeas corpus petition arguing that he'd been improperly seized that February in Oregon, for he was no more a fugitive from Idaho than Haywood. Any judge who hadn't been bought would free him, at which point Darrow and his colleagues hoped to get him as far away from Idaho as possible.

To foil any such attempt, McParland and Hawley ordered a detective to shadow Darrow wherever he went—in Boise, to Oregon, or to Washington. Moreover, they agreed that under no circumstances should Sheriff Sutherland venture into Oregon or Washington. This meant the sheriff would have to stay off the major railroad lines north, instead taking Adams overland—by buggy, horseback, riverboat, and branch railroads—the length of the state to Wallace.

At 2:00 p.m. on Tuesday, September 11, the authorities produced Adams before William C. Dunbar, a justice of the peace, ostensibly for arraignment on the Colorado charge, after which he would presumably be turned over to the Colorado deputies. The Colorado deputies weren't present. Swiftly, the prosecution moved to dismiss the Colorado charges, but as Adams was about to leave the courtroom, Deputy Sheriff Shadrach "Shad" Hodgin of Ada County placed him under arrest—this time on the charges of murder in the woods of northern Idaho. Hodgin immediately turned the prisoner over to Sheriff Sutherland of Shoshone County, who snapped a heavy pair of cuffs on Adams's wrists and placed him—for temporary safekeeping—right back in the penitentiary, which he'd left with such high hopes two days before.

Unbeknownst to the defense, McParland had slipped into the penitentiary three hours earlier, using the time for a meeting with Orchard. As soon as Adams arrived, the warden ushered McParland into his cell. Things didn't go well. "When he saw me," the detective reported, "I thought he would faint. I talked with him for three hours, using every effort in my power to get him to talk." McParland tried to sow some distrust of Darrow and Richardson, telling Adams that "these lawyers simply wanted to get him out of the way—

whether by hanging or otherwise—so he could not appear as a witness in the Moyer, Haywood and Pettibone cases." But Adams only cried and said that the detective was "his best friend, but he could not talk to me, nor would he look me in the face; therefore, my time was wasted."

Just as McParland finished with Adams, two of his lawyers—Morrison and John Nugent—arrived at the prison asking to see their client. They were in exactly the position that McParland had been in when he'd asked a hostile Sheriff Moseley to see Adams. And they got the same result. Whitney told them that he could not let them see Adams without Sheriff Sutherland's approval since Adams was Sutherland's prisoner. Sutherland, he knew, would surely refuse.

Meanwhile, McParland's suspicion about Darrow seemed accurate. The detective shadowing the defense attorney had tracked him to the St. George Hotel in Pendleton, Oregon, one of the principal rail junctions at which any train from Boise to Wallace would have to stop. Darrow was "closeted" at the St. George all day Monday. McParland assumed that he was arranging with Oregon lawyers to swear out a habeas corpus petition when Adams entered the state. One of the people Darrow met with that day answered the description of Ed Boyce, the former WFM secretary, now a Portland hotel keeper. "No doubt but he will carry out any wish Darrow may make," McParland concluded.

At 4:00 a.m. on Wednesday, September 12, two deputy sheriffs from Denver—Al Watson and Charlie Burkhardt—reached Boise with the requisitions for Adams. Boise was familiar territory to Watson, one of the Denver deputies who'd escorted Haywood, Pettibone, and Moyer on their "extradition" four months before. Watson and Burkhardt already knew full well that they could not get Adams—indeed, that was not the purpose of their trip. Before they left Denver, McParland's old friend Sheriff Nisbet had briefed them on their curious decoy role. Now they were briefed again by McParland, Hawley, and Sutherland. "It was agreed," McParland reported, "that the Colorado deputies should act as though I had deceived them and helped out Sheriff Sutherland. This would come to the ears of Adams' lawyers. ...Messrs. Burkhardt and Watson might get some information from these lawyers."

The plan worked beautifully. The Colorado deputies complained long and hard to the Boise press. "We do not feel that we have been treated right in this matter," Burkhardt told the *Statesman.* "We made a long trip up here.... We think that we are entitled to the custody of the man and we propose to take him back to Colorado with us." But Sutherland was adamant: "We have a charge of murder against Adams and we have been waiting a long time to get hold of him. Our case is just as urgent and important as the one in Colorado."

That afternoon, Darrow, who'd hurried back from Oregon, went to the penitentiary with Morrison and Nugent to see Adams. This time, Sheriff Sutherland permitted the interview but insisted that he and Whitney be present. After the meeting—in which nobody said anything they didn't want the other side to hear—Darrow and his associates asked to see their client alone. This Sutherland refused. The lawyers then demanded that Sutherland tell them when he was taking Adams to Wallace. Again the sheriff refused.

There followed an exchange that in days to come would be recalled differently by the two parties. Darrow promised that if Sutherland would take Adams to Wallace by the regular rail route through Oregon and Washington, accompanied by all interested parties, the defense would agree in writing not to interfere with the sheriff en route. According to Darrow, the sheriff accepted this proposal—and then broke his word. Sutherland said he accepted Darrow's plan, but with an additional condition: that Adams sign a waiver of his right to be released under habeas corpus. The defense's flat refusal of this proviso indicated to the prosecutors that, while Adams's attorneys might do nothing along those lines themselves, they would work through other lawyers poised to strike when the train entered Oregon. Convinced that Darrow had already prepared a legal ambush at Pendleton or elsewhere in Oregon, McParland, Sutherland, and Hawley began to lay out the sheriff's overland route.

Angus Sutherland was a shrewd choice as the expedition's leader. He and his brother had long run Wallace's preeminent livery stable, the Sutherland Barns; he knew the horse trails through much of the state. Moreover, for more than two decades, the fifty-five-year-old native of Scotland had played a leading role in northern Idaho law enforcement. During the 1890s, he had served a stretch as Wallace's town marshal, surrendering the job after budgetary restraints became so severe he had to quarter some of the county's prisoners in his own stable. In 1899—after martial law was declared in the Coeur d'Alenes—Bartlett Sinclair installed Sutherland as Shoshone County's new deputy sheriff and later as sheriff. Once martial law was lifted, Sutherland served two more terms as sheriff, elected as a Republican with close ties to executives of the Bunker Hill and Sullivan mine. One time he got himself in a bit of trouble when he ran a ringer—a speedy horse named Smoothwire —in a Fourth of July steeplechase. On three separate occasions during the county's labor unrest, assassins had tried to kill him, but with luck and uncanny premonition, he'd survived. One newsman described him as "unassuming and modest" but "steel-nerved." Six months before, he'd survived a prolonged hand-to-hand struggle with an armed man, which left him with a bullet in his neck. Opponents saw in him "a bitter and intense partisan [who] had always been antagonistic to the Western Federation of Miners and all of its members." McParland had met him for the first time only five months earlier but already regarded him as "cool, deliberate and...utterly reliable."

At the Idanha Wednesday night, McParland and Hawley decided that Sutherland and Adams should be accompanied by two other trusted lawmen —Warden Whitney, who before becoming warden had been sheriff of Kootenai County and thus knew the north well, and Eugene Johnson, the Boise detective who, since the assassination, had been working virtually full-time for the prosecution. That night, Detective Siringo sneaked the sheriff's grip out of the Idanha, and McParland settled Sutherland's bill privately with the manager so none of the clerks would know of the sheriff's impending departure. Late that night, Sutherland crept out a back door of the Idanha and reached the penitentiary by "a circuitous route."

At 5:00 a.m. on Thursday, September 13, Sutherland, Whitney, and Johnson—with Adams in tow—left the penitentiary grounds on a side road, evading the defense's detectives, who kept watch on the main entrance all night. Mounting a carriage parked in the shadows, they raced across the Boise River and four miles west to Perkins Siding, a desolate spot on the Short Line, where they flagged the early train bound for Weiser.

When the district court opened that morning, Adams's lawyers were on hand with a habeas corpus petition, which Justice Stewart promptly granted. But when Deputy Sheriff Jerry Siggins went to the penitentiary to serve the writ on Warden Whitney, he was informed that the warden wasn't there. Siggins served the warrant instead on James Mills, the deputy warden. Meanwhile, Sheriff Moseley began a fruitless search for Sheriff Sutherland, who could not be found anywhere in town. At 2:00 p.m., Mills told the court he couldn't produce the body of Steve Adams because the defendant was no longer in the penitentiary.

"It then dawned on the defendant's counsel that the sheriff had tricked them," McParland reported. "It is funny to see the prisoner's friends and detectives looking for clues as to the whereabouts of Adams. Darrow cursed his Thiel detectives roundly for allowing Adams and Sutherland to get away as he intended to accompany them."

If Darrow did curse out loud, one can scarcely blame him. Adams's disappearance, in the hands of a sheriff closely allied to the Pinkertons and the prosecutors, was a major blow to the defense. Moreover, Darrow didn't have much faith in Adams's ability to resist Pinkerton pressures. "He is not a smart man," he once said, "he doesn't amount to much." But Darrow didn't indulge himself very long with imprecations. Still believing that the sheriff must take a route through Oregon, Darrow and Nugent resolved to give chase. Rounding up Deputy Sheriffs Burkhardt and Watson—whom he still regarded as allies—Darrow asked them to accompany him north, promising to get Adams for them if at all possible. After consulting McParland, the Colorado deputies agreed to accompany him. At 1:45 p.m. on Thursday the strange quintet—Darrow and his wife, Nugent, Burkhardt, and Watson—boarded a Union Pacific train bound for Pendleton, Oregon.

Had Darrow been utterly bamboozled by McParland and the Colorado deputies? Perhaps. Or perhaps he wasn't quite so naive as they thought. Before his departure he told a reporter he thought both the Colorado officers and Sheriff Sutherland might be "putting up a big game of bluff." He didn't think any of them wanted Adams quite as badly as they were professing.

With the defense forces heading north, McParland shifted the pieces on his board. After conferring with the governor, he sent his aide-de-camp Chris Thiele hurrying toward Spokane, with instructions to meet him on Monday morning in Tekoa, Washington—another strategic intersection on the way to Wallace. On Saturday, McParland and Siringo boarded the same 1:45 train for Pendleton that Darrow had taken two days earlier. It was nearly five hours late, reaching Pendleton at 3:30 a.m., whereupon the detectives took breakfast at the St. George Hotel and fell into bed. At nine the next morning, they left for Tekoa.

Meanwhile, Sutherland and his associates, aboard their Short Line train, churned north along the east bank of the Snake River, which in that sector formed Idaho's boundary with Oregon. Shortly past dawn on Thursday, September 13, they reached Weiser, the junction of the Short Line heading west and the Pacific and Idaho Northern Railroad, which turned north into the timber and mining reaches of the "upper country." Dashing from the Short Line's brick depot on State Street three blocks to the Pacific and Idaho's sprawling wood depot on Washington Street, they caught a train that took them sixty miles north to Council, a town of six hundred in a rich fruit-growing valley, so named because it had once been a gathering place for the Nez Perce and Shoshone Indians.

William Allen White, the Kansas editor, had visited Council several years earlier, calling it "a board-sidewalk town, where the saloons do not screen their bars and the two hotels serve canned tomatoes for dinner in little oval side dishes 365 times a year." Of its hotels—indeed of all those from there on north—he recorded ruefully: "Bedsprings halt at Weiser."

Council was as far north as any Idaho railroad penetrated until one got within shouting distance of the population center around Lewiston and Moscow. For the next 130 miles, in the near wilderness between Council and Stites, travelers depended on the horse or the horse-drawn vehicle.

Sutherland encountered "considerable delay" at Council in hiring a horse and rig for the trip north. Directly across the street from the depot was Clinton J. Arnold's Depot Barn, which claimed, "Good Rigs and Careful Drivers Always on Hand for Commercial and Mining Men." The sheriff masqueraded as neither type; he told the livery stable that he and his three companions—he introduced Adams as "J. P. Fuller"—were traveling to a "political meeting" at White Bird, a town on the Salmon River. Perhaps the livery man was suspicious—these customers didn't look much like politicians—or perhaps he didn't have an appropriate carriage available, but it took several hours to get under way. The travelers picked at an unappetizing lunch—canned tomatoes, no doubt—which came at the bargain price of $1.35 for all four of them. By 2:00 p.m. they were off again in a four-horse conveyance with one of the Depot Barn's crack drivers at the reins.

Striking north from Council, they climbed low foothills spread with tamaracks turning gold in the crisp autumn air. Hour after hour they rode into the evening, when "the lavender haze covers the hills and deepens into purple in the arroyos." In the village of Meadows the Arnold livery wagon turned back and Sutherland engaged another wagon to take them on north. That night the quartet caught a few hours' sleep at a rude inn in the hamlet of Price Valley. On Friday the heavens opened, drenching the open carriage and its occupants, but still they rode through the jade-gray hills. Every eight hours or so, they changed horses at some stable along the way—Sutherland, a shrewd judge of horseflesh from his long livery experience, making sure they got the best animals available. Late Friday, they crossed the Salmon River by ferry at Riggins, once known as Gouge-Eye after a fight in which one pioneer scooped another's eye out during one of the town's raucous dances.

About 4:00 p.m. on Saturday, having covered some 110 miles in just over forty-eight hours, they reached Grangeville, a farmer's, miner's, and stockman's trading point on the high plateau called Camas Prairie. As they pulled up at the Grangeville Hotel, a clutch of newspapermen waiting on the broad front porch found them "heavily armed and wear[ing] a determined look." When the reporters tried to interview Adams, they were rebuffed by Sutherland. Adams, who seemed anxious, was handcuffed to one of the officers and was "constantly under surveillance." Although quickly recognized by newsmen and others, he was again registered at the hotel as J. P. Fuller.

Soon after their arrival, the party repaired to their rooms and slept soundly. The *Lewiston Morning Tribune* reported the next day that "it was Adams' condition that necessitated the all-night rest in Grangeville. His long confinement in the penitentiary has told on his physique, and he was about exhausted." The hard days on the road and the scant sleep had also taken their toll on Warden Whitney, a middle-aged man with bags under his eyes.

The party slept late Sunday morning and, after "a hearty breakfast" at a table apart from the other guests, they strolled through town. Adams wasn't handcuffed "and a casual observer would not have believed that he was under detention." They drew quite a crowd of reporters and townspeople, almost as many as had gathered the week before after the town's "pet bear" gnawed a boy's arm half off (by the time Adams got to town, the bear had been fenced in).

Despite the rigors of their journey, the travelers' chief complaint was the cold. "It is freezing cold in the Idaho woods at night in September," William Allen White had reported. One officer was heard to inquire about getting a warmer overcoat. Adams was shivering so hard, Sutherland bought him a three-dollar wool hat and a vial of unidentified medicine.

It was time for the carriage hired in Meadows to turn back, so Sutherland cut a new deal with a driver for the Grangeville and Meadows Stage Line. Before leaving Grangeville at 1:45 p.m., the sheriff told reporters he'd drive to Cottonwood, twenty miles west, stay there overnight, then go on by train to Lewiston and Wallace. This was disinformation, to throw the reporters—and those who believed their stories—off track.

It often seemed as though there were as many reporters chasing Sutherland through those woods as there were detectives. Most of Idaho's press
adored his exploits. "The slick Sheriff from Shoshone," they called him, "a
tireless and fearless officer." They relished the tactics with which he "completely outwitted" Darrow and his colleagues. "It is believed Sheriff Sutherland has given them the slip," the Spokane *Spokesman-Review* chortled as early
as Saturday. The reporters contrasted the intrepid sheriff's pursuit of "his
rough and weary way" with the self-indulgent defense attorneys, who "came
north in Pullmans."

Sutherland had performed superbly in getting Adams halfway to Wallace already. But if one of his roles was to ingratiate himself with his prisoner
and bring him back into the prosecution fold, he did less well in that regard.
According to Adams, on their trip north the sheriff repeatedly denounced the
WFM and its leaders as "outlaws, thugs and dynamiters," which angered
Adams and led him to grimace at the very mention of the sheriff's name. "He
hates me like poison," Sutherland confessed later.

From Grangeville, Sutherland's wagon headed west toward Cottonwood,
but a few miles out it swerved northeast. The roads north of Grangeville were
notoriously bad, often sinkholes of mud that swallowed carriage wheels. "For
miles along that frequented thoroughfare it would be utterly impossible for
teams to pass each other if they should meet," the *Grangeville Standard-News*
had warned that month, "and this is particularly true of precipitous places
where the road is hundreds of feet above the [Clearwater] river." Somehow,
the driver threaded his way twenty miles through great forests of white pine
to Kooskia, a farming town on the Clearwater branch of the Northern Pacific.
Trains on that branch didn't run Sundays, so the four men spent the night at
the Hotel Stuart, then on Monday morning boarded the Spokane Flyer,
dashing for Moscow.

In the smoker car, Sutherland ordered Adams away from the window, for
fear he'd try to escape. Gene Johnson took the window seat next to the
prisoner, with Sutherland and Whitney on the facing seat. A reporter across
the aisle thought Adams seemed increasingly agitated. "He carefully scrutinized every man who entered the smoking car, many times turning around in
his seat to look behind him, as though fearing an attack in the rear."

Reaching Moscow at 12:05 p.m. Sutherland's expedition had now entered
the relatively populous Lewiston area, hard by the Washington border. It was
here that the sheriff anticipated the major effort to seize his prisoner—either
through a habeas corpus petition or by brute force. Accordingly, Warden
Whitney stayed aboard the train all the way to Spokane to see if the coast was
clear ahead, while Sutherland and Johnson, with their prisoner, disembarked.

After the twenty-five-cent lunch at the Hotel Moscow with the local
sheriff, W. W. Robbins, Sutherland marched down Main Street to the Model
Stables, where he tersely instructed the liveryman: "Have the best four horse

team in the barn on the floor in twenty minutes. Give us a driver with a knowledge of the roads and an abundance of nerve."

"I'll send Larry Burke with you," said the liveryman. "The word *fear* is not in his dictionary."

When Burke, "a nervy little Irishman," showed up, he told reporters: "Larry Burke will drive 'em over the pike if any man in Idaho can."

At 2:00 p.m., they were off in a sporty landau behind a four-horse team, driving twenty-two miles to Kennedy's Ford, where they hitched up fresh horses, then on to Campbell's Bridge, where they changed horses again and made for Farmington, twenty-five miles northwest, smack on the Idaho-Washington border. Two of the town's streets were in Idaho, the rest in Washington, including the dusty lane with the only decent restaurant in those parts, Catherine Cunningham's Hotel Farmington. This was precisely what McParland had feared; a smart lawyer with a habeas corpus petition might be lurking in the kitchen. But Sutherland and his companions were hungry as horses from their afternoon's exertions. Moreover, the sheriff was getting a trifle cocky. ("You can say that I will get Adams into Wallace tomorrow," he'd told a reporter in Moscow.) Under cover of darkness, they nipped across the border, wolfed down a quick supper at the cozy little hotel, and by nine were back in their carriage, disappearing into Idaho.

The road north ran through the rugged "hoodoo country," named for an early gold strike, but Larry Burke kept them moving "as fast as horseflesh [could] carry them." Shortly past midnight, they glimpsed the lights of Tekoa, Washington, glimmering across the border. A shipping point for grain and apples and a rail junction where three lines intersected, the town boasted a number of comfortable hotels, among them the Tekoa. To the weary travelers that sounded irresistible, so Sutherland ordered the "nervy little Irishman" to take them there.

This second venture across the border took nerve indeed, for rail junctions like Tekoa were known that day to be swarming with detectives, some working for the defense, others for the prosecution, but all on the lookout for Sutherland's party. For just that reason, the sheriff had sent Warden Whitney ahead on a reconnaissance mission. Still another lawman, a former sheriff of Nez Perce County named Stannus, was functioning as an advance man. Also ensconced in town that night were McParland and Siringo, who'd pulled in from Pendleton that afternoon. Either they, Whitney, or Stannus may have passed word that the coast was clear.

But was it? At least two detectives—one of them a woman—were said to have spent the night at the Hotel Tekoa. If they were prosecution detectives, they were presumably there to protect the Sutherland party. If they worked for the defense, their powers of detection were meager. For, according to a *Spokesman-Review* reporter who watched, Steve Adams "walked into the hotel bar like an ordinary citizen, took a drink of whiskey, entered the office, nodded to the night clerk when the latter spoke to him—not knowing who he was—watched [Gene] Johnson sign fictitious names and then walked upstairs to bed."

In fact, the defense had given up the chase by then. Darrow and Nugent —detained a full day by a train wreck—reluctantly concluded that they weren't going to catch Sutherland. "Darrow was very much disappointed at Sheriff Sutherland not going through Oregon with Adams," a delighted McParland reported a few days later, "but claimed that neither he nor Nugent would have habeas corpused the sheriff."

In the meantime, Darrow's interest had been engaged by another arrest party headed by one of Sutherland's deputies, Carson C. Hicks, who was off in a remote slice of northern Idaho trying to find Newton "Wall-Eye" Glover, an alleged accomplice of Adams's in the Tyler murder. A boatman who hauled supplies up and down the St. Joe River, Glover was described as "a regular river rat." With a Wallace attorney named John H. Wourms and a guide, Darrow sped north by train and buggy to see if he could reach Glover before Deputy Hicks did. But he lost that race, too.

Finally, on Saturday afternoon, Darrow, Nugent, and Lillard, with their relentless shadows Burkhardt and Watson, reached Wallace. In a foul mood, Darrow denounced Sutherland's overland trip as "horse play of the rankest kind." But the whole experience left him with wary respect for the operation's mastermind, James McParland, whom he later described as "the greatest detective in the West."

Early the next Tuesday morning, McParland and Siringo—and Chris Thiele, who'd met them at the Tekoa depot as arranged—boarded the first train for Wallace. At Harrison, Idaho, Leon Whitsell of the defense boarded the train, "evidently expecting Adams to be on it," the Great Detective chortled.

Instead—after five hours' sleep and a good breakfast—Sutherland, Johnson, and Adams remounted their carriage and, with Larry Burke driving, dashed across the Idaho border to Lovell, a town eight miles out on the Oregon Railway and Navigation line. Only there did they catch the train to Wallace. On board, to their surprise, they found Mrs. Adams and two of her children—a boy, seven, and the ten-month-old baby—as well as Steve's brother Joe. (How they happened to board the train Steve was on isn't clear, though a close reading of northern Idaho newspapers would have given them an idea of Sutherland's route.)

"Hello, sweetheart," said Mrs. Adams, throwing her arms around her husband's neck. After kissing her, Adams took his baby in his arms and during the rest of the ride alternately held his son and his baby on his lap.

There were more surprises to come. At the depot in Harrison—on the southern shore of Lake Coeur d'Alene—waited some fifty persons who'd crossed the lake by boat. Among those boarding the train there were more than a few with compelling interest in Steve Adams's hegira: Captain Swain, the Thiel manager, over from his base in Spokane to keep an eye on the drama (though on whose behalf one can't be sure); Warden Whitney, who, detached from the Sutherland party since Moscow, had now caught up with them; Deputy Sheriff Hicks, two guards, and their prisoner, Newt Glover; and even Idaho's senior senator, Weldon B. Heyburn, who ostensibly made his home in Wallace (though critics contended that the lifetime bachelor really lived out of state, with his mother in Spokane). Himself a mine owner, the senator had represented Coeur d'Alene mining interests during the 1892–93 crisis. According to one report, Heyburn had helped facilitate Adams's "hasty removal" from Boise. Others boarding the train at Harrison included detectives, deputies, and numerous "individuals directly and indirectly interested in the Adams and the Steunenberg cases," most "armed to the teeth."

As this hodgepodge of disparate forces rumbled into Wallace that afternoon, some lawmen on board suspected there might be an attempt to rescue, or even kill, Adams as he disembarked. Dozens of armed men piled onto the platform, looking about for trouble, but there was none. Adams was hustled into a Pinkerton rig and, "with all possible speed," deposited in the county jail. Against all odds, Sutherland had done just what he'd said he would: brought his prisoner across 275 miles of forest and prairie and, despite two forays onto "alien soil," delivered him unscathed to the Shoshone County courts for trial.

8

THE FRIENDS
OF MR. FILLIUS

FROM THE START, Idaho authorities knew that catching and convicting Frank Steunenberg's killers would be an expensive proposition. Six days after the assassination, Judge Frank J. Smith proclaimed from his Caldwell bench: "If necessary to find and convict the perpetrators of this fiendish murder, the state should not hesitate to spend $100,000 or even more."

That was a lot of money—equivalent to $1.8 million today—especially for a young, sparsely settled state like Idaho, whose 1906 budget amounted to barely $1,500,000. Certainly, the state didn't have a spare $100,000, or even $20,000, to allocate for such purposes. Canyon County, where the assassination took place, would pay the two-dollar-a-day witness fees and travel allowances for out-of-state witnesses (twenty-five cents a mile, one way, from the Idaho state line), plus some salaries for jail guards and a few other expenses related directly to the trial. But the governor had proclaimed the trial a "state case," meaning the state, rather than the county, would carry on the prosecution and somehow the state would have to come up with the rest of the money.

What was at stake was not just finance of the trial but control of it. For whoever came up with the bulk of the money would, in effect, be the prosecution's client. Behind the scenes, a fierce struggle was waged for that control.

So skeptical was McParland about Idaho's ability to pay his bills that he took the extraordinary step of seeking a personal guarantee from the governor. Gooding, who'd made a lot of money in the sheep business, was asked for an assurance that if the state was unable to pay the agency's bills they could be collected from his private account. Before the master detective bestirred himself, he got that guarantee in writing.

Accordingly, in mid-January 1906, the state's board of examiners—the governor, Attorney General John J. Guheen, and Secretary of State Will H. Gibson—convened at the statehouse to declare a fiscal emergency. Under Idaho law, this permitted the state to issue "deficiency certificates"—stopgap instruments for short-term borrowing—for the payment of expenses associated with the Steunenberg investigation. The board announced its intention to borrow $25,000 through the sale of such certificates to state banks within the next few months.

Most states issue deficiency certificates very rarely, and then only to meet unexpected expenditures or unanticipated falls in revenue. The certificates resemble bonds, except that bonds are generally redeemed in ten years or more, while certificates are usually paid off in sixty days to a year. While a bond is usually secured by receipts from a specific tax or fee, such as bridge or highway tolls, a deficiency certificate is unsecured, the creditor relying on the "full faith and credit" of the state government. In this instance, that meant believing that Idaho's legislature, when it convened in early 1907—it met in alternate years—would appropriate funds to redeem the certificates. Against the risk that legislators might balk at honoring the debt, such certificates carried a healthy interest rate. If the state issued more certificates than the market could easily absorb, they might also be offered at discount.

Under the governor's scheme, each bank would signify how many certificates it was prepared to take. Then, those working for the state on the Steunenberg investigation—from lawyers and detectives to couriers and stenographers—would present their bills to a designated bank in exchange for cash. Once the legislature acted, banks would be repaid from the state treasury. The governor hoped to spread the burden as widely as possible, with at least two banks in each county assuming responsibility for $1,000 or $2,000 apiece. In the last week of March, Gooding wrote personally to the bank presidents asking that they assume this "imperative duty," by taking the certificates at 7 percent interest, but without discount. The response was encouraging.*

Some banks looked to the Boise banks, which, because of their proximity to power, had the clout to ensure that the legislature redeemed the certificates. The governor leaned on the Boise banks and ultimately the city's five major financial institutions each took $1,000 or $2,000 worth, action that stiffened the spines of other bankers around the state.

But some bank officers only grew more anxious. Though the governor could boast substantial Republican majorities in both houses of the legisla-

---

* The first bank to respond affirmatively was the Citizens State Bank Ltd. of Nampa, whose president, H. A. Partridge, said on March 31 that he would take $1,000 worth of certificates "with pleasure." Others who leaped into the breach quickly were the Idaho Trust Company of Lewiston ($1,000), the Bank of Camas Prairie, Grangeville ($1,000), and the Coeur d'Alene Bank and Trust Company of Coeur d'Alene ($1,000). The Citizens State Bank Ltd. and the First National Bank, both of Mountain Home, promised to split a $1,000 certificate, "trusting you will be successful in your prosecution, and that you now have the guilty parties" (H. A. Partridge to F. R. Gooding, March 31, 1906; Frank W. Kettenbach to Gooding, April 9, 1906; W. W. Brown to Gooding, April 18, 1906; Boyd Hamilton to Gooding, April 11, 1906; D. E. Cannon to Gooding, April 11, 1906; Mr. Brown to F. R. Gooding, April 11, 1906).

The Anderson Brothers Bank in Idaho Falls would take $1,000 worth, if other banks subscribed at least $25,000. Several banks—among them the Commercial and Savings Bank of Hailey and D. L. Evans and Company Ltd. of Albion—delayed responding until they could lay the matter before their boards of directors or loan committees or until they saw what other banks would do (C. C. Campbell to Gooding, March 3, 1906; J. E. Clinton, Jr., to Gooding, September 8, 1906; J. N. Givens to Gooding, April 6, 1906; Gooding to Frank F. Johnson, April 16, 1906).

ture, the fall's election would intervene before the banks got their money. Some bankers feared that by then the Democrats might have seized control of the legislature and even, God forbid, have unseated the governor. In the spring the First National Bank of Coeur d'Alene had agreed to accept a $1,000 certificate; by September 5 it had reneged. "We are advised that there is going to be some trouble in getting the legislature to make the necessary appropriations," wrote the bank's vice president. "We want to do our share in matters of this kind, but do not feel like taking any risk."

Snappishly, the governor reminded the fainthearted banker that his original letter had made clear "that the standing of the certificates should rest upon the action of the legislature. Otherwise there would be no necessity of asking for your assistance in the matter." With others, Gooding tried to defuse apprehension. "You will never have occasion to regret your action," he wrote one banker, "I have no doubt but that the certificates will be the subject of action by the legislature at the very beginning of the session."

The governor's plan did stir some outrage. *Appeal to Reason* was aghast at the picture of "the governor of a great sovereign state appealing to private institutions for funds to carry on a prosecution against innocent men!" Another Socialist journal, *Wilshire's Magazine,* put it more bluntly: "An appeal to private bankers for funds wherewith to prosecute labor union officials is about as complete a proof of the reality of the class struggle as could be desired."

More unexpected was the reaction from William J. "Poker Bill" McConnell, the Republican powerhouse who was Steunenberg's predecessor as governor and Bill Borah's father-in-law. McConnell shared Borah's suspicions of Gooding. "Why should the Governor assume the role of prosecutor?" he asked. "Many murderers have been tried and convicted in this state without the chief executive or the state Board of Examiners coming to the rescue of the counties where the trials were held.... It is to be regretted that the Governor found it necessary to make appeal to the banks only for this assistance, thereby giving excuse to those who are charging that the prosecution...is carried on at the instance of the wealthy classes as against the laborers."

Gooding never addressed the ex-governor's complaints directly. If he had, he probably would have said—with characteristic bluntness—that he'd gone to the banks because that's where the money was. In any case, by April 16 he could proudly report that, with half the state's financial institutions still to be heard from, he already had his $25,000. Four days later, receipts reached $30,000.

By far the largest investment in certificates came from one small bank—the First National Bank of Wallace, in the heart of the Coeur d'Alenes. By late autumn, the First National had taken some $8,000 worth of certificates, three times as much as any other bank. The bank paid most of the Pinkerton agency's bills, which were especially sensitive because they often represented confidential undercover operations.

The governor's reliance on the Wallace bank became particularly evident at year's end when several thousand dollars of Pinkerton bills remained unpaid. William A. Pinkerton pressed McParland to collect quickly. "At the conclusion of the case if there, by any bad luck, be an acquittal, it is going to be hard work to get our bills paid," he wrote. "I wish you would explain very thoroughly to Governor Gooding that...our bills must be met promptly, otherwise we cannot go any further." Gooding was in a tight place. Given the guarantee he'd signed, he might have to make up the difference from his own pocket. On December 4, McParland asked James Hawley to remind Gooding that "our bills must be paid. We have the Governor's private guaranty on this matter, but don't wish to push him personally for the amount of these bills." Gooding asked the Wallace bank to take another $5,000 in certificates. After some equivocations—reflecting concern that the appropriation bill hadn't reached the legislature—the First National again paid the governor's piper.

Clearly this was no ordinary financial institution. Founded in 1892, a year after the Mine Owners Association of the Coeur d'Alenes came into being, the First National, from the start, enjoyed an intimate relationship with the owners.

For many years the multitude of competing mines in the Coeur d'Alenes spent almost as much time squabbling or spying on one another as dealing with common concerns; but by 1906 a rash of mergers and consolidations had reduced the rolls of the Mine Owners Association from twelve members to four. For all intents and purposes, the MOA now spoke for the region's two mining giants—Bunker Hill and Sullivan, long the biggest producer of all the Coeur d'Alene mines, and the Federal Mining and Smelting Company, which in recent years had assembled a mining Goliath, comprising the Mammoth, Standard, and Empire State mines in Idaho, as well as the Puget Sound Reduction Company of Everett, Washington.

Not surprisingly, given the dominance of these two companies, the MOA was directed in 1906 by their two general managers, W. Clayton Miller of Federal, who served as president, and Stanley A. Easton of Bunker Hill, the secretary-treasurer. The money the association expended—whether to hire strikebreakers and detectives, contribute to political candidates, or to dam rivers—was traditionally raised through a levy of three to four and a half mills on each ton of ore produced by member companies. By 1906, with its membership truncated, it raised funds more informally, the principals agreeing how much each company should kick in to meet the required sum.

Although Clayton Miller, the MOA president, was once a rising power in the Coeur d'Alenes—he'd served two terms as county surveyor in the 1890s —these days he cut something of a pathetic figure. An able if unspectacular engineer, he'd been promoted to general manager in 1905, though his effectiveness was severely hampered by heavy drinking, bordering on alcoholism. A couple of months after Miller took over the company's active management, the Rockefeller and Gould interests, who'd first bankrolled the conglomerate, sold it to the Guggenheims. Its bibulous manager notwithstanding, the Federal exercised enormous clout in the region through its sheer concentration of mining properties.

But the most influential figure in northern Idaho mining was Stanley Easton, the forty-six-year-old general manager of Bunker Hill and Sullivan. Standing six feet, five inches tall, Easton was "a commanding presence," using his clout as a Republican Party panjandrum to reinforce his standing in the mining community, and vice versa. Austere, positively chilly in personal relationships, he was a formidable figure few men dared to cross.

Frank F. Johnson, the president of the First National Bank of Wallace and a former Republican county chairman, had long been the principal banker to the Mine Owners Association and to many of its individual owners and managers. A WFM lawyer slyly called him "the fellow that generally handled the funds up there, sometimes referred to as the 'slush' fund ... the sinews of war ... the sack, the bag." In 1892, Johnson had circulated petitions urging President Harrison to keep federal troops in the Coeur d'Alenes lest the miners resort to violence again. During the 1899 crisis there, the First National had taken a big slice—90 percent, Johnson later said—of the deficiency certificates the state issued that year. In the current juncture, most of the money that passed from the bank to the state was "guaranteed" by Easton, Miller, or both, thus assuring the First National that, if the state failed to repay it, its friends the mine owners would. In effect, the bank acted as a mere conduit for the passage of money from the mining industry to the state for use in the Haywood prosecution.

The First National extracted a commercial advantage from its pivotal role in this financing. In mid-March, after signaling its willingness to take on a major share of the burden, the small Wallace institution bid for expansion, seeking to charter a state bank in Murray, a gold mining town north of Wallace. On March 9, Frank Johnson wired Gooding: "Wish charter State Bank of Murray. Have wired bank commissioner. Can you help us. Require quick action." Gooding must have acted promptly, for within hours C. S. Loveland, the banking commissioner, wired approval.

But the First National wasn't in the struggle for relatively minor favors like these. Those who stood behind it—Easton, Miller, and the other owners—were clearly committed to the battle against the WFM. On occasion, the bank didn't even wait for Gooding's approach but initiated the contact itself. On April 17, 1906, Frank Johnson addressed the governor: "I write to ask how you are succeeding in getting the banks through Idaho to take up the deficiency warrants.... If you are having any difficulty in this matter, I think I might help you out to some extent if you will let me know just how it stands."

From the start, the northern Idaho mining industry had shown intense interest in apprehending and punishing Frank Steunenberg's killers. Within hours of the assassination, the MOA in Wallace pledged a $10,000 reward for information leading to the malefactors' arrest. This money had never actually found its way into the state treasury. Although George Froman of the Caldwell Citizens Committee and Joe Hutchinson, the former lieutenant governor, might have laid claim to the reward, the $10,000 remained in the mine owners' coffers, untouched but not quite forgotten.

Hawley had ample reason to expect still more from the mine owners. In 1899, when the state needed money for the Coeur d'Alene prosecutions, the Mine Owners Association had come up with $32,000—about a third of it from Bunker Hill and Sullivan—handing $25,000 over to Governor Steunenberg for use at his discretion in the prosecution. Some of this money went to pay Hawley and Borah, then as now the chief prosecutors in the case.

Not surprisingly, on February 4, 1906, barely a month after Steunenberg's assassination and only three days after receiving his copy of Harry Orchard's confession, Hawley wrote Stanley Easton a letter. As lead counsel in the Steunenberg case, Hawley said, he had now "absolutely confirmed" from various sources that

> this crime was not merely the act of an individual incensed against his victim, but part of a premeditated plan to rid the Western Federation of Miners of men supposed to be inimical to that association.... [The Steunenberg murder] is only one of a long series of outrages, and will be followed by others equally monstrous in the future. In my judgment the policy of the leaders of this association has been to commit crimes of this kind in order to terrorize owners of mining property.... As long as [the WFM] exists these [mining] companies will be unable to attend to their own affairs, or run their business and will always be at the mercy of the leaders of this organization.

Hawley's characterization of Steunenberg's murder in these sweeping terms contrasted with the state's official position, frequently enunciated by Gooding, that "there are no political issues involved in this at all. There are no industrial questions. It is simply a trial for murder." In his letter to Easton, Hawley made no such pretense. Indeed, he went on to propose a grandiose scheme "to rid the West entirely of this organization which has done so much to retard our progress, and which is a menace to our future." When the federation's "foul crimes" are known, he said, "it will be easy to raise such a storm that the general public will not countenance the continued existence of the federation." In effect, Hawley was proposing the exact opposite of Gooding's simple little murder trial: a series of great show trials that would not only convict Haywood, Moyer, and Pettibone but utterly discredit, and eventually destroy, the Western Federation, rouse public anger against its form of unionism, and pave the way for a new industrial climate in the West.

To pull off such an enterprise, with extensive investigations all across the Rocky Mountain states and vigorous prosecution of the malefactors, would "require the expenditure of a considerable fund," Hawley wrote. Since raising such a large sum meant "concerted action on the part of the mining companies in the different jurisdictions," he asked, "would it not be well to take measures looking to a union of the companies interested, not only in Idaho, but in the other States affected?"

As Hawley made his pitch to Bunker Hill, his co-counsel, Borah, carried the same message to Federal. Even before Hawley got an answer to his own letter, he received a crossing communication from Clayton Miller, saying, "It has come to my attention that Mr. Borah thinks some funds desirable in connection with suit (Steunenberg). I would like your advice re same. If you think best and necessary please wire F. F. Johnson, Wallace, Idaho thus: 'I agree with Borah' and we will arrange with Mr. J. to send you $3,000 now and $2,000 more if necessary. This is supposed to be used at your and his discretion."

Hawley must have responded as indicated, for on February 21—two days after Haywood, Moyer, and Pettibone were delivered to Boise—Miller informed Hawley, "Mr. Easton yesterday arranged with the Bank here for the deposit to the credit of Gov. Gooding, in conformity with our original offer. . . . We were, of course, greatly pleased with the news that has been received in this matter. . . . We hope that the leaders whom you have arrested will be made an example of for the benefit of all of the mining states. . . . I wish you God's speed in this matter, and assure you that we all appreciate your exertions." The full $5,000 entered the state's account in February and was promptly "used in securing evidence by the Governor."

On February 27, Hawley thanked both Miller and Easton for their "assurances" of financial support. To Easton, he laid the groundwork for further appeals, with a stern warning that the expected indictments would undoubtedly lead to "a series of the hardest fought criminal cases ever tried in the United States. . . . The only thing we fear so far as the prosecution is concerned is lack of means by reason of the State and County not being able under the law to furnish the necessary amounts for the extraordinary expenses that will be entailed."

On March 6, Easton forwarded this letter to his boss, Frederick W. Bradley, president of Bunker Hill, headquartered in San Francisco. Noting that the investigation and trials would be extremely expensive, Easton wrote: "It is a matter of utmost importance that these men must be properly punished and adequate assistance should be forthcoming. The MOA of the Coeur d'Alenes cannot do it all and the prosecution is just as important to the whole western mining field as it is to us. Cannot something be done to enlist assistance from other sources?"

By mid-March, Hawley had a special incentive to raise as much money as he could from private sources. At a meeting with the governor on March 19, Hawley—who two months before had agreed in principle to head the prosecution team—informed Gooding that he would ask $20,000 for the job "provided that said sum will have to be paid by the State of Idaho." But, he wrote, "if help is received from persons interested in the carrying on of these prosecutions so as to enable you to pay the lawyers' fees in whole, or to a great extent from such contributions instead of from the funds supplied by the state, then my fee for such services is to be the sum of $25,000."

The purchase by Idaho banks of deficiency certificates entailed private participation in financing the investigation and trial. Whatever else was afoot, the state relied heavily on these certificates; by August 1906 it had run through the original $30,000 and Gooding went back to the banks for $20,000 more. Given the major role of the First National Bank of Wallace—with its ties to the mine owners—it was at best a questionable arrangement, egregiously mixing public functions and private interests. But since the state would eventually repay these certificates with interest, this was presumably not what Hawley had in mind when he wrote that he expected to be paid more if his salary came in part from corporate or private "contributions."

On the other hand, the $5,000 that the Mine Owners Association presented to the state, to be used at Hawley's and Borah's "discretion," was precisely what Hawley had in mind: an outright contribution to the prosecution by the most interested of parties. It may or may not have been legal, but surely it was not proper. That Stanley Easton felt uneasy about it is clear in the note he jotted to Borah months later: "I hear Frank Johnson of Wallace has been subpoenaed. You remember the financial transactions which went through his hands. Cannot the testimony expected from him be secured from someone else and he be kept off the stand?" And as for private money, that was only the start.

Haywood, Pettibone, and Moyer hadn't been in their penitentiary cells a week before rumors circulated that their prosecution was being subsidized by a private group or corporation. On February 25, a *Statesman* reporter cornered Jim Hawley and asked if he'd "been retained as a private prosecutor in the interests of some individual or corporation."

Hawley responded as follows: "No, sir. I was retained by the state of Idaho to assist O. M. Van Duyn of Canyon County in the prosecution of these cases. I am not in the employ of any private individual or corporation. If such was the case I would not hesitate to say so, for the statute provides that any private party or corporation interested in a prosecution of this nature may employ an attorney, providing the prosecuting attorney is willing to accept such assistance. I am, however, strictly in the employ of the state, and my retainer comes from no other source whatever."*

Hawley's was a lawyer's answer, a shrewd blend of truth, obfuscation, and falsehood. The first sentence was arguably true: ostensibly, at least, Hawley

---

* Earlier, when McParland was asked a similar question, he told Denver reporters, "I was employed by the State, not by the mine owners."

had been hired to assist the inexperienced Owen Van Duyn in Canyon County—though in fact it was Van Duyn who served as a junior assistant to Hawley and Borah. The second sentence is more problematic: on February 25, Hawley might justifiably deny that he was employed by a private party or corporation. But well before that date, he had relentlessly beaten the bushes for corporate contributors to the prosecution; he'd already flushed out some cash in the Coeur d'Alenes, with expectations of more to come; and he stood to benefit by $5,000 if his salary was paid in whole, or in substantial part, from such contributions.

As for the legality of this practice, Hawley's claim that it was explicitly authorized by an Idaho statute went beyond the facts. In 1906, there was no state statute that held, in Hawley's words, that "any private party or corporation interested in a prosecution of this nature may employ an attorney." The practice of hiring private counsel to assist prosecutors was an old one in the West, where it was rare to find competent prosecuting attorneys at the county level and where the mixture of public functions and private interests was endemic. In 1884, a California court noted that the practice "has existed and been acquiesced in almost since the organization of the state." In two highly publicized cases pitting sheep men against cattlemen—the Diamondfield Jack case in Idaho and the Spring Creek raid case in Wyoming—sheep men made no secret of hiring and amply remunerating private attorneys to go after their sworn enemies, the cattlemen and their agents. The more remote the locale, the more visible the case, the more potent the colliding forces, and the more celebrated the defense attorney, the more often another celebrated attorney would be called in to act for the prosecution—paid sometimes by the state, sometimes by an interested corporation or association.*

Traditional, yes; but was it legal? Hawley had reason to know the law on this question, for twenty years before, he'd argued the other side of the matter in a precedent-setting case. In 1885, George Biles was convicted of assaulting a shoemaker named Uhl with intent to murder. On appeal Hawley argued, among other things, that the court erred in allowing a private counsel to assist in prosecuting his client. A three-judge panel conceded that "the statute does not specifically authorize the employment of private counsel to assist in the prosecution of persons charged with crimes," but it pointed to a section of the code that stated: "The district attorney, or other counsel for the people, must open the cause and offer the evidence in support of the indictment." Finding that "the words 'or other counsel' evidently means private counsel; as otherwise there could be no other counsel for the people," the court saw "no reason why counsel may not be employed to assist the district attorney in the prosecution of criminal causes."

---

* In southern states, when a black man was charged with raping a white woman it was long the practice for the family of the "victim," bent on revenge, to provide the "prosecutor" (John P. MacKenzie, interview with author, October 1996).

Those three little words, *or other counsel,* snake through the rulings of Idaho's courts on this question, serving as virtually the only basis for subsequent dicta sanctioning the employment of private attorneys to assist a public prosecutor. If the courts often seemed to be reaching a bit to justify a convenient practice, it was hardly unusual for a judge to construe large principles from small potatoes.

But what of Hawley's further claim that private attorneys might be employed by corporations or other parties interested in the prosecution? At first glance, it would seem that by 1906 this practice was illegal. For six years earlier, the legislature had enacted a statute that read, in part: "No prosecuting attorney must receive any fee or reward for or on behalf of any prosecutor or other individual, for services in any prosecution, or business to which it is his official duty to attend or discharge."* This statute was evidently aimed not so much at a high-profile case like the Steunenberg assassination as at the petty corruption of small-town life. A merchant at odds with another merchant would approach the county prosecutor and offer him a deal: Bring a criminal action against my opponent that will compel him to settle with me; then I'll split the proceeds with you. But if that was the impetus for the legislation, the principle seemed to apply in the larger context. Although neither Hawley nor Borah was the county's permanent public prosecutor, they were exercising his function and any such prohibition on him should have applied to them. But that is not the way the Idaho courts interpreted it. In 1915, for example, the Idaho Supreme Court said the provision applied only to "prosecuting attorneys regularly elected or appointed" and not to private attorneys retained for specific cases. Although there is no mention of this doctrine in 1906, it is quite possible that this interpretation prevailed then as well.

There was one case that stood, in 1906, as an important precedent. It grew out of the state's 1899 hiring of the Moscow attorney J. H. Forney to lead the prosecution of Paul Corcoran for the murder of James Cheyne at the Bunker Hill mill. After his conviction, Corcoran appealed to the Idaho Supreme Court, arguing that the district court had erred in appointing Forney as special prosecutor and acting county attorney, since he'd represented the Bunker Hill and Sullivan Company in a civil case. The Supreme Court rejected Corcoran's appeal, seeing no merit in the argument about Forney's connection to Bunker Hill. "This action," the Court ruled, "is between the people of the state, on one side, and the appellant [Corcoran], upon the other." Even though it was the company's concentrator that was blown up and it was on its property that Cheyne was killed, the Court held that Bunker Hill had no significant "interest" in the case justifying Forney's disqualification as special prosecutor.

---

* The term *prosecutor* here refers not to the prosecuting attorney but to the outside corporation or private individual with an interest in the case.

Never mentioned in the *Corcoran* arguments—because it wasn't known at the time outside a tiny circle—was that Bunker Hill and other Coeur d'Alene mining companies were paying Forney's salary, along with the salaries of all the other prosecutors. In *Corcoran,* therefore, the Supreme Court didn't expressly permit the mining interests to compensate the prosecutor. The precise relationship between Hawley and Borah, on the one hand, and western mining interests, on the other, had never been tested in the Idaho courts. But given the eagerness of Idaho judges to accommodate those interests, it seems likely that it would have passed muster as well.

Ironically, though, the state did slip up in one vital particular. For there was another standard governing appointment of special prosecutors. In an 1897 case, the Idaho Supreme Court noted that "a practice has grown up in some of the counties of the state whereby the board of county commissioners employ counsel at the expense of the county to assist the prosecuting attorney in the prosecution of criminal cases. A board of county commissioners has no such authority under the constitution or the law." It held that in such criminal cases it was the district court's responsibility to name the special prosecutor. Idaho's constitution also gives the governor the power to appoint a special prosecutor. It would thus appear that Gooding's appointment of Hawley as special prosecutor was legal, while Borah's engagement by the Canyon County commissioners was not.

Legalities aside, Hawley knew full well that in the intensely polarized climate of Colorado and Idaho that year, under close scrutiny by the national press, the picture of a prosecution heavily subsidized, and thus controlled, by the mine owners wouldn't look pretty. Whatever the traditions of earlier years —which permitted wool growers to use the bludgeon of the law to belabor their enemies the cattlemen—by 1906 there was a widespread belief that prosecutors, as officers of the court, should be committed not to a conviction at all costs but, in principle at least, to something called "justice."

All that spring, Hawley kept telling the mine owners that their support of the prosecution was entirely legal. "I do not see any reason why financial assistance from outside parties, where the money is to be used for perfectly legitimate purposes, could be an infraction of the rules," he wrote one potential donor. But then he warned: "If it was known that such assistance was being rendered, it would prejudice to a certain extent the prosecution; therefore the necessity of keeping these matters absolutely and entirely secret."

Moreover, Hawley explained, there was still another reason for taking a lot of money from private sources under the table. Expenses "that can be paid by the State will be limited in amounts, and can only embrace certain matters which are absolutely necessary in order to carry on the prosecution." Public expenditures would have to be supported by vouchers and, "as these accounts will be investigated by a legislative committee," only those practices that are "entirely explainable" should be publicly funded. Yet other practices would

clearly be necessary, among them investigations "with reference to the sentiment of the particular community, and amongst particular individuals." This
was clearly a reference to the clandestine investigation of potential jurors,
which at times in that era amounted to jury tampering. "We propose acting
entirely within the law," Hawley assured his donor, adding with a nod and a
wink, "I think you understand the sentiments that are actuating us in the
matter, also the difficulties of the position we are placed in, and the obstacles
we are compelled to surmount."

George H. Kester, a Lewiston banker who bought several thousand
dollars' worth of deficiency certificates that spring, was struck by the governor's mood in those crisis-ridden months. In a letter to Borah, dated March 6,
he wrote: "R. E. Goodwin, who was a guard at the penitentiary returned a few
days ago, and he reports that Gooding is very much alarmed. He says that he
is scared half to death over the dynamiters by night, and the politicians keep
him on the rack by day, so he must be pretty much up against it."

Governor Gooding was indeed tortured by anxiety that the WFM
might kill him or his family, as he believed they had Frank Steunenberg. He
was aghast at the flood of angry letters and death threats, some of them
decorated with skulls and crossbones. One letter contained a drawing of the
governor with his eyes poked out by a pencil. Another, postmarked Los
Angeles, said an avenger was on the way to kill him if he didn't repent. "We
will tear you and all to small bits," said another. "How do you like that?" The
governor didn't like it and his wife, Amanda, liked it even less. So on March 7,
they moved out of the rather grand but isolated residence at 615 Warm
Springs Avenue that the state had rented for him. With Amanda and their two
schoolage children, John and Louise, the governor henceforth occupied a
third-floor suite in the Idanha Hotel, just down the hall from James McParland's similar suite. According to one Socialist reporter, he could frequently
be seen "sliding along the hall to McParland's room to get straightened out."
The governor and his family were closely guarded by a gunman named
William L. "Jack" West, alias Four-Gun Jack, recently released from prison
pending appeal of a six-year sentence for grand larceny in Elmore County,
and Relf Bledsoe, a legendary seventy-five-year-old gunfighter and former
probate judge. When Gooding went out at night, even with his bodyguards,
he was careful not to wander far off the main streets. When he visited his
ranch on weekends, he was accompanied by Eugene Johnson, the private
detective who'd worked for the prosecution since the start of the year. During
the day, armed men escorted John, eighteen, to the Boise Business College
and Louise, thirteen, to St. Margaret's School for Girls (the Goodings were
high Episcopalians). Still others stood close watch in and around the Idaho
statehouse, where the governor worked in a first-floor suite with high windows, graced by brightly colored awnings, that looked out across well-

trimmed lawns (a skilled sniper might, without great difficulty, have put a bullet into the governor through those windows).

Visitors to the statehouse that year found the governor camouflaging his fears with bravado. Implacable and blunt-spoken, Frank Robert Gooding was a formidable adversary—whether out on the public hustings or in the serpentine alleys of criminal investigation. The very picture of the self-made American, he'd been born forty-seven years before in England and educated only through grade school in Paw Paw, Michigan. After four years farming in California, he settled in the mining town of Ketchum, Idaho, where he built a tidy business supplying wood and charcoal to the smelting works there. When labor later assailed him for persecuting the workingman, he invoked his days as a laborer "with pride and satisfaction." Taking his turn with the shovel as they'd searched for Pettibone's Hellfire, Gooding had turned to Harry Orchard's alleged co-conspirator, Steve Adams, and said, "This isn't the first time I've done this work."

In 1888, he carved out a homestead in Shoshone, Idaho, and began raising sheep, becoming so prominent in that industry he served as president of the Idaho Wool Growers' Association three times. Elected to the legislature in 1898, he grabbed the chairmanship of the Republican State Committee by 1902, using that position to wrest the 1904 Republican nomination for governor from the incumbent, Caldwell's own John Morrison.

Along the way, he'd picked up few of the social graces. Secretary of War William Howard Taft, on a political mission to Idaho, reported back: "Gooding is a man without much tact, and has made a good many enemies in his own party. He is a courageous man, a direct man, an honest man, and a pushing man, not refined, not very well educated. . . . He forced his way to the front, so that now he owns some fine farming lands, some great flocks of sheep and is worth about half a million dollars."

Short and portly, with a sunburned face, frowsy reddish-brown hair, and black beady eyes, Gooding reminded observers of a bull mastiff. On one occasion, James McParland found himself apologizing to the governor for a canine comparison in an article, for which the detective had evidently been the principal source. "I hope you will not take an exception to where the article refers to you as a bulldog," he wrote, "because I know the word 'bulldog' was not meant as an insult but was meant to convey to the public that you had the courage and tenacity of a bulldog." A sometime ally who well knew Gooding's graceless style once described his confrontation with Idaho sheep men: "The governor got in with his bludgeon (his only weapon) and clubbed them into being a convention of lambs."

Gooding's blunt style quickly got him in a lot of trouble in the Steunenberg case. Scarcely had the three labor leaders been stashed away in the state penitentiary than he began pronouncing them guilty. "Personally, knowing what I do of the case and of the evidence that is to be presented against the men, I firmly believe that all three—Moyer, Haywood and Petti-bone—are guilty of planning the assassination of Frank Steunenberg," he told one reporter. The three leaders, he said, "in secret and with dynamite have murdered by wholesale while they sat in their luxurious offices directing some fanatical dupe how to do the work." And again: "There has never been any doubt as to the truth of Orchard's confession," he said as early as Febru-ary 26, 1906. On several other occasions, reporters—generally on the left—quoted him as saying the same thing. Critics argued that such statements utterly ignored the presumption of innocence. Strictly speaking, this doctrine doesn't bind a public official in his public pronouncements. At its core, the presumption means simply that the burden of proof in judicial proceedings rests with the prosecution, not the defense. But statements like the governor's make it harder to find impartial jurors and thus to give defendants a fair trial.

Gooding's careless judgments, tossed to grateful reporters like bags of candy, drove his colleagues wild. At a press conference on February 25, Gooding had burbled on about Orchard's confession, saying that it seriously implicated the three WFM officials in no fewer than twenty-six murders—a claim well beyond that made by any prosecution spokesman. Though he'd been sitting in a corner while the governor spoke, Hawley gruffed: "I had nothing whatever to do with the statement. It was prepared and given out contrary to my advice and against all rules of decency and good taste, which I have tried to observe in my professional conduct." He broadly hinted that unless the governor kept his mouth shut he might retire from the case.

Gooding's critics in Boise were alternately horrified and amused. The *Capital News*, Democratic in politics but generally behind the prosecution, wrote that spring: "Somebody ought to muzzle the big chief. . . . His constant fear that the public will lose sight of him and will not realize that he is the whole thing, has made a laughing stock of the prosecution." At ordinary times, he might "be allowed to make an ass of himself with impunity," but when great interests were at stake, Idaho could no longer indulge Gooding's "opera bouffe habit of individual vanity."

While the governor was pictured by his Democratic opponents as "an uncouth sheep-herder," Socialists were somewhat harsher. A writer for *Wil-shire's Magazine* described him as "the dull, blundering creature that sits in the governor's chair." An *Appeal to Reason* reporter wrote that spring that Gooding "possesses no traits of personal refinement and knows not the mean-ing of the word aesthetics. . . . [He is] a close, calculating, energetic, unscrupu-lous commercial proposition, ready to turn a dollar at any time, regardless of the means employed." Even a mainstream lawyer noted Gooding's "lurid vocabulary composed of a complete glossary of profanity and a malaproprian ineptitude in the choice of language." But his supporters dismissed his lack of drawing-room politesse as mattering very little in the "arena of practical, every day common sense business affairs" in which the governor excelled.

•

That winter, like any other prudent merchant, Gooding tried to lay in some insurance against the hazards that he feared lurked just around the corner. On March 17, he wrote Secretary of War Taft—it was the first time he'd corresponded with this august personage.

> We are confronted with a condition in the state of Idaho which may at any time require the services of troops to sustain the law and its civil officers. The labor unions are being prejudiced against the legal authorities owing to the arrest and expressed intention of trying several members of the Western Federation of Miners for the murder of ex-Governor Steunenberg. This feeling of prejudice is being augmented in every possible way by the radical leaders in socialistic thought. Although not especially fearing any serious demonstrations, I feel that it is only proper for me to prepare for a serious emergency.

Gooding asked that "the regular troops at Boise Barracks be placed under my orders if possible, or that such other action be taken as will enable the speedy movement of the troops here."

After conferring with the president, Taft responded in legalistic language. He drew the governor's attention to the U.S. statute which provided that in case of an insurrection in any state, and on the appeal of that state's legislature (or, if the legislature could not be convened, the state's governor), the president could use army or naval forces to suppress such a revolt. In so doing, however, "the President has no power to turn over the command of the military forces to the Governor of a State. The United States military forces must always act under the President, as Commander-in-Chief." The war secretary added, almost as an afterthought: "Should there arise in your State an insurrection (which the President sincerely hopes may be avoided), I am directed by the President to say that ... he will promptly employ a sufficient force of the army of the United States to suppress such insurrection and restore order."

To Frank Gooding, this may have seemed a condescending rebuff from the president. In fact, Theodore Roosevelt was anything but sanguine about the events taking place nearly a continent away. He'd known Frank Steunenberg slightly, having briefly met him at the White House a few months after becoming president. Though Steunenberg was a Democrat, Roosevelt liked him, and three weeks after the governor's death, he'd written a brief introduction to a memorial volume in which he said, "The man himself belongs to that type which found its highest expression in Abraham Lincoln. ... He was emphatically a man of the people." Deeply anxious, as always, about the maintenance of public order and alarmed by the activities of "agitators" whom he believed were acting in the interest of an economic class rather than of the nation, Roosevelt had paid close attention to the uproar in labor circles over the "kidnapping" of Haywood, Pettibone, and Moyer.

In mid-March, the Reverend Llewellyn D. Crandall of Filley, Nebraska, sent the president Eugene Debs's article in the March 10 edition of *Appeal to Reason*. It resounded with rhetorical overkill. Arguing that Frank Steunenberg had "simply reaped what he had sown," it condemned American capitalists— "these gory-beaked vultures are to pluck out the heart of resistance to their tyranny and robbery that labor may be stark naked at their mercy"—and warned them: if they sought to kill Haywood, Moyer, and Pettibone, "a million revolutionists" would rise to confront them.

On March 19, Roosevelt sent the clipping to his attorney general, William H. Moody, with a note: "This is an infamous article. Is it possible to proceed against Debs and the proprietor of this paper criminally?... Please notify the Post Office Department so that the papers may not be allowed in the mails," adding in an inky scrawl, "if we can keep it out."

The president couldn't have been pleased by the coldly correct response he received from one of eight assistant attorney generals, Charles H. Robb, on March 22: "I am sorry to say that notwithstanding the infamous nature of the article, there is no law of which I have knowledge authorizing the exclusion of the paper containing it from the mails, neither is there any statute authorizing the prosecution of Debs for sending such matter through the mails." Robb went on in his reply to propose legislation making it a crime to use the mails in disseminating a criminal libel.

Four days later, with Debs's screed still clanging in his head, the president sat down to write Attorney General Moody: "As you know, the Governor of Idaho has asked us to be ready to aid the state authorities by the use of Federal troops in the event of their being unable to keep order and suppress armed resistance.... In view of the extraordinary interest attending to the case and the widespread commotion that has been caused, I wish very much that you could instruct the [U.S. Attorney for Idaho] to forward to you, confidentially, as full a report as possible upon certain phases of it."

Then, in one blunt paragraph, he went on to state his understanding of the case against the indicted labor leaders:

> That Haywood and Moyer have been at the head of a labor organization, the members of which have practiced every form of violence, including assassination, during a period extending over many years, is not to be disputed. That Haywood and Moyer themselves have been guilty of language and conduct which amounted to incitement to assassination in the past is also not to be disputed. Furthermore, that ex-Governor Steunenberg was assassinated for conscientiously doing his duty in putting a stop to the murders and other infamies perpetrated by the Coeur d'Alene rioters, who were the associates and henchmen of those men, is, I am afraid, unquestioned.

Assuming a more judicious mien, the president went on: "This in no way affects the duty of the State authorities and of the Federal authorities, if it should ever happen that we had any power in the matter, to see that exact justice is done these men. There must be no condonation of lawlessness on our part, even if the lawlessness takes the form of an effort to avenge the wrongs committed by the lawlessness of others. The sole question as regards Haywood and Moyer must be the question whether or not they can be shown to be guilty of this particular act."

To that end of impartial justice, the president asked that the U.S. attorney inform him promptly "whether or not there has been the slightest disposition shown by the authorities in Idaho to act toward these men in an unfair or improper manner, or to deny them their legal rights." On the other hand, he wanted to know whether there was "any symptom of a miscarriage of justice in their favor," given the "tremendous pressure being brought to bear upon the authorities of Idaho to discharge or acquit them whether guilty or innocent."

The attorney general chose not to give this assignment to the U.S. attorney for Idaho, Norman Ruick. Perhaps because he believed that Ruick might not be entirely impartial or perhaps because the matter's sensitivity required a more seasoned lawyer, he handed the job instead to Assistant Attorney General Robb, the very man who'd informed the president there were no grounds to prosecute Eugene Debs.

A thirty-nine-year-old Vermonter who'd often served as a roving Justice Department investigator and prosecutor, Robb wasted no time in addressing the president's questions. Reaching Denver on April 5, he conferred there with Earl M. Cranston, the U.S. attorney for Colorado. Together they met with Governor McDonald to review the disputed extradition of the labor leaders. McDonald told Robb he'd spent "the greater part of two days" examining the requisition papers and accompanying affidavits from Idaho—when, in fact, he'd spent barely two hours on the matter. In his report, Robb also passed on the inaccurate assertion, so favored by McParland, that Haywood had been arrested "in a house of prostitution." From Denver, Robb went on to Boise, where he conferred with Gooding, Hawley, and Borah, who explained that the extradition had to be implemented with extreme speed and secrecy for "fear that the agents of the State of Idaho would receive the same treatment meted out to Mr. Steunenberg or that the train used in transporting the defendants would be interfered with."

Robb—whose political experience had been largely confined to Windham County, Vermont—was much impressed by the forceful governor, whose every official act in these cases, he said, had been "actuated by unselfish and patriotic motives" and "his desire that every legal right of these men be carefully protected." Robb concluded: "The authorities of Idaho are engaged in a gigantic struggle to uphold the law, and I am fully convinced that they possess the requisite courage and ability. Too much cannot be said in praise of the manner in which this crisis has been met by them. That the defendants will have fair and impartial trials before fair and impartial juries, no one at all cognizant of the facts will attempt to deny."

The president had just finished digesting this credulous report when a

letter from Governor Gooding landed on his desk—the first direct communication between the two men. Thanking the president for words of support
passed to him through Idaho's Republican congressman, Burton L. French,
Gooding went on to express his outrage at an editorial called "Idaho on
Trial" in the May 5 issue of *Collier's Weekly*. Written by Norman Hapgood, the
editor, the piece noted that "if the miners are a violent lot nothing better can
be said for the owners." Indeed, it went on, "Idaho has the opportunity to
earn considerable credit or immense disgrace [from the trial].... There are
circumstances which raise suspicion of collusion between the mine owners
and the authorities, and Idaho owes it to herself that this suspicion should be
removed."

The editorial, Gooding told the president, "will present the situation
here to the nation in a very bad light." In that connection, he was sending an
emissary to Washington in the person of Calvin Cobb, owner and publisher of
the *Idaho Daily Statesman*. Cobb was coming, the governor said, "to ask for your
assistance in inducing the great journals of the east to send representatives
here at the time of the trial of the accused persons, for the purpose of making
a full and fair presentation of the facts to the nation. There has been so much
misrepresentation of the situation here by a class who are malicious enemies
of the government, believers in the doctrine of assassination, that an urgent
demand exists that the people throughout the nation should know the truth."

Saying he would "gladly see Mr. Cobb," though doubtful he could help
much with the press, the president agreed there had been "a deliberate
attempt to misrepresent what you and those associated with you have done,
and to bring coercive pressure upon you and upon all other officials in Idaho,
and the attempt cannot be too severely reprobated."

That Gooding should have turned for this quasi-diplomatic mission to
Calvin Cobb reflected not only the ties of personal trust and political self-
interest that bound the two men but the press's equivocal role at the turn of
the century. Neither the creed of "objectivity" nor the separation of editorial
and news operations had yet become established at the nation's major newspapers. Through the nineteenth and into the twentieth century, publishers,
editors, and senior correspondents became mouthpieces of parties and politicians, sometimes serving as outright political agents. Donn Piatt, of the *Washington Sunday Capital*, once regarded as "the most successful correspondent of
the age," performed a host of services for Congressman (later President)
James A. Garfield, then used Garfield's influence to win friends of his a
lucrative War Department contract mothproofing army uniforms. Ben Perley
Poore, the plump correspondent of the *Boston Morning Journal*, wrote speeches
and letters for the congressmen he covered and even swung caucuses behind
them at election time, while taking their "loans" to tide him over. "Half the
great newspapers in our cities are bought up by some political or other great
interest," one observer wrote in 1871.

To Frank Gooding, Calvin Cobb was the logical choice for his confidential agent. As publisher of the state's principal Republican newspaper—so staunchly Republican it was one of a handful of Idaho papers to endorse McKinley in the silver-crazed election of 1896—Cobb not only served as his party's most important instrument of publicity within the state but took an active role in framing the policies he communicated. One eastern paper dubbed him "the chancellor of Republican politics" in Idaho. In the factional battles among Idaho Republicans, Cobb had generally aligned himself with Bill Borah rather than Frank Gooding, but the governor assiduously wooed him, funneling $11,000 in state printing contracts to the *Statesman.*

Calvin Cobb descended from a New England family long steeped in the classics. His paternal grandparents had nine children: Lucius Marcius, Marcius Lucius, Junius Brutus, Brutus Junius, Caius Cassius, Cassius Caius, Lucia Marcia, Marcia Lucia, and—here, with their last born, the classical impulse seems to have expired—Daniel Wells.

The eldest, Lucius Marcius, moved to Chicago at midcentury, establishing a circulating library that preceded the foundation of the Chicago Public Library. Located downtown on Washington Street, Cobb's library boasted some five thousand volumes—all of which were destroyed during the great Chicago fire of 1871, when its building was dynamited in the vain hope of saving a nearby department store. After the fire, Cobb rebuilt and over the next three decades operated a number of libraries, bookstores, and small publishing houses.

Lucius's fourth son, Calvin, worked for a time in his father's publishing house. In 1886, he entered the cattle trade, which took him to Boise the next year. He must have been impressed, for some months later, he purchased the twenty-two-year-old *Idaho Daily Statesman* with two other investors. Later, Cobb and his brother-in-law, Jack Lyon, gained full control of the paper.

In truth, they had a virtual monopoly of Boise's daily press. For some years the city had boasted another paper, called the *Daily Capital,* which in February 1901 converted to afternoon publication, becoming the *Evening Capital News.* That Calvin Cobb resented this flanking attack was evident three months later when the *Statesman* founded its own afternoon paper, the *Bulletin,* for which it obtained a valuable Associated Press franchise to match its own morning franchise. For three years, the two evening papers warred in Boise's small afternoon market, the *News* calling its rival the *Evening Effort,* the *Bulletin* dubbing its competition the *Evening Snooze.* Both papers seemed to be losing money. Then, in July 1904, Cobb negotiated a shrewd deal. The *News* obtained the *Bulletin* and its valuable evening AP franchise; in exchange, the *Statesman* received two-fifths of the *News's* stock. Though not strictly speaking a controlling share, it gave Cobb the balance of power between squabbling stockholders and thus a voice in the evening paper's management.

The *Capital News* was nominally Boise's Democratic paper. It generally supported the party's national ticket, but so lethargic was it in backing Idaho's Democratic candidates and policies that the party suffered acutely from the lack of a vigorous flagship paper. Since the paper was chronically short on cash, Republican politicians—notably Senator Borah and James Brady, the party chairman—provided the *Capital News* with desperately needed loans, thus buying support for themselves and grief for their enemies. It was, in effect, "editorially mortgaged" to Cobb and his Republican allies.

Over the years, both the Dubois and the Steunenberg factions of the Democratic Party had tried to buy the *Capital News* stock held by the *Statesman,* but Cobb had consistently declined to sell. For some time there'd been talk that William Randolph Hearst might buy the paper, or start his own evening paper in Boise, to spearhead his presidential campaign in the Rocky Mountain states. But as nothing came of that either, Calvin Cobb remained the uncontested ruler of Idaho's press.

His wife's family, the Lyons of Mississippi, had a private fortune rooted in rice and sugar cane, guaranteeing the Cobbs a comfortable life. After a 1906 visit with Cobb in Boise, Secretary of War Taft gave the president a capsule portrait of the publisher: "A fine fellow. He is the editor of a paper that any man can be proud of. It has none of the yellow journal characteristics, and he exercises an independent influence that it is very gratifying to see. Nobody owns him. He has a patrimony of his own. He has a very delightful family, lives ... like a gentleman, and with every evidence of refined and cultured breeding. His son is a graduate of Harvard, and I think both he and his wife come from Ohio. They believe in the higher things of life."

Now and then, in mock humility, Calvin Cobb assumed the pose of "the poor country editor," but that wasn't how he saw himself. His own paper was closer to the mark when, after his death, it described him as "erudite, progressive, aristocratic, civic-minded and something of a snob." A former *Statesman* editor called him "an autocratic guardian of the destinies of Boise and Idaho." To the Socialist *Appeal to Reason,* he was only "a violent Republican politician." Year after year he could be found in his publisher's sanctum, erect in a straight-backed Windsor chair, his steel-gray hair parted in the middle, his thoughtful brown eyes above a prominent nose and strong jaw, a cigarette drooping from his pursed lips. On the newsroom wall he had hung his credo: "The *Statesman* in a general way follows the teachings of Hamilton rather than Jefferson. . . . It believes in the rights given us by the Constitution to prevent the tyranny of the mob." His Chicago friends ribbed him about his penchant for the status quo. When Cobb contracted for a column by the Chicago gadfly Finley Peter Dunne, Dunne thanked him for accommodating a dissident in his "valued organ of plutocracy" and said, "It would give me great personal pleasure to know that the stuff was being printed in Boise where I have so many friends among the lower classes."

With his wife, Fannie, and their two children, he lived in a handsome forest-green bungalow—a former stagecoach station—occupying a whole city block. It was tastefully furnished with heirloom furniture and objets d'art, mingling "the fragrance of esthetic culture with the plebian odor of desert sagebrush." The Cobbs built one of Boise's first private tennis courts, on which they entertained the capital's tennis set. The publisher could be a tyrant at home. A list of "house rules" specified: "All members of this family must appear ready for morning prayers at 7:30 A.M.," "Prompt attendance at meals is obligatory," "All horse and jockey talk is prohibited," and, perhaps only half jokingly, "Consider a request from the master of the house as a command."

Fannie was widely regarded as the doyenne of Boise society, a leader of its elite women's club, the Columbian, and a frequent host of the Wednesday Bridge Club. She rode about town in a gay little victoria, with a uniformed coachman at the reins and a parasol to shield her—and her dazzling head of prematurely white hair—from the elements. Calvin walked to work—a scant four blocks to the *Statesman's* single-story office of whitewashed brick at Sixth and Main Streets—so preoccupied with his own concerns he rarely acknowledged other pedestrians. Cobb, a former editor recalled, was "never a 'mixer' with either townspeople or employees." The Cobbs rarely went out at night; instead, people came to them, prompting one wag at the paper to adapt an old Boston adage about the Cabots and Lodges to read: "And this is good old Boise / Where the first families number seven / Where the Ormsbys go to the Cobbs / And the Cobbs go only to heaven."

If he didn't tarry long with the average Boisean, Cobb was well connected back East. From his active role in the Associated Press—he was later a vice president—he knew most of the nation's prominent editors and publishers. A member of the Chicago Club, with reciprocal privileges at clubs in New York and Washington, he traveled in the country's best circles. Moreover, he had a special qualification for the mission: he was among the few Idahoans who could claim to "know" the president. On March 1, 1902, Senator Fred Dubois had taken him by the White House, where Cobb and Roosevelt had a pleasant chat about Idaho politics and forest conservation. Back in Boise, the publisher liked to tell neighbors about his talk with Teddy.

As Cobb prepared to head east about May 15, he had three items on his agenda. On a stopover in Chicago, he would talk with officials of the Associated Press about coverage of the upcoming trial. After thirty-five years of bitter skirmishing with competitors and rebellious members, the AP had emerged as the nation's preeminent wire service—supplying news to, and drawing it from, more than seven hundred daily newspapers. With a few flicks of the telegrapher's key, it could make a story headline news in San Francisco, Duluth, and Baltimore. Gooding, Hawley, and McParland desperately wanted to get their side of the story into a sympathetic ear at the wire service. Cobb could do that.

Then, in Washington, the publisher was to put before the president the governor's concerns about "misrepresentation" of the Idaho situation in the nation's press, from *Collier's Weekly* to Hearst and Pulitzer. Finally, he'd talk with Secretary Taft about the governor's fear of assassination and his growing anxiety about security in Boise.

After their calculated rebuff to Gooding's March 14 request for direct command of U.S. troops in Idaho, the president and his war secretary had edged toward a limited—and very quiet—intervention in Idaho. In early April, they decided to assuage the governor's anxiety by surreptitiously reinforcing the garrison at Boise Barracks, perched on a hillside five blocks north of the capitol. As 1906 began, the barracks were manned by Troop L of the Fourteenth Cavalry, at full strength sixty-five officers and men—though, with desertions and other vacancies, more like fifty. Now Roosevelt and Taft agreed in principle to triple that.

When nothing happened by April 18, Roosevelt jotted Taft a note: "What have you done about getting some more troops quietly into Idaho—or even not quietly if necessary?" Two days later, Taft ordered Troops A and B of the Fourteenth Cavalry on a practice march from Walla Walla, Washington, to Boise—some 350 miles across heavily wooded mountains and grassy plateaus. The troops—both substantially understrength—reached Boise Barracks on May 4, adding seventy officers and men to the garrison.

On May 8, the captain commanding Boise Barracks informed his superiors that Troops A and B were "thoroughly rested and ready for return march" to Walla Walla. The War Department temporized, Taft ordering the army to "hold these troops at Boise Barracks until further orders." But pressures mounted—from the State of Washington's congressmen as well as the commander of the Fourteenth Cavalry—for the return of the two troops to Walla Walla. As Cobb left Boise, Gooding asked him to call on Taft and make sure those troops stayed in Boise.

From the Chicago Club in the third week of May, Cobb reported to Borah on the first leg of his mission, his meeting with officials of the Associated Press. Although the AP's central office was in New York, Chicago was an important base of operations, headed by Charles S. Diehl, the assistant general manager. Victor F. Lawson, editor of the *Chicago Daily News,* was a powerful director. From his days in Chicago publishing, Cobb knew them both. Now he told Borah, "I did well with Associated Press and we will have their crack man and one other."

Late in May, Cobb entrained for Washington, where he had an initial meeting with the president. Thereafter he met Taft, who seems to have been impressed by his arguments on the troop matter, for on June 16, the secretary wrote the president's secretary, William Loeb, asking that the president see Cobb once more, this time "with reference to troops at Boise City." Later that same day, Loeb informed Taft, "In view of Mr. Cobb's statement to the President, the President directs that the troops be retained at Boise City."

The president was feeling warmly that day toward Governor Gooding and the Idaho prosecutors. In a "Dear Mr. Cobb" letter that he handed to his visitor but that was clearly intended for Gooding's eyes, the president sought to reinforce the governor's determination by expressing his "hearty and deep sympathy" for his efforts to bring the men charged with Steunenberg's murder to trial. "I appreciate that he is doing this literally at the peril of his life. ... They [the WFM] will, if they are given the chance, and unless they are cowed, certainly endeavor to make Governor Gooding another victim. I wish to assure Governor Gooding that every honorable and decent man, whether wage worker or capitalist, who has taken the trouble to find out what the facts are, is his hearty supporter." He couldn't resist expressing his "keen indignation" at "certain men of good position" who hadn't troubled to find out the facts.

To these sentiments, calculated to refresh the governor's spirits, he added a note of caution:

> I wish you would tell the Governor that I do hope he will most carefully guard against falling into the grave error that the Governor of Colorado fell into in 1903 and 1904. If I had been in Governor Peabody's place I would have cinched the Western Federation of Miners until it looked like an hour glass, but I would have cinched the big corporations on the other side just as tight. For instance, the failure to insist that the legislature should obey the will of the people and pass the eight hour law, and if it did not do so to keep it in session every day of the whole time for which it was elected, was in my judgment unpardonable.

The last admonition notwithstanding, the letter was as forceful an endorsement of his position as any embattled governor could have asked from a sitting president. But sometime in the next four days, Roosevelt received word that Governor Gooding was financing the investigation and trial of Haywood in part through funds provided by the mine owners. How this information reached Roosevelt is not entirely clear, although it probably came from Assistant Attorney General Robb. There is a hint of this in an exchange of letters between Roosevelt and his closest confidant in the press corps, Lyman Abbott, editor of the *Outlook*, a New York journal of progressive but sober judgment that the president would join as a contributing editor after he left the White House. A former Congregational minister, Abbott had succeeded the celebrated Henry Ward Beecher at Brooklyn's Plymouth Congregational Church in 1887. Roosevelt used Abbott as a sounding board, while the editor made what use he could of his highly placed friend.

Earlier in June, Roosevelt had sent Abbott confidentially a copy of Robb's report. On June 20, Abbott wrote the president, saying that he found the document "authoritative" and asking permission to publish it as part of a series the *Outlook* was running on the Idaho situation.

On June 21, Roosevelt wrote back: "I do not think it best that Mr. Robb's report should be published as yet, partly because there is a matter about the conduct of the case by the State authorities of Idaho which I am at present looking into on my own account." It is only a surmise, but it seems likely that Robb came back from the West bearing word of the state's curious financing of the case, particularly the $5,000 donated by the Coeur d'Alene mine owners; that he did not include it in his report for fear of adulterating the wholehearted endorsement of Gooding that the president plainly wanted; but that sometime after June 16 he mentioned it privately to the president, who determined to take it up with Gooding first before allowing any further dissemination of Robb's findings.

On June 20—the very day Abbott asked permission to publish the Robb document—Roosevelt summoned Calvin Cobb back to the White House and presented him with a second letter. Like the first one, it was addressed to the publisher, but once again it was directed at the governor. In case there was any confusion, this time it explicitly asked Cobb to "please show this letter to Governor Gooding." The president wasted no time in getting to the point: "I have been informed that the Governor of Idaho has accepted contributions from the mine owners to aid the State in the prosecution of the alleged murderers of ex-Gov. Steunenberg. I can not believe that this is true. Such action would be the grossest impropriety, and there would be no warrant whatever for receiving or retaining such contributions." Idaho's government, he went on, would

> make a fatal mistake—and when I say fatal I mean literally that—if it permits itself to be identified with the operators any more than with the miners and if it fails to act as drastically against any corporation or rich man which or who does anything wrong as it acts against the Western Federation of Miners or any of its members or any wage workers who do anything wrong. If the Governor or the other officials of Idaho accept a cent from the operators or from any other capitalist with any reference, direct or indirect, to this prosecution, they would forfeit the respect of every good citizen and I should personally feel that they had committed a real crime.

Roosevelt would give his support to the "constituted authorities of any State, whatever I may individually think of them, where under the constitution it becomes my duty so to give it. But it will be given wholly without sympathy and with a profound contempt for those asking it, if they or their attitude deviate one hand's breadth from the course of fair and equal justice."

It is difficult to imagine a president's giving a governor a more severe dressing-down than this, particularly in contrast to the letter of exaltation that Roosevelt had handed Calvin Cobb just four days before. If ever there was a meal of sweet and sour it was in the briefcase that the publisher carried back to Boise on July 2.

Promptly on the morning of the third, Cobb was in the governor's office, where he read both letters to Frank Gooding. One can only imagine the stunned look on the governor's face as the publisher read him the opening lines of the second letter. Given to bouts of anxiety for far less reason, he now stood in peril of losing the president's support—indeed earning his contempt —just as the worst crisis of his life threatened to engulf him.

In response, the governor shrewdly chose to shake the president's glad hand first. "Your kind words will always be remembered," he wrote that afternoon.

> I am glad to know that you so thoroughly understand the situation that exists here in the west, and to learn that the better class of our citizens in the east, regardless of their positions in life, who have taken the trouble to inform themselves, are in hearty accord with the stand I have taken, looking to the punishment of those guilty of the murder of ex-Governor Steunenberg. I wish to assure you, Mr. President, that I have only one thought in this matter—the punishing of those guilty of that fearful crime, and the wiping out of the stain cast on the fair name of my state.

As for the back of the other hand he'd gotten across the face, he wrote: "I note what you say in regard to the mine owners having anything to do with putting up money for the prosecution of these cases. I am in full accord with you in this matter, and wish to assure you that so far as Idaho is concerned, the mine owners will not be asked for a dollar, nor permitted to take any part in the prosecution."

He then gave a distorted history of the money pledged by the Coeur d'Alene mine owners. "When the news of the assassination of ex-Governor Steunenberg reached me, I at once offered a reward of $5,000 for the arrest and conviction of the guilty parties. The mine owners of Shoshone County, without any solicitation on my part, offered a reward of $10,000." After Harry Orchard's arrest, he explained, he withdrew the reward and advised the mine owners to do the same, at which point they gave the governor $5,000 to pay for preliminary expenses. "At this time," he argued, "it was not known that the Western Federation of Miners was implicated in the murder of the ex-Governor."

What this disingenuous account omits were James Hawley's and William Borah's explicit appeals, as early as February 4, to Stanley Easton, W. Clayton Miller, and other mine owners to help fund the investigation. Moreover, Gooding's version severely distorts these events by contending that the WFM hadn't been implicated at the time the mine owners handed over the $5,000. By January 10 at the very latest, and almost certainly earlier, James McParland had concluded that the assassination was the work of the WFM. In succeeding weeks, Hawley and Borah explicitly invoked the WFM's "foul crimes" as their principal instrument in prying money out of the mine owners.

However he might seek to justify taking this money, Gooding knew the game was up—so far as the $5,000 was concerned. Even then, he claimed to be acting on his own twinges of conscience: "I expressed myself to Mr. Cobb on more than one occasion that I was sorry I ever used a cent of this money. After reading your letter I am convinced that I was right in this matter. I shall return this $5,000 at once.... I feel that the return of this money will leave the state's record clean in the prosecution of these cases."

As soon as he got the governor's pledge, the president fired off a response, brimming with satisfaction: "Three cheers! I can not say how pleased I am with your letter.... You are taking just the stand that an upright, high-minded and fearless Executive should take in refusing to accept any aid from the corporation men. With hearty congratulations, and still more heartily congratulating the American people upon having an Executive of your stamp."

As Roosevelt saw it, he'd saved the mine owners and their captive governor from the consequences of their own blundering (much as he had in the anthracite strike, when, as he said, "I was anxious to save the great coal operators and all the class of propertied men, of which they were members, from the dreadful punishment which their own folly would have brought them if I had not acted"). So pleased was he with his clandestine operation, he jotted a note to Lyman Abbott, enclosing his letter and Gooding's response. "What a queer time I have had in some ways!" he wrote. "A goodly number of the things I have done which I regard as most important will probably never see the light and will be known to only a few people, including yourself." Citing his role in the Russo-Japanese peace negotiations (for which he was soon to win the Nobel Peace Prize), in the "Algerian negotiations," and in the "Alaskan boundary dispute," the president proudly declared: "This Idaho business is one."

Within weeks, the governor kept the narrowest construction of his promise to the president by returning the $5,000 to the Coeur d'Alene mine owners. After consulting McParland—who thought the idea "a good one," since "we have taken the stand that the State of Idaho is prosecuting these cases"—Gooding mailed a check for $5,000 to W. Clayton Miller at Federal Mining and Smelting. Moreover, in the weeks to come, as he campaigned for reelection, he publicly addressed rumors purveyed by the Democrats that the Haywood-Moyer-Pettibone investigation was secretly subsidized by the mine owners. At the Republican convention in Pocatello in mid-August, Gooding proclaimed: "It is charged that the mine owners of the Coeur d'Alenes are furnishing the money to prosecute these cases. The charge is untrue. No individual or corporation will be allowed to pay one dollar toward the prosecution of the accused men." Six weeks later, at the Opera House in Hailey, he repeated the pledge in much the same language: "It has been charged that the mine owners of Idaho and Colorado are furnishing the money for the prosecution of this case. This, too, I deny. No individual, company or corporation will be permitted to furnish one dollar toward the prosecution of those men." The state legislature evidently believed him, for when it expressed its full support of the governor's policy in the WFM case, it said, "No dollar has been or will be supplied from any private source or organization whatsoever." Over the next several months, Gooding would mouth the same words at every opportunity. "Not one dollar," he'd say, or sometimes, "not a single penny."

These solemn pledges to the president and to the people of Idaho notwithstanding, Frank Gooding went right on taking money from the mine owners. Indeed, well before he declared that the return of the $5,000 would "leave the state's record clean," he had opened up a second major channel of private financing—this time from the mine owners of Colorado.

When McParland went to Denver in mid-February to prepare removal of the three union leaders, Associate Justice Luther J. Goddard of the Colorado Supreme Court had offered to provide the renowned Denver trial attorney John M. Waldron as Hawley's trial deputy and the prosecution's Colorado liaison. Ultimately, Waldron—who took only two or three major cases a year—backed out, whether because he had a "disinclination to engage in any criminal cases" or because he had grave doubts about the sufficiency of the evidence, as he hinted later. But these discussions established that Colorado's mine owners would pay Waldron's fees. As early as February 15, Bulkeley Wells and the mining attorney James Williams said they'd provide $25,000, or even $50,000, if necessary. On February 26—days after he'd "escorted" the prisoners to Boise—Wells wrote Hawley that "there is no difficulty whatever about raising funds for this, or other purposes, which may promote the effective prosecution of this matter."

For a time in March, Hawley thought he'd found his principal source of funds in Floyd R. Thompson, secretary of the Cripple Creek Mine Owners and Operators Association. It isn't clear who initiated this connection. On March 26, Thompson acknowledged a letter from Hawley "informing me that some cash would be very acceptable to the prosecution," while Hawley in a letter three days later said, "Our correspondence in regard to this matter was commenced by your very kind offer to advance funds to be used in assisting the prosecution."

In any case, the Cripple Creek mine owners were not only willing but impatient to deliver cash to Idaho. On March 21, Thompson set off for Boise carrying a first installment of a thousand dollars. He hoped, he wrote Hawley, "to furnish what money [the prosecution] would need in these cases." But Thompson got only as far as Pocatello before receiving an urgent telegram from his people in Cripple Creek advising that Hawley "did not want any of us to come there at the present time." He promptly caught a train for home, where he and his colleagues determined that "in consequence of this we will handle all funds through the State Association [presumably the Colorado

Mining Association] until further advised." Undaunted, Thompson assured Hawley: "Our hearts and purses are with you."

Given the prosecution's strictures about keeping all private funding secret, one can understand why Hawley would discourage Colorado mine owners or their spokesmen from toting satchels full of cash to Boise. Pullman cars and hotel lobbies in both states were crawling with detectives who might quickly identify such couriers. Moreover, there were special reasons for keeping Floyd Thompson away from Boise. McParland simply didn't trust Thompson to keep his mouth shut. Warning a Pinkerton colleague not to share documents with him, he said the former undersheriff "would publish the whole matter in the papers."

These misgivings notwithstanding, Hawley tried hard to arrange with Thompson for a regular cash flow from Cripple Creek. "The main drawback of the prosecution, I will frankly say, is the lack of funds," Hawley wrote him on March 29. "A great deal of money is necessary in a case of this magnitude to successfully carry on a prosecution." By then, Hawley seemed to have lost faith in the Idaho mine owners. "It does not look as if interested parties here were going to do anything substantial," he wrote. "In fact, I do not depend on such in the future. If your Association, or the individuals composing it, think it proper to help us out in this matter, I would say in my judgment it would be a proper thing to do, and we would be privileged to accept such aid." Now three months into the case, Hawley had grown impatient about funding. "I would want to know, however, at once, what can be done in this regard; whether we can depend, and what we can depend on. Time is pressing."

But before any deal could be cut with Floyd Thompson, a more reliable —and discreet—channel was established between Colorado's mine owners and Idaho's prosecutors. Writing Hawley on March 29, Bulkeley Wells announced somewhat portentously: "The various parties in interest in Colorado have retained in the interest of you gentlemen in Idaho, who are prosecuting these cases, Mr. Jacob Filius [*sic*] of Denver, an attorney of long and large experience and one in whom we all have the greatest confidence. Not only for good judgment and sound counsel, but quite as much because we know that he can be absolutely relied on to handle all matters relating to these cases with absolute secrecy."

At fifty-nine, Jacob Fillius was a canny veteran of Colorado's labor and political wars. With shrewd black eyes peering out on either side of his great beak, he resembled a wise old bird who'd been watching the world go by so long nothing surprised him. Born in Hudson, Ohio, he'd attended Western Reserve College, then struck out for the West. Settling in the booming silver camp of Georgetown, Colorado, and believing that "sure and speedy riches would accrue" to those who sought the white metal, he prospected for several years without striking it rich. Eventually, he decided to do the next best thing and practice mining law, and before long he was one of the town's leading attorneys, while serving several terms as Georgetown's mayor. Since the mayoralty carried with it the position of police judge, his associates took to calling him Judge, an honorific that stuck for life. In 1893, he moved to Denver, plunging into Democratic Party politics in the circle around "Boss" Robert W. Speer. From 1899 to 1902, Fillius served as president of the city's board of supervisors, then helped draft the city charter. When Speer became mayor in 1904, he appointed his valued lieutenant president of the park board, which later named one of its greenswards Fillius Park.

For a man with a steely determination to beat back the "dangerous classes," urban parks may have had some of the meaning they had for the landscape architect Frederick Law Olmsted: not only pastoral enclaves in the tumultuous city but bastions of "courtesy, self-control, and temperance," of discipline appropriate to the new corporate ethos of cities like Denver.

Fillius's most significant affiliation, however, wasn't at City Hall, but with the dashing polo player, mine manager, and state adjutant general, Bulkeley Wells. For seven years, Fillius had been general counsel to the Smuggler-Union Mining Company and other mines under Wells's management; so close was the relationship that Wells and Fillius shared a suite of offices in Denver's Cooper Building. Not surprisingly, then, Fillius had been drawn into the activities of the Telluride Mine Owners Association and thence into the statewide Colorado Mining Association, the umbrella group encompassing the Telluride, Cripple Creek, and other mine owners organizations. Gradually, he assumed the role of the mine owners' principal attorney, long performed by the Cripple Creek lawyer Samuel Crump, whom Haywood regarded as "the most unscrupulous attorney in the legal profession." When Wells and other owners needed a liaison with the Idaho prosecutors, they turned to Fillius.

James McParland—who was on retainer to many of the Colorado mine owners—knew Fillius well. "A very safe lawyer and an old friend of mine," he wrote on April 4. "There is no doubt but what Mr. Fillius can be trusted." At the suggestion of Frank Cary, the Pinkertons' Denver superintendent, McParland agreed to send Orchard's and Adams's confessions, along with a stack of highly confidential agency reports, to Fillius's office "with the understanding that nobody but himself sees or knows contents of documents." Given McParland's fetish for secrecy and his distrust of outsiders, it was a favor he would have done few men.

Hawley was pleased with the choice of Fillius as well. Writing Bulkeley Wells on April 3, he said, "I had a letter from him, and I like the ring of the letter." He ended by reminding Wells that Idaho's prosecutors were "dreadfully handicapped" by lack of funds.

Two weeks later, on April 17, during a trip to Denver, Hawley met Fillius for the first time at the Brown Palace Hotel. They were joined in Hawley's room by Bulkeley Wells and James McParland for several hours of talk about the confessions, the need for more evidence, and "other matters." McParland was "very pleased" that Fillius had "grasped the idea of what is wanted." By then the prosecutors had made clear they didn't need Fillius as deputy trial counsel; the golden-throated Billy Borah could handle that job quite nicely, thank you. What the prosecutors needed was (1) someone to locate Colorado evidence and witnesses, funneling them north for the trial, and (2) money. Of those, the greater requirement by far was money.

The Pinkertons and the Idaho prosecutors had had their eyes on Colorado money from the start. Their expectations were awakened when the February 16 meeting in Governor McDonald's office, which sanctioned the seizure of Haywood, Moyer, and Pettibone, was attended by James Williams as representative for David H. Moffat and William G. Evans. The Moffat-Evans presence was significant in two respects: it signaled the full support of the state's Republican Party, controlled behind the scenes by Evans, Moffat, and Simon Guggenheim, and it demonstrated that much of the state's corporate elite would welcome Idaho's taking the WFM leaders off their hands and, if possible, hanging the trio.

In the heyday of union power in Colorado—from 1894 to 1904—"it became almost impossible to convict a union man of any offense," wrote an acute observer of Cripple Creek. "Juries could not be secured that would bring in verdicts of guilty. The defense of a union man might consist almost entirely in showing his union record and man after man of whose guilt there was the strongest evidence went scot free." Governor Peabody's increasing reliance on martial law and his defiance of habeas corpus reflected a perception, shared by his corporate allies, that the state's routine legal process didn't permit effective prosecution of union malefactors. By exporting their problem to Idaho, then financing the trial on a capital offense that carried the death penalty, Colorado's mine owners hoped to rid themselves forever of these apostles of disorder. Their message to their counterparts in Idaho was blunt: Here are the bodies, here is the money, please kill them for us.

All this was a bit distasteful to say aloud, but occasionally some plainspoken fellow blurted it out. Three days after the union leaders were put on the special in Denver, Floyd Thompson, the mine owners' secretary in Cripple Creek, told reporters that "the utmost satisfaction prevail[ed] among the mine owners of Colorado" because the union men's arrest promised an end to the "reign of terror" in Colorado mining camps. "Conviction has never been possible in that state, no matter how strong the evidence, because the organization [the WFM] was so thoroughly entrenched that one or more members would secure a place on every jury impaneled, so that if an acquittal was not had, the jury would fail to agree."

Sherman Bell, Colorado's former adjutant general, was both blunt and bitter. Now on the vaudeville stage in a melodrama called *Ding Dong Bell,* a rendition of his Colorado exploits, Bell nursed grievances against many Coloradans still in power—notably Bulkeley Wells, who'd taken his job ("a kindergarten cadet commander," he called him, "a blankety-blank pinhead").

But whatever Bell's motivation, he asked some inconvenient questions. "Why should they try these men in Idaho?" he asked a Denver reporter. "During the troubles here and before the murder of Steunenberg, there were 75 persons killed in Colorado.... One man was killed in Idaho and yet they take men from Colorado to Idaho to try them for crimes committed in Colorado. Why don't they try them here? We have courts. Is it because they are afraid? ... The whole thing is a farce. I detest the principles of Moyer and Haywood, but I think they should get a square deal.... You can say for Sherman Bell that those men are in reality being tried in Idaho, not for the murder of Steunenberg, but for murders in Colorado."

Bulkeley Wells tried mightily to put the best face on the kidnapping he'd overseen. "In my opinion," he told reporters in Boise, "Idaho is the place to try these men, and give them a chance to establish their claim of innocence. Conditions [in Colorado] are such that it is almost impossible to obtain a verdict, the difficulty being to secure juries that are not prejudiced one way or the other.... It will be different with a jury obtained from among the farming class, who are not identified with either the prosecution or the defense, nor concerned in the result save that justice be done."

Paul Thieman, the *Denver Post's* erudite editorial writer, found it a bit shameful: "They are examining the bloody Colorado finger marks and the Colorado blood clots and the tufts of gory hair left for sleuths in the course of Colorado crime, in Idaho—in IDAHO, mark you—let it sink deep—in IDAHO."

Even Jacob Fillius privately conceded that Idaho was doing Colorado's dirty work. "Had Colorado done its duty, as Idaho has done its duty," he wrote Hawley, "this trial at Boise would not and could not have taken place and the ex-governor would have been living today. I cannot but feel that it is a discredit and a shame on Colorado statehood and Colorado citizenship." Whatever his misgivings, Fillius did his best to make sure that Haywood, Moyer, and Pettibone never returned to Colorado alive. It was he who kept cash flowing to Boise to fuel the investigation. The quintessential inside man, he never talked to reporters and none ever smoked out his role. Moreover, he assiduously shielded his contributors. In letters to Hawley and McParland, the lawyer was exquisitely discreet about his donors. "The friends of law and order in Colorado," he called them, or "the parties directly in interest," or "those who are principally interested," or sometimes simply "we."

But their identities aren't much of a mystery. Three days after Hawley and Fillius met for the first time at the Brown Palace, McParland had "quite a long confidential talk" at the First National Bank with its president, David Moffat, a large, balding man with a fringe of white hair and a drooping white mustache. Present at the meeting were Moffat's close associate Walter Scott Cheesman, president of the Denver Union Water Company and vice president of the First National Bank, and James H. Wilkins, a prominent Denver real estate man. "Mr. Moffat congratulated me on the success we had made so far and wished me to convey his congratulations to Gov. Gooding for the noble stand that he was taking on this case," McParland reported. "He also expressed himself to the effect that he had talked with General Wells, and that the people in Colorado including himself would see to it that the State of Idaho should not lack for funds to carry on this prosecution."

In eliciting Moffat's support for his project, McParland surely mentioned that the tycoon figured on Orchard's target list. As the meeting ended, Moffat asked McParland to come see him again before returning to Idaho. So on May 8, McParland met for another two and a half hours with the bank president and William G. Evans, the president of the Denver Tramway Company, at Evans's office. "They both feel highly pleased at the condition of this case as it now stands," the detective recounted, "and informed me that when any financial help is needed Mr. Filius [sic] by making application to Mr. Evans or Mr. Moffat can secure the same."

Plainly, then, one source of funds available to Fillius was this cluster of powerful men who largely controlled Denver's public utilities, finance, and machine politics. Yet, as a mining attorney and close associate of Bulkeley Wells, Fillius drew his funds principally from Colorado's mine owners. If men like Moffat, Cheesman, and Evans had good reason to want Haywood, Moyer, and Pettibone out of the way, the men who operated the state's mines had still greater motivation. Wells himself and Moffat were large contributors to Fillius's fund. So, presumably, were most of the following: Eben Smith, Moffat's partner in his extensive Cripple Creek holdings, which included the Granite, the Anaconda, the Victor, the Antlers, and the Grey Eagle mines; Charles M. MacNeill, a dapper Chicagoan who, as vice president of the United States Reduction and Refining Company (better known as the mill trust), had impressed Bill Haywood as a "wretched little autocrat"; and MacNeill's partners in the Mill Trust, Spencer "Spec" Penrose, a Philadelphia blue blood whose brother was Boies Penrose, the powerful senator from Pennsylvania, and Charles Leaming Tutt, another Philadelphian, who'd found his way to Colorado Springs to sell real estate and insurance. Finally there was Albert E. "Bert" Carlton, a pale young man with "ice cold eyes" and a near monopoly on wagon transport in Cripple Creek. Carlton, MacNeill, Tutt, and Penrose had been known as the Socialites, a quartet of lusty young men who'd caroused through the night in Cripple Creek, playing poker or faro in the Bennett Avenue saloons or tasting the fleshier pleasures along Myers Avenue. By 1906, the Socialites were businessmen, and wealthy young men, with money to spare for a good cause up in Idaho.

Fillius dealt both collectively with the Colorado Mining Association and separately with individual donors, pooling the contributions at his office, then forwarding the money periodically to Boise. His deliveries were more sophisticated than Thompson's: always in cash, carried by couriers who could not be connected with the mine owners or other corporate interests. Indeed, at times the deliveries passed through such convoluted channels that the parties themselves couldn't be sure whether they'd been completed. "It is a surprise to me that the money of which I wrote you did not reach the party referred to," Fillius wrote Hawley on September 17, 1906. "I do not understand it, since the information as it came to me was entirely reliable. It is possible that the money has been placed in the hands of third parties for the present, and that it has not actually come to the hands of the party." The mine owners insisted on absolute secrecy and what in later years would be called "deniability." And, in that respect, they succeeded. As late as March 31, 1907, the *Denver Republican*—the voice of Colorado's business community—could blithely declare: "It is claimed by the defenders of the federation leaders that the Colorado mine owners or their association have contributed largely to the fund for the prosecution. This is an unqualified falsehood. The mine owners of this state have not given a cent, either directly or indirectly. Whatever is being done comes from the State of Idaho."

The mine owners' contributions were divided into two categories, one earmarked for the investigation and trial, the other for "political" purposes. The political contributions were intended to offset a determined effort by the WFM and its allies to defeat Governor Gooding in his reelection campaign. Fillius seemed satisfied that the Democratic candidate, Chief Justice Charles O. Stockslager, would, if elected, proceed with the WFM trials. Hawley, himself a Democrat, agreed that Stockslager was "a law and order man." A Socialist editor concurred, calling the Democratic candidate "a goody-goody old gentleman, who hasn't convictions enough to disagree with anybody." Nonetheless, a defeat for Gooding would be a major blow to the prosecution and could only sap the prosecutors' elan.

At times, Fillius reported difficulty in raising the political money. On June 26, 1906, he held out "little hope" for political contributions since the Coloradans had already given heavily for tough races in their own state. Similarly, on September 17, he wrote, "We are in the midst of political turmoil here, as you are there, and it is rather a bad time to raise additional funds." Later he warned, "Finances at this end are not in good shape."

But sometimes money flowed briskly into Fillius's coffers, particularly funds earmarked for the trial and investigation, a matter to which the Colorado donors assigned high priority. "Collections have been better than expected," Fillius wrote Hawley on one occasion.

It is difficult to say how much money passed through Fillius's hands destined for Idaho. But hints scattered through the surviving correspondence suggest that the total for both categories of contribution between April 1906 and August 1907 was between $75,000 and $100,000—some $1.4 to $1.8 million in today's money. And that wasn't all. In pursuit of Hawley's grand scheme for a united effort by the entire western mining industry, efforts were made to raise money outside Idaho and Colorado. On June 25, 1906, for example, McParland met in Salt Lake City with Roscoe H. Channing Jr., general manager of the Utah Consolidated Copper Mining Company (in which the Guggenheims had a substantial interest). Mr. Channing heard the detective out, then heartily agreed that "Utah ought to do its share." To that end, he said, "he was going to communicate with Mr. Fillius in Denver as it was as much their cause as it was that of the mine owners of Colorado." During the same trip, the detective also saw officials of the American Smelting and Refining Company and the United States Reduction and Refining Company, who "also expressed a desire to assist either financially or otherwise in this prosecution." In April 1907, Hawley wrote to J. W. Finch, manager of the Goldfield Consolidated Mines Company in Goldfield, Nevada, with his familiar pitch: "The lack of funds is our worst drawback." How much Channing or Finch chipped in is not clear, but the prosecution's war chest was almost certainly swelled by contributions from the other western mining states.

The prosecutors' favorite technique for raising money among the mine owners was to contrast their own perilous finances with those of the defense. "The defense will have unlimited money to carry on their end of the contest," Hawley wrote Stanley Easton on February 27.

"Unlimited" was a bit of calculated hyperbole, but there was ample reason to respect the WFM's fund-raising capacity. With nearly forty thousand members in two hundred chapters scattered across twelve states and parts of Canada, the union had a cadre passionately committed to the cause, which it could tap at will. From the start there was talk of assessing each member a dollar a month, and eventually the union did just that, producing something approaching $40,000 each month. But initially it depended on voluntary contributions to the defense fund, and for a time those poured in at an impressive rate.

Some of the bigger WFM locals made substantial contributions during 1906: $6,500 from the Goldfield (Nevada) Miners Union, $3,511 from the Butte Miners Union, $5,000 from the Butte Mill and Smeltermen's Union no. 74, $1,000 from the Tonopah (Nevada) Miners Union. In Silverton, Colorado, the miners union mortgaged its hall to come up with several thousand dollars for the defense fund. More money came from industrial unions in related fields: $5,000 from the Illinois district of the United Mine Workers of America, $1,000 from the American Flint Glass Workers Union in Toledo, Ohio.

In many mining camps, the union put the arm on local merchants who depended almost entirely on union members for their revenue. According to Thiel Operative 53 in Wallace, the Klondike saloon, Madden's saloon, Stillman's saloon, and "all of the gamblers except Sweet and Cault" had "contributed freely" to the union fund during April 1906. Three months later, the same operative reported that all the unions in the Coeur d'Alenes had assessed every member in good standing three dollars toward the defense fund. This produced $3,000 from the one thousand union men in Mullan, Burke, Murray, and Wallace. Across the country, union locals held dances, picnics, raffles, and other events to raise money for the fund. In New York City, a group of professional actors put on Julius Hopp's play *The Friends of Labor*, the proceeds earmarked for the fund.

Initially, the WFM harbored grandiose hopes for support from the IWW, of which Haywood had been a founder. With much fanfare, the organization set out to raise big money under the slogan "Shall our brothers be murdered?" But the fund drive foundered in the growing gulf between the WFM and the IWW. The WFM's acting secretary-treasurer, James Kirwan, told the national convention in 1907: "At one time I believed the IWW was doing good work in raising funds and in creating public sentiment throughout the country, but since that time I have learned that for every dollar they have collected we lost twenty or twenty-five." Ultimately, the IWW raised a modest $11,000.

The Socialist Party provided ample moral support. Two days after the three union men were arrested, its national secretary, J. Mahlon Barnes, sent them a telegram that said, in part, "The purchased confession, the secret special train makes the conspiracy of capitalism complete. Russian methods make pertinent the question: Is Colorado in America?" In March, the national executive committee called on all locals to hold "public indignation meetings" and collect funds for the defense of the imprisoned leaders. It promised to "tear the mask of respectability from these capitalist conspirators and reveal them for what they really are: adepts in small thievery as in grand larceny; skillful in purchasing a jury as in packing a jury; as smooth a set of pirates as ever cut a throat, stole the widow's mite or robbed the schoolhouse." Debs was unstinting in his support of the three prisoners, lending his powerful pen to the cause, racketing around the country giving hundreds of speeches in barns, at skating rinks, and in grange halls.

But several newspapers associated with the party's right wing, notably Milwaukee's *Social Democratic Herald* and the *Chicago Daily Socialist*, downplayed the case, often burying it deep on inside pages. For a time at least, the editors of both papers—Frederic Heath and Algie Simons—believed that Haywood, Moyer, and Pettibone were guilty and feared that support of them could prove embarrassing. This segment of the Socialist press emphasized the defendants' affiliation with the IWW and the WFM, ignoring their membership in the Socialist Party.

In the end, the party's fund-raising efforts proved meager. After a good start—nearly $2,500 in March and April 1906—contributions declined rapidly to $53.05 in September and $26.25 in October. In total, through 1906–07, the party raised almost exactly what the much smaller IWW had—about $11,000. Almost a third of this came from the party's Local New York. Local

Boise contributed $21.69, Local Caldwell $6.15. Northern Idaho mining camps did a bit better—Burke $35, Wallace $50.

Thomas A. Sladden, state secretary in Oregon and a prominent member of the party's left wing, chided his colleagues for their stingy support of the men on trial. "The Socialist Party," he wrote, "has been skulking in its tents while others bore the brunt of the battle. We have been long on sympathy and short on material aid. . . . Five cents of your loose change will buy more justice than a basket full of sympathy." Sladden wondered why the party hadn't simply assessed each member a dollar. "The Socialist Party is a dues-paying organization of at least 30,000 dues-paying members. Deducting for those who might be unable to pay, we should have raised $25,000. . . . I would hate to have my neck in a noose and my party depending upon raising funds in a basket like the Salvation Army on a street corner raising funds to save the unwashed."*

The American Federation of Labor wasn't much more forthcoming. Sam Gompers still regarded the WFM as "antagonistic to the trade union movement." He wasn't in close touch with the miners and had to get the proceedings of their 1906 convention from John Mitchell of the United Mine Workers, who obtained it through the Thiel Detective Service. Nonetheless, he felt American labor "could not abandon the labor men helpless to the vengeance of employers who were in control of the machinery of the state."

In April 1906, he wrote in the AFL's journal, the *American Federationist:* "It is well known that we have markedly differed and still differ from the policy of the officers of the Western Federation of Miners. . . . Their conception and ours of the work and tactics of labor are as far apart as the poles, but this can not and will not interfere with our conception of and standing for the lawful rights to which they are entitled equally with any other men under the sun. Nor is it right or fair to regard these men as already guilty because some hireling of a detective agency, anxious to make a record, so as to earn his blood money, so charges." At his request, the executive council appropriated a relatively small sum—the Pinkertons said $5,000—for the defense fund. McParland thought he knew why the AFL had been so stingy: "Gompers is well aware that the Inner Circle of the Western Federation of Miners is simply a crowd of murderers."

Certainly, Gompers resisted further public identification with their cause. In December 1906, following the Supreme Court's refusal to grant

---

* In fairness to the party, it should be noted that it had fewer potential contributors than appeared on its membership rolls, so heavily had it been infiltrated by private detectives and other agents. A St. Louis detective named Charles F. Evers wrote Hawley that the three-man Socialist delegation that approached the Denver AFL asking it to join demonstrations against Haywood, Moyer, and Pettibone's kidnapping had consisted of himself (then operating under cover for the Master Brewers Association), a man named Charles F. Heintz ("who I later discovered was a detective employed by a firm in Cleveland"), and "a Mr. Sullivan, a radical Socialist who drove a one-horse express wagon" (Evers to Hawley, June 21, 1907).

habeas corpus to Haywood and his colleagues, J. Mahlon Barnes asked him to convene a national conference of labor organizations "to provide means of protection, methods of defense and channels of publicity on behalf of Moyer, Haywood and Pettibone." This request was supported by petitions signed by twenty-seven labor leaders in Chicago, Cincinnati, and Indianapolis. Gompers wrote the AFL's Executive Council of his "grave doubt" that such a conference would "accomplish any good results for the men"; after all, he wrote, "agitation is one thing; tangible and practical results are another." The eleven-man council was polled by telephone. Three members favored a conference, among them John Mitchell of the United Mine Workers, who'd promised Darrow his support in the case. But seven others rallied round the AFL president, and the motion was defeated.

When New York City's Central Federated Union asked again for a conference in January 1907, Gompers rejected it again, prompting a Socialist delegate to charge that the AFL president was "lukewarm" about the WFM's cause. An angry Gompers shot back, "I have not stood on soap boxes in the streets and shouted about this affair, but I have done all that could be done."

In April 1907, the Cigarmakers International Union asked Gompers to raise more money for the WFM's defense fund. In turning it down, he said the request followed too soon on the AFL's appeal to American workers to donate a day's pay for the working men of devastated San Francisco. If the earthquake had not occurred, he replied, the AFL might have done something for the WFM, but a call now "would yield little or nothing."

Relations between Gompers and the WFM men were strained enough by mid-June when Edmund Richardson received a letter, purportedly from Gompers, that threatened to widen the breach. "Dear Sir," it read, "You certainly have shown the utmost incompetence in the management of your case, and have made a horrible mess of the whole thing. If you had been the prosecution's own lawyer you could not have been of more use to them, in delivering halters to your clients. Disgustedly yours, Samuel Gompers."

Though they knew Gompers wished to keep his distance from the defense, the attorneys and their clients could scarcely believe that he would deliver his message so crudely. Richardson sent the letter to Gompers in Washington, asking if he was the author. In reply, the AFL chief was stunned that "you should have even harbored the thought." He promptly assured both Richardson and Darrow that it was a forgery. Whoever sent it clearly wished to increase the bad feeling between Gompers and the defense. That would have served the prosecution's purpose and it may well have been one of McParland's gambits, but the author was never traced.

Far and away the most effective means of mobilizing support for the imprisoned men were the so-called Moyer-Haywood conferences, umbrella groups organized in many communities around the country by patchwork coalitions of Socialists, unionists, Wobblies, Prohibitionists, reformers, radicals, and food faddists. The conferences staged rallies, marches, forums, and discussions; distributed literature; and undertook a wide range of fund-raising activities. Some groups—notably in Boston and New York—were remarkably effective; others—as in Chicago—were ineffectual. Usher Solomon, secretary of New York City's Socialist Party, told the press that across the country, as of April 1, the conferences had raised $101,587 and had already forwarded $92,000 to the defense fund. Since then, many large contributions had been received. "There are 3,000,000 organized workers in this country alone," he said, "and we expect to eventually raise $1,000,000." This was a trifle optimistic. One authority concludes they probably raised "tens of thousands of dollars."

Operating out of WFM headquarters in Denver, the Moyer-Haywood Defense Fund was a well-staffed, shrewdly managed undertaking. The official WFM accounting showed $262,727.85 raised between February 1906 and March 1908, a figure that more or less jibes with Elizabeth Gurley Flynn's later estimate of $300,000. As early as April 1906, *Wilshire's Magazine* asserted that "$200,000 has been subscribed for the defense fund, and $1,000,000 can be had if necessary." In February 1907, the *Idaho Daily Statesman* talked of a fund of "gigantic proportions," which would soon reach $300,000. A Pinkerton operative overheard George W. Goebel, national organizer of the Socialist Party, say that by March 1 the defense fund was expected to reach $500,000.

According to McParland, there was a clear channel for all funds flowing into the defense camp: the WFM turned its money over to Horace W. Hawkins, Edmund Richardson's law partner, who passed it by courier to Richardson in Boise, who in turn passed it through John Nugent to Leon O. Whitsell, a twenty-six-year-old Coeur d'Alene lawyer who was the "dispensing agent" for all funds expended in Idaho. We can't be sure how much money passed through this channel, but the defense never seemed strapped for cash.

All the aid and comfort supplied by labor and its allies seemed for a time as if it would be overwhelmed by the personal intervention of the president of the United States and the resources at his disposal.

If Theodore Roosevelt had an industrial policy, one critic thought, it was "to cuff the radical on one ear and the conservative on the other, without enlightening either." The president's habit of "balancing the blame"—between tyranny on one side, anarchy on the other—once appealed to the muckraker Ray Stannard Baker as a judicious response to industrial strife. How, after all, could one argue with an evenhanded formulation like this: "I believe in corporations; I believe in trade unions. Both have come to stay, and are necessities in our present industrial system. But where, in either the one or the other, there develops corruption or mere brutal indifference to the rights of others, and short-sighted refusal to look beyond the moment's gain, then the offender, whether union or corporation, must be fought."

But Baker came to regard the president's reflexive balancing—which led some newspapers to call him "the man on two horsebacks"—as a way of skirting the hard issues in labor-capital relations. Roosevelt could be found on all sides of these questions. As a state legislator, he supported a controversial bill to abolish cigar manufacturing in tenements but opposed legislation setting a twelve-hour limit for horsecar drivers. As governor, he pushed through a raft of social legislation, much of it favored by labor, but any strike was apt to prompt a call for troops. As president, he railed against the trusts but, by his own admission, "let up in every case where [he] had any possible excuse for so doing"; he championed reform but detested many reformers. Over a long public career, he was neither as supportive to the corporation men as they felt was their due from one of his social standing nor as compassionate to the workingmen as they felt was justified by their grievances.

While he distributed praise in equal dosage, it was excoriation—scrupulously impartial excoriation—that he relished. Rare is the president who doesn't discover the pleasures of seizing the middle ground while lustily reviling marginal voters on both flanks. But for Roosevelt, these maledictions flung left and right, with "a newspaperman's crispness and a boxer's punch," were as much temperamental as tactical. (One evening of this fulmination sent Henry Adams from the table muttering, "The very buffalo must run.") His choice of classical allusion was inevitable when he exhorted Americans to steer a middle course between "the Scylla of mob rule and the Charybdis of subjection to a plutocracy." As one historian has written, "The straddle was built like functional furniture into his thinking."

In early 1906, he applied this frame of mind to the Haywood case: "We can no more and no less afford to condone evil in the man of capital than evil in the man of no capital. The wealthy man who exults because there is a failure of justice in the effort to bring some trust magnate to account for his misdeeds is as bad as, and no worse than, the so-called labor leader [Debs] who clamorously strives to excite a foul class feeling on behalf of some other labor leader who is implicated in murder [Haywood]. One attitude is as bad as the other, and no worse."

The president's chronic balancing drove some of labor's partisans to distraction. When the socialist writer Robert Hunter told Mother Jones of a visit to the White House in which the president said all the Western Federation leaders as well as the beef trust men should be hung, she wrote, "If I had been there I would have told him to go down to the Senate of the United States and take a rope with him, and hang some of those commercial pirates."

Nonetheless, Roosevelt believed it was his role to buffer the collision of capital and labor, to stave off the class war that the ideologues on either side loved to invoke. "It would be a dreadful calamity," he wrote Philander Knox, his attorney general, "if we saw this country divided into two parties, one containing the bulk of the property owners and conservative people, the other the bulk of the wageworkers and the less prosperous people generally; each party insisting upon demanding much that was wrong, and each party sullen and angered by real and fancied grievances."

Increasingly, Roosevelt rationalized his instinctive burrowing toward the middle with a more abstract notion of building a national community, in which class, racial, and sectional interests would converge in pursuit of the common interest. Indeed, as the years went by, he saw himself as representing a kind of golden mean transcending the contending classes, an impartial arbiter devoted to the national good.

To his friend Cecil Spring-Rice, the British minister in Teheran, he wrote, "Here at home I am engaged in the pleasing task of trying to prevent the plutocracy on the one hand and the anarchistic labor group on the other from traveling exactly the same paths that in Russia have made the autocracy and the wild-eyed radicals almost equally impossible and equally dangerous to the future of the country."

Many of those on whom Roosevelt relied sprang from great wealth, inherited or earned: Elihu Root, Philander Knox, Nelson W. Aldrich, Robert Bacon, James Stillman, and George W. Perkins. Nonetheless, he was convinced that other financiers and industrialists were determined to frustrate his reforms. His evisceration of such capitalists could be fierce. He spoke of "the dull, purblind folly of the very rich man," of their "swinish greed," of "the representatives of predatory wealth, of wealth accumulated on a giant scale by iniquity, by wrongdoing in many forms, by open swindling, by manipulating securities, by unfair and unwholesome competition, and by stockjobbing, in short by conduct abhorrent to every man of ordinarily decent conscience."

In these indignant ventilations one senses less fear or hatred than contempt. It is the disdain of an aristocrat dedicated to public service toward men who devote their lives to the accumulation of wealth. When only twenty-eight, he noted that the commercial classes "regard everything merely from the standpoint of 'Does it pay?' and many a merchant does not take any part in politics because he is short-sighted ... and too selfish to be willing to undergo any trouble for the sake of abstract duty; while the younger men of this type are too much engrossed in their various social pleasures to be willing to give up their time to anything else."

To Roosevelt, these "Bourbons" were great vulgarians. "I know the banker, merchant and railroad king well," he wrote the critic and essayist Brander Mathews, "and they also need education and sound chastisement." Later he would say, "Of all forms of tyranny, the least attractive and the most vulgar is the tyranny of mere wealth, the tyranny of plutocracy." At the root of these denunciations lay an aesthetic judgment, a fine distaste for men who might have led graceful lives and instead sullied them by loutishness. And such men, he lamented to the novelist Owen Wister, had somehow mobilized virulent support among the people who should have been his allies, "the gentlefolk, the people whom you and I meet at the houses of our friends and at our clubs; the people who went to Harvard as we did."

His instinctive response to aggressive labor has a different smell—the high, acrid tang of fear. One historian aptly calls it "a morbid fear of social violence," a "jagged dread of violent revolution." For Roosevelt, John Altgeld was a traitor, Thomas Paine "a filthy little atheist." To his friend John Strachey, he confessed, "At times I feel an almost Greek horror of extremes." Confiding in the diplomat Henry White, he imagined that some blundering official "would by his actions awake the slumbering popular distrust and cause a storm in which he would be as helpless as a child."

This anxiety, in turn, elicited Roosevelt's most preposterous rodomontade. During the social convulsions of the 1880s and 1890s, when politicians of all stripes revealed themselves, Roosevelt postured and pontificated. After the Haymarket affair, he blustered from his ranch that his cowboys would like "a chance with rifles at one of the mobs." To a New York audience, he noted "there is but one answer to be made to the dynamite bomb, and that can best be made by the Winchester Rifle." The Pullman strike evoked a sanguinary vision: "I like to see a mob handled by the regulars, or by good State-Guards, not over-scrupulous about bloodshed." In his gut, he knew that sooner or later there would be "a riotous, wicked, murderous day of atonement." According to a report by Willis J. Abbott, an avid Populist, in Hearst's *New York Evening Journal*—which Roosevelt would later call "a tissue of lies"—his response to 1896's great Free Silver crusade ran as follows: "The sentiment now animating a large proportion of our people can only be suppressed as the Commune in Paris was suppressed, by taking ten or a dozen of their leaders out, standing . . . them against a wall, and shooting them dead. I believe it will come to that. These leaders are plotting a social revolution and the subversion of the American Republic."

This, by the way, while that "arch conservative" Mark Hanna was chuckling to his terrified friends at the Union Club: "There won't be any revolution. You're just a lot of damn fools!"

Much has been written about young "Teedie" Roosevelt's conquering infirmity through pure grit. The story is vastly appealing: the frail child who suffered nausea and fevers, vowing at age twelve, "I'll make my body," and pursuing that course with "bulldog tenacity" in daily sessions at Wood's Gymnasium. The results of this regimen have been celebrated as well: the robust stalwart, his chest filled out, his arms newly muscled, battling the western rapids, riding the Dakota badlands, hunting big game, knocking down a barroom tough, eventually leading his own cavalry regiment up Kettle Hill and into history.

It has been widely assumed that this physical transformation was matched by a psychic one, in which young Roosevelt's childhood fears and adolescent doubts were brushed aside by a bristling self-confidence, a virile gusto for life in all its guises.

But had those phantoms of the nursery really vanished so quickly? Wasn't there something about the Haymarket rioters, the Pullman picketers, the Free Silver men of 1896, the miners of the WFM—all those bullyboy whose muscular vitality he tried so hard to ape—that made him feel again like the sickly Teedie enduring the jibes and jabs of his streetwise contemporaries? Why else did he denounce "any kind of class animosity" as positively "wicked"? Why else was he obsessed by the prospect of turning his Winchester on the rabble?

From the start, Roosevelt was predisposed to believe the worst about Haywood, Moyer, and the WFM. Despite his admonitions to Gooding about neutrality and fairness, his letters make plain he'd already concluded that the three union leaders were guilty. Over and over, he referred to them as "thugs and murderers," "infamous creatures," and "infamous scoundrels." In a draft of his first letter for Governor Gooding's eyes, he called them "the murderers of ex-Governor Steunenberg"; only after William Loeb, his secretary, had typed the letter did the president prudently revise it in ink to read "the men charged with the murder of...." This kind of slip occurred several more times in the next few months.

But he could be more explicit. "That Moyer and Haywood are morally guilty for not the occasional murders but the hundreds of murders perpetrated under the foulest and most infamous circumstances by the members of the WFM is so clear that no honest man who knows the facts and is not blinded by disqualifying prejudices can contradict it," he wrote Lawrence Abbott, Lyman's son, in 1906. To William Allen White, he wrote of his effort to "back up the party of law and order, of elementary civilization, in Idaho, against the thugs and murderers who've found their typical representation in Moyer and Haywood."

On one crucial question—the propriety of the union leaders' "extradition" to Idaho—the president had made up his mind long before he received Robb's report. To Lawrence Abbott on April 28—twelve days before the assistant attorney general submitted his report—the president wrote, "It is absolutely certain that they ought to have been extradited from Colorado to Idaho; and any failure to comply with ordinary formalities, if such exists, is of no consequence whatever."

The president wholly accepted James McParland's leitmotiv. "I think the Western Federation of Miners is a body just exactly like the Molly Maguires of Pennsylvania," he wrote Lyman Abbott. "That there are a number of good, honest and stupid men in their ranks I have no doubt, just as I have no doubt that this was true of the Molly Maguires." Their moving spirit could be seen as a revolt against economic or social injustice "only in the sense that we thus describe a band of road agents who rob a coach."

In the summer of 1906, Roosevelt had outrage left over for plenty of others. Some of his most scathing polemics were reserved for class traitors, those men of breeding and taste who broke ranks in a crisis to join the ragtag mob at the gates. To his friend Henry Cabot Lodge, he wrote: "You and I have now been in active politics together for about a quarter of a century, and during that time if I were asked to single out the people whom, for moral and intellectual dishonesty, I thought lowest, I should single out the professional mugwump, the goo-goo class, the professional followers of the *Nation,* the *Evening Post,* and the like; the men who naturally become anti-imperialists, just as they naturally become mugwumps; the men who idealized [the re-former Carl] Schurz, [E. L.] Godkin [editor of the *Nation*], and the other precious scoundrels whose hypocrisy, mendacity and venom naturally at-tracted them."

For Roosevelt in 1906, the very model of the goo-goo who dabbled with revolution, the mugwump who should have known better was Norman Hapgood. Born into a distinguished American family, educated (with his brothers, Hutchins and William) at Harvard, blessed with a felicitous writing style and broad cultural background, renowned for a time as a shrewd critic of the Broadway stage, now the editor of *Collier's,* a participant in the era's muckraking journalism, Hapgood had become a burr under Roosevelt's sad-dle during the 1904 campaign. Then, in early 1906, he became passionately interested in the events that flowed from Steunenberg's assassination. When, in his May 5 "Idaho on Trial" editorial, he suggested "collusion" between Idaho's authorities and the mine owners, he drew Roosevelt's fire, a thunder-ous cannonade all spring and summer.

To Calvin Cobb, the president wrote: "I cannot express my contempt and indignation for the men like Norman Hapgood who, sitting in their editorial sanctums, wholly without any experience with the rough and dan-gerous side of life, and with to their account the minimum credit of manly work, yet condemn explicitly or implicitly, men like the Governor, who is doing the work of civilization on the dangerous frontier of our social life." To Lodge, the president described Hapgood as a "conceited and insincere jack of the advanced mugwump type."

Roosevelt was obsessed with Hapgood's class betrayal. When the editor struck back, accusing the president of a habitual practice of "calling newspa-per men before him to tell them something, and then later denying the statement," Roosevelt responded in two disdainful letters. His ultimate in-dictment of this fellow Harvardian was that he had not abided by "the usages which obtain among gentlemen." The characterization was a curious one because many of those who knew the lean, beak-nosed Hapgood thought he was simply too cerebral and refined for the muckraking life.

But none of that mattered to the president once his dander was up. He couldn't dislike without detesting, exhilarated—as Booth Tarkington noted —by the sheer "fun of hating." Upton Sinclair recalled a visit to the White House when the president began talking about Senator Eugene Hale of Maine, whom he called "the Senator from the Shipbuilding Trust." Sinclair suggested that "if you want to get the full effect of it, sit at a table, clench your fist and hit the table at every accented syllable: 'The most in-*nate*-ly and es-*sen*-tial-ly mal-*e*-vo-lent *scoun*-drel that God *Almight*-y *ev*-er *put* on *earth!*' "

The other comment the Roosevelt-Hapgood correspondence inspires is that of his good friend Cecil Spring-Rice: "You must always remember that the President is about six."

That autumn, Roosevelt's attention was diverted to another target—a titan of industry who, in the president's resonant iconography, had become the personification of the "malefactor of great wealth" and who, ultimately, would serve as the perfect counterweight in the president's campaign of denunciation against Bill Haywood.

Edward Henry Harriman was the son of a threadbare Episcopal clergyman. Quitting school at fourteen, he found his natural habitat on Wall Street. As if bred for the harum-scarum of the financial markets, he snatched his prizes on the run. Starting as a broker's clerk, he had a partnership by eighteen and his own seat on the exchange at twenty-two; by thirty-five he presided over the Sodus Bay and Southern Railroad; by forty, thanks to keeping his nerve while others were losing theirs, he was a millionaire several times over; by fifty, he'd gained control of the Union Pacific, which he soon made the nation's prime railroad property.

Along the way, he made few friends and many enemies. "A cold-blooded little cuss," an associate called him. "At the present moment, Mr. Harriman enjoys more genuine ill-will than any other man in the country," a commentator wrote in 1907. A reporter summed up his reputation: "a thing cold as ice, hard as steel, morally insentient as a granite boulder, a brain of machinery, precise and tireless and, in lieu of two hands and ten fingers, an infinitude of restless tentacles reaching into myriad pocketbooks, spreading resistlessly over public lands, absorbing public grants and public franchises and public property wherever it is not strongly fastened." To a rival, he "would have been a wonderful character if only he had a heart."

The flesh-and-blood Harriman proved less forbidding. A stooped little man, with rimless glasses and a walrus mustache, he reminded one interviewer of "a Frenchman of the small professional type." His manner was "cold and dry," reflecting perhaps "a studied reserve, a careful holding of himself in leash, a fixed resolve that no man should be able to guess the real thoughts and motives which lay within his mind." By some accounts he was a tender husband, a model father of five, an avid hunter and hiker at Arden, his estate near Tarrytown, New York.

The private Harriman may have been harmless enough, but set loose in the financial world, he was a holy terror, a pitiless antagonist who tightened the noose on his adversaries until they cried uncle. Otto Kahn, the financier, once tried to persuade him that he could achieve the same goals by "less combative, more gentle methods." The magnate refused: that would be to "compromise with my nature." When Jacob Schiff of Kuhn, Loeb and Company sought to reorganize the Union Pacific, he felt hemmed in at every turn. Seeking the source of his troubles, he consulted Pierpont Morgan, who reported: "It's that little fellow, Harriman, and you want to look out for him." That was the word on Harriman: Look out.

As prominent New Yorkers, Harriman and Roosevelt had long enjoyed amiable relations. A committed Republican, the financier furnished Roosevelt and his party with money and advice. The two attended each other's receptions, dined at each other's table. Yet, as each grew in ambition, collisions were inevitable.

The first came with the 1901 incorporation of the Northern Securities Company, the vehicle designed to end the war for control of northwestern railroads between Harriman's Union Pacific interests and James J. Hill's Great Northern group. The object was clear: a vast new railroad monopoly dominated jointly by Harriman and Hill. An argument could be made for rationalizing railroad ownership into a few transcontinental lines. But, suspicious as always of these rich men, Roosevelt wouldn't hear it. In February 1902, without consulting anyone except Attorney General Knox, Roosevelt unleashed "a thunderbolt out of a clear sky," ordering his Justice Department to seek dissolution of Northern Securities under the Sherman Antitrust Act. In April 1903, a district court ruled for the government. Finally, in March 1904, by a narrow five-to-four margin—with Holmes, to the president's fury, dissenting —the Supreme Court upheld the lower court and ordered the company dissolved. James Hill vented his spleen: "It seems hard that we should be compelled to fight for our lives against the political adventurers who have never done anything but pose and draw a salary." Harriman glowered silently.

Then, in December 1905, Roosevelt drove another spike in the relationship when he sought new powers for the Interstate Commerce Commission to regulate the railroad industry. Like other railroad men, Harriman deeply resented this effort and fought tenaciously to defeat the measure in Congress.

But the two were, as the president wrote, "practical men." They still talked and corresponded. The president consulted Harriman on policy and drafts of legislation. Harriman was always ready to deal. After all, Roosevelt was still president and Harriman's far-flung interests needed government favors. But Roosevelt remained deeply wary of the grandee whose resistance to regulation was fierce and whose thirst for new railroad properties was well-nigh unslakable.

The president was uncomfortable when his daughter Alice struck up a friendship with Harriman's daughter Mary. As usual, Alice did just as she pleased. The president's sister Bamie was more sensitive to her brother's feelings: when the elder Harriman came to call, bringing her son Sheffield an elaborate model train set—of all things!—Bamie sensed that the present could put the president in an awkward position and ordered it returned to the Union Pacific.

Four months later, another contretemps exacerbated these tensions. At the Harvard-Yale regatta, while thousands watched from the river banks, Harriman and three guests left his yacht to board a small motor launch. With the magnate himself at the helm, it sped after the shells. This was a violation of federal safety regulations, for a crew could be capsized by the heavy swells. Regatta officials signaled Harriman to drop back, but he ignored their warnings. Ultimately, Roosevelt's naval aide—aboard the committee boat— ordered the speedster placed under arrest. His brief detention put Harriman in "a very ungracious mood."

But the most serious breach was rooted in a misunderstanding—perhaps willful—during Roosevelt's 1904 reelection campaign. The episode began shortly after the GOP convention, at which Roosevelt won the presidential nomination for a full term and Harriman served as a Roosevelt delegate. Having sent the president a congratulatory note, Harriman left for Europe. During his two-month absence came the president's reply, thanking him and asking to see him as soon as he returned. Back from Europe, Harriman wrote that he would be glad to see the president. "The situation," he reported, "could not be in better shape." But the "situation"—Republican electoral prospects in New York—wasn't so good. The Republican gubernatorial candidate, Frank W. Higgins, a Harriman ally, was plainly in trouble. The Republican State Committee pleaded for $200,000 from the National Committee, which said it couldn't afford it. In early October, a committeeman, Senator Nathan B. Scott of West Virginia, warned the president about the probability of a gubernatorial defeat but assured him there was no danger of his losing New York. Roosevelt said, "I would rather lose the election in the country than be defeated in my own state."

Shortly after this conversation, the president wrote Harriman: "In view of the trouble over the State ticket in New York, I would like to have a few words with you. Do you think you can get down here within a few days and take either luncheon or dinner with me?" Four days later, Roosevelt wrote still again, noting rumors that Harriman was reluctant to see him in the closing weeks of the campaign and offering to defer the meeting until after the election. In this veiled manner, Roosevelt seemed to be reacting to charges made by his Democratic opponent, Judge Alton B. Parker, that the White House, through the Republican National Committee, was extorting money from corporate trusts by "blackmail" as well as with promises of certain immunities or favors. But the letter served another purpose, creating the documentary evidence that any visit Harriman might make to Washington was on his initiative and for objects of his own.

If Harriman was sensitive about appearing at the White House, he gave no sign of it. For in the last week of October, he went to Washington and met with the president.

Here the president's version and Harriman's diverge dramatically. According to Harriman, the president told him "he understood the [New York] campaign could not be successfully carried on without sufficient money and asked if I would help them in raising the necessary funds." Harriman said he told the president that "the difficulty here" was mainly caused by a revolt of upstate leaders unwilling to support Chauncey M. Depew, the railroad lawyer turned president of the New York Central Railroad, for reelection as United States senator. "If he, Depew, could be taken care of in some other way I thought matters could be adjusted and the different contending parties brought into close alliance again. We talked over what could be done for Depew and, finally, he agreed that if found necessary he would appoint him as Ambassador to Paris.

"With full belief that he, the President, would keep this agreement," Harriman returned to New York, called "an intimate friend" of Senator Depew's and told him that it was necessary to raise $250,000—$200,000 of it for the Republican State Committee—and that, if he would help, "I would subscribe $50,000." Within three or four hours, the $200,000 was raised—reportedly from J. Pierpont Morgan, the railroad magnate William K. Vanderbilt, Sr., and the banker Hamilton Mck. Twombley—and the checks handed over to the National Committee. "This enabled the New York State Committee to continue its work, with the result that at least 50,000 votes were turned in the city of New York alone, making a difference of 100,000 votes in the general result." Although Harriman never quite said so, the implication was that the president's real motive in calling him to Washington was not so much to save Higgins as to rescue his own position in his home state, a state critical to his reelection.

After New York went for both Higgins and Roosevelt, Harriman stopped off at the White House, where, he said, the President "told me that he did not think it necessary to appoint Depew as Ambassador to Paris, as agreed."

If this transaction took place as Harriman alleged, one newspaper later noted, "Mr. Roosevelt was guilty of corruptly inducing Harriman, a great railway magnate, to contribute, and induce others to contribute, a large sum of money to elect him to the Presidency." Moreover, the president would also have engaged in a blatant double-cross.*

Although the whole story of the Harriman-Roosevelt imbroglio was to become public later, the first inkling the president had of these charges came two years later, on Sunday, October 7, 1906. Roosevelt had spent a busy Sabbath afternoon conferring with Senator Albert J. Hopkins of Illinois,

---

* Whatever the quid pro quo, there is ample evidence that industrialists and financiers contributed heavily to the Republican campaign that fall: J. P. Morgan, $150,000; H. H. Rodgers and John D. Archbold of Standard Oil, $100,000; C. S. Mellon, $50,000; George W. Perkins of New York Life Insurance, $50,000—in total $2,195,000 poured into the Republican campaign coffers, 72 percent from corporations. According to authoritative accounts, a desperate president summoned a group of monied men—including Harriman, Twombley, Henry Clay Frick, and Thomas Lamont—to a hush-hush White House breakfast where he told them that if they gave him the money he needed they'd have nothing to fear from him during his second term. When the reelected president promptly renewed his denunciations of the "malefactors of great wealth," Frick, who'd kicked in $100,000, said, "We bought the son of a bitch and then he didn't stay bought" (Harbaugh, *Power*, 227; R. O'Connor, *Courtroom*, 263; U.S. Senate Subcommittee, *Campaign Contributions*, 438–39; Villard, *Fighting*, 177–82; Wiebe, *Search*, 182).

chairman of the Senate Fisheries Committee, described by *Harper's Weekly* as "a rustic lawyer and an enemy of enlightenment," and Senator Boies Penrose, Pennsylvania's unsavory Republican boss. That evening he met for dinner with James S. "Sunny Jim" Sherman, an influential New York congressman then chairing the Republican congressional campaign committee. The subject was the off-year election, now barely a month away, "the President being anxious to know how things were going," the *Washington Post* reported the next day, "and Mr. Sherman being equally anxious to take advantage of the excellent political advice of the President."

In the president's account, the discussion was anything but a routine survey of the political landscape. It was largely devoted to Sherman's report on Harriman's unexpected response when asked to contribute to the campaign of Charles Evans Hughes, the Republican candidate, against William Randolph Hearst, the Democrat, for governor of New York. The flamboyant publisher, with his "yellow" tabloids, his "rabble-rousing" advocacy of municipal ownership of utilities, and his overweening ambition, was a man the president specially detested, regarding him as "the most potent single force for evil we have in our life." Roosevelt feared there was "literally nothing at which [Hearst] would stop in the way of adding fuel to the fire of discontent, reasonable or unreasonable, innocent or fraught with destruction to the whole body politic." Bad enough that Hughes might lose to the vulgar Hearst; worse yet, the publisher threatened to use his victory to launch his own radical pursuit of the presidency. "The producing classes should stand shoulder to shoulder against the exploiting corporations," Hearst had thundered in New York that fall, to the dismay of most men of means. He'd urged an eight-hour workday, a two-cent railroad fare, control of monopolies, and "Americanism." When Sherman called on Harriman early in October, he had every reason to expect a substantial contribution to slam the door on the bolshevist upstart. Instead, the railroad magnate bluntly refused and in explanation, read him a letter he'd written in January 1906 to Sidney Webster, a New York lawyer, describing his dealings with the president.

What Sherman claims to have heard that day—and what he passed on to Roosevelt on October 7—was so extraordinary that the two men hashed it over until well past midnight. Even after the congressman left, the president brooded through the early morning hours. Writing to Henry Cabot Lodge later that day, he described himself as "more shocked than I can say" at the tone, the sheer "naked brutality" of Harriman's remarks to Sherman. Moreover, they echoed what he'd heard Sunday afternoon from Boies Penrose about similar threats by "the Standard Oil people" unless Roosevelt dropped antitrust suits against them. "Do you wonder that I feel pretty hot with them?" he asked "Pinky" Lodge.

At dawn on October 8, the president rose to dictate to his secretary, William Loeb, a long letter to Sherman summarizing the congressman's report of the night before. It was less a letter than a form of record keeping.

Roosevelt routinely wrote these "posterity letters" (what would later be called "memos to the file"), preserving the material for future use. So dedicated was he to this technique that people said that, if the mutilated remains of his grandmother were to be found in his basement, he would at once be able to produce a letter utterly proving his innocence of the crime.

> You informed me that [Harriman] expressed great dissatisfaction with me, and said, in effect, that as long as I was at the head of the Republican Party or as it was dominated by the policies which I advocate and represent, he would not support it, and was quite indifferent whether Hearst beat Hughes or not, whether the Democrats carried Congress or not. He gave as a reason for his personal dislike of me partly my determination to have the railroads supervised, and partly the alleged fact that after [asking him to raise $250,000] and promising him to appoint Depew Ambassador to France, I failed to do it.

As for Harriman's characterization of their 1904 conversation, the president heatedly denied that he'd ever asked him to raise $250,000 for the presidential campaign. "Any such statement is a deliberate and willful untruth —by rights it should be characterized by an even shorter and more ugly word." In fact, the president said, "our communications as regards the campaign related exclusively to the fight being made against Mr. Higgins for Governor of New York, Mr. Harriman being immensely interested in the success of Mr. Higgins because he regarded the attack on Higgins as being really an attack on him." Finally, Harriman had indeed asked him to appoint Chauncey Depew ambassador to France, to which the president had said he "did not believe it would be possible."

"Far more important," the president told Sherman, "are the additional remarks [Harriman] made to you, as you inform me, when you asked him if he thought it was well to see Hearstism and the like triumphant over the Republican Party." These remarks—according to Sherman—were that "he did not care in the least; because those people were crooks and he could buy them; that whenever he wanted legislation from a State Legislature he could buy it; that he 'could buy Congress,' and that if necessary he 'could buy the judiciary.'" Roosevelt went on: "This was doubtless said partly in boastful cynicism and partly in a mere burst of bad temper because of his objection to the interstate commerce law and to my actions as President. But it shows a cynicism and deep-seated corruption which makes the man uttering such sentiments, and boasting, no matter how falsely, of his power to perform such crimes, at least as undesirable a citizen as Debs, or Moyer, or Haywood."

The last sentence was a formulation dear to the president's heart— precisely the kind of balanced excoriation in which Roosevelt reveled. To embrace four of his antagonists in one omnibus phrase must have struck him as a nifty piece of work.

One of the president's closest advisers had chastised him of late for dwelling on the dangers of the great trusts while letting the anarchists and the demagogues off lightly. In a major address in Harrisburg, Pennsylvania, on October 4, Roosevelt had once more denounced the "grave abuses" of giant corporations, proclaiming "our clear duty to see, in the interest of the people, that there is adequate supervision and control over the business use of the swollen fortunes of today, and also wisely to determine the conditions upon which these fortunes are to be transmitted and the percentage that they should pay to the Government whose protecting arm alone enables them to exist." To anxious old money, that sounded like the dread inheritance tax. Henry Cabot Lodge, one of the few men in the world the president allowed to call him Theodore, had written Roosevelt in a gently chiding tone. Warning of the grave danger from radical candidates like Hearst in New York and James B. Moran in Massachusetts, whose "crazy" pronouncements reminded him of "the Jacobin Club," Lodge said, "You made a capital speech at Harrisburg with which I cordially agree, but I wish that you would sometimes bear down a little harder on the Hearsts and Morans, for bad as the other fellows are, I think they are more dangerous." Lodge's letter may have been on the president's mind as he drafted his letter.

For un-American activities, Roosevelt had a rich store of invective: "base," "low," "selfish," "silly," "evil," "noxious," "despicable," "unwholesome," "shameful," "flaccid," "contemptible," among others. But the striking term he chose this time to bracket his enemies—"undesirable"—was one of his current favorites. Both as noun and adjective, it speckled his correspondence of this period. Writing to the Washington Playground Association, he cautioned that public yards needed close supervision if they were not to "become the rendezvous of the most undesirable elements." To Harvard's president, he noted that a recently deposed corporate mogul was "an undesirable, because futile, representative of college men in public life." (He wasn't alone in his fascination with the word. Henry Cabot Lodge often inveighed against "undesirable"—Italian and Slav—immigrants, while Senator Fred T. Dubois of Idaho preferred for his state to grow slowly "rather than for its new comers to be undesirable citizens.")

The term was drawn from the arena of immigration policy—as in "undesirable alien"—which had become one of the president's obsessions. It was a concern he shared with many others: Henry James, aghast at the hirsute newcomers, called them "inconceivable aliens." Roosevelt stewed over the huge influx of so-called new immigrants from eastern and southern Europe. "The best three stocks" who came here, he believed, were the Huguenots, the Puritans, and the Germans who emigrated after the failed revolution of 1848 —the Germans were the best of all—while the hardest to assimilate were the Latins and the Filipinos. Roosevelt derided "the jack-fools who seriously think that any group of pirates and head-hunters need nothing but independence in order that it may be turned into a dark-hued New England town meeting." The president once told John Fox, only half jokingly, that he divided the human race into "two great classes—white men and dagoes."

One must agree with a Roosevelt biographer who concluded that "a mild undercurrent of racism seems to have lingered in his unconscious." Steeped in the pseudoscience of eugenics and its language of "inferior races" and "backward peoples," he'd privately voiced concern about "race suicide" and warned that "racial extinction faced the 'higher races' if they did not increase procreative activities." He wanted families of four to six children, rather than the one to three favored by the middle class. In 1903, he called anyone who hesitated to have children "a criminal against the race . . . the object of contemptuous abhorrence by healthy people." To the Reverend Franklin C. Smith, Roosevelt wrote in 1906, "You say that your ministry lies among well-to-do people; that is, among people of means and upper class workers. I assume that you regard these people as desirable elements in the state. Can you not see that if they have an insufficient quantity of children, then the increase must come from the less desirable classes?"

On that Monday morning, October 8, the president's letter had, as yet, an audience of only one, William Loeb, who'd typed it. Later, Roosevelt would admit how much he had "enjoyed" writing the "undesirable citizens" sentence, "even to the crossing of the T's and dotting of the I's." One imagines the president, delighted with his new formulation, stumping around his office —gleaming teeth, flashing pince-nez, voice raised to falsetto—impatient to read it to someone. As luck would have it, a distinguished audience was at hand. At 12:45 p.m. the Supreme Court of the United States would be gathering in the Green Room to pay its respects to the president. For that Monday marked the start of the Court's fall term and, by tradition, the justices' annual call on the president.

From their marbled chamber on Capitol Hill, they rode up Pennsylvania Avenue in horse-drawn carriages, two to a vehicle (there were only eight justices, since Henry Brown's successor hadn't been named). Decked out in black morning coats and striped pants, they filed into the Green Room, recently redecorated in tones of green and pink by Charles F. McKim, the New York architect. J. M. Wright, the marshal of the Court, announced each justice in turn. First came the amiable moderator, Melville Fuller, followed by the associate justices: Harlan, "the great gnarled oak"; the severe Brewer; "the jovial monk," White; the brooding Peckham; the magisterial Holmes, with his flowing mustache; the birdlike McKenna; the solemn, wizened Day.

Warmly greeting his guests, the president encouraged them to sample refreshments spread out against a velvet-covered wall and bathed in light from a cascading chandelier. The more elderly justices took their ease on chairs and sofas covered in a floral chintz of rose and green. After a few welcoming remarks, the president pulled the letter from his waistcoat. Some people, the president noted, had told him he too often denounced the reactionary Bourbons and ignored the union thugs. He'd like them to hear a letter he'd just written. Then he read it or, more likely, parts of it.

How the justices may have reacted we don't know. Perhaps there was a wry chuckle at Harriman's claim that he could "buy" the judiciary whenever he pleased. There may also have been an uneasy stirring when the president reached his little clutch of "undesirable citizens." For one of the first items on the Court's docket that week was the oral argument in *Pettibone v. Nichols,* the appeal from the denials, by the Idaho Supreme Court and the federal district court, of the petitions for release of the three "kidnapped" labor leaders under habeas corpus. The hearing was scheduled only three days hence, on October 11.

Had the president contrived this juxtaposition to leave the justices in no doubt how he wanted them to deal with the union men's appeal? Probably not. With no advance notice of what message Sherman would bring him that Sunday evening, he had little time to devise such a strategy. More likely, Roosevelt was so delighted with his balancing act—this would show Cabot! —that he couldn't resist performing it for the justices.

But plotted or spontaneous, it was a gross violation of the separation of powers. Presidents were expected to direct the executive branch, submit legislation to Congress, and deal with the Supreme Court at arm's length through the solicitor general. They weren't supposed to lean on the justices, individually or en masse, for specific results. Turn-of-the-century standards, to be sure, were less stringent than today's. It had been common through the nineteenth century for justices to confer with officers of the executive branch on policy and to draft legislation or treaties on which they might later pass. And there'd been flagrant transgressions of the separation of powers before.*

By 1906, though presidents still tried to influence justices, it was no longer considered good form. Whether the president's harsh judgment of Haywood and Moyer influenced the Court in its ruling on habeas corpus two months later is difficult to say, but at least one justice had reason to feel under special obligation to the president that fall.

John Marshall Harlan had long used his influence in a vain effort to put his son James, a Chicago lawyer of modest ability, on the federal bench. In 1892, at the justice's prompting, several prominent Chicago judges and attor-

---

* In 1857, the Court grappled with the case of Dred Scott, a slave who'd sued for his freedom on the grounds that he'd spent time in a territory from which slavery had been excluded by the Missouri Compromise. President-elect James Buchanan, a Pennsylvanian whose sympathies lay with the South, sought a resolution of the thorny question of slavery in the territories so as to quench abolitionist agitation on the eve of his assuming office. In this he was supported by the five justices from slaveholding states, led nominally by Chief Justice Roger B. Taney of Maryland. But if the Court was to settle the issue definitively, it couldn't divide along regional lines; the majority needed at least one Northern justice. Buchanan's friend Justice John Catron of Tennessee suggested that he write Justice Robert C. Grier, a fellow Pennsylvanian, emphasizing—in Catron's words—"how good the opportunity is to settle the agitation by an affirmative decision of the Supreme Court." Buchanan wrote Grier, who assured Buchanan of his cooperation. Ultimately, seven justices—five Southerners, Grier, and Sam Nelson of New York —held that Scott had not become a citizen by virtue of crossing the Missouri Compromise line. The ruling was a major, if temporary, triumph for slavery (B. Schwartz, *Supreme Court,* 54–59).

neys asked McKinley to put James in a vacant Illinois district judgeship, but the seat went to someone else. In 1900, McKinley named him attorney general of Puerto Rico, but when Roosevelt succeeded to the presidency, young Harlan's supporters renewed their quest for the judgeship, enlisting the aid of William Howard Taft. After talking with the president, Taft wrote the justice that he was "not greatly encouraged" by James's prospects.

By mid-1906, James—again vigorously backed by his father—resolved instead to seek a seat on the Interstate Commerce Commission. A seven-member body formed in 1887, the commission had been relatively ineffectual over the intervening years; but with the president pressing to give it increased regulatory powers over the nation's railroads, it seemed destined to bulk larger on the national scene. Each commissioner earned ten thousand dollars a year with liberal expenses.

When several senators opposed the appointment, Roosevelt found himself in an awkward spot. On June 28, he wrote Justice Harlan: "I am having a little trouble about your son James. There is a good deal of feeling, I find, against putting on the Interstate Commerce Commission a man whose father on the Supreme Court will pass on his actions. I have been a little puzzled about it."

Harlan was summering at Pointe-au-Pic, a Quebec resort where, by coincidence, Taft also took his holidays. On July 5, the justice wrote Roosevelt to express "great surprise" that anyone should think his seat on the Court stood in the way of his son's appointment. "The possibility that a Justice of the Supreme Court would be controlled by the fact that his son was a member of the Commission is, I take leave to say, entitled to no consideration whatever." One should assume that each justice "recognizes the responsibilities attached to his high position and, in deference to his conscience, will do his duty."

On July 9, the president sent Harlan's letter to Taft at Pointe-au-Pic. Ten days later, the secretary suggested an ingenious solution. Harlan had been on the bench for twenty-nine years; he was now past seventy-three; the next administration might well be Democratic. "Does he not owe it to the party if his son is to be given what is practically a life office by another Republican president, to retire so that the present Republican administration may appoint his successor and secure the Bench against the appointment by Mr. Bryan of his successor?" Taft offered to raise the matter gently with Harlan during one of their Pointe-au-Pic golf matches, in which the lumbering secretary regularly overwhelmed the aging justice.

The president wasn't averse to shaking loose from the justice he'd describe the following year as "that fine old American patriot." But if Taft raised the matter with Harlan, the justice was disinclined to retire. The president temporized. Then, on August 18, he gave Harlan *fils* the job, without mentioning anything he expected in return. He wrote Harlan *père:* "It was a very real pleasure to appoint your son. I considered carefully, and went over with the Attorney General, the protests made by certain Senators against your son's appointment.... I came to the conclusion that they did not justify a failure to appoint James."

Barely a month later, the Court paid its call on the president. Could this conjunction of events have shaped Harlan's approach to the Idaho case? All one can say is that the president left the Court in no doubt how he felt on the matter, and Harlan—who wrote the majority decision in the habeas corpus case—had reason to feel grateful to Roosevelt.

In the weeks to come, the president focused relentlessly on the midterm elections. In New York, he remained obsessed by the real possibility that Hughes might lose to Hearst. To James Sherman, he wrote: "We must win by a savage and aggressive fight against Hearstism and an exposure of its hypocrisy, its insincerity, its corruption, its demagogy, and in general its utter worthlessness and wickedness."

The political etiquette of that era held that it was "unseemly" for a president to take to the hustings. Straining at this anachronistic straitjacket, Roosevelt felt as if he were "lying still under shell fire" at Santiago. Reluctantly, he assigned the counterattack to cabinet surrogates.

With New York's race still desperately close in its final week, Roosevelt dispatched Secretary of State Elihu Root on a last-minute mission to slay the Hearstian dragon. The former Wall Street lawyer needed little prompting; privately that week he'd denounced Hearst as an "incredible blackguard." On November 1, before three thousand persons overflowing Utica's Majestic Theater, he assailed the press lord as a greedy capitalist posing as a friend of labor, a boodler "covered all over with the mark of Tammany." Then he reminded his listeners of Roosevelt's remark after McKinley's assassination, that those in the press who "appeal to dark and evil spirits" wouldn't "escape their share of responsibility for the whirlwind that is reaped." Roosevelt was referring to Hearst's vilification of McKinley, complete with doggerel by Ambrose Bierce, in the San Francisco *Examiner* a few days before McKinley's assassination: "The bullet that pierced Goebel's breast* / Cannot be found in all the West / Good reason! It is speeding here / To Lay McKinley on his Bier." Now—interrupted by Hearstian hecklers—Root proclaimed that he could say, "by the President's authority," that when Roosevelt excoriated the press, "he had Mr. Hearst specifically in mind. And I say, by his authority, that what he thought of Mr. Hearst then he thinks of Mr. Hearst now."

All fall, the president fielded urgent messages from Republicans in other states asking for his presence or that of his emissaries to swing close contests. To his friend Owen Wister, he explained: "Of course I can not go into State contests save in some wholly exceptional case like that of Hearst. I am dealing with national issues."

---

* William Goebel, Kentucky's governor-elect, had been shot and killed in February 1900.

To Roosevelt's mind that fall, there were two other exceptional cases that demanded presidential intervention. One was Colorado, the other Idaho. In Colorado, the exceptional situation was the gubernatorial candidacy of his good friend Philip B. Stewart. The two men had met in January 1901 when Roosevelt took five weeks off on the eve of becoming vice president to hunt cougar in Colorado. One of his companions was Stewart, a thirty-six-year-old Colorado Springs stockbroker, sportsman, and budding politician. After returning to Washington, Roosevelt confided to another friend that Stewart was "as fine a fellow as it seems to me I have ever met," adding, "I greatly admire strength, both moral and physical; but I do not admire it at all unless it is combined with the sweetness and highminded disinterestedness which Phil Stewart possesses to such a high degree." Soon Roosevelt made Stewart his political agent, and distributor of federal patronage, in Colorado.

Stewart and Roosevelt had grown dissatisfied with the state's Republican leadership, as exemplified by Governor Peabody, who the president thought "manfully did his duty" in confronting the "murderous conspiracy" of the WFM but also "let himself be put in the position of seeming to do this not in the interest merely of law and order, or evenhanded justice to wageworker and capitalist, but as the supporter and representative of the capitalist against the laborer." Worse yet, the president felt, "our people have made the great error of permitting lawlessness on their side to offset lawlessness on the other."

Roosevelt saw Stewart as the leader of a new force in Colorado politics, still staunchly opposed to the WFM but less identified with the most reactionary forces and more responsive to the White House. On the eve of the Republican state convention in September 1906, Stewart had the gubernatorial nomination locked up. Behind him, ironically enough, were arrayed many of those who'd backed—or controlled—the old leadership, including William G. Evans, Denver's tramway king and political boss; and David H. Moffat, the bank president and mine owner. But to give himself latitude to chart a new course, Stewart had set several conditions for his candidacy. One was an understanding that Chief Justice William H. Gabbert of the Colorado Supreme Court, now widely discredited for his lockstep allegiance to Peabody and the mine owners, would not be renominated to the bench.

Even with his impressive backing, which assured him the Republican nomination, Stewart would need plenty of help in the general election. To that end, in September 1906, Roosevelt determined that somebody should place the White House imprimatur on Phil Stewart. His choice was Secretary of War William Howard Taft, the cabinet's heavyweight, both in avoirdupois (he tipped the scales that summer at 250 pounds) and in clout (Washington insiders had already identified him as Roosevelt's successor). On both grounds —like the man imprisoned in Boise—he was often called Big Bill. Moreover, Taft was rapidly developing a reputation as the president's fireman, rushing from war to coup d'état to industrial unrest with the agility of a much slimmer man. "I have never been quite so busy with various things," he wrote his brother that year. "I am overwhelmed with work." As that year's Gridiron Club show put it:

> *Boom, boom!*
> > *If there's trouble down in Cuba*
> *Boom, boom!*
> > *Or a row in Panama*
> *Boom, boom!*
> > *Should a railway insurrecto*
> > *Start to violate the law*
> *Boom, boom!*
> > *If there's graft to be uncovered*
> *Boom, boom!*
> > *Things made light that now are hid*
> > *You must call on Taft, send for peaceful Bill*
> > *to sit upon the lid!*

In mid-September, Roosevelt asked the peripatetic Taft to add another crisis point to his itinerary, Idaho. The immediate impetus for this decision was a letter from Gifford Pinchot, the chief forester of the United States, who had close ties to many Idahoans, among them Calvin Cobb and William Borah. Cobb warned of the WFM's "secret, insidious and determined campaign" against Governor Gooding and argued that "we stand in need of a masterly presentation, by a man of national reputation, of the reasons why it is necessary to show our support of the governor." Later, Cobb would explain the diabolical forces besetting Gooding: "In some counties he was fought as a sheep man; in sheep counties he was fought as a Pinchot man and in league with him to drive the sheep out of the country. In church societies he was called a saloon man, and the saloon men were assured he was for local option. He was accused of being a Mormon, a grafter—anything that would take hold."

In early September, Cobb, Borah, and Gooding had all urged Pinchot to take their case for high-level help to the president. Pinchot's September 9 letter argued for a presidential envoy much as Cobb had. On September 15, the president concurred with his good friend the forester: "There is no issue at this election so important as to support Gooding against those dynamiters and thugs. Taft is going to Colorado to speak for Phil Stewart at my request, he can go on to Idaho."

Two days later, Roosevelt asked Taft "as a personal favor" to speak for Gooding, who was being attacked "by an immense majority of the labor men of the State for his proceedings against the infamous creatures at the head of the Western Federation of Miners."

In picking Taft for this mission, Roosevelt called on a man who already had a reputation for hostility to organized labor. In 1894, while a federal judge in Ohio, Taft had been deeply alarmed by the Pullman strike. His correspondence reveals a fierce hatred of the strikers. "Affairs in Chicago seem to be much disturbed. It will be necessary for the military to kill some of the mob before the trouble can be stopped," he wrote on July 6. "The Chicago situation is not much improved," he wrote two days later. "They have only killed six of the mob as yet. This is hardly enough to make an impression." In other circumstances he'd shown more understanding of labor's point of view, notably on the despised doctrine of assumed risk. He was nonetheless seen as an enemy of labor and his dispatch to Idaho as further evidence of the White House's animus toward aggressive unionism.

Roosevelt's September 17 letter caught up with the war secretary in Cuba, the site of his latest crisis. Insurgents had ousted the new republic's first president, Tomas Estrada Palma. Anarchy loomed. In mid-September, the president dispatched some marines and Boom, Boom Taft, who, working long days in the scalding sun, assumed the job of provisional governor, appointed a new cabinet, persuaded the insurrectionists to disband, and restored a semblance of order.

With the Cuban emergency abated, Taft embarked for home on October 13. By then, the Colorado stop had been canceled. For after Colorado Republicans nominated Stewart for governor, his principal backer, William G. Evans, reneged on his agreement to drop Justice Gabbert from the ticket. Denver's public-utility corporations, for whom Evans was the political agent, had shrunk from alienating the state's supreme court, soon to hear franchise cases worth $50 million to those corporations. Phil Stewart felt honor-bound to decline the nomination. The president congratulated his friend for his ethical standards, while condemning Evans and his "corrupt" colleagues for "improper influence." In sum, Roosevelt wrote, "The Republican Party made a fool of itself."

In the wake of these events, Taft's western swing had two principal objectives: to deliver an unmistakable snub to Colorado's Republican leadership and carry a presidential endorsement of Gooding and his brave fight against the miners. The snub to Colorado was artfully contrived. Originally, Taft's eight-day "stumping trip" was to have taken him from Baltimore, through Chillicothe, Ohio; Decatur, Illinois; Omaha; and Denver, to Pocatello and, finally, to Boise on November 3—three days before the election. Now Taft told his staff to cancel the Denver stopover and alter his route so he never passed through Colorado. At first, a scheduler reported that it was "impossible to avoid passing through Denver," but ultimately another aide found a route that "evades the beautiful—though perhaps not at this time to you attractive—city."

Then Taft's staff leaked a story to the *Denver Times* saying the secretary was avoiding Colorado because the state's Republican Party was "in the hands of trusts." In the next week, Taft received no fewer than four letters from Horace G. Clark, the clerk of the Colorado Supreme Court and Justice Gabbert's political operative, protesting against the "malignant and malicious" interpretations being put on the schedule change, reminding Taft that "the issue in this state is, law and order and the protection of life and property on the one hand, against Democracy, Socialism, the Western Federation of Miners," and urging the secretary to come to Denver or at least to issue a statement clarifying his decision. Taft remained mute.

Equally distressed by Taft's itinerary was Idaho's Democratic senator, Fred Dubois, who feared that the secretary's Idaho appearance would so bolster Republican forces in the state legislature as to imperil his reelection in February (U.S. senators were still elected by state legislatures). Dubois campaigned that year almost exclusively on his contention that the polygamous Mormons represented a threat to American family life and freedoms. For Taft to ignore the Mormon issue and suggest the real threat in Idaho was the WFM could only undermine the senator's credibility.

Taft and Dubois were both Yale graduates fiercely loyal to their alma mater, and over the years the college tie had transcended their political differences. Now, on the eve of Taft's departure, Dubois wrote his fellow Eli a "Dear Billie" letter. "You will find no subject in Idaho which interests the people at all excepting the Mormon question," the senator said. "There are some things higher than politics and I want you to consider well before making this speech in my capital town." Dubois's distress was perhaps excessive, but such campaign trips by cabinet officers, either on their own initiative or as surrogates for the president, were much rarer at the turn of the century than they are today, and Taft was the first cabinet member ever to stump Idaho.

In any case, Taft responded with a brisk little note saying he was going to Idaho "at the instance of the President to speak on law and order and in favor of the election of Governor Gooding." Dubois could rest assured that the secretary would "say nothing of a personal or political character which will trouble you." Unwilling to accept this rebuff, Dubois dispatched his cousin and private secretary, Albert T. Ryan—yet another Yale man—to board Taft's train with a desperate last-minute plea to cancel the Idaho stops. That, too, failed. "I have a right to enter any State in the Union and address my fellow citizens," Taft wrote from the train to his brother Charles.

The secretary didn't look forward to this bout of stumping. Not only was he physically exhausted, he loathed campaign hurly-burly. "Politics, when I am in it, makes me sick," he confided during this trip. Nonetheless, relishing his reputation as the administration's warhorse, he got his massive shoulders into the job.

"I am now on the Illinois Central between Chicago and Omaha, in a very nice private car," Taft wrote his wife, Nellie, on October 31. "My voice was subject to a great deal of strain yesterday, and it still retains the hoarseness that I gave it by too great an effort at Baltimore.... I feel a bit awkward in going to Idaho, because I do not understand the issues that prevail there, and shall certainly not be able to say anything with respect to

Mormonism, but the President was so insistent on it that I could not escape.
. . . I wish the trip were over, especially the Idaho part of it which I do not look
forward to with any pleasure; but I am in for it and must make it go."

As they cruised the plains, Taft kept busy with revised speeches and a
blizzard of cables to Cuba, the Philippines, and Washington. The secretary
had received a letter from Pinchot briefing him on Idaho politics, "which he
thinks he knows," Taft remarked sourly, adding, "I could have a somewhat
wiser adviser on politics than Gifford." Still, needing fresh intelligence, he
looked forward to meeting with Calvin Cobb, who'd board the train at North
Platte, Nebraska, to brief him on the "condition of things" in Idaho.

On the evening of November 2, the "ponderous pachyderm," as one
Idaho editor described him, addressed an enthusiastic crowd of two thousand
in Pocatello. The following morning, as his train advanced toward Boise, it
stopped several times so Taft could speak briefly to the beet farmers and
sheep drovers gathered at sidings and water tanks. "At one place," he wrote
the president, "as we were moving out I heard someone call out, 'Hurrah for
polygamy and Mr. Taft,' which indicated there was some friend of Mr. Dubois
in the audience." Near Shoshone, Governor Gooding's home, the train
stopped again so the governor could give him a tour of his sheep ranch.
Finally, at Nampa, Taft addressed a thousand more persons from the broad
veranda of the Dewey Palace Hotel.

The ride up the branch line to Boise left the secretary impressed. "The
growth of this country is marvelous," he wrote Nellie. "The number of people
that are traveling exceed anything I had supposed. The railroads are loaded
down with both freight and passengers, and the trains are delayed because the
tracks cannot be cleared. The prosperity of the country is something marvelous. On these deserts one sees herds of magnificent looking cattle, fat and
large, and one wonders where they get the feed. The introduction of irrigation makes a blooming country out of what seems most desolate."

Reaching the capital, the governor and Taft went to the Boise Barracks,
where they reviewed the troops of the Fourteenth Cavalry, still on duty there.
The ubiquitous Calvin Cobb next took custody of the visitor, escorting him
to the green family bungalow in the shadow of the capitol, where—not
having slept much the night before—the secretary had a sulfur-water-and-
soda bath, an hour's nap, and "a nice dinner" with the "refined and cultured"
Cobb family. From there he was off to the Columbia Theater to pronounce
the centerpiece of his western trip.

The theater was filled to capacity as Borah rose to introduce the visiting
personage. Then, like one of the heavy cruisers riding at anchor in Havana
harbor, Taft lumbered into firing position behind the podium and delivered
Theodore Roosevelt's salvos to the people of Idaho.

First came support for the governor: "The President believes that the
election of Governor Gooding is one of the most important issues of the

campaign. The question is whether an executive officer, charged with the execution of the law, who attempts to bring to trial men charged with a heinous crime shall be marked for defeat at an election because those men can awaken sympathy the country over because of their affiliations."

Then came the issue that for a time had roiled relations between Gooding and the president but that Roosevelt now regarded as firmly settled: "This is not a prosecution by a corporation. This is a prosecution by the state of Idaho, to vindicate it and its community and to punish a heinous crime. It is not an incident in any war between capital and labor. It is merely for the punishment of crime."

Then the president's slap at the Colorado Republicans who'd defied the White House and double-crossed his friend Phil Stewart: "In the neighboring state of Colorado, they had for years a condition in which both miners and state officers and the heads of mining corporations violated the law in a war against each other, and the president is thoroughly out of patience with them all. They brought disgrace upon the state of Colorado, and what he is hoping and praying for is that conditions may not arise in Idaho which shall lead to the same result."

Finally, scathing presidential contempt for the WFM and its allies: "I assume that the opponent of Governor Gooding is a law-abiding citizen and would obey the law, but he cannot be elected without the aid of those who are opposing Governor Gooding on the ground that he did his duty. Therefore, I do not care what is said with respect to other issues. The issue is the supremacy of the law, the standing up for your officials who have the courage in the face of explosions, in the face of hostile and powerful interests, to uphold the law."

People told Taft that the speech was the most effective one he'd ever given. But he wasn't so sure. After a reception at the Commercial Club, where he met "some of the solid men of Boise City," he returned to his special car and tried to sleep, but his slumber was "somewhat disturbed." On the Overland Limited to Cheyenne the next day, he wrote the president: "This letter will not reach you until after the Idaho election, so that you can read it in light of the event." But for himself, "I regard the question of Gooding's election as very doubtful. . . . I do not know what the purchasable vote is, but I am certain that the Western Federation of Miners will shock the entire country." To Idaho's Senator Heyburn, he wrote: "I am very anxious about Idaho, and especially about the election of Governor Gooding. It would be a national calamity if he were defeated."

But he was not. Root and Taft, the two cabinet stalwarts, who addressed each other as Athos and Porthos, had worked wonders again for their senior partner, naturally dubbed D'Artagnan. On the evening of November 7, Roosevelt started a triumphant note to his daughter Alice after Hughes had defeated Hearst in New York—by 58,000 votes out of 1.5 million cast—but before the Idaho results were in. A few hours later, he completed it: "P.S. Yes, we have elected Gooding Governor in Idaho; it is a big victory for civilization."

The trade union and Socialist effort to defeat Gooding—backed by what McParland described as "unlimited quantities" of cash—had taken its toll. In relatively urban Ada County, where Gooding had a 3,000-vote margin two years before, he lost by 516 votes. He suffered reverses in other labor strongholds—Canyon, Washington, Owyhee, and Elmore Counties. One victim of the labor onslaught was Caldwell's own Frank J. Smith, who, as judge in the Seventh Judicial District, had been slated to preside over the Haywood trial. "It is to Canyon County's everlasting disgrace that the vile influences at work were successful," chided the *Nampa Leader-Herald.*

Nonetheless, Gooding scored heavily in the five southeastern counties where Mormon voters predominated, and the statewide results delighted the Republicans. When Roosevelt learned that Gooding had triumphed by ten thousand votes and that Idaho's legislature would be Republican, fifty-five to seventeen, he dashed off a note to Taft: "Upon my word, I do not know which to be the more proud of, what Root did in New York or what you did in Idaho!" Writing the U.S. attorney in Maryland, he was unable to contain himself. "By George," he exclaimed, "it is a big triumph!"

And to Frank Gooding—who'd so graciously returned that $5,000 to the Coeur d'Alene mine owners, so as to keep Idaho's record "clean"—the president wrote with real warmth: "I most heartily congratulate you (or rather, not you, but the people of Idaho and the people of the United States) on your re-election.... I do not regard your victory in Idaho, any more than I regard the victory of Mr. Hughes in New York, as a mere party victory, but as a victory for our democratic civilization, a victory for that system of personal freedom, personal liberty, under and thru the law, which we hail as typically American."

9

OPERATIVE 21

ON APRIL 30, 1906, a barn belonging to the editor of the *Parma Herald*, a Canyon County newspaper that plumped for the prosecution, caught fire and burned to the ground. Soon afterward, the editor of the *Caldwell News* received a letter warning him to halt his denunciations of Haywood and the others. Alarmed by these developments, James McParland issued an alert to the governor and his own agency: "It now appears that Socialists and anarchists have taken entire possession of Caldwell. It looks to me as though they are going to inaugurate a reign of terror not only in Caldwell but in Canyon County in general.... I would like to be Sheriff of Canyon County for one week or for twenty-four hours and this gang ... would either be in the County jail, run out of town or as a last resort there would be a job for the Coroner."

It was an uncharacteristic eruption from the master detective, usually able to conceal his feelings behind a mask of icy dispassion. Whether it was mounting exasperation at Sheriff Nichols, whom he regarded as a gutless wonder and perhaps a traitor, fresh warnings of arms shipments and paid killers on the loose, or fatigue, by late spring McParland was suffused with rage.

Anxiety that the WFM would slip dangerous men into Caldwell had been with him from the start. On January 10, the very day he'd arrived in Boise to confer with the governor about taking the case, McParland had warned that "this conspiracy is so widespread and so well and secretly conducted that it would not surprise me to find out that the WFM has one or more men posing in Caldwell as *bona fide* residents, for the purpose of proving an alibi. Such men may have their wives or women posing as their wives, to help them out in the plot."

In the weeks after Steunenberg's assassination, the search for conspirators was so thorough that even labor sympathizers in town for years found themselves under suspicion. Bill Williams had been a close friend and union colleague of Haywood's while both were miners in Silver City. About 1900, with his wife and son, Williams moved to Caldwell, buying a house on Dearborn Street catty-corner from the Steunenbergs. For five years, the Williamses lived in amicable concert with their neighbors. But once the bomb blew up the governor barely a hundred feet away, Williams found himself on a list of suspicious characters, although never formally a suspect. He reacted, his son recalled, by withdrawing from all organized activity—including the union—shunning intercourse with his neighbors for fear it would be hostile.

By early March 1906, some of Caldwell's leading citizens detected a new element in town, an organized gang of "tough characters" said to be intimidating citizens and threatening more violent acts. On March 6, the *Statesman* reported "the presence in and around [Caldwell] of many men who do not seem to have any legitimate business." A number of these men, the newspaper said, "have been recognized as persons who were well known in the Coeur d'Alenes during the turbulent period there, and others have been recognized as characters from Cripple Creek." This in turn had "given rise to the fear that they are misguided friends of the men accused of the murder and that they might attempt some desperate move."

The move authorities feared most was a raid on the Canyon County jail. For a few of Caldwell's leading citizens had been alerted that Governor Gooding—irritated by repeated defense complaints about conditions in the state penitentiary—had decided to transfer Haywood, Moyer, and Pettibone back to the tiny Caldwell jail, where the defense contended they should have been kept all along. Some people speculated that the defense strategy had been to force such a transfer, then to use the gang of "tough characters" to raid the jail and free the trio. After a personal inspection of the Caldwell facility, McParland believed a prisoner "could easily walk out without much of an effort."

Accordingly, in days to come, the town's "law and order" element resolved once again to mobilize its forces. A large committee was formed, the *Statesman* reported, "to assist in guarding against any possible disorders." Not surprisingly, the group was headed by George Froman, the renowned Indian fighter and former town marshal who'd helped apprehend Harry Orchard two months before. "Prepared at all times to render instant assistance in the event of trouble," the committee would also "assist in guarding the prisoners wherever these might be where, by a sudden rush, misguided, desperate men could reach them."

On March 13, Sheriff Nichols, assisted by Chris Thiele of the Pinkertons and Rube Robbins, the traveling guard, escorted the three men back by train to the Caldwell jail. As it had been during Harry Orchard's January incarceration there, the jail was intolerably crowded that week with twelve prisoners even before the three men arrived. During the day, all fifteen shared the fourteen-by-eighteen-foot front room where meals were prepared and eaten. But of more concern to the citizens of Caldwell and the governor, the tiny, ill-constructed brick building was clearly vulnerable to attack.

Two days later, when Harry Orchard was brought from Boise to Caldwell for arraignment, the governor made "a show of force," issuing Winchester rifles to Orchard's four guards. Orchard was carefully kept away from Haywood, Moyer, and Pettibone at the jail—he was lodged instead in his old room at the Saratoga Hotel—but he was visibly ill at ease as he puffed on a Havana perfecto cigar. Later he told McParland that he had been so convinced that day that the union leaders would break out of jail, leaving him to face the retribution of Frank Steunenberg's friends and neighbors, that he contemplated suicide. Planning to take the crystal out of his watch, chew it up, and swallow the broken glass or—if the pieces were large enough—to cut his wrists, he shrank from self-destruction only at the last moment. McParland seemed convinced that his volatile prisoner and client had meant to kill himself, though others suspected the clumsy melodrama was designed to convince authorities of the depth of his sincerity. A Denver reporter who saw Orchard that day wrote: "His thin lips were tightly drawn, the bronze hue had left the cheeks, leaving them pale, though not emaciated.... He seemed the picture of abject despair." This report and others from the same time gave rise to a spate of sloppily reported yarns that portrayed Orchard as sick, depressed, deranged, or flatly insane.

That evening, a high-level meeting convened at the Idanha to assess all four prisoners' security. Present were Gooding; Hawley; Montie B. Gwinn, vice president of the Steunenberg brothers' bank in Caldwell; and—reflecting Calvin Cobb's continuing influence in these circles—William Balderston, editor of the *Statesman*. Representing Caldwell's Citizens Committee as well as the Steunenberg family, Gwinn reported that the "gang of tough characters" was so formidable that, if they attacked the jail in an effort to free the prisoners, "the resisting powers of the citizens of Caldwell ... is not to be relied upon." The governor said he'd urge other towns along the Short Line to organize citizens groups that would be ready, in the event of trouble, to come to Caldwell's assistance.

In late March, Caldwell's Citizens Committee detected still other threats to the orderly course of justice in the Steunenberg case. Convening at the Odd Fellows Building, it passed a lengthy resolution denouncing "the efforts being made to corrupt and intimidate the people of Canyon county, to disqualify them from Jury duty. We have positive knowledge that paid emissaries of the defense are at work among the farmers who might be called for jury duty, trying to poison their minds against the State and County officials, and we ask all law abiding citizens not to talk with strangers about the case. We also warn the wives and daughters against female agitators, which we know are at work among the women of Canyon County."

The resolution also called "attention to the inflammatory literature with which the county has been recently flooded, from the bloodcurdling threats of Debs down to some of the daily papers. We resent the insinuation that the citizens of Canyon County would not give the accused men a fair trial, and we openly charge that there is an element at work in our midst who do not want a fair trial, but who are clamoring and working to have the accused men released without any trial at all."

About this time, the governor persuaded Sheriff Nichols to deputize eight of Frank and A. K. Steunenberg's "personal friends"—the sheep rancher James Dement, the landscaper Henry Babb, the former Texas Ranger Ed Morgan, Leon Golder, L. G. Smith, S. A. Wells, J. T. Morrow, and James Merritt—as guards at the jail. According to one account, A. K. Steunenberg —determined that the men who'd ordered his brother's murder should not get away—dipped into his own bank account to provide the guards with shot-guns and Winchester repeating rifles.

A.K.'s efforts proved unnecessary, for soon thereafter the authorities, worried about overcrowding and security at the jail in Caldwell, moved Haywood, Moyer, and Pettibone to the Ada County jail in Boise.

In those grim winter months, A.K. had continued to brood about his insupportable loss. To a friend, he wrote: "I am mechanically going through my duties, but my thoughts are ever on Canyon Hill, where sleeps the bravest, tenderest, gentlest intellect that ever graced this earth. I can't hear a train come in but I go to the window expecting to see his big handsome person coming down the street with his grin which I knew so well and to hear his cheery 'hello' as he stepped to the door."

The prosecutors and the Pinkertons had a peculiar relationship with A.K. As his brother's closest confidant, he received their condolences, their respect, and occasionally even a pro forma consultation. On occasion, they asked his help in controlling Caldwell authorities who threatened to go off on some tangent of their own. But he was not entirely trusted. On February 2, for example, James McParland met with A.K. and Pete Steunenberg for about an hour and a half in his room at the Idanha. A.K. "seemed to be satisfied with what Governor Gooding was doing in this matter," McParland reported, "although he has no knowledge of the work that has really been done in the case, as we do not consider it safe to allow any persons except those we cannot help into this secret."

Lonely and morose, largely excluded from the investigation, A.K. turned that winter to surveillance of the Socialists and unionists who'd begun arriv-ing in Caldwell in anticipation of the upcoming trials. He made it his business to keep track of these interlopers and, when possible, to make life uncomfort-able for them. After all, these were the "dynamiters" who, in killing Frank, had cut off A.K.'s "right arm." In his ever-mounting grief and rage, he re-solved to pay them back.

Canyon County, unlike much of rural Idaho, had long nourished a small but tenacious band of radical reformers. The election returns of November 1906, in which the governor lost the county and Judge Smith his seat, reflected that maverick streak. Some of the county's political awareness could be traced to its location, hard by the capital city of Boise; some to its relative population density; some to an outpost of Eugene Debs's American Railway Union, formed in the early 1890s in Nampa. In 1907, the Pinkertons recorded at least six hundred Socialists residing in Canyon County.

Like many of the county's other leading citizens, the Steunenbergs had difficulty comprehending what could drive disenfranchised men to desperate measures. Caldwell's own politics were generally unruffled by the class passions that prevailed in the mining district to the north. For state and national offices, Caldwell generally voted Republican; its local elections were nonpartisan, pitting the Citizens Ticket against the Municipal Improvement Ticket, with candidates moving back and forth as factional alliances shifted.

In 1894, following the devastating depression of the year before, Caldwell did have a brush with a band of desperate men, when a contingent of Coxey's Army, the tattered legion of the unemployed that set out for Washington that spring, passed through town. Five of Jacob Coxey's twenty "armies of protest" originated in the economically ravaged Northwest. While a thousand men set off from Spokane into the Coeur d'Alenes, hundreds of unemployed miners, timber jacks, and railroad workers, led by S. L. Scheffler, a stonemason, struck east from Portland. On April 28, elements of Scheffler's force seized a special train belonging to the Union Pacific's general manager, Edward Dickinson, then steamed east for 120 miles before they were arrested by U.S. cavalrymen (only to be released, with a slap on the wrist, by Oregon's federal judge).

Other elements of Scheffler's force forged across southern Idaho, following the Oregon Short Line through Weiser, Caldwell, Nampa, and Pocatello. But if authorities to the west had treated the Industrials with surprising leniency, Idaho's federal judge James H. Beatty regarded them as "deluded people" whose faces "bore the indelible stamp of the criminal." Resolving to halt their "wild crusade" with a force of deputy U.S. marshals, he issued an order on May 8 enjoining them from stealing rides on, or commandeering, Short Line trains.

The next day, thirty-seven men from Company 11 of the Portland contingent of Coxey's Army—led by "General" R. B. Breckenridge—reached Caldwell aboard such a train. The stop was to have been brief, but then came orders from Union Pacific headquarters that, as long as the "army" remained aboard, the train was to go no farther. At this, the well-disciplined contingent —each man sporting a badge of red, white, and blue—set up camp on an old circus ground back of the Pacific Hotel, where they unfurled the American flag, saluted, and swore to protect it.

Soon a deputy U.S. marshal arrived from Boise to read the Industrials Judge Beatty's order, to which, he reported with broad sarcasm, the men paid as much attention "as they would to the reading of a passage from the Bible." But the *Caldwell Tribune*—now edited by Rees H. Davis, a McKinley Republican—reported that the men were "orderly and well-behaved throughout." William Borah, who happened to be in Caldwell, described them as "very determined" to reach Washington but "peaceable and quiet." Borah had expected to see a mob of hobos and was "surprised" to find them educated and well-dressed. When it became clear that the Industrials would be with them for a time, Caldwell citizens convened a meeting in Isham's new Opera House, expressing sympathy for the Industrials and condemning the Union Pacific for abandoning them.

The next day, the railroad relented and a locomotive backed down the line from Nampa to pull the sidetracked cars, with the Industrials aboard, out of town. But not before merchants and prominent citizens alike proved "extremely liberal in their donations," many contributing ten to twenty-five dollars' worth of flour, bacon, and potatoes or like amounts in cash. "The Coxeyites will have no occasion to complain of their treatment in Caldwell," said the *Tribune*. "Everything possible was done for their comfort and they went away well fed and hopeful.... That public sentiment is largely with them there is no question."

The *Index* of Emmett, Idaho, believed many people in the state shared the army's rage at "unwise, unjust and class legislation" passed by Congress of late. "It is not strange that Coxeyism is here," the paper said. "It is strange that it delayed its coming so long." Plainly the Coxeyites found substantial support of that kind in Caldwell among those who resented the growing power of the railroads and other corporate trusts.

But some of the kindness that mainstream Caldwell heaped on the Industrials may have been rooted less in approval of their cause than in fear of looting while they were there and in an urgent desire that they leave town as quickly as possible. In turn, the Union Pacific—never popular in town—aroused Caldwell's ire precisely because it had dumped the destitute men there, with no provision for their care. For much of the merchant class, at least, the overriding concern was probably that this burden be moved farther east as quickly as possible—to Nampa or, as the *Tribune* put it, "some neigh-boring town, which had not had the honor of entertaining these distinguished guests of Idaho."

It is difficult to assess the relative strength of these viewpoints. The *Tribune* expressed skepticism about the Industrial Army's aims. While ap-plauding sympathy with the unfortunate men, it warned citizens not to em-brace their cause with "incendiary utterances" against government. "There has yet been no usurpation of the people's prerogatives, no invasion of their rights, no unwarranted exercise of authority; no wrong has been perpetrated which the people are powerless to remedy by peaceable and lawful methods. People who talk lightly about insurrection and revolution do not appreciate the consequences."

By 1896, the great "Popocratic" insurgency had captured Idaho. Some of Caldwell's sturdiest citizens—like the barber William H. Snodgrass, the tin-smith Sam Hartkopf, and the lumber dealer Collister W. Cooper—led the

Populist Party there. But much of that year's enthusiasm grew less from a passion for the Populists' progressive platform than from the Free Silver craze that had utterly scrambled Idaho's politics and put Caldwell's native son, Frank Steunenberg, in the governor's seat.

After Bryan's loss to McKinley that year, Populism's drawing power nationwide was on the wane. An editorial in *Appeal to Reason* proclaimed: "The People's Party has run its course, performed its mission and helped prepare the way for a party of scientific principles...the Socialist Party." In some states, radical "Pops" broke the trail for a brand of Socialism that often retained a broad Populist streak.

American Socialism of that era was less a unified movement than an unruly assembly of sects, sharply divided along ideological and regional lines. At one extreme was the Socialist Labor Party, a small doctrinaire group of Marxist purists—most of them Germans, with a scattering of Poles and Bohemians—led by the strident polemicist Daniel DeLeon, known to his critics as the Pope; at the other was Victor Berger's sober, one-step-at-a-time "gas and water" Socialism, so named because its program emphasized the ownership of municipal utilities. In between ranged a "confederation of re-gional baronies": the immigrant Jews of New York's Lower East Side who were refining a unique amalgam of Socialist politics and Yiddish culture; the struggling farmers of the Southwest—notably Oklahoma—whose Socialism had a powerful dose of agrarian Populism mixed with the natural-rights philosophy of Tom Paine and Thomas Jefferson; the "direct action" Socialism of Bill Haywood's Western Federation of Miners and the IWW, bred in the confrontational climate of the Rocky Mountain mining camps; the generous impulse of do-gooders dedicated to prison reform, vegetarianism, and birth control; and, finally, the warm, even sentimental Socialism of Eugene Debs, which combined an appealing strain of American idealism, invoking justice and brotherhood, with the eloquence to bring it alive for audiences all across the land.

Often it seemed that these factions had little in common except a hatred of "the bosses," a hazy notion of class solidarity, and a quixotic faith in the inevitability of triumph, bred in Marx's conviction that history is on the side of the working class and reflected in the slogan of *Appeal to Reason,* "Socialism is not just a theory—it is a destiny." But at Indianapolis in August 1901, the squabbling chieftains buried their differences long enough to form the Social-ist Party of America, embracing all Socialist factions except DeLeon's haughty purists.

Ironically enough, Idaho had occupied a special place in the plans of early American Socialists. In January 1897, a handful of utopian Socialists and reformers formed the Brotherhood of the Cooperative Commonwealth, enlisting Debs as an organizer. The brotherhood planned to convert America to Socialism by colonizing a sparsely populated western state with small agricultural, timber, and mining settlements. As soon as the Socialist colonists outnumbered other residents of the state, they would frame a Socialist constitution and elect Socialist officials. With that state as their laboratory, they would demonstrate the superiority of their system and gradually win over the rest of the country. The Colonizing Commission, "with a devotion to principle that laughs at death and a will that cannot be broken," designated two northwestern states—Idaho and Washington—as the prime candidates, because they were rich in resources, lightly populated, and "in friendly hands." Two small colonies with a total population of 110 were established in Washington, but none ever reached Idaho. The colonizers frittered away their energies in factional infighting.

When Socialism did come to Idaho, it came more haphazardly and with wide regional variations. The Socialism of southern Idaho was chiefly an agrarian movement, grounded in the early organizing of the Farmers' Alliance, feeding off the resentment of farmers and ranchers at the slow pace of reclamation projects and irrigation and the low prices that creameries paid for milk and flour mills for grain. When S. S. Foote's Caldwell Milling Company burned to the ground in May 1905, the authorities suspected arson. It was later reported that Caldwell's volunteer firemen suddenly came into a supply of liquor that night, guaranteeing that they were late in getting to the blazing mill and that most of them were in no condition to battle the fire. Nobody was ever arrested in the case, but suspicion focused on several "radical" farmers.

To the north, Socialists tended to be affiliated with labor unions—the AFL in urban centers like Lewiston, the WFM in the Coeur d'Alenes. But by and large, Idaho's brand of Socialism kept its distance from the truculence of the IWW and WFM, preferring to concentrate on electing people to local office and running schools, libraries, and newspapers.

Socialism made its debut in Caldwell in 1903 with the formation of the American Labor Union branch. Like the Western Labor Union, which preceded it, the ALU was a creature of the Western Federation of Miners and an immediate forerunner of the IWW. Soon after the federation moved its headquarters from Butte to Denver, it moved the seat of the Western Labor Union to Chicago, renaming it the American Labor Union. The new label signified that the union was now prepared to do battle nationwide for Gompers's constituency in the American Federation of Labor.

The Western and American Labor Unions wholeheartedly committed themselves to Socialism, as the WFM had never done. The ALU's preamble began: "Believing that the time has come for undivided, independent working class political action, we hereby declare in favor of International Socialism, and adopt the platform of the Socialist Party of America."

Those words provoked the *Caldwell Tribune* to a stern warning. It was upon "the shoals of politics," the newspaper admonished in February 1903, that "the great ship of labor unionism has been so many times stranded and often wrecked." If the ALU's object was to "injure or destroy the welfare of capitalists or employers, then unionism [in Caldwell] will prove a curse." But "if the object of the unionizing is to promote the welfare of the working men, and the working men themselves have a correct understanding of their interests, then the union will certainly succeed."

Stung by this rebuke, the new union informed the *Tribune* it wanted it "distinctly understood that there is no Socialism connected with [this] institution. It has no politics concealed about it in any way, shape or form, and won't have 'em." But a few months later, the visit of a Socialist lecturer to nearby Silver City prompted the *Tribune's* editor, Rees Davis, to return to that freighted subject. A stylish rhetorician and biting satirist—regarded by some as "the most gifted literary man in the State"—the Welsh-born Davis marshaled all these gifts in a send-up of Socialist ideology, which he defined as the "Reconstruction of Human Nature by Act of Congress." Socialism, he suggested, contemplated

> the extinction of selfishness, thriftlessness and laziness; it wipes out individual endeavor and individual responsibility; destroys social, political and economic distinctions; overcomes natural idiosyncrasies and acquired peculiarities, and reduces mankind to a smooth, oleaginous, homogeneous paste.... When a child is born, the Government at Washington, D.C. enters him for rations and duty.... The food he eats will be prepared by the Secretary of the Flesh Pots, and served by the fourth Assistant Scullion. The clothes he wears will be designed by the First Lord of the Fashion Plate, and constructed by the Eleventh Assistant to the State Tailor.... When the slobby period in the age of swain and maiden arrives, and thoughts of love bump around their diaphragms, the trouble can be relieved by merely making out an application blank to the Bureau of Matrimony. The First Assistant Match Maker General will tend to all the details. Socialism is a fine thing, especially for wooden Indians.

When someone read this acid spoof to Eugene Francis Gary, a blind tobacconist-newsdealer—and fervent Socialist—in Silver City, he was moved to reply. "Good old Horace Greeley, of honored memory, who founded the *New York Tribune*," Gary wrote, "once during his career was tempted to write a book entitled: 'What I Know About Farming.' Much good natured fun was poked at poor old Horace, and many pretended quotations from the book went the rounds of the press, such as 'if you want to raise good crow-bars plant selected darning needles.'" Greeley on farming was much like Rees Davis on Socialism, Gary concluded. For both editors, recording what they knew was easy, because each knew so little about his subject.

Not only had Davis "successfully advertised his ignorance of all that appertains to Socialism," the newsdealer went on, he had also proved himself ill-equipped to carry out his principal role "as a disseminator of correct information." Gary advised that Davis "look up once in a while out of the rut he is following and read the signs of the times. Let him put his ear to the ground and listen to the tread of the oncoming hosts of the industrial army."

Davis wouldn't publish this letter, he told Gary, because it committed the ideologue's characteristic error of "complacently affirming a superior knowledge and virtue in yourself and utter ignorance and depravity in the opposer.... You are very severe in exposing my ignorance of Socialism, and you have a right to be. Now will you please tell me what *you* know about it? Tell me what you, as a Socialist, propose to do for mankind and how you are going to do it."

To Davis's astonishment, Gary accepted the challenge. There ensued a remarkable exchange in the *Tribune* between these two clever men, disputing a central issue of their time.

A fifty-two-year-old native of Massachusetts, Gary had emigrated to Silver City in the eighties, working as a miner until an explosion in 1891 cost him his eyesight. Henceforth, he wore smoky steel-rimmed glasses to cover those dead eyes and the scarring of his upper face, while the drooping tips of his snow-white Fu Manchu mustache brushed his lapels. Unmarried, Gary lived alone, with plenty of time to polish his rhetoric. "You have ... demanded to know what I know about Socialism," he wrote. "Sufficient, my dear Sir ... to know that [the principles of our party] are founded on right, liberty, truth and justice." Davis had said Socialism would lead to the "centralization" of power in the hands of an oligarchy, to which Gary responded by pointing to the rapid growth of the beef trust, the railroad trust, the mine and smelter trust, and other industrial concentrations. "Do you see centralization going on around you in the country today under the competitive system?" he asked. "Assuming that your answer cannot be otherwise than in the affirmative, which do you consider best conserves the best interests of the whole people, industries, wealth and power placed in their hands, or taken away from them and placed in the hands ... of a small and arrogant class ... whose wealth and power are increasing in exact ratio to the decrease of their numbers?"

In his reply, published in the same issue, Davis abruptly jettisoned his air of lofty condescension, praising his interlocutor as "a gifted writer." The *Tribune*, he said, "is always pleased to present the serious views of others on public questions and accepts the truth always. As Mr. Gary has approached the discussion in a serious and respectful manner, he is entitled to most courteous treatment."

Davis conceded "the injustice and crying sin of the social system which, under the eye and direction of Heaven, has grown up to crush the weak and enslave the poor." The objection to Socialism, he argued, "is not that its teachings are vicious, but that it is impracticable, impossible," a point he illustrated with earthy examples. "Every last one of us is willing to divide share and share with the man above, but we have yet to find the man who is willing to share with the fellow below. It is a fine thing to own a riding share in the rich man's carriage, but who the devil wants a working interest in the poor man's wheelbarrow?"

Even if human nature could be altered—which Davis doubted—how would Socialism go about ameliorating the lot of man? The editor framed his question in terms that the fruit and vegetable growers of Canyon County could understand: "We put a man on a farm. The land is owned collectively by all the people of the world; the plow is owned collectively, the mower and the reaper, the wagon and the horses are the property of the community." Now for the reckoning. "In the fall, he gathers a crop of turnips and artichokes, and starts out to make first payment on his tools and teams. Now who is to say how many artichokes it takes to pay for a bay horse, or how many turnips for a sulky plow, and how are the artichokes and the turnips to be distributed so that every member of the great community shall have artichokes and turnips in just the desired quantities at exactly the right time?"

This missive elicited Gary's longest and most passionate response, a letter that so impressed Davis that he gave his entire front page over to it. "Mr. Gary is afflicted with that greatest of physical misfortunes, blindness," wrote Davis, "but his mental vision, though, as we think misdirected, is certainly very clear. His article should be read with care."

Though giving no ground on his central tenets, Gary was conciliatory. "In your former article you practically denied conditions and stated that Socialism was good only for wooden Indians. You have now admitted that conditions are about as bad as they could be, and that Socialism would be delightful for everyone, but have fallen back on the assumption that it is only a theory and therefore impracticable and impossible."

Gary never quite came to grips with Davis's uncomfortable question about the distribution of turnips and artichokes. The editor's essential error, he contended, was to adopt "the fallacy of the natural depravity of human nature." Socialists, he said, "have always claimed that the human race, under normal conditions, was and is more prone to good than to evil." According to Christian propaganda,

> every small and mean action that comes to light is cited as an evidence of the depravity of human nature, and yet, I dare assert without fear of contradiction, that there are more good actions occurring before us every day and every hour, than there are bad ones.... Once remove the incubus of this cut-throat system ... and the advancement and development of the race will, we firmly believe, be more rapid on its onward and upward career than the world has ever witnessed or dreamed of....
>
> Now my dear sir, I have great hopes for you. You have made more than rapid progress since this Socialistic tournament began. I consider there is excellent timber in you for a Socialist, and predict that you will soon be found in the front rank of the army of Socialism, if not leading the procession.

In his remaining years of life, Rees Davis never became a Socialist. But perhaps it wasn't altogether coincidental that two months after completing his colloquy with Gary, while writing on "Capital and Labor," Davis concluded that capital "dwells in palaces, lolls on velvet cushions, has carriages and servants at beck, railroads and yachts at command ... breathes the very air of luxury, and voluptuousness, until sick and satiated.... It is of the nature of capital to be cold, calculating, unfeeling and overbearing."

Or perhaps Davis had been influenced by the formation in 1903 of a full-fledged Socialist local in Caldwell. The American Labor Union had made little headway in the town, probably because Caldwell never boasted a sufficient industrial proletariat. But a branch of the Socialist Party didn't require large numbers of proletarians, and at the turn of the century, a significant portion of the party's strength lay with members of the petit bourgeoisie in small towns much like Caldwell.

Socialist Party regulations decreed that a local could be created by five or more persons, providing they signed a pledge: "I, the undersigned, recognizing the class struggle between the capitalist class and the working class constituting itself into a political party distinct from and opposed to all parties formed by the capitalist class, hereby declare that I have severed my relations with all other parties, and I endorse the platform and constitution of the Socialist Party, including the principle of political action."

Unlike the fraternal lodges that were such a large part of Caldwell's communal life, Local Caldwell—as it was always called—had no ritual, no grips, passwords, or signs. All of its meetings, the regulations specified, should be open to the public. Members would be required to pay monthly dues, shared with the party's national office (in Chicago) and the state office (in Boise). These dues would "give every member an equal voice in the affairs of the party, as it is a well-known fact that 'he that pays the fiddler calls the tune.'" Whenever possible, the local should meet weekly: "If the Local meets every week there will be no doubt in anybody's mind as to whether there will be a meeting or not. If meetings are held bi-monthly or monthly, the members forget the night of the meeting and there is a small attendance." The local should not meet in the home of any member, because the host sometimes felt "the Local owes him something in the way of a nomination or otherwise." Nor should meetings be held above or behind a saloon: "This has been the cause of the failure of many Locals. The women will not go to such a place, and you will find that your women are your best money-getters." Calm deliberation should prevail at all meetings: "If we are to rule the world, we must train ourselves to think clearly, talk calmly, debate kindly but forcibly, and this training can be obtained in the Socialist Local as nowhere else." The local should elect a new chairman at every meeting, "so that no one gets too much power and becomes the 'boss' of the Local." But it should elect a long-term secretary, who was vital to the local's future: "a live secretary will keep the Local alive, a dead one will kill it."

By early 1907, Local Caldwell would claim forty members—not bad for a town of barely two thousand persons—though the dues-paying working membership was barely half that. The local's secretary and all-around workhorse was W. Herman Barber, a ranch hand then living with his wife, Mellana, on a spread in Deer Flat, six miles from Caldwell. Among its leading members were Thomas F. Kelley, a thirty-one-year-old stonemason who'd worked for the past two years cutting stone for the new Canyon County courthouse— becoming known in Socialist publications as "the noble stonecutter"—and two other stonemasons, Rufus B. Newton and William E. Cavanaugh, employed on the same project; Collister W. Cooper, the lumberyard owner; Frank P. Kipp, who ran a Caldwell brickyard, moved houses, and drilled wells; Harry H. Compton, who sold and repaired bicycles at Compton's Cyclery; a rather mysterious figure named J. R. Nicholson, and George W. Snodgrass, a farmer, whose wife, three daughters, and son, all Socialists, made up the Snodgrass Family Orchestra, which regularly performed at Socialist meetings.

On March 14, 1906, convening under Nicholson's chairmanship, Caldwell's little band of Socialists had sought to diffuse some of the anger and suspicion with which their neighbors viewed them. In a remarkably conciliatory statement, Local Caldwell said:

> As friends and neighbors of the late Governor Steunenberg, we wish to express our horror at his assassination, and to extend to his bereaved family our heartfelt sympathy. We also declare, as Socialists do the world over, against the use of violence and against bloodshed in the struggle of labor with capital. But we must enter our most emphatic protest against the methods employed by the executives of the Capitalist Class in Colorado and in Idaho, to convict our fellow workingmen and comrades.... We especially denounce the violation of the U.S. Constitution and the Federal statutes in the secret extradition from Colorado....
>
> More than all, we denounce the attempt of the Capitalist press of the country, with very few exceptions, to pre-judge the case by calling our comrades "assassins," "murderers," "conspirators," etc. before the evidence has been heard. We demand that these working men, as with all other citizens, shall be presumed innocent until proven guilty.... And we unite with the whole working class of America in their present uprising in a universal protest against what appears to be an attempt of the Mine Owners' Association of the Rocky Mountains to crush out the Western Federation of Miners by railroading their officers to the gallows by the most extraordinary and unconstitutional methods.

Just how moderate this was for the time can be judged by contrasting it with the statement of Benjamin Hanford, Debs's running mate two years before, who declared in March that Steunenberg "got what was coming to him." Even the *Caldwell Tribune,* a Republican paper that generally supported Gooding, greeted Local Caldwell's statement with a combination of surprise and pleasure: "It is a matter of pride and gratification to the *Tribune* to learn that the Socialists of Caldwell are not the Debs stripe. Their resolutions ... with one or two small changes, might easily be mistaken for an orthodox Democratic platform. At any rate, they would suit the Populists to a tee." Nonetheless, it chided the Socialists for doubting that the union leaders could get a fair trial in Canyon County: "The Socialists have not absorbed all the justice in the county. The citizens of this county are largely farmers, stock men, business men and laborers. There is not a capitalist in the county, in the sense in which Socialists use the word capitalist. . . . We believe that 99 out of every 100 people in the county sincerely hope and trust that the men under arrest are innocent. . . . It is true, a great many fear they are not."

The moderation of Caldwell's Socialists may have reflected, in part, the cultural baggage they brought with them from the Midwest, as well as their ambition to become landholders and get rich from irrigated farming as soon as water became available. It also reflected the delicacy of their position. Canyon County was scarcely a Socialist stronghold. In 1904—when Debs, as the party's first presidential candidate, polled 402,283 votes nationwide and fully ten states gave him more than 10,000 votes apiece—the county contributed a barely respectable 236 votes out of 1,919 statewide. Most of the party's strength in Idaho was concentrated in Shoshone and Kootenai Counties to the north, Cassia County to the southeast, and the capital city of Boise.

Nowhere in Idaho had Socialism sunk deep roots. At the height of radical agitation over the Haywood-Moyer-Pettibone kidnapping eight Socialists were lecturing all over the state. One was Ida Crouch-Hazlett, editor of the *Montana News,* the organ of Montana's Socialist Party, who combined her lecturing with extensive reporting on the Idaho scene. Born to an Illinois farm family, Ida Crouch had attended the State Normal School in Bloomington and studied economics at Stanford before marrying Valentine Hazlett in 1892. She became a national organizer for the Woman Suffrage Association, then moved to Colorado at the turn of the century, becoming a Socialist organizer and lecturer and covering the labor wars of 1902–04 for Socialist papers. In 1905 she became editor of the *Montana News* but preferred the role of roving correspondent, in which she displayed courage and shrewd judgment.

She came to Caldwell and Boise expecting to witness great things, but her dispatches reflect deep disappointment. In town after town, she found the leading Socialists were "not those that command the respect and attention" of the community. Good people they were, to be sure, but "largely dreamers and sentimentalists," not men who could mobilize the working class. "There is practically no socialist organization in the state, and practically no one who has any conception of what real socialism is. There are a few vague sentimentalists, quite a number with anarchistic ideas, who think because they are radical and wild talkers they are socialists."

In Van Wyck, a tiny agricultural community, she felt the farmers "know practically nothing about the first principles of socialism." The Socialist Party in Idaho, she concluded, was "simply a disorganized mass of people with vague longings for a better day." Reaching Canyon County, she found Nampa "in the same condition as most of our country towns are relative to the socialist movement—fifty votes, and no organization." These sentiments were echoed about this time by a scorching memo from Thomas J. Coonrod, the party's state president. "Comrades," he wrote, "the good work our state organizer did this summer has been largely nullified by your indifference.... The Socialist Republic can come only through organization, and you never profit by inactivity."

In Caldwell, Crouch-Hazlett found a bit more political awareness, a heightened level of activity. As the site of the approaching trials, the town was filling up with Socialists and other labor sympathizers, flocking there from other Idaho towns as well as from neighboring states.

One of the first to arrive was George Francis Hibner, a farmer, school-teacher, and lecturer from Concordia, Kansas, an active Socialist who would soon run for governor of that state. Hibner belonged to a remarkable mid-western family deeply immersed in radical politics, social causes, and food faddism. His brothers, Lon and Willis, were accomplished minor league ballplayers. A skilled fiddler, Lon also traveled with a circus as a juggler and ventriloquist.

At thirty-two, George was the family intellectual, steeped in the classics, and a poet in "the Walt Whitman tradition." Stirred by the incendiary coverage of the Haywood-Moyer-Pettibone kidnapping in *Appeal to Reason,* he resolved to get into the fight at the red-hot center. Early in 1906, he settled in Caldwell with his wife, Mary, and their three young children. Before long, he was a stalwart of Local Caldwell, immersed in its efforts to support the imprisoned unionists.

Another impressive newcomer was Hermon F. Titus, the grand inquisitor of western Socialism, the principal theoretician of the party's left wing, a heretic-hunting purifier of the true faith. Narrow-minded in doctrinal matters, Titus nonetheless brought to his crusade an unusual breadth of practical experience. Born in Massachusetts, he worked as a clerk in New York, then became a Baptist minister for eleven years, leading congregations in Ithaca, New York, and Newton, Massachusetts. Concluding that the Church did not serve Christ, he resigned from the ministry and, at the age of thirty-five, took up medicine as "a more useful way to minister to man's needs." After graduating from the Harvard Medical School in 1890, he went West as a contract physician for the Great Northern Railway, eventually settling in Seattle, where he gained prominence as a "mugwump" reformer. It was while serving unemployed lumberjacks and other migratory laborers on Seattle's skid row that he read—in the original German—Karl Marx's *Das Kapital,* which persuaded him that "reform was impractical and revolution necessary." Elected state organizer of Washington's Social Democratic Party, he tried to mount a general strike in support of striking telephone operators, but the Western Central Labor Union, a federation of local unions, refused to support him and the strike of the "hello girls" collapsed.

Soon thereafter, in August 1900, a frustrated Titus launched the *Socialist* to "Organize the Slaves of Capital to Vote Their Own Emancipation." Within three years, the Seattle-based paper had seven thousand subscribers across the country, making it the nation's third-largest Socialist publication (after

Appeal to Reason and *Wilshire's*) among about a hundred English-language Socialist weeklies and monthlies that had sprouted in the past decade. "Our work," said Titus, "is to enlighten, to teach, to drive the truth into hard heads." As rigid as Daniel DeLeon, he argued for an uncompromising "revolutionary socialism" (which the Socialist Right burlesqued as R-r-r-evolutionary Socialism). Despite his own middle-class status—or precisely because of it—he railed against "opportunists" like Victor Berger and Walter Thomas Mills, who would turn American Socialism into a middle-class reform party (it was Berger's followers who inspired Trotsky to remark that a gathering of American Socialists resembled a convention of dentists). Though an apostate minister, Titus never abandoned his theological vocation, infusing his Socialism with missionary zeal.

Titus's fervor often outran his resources. By mid-1904, the *Socialist* had shrunk to two pages, without its popular cartoons because it could no longer afford engravings. Seeking a larger audience, in 1905 Titus transplanted the paper to Toledo, Ohio, which he regarded as the center of the industrial heartland. Then, in July 1906, he moved it once again—this time to Caldwell, which he expected to be the crux of the nation's Socialist activity until Haywood, Moyer, and Pettibone were either convicted or set free.

With Titus came Erwin B. "Harry" Ault, his precocious deputy. Ault had gotten his journalistic start as editor of a journal at Equality, a utopian colony on Puget Sound; then, in 1904—when he was barely twenty-one—he'd managed Gene Debs's national campaign tour. Now all of twenty-three, he brought an unusual mix of youthful energy and national experience to Titus's Idaho operation. Thanks to a special fund raised in Seattle, the *Socialist* sent its coverage of the Idaho cases to every union newspaper in the country, which, Titus estimated, put its front-line reporting in the hands of two million union men each week. A clean-shaven middle-aged man with a shock of brown hair falling over his right brow, he'd arrived in Caldwell on March 9, 1906. In establishing himself at the site of the assassination—"at the seat of war," as he portentously put it—Titus and the *Socialist* threw down a challenge to *Appeal to Reason,* the pugnacious Socialist weekly published in Girard, Kansas.

The *Appeal*—whose name derived from the rhetoric of Thomas Paine— had been founded in 1895 by Julius A. Wayland, a peripatetic editor and job printer who had accumulated some $80,000 in gold bullion speculating in Colorado real estate. Wayland was by no means steeped in the movement's great texts; Daniel DeLeon dismissed him as "a Salvation Army sentimentalist." But he had great charm. With engaging deprecation, Wayland called himself the "One Hoss Editor" as he set out to "Yankeefy" Socialism. He richly succeeded, capturing in the twang of his essays the wry humor and feisty independence of authentic American radicalism: "People don't have titles in America! 'Gin the law, you know. Titled people make people work to keep 'em in luxury, you know, and Americans would never stand for that. No

Sirree! Not while the Declaration is read every fourth, and the names of Lexington, Bunker Hill, Homestead and Coeur d'Alene are remembered! No oppression in America, if you please. We are free. We are the great people. The American eagle soars." An occasional column called "Society Doings," in parody of similar columns in countless small-town newspapers, reported items like: "Mrs. Edwin T. Warren, wife of a retired millionaire bridge builder of Chicago, has killed herself and a 4-year-old son" and "Miss Helen Marcelle Dickinson, a society belle of South Side, Chicago, has left the teas, receptions, bridge parties and home of her wealthy parents to go on the stage."

Under Wayland and his slight but fiery managing editor, Fred W. Warren, the *Appeal* had been an enterprising sheet. It was the first journal in the land to publish excerpts of *The Jungle,* Upton Sinclair's exposé of the meat-packing industry, which it called "The Uncle Tom's Cabin of the class war"; it ran lively exposés of white slavery and muckraked the Supreme Court. From the moment of the Haywood-Moyer-Pettibone kidnapping that February, the *Appeal* had made their case a holy crusade. Although Eugene Debs had contributed his first article to the *Appeal* in October 1865, he was not yet officially a member of the newspaper's staff. But with the kidnapping he told Wayland, "I want to do something in this crisis. It must be something far-reaching." He began writing some spectacularly defiant journalism, exemplified by the bravado of the piece that had so infuriated Theodore Roosevelt, with its inflammatory reference to "a million revolutionists."

When that manuscript first reached the *Appeal* office—according to one who was there—Warren summoned Wayland, who read it quickly, paced the editorial room for a moment, then dropped it back in front of Warren. "Fred," he said, "you've been doing most of it lately, and I guess you'll have to do as you please about this."

"J.A.," Warren replied, "you realize that the publication of this article may mean the suppression of the *Appeal* and the arrest for feloniously inciting to armed rebellion, of every one of us, followed by imprisonment and possible execution."

Yes, said Wayland, he understood. But all that mattered was that it would advance the cause of Socialism. "If so, regardless of consequences, publish it!"

Such bravado was contagious that spring of 1906. Ernest Untermann, who regularly contributed material to the *Appeal,* wrote Warren a couple of weeks after the kidnapping: "If the plutes kidnap our organizers and thinkers, we will kidnap theirs. If they murder our men, off come the heads of theirs. If they send their thugs and militia against us, forward the Red Volunteers!" Buoyantly he added: "Fred, this is for publication!"

Wayland and Warren were also influenced by the sensationalist practices of Hearst and Pulitzer, then going head-to-head in New York. In building the *Appeal,* they made frequent recourse to the yellow journalism of the day, including the "sob sister" story, which added human warmth and sentiment to the recital of dry facts that so often passed for reporting in some of the more staid organs of the eastern press. In December 1906, for example, the *Appeal* ran a piece by Luella Twining, a Socialist reporter in Denver, entitled "Will They Hang My Papa?" Under a linecut of Bill Haywood's nine-year-old daughter, Henrietta, Twining wrote:

> "Will they hang my papa?" This is the question William D. Haywood's beautiful golden-haired baby daughter asked a friend who was calling on her mother. Tears hung on her long lashes, and her voice was pitifully pleading. . . . When Comrade Haywood was stolen away, denied the right even of sending word to his invalid wife, who he knew would be frantic with fear, little Henrietta was almost crazed with grief. Every sound that broke the stillness of the succeeding nights sent thrills of terror to her little heart. . . . James McPartland [*sic*], the inhuman monster, . . . pretends to possess a tender heart for little children. . . . Oh, Sleuth McPartland! Here is one of flesh and blood! If you must rain bitter tears for innocent children, shed them for this beautiful little creature. Weep for this baby girl, whose father you are attempting to railroad to the gallows.

The weekly's rousing calls to action on the Idaho "outrage" were, for a time at least, a tonic for its sales. In March 1906, it had a circulation of nearly 300,000, a figure that mounted steadily with the exertions of some forty thousand members of the "Appeal Army," one of the most extraordinary bands of proselytizers this country has ever known. Many of these "salesmen-soldiers" were middle-aged artisans and craftsmen in small cities and country towns throughout the Middle Atlantic, Midwest, and Far West—men like Finley Bickford, a stonemason from Eddyville, Iowa; S. O. Cable, a carpenter from Newton, Kansas; and John Dimond, a shoemaker from Keokuk, Iowa. Some of them sold subscriptions to the *Appeal* out of enthusiasm for the Debsian brand of American Socialism and even organized Socialist locals on the run. Wayland spoke for these ardent spirits when he suggested that the Cooperative Commonwealth was just around the corner. "Socialism is coming. It's coming like a prairie fire and nothing can stop it. . . . You can feel it in the air. You can see it in the papers. You can taste it in the price of beef. . . . The next few years will give this nation to the Socialist Party."

Others peddled subscriptions out of a thirst for cash in America's emerging consumer society. For individuals, a year's subscription cost twenty-five cents, but by submitting a list of twenty or more names that could be delivered to a single address, one got the paper at the "club" rate of fifteen cents a year. A few salesmen, garnering hundreds of subscriptions each year, managed to live on the difference between the two prices; for thousands more, it was an important supplement to their incomes. Wayland and his colleagues viewed the Haywood-Moyer-Pettibone kidnapping, and the ongoing story of the men's incarceration and trial, as an ideal opportunity to build circulation. To labor unions, Socialist locals, and utopian colonies, a flood of letters went out on this model: "You and your brother unionists are no doubt awake to the importance of the approaching trial of Moyer, Haywood and Pettibone, the persecuted victims of the Mine and Smelter Trust. The *Appeal to Reason,* having made every possible preparation to report this trial in a most thorough fashion, now offers your Union the special and extremely low rate of fifteen cents per year, provided the Union subscribes in a body, or at least 20 names are sent on the enclosed list."

The paper had its devoted readers in the county, all right. One was John Gordon, the Socialist proprietor of a pool hall in Payette. "I'll always stand by the 'little old Appeal,'" Gordon told an undercover Pinkerton operative. "They know how to roast that dirty son of a bitch McParland. If what they say about him wasn't true, he'd of brought suit against them long ago."

Another national Socialist magazine had also hoped to use the Haywood case as a means of rallying American workers to the class struggle and, not incidentally, increasing its own circulation. Gaylord Wilshire, publisher of the magazine that bore his name, was one of the most flamboyant—and one of the wealthiest—Socialists of his day. The son of a Cincinnati industrialist, Gay—as he was known to his friends—prospered in the California land boom, developing the Wilshire district of Los Angeles and proposing its grand boulevard. During four years in England, he hobnobbed with George Bernard Shaw and the Fabian Socialists, thereafter trimming his beard—and his ideas—in the Shavian manner. In 1895, Wilshire returned to Los Angeles, built an outdoor billboard empire, ran unsuccessfully for Congress, and then founded a Socialist monthly called the *Challenge,* which he rechristened *Wilshire's Magazine* when he moved it to Canada in 1902 to evade harassment by U.S. postal authorities. In October 1904, it resumed publication in New York, becoming the most literary and intellectual of this country's Socialist journals, publishing the left's most glittering stars: Shaw, Leo Tolstoy, Jack London, Upton Sinclair, William English Walling, Charles E. Russell, and Eugene Debs. Sinclair, who met Wilshire at a party in 1902 and became one of his closest friends, recalled him as "a small man with a black beard and a mustache trimmed to sharp points, and twinkling mischievous eyes—for all the world the incarnation of Mephistopheles." Gregarious, self-promoting, a dude and a dandy, he was, in some respects, a Socialist P. T. Barnum.

For all its literary style and intellectual substance, *Wilshire's* never became self-sustaining. In December 1905—the month of Steunenberg's assassination—it claimed 280,000 subscribers. The next year marked the high tide of Wilshire's standing in the American Socialist movement, built on his magazine, his lectures, his articles, and his courageous defense of anarchists like Emma Goldman and Carlo de Fornaro. But the publisher still had to pour his own—and his mother's—money into his beloved journal, which he called the "Greatest Socialist Magazine in the World." Pressure mounted on him to increase circulation and, thus, augment advertising. To these ends, he

offered lush prizes to lucky subscribers: silk shirts, fountain pens, gramo-
phones, billiard tables, player pianos, collie dogs, automobiles, even a California fruit ranch.

The kidnapping of Haywood, Moyer, and Pettibone seemed to offer
exactly the kind of crisis in American capitalism that Wilshire had long
predicted, a revolutionary moment that would put his magazine at last on a
sound financial footing. "Let us show the world that the workingmen of
America are not lost to shame," he urged his readers in April 1906, "not so
devoid of the red blood of courage, that they will allow one of their comrades
to suffer death at the hand of their enemies, when they have at their command
a weapon which will set him free."

That same month, Wilshire found what looked like a custom-made
publicity vehicle for him, his magazine, and the Boise prisoners as well.
Maxim Gorky, the celebrated Russian novelist, was coming to the city on
April 10 to raise money for Russia's revolutionists. Wilshire invited Gorky to
be his guest, and the writer gratefully accepted.

At the Hoboken pier where he disembarked, Gorky was greeted by
thousands of admirers whose warmth the *Times* thought "rivaled the welcome
given to Kossuth, Hungary's champion of freedom, and Garibaldi, the Father
of a United Italy." He was then conveyed to New York's Hotel Belleclaire. At
a small dinner in his honor at a Fifth Avenue intellectuals' club, Gorky—
wearing boots and a blue peasant blouse—was flanked by Mark Twain and
William Dean Howells, who told him they represented a committee—including Jane Addams, S. S. McClure, and Finley Peter Dunne—that wished
to organize a banquet in his honor. A cartoon in the New York *World* depicted
the Statue of Liberty bending to light Gorky's torch.

Later that week, during a reception at the Belleclaire, Wilshire hurriedly
scribbled a telegram to Haywood and Moyer in Boise and—not wishing to
interrupt the writer while he was besieged by admirers—signed Gorky's
name to it. "Greetings to you, my brother Socialists," it read. "Courage! The
day of justice and deliverance for the oppressed of all the world is at hand.
Ever fraternally yours, Maxim Gorky." When it reached Boise, Haywood
composed an appropriately warm response: "Brother: The class struggle,
which is worldwide, the same in America as in Russia, makes us brothers
indeed. Convey our best wishes to fellow workers in your native land. We are
with you in spirit."

The next morning, when the newspapers published the telegram to
Boise, there was a fuss over the propriety of such intervention in America's
criminal process. Some of Gorky's advisers thought that, in the light of his
mission to raise funds for a Russian revolution, it was unwise to antagonize
those Americans who regarded Moyer and Haywood as murderers. To take
the heat off Gorky, Wilshire confessed that the telegram was his idea. But he
doubted it would cost his guest any dollars. "After all," he told reporters, "it
will not be the wealthy who will contribute to the cause of the revolutionists,

but the poorer classes"—by inference, WFM supporters—"who have less to give but will give of their less abundant resources."

But that controversy, which preoccupied New York's press that morning, was soon overshadowed by a page 1 story in Joseph Pulitzer's New York *World,* which "revealed" that the woman introduced in New York as Mrs. Gorky was actually the Russian actress Maria Andreieva, with whom Gorky had lived since separating from his wife three years before.

This fact was hardly a secret; well-connected reporters knew it and knew, as well, that divorces were difficult to get in Russia—for an agitator like Gorky, well-nigh impossible. But the story served the purposes of two institutions: the Russian embassy in Washington, intent on disrupting Gorky's fund-raising, and the *World,* which resented Gorky's agreement to write exclusively for Hearst's Sunday *American.*

In any case, Milton Roblee, the Belleclaire's manager, ordered the couple out of his hotel. When Wilshire told him that such prissiness would be ridiculed in Europe, Roblee snapped, "This is not Europe. I am running a family hotel and I can't have these people in my house any longer." Supporters found the couple a suite at the Lafayette-Brevoort, but when the manager there discovered who his guests were, they were expelled again. The same story was repeated at the Rhinelander Apartments. Finally, they took refuge at the Staten Island home of the Fabian Socialists Mr. and Mrs. John Martin.

But that was only the start. The *Sun* applauded the expulsions, contending "the purity of our inns was threatened." Senator Knute Nelson of Minnesota said: "That horrible creature, Maxim Gorky—he is about as immoral as a man can be." Plans for an invitation from the White House were scrapped.

Most hurtful of all, because they were his peers, the American writers withdrew their offer of a banquet. Mark Twain explained: "Every country has its laws of conduct.... When anyone arrives from a foreign land he ought to conform to those laws." To a friend he exclaimed, "Gorky has made an awful mistake. He might as well have come over here in his shirt tail!"

H. G. Wells was among the few writers—albeit a visiting Englishman—who stuck by Gorky. "On one day Gorky was at the zenith," he wrote, "on the next he had been swept from the world. To me it was astounding—it was terrifying." One evening, Wells went to Staten Island for dinner with the Martins, Gorky, and Mme. Andreieva. After the meal, they sat in the deepening twilight on a veranda in sight of the torch held high by the Statue of Liberty, which only days before the *World* had depicted lighting Gorky's torch. "[Gorky] had come," Wells would write, "the Russian peasant in person, out of a terrific confusion of bloodshed, squalor, injustice—to tell America, the land of light and achieved freedom, of all those evil things.... And to him she had shown herself no more than the luminous hive of base and busy, greedy and childish little men."

•

The Gorky fiasco could hardly have aided *Wilshire's* subscription pitch, which produced disappointing results. On May 15, 1906, Wilshire wrote Julius Wayland in perplexed commiseration: "Our subscription list is something like yours, not booming as much as it might, although of course we are doing fairly well, seven hundred to eight hundred a day, although some days of course it runs down to three or four hundred. What do you think is the reason subscriptions are not doing as well? My own idea is that it may be possible that this Moyer-Haywood business is not so conducive to getting up subscribers as a good many of the socialists seem to think. On the other hand it may be simply the general stagnation."

Whatever Wayland replied, he surely had reason to expect a greater response, especially in some of the Rocky Mountain states. In March 1907, on the eve of the Haywood trial, *Appeal to Reason* had 2,867 paid subscriptions in Idaho, compared to 21,179 in California and 18,446 in Oklahoma. Expirations in Idaho were running slightly ahead of new subscriptions. There are no figures available for the previous year, before much of the agitation over the case, but presumably they were still lower.

With a bare dribble of *Appeals* reaching Idaho in that bleak winter of 1906, Wayland and his managing editor, Fred W. Warren, made a bold decision: to seed Canyon County with their paper as a means of raising the community's political consciousness, sowing the defense's outlook among potential jurors, and, to be sure, harvesting some valuable attention for the *Appeal*. Warren gave instructions that, for the next eight weeks, five thousand copies of the paper should be dispatched free of charge to W. Herman Barber, secretary of Local Caldwell. Barber would distribute the paper as he saw fit in Caldwell, Nampa, Parma, Meridian, and other Canyon County communities.

The newspaper began arriving in Caldwell in April. Warren was delighted with the prospects. "The boys are thoroughly aroused in Idaho and they propose to see that the Federation officials have a fair show," he wrote a colleague. "The *Appeal* is cooperating at this end and we have agreed to furnish them with all the literature they can distribute with advantage without charge."

But Warren's ebullience was short-lived. A few days later, he received a communication from I. Wilson Wright, state organizer of the Idaho Federation of Labor. It was his sad duty, Wright wrote, to request that the five thousand copies be "discontinued." The reason, he said, was a note from the comrades in Caldwell that read: "You had better order the *Appeal to Reason* stopped for the opinions of all the workers is that the *Miners' Magazine* and the *Idaho Unionist* are the only ones that are doing any good, and the *Appeal* injects the Socialist question too prominently without carrying much matter bearing on the questions in the minds of the people."

Assuring Warren that "the *Appeal* is all right and no kick coming," Wright justified the decision: "It is a hard nut to crack to get the people to read about the case at all and we want to give them just now that which we can induce them to read and we would cut out any and every thing if it would benefit our imprisoned brothers. The Socialists and many outsiders stand by the Old *Appeal* and we will continue working for private subscriptions harder than ever."

It was a rude shock. On May 22, Warren wrote William Mills, secretary of the Globe (Arizona) Miners Union, who'd wanted to send a thousand copies of the *Appeal* to Idaho: "I am at a loss to understand this action as just a few weeks ago the boys were very enthusiastic over the work the *Appeal* was doing and ordered ... five thousand copies every week. I rather surmise that there is some politics and some prejudice back of this matter. However, it does not worry the *Appeal* in the least. We shall continue to hammer away to the bery [*sic*] best of our ability."

The decision should scarcely have been a surprise. In the propaganda war that had broken out in and around "the hostile farmer community" of Caldwell—a war, in essence, for the minds of potential jurors—both sides flooded Canyon County with newspapers, petitions, handbills, flyers, and circulars of all descriptions. One Socialist journal had explained its strategy in this way: "We must deluge Canyon County and the entire district with our literature despite the shrieks and howls of the opposition about 'poisonous Socialist doctrines.' Poison be it, then. Poison as an antidote for poison— Socialist poison for Capitalist poison." Among the papers that the defense distributed in large numbers were the *Miners' Magazine*, the monthly journal of the WFM, published in Denver; the *Idaho Unionist*, a weekly published by the Idaho Trades and Labor Council; *Appeal to Reason*; and, in midsummer, the *Socialist*.

Shorty Martin, operator of the Caldwell Steam Laundry, recalled that "you could get up in the morning and there would be one of those papers on your front porch." Some mornings, two or three. McParland was appalled. "The defense has just flooded the town of Caldwell with Socialist and anarchist literature," he said. "You can easily see what yellow literature will do with people who have no minds of their own." There was simply too much paper floating around the county. A backlash among the nonpolitical majority was inevitable.

But, as Warren correctly surmised, the *Appeal*'s problem in Idaho was, at base, political. The essential judgment came not from the rank-and-file "comrades" in Caldwell—the message quoted in Wilson Wright's letter was probably bogus—but from Darrow, Richardson, and their team, who felt the union men's defense could only be encumbered by association with the *Appeal*'s brand of socialism. Fred Miller of the defense put it quite explicitly in the spring of 1907: "This case has no connection with the Socialists in any respect, and the Socialists who have insisted on making it an issue have done much more harm than good. We have in a great measure headed off many of the Socialist publications from circulation in this part of the country."

Wilson Wright was more than the bearer of bad tidings. A former secretary of Idaho's Socialist Party, onetime recording secretary of Local Boise, currently president of Boise Local 635, United Brotherhood of Carpenters and Joiners of America, and, since January, principal organizer for the AFL in Idaho, Wright was a power in the state's labor circles. Lately he'd converted from Socialist orthodoxy to the revisionist notion of a labor party. A contested concept in radical circles, it derived from the work of the German Socialist Ferdinand Lassalle, who argued that emancipation of the working class would be achieved principally through the ballot, specifically through formation of independent labor parties such as those formed in Massachusetts in 1869 and Illinois in 1873. According to Ida Crouch-Hazlett, Wright was so "enamored of its charms" that he'd "forsaken his first and safe love [presumably Socialism], returned like a hog to his vomit, and is gyrating around with the phantom illusion that the 'good' capitalist system will give him something if he doesn't oppose it too hard." Now an informal member of the defense team, with responsibility for liaison with the Idaho labor movement, Wright, one suspects, had a voice in turning back the ideological Kansas weekly.

Certainly, unionists like Wilson Wright could argue persuasively that potential jurors would only be antagonized by Gene Debs's florid rhetoric about a million gun-toting revolutionists embarking for Idaho.* Evidently some prominent Idahoans took Debs's bluster with deadly seriousness. At a businessmen's banquet in Weiser, the editor of the *Weiser Signal* assured the waiting world that every man in the room was ready to "shoulder a gun and march to the border of this state and give up his life if need be to protect the commonwealth, its honor, its civilization and its laws." Others mixed indignation with ridicule.

"Remember, Gene," admonished one contributor to *Idaho Magazine*, "that Idaho is the largest lead producing state in the Union, that liberality is one of the cardinal virtues of the state, and that if you and your legions do come we guarantee to generously distribute our chief metal product among you, and it will be our unerring aim not to miss a solitary one." In conclusion, it said, Debs's threat had simply thrown many Idahoans into "spasms of laughter" and had made "even our most circumspect and sedate citizens laugh—laugh one of those gurgling, throaty, infectious laughs, like a baby playing with its toes, you know, Gene?"

The *Appeal's* portrayal of Caldwell may have had something to do with Idaho's rejection of the newspaper. On April 7—just a month before Wright's stinging letter—the *Appeal* had published a portrait of the little community,

---

* Debs wasn't the only one to engage in such bravado. After the Supreme Court upheld dismissal of the union leaders' habeas corpus petitions, C. E. Rolfe, a leader of the coal miners, told a Kansas rally: "The Dred Scott decision was followed by the civil war. The Moyer-Haywood decision will be followed by a rebellion of the working class. Arm yourselves, keep a steady nerve and get something to kill squirrels with, for the woods are full of squirrels, and there is going to be killing" (*Idaho Daily Statesman*, February 20, 1907).

now so much in the national spotlight, by George H. Shoaf, a special correspondent recently dispatched to Idaho.

"Caldwell is a small town of perhaps two thousand," he wrote.

> It is the center of all the sheep raising district, and there are numberless farms flourishing all around made so by reason of the irrigation system recently installed. The people therefore are a pastoral people...simple country folk from the farms and rural communities of the Mississippi and Ohio valleys.... This class of people are generally antagonistic to union labor. The farmer who gets up with the sun and works far into the night ordinarily does not like to see the wage-earning workingman demand and secure the eight hour day. He considers miners' wages of three dollars a day exorbitant and outrageous.... Such are the people who inhabit Caldwell and vicinity. They are simply, unsuspecting, honest country people, who do not understand the trade union movement.

Not surprisingly, many in Caldwell took umbrage at this brand of condescension. "It will be interesting to Caldwell people to learn from the *Appeal to Reason* that they are a 'pastoral people, honest but simple,' " the *Tribune* noted laconically. "In other words we are harmless sheepherders."

The *Appeal* faced at least one other obstacle in attempting to capitalize on the Haywood case: overt retaliation by employers against workers who subscribed to the newspaper. In Salt Lake City, a detective named C. W. Shores, who worked for the Denver and Rio Grande Railway, boasted to McParland that when Socialists began to flood the Utah coal camps with the *Appeal,* the *Socialist,* and other "anarchistic literature" featuring the Steunenberg matter he had obtained a list of subscribers from local postmasters and then—to use his expression—taken the subscribers on a "walk down the canyon." In other words, he simply had them discharged, giving them to understand that "neither an anarchist nor a socialist could work in any of the camps belonging to the Utah Fuel Company [or the] Denver & Rio Grande Railroad." Shores, whom McParland described as "one of the best officers in the West," told the Pinkerton man that "his action had had a wholesome effect." Some of the same effect was probably felt in Idaho.

As the spring wore on, Caldwell grew ever edgier as the reports mounted of Socialist organizing in and around the town. On April 25, came a warning from a long-lost voice, that of Captain Swain of the Thiel Detective Service, who was still fluttering around the edges of the case. He may have been doing some work for the defendants, as McParland suspected, but he prudently kept his hand in with the other side as well. Swain wrote A. K. Steunenberg that

> reports from our operatives throughout the Northwest show that the Socialists and friends of Moyer, Haywood et. al. are collecting considerable money for the purpose of establishing an information bureau at Caldwell during the trial of

the cases.... I should be very much pleased to see the authorities of Canyon County take some action in regard to these fellows and when the proper time comes see that their efforts are properly checked and controlled while the trial is in progress, as in my judgment if they are not, the outside world will be misinformed by their foul reports.

In May, the burning of the barn in Parma and threats to George P. Wheeler, an editor at the *Caldwell News*, provided fresh evidence that somebody was trying to intimidate the county's press. Then, in June, Caldwell's Socialists announced plans for a two-week series of street meetings to "educate" the town's citizens on what was at stake in the upcoming trials.

Street meetings were scarcely unusual phenomena in American cities; Republicans, Democrats, Populists, and Prohibitionists regularly sent their candidates out to speak under the stars—as did the Socialists. In the spring of 1901, for example, an "open-air circuit" was organized in fifty northeastern cities and towns for speakers dispatched by Socialist Party headquarters. But the prospect of Socialists venting their noxious opinions on the streets of Caldwell deeply offended James McParland. To Governor Gooding, he wrote:

> These meetings have been stopped in Chicago, Cincinnati, Denver and other places, and I see no reason why they should be given so much rope in the City of Caldwell. They are a gang of cut-throats and murderers and have no right to parade the streets and air their grievances, or in other words, their trumped up grievances, in public, whatever they may do behind closed doors.... It is no use to lie down and let these fellows trample on good citizens that are prosecuting these murderers. Every act of these people should be watched carefully, and when they overstep the law in any way they should be arrested. That is my opinion.

Those wishing to suppress such meetings received extra ammunition that July after the Reverend Ben Holman, a Socialist preacher from Ontario, Oregon—twenty-five miles to the west—addressed several well-attended gatherings in Caldwell's streets. Only later did the sheriff discover that Holman and a Socialist carpenter named Wing had bilked an elderly widow out of $1,100 in a home-building scam. Hermon Titus, in his newspaper, conceded that Wing and Holman were "two Socialist rascals" whose depredations were "so rare that everybody talks about them," while titans of industry routinely "rob their Millions."

But even such felonies were put in the shadow by disturbing reports that reached the authorities' ears later in the summer. According to a Thiel detective in the Coeur d'Alenes, the Western Federation was shipping guns into northern Idaho. "I have had some of these guns in my hands and know that they are there," the detective reported. One thousand weapons were said to have been stockpiled in the tough mining town of Burke, from which they might find their way into a statewide uprising.

And about this time, McParland received a more personal warning. A man named Guy Caldwell, a newly elected member of the Socialist Party's state executive committee who lived in the Canyon County hamlet of Falk's Store, was said also to be "a slugger [hit man] for the Socialist members of the Western Federation." According to a confidential source, he had two principal targets that summer. One was George Wheeler, whom the Socialists regarded as a mouthpiece for A. K. Steunenberg, who by then evidently owned part of the *Caldwell News*. The other target was the master detective himself. "This man Caldwell is the man who claimed he had been looking out to get a chance to assassinate me at the time I was in Caldwell," McParland wrote the governor. "I think this man should be very carefully watched."

Shortly thereafter, McParland began traveling with a full-time body-guard, his old friend and colleague Charlie Siringo (who apparently used the aliases Garner and Davies, though he was widely recognized by his old antagonists among the miners). McParland attributed this precaution to the nervousness of the Pinkerton brothers. They would "not allow me under any circumstances to go up in that country [Idaho] any more without somebody to accompany me," he said. As for himself, "I am not in any way afraid of these people that are making threats." Nonetheless, he would accede to his principals' insistence because "the anarchist literature that has been circulated [in Idaho] ... is liable to incite another Czolgosz to attempt to take my life."

For this intelligence, McParland was relying on a unique source: a Pinkerton man planted deep within Local Caldwell.

Barely three weeks after the assassination, Gus Hasson—McParland's early deputy in the Steunenberg investigation—abruptly broke off his Idaho sleuthery and hurried home to Spokane, where he called in one of his most trusted men, a squat, unprepossessing fellow known within the agency as Operative 21. One of the most experienced general operatives in the Spokane district, he specialized in high-risk undercover operations. Now Hasson briefed him carefully on the Caldwell situation and assigned him the name C. A. Johnson as well as the code name Relic. His cover identity was carefully designed for maximum plausibility: a former Coeur d'Alene miner, still a member of the WFM but currently unemployed and seeking a fresh start in Canyon County, now booming with reclamation and irrigation projects. After a weeklong orientation, Hasson sent the agent to Caldwell. In McParland's words, Operative 21's mission was "roping in with," or cultivating, people who were "suspected of being not only friends of Orchard but who might be used as witnesses for his defense." So deep undercover was this agent, so great a risk was he running, that McParland specified, "no person with the exception of the Governor and Mr. Hasson will know of [his] identity." As he dispatched Operative 21 to the town Hermon Titus had called "the seat of war," James McParland may have thought back thirty-three years to the moment when another young Pinkerton operative had gone deep undercover into the heart of a different struggle two thousand miles away.

Dressed in an old wool overcoat and a battered bowler hat—looking for all the world like a down-at-the-heels migrant—C. A. Johnson caught the Oregon Short Line to Caldwell, arriving one wet February morning. Within a few days, he'd found a job as manager of the Calvert Hotel.

The oldest of Caldwell's hotels, the Calvert dated from 1884, when, as the Iowa House, it catered to freighters and drummers at the bargain rate of six dollars a week. In 1891, it was sold to J. B. Sisson, took his name, and for a few years was regarded as the town's leading hostelry. Then, in June 1903, Addison B. Calvert, the former postmaster of Rockville, Oregon, and his wife, Mary, bought the old place for $2,200 and christened it the Calvert. A two-story frame building, with white clapboards, a pitched shingle roof, and a comfortable front porch, the hotel bestrode the north side of Arthur Avenue, not far from the old city hall and its adjacent firehouse. All too often in a town given to nighttime blazes, the Calvert's guests were awakened by the clanging of the great old firebell.

By 1906, the Calvert had fallen on bad times. The opening of Howard Sebree's spiffy Saratoga Hotel in March 1904 relegated the Calvert to second-class status, while the larger Pacific across the tracks provided stiff competition for the remaining clientele. Increasingly, the Calvert took the leavings—out-of-work miners, struggling farmers, small-time salesmen, all the riffraff of the road.

For that very reason, in the days following the assassination, the Calvert had been a major focus of both Thiel and Pinkerton investigations. The unsavory English "anarchist" who became an early suspect had claimed to be eating at the Calvert when the bomb went off. Then there was a scruffy man, wearing a mackinaw coat with a large collar turned up around his neck and face and "a bright and wild look" in his eyes, who rushed into the Calvert's dining room after the explosion and collapsed on a couch, seemingly out of breath. No one ever discovered who he was, but Thiel and Pinkerton detectives were in and out of the Calvert for days, watching the raffish assortment of tenants come and go, seizing now on one, then another, until all attention shifted to Harry Orchard.

To McParland and his Pinkerton colleagues, the Calvert must have looked like a perfect outpost for Operative 21. It was just the kind of place at which radical agitators might put up, hoping to blend into the background. Although Mrs. Calvert happened to be at the hotel the night of the assassination, the Calverts were essentially absentee landlords. The hotel was leased to a Mrs. Lucinda Jones, a widow, who may have doubled for a time as manager. It was to Mrs. Jones that C. A. Johnson applied in early February seeking work. From the beginning, they seem to have struck it off—Mrs. Jones had Socialist leanings herself—and Johnson went to work at the Calvert almost immediately. From his post behind the reception desk, he kept a close but unobtrusive eye on the scruffy traffic that milled among the lobby's potted plants and overstuffed furniture.

For several weeks in March, one of the hotel's guests was a New York journalist in Caldwell to prepare a report on the Steunenberg assassination and its aftermath. Associate editor of *Wilshire's Magazine,* Joseph Wanhope was a darkly handsome young man with a flamboyant pompadour and the style of a riverboat gambler. Even before his investigation began, Wanhope had reached some sweeping conclusions. On March 12, while passing through Denver, he filled in for an absent Gene Debs, the scheduled speaker at a rally in the city's Coliseum. On the platform before the speech, W. M. Hesener, secretary of Denver's Socialist local, told Wanhope to "hand them a heavy bunch"—give them the full treatment—and he did. The youthful orator—whom a colleague, in a surfeit of enthusiasm, once hailed as "the Wendell Phillips of the East"—told the crowd of four thousand Socialists and unionists that the Pinkerton-engineered kidnapping was evidence of the "desperate measures to which a dying system is reduced in an attempt to avert its inevitable doom." Whatever sugary frosting might be smeared over the crime, he assured his listeners, American workers now boasted a courageous press that would rebut "the flood of lies and falsehoods continually vomited forth from the capitalist organs in this case."

His preconceptions notwithstanding, Wanhope was an energetic reporter, and once he reached Caldwell he quickly sought out his fellow Socialists. On March 25, Wanhope wrote his publisher, the mischievous Mephistopheles, Gaylord Wilshire, in New York: "Last night, having heard a rumor that there really were some Socialists in Caldwell, I got on the trail, and to my great surprise succeeded in unearthing a nest of the vipers. There are more than I thought and they tell me there are five or six locals in the neighboring towns.... The Socialists here are going to get an organizer from the National Office in this place if possible and promise to become very active soon."

From what Wanhope could tell, Caldwell's population was broadly divided into "the new and the old." The old-timers, who'd been there several years or more, tended to be Republicans, conservative in their views, and hostile to the WFM and its leaders, while many of the relative newcomers—in Caldwell less than five years—were Socialists, Populists, or "radicals of various kinds." Some Socialists, he noted, had been drawn to the area by the prospect of government irrigation projects. For the time being, though, many were still camped out on the sagebrush desert, living in shacks, working as handymen, waiting for the promised water.

"I am going to cultivate one or two of these Socialists, who seem to be overflowing with political pointers and other information that may be of use to me," Wanhope wrote. One of those he cultivated was the manager of his hotel, C. A. Johnson.

Wanhope's lengthy article was scheduled to appear in the April issue of

Wilshire's, and, hard pressed to finish, he was happy for assistance from the friendly radical behind the reception desk. On winter evenings, around the potbellied stove in the Calvert's lobby, C. A. Johnson and Joseph Wanhope got to know each other, Johnson cleverly playing the neophyte Socialist eager to learn from the seasoned big-city agitator. Flattered by Johnson's attentions, Wanhope spent hours spinning tales of Gene Debs, Mother Jones, and other legendary Socialists he'd known.

One day, a Caldwell Socialist—perhaps Operative 21—took the correspondent to look at Steunenberg's blasted gate. "S. was literally torn to pieces and there are bits of him still in the debris," Wanhope told Wilshire. "I picked up an inch square of muddy cloth, which my guide (an active Socialist) said was a piece of the deceased's pants. Am keeping it for a souvenir."

But Wanhope spent many evenings alone in his room writing his article, which would be entitled "The Haywood-Moyer Outrage." If he showed some of it to his new friend, the hotel manager might have been struck by the highly colored style characteristic of that era's radical journalists. To capture Idaho's mood in the weeks after the February kidnapping of Haywood, Moyer, and Pettibone, he began with a Kipling poem:

> *Now is the hour of pride and power,*
> *Talon and tusk and claw;*
> *O, hear the Call! Good hunting all,*
> *Who keep the Jungle Law.*

"In the capitalist jungles of Colorado, Idaho and the mining localities of the western part of the continent," he continued, "the hunting season is now in full swing. The quarry has been stalked and shadowed and tracked and driven and rounded up, and the beasts of prey are crouching for the final spring.... Sinuous and catlike, the hunting leopards of the detective bureaus sneak through the underbrush on their bellies, their senses sharpened by the scent of the blood money.... And on the outskirts of the chase, hover packs of little capitalist hyenas, waiting to pick the bones after their superiors have gorged themselves on the expected prey."

Along with his jugular journalism, Wanhope functioned as a Socialist Party organizer and, in that capacity, addressed several meetings in Caldwell and Boise, among them the street meetings that had so outraged McParland. Wanhope brought a touch of irony to his rabble-rouser role; he knew that many Americans saw organizers like himself as "deep-dyed and tyrannous conspirators" who were saying to society, "Tremble, we have a menace for you." But he was an effective orator and Caldwell's Socialists rented Isham's Opera House for a major speech on March 27. Wanhope assured Wilshire he would go after the town's conservative businessmen, "put it to them straight and strong," demonstrate that "what they are really doing is to bring this very Socialism that they so dread, all the sooner." Later Wanhope claimed his meeting was not only the largest Socialist gathering ever held in Caldwell but "the biggest meeting of any sort in the history of that burg." The Boise meeting was "still bigger." His claims should be taken with a pinch of skepticism.

In his letter to Wilshire, Wanhope mentioned being shown around town by a Socialist "guide" who lived six miles out of Caldwell and "has been waiting three years for the water and expects to wait three more." This was almost certainly Herman Barber, the recently married Deer Flat ranch hand, and secretary of both Local Caldwell and the Canyon County central committee of the Socialist Party, who was often desperate for money. Barber frequently walked the six miles into town after his day's work, proving an "earnest, faithful and active" leader. He introduced the visitor to Caldwell's other leading Socialists—Kipp, Kelley, Newton, Snodgrass, Nicholson, and the rest.

If Operative 21 hadn't already penetrated Local Caldwell before Wanhope's visit, he surely did during the correspondent's weeks in town. Neither Wanhope nor Caldwell's Socialists seem to have entertained any suspicions about the hotel man, for sometime in March he was admitted to membership in the local. Henceforth, he religiously paid his forty-five cents in monthly dues (as he did his dollar-a-month dues in the Western Federation and a one dollar WFM assessment for the Moyer-Haywood Defense Fund).

Not surprisingly, the Calvert's new manager soon drew the attention of those on the outlook for suspicious strangers. It may well be that it was the operative about whom the *Statesman* wrote on February 27: "For some weeks —since a short time after the murder—a man has been in Caldwell who is an entire stranger and whose identity has not been discovered. He seems busy, but those with whom he busies himself are all strangers."

He certainly attracted the quizzical eye of A. K. Steunenberg. The little newcomer was so brazen, attending the radical street meetings, gobbling Chinese food with the Socialist editor from New York, consorting night after night with known Socialists in the town's cheap dives! He often seemed to be flaunting his obnoxious presence. On several occasions, A.K. and his allies approached Lucinda Jones, advising her to get rid of Johnson. But, as he was an excellent manager, she declined. Evidently, the Calverts refused to countermand her.

Then God's hand seemed to intervene. In late February, Addison Calvert was felled by appendicitis and spent a week recovering in a Boise hospital. No sooner was he released than his wife, Mary, fifty-eight, who'd been in ill health for some time, took a turn for the worse. Addison Calvert put his hotel on the market. It was promptly snapped up by John C. Rice and his partner, J. M. Thompson, friends and business associates of the Steunenbergs. They closed the deal, for $4,250, on March 29, two days before Mary Calvert died.

One of their first steps was to call in Mrs. Jones and order her, with no equivocation this time, to get rid of "that Socialist" Johnson. Once she reluctantly complied, they fired her as well, paying her three hundred dollars for the remainder of her lease on the hotel. One needn't look too closely to see A.K.'s fine hand in these moves. Or so thought James McParland, who on April 22 reported: "I regret to note that through the action of A. K. Steunenberg, No. 21 lost his position in the hotel. I would much rather that he should lose his position than to have this man pointed out to Mr. Steunenberg."

Renowned for keeping his head in a crisis, Operative 21 stayed cool in this one. Using his dismissal to reinforce his cover as a resolute Socialist, he wrote Joseph Wanhope, now returned to New York:

> I will drop you a few lines just to let you know how things are going. Caldwell business men have concluded to drive me out of the place. Yesterday the owners of the "Calvert Hotel" called the proprietress up over the phone and asked her to come to their office. They told her she must get rid of me or they would cancel the lease. She told me about it and I agreed to quit. I then asked to be allowed to pay my board at the hotel, but they objected to that, saying they did not want me around the place at all, and they also attempted to bar me out of the "Pacific Hotel." I guess now that I will stay in town just the same. I was ready to leave and go home, but think now I will stay just a few weeks just to show them I can. The town is considerably stirred up over the event. It is reported here that two companies of troops are stationed at Boise and that another is on the road there from Walla Walla, Wash. I look for a hot time next month, as everything seems to be pointing that way.

Just as the operative had hoped, Wanhope published his letter in the May issue of *Wilshire's,* followed by an editor's note expressing deep sympathy for this honest workingman harassed by "the petty tyrants of this rustic burg."

Johnson's crime, Wanhope explained, lay

> in the fact that the local powers have discovered that he was at one time a member of the Western Federation of Miners. Several times previous to this incident, his employer had been secretly approached and advised to get rid of him on the plea that he would "ruin her business." Until now she had declined on the ground that she herself was inexperienced in the hotel business, that Mr. Johnson was a competent manager, that the business had prospered under his charge, and that he could not easily be replaced. All of which though perfectly true availed nothing. From what I know of Mr. Johnson, however, the business element are likely to have an exciting time trying to run him out of town.

McParland was determined to resist all efforts to drive Operative 21 out of Caldwell. The agent's growing acceptance by the Socialist-unionist community coalescing around the trial was too valuable to sacrifice. Days after Johnson lost his job, McParland ordered Chris Thiele, now supervising agents in the Steunenberg case, to "instruct the operative to get a job somewhere else so he can cover matters while in Caldwell." Within weeks, McParland was pleased to hear that Operative 21 had stuck it out, finding at least temporary lodging with Frank Kipp, the brickyard operator, and his wife, Lulu. Kipp was one of Caldwell's most flamboyant radicals—"a hot Socialist," the operative called him—and the friendship only augmented Johnson's standing in Local Caldwell.

Moreover, Johnson had found another job, a position that delighted McParland. Through his Socialist comrades, he'd come to know Leon O. Whitsell, the Coeur d'Alene attorney who in February had assumed a variety of tasks on the defense team, notably as the principal "dispensing agent" for funds. In the weeks since, McParland had also identified Whitsell, along with Billy Cavanaugh, one of the Caldwell stonecutters, as leaders of the "gang of tough characters" who increasingly worried the Pinkertons. The detective had long yearned to tap into the young lawyer's clandestine activities. Now Whitsell, a young man with an ample shock of brown hair and a penchant for jaunty bow ties, asked Johnson to canvass Canyon County's farmers to learn their political outlooks and their views of this case, looking toward the time when some of these men would be summoned to serve on the trial jury.

For the prosecution, this was an astonishing bonanza. Hawley and McParland had long regarded the canvass of potential jurors as among the most sensitive clandestine operations to be undertaken by both sides. Even if the canvasser made no offers to a potential juror, no effort to influence his opinion of the crime or the defendant, such contact, in and of itself, might be seen as jury tampering. The whole subject was so sensitive that Hawley insisted that it not be financed with public money, because state officials would have to account to the legislature for the funds; when reports surfaced in the press that the prosecution was conducting such an operation, Hawley flatly denied it, saying, "No attorney for the prosecution has authorized anyone to make such canvass; we are not hiring men to approach any citizens to get their opinions regarding these cases." On the defense side, the activity was equally clandestine. For each side, the stakes—a jury sympathetic to its case—were high indeed.

But, quite apart from his specific assignment, Whitsell's decision to use Operative 21 in the canvass meant that the agent was now a trusted member of the defense team. The report relayed to McParland in early May said he had "stronger standing than ever" among Caldwell's Socialists and unionists. McParland had good reason to hope that this skilled operative would capitalize on that confidence to draw even closer to the heart of the Darrow-Richardson operation.

But McParland remained anxious at fresh reports that A. K. Steunenberg, John Rice, and their allies—very likely Harry Lowell, George Froman, and Dan Campbell—were still trying to drive the man they knew as C. A. Johnson out of town. Surely there were few Idaho citizens who more desperately craved conviction—and execution—of the union leaders than A.K.; yet here he was striving to displace the most valuable of the prosecution's operatives. On May 7, McParland in Denver wired Hawley in Boise asking whether there wasn't some way to "shut off" the Caldwell businessmen hounding the operative and thereby "allow twentyone [to] continue as he is now doing."

Later that day, McParland spelled out his concerns to the agency:

> The only thing that bothers me now is that some of the good citizens of Caldwell who are hot on the operative's trail—and we can not blame them as they are not in a position to know what the operative's business is—may attempt to run him out of town. I therefore would suggest that without giving the operative away that Mr. Rice or somebody that can be depended upon should be instructed to let this man alone as I can see the importance of the position that Whitsell has now placed him in. In this way the operative may be employed by them during the whole trial if the thing is worked right.

But McParland knew the perils in alerting anyone to the operative's identity: "It is very dangerous even to make any suggestion such as I have mentioned to Mr. Rice or to anybody else for the simple reason that Mr. Rice might confide to some of his friends and the operative might be uncovered. I will leave this matter to Gov. Gooding and Mr. Hawley." For the time being, the governor and the prosecutor opted for safety, saying nothing to Steunenberg and Rice, hoping that ultimately their fervor would slacken.

In midsummer, Operative 21 moved out of Kipp's place into a new boardinghouse that his old boss, Lucinda Jones, had opened. And in August, his penetration of the Socialist community was capped by election to the party's six-man Canyon County central committee, along with Herman Barber, J. R. Nicholson, Charles D. Cannon, A. J. Howd, and Hastings M. Whitney. Since all but Howd—a prominent Emmett peach grower—were citizens of Caldwell, it may well be that the county committee duplicated, or at least heavily overlapped, leadership of Local Caldwell. In any case, C. A. Johnson was now solidly installed in the inner circles of both.

Indeed, efforts to drive him out of town had only added to his prestige in Socialist circles. "I see you are still having laurels crowded upon you," a colleague wrote in February. To Ida Crouch-Hazlett, the Montana editor who had a low opinion of most Idaho Socialists, he was nothing short of a working-class hero. A "fortunate circumstance," she wrote, had strengthened Socialist forces in Caldwell, namely the arrival in town—on a "homeseekers' excursion"—of one C. A. Johnson, a Seattle Socialist and old WFM member who'd mined in the Coeur d'Alenes.

> The detective-cursed town of Caldwell had his baggage searched by Pinkertons before he hardly had time to turn around, and the good citizens of the Canyon county seat tried to bar him from hotels and all places of lodging, attempted to persecute Mrs. Jones, his landlady, for harboring him.... But Johnson proved to be the big Swede when it came to handling him. In spite of threats on his life, shadowing by detectives and other dark and gruesome accompaniments that

have followed the melo-dramatic grand stand play that the lords of misrule have employed in the fateful struggle, he stayed, he saw, he worked, and he has practically conquered so far. The attorneys for the Federation employed him on the case and he has been here ever since.

All through 1906 and into early 1907, the operative labored at the juror canvass with his staff of six or eight. These "scouts"—mainly Socialists and union members—were paid $3.50 a day, the miners' daily wage demanded by the WFM. Armed with lists of registered voters in each precinct, they fanned into Canyon County's alfalfa fields and fruit orchards, pretending to sell book or magazine subscriptions, livestock insurance, or sewing machines. Some, with bedding rolls over their shoulders, posed as laborers looking for farm work. Often showing up in pairs, they'd take their time, ambling down all sorts of conversational byways until they reached the upcoming trial, trying to draw from the unsuspecting farmer a comment revealing his attitude toward the case.

Sometimes the visitors expressed a strong opinion to provoke a response. "A farmer whose name is withheld tells a story of a man coming to his farm asking for something to eat," the *Portland Oregonian* reported in February. "While he was eating he said that he had been employed at a farm ten miles away and had been discharged because he had expressed himself too openly regarding the assassination of ex-Governor Steunenberg. Then he told a horrible tale of tortures and misery meted out to prisoners of the sweat box. This farmer failed to be in sympathy."

If the potential juror revealed his views, his name would be entered on an alphabetical list by precinct, followed by notations like "Republican N.G. [No Good] for defense," or "Socialist, O.K. for defense," or "Rep., anti-Gooding, favor of defense," "believes this is a case of graft to elect Gov. Gooding, but thinks the prisoners innocent," "expressed opinion against men, would like to see them hung," and occasionally "unfit for serve account ignorance," "gone," or "deaf," or simply "idiot." These lists would be on the defense table before Darrow and Richardson when it came time to pick a jury.

Such contacts were full of pitfalls, difficult enough for the professional, risky for the amateur. For there was a thin line between smoking out a potential juror's attitude and seeking to change that attitude or otherwise purchase a potential juror's support in the upcoming trial.

Several of the operative's staff soon found themselves in trouble with the law. One was Jesse Davis, a Caldwell Socialist with boundless energy and determination. Out on the boggy roads of Canyon County seeking affidavits, he wrote Johnson: "I have had one hell of a time. No bottom to the roads. Yet I have pounded them hard. Emmett to Payette, Payette to Emmett. But thank God the outlook is good. Let us ever remember the world loves a fighter, even though a few Sons of Bitches pound us on the back. Am going to pound them over the back to Caldwell tomorrow."

Davis and his brother-in-law, Orlando Hudson, were accused of trying to bribe two members of the Canyon County grand jury that indicted Haywood, Moyer, and Pettibone. Evidently, he and Hudson were seeking confidential information presented to that jury—the contents of Harry Orchard's confession and any letters that Orchard might have received from Bill Haywood—information that would have been critically important in preparing the defense case. According to testimony offered in the county's courts, Hudson approached H. M. Day, a farmer, and said Day could earn at least a hundred dollars by providing such material. Hudson was said to have visited Day's ranch and, after sitting around the house for a time, to have suddenly asked, "Day, how's your conscience? Have you any scruples against making a piece of money?"

"Not at all," replied Day, in the county's time-honored spirit. "I am after the money." But when Hudson explained what was involved, Day said he didn't want to make money that way.

According to prosecutors, Jesse Davis's encounter with J. R. Vasser, another Canyon County farmer, was similar. But the tampering allegations were difficult to prove and ultimately charges against Davis and Hudson were dropped.

The operative soon realized there might be another agenda in these contacts with real or potential jurors. One day, when he had said he might be moving on, Davis had said he mustn't go. According to Davis, Fred Miller of the defense team had recently told him that "there would have to be some 'firing' [this may be a misprint for 'fixing'] of the jury done in this case and that he looked for Davis and Johnson to do it; that it did not matter if it cost $2,000 to the man, they must have the right kind of a majority on this jury." Davis had urged Johnson to stay, foreseeing their making "a few hundred" dollars for their efforts. "He said that was the way Miller and Robertson won a great many of their cases . . . that was the way they won the Sloane murder case in Spokane and that Whitsell went there on purpose to deal with prospective jurymen."

A few days later, after dinner with Barber and Johnson, Davis came back to the subject, telling of his experience in a Missouri case. "After the evidence was all in and the Attorneys had made their arguments," the agent recounted, "they were afraid the case was going against them, so he and another man climbed a ladder to the Jurymen's window, at 1 o'clock in the morning, broke the window and bribed the jury, by paying them $2,500 apiece to bring in a verdict of 'not guilty.' He said there was more than $40,000 spent during that trial and that was the way in which most of these celebrated cases were won; that he believed the same methods would have to be employed during the Moyer, Haywood trial. He cautioned us to say nothing about this to anyone."

Four days later: "[Davis] has the idea that the defense will bribe the jury, when the Moyer, Haywood trial comes up. He said there would be thousands of dollars here then and we would be able to make a good piece of money out of it; that it was a graft and we might as well have a part of it as not; that the Attorneys for the defense were making a fortune out of it.... He said he had done such work before and would do it again if there was money in it, but would like to have me to help if the thing came off, which I promised to do if I was still here at the time."

Finally, the operative reported on Davis's account of a meeting with John Nugent, the third-ranking member of the defense team: "Nugent had acknowledged that the prosecution had a strong case and his only hope for winning was to bribe the jury; Davis said he had told Nugent that would be a dangerous piece of work, but that he believed it could be accomplished; that he had done such work before." After telling Johnson of another trial—this one in Nebraska for "deliberate, cold-blooded murder"—in which the jury had been bribed with fistfuls of cash, Davis expressed his confidence that "the same thing could be accomplished in this case if the funds were forthcoming."

In the grand tradition of Pinkerton undercover men, Operative 21 spent hours every evening in Caldwell's saloons, treating the patrons to drinks, trawling for flotsam and jetsam. He'd drop in at Dan Brown's Caldwell Club to swill watery beer at the battered wooden bar with stable hands and sheep men; move on to the Board of Trade saloon for several shots of Kellogg's Old Bourbon, the house specialty; then on to the Exchange saloon or Gordon's, invariably winding up at the Palace saloon.

Caldwell's first Palace saloon had opened in 1884, advertising itself as "Headquarters for Politicians. Who Are Supporting the Republican Ticket. And the only place where the Leading Republicans of the Territory go when they come to town." It had moved several times in the past two decades, presently occupying the ground floor of the Masonic Building, sandwiched between Isham's Opera House Pharmacy and Howard Sebree's First National Bank and just a couple of steps off Caldwell's principal intersection, Seventh and Main. On warm summer evenings, when they threw open the windows, a patron had a front-row seat on Caldwell's renowned cornet band, rendering Verdi's "Aria from *Il Trovatore*" or Sanglear's stirring march "The Belle of Indiana" on the ornate bandstand just outside. And any day of the year, a man seated at the spacious bar sipping a Gund's Peerless Beer and spitting tobacco juice into one of the polished brass spittoons could turn on his stool and get a first-class view, out one window, of guests pulling up to the Saratoga Hotel or, out another, of A. K. Steunenberg and his colleagues bustling in and out of the Banking and Trust Company. It was about the best vantage point an inquisitive fellow could have on Caldwell's movers and shakers.

But the operative had another reason for choosing the Palace as his nocturnal headquarters. For some reason, the once stoutly Republican establishment had become the favorite haunt of Caldwell's Socialists. Perhaps it was George Wattles, the new proprietor, or Frank Blake, the garrulous bartender, or C. E. Hayward, the "hash man" behind the lunch counter, who'd made it clear that the "lunatic fringe"—as Theodore Roosevelt liked to call them—were welcome, as they weren't at many other bars in town. A man could wander into the Palace any night, and before long, Local Caldwell would produce its quorum right there.

All Operative 21 had to do was keep his ears open. One winter's night, as snow drifted up the sidewalk and a north wind rattled the windows, it was Rufus Newton, one of the stonemasons working on the new courthouse, talking about the assassination. "The man who killed Steunenberg was deserving of a medal," he said. "The only fault he found with the affair was that it was not done long before it was," the operative reported. Newton went on to say, "The entire Steunenberg family are grafters. They came to Caldwell with nothing and grafted themselves rich, while they had a chance at the State Treasury."

These were brave words to speak anywhere in Caldwell, much less thirty yards from the governor's old bank. E. E. Perry, a Socialist from Deer Flat, was ejected from the Saratoga Hotel one night for mouthing off in the same fashion, but Operative 21 figured "he was so drunk that he didn't know what he was saying."

There was a lot of bold talk around the Palace of a winter's evening. One January night, the operative had a long talk with Sam Vasser "about the prisoners," during which Sam declared himself willing to do anything in his power to aid them.

"Yes, Sam," said the operative, "I believe you would do anything, as long as it is honorable, for them."

"Yes," said Sam, "and it would not make much difference about it being honorable or dishonorable as long as it was a help to them, and I did not have to run too big a chance."

That same evening, the operative met, for the first time, the notorious Guy Caldwell from Falk's Store, who'd vowed to kill McParland. The Great Detective wanted Operative 21 to hear Caldwell's murderous plans direct "from his lips." A Mormon and a Socialist, Caldwell carried a revolver he fondly called Old Betsy. He told Operative 21 he planned to attend the trial and to have Old Betsy with him, "ready for use" at all times. "A man would be doing an act of humanity," he said, "to kill Governor Gooding or Detective McParland."

The operative was such a steady customer at the Palace that occasionally Frank Blake asked him to step behind the bar while he ran an errand or two. The operative was happy to oblige. Customers with something on their minds felt comfortable sharing it with the man behind the bar. He got his best stuff that way. Moreover, as bartender, he was well positioned to get a good look at all the new faces that kept popping up in town. "It is supposed that they are land lookers or homestead seekers," the operative reported, adding pointedly, "although most of them are miners or have been at some time." George Wattles, the Palace's proprietor, had told the detective that "there was hardly a day passed but what there were strangers coming in the saloon; that he had never seen them before, and that they pretended to be looking for land, but that he believed that was only a 'bluff,' and that they were coming in here for a purpose. He said that he believed that there would be other people sent in here too; that martial law would be declared and [he] was afraid the saloons would be closed if martial law was declared."

Its Socialist clientele notwithstanding, the Palace was popular with townspeople of all stripes. One day, Bert Fuller, the city marshal, came in and spent an hour drinking and chatting with Operative 21. Fuller wasn't well liked by Caldwell's Socialists. Once he'd arrested "Red" Welsh, a brick molder and member of Local Caldwell, for public drunkenness after a night of heavy drinking at the Palace. On the way to jail, Fuller hit Welsh several times with his meaty fist and, once inside the jail, knocked him down again for good measure. The Socialists wanted Fuller removed from office, partly in retribution for this assault but mostly so they could replace him with Fred Davis, the town's night marshal, who was also a Socialist.

Nonetheless, Fuller didn't hesitate to drop by the comfortable little bar for a quiet drink. Perhaps he was gathering intelligence, for he asked C. A. Johnson, the man he regarded as a Socialist organizer, whether he thought the Haywood trial would really take place in Caldwell. The operative said he didn't know. Fuller said he'd heard that troops would be brought in during the trial and the town would be under martial law. "If this was done," he said, "it would be done in order to prejudice the public against the defendants." The operative reported Fuller as saying that "he had talked the matter over with Mayor [Roscoe] Madden, and that the Mayor was not in favor of martial law, but thought the town could be controlled by swearing in a few extra policemen." At which Herman Barber of Local Caldwell piped up to say that "the Steunenberg people might influence Madden to ask for troops, as he was pretty well tied in with them in his financial affairs."

Another of the operative's favorite hangouts was Gordon's, a dimly lit dive a few blocks down Main Street. One evening in September 1906, while he nursed a whiskey at the bar, he fell into conversation with one of those "desperate men" for whom he'd been instructed to keep a special lookout. To the agency, he described John Victor as about forty-two years old, with "sandy complexion," hair and mustache slightly streaked with gray, "the skin on his face hang[ing] in folds, making him look older than he is, and dressed in a plain, neat, gray suit." Victor confessed to being an ex-miner who'd worked at Cripple Creek "just before the trouble." He'd been forced to leave and now he was "very bitter against the officials of that part of the country." Victor showed the operative "a dirk knife, and said that he always carried it and a gun, and that if the occasion ever came, he could use them. He said that he was glad when he heard of Ex-Gov. Steunenberg's death; and that we would hear some more 'good news' before long." When the operative asked him what that news was, "he said that Gov. Gooding would cross over the divide as soon as this case was over; that there were men who would kill the governor now, would it not hurt the prisoners' case." Whether the operative took him at his word, he does not say, but Victor was "quite drunk" when last seen that evening.

Operative 21 was a careful, dispassionate reporter of what people were saying in Caldwell's bars and bagnios, but only rarely did he reveal his own assessment of their boasts and threats. Another Pinkerton operative in town that winter reported that one Socialist meeting he attended drew "about twenty-five people" and noted that "all of them were the poorest working people in town. I looked pretty tough myself, but I was ashamed to be there with that crowd." Later the same agent wrote: "From what I've seen of the Caldwell socialists they don't amount to anything. They are nothing but a few hoboes and saloon loafers." That went farther than Operative 21 ever went in dismissing the bar talk as drunken bluster, but few secret agents went out of their way to denigrate the value of their own intelligence.

In the saloons, he matched his interlocutors drink for drink but somehow managed to keep his wits about him. In his room at Mrs. Jones's house, he'd scribble his report in pencil on plain white paper, stuff it in an envelope with no return address, and the next morning mail it from Caldwell's post office. One wonders if Clara Maxey, who ran the office, ever wondered why this knockabout fellow had such an active correspondence, for almost every day the energetic operative had something to report, if only his nightly round of the saloons, a conversation with Kipp, Barber, or Davis, a tidbit of gossip picked up in the Palace or Gordon's. Rarely did he confess, as on April 16, "I did not do anything today." What little mail he received—the occasional note to meet Assistant Superintendent Thiele for special instructions or a debriefing—he picked up from a locked box he rented at the post office.

To defuse suspicion, he tried not to look too purposeful in his intelligence gathering. Along with visiting the saloons and low-down dives, he found time for the innocent pleasures of small-town life: the bowling alley, the pool hall, the skating rink, the strawberry-and-ice-cream socials, and the weekly band concerts. With other Socialists, he attended the Canyon County socialist picnic at John Green's Grove on August 31 and sat on the grass listening to the Snodgrass Family Orchestra. When the county fair opened in October, he bought a one-dollar pass so he could get out there and see the donkey race and the best ladies single driver, as well as competitions for the best loaf of bread and the best Indian beadwork. Like many other Caldwell men, he whiled away the hours smoking, spitting, and grousing at one of the town's livery stables—in his case, Van Housen's Pioneer Barn. Van Housen, a former officer of the American Labor Union and still a Socialist, liked to rail against detectives. "He said he always went prepared for the Pinkertons and if they ever fooled with him there'd be a funeral; that there were six or seven of the 'Blood-suckers' in town now," Operative 21 deadpanned.

By late autumn of 1906, the operative had been away from home nearly a year. A happily married man, he hankered for his wife. Things were quiet enough in Caldwell that McParland thought he could spare him awhile. So, giving his Socialist colleagues some excuse about a sick relative, he entrained on November 18 for Seattle, where he spent nearly three weeks.

The hiatus gave the Great Detective time to study reports from his other star undercover man. Code-named Operative 28, he was Arthur C. Cole, a "well-educated and intelligent" man who for years had been a visible partisan of Colorado's Mine Owners Association. From December 1903 to June 1904—during the state's bitter labor wars—Cole had been secretary of the Citizens' Alliance of Cripple Creek, a virtual auxiliary of the MOA. During 1904, while serving as lieutenant of Company L of the Colorado National Guard, he'd ordered the firing on the union hall at Victor and forcibly deported many union miners. Cole also did "secret work" for the MOA and various mining companies. In September 1905, the Pinkertons engaged him to work on behalf of James F. Burns, former president of the Portland mine, who was engaged in a bitter struggle for control of it.

Within days of Steunenberg's assassination, McParland brought Cole into that case as well, at first to investigate Harry Orchard's background in Colorado and eventually to become the lead agent in a major operation designed to entrap the Haywood defense.* Given his history on the other side, Cole might have seemed an unlikely instrument for Darrow and Richardson. But to prove a mine owners' conspiracy to destroy the WFM, the defense attorneys needed some defector from the owners' ranks—and Cole persuaded them he was their man. Under McParland's active guidance, Cole promised to testify in Boise about the mine owners' plans to blow up the Independence depot and assassinate public figures in Colorado and Idaho so as to blame these atrocities on the WFM. Ultimately, the plan called for Darrow to bring Cole to Boise as a defense witness, then have him appear for the prosecution, testifying to the "lies" Darrow had paid him to advance.

In this year-long effort to infiltrate, and ultimately betray, the Haywood defense, Cole dealt principally with two representatives of the Darrow-Richardson team. One was Frank Hangs, forty-six, a former Denver justice of the peace and city attorney of Cripple Creek, who now represented WFM interests in that troubled community. The other was Walter McCornack, one of Darrow's most remarkable agents.

Walter Edwin McCornack was among the greatest football players the young sport had yet produced. Between 1893 and 1896, he'd been an outstanding Dartmouth quarterback, elected captain his last two years and becoming

---

* The priority McParland gave this operation is reflected in a letter he sent from Denver to the Pinkertons' superintendent in Portland early in 1907: "I am at present engaged on a very important matter in connection with this case. The matter in question is second in importance to the confession of Orchard, and of such importance that . . . I want to devote most of my time to the matter" (McParland to Kemble, January 11, 1907).

the first Dartmouth player selected as a Walter Camp All-American. After coaching at Exeter, he returned to Dartmouth in 1901, rapidly transforming his alma mater into a regional powerhouse. In 1903, he resigned to study law at Northwestern while coaching that university's team in what was then known as the Big Nine.

His three-year record at Northwestern—twenty-six wins, five losses, and four ties—was superb. But early in 1906, the university stunned its alumni and rooters by withdrawing from intercollegiate football. In part this decision —following similar moves by Columbia, Stanford, and California—reflected an outcry against the game's "professionalization." Scholars decried the "undignified chase among the colleges after men of muscle," the schooling of "powerful animals." In November 1905, McCornack himself was accused of paying boys to play, giving bonuses for each victory. He denied the charges, but suspicions persisted.

But the immediate trigger for these withdrawals was rising concern about the game's "brutality." In the era before the forward pass, coaches relied heavily on the so-called mass play, exemplified by the "flying wedge," the "forcing of a solid triangle of vigorous men upon one or two isolated but sternly resisting players." In 1905 alone, 145 football players suffered serious injuries and 24 were killed, prompting Professor Shailer Mathews of the University of Chicago Divinity School to protest against "this boy-killing, man-mutilating, money-making, education-prostituting, gladiatorial sport."

Theodore Roosevelt took great interest in this controversy, calling a meeting of football's Big Three—Harvard, Yale, and Princeton—at the White House in October 1905, which produced a promise to honor "in letter and in spirit" the rules on roughness, holding, and foul play. That Roosevelt worried about the game's roughness was evident in his warning to his son Ted about playing football at Groton against older and heavier boys: "Athletic proficiency is a mighty good servant, and like so many other servants, a singularly bad master." But his public tirades on the subject became notorious: "The time given to athletic contests and the injuries incurred on the playing field are part of the price which the English-speaking race has paid for being world conquerors."

In any case, by early 1906 "Mac" McCornack, having earned his law degree and without football responsibilities, was free to take up other assignments. During law school, he'd worked part-time in Darrow's office. When Darrow took on the Haywood case—and needed someone to head up his investigation in the tough mining districts of Colorado—he thought of McCornack. Though not a large man as football players went—only five foot ten and 160 pounds—he was wiry, bold, and tenacious. Darrow needed an investigator in Cripple Creek and Telluride who wasn't easily pushed around. He sent McCornack, and all through 1906 and into 1907, the All-American quarterback bargained with Operative 28 and other management bullyboys, trying to build a case for a mine owners' conspiracy against the WFM.

•

Shortly after Operative 21 returned to Caldwell on December 15 an incident occurred—or didn't occur—that was to occupy much of the operative's time for weeks to come. His principal deputy, Jesse Davis, told the outgoing sheriff, Jap Nichols, that just before midnight on Saturday, December 29—more or less the first anniversary of Governor Steunenberg's assassination—several masked men had tried to kill him, his wife, Lucy, and his sons. Davis contended the attackers had been "Pinkerton people" bent on retaliating for his denunciations of Governor Gooding and Judge Frank Smith the autumn before and on dissuading him from "doing further work for the WFM."

Davis said that he'd been awakened that night by the "violent barking" of his dogs. Looking out the window, he and his wife saw two men with black handkerchiefs tied over their faces riding toward the house. Suddenly, the men pulled revolvers and fired two shots in the direction of the building. One bullet crashed through the Davises' bedroom window. The other went through a tent in the backyard, where their consumptive son took the "open-air treatment" with one of his brothers. Davis went for his shotgun; unable to find cartridges, he struck a match, which brought another volley of gunshots crashing through the window. Finally, Davis managed to load his weapon, but by the time he got outside the attackers were well out of range.

From the start, there was plenty of skepticism in Caldwell about Davis's allegations. The *Caldwell Tribune* found the story bearing "all the earmarks of improbability." At the time of the alleged attack, it said, "it was raining and very dark, and it would have been impossible for Jesse Davis or any other man with ordinary eyesight to have told whether the men were masked or not." The *Tribune* concluded that Jesse Davis and his "confederates" had concocted the whole episode as part of the defense's campaign for a change of venue, since such a motion would benefit if it could be shown that Caldwell was unsafe and its people unlawful.

The county's new sheriff, William H. Thorp, and his deputy Frank Breshears inspected Davis's place and found "bullet holes in the house and the tent" but "could not find evidence to fix the blame on any particular person or persons."* The Pinkertons were even more skeptical. "There is no question in my mind but what Davis is guilty of this so-called outrage upon himself and his family," McParland wrote on January 7. "As to whether he fired the shots from the inside or outside of the house, I think this could be easily determined by an expert."

But if the Davis episode was theater, it seems nevertheless to have persuaded Caldwell's Socialists. On January 5, Herman Barber—still secretary of both the town and the county Socialist organizations—showed Opera-

---

The outgoing sheriff, Jap Nichols, had decided that the job was "too strenuous" for him and he didn't want a second term (*Caldwell Tribune*, May 19, 1906).

tive 21 his "automatic gun" and "how fast it would shoot." He said that he had bought it "as soon as he heard of the shooting at Davis' and that he intended to carry it all the time, as he didn't consider anyone safe who had ever worked for the W.F. of M. He said if anyone started to following [*sic*] around when he went to work this time, that the Coroner would have a job; that he believed it would be an honor to kill a Pinkerton."

But the principal Pinkerton in town wasn't worried, for his cover was holding fast. In mid-January, Operative 21 heard from his friend Joseph Wanhope at *Wilshire's Magazine*, thanking him for a letter the operative had recently sent. The editor was "glad also to see that you have stuck by your guns and they have not been able to drive you out." Wanhope doubted whether he'd cover the Haywood trial for *Wilshire's*, noting that the full weight of editing the magazine and several sister publications had fallen on his shoulders. "However, we will not be without a representative at the trial. I see the 'Appeal' has engaged Debs, and that certainly is an excellent move. Our man is not selected yet, but I can tell you in confidence that we are negotiating with an equally well known Socialist writer who can perhaps even surpass Debs in descriptive work. I am not at liberty to give his name."

The man *Wilshire's* had in mind was the twenty-eight-year-old Upton Sinclair, who, after years of penury, was an overnight sensation following the 1906 publication of *The Jungle*, which portrayed the world as "a slaughterhouse where the many were ground up into sausages for the breakfast of the few." Sinclair followed events in Boise closely in the press, firmly believed the defendants were innocent, and even worked some perfervid paragraphs on the case into the closing chapters of *The Jungle*. (He toned them down at the urging of Fred Warren, his editor at *Appeal to Reason*, but not sufficiently to satisfy Theodore Roosevelt, who wrote Sinclair's publisher to denounce his "ridiculous socialistic rant.") He had just finished a book called *The Industrial Republic*, which *Wilshire's* was excerpting that spring, explaining in an introductory note that "Mr. Sinclair asserts that his studies have led him to the positive conclusion that the revolution which will displace capitalism as the form of economic society will begin immediately after the presidential election of 1912." A close friend of Gaylord Wilshire's, Sinclair apparently accepted the assignment at the editor's urging. *Wilshire's* announced proudly in February 1907: "We have engaged one of the best Socialist writers in the country.... A man who could write *The Jungle* can write the history of the trial in a manner to shake capitalism once more to its very depths." As late as April, the magazine said Sinclair would leave for Boise as soon as a trial date was set.

In his letter to the operative, Wanhope went on: "Glad to know that the boys [Haywood, Moyer, and Pettibone] are in good health and spirits. I hope the outcome will be such that they will be free men before many more weeks have passed.... Are you still in the Hotel business? If so, let me know, and i will post the man we send out, and you may be able to find him a room in advance.... How is the Socialist local getting along in Caldwell. It should be fairly large by this time. Give my best regards to Barber, Kipp, Snodgrass, Kavanaugh [*sic*], and Kelly [*sic*]."

The operative showed the letter to Frank Kipp, who was "well pleased at the mention of his name" and "thought we ought to reorganize the Caldwell local and get it in good working order again before the trial of Moyer, Haywood and Pettibone." Kipp's comment suggests that, despite their surface activity, the Caldwell Socialists were no more rigorously organized than those elsewhere in the state who had so dismayed Ida Crouch-Hazlett.

In mid-January, Leon Whitsell handed the operative a fresh responsibility. Even as C. A. Johnson and his staff continued to canvass the county's male population eligible for the jury, he was asked to lead the affidavit drive seeking a change of venue. Darrow and Richardson had concluded that, their best efforts in jury selection notwithstanding, Canyon County was simply too obsessed with the tragedy of Frank Steunenberg's untimely death. They wanted a site—preferably the Democratic stronghold of Washington County —where they wouldn't have to try the case before the dead governor's relatives, friends, and neighbors.

In the affidavits that the operative now hauled back and forth across the county, men were asked to swear that, since the assassination, "a strong prejudice" existed against the defendants in Canyon County and that so many men in the county believed the defendants guilty of Steunenberg's murder "that defendants cannot have a fair and impartial trial in said county." If possible, Whitsell said, Johnson's canvassers should collect six hundred affidavits. But no affidavit should be sought from any prospective juror known to be favorable to the defense, for fear his signature might disqualify him from the panel.

For weeks that winter, the drive for affidavits was slowed by an infuriating obstacle. The documents had to be signed before a notary public, and most of Canyon County's notaries were lawyers, who flatly refused to perform even this small service for the defendants. A few years later, the Caldwell lawyer Ralph Scatterday recalled that time: "The city became overrun with detectives. Nobody knew for whom they were working. One of the detectives was an offensive fellow, potbellied, who went around contacting everybody and insulting everybody. He came to my office and offered me twenty-five dollars a day for the simple task of witnessing signatures for a change of venue. When I refused to work for the union, he snarled, 'The union will get you for this.'" Later still, his partner, Owen Van Duyn, told him the man who'd approached him was C. A. Johnson, a prosecution detective posing as a defense agent. "My partner showed me the dossier in which my reactions to the bait of twenty-five dollars a day had been recorded."

For notaries, the operative ultimately fell back on Henry and Walter

Griffiths, Caldwell attorneys who'd done the unthinkable—actually joined the defense team; A. A. Sissons, a lawyer in Parma; and Ira Kenward, a Payette attorney.

On January 16, the operative took a day off to go wolf hunting with Jesse Davis. Hiring a saddle horse from the Pioneer Barn, he rode out to Davis's place and thence about five miles across country, noting for his employers that Davis was heavily armed with a 28–30 Winchester rifle, a .22 Winchester, and a 12-gauge shotgun. Had any of these weapons, he wondered, been the ones fired into Davis's house and tent in December, and, if so, who had pulled the trigger? Without spotting any game at all, they returned to town.

After a ritual visit to the Palace saloon, the operative ambled across the street to check his post office box. On the way out, he encountered Herman C. Carrier, the new proprietor of the Calvert Hotel, the man to whom John Rice and his law partner, J. M. Thompson, had leased the hotel after getting rid of both the operative and Lucinda Jones. Carrier was a professional hotel man who had until recently held a lease on Caldwell's Commercial Hotel.

There was no love lost between Carrier and him, but the Pinkerton man seemed surprised when Carrier accused him of "keeping people away from his house, giving it the name of 'scab' house." The operative said he'd done no such thing; Carrier insisted he had, finally calling him a liar. "I promptly knocked him down," reported the operative. "He got up running and left his hat behind him."

Caldwell didn't wink at casual violence on its downtown streets. The very next day, Operative 21 was served with a warrant and ordered to appear two days hence in Canyon County District Court. One would have expected the Caldwell establishment to rally behind the proprietor of John Rice's hotel and against Johnson, the notorious Socialist. If nothing else, this incident might have provided the long-sought occasion to run the operative out of town. But, quite the contrary, people took the operative's side of the matter.

When court convened on January 19, Judge Frank Smith fined him ten dollars for knocking the hotel keeper down on a public street. Then the city attorney—we do not know whether it was Rice or Thompson—announced that he had conclusive evidence that Carrier was carrying a concealed weapon. Concealed weapons were not all that unusual in Caldwell; if the operative is to be believed, at least a half dozen Socialists carried them. (On one occasion, Leon Whitsell showed the operative a Colt automatic .32, with its magazine of eight cartridges, "a handsome little gun" that he said he and all the defense lawyers, Darrow among them, were carrying.) Nonetheless, Judge Smith ordered Carrier searched then and there. When a revolver was unearthed, stuffed in an inner pocket, the spluttering hotel keeper was fined fifty dollars on the spot.

That wasn't all. Eleven days later, the town marshal found the Calvert Hotel to be "a house of ill fame," closed it down indefinitely, and ordered H. C. Carrier to get out of town at once—which he apparently did.

Operative 21 quoted the marshal as saying, "It was a good joke on the proprietors of the place, as they ran Mrs. Jones out of the place, because it was not run to suit them, and then got in a party who turned it into a house of ill repute." But if it was a joke, it was a joke that Rice and Thompson, as the city's attorneys, played on themselves, as the hotel's owners. Indeed, the more one ponders this sequence of events, the more one is inclined to believe that the governor or James Hawley had finally found some way to get word through to A. K. Steunenberg and John Rice that Operative 21 had to be kept on the job in Caldwell. Years later, Pete Steunenberg told an interviewer that people had come to him and said there was a man going all over town saying, "Governor Steunenberg got what was coming to him." Friends offered to run the fellow out of town. "Then we found out he was a Pinkerton, working for the State, as an agent provocateur trying to find out who in town was sympathetic to labor." That sounds like Operative 21.

If the Steunenbergs were tipped off, perhaps Carrier, though he was Rice's lessee, had simply not gotten the message. When he pursued his vendetta against the operative, it became necessary—for reasons of state—to shut the hotel down awhile and hustle its misguided proprietor out of town.

Maneuvering by both sides accelerated as they neared the March 12 start of the spring term in Canyon County's courts. Since the Socialist-WFM agitation had claimed Judge Smith as its prime victim the autumn before, the cases against Haywood, Moyer, and Pettibone now rested with the Democratic victor in that race, a small-time lawyer from neighboring Payette named Edgar L. Bryan. But the court had appointed Bryan a year before to represent Harry Orchard, and many felt it would be a conflict of interest for him to preside over the Haywood-Moyer-Pettibone trials. Although Hawley thought Bryan "a good man," McParland, for one, was "very doubtful" as to whether he could be depended on. After all, the detective noted, "he was elected by Western Federation of Miners money." Bryan saw no reason to disqualify himself, but he reluctantly bowed to pressure, asking Judge Fremont Wood of the Third Judicial District (Ada County) to take his place.

Wood was a fifty-year-old Republican elected to the bench just the previous fall, replacing George H. Stewart, who at the same election was elevated to the Idaho Supreme Court. Born in Maine, he was the son of an abolitionist legislator and close friend of Hannibal Hamlin—Lincoln's vice president, who campaigned for the use of black regiments during the Civil War. Wood attended Bates College for two years before his father's death compelled him to support the family. After reading law in two small-town law offices, he'd gone West in 1881 with a friend, Wallace R. White, who'd been appointed United States attorney for the Territory of Idaho. Shortly after their arrival in Boise, White appointed his friend as assistant U.S. attorney, a job Wood held concurrently with the post of Boise city attorney. When Idaho became a state in 1890, Wood was named U.S. attorney and, in that capacity, prosecuted the Coeur d'Alene defendants of 1892, convicting thirteen men for contempt of court and four—among them George Pettibone—for criminal conspiracy.

One might imagine that his role as a prosecutor in 1892 would have alarmed the Haywood defense team, but such was Wood's reputation as a fair-minded man that the defense actually welcomed his assuming jurisdiction—as did the prosecution. McParland informed Gooding that the judge was "a man of strong character and will show no favors." Something of a country gentleman, the judge owned extensive apple orchards on Boise's outskirts and was acknowledged to be one of the state's leading horticulturists, specializing in dazzling red roses.

On March 25, after hearing arguments by both sides, Wood granted the change of venue for which the defense had been plumping. But instead of its preferred site in Washington County, Wood brought the trials to his own bench in Boise, setting May 9 for the start of jury selection. The three men would be tried separately, with Haywood—the prosecution's principal target —coming first.

Both sides accepted this resolution with equanimity—though, for Haywood, there was one ironic note in the decision. Some months earlier, Billy Cavanaugh, the Caldwell Socialist working on the Canyon County courthouse, had sent word to Haywood asking if there was anything he would like to put in the courthouse cornerstone that would be laid on April 4, 1906. Haywood smuggled out his WFM membership card and a copy of the union's constitution, which Cavanaugh placed in the cornerstone—a talisman, perhaps, for a favorable verdict.

Haywood, Moyer, and Pettibone hadn't been held in Canyon County since late March 1906, when the authorities had moved them to the Ada County jail in Boise. Now their trials would be held in the courtroom two floors above their heads.

For the defense, anything was better than Steunenberg's hometown, where "the very air"—as Ida Crouch-Hazlett put it—was "surcharged with prejudice." For that very reason, McParland preferred Canyon County as the trial site; a change, he wrote the Pinkerton brothers, would be "very unfortunate." But so far as Hawley and Borah were concerned, Boise had the benefit of being home: they could operate out of their own law offices and sleep in their own beds instead of in some country hotel with suspect plumbing and indigestible food.

Ida Crouch-Hazlett noted that Caldwell's businessmen—eager to make "a good thing off Steunenberg's death"—were much disappointed over the court's decision. "Hotels, restaurants, stores were holding their breath over how much they would make off that trial," she reported.

Wood's decision carried with it one serious problem for both sides. All the canvassing work designed to identify sympathizers and enemies among Canyon County's potential jurors would go for nought. With barely six weeks left before the trial started, the lawyers would have to work quickly indeed if they were to find out much about Ada County's jury pool.

The prosecution could only hope that the defense would bring Operative 21 to Ada County to assume the same responsibilities he'd shouldered in Caldwell. But McParland, through Thiele, warned his star undercover man against showing any eagerness for such a move. The operative was "not to even hint to the lawyers for the defense that he was willing to leave Caldwell and go to Boise in the interest of the defense, but let that request come from the defendants' lawyers." Moreover, he was advised to seek payment for his work—until then, Whitsell had handed him a twenty-dollar bill now and then to defray expenses. McParland warned that a working man like C. A. Johnson would surely want to be paid, while a man willing to work for nothing would be suspect. About April 1, Whitsell brought up the move himself, asking Operative 21 to head up the canvass in Ada County, as he had in Canyon. McParland was "very much pleased" that his strategy had worked. Hawley found it "rather hard to go through this trouble the second time" but was delighted to learn that the operative was on the job in Boise, remarking, "I have more confidence in him than any other man ... and feel assured now that the other side will get no advantage."

So delighted was Frank Gooding with the way things had turned out that on April 10 he couldn't resist forwarding five of the operative's reports to the White House for Theodore Roosevelt's perusal. "I am sending you several reports of No. 21—secret operative of the Pinkertons—who has been in the employ of the state for more than a year last past," he wrote. "He has reported to me every day, and I have absolute confidence in him. His work has been of extreme value to us. He has so fully gained the confidence of the attorneys for the defense that he has been put in full charge of the work of polling the county, for the jury that will try the Heywood [sic] case next month."

With no record of a presidential reply to this letter, one is left to wonder how Roosevelt reacted to such a boast. Repeatedly in weeks gone by, he'd urged on Gooding the "course of fair and equal justice." But could the defendants really get a fair trial if spies in their midst passed on their attorneys' every deliberation—and, most important, their attorneys' assessment of potential jurors—to the prosecutors?

In the prosecutors' delight at Operative 21's transfer, there is no sign that they were troubled by ethical considerations. For McParland, months of careful preparation had yielded a big payoff: an agent in place at the very umbilicus of the defense team, Suite 323 on the third floor of the Overland Block, a four-story Italianate building with a cornice of roaring lions' heads, the most expensive office space in Boise, where Darrow, Richardson, Nugent, and the other attorneys and detectives had established their headquarters. An operative who kept his eyes and ears open—and Operative 21 was surely that—could hardly fail to pick up armloads of useful intelligence.

In the weeks to come, the Pinkertons exercised exquisite care about contacting the operative. "I will not attempt to connect with #21 at this time," Thiele wrote McParland on April 20, "as it would be taking a big chance of uncovering him, owing to the fact that if he were absent from his work he would be suspected and I am being closely watched by the spies of the W.F. of M."

For the time being, the operative remained undetected by the defense, but abruptly his own libido threatened to destroy his usefulness to the prosecutors. In late April, he wrote to Thiele reminding him that he'd been undercover almost without interruption for seventeen months, away from his lovely wife in Seattle, and asking that she be allowed to join him in Boise. If this request was denied, the operative warned, he'd have to go back to Seattle. Thiele hesitated, for the notion of a wife's joining her husband during an undercover operation was anathema to the Pinkertons.

Then on May 4, McParland was reading agents' reports in Hawley's office when he came across the operative's plea. Stunned by its implications, McParland addressed the problem with characteristic dispatch, ordering P. K. Ahern, the general superintendent in Seattle, to purchase a ticket to Boise for Operative 21's wife. "It is needless to say No. 21 holds the most important position of any operative we have detailed on this matter," he wrote his agency. "It will be much more satisfactory to have No. 21's wife here than to have him go to Seattle at the present time. We cannot afford to lose his services."

So successful had been Operative 21's infiltration of the defense that in that winter and spring of 1907, McParland sent two more undercover men into the defense ranks. One was Operative 10D, whose instructions were to join the ranks of Socialists and labor men in Caldwell, Nampa, and Payette. "His grammar is not of the best," one Pinkerton superintendent informed another, "but he writes good full reports." The other, 24A, did the same kind of work in Boise. While neither of them got as close to Darrow and Richardson as Operative 21, they both contributed valuable intelligence on the opposition's activities.

If part of the operatives' responsibility was to keep a close watch on overtly suspicious characters, another was to observe ostensibly respectable citizens, for fear that some of them might be cleverly disguised agents for the other side. On one occasion, Operative 21 had reported on the suspicious activities of Dr. John A. Myer, one of the three Caldwell physicians who'd attended Frank Steunenberg in the last terrible minutes of his life. Myer enjoyed a good reputation in Caldwell, but some of his doings that spring— unspecified in extant reports—suggested to McParland that he was a "traitor." This prompted the detective to ruminate: "If Myers [sic] is a traitor we may find a number of other citizens in Canyon County and more especially in Caldwell that are traitors at heart although on the outside they appear to be good citizens."

Early in 1907, Operative 21 reported on a bold attempt to infiltrate some of the community's "respectables" on the defense's behalf. The target was the Independent Order of Odd Fellows, one of Idaho's most active fraternal organizations. Ralph Gilbert, a tender of irrigation ditches in Parma and a "sympathizer with the prisoners," had long been an Odd Fellow in Parma. Operative 21 reported that Gilbert had agreed, "on condition that his name was never brought into the affair," to make regular reports to the defense on the conversations of Fred E. Fisk, chairman of the Canyon County Board of Commissioners, and other prominent Odd Fellows. If the Parma lodge was replete with local muck-a-mucks, Caldwell's boasted an even showier roster of Odd Fellows whose casual confidences at the clubhouse bar might prove useful to the defense. A. K. Steunenberg held high rank, having served successively as grand secretary, grand master, and grand representative to the Sovereign Grand Lodge. John, Will, and Pete Steunenberg also belonged, as did their confidant Montie Gwinn, John Rice, Albert F. Isham, and Sheriff Nichols. Moreover, as of January 1907—thanks to A.K.'s efforts—the Caldwell lodge, in its brick building by the railroad tracks, became the headquarters of Idaho's Odd Fellows. If Ralph Gilbert kept his ears open around the lodge bars in Parma and Caldwell, there'd be no end of information he could pass on to Darrow's defense team.

McParland had turned up a similar plot, which threatened to bring the defense even more valuable intelligence. One evening, back in Denver, he wandered into a favorite haunt, Walker's saloon on Fourteenth Street, where he fell into conversation with Frank Tarkington, "a very nice gentleman" who tended bar there and occasionally passed on useful tips to the master detective. Tarkington told McParland that a man named Charles H. Libby, a longtime court stenographer well known to many Denver judges and lawyers, had come by several times in the past week inquiring after McParland. In the course of his bar chatter ("Has McParland been in here today. Well you and he are friends, aren't you? Do you ever hear him talk about this Idaho affair?"), Libby had mentioned that he had a good contract with Edmund F. Richardson, the defense attorney, who was taking him to Boise to make a stenographic record in the Haywood trial.

"I can guess why Richardson picked Libby," said Tarkington.

"How's that?" asked McParland.

Tarkington reminded the detective that all three of them—the bartender, the detective, and the stenographer—were Elks. "As you are aware, Mr. McParland, they have a very select lodge of Elks in Boise, the best business men and professional men in the city all belong. Richardson must expect that Libby can get a great deal of information on the strength of Elkdom."

McParland was "inclined to think Tarkington's views are right." For McParland had discovered that Boise's Capital City Lodge no. 310, BPOE, numbered among its members the Pinkertons' principal client, Governor

Gooding; the prosecutors, Hawley and Borah; Owen M. Van Duyn, the Canyon County attorney; the trial judge, Fremont Wood; the new Ada County sheriff, Shadrach Hodgin; the defendants' principal guard, Erastus M. Beemer; Charles F. Koelsch, the Ada County prosecutor; Pete Steunenberg; Ralph V. Sebree, manager of the Saratoga Hotel; and Montie Gwinn. James Hawley had long been one of the state's most prominent Elks, having served as Exalted Ruler—his grandchildren, unable to get their mouths around that title, called him the Exhausted Rooster.

Accordingly, the Exhausted Rooster and other prominent Elks were warned to watch what they said around the busy bar at the BPOE Hall.

10

UNDESIRABLE CITIZENS

On the morning of April 2, 1907, two stories calculated to discomfit the city's gentility and delight its hoi polloi appeared side by side on page 1 of the vastly popular New York *World*. One article reported that fashionable equestrians boarding horses at Durland's Riding Academy on West Sixty-fifth Street in preparation for its annual horse show opening that night had been compelled to clean out the animals' stalls because of a strike by grooms and stable men. As befitted a newspaper that found its way onto thousands of breakfast tables across the city, the *World* did not spell out the "disagreeable tasks" that several exquisite debutantes and at least one member of the Tiffany family had been required to perform.

The other piece that unsettled the haut monde over their coddled eggs and kippers that morning was the bold two-column lead story headlined in oversized black type, "Roosevelt Begged Me, Wrote Harriman, to Raise Campaign Funds." Several aspects of this tale were particularly offensive to the wellborn. First, the letter at issue was drawn from the private correspondence of two of society's leaders; indeed, it was the letter E. H. Harriman had written on January 2, 1906, to his friend Sidney Webster describing his unfortunate dealings with the president. Second, Harriman alleged that the shorthand notes for the letter had been purloined by his discharged stenographer, Frank W. Hill, then sold to William Randolph Hearst's *New York American*, which had dithered for several days about publishing it. Finally it was resold to the *World,* the flagship of Hearst's arch rival, Joseph Pulitzer, which had a special interest in the story since it seemed to confirm the *World*'s own 1904 charges of a corrupt relationship between Roosevelt and the great trusts. Needless to say, such breaches of trust by personal retainers were a practice disdained by men and women of good breeding.

The story's substance was, in any case, repugnant to all who cared about ethical standards in government. Harriman's letter to his friend, written fifteen months before, recounted the railroad tycoon's allegations that Roosevelt had pressured him and other wealthy New Yorkers to contribute handsomely to the 1904 presidential campaign; that in exchange for those contributions the president had promised to appoint Harriman's ally Senator

Chauncey M. Depew of New York as ambassador to France; and that after the
$250,000 had been delivered, the president had brusquely repudiated his part
of the understanding. Until that bright spring morning in 1907, these allegations—which Congressman James Sherman had recounted to President Roosevelt over dinner at the White House the October before—had been known
only to a handful of Washington insiders and the tycoon's intimate circle.
Abruptly, it was the talk of the town—and, soon, of the nation.

Harriman quickly conceded the letter was his but deplored "that the
sacredness of a private correspondence should thus be violated," all the while
assuring reporters, "I did not authorize it to be published." With earnest
regret he nonetheless added, "I cannot withdraw anything contained in the
letter." The furor was heightened by reactions from several of the tale's
principals. "Well," quipped Depew, "these disclosures certainly add to the
gayety of nations." He contended that "all of the rich men whom I call my
personal friends contributed to that campaign. They did so, not that they
hoped to secure any favor for me; they wanted to see Roosevelt elected."
Alton B. Parker, the Democratic candidate for president in 1904, greeted the
revelation as "a measure of confirmation of my statements during the campaign" that certain corporations had been compelled to contribute to Roosevelt's 1904 campaign by a combination of threats and promises.

According to one account, when the *World*'s story reached the White
House, the president flew into "a towering rage." After a previously scheduled cabinet meeting, now largely devoted to the Harriman matter, Roosevelt
huddled with Secretary of State Elihu Root and Secretary of the Treasury
George B. Cortelyou. Quickly they retrieved the letter to Congressman
Sherman that the president had written the previous October for use at the
appropriate moment. Plainly, the moment had arrived. That afternoon, when
a hundred members of the Washington press corps filed into William Loeb's
office, they found the president perched on the edge of his secretary's desk.
After a few preliminary quips, Roosevelt handed out copies of the Sherman
letter. In it was his assertion that Harriman's version of their dealings during
1904 was "a deliberate and willful untruth," along with his own description of
those events, documented by texts of letters exchanged between the parties.
Toward the end was the sentence that had so pleased Roosevelt the fall before:
Harriman's boast about buying state legislatures, Congress, and the courts
showed, he'd written, "a cynicism and deep-seated corruption which makes
the man uttering such sentiments, and boasting, no matter how falsely, of his
power to perform such crimes, at least as undesirable a citizen as Debs, or
Moyer, or Haywood."

Initially, the press focused on the extraordinary spectacle of the president of the United States and the vastly rich president of the Union Pacific
Railroad publicly calling each other liars. For days to come, this pitched
battle dominated front pages. But so complex was the imbroglio, so hard to
sort out charge and countercharge, that some found it wearying. "Who cares?"

wrote Hugh O'Neill in the *Denver Post*. "Who cares what Harriman wrote of Roosevelt, or said to Roosevelt? Who cares what Harriman wrote to Webster that Roosevelt said to Harriman? Nobody. Nobody in the West, at least."

Gradually, attention shifted to a much starker, more easily comprehended aspect of the president's letter: his public condemnation of two men facing charges of murder who, if convicted, would undoubtedly face the gallows.

Privately, some of the president's friends applauded his frankness. "Bless you, my dear Theodore," wrote Owen Wister. "Bless you for the Undesirable Citizen letter. If I may be so bold as to say to you—you've never surpassed this in the way of a public document." An Illinois lawyer wrote Loeb: "The President said what he meant, and meant what he said, and we are proud of him that he did not craw-fish."

From the Ada County jail came Bill Haywood's carefully drafted comment: "The President says that I am an undesirable citizen, the inference being that as such I should be put out of the way. His influence is all-powerful and his statement, coming as it does on the eve of my trial for life, will work me irreparable injury and do more to prevent a fair trial than everything that has been said and done against me." This doesn't sound like Haywood and was probably drafted by Darrow or Richardson. Haywood's real reaction can be inferred from a comment made to a reporter a year later: "It was while my two comrades and myself were put in cells, our hands shackled behind us, that this idol of yours in the White House wrote a letter denouncing us as 'undesirable citizens.' That was not the work of a great man. It was the work of a coward."

It was also a boon to the defense camp, for it gave them a brand-new organizing tool, a specific target at which to direct the public's rage. Austin Willard Wright, a friend of Clarence Darrow's in Chicago, chortled to another Darrow friend, Charles Erskine Wood, in Seattle: "It seems to me that the ailment of Roosevelt is mental and consists in an inability to organize and coordinate the changes of consciousness which constitute thought." Mother Jones couldn't restrain her delight, writing to Terence Powderly, now with the Bureau of Immigration: "How the spectacular performer in Washington has put his foot in it. The words 'undesirable citizen' will go down in history. He and his crew of pirates would no doubt give a great deal to undo that."

From New York came a letter to Roosevelt by Thomas Crimmins, chairman of the executive committee of the Moyer-Haywood Conference of New York, one of the defense committees charged with raising money and rallying public sentiment in the nation's major cities. New York City's conference claimed some three hundred labor leaders, representing more than 200,000 workers. "Are you not aware," asked Crimmins, "that words like yours coming from the Chief Executive of the nation may poison not only the mind of the general public, but also of a possible jury, against men who are yet awaiting their trial?" From Eugene Debs—another of Roosevelt's "undesirables"—came the harshest denunciation of all. Writing in *Appeal to Reason*, he said that the president had "uttered a lie as black and damnable, as foul and atrocious as ever issued from a human throat.... The man in the White House, who with the cruel malevolence of a barbarian has pronounced [the defendants'] doom,... is the friend of the enemies and the enemy of the friends of this republic."

As the denunciations crashed around his ears, the president kept his own counsel, steadfastly—and uncharacteristically—declining to rise to the bait. But in mid-April, he could resist no longer. To his son Kermit, he wrote: "The labor people insisted upon having a row with me, and after having made every effort to avoid it, I concluded that it could not longer be avoided and that I had better meet the attack aggressively and fearlessly."

Of the hundreds of protests the president had received, he chose to answer one from the Moyer-Haywood-Pettibone Defense Conference of Chicago and Cook County, in the person of its chairman, Honoré Joseph Jaxon.

Although Roosevelt didn't know it, Honoré Jaxon was one of the most remarkable figures ever to exchange letters with a president. Born William Henry Jackson in Toronto, he studied classics at University College there before dropping out to help his family through hard times, ultimately moving to Canada's Northwest Territories, where he became secretary to a radical farmers union. Soon he fell under the spell of Louis Riel, self-proclaimed "Prophet of the New World" and leader of an uprising of métis, or mixed-blood Indians, against the territories' white settlers. Jackson served as secretary of Riel's "provisional government" until the uprising was crushed by a force of seven thousand Canadian troops at the battle of Batoche in 1885. Riel was tried for high treason and executed that November, but Jackson's life was spared when he was declared insane and sent to a lunatic asylum. Escaping some weeks later, he crossed into North Dakota and, after a brief detention, drifted to Chicago, where he adopted the manner and French-style name of a métis. Becoming active in the Chicago labor movement, he served as secretary of the city's Carpenters' Council, but only with the Haymarket riot in 1886 did he find his niche as a philosophical—though not a violent—anarchist.

Over the next several decades, Jaxon led the life of a social and political adventurer, organizing a World Conference of Anarchists during the World's Columbian Exposition in Chicago; joining Coxey's Army on its march to Washington, dressed flamboyantly in a white sombrero, leather breeches, and a decorated blanket; enrolling in the exotic new Baha'i cult. With his wife, Aimee Montfort, a French Canadian schoolteacher, he occupied two rooms in back of a vinegar factory, cluttered with books, papers, scientific apparatus, firewood, and old clothes. The *Saturday Evening Post* described him in 1907 as a "labor leader, doctor, occultist, chemist, trapper, architect, hunter, lawyer,

solicitor, non-resistant, philosophical anarchist, spirit-fruitist, colonizer, revolutionist, letter writer and half-Indian."

Jaxon wrote a florid, grandiloquent prose, warning the president that to
place the imprisoned men

> in the same class with the railway magnate is in reality and to that extent
> equivalent to investing the latter gentleman with the commendation rather than
> the censure of the author of the criticism referred to; and whether that author
> shall prove to have been yourself or some other person endeavoring without
> authority to place his own words in your mouth, our own criticism of that
> particular phrase of the letter attributed to you is that the comparison confers
> altogether too high an honor upon a financier who would himself be among the
> first to admit that his activities as thus far revealed to the public have been
> inspired by purely selfish motives rather than by the overmastering love for
> humanity which is the most striking characteristic of Moyer, Haywood and
> Pettibone.

The president sought to put Jaxon on the defensive. "I entirely agree
with you," he wrote, "that it is improper to endeavor to influence the course
of justice." For that reason, he regretted the inscription on the conference's
stationery: "Death—cannot—will not—and shall not claim our brothers!"
This showed "that you and your associates are not demanding a fair trial, or
working for a fair trial, but are announcing in advance that the verdict shall
only be one way and that you will not tolerate any other verdict. Such action
is flagrant in its impropriety, and I join heartily in condemning it." Jaxon's
comments were "designed only to coerce court or jury" and should therefore
be condemned.

Turning to his own much-disputed phrase, Roosevelt argued that "it is a
simple absurdity to suppose that because any man is on trial for a given
offense he is therefore to be freed from all criticism upon his general conduct
and manner of life," though he added hastily, "I neither expressed nor indicated any opinion as to whether Messrs. Moyer and Haywood were guilty of
the murder of Governor Steunenberg."

If this obduracy was meant to defuse the protests—and one wonders if
that was ever Roosevelt's aim—it had just the opposite effect. On the day the
White House made his response to Jaxon public, James Sheehan, a leader of
Milwaukee's Federated Trades Council, called for a national day of protest
in early May at which laboring men and women could demonstrate their
indignation at Roosevelt's "undesirables" statement and its reiteration. "Coming from the chief executive of the nation, such utterances could not but have
the effect that Roosevelt affects so deeply to deplore—inflaming the public
against the imprisoned officials," he said. Sheehan promised to press his call
for a demonstration at the next meeting of the council.

Two days later, the council endorsed the idea, which picked up support
in labor strongholds across the land. In Pittsburgh, P. J. McCardle, president

of the iron, steel, and tin workers, called the president's letter a "childish outburst." In San Francisco, the carpenters union accused Roosevelt of working in the interest of "capitalist bandits."

In New York, the Moyer-Haywood Conference invited the Central Federated Union to join in a massive demonstration in early May. An umbrella group, embracing both the cautious machinists and the militant riggers, the CFU had difficulty in framing its position at a couple of boisterous meetings. Its indecision was exacerbated by Roosevelt's last-minute effort to siphon off the anger building behind the protest. Agreeing to receive a small CFU delegation, the president met with three unionists for nearly two hours at the White House on May 2, taking his most conciliatory stance yet, then following up with a cordial letter. Only partially mollified, the CFU resolved to join the demonstration anyway.

The date was set for May 4, the Saturday before the trial began. Across the land in succeeding weeks, representatives of labor, of the Socialist Party, and of the several Moyer-Haywood conferences mobilized their forces for the largest possible turnout.

The day's centerpiece was to be New York City's great procession, designed to culminate in a mass rally at Grand Central Palace. The focus on New York seemed natural enough, for Socialists had a greater presence in the nation's largest city than anywhere else in the land. Over the last decades of the nineteenth century and the first years of the twentieth, New York had been a powerful magnet to Jewish immigrants from central and eastern Europe, carrying with them a revolutionary cast of mind grounded in a synthesis of Talmudic and Socialist doctrine.

Jewish emigration to New York took place in stages, depositing settlers like mineral layers on a mountainside. The first Jews to arrive were Sephardim from Spain, Portugal, and Holland, reaching the New World in the seventeenth and eighteenth centuries, gradually dispersing to some of the city's most comfortable neighborhoods. Next came German Jews, who reached these shores in the mid–nineteenth century. Most Germanic Jews tended to remain within New York's German community, for years centered on "Dutchtown," just north of Houston Street, until the more socially mobile settled uptown in Yorkville.

Beginning about 1870, the German impulse to emigrate spread from the Silesian plains into Poland. All through the seventies, Polish Jews—many of them skilled tailors from Suvalki province—streamed into lower Manhattan, settling first around Bayard and Mott Streets, later at the foot of Canal Street where it converged with Essex Street and East Broadway to form Rutgers Square. They were followed by Hungarians, Rumanians, and Galicians, each group finding its niche in this polyglot neighborhood; but their combined influx was as nothing compared to the staggering migration, about to begin, of Russian Jews.

A wave of anti-Jewish pogroms, beginning in Elisavetgrad in April 1881, triggered a Jewish emigration from Russia that mounted steadily over the next two decades. A terrible massacre on Easter Sunday 1903 in the Bessarabian capital of Kishinev—costing the lives of fifty Jews—set off a new wave of emigration, soon swelling into panicky flight. By 1904, annual Russian-Jewish migration to the United States reached 77,544; in 1906, it peaked at 125,832—many immigrants settling within a peddler's shout of Rutgers Square.

By then, the Lower East Side was dressed out in a coat of many colors, as richly variegated as the eastern European society it replicated. To the Russian intelligentsia, East Broadway was New York's Nevsky Prospect, the grand boulevard of imperial St. Petersburg. It was there that physicians and dentists practiced in spacious brownstones shaded by leafy trees. A few blocks north, Grand Street was the community's principal shopping thoroughfare, where great department stores like Lord and Taylor and Lichtenstein's got their start. At cafés along Canal and Houston Streets, the immigrants sat for hours sipping tea from tall glasses and talking of Kropotkin and the Yiddish theater.

Many of the newcomers found work in the city's garment, tobacco, and furniture trades or other light industries. Of these, apparel work was supreme, centered in the loft workshops established during the area's German settlement. As Russian and east European Jews, many of them fresh from the shtetl, invaded German Jewish turf, they aroused resentment among the earlier immigrants, jealous of their reputations for erudition and respectability. The German Jews sneered at the newcomers' Yiddish language as "piggish jargon," at their socialistic convictions as "dangerous principles innate in the Russian Jew," at their religious doctrines as "the shackles of medievalism," and finally at the Russian Jews themselves, whose names so often ended in "ki," as "kikes."

Moreover, as Russian Jews entered the garment industry, many became independent "clothing contractors," cutting and stitching in their homes and hiring their help in a daily "shape-up" at Hester and Ludlow Streets, which, from the din of haggling, became known as the Pig Market. The muckraker Jacob Riis followed one such contractor "up two flights of dark stairs, three, four, with new smells of cabbage, of onions, of frying fish, on every landing, whirring sewing-machines behind closed doors betraying what goes on within, to the door that opens to admit the bundle and the man." Inside were five men, a woman, and three children—a typical "sweatshop."

By century's turn, much of the Lower East Side resembled the Jewish quarters of Warsaw or Minsk, only magnified by the immensity of the Jewish population compressed in this narrow corner of the metropolis. The Tenth Ward—at the district's heart—was the city's most crowded, with over seven hundred inhabitants per acre, denser than Calcutta's slums. On Rivington Street, it was said, "the architecture seemed to sweat humanity at every window and door." So stultifying was the damp of these tenements that one girl told a settlement worker, "It seemed as if there wasn't no sky." An investigator heard the same plea over and over: "Luft, gibt mir luft"—"Air, give me air." Tuberculosis—with its telltale splatters of crimson spittle—was endemic to these pestholes, "the very walls reeking with it." They called it "the shop sickness, the plague of Dollar Land."

Yet many of this quarter's residents transcended these conditions with a restless energy, a compulsion not only to survive but to prevail. The most willing to shuck the older ways were known sarcastically as allrightniks. In the old country, leadership had come from the rabbinate, scholars of genuine learning but often with a tendency to obscurantism. In the upheaval accompanying the flight to the New World, no sector of Jewish society lost status more thoroughly than the rabbis. In their place emerged the proletarian intellectuals, many finding in shirtmaking and button stitching undemanding tasks that gave them time to converse and speculate—not unlike the cigar makers from whose ranks emerged the trade unionist Samuel Gompers.

The intellectuals who rose within the garment trades were often Socialists, working-class savants mixing up a rich stew of Talmudic doctrine and Marxist dogma. Tracts of that era saw a congruence between the two beliefs: the coming of the Messiah became the social revolution; Israel's liberation from Egypt symbolized the workers' liberation from class oppression; Socialism was the Torah of the workingman. This was more than clever packaging; Socialism's emphasis on social justice and universalism, its prophetic message and apocalyptic vision echoed Judaic themes. One devout workman recalled his feelings when he first picked up a Yiddish Socialist newspaper: "I liked it because its ideas were hidden in my heart and soul long ago."

By the first decade of the twentieth century, the most forceful spokesman for this hybrid faith was Abraham Cahan. Himself the grandson of a rabbi, Cahan was born in 1860 in Vilna, the Lithuanian city that had such a rich rabbinical tradition that Napoleon, on his doomed road to Moscow, dubbed it the Jerusalem of Lithuania. Cahan's family expected him to become a rabbi—and for a time he proved an apt Talmudic student—but from an early age he was pulled toward more secular concerns. Enrolling at Vilna's Jewish Teachers' Institute, he dabbled in revolutionary activity. When some friends were arrested and police searched his room, Cahan, at age twenty-two, joined the 1882 exodus to New York, where he promptly plunged into the political ferment of the Lower East Side.

As the Haymarket case of 1886 proved a turning point in the lives of Bill Haywood, Clarence Darrow, and Honoré Jaxon, so, too, for Abraham Cahan. Following the anarchists' execution, he was suffused with ill-defined rage. Plunging into the manuscripts of disaffection, he reread Marx and Plekhanov, while seeking instruction from a German-born anarchist. By year's end, he'd decided to join DeLeon's Socialist Labor Party. "When I got my membership card," he wrote, "I felt as if a stone had been lifted from my heart." But before long, he'd broken angrily with the authoritarian "Pope" and moved steadily into the party's Social-Democratic wing, taking up cudgels to combat De-Leon's vast influence in the Jewish labor movement.

Cahan helped found the Russian Jewish Workers Union; for a time headed the cloakmakers union; edited a Socialist daily called the *Arbeiter Zeitung;* and, in 1897, with other leaders of New York's Yiddish press, founded a new paper called *Vorwarts (Forward),* after Berlin's great Social Democratic journal.

Cahan's Socialism was a long way from DeLeon's icy dogmatism. Brimming with self-assurance, he could be more than a bit domineering himself, but he had no taste for the SLP's sterile polemics. Instead, he sought to create a popular workers' paper breathing the streetwise pragmatism of the American city. When some of his new colleagues resisted, he resigned. For nearly five years, he went into a remarkable self-imposed exile, out in the Yankee world of the New York *Commercial Advertiser,* where he learned the reporter's trade—until then he'd been more a polemicist and a feuilletonist —under a master of the craft, Lincoln Steffens, the paper's city editor. There, too, he worked with the talented Hapgood brothers, Norman and Hutchins. Then in March 1902—after Steffens went off as muckraker in chief for *Mc-Clure's* and Norman Hapgood became editor of *Collier's Weekly*—Cahan won over some old colleagues and resumed his editorship of the *Forward.*

During his second turn as editor, the paper more fully realized Cahan's evolving journalistic, political, and social views. No longer an orthodox Socialist newspaper, not even, strictly speaking, a labor paper, it was an uncommon hybrid, a Jewish-Socialist-labor paper heavily laced with the "human interest" journalism of Lincoln Steffens and the Hapgoods, to which had been added dollops of Hearst's and Pulitzer's yellow journalism. As Oswald Garrison Villard, editor of the *New York Post,* put it, the *Forward* was "a striking American newspaper in the Yiddish language." By 1903, it claimed a circulation of a hundred thousand.

A fine-boned man with dark eyes boring through steel-rimmed glasses, Cahan seemed reserved and meticulous. Beneath his cerebral exterior lurked a passionate interest in the life of the streets, the powerful pulse of immigrant life. He prowled the alleys, frequented the cafés along Grand and Division Streets, surveyed the pushcarts and tenements of the garment district. He was seeking stories for his paper, but he was up to something more, immersing himself in the teeming life of the Jewish quarter like the *narodnik*—man of the people—he was. Forswearing abstractions, he strove to make the *Forward* "interesting to all Yiddish-speaking people, big and little"—women certainly included. Indeed, much of Cahan's newspaper—notably the famed advice column, the "Bintel Brief"—was aimed at a female audience, a readership that its competitors had largely ignored. It would be written in "pure, plain *Yiddishe Yiddish,*" by which Cahan meant Yiddish the way ordinary Jews spoke it, not the intellectualized Germanic version known as *Deitshmerish.* Certainly the *Forward* was the most "gele" ("yellow" or, by extension, "sensational") of the Yiddish papers, sometimes "to the edge of the salacious." His critics accused Cahan of "lowering himself to the masses instead of lifting them up," to which the editor responded: "If you want to pick a child up from the ground, you first have to bend down to him. If you don't, how will you reach him?"

In 1904, the *Forward* bought a three-story building at 175 East Broadway, facing Rutgers Square and the new Seward Park, at the very heart of the Jewish community. A year later, it began to address a thrilling and terrible story at the core of the Russian Jewish experience. On Bloody Sunday, January 9, 1905, a procession of 200,000 workers, many of them carrying religious icons and pictures of Czar Nicholas II, converged on the Winter Palace in St. Petersburg. At its head was the charismatic priest-reformer Father George Gapon, bearing a petition asking an eight-hour day, a minimum wage of one ruble per day, and a constituent assembly. When the workers refused orders to halt, the czar's troops opened fire. Between two hundred and five hundred marchers were killed outright, perhaps a thousand more wounded. After the first volleys, Father Gapon jumped to his feet, shouting—half in anguish, half in exalted defiance—"There is no God anymore, there is no czar!"

The cry echoed thunderously on the Lower East Side, home to so many of the czar's former subjects. It reverberated in the months to come, as thousands of Russian workers laid down their tools in protest, university students boycotted classes, and the czar's forces continued their slaughter of protesters (seventy in Riga in January, ninety-three in Warsaw that April; then, in mid-June, the worst yet, two thousand killed, three thousand injured in Odessa). Day after day, the *Forward* chronicled the mother country's descent into chaos.

Cahan's editorials mourned the dead while thrilling to the political upheaval. "The hand shakes, the heart leaps with joy and enthusiasm," he wrote. "Revolution! We have a revolution in Russia! A real, general people's revolution. A proletarian worker's revolution." Even the next round of czarist repression and the exile of Socialist leaders to Siberia didn't dampen the *Forward*'s enthusiasm for the changes under way in the homeland.

While the czar exaggerated when he said "nine-tenths of the revolutionaries are Yids," there was enough truth in the statement for the readers of the *Forward* to identify proudly with their coreligionists. Time and again, the Jews of the Lower East Side went into the streets to demonstrate their solidarity with the martyrs of the Russian Revolution.

Cahan served as a crucial intermediary between Jewish revolutionists in Russia and the desperately needed funds of New York's Jews. The General League of Jewish Workers in Russia, Poland, and Lithuania, commonly known as the Bund ("the League"), was an umbrella organization of Jewish Socialist groups founded in 1897. Gradually, Cahan became its principal spokesman in the United States. Starting in 1903, when the Bund first sent delegates to raise money in New York, the *Forward* devoted lavish space to these romantic figures, assuring they didn't return to the homeland empty-handed.

In autumn 1906, Cahan found himself in a squeeze between three men he didn't much care for: Theodore Roosevelt; Oscar Straus, a prominent German Jew and former U.S. minister to Turkey; and William Randolph Hearst, the Democratic candidate facing off against the Republican Charles Evans Hughes for governor of New York.

Warned that the gubernatorial contest was desperately close, Roosevelt worried that Lower East Side Jews would go for Hearst, who'd cultivated them with his Yiddish-language journal, the *Yiddisher Amerikaner,* his thunderous denunciations of Russian barbarism, and his drive to aid pogrom victims. On October 9, the president asked Straus, whose family owned R. H. Macy and Company, the giant department store, to "see if there is not some way in which you could be of assistance in preventing the East Side vote—notably among the Jews—from going for Hearst. He has completely misled those poor people over there." Three days later, Straus reported that his hand was on "the pulses on the Eastside. I think you need have no fear that Hearst will mislead your constituents over there." The year before, Straus conceded, Jews had supported Hearst for mayor. But that was when Tammany lined up behind Hearst's opponent. "Today Tammany and the devil are behind Hearst," he assured Roosevelt, "and our Eastside friends I am sure will show a wise discrimination." A few days later, Straus went public, denouncing Hearst as "an unconscionable, sensational, insincere sham." He told a Jewish reporter he'd vote for Hughes because, "like Gideon of old, he was summoned by the righteous voices of the people."

Roosevelt had shown bad judgment in asking an uptown German Jew to intervene with Lower East Side Jews, many of whom resented the lofty condescension of these grandees. Later that month, Roosevelt upped his ante for the Jewish vote by appointing Straus his new secretary of commerce and labor, the first Jew ever named to a presidential cabinet. At a banquet in the new secretary's honor, Roosevelt insisted that Straus's religion hadn't been a consideration, turning to the patriarch Jacob Schiff of Kuhn, Loeb and Co. for confirmation. Schiff, who was growing deaf, hadn't quite heard the president and chimed in: "That's right, Mr. President! You came to me and said, 'Jake, who is the best Jew I can appoint Secretary of Commerce?' "

From a capitalist standpoint, wrote Cahan, Straus was "a fine man." Roosevelt was mistaken, however, if he thought he could buy Jewish votes with this appointment. "The Jewish masses will not forget that Mr. Roosevelt has in no way used his might and his moral power, as president of the Republic, to raise his voice in protest against the Russian murder of Jews."

But if Cahan had little use for either Roosevelt or Straus, he reviled "the faker" Hearst. All fall, he belabored the magnate who had the gall to call himself a friend of the Jew and the workingman. As Straus had predicted,

Cahan was angered by Hearst's alliance with Christy and Tim Sullivan, notorious chiefs of Tammany Hall. "Even a blind man can see that Hearst's entire 'Independence' movement was no more than a bluff, in order to entice Tammany Hall to nominate him. Now he has done this he is a Tammany man, the boodler-general, an ex-independent."

Ultimately, Cahan supported the Socialist candidate for governor, John C. Chase, and worked even harder for Morris Hillquit, the Socialist making a strong challenge to the Tammany- and Hearst-backed incumbent, Henry M. Goldfogle, in the Ninth Congressional District. But Cahan's influence wasn't sufficient in either race. Oscar Straus had underestimated the pull of Hearst and Tammany. In the Eighth Assembly District—the heart of the Lower East Side—Hearst beat Hughes 5,387 to 1,623, the Socialist candidate drawing only 452 votes. Hillquit beat the Republican Charles Adler but finished a close second to Goldfogle.

Thus, then, as 1907 began, Cahan nursed a grievance against the conniver in the White House. And as Haywood's trial approached, he saw the great march of May 4, 1907, as an opportunity to play, once again, a leading role in the international struggle for workers' self-determination.

On April 30 and May 1, the *Forward* ran page 1 notices urging its readers to join the protest: "A Quarter of a Million in the Coming March.... Never has there been such a May Day Parade in twenty years. All the unions of New York, conservative as well as radical, American and Irish, as well as German, Jewish and others. The entire country waits to see the protest march." On the morning of the march, the story climbed to the top of page 1, summoning readers to "the holiest cause": "Workers! Sisters and Brothers! Today is the day when the cause beats an alarm.... From many thousands of throats must respond the cry this evening: 'Justice and freedom for our innocent perse- cuted brothers, Moyer, Haywood and Pettibone!' "

In an editorial, Cahan noted that Roosevelt had asked why they were "inciting" people to support "undesirable *(unerwunscht)* citizens." This dem- onstration, the editor explained, would respond that "workers cannot have any trust in the courts in America to render nonpartisan justice! They know that the courts, and the entire government today, are in the hands of the capitalists." The president had intervened "because he is partisan, for the capitalists and against the workers!"

The march's organizers—Socialists and unionists in the Moyer- Haywood Conference—devised an unconventional route. Of late, Jewish and labor organizations had refused to join the annual Labor Day parade along Fifth Avenue because they objected to marching up the "avenue of the enemies." Fifth was New York's grandest boulevard, particularly along "the line" between Twenty-third and Forty-second Streets, flanked by the marble palaces of the rich and the cafés and restaurants where theatrical and literary celebrities convened. Many immigrants resented this ostentatious display.

Some years before, a less prudent Abe Cahan had urged his proletarian audience to "charge up Fifth Avenue with axes and swords," which a biographer concludes was meant "as an intoxicant for the soul rather than as a real call to action." At a May Day Moyer-Haywood rally, Elizabeth Gurley Flynn, president of the Socialistic Women of Greater New York though still in high school, told demonstrators in Union Square, "We have not marched today as labor does on Labor Day. Then it goes up Fifth Avenue and is reviewed like so many cattle by the forces of capital. Today we review ourselves and note our own power."

This time, the procession would be divided. A "downtown march," principally of Jews, would leave Rutgers Square and head uptown along Second and Third Avenues. The "uptown march," made up largely of German- and English-speaking Socialists and unionists, would step off from the city's nerve center of Socialist-labor activity, a hundred feet of East Eighty-fourth Street between Socialist Party headquarters at number 239, where Usher Solomon, the state secretary, answered reporters' questions at his desk between portraits of Karl Marx and Ferdinand Lassalle, and the Labor Temple at number 243, a yellow-brick building with "Knowledge Is Power" emblazoned above the swinging doors and inside a busy saloon where German unionists hoisted schooners of pilsner.

From there, the marchers would head downtown along First and Third Avenues. Only when they reached Fifty-seventh Street would the uptown contingent cross onto Fifth and march defiantly down the "avenue of the enemies" to Fortieth, where it would turn east, converging with the downtown contingent at Lexington Avenue for a mass rally in Grand Central Palace and on nearby streets.

Several considerations governed this division: tensions between Jews and Gentiles; lingering resentment between eastern European Jews downtown and Yorkville's German Jews; an effort to involve a broader swatch of the city in the day's events.

Saturday, May 4, dawned gold and blue, a warm spring sun burning in a cobalt sky. At 2:00 p.m., Jewish garment workers, labor groups, and Socialist societies began forming ranks at assembly points in and around Rutgers Square. The Eighth Assembly District of the Socialist Party, for example, gathered at their clubrooms at 106 Ludlow Street, a block west of the Pig Market, where, to the martial rhythms of a crimson-jacketed band, they strutted their stuff through the twisting cobblestoned streets. At intersections, they were often compelled to wait for other groups marching to their own bands. As the cacophony reverberated off brick walls, the deafening noise did nothing to deter the spectators, massed six-deep on the sidewalks.

About 5:30 p.m., the downtown marchers massed into three divisions. Promptly at 6:15, with a crash of cymbals and a blare of trumpets, the First

Division swung onto Canal Street heading for Ludlow Street. Leading the way, with a broad red sash across his chest, was the downtown parade's grand marshal, John C. Chase, the unsuccessful Socialist candidate for governor that past November, now the party's state organizer. Strung out behind him were the First Agitations District of the Socialist Party, accompanied by its own band; the Eighth, Sixth, and Second Assembly Districts of the Socialist Party; the *Forward* Association; the Socialist Federation; the Semitic Progressive Society; the Socialist Educational Alliance; the Progressive Workingmen's Association; and the Ever Young Men's and Young Ladies' Progressive Benevolent Society.

Many marchers represented the eastern European shtetls from which the immigrants came. In the First Division came, among many others, the Progressive Young People of Yekaterinoslav, of Kopy, and of Slutzk; the Young Men's Benevolent Association of Tahzitz, of Tcherninow, and of Kartuzh-Berez; the Aid Society of Choloptz; and the Progressive Association of Mir—organizations deeply comforting to the city's uprooted greenhorns.

In the Second Division came the Jewish unions: the retail clerks, the paper bag makers, the knee pants makers, the waist makers; the suspenders makers, the mineral water bottlers, and the waiters. The Third Division was led by units of the Russian revolutionary Bund from Dvinsk, Bobroisk, Homml, Lodz, and Minsk, followed by six branches of the Workmen's Circle, a benevolent society of Jewish trade unionists, with the rear brought up by more trade unionists: the cap makers, the cloak, skirt and waist makers, the furriers, the shoe fitters, the neckwear makers, the sailor suit makers, and the lace makers.

About 40 percent of the marchers from Rutgers Square were women, reflecting the heavy proportion of women in the sweatshops of the garment industry. Many were shirtwaist makers, then on strike against their employers. "Hurrah for the Jewish neighborhood," proclaimed the *Forward*, "... the first to show that the woman is not valueless in the struggle."

As the downtown contingent got under way from Rutgers Square, the uptown marchers gathered outside Socialist Party headquarters on Eighty-fourth Street. They had a problem: a livery stable that had contracted to supply horses for the marshals still hadn't delivered them. An emergency council concluded that the marshals would simply have to "foot it." But the chief marshal of the uptown parade, Daniel H. Featherstone, secretary of the Brotherhood of Carpenters, couldn't be found—he'd gone in search of a horse. Finally he showed up—without a mount—and, an hour late, the parade set off down First Avenue. After a mile or so, there was a sudden commotion at the rear and a group of hostlers came galloping down the line with the missing horses.

The uptown parade consisted of nine divisions, the first headed by the Central Federated Union, the city's principal labor organization, created in a turn-of-the-century merger of the German-dominated Central Labor Federation and the Irish-run Central Labor Union. But of 250 unions in the Central Federated Union, only fifty or so were represented in the march, led by the housesmiths and bridgemen's union in bright red vests.

At the assembly points, the marchers had been issued badges bearing a single phrase, "I Am an Undesirable Citizen," which thousands of them wore pinned to their lapels or blouses. They'd also been issued hundreds of banners and signs bearing, in Yiddish and English, the approved slogans of the day—as many critical of the president as supportive of the three unionists:

"Roosevelt constitutes himself prosecutor, court and executioner."

"He can show his teeth. We are not afraid."

"Special trains for kidnappers. Special trains for the President. Furnished by the same people."

"Haywood is in jail for not contributing towards Roosevelt's Campaign Fund. Harriman did and he is at large."

"Colorado and Idaho? Two New Russianized Provinces."

All through the soft light of evening they came—Rumanian pants makers, Polish purse makers and furriers, Hungarian vest makers, Galician tie makers, Russian cloak makers and shirtmakers—by the thousands they came, shouldering their placards, brandishing their banners, singing along with the thump and crash of the bands. By 7:00 p.m., as darkness began to fall, the marchers lit Japanese lanterns that they carried at the ends of flexible bamboo canes, forming "a long bobbing column of dancing flamepoints, fading away in the distance."

Most of the workers had decked themselves out in their holiday clothes —appropriate to this "holiest cause." With earnest faces, their bodies proudly erect, they marched in dark suits, detachable collars, string ties, and bowler hats, the boys in knee pants, high socks, and cloth caps. Women wore ankle-length dresses with high collars and long sleeves; the older women had their hair done up in buns at the backs of their heads, the younger ones wore pigtails or braids, but all wore hats, in black or dark blue. Although respectable Jewish women normally eschewed red—a "harlot's color"—in their clothing, today was different; many sported a red sash, or scarf, or scrap of red cloth attached to their hats, in this context a show of support for international Socialism.

The black flag of anarchism was entirely missing. The Moyer-Haywood Conference told the press that both the anarchists and the IWW had asked to march but had been rejected in order not to offend Gompers's AFL, which was supplying many marchers. Officially, Herman Robinson, the AFL's New York State representative, kept his distance from the event. "Some of these men have apparently taken it upon themselves to speak for labor," he said. "I'm not sure whether they're laboring men or not."

Many marching units had their own musicians to spur them on. In all, more than forty brass bands and fife-and-drum corps marched that evening, their favorite tune, by a wide margin, that theme song of international Socialism the "Marseillaise."

Socialist songwriters had recently turned out another ditty, this one derived from the Luella Twining piece in *Appeal to Reason*. Its lyrics, placed in the mouth of Bill Haywood's nine-year-old daughter, Henrietta, went in part:

> *"Are they going to hang my papa? He's innocent, I know.*
> *He never could do any wrong; he is so good and true.*
> *It surely will kill dear Mama, and break my heart in two.*
> *Are they going to hang my papa?" pled this babe with eyes of blue.*

Another song popular among the marchers went as follows:

> *And shall Moyer, Haywood, and Pettibone die?*
> *And shall Moyer, Haywood, and Pettibone die?*
> *Here are 60,000 workingmen*
> *Who will know the reason why.*

How many really marched that day? There was no consensus. The "quarter of a million" earlier invoked by the *Forward* was pure chimera. Closer to reality was the seventy-five thousand predicted by the Socialist organizers or the sixty thousand in the marching song. Afterward, the *Forward*, as much participant as observer, dutifully claimed seventy thousand. *Wilshire's* and the *Herald* both picked fifty thousand. Most of the establishment press put the figure far lower: the *Times*, the *Sun*, *Harper's Weekly*, and the Associated Press all hit on twenty thousand. Pulitzer's *World*, friendly to the protesters, offered forty thousand, a figure echoed by Norman Hapgood in a piece for the *American Magazine* and—surprisingly enough—by the *Worker*, a Socialist Party organ. That seems about right.

But whatever the actual number of marchers, everybody agreed there were several times that many thronging the sidewalks or leaning on windowsills and rooftop ledges. The *World* put the onlookers at "hundreds of thousands," reporting that "all the East Side was alive with working people, pushing, pulling, tugging at one another to get somewhere." Hawkers sold walking sticks with small red flags on them and copies of a twenty-five-cent booklet called "The Pinkerton Labor Spy," written by Morris Friedman, a former stenographer in the Pinkerton's Denver office, and largely devoted to the iniquities of James McParland.

With authorities concerned that disorders, even full-scale rioting, might break out along the parade route, police in their new blue-and-gold uniforms kept watch on the proceedings. A Captain Martin of the Eighty-eighth Street station house, with a Sergeant Gordon and ten patrolmen, marched at the head of the uptown parade, while another fifty policemen stood guard along the route. Downtown, security was tighter. Inspector Murphy had 250 policemen at the head of the parade and another 250 along the line of march.

Perhaps because of the large police presence, the marchers were disciplined, even subdued, but their mood did not suit all participants. One marcher was heard to complain, "This is like a ginney funeral." The *Worker's* correspondent concluded that "those high in authority would have welcomed the slightest pretext for ordering the nightsticks into play," but no pretext was offered.

When the parades fused at Fortieth and Lexington, "the marchers perked up their courage and let loose their voices," accompanied by the massed bands. Fifteen thousand Japanese lanterns flickered in the night, while Roman candles and Greek fire arced over the assemblage.

By eight, the huge throng pressed toward the Lexington Avenue entrance to Grand Central Palace, beneath a sign blazing that name in the night sky. The six-story brick palace was one of turn-of-the-century New York's most impressive structures, occupying the entire block bounded by Lexington Avenue, Depew (now Vanderbilt) Place, Forty-third, and Forty-fourth Streets. Completed in 1893, at a cost of $1.5 million, it could accommodate fifty thousand persons in its 310,000 square feet of exhibition halls and theaters, restaurants and cafés. Passing through the front portals, one ascended a curving stairway to the second floor, which opened onto a great central hall— three stories high and topped by a glass dome—that seated four thousand.

Earlier that evening, the Socialist leadership had difficulty in gaining entry. According to the *Sun,* whose reporter smoked out more than a few embarrassing incidents that day, there'd been "some trouble" over a certified check that had to be delivered to the management before anyone could be seated. After a considerable delay, a functionary arrived with the check, and the central hall quickly filled up.

For a time, police feared that frustrated marchers pressing toward the entrance might turn violent. But Inspector Walsh and his men dispersed the throng to five "overflow meetings" on side streets between Forty-third and Fiftieth Streets, where speakers addressed them for hours. Only now and again did police have to clear the way for a passing streetcar.

Inside, those fortunate enough to have gained entry relaxed in the buff-and-gold splendor of the central hall, lit by seven hundred incandescent bulbs in seven crystal chandeliers. Despite this imperial decor, the building was one where many in the audience felt at home, for it was there that the *Forward* held its annual masquerade ball—proletarian garb required—and there, too, that the Bund had mounted its first American convention in 1903.

The spacious stage was draped with an American flag flanked by two red banners. Nearby, crimson placards proclaimed: "If they hang our Western brothers for being union men, they will hang us next" and "We don't beg for justice, we demand it." The throng was in a holiday mood. One man jumped on stage, shouting, "Three cheers for the hostlers' union," and the crowd gave it back to him: one, two, THREE!

The speakers included Abraham Cahan; Alexander Jonas, a leader of the American section of DeLeon's Socialist Labor Party; William A. Coakley of the Central Federated Union; and Ben Hanford, Debs's vice presidential candidate in 1904. Presiding that evening was the Socialist attorney Morris Hillquit—the former Moses Hilkowitz of Riga, Latvia—who'd come surprisingly close the previous fall to taking the congressional seat in the Lower East Side's Ninth District.

"Ladies, gentlemen, and fellow undesirable citizens," Hillquit began, eliciting a roar of derisive laughter. Because of recent events, he said, the meeting "incidentally and accidentally" had turned out to be a reply to "that infamous criticism on the part of our President." Sitting nearby, the Socialist John Spargo remembered Hillquit as "like a wild cat" in the ferocity of his assault on the president.

"One great capitalist merely tightened his purse strings and the President got provoked," Hillquit rasped, so Roosevelt "hastened to brand him as an 'undesirable citizen,' and in order to illustrate his depravity he added that he was as undesirable as Debs, Moyer and Haywood.... To us the man who has received the highest trust in the gift of the people, and who abuses it to poison the nation against the men whose lives depend upon an unbiased public opinion, in violation of his oath—to us, that man is an undesirable citizen." More thunderous applause and shouts of approbation.

Then Hillquit introduced the evening's principal speaker—none other than Joseph Wanhope, the *Wilshire's* editor, handed the assignment because he was the only New York Socialist who'd actually been to Caldwell, Idaho, and examined the site of Steunenberg's assassination. Sensing that the audience was thirsting for more ridicule of the president, Wanhope got right to work. "How is it that this man has been allowed unchallenged to lay down for your guidance a code of morality and action, to lecture you like pupils of an infant school, and denounce and insult you if your conduct does not square with the rules he has promulgated for you?" With satisfaction, Wanhope proclaimed that *Wilshire's,* like other bastions of the Socialist press, would be in Boise to cover the Haywood trial. For the first time, Socialists would have their own reporters at a major trial, "unshackled from the capitalist press."

Then, his black pompadour bobbing in the spotlights, Wanhope swung into his peroration. "Let us serve notice upon the capitalists, upon Wall Street, from which Idaho is governed, that we are going to watch this trial, and that if in the course of it our suspicions are justified, we are going to take the necessary steps to do away forever with an industrial system that depends upon murder for its continuance." After a dramatic pause, he added, "I want to tell the gentlemen of the press that if this be treason, let them make the most of it."

Controlled pandemonium ensued, the workers—Jewish, German, Italian, Greek, Irish, and American—cheering the sheer audacity of this challenge to the president. But in the days to come, New York's press made clear that it did indeed regard Wanhope's remarks as seditious, if not treasonous. The *Sun's* reporter, better at sly irony than at indignation, noted only: "No details of the impending revolution were given out." Arch ridicule of the day's events was in vogue at the uptown papers. "If a big proportion of the residents of this city sympathize with Moyer, Haywood and Pettibone," wrote the *Tribune,* "they made no blatant demonstration of it yesterday afternoon." The *Post* turned up news unreported by others: "As a precaution against the impressiveness of the demonstration being impaired by lack of enthusiasm and spontaneity, most of the organizations have voted to impose a fine of five dollars on every member who fails to march. This fact will be of importance to the spectator who may wish to speculate from the curb as to the real significance of the procession."

The account in the *Forward,* apparently written by Abe Cahan himself, more than made up for the laconic dismissal by the establishment press. "The Entire Neighborhood in the Parade" was the headline stretched across page 1. "Glorious, unforgettable, rapturous and heart-rending pictures. Huge mass gatherings in Grand Central Palace. The martyrs of Workers' America and of the Yiddish Neighborhood" read the subheads. In his story, Cahan called the historic march "large, elevated and touching."

But nobody captured the significance of the day's events quite as shrewdly as Norman Hapgood, the editor of *Collier's,* who had already locked horns with Theodore Roosevelt on the meaning of the Haywood case. For Hapgood, the march of the Yiddish-speaking garment workers from Rutgers Square to Grand Central Palace had special meaning. He'd worked for nearly five years on the *Commercial Advertiser* with Abe Cahan and although he was the paper's theater critic and Cahan a reporter on the city desk, the two men had achieved a remarkable rapport. With his brother Hutchins and Steffens, he'd listened for hours at the city-room table as the older man talked of Socialism, anarchism, and literature. Moreover, Cahan had introduced his colleagues to the life of the Lower East Side, which Hutchins Hapgood later memorialized in his remarkable work *The Spirit of the Ghetto.* Norman Hapgood, too, found himself powerfully drawn to this vivid, animated quarter, often writing about the Yiddish theater, of which he became a passionate devotee.

Did Cahan induce Hapgood to write an article about the May 4 march? Perhaps. In any case, the July issue of the *American* carried a remarkable piece, unsigned but clearly by Hapgood, in which he identified strongly with the marchers and their cause. "So this was the Socialist parade to which the papers had referred! I had no idea that it was to be such a tremendous and impressive affair. As I stood there, the solid column swept past—painters, carpenters, hod-carriers, masons, iron workers—every sort of trade-union, each with its own banners—and an extraordinary number of bands all playing the Marseillaise," he wrote.

The thundering big brass band ... the strains of the Marseillaise ... the steps of the marching men, gave to the scene an indescribable color of martial zest and enthusiasm. ... I looked up once or twice to see if the palaces were quaking; but they stood perfectly firm and dark. Presently the parade stopped. I stepped out into the street and approached two or three of the marchers.

"Do you have a meeting after the parade?" I inquired.

They all turned to me questioningly and I repeated the question. They shook their heads: not one of them understood English. So I walked down the line and tried again, with the same result. ... It struck me as being highly significant, this demonstration. Here were 40,000 men marching in New York City ... because three labor leaders are on trial for murder in a state two thousand miles away. Isn't it extraordinary when one comes to think of it? For one thing it presupposes, doesn't it, a remarkable substratum of common interest and intelligence? No one, even a conservative like myself, could see it without feeling how effective it was as a demonstration. It must have had both brains and money behind it, and brains and money are always to be reckoned with. Moreover, it had real enthusiasm—a sort of contagious fervor which is in one way more to be considered than brains or money.

Hapgood had shrewdly zeroed in on the most astonishing aspect of the day's events: that these tens of thousands of eastern European immigrants—many of whom did not speak or read English—should have managed to identify with the travails of a western roughneck, the son of a Pony Express rider, a man who—in most outward respects—was as different from them as he could possibly be. Labor solidarity was hard enough to achieve in New York itself, where the feuds between the "pure and simple" unions of the AFL and the DeLeon faction of the Socialist Labor Party, not to mention the divisive influence of the IWW and the anarchists, constantly threatened to tear the house of labor apart. Indeed, most self-conscious Jewish Socialists weren't drawn to the IWW, whose radical unionism reminded them all too much of their unhappy experiences with DeLeon's party in the 1890s. And yet here these thousands of immigrants in their cloth caps had marched for a man about to go on trial for his life in a western state few of them could pronounce, much less locate on a map.

What accounted for this? To Hapgood, it was a matter partly of brains, partly of money, partly of a "contagious fervor" that united these men of disparate backgrounds and programs. But to Abraham Cahan, this reaching out to the hero of the western miners, this identification with the broader American labor movement, was one more step in the Americanization that he so devoutly sought for the immigrants of the Lower East Side (but that many Orthodox Jews bitterly resented, seeing it as an extirpation of their religious and cultural roots). In the pages of the *Forward*, Cahan wrote repeatedly on American themes: from the U.S. Senate to baseball to the Fourth of July. As subscription premiums, he gave away thousands of Yiddish-English dictionaries so his readers could learn the language of their adopted land. At home he worked away on a giant Yiddish history of the United States, writing on subjects as different as the voyage of Columbus and the Pueblos of the Southwest. But he wanted his people to know more than American history; he wanted them to know the secrets of the American heart. "We have to be Americans," he wrote in one editorial. "We shall love America and help to build America. We shall accomplish in the New World a hundred times more than we could in the Old."

So it was all the more ironic that many onlookers regarded the parade as evidence of precisely the opposite: how un-American the marchers were. On May 4, The Reverend Henry A. Brann, pastor of St. Agnes Roman Catholic Church, had watched from the steps of his church as the parades converged barely a half block away. The next morning, at high mass, he loosed a scathing denunciation of the men and women he'd seen in the streets the night before. "It was enough to make the blood of an American citizen boil to witness this un-American demonstration," he told his parishioners.

> I watched the crowd pass back and forth and hardly heard an English word spoken. There was not an American flag carried and most of the banners bore inscriptions printed in foreign languages. The hired bands in general ignored our good old American airs like "The Star-Spangled Banner" and "Hail, Columbia" and instead habitually played the Marseillaise which is a national air identified with blood, murder, rapine and violence. Are we going to substitute a foreign hymn for our national anthem? . . . The demonstration last night was in bad taste, to say the least, and leads one to suspect that some unprincipled politician paid for the hall, flags and bands from his own sinister motives. That horde could hardly have paid the expenses of last night's celebration. . . . This horde abused the privileges they got by being permitted to land on our shores. We ought not to become the dumping ground for the refuse of Europe.

The next day, in an editorial titled "Unworthy and Undesirable," the *New York Times* declared, "Father Brann deserves the thanks of the community for his denunciation of the Socialist parade." Calling the march "an uncalled for and un-American demonstration," whose participants "do not understand or appreciate their privileges as citizens or denizens of the United States," the *Times* said, "A parade of Socialists bearing red flags and employing bands to play the 'Marseillaise' is in this country . . . profoundly asinine. It has no meaning reconcilable with human reason. It represents no sane aspiration. . . . The Rector of St. Agnes has performed a public service."

Throughout the country that weekend, tens of thousands of other workers marched on Haywood, Moyer, and Pettibone's behalf. In Brooklyn, twenty thousand paraded through the borough to several mass meetings outside the Labor Lyceum. In Rochester, New York, demonstrators filled the Cook Opera House, where they raised $744 for the defense fund, after subtracting $3 for a drummer. At Fair Hope, a single-tax colony near Mobile, Alabama, Socialists held a "largely-attended" meeting on the shores of Mobile Bay and raised several hundred dollars for the defense fund. Three thousand citizens assembled at the baseball grounds of Lynn, Massachusetts, to hear a speech by Miss Luella Twining of Denver, special correspondent of *Appeal to Reason,* now on the WFM payroll as a "solicitor" for the defense fund.

But perhaps the most surprising demonstration of all took place in Boston. Since the city was scarcely known as a radical labor town, the police and the press were astonished by the crowd that massed on Boston Common that Sunday—estimated at a hundred thousand. That didn't include the twelve thousand unionists and Socialists who paraded through the city from the South End, down Tremont Street to the Common, or the many thousands more who lined the route to cheer or gawk. The *Boston Globe,* a journal friendly to labor, published a sympathetic piece—probably by its labor reporter, John F. O'Sullivan—that expressed awe at the sheer breadth of the working population represented in the parade: "There were sturdy teamsters, self-reliant carpenters and riggers and those of other stalwart trades, while behind them there trudged resolutely dainty garment workers and tailors, trig and trim in the spring suits which were convincing examples of the technical skill of the craft."

Reporters speculated that recent labor strife in Boston, notably the use of strikebreakers to defeat a teamsters strike—and some accompanying gunplay—may have swelled the crowds that day. Nonetheless, so cautious was Boston's labor leadership that the Central Labor Union—an umbrella group similiar to New York's Central Federated Union—banned the red flag of Socialism from the march. Here and there a red scarf or sash could be seen, but the crimson banners and other Socialist paraphrenalia so evident in the New York parade were absent in Boston.

Once the marchers joined the assemblage on the Common, they heard Joseph Spero, the parade's chief marshal, denounce the president's intervention. "More than 2,000 years ago, Jesus Christ was termed an 'undesirable citizen' and was crucified," he told his largely Catholic audience. "In Boston, Wendell Phillips and Garrison were called 'undesirable citizens' who freed the human slaves of the south. It was the 'undesirable citizen' who established the American Republic and it will be the 'undesirable citizen' who will yet bring freedom to the human race."

Comparing the president's denunciation of Haywood and Moyer to the act of a bully, Spero asked: "What would you think of my taking a helpless man, a man whose hands and feet were bound, who lay on the ground, while I raised my hand to strike him?"

"Coward!" chorused the crowd. "Coward!"

Not everywhere was the enthusiasm of workingmen as high as it was in New York and Boston. In St. Louis, the Central Trades and Labor Union refused to endorse a resolution passed by the pattern makers deploring the president's statement. "No matter what we may think of Mr. Roosevelt," said its executive council, "we must, as good citizens, respect the office of the Chief Magistrate of our Republic."

The Chicago Federation of Labor was as reluctant as its St. Louis counterpart to take on the president. In Honoré Jaxon's own city, the federation declined to respond to the president's letter. Indeed, its leaders seemed more than a little embarrassed by the lèse-majesté of the exotic half-breed. When the Cook County Moyer-Haywood Conference, of which Jaxon was chairman, announced a public demonstration on May 10, the federation's secretary, Edward Nockels, told reporters: "We have not a word to say and, therefore, he will have to face his own troubles alone. Labor cannot be held to account in any way for Jaxon's protest to the President, nor for what follows."

A protest march was eventually organized in which both the Moyer-Haywood Conference and the Chicago Federation of Labor took part. But the impetus behind this demonstration came from neither group but from an intense thirty-seven-year-old New Yorker named Margaret Dreier Robins.

Margaret Dreier descended from a long line of merchants and civic leaders in Bremen, a Hanseatic city that the Dreiers saw as embodying "the golden thread of democracy." In 1849, her father, Theodor, emigrated to New York, part of that flood of German "Forty-eighters" whom Theodore Roosevelt regarded as the best immigrant stock ever to grace these shores. Through hard work and ingenuity, he ascended from clerk to partner in an iron company. Returning to Germany on a visit, he brought back a younger cousin as his bride. "Eager to know Americans," Dorothea Dreier declined to settle in the German community of College Point. Instead, the Dreiers bought a row house in Brooklyn Heights, Brooklyn's most fashionable neighborhood, offering both "elbow room and a hush at night." Perched atop a bluff overlooking the East River, it was easily accessed from the big city by ferry and, after 1883, by the Brooklyn Bridge; when the Dreiers moved there it was populated principally by New England Protestants. Later they moved to a handsome three-story brownstone on Monroe Place, where their four daughters—Margaret, Dorothea, Katherine, and Mary—and son, Henry, were raised. Though all spoke German at home, the Dreiers—just as determined as Abraham Cahan to become real Americans—hired an English governess to educate the children in the language of their adopted land.

It was a grand household of wealth and taste, a family of eight tended by seven servants. If the Dreiers were resolutely assimilationist, the house brimmed with German gemütlichkeit. Dorothea Dreier adored music. "She arranged to sing with us every afternoon from five to five-thirty," Mary recalled. "Mother's lovely voice rang through the house, and the high treble voices of the childen joined in the songs ... of Schubert, Schumann, Franz and Brahms, the great hymns and chorales of Bach and Martin Luther." Between Christmas and New Year's the family gathered every night to sing. "We would light the candles," Mary recalled, "and with no other light sit around the Christmas tree, surrounded by such dear loveliness that the world seemed a bit of heaven."

The family prided itself on good citizenship. Theodor was a trustee of the Brooklyn Hospital and Dorothea took up social work, helping to manage the Brooklyn Industrial School and Home for Destitute Children. But they could also be class-bound. Educated by tutors and at George Brackett's exclusive School for Girls, the Dreier girls regularly attended Sunday School at the German Evangelical Church, but their attendance slacked off because "the poor German children used their Sunday dresses which were not thoroughly aired and therefore the smell of stale clothing permeated the air."

The four sisters didn't go to college, as their mother thought American colleges put too much emphasis on the intellectual at the expense of the artistic. But eventually Margaret read philosophy under Dr. Richard Salter Storrs, minister of Brooklyn's Church of the Pilgrims and second only to the late Henry Ward Beecher on the roster of great Congregational clerics. The four girls grew into extraordinary young women. Katherine became a well-known painter and a founder of the Société Anonyme, which promoted avant-garde art; Dorothea became a painter as well, though less celebrated; Margaret and Mary both followed their mother into social work.

For Margaret, there were "dark hours" along the way. By her twelfth birthday, she was a "glowing girl," with "raven black hair...flashing dark eyes, high coloring and fine features." But she suffered from the cluster of symptoms—headaches, fatigue, and depression—often diagnosed in those years as neurasthenia. When she was in her late teens, a British physician provoked her rage by suggesting she was destined, like many similiarly afflicted women, to live "the life of an invalid."

With the study of Emerson, Kant, and Descartes, she pulled out of the slough. Stirred to religious idealism by stories of the abolitionists, craving a life of service, at nineteen she joined the Women's Auxiliary at Brooklyn Hospital, soon becoming its secretary-treasurer. For fifteen years the hospital —particularly the care of women and children in its charity wards—became the principal focus of her civic energies. Then, through the influence of Josephine Shaw Lowell, a founder of the Women's Municipal League, she was introduced to the wider world of social reform, especially the plight of the woman wage earner. In 1902, she joined the Women's Municipal League, serving for two years as its legislative chairman, focusing on the role of so-called employment agencies in leading working women into prostitution.

In 1904, a former garment worker named Leonora O'Reilly recruited Margaret and her sister Mary for the Women's Trade Union League, founded that year on the model of the decades-old British Women's Trade Union League. Some such organization was clearly needed in this country: of five million American women working for wages in 1905, a tiny minority belonged to trade unions, while only 4 of the 496 delegates to that year's AFL convention were women. From the start, the U.S. league was conceived as a coalition of women wage earners and social reformers, its twin goals to improve the lot of women workers by organizing them in trade unions and to educate the middle-class reformers, known as allies, about the conditions of working-class life. By 1904, it had embryonic branches in New York, Chicago, and Boston but virtually no money.

Thus, it was scarcely coincidental that the New York league prevailed upon Margaret to become its treasurer, and the National League soon followed suit. When her parents died, they'd left her a $600,000 trust fund, ensuring she'd never have to worry about money. Soon she was putting chunks of her legacy into the WTUL. If that troubled her at times, she was nonetheless thrilled to be participating in an era of momentous social change. To Mary, she wrote: "History is making fast."

Her personal life was stagnant. By her late twenties, Margaret was reconciled to spinsterhood, signing letters to her sisters, "Your Old Maid." Then in April 1905, at age thirty-six, she met Raymond Robins, a sociologist and municipal reformer, at a dinner party after he spoke on the "Social Gospel of Jesus" at the Plymouth Church.

Tall, handsome, with a natural eloquence and forceful personality—but subject himself to insomnia, moodiness, and, eventually, emotional breakdowns—Robins was head resident of Chicago's Northwestern University Settlement. He'd come to that position after years of working in Florida phosphate mines, Tennessee coal mines, and Colorado lead mines, during which he'd joined the Western Federation of Miners. Later he earned a law degree, followed the Alaska gold rush, was ordained in both the Congregational and Methodist churches, and set out to clean up the boisterous mining community of Nome. In 1901, he moved to Chicago, where he became a confidant of some formidable social reformers, including Jane Addams; Graham Taylor of the Chicago Commons Settlement; and Mary McDowell, known as the Angel of the Stockyards for her work with slaughterhouse workers. During the 1902 anthracite coal strike, in which Darrow served as attorney for the mine workers, Robins was part of his team, winning both Darrow's and Roosevelt's admiration.

Margaret and Raymond were married in June 1905 and settled in Chicago. With her trust fund they could have bought a house on burgeoning Lake Shore Drive but moved instead to a third-floor cold-water flat on West Ohio Street, in the heart of the Seventeenth Ward's tenement district, notorious for labor unrest and election violence. It was a vast change from the home in which she'd been raised, but Raymond thought she could only slip the bonds of class and "find her true freedom and power" in the "bloody Seventeenth," where they could be on intimate terms with Chicago's urgent social problems. "I am in it thick!" she joyfully wrote her sister.

In early 1907, Margaret Robins became president of both the Women's Trade Union League of Illinois and the National Women's Trade Union

League. She was more than an administrator; for years to come she was the organizations' driving force and their principal source of funds, not only covering the entire budget of the national organization (between $4,000 and $10,000 a year) but running both leagues from an office in her flat, paying her own expenses and the salaries of two employees.

Her rescue of the national organization from bankruptcy allowed her to put her stamp on it, becoming known to its members as the Great Mother. Soon she took her place in Chicago's social-justice movement, alongside Jane Addams (whom Robins, like others—not without a touch of irony—called Saint Jane), Ellen Starr, and Mary McDowell. On the second Sunday of every month, she presided over public meetings at Hull House, addressing such pressing questions as "The Immigrant Woman" and "The Conditions of Women and Children in Industry." Following the program, there were re-freshments, music, and a chance to mingle with the social workers. But knowing she couldn't rely solely on social workers and their clients, she strove to earn the trust of the leaders of the Chicago Federation of Labor—men like Edward Nockels and John Fitzpatrick—aided by her husband, who'd long enjoyed the federation's confidence.

But now, in the spring of 1907, she faced an exquisitely difficult decision: how to respond to an invitation from the Moyer-Haywood Conference, headed by Honoré Jaxon, to march for the imprisoned labor leaders and in protest of President Roosevelt's intervention. Powerful forces lined up against such participation. Not only did the Chicago Federation of Labor spurn Jaxon and hew to Sam Gompers's more moderate line, but so did Jane Addams, an influential member of the Illinois league's board. Although Addams supported the AFL, she was suspicious of the IWW and Haywood's "direct action" program. "It is only occasionally that I get a glimpse of the chivalry of labor," she once wrote. "So much of the time it seems so sordid."

There were formidable pressures from the other side as well. As a former WFM member, Raymond Robins knew and admired Bill Haywood. He un-derstood how high the stakes were in the approaching trial. In the winter of 1906, Mother Jones, the labor organizer, then on the WFM payroll as a speaker, attended a meeting with Ray Robins. Abruptly, she put her head down on the table, "sobbed like a child," and blurted out, "They are going to hang Bill Haywood, and you men are sitting still."

"Oh no," Ray said. "We are shouting from the street-corners, and he will not be hung."

Knowing that whatever she did on this issue would stir fierce contro-versy, Margaret Robins studied the matter carefully. Through John Marshall Harlan, Jr., a Chicago lawyer and a son of the Supreme Court justice, she obtained a copy of his father's majority opinion on the habeas corpus plea, as well as Justice McKenna's dissenting opinion, whose exposition she found "a magnificent arraignment of legalized kidnapping."

As she wrote her friend Carrie Reid when the Supreme Court ignored its constitutional duty in *Pettibone v. Nichols,* "it became the duty of all those who desire an impartial administration of the law to make such solemn and commanding protest as means and opportunity would permit," just as protesters from Maine to California had spoken out after the Court's infamous Dred Scott decision. "Is it only the struggles of the past, Carrie, that can command our loyalty, or will we not rather pray God that today . . . in the heat of the battle, under abuse and public obloquy, we will have courage to be true to the right as we see it?"

Robins was attracted to the march by a long-standing personal disposition as well. As a child, she'd directed her siblings in playlets, and from the moment she took charge of the leagues, she'd infused them with her love of theater, music, and pageantry. Under her direction, they produced many plays celebrating the powers of women. For Robins, the march would be more than an act of solidarity with Bill Haywood and a repudiation of Theodore Roosevelt; it was to be a grand pageant symbolizing working-class unity, women very much included.

Robins could be willful and domineering. Having made up her mind by late April that Haywood and his colleagues had been treated unjustly, she determined that the Illinois league would take part in the march. As one of two league delegates to the Federation of Labor, she felt empowered to commit the league to a leading role in the parade. When others dissented, she stood her ground. Her sister Mary—who knew her better than anyone else— wrote of Margaret:

> *Her heart ran out in a consuming flame*
> *Against injustice where she saw it rise.*
> *She met betrayed young lives, heard anguished cries,*
> *Demanded justice as their rightful claim.*
> *With voice and spirit which she would not tame*
> *She chose words flaming, passionate yet wise*
> *And called indifferent hearts to strange surprise.*

As the spring wore on, Robins took an ever-larger role in planning the Chicago march, now scheduled for Sunday, May 19. Hampered by city officials who refused to grant a permit for a postparade rally on the lakeshore, the organizers had to wrestle as well with doubts and inhibitions in their own ranks. Among many of the trade unionists there was profound skepticism that Chicagoans would join such a protest, particularly when it was conceived as an open affront to Theodore Roosevelt. After a motion was made to purchase fifty thousand buttons bearing the phrase "I Am an Undesirable Citizen"— the same button worn by marchers in New York—a federation man said, "I don't believe you can get that many union men in Chicago to wear them." The button order was reduced to five thousand.

Nowhere in the nation was the labor-Socialist community so badly fractured as it was in Chicago. This was partly due to the presence there of

IWW headquarters, which was an endless source of squabbling among the city's left wing. In the immediate wake of the Haywood-Moyer-Pettibone kidnapping, the IWW took the lead in inviting Chicago Socialists and certain labor unions to a mass protest meeting in Apollo Hall on Sunday, March 4, 1906. The Cook County Committee of the Socialist Party responded with a letter to its affiliated locals advising them that "in view of the party's position in the matter of trade unionism"—a reference to the party's opposition to "dual unionism"—it was "deemed wise not to comply with the request." Instead, the committee summoned Socialist locals to a meeting of its own the same day. The IWW meeting—cosponsored by DeLeon's Socialist Labor Party, the *Arbeiter Zeitung,* and the Jewish Bund—drew 1,500 persons and raised $203 for the defense fund. The poorly attended Socialist meeting raised a scant $50. That was only the start of the quarreling. When the IWW called another meeting to set up the Moyer-Haywood Conference, the Socialist committee again advised its locals not to attend. Thus, the conference didn't bear the party's imprimatur, though individual members and locals partici-pated.

In the week immediately preceding the May 1907 march, a fierce strug-gle raged within the Chicago Federation of Labor over whether to join in. Such participation was critical to its success, for the march had been sched-uled to coincide with a meeting of the federation's assembly, a body of five hundred labor leaders representing the 175,000 union workers in Chicago. Margaret Robins was relying on them to swell the marchers' ranks, a visible manifestation of organized labor's support.

But as the march drew closer, labor's sachems stewed and fretted. The struggle was particularly intense among the city's powerful building trades. On May 12, the Building Material Trades Council, comprising thirteen trade unions, voted to participate, while the rival Associated Building Trades, with a membership of some fifty thousand workers, declined to join as a unit, though it permitted individuals to march if they wished.

It became clear that the relatively conservative Federation of Labor would participate only if it, rather than the Socialists, controlled the event. Literally on the eve of the march, it appeared that labor had won out. Ernest Berger of the brewery workers was elected chief marshal, with the details of organization placed in the hands of three unionists. Honoré Jaxon was explic-itly told to stay away. Moreover, the labor delegates agreed that red banners and even the red neckties that hundreds of Socialists planned to wear should be prohibited. Not everyone concurred. In an impassioned address to the delegates, T. P. Quinn declared: "Every schoolboy knows that the red flag floated over battle fields from Bunker Hill to Yorktown. I regret to see the red flag sacrificed to the superstitions of the hour. We should act like free men." But pressure from city officials and the anxiety of many unionists converged to uphold the ban. Moreover, placards attacking President Roosevelt were banned as well, the sole exception being the button "I Am an Undesirable Citizen," which sold for five cents, the proceeds to go to the defense fund.

Overnight the Socialists mounted a countercoup. For when the marchers assembled the following afternoon outside the Federation of Labor Hall, the followers of Debs and DeLeon had turned out in significant numbers, many of them brandishing the very red flags that had been proscribed by the labor delegates the evening before.

Over that last weekend, Margaret Robins had endured her own trial by fire. On the Friday before the march, she gave a luncheon for eighteen to honor the newly appointed head resident of the Northwestern University Settlement. The luncheon was held in the Hull House dining room, and just as guests began arriving, Margaret was summoned to Miss Addams's study. There she found Saint Jane with Ellen M. Henrotin, Margaret's immediate predecessor as president of the National Women's Trade Union League and still a member of its executive board. Henrotin was a woman to reckon with: the wife of a prominent banker, she was serving her second term as president of the General Federation of Women's Clubs of the United States. As Robins recalled it, Addams told her "how serious a blunder I had made in permitting the League to participate in the Moyer-Haywood parade." She was "very sweet and very gentle," and Robins concluded that Henrotin had asked her to deliver this reprimand. Henrotin was "fearfully excited and wrought up and refused to stop discussing the question even though the guests had arrived."

Robins was portrayed to her own guests as someone who had "over-stepped her rights and by an individual act had placed the League in an unwarranted position." Unable to answer back and "cut up by the demand to quit at this last moment," she found it hard to act the "happy hostess." But things became more uncomfortable yet when Henrotin insisted that the Illinois league's executive board be summoned into special session at Hull House Saturday evening—the night before the march—to vote on the organization's participation. "It really was a battle royal, and I felt as limp as a rag when it was over," Robins wrote later. "The [working] girls stood by me like a stone wall and were amazed to think that there could be any question regarding the action of the League. Mrs. Henrotin again was very much wrought up and after having asked for a vote in the beginning, refused to let a motion be made when she saw that she was entirely alone in her position. Miss Addams was complete [*sic*] won over by the fact that the girls were so strongly for the parade and by my showing her how carefully I had studied the question."

Though Robins understood working girls better than Saint Jane did, she knew she was still a prisoner of her class. Months later she would confess to her sister: "Yesterday afternoon I spoke to the striking glove workers, and the evening before to the waitresses. I wonder how I am ever going to learn to speak to the type of women such as the average waitress is. She really is a 'hobo' girl....I have decided to take a course of reading to help me in this work. I think perhaps if I read Adam Bede and see what Dina says to the people, I may get somewhere."

Sunday afternoon, minutes before leaving for the march, she jotted a quick note to Mary: "These are hot days.... Dear St. Jane gave me a jab and Mrs. Henrotin went agin me, but the labor girls stood with me.... We must [leave] in a short time to form the march—the day is glorious."

For Robins, at least, the next few hours *were* glorious. In recognition of her central role in organizing the procession, she was accorded a position of honor near the head of the parade. First came an American flag, followed by a brass band rousing the crowds with anthems; then Chief Marshal Berger of the brewery workers proudly erect in his carriage, followed by Robins in a carriage of her own, her arms filled with American Beauty roses. Her photographs in the paper had made her instantly recognizable to many along the route, who greeted her warmly. "I wish you could have heard the way the Yiddish bakers cheered us," she wrote Mary.

In the next carriages came other league officers and trade union members of the executive board, though the middle-class "allies" stayed home. The WTUL contingent was followed by thirty-two girls in pinafores—the daughters, aged eight to fifteen, of Chicago union men—carrying a banner bearing Henrietta Haywood's apocryphal question: "Will they hang my Papa?" This feature of the march, proposed by J. Edward Morgan, the WFM's Chicago spokesman, made a striking tableau. But it struck the league's most sophisticated members as "maudlin," prompting Robins indignantly to deny responsibility for it.

Just as in New York, the number of marchers became a matter of dispute. The *Chicago Record-Herald* put it at thirty-seven hundred, the *Chicago Tribune* at four thousand. But Robins described for Mary "that moment of exaltation which came when I saw the line of 20,000 to 30,000 men and women ready for the march." There was disagreement, too, as to how many red flags appeared in the parade—in violation of police orders and the Federation of Labor's resolution. According to several news accounts, when the head of the parade reached Madison and Union Streets, a woman leaned from a window with a bright red flag in either hand, shouting, "Down with government and governors," to which Robins responded with a vigorous wave of her pink roses—a story she dismissed as "absolutely untrue."

Robins would also insist that "not a single red flag was carried in the parade," but the weight of journalistic testimony was against her. According to the *Daily Inter-Ocean*, the parade was "a trail of the red flag from start to finish," a scarlet "taint of anarchy." The *Record-Herald* found "a sea of red flags" and "red badges, sashes and ribbons," the *Tribune* "hundreds of red flags and banners." As her biographer noted, perhaps Robins was "unable or unwilling" to see the red banners. After all, she was seated in the second carriage, looking "figuratively as well as physically" toward the American flag up front. To her, the marchers were in "a line of American ancestry going back to the Minute Men of the Revolution." George M. Shippy, Chicago's police chief, didn't see it that way. He considered wading into the marchers and seizing the flags but held back, fearing it might set off a riot.

The ocean of red, the *Tribune* contended, helped mark the parade as "almost wholly a socialistic affair." That, too, was a matter of dispute between Robins and the establishment press. According to Robins, the twenty thousand to thirty thousand marchers included "every trade in the city but the building trade." According to the *Tribune,* it was "little patronized by the trade unions." The *Record-Herald's* longtime labor reporter, Luke Grant, wrote: "A feature of the parade was the almost total failure of the delegates to the Chicago Federation of Labor to participate. The meeting of the federation in the Omaha building was adjourned at 2.43 o'clock, in order that the delegates might get in line, but most of them ignored the opportunity." Among the unions that did march were the woodworkers, the cigar makers, the bakery workers, the skirt makers, the beer bottlers, and the "ladies tailors."

Even if the union turnout was relatively sparse, it was nonetheless an impressive procession, a gorgeous pageant in Robins's terms. By Luke Grant's watch, it took thirty-five minutes for the marchers to pass. The void created by absent unions was evidently filled by "anarchists, socialists and other free-thinking advocates." A conspicuous—and controversial—figure in the march was Lucy Parsons, widow of the anarchist executed for his role in the Haymarket riot.

On one point organizers and critics agreed: "the parade was one of the most cosmopolitan...held in Chicago in years," the marchers including Russians, Poles, Serbians, Lithuanians, Germans, Austrians, Italians, and more, all but a few wearing their five-cent button. Here and there in the march, workers held bedsheets into which spectators were encouraged to throw change for the defense fund.

As the procession turned into the West Side baseball grounds—which Robins described as "nothing but a huge dirty field with no stands and no trees and no grass"—it began to rain. The crowd split into six different language groups as a half dozen orators mounted wagons in the mud, producing "a babel of voices." That evening, the Socialists held a dance in the Wicker Park Hall.

In the days that followed, Robins drew some scathing attacks for an event many people regarded as a fiasco. The Gompers wing of organized labor was particularly hostile. John Matz, president of the Carpenters District Council, warned, "If the Federation continues to recognize such movements as that of Sunday, a number of strong units will be obliged to withdraw." George J. Werner, secretary of the International Blacksmiths Union, said union men should protest against anything savoring of "revolution or physical violence, such as Sunday's parade."

Robins continued to hear criticism as well from inside her own circle. Shortly after the parade, word circulated that she was so obsessed about organizing women in trade unions that she had allowed her baby to freeze to death on the fire escape—"she who, to her unending sorrow, never had a baby," as her sister Mary noted. She was blackballed for admission to the Chicago Women's Club, of which Ellen Henrotin had recently been elected president.

There'd been gentle words from Jane Addams, a conciliatory letter from Henrotin telling Robins how much she admired her and how fond she was of her, and a class-conscious comment from the president of the Woodlawn Women's Club: "To sink your own personality with your natural sense of refinement and taste so completely with the common lot is the finest heroism I know and I offer before it my humblest homage."

Nonetheless, Robins's relations with Hull House quickly deteriorated. In 1905, before she knew Addams well, Robins had written Mary: "Miss Addams is the greatest woman I know, large-minded, great-hearted, generous and forgiving." Now the relationship was in shambles. What did the greatest damage, besides their differences over Bill Haywood, was Addams's actions that spring as a member of Chicago's school board.

Raymond Robins and seven other insurgent board members had put forward a plan to insulate the evaluation of teachers from political pressures, a plan vigorously resisted by the city's new mayor, Fred A. Busse. The press denounced the proposal. "Why have all the privileged interests of the city combined to make this attack and make it so venomously?" Margaret Robins asked Lincoln Steffens. Now to Raymond's and Margaret's astonishment, Addams voted against the plan. On May 27, Margaret wrote Mary: "St. Jane has given me such a blow, I can hardly see straight." Margaret found Addams's positions on the parade and the Board of Education simply "incomprehensible." By autumn, the chasm between the two women, and their institutions, was unbridgeable.

But Robins stayed the course. To a friend who wondered how she could bring herself to march on Haywood's behalf, she wrote: "Behind Haywood, I see the great army of the toilers of the world. Himself a simple miner, deriving his free spirit and unflinching courage from a line of American ancestry...he has fought for an eight-hour day, against child labor in the deadly smelters.... He is rough, hard-handed and none-too-careful, doubtless, of men and methods." Behind the prosecution Robins saw "the able and powerful attorneys of the Mine Owners Association and the Pinkerton Detective Agency, supported by the millions of the Smelter Trust and those industrial robber barons that have prostituted to selfish ends sheriffs, legislatures, courts and governors of sovereign states in pursuit of the satisfaction of their inhuman greed."

Finally, she asked: "Is it so strange that I, a free woman, whose fathers fought for their faith and founded the free cities of Germany, should take sides with those who are fighting for the fundamental right of personal liberty as guaranteed by our Constitution?"

Nor should anyone have been surprised when Mary Dreier took up the same cudgels in New York. Seven years Margaret's junior, Mary had modeled her career after her older sister's. For a time she worked with Leonora O'Reilly at Asacog House, a Brooklyn settlement whose name stood for "All Sorts and Conditions of Girls." When Margaret decamped for Chicago, Mary took her place as president of the New York Women's Trade Union League. But Mary's style was different from her sister's. Eschewing Margaret's head-on attack, Mary addressed Haywood's plight obliquely as a high-minded pursuit of truth. In late spring of 1906, she took the lead in forming the Moyer-Haywood Inquiry Committee of New York, which met through the summer and autumn of 1906 at her Brooklyn Heights home.

The committee's twenty-four members were a curious amalgam of social workers and accomplished men from the world of business and the professions. On the social-work side of the ledger, there was Leonora O'Reilly, Margaret and Mary's friend who'd brought them both into the WTUL; Lillian Wald, a public-health nurse who'd founded the Henry Street Settlement, a neighborhood center on Manhattan's Lower East Side; Jane E. Robbins, a social worker who had headed the New York College Settlement on Rivington Street; Charles B. Stover of the University Settlement on Eldridge Street, known for his development of urban parks; and Lucy Whitlock, a church worker.

Among the men of the world, two held public office in Brooklyn: Alfred J. Boulton, a former leader of the stereotypers union just elected Kings County register on the Hearst ticket, and his deputy, a chemist named Gustave W. Thompson. There was a prominent newsman, Roscoe C. E. Brown, editorial writer for the *New York Tribune;* a stockbroker, Herbert H. Knox; an architect, Alexander Mackintosh; an attorney, James McKeen, who had served as Charles Evans Hughes's assistant in the insurance investigations and was now general counsel to Mutual Life.

The clergy was well represented: a Catholic priest, the Reverend William J. White, charities administrator in the Brooklyn diocese, and no fewer than four Episcopal rectors from Brooklyn—the Reverend Reese F. Alsop of St. Ann's, Canon William Sheafe Chase of Christ Church, the Reverend John Howard Melish of Holy Trinity, and Charles F. J. Wrigley of Grace Church, archdeacon of southern Brooklyn, who served as the committee's chairman, while Mary Dreier was its secretary.

One curious feature was the inclusion of four wives—Mrs. Alsop, Mrs. Boulton, Mrs. McKeen, and Mrs. Melish—traceable perhaps to the feminist principles of Leonora O'Reilly, Lillian Wald, and Mary Dreier. Mary never married. But in June 1907, a month after the Chicago march, she confessed her love to her sister's husband, an explosive situation that Raymond deftly defused by enlisting Mary in a secret compact, "the Order of the Flaming Cross," in which her romantic passion was transmuted into social service. Lacking a spouse, Mary put her sister Katherine on the committee.

The Moyer-Haywood Inquiry Committee shouldn't be confused with the Moyer-Haywood Conference, the socialist-unionist coalition, openly supportive of Haywood, that organized New York's parade. In forming her committee, Dreier excluded Socialists and union members, seeking out substantial men and women who could hardly be accused of fostering anarchy. In its statement of purpose, the committee emphasized that it sought only "to secure unbiased information, in face of the present conflicting reports."

For weeks, in Dreier's living room, the members debated a letter asking clergymen and editors in Idaho and Colorado to supply facts. The first draft proclaimed them "neutral" on the case, but that was removed from the final version. Behind the facade of dispassion, there can be little doubt that Mary and most of her colleagues were devoted to Haywood's defense.

In August, the group agreed on a letter noting that Steunenberg's assassination and the events that followed had aroused "a great deal of interest here" in what would be "the most important criminal trial ever held in our country." New Yorkers were concerned about reports that "these men were extradited illegally, and that they may not receive a fair trial." Believing that an enlightened public opinion was an essential safeguard of justice, the committee invited replies to the enclosed questions, so the committee could "direct public opinion, in our city, in accordance with the facts."

Among other things, the committee asked: "To what extent is public sympathy in your neighborhood for or against the three men, Moyer, Haywood and Pettibone? What is believed to be the motive these three men had in seeking the death of Ex-Governor Steunenberg? Has any motive for killing him been ascribed to anyone else?"

No record remains of the answers the group received or of any conclusions based on the "facts." Perhaps it got so few responses the members were unable to draw conclusions. Or perhaps this diverse body was unable to agree on their meaning. But the committee's very existence raises interesting questions. How, for example, does one explain the preeminent role that Brooklyn played in the response to the Haywood case?

The answer probably lies in the airs that New England Protestants on the Heights had long given themselves. In part, they were protecting their real estate, promoting their borough of "homes and churches" as opposed to the slough of depravity across the river, not to mention the cluster of lower-status Catholics in the Brooklyn lowlands. In part, though, they were responding to Brooklyn's renowned Congregationalist ministers like Henry Ward Beecher, Lyman Abbott, and Richard Salter Storrs, who had long preached a kind of moral stewardship, the notion that Brooklyn was called to serve as a moral beacon to the nation.

Striking, too, was the heavy participation of the borough's Episcopal clergy—four rectors and two of their wives, fully a fourth of the committee. Whatever their other motives, these Brooklyn rectors had been drawn by the Social Gospel, a movement summoning Christians to seek social justice for the poor.

The Social Gospel was born as lonely dissent in the 1870s, when a different spirit reigned among many American churchmen. Under the impact of the 1877 railroad strikes, the *Independent,* a nondenominational organ of the nation's Protestant churches, editorialized: "If the club of the policeman, knocking out the brains of the rioter, will answer, then well and good, but if it does not promptly meet the exigency, then bullets and bayonets, canister and grape—with no sham or pretense, in order to frighten men, but with fearful and destructive reality—constitute the one remedy and the one duty of the hour." That same summer, the *Congregationalist* said: "Bring out the Gatling guns. Let there be no fooling with blank cartridges. But let the mob know, everywhere, that for it to stand one moment after it has been ordered by proper authorities to disperse, will be to be shot down in its tracks."

Such tough talk dismayed Henry Codman Potter, New York's Episcopal bishop, who warned: "We shall not finally silence the heresies of the communist with the bullets of the militia." Potter contested the view of labor as a commodity, an outlook that had reigned supreme ever since enunciated a half century before by his own father, the Reverend Alonzo Potter. In an 1886 pastoral letter, the junior Potter argued that only the principle of "a joint interest in what is produced, of all brains and hands that go to produce it" could heal "those grave social divisions" that plagued America at century's close.

Soon the Social Gospel amassed a considerable following in Protestant denominations. Though the Baptist theologian Walter Rauschenbusch developed the most coherent justification, in no branch did it find more followers than among Episcopalians. In 1883, the General Convention of the Episcopal Church noted that of late "this Church has been awakened to increased practical sympathy with the worker and suffering classes."

In part, the movement's strength among Episcopalians was due to the social assurance of that church's members: they could afford to identify with the poor without fear of losing status. And nowhere were the social evils bred by the industrial revolution more evident than in New York. It was there that the Reverend Edward A. Washburn condemned the swarming ghettos where "thousands are bred in the sunless dens of vice and seemingly doomed to moral death." Over the next forty years, Episcopalian bishops and rectors in New York played a central role in the evolution of the Social Gospel.

In 1887, they founded the most effective of all Social Gospel institutions, the Church Association for the Advancement of the Interests of Labor. Defining labor as "the exercise of body, mind and spirit in the broadening and elevating of human life," CAIL campaigned against child labor and sweat-shops and, beginning in 1890, persuaded many New York Episcopalians to dedicate one Sunday a year to the cause of labor.

One of those heavily influenced by CAIL was the Reverend Frederick Burgess, rector of Grace Church, Brooklyn Heights, from 1898 through 1901. In 1902, he was consecrated the second bishop of the Long Island diocese, which included Brooklyn, and in his diocesan address a year later, he spelled out his vision of the Episcopal Church's mission: "Let the Church go on and fight its battle with the world...let it speak in the midst of labor strifes, whenever it can protect the cause of justice, impartially to the workingmen or to the threatened contractors; let it refuse the large fights which come from men whose moral life has been notoriously corrupt, or from fortunes won by child labor, or by grinding the face of the poor in the gloom of the mines or amid the clatter of the mills."

Soon the bishop formed—and chaired—a Social Service Committee, the first of its kind in the Episcopal Church. Among its ten clerical members were three Brooklyn rectors from the most urban segment of the diocese: Charles Wrigley, John Howard Melish, and William Sheafe Chase. In its wide-ranging work, the committee addressed marriage, divorce, law enforce-ment, political reform, labor and capital, commercial ethics, intemperance, and gambling.

In grappling with labor questions, it leaned on Melish, who in 1906 it named its fraternal delegate to the Brooklyn Central Labor Union as a way of "endeavoring to remove mutual distrust between capital and labor." Melish's devotion to the cause of labor had been stirred when he attended the AFL convention, where Samuel Gompers struck him "like one of the Hebrew prophets as he pleaded for justice and fair play." Now, attending the CLU meetings each Sunday afternoon at the Labor Lyceum, he was impressed once more. "In no body of men with whom I am associated," he noted, "have I heard more vital subjects discussed or treated with greater fairness." He was pleased to report that, "though the meetings are held on Sunday, in a room over a place where liquor is sold, the moral atmosphere of the place is as wholesome as that of any fashionable club.... The ethical value of such meetings on Sunday is vastly superior to the social club and not unworthy of comparison with the Church."

It was at one such meeting that Melish met Mary Dreier, a delegate from the Women's Trade Union League. Polish and Lithuanian workers had struck one of the borough's jute mills, but with no strike fund and no real organiza-tion, they'd been routed by a determined management. That afternoon they appealed for help from the CLU, but aroused little sympathy among the Anglo-Saxon delegates until Mary stood up and, "with blazing eyes," ex-claimed, "You have never given them a chance!" Melish rallied to her support and they soon became close friends. Many years later, Mary reminded the rector of "those extraordinary days of long ago when we ... sat in the smoke filled room all afternoon."

The friendship forged at those meetings was the first building block of the Moyer-Haywood Inquiry Committee. Melish appealed to Bishop Burgess and his colleagues on the Social Service Committee, notably Rectors Wrigley and Chase, the three of them then bringing in the fourth rector, the elderly but influential Reese Alsop of St. Ann's. All through 1906 and into 1907, the committee sought to mobilize public opinion behind Bill Haywood and his imprisoned colleagues.

The Inquiry Committee may have had yet another purpose: to counteract the influence emanating from perhaps the most renowned pulpit in the land. For forty years, from 1847 to 1887, the Plymouth Congregational Church at Hicks and Orange Streets in Brooklyn Heights had been pastored by Henry Ward Beecher, a powerful preacher, ardent abolitionist, and early advocate of temperance, women's rights, and educational reform—in short, many of the notions that, before long, would coalesce into the Social Gospel. Beecher was succeeded by another towering figure in the Protestant community, Lyman Abbott, who served until 1899, when he became the editor of the *Outlook,* remaining all this time one of Theodore Roosevelt's closest confidants. That same year, Abbott handed Plymouth Church over to the Reverend Newell Dwight Hillis, a native of Magnolia, Iowa, who'd pastored Presbyterian churches in Peoria and Chicago before entering the Congregational fellowship to accept the prestigious pulpit.

A vigorous forty-seven in 1906, Hillis was a tall, commanding figure with "dashing, showy abilities," who reminded audiences of Rudyard Kipling. A prolific writer of articles and books, he produced such popular works as *Quest of Happiness* (1902) and *Success Through Self-Help* (1903). Each week for twenty-five years his sermons—delivered in the barnlike two-thousand-seat Plymouth Church—were published in the *Brooklyn Eagle.* A powerful preacher and skilled lecturer, with a rich baritone voice and formidable rhetorical skills, he could be very persuasive. The Reverend Charles F. Aked of the Fifth Avenue Baptist Church effused in a 1907 letter, "You are the most interesting personality in America." Another observer described his sermons and lectures as "a swift, steady stream of well-cadenced, parse-able sentences that shimmered with many lights and bore innumerable facts and fancies and apothegms to the mind."

Hillis regularly accepted speaking invitations all over the country. In the winter of 1906–07, he toured the Pacific, speaking in dozens of communities along the way, accompanied by the Apollo Glee Club. On February 26, he spoke on "John Ruskin's Message to the Twentieth Century" at Boise's Columbia Theater in a series sponsored by the Young Men's Christian Association. During his stay, he became fascinated by the Haywood case as it moved toward trial.

It occurred to someone in Governor Gooding's entourage that Hillis might prove helpful in explaining the governor's position to the nation. A sign of how seriously Gooding took this recommendation was his decision to let the visiting cleric spend an hour with Harry Orchard out at the penitentiary —a privilege extended to very few persons not associated with the prosecution. The assassin impressed Hillis with the sincerity of his confession. Shortly thereafter, Hillis also met with the Reverend Edwin S. Hinks, dean of Boise's Episcopal Cathedral and Orchard's "spiritual adviser."

Dean Hinks was a relatively new recruit from secular to clerical ranks and remained as effective in one realm as in the other. Born in Baltimore on the eve of the Civil War, he'd received a law degree from the University of Maryland in 1880 and practiced for a time in the city of his birth. In 1884, he married Lizzie Lee Funsten, a cousin of James B. Funsten, an Episcopal priest from Virginia who was eventually dispatched to serve as bishop of the church's Seventh Missionary District, based in Boise. Under the Funstens' influence, Hinks abandoned the law and entered the Virginia Theological Seminary, graduating in 1890. For twelve years he pastored churches in Upperville and Leesburg, Virginia, and in 1903 he accepted Bishop Funsten's invitation to join him at Boise's cathedral. A lanky priest with a zest for shooting quail and other wild game, Hinks was described by one correspondent as "a man's man, and one of the noblest and most devoted Christian characters." Unlike the four rectors of Brooklyn Heights, he had no patience with the liberal pieties of the Social Gospel; in Harry Orchard's terrible tale, he and Hillis read the same powerful lesson, the same strenuous call to action.

In early June 1906, it was Hinks's turn to preach at the penitentiary in a cycle of ministers from all denominations. When he was unable to go, his place was taken by an Episcopal clergyman from Pocatello, though Hinks's name remained on the blackboard as officiating. Mistaking the two priests, Orchard asked to see Hinks, and the real one, naturally curious about the celebrated prisoner, spent two hours with him. Orchard had been reading a Bible sent him by an Illinois physician, and he wanted to know whether it said anything that would preclude his hopes for everlasting life.

"I am not his father confessor in a religious sense," the dean told a reporter. He saw himself more as a counselor, guiding Orchard's reading of the Bible and recommending other religious reading. When McParland suggested that Orchard put his confession into narrative form—to straighten out its elusive details and gnarled chronology—Dean Hinks served as the first reader and editor of the "autobiography."

Hinks didn't regard Orchard as inherently criminal; sounding a bit like Clarence Darrow, he held that the accused was "a creature of conditions," his crimes "the result of his environment." He was "like one of Quantrill's guerillas, or one of Mosby's men. He was enlisted in war, as he believed, and his share of the fighting was not in the front rank facing the enemy, but skulking at night, killing the pickets on the outposts and getting inside the enemy's lines to do all the injury he could. Human life meant no more to him than it did to one of Mosby's followers." *

But that was over now. "In all my life, I have not seen such a complete and radical change in a human being within the period of a year," Hinks said. "I believe Orchard is genuinely repentant. When I first saw him he was afraid to read the Bible, afraid to talk, afraid of everything. Now he is composed and apparently willing to make such amends as he can for a life of crime and sin."

Hinks properly disclaimed any credit for reawakening Orchard's Christian faith. James McParland probably deserves the credit for that, through his shrewd use of biblical lessons and the forms of the confessional to extract his prisoner's admission of guilt. Before long, Orchard seems to have treated him as a father confessor. On July 22, 1906, for example, he wrote the detective, "I shall always feel and do believe that God sent you as his messenger to warn me and cry unto him for mercy before I had made the last desperate plunge into the great beyond where all hope of the future life is past."

Belle Steunenberg may also have played a role here through her Christian charity and public forgiveness of her husband's assassin. In several early interviews, she made clear that she had no bitterness in her heart for Orchard. "Poor fellow," she said on one occasion. "No one can tell what influences may have been brought to bear on him." On another occasion she sent him an Adventist tract called *Steps to Christ* and some religious periodicals. But the persistent legend that she visited him in prison and pleaded with him to become a Christian is evidently not true.

At least two other Boise clergymen enthusiastically endorsed Orchard's Christian rebirth, but not everyone was dazzled by the splendor of his transformation.

Years before, the Unitarian Church had put out a feeler in Boise, but the frail New England transplant never sank deep roots in Idaho and before long the outpost was abandoned. In the autumn of 1906, the Reverend Samuel A. Eliot, son of Harvard's president and himself president of the Boston-based American Unitarian Association, decided the time had come to revive the church in Boise. He induced the Reverend John C. Mitchell, then heading a prestigious parish in Lebanon, New Hampshire, to assume the mission. A fifty-three-year-old graduate of the Yale Divinity School, Mitchell arrived in Boise in October 1906, and by the following May the parent association was so pleased with his work that it appropriated funds to construct a church building in the city.

For the time being, though, Mitchell's flock was only the Boise Unitarian Club, holding evening services in a rented hall. One Sunday night, the minister rose in his improvised pulpit and bluntly assailed the prevailing clerical

---

* John Singleton Mosby and William Charles Quantrill were Confederate cavalry officers in the Civil War, commanding irregular "rangers," or "raiders," who killed and plundered behind Union lines. Regarded as heroes in the South, these troops were declared outlaws by the Union and, if caught, were generally hung without trial.

view of Boise's most celebrated criminal: "A deep-dyed, cold-blooded murderer is reported all of a sudden to have been miraculously converted. I
am informed three clergymen of our city have publicly made the startling
announcement that this murderous villain is saved, has been born again, that
he is all ready for the golden harp of glory and a crown of Paradise." To
pronounce such doctrine, Mitchell said, was "a miserable travesty of morality
and of Christian religion." Worse still, the murderer proposed to publish in
book form "the bloody horrors conceived in his own heart and executed by
his own hand. He hopes thus to immortalize his name. Such a book ought
never to see the light. It ought to be suppressed by law. It could but corrupt
and debase morals."

Though it flew in the face of the public religiosity employed by Gooding
and McParland to rehabilitate the assassin, Mitchell's sermon found an echo
in some quarters. More than a few Idahoans were skeptical of a man who
transited so quickly—as the *Socialist* said—from arch criminal to arch Christian. "New road to heaven," wrote Hermon Titus. "Commit twenty-six murders. Confess, charge them to some innocent men. Read ecclesiastial history.
Be canonized, pardoned, become a famous preacher of salvation and a hero to
sentimental women of both sexes."* Among the skeptics was William Borah,
who never relented in his hostility to the man who had slaughtered his friend.
Another was the dead man's brother John, who wrote Hawley, "I don't have
much use for a man that never thinks of doing the right thing till he is
caught."

On the afternoon of February 26, 1907—following his meetings with
Orchard and Hinks—Dwight Hillis met with the governor in his statehouse
office. Evidently Gooding asked the clergyman to perform some services for
him back East, for the next morning Gooding wrote Hillis in Brooklyn
enclosing a copy of a letter and some other documents bearing on Steunenberg's murder and "the persons accused of the assassination."

"I am sending these for the express purpose of having you show them to
Dr. Lyman Abbott in the strictest confidence, it being understood that he is
not to quote from these documents or make their contents public," the
governor wrote Hillis. The documents apparently included a rough draft of
Harry Orchard's confession, which hadn't yet been made public, but was the
core of the government's case and the material most likely to have an impact
in the East. "From the many resolutions and letters I have received since this
dreadful tragedy's occurrence," the governor wrote, "I am satisfied there are a
great many good people who have been and are being misled as to the true
conditions existing in Idaho. No greater service could be done the American
people than to make it plain"—and here he sang his old refrain—"that this is
only a murder trial."

---

* The figure of twenty-six was sometimes used as the number of murders to which Orchard
confessed, but eighteen is the figure the prosecutors generally used.

He repeated the assurance he'd given the president, which, though narrowly accurate, was misleading as to the trial's financing—"I have refused the assistance of the mine owners of Idaho and the State alone stands behind this prosecution"—and he closed by hoping that the information Hillis had received in Idaho, plus the documents now forwarded, would enlist Abbott's help "in placing our troubles honestly and fairly before the people of the East."

When he reached New York, Hillis did show these materials to Abbott, who, in turn, may have passed them on to his friend in the White House. But Hillis didn't stop there. In the months to come, he functioned as an intermediary between Idaho's authorities and eastern figures who might prove helpful to the prosecution. He was especially active in efforts to influence the eastern press, performing much the role that Gooding had once asked of the president himself: inducing eastern newspapers and wire services to send their best men to cover the trial.

He carried his message into his distinguished pulpit, where one Sunday he proclaimed: "It has become almost certain that [Orchard] has told the truth, the whole truth." Likening the assassin's conversion to the metamorphosis that Saul went through on the road to Damascus, Hillis said "the whole tranformation which [Orchard] has undergone carries in it no surprise" to "the student of the moral wonders and of the spiritual marvels of the human race." He had simply moved from one organization, a labor union, which sought to "bull its way in this world by force and slaughter," into another organization, the church, which commanded "by faith and truth and prayer and mutual help [and] assurance of eternal blessedness in the world beyond."

But Hillis's "facts" were so selective and the gloss he put on them so heavily weighted toward the prosecution that his counsel often lacked credibility. Thoroughly in tune with his wealthiest parishioners, he could no longer summon much empathy for the workingman. By no means a consistent conservative, he vigorously resisted calls for shutting off the flow of European immigrants, cautioning: "The best folk of other lands are coming to us." But Hillis had become increasingly anxious about social unrest. "Of late, public life has been full of harshness," he wrote in May 1906. "What bitterness one hears occasionally in public meetings! All rich men are represented as monsters. 'Save your money, boys, and buy a gun,' was the last word of advice one poor man had to give a crowd of listening laborers. Our leading Socialist in the realm of fiction is now pointing all the poor workingmen to the avenues and palaces, while he urges them to carry their hammers home at night that they may be ready for the signal to march up Fifth Avenue."

This defense of the comfortable against the urban poor and disaffected was a reflex that had a precedent a half century before. When Beecher first came to Plymouth Church in the 1840s, he was a fiery advocate of the antislavery position and its accompanying reforms. But as time went by he increasingly identified with the business and professional men in his

congregation who lived on the tree-shaded streets of Brooklyn Heights, behind the bluestone-paved walks and decorative iron fences, ensconced in fine
old brick and brownstone houses decorated with hand-rubbed antiques, fine
works of art, and other accoutrements of the good life. These prosperous
merchants had taken care of Beecher, building a more commodious establishment after his church burned in 1849 and lavishing money and comforts on
him. "Henry's people are more than ever in love with him," wrote his sister
Harriet, the author of *Uncle Tom's Cabin,* in 1855, "and have raised his salary to
$3,300, and given him a beautiful horse and carriage worth $600."

Not surprisingly, Beecher reciprocated. "Natural aristocracy," he wrote,
"is the eminence of men over their fellows, in mind and soul." Such natural
aristocrats could spend their money as they pleased. "The question is not
what proportion of his wealth a Christian man may divert from benevolent
channels for personal enjoyment through the elements of the beautiful. For, if
rightly viewed and rightly used, his very elegancies and luxuries will be a
contribution to the public good." Beecher's position, one historian has
pointed out, "made luxury and extravagance not only respectable but pious."

Lyman Abbott, who succeeded Beecher, was a Social Gospel man in
good standing. Recognizing that the workingman had genuine grievances, he
promoted a partnership of labor and capital in a system he called "industrial
democracy," exemplified by profit sharing and cooperatives. The use of the
Pinkertons to break the Homestead strike struck him as immoral. "We cannot
suppress this growing discontent," he declared, "we must remove its cause."
But his close friendship with President Roosevelt brought him into full accord with the president's politics. Increasingly he joined in the president's
fierce animus toward Haywood and the WFM.

Hillis took these tendencies still further, becoming virtually a member
of the prosecution team. After a small part of his role surfaced later, Ida
Crouch-Hazlett wrote of him: "This 'divine' had proved the biggest toady and
lick-spittle that a capitalist could employ to give its filthy deeds prestige. He
gave it as his sacred opinion that these men were guilty and hoped they would
hang. Thus do the priests of the world bolster the immoralities of the ruling
class."

It was precisely this alliance between the church and the powers that be
that the Episcopal clerics in Mary Dreier's committee had disavowed. In
stately Brooklyn Heights, all through 1906–07, these two clerical camps did
battle for the allegiance of the social and cultural elite.

But these eastern engagements were only skirmishes. The real battle
back in Idaho was rapidly approaching and James McParland grew ever more
apprehensive about his case. It had been a bad winter for the Great Detective.
After months of preliminary sparring, Steve Adams was to go on trial February 11 in the northern Idaho city of Wallace on charges of murdering the
alleged claim jumper Fred Tyler in 1904. This was the charge on which

McParland had succeeded in holding Adams the previous September after he'd repudiated his confession. In the months since, Adams had remained "wholly in the power of his lawyer, wife and uncle," McParland concluded. But now the prosecution hoped it could use a conviction in the Tyler trial as a bargaining counter to persuade Adams to reaffirm his confession corroborating Harry Orchard's testimony. Months before, McParland had recounted a conversation with Governor Gooding on how to bring Adams around in which the governor had said: "If Adams were convicted and brought to the penitentiary to be executed no doubt he would make a full break as to what had induced him to act as he has done recently."

At 4:00 p.m. on February 9, McParland; his bodyguard, Charlie Siringo; his new stenographer, Robert P. Shollenberger; and Warden Whitney of the state penitentiary boarded a Union Pacific train on the circuitous route to northern Idaho through Oregon and Washington, which usually took twenty hours or so. Arriving in Pendleton, Oregon, at five on Sunday morning, they discovered that heavy snows, landslides, and washouts had blocked the major routes north. Hoping to reach Spokane via Portland, they entrained on the Northern Pacific only to find that route blocked by a freight wreck. With four hundred other delayed passengers, they boarded a cargo ship on the Columbia River, which reached Portland at 10:30 p.m., and the next morning caught a train for Seattle, where they were delayed another day. Weary, hungry, and anxious, they pulled into Wallace at 2:30 p.m. on February 14—three days after jury selection had gotten under way.

McParland's frustrations had only begun. Chris Thiele had booked rooms for him and Shollenberger at the Wallace Hotel, but the detective, accustomed to certain minimal creature comforts, was outraged at his accommodations. With "lots of snow and ice in and around Wallace," he wrote the Pinkerton general manager, George Bangs, "the room I am occupying is 8 x 8 without any stove or heat." And that wasn't all: "For a place like Wallace, the county seat with some of the greatest mines on earth surrounding the town, it is a wonder to me that somebody does not build a hotel and start a dining room wherein a man could get a decent meal. There is one restaurant in town and that is run just as the restaurant keeper pleases, and you must take whatever you get."

Soon other matters reinforced his black mood. When he arrived in the courtroom on February 15, he was aghast at what had transpired there without him: "As there is no industry in this country except mining, not even farming to any extent, the jury is composed, as it were, of miners and people that are depending on the miners for patronage." Some of the potential jurors summoned on the original panel were partisans of the WFM, mining men from the village of Mullan chosen by a county commissioner named Gearin. With the prosecution exhausting their five peremptory challenges on these people, the result, he reported, was "nine good jurors, two very doubtful, and one we are sure will never fetch in a verdict of guilty as he is a brother-in-law of the notorious Paul Corcoran who led the attack on the Bunker Hill & Sullivan mine and mill in '99."

As presented by Jim Hawley and the Shoshone County special prosecutor, Henry P. Knight, the state's case against Adams for Tyler's murder rested, in considerable part, on a confession he'd allegedly made to the Pinkertons' Chris Thiele in the back room of the warden's office of the state penitentiary in mid-April 1906. According to Thiele's testimony, Adams told him that he and Jack Simpkins had gone up to the heavily timbered Marble Creek district of northern Idaho. Simpkins had left, but Adams had fallen in with two other settlers in the region, Newt "Wall-Eye" Glover and Alva Mason, who were agitated about newcomers to the district who they figured were actually "cruisers" (timber locators) for the big lumber companies or, worse yet, claim jumpers seeking to deprive the old-time settlers of their land.

One of these interlopers was Fred Tyler, a thirty-four-year-old Michigander, who'd come to northern Idaho in the late winter or early spring of 1904, settled first in the city of Coeur d'Alene, but toward the end of May gone into the Marble Creek country to locate a homestead. He found some property he liked and built himself a cabin.

According to Chris Thiele, Adams told him that, on or about August 10, he, Glover, and Mason had resolved to kill Tyler, a crime that would not arouse much stir in those parts, where claim jumpers were regarded as human jackals; as far as anyone could remember, there had never been a successful prosecution for killing one. Failing to find Tyler at his cabin, they laid in wait for him on the trail. After sundown, as Tyler came whistling through the woods carrying a gunny sack full of trout he'd caught in the creek, Adams stepped from behind a tree and held a Winchester rifle on the suprised young man. After questioning him without avail as to who had sent him into the north woods, Adams shot him. Later, he also killed another alleged claim jumper, Ed Boule—although Adams was not currently charged with that killing. In sum, said Thiele, this had been Adams's confession to him.

Nearly a year after the events recounted—on July 23, 1905—a corpse was found in the woods, badly decomposed, gnawed by scavenging beasts, but ultimately identified as that of the missing Tyler. The prosecution brought in several members of the party that found the body to testify about a horseradish bottle, a black hat, and brown handmade shoes found nearby.

On Adams's behalf, Darrow and Richardson put on a vigorous defense, exploiting every ambiguity and contradiction in the prosecution's evidence. But the heart of the defense case was Adams's own appearance on the stand, during which he admitted talking with Chris Thiele the previous April but vehemently denied confessing to the murders of Tyler and Boulé.

For James McParland, however, the most memorable—and painful—part of the trial was his own appearance on the witness stand and particularly the combative cross-examination by Edmund Richardson. At one point, Richardson attempted to ask the detective about his strange activities in Parsons, Kansas, in 1886, which had recently prompted some prominent citizens of that community to label him "low and vile...a conscienceless and desperate criminal." Judge William W. Woods had deemed the questions irrelevent to the current case, but as McParland was leaving the witness stand, Richardson said ominously: "I have the affidavits relative to the Parsons affair."

Whirling in his tracks, McParland challenged the lawyer to produce the men who'd made the affidavits.

A bit sheepishly, Richardson said he didn't want any altercation with the detective.

"I didn't think so," crowed McParland.

"I am not afraid of you," Richardson shot back.

"Well," the detective replied, "that is the way I feel in regard to you."

This mutual bravado reflected the testiness between the two men, but what particularly enraged McParland was a report in the Spokane *Spokesman-Review* and then, through the Associated Press, in papers across the country that after this exchange, spectators had cheered Richardson and hissed the Great Detective. For days, McParland fulminated over the report, charging that the reporter had been "paid" to manufacture this lie. "While I am well aware that the defense would resort to nearly all matter of dirt," he wrote, "I did not hardly expect they would resort to a low trick as this." The detective insisted to his superiors that he was "not at all disconcerted about this matter, but merely wish to draw your attention to what we may expect during the trials of Moyer, Haywood and Pettibone."

Through much of the Adams trial, the bleached skull of the corpse identified as Tyler's had rested on the prosecutor's table, a reminder of "the terrible deed" committed up on Marble Creek. But neither the skull nor the supporting testimony did much to alter the jury problem that McParland had recognized from the beginning. The jurors began their deliberations at 10:45 on the morning of March 6. Some "loud talking" could be heard from the jury room, but no verdict emerged that day or the next. At seven the following evening, the foreman informed Judge Woods that the jury was hopelessly deadlocked, and the judge promptly discharged it. In conversation with one juror sympathetic to the prosecution, McParland learned that the jury had stood five for conviction and seven for acquittal. At the last moment, one juror switched his vote, creating the apparently irreconcilable deadlock.

It was a terrible blow to the prosecution. McParland had felt all along that, with the shadow of the noose hanging over him, Adams would see that he had aligned himself with the wrong side. Now the detective did his best to be optimistic. "Mr. Hawley in his closing argument for the state, I think, has left the bars down for Adams to return to the fold if he has any thinking power," he wrote Gooding. Adams having on cross-examination "admitted every word to be true in his written confession except the fact that when he said he murdered Tyler and Boulé he lied, if he should come back to the state he has not in reality injured himself as a witness in the Moyer, Haywood and Pettibone cases."

On the evening of the verdict, McParland reported: "Adams has felt very blue all day, but there is no doubt he will pick up courage now as the jury has hung. He has claimed right along to Deputy Sheriff Hicks that it is much better to hang the jury than to hang the prisoner."

The next day, McParland, his three Pinkerton aides—Siringo, Thiele, and Shollenberger—and Warden Whitney boarded a train for Spokane. Thiele told his boss that on the same train was Harvey K. Brown, the former sheriff of Baker City, Oregon, who'd been in Wallace during the trial with "old man Lillard," Steve Adams's uncle. McParland perked up, asking Thiele to introduce him to Brown. The two lawmen had a chat, and since they both had to lay over in Spokane, McParland asked Brown to dine with him that night. They went to Davenport's, Spokane's best steak house, where they had "a very nice dinner," then adjourned to McParland's room and talked for a couple of hours.

"In all my experience in [the] detective business," McParland told Brown, "I never regretted anything more than I regretted to have to take the witness stand and assist in prosecuting Steve Adams, notwithstanding the fact that Steve Adams is a notorious criminal." For, McParland said, "I did not consider Steve a criminal at heart; he was easily led and a few designing men had led him to do those things."

Having polished up Adams a bit, the detective went on to blacken the names of Darrow and Richardson, telling Brown that he "had never seen men who had called themselves reputable lawyers take a man who was a state witness and on a pretext of being his best friend get him to go back on the state and then, while ostensibly appearing to defend him, place him in a position where he would be convicted of a capital offense: that it was the most cold-blooded, high-handed injustice [he] had ever seen."

Moreover, Brown should warn Lillard that in the fall, unless Adams helped the prosecution in the Haywood case, the prosecution was sure to get a change of venue, removing Adams's case from the mining territory and putting it before "a jury of American farmers, men that are true, loyal citizens . . . and such a jury would convict Steve in about two minutes."

Before the evening was over, McParland enlisted Brown in a plan to persuade Lillard to reverse field once again, convincing his nephew that his best interests now lay in "returning to the fold" of the state and reaffirming his confession, which would seal Bill Haywood's fate. Brown had earlier confided that since leaving office as sheriff the year before he'd been doing "a little detective work" himself, charging five dollars a day. McParland said the state would be happy to pay his fee if he'd take care of this little matter for them. Brown seemed pleased by the Great Detective's attentions and said he'd see what he could do.

For more than a month, as the Haywood trial drew ever nearer, McParland waited impatiently for Brown's report. Finally, on April 17 came the answer he'd dreaded: The old man says he would rather see Steve hung than return to the McParland gang."

The very next day, the chief of the "McParland gang" launched the second stage of his Adams operation in a five-page single-spaced "Friend Tom" letter to Tom McCabe, first deputy sheriff of Shoshone County under Sheriff William J. Bailey. Over some good whiskey in Wallace, McParland had come to know McCabe, finding him "a very smart man" and "a warm friend of the Agency," who "seems to take a personal interest in me." Now the Great Detective proposed an ingenious scheme.

McParland began by noting that the only official in Wallace whom Adams seemed to trust was another deputy sheriff, Carson C. Hicks. On a number of occasions, as Hicks, an acting jailer, escorted him from his cell to the courtroom and back, Adams had confided in him his worst fears and dearest hopes. One link between the two men was that both hailed from Missouri. Missourians weren't popular among northern Idaho miners, because their state was the principal source of scabs employed by the mine owners to break strikes in the Coeur d'Alenes. Regarded as pariahs by many other Idahoans—who called them Missukes, not a nice word—Missourians tended to stick together up there. As an alleged hit man for the Western Federation of Miners, Adams was an unlikely scab. Hicks, a former miner who came from Joplin, Missouri—the center of scab territory—had worked as a miner in Colorado and run a saloon in Kansas, where he was convicted of assault to kill and spent four years in prison. When he came to Idaho after the troubles of 1899 it may have been as a strikebreaking mercenary at the Sixteen to One mine. In any case, he and Adams seemed to get along.

McParland knew that Darrow had assigned another member of the defense team, the Wallace attorney John H. Wourms, to stick close to Adams and shield him from prosecution advances. Hicks would have to make his overture indirectly through Mrs. Adams, known to be the greatest single influence on her husband and also seemingly friendly with Hicks.

"Therefore," McParland wrote Tom McCabe, "I would suggest that Mr. Hicks throw himself in the way of Mrs. Adams." He should then tell her: "I have done all I could for Steve. It is not because I think he is innocent.... However, seeing how the counsel for Moyer, Haywood and Pettibone have duped Steve's uncle into offering Steve up as a sacrifice in order to free the men that led him to commit crime and then allowing him to be convicted, which he surely will be, I don't like to see a man born and raised in the same state as myself...offer up his life for the very men that are the cause of his separation from his wife and family."

Hicks should make sure Mrs. Adams didn't misunderstand him. He should say: "I am not a detective nor is it anything in my pocket, nor will I receive any financial benefit no matter what may become of these people or your husband. Now I would not go to your rooms to talk with you, but if you walk down to my house where Mrs. Hicks will be present, I will follow you down there in a short time and have a long confidential talk with you." As for the presence of Mrs. Hicks, McParland thought "it would do Mrs. Adams good to have a talk with a decent, respectable woman, something she had not had a chance to do for a long time." For months, while Adams had been held in the penitentiary, his wife had been lodged in the women's wing, conversing with prostitutes and shoplifters.

If Hicks got her down to his house, he should come on more strongly, telling her, "Mrs. Adams, it is your duty as a wife and mother to put Steve on his guard as to what the outcome of his case will be," and then flat out, "The State is the only one that can befriend Steve now, neither his uncle nor his array of counsel can do it."

Toward the end, McParland backed off a bit, assuring his friend Tom he was offering "simply an outline of suggestions." On its receipt, he hoped that Sheriff Bailey, Hicks, Angus Sutherland (now serving as a deputy sheriff), and McCabe would give it serious consideration. "If you . . . can see some better way to accomplish the purpose we have in view," he proposed, "why go ahead and try it your way. If Mr. Hicks can succeed in getting Steve to recant what he has done, I think I can guarantee you will all be well paid for your trouble."

In a postscript, the Great Detective, attentive as always to the smallest details, suggested that Hicks "supply himself with a few cigars and give Adams a cigar once in a while." Adams was addicted to cigars and pipes— McParland had tried to soften him up some eight months before by sending him a $3.65 briar pipe and a sack of tobacco—and the Pinkertons guaranteed that Hicks would be reimbursed for his tobacco expenses.

As requested, McCabe, Sutherland, Bailey, and Hicks gathered shortly after McParland's letter arrived and discussed the detective's plan. They were "trying to get everything shaped up" when other events intervened.

The Wallace Hotel, the third-rate hostelry where McParland had spent some unhappy nights during the Adams trial, may not have had much of a restaurant, but its commodious saloon was a popular gathering spot for northern Idaho law-and-order men. Indeed, when he wasn't serving as deputy sheriff, Tom McCabe was the principal bartender there.

On April 24, William "Billie" Quinn, thirty-eight, the former Wallace police chief and now a mill man at the Hercules mine up the mountains in Burke, had just been released from the county pesthouse, a quarantine spot for those suffering from infectious diseases. Vastly popular in the area, Quinn was known as "a jolly, good-natured fellow." Certainly he was feeling jolly that day. To celebrate his release, he began drinking in the morning at Zeitfuch's saloon, moving on to Moore's saloon and, later, the bar of the Wallace Hotel.

About eleven that evening, after many drinks had been consumed by all parties, Quinn got into a heated argument with H. W. C. Jackson, a pugnacious little fellow with a bushy brown mustache, who edited the *Wallace Miner*. According to several eyewitnesses, the subject under discussion was President Roosevelt's statement that Bill Haywood and Charles Moyer were "undesirable citizens."

Ironically enough, Quinn—a former miner and still a member of the WFM—knew the president. Once a cowboy, he'd worked on Roosevelt's ranch in the Dakota badlands and several years before, when Roosevelt had visited Wallace, he'd asked after Quinn and shaken his hand. Quinn had voted for the president and said he would do so again.

All this notwithstanding, as a loyal union man, Quinn took high umbrage at Roosevelt's remarks about Haywood and Moyer. "Neither the President nor anyone has the right to convict a man who hasn't been proven guilty," he was said to have told Jackson. The president's letter, he added, "did not suit him."

"Well, it suits me," Jackson said.

"That's what I stand for," Quinn said stubbornly. As if to demonstrate his other allegiance, Quinn pulled a WFM union card out of his pocket and held it there, tapping it with his thumb, saying he was fully paid up to June 1 and was therefore "fighting" for Haywood, Moyer, and Pettibone with his money. Some witnesses said he scraped the card along Jackson's nose.

When Jackson dissented, Quinn said he'd just gotten out of the pesthouse—where evidently he'd suffered from a mild case of smallpox—and his back was covered with scabs, adding that Jackson was "a scab son of a bitch."

So vehemently did Jackson take exception that Norman MacAuley, the manager of the Wallace Hotel, ordered him to leave because they "wanted no trouble in the place."

Toward midnight, at Bank and Sixth Streets, Jackson encountered Carson Hicks, who was wearing a black overcoat with a slouch hat pulled down over his eyes. Hicks had departed his duties at the county jail on the first floor of the courthouse about nine-thirty, leaving Frank Rose in charge of the prisoners, and had spent two hours drinking in the Office saloon. (When Hicks was drinking, one policeman said later, he could be "quite radical," referring to his demeanor, not his politics.) After Jackson told the deputy about his fierce argument with Quinn, Hicks set off down the street, stopped briefly at the Comet Saloon, then entered the Wallace Hotel saloon through the side swinging doors. He spotted Quinn—who was six foot three—standing by a slot machine, with one long arm slung over it.

Here the testimony of the participants, and of eyewitnesses, sharply diverged. According to Hicks himself, he heard Quinn say—with a "sneer"— "Here's one of my Missouri friends."

According to Hicks, he replied noncommittally, "I don't know," at which Quinn flared up, calling him a nasty name and swearing, "I'll show you." As

Quinn swore at him, Hicks said, "his right arm shot off the machine and both of his hands went toward his pistol pocket." He looked "pretty fierce," the deputy would testify.

At that, Hicks pulled out a .33-caliber automatic revolver and fired a shot into Quinn's chest. Gravely wounded, Quinn slumped to the floor. His friends placed him on a pool table in the billiards room, where a doctor examined him and concluded he was a "goner." Then he was taken to the city hospital, where he died twenty-four hours later after giving the police a full statement.

William A. Judkins, the night clerk at the nearby Ryan Hotel, who'd stopped in for a drink at the Wallace that night, told a very different story of the shooting: "Unless my eyes deceived me, Hicks must have come into the saloon with the purpose of murder in his heart. The whole affair was so deliberate that I could hardly realize what had happened. After Hicks entered and Quinn made the remark that 'Here comes my friend from Missouri,' Hicks turned toward Quinn with the words, 'I'll fix you.' Then Quinn replied, 'You'll have to show me.' Next Hicks' gun cracked."

The state's witnesses at the later trial insisted that Hicks had drawn his gun from the pocket of a black overcoat, as though he had placed it there knowing full well he was going to use it. Hicks insisted he drew the gun from a special gun pocket he had in his trousers.

On his deathbed, Quinn said he'd never had any trouble with Hicks before: "I thought it was a joke when he pulled his gun. I always thought he was my friend." Quinn denied reaching for a gun, saying he didn't even have a weapon on him at the time; his gun, he said, was at home locked up in his trunk. The state's witnesses agreed unanimously that Quinn was unarmed, while Hicks said he'd heard that a pistol may have dropped out of Quinn's pocket after the shooting and been picked up by a bystander.

Everyone agreed on what happened then. George Young, Wallace's night officer, was standing at the bar munching on a tamale. Young pulled his gun and advanced on Hicks. But Hicks said, "Don't you butt in," and with his gun covering Young and the others at the bar, he backed out of the saloon. Out in the street, Francis Xavier Patrick Scully, a "floral designer," came running up to him and said, "Hicks, you shot a man. Give me your pistol." Hicks told him, "You little bastard, get away." But when Sheriff Bailey came ambling up, Hicks quietly surrendered. According to Bailey, Hicks said he'd killed Quinn because he was "cussing Roosevelt." Hicks later denied saying that.

The shooting was the year's biggest event in Wallace. The *Wallace Times* of April 26 said, "It has been long since the city of Wallace has been so stirred up over anything as the murder of Quinn. The news spread quickly after the shooting and from early morning little groups could be found gathered together all over the city, in saloons and restaurants and business houses discussing the latest phase of the affair.... Quinn was known all through the Coeur d'Alenes and the excitement was intense. Friends of the murdered man united in severe condemnation of what they termed 'such a cowardly act.'"

But Hicks's colleagues and friends stood by him—as did James McParland. On May 7, writing Henry P. Knight, the former prosecutor of Adams, who was now Hicks's lawyer, the detective said he had just "learned with much regret the trouble that our mutual friend, C. C. Hicks, has gotten into. ...I wish you to extend my sympathy to Mr. and Mrs. Hicks, and tell them if there is anything that either I or any of our employees can do for him, we will be more than willing to do it, and hope he will come out of this trouble all right." Indeed, the detective went out of his way to emphasize that the State of Idaho at the very highest levels continued to stand by the accused murderer. "I have taken the matter of Mr. Hicks' trouble up with Mr. Hawley and Governor Gooding, both of whom sympathize with Mr. and Mrs. Hicks, and both desire me to say that while they would do everything in their track, he can depend upon it, an extra effort will be made on the part of the state to see him through this trouble."

McParland then got more explicit, making it very plain that the unfortunate murder should not interrupt the assignment he had given Hicks.

"Of course," McParland conceded to Knight, "the trouble that Mr. Hicks has gotten into alters matters to a great extent as he would not be able to carry out the instructions so far as they relate to Mrs. Adams." Hicks's arrest, however, had one distinct advantage: it put the former jailer on the other side of the bars, in the very holding cell with his ex-prisoner, Steve Adams. Four other men were in adjacent cells. This, said McParland, "would not interfere with his carrying out the instructions given in that letter as to how to work on the feelings of Adams."

Becoming still more explicit in his letter to Knight, McParland held out the prospect of cash payments to Knight: "The State is more than willing to deal liberally not only with Mr. Hicks and the Sheriff's office but yourself, if you can be the means of getting Adams back in time to appear as a witness in the cases of Moyer, Haywood and Pettibone."

Hicks couldn't write directly to McParland for fear that some unauthorized person not in on the plan would intercept the letters. So he gave the gist of his message to his wife, who then wrote it up for her husband. On May 12, the Hickses communicated as follows: "Steve is on the fence and don't know which way to 'jump.'... Wourms is here pretty regular telling Steve not to talk to me." Later in the day, apparently after Hicks had talked with Knight, came another letter: "I am more than gratified to learn of the way things are shaping themselves in Boise in my behalf. I will say that Steve is square on the fence, if handled I believe he will come through, but I am afraid those lawyers will get to him and change him, that is to keep him where he is now. ...I have told him that his big lawyers will not be on hand to defend him after they are through with [Haywood, Moyer, and Pettibone] in Boise."

On May 14, McParland wrote back, noting what Hicks had to say about Adams being on the fence. "Well all that is wanted is to have him jump the right way.... Owing to the fact that the defendants' lawyers know Adams and you are confined not only in the same jail but in the same cell, I am somewhat surprised that a proposition from that side has not been made to you as they have approached nearly everybody else that they think could help them out."

In September, when Hicks stood trial for the Quinn killing, Henry Knight asked Thomas Corra, secretary of Burke's WFM local—to which Quinn had belonged—"Did you know that Mr. Quinn was a member of the Thiel Detective Agency?" Corra said he did not. The same question was asked of every prospective juror, all answering in the negative. The very fact that the question was asked so often suggests that the former chief of police, like other former police officers, may well have been secretly working for Thiel. Correspondingly, if Hicks wasn't a Pinkerton, he was surely working at McParland's direction.

This raises some intriguing possibilities. Was Billie Quinn a casualty of the Thiel-Pinkerton feud? Was he a victim of Theodore Roosevelt's penchant for invective? Or had Quinn's murder been a setup all along, designed to put Hicks in Steve Adams's cell, where he'd have maximum opportunity to bring his fellow prisoner back into the prosecution camp?

We shall probably never know for sure, but the conduct of the trial suggests an answer. Each day of the trial, Hicks entered the courtroom through the front door and down the center aisle, accompanied by his wife and his close friend Deputy Sheriff Frank Rose, now his jailer; he did not come through the prisoner's entrance behind the rail. When he told his own story of the shooting, it was "with never an indication of remorse, but just as if he were relating the details of an incident in which he was not particularly interested." As other witnesses testified, he sat in court idly paring his nails and cutting his tobacco with a penknife, seemingly unconcerned with the result. He was quite right not to worry. Although the county prosecutor, Walter Hanson, said he'd never seen a murder case in which the testimony was so "overwhelming," the jury seemed underwhelmed. It required two ballots. The first was eleven for acquittal and one blank. The second was unanimous for acquittal, on the grounds that Hicks had acted in self-defense. By the big clock on the courthouse wall, the jury's deliberations took exactly two minutes.

11

ONLY A MURDER TRIAL

THE MOST CELEBRATED BOOK of 1907 was *The American Scene*, the fruit of Henry James's year-long sojourn in his native land after an absence of twenty-two years. Twined in a dense thicket of Jamesian prose was a cranky if original view of America at century's turn. Mildly apprehensive as he toured the Hudson River Valley in Edith Wharton's new motorcar, offended at the "invalidities, hideous and unashamed," disfiguring the American landscape, the expatriate had come in search of the essential "spirit" of this crude, pushy land that once he had called his own. It was Theodore Roosevelt's land now, and James couldn't abide the president ("the mere monstrous embodiment of unprecedented and resounding noise") any more than Roosevelt could stand him ("What a miserable little snob Henry James is!"). But he was an inquisitive little snob, poking into all the quirky corners of American life, and soon he found its "supreme social expression" in "the Pullmans that are like rushing hotels and the hotels that are like stationary Pullmans." Of the two, he wondered "if the hotel-spirit may not just be the American spirit most seeking and most finding itself."

What James had shrewdly discerned was the new willingness, even eagerness, of comfortable Americans to live their lives in public. The urban poor had always lived in public, crowded stoops and swarming streets seeming the natural habitat of "the inconceivable alien" he'd glimpsed downtown on Rutgers Square. But his own class, and those of whom he wrote, had perfected "the private life"—the title of one of his short stories—often sequestered behind high walls and iron gates.

Some dated the sea change to an evening in the late 1890s when a former champagne agent named Henry Lehr induced Mrs. William Astor, the diamond-tiaraed queen of New York society, to attend a dinner at Sherry's restaurant. The next morning, a society reporter exclaimed, "I never dreamt it would be given me to gaze on the face of an Astor in a public dining room." Henceforth, it was permissible for even the most exquisite members of the Four Hundred to dine out, and increasingly those outings took place in hotel ballrooms or hotel restaurants.

The notion of a gentleman's confronting his fellow man in public may have originated on the Pullman, and particularly in the smoking car, where, "under more democratic traditions than are to be found in any other spot on the continent," travelers of all social conditions shared confidences through a tobacco haze. One commentator wondered how much of this fellowship stemmed "from the fact that the men have never seen one another before, and will never see one another again, and just how much arises from the subtle influence of tobacco as a social solvent." George Pullman thought the lavish accoutrements of his smoker cars tended to civilize even louts and ruffians. "Take the roughest man," he wrote, "and bring him into a room elegantly carpeted and furnished, and the effect on his bearing is pronounced and immediate." It was said that James Bryce, the British author of *The American Commonwealth*, came to know the New World by talking with men in smoker cars. In that intimacy, travelers shared confidences with those they'd never invite to their own dinner tables.

"Living in public, eating in public, and all but sleeping in public" was the essence of the hotel experience, reaching fruition in the Gilded Age. Through the eighteenth century and into the nineteenth, American wayfarers found food and shelter at modest inns—especially indifferent in the West, where so-called road ranches sprang up along stage routes. Touring Texas in the 1850s, the landscape architect Frederick Law Olmsted found these "ranches" to be nothing more than foul-smelling cabins, where breakfast was "a succession of burnt flesh of swine and bulls, decaying vegetables and sour and moldy farinaceous glues," whiskey a concoction called "tangleleg" made of tobacco, molasses, red peppers, and alcohol, potent enough to "make a hummingbird spit in a rattlesnake's eye."

The first stab at something more refined came in 1829 with the opening of Boston's Tremont House, which offered hitherto unimaginable comforts: free soap and a pitcher in all 170 rooms; in the basement, eight baths with cold running water. But it was the midcentury spraddle of railroads across the land that prompted a mushroom of hotel development. Often hotels erupted at the end of the tracks as an accommodation to construction gangs, then moved on when that section was complete: one moved so often it was dubbed the Wandering Hotel. As time went by, these structures got vaster and grimmer, aping the coal-blackened "warehouse" style of British railway hotels.

With the century drawing to a close, a new taste for luxury ushered in the grand hotel. In 1888, Chicago cheered Louis Sullivan's Auditorium Building, embracing a four-hundred-room hotel, an auditorium seating four thousand, even an opera house. In the mid-1890s came New York's thousand-room Waldorf-Astoria, that "great glittering, costly caravansary," replete with galleries, ballroom, theater, and Palm Room restaurant, which had prompted Henry James's ruminations on the "hotel-spirit." The New York hotels of this era positively wallowed in voluptuous swank: "Pompeian conceits in color and subject, tapestries superb enough for an oriental queen, and a glitter of gold and silver." In 1875, the *Building News* concluded: "Railway terminals and hotels are to the nineteenth century what monasteries and cathedrals were to the thirteenth."

The thirst for extravagance swept some patrons beyond all limits of good taste. When the Bradley Martins spent $369,000 on a grand ball at the Waldorf in 1897, the stark contrast with the misery of other Americans, still recovering from the nation's worst depression, was too blatant; protests drove the Martins into permanent exile in England. But the quest for luxury persisted. In 1907 came eighteen stories of sumptuous display called the Plaza, where the only limit placed on decoration was "the human limit on the ability of the designers to suggest anything more beautiful and rich." The Plaza was a "composite residence," housing short-term visitors as well as those who chose to live there full-time. Some sneered at the notion: "Gentlemen will never consent to live on mere shelves under a common roof." But among the luminaries settling at the Plaza were Alfred G. Vanderbilt and the financier John W. Gates, who leased a thirteen-room suite for $42,000 a year.

Though such extravagance satisfied democratic America's repressed craving for palaces, critics found the new hotels vulgar. When Rudyard Kipling visited Chicago's Palmer House, he found it a "gilded and mirrored rabbit warren . . . crammed with people talking about money and spitting about everywhere." To Henry Adams, Lizzie Cameron wondered at the summer version on beaches from Bar Harbor to Cape May: "Why do we like feeding in long trough-like rooms, black with flies and negro waiters? And sitting infinite hours, in infinite dozens of rocking chairs rocking infinite miles, on a piazza half a mile long? And the coarseness, the loudness, the cheapness. . . . It is appalling." Charles Dickens didn't care for American hotels "in which we can get anything we want, after its kind, for money; but where nobody is glad to see us, or sorry to see us, or minds (our bill paid) whether we come or go."

In *The Common Lot,* the novelist Robert Herrick made the "Glenmore Family Hotel" stand for all that was tawdry and meretricious in American life. It was "one of those shoddy places, where flock young married people with the intention of avoiding the care of children and the trials of housekeeping in modest homes; where there is music twice a week and dancing on Saturdays." When it catches fire, it crumbles like "rotten cheese," killing ten. Its architect, who'd just wanted to "make some money," is haunted by the "horrid" wails of the dying.

Noting that suicide was rampant in cities with many long-term hotel guests, another critic suggested that self-destruction was "sometimes the tragic climax of the demoralizing lonesomeness" associated with hotel life. Others feared its subversive effect on American womanhood: "A place with so many beds could not be pure." But if sex and drink were associated with the hotel, it was less a sink of corruption than a stage on which guests indulged their penchant for make-believe, whether strutting their stuff on the polished dance floor or reclining in Lucullan luxe on the veranda.

The core clientele of the new hotels were traveling salesmen, first known as "bagmen" after the carpetbags in which they carried their samples, later as "drummers," after the business they "drummed up" for their firms. In gay waistcoat, splashy necktie, and gold watch chain, the drummer was instantly recognizable. "Who puts oup at der behsht hotel," asked a newspaper poet of the 1870s, "Und dakes his oysters on der shell / Und mit der frauleins cuts a schwell? / Der Drummer." As he donned the more dignified title of "commercial traveler" around the turn of the century, he still struck a dapper figure, slaking his thirst of an evening at the bar off the lobby.

By the turn of the century, hotels were linked with the shadier sort of political deals. In Washington, the "smoke-filled rooms" were at Willard's and the Ebbitt House; in New York, at the Fifth Avenue Hotel. Swarming in the corridors, reporters chased the latest rumor. To one newsman, on a winter's day in 1885, Albany's political hotel, the Delavan, "buzzed like a fly trap in a butcher's shop in midsummer." To some, the hotel, in its gratuitous heterogeneity, threatened public order. Alarmists saw it as a playground for "the cleverest criminals, the gentlemanly and ladylike rascals attracted to New York from the great capitals of Europe, saying nothing of our own gifted swindlers." Flimflam artists, jewel thieves, gigolos, second-story men, forgers, rogues, and blackguards were said to lurk in its gorgeous galleries. The answer in this detective-crazed land was the omniscient house detective.

Its perils notwithstanding, by 1900 the grand hotel was an indispensable ingredient of America's urban scene. In Baltimore, it was the Belvedere; in Seattle, the Savoy; in Cleveland, the Euclid; in St. Paul, the Ryan—and so forth across the land. Hotels filled American needs, and not just for display and dissipation. This was particularly so in smallish western communities, where life's amenities weren't so thick on the ground as they were back East. Here a hotel wasn't just a place with a lot of beds but one of the few spots in town where one could get a decent meal, where the Elks or Ladies Reading Circle could gather, where one could get a shave and a haircut, buy a new shirt, send a telegram, shoot billiards, obtain theater tickets, or—if one was a drummer, a reporter, a jewel thief, a detective, or a prostitute—lounge about the lobby smoking, watching and waiting for professional opportunity to strike.

"Livestock, Political and Social Center," the Idanha called itself. "Not only a hotel, but a home." Both claims were amply justified. For in 1907, Boise's grand hotel was a sheep-and-cattle mart, town square, public forum, fraternity, political club, secular cathedral—and, abruptly, in early May, the pulsating heart of the Haywood trial.

Its architect, a Boise Scotsman named Walter Stewart Campbell, had approached this prized commission with earnest deliberation, visiting most modern hotels between Boise and New York. He might have ended his tour at Caldwell, for ultimately he settled on the French château style of the

Saratoga Hotel, which resembled structures—notably Quebec's Château Frontenac—erected across the continent by the Canadian Pacific Railway. The Idanha's red-brick and sandstone bulk towered over the buildings around it; at six stories, it was Boise's first "skyscraper." All but three of its 140 rooms —even bathrooms—had outside views. Emphasizing its civic function was a steel canopy over the main entrance from which politicians could address their constituents in the street below. Its crenelated roofline dominated by four shapely turrets surmounted by flagpoles, weather vanes, and other spiky ornamentation, its facade enlivened by striped green-and-white awnings fluttering at every window, the Idanha from afar had the look of a fairyland castle.

The "acme of perfection," the *Statesman* had called it when the hotel opened, with calculated symbolism, on the first day of the twentieth century. Some $125,000 had been spent to equip the Idanha with all the latest contrivances. An elementary intercom system called the "enunciator" connected all rooms with the bell captain in the lobby so a guest could order eggs Rockefeller or Welsh rarebit delivered in a silver chafing dish by one of the hotel's seventy employees (many of whom lived on the hotel's top floor). Private telephones were available at a daily fee. One turned on the room lights by pushing pearl buttons that shone in the dark. Guests were whisked to and from their floors by the hotel's most spectacular contraption, an electric elevator, the first of its kind in the Northwest, built by the Otis Elevator Company and powered by a fifteen-horsepower motor, covered in glass so a delighted public could watch it run. In one corner off the lobby gleamed the tiled walls of the Idanha Pharmacy, which offered a state-of-the-art soda fountain and an ample cigar counter. In the basement, Schmelzel and Gallap plied their barbering trade. To the right of the main entrance, marble steps led to the Idanha barroom, with its ornately carved mahogany bar and profusion of brass, also entered through a doorway from the lobby. All this was available on the European plan for one to three dollars a night.

All sorts of people stopped at the Idanha: politicians of every stripe (though its owners were staunchly Republican, the Democratic State Committee met there), stars and featured players in theatrical companies (ordinary actors stayed at the seedy Mitchell Hotel by the depot, which advertised "Special Attention to Theatrical Folk"), itinerant ballplayers and their hangers-on, lovers consummating their desire, licit and illicit.

One weekend that spring of 1907, Mrs. Ralph M. Hedges, the wife of a prominent Caldwell civil engineer, came to Boise with a lady friend on the morning train. On the same train was A. S. Whiteway, a Boise contractor then completing the Canyon County courthouse. Checking into the Idanha, Mrs. Hedges may or may not have been joined by Mr. Whiteway for an hour of mutual delectation. That evening her husband arrived and the Hedges, the lady friend, and Mr. Whiteway dined together. The next day, after attending a ballgame, Whiteway and his wife were strolling along Main Street when

Hedges stepped out of the Idanha and asked for "a few words" with Whiteway. Leading the way to Suite 5, Hedges abruptly demanded to know what was going on between his wife and the contractor. When Mrs. Hedges denied everything, her husband pulled out a .32-caliber automatic and shot the contractor four times. Rushed to the hospital, he survived his wounds. The police said Hedges, "crazed with jealousy," had intended to kill his wife as well but had lost his nerve. Among the first persons to rush to the scene were Governor Gooding, James McParland, and a passel of Pinkertons.

In the first days of May 1907, scores of newcomers shouldered their way through the brass doors opening onto Main Street and strode across the gleaming Italian marble floor of the Idanha's rotunda-lobby to the reception desk, where the manager, E. W. Shubert, presided in black cravat and gray morning coat. There were defense attorneys (the prosecutors were home-grown), detectives from both camps, witnesses for each side, reporters from New York, Chicago, Portland, and Denver, and a motley crew of stenographers, bailiffs, retainers, informants, grifters, courtesans, hookers, and all the other riffraff that public entertainments of that era invariably attracted.

For fifteen months—since the governor and his family, in fear for their lives, fled to a third-floor suite in the care of bodyguards—the hotel served as prosecution headquarters. The governor enjoyed a close relationship with the place. His inaugural ball had been held at the Idanha in January 1905, eight hundred of the state's elite waltzing in the glow of Japanese lanterns. The Goodings did all their entertaining there; indeed, one Sunday on the eve of the trial, Mrs. Gooding presided at a luncheon at the hotel, as if to demonstrate that she and her husband were unafraid of assassination.

But the Idanha cultivated all of the capital's panjandrums. When Justice Stockslager, about to challenge Gooding for governor, wished to throw a bash for three hundred persons, he did so at the Idanha, a supper served in a private second-floor dining room gay with scarlet carnations and red-shaded candles, with Christiansen's orchestra playing at the head of the stairs. And when Borah, already serving as a special prosecutor, was elected to the U.S. Senate in January 1907, an extraordinary "citizens' reception" was held at the Idanha in which "dress suits jostled coarser garments, cutaways rubbed elbows with well frayed sacks; Paris gowns and home made frocks were in line."

As early as January 1906, James McParland had settled a few doors from the governor's suite, in Room 35. Although he'd shuttled back and forth to Denver during those months, the hotel remained his base for this operation. On May 5, 1907, he returned with his entourage, ensconcing himself at the Idanha for the trial's duration. Most detectives were finished with a case once they'd turned the malefactor over to constituted authority. Not McParland. He was master not just of the Steunenberg investigation but of the trial as well. Even the governor and the prosecutors, who theoretically outranked him, heeded his every suggestion. According to Hermon Titus, "when

McParland speaks, all civil officialdom in the capital of Idaho listens and quakes."

Ready at a moment's notice through a connecting door was his private stenographer, Robert P. Shollenberger. For the past year, McParland's eye on the Boise scene, Deputy Superintendent S. Chris Thiele, had occupied a room across the hall. Charlie Siringo, McParland's bodyguard, had another room nearby. Though James Hawley and William Borah maintained their own offices elsewhere in the city, it was in Gooding's or McParland's rooms at the Idanha that the prosecution met to devise its strategy. Anyone wandering onto the third floor was immediately taken in charge by an armed Pinkerton demanding to know what his business was.

On other floors, the Idanha remained a farrago of strange bedfellows, its lobby a cockpit of intrigue. Though McParland spent most of his time closeted on the third floor, he took his daily constitutional along Main Street with the faithful Siringo at his side, the Great Detective wearing a high-peaked white Stetson, Siringo a similar model in black, both men swinging their polished canes. And he condescended to spend an hour or two each day holding court in the lobby—"like a major general," wrote Hermon Titus. "Here he sits and smokes and receives homage. Most pass by with awed looks, while some few are proud to be seen sitting alongside and basking in the great man's halo." Occasionally a union man or radical journalist approached too closely—like George Shoaf of *Appeal to Reason,* constantly seeking a snapshot —but Charlie Siringo quickly interposed his body, shouldering the intruder away from the Great Detective. McParland resisted all efforts to take his photograph, and when Socialist newsmen persisted, he and his bodyguards broke three cameras.

At times, the spacious lobby didn't seem large enough to contain all the gunslingers in the prosecution camp. One day, two of the deadliest—Charlie Siringo and Bob Meldrum—confronted each other by the mahogany bar. Hawley had imported Meldrum and his sidekick, Rudie Barthell, ostensibly under subpoena as prosecution witnesses, actually as insurance against federation "thuggery" or other contingencies. Ten years before, as sheriff of Carbon County, Colorado, Meldrum had pursued a gang of horse thieves headed by "Kid" Curry, while the Pinkertons sent Siringo to infiltrate the bunch. Unaware of the desperado's identity, Meldrum had almost killed Siringo. Now, as they eyed each other grimly, Meldrum's hand jumped toward his revolver pocket. "I've felt worst about not getting you than any man I ever missed," he growled. "It's all right, Bob," said Siringo. "I call it all off." Ultimately, they downed a whiskey together.

Surprisingly, given all the Pinkertons crawling its corridors, when Clarence Darrow, his wife, Ruby, and a stenographer named Miss Terry reached Boise on April 26, they checked into the Idanha as well. Darrow was as jumpy as a prizefighter on the eve of a championship bout. "I am going back to Idaho the last of this week to begin the fight of my life," he'd written Brand

Whitlock on April 8. Whitlock fed Darrow's grandiosity, assuring him, "You are making history out there in Idaho."

Though other of the defense attorneys, among them Ed Richardson and Fred Miller, had quit the Idanha after they found their rooms "patrolled at all hours by rubber-heeled sentinels," Darrow found the hotel to his liking. Relishing its new café, done up in lemon and varying shades of green, he took a particular fancy to the black waiters, and they to him. (A dignified lot, in the upper echelon of Boise's black society, the waiters held an annual ball at the Grand Army of the Republic Hall, with four of them harmonizing as the Idanha Quartet.)* For a time at least, Darrow and McParland both took their breakfasts in the café, sipping their coffee and perusing the *Statesman* at nearby tables. (Ida Crouch-Hazlett, who may have joined them now and again, said of McParland at his coffee, "He sucks it up so that you can hear it all over the room.") In this curious calm before the storm, the two sides studied each other more with curiosity than animosity.

One Sunday evening in May, Darrow lectured at the Columbia Theater under the auspices of the Unitarian Club, the most progressive of Boise's congregations. Since the "church" as yet had no building to call its own— holding weekly services in the same hall where the black waiters held their ball—it had leased the 829-seat Columbia, the city's principal theater, for this widely anticipated event. The twenty-five-cent admission fee went to the church's building fund. It was the feisty new Unitarian minister, John C. Mitchell, who dared lavish praise on the unorthodox visitor.

The Unitarians took a calculated risk in presenting the itinerant atheist in a community largely hostile to both his ideas and his client. But Boiseans turned out by the bevy to see what Darrow was like. Though Darrow had just turned fifty, he was not yet a household name in America; many Idahoans had heard of him, vaguely associating his name with Chicago, Debs, and the Pullman strike, but weren't quite sure who he was.

The trial community was amply represented in that evening's audience, which filled the theater "from pit to dome." At least two Pinkertons were spotted in the orchestra. Judge Fremont Wood attended, as did Senator Borah. On the defense side, Fred Miller, the attorney from Spokane, and his wife occupied one box. Visiting reporters of all stripes were there. The Socialists —among them Ida Crouch-Hazlett of the *Montana News,* Wade R. Parks of the *Daily People,* and Ernest Untermann of *Wilshire's Magazine*—clustered just beyond the footlights, prompting one mainstream journalist to complain of a "claque" seeking to exaggerate Darrow's following. Bill Haywood's

---

* The saga of the Idanha's black waiters was a sad one. When the hotel opened in 1900, it employed Chinese waiters, but by 1906 threatened boycotts by many whites forced them to dismiss the Chinese and hire black men and women instead. Then, when a new manager took over at the Idanha in 1908, he replaced the black waiters with white women. "The hungry traveler who steps into the attractive café now," he said, "will be served by deft-handed maids in pretty uniforms of black and white" (d'Easum, *Idanha,* 124).

invalid wife entered the theater in her wheelchair, pushed by another Socialist correspondent. A. E. Thomas of the New York *Sun* noted with amusement that Socialist George Shoaf shared a box with a man from "a capitalistic
organ *par excellence,*" probably Oscar King Davis of the *New York Times.* "The
lion and lamb lay down together" in the audience that night, Thomas concluded.

Darrow may have been a trifle apprehensive, for he had his flowing locks
sheared back a bit and his boots polished, and he delivered a speech he'd
given many times before—one, he hastened to point out, that had "no application whatever to present conditions"—a surefire crowd pleaser. "Walt
Whitman was not a business man," he began, drawing the same burst of
laughter the line elicited back East. "He didn't know how to get money out of
his poems. No one ever would get money out of good things. It is only the
worthless things that bring cash."

If the Pinkertons were "looking for seditious utterances," as A. E.
Thomas speculated, they found none, and "it wasn't long before they were
applauding with the rest." Wood and Borah leaned forward in their seats "so
as not to lose a word" as Darrow swung into his peroration: "And so to the end
Whitman sang his optimistic song, died an optimist, looked out into the night,
and seeing the rising sun, he saw it because of his gentleness, kindliness, and
good will to all mankind, [for it] dwelt in his soul, and his soul was the only
real thing to him."

The Pinkertons, the judge, the prosecutor, and the heterogeneous press
corps joined in a rousing ovation. "Then," wrote the man from the *Sun,* "the
whole bloodthirsty crew poured out of the theater and strolled slowly home
under the stars, discussing the philosophy of Walt Whitman."

Ida Crouch-Hazlett found the lecture elating, convinced that it had "put
the socialists and the demanders of working class justice on a superior plain
[*sic*] with the world's pure and ideal thought." And that, it seems, is precisely
what Darrow intended—to defuse the air of anarchistic terror that hung over
the defense team and show Boise's opinion makers that he and his colleagues
were capable of refined moderation.

Ultimately, the prosecution's grip on the Idanha proved oppressive for
the Darrows. Even the hiring of a bodyguard—Billy Cavanaugh, the Socialist
stonecutter who'd known Haywood in Chicago but now lived in Caldwell—
didn't give them a sense of security at the Pinkerton-ridden hotel. In mid-
May, they rented a furnished bungalow at 103 Warm Springs Avenue, surrounded by apple trees, lilacs, and yellow roses, with a few chickens
scratching on the lawn. Pinkertons, hired guns, and corporation agents notwithstanding, Darrow was getting to like this pretty little town on the irrigated desert, which he called "the Athens of the Sage Brush."

The Ada County courthouse, where Haywood's trial would take place,
was a square, Italianate red-brick building topped by a wooden cupola, home

to cooing pigeons and large black bats.* Built in 1882 next to Idaho's state-house, its quarter century of hard service had left it a bit down-at-the-heels, signifying to one Boston correspondent the "frontier conditions" in which the case would be tried. Its basement housed the county jail, where the three defendants had been held for more than a year. A stairway brought those seeking justice into an austere second-floor lobby, from which one climbed an interior staircase to the third floor and a pair of battered doors, covered with green billiard-table felt, opening into Judge Fremont Wood's courtroom.

It was a middling chamber—some seventy feet long and forty-five feet wide—with bare plaster walls and hard wooden benches resembling the pews of an old-fashioned country church (but not half so comfortable as the benches on Boston Common, thought the Boston correspondent). It usually accommodated 250 persons, but, anticipating a heavy demand from the jour-nalistic and legal fraternities, the judge had made room for fifty additional seats inside the rail. The courtroom had an unorthodox configuration. At its eastern end, from a bench resembling a pulpit, presided Judge Wood—a dignified presence described by one Socialist reporter as "a man in a well-cut black frock coat, turned-down collar and white-linen tie, silver grey at the side temples, calm yet alert eyes and a voice rather deep but distinct"—usually flanked by a glass water pitcher and a stack of leather-bound law books. The elevated witness box stood facing the judge about twenty-five feet down the center aisle, reached by three shallow steps and lit by two brass chandeliers. Instead of being set off to one side, as was customary, the jurors were ranged before the bench, their high-backed oak swivel chairs allowing them to pivot east to face the judge or west to observe the witness and, beyond him, the spectators' section, which sloped down a bit toward the bench like a theater orchestra. At a pine desk to the judge's right sat the stolid clerk of the court, Otto Peterson; to the left, in a chair perched atop a platform, so he could survey the entire assemblage, loomed the county's newly elected sher-iff, the imposing Shadrach Hodgin. The prosecutors occupied a long table to the right of the witness box, the defense attorneys to its left. Directly in front of the witness sat the stenographers, Boise's W. L. Phelps and Denver's C. W. Libby (whom McParland still suspected of being an agent for the defense). So cramped were all parties in the little amphitheater between the jury and the rail that Bill Haywood could reach out and tap the knee of the nearest juror, barely three feet away. On the front wall hung a real estate company's garish calendar, nearby a sign warning that "Spitting on the Floor, Smoking in This Room" were strictly forbidden. Spitting was permitted, if not actually encouraged, in the blue-and-white cuspidors that squatted beside each juror's

---

* The defendants were to be tried separately, and it was widely believed that Moyer's case would come second and Pettibone's third. Harry Orchard wouldn't be tried until he'd testified against his alleged co-conspirators.

chair and by the attorneys' tables. Along the north wall ran a hat rack on which, at any given time, would hang a half score of black bowlers, a few Stetsons, and, as the spring wore on, the straw boaters wrapped with boldly colored ribbons favored by the press boys. In the heat of May, the tall shuttered windows along the side walls, shaded by striped awnings, would be flung open to encourage at least the rumor of a breeze, and through the cupola the spring sun cast a gaudy light on the solemn proceedings below.

On May 6, the parties assembled to deal with preliminaries, Hawley and Borah for the state, Darrow and Richardson flanking Haywood. The defense wanted a "bill of particulars" spelling out the detailed charges against their client. Having chosen indictment by a closeted grand jury rather than a public hearing, the prosecutors had kept the exact nature of their case from the defense, riling Darrow and Richardson.

Conceding that Idaho had no statutory requirement for a bill of particulars, the impeccably dressed Richardson reminded Wood that it was within a judge's "sound discretion" to insist on one. It was particularly appropriate in this case, he argued, because Haywood—and his two compatriots—had been out of state when the murder was committed. Given his absence, it was unclear how the state proposed to connect Haywood to Steunenberg's assassination. "The defendant," Richardson said, "is entitled to know the overt act charged against him." What the defense wanted most was Harry Orchard's confession, whose exact contents hadn't been made public (though Gooding had provided it to clerical supporters like Lyman Abbott, Dwight Hillis, and Edwin Hinks, and McParland had leaked general summaries to friendly journals like the *New York Herald* and the *Denver Republican*).

Borah held that the defense was seeking not to flesh out the charge but to know the evidence against the defendants—evidence that the prosecution was entitled to keep confidential until it was presented in court. Judge Wood found for the prosecution. By repeatedly reporting itself ready for trial, he ruled, the defense had waived any right to such particulars. He put the parties on notice that the trial would begin at ten Thursday morning.

On May 9—some sixteen months after Steunenberg's assassination— *The State of Idaho v. William D. Haywood* opened to weighty expectations. "The eyes of the civilized world," wrote the *Statesman*'s Harry L. Crane, would be focused on "these great proceedings." As a "determined struggle between labor unions and capital," said John W. Carberry of the *Boston Globe,* it was "one of the great court cases in the annals of the American judiciary." The *People*'s Wade Parks did not hesitate to call it "the greatest trial of modern times."

For the first time, most of the lawyers on both sides were present in the courtroom. At the prosecution table sat the compact four-man team of Hawley and Borah, representing the state; the dandified Owen Van Duyn, speaking for Canyon County; and the hawk-faced William A. Stone, Frank

Steunenberg's old friend, for the Steunenberg family and other Caldwell interests.* The facing table wasn't large enough to encompass the entire defense team, which by then had ballooned to eleven. But present that morning were Darrow, Richardson, Miller, Nugent, Murphy, and a new attorney whose presence in the courtroom stirred a furor in Boise's better circles.

One of Boise's leading citizens, Edgar Wilson was an accomplished attorney and banker who'd served as the state's lone congressman—once as a Republican, once as a Silver Republican—and also as Boise city attorney and Ada County attorney. For a man of that rank to throw in his lot with Darrow and Haywood would certainly have aroused Boise's comfortable citizens in any circumstance. But what had people buzzing that morning was another of Wilson's credentials, his eleven years (1884–95) as a law partner of Fremont Wood's before Wood went on the bench. As Edgar Lee Masters handled much of the office work while Darrow performed in court, so Wilson had been the "inside man" to Wood's "outside man." Nobody could remember the last time he'd tried a criminal case. Surely his principal value to the defense wouldn't be in the courtroom, and many people believed he'd been engaged as a pipeline to the judge.

Darrow denied any such intent. He'd approached a good friend, Richard F. Pettigrew, the Populist senator from South Dakota, asking for an introduction to Pettigrew's old ally in the Free Silver ranks, Senator Dubois of Idaho. At a dinner arranged for that purpose in Chicago, Darrow asked Dubois to recommend prestigious local counsel in Boise and Dubois said the only man for the job was his longtime friend Edgar Wilson. So highly regarded was Wilson in Boise that he'd been the leading candidate that winter to succeed James Beatty on the federal bench. Only his penchant for heavy drink—and a persistent story about the night he and a friend had broken some furniture in a Boise bordello—caused President Roosevelt to seek his new judge elsewhere. But such considerations were largely irrelevant to Wilson's role in the Haywood defense.

By then, to be sure, the defense team already included a slew of Idaho attorneys. There was Nugent, the former Owyhee County prosecutor, counsel to the Silver City Miners Union, and youthful friend of Bill Haywood's; Leon Whitsell, the Coeur d'Alene lawyer and espionage commander; and Thomas D. Cahalan, a Boise criminal lawyer with extensive knowledge of potential jurors. There were also the father and son Henry and Walter Griffith from Caldwell, whom McParland believed the defense had hired some months before, at a joint fee of $5,000, precisely because they were on good terms with Judge Edgar L. Bryan, who'd originally been expected to try the case.

If Darrow now felt the need for still another Idaho lawyer—and paid

---

* Stone was famous in those parts for winning a rape case after telling the jury: "I don't believe a man can run as fast with his pants down as a woman can with her skirts up."

him, as rumor had it, a whopping $15,000—McParland and others concluded his object must be to curry favor with the new presiding judge, Fremont Wood. Wilson and Wood had dissolved their partnership in 1895, when Wilson took up his congressional duties, but they'd still shared a well-appointed Boise office and seen a good deal of each other until Wood was elected to the Third District bench in November 1906. When Darrow invited Wilson to join the defense, Wilson called on his old partner to ask if that assignment would embarrass him.

Wood was "somewhat stunned" at the question, particularly since Wilson had been among the most virulent critics of John Morrison, the former governor, when that stalwart agreed to join Darrow in representing Steve Adams the previous August. Yet, concluding that "our previous association could in no way affect my ability to try the cases and do exact justice," Wood assured his ex-colleague that his taking the job wasn't a problem.

But Wilson's presence at the defense table was to cause the lawyer himself much grief in succeeding months. Until that day—despite his well-known taste for "loquacious juice"—the Wilsons had been prominent members of Boise society. The husky former congressman with the extravagant handlebar mustache, his wife, Laura, and their two children lived in a Queen Anne–style villa set on a full-acre lot along Warm Springs Avenue. Once they had entertained—and been entertained by—the town's very best people. But soon after he agreed to help in Haywood's defense, Edgar and Laura were ostracized by their social peers, given the cold shoulder at public receptions, and struck from the invitation lists for private affairs. Business organizations that had retained him in the past vowed he'd never get their patronage again; civic organizations asked him to drop from their rolls; old friends cut him dead on the street.

From his suite at the Idanha, McParland worked hard to embellish the courtroom scene. His top priority was to persuade Belle Steunenberg, the governor's widow, to take a regular seat within the rail, where she would serve as a poignant reminder that a real human life had been snuffed out in these class wars. On May 6, he asked William Stone, Caldwell's representative on the prosecution team, to see if he could arrange Belle's presence, but Stone doubted he could. "As I understand it," the detective reported on their conversation, "Mrs. Steunenberg is rather a peculiar character and is somewhat of a religious fanatic of the Seven Day Adventist type and looks at all matters that might transpire in a philosophical way, even to the death of her husband." McParland then requested Owen Van Duyn to approach an elder of the Adventist Church to see if someone armed with religious authority could "induce" Mrs. Steunenberg to attend. Van Duyn did his best, but Belle —who'd become something of a recluse since her husband's murder—firmly declined.

For similar considerations, Darrow had urged Haywood's wife and daughters to attend the trial, and they'd readily agreed. Nevada was there that morning—a fanciful bonnet atop her brown hair, a shawl drawn over her shriveled shoulders, in her arms a bouquet of red roses given her by Mrs. Steve Adams—seated in a wheelchair between her husband and her nurse, Gertie Wesselman. Vernie, sixteen, sat to her mother's right, while the red-haired, freckle-faced Henrietta, nine, clung to her father, not infrequently climbing into his accommodating lap. To one mainstream correspondent, Henrietta was "an unaffected, lovable, sunny little girl whose presence makes a man think of boyhood days and sweethearts and school companions." She and her father made an affecting tableau, which the jurors couldn't fail to notice. For much of the trial, Haywood's mother, Etta Carruthers, and his thirty-year-old half sister, Mary, also sat nearby. To Ida Crouch-Hazlett, this clump of Haywood women in their bright dresses looked "attractive as daisies" in that grim courtroom.

The pretty scene Darrow had contrived at the defense table drove McParland wild. Scorning the defendant, "this model and moral man Haywood, the man that was so kind to his wife and family," the detective longed to produce the three officers who'd arrested Haywood at the Granite rooming house in bed with Winnie Minor. Only they—Undersheriff Thomas Baird, Deputy Sheriff Leonard De Lue, and Glen Duffield, the deputy sheriff and city jailer—could testify that "Haywood, who was written up as one of the most model men in the city of Denver, was found stripped naked in a room in an assignation house with a woman" not his wife.

McParland seems to have specialized in this sort of revelation. In 1904, he was evidently the source for an item in *Polly Pry*, a Denver newsletter, about the labor organizer Mother Jones. The scandal sheet, which spoke for the Peabody administration, was operated for a few years by Mrs. Leonel Campbell Anthony, who'd formerly written as "Polly Pry" for the *Denver Post*. In her newsletter of January 1904, she cited records "down in the 'Pinkerton office'" as showing that Mother Jones had been "a vulgar, heartless, vicious creature" as a prostitute and/or madam, in Denver's red-light district and in similar quarters in Omaha, Chicago, and San Francisco. Though Mother Jones ignored the accusation, it damaged her reputation in some circles.

If McParland could have managed it, he would have tarnished Clarence Darrow's reputation as well. On March 5, 1907, he wrote the governor: "My informant also told me that in addition to Darrow being a Socialist, both he and his wife are free lovers. The wife made the statement this evening that a man has a right to desert his wife and family if he felt like it and that her husband agreed with her views on this subject. However, Darrow said while a man had a right to leave his wife if she didn't suit him, if he had any family he should take care of the family. The woman that Darrow is living with is a Swede and is his second wife. As to whether his first wife is dead I don't know."

Preparing to disclose Haywood's concupiscence, McParland had cleared the notion in May 1906 with Sheriff Alexander Nisbet of Denver. "We also talked with the deputies to that end," McParland told his agency at that time, "and they are willing to go." But in the interim, something—or somebody —had changed their minds. On May 16, 1907, Frank Cary, the Pinkerton superintendent in Denver, reported to McParland: "De Lue and Baird are sworn enemies, and each is trying to throw the odium of testifying as to who was with Haywood at the time of his arrest on the other. As you know, both of the men are politicians, and each thinks that by refusing to go to Boise the other would go and he would be prepared to say to the working men that he was too much of a friend of the working man to testify against their champion and thus belittle the one who goes to testify." De Lue, now in charge of the sheriff's detective squad and widely regarded as on the take, had told Cary that "Haywood's wife is an invalid and a cripple and that it would not be right for her to know that her husband was laying up with other women." This, Cary remarked acerbically, "is the first time I have ever known De Lue to have any moral scruples." As for Duffield, McParland reported, the jailer didn't want to take the stand in Boise because he would be vulnerable on cross-examination for lying to Horace Hawkins, Ed Richardson's partner in Denver, when the attorney asked if the three men were in custody the night of the "extradition." Finally, Cary suggested, even Sheriff Nisbet was now play- ing "peanut politics," afraid that if he permitted his deputies to testify "it could cost him labor votes at the next election."

Ultimately, McParland had no doubt what lay behind the deputies' sudden change of heart. "I believe these men have been bought over," he reported on May 24, "as Haywood has been afraid that this [his tryst with Winnie Minor] would be brought out."

Still seething at saccharine reports of Haywood smiling at his crippled wife or taking Henrietta on his lap, the detective turned his considerable powers to getting a jury that would send the "hypocritical" labor leader to the gallows.

In the century's first decade, America's jury system was in bad odor. Once it had been deemed "the palladium of liberty," the bedrock guarantee of equal justice under the law. But now the eastern and southern European immigrants flooding the cities, and concomitant fears of "mob politics" and public disorder, had set off a chorus of high-minded demands for the system's reform or even abolition. A city jury, warned the *Arena* in 1905, was "fre- quently corruptible"; plainly put, "you can 'do business' with it, if you have the money." Though a country jury was "rarely corruptible," it was "densely ignorant and stubbornly bigoted." The *Nation* held that "nobody but the criminals and the 'jury fixers' are interested in the continuance of the present state of things.... We cannot go on much longer picking out imbeciles, knaves and ignoramuses to bring our malefactors to justice." To *Munsey's Magazine,* a jury's task was "expert work and should be done by those educated, trained and experienced in such matters," in other words, "a professional jury bench."

Though both sides worried about purchase or intimidation of the Haywood jury, Judge Wood moved doggedly to find twelve honest men and true. Following the so-called California system of jury selection, Idaho courts filled the jury box with talesmen (potential jurors), then subjected them to questioning, first by the prosecution, then by the defense. Each time a talesman was removed for any reason, his place was immediately taken by the next man on the roster, the jury box remaining filled until both sides had accepted twelve men.

To find his way onto a jury, a male citizen of Ada County had to pass through three successive screens, each of which might remove him from the panel. The first was his own plea to be excused—which, according to law, could be granted because of one's own (or a close relative's) ill health, a position of public trust, or the press of private business to which no one else could adequately attend. A potential juror might have other motives for seeking release from this obligation. The trial promised to be lengthy and arduous, with seclusion from friends and family. Finally, there was a consideration that no juror dared speak out loud. As the New York *World* put it, with only modest exaggeration, "This has been a man-killing country and, under the shadows of a strong suspicion that there may be avenging murders by cranks or others, it may prove difficult to secure twelve men for the jury willing to run the suspected risk."

Available to the attorneys that first day were twenty-eight talesmen left over from the regular April venire, a 150-man panel drawn by the county commissioners from the county's registered voters who were also "of fair character, of approved integrity and of sound judgment." Even before jury selection formally began, a well-connected talesman named Ben F. Eastman had been excused on unusual grounds. Eastman, it seemed, was treasurer of the Boise Gun Club, currently hosting visiting sportsmen at the annual shootfest of the Idaho State Sportsmen's Association. An ardent sportsman and dandy-about-town, Eastman begged the court to let him compete. Idahoans took their shooting seriously, and so, by mutual consent of the parties and the judge, young Eastman departed "with every manifestation of joy."

To others who pressed around the judge's bench clamoring to be excused, Wood was more exacting. "You understand, gentlemen," he said, "I don't want any but legal excuses." Brandishing physicians' notes certifying to their lumbago, hemorrhoids, and carbuncles, a platoon of men tried to get off on health grounds; few succeeded. The chairman of the county's board of public works, a probation officer, a road overseer, and a rural mail carrier were released because their jobs were "in the public interest." Others were let go because their work was irrigation, the lifeblood of Ada County's parched acres; one man couldn't leave his sheep at shearing time.

By then, the original venire was virtually exhausted. Judge Wood promptly instructed Sheriff Hodgin to summon a special venire of a hundred "good and lawful persons." All weekend long, Hodgin—who, with his lean good looks, reminded onlookers of Owen Wister's Virginian—and seven of his deputies rode the sagebrush flats and irrigated farmlands of Ada County delivering summonses to their quota of good men, primarily in the rural precincts southeast, north, and west of Boise.

On Monday, May 13, the designated talesmen—most of them farmers and ranchers—showed up in court, some spruce in their Sunday best after a genteel train ride, most speckled with dust their ponies had stirred up on the road, virtually all sporting elaborate whiskers. There they sat, row after row of them, the white dust powdering their bushy mustaches and flowing beards, sifting gently onto the benches and floor.

Every attorney had his own criteria for picking a jury. Darrow had developed rules of thumb that he recorded for the benefit of lesser practitioners. If one represents the underdog, as Darrow invariably did, one should always take the Irishman. He is "emotional, kindly and sympathetic," and "his imagination will place him in the dock." An Englishman isn't as good, but he has a tradition of "individual rights" and isn't afraid to stand alone. The German is worse still, but if he loves music and art, he is emotional and will want to help you.

As for pious men, Darrow had little use for most of them. Worst of all is the Baptist, for he thinks all outsiders are doomed to perdition. The Presbyterian is almost as bad; if he "enters the jury box and carefully rolls up his umbrella," let him go, "he is cold as the grave." The Methodists are "nearer the soil," not half bad, though they won't take a drink. "If chance sets you down between a Methodist and a Baptist, you will move toward the Methodist to keep warm." Lutherans, especially Scandinavians, are "almost sure to convict." But if you draw a Unitarian, a Universalist, a Congregationalist, a Jew, or an agnostic, "don't ask them too many questions," let them stay.

The defense lawyer should never take a wealthy man; he'll convict "unless the defendant is accused of violating the anti-trust law, selling worthless stocks or bonds, or something of that kind." After the board of trade, for him the prison is the most important public building. And "do not, please, accept a prohibitionist: he is too solemn and holy and dyspeptic. He knows your client would not have been indicted unless he were a drinking man, and any one who drinks is guilty of something."

In the Haywood case, however, both defense and prosecution went well beyond such rough measures of a juror's likely opinion. They were amply equipped with precise intelligence gathered during the massive effort both sides had expended to compile the preferences, affiliations, and dirty little secrets of hundreds of potential jurors. Both sides had sent small armies of scouts into the countryside posing as insurance men, encyclopedia salesmen, and other itinerants. Now, on the defense and prosecution tables, lay the fruits of that undercover work, typewritten "dope sheets" listing each jury man, his political and other affiliations, and a brief assessment. The situation was further complicated by the penetration of the defense's juror-vetting process by the Pinkerton master spy, Operative 21, who eventually supervised that undertaking. Thus, on the table before Borah and Hawley were copies of the defense's dope sheets, as well as their own.

The second screen through which jurors had to pass was the "challenge for cause," an accusation by either the prosecution or the defense that a potential juror was so infected by bias—either actual or implied—that he could not deliberate impartially. The prosecution examined a potential juror first to see if there was bias that would justify excluding him for cause (though the talesman was always warned not to say which side he was biased toward, it was rarely difficult to discern). If he survived that scrutiny, he was "passed for cause" and remained provisionally in the jury box. When the prosecution had passed twelve jurors for cause, the defense took over the questioning until it had passed twelve for cause. Occasionally, one side or the other would reserve its right to come back and question the talesman again at a later date, and the talesman would retain his seat in the box until then.

The difficulty was that many talesmen, not wishing to serve but knowing they didn't have grounds to be excused, could simply claim an opinion hardening into bias, which would assure them quick passage back to the ranch. Indeed, so many talesmen were eager to confess that their minds were made up that reporters regarded the process as farcical. "God's truth, but they were liars!" wrote a man from the *Denver Post.* "They came in and sat in the vacant chair, one by one, and perjured themslves blatantly, freely and eloquently."

Ironically, when a juror didn't declare bias, the attorneys often grew suspicious. If he wasn't a man they knew to be solidly in their camp, why did he want to serve? If such a juror declared he had an open mind, that meant ipso facto he had a closed one—and in the wrong direction.

Thus, day after day, through May and into June, defense and prosecution bent every muscle to discredit such jurors. Armed with information gathered by their scouts, the parties tried to smoke out what they knew to be the talesmans' true feelings by asking their reaction to the president's "undesirable citizens" letter, Secretary Taft's speech in Boise the previous November, Governor Gooding's assertion that the defendants were guilty, Gene Debs's screeds, and *Appeal to Reason's* polemics. They asked what party the potential jurors belonged to, what church they worshiped in, what unions they'd joined, what newspapers and magazines they read.

One of the first men Darrow took on was Allen Pride, a thirty-six-year-old farmer listed on the defense's dope sheet as "Rep., N.G. to defense." Unlike the other lawyers, who stayed seated at their table, Darrow got up close, hooking his suspenders and tilting into the jury box like a small-town druggist leaning across the soda counter.

"Imagine yourself in the defendant's shoes," he said to Pride. "Would you want a man on the jury whose mind is in the same condition as your own?"

"I'd hate to be in such a predicament."

"You'd want a fair jury?" asked Darrow.

"Yes."

"And you think you could be fair?"

"He might do worse."

The attorney and the talesman paused for a moment, looking each other straight in the eye.

"And he might do better?" said Darrow. "Isn't that so?"

"Perhaps," said Pride, "but I think not."

For the moment at least, Pride had stood off his shrewd inquisitor.

Now and again, the report on a talesman was so unequivocal that the attorneys would put their undercover investigator on the stand to discredit him. Consider D. W. Henry, a slim, swarthy carpenter from south Boise.

Henry, who claimed not to know what the WFM was (except that "it ain't a religious organization"), was asked whether he'd spoken with a defense investigator named R. Z. Lovelace. Henry conceded he had but denied he'd told Lovelace that the labor leaders were guilty, otherwise they wouldn't be on trial.

Then Darrow produced Lovelace, who told the court he was an engineer originally from Chicago, who'd come to Boise in early 1906, just after Darrow entered the case—which strongly suggests he was a private detective brought to Idaho by Darrow for just such work. Lovelace testified that Henry had certainly told him that if the trio wasn't mixed up in the Steunenberg murder they'd never have been arrested. Moreover, he was "running down Socialists" and other "radicals."

At that, Darrow brought Henry back to the stand. What did he mean by "radical"?

"When a man says he can get out and kill off half a town in half a day, I would call that a radical statement," Henry said to a burst of laughter. Darrow returned to the statement Henry had previously denied making. "Mr. Henry, you have heard Mr. Lovelace's statement. What do you say about it?"

A bit sheepishly, Henry now admitted he probably had told Lovelace that the defendants must be connected with the Steunenberg murder.

"I think that's all," Darrow said with a little smile, glancing toward the judge.

"The court will allow the challenge," said Fremont Wood. "Step aside, Mr. Henry."

From his seat at the defense table, Bill Haywood admired the way

Darrow went after dangerous men in the jury box. "It was like killing snakes," he wrote. But when the final decision had to be confronted, whether to challenge a man for cause or not, he was no bystander. His head was always prominent in the circle of defense lawyers grappling with the problem.

Jim Hawley, in turn, went after L. M. Campbell, a studious young man with slickly combed hair, a high collar, and gold-rimmed nose glasses, who read more widely than the average talesman—in the *Statesman,* the *Gem State Rural,* the *Twin Falls News,* and several Socialist papers that had been tossed on his porch. At first, Campbell insisted he could render a fair decision but under questioning conceded that he had formed a "certain prejudice" against one of the parties. Was it against the defendant? Hawley wanted to know. When Campbell said it was not, Hawley—a toothpick working in his mouth— promptly challenged him. Judge Wood let the studious young man go.

Such triumphs were rare. Most of the time, it was difficult to get a juror to admit his bias, particularly if he'd been prepared by the attorneys to rebuff such suggestions. So when both prosecution and defense had passed twelve men for cause, the two sides fell back on the third screen in the selection process, the peremptory challenge, which could remove a juror with no reason cited. In federal criminal cases and in most state trials, the defense had ten peremptories to the prosecution's five—a tacit acknowledgment that the prosecution started with a leg up, since many people assumed a defendant was guilty merely because the government had charged him.

But so intense had been the pretrial investigations of potential jurors in the Haywood case that McParland was unwilling to cede the defense even that small advantage. Hawley, who thought the trial would be "as hard a fight as ever took place in a courtroom," agreed. In early winter, McParland, Gooding, and Hawley had decided to seek legislation increasing the prosecution's peremptory challenges to ten. On January 14, 1907, with the legislature a week into its biannual session, the detective wrote Hawley to jog his memory. "That matter should be looked into and disposed of at as early a date as possible," he said. Two days later, Hawley reported that he'd "taken this matter up with several of the members and they seem inclined to favor it." But he went on: "We have got to be very careful in doing anything of this sort, because if the attention of the defense was called to a bill for this purpose, they will at once conclude that it is done to affect their case, and possibly make a fight."

Evidently, Darrow and his team failed to smoke out the prosecution's gambit, for the bill moved smoothly through the legislature and went into effect, with other new legislation, on May 7, 1907. Even then, there was some question as to whether the new rule could be applied to the Haywood trial. Since the crime that gave rise to the case had taken place more than a year before the law was enacted, the defense argued strenuously that it was ex post facto legislation. "It might have been well labeled as 'an act passed as an emergency to assist the state in [these] trials,'" argued Richardson. Fremont

Wood listened carefully in his characteristic pose—a pencil in his right hand, its eraser pressed lightly against his upper front teeth—then held for the prosecution: both sides would have ten opportunities to rid themselves of an otherwise qualified juror who threatened their interests.

There were those—among them, Roosevelt's attorney general, Charles J. Bonaparte—who thought that peremptory challenges should be abolished altogether, that jurors ought to be challenged only for reasonable cause. But to both sides in the Haywood case, the peremptories were precious bullets to be guarded jealously. If a juror had been approved for cause by both sides, he might remain in the jury box for weeks and still be excluded by one side or the other on a peremptory challenge.

On May 9, McParland reported: "All of the jurors that we considered were favorable to the defense made sure to qualify. However, later on, these men will be challenged peremptorily." One lawyer for the state, hinting at what was in store for these jurors, drew his hand across his throat in "a motion suggestive of decapitation." Sure enough, the state used its first peremptories against A. L. Ewing, a white-bearded carpenter, and William van Orsdale, a hardscrabble farmer. Not surprisingly, the defense used its first peremptory to get rid of the stubborn Mr. Pride.

Within a week, the struggle over the jury had settled into a grim war of attrition, which some found tedious. Hermon Titus said he thought it "about as bad as a ride across the sage brush benches of this Southern Idaho Country." But, he noted, "sage brush land with proper irrigation becomes brilliant with rich vegetation. So with these long hours...if you only bring a keen understanding to your task you will see here the most important work of the whole trial."

To Crane of the *Statesman*, "Every inch of ground is now being fought by the attorneys on both sides. No juror is accepted for cause until every possible question has been asked in an effort to learn his true state of mind.... Nearly every [peremptory] challenge from now on will be resisted if there is a shadow of a chance for a favorable ruling by the court." Crane, who spoke for Boise's establishment, noted "the preparation for this test has been as near perfect as could be. It would seem, in watching the examinations, that the attorneys have the life history of almost every available man for jury duty in Ada county, from the cradle to the minute his name is called."

As the attorneys jockeyed for advantage, their tempers frayed. After Richardson posed a long, complex question to a farmer named Sam Jones, Bill Borah interposed: "I'd like to know if that was a question?"

"If you'd been paying attention," snapped the haughty Denver lawyer, "you would have known it was a question."

"I couldn't follow your mind," Borah shot back.

"Well, sir," drawled Richardson in his most condescending style, "I'm not to blame for that. All I can furnish is the mind. I can't furnish you with the capability of comprehending it."

Borah and Darrow tangled during the latter's fierce examination of a retired rancher named Harmon Cox. On the table in front of Darrow was a report from a defense agent who reported that the talesman was "opposed to organized labor." His nineteen-year-old daughter was among the scabs replacing the striking "hello girls" at Boise's Independent Telephone Company.

In response to Darrow's questions, Cox saw nothing wrong with his daughter's taking a striker's job and acknowledged that she'd spoken with him before she did so.

"Have you ever formed an opinion regarding the guilt or innocence of the accused?" Darrow asked under furrowed brows.

"No, sir," replied the Civil War veteran, whose gray beard hung on his chest "like the sporran of a highlander's kilt."

"Is that right?" Darrow asked disbelievingly as he leaned on the defense table, twirling his gold spectacles.

"That's what I said."

Darrow wouldn't give up. "How much evidence would it take to change the opinion you have?" he asked.

"That's an improper question," objected Borah. "The juror has not said he had an opinion to be changed."

"Are you stuck on this juror?" demanded Darrow.

"I am stuck on you, sir," snapped Borah, rising to his feet.

Unmoved by Borah's objections, Darrow hammered away at the grizzled veteran of the Grand Army of the Republic, who finally erupted. "I have answered those questions again and again," said Cox. "I can't see the sense of asking them over and over."

Darrow's face grew purple as he declared through clenched teeth: "I challenge this juror for incompetency. He is ignorant and no man should be tried for his life by such a man."

"State your challenge and cut out your stump speeches," said Borah, swinging one foot jauntily, clearly enjoying himself.

"You don't want to force this juror on us, do you?" Darrow asked Borah. "You wouldn't want a client of yours tried by a juror like that, would you?"

"I object to counsel making such remarks to us," put in Borah. The challenge was denied.

The next morning, Hugh O'Neill of the *Denver Post* took Darrow to task for that performance. "If it had been a fight with bare knuckles or light gloves instead of a contest of brains and wits and words, [he] would have been counted out in the first round. He did not succeed in disqualifying Harmon Cox; he lost his self control. He came out of the conflict with Borah a sadly beaten gladiator, and all his 'brother counsel' of the defense turned their backs upon him and stared angrily at the wall."

Darrow's behavior that day was difficult to understand since the term *incompetency* in this regard meant lack of education. True, Cox had little formal education. He'd been a carpenter and a teamster and, more recently, a farmer, but he was of more than ordinary intelligence and an avid reader. Since none of the jurors had much formal education, Darrow's scorn of Cox might be interpreted as condescension toward the entire panel, an impression that could haunt the defense at verdict time.

So hard-fought was the struggle over every juror that word of the courtroom tug-of-war drew several dozen members of the Boise bar to the courtroom, where they took careful notes on each Darrow thrust and Borah parry. "The younger lawyers particularly regarded this opportunity as one of the most fortunate that could come their way," the *Statesman* reported.

Despite their angry encounter over Cox, Darrow and Borah soon developed a strangely playful relationship reflecting mutual respect, even sneaking affection.

Once, searching through papers for the dope sheet on a rancher named John Shaffer, Darrow turned to Borah and said, "We can't get this man placed. Let's take your dope, Borah. Our dope seems mixed."

"We found out where this man lived last fall," said Borah with a little smile. "But you won't need any dope on him."

One time they met on Main Street, Darrow with reporters who looked like "hoboes," Borah's gang having "a Broadway appearance." "How is it," asked Darrow, "that you always have a swell looking crowd around you?" "Birds of a feather flock together," said Borah.

By 11:00 a.m. on Tuesday, May 21, the hundred-man special venire had been exhausted, and Judge Wood ordered Sheriff Hodgin to ride his buggy into the countryside once again and find sixty more men by 2:00 p.m. the next day. But even that didn't prove sufficient. By the following Monday, the attorneys had chewed their way through the second special venire, and the judge ordered up a third panel of sixty-one men.

Evidently struck by the interminable length of these proceedings, during which they would make only the three-dollars-a-day jury fee, many of the new talesmen sought to evade the sheriff's deputies. One man was found hiding in a cellar, another had to be prodded from a haystack with a pitchfork, a third took to the hills for a couple of days, only to walk into the hands of a tenacious deputy when he returned.

But nobody gave the authorities quite so much trouble as John E. Tourtellotte, the flamboyant architect who'd designed the Steunenberg brothers' bank in Caldwell, among many other distinguished Idaho buildings. On May 25, Tourtellotte—"a handsome, self-confident, bowler-hatted fellow" with a "wonderful gift of gab"—cropped up in the jury box. Questioned by Borah, he declared himself conscientiously opposed to capital punishment and said he could think of only two instances in which he could vote to hang a man: first, if the defendant was convicted of belonging to a group that menaced society, a group that had taken lives, as he put it, "by the wholesale, like anarchists"; and second, if the man was convicted during wartime of being a traitor to his country.

When Borah accepted Tourtellotte, Darrow gasped. Their eyes met. "You pass this man for cause?" he asked in astonishment.

"He is up to you," Borah said with a little smile.

Somewhat bemused, Darrow asked the architect: "Have you thought in your mind that this defendant may belong to such an organization as you have said came under your exceptions—an organization which has menaced society, as you described?"

"I hadn't thought of it, until you spoke of it," said Tourtellotte. "But now I can see how it might be."

It seemed as if the dashing architect had cleverly managed to raise severe difficulties for both parties simultaneously—for the prosecution because he claimed scruples about capital punishment, for the defense because one of his exceptions might fit Haywood.

Borah, to be sure, had accepted him, but that looked to many like a ploy, an attempt to make Darrow use one of his precious peremptory challenges. So it was to the onlookers' astonishment that Darrow, with a "jovial smile," passed Tourtellotte as well. All of a sudden, the architect was on the jury and it was apparent from his face that "he did not relish his position." Perhaps it had occurred to Tourtellotte that, were he to find the wrong way, he might no longer have such lush pickings among state contracts. Two years before, the Capitol Building Commission—composed of Governor Gooding as chairman; Secretary of State Will H. Gibson; Henry C. Coffin, the state treasurer; Judge James H. Beatty; and a prominent Boise real estate man, Walter E. Pierce—had awarded Tourtellotte's firm the much-sought commission to design the new Idaho statehouse, for the handsome fee of $10,000. Curiously, the defense never used this connection to challenge him, but evidently it weighed on the architect's mind.

For after lunch he rose in the jury box to tell Fremont Wood, "Your honor, I cannot take the oath as a juror. I cannot vote to find this man guilty if it is understood that the penalty is death if he is convicted." The judge refused to excuse Tourtellotte, whom he knew well. The defense and the prosecution held back as well, each hoping to compel the other to use a peremptory. Meanwhile, agents of both parties were hard at work seeking to divine the architect's true feelings. On May 26, Operative 24A reported to McParland that Darrow was claiming to have tricked the prosecution into accepting Tourtellotte, since the architect secretly favored Haywood; "the defense are going to try to keep him on the jury," the operative reported, "as it is a certainty that he will never vote to convict." From a Hearst reporter, McParland picked up the story that "there was insanity in the Tourtellotte family and that the architect had been tried for insanity," a baseless canard.

Finally, on May 31, Tourtellotte forced the issue by rising to say that he was prejudiced against the WFM and "against Haywood as an officer of that organization" if it was responsible for all the troubles in the Coeur d'Alenes. Thoroughly exasperated, the judge and the parties agreed to let him go.

On May 25, the prosecution dealt the defense a heavy blow when it exercised one of its three remaining peremptories against George H. McIntyre, a Quaker farmer whom Darrow and Richardson had regarded as one of their staunchest friends in the emerging jury. McIntyre had been in the very first batch of jurors to take their seats in the jury box on May 9, had sailed through the initial scrutiny by prosecution and defense, and had stayed there day after day until May 25, while virtually all the faces around him changed several times.

The defense had a report—evidently favorable—on McIntyre from a scout named R. P. Smith. But since it had been passed along by Operative 21, a prosecution spy, Hawley and Borah, too, had the defense's assessment. Evidently, the prosecutors had been toying with the defense, raising their hopes that McIntyre might just survive and then, at the last moment, knocking him out with a peremptory.

So disappointed was the defense team at McIntyre's removal that John Nugent asked Operative 21 to find the man and bring him to the office. Darrow welcomed the talesman, saying how sorry he was to see him go, then took him to his private office for a chat, evidently to pump him for intelligence about others on the panel. Later, Darrow told Operative 21 that McIntyre knew nothing about the other jurors because, as the judge had insisted, "they did not talk among themselves" about the case.

This was one of the last tasks the operative performed in his role as C. A. Johnson. For about this time, the defense at last discovered that he was not who he claimed to be.

In the course of that spring, Darrow and his colleagues had become increasingly convinced there was a spy in their ranks. Information held very tightly was getting to the prosecution and even into Boise's newspapers. By May 11, suspicion had fallen on a recent arrival named Warren, a smooth-shaven six-footer in a black suit and stiff hat who claimed to have been sent to Boise by the Federal Trades and Labor Union of Chicago to aid the defense. From the moment he arrived, some members of the defense team regarded him as "a traitor," as he'd been seen "talking to the police in a friendly way." McParland told his colleagues that Warren was actually W. J. Turner, assistant superintendent of the McGuire and White Detective Agency of Chicago, who was working for the defense, perhaps in bribing the jury. If so, his true identity was a dark secret to some of the defense attorneys. As late as May 26, Nugent told Operative 21 there was "still a leak in the office," that he was still "suspicious of Warren," and that the operative should say "nothing about the case in any way to Warren or any of his friends."

At some point suspicion turned from Warren to Operative 21 himself. That happened after Pinkerton expense statements, submitted to the state for reimbursement, somehow found their way to the defense team. Idaho's state auditor, Robert Bragaw, had long been at odds with Governor Gooding over how to handle the Pinkerton submissions. Ordinarily, they would have gone directly to Bragaw for examination. In this case, however, the auditor had received only the gross amounts, while the detailed statements, showing day-by-day expenses of each Pinkerton operative, were initially locked away in the governor's office. Then on January 23, 1907, Ravenel Macbeth, a state senator from Custer County, introduced a resolution calling for a detailed list of all claims against the state paid by state deficiency warrants. It passed unanimously.

A native of South Carolina descended from French Huguenot and Scotch ancestry, the debonair Macbeth was a cousin of the novelist, and Roosevelt confidant, Owen Wister. Emigrating to Idaho in 1894, he served as federal agent of an Indian reservation for a time before his election to the senate, where over seven terms he became "a recognized leader in democratic circles." As a Democrat, he could well be expected to accuse the Republican Gooding of poor fiscal management. But Gooding and McParland both perceived a more sinister motive behind his motion.

Macbeth's fellow Democrat, James Hawley, pressed the senator to relent, warning him that "under no circumstances would the prosecution consent to let the Idaho State Legislature pry into reports which were rendered by the Pinkerton Detective Agency." Eventually, it was agreed that the expenses could be reviewed by an ad hoc committee of the senate. To this end, Bragaw was given custody of the reports on condition that he share them with nobody except the committee. Somehow, the reports fell into the hands of the defense. Who leaked them—Senator Macbeth, others on the committee, or Bragaw—we do not know. Gooding, however, plainly blamed the auditor, whom he all but accused of treason. Behind closed doors, Gooding denounced Bragaw as "a God Damned Pig Head." In a public tirade at him, the governor revealed that the detailed comings and goings of the operatives listed in these reports enabled the defense to identify "every secret service agent of the state."

Some years later, Darrow told a government commission that "one man closely associated" with the defense had been identified "at the last minute" as "a detective who was in the employ of the other side all the while." If this was Operative 21, as seems likely, one can imagine the shock and rage Darrow and his associates felt when they realized that the man who'd directed their critical juror canvass was, in fact, a Pinkerton spy. If some hotheads wished to harm the traitor then and there, cooler heads prevailed. According to Gooding, the operative was "warned to leave the state or suffer the death penalty."

At about the same time, the defense discovered the identity of Operative 28—A. C. Cole, the former Colorado National Guardsman. Cole had arrived in Boise on May 18 and checked into the Idanha Hotel. Presumably he was there as a defense witness, in conformity with Walter McCornack's operation. But he never appeared on the stand. On June 30, Darrow and Richardson summoned Cole to defense headquarters and showed him copies of his confidential reports (evidently filched from the Pinkertons), after which Cole was "shown the door and told not to come back."

The uncovering of Operatives 21 and 28 seems to have prompted both sides to redouble their security, for not long thereafter the prosecution discovered two men believed to be spies for the defense, one a Boise policeman named Willard Gibson, the other a private detective named Matt Gillam, who'd ostensibly been working for the state. They were both dismissed forthwith.

Barely a week later, defense staffers became concerned by the disappearance of some important papers held at defense headquarters in the Overland Block. Suspicion fell on a cement worker and defense operative named Dell Williams. Leon Whitsell, whose task it was each day to carry the defense's papers back and forth to court in a large leather grip, announced in Williams's hearing—perhaps to test his reaction—"We have a good line on who has been taking papers from the office and think in a little while we will have him behind bars." Williams never reported to the office again. After drinking at the Montreal saloon, he packed his belongings and left town, taking every cent his wife had in her purse and telling her, "Good-bye, you will not see me again."

But it was the uncovering of Operative 21 that dealt the prosecution its heaviest blow and posed the most excruciating dilemma for the defense. Should Darrow and Richardson trust any of the reports on talesmen the operative had submitted? Were these honest assessments of the jurors' predilections or were they aimed at persuading the defense to fill the jury box with men favoring the prosecution? To have falsified all his assessments—systematically listing friends as enemies and enemies as friends—would have discombobulated the defense team but would also have imperiled the operative, inviting other defense scouts to flag this gross distortion of the canvass results. Apparently, most of the assessments he'd reported to the defense—and later to the Pinkertons—were honest. For when he did falsify his assessment, he plainly identified it as such to the prosecution. In his April 14 report to the Pinkertons, for example, he wrote: "The following is a list of the voters of Meridian precinct as checked up by the Attorneys for the defense, except where their list shows W. J. Davison friendly to the defense instead of the prosecution." In the body of the report, the operative wrote of Davison, "friendly to prosecution, thinks prisoners guilty (I have marked this man on the [Defense] Attorneys' list as favorable to defense, very prominent man, well educated, has served several times as juror)."

On June 3, the painstaking process of jury selection—which the *Statesman* had called "pouring the venire sand through the jury knothole"—moved toward conclusion when the defense used its last peremptory against Alfred A. Eoff, retired cashier of the Boise City National Bank. Eoff was the ninth banker summoned in the four venires, a statistic that the defense attorneys cited with some incredulity, and from the moment he entered the box it was clear that the defense would either remove him for bias or with its last peremptory.

With Eoff gone, a critical juncture had been reached; both sides having exhausted their peremptories, the next man called would have to be disqualified for bias or would remain on the jury. The clerk drew a slip from the box and the man called as juror 12 was a long, lean cattle rancher named O. V. Sebern. Operative 21's report on White Cross precinct showed an "O. V. Seberson" (given the unusual initials, almost certainly the same man) as "N.G. to defense." That accounted for Richardson's searching examination, which meticulously sifted the talesman's background, looking for anything that might justify a challenge for bias. A sallow-complexioned fellow who lived on a small ranch a mile north of Boise, Sebern said he was a Methodist and a Republican but wouldn't "care a hurrah" whether Bill Haywood was a Socialist or a Prohibitionist. When Richardson asked the defense's favorite question—whether he would be willing to be tried by a juror whose mind was in the same state as his own—Sebern said, "I would not like to be tried at all, but if I had to be tried, any square, honest man who wanted to do exact justice would satisfy me for a juror, regardless of what opinions he might have." That seemed to satisfy both sides.

By 12:30 p.m., the jury was complete. In addition to Sebern, its members were Thomas B. Gess, Finley McBean, Samuel D. Gilman, Daniel Clark, George Powell, H. F. Messecar, Lee Schrivener, J. A. Robertson, Levi Smith, A. P. Burns, and Samuel F. Russell. The most remarkable aspect of that dozen was their relative homogeneity. All were or had been farmers. Nine still tilled the land, while one was a real estate agent, one a building contractor, and one a foreman of fence construction. Eight were Republicans, three were Democrats, and one was a Prohibitionist. All but one were over fifty years old; most were in their late fifties or their sixties. All wore beards, chin whiskers, or mustaches, or a luxuriant combination of the three.

Sequestered for the trial's duration, the jurors were housed in a private home rented from a Boise shoe salesman named Henry Konrad, across the street from the courthouse's rear door. The frame dwelling, with its broad wrap-around veranda, climbing roses, and spacious lawn, was furnished in gemütlich style, with soft beds (two jurors to a bed), deep easy chairs, and sturdy tables on which a man could hoist his feet at the end of a long day in the jury box. The jurors were under constant observation by four bailiffs— John A. McGinty and William Bryon by day, Frank Breshears and Thomas H. Pence by night. The food—prepared by Mrs. Pence—was said to be good and plentiful. Though strictly prevented from talking with outsiders, the jurors were permitted early-morning strolls into the Boise foothills and outings on the river and to the circus. They could read the newspapers, but only after the bailiffs had cut out any reference remotely connected to the trial; given the heavy coverage of the trial by both Boise papers, the result was often a sorry mess of mutilated newsprint.

Some years later, Judge Wood would regret that he'd permitted the jury selection process to drag on quite so long. Because of the case's importance, he'd granted "great latitude" in the examination of talesmen and "probably allowed challenges for cause where a more strict interpretation of the law would have suggested denial of the challenges." But then, he reflected, "every movement was being scrutinized by more interested people than had ever before followed the trial of an individual case in the history of the country," and the unfortunate intervention of the labor and Socialist community, on the one hand, and of President Roosevelt, on the other, "could not be kept out of the case while examining prospective jurors."

To establishment reporters from the East, the jury was the very essence of the West. "A hard-headed common sense dozen of middle aged farmers," wrote A. E. Thomas of the New York *Sun*. "They are the sort of men who have built this country out of sage brush and alkali and lava rock. They are the true architects of the West."

Although the parties' public statements should probably be received with some skepticism, the prosecution seemed happier than the defense about the dozen they'd chosen. "We are thoroughly satisfied with the jury," Hawley told reporters that afternoon. "We have twelve fair-minded men who will do even justice between the state and the defendant." Borah put it more boldly: "If we cannot convict before this jury, we are not entitled to a conviction."

A statement released by Darrow and Richardson noted: "There is no man on the jury who works for wages or has ever belonged to a labor organization—excepting Burns, who was a member of a carpenters' union 14 years ago." The defense attorneys went on to point out that from a county of 12,000 inhabitants, with 5,000 subject to jury duty and 249 summoned in four venires, there had been only three trade unionists. As a result, the attorneys contended, the jury was "uniformly made up of a class to which none of the defendants have ever belonged and who have no natural kinship to labor organizations." In addition, "they are drawn from a small county almost wholly agricultural and each member for a year and a half has read little about the case except what has been contained in the Boise daily papers and this has uniformly been hostile to the defendants." Although the jurors appeared to be "men of honest purposes," the defense felt the panel was heavily stacked against them from the start.

To many urban observers, a jury of farmers was a nightmare. "To such men," the *Arena* had written in 1905, "the town meeting, the circus, election day and attendance at court, constitute the only breaks in a monotonous round of daily vegetation. For these men cannot be said to live. They vegetate. ... To the bucolic mind jury duty is a great honor conferred by the government, in return for which the juror believes that his verdict should accord with the wishes of the district attorney, whose utterances he regards as oracular." A. E. Thomas observed: "The rural mind is ill-adapted to resisting legal wiles." John R. McMahon of *Wilshire's Magazine* could scarcely suppress his disdain for the Idaho farmers. "Some are untidy and bucolic, with alkali dust on fringed trousers and heavy shoes," he wrote. "It is an ironic commentary on our society to see 'successful' farmers and business men who have not succeeded in the least cultivation of their minds." The whole proceeding struck McMahon as "a badly arranged farce enacted by bucolic thespians." Not everyone agreed. One Colorado newspaper commented, "Farmer juries are the best kind. They are a law-abiding, peaceable and justice-loving class and will give the accused a square deal if any American jury can."

Privately—as well as publicly—Haywood's defenders regarded the jurors with deep misgivings. As late as May 26, when all but three members of the final panel were in place, John Nugent told Operative 21 he was "not pleased with the jury as it now stands" and "the best [the defense] could hope for was a hung jury."

On May 28, while the court was preoccupied with jury selection, a man appeared on Boise's Main Street whose straw-colored beard, mustache, and eyebrows presented an incongruous picture, since his hair was a bright shade of red. When the man emerged from a saddlery where he'd had some holes punched in his gun belt, a police officer, Fred Andregg, stopped him. The city's fifteen patrolmen were under strict orders to pick up all vagrants or "suspicious characters" they found on the streets that summer (some fifty such types had been quietly put on trains and shipped out of town). Now Andregg searched the flour sack the red-haired man had slung over one shoulder. In it he found a .32 automatic Colt revolver, a box of cartridges, brass knuckles, a dirk with an eight-inch blade, a bunch of skeleton keys, some Socialist pamphlets, and a paid-up membership card in Local 22, the IWW, Spokane, Washington.

Not surprisingly, the man—who gave his name as Carl H. Duncan and his age as thirty-four—was arrested as a "suspicious character" and confined in the city jail. The next morning, in a lengthy interrogation by the county attorney, Charles F. Koelsch, he claimed to be a 1894 graduate of the University of Michigan at Ann Arbor, where his mother and brother still lived. He admitted to being a member of DeLeon's Socialist Labor Party and said he'd come to Boise to attend the Haywood trial and to learn "cow punching," but knowing the stern suspicion there toward Socialists, he'd disguised himself as a farmer.

Several days after the arrest, a letter arrived from Ann Arbor, purportedly from Duncan's mother. "Dear Charlie," it read. "Can it be that all this in the paper means you? It is so terrible that it seems it will kill me. Why do you do it? Why join yourself to the plans and schemes of foreign outcasts? Oh! Stop right where you are and remember the better things of life to which you were accustomed in past years."

But that same day a less endearing letter was slipped under the door of Boise's mayor, John M. Haines, which read: "C. H. Duncan is a desirable citizen, and we demand that you order the police to turn him loose. We also demand that you remove Chief of Police [Benjamin F.] Francis at once because of his unjust action in persecuting this man. If you do not remove him, we will do it for you." The next day, Duncan appeared in police court, charged with carrying concealed weapons. Given a choice of a hundred-dollar fine or sixty days in jail, the drifter—with only thirteen dollars to his name—went to jail, where he passed the time reading J. R. Monroe's antic poetry in *The Origin of Man*. But Duncan's incarceration did little to dampen the mild case of hysteria that his sudden materialization on Main Street had triggered in Boise.

For more than a year, Frank Gooding had stewed about threats of a labor or Socialist insurrection during the upcoming trials. In early 1906, he'd persuaded Roosevelt and Taft to triple the cavalry force stationed at the Boise Barracks, bringing Troops A and B of the Fourteenth Cavalry from Walla Walla to reinforce Troop L. When pressures built for returning the reinforcements to their home base, the governor and Calvin Cobb had convinced the White House to retain them in Idaho. Only in late fall—with winter approaching and the troopers squeezed into "inadequate quarters"—did the War Department finally withdraw Troops A and B, replacing them with Troop K from the Presidio at San Francisco. On the eve of the trial, some 106 enlisted men, five officers, 110 cavalry horses, and four newly arrived "machine guns" were posted at the barracks.

Though that useful force was bivouacked a half mile from the statehouse, the governor had no direct claim on its services. A year before, the secretary of war had rebuffed Gooding's artless request to take command of the cavalry at Boise, reminding him that all U.S. forces owed their sole allegiance to the president. Now the governor sought to clarify the conditions of their employment. On May 1, he wrote Taft informing him that "the Heywood [*sic*], Moyer and Pettibone trials will begin in Boise, on the ninth of this month, and our little city is already filling up with 'Red Necks.' Of course we know that they are not here for any good purpose." Insisting that he was "not alarmed at the situation," the governor felt "we should prepare in every possible way for the worst, so as not to be taken unawares." Though he knew that "an appeal to the general government should be the last resort," he suspected that "if there is need for the use of troops, it will come without a moment's warning, so that quick action will be necessary." In reply, Taft noted that—since Idaho's legislature wouldn't meet during the trial to issue a call for troops—Gooding should apply directly to the president, "stating the necessities of the case and adding that the forces at your disposal were not adequate to maintain order."

The army's original decision to establish a base at Boise had developed in response to a different danger: the threat, explicit and implicit, of the Bannock and Shoshone Indians to drive gold miners from the Boise Basin. On Independence Day, 1863, the War Department formally dedicated an outpost in the foothills north of the Boise River. Fort Boise, as it was known then, was laid out around a spacious parade ground. Sentries flanking the whitewashed gateposts stood barely half a mile from Boise's nascent business district, providing the young community with a reassuring sense of security. Every dawn, the city was reminded of the cavalry's presence by the bold flourish of a reveille bugle; at every sunset a howitzer boomed across the hills, the garrison standing with bared heads as the flag descended.

From the start, officers at the barracks formed the nucleus of Boise's social life, squiring its eligible daughters to cotillions and balls along Warm Springs Avenue, entertaining the city's merchants, politicians, and their ladies at receptions and band concerts on the post's manicured lawns. In summer months, the officers wore dazzling white uniforms garnished with gold braid, a striking contrast with the handsome blue-and-yellow uniforms of the troopers as they paraded through town on their regular training rides. But the enlisted men could be a rambunctious lot, storming downtown of an evening to fill the brothels and saloons along West Main Street. All too often, fueled by strong drink, high-stakes gambling, and lively women, violent incidents broke out between soldiers and civilians, such as the one in which Private Marshall Garrett of Troop L had his nose broken by an angry citizen armed with brass knuckles.

The troopers found their principal recreation in Boise's red-light district, perched brazenly at the post's doorstep. A two-block area, it centered on Levy's Alley, a narrow thoroughfare paralleling Main Street. The alley took its name from Davis Levy, a Polish Jew who'd come to America in 1847 at the age of fifteen, arriving some twenty years later in Boise, where, in a building at Sixth and Main, he established the California Bakery. Soon Levy expanded, erecting several two- and three-story brick buildings in the 600 block of West Main Street, filling the alley in the rear with a number of wooden "cribs." By the 1890s, all these buildings were bordellos, the brick buildings for relatively expensive prostitutes, who charged five dollars a session, the wooden cribs for those whose going rate was two. For a time, the area was called Whitechapel, after London's most depraved district, but soon it became known simply as Levy's Alley or, in the *Statesman's* vivid language, "Levy's reeking haunt of vice."

A notorious figure in town for his emaciated form, his tattered clothing, his pungent odor, "the way he swore and blasphemed," Levy was said to have secreted thousands of dollars somewhere in his warren of interlocking bordellos. On October 5, 1901, his body was found on a bed in the lodging house at 612½ Main Street where he lived and did business. He'd apparently been attacked while eating his dinner, strangled with the food still in his mouth. Then he was taken into the adjacent room and laid out on the bed with a bloodstained towel over his face. The authorities believed the motive was robbery, since Levy was known to have had five hundred dollars in his pockets that day—receipts from his stable of whores. Within a month, police arrested one George Levy, a French pimp who lived nearby with his two prostitutes. Not related to Davis Levy, George rented one of the cribs as working quarters for his women. Found guilty, he served nine years in the pen.

For a time after these events, Moses Alexander, Boise's reform-minded mayor—and the first Jew to hold high public office in Idaho—cracked down on the city's prostitution, perhaps because he felt personally impugned by the Jewish whoremasters. But before long, they resumed their activities in and around Levy's Alley, enjoying a mutually rewarding relationship with the police. During a 1908 investigation, Boise's police chief, Benjamin Francis, testified that the local Elks had presented him with a "very nice" diamond badge in appreciation of his work, but it was later revealed that the badge came from the prostitutes at Agnes Bush's house, passed through the Elks to maintain the appearance of propriety.

When John F. MacLane, a Yale-educated lawyer, came West in 1906, he found the 600 block of West Main Street to be "a miniature Barbary coast." Every afternoon about four, Levy's Alley disgorged its denizens onto Main Street. The girls were "out in force and in their best clothes," MacLane wrote, "to parade the streets and visit the stores, as conspicuously as on Unter Den Linden in Berlin or the Kartner-Strasse in Vienna."

Needless to say, venereal disease was rampant at the barracks. In September 1906, Lieutenant Henry J. McKenney, the post commander, wrote the War Department noting that his cooking facilities had been strained by tripling the garrison. But the most critical problem was the discovery that the post baker had syphilis. McKenney urged the army to rush him a new baker, and on October 16, Private Edgar T. Brock, a freshly risen graduate of the Fort Riley Bakers School, reached Boise.

Barely ten weeks later, the post surgeon found it his melancholy duty to recommend that Private Brock be relieved as baker for "gross inefficiency." Since Brock had taken over, "the bread has constantly been of an inferior quality . . . dark, soggy and unfit for issue," he wrote. "The man lacks the strength, energy and aptitude to make a baker and is absolutely incompetent." Moreover, the surgeon added, "Private Brock has developed a severe case of gonorrhea." Officers may have wondered whether military bakers had some special affinity for Levy's Alley, the province of the former master baker Davis Levy. In any case, the post surgeon urged that a "competent"—and healthy—baker be sent to Boise forthwith. Ultimately, the baking duties fell to a Private Lanham, who was promptly arrested by military authorities, charged with stealing a suit of clothes from one of his barracks mates.

That winter and spring of 1907, the barracks had a more acute problem—a growing flood of desertions. For some time, seven or eight men a month had deserted the post, some of them recovered by military authorities in cities like Salt Lake and Portland. Then, just as the Haywood trial began, the rate sharply increased—twelve men defecting in one week alone.

On May 19, 1907, in an interview with the *Denver Post,* Captain Clark D. Dudley, the barracks commander, conceded that an unusual number of men had recently absconded. Moreover, the captain believed that some outside force—presumably allied with the WFW—was encouraging this wholesale defection. Some of his soldiers had told him that "strangers in town" had offered them "a number of inducements" to desert. These people—whom the *Denver Republican* quickly identified as Socialists—had "redoubled their efforts during the last few days."

In a letter to the army's adjutant general, Dudley said that low pay, bad food, and hard work were "minor factors" contributing to the high rate of desertion. He put greater stress on "the absolute disregard of the obligations of an oath becoming inherent among the people of the present generation." Such faithless young men "would think several times" about deserting, the captain recommended, if photographs of each deserter were posted in every town with a fifty-dollar reward for his capture.

Another factor contributed to the desertion rate, one that Captain Dudley didn't care to mention—his own arbitrary administration. According to charges later leveled at a court-martial, the captain had ordered nineteen-year-old Private Fred C. Lang, who'd missed a practice march, to parade for three hours on the veranda of his quarters with a placard on his back reading "Bad Boy." Indeed, after this experience, which earned him the jeers of his fellow troopers, the young private did desert.

For being absent without leave in Boise saloons for forty-eight hours, Dudley had also ordered Private Harry Strong to be shut up for five hours in a small shed that had been used as a latrine and then, for four days, in a five-by-five-foot closet filled with old horse bones, where he subsisted on a diet of bread and water. Similarly, Private Robert E. Baylor was held four days on bread and water in the "solitary cell" of the post guardhouse. Arguing the army's case, the judge advocate contended that these punishments were "barbarous, and cruel and tyrannical," like "a tale from Russia, the land of the oppressed." The board evidently agreed, for they found "this misguided commander" guilty, sentencing him to four months of confinement on post and issuing an official reprimand. In approving the board's finding, the Third Infantry's commander noted that Dudley's "unjust and tyrannical treatment of enlisted men" was presumably responsible for the fact that "desertions were excessive and discontent prevalent at the post while Captain Dudley was in command." Late in June 1907, A. C. Smith replaced the discredited Dudley in command of Boise Barracks, but it was too late to bring esprit de corps to this deeply troubled installation.

At times, the Socialist and labor press worked itself into a fever about the cavalrymen at the barracks, whom it regarded as a savage band of cossacks about to wreak havoc on honest workingmen in the streets. One summer afternoon, Ida Crouch-Hazlett and George Shoaf wandered out to the barracks to inspect the big guns and the battery of Gatlings, their barrels seemingly trained on the streets before the courthouse, "ready for deadly action." The two Socialists prowled the base, ignored by the troopers as they "siz[ed] up these instruments of death." Weeks later, Shoaf expatiated in *Appeal to Reason* on what he'd seen that day: "Nothing would give Gooding greater delight than to have the opportunity of turning half a dozen gatling guns on a mob of unorganized and undisciplined wage slaves.... Outwardly Boise appears pacific, but beneath the surface warlike preparations are going on night and day."

Such anxiety—some might say paranoia—ignored conditions at the barracks. Had the War Department sent the Fourteenth Cavalry into action in Boise's streets, one wonders how effective these discontented, venereal troopers would have been.

In case of serious unrest, Gooding would have been required by law to look first to his own resources, namely, the Idaho National Guard. After performing creditably in the Philippines, the Second Idaho Regiment had returned to its home state, twelve companies with an authorized strength of forty citizen-soldiers and three elected officers each, a total of about five hundred, scattered across Idaho. The late war had convinced the president and influential members of Congress that, in state after state, the National Guard was in desperate need of modernization. In Idaho, for example, lax administration, a shortage of funds, haphazard training, and a heavy reliance on teenaged farm boys had often caused the guard to be dismissed as "tin sword play soldiers." In 1903, Congress had provided for disciplining, arming, and organizing the various state militias into a national reserve force up to regular army standards. Henceforth, each guard unit would train with the regular army, participate in at least twenty-four encampments a year, and receive much-needed federal funds and equipment—which could, in turn, be withdrawn if such units fell below national standards.

Accordingly, in mid-1905, Governor Gooding had engaged the services of a forty-four-year-old officer, recently retired from the regular army, to bring the Second Idaho Regiment up to snuff. A veteran of twenty years' service, Major Lorenzo P. Davison had graduated from West Point in 1885, then gone West to chase renegade Indians. His early fitness reports were outstanding: "Of unusually marked ability," wrote one commander. "Bids fair to be a very distinguished man."

Then came assignments to Puerto Rico and the Philippines during the Spanish-American War. In striking contrast to the so-called immunes, who had varying degrees of resistance to tropical diseases, Davison seemed especially vulnerable to them. Shortly after his arrival in Puerto Rico in 1899, he suffered severe bouts of "fever, malaria and dysentery." Apparently recovered, he was dispatched to the Philippines, where he was felled once again by malaria, so acute this time that doctors at Corregidor declared him "totally unfitted for tropical service." Over the next five years, he was in and out of army hospitals suffering from minor strokes, paralysis of the right arm and leg, speech impairment, temporary blindness of the right eye, rheumatism, herpes, nausea, hallucinations, "loss of nervous control," and "mental confusion." In September 1904, a board of officers—after hearing testimony that "his mind gets confused when he gets excited"—recommended that he retire from active duty, which, in December 1904, he did.

Once he'd returned to civilian life, his ailments improved somewhat, so that when friends put him forward for the Idaho job, he was eager to begin a new life in the bracing air of the great Northwest. But no sooner was he settled in Boise than a long-festering domestic dispute began to preoccupy him. Davison and his wife, Carolyn, hadn't lived together for five years, though the major had furnished her funds to support herself and their four children. Later he'd learned that instead of spending this money on necessities, Carolyn had squandered it on "fine raiment, jewelry, liquor and extravagant entertainment." Moreover, at her Illinois home she'd run with what Davidson described as "a rich, fast, smart set that no officer of my rank could afford." In February 1905, after Carolyn made clear she had no intention of living with him again, he removed his children from her home, settling with them in Boise. Now his wife was attempting to correspond with the children for the purpose of "enticing them away from home." As she filed for divorce and pressed for custody of the children, Davison warned the War Department that a "scandalous" divorce trial would ensue.

Somehow, amid all his troubles, Davison found time to execute his military duties, advising Colonel John McBirney, Idaho's National Guard commander, and instructing each of the companies in tactics and logistics. But very soon Davison encountered a considerable stumbling block in his efforts to bring the Idaho guard up to national standards—"the persistent idea that the organized militia [an informal name for the guard] are primarily intended for the suppression of labor troubles."

There were those in Idaho, he reported, who felt that "men united as closely as are all the inhabitants of a single state, especially in Idaho, should not be subject to calls to suppress disorders arising from labor troubles where presumably the men engaged in such protests (strikes, etc.) have some grounds for dissatisfaction." Many Idahoans who might have made good guard material refused to enlist under these circumstances. That liability, Davison argued, could be removed if the War Department made clear its determination to intervene with federal troops in such a crisis. But the department demurred. "While the status of affairs, as presented in your letter, is to be deplored," the military secretary replied, "the War Department is wholly without legal authority to act in the manner suggested."

As the Haywood trial approached and Frank Gooding made clear that he might have to mobilize the guard if labor and its Socialist allies caused trouble in Boise, Davison felt squeezed between the exigent governor and the reluctance of many of the guard's officers and men to be drawn into any such conflict.*

The governor and his associates weren't depending entirely on either U.S. troops or the National Guard. In the spirit of western vigilantism, they relied as well on a body of freebooters. Among them were the host of Pinkerton detectives—some said upwards of thirty—by now assigned to Boise. Then there were the hired gunslingers like Bob Meldrum and Rudie Barthell, whom the prosecution had brought to town as insurance against labor agitation and violence. McParland knew that notorious pair all too well and warned that they "must not drink" and should "keep their heads level." Such admonitions notwithstanding, Meldrum soon got into several brawls with labor sympathizers. So blatant was his pugnacity that Boise's police chief had to call him in for an ultimatum: either he behaved himself or he'd be shipped back to Colorado. Finally, in case of serious trouble, the prosecutors could call on law-and-order men from Caldwell and Boise, who were eager to be in on any shoot-out during the trial.

One of the deepest secrets in town was the formation of a Boise Citizens' Alliance, patterned after the group of that name that had reinforced the business-oriented administration of Governor James H. Peabody during Colorado's labor wars. With tactical support from McParland's Pinkertons, the alliance had organized stealthily among Boise's merchants and professional men, many of whom secretly took rifle and pistol practice. At least a hundred to two hundred men were reported ready to go into the streets at a moment's notice. Chris Thiele, McParland's semipermanent man in Boise, served as liaison with the alliance. On May 11, Thiele met with Charles J. G. Hass, one of the merchant organizers, to warn that "it behooved him to be very careful that no leak occurred in their meetings, as at the present time the labor unions would cause considerable agitation about anything the Citizens' Alliance would contemplate doing in Boise. Mr. Hass assured me he would be very cautious regarding this matter." So careful were the Pinkertons on the subject that James McParland, who seems to have written about everything else, never once mentioned the alliance.

One of the few occasions on which the alliance's activities threatened to become public was in early May—around the time of Thiele's warning—when the merchants became deeply concerned about street meetings similar to those in Caldwell that Hermon Titus, editor of the *Socialist*, was scheduled to hold in Boise. A secretly convened gathering of Boise merchants—almost certainly the alliance—told Mayor John M. Haines that the business community would tolerate no street meetings; when Titus reached town on May 8, Haines summoned him to City Hall and delivered the message. Titus held no

---

* Coming on top of his continuing health problems and his wife's harassment, these problems proved too much for Davidson, and by October 1907, he asked Gooding to relieve him of his military duties, which the governor promptly did. (Davidson to Gooding, October 1, 1907; Gooding to Adjunct General, October 1, 1907).

street meetings, though he did deliver one speech at the Columbia Theater (which the *Statesman* starchily refused to advertise). James Noland of the *Denver Post* wrote: "I have it from reliable authority that these merchants will go to any extreme to preserve quiet in Boise. To this end their organization is compact and its existence bodes evil for that person who presumes to defame this community by word or deed."

Within the courtroom, and in the dingy corridors outside, order was maintained by a dozen deputy sheriffs, a mix of men already on Sheriff Shad Hodgin's staff and men engaged specially for this purpose from Canyon and other nearby counties. Chief among these was a hulking, blunt-spoken deputy sheriff named Erastus M. Beemer, known to one and all as Ras. At age forty-nine, Ras was a veteran of Idaho law enforcement, having served as an Indian scout under the legendary Rube Robbins, then as a deputy sheriff under his uncle, Joe Wilson, and finally under Hodgin. A prominent Elk and Eagle, he'd worked now and again—between lawman stints—as a cattle and horse dealer. Some years later, Hodgin would say of Beemer, "He was my right hand man during those trying times [the Haywood trial]. He could neither be bought, persuaded nor frightened from his line of duty." Among others assigned to the courthouse was Jerry Siggins, another Hodgin deputy; Frank M. Breshears, a dapper Canyon County deputy who favored colored vests and bow ties; and "Colonel" Elias Marsters, a veteran of the Spanish-American War.

Still another recruit for courthouse duty was James Hawley's eldest son, Edgar, a lawyer by training if not by temperament. Like Marsters a veteran of the late war, he was rangy and tough and quick on the draw. His father, the special prosecutor, publicly dismissed Frank Gooding's fear of assassination. "Rot!" he told one reporter, insisting he carried no weapons, had no bodyguard, and felt the need for neither. Nonetheless, at the elder Hawley's insistence, one of Edgar's jobs every morning was to scan the courtroom for the number and location of the defense's gunmen. Though side arms were supposed to be checked outside, there was no elaborate search of lawyers and spectators and there was always concern that somebody might smuggle a six-shooter inside. On occasion, spectators slipped into the courtroom carrying packages feared to be bombs, but all these people turned out to be harmless—two women carrying their lunches wrapped up in scarves, a sheepherder with his soiled overalls covered by brown paper.

To ensure against mayhem in the streets around the courtroom, the prosecution placed a sniper in a garret atop a grocery store at the northwest corner of Bannock and Eighth Streets. From his perch, this sharpshooter had an unobstructed view of the courthouse two blocks east and one block north. He never found it necessary to pull the trigger. But at least one other sniper was loose in town: one soft spring evening, a bullet from an unidentified gunman crashed through the window of a room in which Senator Borah's wife, Mary, sat talking with Eva Dockery, the *Statesman*'s society editor. The bullet was presumably meant for Mary's husband.

All through the spring and summer, rumors of imminent trouble reached the authorities. One report, from a Professor Jenks, warned that, if Haywood was convicted, Socialists, anarchists, and unionists might retaliate with massive demonstrations in Boise or, worse yet, assassination of state or federal officials. After an investigation, John E. Wilkie, chief of the Secret Service, pooh-poohed the idea in a report to the White House. "We must give the radical branch of the Western Federation credit for having at least common sense," he wrote, "and it does not take much of a prophet to imagine the plight in which they would find themselves were there to be even a demonstration or attempt upon the life of the President or one of his cabinet officers. ... Every interest they have in the world would be centered in preventing an act of that kind."

At 9:20 a.m. on Tuesday, June 4, as the trial proper got under way, every seat in the courtroom was filled to hear Jim Hawley open the prosecution case. Rising to his feet, this "representative citizen of the sagebrush"—a formidable figure at six foot four and 215 pounds, a walrus mustache bristling under his nose, a thick watch chain draped across his substantial belly—lumbered toward the jury box to open the most important trial of his long career.

> We will prove to you, gentlemen of the jury, that at the inception of this organization [the WFM] a conspiracy was formed by the members of the "inner circle," the object of which was to perpetuate their own power, influence and control both in the Federation itself and in the governmental matters of the different sections of the mining country wherein they had control by employing, gentlemen, desperate criminals to commit murders and other atrocious crimes by unusual and alarming methods against those who in official position refused to be influenced by their wishes and those who in private life ran counter to their interests.

Hawley took all sorts of liberties with the English language, especially the rules of grammar and syntax. He was famed for coining words and phrases never before heard in the law courts, known to the press as Hawleyisms; he once described how a man "clamb" from one level of a mine to another. In his mouth, his beloved state came out "I-dy-ho."

From his hard wooden chair inside the rail, lanky, bespectacled Hugh O'Neill of the *Denver Post* found Hawley's rustic style and mining-camp humor unimpressive. "He droned on for almost twenty minutes unnoticed. He was reciting, formally, dry facts. In the warm, shaded room, they seemed dull and uninteresting.... He spoke on and on, and on, and on and we were weary. We had heard it so often before.... The court yawned. It was so warm and drowsy and—Bang! Darrow was on his feet, thumping a book, his voice husky with protest."

"Wait a minute, Mr. Hawley," Darrow interjected. "Your Honor, if an opening statement has any function, it is to tell a jury what evidence they propose to offer in a case." Hawley's statement had nothing to do with the state's evidence, Darrow suggested, but was "thrown in for the purpose of prejudicing the jury about a matter which could not be in evidence."

"The Court will permit nothing here in the shape of argument," Wood admonished Hawley. "You must make a statement of what you expect to prove."

"That is what I am trying to make, Your Honor, and I think I understand my rights and my duties as well in this matter."

"It doesn't look as though you did," put in the pesky Darrow.

"I don't care, sir, what it looks to you," Hawley snapped, clearly nettled now. "I am not running this case to meet your wishes or your ideas; and I ask, Your Honor, not to be interrupted by this counsel—"

"You will be interrupted every time I think you are trespassing," Darrow shot back.

After Judge Wood gaveled the squabbling attorneys to order, Hawley sought to address the heart of Darrow's objection: that the prosecution's broad opening statement had nothing to do with the crime that had been committed in Idaho, the assassination of Frank Steunenberg. The state, Hawley declared, held that "the killing of ex-Governor Steunenberg was not the primary object of this conspiracy but was only an incident of it and a part of their general policy."

When Hawley came to the examination of Harry Orchard by James McParland and referred to them as "gentlemen," Darrow broke in again to ask with a puckish smile which of them was a gentleman.

Reddening above his wing collar, Hawley muttered, "That may be very cunning, these kind of remarks, but they are entirely out of place, Mr. Darrow, and if you choose to interrupt with those kinds of expressions you will be answered in kind."

Hawley's exasperation was precisely what Darrow had sought. Behind it was his deliberate strategy, evident in virtually all his trials, of selecting one of the prosecution's attorneys as a scapegoat against whom to employ his considerable weapons of scorn and sarcasm. So venomous were Darrow's sallies against the verbose and syntactically muddled Hawley, so wounding were they to the attorney's pride, that Hawley's twenty-five-year-old son, Jess, who assisted him throughout the trial, occasionally threatened—out of court —to punch Darrow in the nose if he didn't cease and desist.

Edmund Richardson joined occasionally in the harassing fire against Hawley. When the prosecutor referred to McParland as "the terror of the evil doers throughout the west," Richardson quipped sarcastically: "That will be proved, I suppose."

By now, the defense tactics had so rattled Hawley that he felt compelled to apologize to the jury. "I don't know, gentlemen of the jury, as I make myself intelligible, with these numerous interruptions which my friends on the other side seem to think it is necessary to interpose."

But he slogged along for an hour and twenty minutes, recounting an assortment of bombings, assassinations, and attempted assassinations in Colorado, Wyoming, California, and Idaho—"the most fiendish crimes that were ever perpetrated anywhere"—to which Orchard had confessed. Insofar as the Steunenberg murder was concerned, Hawley conceded Haywood hadn't been in Idaho at the time—and Pettibone and Moyer hadn't either—but he expressed confidence that, under the statutes of the state, "we will be entitled to a verdict at your hands because the proof will satisfy you beyond all reasonable doubt as to the guilt of these defendants."

When Hawley concluded, Darrow informed the court that he would postpone his opening until after the prosecution had put in its case. This rare ploy seems to have been grounded in two considerations. Since Hawley had held back so much detail, he hadn't given the defense much of a target to shoot at; likewise, Darrow wanted the prosecution to present its evidence knowing as little as possible about the defense strategy.

With these preliminary maneuvers out of the way, the prosecutors launched their case by asking citizens of Caldwell to describe the events of that snowy day on which Frank Steunenberg had lost his life. Among those who testified briefly were C. F. Wayne, the Steunenbergs' neighbor who had milked the governor's cows and fed his chickens only minutes before the bomb went off; John Gue, one of the physicians who attended Steunenberg on his deathbed; the attorney John C. Rice, the governor's close friend and neighbor who'd noticed the man called Thomas Hogan strolling Cleveland Boulevard examining the Steunenberg residence through binoculars; Alex Ballantyne, who'd seen Thomas Hogan emerging from the hotel that night and Frank Steunenberg following a few minutes later; Julian Steunenberg, the governor's eldest son, who recounted a conversation with Hogan at the Caldwell depot in which Hogan said he wanted to talk with Julian's father about buying some sheep. Some of these witnesses also testified to encountering Hogan's partner, a man who registered in hotels as "Simmons" but who was believed to be the elusive L. J. Simpkins.

By midmorning on June 5, as the last of these witnesses completed his testimony, there was a pause in the proceedings. Senator Borah told the court sotto voce, "The next witness will be here in a few moments." After five minutes, during which the crowd murmured and rustled in anticipation, Hawley broke the silence in his resonant bass:

"Call Harry Orchard."

Instantly, the door leading to Judge Wood's chambers swung open and through it came Ras Beemer, the hefty deputy sheriff in charge of courtroom security, followed closely by the witness whose astonishing confession had led to the indictment of the three labor leaders and whose testimony here would likely determine whether Bill Haywood lived or died.

For months there'd been rumors that Harry Orchard would never survive to take the witness stand. The previous autumn, McParland had heard reports that the WFM was going to slip poison into Orchard's food at the penitentiary; he'd warned Warden Whitney "to be on your guard to see that Orchard does not come in contact in the penitentiary with any person that could injure him." There was talk of sharpshooters stationed on Table Rock, a mesa above the penitentiary, who'd sworn to shoot him on his way to the courtroom.* The state assigned guards to man those heights night and day, while Hawley sent word to the defense: "The second man to be shot will be Darrow."

For the first time since March 1906, when he'd testified in Caldwell before the Canyon County grand jury, Harry Orchard had spent a night outside the penitentiary's beige sandstone walls. Because the prosecutors couldn't be sure how much time the preliminary witnesses would consume, they needed Orchard close at hand. Normally, he would have been kept in the county jail beneath the courthouse, but that was obviously unfeasible, since the men against whom he was testifying now occupied that space. So about seven the previous evening, Warden Whitney himself, accompanied by his wife and daughter, had driven the assassin to the offices of Hawley, Puckett and Hawley on the second floor of the Odd Fellows Block, where he spent the night on a leather couch, closely guarded by a heavily armed squad of penitentiary guards and prosecution gunmen. All morning, he'd been held in readiness at the law firm until, shortly past ten-thirty, the guards hustled him the four blocks to the courthouse, then up the back stairs into the judge's chambers.

Now, dressed in a gray checked tweed suit, his unruly hair carefully barbered, a newly grown mustache blooming on his upper lip, Orchard walked purposefully toward the witness stand. From his seat nearby, John E. Nevins of the Scripps-McRae News Service, ruminated on the contrast between Orchard the criminal and Orchard the witness.

"Orchard the criminal," he wrote that evening, "wore a badly fitting coat, no natty collar, no well-tied scarf, no jaunty negligee shirt. His hair was hacked, not trimmed. He was unshaven, not well-groomed.... The eyes were shifty and watery. A life of indulgence and intimacy with crime had left its

---

* One man who believed these rumors was John H. Murphy, the WFM's veteran lawyer, now deathly ill with tuberculosis. On May 8, his thin lips so bloodless one could almost see the teeth behind them, he told a reporter he'd heard "many whisperings of possible unlawful outbreaks, of plots laid in secret to assassinate Orchard, or perhaps some officers of the law." A Denver man had told him that he'd be in Boise for the trial and that Orchard would never live to testify. "The officers have his description and our agents have it. If he comes here he will be arrested. ... I heard there might be rioting here and I came to Boise to lead the mob. And if there should be [a riot], I'll be at its head, pointing the way, not to lawlessness and deeds of violence, but to paths of peace that lead to happy homes and contentment" (*Denver Post,* May 8, 1907).

unmistakable impress upon the sodden face. This man might be guilty of anything."

Whereas, "Orchard the witness might be a Sunday school superintendent. He is carefully attired—collar, cuffs, scarf, even to the quietly displayed watch chain, which lies across his benevolent breast. He affects dark colors, as becomes one contrite and oppressed with a sense of his own wickedness. His hair is cut in the mode, well-trimmed. The mustache is carefully arranged. His hands are perfectly kept, his nails manicured."

To a sardonic Hattie Titus, writing in the *Socialist*, he was the best-dressed man in the room, "a regular matinee idol." Pretty soon, she thought, "the ladies will be throwing bouquets at him."

As he passed the man whose life he was about to put in jeopardy—and whom he hadn't seen for nearly two years—Orchard kept his eyes discreetly on the floor. But as he turned in the witness box, Harry Crane, the *Statesman* reporter, thought he saw the assassin's pale blue eyes lock for one terrible moment with Bill Haywood's single sighted eye. Beneath that unflinching glare, Crane detected on Haywood's face the curled lip of scorn. But even Haywood soon recognized how effective a transformation had been worked on the prisoner. "Far from being the furtive weasel of a man that his story would lead one to expect, Orchard was well-set-up, bluff, with an apparently open manner."

As Orchard raised his hand to be sworn, Ras Beemer and a penitentiary guard assumed their places on either side of him and two feet to the rear; known to be an excellent shot, Beemer carried a heavy weapon prominently displayed under his wide leather belt. At the same moment, the courtroom doors were locked from the inside, and extra guards, among them the dread gunfighter Bob Meldrum, took up positions at all entrances and along the side walls, their eyes "on roving commission," scanning the spectator section for a hostile move against the witness. Other deputies and detectives sat in plain clothes among the onlookers. Inside the rail, a woman dropped her parasol, and brave men flinched. Far back in the room, a man stood to get a better view. "Sit down!" bellowed a deputy, and the other guards trained their weapons on the abashed spectator until he took his seat.

"Mr. Orchard, where do you reside?" Hawley began.

"Up at the state penitentiary," the witness murmured.

"What charge, if any, has been made against you?" Hawley asked.

"I was charged with the murder of Ex-Governor Steunenberg."

"Is Harry Orchard your real name?"

"No, sir."

"How long have you been known by the name of Harry Orchard?"

"About eleven years."

"What is your real name?"

At this question, the entire courtroom—attorneys, reporters, bailiffs, spectators—seemed to lean forward, eager to catch the name on the witness's lips. Nobody was more intensely interested than Darrow, Richardson, and the rest of their team, for over the past year the defense had mounted a major effort to discover the real identity of the man who sat before them now—a search that had carried their agents through much of the United States and Canada, from close to the Arctic Circle to the Rio Grande. Their effort had garnered all sorts of incidental information about the man in recent years but ultimately had failed to answer the riddle of his true identity.

The principal defense agent in this endeavor was the Chicago lawyer George E. Dickson, president of the Workmen's Legal Security Company, which investigated accidents and filed suits for workmen injured on the job. At the Chicago Federation of Labor, questions had been raised about the working methods of the Legal Security Company, particularly whether they might involve some sort of bribery. It is not clear if Dickson had ever dabbled in the time-honored Chicago art of jury bribery, but that he was something of a sharp operator in Chicago's legal-labor-political jungle seems evident. He'd worked for Darrow before, and shortly after taking on the Idaho case, Darrow turned to him once more as one—perhaps his principal—investigator.

In mid-April 1906, Dickson had launched his search for the real Harry Orchard with a visit to the Coeur d'Alenes. At the county seat of Wallace, he sought out May Awkwright Hutton, the wife of Levi W. Hutton, the engineer of the Northern Pacific freight train that had been hijacked by union miners on their way to blow up the Bunker Hill and Sullivan concentrator on April 29, 1899. Hutton and his conductor had claimed perfect innocence, but attorneys for the state didn't believe them and the Huttons were for some time regarded as outcasts in "respectable" northern Idaho circles. But then, in June 1901, the Hercules mine in which the Huttons had a stake hit the richest silver-lead vein yet discovered in the Coeur d'Alenes and they, like Ed Boyce, first president of the WFM, suddenly found themselves wealthy. Henceforth, they occupied a kind of limbo between the world of disaffected miners, with which they had once identified, and the comfortable classes who drew a good living from western mines.

Ironically, Harry Orchard—who now stood accused of being the demon of radical unionism—had once owned a one-sixteenth share in the Hercules mine. Had he not sold it before the mine hit pay dirt, he—like Ed Boyce and May Hutton—might have made the transition to respectable society. Now Dickson hoped that May and Levi Hutton could help him understand just who Harry Orchard was.

On April 17, Dickson found Mrs. Hutton "true blue," eager to help Bill Haywood's defense and brimming with information about Orchard's activities as a union miner and activist in the Coeur d'Alenes from 1895 to 1899. But her husband, Levi, still traumatized by the events of 1899, was determined to "have nothing whatever to do with the [Haywood trial]." After several days with the Huttons, Dickson reported to Darrow: "I am becoming convinced that Orchard is the real name of our subject."

According to May Hutton and several Coeur d'Alene miners, Orchard claimed to have worked at a cheese factory near Napanee, in the Canadian province of Ontario. So Dickson entrained for Napanee, where he found no fewer than five cheese factories in the immediate area. The factories had changed hands from one to half a dozen times in the past fifteen years, but with dogged persistence he interviewed all the present and former proprietors, some workers, as well as the Canadian government's inspector of cheese manufacture. Though none identified Orchard's picture, two men thought it looked a bit like Robert Washburn, a man they'd known at the cheese factory in Morvan. Convinced he'd finally unmasked Orchard, Dickson sped to the town, only to find Washburn still stirring up a tasty goat cheese nearby. For a time, the defense followed the decade-old tracks of a man named Frank Moore, who'd also worked at a cheese factory, but ultimately abandoned him as well.

Finally, on May 16, Dickson wrote Darrow, "I have investigated all the clews we had as to Orchard's alleged career in the East and find all of these stories to be without foundation in fact. . . . It is too bad we have not got his right name, but even then it would probably be very difficult to trace his movements so long ago, especially as he was a man of no prominence—simply an ordinary laborer and cheese maker."

Jim Hawley's question—"What is your true name?"—hung for a moment in the silent courtroom, the only sound the whir of the wooden fans paddling the muggy air. Then, leaning forward ever so slightly and enunciating with great precision, the witness said, "Albert E. Horsley."

With that, he began his mesmerizing tale, purporting to be the story of his life, while a full house of spectators listened "tense-nerved, rigid, gaping-mouthed." Through his days on the stand, the courtroom was packed as never before, as many as a thousand would-be spectators—among whom women predominated by as much as two to one—besieging the courthouse, blocking the interior staircase, and spilling onto the lawn. Women fainted in the crush, men jostled for position, provoking occasional fistfights. The guards had their hands full controlling the multitude who wished to see and hear the famous killer.

Under Hawley's gentle prodding, Orchard told the court he'd been born forty years before, the second oldest of eight children born to a farmer named Lyman H. Horsley and his wife, Margaret, in Northumberland County, Ontario. Educated only through the third grade, he went to work on his father's farm and then, at age twenty-four, turned his hand to cheese manufacture (Darrow's man had at least been looking in the right county and the right industry). In 1896, at age thirty, he left Canada, traveling to Spokane and then to Wallace, Idaho, where he drove a milk truck for a while, then ran a wood and coal yard in Burke.

In March 1899, the man who by then called himself Harry Orchard left the wood yard and went to work as a mucker in Burke's Tiger-Poorman mine. He joined the Wardner Miners Union, thus becoming a member of the Western Federation of Miners on the eve of the most tumultuous moment in Coeur d'Alene history. According to his testimony, on April 29 he was among the thousand miners who hijacked the Northern Pacific train, diverting it to Wardner, where some of them blew up the Bunker Hill concentrator.

Orchard's tale did more than connect him to those historic events; it put him at the center of the day's action, not far from William F. "Big" Davis, a burly miner whom Orchard identified as the operation's leader. Orchard claimed to have been in the small group that penetrated the concentrator and planted the dynamite in three separate locations.

"Who lit the fuse?" asked Hawley.

"I lit one of them," the witness said with laconic understatement. "I don't know who lit the rest."

"After the fuses were lit, what was the result?"

"The mill was all blown up—blown to pieces."

"After the blowing up of the mill," asked Hawley, "what was done?"

"Got on the train and went back to Wallace."

"Anybody killed during the affair?"

"Yes, sir.... Two men killed."

As remarkable as his tale was the manner of its delivery. Orchard's voice was strong, steady, and carefully modulated; his answers came without hesitation; he never failed to call his interlocuter "Sir"; his bearing, wrote the *Denver Republican,* was "as placid as a summer lake."

When the Fourth Cavalry rode into Burke and began arresting the town's entire male population, Orchard went on, he and other principals in the "riot" were up in the snowy hills overlooking the town, watching as troops went door-to-door taking the men's friends into custody. "We made arrangements with Dr. Collins [a Burke physician] that, if it was alright for us to come down, he would put a sign out on his house, put a flag out. We didn't see any ... [so] after it got dark we sent two men down and they found out through the women, some of the women of the place, that they had arrested every man there was in the place and taken them to Wardner."

Orchard and several mates made for sanctuary across the Montana border, about forty miles due east. For a while, he holed up with a friend in the Bitterroot Valley, then went on to Butte, the bastion of mining labor and, at the time, the site of WFM headquarters. There he met briefly with Ed Boyce, the union's president. Boyce gave him a "withdrawal card" certifying that he'd been a member in good standing of the Burke local and in effect asking unionists to treat him as a brother.

For several years, Orchard drifted through mining and dairy jobs in Utah, Arizona, Idaho, and California. In July 1902, he found himself at Cripple Creek, Colorado, on the eve of the strike that would paralyze that community's mining industry. He joined the Free Coinage Union in neighboring

Altman, whose president was none other than Big Davis, the man who'd led the expedition to blow up the Bunker Hill and Sullivan mine in 1899.

Over the next three years, under the tutelage of Davis and of Sherman Parker, the union's financial secretary, Orchard launched his career as a union terrorist. His first job in November 1903—undertaken for a fee of five hundred dollars—was blowing up the Vindicator mine, an explosion that killed a superintendent and a shift boss. Six months later, he testified, he blew up the Independence depot, killing thirteen. Later, he said, he took his orders from Bill Haywood and George Pettibone, who assigned him to kill Governor Peabody, Justices Goddard and Gabbert, Fred Bradley, president of the Bunker Hill and Sullivan Company, and others. These assassination attempts failed for a variety of reasons. Judging from Orchard's testimony, his motivation was cloudy: a pinch of union loyalty, some anger at stiff-necked mine owners, a dollop of resentment against the scabs who took the strikers' jobs, and a big hunger for the money—two hundred to five hundred dollars a job —the union paid him for these bombings.

In the summer of 1905, Orchard testified, Haywood, Moyer, and Pettibone assigned him to kill Frank Steunenberg. They said that four other men —Steve Adams, two Cripple Creek miners named Art Baston and Ed Minster, and a man named McCarthy—had been sent to kill Steunenberg, but all had failed. Now they wanted him to try it. Haywood said, "Steunenberg has lived seven years too long." In return, they promised a fee of several hundred dollars and a ranch where he could retire from his life as a union killer.

Haywood had laid out the rationale behind the Steunenberg assassination:

> He said if we would get Governor Steunenberg after letting him go seven or eight years and then go back to Paterson, New Jersey, and write some letters from there to Mr. Peabody, Mr. Bell and Judge Goddard and Judge Gabbert and some of the mine owners that had been fighting the Federation, and tell them that they would get what Mr. Steunenberg got, that we hadn't forgot them, and that he thought if we wrote the letters from there to these men, if we got Mr. Steunenberg, and tell them they'd get the same as he got, it would be worse than death itself, it would be like a living death to think somebody was after them to kill them and didn't know who it was.

Moyer believed that the assassination would have "a good effect," that "it would scare the rest of these men" who opposed the WFM. Haywood described Steunenberg to Orchard, told him "what kind of a looking man he was, how he usually dressed, said he was engaged in the sheep business and he understood that he took a buckboard and drove out into the mountains." Though Haywood thought "it would not be hard to get" Steunenberg, Pettibone thought it would be "a very hard job down in a little country town like Caldwell was." They "talked a good deal on that," and about two days later he started for Idaho. There he teamed up with Jack Simpkins, the WFM board member responsible for Idaho. Reaching Caldwell, they checked into the Pacific Hotel, registering as "Thomas Hogan" and "J. Simmons." Lounging around town for several days, they finally found the governor at the Saratoga Hotel on the afternoon of November 6.

Quickly returning to their room at the Pacific, they assembled the bomb from the ingredients in Orchard's grip. It consisted of a wooden box about eight inches square and four inches high. In the box they packed ten pounds of "giant powder of dynamite" and about a hundred fulminating giant caps, over which they placed a piece of cotton saturated with cyanide of potassium and sugar. Slanting over the cotton was a bottle containing sulphuric acid sealed with a cork. In the cork was a pin, and attached to the pin was a piece of wire, the end of which was stretched across the footpath just outside the governor's residence about four inches off the ground. When the governor passed on his way to his garden gate, his foot would trip the wire, which would draw the cork from the bottle, discharging the acid, which, mixing with the saturated cotton, would cause the caps to ignite and explode the dynamite.

Quickly they raced to Steunenberg's residence, where they installed the bomb, then returned to the Pacific Hotel to wait. When, after an hour, they'd heard no explosion, they sidled past the gate and found that somehow the wire had snapped. Removing the bomb, they hid it in weeds and manure along the railroad tracks by the hotel.

That fiasco persuaded Simpkins he better not hang around Caldwell any longer. He'd recognized several men on the street the day before and was afraid they'd seen him. If Orchard was arrested, he said, it would go worse for him if Simpkins was taken with him. He left for Silver City, telling Orchard to finish the job alone.

That day Orchard checked out of the Pacific, finding a sunny front room in a boardinghouse run by Mrs. William H. Schenck at 1004 Cleveland Boulevard, about halfway between Steunenberg's house and the Christian Church. For several weeks, he tried to locate the governor, who seemed to be away much of the time. On November 22, Orchard left for Salt Lake City, where he hoped to find a friend who could help him with his assignment. But the friend wasn't there, so Orchard returned alone to Caldwell on December 13, checking into the Saratoga Hotel, registering once more as Thomas Hogan.

For the next few days, he tried to get a fix on the ex-governor's schedule. He didn't catch up with him until Christmas day, when he saw him with his family on his way to his brother A. K. Steunenberg's house for the holiday dinner.

"After it got dark, I went up to his residence and took a pump shotgun with me and thought I would try to shoot him when he was going home. . . . I was there an hour or so before I heard him coming home, and he come soon after I got up there but he got in the house before I got my gun together."

In Room 19 at the Saratoga, Orchard then fashioned a second bomb, nearly identical to the one he and Simpkins had made. He wrapped it in newspaper so that it looked like an innocuous parcel, and kept it in a drawer ready for instant use. He didn't find the governor out in public again until late on the afternoon of December 30. "I located him just before evening. I was in the saloon part of the hotel playing cards and I came out into the lobby and I seen Mr. Steunenberg sitting in the hotel talking to another man."

"Do you know who it was he was talking to?" asked Hawley.

"A man I think they called Mike Devers."

"Go on and state all you did from that time on, Mr. Orchard."

"I came out of the saloon and I went over to the post office and asked if there was any mail for me, and when I came back he was still sitting there. I went out and went up to his residence as fast as I could walk—as fast as I could go—and I placed [the bomb] at his gate in such a way that when the gate was opened it was fastened there with a string [actually a three-foot piece of fishing line] and it would explode the bomb.

"When I was going back about two blocks and a half farther returning towards the hotel I met Mr. Steunenberg and I ran as fast as I could to get back to the hotel and I was about a block and a half from the Saratoga Hotel on the footbridge when I heard it go off, and I hurried on to the hotel as fast as I could and went into the saloon part of the hotel first and met the bartender there and helped him tie up a little parcel he was trying to tie up, and then went up to my room. . . . I stayed there until the next day and Monday afternoon I was arrested and charged with the murder of Governor Steunenberg."

As Hawley began to wind up his direct examination of Orchard on June 6, rumors circulated of fierce differences within the defense camp about who would cross-examine this all-important witness. So precise, so unruffled, so convincing to many had been Orchard's presentation that the defense realized more than ever how critical would be the effort to break the self-confessed assassin's composure and open holes in his seamless account of WFM-sponsored murder and mayhem. Whoever succeeded in doing that would be the defense's star performer and, not surprisingly, both Darrow and Richardson coveted that role.

This wasn't the only point of friction. Defense attorneys as a rule have large egos, and in this flamboyant fraternity, Darrow and Richardson were known for their outsize self-regard. Both were accustomed to being lead lawyers, neither had ever voluntarily taken a backseat to anyone, and neither was about to do so now. "Two stars of the same magnitude cannot occupy the same orbit," the *Denver Post* announced portentously.

Their styles were in stark contrast. Though hostile to both men, the *Denver Republican*'s man at the trial captured part of the difference when he wrote: "Darrow, the loose-jointed, beetle-browed lawyer, [was] literally the antithesis of Richardson, the straight-backed, austere lawyer. . . . Richardson stood just as far from the jury as he could and spoke to them as if they were children and he the schoolmaster. Darrow got so close to the front row with his primitive features that the jurors could not conceal their discomfort, some their apparent disgust at such uncouth familiarity." Crane of the *Statesman* noted that, after Richardson's "fiery, fierce eloquence," Darrow's "plain, old-fashioned, easy, quiet manner . . . was resting, refreshing . . . [making] one think of the 'pie that grandmother used to make.' " Darrow thought Richardson was "an able man" but "lacking in subtlety."

Moreover, the two men clearly had political differences. Darrow was widely perceived as a Socialist, though the attorney insisted that he wasn't. But Darrow certainly shared many Socialist convictions and felt quite comfortable defending Socialists, while Richardson was a more conventional western Democrat with Free Silver leanings. "I don't sanction Socialism," he said, "at least not when it is coupled with the trying of a legal suit—especially when that case is a murder case and means a man's life. Preaching Socialism and trying a law case are entirely different matters."

In November 1906, their differences nearly led to Darrow's withdrawal from the case. The focus of this dispute was Darrow's investigator, George Dickson. On November 1, Richardson reminded Darrow that Dickson had become persona non grata with Charles E. Mahoney and James A. Kirwan, the WFM's acting president and secretary-treasurer, who wouldn't spend "another cent" on him. Conceding Dickson may have been blamed unfairly for what he'd said and done, Richardson demanded his dismissal.

Four days later, Darrow replied in heated defense of Dickson, charged that Richardson and Nugent were "prejudiced" against him, and said, "So far as my connection with the case is concerned, I would be glad to be relieved of it, excepting I feel that the men themselves may think I can do them some good. So long as they think so I must try the best I can that there shall be no friction." Richardson could dismiss Dickson "on [his] own account," but Darrow would not do so without "explicit orders from Moyer, Haywood and Pettibone."

Richardson's reply, which does not survive, was evidently very strong, for on November 9 Darrow wrote the prisoners in the Ada County jail, saying, "Under the circumstances I do not see how I can stay in the case. I certainly can not stay in it with the understanding that he [Richardson] is leading counsel and that he will give directions. I would not have undertaken the case on those terms in the first place, and can not do it now. The only thing I consider in this connection is its effect upon you. . . . I cannot yield my opinion as to what ought to be done to any one but you three men."

Evidently, the prisoners found a solution with which both jealous attorneys could live. It isn't clear precisely what the WFM leaders had against Dickson—or whether he stayed on the case in any substantial way. The union's records show he was paid through July 1906 but then received no more money until June 1907, when he got $1,535, which may have been a settlement for past salary and/or expenses.

But bitter differences persisted. One developed in early June when yet another lawyer joined the defense team. The Butte Miners Union, the WFM's largest constituent union, had engaged and fully paid for the services of Peter Breen, forty-six, an ex-miner and former inmate of the 1892 Coeur d'Alene bullpen who had served as prosecuting attorney of Silver Bow County (Butte), Montana, from 1900 to 1904 and was now a criminal attorney there. A renowned wit and storyteller, Breen was also known as a hothead (he was much closer politically to the Ed Boyce of the 1890s than he was to the moderate leadership of the Butte Miners Union, which makes his dispatch to Boise a bit of a mystery). When asked for his reaction after Steunenberg's assassination, he said, "Well, as J. M. Kennedy [a Butte labor leader] once remarked on a similiar occasion, 'You can't make a dead saint out of a live scoundrel,' and Frank Steunenberg was as loathsome a reptile as ever crawled the earth."*

When the florid, restless attorney took his seat at the defense table on June 2, Hugh O'Neill of the *Denver Post*—a hard-nosed Irishman if ever there was one—recognized in Breen "a potent, indomitable fighting man" with "muscular arms" and "threatening eyes." He sat in court "looking as if he wanted to jump into the fray and show the rest of them the only real way to fight the case." As to the rumor that Breen had been sent to Boise to reconcile the squabbling defense attorneys, O'Neill said he was "the kind of a man to reconcile a row by expeditiously knocking half the fighters on the head." Indeed, his presence only exacerbated tensions between the lawyers, Darrow welcoming him while Richardson openly snubbed him.

Darrow and Richardson tried, desultorily at times, to disguise their differences. Asked who was the lead defense attorney, Darrow told the *Statesman:* "There is no chief counsel on our side. We are all on equal footing." When Frank L. Perkins of the *Portland Evening Telegram* and Hugh O'Neill of the *Denver Post,* both friendly to the prosecution, refused to buy this story and wrote of the tensions on the defense team, Darrow and Richardson issued a statement contending that "at no time has there ever been any disagreement between us upon any point in the case we are trying," a disclaimer so sweeping it was widely ignored.† As Orchard's critical cross-examination neared, loud voices could be heard from behind closed doors in the conference room at the Overland Block.

Ultimately, Richardson—widely regarded as a tough, effective cross-examiner—simply seized the Orchard assignment by fiat, and Darrow, in a

---

* Borah sought to subpoena the reporter to whom Breen gave that interview, in hopes of putting him on the stand in Boise and thus underlining the implacable hostility of the WFM and its allies toward Steunenberg. Either he was unable to find him or he thought better of the idea (Borah to A. B. Keith, June 1, 1907).

† When it was all over, Darrow cut loose, telling the *Statesman* that Richardson was "very hard to get along with, ... very egotistical, arrogant and exceedingly jealous" and adding, "we never could travel double again" (*Idaho Daily Statesman,* August 2, 1907, 1).

gesture at collegiality, ceded the field to him. Over the next five days, Richardson proved every inch the fierce inquisitor. He lost no time emphasizing the seamiest sides of Orchard's character, showing him to be a womanizer who had run away with another man's wife, deserting his own wife and young daughter; a bigamist who had married a woman named Ida Toney in Colorado in June 1903 though still married to his first wife in Canada; a compulsive gambler who lost heavily at poker and roulette, leaving him with a persistent need for cash; a frequenter of low saloons, where he often drank to excess; a thief of ore; even a cheat at weighing cheese.

Richardson took special pains to emphasize the witness's indifference to the loss of human life. In revisiting the Vindicator mine bombing, he asked: "You expected to kill fifty or sixty men that night?"

"I did not know how many we would kill," Orchard replied.

"The more the merrier?"

"I did not think about that."

"And you did not care?"

"I don't know as I did."

"Just as soon kill a hundred men as one?"

"I was not thinking about that."

On cross-examination, Orchard testified to one abortive assassination attempt he hadn't mentioned on direct. It occurred on September 5, 1905, when Steunenberg made one of his frequent trips up to Boise and stayed, as usual, at the Idanha. Orchard followed with a bomb in his valise and, by sheer chance, was assigned a room adjacent to Steunenberg's. Using a skeleton key, he gained admission to the governor's room and decided to place his bomb under Steunenberg's bed, where it would be sure to blow him—and, with him, Boise's secular cathedral—to little pieces. But listening to the loud ticking of the clock, he got worried. "I thought it would be too risky . . . after having got a room next to him and then going away, I'd be apt to be suspected."

"That particular bomb would have blown the hotel all to pieces, would it not?" Richardson asked.

"Yes."

"And you were willing to do this?"

"Yes."

"Did you expect to stay in the hotel that night?"

"No, sir."

"You were willing to kill everybody but yourself?"

"Yes."

By the next morning, June 13, the cross-examination was winding down. On what promised to be his last crack at the assassin, Richardson now turned on him with a final assault of unusual ferocity.

"So you thought you could make your peace with the future by having someone else hanged, did you?" he asked in a harsh, angry voice.

Orchard trembled, his lips quivered, his body shook with sobs, and he reached for a handkerchief with which to stanch the tears.

"No, sir. No, sir," he stuttered, struggling to regain mastery of himself. "I had no thought of getting out of it, by laying it on anybody else. I began to think about my past life and the unnatural monster I had been.... It was after I received a Bible from a missionary society in Chicago that I came to the conclusion that I would be forgiven if I truly repented and I decided to make a clean breast of it all."

In those closing minutes, Richardson rang changes on a persistent theme of his cross-examination: that Orchard was a puppet at the end of a string held by the Great Detective himself. "I noticed that many times Mr. Hawley told you to go on in narrative form," he began. "Have you got this matter written up in narrative form?"

"I have got the history of my life written up."

And a minute later: "It was at Mr. McParland's suggestion that you prepared it?"

"No, sir."

"Did you ever hand one of your narratives to him that you had prepared?"

"I think I did."

"Yes, and hasn't he edited your narrative—gone over it and suggested that some things should be stricken and others put in?"

"No, sir."

"And haven't a good many of those changes which you have made been made with reference to making it so that it would connect up Moyer and Haywood with different transactions which you have been in?"

"No, sir."

"Mr. McParland has been the man who has been the mentor of your testimony at all times?"

"I don't know what you mean by that."

"The man who has been guiding and directing you as to how you should testify."

Orchard glared at Richardson for a moment and then, in a cold, even voice, said, "He has *not* been directing me."

Finally, on June 13, the twenty-six hours of cross-examination were over, widely regarded as a resounding failure. On balance, Orchard had stood up to Richardson's harsh grilling better than anyone would have predicted. Darrow, in a caustic aside to a reporter, said Orchard could think four times while Richardson was thinking once. At only one moment in that final day had the witness briefly lost his astonishing composure, and this in such a way that it well may have aroused the jury's sympathy. Christopher Powell Connolly of *Collier's,* himself a lawyer, concluded at the end of Orchard's stint on the witness stand that he was "the most remarkable witness that has ever appeared in an American court of justice."

Now, with the heart of their case before the jury, the prosecutors had to buttress it with as much corroboration as possible. Hopes of putting their one solid corroborative witness, Steve Adams, on the stand were fading, as Adams refused to revive his repudiated confession. On June 14, armed guards brought him into court briefly so a witness could identify him, but he seemed in such a "defiant humor" that he never appeared again.

Thus, Hawley and Borah had no choice but to fall back on a considerable mass of circumstantial evidence, which, seen together, they argued, would connect Haywood with Steunenberg's assassination. First came an effort to establish motive, to prove that Haywood so loathed the former governor of Idaho, as the author of the bullpen and other oppressive measures in the Coeur d'Alenes, that he might contemplate his murder.

Here the prosecutors relied on a series of articles that had appeared over the years in the *Miners' Magazine,* the official journal of the Western Federation of Miners. One of the first articles Bill Borah read into the record had been published in February 1900, before Haywood became an officer of the WFM, but it illustrated the rage many in the labor movement felt toward Steunenberg and his allies for the events of 1899. Written by Eugene Debs, it warned Steunenberg, General Merriam, and Bartlett Sinclair, "We have an account to settle with you." The outrages perpetrated by such men "in servile obedience to their mercenary masters will be remembered, and in good time they will find themselves in the pillory where every honest man can scorn them and every decent dog can bark at them."

Another article ran on the eve of Steunenberg's leaving office. "On the 10th of January, 1901," it read, "Frank Steunenberg, Governor of Idaho, will sink into obscurity from public view, where he shall forever lie buried, damned for the outrages he committed upon the workingmen of the Coeur d'Alenes.... Your ambition was money, which in your estimation was superior to honor, but you are gone and your political tombstone shall be inscribed in indelible words, 'Here lies a hireling and a traitor!' "

Later, the state introduced several articles that appeared in the magazine after Steunenberg's assassination. The magazine's first reaction in January 1906 was brief and sardonic: "Former Governor Frank Steunenberg of Idaho met his death last Saturday evening at his home at Caldwell, Idaho. The press dispatches report his dissolution via the bomb route." Another was a brief editorial reprinted from the *Western Clarion* that noted, "A chap by the name of Steunenberg was blown up the other day at Caldwell. He came into fame as the inventor of that revered institution known as the Bull Pen. The bomb had been carelessly left, presumably by some Russian revolutionist, in the gateway leading to the Steunenberg habitation. Such carelessness should be frowned on. The gate was completely wrecked."

But fulminations against Steunenberg, even sardonic satisfaction at his death, didn't prove an overt act, as part of a conspiracy, to bring that death about. Here the prosecutors fell back on a number of different acts—murders, bombings, holdups, and the like—that, seen as part of a pattern, might link Haywood to a conspiracy.

One was a letter postmarked Denver, and dated the very day Steunenberg met his death, that Orchard had received in the Canyon County jail at Caldwell. Although it was not signed, Orchard swore it was in Pettibone's handwriting. It read, in part: "Friend Tom—Your letter received. That was sent to Jack December 21 for you. He should send it so that you ought to have it by this time." According to Orchard, this referred to two hundred dollars that Jack Simpkins had sworn to secure from Pettibone when he left Caldwell for the north country.

Another was the letter from Robertson, Miller and Rosenhaupt in Spokane announcing that Fred Miller would start for Caldwell in the morning. Orchard had testified that on several occasions Haywood, Moyer, and Pettibone had told him that if ever he was arrested he shouldn't communicate with them, but they'd make sure an attorney reached him as soon as possible. Now Jasper Nichols, the former Canyon County sheriff, was called to establish that Orchard had sent no telegram or other message to Spokane summoning Miller. To some, this letter, and Miller's arrival at Caldwell shortly thereafter, was the strongest corroboration of Orchard's testimony about his dealings with Haywood. As this letter was introduced, Hawley turned to Richardson and asked pointedly if he knew when Miller would return from San Francisco, where he was gathering information on Orchard's alleged attempt on Fred Bradley's life.

"He will be here when he gets those depositions he went after," Richardson snapped, apparently resenting the implication—widely spread by the mainstream press—that the defense intended to keep Miller out of town as long as necessary to prevent the prosecution from calling him as a witness.

On June 21—after the prosecution called a Negro trader who swore he'd sold a horse and buggy to Orchard in June 1903 and had seen Haywood and Orchard riding in it together—Borah told the judge, "The State is ready to close its case."

The prosecution wasn't altogether pleased with its case. Seventeen witnesses had been sent home a few days before without having been called to the stand, because they didn't fit the state's pattern of evidence. Boise abounded with rumors that the prosecutors were dissatisfied with McParland and the Pinkertons. Borah, in particular, was said to be grumbling that he'd come into the case only because the Great Detective had assured him they'd have the corroboration they needed. Hawley insisted they had plenty. Borah wasn't so sure.

At this juncture, Ed Richardson rose to make just that point. It was the copybook argument that the prosecution's case didn't add up to enough evidence to convict the defendant. But this time, given Idaho's requirement for corroboration of a co-conspirator's testimony, the motion was more than routine.

"I would say to your honor," Richardson began, "that if Haywood were guilty of blowing up the Vindicator mine, which he is not; if Haywood were guilty of the attempt upon Gabbert, which he is not; if Haywood were guilty of the conspiracy on the life of Peabody, which he is not; if he killed Walley,* which he did not; if he killed Bradley, which he did not; even if all these things were true, which they are not—all this would be insufficient to convict him of a crime on the body of Steunenberg. These were all crimes committed in states other than the state of Idaho and this man Haywood stands charged only with a crime committed within the borders of the state of Idaho.

"We come therefore to the proposition—by whom does this man stand connected with the murder of Steunenberg except by the mouth of the man who sat in that witness chair and whose unsupported word is not worthy of belief by any living person?" To leave the case to an Idaho jury was "to leave it to passion and prejudice," when law should dispose of it now. "Here is a case that has fallen flat without Orchard and all the testimony falls to the ground without the aid of this foul fiend of crime, and this is all the Pinkertons can produce to us after more than a year of work. Your honor, this motion should be sustained."

When Richardson sat down after two and a half hours, Borah rose to argue against the motion. "If your honor please, the contention of the state in this case is that some years ago there was formed or grew up what we may call and what we should call a conspiracy.... It is only necessary to show, after we have shown the existence of a conspiracy, that some members of that conspiracy went to Caldwell and committed the crime, although every other member of the conspiracy might have been in Europe at the time." If the evidence showed the existence of a conspiracy, "every particle of evidence that tends to show the conspiracy tends also to corroborate the testimony of Harry Orchard."

The question before the court, Borah concluded, "is whether or not the state is correct that there was a general conspiracy and whether or not the evidence in this case tends to show that general conspiracy, and the defendant in this case as a member of that conspiracy."

As the parties looked to the judge for his ruling, Fremont Wood—stroking his clean-shaven chin—was in a quandary. As he later explained, he had listened with great care to Harry Orchard's testimony and "as merciless a cross-examination as was ever given a witness in an American court" and had concluded that Orchard was "speaking truthfully and without any attempt to misrepresent or conceal." Accepting Orchard's testimony, he leaned toward believing that Haywood was guilty. On the other hand, he didn't believe the state had presented sufficient corroboration to justify a guilty verdict.

Thus, he might ordinarily have granted the defense motion for a di-

---

* An innocent passerby killed by a bomb intended for Chief Justice William H. Gabbert of the Colorado Supreme Court.

rected verdict of not guilty were it not for the presence of his old partner, Edgar Wilson, on the defense team. From a strictly personal point of view, he attached "no importance" to Wilson's role in the case, but he was clearly worried about appearances.

Without explaining his reasoning—for Moyer and Pettibone remained to be tried—Wood brusquely rejected the defense motion. "The court is thoroughly satisfied that this case should be submitted to the jury," he said, ordering the defense to begin presenting its evidence in the morning.

12

QUARTET

WHEN ETHEL BARRYMORE checked into the Idanha on the morning of June 24, there was a "very strange atmosphere" in the lobby. It was "full of extraordinary-looking people," most of whom seemed to be armed. A big man shuffled over to introduce himself. "I was a great friend of your father's," he said. "My name's McParland. I'm a Pinkerton man."

"What's happening here?" she asked.

"Don't you know? This is the Haywood trial. The whole town is a fort."

McParland wanted to show her something in his room and the twenty-seven-year-old actress followed, full of gumption and curiosity. McParland lifted his mattress, revealing several Winchester rifles concealed beneath. "There are rifles under every mattress in the hotel," he proclaimed.

A chill skittered up Barrymore's spine, probably just what McParland had tried to provoke with his hyperbole. Thanking the detective—with whom she pronounced herself "wonderfully pleased"—she went to her suite, where her Swiss maid, Berthe, helped her dress for lunch with Calvin Cobb and his family.

Barrymore knew the publisher's daughter, Margaret, through mutual friends back East: Alice Roosevelt, the president's high-spirited daughter, and Ruth Hanna, the introspective child of the late Republican kingmaker, Mark Hanna. Ethel, Margaret, Alice, and Ruth—along with Eleanor Medill "Cissy" Patterson, daughter of the *Chicago Tribune's* editor—made up a remarkable circle of beauty and intelligence. Margaret, Ruth, and Alice were great talkers, downed gallons of iced coffee, and adored their "monkey act," in which they'd crouch on chairs, make simian faces, utter screeches, and gleefully pretend to pick lice off one another. That wasn't what the schoolmarms had tried to instill in Ruth, Cissy, and Margaret at Miss Porter's, the school in Farmington, Connecticut, devoted to the refinement of highborn young women. Alice had been educated by private tutors, while Ethel's schooling—at Philadelphia's Academy of Notre Dame—was truncated when she went on the stage at fourteen. Of them all, Cissy was the most dazzling: "Watch the way that girl moves," Theodore Roosevelt told his daughter as Cissy came down a reception line. "She moves as no one has ever moved before." We don't know what the president thought of Ethel, but when a cousin of his married a French actress, he wrote in his diary: "He is a disgrace to the family—the vulgar brute." The five young women had gone off in different directions, but they'd stayed in touch, passed friends and suitors around their circle, and determined to enjoy life while they were young and gay.

Barrymore stayed with Cissy and her husband, Count Gizycka, when she played Washington, dined with Ruth and her husband, Medill McCormick, in Chicago, and when she learned that her road company of *Captain Jinks of the Horse Marines* would make a one-night stand in Boise that June, wrote Margaret Cobb, who promptly invited her to lunch.

Up in her spacious suite, Barrymore put on her tan linen suit with its touch of turquoise on the collar and cuffs and, to top it off, a large black Milan straw hat trimmed with bird of paradise feathers—a hat, noted the *Statesman*'s society editor, "which, on anyone less beautiful, would have been most trying." Dabbing Atkinson's White Rose behind each ear, she was off in a horse-drawn cab to the Cobbs' elegant bungalow, the house where the secretary of war had spent the night eight months before.

To the president, Taft had described Margaret Cobb as "a bright society girl," which was about right. Scarcely a great beauty, at twenty-five she was petite, with dark eyes, long tapering hands, aristocratic bearing, and a sense of the ridiculous that echoed Barrymore's. So the actress felt right at home as she sat down in the Cobbs' dining room for a *déjeuner à quatre*, served by their Chinese manservant, Hong.

As Idaho's preeminent publisher and a presidential confidant, Calvin Cobb felt it was incumbent on him to frame the issues of the day for his guest. So he hurriedly briefed her on the trial under way down at the courthouse. More politically aware than most actresses—after all, she'd dined at the White House and breakfasted with Mark Hanna just across Lafayette Square —she was fascinated. This was a banner day at the trial, Cobb explained. The defense was calling Harry Orchard back to the stand for impeaching questions. The assassin? Barrymore exclaimed. Would she like to go? Cobb asked. Very much!

Though it was more crowded than it'd been for weeks, Cobb's man Harry Crane had found the publisher, his wife, and their guest places inside the rail. As they took their seats, they discovered that Harry Orchard wasn't on the stand after all. Clarence Darrow was opening for the defense. The defense attorney had reason to expect that all eyes in the courtroom would be on him that afternoon, as they'd been that morning. One can imagine his irritation when into the courtroom strolled one of America's most beautiful women. A. E. Thomas of the New York *Sun*, a prospective Broadway playwright, concluded that the actress had "divided with Mr. Darrow the attention of the spectators."

Nonetheless, Darrow put on quite a show. Oscar King Davis of the *New York Times* found it "a clever, striking performance . . . a shrewd forceful presentation of his case." Thomas thought it was "even brilliant at times and replete with those touches of sarcasm and irony of which the Chicago lawyer is such a master."

Darrow began with some fine sport at Jim Hawley's expense. "It's the Western Federation that's on trial here," he said. In fact, it was right downstairs, where the three defendants were incarcerated, that the great federation had been formed. "Of course," he said with a broad smile, gesturing toward Hawley, "they had to have an attorney. They did the best they could [laughter]. They hired Mr. Hawley [louder laughter]—the man who is now taking the leading role in the prosecution of these men; he counselled them and advised them regarding this new organization . . . the organization he is now trying to kill.

Much of Darrow's address was a systematic effort to strip Harry Orchard of his mystique, portraying him as "this leper," "this shoestring gambler," "the most monstrous liar the world has ever seen." Darrow sought to rehabilitate the WFM, painting it as a genuine labor organization unfairly saddled with a reputation for violence. "We propose to show you that every illegitimate child of violence that has been born west of the Missouri river since 1895 has been done up in swaddling clothes and rushed off to Butte or Denver to be deposited on the doorstep of the Western Federation of Miners headquarters," he said.

Barrymore followed Darrow closely but distrusted his slick performance. She recalled later: "He had all the props: an old mother in a wheelchair and a little girl with curls draped around Haywood"; she found herself wondering whether Henrietta was even Haywood's daughter. The actress *was* enormously impressed by the jury, "the most wonderful-looking men I've ever seen. They were all ranchers with the bluest eyes, like sailors' eyes, used to looking at great distances. They made me think of Uncle Sam as Uncle Sam ought to look without the goatee. They were magnificent."* Even their names implied honesty, she thought. "Often there's a touch of dishonesty in a jury, you know, a 'fixing' thing, but it is not so with these men. It will be an awful blow to organized labor if they convict Mr. Haywood."

Delighted to have one of America's leading actresses in his courtroom, Judge Wood adjourned early to host an impromptu reception in his chambers. Among those in attendance were Darrow, Richardson, Hawley, Borah, Charlie Siringo, Sheriff Hodgin, the Cobbs, some of the leading press "boys," and two other visitors: S. S. McClure of *McClure's Magazine,* in town on a mission for his magazine, and Gifford Pinchot, the chief forester of the United States,

---

* An awful lot of nonsense was written about this "great American jury." The very same day that Barrymore was in the courtroom, Hugh O'Neill of the *Denver Post* wrote: "The twelve jurymen trying this case are essentially and altogether Western men. They are frontiersmen, hard-bitten in the life of the frontier . . . men of their hands, sun-baked, hard-gripped, deep-bitten men, small ranch owners mostly, who thought for themselves and believe above everything in the individual freedom of individual Americans" (*Denver Post,* June 24, 1907, 1).

who'd arrived in Boise that very morning on a tour of western forests. Barrymore had sat next to Pinchot that afternoon and found him "dreamy-
looking." Whether she meant that he was wonderfully tall and lithe—as he
was—or that he seemed to be focusing on some far-off woodsy realm—
which he often did—isn't entirely clear.

Another sinewy figure had been watching Barrymore that day. Slim and
darkly mustachioed, Charlie Siringo was a congenital romantic who enjoyed
considerable success with the ladies; his memoirs are spiced with occasions
on which "Little Cupid shot my system full of darts." Fifty-two years old, his
boyish countenance stained brown as saddle leather, he was still a natty
dresser. A photograph taken during the trial showed him decked out in a
well-tailored suit and a narrow-brimmed Stetson, a boutonniere blooming in
his lapel, a stickpin piercing his silk cravat, his left hand grasping a carved
walking stick, in which he concealed a twenty-inch throwing knife, his right
curled around an engraved silver-plated Colt .45. Holding the pistol at his
right hip and fanning the hammer with his other hand, it was said, he could
put six shots in a pattern two inches wide from thirty feet away. Between
wives at the time, though engaged to an Oregon girl he'd soon marry, he
was interested less in combat than in romance. Beneath his neatly trimmed
mustache twitched a mischievous smile.

In the drowsy heat of that summer afternoon, Siringo couldn't keep his
eyes off Barrymore. At the reception, he approached her to confess himself a
dedicated fan. Once she smiled that devastating smile, he was "kneeling at her
feet, figuratively speaking." He'd heard she was disappointed at not seeing
Harry Orchard. Yes, she'd set her heart on that. Well, said Siringo, it wouldn't
be easy—no one except officers of the court, Pinkerton detectives, and guards
were supposed to see him—but perhaps it could be arranged, assuming she'd
"act her part."

"I had learned," Siringo recalled, "that all men, no matter how old, have
a weak spring in their make-up, which can be snapped asunder by fair women,
if they only go at it right. Of course I hated to put up a 'job' on [McParland],
but who wouldn't to make a pretty girl happy?" Siringo took Barrymore back
to the Idanha. "The play started when the young actress moved her chair
close up to the gentleman, so that she could look him in the face. When the
one-act drama was over we all started in a carriage for the penitentiary."

By then, "all" included Siringo, Barrymore, Fannie Cobb, S. S. McClure,
and the "dreamy" Mr. Pinchot. They met Orchard in the back room of
Warden Whitney's office, the very room in which McParland had taken his
confession. Ethel thought he looked like "a respectable grocer . . . very polite
and quiet."

"I've heard a lot about you, Miss Barrymore," said the assassin.

"I've heard a certain amount about you," she replied.

They chatted about the theater and journalism; the warden wouldn't let
them discuss the case itself. That didn't stop Barrymore from rhapsodizing to

a Spokane reporter two days later: "I don't see how [Orchard] could have done such things as he claims he did and look the way he does. I don't see how he could have kicked a dog and have the look he has out of his eyes. Why, I was as close to him as I am to you. He has the most straightforward look and can give you glance for glance.... Of the two men, Orchard and Haywood, the former is by far the better and cleaner looking man. I shuddered when I looked at Haywood."

Before long, it was time for Barrymore to get back to town and prepare for the evening's performance. No passerby glimpsing her willowy figure breezing in the stage door of the Columbia Theater could have guessed that this captivating creature was suffering a cruel bout of depression.

All spring, Barrymore had brooded on the quagmire of her career. It wasn't that she lacked for roles. Her producer, Charles Frohman, had kept her hopping those past months at the Empire Theater, that "aristocrat of all New York theaters," on West Fortieth Street. Starting in February, she'd done the *Captain Jinks* revival, played the charwoman Mrs. Jones in John Galsworthy's *The Silver Box*, the adventuress Jessie Milward in Robert Marshall's *His Excellency the Governor,* and in May taken on the title role of Hubert Henry Davies's sentimental *Cousin Kate.*

No, it wasn't her billing or her leading men, the usual complaints of headline actresses, but the vacuous plays Frohman kept putting her in—what one critic called "invariably pretty, delicate dramatic watercolors, but of no actual account, save to display her personality to the best possible advantage." She wanted to play Lady Teazle in Sheridan's *The School for Scandal,* which she thought "the finest comedy ever written," or an ancient Greek drama, or a modern adaptation, like Racine's *Phèdre,* at Berkeley's Greek Theater. She'd begged Frohman to let her play Shakespeare's heroines—Beatrice, Juliet, above all Rosalind in *As You Like It.* But he wouldn't hear of it. He didn't care much for Shakespeare. The American theater's most successful producer, with ten thousand employees, an annual payroll of $35 million, and a record of producing some of the world's finest playwrights, Frohman hadn't built his empire by catering to the whims of his darling ingenues.

When he let her play the charwoman in Galsworthy's play, critics were incredulous. "Why on earth so pretty and clever a girl as Miss Ethel Barrymore wants to waste her time and talent and throw her beauty into entire eclipse by playing the role of the downtrodden cockney charwoman is beyond comprehension," said the *Sun.* "It represents just the sort of thing which people go to the theater to get away from." When he allowed her some matinees as Nora in Ibsen's *A Doll's House,* her public revolted. "Let those who are fond of issues of discordant and nightmarish problem plays hack away at Ibsen's 'messages'—those awful questions of sex and madness and disquieting stage discussions," wrote a group of her admirers. "For the love of those who love you as a woman, and not as a streak of feminine perversion, leave Mr. Ibsen alone—completely, now and evermore."

Critics and audiences preserved, as if stamped on a cameo, an image of the Ethel Barrymore they idolized: "that winsome slip of a fascinating girl," that "belle ideal of the Gibson girl," that "crowned and sceptred, adulated and adored, queen of the high joint lands of Bohemia and Smartdom." Her kittenish giggles, the petulant tosses of her ash-brown hair, the widening of her enormous blue eyes, her "voice of coo and her air of wheedle," that languid, husky, breathless drawl with which, in a play called *Sunday*, she'd delivered her memorable exit line, "That's all there is, there isn't any more" —all these endearing mannerisms had made her father, the matinee idol Maurice Barrymore, exclaim to the playwright Augustus Thomas: "My God, isn't she sweet!" and led the American public to take this radiant Anglo-Saxon beauty to their hearts, cherishing her as "our Ethel, the American girl."

Her very popularity threatened to strangle her. Tabloid reporters invented romances where none existed, demonstrating their ingenuity at keeping her on page 1 ("Miss Barrymore Sees Vessel Sink" was the headline when, aboard a yacht, she watched a passenger liner go under). Even the left, usually scornful of commercial theater, loved her. William Mailly, the Socialist Party's former national secretary and now the theater critic for the New York *Worker*, while deploring the fluff she played in, extolled her "personality that has heart and soul behind it, and that gets over the footlights no matter what sort of part she plays." But Barrymore wanted desperately to slip from her admirers' embrace and plumb her dramatic depths.

Her ambitions were large: to follow the path of the remarkable Barrymore-Drew family, the aristocracy of the American stage—specifically, to achieve the comic skills of her actress mother, Georgie Drew Barrymore, the suavity of her uncle John Drew, the consummate artistry of her grandmother, Louisa Lane Drew. There was plenty of competition from her brothers—Jack would go on to fame as John Barrymore, while Lionel was a skilled character actor. In his youth, Lionel hadn't been so sure about a theatrical career but never breathed his misgivings to Ethel, for "to doubt the sacredness of the theater arts in the presence of Ethel Barrymore would have been comparable to the impiety of demeaning Holy Writ in the presence of a nun."

The question bedeviling her that spring—as one writer put it—was "whether this young woman is to be permanently cursed by the insatiable desire of her chocolate-cream following for theatrical goo-goo." Her dilemma was scarcely unique. Sarah Bernhardt once said acting—making up, emoting, yielding to the audience—was a feminine craft. In the winter of 1906–07, the leading figures at the nation's box offices were almost all women: Maude Adams (the top money earner), Mrs. Nat Goodwin (the runner-up), Lillian Russell, Olga Nethersole, Minnie Maddern Fiske, Amelia Bingham, Annie Russell, Henrietta Crosman. But little artistry was demanded of them. Audiences loved a pretty girl "with dreamy eyes, spun gold hair and peach-glow complexion," wrote one critic. "If to these qualities she adds even the semblence of talent, temperament and personal magnetism, she is, indeed, gifted by the Gods."

If her pigeonhole was claustrophobic, Barrymore's misery went deeper still. She'd been a darling of society on two continents. In her native Philadelphia, she was taken up by Mrs. Alexander Van Rensselaer; in Chicago, she was a belle of Mrs. Marshall Field's balls; in New York, she lunched at the Waldorf's Palm Room with her friends Frances Rosengarten and Dora Harris (they called the Waldorf the Habit because they were there so often). In London, she dined with the duke and duchess of Connaught, charmed the painter James Whistler, and waltzed with Lord Kitchener. Upon her roll of suitors were emblazoned the duke of Manchester, the earl of Ava, Sir Robert Peel, Charles Devalen Wetmore, and Prince Kumar Shri Ranjitsinhji (unable to pronounce that, she called him Prince Ragtime). She'd been engaged to two well-placed men—Laurence Irving, son of England's leading actor-manager, and Gerald Du Maurier, the son of the novelist George Du Maurier —but had broken off with both. Winston Churchill had proposed marriage several times, but he didn't stir her the way he would the British electorate.

Lionized by the best people, she couldn't abide it. To a reporter, she said: "We have to eat luncheon and dinner, don't we? What difference whether one eats alone or in company?" Of high-society gatherings, she said: "I am bored to death.... I don't know what to talk about."

A reporter who visited her apartments overlooking Bryant Park found them "not in the least like those of other favored actresses." The most imposing furniture was a grand piano—once she'd dreamed of being a concert pianist—on which she played Sibelius and Liszt. An easel displayed her sketches. Her bookcases were stocked with Blake, Keats, Whitman, Poe, Henry and William James. She "worshipped" Mark Twain, who was always nice to her; she adored Henry James, who thought she was "rather Gothic." She craved to be taken seriously.

Her unhappiness had manifested itself on stage in episodes of vertigo. Sometimes, she fainted in midscene, the curtain ringing down until she could be revived with smelling salts. In Boston in 1905, an interviewer concluded: "That Miss Barrymore is ill there is no doubt...her face has got a bit haggard. Her eyes are dimmed. The languor that has characterized her every movement is more pronounced." Her physician advised a long rest. Barrymore hinted that she was preparing to quit the theater—perhaps to return as an operatic alto. She even hated her name, wishing to be called Daphne instead.

The critic Burns Mantle captured her mood: "The world is a dark blue and nothing seems worthwhile. The New York play reviewers are determined to ruin her career, there is nothing to be gained in doing one's best, no one appreciates her sincere efforts to succeed and—in a word—nobody loves her. If Miss Ethel were to analyze her mood she would likely discover that she is not really at outs with the world, or with the critics, or with society. She is disappointed in herself."

Though Barrymore's problem seemed to lie with her producer, he was only part of it. For Frohman was a prime mover in the so-called Theatrical Syndicate, which by 1907 had a stranglehold on the American theater—much as the great smelter trust did in the mining industry.

Until the late nineteenth century, American theatrical production was in the hands of resident repertory companies in cities as diverse as Boston, New Orleans, and San Francisco. But as railroads spanned the continent, one could move entire productions—cast, crew, sets, and costumes—by train from city to city. By century's turn, American repertory companies had largely atrophied as the era of the American theatrical road got under way. A play would show in New York for a month or two, but the big money wasn't made in Gotham. It was out on the road, in a succession of one- or two-night stands that went on until the cast dropped from exhaustion.

Some companies had toured the land even before the railroads. Joe Jefferson went trouping with his father in 1838 by wagon and boat: "We traveled from Galena to Dubuque on the frozen river in a sleigh. A warm spell had set in. We would sometimes hear the ice crack under our horse's feet; now a long-drawn breath of relief as we passed some dangerous spot, then a convulsive grasping of our nearest companion as it groaned and shook beneath us." Sol Smith and his company set off down the Allegheny River in two skiffs, the young men going first, "with the understanding that if they came to a town worth 'taking' they were to leave a flag flying on the bank of the river as a signal that . . . they had made arrangements to perform there."

The all-time favorite of the American road was an adaptation of *Uncle Tom's Cabin*, first performed in Troy, New York, in 1852. It was a landmark because it finally brought into all those opera houses the religious folks who'd been waiting for something truly "uplifting" to justify their presence in "the devil's chapel." Actors who played "the Tom Show" often did nothing else and were called "Tommers." Before the show, they paraded down Main Street in full regalia: Simon Legree, flicking his bullwhip; Topsy, making pickaninny faces; gray-haired Uncle Tom and sweet Little Eva; a few scruffy mongrels playing bloodhounds. So popular was the Tom Show it played somewhere in the land for ninety consecutive years. Churchgoers were further accommodated by two dramas on the demon rum: *The Drunkard* and *Ten Nights in a Barroom*. By then the pious folk were hooked.

The next gargantuan road hit belonged to James O'Neill—Eugene's father—playing Edmond Dantès in Alexandre Dumas's swashbuckling romance, *The Count of Monte Cristo*. O'Neill opened it in New York in February

1883, where it ran for a month, then went on tour. After a year the producer sold it to O'Neill for $2,000, little guessing that he would tour it for a quarter century, play Edmond more than six thousand times, and earn $800,000.

Soon he wearied of the role. By 1887, the play had deteriorated into "a bit of coarse theatricalism, that pleases only the more ignorant of theatregoers." O'Neill tried to escape *Monte Cristo* but kept returning because nothing earned the way it did. Bijou Fernandez, his costar, recalled, "We almost died doing it. I don't know where they found all those cities."

One city they found was Wallace, Idaho, where O'Neill encountered something more lethal than ennui. At the Masonic Opera House one night in 1904, a miner named William Cuff violated the law by smoking a cigar. A deputy ordered him to stop and, when Cuff persisted, yanked the cigar out of his mouth. Cuff stormed from the theater, borrowed a Winchester, and laid in wait outside. When a doctor left, Cuff shot him dead. In the ensuing panic, Officer William Quinn killed Cuff with a shot in the head. Three years later, Deputy Carson Hicks would kill Quinn with a bullet through the chest.

When audiences tired of *Monte Cristo*, O'Neill took it on a vaudeville circuit, preserving his sanity "by never drawing a sober breath until the tour had terminated." He knew that in his lust for money he'd destroyed himself as an actor. When he'd played the role 5,678 times, a reporter asked why he kept touring it. "Well," said O'Neill, "because I cannot get rid of the cursed thing. . . . Edmond Dantès is the old man of the sea around my neck. I have carried him twenty-five years, but he won't let go."

Even in shorter stints, the road could be grueling. In the 1860s, one young actress on a trip from Louisville to Nashville was ill all the way from "the ceaseless jolting, the stifling fumes from the stove, the nauseating hawking and spitting, and 'greasy sweat' that pervades the cars." Since they had to be on time for trains, players stayed at hotels near the station, invariably the worst in town. Though auditoriums were often splendid in cream and gold, backstage was a fetid warren.

Rose Eytinge recalled the evening a manager took her to Alexandria, Virginia, to play *East Lynne:* "The entrance to the theater was down a dimly lighted sequestered street, where our footsteps echoed with a melancholy sound. . . . Oh! the dust. It was like the tomb of a mummy at Thebes or Karnak. . . . Only one gentleman in the stalls and two or three boys in the three-penny gallery."

By 1896, more than three hundred "legitimate" road companies crisscrossed the land, with another hundred or so vaudeville, burlesque, or variety shows playing the cheaper circuits. Now the flourishing road tradition led to a revolution in theatrical organization. Originally, dapper straw-hatted managers of local theaters came to New York each summer to negotiate with dozens of producers for "attractions" and dates, haggling like Arabs at the bazaar. But trusts were breaking out all over in steel, oil, railroads, even typewriters and sewing machines. It was inevitable that theatrical producers would join forces, too, bringing "order" to their industry, wringing from the stage every penny it would yield, aggravating the quarrel between capital and labor. This is what happened in 1896 when six theatrical magnates—Abe Erlanger and Marc Klaw, who controlled most of the South; Charles Frohman, the leading producer, who also booked for a chain of western theaters; Sam Nixon and J. Fred Zimmerman, who controlled the Philadelphia stage; and Alf Hayman, who had western theatrical properties—gathered for lunch at New York's Holland House. Before long, they created a syndicate that controlled production at seven hundred theaters from Bangor to San Diego.

Booking was handled by Klaw and Erlanger, whose kingpin was Abraham Lincoln Erlanger, a plump Buddha who got his start in a Cleveland box office and now relished the title of "the theatrical Napoleon." His office was adorned with likenesses of the Little Corporal and, not infrequently, he'd strike a Napoleonic pose, hands clasped behind him, a dark scowl on his face. Erlanger had nearly as many enemies as Napoleon: he was famed for the brusque dismissal of petitioners, an icy indifference toward the rest of mankind. When a theatergoer complained about the two-dollar price for an orchestra seat, he wrote back in full: "In answer to your letter of the 11th, we would suggest that you borrow a dictionary and look up the word 'impertinence.' "

In contrast, his partner, Marc Klaw, formerly a Louisville lawyer, was thin, almost cadaverous, and a "natural diplomatist, suave and easy in his converse with men." Managers from the hinterland who'd been pulverized by Erlanger's imperious edicts could be rehabilitated by Klaw's unctuous attentions.

Each man, in his own manner, was out for the same thing: utter domination of the American stage. This the pair achieved through an elaborate protocol of quid pro quos. If a theater manager wanted one of the syndicate's prime attractions, he had to take a bunch of clinkers as well, each house on the circuit compelled to sign at least thirty weeks of productions from September through May. But while house managers were utterly dependent on Klaw and Erlanger, the producers needed the syndicate just as badly, for the only way a cross-country tour of major cities became economically feasible was to book an unbroken skein of one-night stands in between, and even if a producer managed to find a nonsyndicate house in New York and San Francisco there was no way for him to garner the Omahas and Harrisburgs, whose theaters were, if not owned outright by the syndicate, then invariably under an exclusive operating agreement. To producers, managers, and actors alike —as Norman Hapgood put it—the syndicate's message was: "Nominally, we act as your agents. In reality, we are your absolute masters."

A few stars held out by booking themselves independently. They formed the Association for the Promotion and Protection of an Independent Stage in America, headed by the Shakespearean actor Richard Mansfield, who gave impassioned curtain speeches denouncing the trust (until theater owners, under heavy pressure from K and E, ordered the fire curtain dropped to cut him off). The comedian Francis Wilson said: "A number of speculators have [the theater] by the throat.... We are in the hands of the enemy, God Help Us!" Ethel's father, Maurice Barrymore, helped form another dissenting group, called the White Rats ("star" spelled backwards). As he went mad from terminal syphilis, his war cry became "Death to the syndicate!"

Among the holdouts were two strong women, France's legendary Sarah Bernhardt and the beloved Minnie Maddern Fiske, "the first lady of the American stage." Bernhardt announced an American farewell tour in 1906, but since she wouldn't play ball with him, Erlanger banned her from syndicate houses. So the divine Sarah performed in primitive facilities across the land. In Dallas, she played Camille for eight thousand Texans in a huge tent rented from Barnum and Bailey and erected in a cornfield. In Houston, she performed at a skating rink.

The syndicate despised Mrs. Fiske and her husband and manager, Harrison Grey Fiske, who was also editor-publisher of the *Dramatic Mirror*, which railed against the syndicate's "greed, cunning and inhuman selfishness." On the syndicate's behalf, Alf Hayman warned him, "I'll kill the Mirror, break you, and drive Mrs. Fiske from the stage." The Fiskes fought back, Minnie charging that the syndicate had "killed art, worthy ambition and decency," her husband knocking Erlanger down on the street.

It didn't escape the critics that the syndicate's founders were all Jewish, and a few opponents retaliated with anti-Semitic screeds, aimed principally at Klaw and Erlanger. Chief among the Jew baiters was James S. Metcalfe, the drama editor of *Life* (a magazine unconnected to the one launched years later by Henry Luce). "They are not Jews of the better class, certainly not descendants of the poets, prophets and mighty warriors of Israel," he wrote in 1904. "In their veins runs the blood of Fagin, Shylock and the money-changers who were scourged from the temple.... The two Jews are well clad and have the toad-like appearance which comes from gross feeding." *Life* ran a cartoon, drawn by Metcalfe, ghoulishly depicting a bloated Erlanger in front of Chicago's Iroquois Theater as it went up in flames. The Iroquois, the syndicate's Midwest flagship, had been destroyed in a 1903 fire that killed eighty-seven people, principally because of blocked fire exits. Klaw and Erlanger sued *Life* for libel and banned Metcalfe from all forty-seven New York theaters under their control.

That year, the syndicate engaged in some rearguard skirmishing with an upstart team of New York producers and theater owners, Sam, Lee, and J. J. Shubert. On May 11, Sam Shubert was on his way to Pittsburgh to regain control of a house they'd lost to the syndicate when his train sideswiped a work train filled with blasting powder. Twenty-two persons, Sam among them, died in the explosion. J.J. arrived in time to hear his brother's last words, an excoriation of Abe Erlanger for doing him in.

In 1907, the Shuberts appeared at last to be caving in before the syndicate through a "working agreement" that added twenty-three of their fifty theaters to the trust's network. But Sam's last words still rang in their ears, and before long, open warfare resumed between the Shuberts and the syndicate.

Abe Erlanger once said: "I like Maude Adams in Peter Pan, Julia Marlowe in Twelfth Night and Ethel Barrymore no matter what she does." But the syndicate maximized profit by keeping stars of Barrymore's magnitude in vehicles producing the largest possible revenue. In 1907, that meant something by Clyde Fitch, Broadway's most commercial playwright.

A slender young man-about-town, Fitch sported a black guardsman's mustache, smoked gold-tipped cigarettes, sipped café au lait, wore spats and English hats, and never put on the same suit twice. He lived alone in a Manhattan brownstone embellished by marble statues of Cupid and Adonis. To some, he had "the facade of a dandified ass." But he had an ear for the social twitter of the turn-of-the-century smart set and was just risqué enough to titillate his constituency. The sound of a Fitch play was captured in a ditty by a man from the *Sun:*

> *Swat,*
> *And out of the glittering social grot*
> *Of the very Fitchiest, fetchingest lot,*
> *Stirred in the scorching society pot,*
> *Hot,*
> *He plucks a wild, weird name and plot;*
> *Whiz!*
> *Through all the scenic mysteries,*
> *The gayly appareled fantasies*
> *Likewise the dramatic unities,*
> *He shoves his pen until he makes it sizz,*
> *Biff!*
> *Act I,—Act II,—Act III, as if*
> *The thing were a cigarette to whiff.*
> *Slambang!*
> *The word goes out to the Broadway gang;*
> *Hooray!*
> *Clyde Fitch has written another play."*

Some critics discerned a satirical edge to his work. In the guise of celebrating the fashionable ladies of his era—they said—he applied "an occasional flick of the lash" from a "silken, perfumed whip," suggesting how vacuous these gentlewomen were. Perhaps. But his society audience took his works at face value.

Dramas spewed from his typewriter as fast as producers could mount them. In London during 1900, he began work on the airiest of comedies, described in a letter to a friend: "Thank goodness next sunday I sail for home. I am home sick (which, after all, isn't so bad as being tummy sick!) And I bring a brand new play (PURE, too!) finished. I don't think even the *World* or *Journal* could blush at this play. At the same time I hope it is very amusing. I have called it (so far) 'Captain Jinks of the Horse Marines'; you may know the song."*

Set in New York in 1872, Fitch's "fantastic comedy in three acts" tells the slight tale of Aurelia Johnson from Trenton, New Jersey, who takes on the persona of Madame Trentoni, an operatic prima donna who is "quite the most lovely creature that ever came, like Venus Aphrodite, from the sea!" Returning to her native land aboard a Cunard liner, she is serenaded on the wharf by three young dandies, among them Captain Robert Carrolton Jinks of the Horse Marines, a former Confederate officer from Virginia who—on a lark—wagers a thousand dollars he'll make love to her. They fall in love for real; she learns of the "scandalous bet" and calls the whole thing off; with a siege of flowers, he wins her back.

Fitch wanted a more experienced comedienne to play Madame Trentoni, but Frohman insisted on Barrymore. She worked like crazy and eventually Fitch became her most determined champion, even rewriting sections— for example, the reporters' hounding of the visiting star—to echo Barrymore's own experience.

On January 7, 1901, the play opened in Philadelphia to mixed reviews, including one that began, "If the young lady who plays Madame Trentoni had possessed beauty, charm or talent, this play might have been a success...." Barrymore was devastated and still hadn't recovered by February 3, when the play began its New York engagment at the Garrick. In an "agony of terror," she vomited. The theater was packed with first-nighters, friends, and family. She couldn't fail now.

Knowing that many New Yorkers didn't yet believe the youngest Barrymore was an actress, Fitch wrote just the exchange to disarm them. "But you are an actress?" asks the captain's mother. "There seems to be some question about that," says Madame Trentoni. When Barrymore spoke that line with charming modesty, the first-nighters shrieked with laughter, entirely won over.

Back at Mrs. Wilson's rooming house on Thirty-sixth Street, she sat up waiting for the reviews. There was a bit of everything. The *Tribune's* William Winter, the most celebrated critic of his time, dismissed her as "a juvenile performer, still in the experimental stage." The *Times* thought she'd bear watching. But the man from the *Sun* came through with the encomium for which she'd yearned, finding her "the full equal of Georgie Drew Barrymore." It was the happiest day of her life, she told an interviewer. A few days later, turning the corner, she saw her name in bulbs on the marquee. At last, she was

---

* It was an English music hall ballad of the 1860s—one of the so-called silly-ass songs—written and popularized by a London comedian named William Lingard. It began: "I'm Captain Jinks of the Horse Marines / I often live beyond my means / I sport young ladies in their teens / To cut a swell in the Army" (Spaeth, *Weep*, 208).

a bona fide star, "the newest princess of our footlit realm." The comedy team of Joe Weber and Lew Fields paid her their highest compliment by staging a parody of the play at their music hall. *Jinks* ran at the Garrick for seven months, and when it was finished there, Barrymore led a road company touring the East and Midwest.

Grateful to Fitch for writing her first real hit, she was ambivalent about his work. When other playwrights failed her, she turned back to him. "If you breathe one word of this, ALL is over between us," she confided in 1906. "I hear, on what is known as 'very good authority,' that the play written for me by one Englishman is not to the good.... Now, Clyde, I would give an awful lot if you would write me another wonderful part. There's no one like you— you know—& I know so well you'd do me another great turn.... Do come in here & let us converse madly."

Yet in 1907, she told a reporter that "parts like the lead in 'Captain Jinks' are very nice and pretty and pleasant" but wondered if it wouldn't be even nicer to do something grown up. She knew full well what the most demanding critics thought of Fitch: William Winter had called *Jinks* a "silly, farcical, trivial play," while the *Sun* dismissed it as "fluff and frivol." But it produced huge revenues, so Frohman kept reaching for more Fitch—first a revival of *Jinks*, then in spring and summer a western tour covering the territory they hadn't reached in 1902.

Barrymore and her company of twenty-six kicked off the tour at the Atheneum Theater in Jackson, Michigan, on May 20, 1907, then proceeded west to Battle Creek, Grand Rapids, and Kalamazoo. Battle Creek's Post Theater advertised itself as "Absolutely Safe—28 Exits," attempting to defuse the anxiety still lingering from the Iroquois disaster. The audience was "enraptured." The next night, in Grand Rapids, a critic was surprised to find that "Miss Barrymore did not suffer loss of charm by the wearing of the old fashioned raiments" but thought Bruce McRae as Captain Jinks "somewhat cold in his love-making."

In Kalamazoo, the tour began to click. At the final curtain, the "fashionable, intelligent, appreciative" audience filling the Academy of Music gave Barrymore eight curtain calls—"real, genuine, heartfelt outbursts of applause"—at which "Our Ethel tripped into the limelight" and stuttered, "I— I thank you; but I can't make a speech," a comment so charmingly inadequate that it "brought forth another whirlwind of hand clapping." The *Kalamazoo Gazette* noted that "no actress in recent seasons has so absolutely captivated the theatergoers of this city."

The next night in South Bend, Indiana, things took a turn for the worse. Barrymore was bothered by a head cold precipitated by the contrast between sultry New York and Michigan's chill rains. A doctor warned of its escalating to pneumonia. Barrymore got through the performance, but the tour manager, Robert Eberle, knew she wouldn't make it the next night in Springfield, Illinois. The company headed for Chicago, where Barrymore was installed in a suite at the Auditorium Hotel. (The caste system of the road guaranteed a star the best accommodations in town, while the rest of the cast dispersed to cheaper hotels like the Bismarck and the Briggs House or to theatrical boardinghouses. Many hotels declined to take minor players, still considered part of the demimonde.)

Barrymore stayed in bed all weekend and on Monday her doctor felt the danger of pneumonia had passed. But he and a consulting physician believed she was now suffering a nervous breakdown, requiring another week's rest. Eberle canceled appearances in Peoria, Illinois; Des Moines, Davenport, Cedar Rapids, and Sioux City, Iowa; and Lincoln, Nebraska.

Seemingly recovered from whatever had ailed her, Barrymore picked up the shreds of her tour in Omaha on June 3 and 4. The next night, in St. Joseph, Missouri, a critic thought that "owing perhaps to her recent illness, there was a delicate, fragile touch which made the character even more appealing." The company played Kansas City; Denver; Pueblo, Colorado; and Cheyenne, Wyoming, before pulling into Salt Lake City for two nights. A *Deseret News* reporter aroused interest in her arrival by announcing that she was "soon to be borne away captive by a scion of one of England's leading families." Unimpressed by this impending tragedy, the *Salt Lake Herald* found that *Jinks* was "not a great play and Ethel Barrymore is not a great actress, but somehow the combination seems to hold you."

With this backhanded compliment ringing in her ears, a melancholy Barrymore and her company of players entrained near midnight on June 23, crossing Idaho's great sagebrush desert in the dark, their skin abraded by alkali pelting through the open windows, pulling into Boise shortly past dawn.

Eagerly awaiting her arrival was James Alonzo Pinney, the seventy-two-year-old proprietor of Boise's Columbia Theater. A three-term mayor of the city—his latest stint had just ended—Pinney generally ran for office with the support of those who favored a "wide-open" city ("every gambler, every dissolute character, every saloon man," complained the *Statesman*). He'd started his theatrical career in 1888, managing other people's theaters. In 1892, he erected the 829-seat Columbia, then the Northwest's finest theater and, four years later, the site of the historic compact of Idaho Populists and Democrats that made Steunenberg governor. Its fanciful design—stick-and-shingle towers and upper facade atop a striped brick base—was a curious mixture of Moorish and medieval northern European elements. Inside, illuminated by 1,450 incandescent lamps—more than the entire city had employed five years before—the ceiling was embellished with portraits of Shakespeare, Hugo, Beethoven, and Goethe. The fire curtain sported an "Allegory of Theatrical Arts," Idealism blessing the union of Truth and Devotion. Above the proscenium arch, flanked by a diaphanous odalisque and a fetching Fatima, reigned a portrait of Pinney himself, emblematic of his healthy self-regard.

From its earliest days, Idaho had relished the diversion offered by traveling companies. In 1884, the *Statesman* noted that if the mail from Boise was a half hour late, railroad authorities were furious, but a train crew had "waited four hours Saturday night for the Phosa McAllister Dramatic Company without murmuring." Pinney was after something more than a good road show. Devoted to the classics, he'd opened his temple of culture with Shakespeare's *As You Like It,* starring Julia Marlowe as Rosalind (the role Ethel wanted, above all others, to play). Since then, he'd done his best to interlard commercial potboilers with works of real artistry, importing Louisa Lane Drew, Ethel's grandmother, in Sheridan's *The Rivals* and Helena Modjeska, the Polish tragedienne, in the Bard's *King John.*

As the syndicate tightened its noose, Pinney struggled to keep his productions a cut above those offered by Boise's three vaudeville houses. In 1906–07, there were three Shakespearean offerings, Jane Corcoran in Ibsen's *A Doll's House,* and Rose Coghlan in Shaw's *Mrs. Warren's Profession.* But the season was dominated by frothy musicals like *The Strollers* ("one continuous laugh set to music") and *The Royal Chef* ("the musical cocktail with a menu of music"). Seven minstrel troupes played Boise that year, as well as the obligatory *Uncle Tom's Cabin* ("Two brass bands, Two Funny Marks, Two Mischievous Topsies, Genuine Southern Cake Walkers, buck and wing dancers, male and female quartette, ponies, donkeys and bloodhounds"); *At Yale,* featuring "the real boat race between Yale and Harvard"; and *Kerry Gow,* with "two thoroughbred horses and a flock of wonderful trained carrier pigeons."

Finally, there was a hint of things to come: "A Surprise, A Wonder, A Marvel—miles of moving pictures." Boise's first taste of a dramatic film had come that fall with *The Great Train Robbery,* flashed on a white sheet atop Alexander's Clothing Store—an ominous challenge to Pinney's dominance of the city's entertainment industry.

So the impresario was delighted to welcome *Jinks,* one of the few respectable dramas to play Boise that year, with a star you could unblushingly put in lights. And it was a surefire moneymaker: all 829 seats had been sold a week before. With a $2.50 top for lower boxes down to 75¢ in the kids gallery —a scale considerably higher than the average Boise attraction—*Jinks* would gross $1,114.50, second that season to Frohman's other touring success, *She Stoops to Conquer.* Pinney's 20 percent house split would leave a handsome payoff of $222.90.

In her dressing room, Barrymore changed from her tan suit into the blue moiré silk frock with giant hoop skirt and bustle in which she sashayed down the gangplank in act 1. By act 3 she'd changed again, into a spectacular gown whipped up from a hundred yards of white tulle showered with rosebuds. With a wreath of pink roses in her waterfall curls, she stood center stage and delivered the passionate speech in which Madame Trentoni, fresh from her operatic triumph, proclaims her love for Jinks: "Oh, Papa, you can't understand how I feel—you're only a man! You say the people tonight stood up and shouted themselves hoarse! Did they? I heard nothing but the beating of my poor heart. You say I have been deluged with gifts of flowers, but the only gift I want is missing—one man's honest love!"

When the curtain came down, the audience gave Barrymore five standing ovations. It was an eclectic crowd—the theatergoing elite, prosperous ranchers and miners from the hinterland, and a substantial delegation from the trial community. Out in the orchestra, Barrymore saw several of the impressive men she'd met at the courthouse. In one box purchased by S. S. McClure sat his star reporter George Kibbe Turner and the Associated Press's two aces, Martin Egan and John Russell Kennedy, and their wives. Barrymore found it thrilling, for she'd "never seen such a body of men... lawyers, newspaper reporters, detectives." It seemed to her that "the best of the universe in his particular line [had come] for this one crucial test." And they were out there in the dark, applauding her!

After the last backstage visitor had left, James Kearney, the stage manager, reminded the cast it was time to go; they had a performance the next evening in Walla Walla, eight hours away. But down at the depot, Barrymore felt a sudden urge to talk to Charlie Siringo. She'd glimpsed his chiseled profile in the audience. Was she feeling a touch of what Madame Trentoni felt in act 3, a sense that all the applause was meaningless without someone to share it with? Calling his room at the Idanha, she asked Charlie whether he'd like to come say good-bye.

Always the romantic, Siringo couldn't believe his good fortune. Somewhere in Boise, at a few minutes past midnight, he rustled up a bouquet of roses, ran two blocks down Tenth Street to the depot, and pressed them into the soft white hands of the adorable actress. Years later, Barrymore would forget the detective's name, recalling him only as "a little Pinkerton man, who had been working under cover on the railroads." But Charlie remembered Ethel all too clearly. "Her happy smile and warm hand-shake," he wrote, "linger with me to this day."

Hours after Barrymore left town, the early westbound train deposited another distinguished visitor on the windswept platform of the Boise depot, a hulking bear of a man with a slight forward lunge to his body, a shiny bald pate, rimless pince-nez glasses, and a waxed black Prussian mustache whose pointed bristles thrust boldly up his pallid cheeks.

The newcomer was Hugo Münsterberg, professor of psychology at Harvard University, a protégé of William James's and his successor as director of the Harvard Psychology Laboratory. At age forty-four, Münsterberg was, after James, America's best-known psychologist. He'd come to Boise at the summons of S. S. McClure of *McClure's Magazine* to study Harry Orchard, the enigma at the heart of the Haywood case.

To those who'd observed his Teutonic posturing on two continents,

Münsterberg was a bit of a mystery himself. Born to a prosperous Jewish family in the Baltic seaport of Danzig, he displayed startling precocity, writing a poem at age seven, launching a magazine at twelve. Very early he took aim at an academic career, but the road to a university position was arduous for a Jew, so shortly after his father's death in 1881, Hugo and two brothers converted to Christianity. In 1882, he entered Leipzig University, studying under the experimental psychologist Wilhelm Wundt.

The modern discipline of psychology had been born in Leipzig three years before when Wundt and two students conducted an experiment measuring "the duration of apperception." With a clocklike mechanism, they recorded the time elapsed between a subject's hearing a ball hit a wooden platform and the time he pressed a telegraph key. Before long, Wundt's laboratory had become the principal training ground for would-be psychologists. As the leading proponent of the notion that mental processes could be studied experimentally, the austere Wundt, son of a Lutheran pastor, divorced psychology from theology, creating "a new domain of science." Although trained as a physiologist, he concluded that physiological factors could not explain human perception, which arose through a "creative synthesis of mind." From that, he derived his first principle of the "creative will," a life force central to all human cognitive activity.

Beginning as Wundt's loyal disciple, Münsterberg gradually staked out a dissenting position, which his master came to view as rank heresy. From his laboratory at Freiburg University, Münsterberg denied that mental processes developed by special laws. All human behavior, he held, could be explained in materialistic terms. In 1891, he asserted that consciousness, which controlled human ideas and feelings, had its source in "the muscles, joints, glands, blood vessels, tendons, intestines, etc."

So impressive were Münsterberg's credentials that, when William James planned a sabbatical in 1893, he asked Münsterberg to assume a major part of his responsibilities at Harvard. Conceding that the university "could get younger men here who would be *safe* enough," he said they needed "a man of genius if possible." Such language might be dismissed as insincere flattery had James not written to his novelist brother, Henry, describing Münsterberg as "the Rudyard Kipling of psychology."

William James had launched the Psychology Laboratory in the late 1870s as a "demonstration room." But Harvard's psychological studies lagged behind those of Johns Hopkins, Clark, and the University of Pennsylvania. That, to James, was simply unacceptable. "We are the best university in America," he declared, "and we must lead in Psychology."

But James was at best ambivalent about the academic discipline of psychology. To his brother Henry, he called it a "nasty little subject." He was particularly dubious about its claims to scientific accuracy, noting that it had produced "not a single law in the sense which physics shows us laws, not a single proposition from which any consequence can causally be deduced.

This is no science, it is only the hope of a science." Although he'd performed plenty of laboratory experiments, he'd developed an intense distaste for Wundt's reliance on the "writhings" of decapitated frogs: "The thought of psycho-physical experimentation and altogether of brass-instrument and algebraic-formula psychology fills me with horror."

But if he yearned to devote himself to religious and philosophical speculation, James knew full well that "brass-instrument" psychology must continue, and Münsterberg was the man to carry it on. To his colleague Josiah Royce, James captured the new man's pluses and minuses: "an extraordinarily engaging fellow, not of the heroic type, but of the sensitive and refined type, inclined to softness and fatness, poor voice, vain, loquacious, personally rather formal and fastidious, desiring to please and to shine. . . . His brain never tires; he is essentially a man of big ideas in all directions, a real genius."

As years went by, James saw more faults than assets, accusing Münsterberg of "shallow dogmatism," bad taste, and self-importance. Others agreed. A former student referred to him as "Wotan." A professor's wife quipped, "Ein Münsterberg ist unser Gott," after Luther's hymn "Ein feste Burg ist unser Gott."

Relations between James and Münsterberg hit bottom at the 1905 dedication of Emerson Hall, the new home of Harvard's psychology and philosophy departments. As division chairman, Münsterberg presided and bulked large as well in the program's second half, the annual meeting of the American Psychological Association. James found it unseemly for a German to assume such a dominant role—"five speeches in the course of an hour"—at an American gathering. In a sulk, Münsterberg resigned as chairman, saying: "It is certainly abnormal that the least worthy member of the Department is chairman of it for five years and after all I am merely 'a German.' . . . A born American ought to take my place at once." Harvard's president, Charles W. Eliot, strove mightily to heal the rift between his two psychologists, writing James: "The fact is that Münsterberg, like most men who think rather too much about themselves and their doings, is over-sensitive." He had "a German way of doing things, which is different from our Yankee way. . . . But when you recommended Münsterberg for an appointment here you must have expected he would be different from us. . . . We cannot expect to profit by his merits without ever having to wince at his defects."

Later, Münsterberg told Eliot the incident "changed totally my feelings toward this community." Although he exaggerated the hostility he faced, he didn't imagine it. In 1904, Henry James reminded himself to write something about "the 'sinister,' the ominous 'Münsterberg' possibility—the sort of class of future phenomena represented by the foreigner coming in and taking possession." By 1901, Münsterberg's intense loyalty to the Kaiser and his close relations with the German ambassador, Edmund von Holleben, had prompted rumors that he was a spy.

No spymaster would have recruited such an operatic figure, but the professor did promote Germanic ideals in America; von Holleben called him "a good lever" for influencing American attitudes. In no sector was he more active than in the relation of the sexes. One cliché of the age—trumpeted by the strenuous man in the White House—was the "feminization" of America (witness the dominion of actresses on the nation's stage). Münsterberg argued that it was "the central function of woman to be wife and mother" and of man to put his virile stamp on "public life and culture." As women infiltrated Harvard through Radcliffe, he thundered: "What a calamity for the country if this great epoch in the life of the universities were ruined by any concessions to the feminine type of thinking."

By this time, Münsterberg had aroused a new resentment, a feeling by more traditional academicians that he was unduly popularizing psychology, playing to the gallery in a way inappropriate for a scholar. At Leipzig and Freiburg he'd been a caricature of the *Wissenschaftler*, the scientist burning the midnight candle in pursuit of "pure truth." But by 1907 he argued that "experimental psychology has reached a stage at which it seems natural and sound to give attention also to its possible service for the practical needs of life."

As his thirst for public recognition grew, it struck him as "astonishing that no path led from the seclusion of the psychological workshop to the market place of the world." Even as he wrote, that path opened. Americans were fascinated with the emerging world of psychology. The month Münsterberg arrived in Boise, William Allen White warned John S. Phillips, editor of the *American Magazine*, that the journal was "not holding up." Asserting that it needed a series on some nonpolitical subject, he recalled that the muckraker Ida Tarbell had "once suggested what I think is the crackingest subject for a magazine series that ever was put up. I mean a series of articles by somebody like William James, or some perfectly orthodox psychologist, on the subject of abnormal psychology and multiple personality... thought transference, faith healing.... It is a brand new field; it would... make a great hit."

Serious men had their doubts. Across Harvard Yard, Thurman Arnold—preparing for a distinguished career as a lawyer, judge, and teacher—regarded events at Emerson Hall with lofty disdain: "The study of psychology was something no sound scholar would care to be dabbling in." Some were intrigued by the new science but had difficulty grasping its principles. Jotting questions in his copy of James's *The Principles of Psychology*, and thinking perhaps of his wife's suicide a decade before, Henry Adams wondered how passions overcame the human will: "How can a thought outside the body penetrate and kill the body? Why is will powerless to control it?"

By 1904, several American psychologists were dabbling in practical psychology. "I see no reason," said James McKeen Cattell, "why the application of systematized knowledge to the control of human nature may not in the course of the present century accomplish results commensurate with the

nineteenth-century applications of physical science to the material world."
Münsterberg belonged to a circle of Boston psychologists, neurologists, and
philosophers, including James, Royce, Morton Prince, and James Jackson
Putnam, who were experimenting with the emerging field of psychotherapy
—and were understandably fascinated by the work of Sigmund Freud, whom
they flocked to hear when he spoke at Clark University in 1909.

Another field promising fruitful application of psychological principles
was the law. At the trial of Harry Thaw for the murder of the celebrity
architect Stanford White, which had ended two months before the Haywood
trial began, a half dozen "alienists"—the first breed of psychological thera-
pists—testified for both sides on Harry Thaw's sanity. The press scorned such
expert testimony. Irvin S. Cobb of New York's *Evening World* laughed up his
sleeve at "the scurvy, sweated smear of pseudo-scientific poppycock which
was spread like butter on a hot griddle over the fraud-tinged transcript." One
day,

> good old Dr. J. Mumble Visaversa, the snuffy, owlish ex-keeper of this public or
> that private madhouse in the adjacent area, would be adjusting his double lenses
> and smoothing his waistcoat and demonstrating by a mysterious patter, studded
> thick with infirm Greek and limping Latin, and likewise by quoting substantiat-
> ing extracts from medico-legal authorities, that Thaw had been wildly insane
> when he shot White although now was miraculously and absolutely restored to
> complete sanity. But tomorrow...he'd be proving beyond the scintilla of a
> doubt that the man had never been at any hour of his life insane.

Finley Peter Dunne sounded the same note, recounting expert testimony as
to why a defendant stole a watch: " 'I come to th' conclusion,' says th' expert,
'that th' man, whin he hooked the watch, was sufferin' fr'm a sudden tempest
in his head, a sudden explosion as it were, a sudden, I don't- know-what-th'-
divvle-it-was, that kind iv wint off in his chimbley, like a storm at sea.' "

Such ridicule notwithstanding, Münsterberg was deeply interested in
applying psychology to legal evidence. Convinced that such testimony would
soon be widely accepted, he wrote, "Every day errors creep into the work of
justice through wrong evidence which has the masks of truth and trustworthi-
ness.... To be satisfied with the primitive psychology of common sense seems
really out of order when crime and punishment are in question."

The area in which psychology could contribute most, he thought, was in
distinguishing false testimony from true. Well before development of the
modern lie detector, Münsterberg relied on psychological intuition and such
"brass instruments" as the sphygmograph, which kept the subject's pulse, and
the pneumograph, which measured breathing.

Ironically, some years later, a former student of Münsterberg's, the be-
haviorist Edwin B. Holt, wrote of "a fairly well-educated businessman" who
was "one of the most unconscionable liars who ever lived." So anxious was he
about his lies, Holt contended, that he developed "an almost pitiful emotional

recoil at any mention of deceit and untruth" and to cover this anxiety began many sentences, "I confess frankly that, ..." which invariably led to an "amazing whopper." Münsterberg's associates recognized him in this portrait, as did the professor himself, and Holt was thunderously denounced.

Münsterberg first came to national attention as diviner of a defendant's secrets following a Chicago murder. Barely two weeks after the Emerson Hall imbroglio, a young man named Richard Ivens was arrested for the brutal strangling of a Chicago housewife. Detectives had extracted his confession by dubious means and he soon retracted it. Nonetheless, Ivens—who may have been retarded—was convicted and sentenced to death. At this point, a Chicago "nerve specialist" named J. Sanderson Christison sought to show that the man's confession was bogus. In a self-published pamphlet, he noted that Ivens heatedly denied his guilt at first, changing his mind only after the police insisted on his guilt. The confession, he argued, was the involuntary elaboration of a suggestion put in his mind by the authorities. Seeking the support of recognized authorities, Christison obtained statements from both James and Münsterberg. "Ivens probably innocent," James wired. "Reprieve necessary for thoroughly investigating mental condition."

No uncertainty inhibited Münsterberg. Though he hadn't examined Ivens, relying instead on evidence supplied by Christison, he proclaimed: "I feel sure that the so-called confessions of Ivens are untrue, and that he had nothing to do with the crime. It is an interesting and yet rather clear case of dissociation and acute suggestion.... The witches of the seventeenth century were burned on account of similar confessions."

The oracular judgment from Cambridge did little to assist the convicted man; what it did was stir midwestern resentment. Some argued it was "inconceivable that any man who was innocent of it should claim the infamy of guilt." Newspapers raged at Münsterberg's "long-distance impudence" and "Science Gone Crazy." Psychology, wrote one commentator, was "simply another way of possibly cheating justice." With a vengeful crowd gathered outside the jail, Ivens was hung on schedule on June 22, 1906.

Münsterberg vigorously defended his "much-abused letter" on Ivens but seemed aware that the next time he made such assertions they must follow a personal examination of the defendant. This was the context in which he received McClure's wire asking him to come to Boise to observe and interview Harry Orchard and to write an article answering the question that perplexed the nation: Was Harry Orchard telling the truth?

S. S. McClure edited America's most exciting magazine. Founded inauspiciously during the 1893 financial panic, McClure's had soon been "on the verge of failure." Borrowing from friends, relatives, and contributors, he bought enough time to assemble a team that would later be called "the most brilliant staff ever gathered by a New York periodical," among its members Lincoln Steffens, Ida Tarbell, Ray Stannard Baker, and David Graham Phillips. In January 1903, when Steffens's "Shame of Minneapolis," Tarbell's latest installment on Standard Oil, and Baker's "The Right to Work" appeared in a single issue, McClure would claim it was pure coincidence that all the articles dealt with a single subject: "Capitalists, workingmen, politicians, citizens—all breaking the law, or letting it be broken." Coincidental or planned, a new vogue of American reporting had been born, what Theodore Roosevelt four years later in a fit of pique would call the "muckrake" style. But the president's denunciations of the muckrakers as "potent forces for evil" only lent them panache. Over the next six years, during which its circulation rose to half a million, *McClure's* would prosper on the brio of its muckraking, while a host of imitators—*Collier's, Leslie's, Everybody's*—struggled to keep up.

One might imagine that the cachet of this swashbuckling style, as well as the attention directed at McClure through the president's saber rattling, would have given the onetime peddler a fully realized sense of his own worth. But the burning spotlight only exacerbated his tendency to anxiety and excitation. He responded to every fire bell, running first to St. Petersburg to observe the Russian Revolution, then to Chicago to document the rise in homicides.

Moreover, his occasional infidelity to his matronly wife, Hattie, blossomed in 1903–04 into a full-scale affair with the poet Florence Wilkinson. Some of Wilkinson's banal poetry in the magazine was clearly addressed to McClure: "I took you into my lonely arms / You were the soul of me; / There was no speech between us twain, / There needed not to be." The affair preoccupied McClure until another woman, a rival for his attention, presented the magazine with a manuscript called "The Shame of S. S. McClure, Illustrated by Letters and Original Documents." Ultimately, McClure came to his senses and begged his wife's forgiveness—which she gave, grudgingly at first.

It was too late to save his collaboration with Steffens, Tarbell, Baker, and Phillips. "He's a Mormon," Tarbell wrote, "an uncivilized, immoral, untutored natural man with enough canniness to keep himself out of jails and asylums." In May 1906, the four writers quit *McClure's* and took over a foundering monthly called the *American Magazine*. McClure, in turn, assembled a new staff, made up of such stars-to-be as Willa Cather, George Kibbe Turner, Will Irwin, and George Kennan. Some years later, Ellery Sedgwick would write that a week with McClure "was the precise reversal of the six busy days described in the first chapter of Genesis. It seemed to end in a world without form and void. From Order came forth Chaos."

McClure's journal came through the crisis intact and as influential as ever, but the years of turmoil had taken their toll on "the General." A photograph from this time exhibits a frail man, his tousled blond hair pushed carelessly off a creased forehead, a deep worry line between the brows, dark pouches beneath, and a look of apprehension in the wide, startled eyes. A 1907 article about the editor captured the same dishevelment, describing "a pair of shoes that hadn't been blackened for a month, a coat rumpled in the back; trousers that ought to have been pressed and faultless linen in violent disharmony with all else." Never, it said, had McClure been seen to laugh and only rarely to smile. "The spectre of the ruin which harassed his early years," it surmised, "has left its shadow in his face."

No passive receptacle for his contributors' manuscripts, he prided himself on quitting his Lexington Avenue headquarters and getting out in the world, hobnobbing with politicians, industrialists, and detectives, meeting new writers and artists. With a knack for smoking out stories, he fairly bristled with editorial projects. "If he had been a woman," said one of his editors, "he would have been pregnant all the time."

For months, McClure had been intrigued by Steunenberg's assassination and, specifically, by Harry Orchard's role. His active investigation began when he learned that Orchard had secretly written an account of his criminal activities. In February 1907, Frank Gooding sent a rough copy of the "autobiography" to Dwight Hillis of Plymouth Congregational Church in Brooklyn Heights, hoping the well-connected minister could find it a New York publisher. In March, he followed up with a more polished version. Hillis showed it to his friend Melville E. Stone, general manager of the Associated Press, who agreed it ought to be published and suggested that Hillis pass it on to McClure, which in April 1907 the minister did.

For years, McClure had betrayed an anxiety about labor's "lawlessness." In part his misgivings sprang from an 1896 pressmen's strike against his own company occasioned by his temporarily cutting his press feeders' wages from twelve to ten dollars a week. When the feeders walked out, all of the plant's sixty skilled workers followed. McClure prevailed and refused to rehire any of them. Henceforth, he expressed deep concern about the maintenance of public order and deplored Socialism as one of those "unreasoning, passionate gusts of public opinion." In 1904, he sent Ray Stannard Baker to Colorado to write on "The Reign of Lawlessness" by both capital and labor. Now, regarding Orchard's manuscript as a fascinating glimpse into the mind of a terrorist, he resolved to publish it in installments that summer and fall, then as a book.

Orchard wasn't a writer. He'd need help getting his story into publishable form. To that end, McClure sent George Kibbe Turner racing toward Boise. With the loss of Lincoln Steffens, Turner was *McClure's* new specialist on municipal affairs, but the ex-newspaperman was anything but a typical muckraker. A mild, self-effacing man of thirty-five, "with mousy hair and a mousy personality," Turner had graduated from Williams, then gone to work for the nearby *Springfield* (Massachusetts) *Republican.* In 1899, he'd begun selling short fiction to *McClure's;* not until the first string defected in 1906, though, did he achieve stardom.

In an early short story and a novel, *The Taskmaster,* Turner had tried out the classic crusader's quarrel with the trusts but never felt comfortable in that role. By 1907, he'd concentrated his fire on the traditional targets—liquor,

crime, gambling, and the "white slave" trade—all vices against which merchants and industrialists also inveighed. Toward the trusts that dominated
railroads, steel, mining, and other basic industries, Turner turned a sanguine,
even accommodating, eye—seeming to regard the hard-charging business
community as the salvation of American civilization. McClure liked Turner's
lean, unrhetorical prose, which let events and documents speak for themselves. But sometimes the journalist didn't dig hard enough for facts. If there
was a defect in Turner's writing, McClure wrote Willa Cather, it was "a
certain distaste towards documentation."

As Turner headed for Boise on May 6, his instructions were to gain entry
to Orchard's cell and begin getting the manuscript in shape for midsummer
publication. He wasn't authorized to deal with contractual matters; to that
end, McClure resolved to go to Boise himself. He traveled first to San
Francisco, recently devastated by the earthquake, then to Los Angeles, reaching Boise on May 23. There he met with the governor, McParland, and
Hawley. Finally, he visited Orchard in his cell to agree on the terms of
publication: the assassin got "a good contract," with a cash advance of a
thousand dollars. As always, when out on the road in the thick of the news,
McClure was ebullient, striking a *Statesman* reporter as "jovial."*

On May 25, McClure returned to New York, then came back to see
Orchard on the witness stand. On June 17, he had "one of the most remarkable
interviews of [his] life" with the assassin. Writing the next day to MacKenzie
in New York, he said:

> I got a glimpse into one of the greatest human dramas that ever existed. It
> seemed to me that what I saw yesterday revealed the real Shakespearean drama,
> only a real thing; the thing that occurs only once in a thousand years....
> Orchard has a singularly marvelous mind, and I must say, a most marvelous
> character. His actions on the stand were just the same as if he had been an
> inspired man. His mind worked with extraordinary rapidity. He never hesitated
> for a second; he never got mixed up; he utterly nonplused the defense. Those
> men like Darrow and Richardson believe in no God, do not believe in great
> transformation of character, and were simply helpless before this marvelous
> man, who seemed to be clothed with all the power of God.

McParland had told McClure of a remarkable exchange of letters between Orchard and his first wife, whom he had deserted eight years before as
he set out on his path of mayhem and murder. In the warden's office that

---

* Hugh O'Neill, the rangy Australian covering the trial for the *Denver Post*, didn't think much of
the great magazine editor when McClure "blew in" to the Idanha lobby that night. "He was a
fat little man, with twitching hands and dancing feet, as busy as a bee in a bottle," O'Neill
wrote. Eastern magazine editors were "very superior people and when they die, wisdom will
die with them.... They know nothing of law, their geography is so vague that two of them
thought that the prisoners were chained in silent cells, fed on bread and water, and surrounded
by a park of artillery" (*Denver Post*, May 25, 1907).

afternoon, McClure asked to see the letters and Orchard promptly produced them.

In his letter, dated May 12, 1906, and addressed "My Dearest Wife," Orchard told his first wife, Florence Fraser, that the man she'd been reading about in the newspapers was, in fact, her long lost husband, and he begged her to forgive him for deserting her and their daughter, eleven-year-old Olive May.

In her response, dated May 31, 1906, Florence wrote:

> God only knows how I shall have strength to write this letter. How I have longed and prayed for some word from you. But I was in no way prepared for this terrible news. Oh, if I could only help you in some way or share it with you. Please don't think I ever hated you as you say in the letter or even felt indifferent towards you. It broke my heart when you went away. But there has never been a time when I would not have done anything for you or given the last cent I had for you.... My Dear Albert you are freely forgiven and have been for years. Oh if you had only come back or written all would have been well. I am so thankful dearest to know you have met with a change. And that God has forgiven you all.... Let us pray earnestly that he may open a path for your escape.

Then, after passing on the family news about sister Jennie and Uncle Brigg, she concluded: "Oh that I could fold my arms around you and kiss your lips, and that you could know how freely you have been forgiven. May God bless and sustain you in this great trial is the prayer of your loving wife Florence. I shall never cease praying for you."

On reading this letter, McClure was overcome by emotion. He found Mrs. Horsley "a woman of culture and refinement, of great ability and of the highest character," and her letter struck him as "one of the most beautiful documents in all literature." Having also read a "very touching and pathetic" letter from Orchard's young daughter, McClure concluded that "such faithfulness and love and nobility of character as [is] revealed in these letters is very rarely seen in any literature."[*]

So moved was he that he handed Orchard fifty dollars, asking him to

---

[*] McClure found a still more promising writer in Charlie Siringo. Writing one of his editors in New York, he regretted that Viola Roseboro hadn't accompanied him to Boise. The hard-smoking ex-actress was McClure's reader of unsolicited manuscripts, credited with "discovering" Booth Tarkington, Jack London, and Willa Cather. Now McClure wrote: "There are men here that far transcend in their careers and in their characters any men we have ever published in fiction.... One of them here I would like to bring back with me and add him to our collection. He is a man whom I think has the most marvelous history I have ever met. Turner has seen a lot of him, and when he comes back we must get Miss Roseboro down and have [Turner] tell about him." Roseboro never got her crack at Siringo, which was too bad, because the cowboy detective went on to a considerable literary career, writing a half dozen lively memoirs of detective life in the West (McClure to MacKenzie, n.d. [c. June 18, 1907]; Wilson, *McClure's*, 75–78; Pingenot, *Siringo*, 149).

send a copy of Florence's letter to his own wife, Hattie, then on her way to their favorite spa, the Grand Etablissement Hydrothérapeutique et Grand Hôtel at Divonne-les-Bains, France. Florence Horsley's letter surely was extraordinary in its loving magnanimity, but the intensity of McClure's response suggests that it had a special meaning to him. Did it represent the undeserving forgiveness of which only blind devotion is capable? Was Mc-Clure—himself a philanderer—displaying Florence's uncalculating love for Hattie's edification?

On June 19, Orchard wrote Hattie McClure:

> I promised your dear husband yesterday that I would write to you.... I have been an awfull [sic] sinner and committed awfull crimes.... I was going to end my miserable existence after I was arrested but when I stood as it were on the edge of the precipice and was about to make the last desperate leap into the great beyond, I well knew that down deep in my hear [sic] that I did believe there was a God and a hereafter.... The first thing I did after this was to find out if my Dear wife and Darling little Olive was [sic] alive and when I found they were I wrote to them and told them all.

He enclosed his wife's letter, which S. S. McClure had found so beautiful, but implored Mrs. McClure not to let it reach the public. "My dear wife has asked me several times to destroy her letters but I could never do that. I read them over and over and they are the greatest earthly comfort I have."

On this trip to Boise, McClure sat down for a long talk with Clarence Darrow. They discussed Orchard, whom the lawyer regarded as "one of the most remarkable men he [had] ever seen." McClure later reported to a friend that Darrow thought the assassin "a man whom nothing could touch; he was above all ordinary influences: fear, hope, reward, threats; everything. He was above every human consideration.... He said he would give five hundred dollars to spend a week with him." (Jim Hawley echoed this sentiment, saying about this time of Orchard, "He is a psychological mystery.")

Evidently, Darrow planted a doubt in McClure's mind as to whether the story Turner would get from the assassin would be reliable. One way of dealing with this problem would be to get the other side. So McClure promptly made a bid, through Darrow, for an article by Haywood. Whether it was three thousand dollars for a thousand words or a thousand dollars for three thousand words—Haywood could never remember which—he regarded it as an "enormous sum," and he turned it down. He wouldn't write for a magazine that gave all this attention to Harry Orchard.

Returning to the Orchard enigma, Darrow suggested that McClure bring in somebody who might pierce the assassin's bland facade. Abruptly, the editor decided to put another man on the project—a psychologist who could determine how much of Orchard's story was true. He thought immediately of Münsterberg, whom he'd known since 1902. McClure's had published the professor's articles on popular psychology, while the company's book publishing branch, McClure, Phillips, and Company, had published his portrait of his hosts, *The Americans.* That McClure's dealings with the professor had not always been smooth is suggested by a remark he made in a letter to his subeditor, Cameron MacKenzie, from Boise in mid-June: "In a way Münsterberg is hardly the man. William James would be better." But James didn't write much for the popular press, while McClure was sure Münsterberg would leap at the opportunity. The editor fired off a telegram to Münsterberg.

Hugo Münsterberg had been taking his ease by the sea when he received McClure's urgent summons to Boise. Although the professor and his wife owned a handsome house on Ware Street, a few blocks from Harvard Yard, they spent much of the summer at a shingled cottage in Clifton, which they began renting during the Spanish-American War. "When I selected this abode on the sea shore for the summer," Münsterberg wrote in 1898, "it was mentioned to me as a special feature and attraction of the house that the porch on which I am writing this vacation correspondence would command an excellent view of the movements of the Spanish men-of-war upon their invading Boston harbor. I waited in vain for that interesting spectacle. Instead, only the Boston excursion steamers and merry yachts rode by this rocky coast."

The professor loved drowsy summer afternoons reclining on that porch in thrilling view of the foamy surf pounding the boulders below. But when he received McClure's telegram, the Boise assignment struck him as "a psychological problem of unusual interest," a prime opportunity to test his method for lie detection; indeed, given his claim that psychologists could "pierce the mind," it was his positive "duty to venture the little excursion." As Münsterberg wrote later,

> Whoever claims that he can whistle must finally prove it by whistling; to round the lips is not a sufficient demonstration. This principle holds true, after all, even for experimental psychologists.... That an experimental study of a mind's make-up can be of decisive importance for a court trial when no mental illness is in question still sounds like a fantasy both to the public and to the lawyers; if the psychologist wants to prove it, he must not only promise it with reference to abstract possibilities, but must really prove it in concrete cases before the court.

So on June 21, he left his wife and daughters at the shore and embarked on the four-day train journey to Boise, bringing "a trunk full of psychological apparatus." This was by no means the professor's first trip to the American heartland. He had attended Chicago's World Columbian Exposition and visited Niagara Falls, Kansas, Nebraska, even California, where he spent "a whole night with the Chinese." But raised among the well-tended gardens of northern Germany, he never cared much for the bleak austerity of America's plains and western mountains, the immense fields, the long, straight roads, the clutter of horse-drawn vehicles along the dusty streets of monotonous towns. Even the Adirondacks struck him as so "dusty, dry, foggy and disagreeable" that he cut short a trip there. His was such a Teutonic personality, essentially alien to the American strain, that he always felt out of place anywhere but in the refined acres of his beloved Cambridge and its immediate environs. "Almost everything which is intellectually exalted in this country has come from Boston," he wrote in 1904, "all the best aesthetic and moral and intellectual impulses originate in New England." One can only imagine what he felt as he landed on the Boise railway platform, under the pale arc of that vast western sky.

If the Herr Doktor at first regarded his new surroundings with mild disdain, then Boiseans had an exaggerated respect for things Bostonian. Münsterberg was received with deference, not only by his employer, S. S. McClure, but by Gooding, Hawley, and Borah. Hours after his arrival, he was escorted through the gaping crowd to a seat at the prosecution table and later shook hands with Darrow and Richardson.

Münsterberg's first reaction to Judge Wood's courtroom was purely aesthetic, an instinctive recoil from the primitive look of the place: "My nerves protest, for instance, against twelve jurymen in rocking chairs, each one rocking in his own rhythm. I like still less the prominence of the spitoons, even on the elevated witness chair; to take an oath, to spit and to sit down was indeed the usual beginning for each witness. Least of all did I become acclimatized to the chewing of all concerned: the maximum consumption of gum being at the lawyer's table, Mr. Haywood participating in the gum of the defense." (Here the professor betrays his unfamiliarity with the western country, mistaking the wad in men's cheeks for gum when it was almost certainly tobacco.)

But his extraordinary seat, "a few feet" from the witness stand, gave him a superb vantage point from which to observe the attorneys of both sides (whom he thought "brilliant and strong"), the judge ("a perfect model"), and the day's first witness, Harry Orchard himself. As he described it later, Münsterberg's first reaction to Orchard was "very unfavorable." His profile, especially his prominent jaw, struck the professor as "most brutal and vulgar." Münsterberg marked "the deformation of the ear, the irregularity in the movements of the eyes, and the abnormal lower lip." For a scientist, he appears surprisingly prone to the clichés of phrenology: "That this was the profile of a murderer seemed to me not improbable, but that this man had become a sincere religious convert seemed to me quite incredible."

Turning toward Haywood, he reflected that this was "the head of a thinker and leader." What he saw was "a man who has ideals and is ready to fight for them against this whole commonplace social body, a man of the type who ultimately build up the world and master fate." Münsterberg was emphatic in his preference: "For a real man give me Haywood." Indeed, "No sharper contrast was possible: all my sympathies went to this brilliant face of the defendant and all my disgust to the witness." He felt "almost unwilling to enter into a psychological examination at all as my scepticism of Orchard's so-called confessions was now so intensified by the first personal impression that any further step seemed superfluous. I agreed with Mr. Darrow's repeated statement that Orchard was a monstrous liar."

Nonetheless, the next morning, Wednesday, June 26, the "courageous Governor of the state" drove him to the penitentiary and arranged his interview with Orchard in the warden's back room, where two days earlier Barrymore, McClure, and the others had had their talk with the prisoner. Not surprisingly, given his courtroom impression of the assassin, Münsterberg "shivered" when he shook the man's hand. But soon he set to work on his "scientific inquiry."

Münsterberg acknowledged the view, vigorously expressed by his Chicago critics, that no innocent man would confess to a crime he hadn't committed. But he knew as well that "at all times and in all nations experience has suggested a certain distrust of confessions." It was true, for example, that "promises or threats"—specifically hope of "a recommendation to mercy"—might induce a false confession or "the abnormal, hysterical, neurotic tendency" to self-accusation where none was called for.

To detect such factors at work in Orchard's confession, Münsterberg later claimed that he'd employed "nearly one hundred tests and experiments." But those on which the professor relied most heavily were the word-association tests developed by the Swiss psychologist Carl G. Jung. (He sometimes seemed to forget just where he'd gotten the technique, which ultimately led Jung to write President Eliot of Harvard complaining about Münsterberg's appropriating it without proper credit: "The professor does not mention who the discoverer of this method is, so that, I understand, that some journals have taken for granted that he is the sole originator of all this, and he has not, to my knowledge, taken the trouble to correct these statements. In doing that Professor Münsterberg violates all customs of international literary etiquette." Münsterberg heatedly denied the charges, insisting that everybody knew where the technique originated and, moreover, that such attributions weren't appropriate in popular journals.)

As Münsterberg described it, the experiment depended on a piece of deception. "If he thought that he, the experienced poker-player, could easily hide his inmost mind and could deceive me with cant and lies, I turned the tables on him quickly." He explained to Orchard that he would call out fifty words and at each word Orchard should, with the least delay, name the first word that came to his mind. "I should learn all from the ideas which he would bring up," Münsterberg said he told Orchard. In fact, though, the professor also employed a chronograph that measured in fractions of a second the time between his calling the word and Orchard's reply, and the interval signified as much as—or more than—the word itself. It indicated whether the trigger word was freighted with anxiety or other emotion.

With innocuous words, Orchard answered very quickly indeed. When Münsterberg said "river," it took the prisoner only eight-tenths of a second to shout "water." Between "ox" and "yoke" there was only six-tenths of a second. Between "tobacco" and "pipe" eight-tenths again.

But mixed in with such bland words were some directly related to Orchard's criminal career: "confession," "revolver," "religion," "heaven," "jury," "death," and "blood," as well as the names of some of his victims and his alleged accomplices. The prime issue in the experiment was how much delay followed such loaded words, for if Orchard had something to hide he would be on guard so as not to reveal his secrets.

Münsterberg soon perceived a "remarkable fact"—that "the dangerous words brought, on the whole, no retardation of the associative process." When Münsterberg said "confession," Orchard was back with "truth" in barely eight-tenths of a second. "Heaven" = "God" took less than a second, as did "pardon" = "peace" and "governor" = "executive." Münsterberg reasoned that "a mild, indifferent serenity had taken hold of his mind, and that his criminal life was of no concern to him." Finally, Münsterberg concluded that the experiments "gave a definite reply to a definite question," that they conclusively "proved that the murderer did not try to hide anything."

Münsterberg spent four hours with Orchard on Wednesday. That evening, he shared his impressions over dinner at the Idanha with Governor and Mrs. Gooding, Dean Edwin Hinks of the Episcopal Cathedral (whom the professor found "lovable"), and Hinks's wife, Lizzie. Münsterberg was comfortable in such refined company; he had less patience with Boise's scruffy Socialists, who started "the absurd rumor that I had been called to hypnotize Orchard for the State." The next morning he returned for another three hours with Orchard. On the evening of the second day he took his leave of the assassin. "I pressed his hand as that of an honest reliable gentleman, and, with full feeling of the responsibility, I felt ready to affirm that every word in Orchard's confession is true." His experiments, he said, left "not the slightest doubt of it."

Having solved the conundrum he'd come to answer, the professor left for home early on Saturday, June 29, carrying with him a gift from the governor, an elaborately embroidered cradle board for an Indian papoose. He endured another four-day trip in his Pullman sleeper, arriving at Boston's South Station on the afternoon of July 2. After a short carriage ride across town to North Station, he boarded an Eastern Railroad commuter train for his summer home at Clifton. Suddenly in the aisle materialized a gentleman who said he was from the *Boston Herald,* a straitlaced businessman's paper that Münsterberg sometimes read. Would the professor mind if he sat down? In Boise, Münsterberg had scrupulously eluded the press, sharing his conclusions only with a few newly made friends (among them, apparently, Calvin Cobb). But now, "over-fatigued" from travel—he'd found the heat in Boise particularly oppressive—and more than a bit flattered by the attention, Münsterberg offered only perfunctory resistance to the reporter's request for "a few words" about Harry Orchard. "As I had to sit with him half an hour, we entered into conversation," he said. Before he knew it, he had yielded to what his sister later called the reporter's "third degree," giving the gentleman from the *Herald* quite a few words about Harry Orchard.

According to the account that appeared on the paper's first page the next morning, he said emphatically that "Orchard's confession is, every word of it, true." And he went on: "Orchard is a remarkable criminal mentality. He is the most extraordinary criminal I have ever examined and I do not mean because of the record of assassination to which he confessed. He is complex. In some respects he is very emotional and extremely sensitive to suggestions, while, when approached from other directions, there is an apparent absence of sentiment or feeling."

The reporter kept asking questions and Münsterberg kept answering: "Orchard has a very alert mind, he is singularly keen. My measurements as well as my oral examination of him show that his mind is not only active and accurate, but he has very quick perception; he anticipates. In fact, for mental alertness, few Harvard students would measure up to him." He hailed his hosts, the governor and the prosecutors: "I was very much impressed with the dignity which characterized the whole of the proceedings. The attitude of the judge and prosecuting officers ... impressed me most favorably; and while I say that I regard every word of Orchard's confession as true, I must also say, from personal observation, that Haywood is having an absolutely fair trial."

When the professor saw the *Herald's* front page, he could hardly believe he'd said all that. His telephone jangled with calls from Boston and New York. Soon a reporter from the *Boston Transcript* was on his doorstep, pressing for more. The afternoon paper of Boston's Brahmin elite, the *Transcript* was also the journal read most thoroughly by Harvard's faculty. Since he'd already talked to the *Herald,* the professor—who put a lot of stock in what his colleagues thought—felt he had to clarify things for the gentleman from the *Transcript.*

In its page 1 story that very afternoon, the *Transcript* was careful to give Münsterberg his full credentials—"Ph.D, M.D. and professor"—and full credit for his reluctance to talk: "He was averse today to speaking at length, because of the scientific terms and involved phraseology which a proper exposition of his examination would entail." Nonetheless, "in a nutshell, he declared himself ... firmly convinced of the truth of Harry Orchard's testimony."

His second interview brought the professor some sharp rebukes. The *New York Times,* which had editorially supported the Gooding administration in its handling of the Haywood matter, found Münsterberg's statements "unwise and unfair." As a psychologist, it noted, he was free to say what he wanted, "for psychologists have no responsibility." But he was "a member of the faculty of one of our foremost universities, and in that capacity he should set an example of wise reticence and sober judgment to impulsive and voluble youth." His failure to live up to those standards was serious, since his opinion on Orchard might "influence a juryman if it reached his ears." Another paper mocked the new science by publishing a satirical interview with "Prof. Hugo Monsterwork of Harvard." *Wilshire's Magazine* had a point when it remarked: "The learned professor seemingly neglected to take into consideration the fact that another expert psychologist, Professor McParland, had been previously working on the subject for sixteen months."

The wire services relayed the Boston stories across the land. On July 4, Calvin Cobb's *Statesman* carried a headline on its front page: "Professor Münsterberg Declares Orchard Story True." Haywood's supporters were furious, branding the Harvard professor "an intellectual prostitute" and "a shameful charlatan." Hermon Titus, who had a medical degree from Harvard, had learned there "that no diagnosis should be reached till the fullest examination had been made, all the facts collated and every possible error eliminated. This is the method of science. But this has not been the method of Münsterberg, . . . the isolated prig. . . . Lord! Send a Virgin Professor from Vassar to report on Madame Hook, who has graduated from a Parlor House to a parlor!"

Darrow and his colleagues on the defense team were livid. Not only had Münsterberg assured them he'd have nothing to say about his experiments until the trial was over, but the defense feared that this prominent story might somehow find its way to the sequestered jury, perhaps through a bailiff sympathetic to the prosecution. Darrow's outrage was ironic, since, according to McClure, it was Darrow who'd suggested the hiring of such a savant to plumb Orchard's psychological state. Nonetheless, he and Richardson promptly released a statement bristling with indignation: "Professor Hugo Münsterberg's opinion that Orchard, the self-confessed assassin, is telling the truth, is merely a paid testimonial. The professor came here under hire to rehabilitate a magazine story furnished by Orchard." The gentleman from Harvard had spent "a few days here, the guest of the prosecution, his expenses paid by the magazine publisher. So far as his observations go he might as well have written his scientific analysis of Orchard without the inconvenience of leaving Boston. The professor did not see Orchard on the witness stand; he did not hear a word of his testimony. The professor did not see or talk with Haywood, Moyer, Pettibone, their attorneys, nor anyone connected with the defense."

When Münsterberg saw this statement in a Boston paper, he wrote Darrow, assuring the attorney, "I do not want to quarrel with you," and acknowledging that "you had to do your utmost to weaken the impression of my remarks." But "you went too far in this effort. It is a little strong, for instance, to deny that I saw O. on the witness stand while you yourself called him to the witness stand immediately after shaking hands with me in the courtroom on Tuesday the 25th of June. It is still worse that you rely on such false methods as giving the impression that I was paid for my interviews or for finding material in Orchard's favor. . . . I give you my word of honor that my publisher Mr. McClure never paid me a cent and never will pay me a cent for anything but royalties and honorariums for my articles in the magazine." If asked by the publisher to "adjust or revise my findings or suppress anything in his interest, I should never have spoken with him again."

He took umbrage at "your hint of graft," which he said was "not only unfair to me and Mr. McClure, it was unfair also to Haywood as I did not make a secret of the fact that I had a most unfavorable impression of Orchard and a most sympathetic one of Haywood whom I observed more closely than you think." Finally, the professor said he'd never asserted that what Orchard said was objectively true, only that it was true subjectively, that Orchard believed now in the truth of what he said. "That was the only point which interested me as a psychologist."

Darrow was unimpressed by such protestations. "I don't know," he wrote, "whether you mean to say in your letter that your final article or report was going to be favorable to Haywood or not. Neither do I know whether I care." As a "scientific man," the professor had compromised himself. "You came to Boise at the request of Mr. McClure.... It is entirely possible that you did not intend to boom that article or be used by McClure, but the inference that it was done wittingly or unwittingly will always remain if you proceed further in this matter."

As for the professor's claim that he'd observed Orchard in court, he'd missed the assassin's eight full days on the stand, seeing him only in the thirty minutes when he'd been recalled for impeaching questions, ones that were "unimportant and could in no way test him."

"You consorted with the enemies of the defense and the friends of Orchard and the prosecution. You got no information whatever from us and made no investigation of our witnesses or our clients, and in my humble opinion you are in no more position to give any intelligent judgment upon the truthfulness of Orchard's story than the man in the moon, and whatever you say upon this question... you are saying it at your own risk of your reputation and whatever there may be in the science you profess to serve."

The "one unalloyed joy" in his life, Clarence Darrow used to say, was baseball. "I have snatched my share of joys from the grudging hand of fate as I have jogged along," he wrote, "but never has life held for me anything quite so entrancing as baseball."

Growing up in Kinsman, he'd been the town's star first baseman, so compelling that girls vied for the honor of stitching his uniforms. Sometimes when a trial was languishing on a summer's afternoon, his mind would drift back to that magic moment when he'd won a ballgame with a ninth-inning home run: "Whenever I read of Caesar's return to Rome, I somehow think of this great hit." When a friend's daughter asked him to autograph a book under Babe Ruth's signature, Darrow scrawled, "Clarence Darrow, Pinch Hitter."

The 1906 season had been deeply satisfying for Darrow, an avid Chicago

Cubs fan. Featuring the slick double-play combination of Tinker to Evers to Chance and the dancing screwballs of "Three Finger" Mordecai Brown, the Cubbies had advanced relentlessly to the National League pennant, winning by the largest margin in major-league history. The *Chicago News* called them "the greatest aggregation ever gathered on a diamond." Then they'd confronted their crosstown rivals, the White Sox, the "hitless wonders," in the World Series. Even when the Sox took the series, Darrow's enthusiasm for the "greatest of games" was scarcely diminished.

Now, with the 1907 season getting under way, he missed his Cubs acutely. Destined to spend months in western exile, he craved the fragrance of an infield baking in the midsummer sun, the satisfying plunk that ash makes on horsehide. Reaching Idaho toward the end of April, he was delighted to learn that, weeks before, Boise had joined the new Idaho State League, a semiprofessional circuit made up of teams from eight towns in the Snake River Valley linked by the Oregon Short Line and Pacific and Idaho Northern Railroads: the Boise Senators, the Caldwell Countyseaters, the Payette Melon Eaters, the Weiser Kids, the Nampa Beet Diggers, the Emmett Prune Pickers, the Mountain Home Dudes, and the Huntington (Oregon) Railroaders.

It's not clear how many games Darrow attended. But consider these factors: the court didn't meet on Sundays or holidays; Idaho's new Sunday closing law kept the saloons—of which the attorney was inordinately fond—firmly shuttered on the Lord's day, while also prohibiting Sunday operations of theaters, variety shows, dance halls, racetracks, bowling alleys, and poolrooms; the law exempted baseball, permitting teams to play all their games on Sundays and holidays; as a thoroughgoing skeptic, Darrow didn't attend church; he'd never thought it was immoral to enjoy oneself on the Lord's day; when churchmen sought to close the Columbian Exposition on Sundays, he'd asked the Sunset Club, "If literature is good on Monday, is it bad on Sunday; and if it is well to study and admire works of art on Saturdays, is it ill to look at them on Sunday?"; each Sunday morning during the trial, he visited the Haywood family at their rented house on Twelfth Street but was gone by midday; he was notorious for not spending much time preparing his cases; for many in the trial community, notably the press, the weekly baseball matches were that summer's principal distraction; finally, one player in the league was performing such prodigious feats he must have arrested the attention of a baseball fanatic like Darrow.

His name was Walter Johnson. At age twenty, he was pitching his second season with the Kids at Weiser, seventy-five miles northwest of Boise. Already he'd won a reputation as the most exciting pitching prospect ever to play in any minor league.

Robert T. Small, one of the Associated Press men at the trial, was a baseball addict. During his seven years on the *Washington Star*, he'd zealously supported the cellar-dwelling Washington Nationals, owned by the family that owned the *Star*. Wherever he went, he went out to the ballpark.

He wasn't alone. His colleague Martin Egan had once covered baseball for the *Seattle Post-Intelligencer* and remained a fierce fan. Frank Perkins of the *Portland Evening Telegram,* writing on the trial's press coverage, noted that Sunday was a quiet day for the correspondents: "Baseball games between the local nine and teams from towns in the surrounding territory are well patronized by the newspaper men." Indeed, Small estimated that "two score newspapermen and ten" were in the stands every Sunday.

"No one of the eastern writers," Small wrote, "will ever let fade the memory of the first Sunday that Walter visited the Idaho 'metropolis.'" That was May 26, when the Kids, behind Johnson, beat Boise's Senators 12–0. Johnson shut out the locals, allowing five hits, striking out ten. Not yet a polished pitcher, he didn't have much of a curve or a change-up. But when he reared back and heaved the ball, he threw it faster than the reporters had ever seen. Small thought he was watching "a cyclone."

When the Kids visited Boise, they stayed at the Idanha, and on at least one occasion, the newsmen living there got a treat. Inclement weather one morning made outdoor practice impossible, so Walter got in his pregame warmup in the hotel's second-floor corridor, with a chamber pot as home plate.

Ranging far to catch a good ballgame, the newsmen took advantage of special excursion trains that, for example, charged only $3.20 for the Boise–Weiser round-trip. Early in the season, Jim Noland of the *Denver Post* reported, "A baseball game at Caldwell, twenty miles away, almost denuded the town of its male inhabitants yesterday." Clearly Noland had joined the exodus. A month later, most of the trial's press corps went en masse to Caldwell again, this time as guests of the town's Commercial Club, to inspect the town in which Frank Steunenberg had lost his life. After breakfast, they watched Mountain Home lick the home team 5–4.

A. E. Thomas of the New York *Sun* was another reporter who rarely missed an afternoon at the ballpark. As early as May 12, in a lyrical portrait of a Boise Sunday, he reported on a "right smart" Boise-Emmett game at Riverside Park. He was impressed at the way the fans "exploded at the slightest provocation." A base hit produced chaos. A two-bagger set off a riot. He was enthralled by Emmett's cheerleaders, "five little girls in short dresses and with pigtails down their backs and two old women with gray hair," who "eclipsed anything in the line of rooting that the East has ever seen."

But as the season wore on, it wasn't the cheerleaders or the hotdogs or the summer sun that brought the trial community to the ballgames. It was the astonishing young pitcher from Weiser.

Among the nicknames with which sportswriters showered Walter Johnson, there was one—the Humboldt Thunderbolt—that seemed inappropriate. For while born on a farm near Humboldt, Kansas, he didn't get serious about baseball until 1902, when his family moved to southern California, lured by the discovery of black gold beneath the orange groves. Settling in the sunny hamlet of Olinda, twenty miles southeast of Los Angeles, Walter's father became a teamster with the Santa Fe Oil Company, a partnership between the Santa Fe Railway and Edward L. Doheny, an oil man who would go on to a certain rancid fame as instigator of the Teapot Dome scandal. The Johnsons moved into a house on Olinda's main drag, which—like the wooden derricks rising and dipping all around them—belonged to the oil company.

Southern California's oil boom had prompted a baseball craze, since the balmy weather meant a boy could play the summer game all year long. Among its aficionados were the husky drillers and loaders with the oil companies, whose executives, wishing to associate the company with these games, encouraged the hiring of men with baseball skills. Olinda had no proper ballfield on which to host other town teams, so Olinda's Oil Wells played home games in nearby Anaheim. Among their ardent fans were Frank Johnson and his teenage son.

One afternoon in July 1904, the Wells built such a huge lead over Eureka that their manager gave some local boys a chance. Weeks before, he'd been so impressed by Walter's pitching on a diamond laid out behind a livery stable that now he said, "Go on in, Walt. Let's see what you can do." The seventeen-year-old ambled to the mound and struck out six men in three innings.

After pitching regularly for the Wells the next spring, he got what looked like his big break. A former teammate, now with the Tacoma Tigers of the professional Northwestern League, recommended Johnson for a vacant pitching berth. With a satchel full of his mother's sandwiches, he set off for the northland. But San Francisco had just been rocked by its great earthquake. With fires still smoldering across that city, the Pacific Coast League—which had boasted San Francisco as its flagship team—seemed doomed. Expecting to have his pick of the disbanding players, Mike Lynch, Tacoma's manager, figured he no longer needed the kid from Olinda. In releasing Johnson, the manager told him he had no future as a pitcher, suggesting he try the outfield. This gratuitous advice would haunt Lynch for the rest of his baseball days.

Johnson was devastated by his dismissal. A thousand miles from home, with only a week's pay of forty dollars in his pocket, he was desperate. Rescue came in a telegram from another former Olinda teammate. Clair Head, an infielder who'd caught on with the Weiser Kids, urged Johnson to join him.

This was the heyday of "town ball," an era when every community in the land that could boast a dusty pasture and a chicken-wire backstop managed to field its own team. Many of the game's greatest players got their start on such teams: "Smoky Joe" Wood was sixteen when he pitched for Ness City, Kansas, Christy Mathewson only thirteen when he started with Factoryville, Pennsylvania.

Since townsfolk believed their team's performance reflected the community's character, a winner was a community's best advertisement for investment and emigration. If a town played good ball and supported its team with brio, the reasoning went, it must be "a wide-awake, hustling place." Finally, for many towns, fiercely competing with neighboring villages for mercantile supremacy, baseball was often a sublimation of the instinct for outright warfare—or, as Mark Twain put it, the "visible expression of the drive and push and rush and struggle of the raging, tearing, booming nineteenth century."

Winning wasn't just preferable to losing—it was imperative. Town leaders made perfunctory obeisance to the notion that a team should be composed of local boys—wiry clerks, strong-armed laborers, and husky farmers —but in fact there was an irresistible urge to import reinforcements, brought in for a day, a month, or a season, supported with jobs from the business community and often appearing under pseudonyms to disguise their identity. Such ringers were often paid a salary, while residents had to be satisfied with occasional cash for specific performances. Gamblers in the stands would shout out offers for a home run or a double, then pay off with a shower of silver dollars, even a gold watch or two.

In communities too small to attract road companies to their opera houses, these games were the principal source of entertainment. But they were more than that—elaborate municipal spectacles, enlivened by a parade down Main Street, crimson-jacketed marching bands, concessionaires hawking sausages and beer, cheering sections, spectators pouring in from the countryside on special trains, waving silken banners and hand-lettered placards, and, when night fell on the roiled pasture, a hot-dish supper served up by the town's good ladies at the firehouse or grange hall. The pretense was that this was all healthy old-fashioned American fun for the fans (short for "fanatics") but the town's self-regard and commercial prospects were at stake —and, more often than not, prodigious cash, put up by local businessmen and professional gamblers.

Weiser (pronounced "Wheezer") took its name from Jacob Weiser, an explorer who in 1811 camped at the confluence of the Snake River and a smaller stream. For decades only a camping ground on the Oregon Trail, it later acquired a ferry and a general store. But its birth as a town came in 1884 when the Union Pacific tracks pushed into Idaho. Irrigation opened up the surrounding flats for truck farming and peach orchards. Weiser became a provisioning point for miners prospecting the Seven Devils area to the north and timber cruisers marking off tracts of likely pine and cedar.

Saloons, bordellos, and Chinese opium dens sprouted along its dusty streets, patronized by railroad workers and cattlemen who gave the town a nasty reputation. "All the assaults, drag-outs, knock-downs, dirk carving and pistol practice," a pioneer explained, "has been intimately connected with one or the other of the whiskey mills in Weiser City." But by 1906, its population approached three thousand, and as the seat of Washington County and the headquarters of the Pacific and Idaho Northern Railroad, it boasted six general stores, a racetrack, two hotels, and a theater which that June presented a touring company of *Mrs. Warren's Profession*. Like Caldwell, Weiser wasn't shy about extolling its virtues, claiming "the most beautiful

women, the happiest and most contented men, the most luscious fruits, the
plumpest grain, the sweetest hay, the fattest sheep."

In spring 1906, members of the town's Commercial Club considered
fresh means of promoting their community. "The best advertising medium,"
they concluded, would be membership in the new Southern Idaho League.
Admission to the ball grounds was pegged at twenty-five cents, with another
quarter for a grandstand seat, but that wasn't enough to support the club,
which had to provide six new balls for every game and "police to keep the
field clear."

Once their application was accepted, James B. Coakley, a city councilman, was hired as the team's manager. At the league's organizational meeting,
he specified that all teams must be composed of amateur players and that no
professionals would be recruited. Although Johnson was arguably a professional—he'd been paid for his brief stay in Tacoma—he was too intriguing to
pass up. Perhaps Coakley's violation of his earlier pledge proved embarrassing, for he resigned as manager on May 13, replaced by Sheriff Bob
Lansdon.

On May 18, hungry and broke, Johnson clambered off a day coach at the
Weiser depot and asked the way to "baseball headquarters." On Main Street,
he ran into his friend Clair Head, who took him in charge. Within twenty-
four hours, Johnson had a part-time job with the Bell Telephone Company at
ninety dollars a month. He claimed to have dug a posthole or two, but the job
was a subsidy for the town's baseball enterprise. He belonged to the company's "baseball department," his duties to pitch for the Kids. The *Weiser
Semi-Weekly Signal* announced, "Walter Johnson of Los Angeles was among
city arrivals yesterday."

Two days later, Johnson pitched against the Boise Senators. As he took
the mound at the capital's Riverside Park and began warming up with the
catcher, E. Cornelius Uhl, he struck savvy baseball men in the crowd with his
distinctive delivery: standing ramrod straight, he rotated his arm in a full-
circle windmill windup, then cocked it as far back as it would go and buggy
whipped it in a sinuous arc, sometimes sidearm, sometimes almost underarm.
Johnson's arms were unusually long—a "scientific" measurement determined
that from tip to tip of his outstretched fingers was seventy-eight and a half
inches—giving extra force to his slinging motion. Grantland Rice, the sports-
writer, once called Johnson's "the finest motion in the game"; it was such a
natural delivery, in which his back muscles did all the work, that it spared him
the arm ailments besetting many hurlers, allowing him to pitch with uncanny
frequency for much of his career.

Johnson's first moments on the mound that afternoon were unsettling:
two hits and an error loaded the bases. But from there on he was in full
command, striking out seven, allowing just four hits, winning 17–1.

The *Statesman* was slow to take notice, focusing instead on Uhl, a fifty-
three-year old, 250-pound farmer playing his first game in fifteen years. He'd

long since given up the game because of arthritis, but after seeing Boise whip Weiser the week before, he thought, "I am old and fat and grey-headed, but I can play ball enough to beat that bunch." For some reason—he wasn't a ringer in need of disguise—he played for Weiser as "Miller." (Johnson, who surely was a ringer, played that first game as "H. Smith"; all season Clair Head was "Roy Patterson.") The *Statesman* gave Miller/Uhl—nicknamed Foxy Grandpa—much of the credit for Johnson's success. "He coached up young [Johnson] until the latter kept his head all the way through. Every time a Boise man got on base—and there were very, very few—Foxy would pull off some sort of an unexpected play and catch the runner napping."

Even Johnson's victory over the Payette Melon Eaters the next Sunday —a 12–0, one-hit masterpiece in which he struck out twelve "watermelon boys"—didn't bring him much applause in the Boise papers. But in Weiser, Johnson was already a flat-out sensation as the Kids invaded the territory of their traditional rivals, the Caldwell Countyseaters, on June 10.

Though town baseball ostensibly settled grudges peaceably, in fact the intense competition of the ballfield, exacerbated by heavy drinking on game day, often triggered fisticuffs and brawls. Umpiring was a dangerous vocation. On one occasion, two different Nampa players struck the same umpire after a close play at second base. The ump fought loose and "soundly thrashed" the Nampa first baseman. Caldwell, which had once fielded a club called the Rough and Ready Baseball Team, was known for its two-fisted fervor.*

Several hundred Weiserites accompanied their team to Caldwell that day, filling the visitors' stands at the old ball field behind the courthouse. Hundreds of Caldwell rooters spilled out of the home stands, invading the outfield grass. Pacing in front of the Caldwell bench was their manager, Walt Sebree, proprietor of the Caldwell Power Company and famed for his exploits back East, where he'd pitched for the renowned Pope Manufacturing team.

Even before the game started, the Kids and the Countyseaters snarled at each other. Foxy Grandpa later recalled efforts of the Caldwell band to disrupt Johnson's concentration: "Part of the band got in the stand, the other part got behind me. Whenever Walter started his delivery, the drums, trombones and other instruments would let out an awful howl." Foxy let one of Johnson's fast balls through to clatter into a trombonist. The band retreated to the stands.

Shrugging off the distraction, Johnson had the Champions shut out, 4–0, through the fourth inning. As he took the mound in the fifth, Weiser fans chorused, "Lick Caldwell." Caldwell's faithful were "sore as pups" at an umpire's disputed call and some berated Lafayette "Lafe" Lansdon, Weiser's lanky first baseman. Lafe jawed back. When Weiser's manager, Sheriff Bob

---

* Most of Caldwell's fanatics were law-abiding citizens. Indeed, the most fanatic of all was said to be Gilbert Shelby, the court reporter to Judge Frank J. Smith, who recorded the first systematic interrogation of Harry Orchard on January 3, 1906.

Lansdon, saw that his brother, and deputy sheriff, was about to mix it up with the home crowd, he ran down to back him up.

Both of the Lansdons, Johnson recalled, were "fine big Western types." Bob was something of a local hero, at age thirty-one a former colonel of the Idaho National Guard regiment that had fought in the Philippines. Since then he'd embarked on a political career that first had carried him into the sheriff's office and that autumn would make him Idaho's secretary of state. He was known as Fighting Bob for the "relentless manner in which he made war on his political enemies," and on his ball field antagonists as well. At the Caldwell game, Johnson recalled, Lansdon "sat on the bench armed as if he were out after the James boys." As Sheriff Bob arrived to aid his embattled brother, a Caldwell fan—called "a thug" by Weiser rooters and later identified as the former Iowa state boxing champion Swain Beatty—rushed from the stands "like a mad bull" and took a poke at Lafe. Lafe swung back, Bob decked a Caldwell fan, and soon the "merry villagers" were mixing it up along the first baseline.

On the mound, Johnson gaped at the flying fists. A "hard-looking customer" from the Caldwell benches sidled up to growl, "You ain't much on roughin' it, is you?" The rookie shrugged. "To tell the truth, my friend," he said, "I just joined the club, and I don't know which are our players and which are yours." A minute later, Bob Lansdon and the Weiser police chief hustled out to the mound to make sure their prize pitcher didn't get injured. "Don't budge, kid," muttered the sheriff. "We ain't going to let you hurt your arm swinging on some worthless coyote. You get paid for pitching, but we can get everybody in town to fight for nothing."

Ultimately, Caldwell's sheriff, Jap Nichols, and his deputies restored order. But before the game resumed, Walter Sebree, the Caldwell manager, assumed an "operatic" air in front of the Weiser stands, "not unmindful of Lear arraigning the fates," and berated the visitors in stentorian tones: "There is not a respectable lady or gentleman among you! You are all toughs, hoodlums, rowdies and prize-fighters!"

When the game resumed, Johnson and his teammates humbled the Countyseaters, 8–1. But Caldwell had its revenge. Sheriff Nichols escorted the Lansdon brothers, three other Weiser players and—to give the impression of evenhandedness—Caldwell's Eddie Hammond to a makeshift courtroom, where a justice of the peace required each to post ten dollars' bond for a later trial, at which the Kids never appeared.

Reverberations from the unpleasantness rumbled on for days. The *Statesman* denounced the brawl at Caldwell as "a disgrace to the great national game." The *Caldwell Tribune* invoked national politics, saying: "Sunday's base ball game was of the strenuous type. President Roosevelt would have been delighted, but the people of Caldwell were disgusted." Several Weiser citizens challenged Caldwell to a rematch, pledging to wager a thousand dollars on the result. Mayor Pont Moulton summoned Johnson to his office and asked,

"Young fella, do you think we can lick these fellas if we play another game?" Johnson allowed as how they could. Moulton challenged his Caldwell counterpart, Roscoe Madden, who cooly declined. But when the editor of the *Weiser World* confronted Jap Nichols on a train, Caldwell's sheriff apologized to Weiserites offended by Walter Sebree's comments. "Walt just lost his head, I guess," the sheriff said. He wanted the Lansdon boys to "understand that I arrested them, not because I was sore. There was a fight and 600 people saw it. I had to quell it."

A week later, Johnson learned that the whole fracas had been stage-managed by professional gamblers who'd wagered heavily on Caldwell. They had "agreed that if Caldwell was running behind by the middle of the game, a fight would be started, hoping to remove our best players from the line-up."

When Johnson beat Emmett 1–0 the next Sunday, striking out thirteen Prune Pickers, the Kids (7–3) finished the season in second place, behind Caldwell (9–1).

On July 10, carrying in his wallet a *Signal* clipping calling him "the greatest pitcher in Idaho," Johnson returned to California. He hoped to catch on with a Pacific League team, but he got no bids, so he played for the Oil Wells that winter. In the spring, concluding he was "doomed to shine at Weiser," he returned for a second season, bringing with him two other Oil Wells, Guy Meats, a catcher, and Billy Elwell, a second baseman.

Johnson had grown fond of the "big hearted, two fisted" town. He loved the wild country, the woods fluttering with quail, the mountain streams jumping with speckled trout. With Cliff Nevins, the Kids' twelve-year-old batboy, Johnson fished every creek for miles around.

Over the winter, the Southern Idaho League had become the Idaho State League. After its splendid 1906 season, Weiser was "a sure enough baseball town." People "thought, talked, and dreamed of nothing but the game," Johnson recalled. "I've seen a lot of towns get steamed up over baseball, but the place that went craziest over the game was Weiser." The club improved its financial footing by selling two hundred shares of stock to the public. Gone were the Lansdon brothers, who'd brought the team into bad odor, Bob Lansdon replaced as manager by J. C. O'Toole, owner of the Weiser Hotel. The town had dressed up its ballfield, enlarged the grandstand, and replaced the team's drab gray uniforms with blue flannels stitched in white tracery.

From the new season's start, Johnson pitched like a man possessed, beating Payette 13–1 on April 14 and Huntington 19–0 a week later. Of Weiser's impressive hitting in those two games, the *Signal* preened: "The bombardment was so fierce that jack rabbits cut for the hills."

By then, Johnson had achieved a rare kind of celebrity in the Snake River Valley, not only for his prodigious baseball talents but for his unassuming air off the field. The big galoot was simply too good to be true: tall (six foot one), husky (175 pounds), soft-spoken, poised for his years, ready to lend a hand to an elderly woman in a Pullman or to Weiser's business community in its incessant promotions. Despite ample temptation, he neither drank nor used tobacco—and that at a time when America's most famous advertisement was a photo of Napoleon Lajoie, Cleveland's second baseman, above the slogan "Lajoie chews Red Devil Tobacco. Ask him if he don't." Johnson didn't run with wild women either; when the other players dropped by Nellie Bagley's house in Weiser's red-light district, he stayed at the boardinghouse, "reading a lot." A former opponent called him "a nice clean boy."

Not all of Idaho's players were as mild-mannered as Johnson. There were Weiser's brawling Lansdon brothers and the Kids' outfielder Tommy "Hungry" Higgins, who one day was "so drunk in right field he couldn't find a ball hit at his feet." There was "Duke" Campbell, a bartender at Boise's notorious Hoffman House and the star pitcher for the Boise team, who was sentenced to ten days in the city jail for assaulting his wife. And there were the two Mountain Home Dudes—Thomas Grayson, the team's top pitcher, and Lloyd E. Zimmerman, its hot-hitting center fielder—arrested in midseason for statutory rape of two fifteen-year-old girls. So valuable to Mountain Home were these two athletes that the judge dismissed charges against them after they married the girls.

On April 28, the Kids headed for Caldwell and a rematch of the game that had set off such a brouhaha the year before. With the league pennant fluttering atop the Saratoga Hotel, the Countyseaters had changed their name to the Champions and they meant to stay that way. More than 1,500 persons were in the stands that day, anticipating fireworks on and off the field. But, as the *Signal* later confessed, "the game was cleanly played, there being little rag-chewing and no gab fests or mid-diamond mass meetings." Johnson pitched superbly, striking out seventeen Caldwell batters, only to lose 2–1.

Over the next few weeks, Johnson was nearly unhittable. He beat Nampa 10–2, striking out fourteen; Boise in a 9–0 one-hitter, striking out nineteen; Boise again, 12–0 (the Senators, said the *Signal*, were "unmercifully slaughtered—cut, dried and hung on the fence"); then Huntington 5–0. The next day, he got a last-minute call from Nampa to pitch for them against Mountain Home that afternoon in a "special game." Johnson rushed to Nampa, where he utterly baffled the Dudes 5–0 on a no-hitter. Then he pitched his second straight no-hitter and the only perfect game of his career, beating Emmett 11–0. A week later, he licked Nampa 4–0, striking out eleven, and finally Payette, 17–0, striking out thirteen. Pretty soon, Idaho papers took to using a simple three-word explanation for these lopsided contests: "Too much Johnson."

In this remarkable month—from May 19 to June 23—Johnson had pitched seven consecutive shutouts and, counting the last four innings of the first victory over Nampa, had held his opponents scoreless for sixty-seven straight innings, breaking the record of fifty-four held by "Doc" White of the White Sox. In that span he gave up only fourteen hits and struck out ninety-seven batters. It was a breathtaking performance, never matched in any league. Johnson began hearing from teams like Spokane and Portland, who months before had spurned his services. Still seething over the way he'd been treated in Tacoma, Johnson was having none of it.

But rumors circulated of another kind of offer. "Every now and then," Johnson recalled, "after watching me pitch a game some stranger would tell me that he liked my pitching, that he was from the east, and that he intended writing to the manager of this or that [major league] club." But Johnson thought that possibility "quite too far away to give it any serious consideration."

As Johnson's "discovery" was the most celebrated in baseball history, many people claimed to have been part of the transaction. The Detroit Tigers, the Pittsburgh Pirates, and the Cleveland Indians were all said to have gotten tips but either ignored them or didn't respond in time. Meanwhile, the Washington Nationals were moving in for the kill. Among those who'd tipped the Nationals was the AP's Bob Small. Being a resident of Washington, he wired to the Nationals' president, Tom C. Noyes, telling him Idaho had a "cyclone" who was worth a "once-over." Noyes wired his thanks but said he was already on to the "phenom" and was about to sign him.

"Pongo Joe" Cantillon, Washington's manager, was susceptible to the notion of a fabulous country boy who would somehow rescue his slow-footed, weak-hitting ball club, running last in the American League. So long had the team floundered in the league's depths that some wag took to calling the nation's capital "first in war, first in peace, and last in the American League." But if anyone could lift the Nationals out of the cellar, it was Pongo Joe— named for his simian features—who'd replaced the ineffectual J. Garland Stahl as manager after the 1906 season. Cantillon was regarded as "virile" and "scrappy," a "fighting manager" who could "infuse life into a team."

Who first tipped Pongo Joe to Johnson remains in doubt. The pitcher thought it was a liquor salesman, "a big, red nosed fellow" from Chicago, who "through indiscreet oversampling of some of his own samples" was compelled to lay up in Weiser for a while. According to Cantillon, the tipster was Joe Shea, with whom he'd played ball out West. By 1907, Shea did advertising for the Twenty Mule Team Borax Company. On a trip to Boise, he saw Johnson pitch and wired Cantillon. Pongo Joe ignored the first telegram, but Shea followed up with more wires and letters. One letter was said to have gone like this: "You better come out here and get this pitcher. He throws a ball so fast nobody can see it and he strikes out everybody.... He's a big, 19-year-old fellow like I told you before and if you don't hurry someone will sign him and he will be the best pitcher that ever lived.... He knows where he's throwing because if he didn't there would be dead bodies strewn all over Idaho. So you'd better, Joe, or you'll be sorry."

Pongo Joe didn't have much to lose. Moreover, his second-string catcher, Cliff Blankenship, had broken his finger. So Cantillon sent him hustling west to look at two prospects: Clyde "Deerfoot" Milan, a speedy Wichita out-fielder, and Johnson. The catcher signed Milan, then entrained for Weiser, arriving on Friday, June 28, five days after Johnson had completed his skein of sixty-seven scoreless innings.

On soft July evenings, it was light enough in Weiser to play ball until eight. That Friday, Johnson and some teammates were working out behind the Vendome Hotel, while a clutch of aficionados—among them Cliff Blan-kenship—looked on. What the Washington catcher saw was "a big, husky boy and a green one, too. He knew nothing of the fine points about baseball but he could put more smoke on that old baseball than I ever dreamed possible."

As Johnson strolled home to his rooming house, his way was barred by a hulking figure. "You had a lot of stuff on the ball this evening," the stranger said, "but you were a little wild."

That surprised the pitcher, who thought his control had been pretty good that evening, as it had been all season long: in ten games, he'd walked only three batters. At this juncture, Blankenship introduced himself and asked whether the pitcher would care to go to Washington. To his astonishment, Johnson said he was happy in Weiser. Johnson explained later, "I was suspi-cious of those city fellows."

"Ain't you glad to get a chance in the East?" Blankenship asked.

He'd been East, Johnson said. With what team, the catcher asked. "No team," said Johnson. "I was born in Kansas."

Asking the youngster to think over his proposition, Blankenship said they'd talk later. Johnson shared his dilemma with his friend Guy Meats. "Walter didn't want to go," Meats recalled. "He just couldn't believe he was ready for the big leagues." The "bigs" in those days were the playground of immortals like Ty Cobb, Honus Wagner, and Christy Mathewson, rich com-pany for a kid from Olinda. Moreover, the long shadow of Tacoma held him back: he was terrified of being rejected again, then stranded in a strange city three thousand miles from home, forced to take an expensive journey "back to the chaparral." He wired home, hoping they'd solve the problem for him by saying no, but his mother told him to use his own judgment.

When Johnson saw Blankenship later that evening, the pitcher gave in but said he'd need $250 in extra travel money in case things didn't work out. Blankenship wired the Nationals but the next day gave him only $100. No contract was signed then: "They'll fix your salary up when you land in Washington," Blankenship assured him. The catcher hoped to take Johnson on the train with him the next day, but Johnson felt obliged to play out the last two weeks of Idaho's season. He particularly wanted to pitch in the "big game" against Caldwell that Sunday. Reluctantly, Blankenship agreed, then returned to Washington.

The Caldwell game on June 30 was indeed a big one. There was the traditional rivalry between the two teams, the lingering resentment from the previous year's brawl, and the tight race for the league championship. On the strength of Johnson's phenomenal pitching, Weiser led with a 9–1 record, but the Caldwell Champions were only a game behind. A victory Sunday would leave them tied. Finally, when news leaked out that Johnson had been signed by Washington, the game took on a special mystique because it would be one of his last appearances in a Weiser uniform.

Betting, always furious in Caldwell-Weiser contests, exceeded all bounds. Upwards of $10,000, "everything but the jails and courthouses," was wagered on the game. Going up against Johnson, Walt Sebree and his backers concluded, they'd need to beef up their own pitching and bring in some hitters. So in the week before the great Weiser match, Caldwell went out to load up on outside talent.

Like all the other teams in the league, Caldwell had never relied entirely on its own "locals." They'd recruited John Flynn and given him a job at Tom Little's dry goods store during the week so he could play ball on Sunday. But now they were after bigger fish. Eddie Hammond, Caldwell's captain, went to Butte, Montana, with "an unlimited bank account" to draw on and there obtained the services of three Northwestern League stars: Herwig, a Spokane slugger; Sturgeon, Butte's second baseman; and, most important, Aberdeen's great hurler, Irv Higginbotham, destined for stardom with the Chicago Cubs. Finally, Walt Sebree arranged for Nampa to cancel its game with Payette so he could bring in the renowned "Big Leaguer" Hanson to catch Higginbotham.

As game day approached, the Caldwell-Weiser collision rivaled the Haywood trial as a topic of conversation. Among those who made the trip from Boise were Bob Small, A. E. Thomas, Jim Noland, and half a dozen other reporters covering the Haywood trial. From early morning, the horse-drawn vehicles making their way to the Caldwell ball grounds stirred billows of dust on the roadways. According to that morning's *Statesman*, "the whole town of Weiser is going to Caldwell to see the game."

Another *Statesman* writer captured the moment: "Like the clans of the olden country came pouring in from every nook on their great fete days, so the people flocked to Caldwell today to see the greatest, fastest, and all-important game of baseball yet played in the Idaho State League."

Some three thousand persons filled the grandstands and overflowed onto the playing field. The panting throng was rewarded with one of the year's best games. In the first inning, Johnson walked two Caldwell batters but was saved from a bases-clearing home run by an astonishing catch by Hungry Higgins. From then on, he baffled the Champions, striking out fifteen. But Higginbotham was even more effective, striking out eight of the first nine batters and seventeen overall, the Kids going down "like ripe grain before the sickle."

At the end of ten innings, the score stood at 0–0—"two rows of post holes," as rural papers of the day put it. In the eleventh, Guy Meats singled and reached third. Hungry Higgins—dead sober for once—advanced to the plate, bidding to be the afternoon's unchallenged star. From Weiser's dugout,

C. S. Shirley, the team physician, erupted onto the playing field, brandishing a fistful of cash and shouting, "seven hundred and fifty dollars is yours if you score that man"—but the game remained scoreless as Meats was out at home on an abortive squeeze play.

Into the bottom of the eleventh, Johnson carried a gaudy new statistic: seventy-seven consecutive scoreless innings. But this inning started badly, the ringer Sturgeon beating out a bounder to short, while Hammond followed with a liner, advancing Sturgeon to third. Caldwell's band split the air with a fanfare, but Johnson bowed his neck, determined to keep his scoreless streak alive. Herwig bounced an easy grounder to Wallace Childers at third, who fired a bullet toward home. The ball hit Sturgeon in the back and bounced away as the Butte import skidded across the plate with the winning run.

Not surprisingly, in the days that followed, recriminations rattled along the Snake River Valley. "For low down, unprincipled methods in baseball playing," thundered Weiser's *American,* "we will back the management of the Caldwell Club against the west." The *Signal* grumped: "If you can derive any glory out of this Sunday's game, Caldwell, do so, but remember your actions have wiped out every element of true sport in the game in Southern Idaho and Sebree can wrap the pennant around the baseball coffin of the league and gaze about him with tear-dimmed eyes and say to honest sportsmen, 'Behold the evidence of my handiwork.'" Eddie Gheen, the Weiser left fielder, burned his blue jersey in protest.

Darrow agreed with Weiser's plaints: "The hired players of today," he wrote some years later, "are no more players than mercenary troops are patriots. They are bought and sold on the open market, and have no pride of home and no town reputation to maintain. Neither I nor any of my companions could any more have played a game of baseball with Hartford against Farmington than we could have joined a foreign army and fought againt the United States."

But the league president rejected Weiser's protest, and the *Caldwell Tribune* briskly dismissed such mewling: "There was a question raised by the Weiser team as to the legality of Caldwell strengthening their team by hiring four new men, but as this has been done frequently by others of the league teams, that objection is not well taken."

With Caldwell and Weiser deadlocked in first place, the league descended into a shambles of "loading up" and other shenanigans. Somebody in Weiser left a hose running all night, flooding the Weiser ball field and ensuring the team couldn't play Emmett July 7. Instead, five talented Kids became Melon Eaters for a day. With Johnson pitching, Payette beat Caldwell 4–2— "as easy as hulling peanuts for a cage of monkeys," the *Signal* exulted.

That put Weiser temporarily in the lead. But Caldwell argued that the Kids had flooded their own field, and the league's directors awarded the unplayed Weiser-Emmett game to Emmett on a forfeit. That put the Caldwell record at 11–3, while Weiser was 10–2 with two games still to play against Mountain Home. If the Kids won both, they could still take the championship.

Then someone recalled that Nampa hadn't shown up for an earlier game against Caldwell. When the director gave the game to Caldwell, the best Weiser could do—if they won twice against a loaded-up Mountain Home squad—was tie for the championship. That's what they did, Johnson pitching a splendid two-hit shutout in the second game. The season was over, and Weiser shared the prize with its despised foes.

It was time for its young phenom to move on. At a banquet in the Vendome Hotel, the town's establishment lionized him. The *Statesman* extolled Johnson as "a fine young man" and said his career would be "watched with interest" by his many Idaho fans. On July 23, the young pitcher left for Washington. According to the "All Around the Town" column, which had welcomed him to Weiser fourteen months before, a "host of friends" were at the depot to bid him farewell.

Johnson reached Washington on July 26 with his worldly goods in a cardboard suitcase and his "eyes, ears and hair filled with cinders." Before long, Pongo Joe put his imprimatur on the phenom's acquisition. "Blankenship was sent up into the woods, cut down a tall pine and floated it down the creek," he said, "and it's a mighty good piece of timber, don't you think?"

Late that June, with the town mesmerized by Walter Johnson's streak of scoreless innings, a tall stranger ambled onto the stage of Weiser's Wheaton Theater and temporarily took his audience's mind off baseball.

Two days after attending the Haywood trial—and encountering Ethel Barrymore—Gifford Pinchot told a capacity audience in the eight-hundred-seat theater that Theodore Roosevelt's timber policy was "rather to help the small man making a living than to help the big man to make a profit." He and the president were determined to provide "the greatest possible good to the greatest possible number."

The reason timber barons were so eager to control the nation's forestlands, Pinchot argued, was that, at the current rate of consumption, America had but twenty years of timber left. Knowing this, the timber syndicates were "gobbling up our timberlands at an alarming rate." Thus, the government was compelled to withdraw from sale certain lands, in the form of forest reserves, or national forests, as they were now known. Citizens would be permitted "liberal use" of timber in these reserves, but the syndicates would be shut out.

Aware that "for once they were listening to the government's side of the question from the highest authority," reported the Weiser *Signal*, the audience heard him out with "profound attention" and responded with "liberal applause"—a considerable achievement for Pinchot, who'd come to Idaho seeking to mobilize opinion behind the president's timber policy.

As chief forester of the United States and director of the United States Forest Service, Pinchot ran a department with far-flung responsibilities. But by temperament he was less an administrator than a publicist and dramatizer of the forest story. Delegating the service's day-to-day direction to his trusted lieutenant Overton W. Price, he concentrated on selling sound forest practices to millions of apathetic, skeptical, or downright hostile Americans.

In Idaho, the Roosevelt-Pinchot forest program stirred fierce passions among both supporters and detractors, a struggle that now converged with the Haywood trial in a volatile, and potentially explosive, mixture.

"My own money came from unearned increment on land in New York held by my grandfather, who willed the money, not the land, to me," Pinchot wrote in 1914. "Having got my wages in advance in that way, I am now trying to work them out." An aristocrat with a passion for public service, he was the architect of Roosevelt's conservation policy, the force behind its implementation. He was also a zealot who drove many opponents to apoplexy. Their appeals to the president for relief from the fanatic went for naught, as few men so thoroughly enjoyed the president's confidence as this long, slim woodsman.

Cyril Constantine Desiré Pinchot, a captain in Napoleon's army, was driven out of France for plotting to free his commander from St. Helena. In 1816, he emigrated to the United States, settling in the Pocono woods near Milford, Pennsylvania. There he became a successful merchant and raised his son, James, who made a small fortune in New York manufacturing and real estate, "so much out of proportion with the amount of capital invested" that he retired at forty-four. Constructing a palatial residence, Grey Towers, in Milford, James married an heiress and spent the rest of his life as a country squire and patron of the arts. One artist he subsidized was the painter Sanford R. Gifford, after whom he named his eldest son.

Gifford Pinchot was educated in Europe and later at three of America's best private schools. At Yale, he played varsity football—as substitute quarterback—under the legendary Walter Camp and was inducted into Skull and Bones, the college's most prestigious secret society. His political views were scarcely distinguishable from those of his conventional classmates. "The railroads own the tracks and the cars, don't they?" he asked. "Then why shouldn't they charge what they please?"

Decidedly unconventional was his career choice. Before he departed for Yale, his father—once vice president of the American Forestry Association— had asked him if he might like to be a forester. No American had ever chosen to become a professional forester and Gifford had no idea what a modern forester would do, "since he no longer wore green cap and leather jerkin, and shot cloth-yard arrows at the King's deer."

As a boy, he'd prowled the woods and streams, heard a panther scream in the Adirondacks, roasted his supper on a camp fire. Gradually, his father's suggestion grew on him. Yale offered no forestry courses, so he took astronomy, geology, and botany. By graduation, he knew where he was headed but not how. Since the profession didn't exist in the United States, there was no recognized route to certification. So in 1889, Gifford set sail for France, proceeding down the Rhine to Bonn, where he sought counsel from Sir Dietrich Brandis, the world's leading forester.

At Brandis's suggestion, Pinchot enrolled in the French Forest School at Nancy, which encouraged students to develop *"le coup d'œil forestier,"* the forest-er's eye, the ability to see the forest in all its beauty and complexity. There he spent days examining the National Forest of Haye and the Communal Forest of Vandoeuvres, professionally managed woodlands where timber was har-vested to support forest industries.

Europeans cautioned that, while an autocracy could mandate such pro-grams, they'd be more difficult in a democratic society where most forestland was already in private hands. "Nothing general can be done," Brandis advised, "until some state or large individual owner makes the experiment and proves for America what is so well established in Europe, that forest management will pay."

Coming home in 1890, believing that "forestry is the art of using a forest without destroying it," Pinchot confronted an America obsessed by a "fury of development," which had called forth a "gigantic and lamentable massacre" of trees. "The American Colossus," he would write, "was fiercely intent on appropriating and exploiting the riches of the richest of all continents— grasping with both hands, reaping what he had not sown, wasting what he thought would last forever."

When European discoverers first set foot on the continent, forests cov-ered nearly a billion acres—a seemingly inexhaustible supply of oak, pine, spruce, cedar, redwood, and fir—as thick as quills on a porcupine. But Ameri-cans had been at war with the forest ever since. As Theodore Roosevelt put it: "The American had but one thought about a tree, and that was to cut it down."

Moreover, the government often seemed determined to give away what remained of the public domain as quickly as possible: more than 150 million acres had gone to encourage the building of railroads, 4.5 million to promote the construction of canals, 3.5 million to encourage the building of wagon roads, 2.25 million as an incentive to river improvement—not to mention something approaching 100 million to prospective settlers under the Home-stead Act, which granted a citizen 160 acres of land if he lived on it for five years, and millions more under the Timber and Stone Act of 1878, which permitted individuals, by paying $2.50 an acre, to acquire up to 160 acres containing either timber or stone (provided they swore the land was solely for their own use and they had made no prior agreement to convey the title to another person).

Roughly half of those billion acres of timber had now been cut, and of those that remained, four-fifths were already in private hands. Every day, millions of board feet were tumbling to earth. The results of the timber syndicates' "chop and run" policy were already visible through great sections of the upper Midwest. Within decades, the white pine, once the glory of Minnesota, Wisconsin, and Michigan, had been virtually decimated to feed Chicago's lumber market. For mile after mile, only heaps of "slash"—twigs, branches, and other debris—marked the killing ground of the high timber. Some years later, a timberman wrote: "It was almost a crime against Nature to cut it, but we lumbermen were never concerned with crimes against Nature. We heard only the demand for lumber, more lumber and better lumber."

In the century's last decade, the axes and saws whirred westward, chewing up the vast forests of the Pacific Northwest. Pinchot didn't want to stop them; he wanted to regulate their use. Seeking to prove that professionally managed use was practicable, he accepted, in 1892, a position with just the sort of person Brandis had in mind when he suggested that an individual proprietor might sponsor such an experiment.

George Washington Vanderbilt was a grandson of Cornelius Vanderbilt, the "commodore" who'd built a fortune on steamships and railways. With no racing stables or chorus girls to distract him, the shy bachelor established the Biltmore Estate on tableland in North Carolina's Blue Ridge Mountains. Biltmore House was a French Renaissance château, surrounded by a model farm, an arboretum, a game preserve, and thirty-five hundred acres of woodland. The estate had been designed by Frederick Law Olmsted, the landscape architect and a friend of the senior Pinchot's. When a forester was needed, he recommended Gifford.

Blue Ridge mountain folk called Biltmore "Vanderbilt's Folly" because of the staggering amount spent on it. But to Gifford it was a dream come true —a forest of his own in which to try out timber management. First, he made an inventory of his woodlands, marking the oaks, chestnuts, and yellow poplars he wanted cut.

Americans were accustomed to lumbering by cutting the young growth to permit easy logging of the high timber, which left heaps of slash on the forest floor and exposed the land to erosion and flooding. Pinchot insisted that his men respect the young growth, that they cut only trees marked by the foresters, and that they fell trees in a direction that would least damage surrounding trees. For every tree cut, they planted five or ten. Pinchot knew that the nostrum "Plant a tree for every one cut down" was nonsense: one seedling for every felled tree let sunlight flood the land and produce a park of branching shade trees, not the dense forest of clean trunks fit for lumber. When a leading German forester visited that year, he proclaimed the estate "a perfect piece of work." Pinchot's reputation was made.

Vanderbilt permitted him to accept outside work, so in 1893 he opened a consulting engineer's office in Manhattan. This produced contracts with Columbia University to design a postgraduate forestry course and with the

State of New Jersey to survey its forests. Eventually, Pinchot drifted into New York politics, campaigning with the Citizens Union for social reforms.

Pinchot wasn't all high-minded work. In this period he met a woman he loved, Laura Houghteling of Chicago. When she died in 1894 he was desolate, and for years he remained in her thrall. After testifying to a Senate committee in 1906, he jotted in his diary: "I felt today my Lady's help." He didn't marry until he was forty-nine.

His increasing stature brought him a larger public role. In part owing to his own exertions, the National Academy of Sciences, in early 1896, appointed a seven-man National Forest Commission to examine public timberlands. The government's principal steps to preserve American forests had been the 1881 passage of legislation creating a Division of Forestry in the Agriculture Department and, ten years later, an act authorizing the president to create "forest reserves," land in which the cutting of timber could be wholly or partially prohibited. By 1896, Presidents Harrison and Cleveland had designated nearly twenty million acres of reserves by removing them from the public domain, but there was still no consensus as to how rapidly those reserves should be expanded and what rules should govern their use.

The commission charged with answering those questions was chaired by Charles S. Sargent, professor of arboriculture at Harvard, and dominated by other leading academicians. Its only working forester, and its youngest member, Pinchot became the commission's secretary. From the start, he was at odds with the autocratic Sargent. To his diary, Pinchot confided: "Sargent opposed to all real forest work, and utterly without a plan, or capacity to decide on plans submitted."

The commission considered an inspection trip of western forests; there were no forest reserves in the East, because there were no public lands there. Somehow the tour kept getting put off. Impatient at the delay—he gave off a perpetual air of tensile urgency—Pinchot left in early June, traveling at his own expense and accompanied only by his Yale classmate Henry Graves. Even when the rest of the commission caught up with them in Montana in July, most members preferred to travel by train, prompting Pinchot to another diary entry: "Sargent doesn't fish or hunt or know anything about the mountains." Pinchot and some aides hiked across the Bitterroot Mountains and spent three weeks in Idaho's Clearwater country, his first significant visit to the state. Later that summer, he spent a day—and a bitterly cold night—in the woods with John Muir, a commission consultant and, at fifty-eight, the nation's most influential naturalist and one of Pinchot's heroes (though they would soon be at odds).

When the commission started drawing up its report, the differences between Sargent and Pinchot sharpened. Sargent wanted the forest reserves kept inviolate; Pinchot favored regulated use. Unable to reach agreement, the commission passed along oral recommendations. About to leave office,

Cleveland couldn't wait and issued proclamations creating thirteen new reserves, a total of 21.4 million acres.

Without a report explaining the rationale, the president's action stirred a torrent of outrage. In South Dakota, timbermen dressed as Indians demonstrated at railroad depots to protest what they saw as a presidential effort to halt development and give the West back to the Indians. Pinchot later concluded that the commission's error had been to "pass through the Western country without allowing the Western people to know what was being done." He resolved not to repeat that mistake.

In the McKinley administration, management of the forest reserves fell to Interior Secretary Cornelius W. Bliss, who asked Pinchot to serve as his "confidential forest agent." Traveling widely, Pinchot managed to calm western fears and to spread his own views of enlightened forest policy. In July 1898, McKinley promoted him to chief forester and head of the Agriculture Department's Division of Forestry (later renamed the Bureau of Forestry, then the Forest Service).

It was at this time that Pinchot renewed his acquaintance with Theodore Roosevelt. Their paths had crossed in New York and Roosevelt had sponsored Pinchot for the Boone and Crockett Club, a society of a hundred wellborn sportsmen who had killed at least three species of North American big game "in fair chase." Now Roosevelt, as New York's governor, invited the chief forester to visit him in Albany to discuss the future of the state's forests. Roosevelt asked him to stay in the Executive Mansion. On his arrival, Pinchot found the mansion "under ferocious attack from a band of invisible Indians, and the Governor of the Empire State was helping a houseful of children to escape by lowering them out of a second story window on a rope." That evening, the governor and the forester squared off in a boxing match, in which Pinchot managed to floor Roosevelt.

This was an appropriate start to a relationship that would flower into one of Roosevelt's most fruitful personal-professional alliances. "I have one friend ...in whose integrity I believe as I do my own," he wrote a reporter. "This is Gifford Pinchot." The lean forester towered over the stocky president, but both were robust, determined men. Each saw, and newly appreciated, himself mirrored in the other's eyes.

When Roosevelt advanced to the White House, he brought with him a personal bent for the active outdoor life, an intense interest in the natural world. He could wax rhapsodic about trees. After camping with John Muir in Yosemite in 1903, he told an audience: "Lying out at night under those giant Sequoias was like lying in a temple built by no hand of man, a temple grander than any human architect could by any possibility build." It was, he told friends, "the grandest day of my life."

To shape those predilections into full-blown programs, Roosevelt leaned heavily on Pinchot. The forester and the president shared a sociopolitical analysis of the forest problem that jibed with the progressive side of Roosevelt's persona: the nation's woodlands must be held in trust for the American people, not for powerful timber interests. The forester drafted the forestry section of Roosevelt's first State of the Union message, delivered on December 3, 1901, producing such characteristic formulations as: "The fundamental idea of forestry is the perpetuation of forests by use" and "The forest reserves should be enlarged and set apart forever, for the use and benefit of our people as a whole, and not sacrificed to the shortsighted greed of a few."

Pinchot's influence with the president dismayed Muir, Sargent, and others, who regarded the forester as too political, too opportunistic, too ready to compromise on principle to win support in the Congress and state capitals, too indifferent to aesthetics and to wildlife protection. His willingness to permit lumbering and sheep grazing in the reserves offended the purists who believed in preservation at all costs. "There is no one but you and I," Sargent wrote Muir, "who really love the North American trees." Muir, the bearded Scotsman, was the first president of the Sierra Club and inclined to a certain mysticism about the natural world: "I never before saw a plant so full of life; so perfectly spiritual, it seemed pure enough for the throne of its Creator. I felt as if I were in the presence of superior beings who loved me and beckoned me to come. I sat down beside them and wept for joy." He argued passionately that there were intangible considerations as important as board feet or votes in Congress.

The forester quickly became part of Roosevelt's "tennis cabinet," friends who joined him on the tennis court, for jujitsu in the gym, or on rambles through Rock Creek Park. With his puckish sense of humor, Pinchot became a popular figure on Washington's social scene. Still unmarried, he lived with his parents in their palatial residence at 1615 Rhode Island Avenue, where his mother, Mary Pinchot, served as his hostess at glittering dinner parties for administration colleagues and powerful congressmen. "He was very appealing to the ladies," Alice Roosevelt recalled, "and even my spinster Aunt Emily believed for a time that he was intended for her and had to be disabused of this notion."

His warm support from the White House notwithstanding, Pinchot remained frustrated by what seemed to him an utterly illogical division of powers. The Interior Department, through its General Land Office, controlled the forest reserves but had no foresters; the Bureau of Forestry in the Department of Agriculture had the foresters but no forests. So long as this split persisted, the term *chief forester* was an empty title. Pinchot became increasingly obsessed by this fracturing of his bailiwick—which served the interests of the timber syndicates. For some years, the effort to gain full control of both forests and foresters became his "chief object in life."

In 1902, a bill calling for that transfer was defeated, 100–73, in the House after influential congressmen denounced Pinchot's "so-called scientific forestry." Finally, he conceived the American Forest Congress—ostensibly a gathering of congressmen, lumbermen, railroad men, miners, editors, and educators—which convened in Washington in January 1905. Later, Pinchot proudly confessed that the gathering had been "planned, organized and conducted" by his bureau with the transfer of powers as its central objective. This time it worked. Within weeks, the Transfer Act sailed through both houses of Congress and was signed into law. The Bureau of Forestry became the Forest Service; the forest reserves became national forests.

By at last combining foresters and some 86 million acres of national forests within his service, Pinchot became a still fatter target for westerners profoundly skeptical of "Pinchotism." The dyspeptic Speaker of the House, Joseph G. Cannon, once growled, "Not one cent for scenery." As an eastern patrician, Pinchot riled those with a class chip on their shoulders. "Cecil Rhodes was not within one million miles of exerting the power that Gifford the First claimed to himself," argued a Colorado legislator. "This enormous territory of forest reserves is an empire within a republic, ruled by a despot with as much power as the Czar of Russia."

If such formulations went too far, they reflected a real anxiety on the part of many westerners that the withdrawal of so much land from settlement would restrict the region's development. Washington's governor charged that Pinchot had "done more to retard the growth and development of the Northwest than any other man." The attack on the Forest Service was spearheaded by a determined group of western senators—among them Weldon B. Heyburn of Idaho, Charles W. Fulton of Oregon, Clarence D. Clark of Wyoming, Henry M. Teller and Thomas M. Patterson of Colorado.

Pinchot fought back, waging a bitter struggle for public opinion. "Just so long as I am able to travel and speak, and just so long as the western people are willing to meet me," he said, "I propose to discuss with them face to face any differences we may have." When he wasn't behind his desk at his red-brick headquarters on F Street, more likely than not he was out "at the front" beyond the Mississippi, meeting with western governors and senators or appealing over their heads to ranchers and farmers. In Wyoming, for example, he eventually won over the influential congressman Frank W. Mondell—a considerable prize since Mondell later became Speaker of the House.

Opposition to the Roosevelt-Pinchot forest program was especially fierce in Idaho, in part because of the heavy concentration of national forest reserves in the state. By 1907, of the state's 53,945,000 acres, some 20,336,000 had been designated as seventeen national forests. Resistance to Pinchot's programs was concentrated in the heavily forested north. "Forester Pinchot is an enthusiast, in other words a 'crank' on such matters," wrote J. F. Scott, publisher of the *Coeur d'Alene Press,* "and while such people accomplish things, they need to be held down by the more conservative." The war cry of the western opposition went something like this: "A dude in Washington is to decide whether a man out in Idaho shall cut a stick of timber or not!"

Pinchot had scant hope of converting Senator Heyburn, a native of northern Idaho and longtime ally of the timber interests. In Heyburn's relentlessly confrontational view of the world, the forester's program represented a grievous affront to Idaho's sovereignty. Of Heyburn, Calvin Cobb wrote Pinchot: "He has wonderful energy and personal courage, but no moral sense." After Roosevelt denounced Heyburn's "contrary policy of destruction of the state's future assets in the temporary interest of a few favored parties" and Pinchot published his correspondence with the senator, any hope of accommodation was lost. Henceforth, the florid senator burned with a "deep and malignant" hatred of the forester.

Southern Idaho, with its less-forested farm country, was more friendly. So Pinchot wooed Governor Gooding, a sheep man from the Snake River plain. At long last, on September 5, 1905, Pinchot left the governor's office with Gooding's commitment to support the forest reserves. In the form of a joint interview tendered to Cobb's *Statesman*, the governor insisted he had never opposed the principle of forest reserves, merely the "crude" ancillary regulations, and pledged henceforth to assist Washington's timber policy every way he could.

To his father, Pinchot could scarcely contain his chortle. Gooding's defection, he boasted, "will leave Heyburn absolutely alone, and he will either have to accept the President's policy or get out of the Republican party. ... All organized opposition in the West to the Forest Reserve policy is at an end."

Hardly. In fact, Heyburn only redoubled his attack. At the National Irrigation Congress in Boise a year later, he took Pinchot on. "Forest reserves belong to the land of lazy monarchs," Heyburn declared. "Three times have the strict regulations of English forest reserves precipitated revolution in that country, which ended only when the head of a sovereign was on the block. ... It will do the same thing in this country!"

Then the senator unfurled his "forest reserve map" of Idaho, with more than a third of the state's territory colored black for reserves, removed from the state's productive economy and subject to the "proclamation of desolation." He warned that the Forest Service's dead hand had spread just as far in Montana and Washington, while in Wyoming "the shade is falling fast."

In early 1907, the western senators mounted their most determined assault yet. On February 18, Senator Fulton took the floor to contend that the Forest Service was "composed of dreamers and theorists," but

> beyond and outside the domain of their theories and their dreams is the everyday, busy, bustling, throbbing world of human endeavor, where real men are at work. ... While these chiefs of the Bureau of Forestry sit within their marble halls and theorize ... the lowly pioneer is climbing the mountain side where he will erect his humble cabin, and within the shadow of the whispering pines and the lofty firs of the western forest, engage in the laborious work of carving out for himself and his loved ones a home and a dwelling place. It is of him I think and for him I take my stand today.

Emboldened by his own oratory, Fulton introduced an amendment to the Agricultural Appropriations Bill depriving the president of his authority to create new national forests within Oregon, Washington, Idaho, Montana, Colorado, and Wyoming and reserving that right to Congress. So strong was anti-Roosevelt feeling that the amendment sailed through without a roll call. The president had until March 4 to sign the appropriations bill. To have vetoed it would have left the Agriculture Department and the Forest Service without funds to operate.

Yet the Fulton amendment drove a stake through the heart of the administration's forest reserve policy. Huddling at the White House, Roosevelt and Pinchot quickly devised an audacious riposte. The service had gathered evidence justifying the creation of twenty-one new forest reserves on public land and the expansion of eleven existing reserves—doubling the area under protection to roughly 150,000,000 acres. Working around the clock, the Forest Service's staff—whom the critics denounced as "dudes and invalids"—prepared paperwork for the thirty-two proclamations, which were issued on March 2. Only then did the president sign the appropriations bill. The reaction among many westerners to these "midnight" proclamations was predictably sulfurous. A call went out convening a protest meeting in Denver on June 19; Pinchot made plans to attend and confront his opponents.

But there were other instruments at hand with which to protect the nation's woodlands, notably the criminal law. For years, it had been evident to federal investigators that what one reformer called "sharps, speculators, sharks, land grabbers and other scoundrels" were obtaining vast tracts of timberland through fraud, taking advantage of laws designed to furnish land to the small settler at prices he could afford.

Because of the family-size, 160-acre limit on timberland that could be claimed by any individual or corporation, it was difficult for timber syndicates to assemble large woodland tracts without fraud and bribery. To this end, swindlers in the Great Lakes region, and now the Pacific Northwest, had grabbed thousands of forested acres—which the government had intended to distribute in little parcels to "the small man"—passing them on to huge corporations at a fraction of their value.

Even with the transfer of the national forests to the Forest Service, the General Land Office in the Interior Department retained jurisdiction over thirty-three million acres of public lands, those parts of the public domain not yet granted to private parties or fenced off in national reserves and forests. In late 1902, an informant told the GLO of a ring gobbling up public land in California and Oregon. Binger Hermann, the former Oregon congressman heading the office, tried to bury the lead, but others insisted on following its trail. Agents dispatched to Oregon turned up a major scandal that eventually forced Hermann's resignation. Though indicted for burning his files, he was never convicted.

The Oregon land ring employed several techniques to obtain government timberlands by fraud, most involving the use of dummy settlers to file false claims. One investigator reported "trainloads of women schoolteachers" from Minnesota brought in to file for land they promptly sold to their corporate sponsors. Initially, the ring involved small fry, among them a petty speculator who fled to Europe with the belly dancer Little Egypt. But Francis J. Heney, the aggressive special prosecutor, had larger targets in mind: "I am after the big fish," he said, "and as long as there is a hook and a line or a bit of tackle in the Government box, I will keep after them. Graft is ruining Russia today; graft ruined Rome, the ancient empire of the world, and unless the juries of the Nation sustain the laws of the United States, graft will ruin this country." Aided by the Secret Service's crack operative William J. Burns, Heney netted some big fish, including Oregon's political patriarch, Senator John M. Mitchell, convicted of taking a bribe ("Harry," he told his secretary, "you know they'd hadn't ought to prosecute me for that. All I ever got was some little checks"), a congressman, a United States attorney, a United States commissioner, and three state senators. (Burns suspected that Oregon's other U.S. senator—Pinchot's longtime nemesis, Charles W. Fulton—was also involved in the land frauds.)

The staggering haul of Oregon officeholders—indeed, the revelation that, as Lincoln Steffens put it, the General Land Office was "corrupt to the core"—made popular heroes of Heney and Burns and put the war against land fraud high on the national agenda. To Roosevelt, these frauds subverted his land policy, which "should always be to favor the actual settler, the actual home-maker, who comes to dwell on the land and there to bring up his children to inherit after him." In December 1906, the president delivered a special message to Congress, proclaiming the government's determination to stamp out timber fraud and instructing the interior secretary "to allow no patent to be issued to public land under any law until by an examination on the ground actual compliance with that law has been found to exist." To conduct such investigations, he proposed to increase the General Land Office's corps of special agents.

Indeed, as the president spoke, these agents were tightening the investigative noose about a land ring alleged to be operating in Idaho. By January 30, 1907, Francis N. Goodwin, chief of the GLO's field division, made a full report on the case to W. A. Richards, the office's new commissioner, asserting that there was strong evidence to show that the Barber Lumber Company of Eau Claire, Wisconsin, conspiring with a ring of well-connected Idaho political figures, had fraudulently obtained forty thousand acres of timber in the Boise Basin. In mid-February, Judge James H. Beatty wrote Secretary of the Interior Ethan Allen Hitchcock pressing for prosecution of these cases. On March 11, after Hitchcock and Attorney General Charles J. Bonaparte gave the go-ahead, Idaho's U.S. attorney, Norman Ruick, began presenting the case to a federal grand jury.

By mid-March, disconcerting rumors seeped out of the grand jury, suggesting some major Idaho figures were about to be indicted. Among those said to be implicated were Senator William E. Borah. Gooding was horrified. Though Borah was surely no friend of his, he would rely heavily on the lawyer's courtroom skills and inspired oratory to win the Haywood case.

In late March, Gooding resolved to do exactly what he'd done the year before when he needed intelligence on—and a voice in—Washington decision making. He dispatched Calvin Cobb to the nation's capital to find out what was going on, while wiring Roosevelt to ask that he stay the investigation until Cobb reached Washington and informed the president of things he would "want to know and ought to know." Evidently, Cobb also represented Borah on this trip, for he kept the senator closely in touch with the evolving situation by telegram.

On March 27, from his eastbound train, Cobb wired Pinchot urgently: "Will be at Willard tomorrow Thursday at five. Will you leave word if you can see me that evening?" Pinchot had an engagement on the twenty-eighth but left a handwritten card at the Willard Hotel's front desk saying that he would be delighted to see Cobb at his house after nine.

When the two men sat down in Pinchot's study that night, they represented a curious convergence of disparate interests. Insofar as Cobb represented Governor Gooding, the forester may have felt a bit of a grudge. For the autumn before, during his tough reelection fight, Idaho's governor had publicly reneged on his hard-won pledge to support Pinchot's forest policy. Declaring himself unalterably opposed to "a single acre" of northern Idaho land going into forest reserves, he proclaimed: "If you do not want to see the greater part of northern Idaho in forest reserves, send a man to the United States Senate who will stand shoulder to shoulder with Senator Heyburn." For a time Pinchot considered counterattacking, but—given the president's support of Gooding in the Steunenberg matter—he ultimately decided to ignore the governor's statement, treating it as a temporary political expedient. When Gooding was reelected, Pinchot congratulated him warmly, adding, "Now that the new forest reserves in northern Idaho have been created, I hope the agitation will die down and that we shall be able to get to work together to safeguard the interests along the lines of our joint interview in the *Statesman*."

All this time, Pinchot had elaborately cultivated Calvin Cobb, and that for any number of reasons: because the publisher had established good relations with the president; because he remained a convenient channel to both Gooding and Borah; and because he edited Idaho's most consequential newspaper, an essential organ through which to mold western opinion on forest issues. Indeed, Cobb had vigorously supported Pinchot and the president on timber matters, for which the forester was appropriately grateful. On the same day he congratulated Gooding on his reelection, he dropped Cobb a note hailing the election returns and adding his deep appreciation for the publisher's "admirable" support of the Forest Service.

The publisher, in turn, had ample reason to cultivate the forester: he knew of Pinchot's influence with the president; he valued him as a news source on matters of great moment to his readership; he appreciated Pinchot's assistance on the bundle of issues around the Haywood trial, the biggest local story of his generation; he knew how helpful the forester might be to those facing indictment in Idaho, many of whom were the publisher's friends; and, finally, by then Cobb knew that he might well be caught up in the timber fraud scandal himself and hoped Pinchot would help extract him from that mess.

So each man had gone out of his way to stay in the other's good graces. Both were, after all, representatives of that "better class of men" accustomed to meeting one another in the elite clubs, the fine restaurants, the bars of the most comfortable hotels. When Pinchot attended the National Irrigation Congress in Boise the fall before, Cobb had made sure that the forester stayed with him at the Idaho Street bungalow and took most of his meals with the Cobb family. Pinchot, in turn, had entertained Cobb and called on his wife and daughter during their stays in Washington. Now he was pleased to offer the publisher a seat by the fire, a drink of whiskey, and a sympathetic ear for whatever was on his mind.

Cobb stayed a week in Washington, during which he had at least one audience with the president and one with Attorney General Bonaparte. Eventually, both men agreed to keep the timber fraud indictments formally secret until the Haywood trial ended. Bonaparte wired Ruick on March 29 to avoid all "publicity harmful to [the] murder prosecution."

On his way home on April 9, Cobb wrote Pinchot from the Chicago Club to report troublesome news just received from Idaho: "I heard from home that Ruick and Beatty have examined a list of witnesses to prove that the Barber Lumber Company owned stock in the *Statesman* and even had [my accountant] come in with his stock book and stood over him to see that he read the stubs correctly. I suppose [Ruick] wants to connect me with the lumber deals in that way and then with the Steunenberg case. I think Beatty and Ruick are a bad lot but am delighted to have them make the effort to get me in."

But reaching Boise on April 12, Cobb was not so delighted to discover what his enemies had been up to. The day before, the *Capital News* had published a page 1 item noting, "It is rumored about the Federal Building that Calvin Cobb is a much wanted man." Cobb dashed off a statement in response: "Upon returning home today I find that the *Evening Capital News* has published a statement intended to convey the impression that I was absent from the city because of a fear that I might be 'wanted.' I was here for two weeks after the grand jury met and had no intimation of any nature that I should be wanted."

Ruick, it seemed, had also asked Western Union for all recent telegrams to Washington signed by Cobb. But Ruick's "chief crime against me and my family," Cobb wrote Pinchot, was that "during my absence when he and all department men knew where I was, and without any request for my presence, he had placed continuously about my home three men to watch my house— the object was, of course, to give the impression that I was in hiding and to insult my family." Then Cobb asked Pinchot the favor he'd been leading up to for weeks. "I must ask you as my friend to aid me in getting his [Ruick's] summary removal.... I am sure you will feel that I am justified in asking you to make a fight for me on this issue and I cannot think the President will allow such a [scoundrel] to have the power to vent his personal spite on decent people."

The request put Pinchot in a delicate position. For, ostensibly at least, Ruick was enforcing the very legislation the forester needed to put teeth in his timber policy. How could he ask the president to go easy on the publisher because he was a friend? There's no evidence he did ask.

Pinchot may have hesitated because of some rather curious goings-on in Boise during early April. The grand jury had subpoenaed L. G. Chapman, manager of the Barber Lumber Company operation in Boise, and asked him to produce the company's books. (Cobb's son Lyon had worked for Chapman since 1905.) Chapman, on Borah's advice, conceded that he had them in his custody but refused to hand them over. On April 9, Judge Beatty sent him to jail, where he remained until April 19, when a federal judge in Portland released him. The Secret Service concluded that Borah—as the Barber Company's principal lawyer in Idaho—had told Chapman to "go to jail" before giving up the papers. In a letter to another Barber Company lawyer, in the home office, Borah wrote, "We did not have anything to conceal in our books which I could see or of which I had knowledge. But after full consultation we came to the conclusion that if they wanted an indictment they would have it anyway." The company was under no obligation, Borah thought, to furnish the prosecutors "our entire case in advance."

This may have been a legally sound position, but it did not awaken confidence in Pinchot that Borah—and Cobb—were on the up and up. Nonetheless, Pinchot continued to provide advice and intelligence to his friend the publisher. Writing on April 15, before he received Cobb's latest communication, Pinchot responded to the April 9 letter from Chicago: "It is curious and interesting, but not important except as showing animus, that you have been investigated as to your connection with the Barber Lumber Company. That must have been spite.... That anyone could think of connecting you with land frauds is, of course, ridiculous." But he had more important news. "Things seem to have been moving very fast since you were here," he wrote Cobb. "I learned yesterday that Senator Borah has been indicted, and I have just had a telegram from him asking whether I would be in Washington for the next ten days, to which I replied that I would. I am more sorry than I can say for this development, but am particularly anxious to hear from you just what it means."

As he'd signaled Pinchot, Borah did rush to Washington. He wrote a confidential letter to the president—which, at his request, was kept out of the White House files—and followed up on April 22 with a call on the president. Emerging from Roosevelt's office wearing a thin smile, he told reporters, "The reports that indictments have been returned against me or my clients for alleged land frauds are simply rumors. I know nothing of any such indictments. My call was simply one of respect."

In fact, he confided to a friend, he'd asked the President to suppress the indictment until the Haywood trial was over, then resubmit the matter to another—and presumably fairer—grand jury. The current jury, he argued, had been stacked against him from the start by the U.S. attorney and the U.S. marshal, Ruel Rounds, who'd made sure it was filled with some of his worst enemies in Boise. The president had deferred decision on the second request but granted the first. The indictments of eleven persons voted by the grand jury on April 12 remained sealed in Judge Beatty's office. Accused of timber fraud were eleven individuals: Borah; Frank Martin, Steunenberg's attorney general; James T. Barber and Sumner G. Moon of the Barber Lumber Company; seven other named conspirators; and a mysterious "John Doe."

In a city crawling with detectives of all persuasions, it was impossible to keep such a development secret very long. The indictments were bad news for the prosecutors, but, worse yet, they had reason to suspect that behind the grand jury's action stood the Western Federation of Miners. Eugene Johnson, still a detective on Hawley's staff, staked out Ruick's office and found attorneys for the defense—notably Fred Miller and Leon Whitsell—paying long calls on the prosecutor. "It is common talk among the best men in town," he reported, "that the attorneys for the defense have got next to Ruick with money."

On April 5, Operative 21 weighed in with some intelligence he'd picked up that day at defense headquarters. From a conversation he'd overheard between Nugent and Whitsell, he concluded that "the W.F.M. is interested in the investigation of timber frauds... that the object was to implicate ex-gov. Steunenberg in the land deals of Idaho and discredit him in the eyes of the people in order to help the cause of the defendants and that the district attorney [Ruick] who is conducting this investigation is a friend of Nugent's." James McParland, with his keen eye for pertinent intelligence, plucked out this nugget and rushed it to Gooding. "I think if this could be conveyed to the authorities at Washington," he wrote, "it would enlighten them some on the investigation that is being made at Boise by the United States Grand Jury."

Gooding didn't need much prompting. In his April 10 letter to the president, enclosing Operative 21's reports, the governor drew Roosevelt's attention to the April 5 report:

What I have feared all along... is that the late Governor Steunenberg would be smirched, and that the report of the grand jury making charges against him, at least by implication, would be given out just prior to the trial of the first of his murderers. I do not wish to be understood as expressing a belief that Mr. Ruick is in the employ of the Western Federation of Miners, or of being personally interested in the defense of these men, who are accused of the Steunenberg murder. However, it is very plain to me, that the work of the department of justice in Idaho at this time, is almost entirely in the interest of the defendants.

Hawley, writing to McParland, was even more certain of what was going on: "There is no doubt in my mind in regard to the United States attorney acting [in] collusion with the friends of Haywood. Of course this is a matter that I am not prepared to state openly, but I believe it, and that we will have some proof of it before the matter is through."

For some months, Pinchot had planned a June visit to Idaho as part of his campaign for western support. Cobb did his best to prepare the forester's way. "The purposes of the government have been sadly misrepresented and many people misled," he editorialized in early May. "When Mr. Pinchot shall have explained the entire system and pointed out its benefits, there will be little or nothing left to which to object."

Though careful to cultivate this important ally, Cobb was feeling increasingly out of joint that spring. The indictment of his ally Borah, the surveillance of his home and family, the government's failure to recognize the collusion between Ruick and the WFM had deeply embittered him. Writing Pinchot on May 6, he warned that he was "disposed to give up making any further effort for honest government." Over the course of two decades, "I have been doing all in my power to uphold the administration in its efforts to better conditions of public service.... I have been vilified, abused, boycotted and now, instead of the consideration that I might reasonably expect the administration to give me, I find that this effort to drag my name in the mire by a dishonest official is, so far as I can see, to be condoned."

As Pinchot reached Boise on June 24, he found himself in a tight place. On one flank loomed the U.S. attorney, prosecuting violations of the nation's timber laws, ostensibly designed to preserve Pinchot's—and the president's —cherished forests. On the other ranged his friends Cobb and Borah and his temporary ally Gooding, men whose reputations could only suffer from vigorous prosecution of the timber cases and whose great crusade against the WFM might rise or fall accordingly.

Pinchot had planned to address Boise's Commercial Club the night of June 24. But many members had tickets for Ethel Barrymore's performance, so the speech was put off to the next night. Meanwhile, Pinchot attended the Haywood trial and "saw most of the celebrities, famous and infamous, at close range."

On the evening of June 25, the club's dining room on the fourth floor of the Boise City National Bank was filled with members, their ladies, and their guests as Borah introduced the forester.

"I've just come from Denver," Pinchot began. "Hearing some of the speakers in that city at the land convention, I felt as if I were one of the greatest murderers in the United States. But here I feel that I am in a different atmosphere. . . . You look to the time when you have a million people in Idaho. Why not look to the time when you will have two million, five million? In the forest reserves you are laying the foundation. I believe in the West. I believe in it more and more every year and in a very much greater West of the future."

From his seat in the front row, the recently indicted Senator Borah could be pardoned if he wondered what kind of a future the Roosevelt-Pinchot timber fraud prosecutions were preparing for him.

13

GENTLEMEN OF THE PRESS

ON SARAH BERNHARDT's farewell tour of America in 1906, she played Carson City, Nevada, where she grew fond of a young newspaperman named Sam Davis, who'd interviewed her for the *Carson Appeal,* Hearst's San Francisco *Examiner,* and the Associated Press. As her train was about to leave—so the story goes—the actress put her hands on the reporter's shoulders, kissed him first on one cheek, then on the other, then squarely on the mouth. "The right cheek is for the *Appeal,"* she said, "the left is for the *Examiner,* and the lips, my friend, that is for yourself."

"Madame," exclaimed Davis, "I also represent the Associated Press, which serves 380 papers west of the Mississippi alone!"

Such was the mystique of the AP, the largest news service in the nation, and perhaps in the world. Its ubiquity impressed even the irreverent Mark Twain, who addressed the agency's annual banquet that same year. "There are only two forces that can carry light to all corners of the globe," he said, "only two—the sun in the heavens and the Associated Press down here. I may seem to be flattering the sun, but I do not mean it so; I am meaning only to be just and fair all around."

In 1907, some Americans were aghast at the notion that a "great octopus" like the AP could embrace eight hundred member papers, putting its product before as many as twenty-five million readers every day. "Here," wrote one stupefied editor, "is the most tremendous engine for Power that ever existed in this world. If you can conceive all that Power ever wielded by the great autocrats of history, by the Alexanders, Caesars, Tamburlaines, Kubla Khans and Napoleons, to be massed together into one vast unit of Power, even this would be less than the Power now wielded by the Associated Press."

The AP's puissance was measured as much by organizational rigor as by sheer size, for in an era of trusts, it was one of the nation's most effective monopolies. A newspaper with a precious AP franchise was protected against any competitor in its territory seeking one, while the AP itself had dread powers to discipline a paper that dealt with a rival wire service (the nascent United Press, for example, or the Laffan News Service). In 1898, facing charges of trafficking with an enemy, the Chicago *Inter-Ocean* challenged the

AP's structure in court. When the Illinois Supreme Court upheld the suit, finding that the AP was "so affected with a public duty" that it must provide its news to any applicant, the AP abruptly dissolved as an Illinois corporation and reorganized in New York, this time not as a business corporation but as a "mutual association"—like a literary society or fishing club—permitting it arbitrarily to expel any member who protested publicly against the way the organization was run. Henceforth, all insurgency was doomed.

To its critics, the AP was fond of stressing this "mutuality," arguing that it was merely a "clearing house," drawing news primarily from its members and distributing it to other members. In fact, the AP stood for the notion that news was private property, fiercely retaliating against anyone who poached on its preserve. It was dominated by an inner circle of large metropolitan newspapers that at the time of the service's reincarnation in 1900 had each purchased a thousand dollars in bonds worth forty votes, compared to the single vote held by ordinary members. Buttressed by this margin, old-guard papers like the *Chicago Tribune* and the *Washington Star* were firmly in the saddle. To Will Irwin, a former reporter turned press critic, the AP was run by a "stand pat" crowd unmoved by the grievances of labor or the ills of the teeming cities.

Where it drew news from a member paper, which generally supported the community's most substantial interests, the AP reflected the outlook of that city's power structure. In Boise, from the night of the assassination until the eve of trial, the *Statesman* for all intents and purposes had *been* the AP. As Ida Crouch-Hazlett put it, "Crane, of the Boise *Statesman,* a mine owners' sheet, is attending to the Associated Press dispatches and anything that will benefit the prisoners will not be reported by him."

The pressures on men like Calvin Cobb or his city editor, Harry Crane, were as much social as ideological. "It is embarrassing to meet at the country club a man concerning whose trust company you have published unpleasant news that morning," Irwin noted. "It is distressing to find a department store withdrawing its advertising because you have 'roasted' the bank in which the president of the store is a director."

In large cities and some state capitals, the AP maintained bureaus staffed by its own men, and to cover major events like the Haywood trial, it dispatched its own reporters. But that did little to diversify the AP's menu. For these editors and correspondents tended to share management's mind-set. To them, as Irwin put it, "a movement in stocks is...big news. Widespread industrial misery in a mining camp is scarcely news at all.... The trial which follows, with its illumination on the methods of Tory interests when they have their own way, is not news." To Oswald Garrison Villard of New York's *Evening Post,* the AP had "always bowed down before authority and rarely ever stood up to the government in any controversy." Because of its reliance on local papers, it reflected "every local prejudice and bent," which in the South meant "the white man's side of any race trouble." To Upton Sinclair, the

AP's vast reach ensured that American public opinion was "poisoned at the source."

In 1907, the AP's day-to-day operations were in the hands of its longtime general manager, Melville E. Stone, a former Chicago banker and club man who relished the camaraderie of powerful men and performed unusual services for them. When E. H. Harriman answered Roosevelt's "undesirable citizens" letter—a matter that remained on the front pages for weeks on end —it was Stone who wrote the magnate's response. Correspondingly, the general manager had little patience with the maunderings of the dispossessed or the carping of the AP's critics, like "the noisy young man from Grub Street who, with marked literary mien, half-lighted cigarette and unspeakable cocksureness, is hunting about for something to reform."

Stone stewed over southern and eastern European immigrants, "discontented workingmen ripe for trouble," who didn't comprehend "the spirit of American institutions" and threatened public order. As editor of the *Chicago Daily News,* he'd campaigned—publicly and covertly—for prosecution of the Haymarket defendants, arguing that, even if none was the actual bomb thrower, they were culpable because they'd advocated violence (fearing their influence as martyrs, he later tried to save their lives).

Now, with many of these issues surfacing in the Haywood case, Stone's AP prepared extensive coverage. It had just produced a substantial daily report from the trial of Harry K. Thaw for the murder of Stanford White, which had ended April 12 with a deadlocked jury. But Thaw was tried in fascinating Manhattan and many papers sent their own men to the big city. Given Boise's remoteness from most of the nation's press and the expense of maintaining a correspondent there for months, still more papers intended to rely on the AP during the Haywood trial. Growing in muscle every year, the AP determined to mount a maximum effort for this case, which a spokesman called "so much greater and of such vast importance that it is not to be compared for a moment with the Thaw case or any other great case of recent years."

Indeed, the Haywood case may have been the first trial in American history in which the real target wasn't so much the jurors in the box as the larger jury of public opinion. It bore the signs of a spectacular show trial, a great national drama in which the stakes were nothing less than the soul of the American people. In his February 1906 letter to Stanley Easton of Bunker Hill and Sullivan, seeking to raise a war chest for the vast legal struggle, James Hawley had proposed an ambitious scheme "to rid the West entirely of [the WFM] which has done so much to retard our progress." By tracing these "foul crimes" to the federation, he said, "it will be easy to raise such a storm that the general public will not countenance [its] continued existence."

Surely the mine owners, the governors of Colorado and Idaho, the Pinkertons, and the prosecutors hoped to prevail at the trials and put Haywood, Moyer, and Pettibone on the gallows. But if they failed in that, their larger goal remained to persuade the American people that the WFM was a gang of cutthroats and dynamiters that should be, if not actually annihilated, then prevented from impeding the West's new corporate order.

The defense was no less eager to use the trial as a platform from which to address the American public. Darrow was a past master at such arts, both in shaping the climate in which a trial would take place and, in turn, using courtroom events to form public opinion. Years later he told the Senate Commission on Industrial Relations that in labor's struggles the molding of public opinion was a top priority, an instrument of "the greatest force and value." A Socialist writer in Boise for the trial told a colleague in the mainstream press: "It's all propaganda. We will spread the story of this case all over the country and we will show the masses that they cannnot hope for justice from their masters." Ironically, Theodore Roosevelt had played right into Darrow's hands with his "undesirable citizens" statement; the defense seized the opportunity by organizing the great marches in New York, Chicago, and Boston. The slogan "I am an undesirable citizen," displayed on thousands of working-class breasts, was a masterstroke of public relations.

A few earlier trials—the Haymarket and Pullman cases come to mind—had betrayed some of the same characteristics, but what distinguished the Haywood trial from all that preceded it was that there was now a national public ready, eager, and able to absorb the disparate messages dispatched from the Boise courtroom.

The very notion of public opinion was a product of this period. Through most of the nineteenth century, the nation had been fragmented by region, state, race, and nationality into a multiplicity of "island communities." Journalists served discrete audiences. As editor of the *North American Review* in 1871, Henry Adams was "perversely proud" of its tiny circulation—perhaps four hundred—since he believed that everyone who mattered was on the list. But by 1907, the theatrical or circus press agent in his checked suit, patent leather shoes, and brown derby had given way to the sleek "public relations man," a calling virtually invented at the turn of the century by a young Princeton graduate named Ivy Lee.

Moreover, the very appetite and compass of the American press had been vastly enlarged of late. Given the reach of the Associated Press, the Scripps-McRae News Service, the Publishers Press, and the Newspaper Enterprise Association; the circulation of national magazines like *McClure's* and *Collier's;* the shrill carrying power of the great urban tabloids, all the apparatus was in place with which to put these stirring events before a continental audience. "And what an audience!" a Portland reporter wrote as the trial opened. "Seldom have men played to one so great. The whole American people fill the seats of the vast auditorium, extending from the Atlantic to the Pacific, from the Great Lakes to the Gulf."

And of all the instruments of opinion making, none was the equal of the Associated Press. Now the AP decided to send to Idaho three senior correspondents to report the news and two experienced operators to send the copy from a special installation in the courthouse over a leased line to Salt Lake City, thence to member papers across the country and—through working agreements with the Reuters, Havas, and Wolff agencies—to the world.

Accordingly, on April 19, Stone summoned a stenographer to his desk in the huge red-carpeted boardroom of the AP's executive offices at 195 Broadway, settled his pince-nez glasses on his aquiline nose, and dictated a letter to his old friend Robert A. Pinkerton, six blocks down that storied thoroughfare. Stone informed the agency's coprincipal that he was sending to Boise "three of our best men": John Russell Kennedy, until recently the AP's night manager in New York and interim superintendent of its eastern division; Martin Egan, a star correspondent who'd formerly headed its bureaus in Tokyo and London; and Robert T. Small, an able writer who'd just reported the Thaw trial. "I am impressed that [the Haywood-Moyer-Pettibone] trials are going to be very important from a news standpoint, and it is of great consequence that the Associated Press handle them intelligently and impartially," he explained. "As you know, I have not the slightest sympathy with the sort of journalism which undertakes to sacrifice the ends of justice for a newspaper 'beat,' and the gentlemen who are going out to represent the Associated Press may be thoroughly trusted to betray no confidences, and to do no dishonorable act. I think it would be helpful to them, in the legitimate discharge of their duty, if they could know Captain McParland, and he could be assured of their high character."

Pinkerton sent Stone's letter on to McParland in Denver, adding, "I endorse Mr. Stone's views as expressed in this letter and wish you would arrange it so his representatives will have all proper consideration. Mr. Stone and I were boys together and you are personally acquainted with him, and know how reliable a man he is, that he always keeps his word."

That same afternoon, the general manager wrote another old friend, Secretary of War William Howard Taft. Stone knew Taft had become friendly with Martin Egan while the AP man covered the Russo-Japanese War, and had remained on close terms with him. Now he wrote Taft: "I think you sustain rather close relations with Governor Frank R. Gooding, and a note from you to him commending Martin Egan as trustworthy and decent might be helpful." On receipt of this note, Taft wrote Gooding—whose political future he'd helped assure with his trip to Idaho the fall before—affirming that Egan was "a man of ability and good judgment and worthy of your highest confidence."

Before his men left for Boise, Stone summoned the Reverend Dwight Hillis of Plymouth Congregational Church, who'd already served as an intermediary between Gooding and the eastern press. It was to Hillis that Gooding had sent an early draft of Orchard's confession, and he in turn showed it to his friend Stone and then, at the general manager's suggestion, to S. S. McClure. Now, at Stone's request, Hillis gave the manager, Kennedy, and Egan "an outline of the outrages and murders committed at the instance of the Inner Circle of the Western Federation of Miners." According to McParland, Kennedy said "it was the most thrilling story he ever heard" and "what made it more interesting was the manner in which Dr. Hillis recited it." But Kennedy thought his version somewhat "embellished." Stone instructed Kennedy and Egan to write up Hillis's briefing for distribution to AP members even before the correspondents departed for Boise, but the reporters balked, arguing that would suggest "the Associated Press was partial to the State." After "some persuasion," Stone gave in. The correspondents left for Boise, arriving April 30.

When Kennedy and Egan were ushered into Gooding's office on May 2, they received a "very cordial" welcome. That wasn't surprising since, a year before, Gooding had dispatched Calvin Cobb to urge the eastern press—and the AP in particular—to send their best men to the trial. But Gooding was so effusive that Kennedy said "he never had received the same attention and treatment from the highest official of a state before."

Hours later, Charles Elmer, the governor's secretary, knocked on McParland's door and introduced Kennedy, a slim man with a black Vandyke beard and mustache, to the detective and James Hawley. "We had a very pleasant chat," McParland reported, "and Mr. Kennedy informed us he had to send about two thousand words to Mr. Stone and thought it best to consult Mr. Hawley and myself relative to what they should send out.... We suggested to Mr. Kennedy that while we did not want to censor what he should send out, if he would ... read it to us, we might have some suggestions to make which would be beneficial to him, in other words we might add to it. He thought that was very fair."

Early that afternoon, Kennedy and Egan reappeared and read their story to the detective and the prosecutor. McParland told them it required some corrections, as to certain names and the number of murders attributed to Orchard. But by and large the detective and the prosecutor thought the article was "a good one and very fair." Fair to the prosecution it certainly was. Kennedy assured McParland and Hawley that "every word of that article is based on the information given to me by Governor Gooding."

The two-thousand-word piece was what reporters call a scene setter, describing the players, the issues at stake, the arena in which the contest would be fought. In so doing, it established the framework within which readers would assess succeeding events and, thus, was among the most important stories the AP men would write from Boise. It was easy to see why the piece, which ran across the country the next Sunday, delighted the prosecution. It said the state charged that, "to retain the moral and financial support and fealty of some 32,000 followers, the members of an alleged 'inner circle'" of the WFM had carried out "a long series of murders and acts of violence, medieval in conception and nihilistic in execution."

The piece descended into bucolic pathos when it said that Steunenberg, having "retired from politics, lived the simple life of a sheep farmer" and into melodrama when it noted that the simple sheep farmer had been "stricken down as a traitor to his fellows by a mind that never forgets and an arm that can reach through years to strike when least expected." It flattered the Great Detective in noting that "the case had passed into the hands of the Pinkerton detective agency and James McParland, famous for his part in the Molly Maguire affair." It repeated a critical, and most dubious, claim in saying, "It is alleged that Orchard's confession has been amply confirmed." Only in their final paragraph did the AP men give the defense its due, noting that "the defendants deny their guilt most positively and in turn assert that they are the victims of a giant conspiracy as daring in conception and act as the one alleged against them."

As the two correspondents left McParland's room that afternoon, John Kennedy assured him that, "with the statement Mr. Hawley will give us tomorrow, we will lay the foundation for the public to receive—in fact, to seek—all Associated Press dispatches in future on this case."

With this show of malleability, Kennedy may have been preparing the way for a coup de théâtre. Able diplomatic correspondent that he was, he had a knack for telling people what they wanted to hear. Shortly after his arrival, Kennedy—who'd never been west of Chicago before—gushed to a *Statesman* reporter, "People exist in the east; here they live!" What Kennedy wanted was an exclusive interview with Harry Orchard. There was much curiosity about the assassin back in New York, he said, and the prosecution could dispel all the wild tales about Orchard's deterioration or insanity by displaying him to the AP. At first, the state seemed amenable. But on May 6, McParland and the governor decided that Orchard should see no reporters for the time being, "even representatives of the Associated Press, whom we knew were friendly to us."

One afternoon about a week before the trial began, the phone rang on the desk of Oscar King Davis, a senior correspondent in the *New York Times*'s Washington bureau.

"Do you want to go to Idaho?" asked Carr Van Anda, the paper's managing editor.

"Sure," said Davis, but he couldn't leave until the next day.

"Why can't you go this afternoon?" snapped Van Anda.

"There are several reasons," replied the laconic Davis. "The first is that I haven't any money and the others don't count."

"What do you do with all the money you win at Benning's?" Van Anda replied, reminding Davis of his well-known predilection for Washington's race track."

With such badinage did the *Times* dispatch its man to Boise on the next day's express train.

In his autobiography, Davis cited this exchange as evidence that his reporting was honest. "Some of the supporters of Haywood, who didn't like the dispatches I sent from Boise during the trial, asserted rather loudly that I was writing under instructions," Davis said, "and some of the Socialist newspapers, which have a practical understanding of venality, could think of no other reasons for my views at the trial than that they were paid for." When he told one Socialist reporter in Boise—Hermon Titus of the *Socialist*—exactly how he got his assignment, the reporter was "utterly stumped." He could not conceive of "a newspaper being sufficiently independent and honest to be willing to print the news as it was, regardless of its editorial views, and of having a correspondent whom it trusted enough to get the news absolutely without special instructions."

At forty-one, O. K. Davis was one of the nation's leading political-military correspondents. He'd inherited his calling from his father, a Baptist minister turned newspaper editor in upstate New York and later in Wahoo, Nebraska. Oscar graduated from Colgate in 1888, served on the New York *Sun*'s copy desk, and then in 1898—largely through his own enterprise in obtaining press credentials from Assistant Navy Secretary Theodore Roosevelt—became the *Sun*'s man with Commodore Schley's "flying squadron" in Atlantic waters during the Spanish-American War. Later he accompanied Dewey to Manila and wrote a widely admired piece on the capture of Guam. Though generally a cheerleader for American imperialism, he disliked his countrymen's behavior in the Philippines: "The Americans did not understand the native language, customs or beliefs. They called the natives 'niggers' and treated them as such. They were high-handed, arrogant and often unjust."

After covering the Boxer Rebellion and the Russo-Japanese War, Davis left the paper in 1904 to write fiction, producing a novel set in Japan and a collection of short stories. His style could be overwrought ("Under his silky mustache his white teeth ground against themselves and from between them oozed out a series of Spanish expletives") and the books didn't sell. "The fiction business played out for me last fall and I had to get back into the newspaper business," he wrote a friend in May 1906. "It is a good job, as newspaper jobs go, and I like the work better than any other newspaper work —except war correspondence."

It was indeed a good job, for by 1907 the *Times* displayed some of the virtues that within a generation would make it the nation's preeminent newspaper. It had been largely moribund when purchased in 1896 by Adolph Ochs. A shrewd operator from Chattanooga, Tennessee, Ochs reduced the paper's price from three cents to a penny, thus challenging the popular press on the newsstands, and by the time O. K. Davis joined its staff in 1906, the *Times*'s circulation had risen to a robust 150,000. Its generally upper-middle-class audience was drawn by excellent financial news, thorough coverage of government and politics, Charles R. Miller's nonpartisan but Tory-inclined editorial page, and Ochs's uncommon addiction to accuracy.

The *Times* had already published some ridiculously inaccurate material on the Haywood case, perhaps because it had relied on reporters other than its own. On Sunday, April 21, in its feature section, it ran a long piece about the upcoming trial—apparently from an unidentified news service—which reported, among other things, that after the explosion Frank Steunenberg's head had been found "a block away" from his house. This is curious indeed since the governor was talking only seconds before his death. The same article erroneously reported that, since confessing, Harry Orchard had become "greatly weakened mentally."

The only drawback to his *Times* job, Davis wrote in 1906, was that he had to work nights and didn't get home to his wife, Jessie, and infant son much before midnight. The prospect of months in Idaho meant a longer absence from his family, but otherwise it probably pleased Davis. For it offered a challenging story in a picturesque setting, circumstances that had drawn vivid prose from him as a Far Eastern correspondent. Moreover, Davis was a gregarious man who enjoyed the camaraderie that often develops among reporters on a prolonged out-of-town story.

Davis's account of his assignment has the ring of truth. Surely there was no reason for Van Anda to give a veteran correspondent explicit instructions on how to tackle such a story. Davis knew the *Times*'s position on the case: its editorials had consistently supported the Roosevelt-Taft-Gooding-Pinkerton agenda and dripped scorn for Haywood and the WFM. There is no evidence that Davis disagreed with that position.* In short, his Boise coverage was probably less the work of a venal mouthpiece for a publisher's prejudice than the reflection of unspoken assumptions Davis shared with his editors.

The *Times* recruited a second writer in Boise, whose appearance in its columns may have been designed to mollify those dismayed by the paper's editorial position. During the trial's first weeks, several paragraphs signed by Clarence Darrow preceded O. K. Davis's daily story. The notion of a partisan helping to write his own story, repugnant to most modern editors, was quite common in 1907. Politicians wrote about their campaigns, actors about their dramas, ballplayers about their games—provocative gimmicks in the circulation wars. The pieces that appeared under Darrow's name—one wonders whether he actually wrote them or whether Davis ghosted them—were mostly innocuous accounts of the court proceedings, with a dash of atmosphere. But one day, Darrow's snippet on jury selection contained a piquant insight into Western society: "The number of [talesmen] who have no church connection is remarkably large, and the great proportion of jurors who belong to some secret society is striking. No doubt the lodges have largely taken the place of the churches in the newer western towns, and these furnish a large

---

* Davis would go on to head the *Times*'s Washington bureau and develop close relations with both Roosevelt and Taft. When Roosevelt ran for president on the Progressive ticket in 1912 Davis would leave the newspaper to become secretary of the Progressive National Committee in charge of publicity.

part of the social life which eastern communities find in the church organizations."

Arriving in Boise aboard the same train as Davis was another representative of New York's elite press: Albert E. Thomas of the *Sun*. To those who knew him, his presence in Idaho was a surprise. For Thomas was the only reporter in the land who simply refused to work in the summer—and usually got away with it. For years, he'd appear in the editor's office on June 1 and tender his resignation. He'd disappear for three months—to a rented cottage on the beach in Charlestown, Rhode Island—where he'd sail, fish, and golf until September 1, when he'd stroll nonchalantly into the *Sun* office and apply for a job. Despite the paper's rule that if you left the *Sun* you never came back, management made an exception for Al Thomas. He was that good.

Born in Massachusetts, like O. K. Davis the son of a Baptist minister, Thomas graduated from Brown in 1894. For a decade, he learned the newspaper game on the *New York Tribune,* the *Morning Telegraph,* the *Evening Post,* and the *Times.* In 1906, he joined the *Sun,* where he quickly drew major assignments such as the U.S. intervention in Cuba that summer.

A lean, dark young man, with a well-tended mustache, arched eyebrows, and a pipe invariably stuck in his wry mouth, he carried with him "an unhurried air and a countenance at once so ironical and so urbane." Still a bachelor, he was a familiar figure around the bar at Lipton's, where the waiters all knew his name, or at Jack's, where the *Sun*'s reporters drank highballs with young actresses until three in the morning.

Like Davis and many of his contemporaries, he regarded newspaper work as preparation for a literary career. In 1903, he'd published his first novel, *Cynthia's Rebellion,* hailed as a "sparkling little romance to take with you on a summer outing." And year after year, he turned out plays—fifteen in all—in an unsuccessful effort to crack the Broadway stage. His style was likened to that of Clyde Fitch, both "quizzical and whimsical," his humor coming from "the drawing room and not the sidewalk." His politics were conventionally Republican, even if he harbored doubts about the unpredictable fellow in the White House. His view of Socialism can be intuited from a remark he made when accused of stealing an idea for a play from Upton Sinclair: "Only an abandoned criminal or a prestidigitator would steal a humorous idea from Mr. Sinclair."

The *Sun*'s politics were unpredictable but, of late, bleakly conservative. Though the paper published Jacob Riis's exposés of sweatshops and tenements, it was fiercely antiunion. Theodore Roosevelt may have been exaggerating when he wrote in 1903, "It is extraordinary how vicious the paper has become. It is frankly the organ of the criminal rich, quite as much so as [William Randolph Hearst's] *Journal* is the organ of the criminal poor." As early as May 7, 1906, the *Sun* had proclaimed: "Murders decreed by the Federation's Inner Circle were carried out by its faithful members, men like

Orchard and Adams." But most *Sun* readers probably subscribed to the paper less for its editorial polemics than for the high style of its news pages. For years, under its late editor Charles Dana, the *Sun* had hired supremely talented young men—David Graham Phillips, Samuel Hopkins Adams, and Frank Ward O'Malley—and freed them to write with flair and imagination. It was the newspaperman's newspaper, covering turn-of-the-century New York, its theaters, nightclubs, and raffish underworld, as well as its politics and economy, with such vigor that Edith Wharton once said it was "hard to be good in New York with the *Sun* making vice so attractive in the morning and the *Post* making virtue so dull in the afternoon." Or, in the words of another critic, "The New York *Sun* is to journalism what the can-can is to dancing." It was a "gentleman's shop," the standards for admission being "much the same as those of any metropolitan club." In these respects, Thomas—A.E. to his readers, Al to his colleagues, Tommy to his friends—was solidly in the *Sun* tradition, and it was surely his gift for language, not his politics, that prompted Chester S. Lord, the managing editor, to ask him to go to Idaho.

We don't know what persuaded Thomas to abandon his traditional respite on the Rhode Island strand and accept an assignment that would keep him in Idaho's baking acres for most of the summer. Perhaps he saw the assignment as such a plum he couldn't say no; perhaps he expected the trial to be so brimming with drama that an aspiring playwright had to be there (the *Sun* had assigned another aspiring playwright, Franklin Fyles, to cover the Thaw trial). Or perhaps he thought the stately pace of a long trial, with evenings and weekends to himself, was just the routine he needed to complete his most recent and first successful play, a frivolous comedy presented by Klaw and Erlanger not long thereafter as *Her Husband's Wife*.

To James McParland, following the lead of his agency's promotion-minded founder, the care and feeding of the trial's press corps was essential to his job. For decades, McParland had cultivated the press boys, drunk with them, dined with them, regaled them over and over with the Molly Maguire yarn, itself one of the great news stories of the late nineteenth century. Despite his stern emphasis on secrecy, he'd always fed selected reporters choice tidbits from his investigations, then used these men to mislead his quarry, to rally public or financial support, or to spy on their colleagues. Most reporters rewarded him with favorable coverage, keeping him an oversize figure in the Sunday rotogravure sections.

Now that he was back on page 1, he worked still harder at "staying on the right side of the newspaper boys." In early May, he took time out each day for a drink with the most recently arrived reporters, giving his bosses a capsule assessment of each—Hugh O'Neill of the *Denver Post* ("a very able writer, has traveled a great deal and is a very experienced newspaper man"), the bibulous John H. MacLennan of the *Denver Republican* ("one of those Scotchmen that will not break his word even should it cost him his job"), J. S. Dunnigan of the Hearst papers ("simply here in the interest of the defense"), and Frank L. Perkins of the *Portland Evening Telegram* ("a very smart young fellow I have known for some years").

"As I will meet those men every day," McParland wrote the governor, "I don't intend to quote them further in my reports except something of importance transpires." And then, in an aside intended no doubt for the agency's auditors, he noted that the reporters "are all very liberal and act friendly and at times I must spend a little money with them."

McParland didn't drink with Socialists. Neither did the governor. Miffed over this snub, George Shoaf wrote in *Appeal to Reason:*

> Gooding and McPartland [*sic*] have elegant suites at the Idanha hotel, and to this hostelry the "war" correspondents of the capitalist press are brought as soon as they alight from the train. In Gooding's private parlors the story of the assassination is recounted.... Particular emphasis is placed upon the horrors of the dynamite explosion and the press writers are psychologized into believing that dynamite is hid in chunks all over Ada and Canyon counties.... Then the Socialism of the WFM is painted in deep red colors, and the imprisoned leaders are thrown upon the canvas and made to look like howling war gods.

Such public relations accomplished several purposes. The Pinkerton agency, after all, was a business proposition; it had plenty of rivals, and to find and hold clients it had to keep its name before the public. It needed to cultivate all potential sources. The previous September, on the eve of Steve Adams's trial in Wallace, McParland had spent a whole day at the Republican County Convention, explaining to his superiors, "As we must now prosecute Adams here, we must get all the friends we can."

Then there was McParland's personal vanity. On April 23, learning of the AP delegation's imminent arrival, he wrote Gooding: "As you are aware, Shoaf either through malice or to mislead the public always reports my name as McPartland. In talking with these gentlemen [Kennedy, Egan, and Small], I wish Mr. Borah, Mr. Hawley and yourself would impress upon them the proper way to spell my name is McParland."

But this wooing of the press had more ambitious ends in view. One principal objective as the trial got under way was to get Harry Orchard's confession into magazine and, eventually, book form, so his grisly tale would reach the largest possible public.

On May 10, Idaho's governor escorted George Kibbe Turner of *McClure's* to McParland's rooms at the Idanha. After explaining the magazine's grandiose plans for Orchard's confession—five installments running consecutively from July through November—Turner asked permission to enter the prison and spend weeks with the assassin reviewing the manuscript, clarifying the text, seeking fresh material.

The detective and the governor exchanged dark looks. They wanted to cooperate, McParland would answer any questions put to him, but interviews with Orchard weren't in the cards. "We haven't permitted anyone to see Orchard," Gooding said, "even the Associated Press." While they did not doubt [the AP's] loyalty" to them, they had repeatedly refused Kennedy's requests. Hawley was even more adamant. Only prosecutors, detectives, and Dean Hinks could see the prisoner until he came off the witness stand. "If we let you in," Hawley told Turner, "all the other reporters"—"the fine corps of intelligent newspapermen representing the best newspapers in the country" —"would know that Mr. Borah and I had simply lied to them and we could not expect fair play from men who'd been misinformed."

Turner nodded. "I don't want to interfere with the trial in any way," he said. But McClure wasn't so understanding. Access to Orchard was part of the contract he'd made. No access, no deal.

Gooding was confronted with an excruciating conundrum: how to placate McClure without alienating the press boys, especially the elite quartet— the AP's Kennedy and Egan, Davis of the *Times,* and Thomas of the *Sun.* Finally, Gooding settled on what seemed a simple solution. Since Turner intended to publish between July and November, he wouldn't care who got in to see Orchard first so long as he eventually got in. The men from the elite press cared intensely. So he ordered his secretary to arrange for Kennedy, Egan, Davis, and Thomas to see Orchard at once.

On the morning of Thursday, May 16, the governor personally escorted the reporters by carriage to the pen, where they were ushered to a semicircle of chairs in the warden's anteroom. Gooding didn't stay for the interview but the warden did, to ensure there was no discussion of "the case."

Dressed in his natty gray suit and patent leather shoes, Orchard entered "quietly, smiling a little as he advanced, and looking straight ahead out of a pair of twinkling, blue eyes," according to the AP story. "His greeting was self-possessed and his manner courteous."

"I am a little leary about talking to newspaper men," Orchard said, "so if you ask me anything that I think I should not talk about I'll tell you. I know you'll understand."

Asked whether he had any complaints about his treatment at the pen, he said, "I've been treated very well . . . with the utmost courtesy by everybody. I have a large room with open windows. I exercise every day."

Did he read much? Yes, he read the newspapers, but mostly ecclesiastical and religious works: the life of John Wesley, a book on the Reformation, something on the history of England. He used to read cheap novels.

"Why did you change?" he was asked.

"It is like a man who has been doing wrong all his life and suddenly decides to do right. He cannot undo all the wrong he has done, but he can at least do something to clear things up."

Abruptly, Orchard switched roles, posing questions to the newsmen. He was curious about the Thaw trial. Had the western defense attorney held his own against the eastern prosecutor?

With time running out, one newsman asked a question that trembled on the edge of the impermissible: "Was force or duress of any kind used on you by Captain McParland or anyone else in securing your alleged confession or statement, and have any promises of any kind been made to you in that connection?" Orchard replied: "At no time was I ever subjected to force or pressure of any kind.... Anything I said was of my own free will and accord. It was just as I talk to you here."

At a signal from Whitney, the interview was over. As he left the room, Orchard turned in the doorway and said, "Good-bye, gentlemen. I am very glad to have seen you. I wish you all good health and I hope to see you again."

It was nearly noon and the reporters hurried back to the Idanha to file their stories. Not surprisingly, word of the restricted news conference quickly reached their colleagues and before long a swarm of angry reporters besieged the governor's office, demanding similar access to Orchard. Gooding, whose devotion to the truth was sometimes questioned, later insisted that he hadn't singled out certain correspondents. "I gave my secretary a list of names of all of the correspondents of big newspapers," he said, "and through a mistake of his some were notified earlier than others. As soon as I discovered the mistake, I took pains to see that all were treated alike."

What he did was to give way piecemeal. The first to obtain a dispensation was the *Boston Globe*'s John W. Carberry, who must have been angry indeed, for Gooding arranged a carriage to speed him to the pen, where he enjoyed a full hour alone with Orchard. His gleanings were not unlike his predecessors', and he ended: "Having seen and talked with many men who in murder trials have been the bulwark of the prosecution, and who have consequently been open to the most ingenious and merciless attack by the opposing attorneys, the *Globe* staff man, after an hour with this admitted murderer today, is convinced that he will make a notable witness."

The next man to reach the pen was Hugh O'Neill of the *Denver Post*, a salty veteran who also drew conclusions that could only please the prosecution. "We had thought of [Orchard] as something shambling and despicable," he wrote. "We had imagined him as everything but what he actually was as he sat smiling before me, a healthy and vigorous and strong-limbed man, with no trace of vice in his face and no cloud of fear in his eyes."

By now, cries for equal treatment had grown so insistent that the governor was compelled to "throw down the bars" and arrange an omnibus interview for twelve reporters, representing most of the remaining mainstream newspapers. Originally, this event was scheduled for five in the afternoon, but through a "misunderstanding," the full group didn't reach the pen until eight.*

Under questioning this time, Orchard told more of his personal habits. Asked about his drinking, he said he'd never been "a hard drinker." On his gambling: "I have been a gambler to the extent of putting up money for other men better at cards than I to take away. I have played poker considerably."

The newsmen seemed as impressed by the prisoner as their predecessors, the principal exceptions being J. S. Dunnigan of the Hearst papers and C. N. Landon of the *Cleveland Press,* which had been consistently hostile to the prosecution. "With Warden Whitney sitting at his elbow and censoring all questions," wrote Dunnigan, "Orchard talked generalities. He obeys absolutely the instructions of his keepers and speaks by rote when asked what he expects." Landon saw beneath Orchard's "veneer of polish and sanctimony" the "vengeance and greed" that drove him to kill.

The next morning's *Statesman* not only displayed on page 1 Harry Crane's breathless account of the group interview but reprinted inside the AP story and two brief interpretive pieces commissioned from O. K. Davis and A. E. Thomas.

"Orchard surprised me a good deal," wrote Davis. "His manifest intelligence, alertness of mind, quick comprehension and ready humor are more than sufficient contradiction of the reports of his fading strength and failing mind."

"Harry Orchard has balanced his books," wrote A. E. Thomas. "[He] knows what he owes to the people of America and to his own conscience and he has determined to pay the bill.... Whatever the Harry Orchard of December 30, 1905 may have been, men who look like the Harry Orchard of May 16, 1907 are men who tell the truth. There is a conscience behind those blue, unfaltering eyes of his."

Nobody was more delighted by the day's events than McParland, who after talking with Kennedy, Egan, Davis, Thomas, Carberry, O'Neill, and MacLennan reported that "the State has made a good move in allowing the newspaper men at this time to see Orchard and show the world that he is not an imbecile."

But when the *Statesman* slapped on Boise's doorsteps the next morning, it left some readers deeply aggrieved. Among the disaffected were the defendants themselves, their attorneys and supporters, and a number of newspapermen who'd been excluded from the previous day's interviews, most notably C. A. Broxon of the *Evening Capital News,* the *Statesman's* ostensible competition.

* The group included John Fay of the New York *World,* Luke Grant of the *Chicago Record-Herald,* J. S. Dunnigan of the Hearst papers, E. G. Leipheimer of the *Butte Evening News,* John E. Nevins of the Scripps-McRae News Service, Blaine Phillips of the *Brooklyn Eagle,* Jacob Waldeck of the Newspaper Enterprise Association, Harry L. Crane of the *Idaho Daily Statesman,* John Tierney of the *Rocky Mountain News,* John H. MacLennan of the *Denver Republican,* C. N. Landon of the *Cleveland Press* and the *Omaha News.*

Frank Gooding was punishing the *Capital News* for recent transgressions. To be sure, Calvin Cobb still held the balance of power among the evening paper's stockholders, assuring that the paper backed his Republican friends, but of late that had meant Cobb's ally Billy Borah and not their factional rival, Frank Gooding. On July 18, 1906, for example, the *News* had reprinted an article from the *Salt Lake Herald* that said, in part, "Gooding and graft have become so thoroughly known as synonymous terms that the rank and file will have no more of it." (Joel Priest, the *Salt Lake Herald's* correspondent at the trial, was also excluded from the Orchard interviews.) Gooding had held his fire until after his reelection. Then on Christmas Eve, 1906, a Boise constable called at the *News* office and arrested Richard S. Sheridan, the paper's general manager, on charges of criminal libel. As the Haywood trial opened, the governor's action against Sheridan was still pending, and feelings between the paper and the governor had been rubbed raw.

The others excluded from the "pink tea at the pen" were chiefly those reporting the trial for Socialist and labor papers. On their behalf, George Shoaf of *Appeal to Reason* scorned Gooding's cultivation of the capitalist press. "Like a would-be sleuth he carefully selected the scribes of capitalism, and the exponents of kidnapping and gum-shoed them to the penitentiary, where Orchard had been coached to roll his eyes, display his fresh-born piety, and the meekness of his McPartland-made manners." Much of the anger focused on Davis and Thomas, who—it was said—had been granted places at the first interview after agreeing to show their stories to Gooding before filing them.

Among those seething at the *Statesman's* coverage was Fremont Wood. When court convened at nine, there was hell to pay. In his sternest tone, the judge told the hushed chamber that his attention had been called to articles in the morning paper "calculated to influence the jurors that have not been called in this case." The judge said he "very much question[ed] the propriety of these publications" in the midst of efforts to find an impartial jury. Although the talesmen occupying the jury box had been sequestered overnight and thus prevented from reading about the trial, the fifty talesmen waiting examination were free to read what they wished. Wood conceded that he may have erred in not admonishing them to avoid reading about the trial, but he hadn't expected anything as egregious as what appeared that morning.

With the jurors and unselected talesmen out of the courtroom, he now invited comments from the attorneys stirring anxiously before him. Edmund Richardson was outraged. The governor, he said, had singled out for interviews the Associated Press and others who'd reported "upon the side of the prosecution." This was done, he concluded, to give Orchard "credibility in the eyes of this jury and in the eyes of the world, and it was a dastardly outrage." Darrow called it "the most flagrant attempt to influence a jury" he'd ever heard of, prompted, he thought, by talesmen's statements that they couldn't trust testimony from such a debased murderer. The reporters had fallen for "a lot of stuff which upon its face was manufactured, a lot of maudlin religious idiocy." Darrow saved his harshest words for Calvin Cobb, who, in lending himself to this operation, had ignored his responsibility as "the chief educator of the public and the molder of public opinion."*

Darrow and Richardson expressed confidence the prosecutors had nothing to do with this "travesty." But Gooding, Darrow said, "should be called in and examined, and if this matter calls for punishment for contempt, should be punished."

Hawley insisted he'd first heard of the interviews after they'd taken place. Having had his own differences with the governor, he offered half-hearted assurances that Gooding hadn't "the remotest idea" the interviews might prejudice the jury pool. While conceding that the interviews were "not in good taste," he argued that, given the charges of prosecutorial misconduct, all this had injured the state more than the defense.

The newsmen who'd conducted the interviews listened with an exasperation bordering on incredulity. They'd only done their job, they insisted; if it had served somebody else's interests, that wasn't their concern. Davis and Thomas, in particular, were outraged at the defense and the judge for raising the issue of contempt. One reporter thought the press had been "handed a lemon"—and if by that he meant they'd been shrewdly used for others' purposes, he was surely right.

Borah, who assiduously cultivated the national press throughout his career, now rode to the reporters' defense. He refused to believe that these newsmen, "men of standing and character," would enter a conspiracy to influence the jury. Moreover, whether their articles were "colored" toward the prosecution or the defense, they would be "ninnies and fools" if they came there without opinions.

Maybe so, the judge said, but he wanted to know what all the parties to this incident had intended. Referring the matter to the Ada County attorney, Charles F. Koelsch, Wood instructed that if Koelsch found "there has been an attempt in any way to influence the jurors who are about to be examined in this court, I want him to take such action as the law may seem to justify."

Koelsch was Borah's protégé, having trained in his office, so it was no surprise that by noon the next day he had on the judge's desk a report exonerating both the governor and the reporters. The correspondents had been "so insistent to see [Orchard] that their request was finally granted." Those who'd acceded to it never contemplated that "there could be anything improper in their action." When the newsmen were accorded the interview at last, they "seized it with avidity, and with no thought other than that it would be front page, scare-head-line matter."

Nonetheless, Koelsch recommended that the judge issue an order "for-

---

* Wade Parks of the *Daily People* reported that J. R. Kennedy of the Associated Press told him that Darrow approached him with "tears in his words" and begged the Associated Press to balance the scales by doing an interview with the defense. This seems unlikely (May 23, 1907).

bidding any publication that would in the slightest degree tend to obstruct the proceedings of this court" or that expressed "an opinion as to the merits of the cause on trial." Wood declined, perhaps because he knew that many dispatches would run afoul of the second clause or perhaps because he felt the issue had been sufficiently aired and he could look now for voluntary restraint by the "gentlemen of the press."

From the start, that honorific was freighted with irony. Through the nineteenth century, news gathering was considered a lowly occupation, its practitioners on a par with actors and acrobats. Not yet a profession or even a dignified craft, it was the "haven of shipwrecked ambitions," sought by men who'd failed in other endeavors, by bohemians who scorned the conventional life, by petty grafters hungry for free theater tickets or railroad passes. To Harvard's president, Charles W. Eliot, in 1890, reporters were "drunkards, deadbeats and bummers." When Charles Edward Russell was city editor of the New York *World* in 1894–96, a reporter was "a harum-scarum, irresponsible person with soiled cuffs and the lees of last night's drunk still upon him." To O. Henry, the reporter was "a man about half shabby, with an eye like a gimlet, smoking cut plug, with dandruff on his coat collar."

At banquets, the "cattle of the press" were frequently seated behind a screen so diners wouldn't spoil their appetites by gazing on them. One newsman, covering a literary society at a great home, was told to wait. The lady of the house inquired who he was; "a reporter," said her husband. The lady gathered the silverware from the dining room and hid it in a safe place.

Some prospective reporters must have been slovenly indeed. For in 1889, a newsman published *The Ladder of Journalism: How to Climb It*, a primer for aspiring reporters that didn't shrink from instruction in personal hygiene: "Neatness in dress, cleanliness in habit and propriety in general conduct never fail to gain respect.... Vulgar language creates disgust."

But reporters were scorned because decent people—even decent editors—regarded news as inferior to opinion. Through the 1820s, what passed for newspapers were politically subsidized pulpits from which editors preached, rarely dirtying their hands with mere facts. Their audience—partisans and intellectuals—hoisted their pantaloons above the offal of the magistrate's courts and jails, poor houses and asylums where less fortunate folk endured the indignities of the industrial city.

In the 1830s, a new breed of paper made its appearance: the penny press, so-called because the papers reduced their price from the six cents standard among the elite press to a single penny, thus opening up a new working-class audience. Centered in New York, Philadelphia, and Boston—and identified with Jacksonian democracy's demands for a reduced work week, expanded suffrage, and free schools—such papers concentrated on delivering news, not opinion. Indeed, James Gordon Bennett's *Herald* and Benjamin Day's New York *Sun* invented the modern concept of news as they turned their attention, for the first time, to the lives of ordinary people in the courts, markets, theaters, and sporting arenas. To older New York papers, such coverage was "indecent" and "blasphemous"—epithets flung by a fading elite at the free-market society led by the emerging middle class. Bennett himself was dubbed "the prince of darkness."

As the penny papers' coverage expanded, so did circulation. If the old-guard papers were rented by political parties, the new ones sold their product to the public—for the first time it was hawked by newsboys in the streets—then sold their readership to advertisers. The trend toward a general audience accelerated during the Civil War. Across the land, farmers and mechanics waited for the latest edition with its lists of dead and wounded, its stirring accounts of actions at Antietam or Manassas. By war's end, we'd become a nation of newspaper readers.

Reporters had showed what they could do with a great story, but for some years to come the press still functioned largely as the megaphone of imperious editors like E. L. Godkin of the *New York Evening Post* and Horace White of the *Chicago Tribune.*

Three forces combined to change all that by century's end. First was the flood of immigrants who transformed the nation from an Anglo-Saxon land to a tumultuous hodgepodge of cultures. The second was technology. In 1886, Ottmar Mergenthaler invented the "line-o'-type" machine, which set type five times as fast as the old-time printer with his box of precast characters. By 1891, one of R. Hoe and Company's quadruple presses could fold, cut, and paste seventy-two thousand eight-page papers an hour. Finally, new advertising supplied funds needed to foot increased editorial expenses.

Until the 1880s, most editors were apathetic, if not hostile, to display advertising, which usurped space they coveted for editorial matter. Since most early papers were subsidized by special interests, advertising hadn't bulked large on their balance sheets. What ads they ran appeared in agate type, stacked in long gray columns. This practice changed with the arrival of brand names and department stores. Dry goods stores, which had always advertised, now concentrated in multistory buildings, absorbing other retailers. Increasingly, these vast emporia trumpeted merchandise in large display ads. In 1904, the *Dry Goods Economist* noted: "The newspaper of today is largely the creation of the department store."

Dependence on their advertising lent the department stores leverage. Since shoppers craved security, store managers asked papers to omit a store's name from reports of shoplifting or other on-site crimes. Management resented suggestions that the low wages it paid shopgirls pushed them into prostitution; with an eye to such sensibilities, the Sunday *World,* which regularly ran O. Henry's stories, declined to publish "An Unfinished Story," his tale of a salesgirl who weighed her virtue against her empty pocketbook. When bubonic plague hit San Francisco in 1901, department stores exacted a pledge that the press would suppress the news lest tourists shun the city.

Advertisers of all kinds felt they'd earned suppression of news harmful to themselves or their family. It took a courageous editor to respond as Lincoln Steffens did when called by an advertiser: "You have the wrong number. This is the news department. We have a business department that attends to business."

Increasing dependence on advertising didn't reduce pressure for circulation; indeed, the number of readers became the prime measure of the rates papers could charge for ads. The craving for circulation posed a dilemma: was it a paper's duty to lead readers toward the moral life or wasn't it perfectly professional to give readers what they wanted? In 1882, William Dean Howells grappled with this question in his novel *A Modern Instance*. Bartley Hubbard, an ambitious Boston editor, wanders into a tavern, where he hears a man questioning the manager of a popular variety show.

> "What's that new piece of yours, Colonel?" he asked after a while. "I ain't seen it yet."
> "Legs, principally," sighed the manager. "That's what the public wants. I give the public what it wants. I don't pretend to be any better than the public. Nor any worse." . . . [So] said the manager of a school of morals, with wisdom that impressed more and more the manager of a great moral engine.
> "The same principle runs through everything," observed Bartley.

Although Howells yearned for the days when newspapers were great moral engines, by the 1880s the trend was decisively in Bartley Hubbard's direction. Charles Dana of the *Sun* said, "I have always felt that whatever the Divine Providence permitted to occur I was not too proud to report." The *Sun*'s motto—The Sun Shines for All—proclaimed that it addressed all classes and all tastes. Dana admonished his reporters, "Make it interesting!" —a compendious category that included "the exact weight of a candidate for President, the latest style in whiskers, the origin of a new slang expression, the idiosyncrasies of the City Hall clock, a strange four-master in the harbor, the head-dresses of Syrian girls." The *Times*'s motto—All the News That's Fit to Print—was a direct rebuke to the *Sun*'s, asserting that some phenomena the *Times* was too proud or too scrupulous to report.

Soon there sprang up a journalism with no scruples whatsoever. Dubbed "yellow journalism" after a comic-strip character called The Yellow Kid, it got its start in the 1880s in St. Louis and San Francisco, where two young publishers took Dana's principle to its logical—or illogical—extreme.

A Hungarian immigrant and onetime mule hostler, Joseph Pulitzer had made a huge success of the *St. Louis Post-Dispatch* with stories that tweaked the noses of the city's Bourbon elite, like "Well Known Citizen Stricken Down in the Arms of His Mistress." But when his enemies exploited a murder at the paper's office to build sentiment against him, Pulitzer grabbed his chips off the table. In 1883, he plunked them down in New York, purchasing the *World*, which ran stories like "Election of an Executive Committee of the American Cocker Spaniel Club."

The publisher resolved to go after elements of New York's population who'd never read an American paper with any regularity, perhaps because none had ever paid much attention to them: immigrants from eastern and southern Europe, jostling for a place in this strange New World, and women, long accustomed to passive acquiescence in their men's requirements but now seeking the suffrage, jobs, and social equality.

Pulitzer appealed to the most elemental human passions—as one competitor said, "Sport for the man, love and scandal for the woman." There'd never been a sports department until Pulitzer introduced one at the *World* in the late 1880s, covering horse racing, boxing, and baseball. Chicago baseball writers pioneered a colloquial style—comparing a ground ball ripping through the infield grass to "the hired man eating celery." Soon that lingo spread to New York. The first women's advice column—letters from a "city cousin" Edith to her "country cousin" Bessie—appeared in the *World* in 1883, the first romantic fiction later that year.

Pulitzer's genius lay in his bold blend of sensationalism and idealism. He routinely offended good taste in his brazen display of sex and scandal but combined it with a warm concern for underdogs and a crusading zeal for bettering their living conditions. This concoction was an instant success. In his first three months as the *World*'s ruler, the paper's press run went from nineteen thousand to thirty-nine thousand—almost none of it at the expense of other morning papers, suggesting that Pulitzer was indeed tapping into new sources of circulation.

In 1886, the *World* hired an unlikely reporter just expelled from Harvard, where he'd sent each of his professors a chamber pot with the recipient's name inside. William Randolph Hearst had admired Pulitzer's own stunt the fall before when, after Congress failed to appropriate money for the Statue of Liberty's pedestal, the *World* raised $100,000, much of it in children's nickels and dimes. So fascinated was Hearst by the *World*, it became his model for the San Francisco *Examiner* after his father bestowed that paper on him in 1887.

Eight years later, Hearst was back, purchasing a languishing "chambermaid's paper," the *Morning Journal*, challenging his former idol for circulation, riches, and fame in the big city. No American community had ever witnessed the journalistic warfare the yellows waged in the 1890s, matching one another turpitude for turpitude. "What we're after," said one of Hearst's editorial writers, "is the gee-whiz emotion." It wasn't necessary to tell an outright lie; a small shift in emphasis could transform an ordinary event into a heartrending drama.

Under Arthur Brisbane, Hearst's editorial page translated its prolabor stance into vivid passages simple enough for a child to comprehend: "You see a horse after a hard day's work grazing in a swampy meadow. He has done his duty and is getting what he can in return. On the horse's flank you see a leech sucking blood. The leech is the trust. The horse is the labor union."

Hearst wouldn't be outspent or outdone. Admiring the magazine of the Sunday *World,* he hired its editor and entire staff. After Pulitzer lured them back, Hearst—dickering from his office in the Pulitzer skyscraper—raised the ante 25 percent and won them back again. Pulitzer evicted Hearst, thundering, "I will not have my building used for purposes of seduction!"

This competition reached a crescendo in the Spanish-American War, a conflict Hearst and Pulitzer helped precipitate. For two years, while Hearst decorated his front page with spread eagles and cannon, the *Journal* built America's war hysteria with stories of unauthenticated atrocities. Though lacking Hearst's undiluted enthusiasm for war, Pulitzer wasn't far behind. Once the *Maine* exploded in Havana harbor, the *World* beat the war drums, giving prominent play to Buffalo Bill Cody's idle boast that thirty thousand Indian fighters could chase the Spaniards out of Cuba in sixty days.

When McKinley finally declared war on Cuba in April 1898, Hearst and Pulitzer outdid each other in bravado. Though he already had Richard Harding Davis on the scene, Hearst chartered a launch and steamed south to cover the war with his star correspondent James Creelman. Pulitzer engaged Stephen Crane and the swashbuckling Sylvester Henry Scovel.

If the Civil War elicited the full-blown American newspaper, the war with Spain ushered in what the newsman Irvin Cobb called "the time of the Great Reporter." The exploits of Davis, Crane, and Scovel captured the public imagination. All of a sudden, one of America's most despised professions had become one of its most glamorous. For years, reporters had been virtually anonymous, their bylines as rare as cucumber sandwiches at the city desk. Owners liked it that way because it prevented newsmen from gaining a following of their own, useful in haggling for higher wages. Now names like Richard Harding Davis and Stephen Crane were coin of the realm, exploited by management to build circulation, by reporters to build independent careers.

For the cub reporter—often a rube from the countryside or an immigrant fresh off the boat—covering the teeming city could be a thrilling enterprise. Joseph Ignatius Constantine Clarke of the *New York Herald* thought "it would be hard to hit upon a career more seductive, more satisfying than that of a footloose reporter on a great paper, whose compensation was mainly in what fine things he saw."

With reporting's new glamour and rising salaries, many reporters came from American colleges. As late as 1870, when Julius Chambers sought a job at the *Tribune* and told Horace Greeley he'd just graduated from Cornell, the editor growled: "I'd damned sight rather you had graduated at a printer's case!" But Dana, himself a Harvard graduate, disagreed; to cover a prizefight or a murder, he preferred "a young fellow who knows the 'Ajax' of Sophocles."

A few college men trickled onto papers in the seventies; by the nineties, there was a steady flow; by 1907, half the reporters and three-quarters of the editors on big-city dailies were bachelors of arts, convinced that newspapering was what Godkin of the *Evening Post* had lately described as "a new and important calling."

These graduates helped transform the stilted language of journalism. Steffens felt he'd been "permanently hurt" by his years on the prissy *Post,* where newsmen were to report "like machines, without prejudice, color and without style." Now, as the age of the reporter opened, Will Irwin, Julian Ralph, and Julius Chambers developed colloquial styles rich with telling detail.

Many reporters of this generation were the bad-boy sons of Protestant clergymen, among them A. E. Thomas, Oscar King Davis, Stephen Crane, Sylvester Scovel, the *Journal's* Ralph D. Paine, and the *Herald's* Harry Brown. Such men fled the conventional pieties for what Theodore Dreiser called the "pagan or unmoral character" of the reporters' room. "While the editorial office might be preparing the most flowery moralistic or religionistic editorials regarding the worth of man," he wrote, "in the city room the mask was off and life was handled in a rough and ready manner."

Reporters now put their faith in "scientific method," empirical observation, precision, and quantification. After graduating from Berkeley, Lincoln Steffens did graduate work in Germany with Wilhelm Wundt, the psychologist who'd trained Hugo Münsterberg. Herbert Spencer's social Darwinism enjoyed a vogue among many reporters of that era, including Dreiser, Ray Stannard Baker, and Abraham Cahan.

The mystique of "facts" hung in the air. To the First International Congress of Historians in 1900, the scientist Henry Houssaye declared, "We want nothing more to do with the approximations of hypotheses, useless systems, theories as brilliant as they are deceptive, superfluous moralities. Facts, facts, facts—which carry with themselves their lesson and their philosophy." It was a theme Darrow had sounded in 1893 when he said, "The world has grown tired of preachers and sermons; today it asks for facts." Wundt, too, called for "facts, nothing but facts," and Ray Stannard Baker echoed, asserting, "Facts, facts piled up to the point of dry certitude, was what the American people really wanted."

In this quest, newspapers often relied on a class of journalist known as detective-reporters, whose techniques were not unlike those of professional sleuths. At taverns where newsmen congregated, the feats of such specialists were recounted with awe. There was the man with a bomb who'd walked into the office of the financier Russell Sage and demanded a million dollars. When an alarm sounded, he dropped his bomb, blowing himself and Sage's clerk to pieces. The bomber's identity puzzled police until a *World* man traced a button and a scrap of trousers to a tailor who identified him as a Boston note broker.

Such yarns had a self-serving subtext: that a good detective-reporter could run circles round a city detective. As Conan Doyle hymned Holmes's superiority to the clods from Scotland Yard, so Julian Ralph held that, compared to the resourceful reporter, detectives were "a lower order of men." To Dreiser, "the detective had no brain at all, merely a low kind of cunning, often red-headed, freckled with big hands and feet...with a ridiculous air of mystery and profundity in matters requiring neither, dirty, offensive, fish-eyed and merciless...whereas the average reporter was, by contrast anyhow, intelligent or shrewd, clean nearly always, if at times a little slouchy, inclined to drink and sport perhaps but genial, often gentlemanly, a fascinating story teller, a keen psychologist." The reporter would solve any case, then "at the great moment" the cops would step forward "to do the arresting and get their pictures and name in the papers."

To the public, though, reporters and detectives often seemed cut from the same repellent cloth. A reporter for the *Statesman* assigned to interview people at the Boise depot found that when he asked them their business he received a "haughty look" and a cold no, followed by a blunt question: "Are you a detective?"

The turn-of-the-century reporters most celebrated as investigators were the muckrakers. In a 1907 interview, S. S. McClure called that notion into question. From Paris, he insisted that his magazine "had never made a single exposure in all the years of the publication. It never employs detectives and has never made original investigations. It has never given the public a single fact that had not already been made public either in the big newspapers, in court records or through the investigation of different government bodies. It has simply presented and explained as vividly and concretely as possible certain masses of facts that were already common knowledge." In disclaiming original investigation and all facts not certified by authority, McClure was approaching an old question in American journalism: how does one distinguish between fraud and reality?

The 1830s saw not only the rise of the penny press but the emergence of that master of humbug P. T. Barnum. In 1836, he toured with a black dancer he declared to be George Washington's 161-year-old former nurse. Soon his American Museum on Broadway displayed Dr. Griffin's famous "mermaid," whom Barnum boomed as "the most stupendous curiosity ever submitted to the public for inspection." In fact, the curiosity was the head and hands of a monkey skillfully sewed to the body and tail of a fish. When scientists debunked the mermaid, Barnum advertised piously: "Who is to decide when doctors disagree?" The answer was the public, invited to pay their admission to make up their own minds, which many thousands did. Over the years, Barnum proffered a dazzling array of deceptions: the chess-playing automaton (with a man hidden inside); Santa Anna's wooden leg (which was somebody's leg, but not the general's); all sorts of anatomical monstrosities; hats and jewelry offered as sacred relics of famous men and women.

At the same time, fraud was endemic in the American press. In 1835, the *Sun* published articles, supposedly reprinted from the *Edinburgh Journal of Science*, about the strange inhabitants of the moon viewed by a powerful telescope: blue goats with a single horn, biped beavers, short, hairy men with bat wings. The story was soon exposed as a hoax written by Richard Adams Locke, the *Sun's* star reporter. The unrepentent editor, Benjamin Day, invited every reader "to examine [the moon story] and enjoy his own opinion." The "disclosure" greatly boosted the paper's circulation. When Locke quit the *Sun* to found the *New Era*, he published the "lost manuscripts" of the Scottish explorer Mungo Park, who'd disappeared thirty years before while trying to reach Timbuktu. They were, of course, as bogus as blue goats.

In 1874, the *New York Herald* devoted its first page to a widely accepted hoax about the escape of lions, tigers, and elephants from the Central Park Zoo and their rampage through the city, killing forty-nine and mutilating many more. The *Philadelphia Press* wrote of the gentleman who bought a bundle of toy balloons and gave them to a girl on the beach. The child wrapped the string around her waist, and the wind whisked her away. She would've been lost at sea had a hunter not shot the balloons, returning her to earth.

The art of faking it worked its way into the journalistic canon. In 1887, *Writer* magazine said such deception was "an almost universal practice." Reporters were advised not to invent "the important facts of a story" but to supply with "healthy imagination" the "descriptive details," which might "serve an excellent purpose in the embellishment of a despatch."

One form particularly susceptible to faking was the interview. A relative latecomer in American journalism, it wasn't highly regarded, even when genuine, because it smacked of sycophancy. In 1869, the *Nation* saw it as "generally the joint production of some humbug of a hack politician and another humbug of a newspaper reporter." When a yellow reporter was refused an interview, he often wrote it anyway. Many celebrities, eager for publicity, blithely went along. When Dreiser asked John L. Sullivan what he thought of exercise, the prizefighter roared: "Exercise? What I think? Haw! Haw! Write any damned thing yuh please, young fella, and say that John Sullivan said so. That's good enough for me. If they don't believe it bring it back and I'll sing it for yuh."

Why did Americans take such satisfaction in deciphering Barnum's and Locke's humbugs? In the tumultuous cities of the mid–nineteenth century, swarming with yokels from the country and greenhorns off the boat, the ancient hierarchies had been scrambled beyond recognition. In this fluid social order, nobody quite knew who their interlocuter was. The archetypal villain of the era was the confidence man who preyed on newcomers with his bundle of shell games and thimblerigs, while false identities and disguises were a consistent theme of the early dime novels. It took keen wits to decipher a bunco artist and a Barnumesque humbug. As one historian has written: "Those who managed to solve the puzzle . . . could pride themselves on possessing sharper perceptions and keener insights than those ordinary mortals who had been taken in."

Perhaps this was part of the satisfaction the American press found in peeling identities off the mysterious figure known first as Tom Hogan, then as Harry Orchard, then as Albert Horsley. McParland, the impresario of investigations, proclaimed him the most remarkable witness ever produced in an American courtroom, while Darrow, the great debunker, declared him the biggest fraud ever perpetrated on the American public. Like Barnum's mermaid and Locke's blue goats, Orchard was examined in relays by sheriff's deputies, Pinkertons, reporters, scientists, and the clergy. Ultimately, the decision would lie with the jury of Idaho farmers, who represented the greater jury of all Americans, the court of public opinion.

For years, the genteel press had shunned criminal trials. "In order to preserve the vigor of the moral faculty," the Philadelphia physician Benjamin Rush wrote in 1786, "it is of the utmost consequence to keep young people as ignorant as possible of those crimes that are generally thought most disgraceful to human nature. . . . I should be glad to see the proceedings of our courts kept from the public eye, when they expose or punish monstrous vices."

The penny press, by contrast, lustily embraced crime coverage. The 1836 ax murder of a prostitute named Helen Jewett ushered in the new era. A clerk named Richard Robinson had regularly visited the house of Mrs. Rosina Townsend, where he'd become infatuated with "the Jewett woman." Now he was marrying a respectable girl and wanted his letters to Miss Jewett returned. He'd last been seen in her room about 11:00 p.m., when he'd ordered champagne. The police arrested him at his lodging house.

The case triggered an unprecedented orgy of lurid stories and fictionalized episodes in the penny papers. Reporting on a glimpse of Jewett's body—very likely invented—James Gordon Bennett of the *Herald* expatiated: " 'My God,' exclaimed I, 'how like a statue! . . . The body looked as white, as full, as polished as the purest Parian marble. The perfect figure—the exquisite limbs—the fine face—the full arms—the beautiful bust—all—all surpassed in every respect the Venus de Medici."

Aroused by this journalistic debauch, six thousand persons converged on the courtroom in a pounding rainstorm to seek seats as the trial began. It took sheriff's deputies and thirty special constables to clear a path for the judge and his clerk through the unruly crowd. For days, the penny papers ran verbatim transcript until Robinson was acquitted. Nauseated by the episode, the high-minded William Cullen Bryant of the *Post* was "glad that our columns are relieved from this disagreeable subject."

But readers were hooked. Henceforth, murder trials were the acme of public entertainments. The 1842 trial of John C. Colt for murdering a printer named Samuel Adams aroused such fierce interest that Greeley's *Tribune* put out several extras a day, with verbatim coverage by a twenty-two-year-old reporter named Henry Raymond, whose daily product of six columns would have done credit to a court stenographer. A decade later, he wrote in his prospectus for the *New York Times:* "The law courts should be carefully, accurately and more fully reported than is usual, as they relate to the business, and thus enlist the attention and interest, of a very large class of people."

The most heavily covered trial of the century wasn't about murder but about the other enthralling subject: love, sex, adultery, and their heartrending consequences. The defendant was the Reverend Henry Ward Beecher, one of Dwight Hillis's predecessors at Plymouth Church and for decades America's most renowned cleric. His bed partner was Elizabeth Richards Tilton, wife of Theodore Tilton, Beecher's longtime colleague. When Tilton's suit for alienation of affection came to trial in Brooklyn City Court in 1875, it became the hottest ticket in town. Members of Beecher's flock deluged him with roses and lilies, while Tilton's admirers buried him in bloodred tulips.

Packs of reporters stalked everyone, however slightly involved—even the families' grocers and shoemakers. One reporter at the Tilton residence was reduced to watching the flowers grow, or not grow: "The house looked desolate, the English ivy and smilex were withering in the rustic hanging baskets...." A reporter on duty in a tree had food pumped up to him through a garden hose. When the jury deliberated for eight days in stifling heat, reporters crawled onto window ledges, scouring the jury room with spyglasses. The trial ended in a hung jury, which didn't stop the *Louisville Courier-Journal* from labeling Beecher "a dunghill covered with flowers."

The Beecher story had a particular grip on women, mesmerized by a preacher in passionate embrace with a church lady. Over the years, women became a principal audience for any trial that had at its center an abandoned or traduced woman. One that particularly engaged their attention involved a Floradora girl named Nan Patterson charged with killing her lover, a bookmaker named Caesar Young, in June 1904, hours before he was to leave with his wife on a European tour. When Patterson's trial began, men and women alike fought for admission. "Women, many of them dressed in the height of fashion," reported the *Times,* "could not understand why officers barred their way, and returned again and again to the storming of the doors." Ultimately, many got in and came back for weeks, until this trial, too, ended in a hung jury.

Nothing restrained New York's press in January 1906 when it realized the lubricious possibilities of the Thaw trial. To Irvin Cobb, the Kentucky-born wit who covered it for the evening *World,* the story had everything: "wealth, degeneracy, rich old wasters; delectable young chorus girls and adolescent artist's models; the behind-the-scenes of Theaterdom and the Underworld, and the Great White Way, as we called it then; the abnormal pastimes and weird orgies of over-aesthetic artists and jaded debauchees." It was a "bedaubed, bespangled Bacchanalia."

From the moment Harry Thaw put three bullets into Stanford White's starched white shirt on June 25, 1906, the case dominated the front pages as no murder had since Lizzie Borden put down her hatchet. In New York, the yellow press took aim at the same shirt front. For, though Stanford White had been the most distinguished architect of his time, he was also a wealthy "libertine," fair game for papers that specialized in exploiting working-class resentment of the decadent rich. The *Journal* and the *World* portrayed him as a monster of depravity who'd entrapped Evelyn Nesbit with drugged champagne in a love nest with velvet draperies and mirrored ceilings. From his self-imposed exile in Paris, James Gordon Bennett Jr. cabled his editors at the *Herald:* "Give him Hell!"—and they did. For New York's press, the story was pure gold: the *World* had 537,734 readers the day White was shot; over the next week, it gained 100,000.

When this "trial of the century" began in January 1907, the press benches were jammed with a hundred reporters, many of them celebrities in their own right: Cobb for the evening *World,* Samuel Hopkins Adams for the morning *World;* Roy Howard for Scripps-McRae, Alfred Henry Lewis for Hearst. Writing commentary for the *Herald* was Roland B. Molineux, a convicted murderer. Largely uneducated but infinitely debonair, Molineux belonged to the Knickerbocker Club in 1899 when he was charged with killing a fellow member, convicted, then—after an appeals court overturned the conviction—acquitted in a second trial in 1902. He'd written a book on life in the death house and dashed off fiction for the Sunday supplements. His assignment was to give the reader a sense of what Thaw was going through, which he did in prose like this: "No poor wretch whose life depended upon the issue of hand-to-hand encounter between Knights of old ever looked upon the tilting ground with greater dread than does the defendant." *

But the trial's most celebrated reporters were the four women who occupied a front table: Winifred Black (aka Annie Laurie), Elizabeth Meriweather (aka Dorothy Dix), Ada Patterson, and Nixola Greeley-Smith (Hor-

* Paul Thieman, the *Denver Post's* shrewd editorial columnist, later compared the defense's tactics in the Thaw trial to the prosecution strategy in the Haywood case. Thaw's attorneys presented him to the jury as "a dissipated young man [who] after many amours, fell truly in love with a girl who had grown as a flower in a moral truck heap. Himself regenerated by his own honest love, the once erring young man strove to transplant his beloved flower from sin to virtue and, in fighting with a man of the muckheap for a woman's soul, he killed the man." Similarly, the prosecutors had depicted Harry Orchard as "a bloody assassin, a fiendish dynamiter, [who] once was a boy taught virtuous and holy things by a good mother.... Taken red-handed and put in prison he had time to reflect....Good books were given him....He remembered the teachings of his mother....His soul stirred within the scab of coagulated crime." To be sure, Thieman conceded, this tale of "spiritual salvation" presented "great" possibilities of attack to Darrow's "brilliant, sardonic, pitiless defense" (*Denver Post,* May 18, 1907).

ace Greeley's granddaughter), the first three covering for Hearst, the last for Pulitzer. Irvin Cobb dismissed them as the "sob sisters" because they were there to capture the tear-filled eye and quivering lip. Newsmen regarded the sob sisters as intruders, calling them variously the "sympathy squad," the "pity patrol," and the "pathos brigade."

The "sisters" focused on the poignant figure of Evelyn Nesbit. Patterson described that "poor, beautiful, foolish, ignorant girl of sixteen pursued with the wealth and ferocity of a panther, by a man old enough to be her father." To Dix, Nesbit had been "the gay little butterfly of the studio, dancing down every wind of pleasure, blown hither and thither at a breath of caprice or desire. Now the butterfly has found a soul."

Some papers cleaned up their accounts, referring to "conditions which cannot be described in a family paper." Others ladled up every salacious detail, stirring a tempest of indignation, which embraced the nation's first reader. "It is disgusting that people should be willing to read such loathsome matter," Roosevelt wrote George Cortelyou, his postmaster general. "Can not we keep them [*sic*] out of the mail?" As with his earlier query to Attorney General William Moody about banning *Appeal to Reason*, the answer was no. Stung by such criticism, the *World* objected: "It is easy enough to rail at the newspapers for printing stenographic reports of the case, but what ought they do? Garble the testimony? Suppress the evidence upon which Thaw's life depends?" All of which handwringing prompted Finley Peter Dunne's Mr. Dooley to eulogize those "des'prit journalists, that has pledged their fortunes an' their sacred honors, an' manny of thim their watches, to be prisint an' protect th' public again th' degradin' facts."

The men and women representing the Socialist press in Boise regarded themselves as desperate journalists struggling against formidable odds to bring suppressed facts to a waiting proletariat. At public rallies, Joseph Wan-hope had repeatedly pledged that Socialists would have their own reporters at the trial, ready to rebut the "lies and falsehoods vomited forth" by the plutocratic organs. Individual Socialist reporters had covered earlier court-room dramas, notably the Debs trial in 1894, but never before had an American trial drawn such a phalanx of Socialists, representing every slice of that fragmented movement.

These ranks were less glittering than anticipated owing to last-minute withdrawals by two of the party's celebrities. On May 23, with the jury's completion in sight, Eugene Debs was preparing to leave Girard, Kansas, for Boise—where, along with George H. Shoaf and Ryan Walker, a cartoonist, he was to represent *Appeal to Reason*. But he had other plans as well. As early as February, Debs had informed his Idaho supporters that he would also hold meetings in Boise's streets to rally support for the defendants. The defense attorneys wanted none of that. Just as Debs was about to leave for Idaho, he received a letter from Darrow and Richardson that, according to *Appeal to*

Reason, earnestly requested him not to come "on the ground that his presence would inflame the public, prejudice the jury and jeopardize the lives of the defendants." A "consultation"—presumably with Julius Wayland, the editor, and Fred Warren, his managing editor—took place and "it was concluded that neither Debs nor the *Appeal* could afford to assume such a responsibility." Boise's Socialist community denounced Darrow and Richardson for "showing the white feather in the face of the enemy." Though Debs insisted he was not disgruntled, he may have shared some of Haywood's suspicion that Darrow had deflected his former client out of a "desire to be recognized as the most prominent person in the trial."

About the same time—and for much the same reasons—Upton Sinclair bowed out as representative of *Wilshire's Magazine.* He was replaced by no fewer than three pinch hitters: the ponderous German-born theorist Ernest Untermann, and the husband-and-wife team of John R. McMahon, whose novel *Toilers and Idlers,* about a life-weary young man of wealth, had been serialized all that spring in the pages of *Wilshire's,* and Margherita Arlina Hamm, who'd covered the Sino-Japanese and Spanish-American Wars and written eleven books on everything from *Chinese Legends* to *Eminent Actors in Their Homes.*

A third celebrity of the left had been approached to cover the case but declined. In April 1906—when the trial seemed imminent—Jack Barrett, news editor of Hearst's San Francisco *Examiner,* called Jack London in Oakland to ask if he'd go to Idaho for them. London said he was "too busy" working on his new book, *The Iron Heel,* "a socialistic-capitalistic novel." Barrett then asked him to knock out an opinion piece, which he did. Hearst never published it, but it appeared in the *Chicago Socialist* as "Something's Rotten in Idaho."

In addition to Shoaf, Walker, Untermann, McMahon, and Hamm, the left was represented at the trial by Wade Roscoe Parks and Olive Johnson of New York's *Daily People,* the organ of Daniel DeLeon's Socialist Labor Party; Hermon Titus, editor of the *Socialist,* variously of Seattle, Toledo, and Caldwell; Ida Crouch-Hazlett of the *Montana News,* who also wrote for the *Social-Democratic Herald* of Milwaukee, the moderate voice of Victor Berger's "gas and water" Socialism; J. C. Dalby and W. J. Scott of the *Seattle Union Record;* J. E. Roberts, editor of the *Idaho Unionist,* the twice-weekly organ of Boise's Trades and Labor Council; and W. Herman Barber, the secretary of Caldwell's Socialist local, who'd signed on as special correspondent of the *Pittsburgh Leader,* a paper with unionist-Socialist leanings.

One might have expected some solidarity in the Socialist camp, not only because three of its members were on trial for their lives but because the Socialist correspondents encountered so much discrimination and harassment in Boise. The governor and McParland had excluded them from the special briefings at the Idanha as well as from the Harry Orchard interviews. Sheriff Hodgin made sure they had the worst press seats in the courtroom: while the

AP and mainstream newspapers were assigned choice places at tables inside the rail, the Socialist-labor contingent all sat outside that privileged enclosure, writing on a two-foot-wide shelf affixed to the rail. Ida Crouch-Hazlett found such petty discrimination "embarrassing," if not downright humiliating.

Worse indignities were encountered outside the courtroom, incidents that lent some support to Darrow's subsequent charge that Boise was "a community where feeling and sentiment and hatred have been deliberately sown against [Haywood]." According to Margherita Hamm, who summed up these incidents for *Wilshire's Magazine*, through June no fewer than seven Socialists had been physically "assaulted." Hattie Titus, Ida Crouch-Hazlett, and she had been "spat upon in the streets and hissed." They and others had been trailed by detectives and Colorado gunmen, had had their mail tampered with* and had found notes dubbed "skiddoo postals" pushed under their doors inviting them to "get out of town" quick. "The girls who sell us rolls at the bakery," wrote Hamm, "said they had been promised free tickets to the hanging of Haywood, by Hawley, and hoped I would stay to see it as it was the first Socialist hanging ever held in Idaho, and they thought it would be a lesson to Socialists." Since Socialist women seem to have drawn more scorn than their male colleagues, they may have received a double dose—for stepping out of a woman's role as well as for their politics.

The one place the visitors felt at home was the cigar store operated by Eugene Francis Gary, the blind tobacconist-newsdealer from Silver City who'd debated Socialism with Rees Davis in 1903. Gary had moved to Boise in 1905 and, as the trial opened, had been elected chairman of the city's Socialist local. His newsstand at 215 North Eighth Street, two blocks from the Idanha, offered "Cigars, Tobacco, Confectionery, School and Office Supplies, Fruits and General News." Since it also carried Socialist periodicals and plenty of Socialist gossip, it became the Socialist reporters' favorite gathering place, where they mixed with Boise's homebred radicals.

Boise was "not a good town for socialists," Local Boise's secretary conceded. Ida Crouch-Hazlett thought it "a good place for capitalists to gather and plot against working men." Nonetheless, twenty-one Socialists had applied for the local's charter in December 1905, a few days before Steunenberg was killed. By the next April, it had fifty-two members. That spring, the local had issued a "manifesto" on the assassination that was both balanced and fair. It condemned the "class war" between mine owners and miners and regretted that Steunenberg should have been one of its victims "as many an unknown

---

* Even the Hearst correspondents had their mail intercepted. In one case, the Pinkertons took a postcard from Denver directed to Hearst's Clement J. Driscoll and showed it to the governor as evidence that Captain Swain of the Thiel agency was in league with Hearst and the defense (McParland Report, April 12, 1906, Idaho State Historical Society).

miner has also fallen." Despite the manifesto's moderate tone, the *Statesman*—whose slogan that year was The Whole Story—refused to print it.

Organizing around the approaching trial may have increased the local's membership somewhat, but it was still shy of a hundred. Among the Socialists who frequented Gary's were William F. Bradley, the local's secretary and its nominee the previous autumn for judge of the Third Judicial District, the very seat now held by Fremont Wood, and Louis E. Workman, a lawyer and farmer, who'd been the party's candidate for state attorney general.

Gary's also drew the city's leading labor leaders, among them I. Wilson Wright, the local's former recording secretary, now president of the carpenters union and organizer for all Idaho's labor unions; C. Underwood, business agent for the Boise Federation of Labor; and William Greenberg, its secretary.

Boise wasn't a labor town. Fewer than a thousand men and women and a dozen floats had participated in the city's 1906 Labor Day parade, a number swelled by delegations from Caldwell, Nampa, and nearby towns. Moreover, most of Boise's unions—carpenters, teamsters, painters, stage employees, and bartenders—were affiliated with Gompers's AFL, their stance on industrial-political questions far more cautious than the WFM's.

This circumspection was evident in their reaction to the Bloody Sunday parade of union miners of Goldfield, Nevada, on January 20, 1907, to commemorate the massacre of Russian revolutionists at St. Petersburg a year before and to protest the impending Haywood trial. Three thousand WFM and IWW marchers, brandishing red flags and a banner proclaiming, "If they pack the jury to hang our men, we will pack hell full with them," listened as Vincent St. John of the WFM promised, "We will sweep the capitalist class out of the life of this nation and then out of the whole world."* Stunned by such audacity, Boise's Federation of Labor passed a resolution condemning Goldfield's extremism.

Boise's "safe, sane and conservative" union men didn't inspire confidence in George Shoaf, who in April 1907 suggested that they were in the union "not because they realize the existence of the war between the robbers and the robbed, or because of their desire to effectively participate in the class struggle, but because it is . . . a little harder to stay out than it is to get in. Should a class war occur, I would not give thirty cents for the loyalty of all the union men in Boise."

On that point—and practically no other—McParland agreed with Shoaf. In March, he told Gooding that Gary's was where "the handful of resident anarchist malcontents hang out," a crowd that neither the WFM nor the IWW would trust "with anything." And yet, conscientious to a fault, he kept these malcontents under surveillance. A Pinkerton from Denver named

---

* Arrested in February 1906 as an accomplice in the WFM "conspiracy," St. John had since been released for insufficient evidence of his guilt.

L. D. Alexander, as Operative 24-A, stopped in at Gary's twice a day all winter and spring. "I visited E. F. Gary's and met Smith, Claire, Robinson, Cope, Jones, Bradley and Workman," he wrote one day. "I stayed there about three hours and all they did was curse Gooding and his Pinkerton 'thugs' and the Mine Owners Association, and hope they'd never be able to hang Moyer, Haywood or Pettibone." On one occasion, he met Bill Greenberg of the Federation of Labor, a friend of Moyer's. "He would not give one hair off of [Moyer's] head for the whole carcass of 'Sheep-thief Gooding' or Hawley or all the rest of the bunch. He said 'To hell with the flag, I used to have some respect for it, but have none now.'"

Now and then, Chris Thiele would wander into Gary's, browse the Socialist journals, and "ask all kinds of questions." He made no effort to disguise his identity and Boise's Socialists saw his presence as pure harassment. They particularly resented Thiele because, as he'd admitted on the witness stand at the Steve Adams trial, he'd served in 1904 as an undercover labor spy at the Butte Reduction Works. It had only been for ten weeks, he insisted, and all he'd done was report on mill men who were stealing ore, but the WFM regarded him as a sneaky informer. One day at Gary's, Underwood of the Boise Federation of Labor denounced him as "that little stinker of a thug," adding "it's too bad that some one doesn't choke him to death!"

Whatever solidarity these rigors fostered, the Socialist camp wasn't a happy one. So riven were its members by ideological, tactical, and personal differences that they spent almost as much time jousting with one another as dueling with the class enemy or, for that matter, reporting the story.

Some of the trouble dated back to the bitter 1906 campaign during which Haywood's defense team had sought, at all costs, to unseat Judge Frank J. Smith in the Seventh Judicial District, where Haywood had been slated for trial. Hermon Titus, then publishing the *Socialist* in Caldwell, grew outraged when John Nugent helped nominate and support the Democratic challenger while seeking to persuade the Socialist to withdraw from the race. The result would have amounted to fusion between the Democratic and Socialist tickets, an "opportunistic" act that was anathema to an uncompromising left-wing Socialist like Titus.

The May 11 issue of *Appeal to Reason* noted that "a certain individual, prominently connected with the Socialist party, is preparing to get his reward of perfidy by deserting Moyer, Haywood and Pettibone in their unequal fight against the power of combined capital." It admonished all Socialists "to be prepared for the Judases and Arnolds that manage to worm their way into every labor movement only to desert when desertion pays."

Any doubt about the putative traitor's identity was soon removed when the article's author, George Shoaf, encountered Titus on a Boise Street and told him bluntly he was the scoundrel. In the next issue of Titus's *Socialist*, the editor struck back. "I denounce the whole accusation as an infamous lie, a damnable insinuation, the most contemptible journalistic trick to ruin a fellow editor and comrade that was ever executed," he wrote, demanding a retraction from Shoaf and his paper. "With John F. Nugent, who is not a Socialist and of whom nothing better could be expected," Titus added rather ominously, "I shall deal otherwise." When Titus strolled into defense head-quarters in the Overland Block on May 10, Nugent used some "harsh names" in ordering the editor thrown into the street, which only stoked the fires of contention.

The following week, Shoaf struck again, accusing Titus and his wife, Hattie, of taking their meals at one of Boise's Chinese restaurants, an odious act for a Socialist since it could be seen as discriminating against union members of American birth.

Hermon Titus had two pulpits from which to preach his brand of left-wing Socialism. Between major set pieces for his weekly *Socialist,* he contributed a daily article to the Yiddish-language *Forward* in New York. These pieces were highly opinionated and relatively short, usually introduc-ing a wire-service account of the day's events in court. It was a sign of Abraham Cahan's identification with the very American struggle taking place in Boise that he recruited his own man there, despite ruinous cable charges and the expense of translation.

"The telegrams which the *Forward* prints from the Haywood trial come to us every day direct from the courtroom in Boise, Idaho, from the extremely important Socialist editor, Doctor Hermon F. Titus," Cahan told his readers. "Comrade Titus sits in court at the trial, near Haywood and his lawyers. His telegrams are written to us with his own Socialist pen." Despite the heavy cost, he said, "a newspaper like ours, published for socialist instruction, must make a maximum effort to obtain the clearest, mightiest and most convincing articles about this world-historic socialist trial."

Titus's dispatch on June 6, 1907—dealing with Orchard's first appear-ance on the witness stand—was headlined "Orchard's Bubbe-Mayses," which may be translated "Orchard's Old Wives' Tale" or "Orchard's False Story." In a heavily colored account, Titus said Orchard's testimony was "too wild to believe," sounding more like "a melodrama or a bloody detective story." More likely than the old wives' tale, he argued, were two other possibilities: that Orchard was "a murdering devil, like Jack the Ripper," who'd committed the crimes on his own, or that he'd been hired by the Pinkerton agency "to break the back of the miners' union."

After Hugo Münsterberg's findings reached the press, Titus wrote an impassioned piece from Boise headlined "How 'Science' Confirms Orchard's Truth," in which he argued that "Capital, the mighty owner and exploiter of labor" had used Münsterberg's bogus science to "save the skin" of the lying witness. First, the capitalist organ *McClure's* had imported the German Jew Münsterberg to "explain in the name of science, that Orchard is sound of mind and an honest man." Then "the greatest capitalist newspapers have instructed their correspondents in Boise" to accept Münsterberg's findings and thus "to create falsehoods for the world and to present the trial exactly as the prosecution does."

Titus's dispatches were only part of the massive coverage Cahan devoted to the trial: virtually every day for three months, he put Titus's telegrams and wire-service stories on page 1, often side by side with his own lengthy editorials. Day after day, this Lithuanian immigrant—who'd never set foot west of the Ohio River—strove to connect these events in far-off Idaho with the concerns of his readers on Essex and Mott Streets.

On July 4, he extolled the most American of holidays. What did one find that day, he asked, when Americans "celebrate their nation of free, equal citizens? . . . A nation divided in two, that's what we find!" The "mining millionaires of Idaho and Colorado" were celebrating the Fourth on their lush estates, while Haywood, Moyer, and Pettibone were celebrating it in the Ada County jail. "Not Haywood," he concluded, "but the capitalist class of America is the one on trial, not just a murder trial of a union man, but a trial of the entire modern world."

Ida Crouch-Hazlett, perhaps the most evenhanded of the Socialist correspondents, was disturbed by all the squabbling in Boise. Part of the problem stemmed from the internecine battles between genuine Socialists. But part, she noted, was the presence of "a number of queer-acting and decided cranks calling themselves Socialists in Boise during the trial. Some of them have acted with great impudence."

One of those Crouch-Hazlett had in mind was Carl Duncan, the young man arrested on Main Street on May 28 wearing a false beard and mustache and carrying a revolver and brass knuckles.

Another troublemaker was Wade Roscoe Parks of New York's *Daily People* and the IWW's *Industrial Union Bulletin*. The *People*, a slim four-page sheet always on the brink of bankruptcy, could never have afforded its own correspondent in Boise had the IWW, now run by its DeLeon faction, not subsidized Park's rail fare and hotel bill. To Crouch-Hazlett, Parks seemed "a weird, lank, intense looking individual that strides through the town like a race horse, always carrying a mysterious and cavernous bag."

At lunch hour on May 17—as Koelsch prepared his report to Judge Wood—Parks entered the Women's Exchange, a cooperative restaurant in the basement of the First National Bank. The exchange sold dishes prepared by fifteen Boise women to other women wishing to take home ready-to-eat food. The genteel establishment also served breakfast, lunch, and tea on its premises. Priced at only thirty-five cents, the lunch drew some of the trial's most impecunious reporters.

When Parks finished his meal, he went to the cashier's desk, where the manager, Mrs. J. C. Dressler, was working. Placing his grip on a stool and leaning toward her, he confided that it was full of "Pettibone dope," the explosive Steve Adams allegedly planned to toss into trains carrying scabs to Colorado. The "dope" would "open any combination in the world," he told her.

Thinking he was joking, Mrs. Dressler laughed. But Parks asked, "Haven't you heard the big doings? They've discharged the jury in the Haywood case and the governor and attorney general will be in jail before night. They've discovered that the *Statesman* and other capitalist newspapers have conspired against Haywood, Pettibone and Moyer, and they're all to be properly 'fixed.' You shall know the truth and it will save you!" the *Statesman* reported. According to another account, he said he was prepared to "blow hell out of these men who denied the truth of the brotherhood of man." The first of his victims would be Governor Gooding; the courthouse and the *Statesman* would be next.

At this, the young man grabbed his satchel and rushed from the restaurant. Thoroughly alarmed, Mrs. Dressler informed the bank president's son, who in turn hailed the chief of police, Ben Francis, who happened to be strolling nearby. Francis shadowed Parks to the courthouse, where he informed Sheriff Hodgin of the incident. Hodgin confiscated Parks's suspicious grip but found nothing inside but copy for Parks's newspaper and a few Socialist pamphlets. When questioned about his remarks to Mrs. Dressler, the reporter said he'd meant only that the explosive manuscript in his grip would blow people up, figuratively speaking. Henceforth, he promised to quote only poetry. The sheriff concluded he was "a harmless crank" but, given the tensions in town, resolved to keep him under surveillance.

His pranks notwithstanding, Parks wasn't the most flamboyant of the Socialist correspondents. That distinction surely belonged to George Shoaf, who liked to call himself the "war correspondent of the Class War."

Born in 1875 in Lockhart, Texas, Shoaf had—according to his own testimony, which must be received with some skepticism—a most unorthodox upbringing. At age seven, he'd watched as his father, playing poker in a saloon, pulled a revolver and shot a Mexican, who'd been brandishing a bowie knife, squarely between the eyes. Then father and son went home to dinner.

In a lifetime of gunplay, the elder Shoaf—whom his son described as "a terror to peace loving citizens"—claimed to have killed twenty men. For some years, he ostensibly put his marksmanship at the service of the people, serving as marshal of Lockhart and as San Antonio's chief of detectives. His son "idolized" him, in part perhaps because, flush with profits from his gambling operations, his father indulged his every whim. George claimed to be the first San Antonio boy to ride his own bicycle.

His radicalism was acquired from a great uncle, John "Dirty Shirt" Davis, a Populist member of the Texas senate. Named for his scruffy attire, Dirty Shirt was an orator of the old school, a voracious reader who educated his grandnephew in the literature of dissent. Shoaf joined the Socialist Labor

Party, but when Gene Debs spoke at the San Antonio Opera House in 1898, Shoaf was seized by enthusiasm and Debs replaced the trigger-happy father as the "god of my idolatry." Quitting the SLP, he helped found a San Antonio branch of the Social Democratic Party and mounted a quixotic campaign as a Socialist candidate for lieutenant governor.

Shoaf broke into journalism on the *San Antonio Express,* under the colorful William C. Brann, later editor of the *Iconoclast,* one of America's great radical journals. Brann's ferocious assault on conventional pieties became a model for Shoaf's own journalism, but the master's invective was rooted as much in shrewd marketing as in outraged principle.

Following his apprenticeship with Brann, Shoaf found a new leader, Walter Vrooman, founder of Ruskin College, a labor institution in Trenton, Missouri, that tried to produce Socialists through education. Taking Shoaf with him to Chicago, Vrooman launched a harebrained scheme to incite Americans to violent revolution by exploiting their anxiety over Oriental immigration. He sent radical agitators—among them Shoaf and Honoré Jaxon, the Canadian-born rebel who later corresponded with Theodore Roosevelt—into Chicago neighborhoods to warn of the yellow peril. On several occasions, Shoaf claimed to have dressed as a Chinese man—pigtails and all—in order to rouse a xenophobic mob. The conspirators had begun to recruit a private army, while rifles piled up in a Chicago warehouse, when McKinley was shot in 1901. Vrooman, fearing he might be implicated, decamped for Florida. The revolution died aborning.

Adrift again, Shoaf played piano for a time in a Wabash Avenue whorehouse, but he was still "bent on revolution." Becoming a conductor on the Chicago street railway, he set out to organize a transit workers union, a goal that had long defied Sam Gompers. The company was unremittingly hostile, so Shoaf assembled a "secret organization" but made the mistake of recruiting a company spy, who turned him in. Suspecting he was about to be fired, Shoaf wrote a letter—exposing the miserable working conditions of the streetcar workers—to Hearst's *Chicago American,* where it appeared on the front page. When Shoaf was fired, Hearst, Gompers, and Darrow, among others, rode to his support, and in late 1901 he succeeded, with their help, in organizing the Amalgamated Association of Street Railway Employees, embracing twenty thousand workers. During these years, Shoaf and Darrow often collaborated and Shoaf played a prominent role in the unsuccessful effort to persuade Darrow to run for mayor of Chicago on a Populist-Democratic ticket.

Early in 1902, Shoaf became editor of the transit workers' paper, the *Union Leader,* and shaped it into an ardent voice for Socialism. The Irish Catholic Democrats who ran the union, backed by Gompers, vigorously resisted, and Shoaf joined the Hearst paper that had supported his union organizing. The *American* was Hearst's midwestern outpost, established in 1900 as a stepping-stone to the presidency. Its city editor was Moses Koenigsberg, who'd worked for Brann in San Antonio and knew Shoaf well. "George," he said, "you should now know you can't get anywhere with your Socialist agitation. Cut out that foolishness . . . [and] in time you may be able to make your mark."

The *American* practiced Hearst's brand of yellow journalism with prodigious gusto. "Every story with [Koenigsberg] was a sensation, had to be a sensation, or it was not a story," Shoaf recalled; nor did the city editor scruple much over how his men got their daily dose of delirium. As a principled Socialist, Shoaf claimed this bothered him at first, but ultimately he determined to "sidetrack idealism, and pursue the capitalist newspaper game to the reprehensible end," a pursuit he thought compelled him "to degenerate into a moral scalawag, ready to violate any law and perpetrate any crime in furtherance of my efforts to 'get ahead.'"

When Koenigsberg assigned him to get a photograph of a Chicago woman who was suing her husband for divorce—no paper had been able to get one—he wangled an introduction to her maid, took her to dance halls and shows, made love to her, won her undying affection—and procured the photo.

By then, he was a practiced "yellow kid." With his Texas brogue, one acquaintance thought he resembled a Methodist preacher—he had, in fact, attended a Christian college and for a time pastored a small Christian church. "Hayseed seemed to drop from him. He was pure corn. But turn him loose on a story and he'd shake the world." To Moses Koenigsberg, he was "one of the most tenacious diggers that ever gladdened a news editor's heart."

Shoaf loved the reporter's life in Chicago—the tumultuous bars and cafés, the lofty talk of intellectuals like Darrow and Brand Whitlock, the heady access to power. But he remained a Socialist, and when Fred Warren offered him a job in the summer of 1903 reporting the Colorado mining wars for *Appeal to Reason*, Shoaf couldn't resist. "I knew the system which generated and upheld the putrid mess called the American way of life could not last, and that if I remained a capitalist newspaper man, I would degenerate into a contemptible prostitute." The *American* was loath to lose him and ultimately he agreed to report the story for both papers.

Depositing his wife, Sallie, and their three children in Texas, Shoaf set off that fall for Denver to investigate the struggle between the WFM and the mine owners. Hanging round the Mining Exchange Building, he fell under Haywood's spell. Always prone to hero worship, Shoaf now attached himself to Haywood. "Was there ever another precisely like him!" he wrote. "He was the mental and physical incarnation of Spartacus, the Roman gladiator, Simon Girty, Irishman turned Indian, and Osceola, the Seminole warrior. He had the courage of a lion, the audacity of the devil. . . . He became the god of my idolatry."

Shoaf hadn't been in Colorado long before he became convinced that Pinkerton gunmen were out to kill him. So Shoaf began carrying his own .38-caliber revolver. On one occasion—still according to Shoaf's own account

—he was trapped in a Denver saloon by Charlie Siringo and two other Pinkertons. Approaching the trio, he leveled his revolver at Siringo and rasped, "Up with your hands, gentlemen, belly the bar, and keep your hands raised, or I'll start shooting now!" as he escaped through the swinging doors.

Then, Shoaf claimed, he and an ally, the WFM stalwart Vincent St. John, set out to assassinate McParland, an act they believed would "put the fear of God" in Colorado's capitalists. "For days and nights we camped on the trail of the detective chief, but his ever present bodyguard of several huskies prevent us from getting near enough to accomplish our purpose." How much of this has any basis in reality is difficult to say. Surely Shoaf was a figure out of the most preposterous dime novels. Indeed, his Colorado exploits inspired not one novel but two—his own *Love Crucified: A Romance of the Colorado War,* which the *Appeal's* book division brought out in 1905 under the pseudonym George Henry, and one by his admiring *Appeal* sidekick, Walter Hurt, entitled *The Scarlet Shadow,* which appeared in 1907 on the eve of the Haywood trial.

In *Love Crucified,* Shoaf appears early in the guise of Charlie Harding, a Texas reporter who finds his way to Colorado, where he meets William Hayworth, a labor leader with "a big head, a square jaw and the physical strength of an ox." Becoming Hayworth's assistant, he plunges into "the most tremendous industrial tragedy that has yet occurred in the economic development of the world," Colorado's labor wars.

Intertwined is the drama of Charlie's love for Margaret Miller, "a young person of high breeding . . . elegance and intellectual accomplishment." Margaret, in turn, regards Charlie as "a young man of more than ordinary culture —one from whose eyes shone extreme kindness." Caught up in the diabolic machinations of the Colorado mine owners, Margaret is held captive for a time in an abandoned mine shaft but escapes and makes her way to Denver, where she is reunited with Charlie. At this juncture, she testifies to the power of love: "Love racks the brain till the world reels, but the shock of it opens the gates of paradise and pours the floodtides of life over the miasmic deserts of human existence, burning up the dross and refining the gold."

Hurt's novel is explicitly based on the Steunenberg assassination and the Haywood trial. When the WFM leaders are kidnapped from Denver by a "crafty, cruel, conscienceless" sleuth named "Tim MacFarlane, manager of the western division of the Thugerton Detective Agency," the editor of the Chicago *Express* exclaims: "Send Shoforth!" "Alert, expectant and ready for any emergency, Gordon Shoforth is "the ideal correspondent, vigilant as a weasel and virile as a live wire." Possessed of a body "as resilient as rubber," he walks "as if shod with steel springs," and anytime the "social volcano" erupts, he is the man "despatched to the place of disturbance."

So threatening to Colorado's mine owners is Shoforth that he, too, is kidnapped and held in a deserted mine, guarded by a "vile visaged Mexican half-breed . . . with a smile upon his lupine lips." But he escapes and finds time for a dalliance with a mine owner's daughter. While he converts her to

Socialism, "as a born voluptuary" he admires her "bursting fullness of bust and hip."

In Boise, Shoforth listens with mounting revulsion to Orchard, "the professional perjurer," throw the blame for Steunenberg's death on the innocent Haywood: "Cruelty crouches in his heart, and his foul lips are fondled by the Father of Lies to whom he has sold as provender for hell's carrion-crows his festering and fly-blown substitute for a soul." As the jury deliberates Haywood's fate, most of the reporters congregate in the Idanha's lobby. But one is missing. Dick Walton of the Chicago *Clarion*—an "aristocrat" clearly patterned after Richard Harding Davis—is in his room upstairs committing suicide, but not before he leaves a note for Gordon Shoforth containing enough final-act switches and discoveries to satisfy the most demanding Restoration playwright.

"Orchard is a liar and a hired tool," the note says,

> and is entirely ignorant of the real facts in the case. I killed Steunenberg. It was easy. As a newspaper correspondent, I was able to cover my tracks completely. . . . To make the whole matter clear to you, I must tell you who I am. I am not really a Walton by birth, and a patrician. I am of the proletariat. My father was one of the "Molly Maguires" hanged through McFarlane's machinations. I had learned—in what manner is not of consequence—that Frank Steunenberg, like myself, was an adopted child whose origin was a secret save to a few. He was the son of Tim McFarlane.

Adopted by the Steunenbergs, Frank had risen in Idaho politics, helped along by McFarlane's chicanery. "Knowledge of all this," Walton concludes, "was the key to unlock the door of my heart's desire—revenge. I selected Frank Steunenberg as the object of death." Approving the choice, "in view of his record during the Coeur d'Alene labor disturbances," is a committee of the Russian revolutionary party whose agent Walton now turns out to have been.

When he has finished reading Walton's astounding letter, the ever-alert Shoforth exclaims: "It's a scoop!"

None of the prose in these novels is any more hyperbolic than Shoaf's, and Hurt's, language in *Appeal to Reason*. It was James McParland who roused the two reporters to their wildest excess. To Shoaf, he was "the greatest and most horrible Gorgon of this monster-bearing age. . . . It requires no stretch of the imagination to see the fires of hell in the depth of those eyes. . . . As a brute he is splendidly developed. . . . Fiend incarnate . . . the leer of Satan on his face." But, writing in the same issue, Hurt may have trumped his colleague: "Were the world's supply of emetic poured down the hot throat of hell, the ultimate imp of the last vile vomit would be an archangel in good standing compared with this feculent fiend."

The slim, dark-haired, "disarming" Shoaf was a bit of a scoundrel with women. "You couldn't help liking the rogue," said one of his editors. "Ladies fell for him in rows." He'd been married to Sallie for two decades but was frequently unfaithful. When Shoaf first arrived in Boise, he and some other Socialist reporters found rooms in a boardinghouse run by a Mrs. Deems at 422 Idaho Street. It is unclear whether Sallie was with him at the start, but eventually she joined him with their six-year-old son, Gordon, in tow. Nonetheless, it appears that Shoaf formed—or perhaps resumed—a relationship with Ida Crouch-Hazlett during the trial's early weeks. At forty-five a "large and handsome woman," she had been married to Val Hazlett since 1892, but by 1907 they may have been estranged. She'd known Shoaf well since both reported the Colorado labor wars in 1902–04. In Boise, they not only lived under a common roof but often dined together, with or without the other Socialist reporters.

Also living at Mrs. Deems's house were several teenage girls who attended a Boise business college, among them a fifteen-year-old named Florence Abbott from a farming family in Yale, Idaho. According to a complaint filed by the girl, Shoaf at some point shifted his attentions from Crouch-Hazlett to Miss Abbott and had sexual relations with the girl first on July 9 and on several other occasions. Mrs. Deems told police Shoaf hadn't been in her house very long before she noticed him talking with Miss Abbott "on the sly"; she'd warned him to stop and reminded Florence she was there "under her charge." But neither paid her much heed. A few nights later, Mrs. Deems found them strolling together on the statehouse lawn.

Some weeks after the Shoafs came to her house, Mrs. Deems moved nearby, taking with her some of her boarders—among them Miss Abbott— but barring Shoaf, who then found quarters at a Mrs. Martin's rooming house. There he resumed his surreptitious relations with Miss Abbott, eventually persuading her to move to Mrs. Martin's too.

Soon after the charge of statutory rape surfaced in the Boise press, however, Miss Abbott repudiated her statement, saying that she wished "to exonerate [Shoaf] entirely" and to say that the earlier statement she'd signed was "false in every particular." She went on:

> Since Mrs. Ida Crouch-Hazlett of the *Montana News* figured so prominently in "exposing" this affair, I desire to say something about her in this connection. When Mrs. Hazlett imagined that Mr. Shoaf was playing fast and loose with my affections and was preparing to give her the "double cross" her attitude changed. She grew cold toward him and warmed up toward me. She tried to induce me to embrace the doctrines of Socialism. She announced that she was an atheist and a free lover, saying that all scientific Socialists were atheists and free lovers. [Another version reported that Crouch-Hazlett told Miss Abbott that Shoaf was only a "half-baked" Socialist, in that he was "neither an atheist nor a free lover yet."] Her malignant attacks upon Mr. Shoaf and her willful efforts to effect my disgrace were prompted purely from jealousy, and were as cowardly as they were devoid of truth and principle. When she thought she saw him slipping from her affections, she delib-

erately manufactured the story that was calculated to place him in the hands of enemies.

Some who read Miss Abbott's statement doubted that it was the work of a fifteen-year-old girl and thought it sounded like the lusty prose of George Shoaf. James D. Graham, secretary of the Montana Socialist Party, was so outraged by what he read in the papers that he came to Boise and personally investigated the case, concluding that Shoaf was indeed the author of Miss Abbott's second affidavit. "Not content with endeavoring to clear himself," Graham charged, "he stoops to the lowest act a man can be guilty of, that of endeavoring to ruin a woman's character and reputation. Instead of Shoaf being the victim of a conspiracy, it is Mrs. Hazlett who is being made the victim by Shoaf and his friends, for no other purpose than that they are all jealous of the work she had done in reporting the trial at Boise."

Just where the truth lies in this snarl of accusations is difficult to say. All through the trial, Shoaf juggled relations with three women: his wife, Ida Crouch-Hazlett, and Florence Abbott—a tangle that was bound to end badly. But there were others besides Crouch-Hazlett with reason to wreak vengeance on Shoaf who might have used the alleged rape to do so.

The *Appeal* wasn't popular with its competitors—on the left or the right. The *Statesman* liked to call it *Appeal to Treason*. Even those who defended Shoaf himself—as Ida Crouch-Hazlett did for months—condemned the paper. "True Socialists despise the *Appeal*," she told a reporter. "It is printed to sell, not to help the party. It is making dupes of those who subscribe to it and it is doing great harm to the workers to whom the real interests and purposes of the party are dear."

Shoaf was the *Appeal*'s boldest swashbuckler—and its biggest liar. Emanuel Haldeman-Julius, a Socialist editor who knew him well, thought he had "a prejudice against facts." A "natural born romancer," he practiced in the great American tradition of journalistic humbug, but his strategy, according to Haldeman-Julius, was precisely the opposite of what *Writer* magazine had suggested in 1887: instead of getting the important facts right and inventing the details, he'd "build a story on a vast hoax, but saw to it that it was supported by the nicest regard for factual details." Shoaf himself, in the guise of recounting journalistic practice, captured his attitude pretty well: "If the facts do not accord . . . get up the story, anyway. Use the names of the parties involved in the plot, give dates, places and such other incidents as will lend a semblance of truth to the proposition, crowd the story with fictititous names and characters, throw ginger and insinuative suggestion into the article, write it up 'red hot,' and send it in."

Sometimes Shoaf even lied about lying. After he and his Socialist colleagues were excluded from the Orchard interviews on May 16, he announced one day in the courtroom, "You fellows thought you all had me scooped, but your interviews can't compare with the interview I sent my paper the other day with Orchard."

"Did you see Orchard?" a reporter asked.

"I saw him in my mind," Shoaf shot back. "Anyhow, I certainly did send a swell interview—one that will make a sensation when it comes out." None appeared. And unless the *Appeal* declined to print it—which seems most unlikely—Shoaf was simply having some sport with his colleagues.

He did print some whoppers—such as the report that the prosecution had a $60,000 fund ready to bribe the jury. When a *Statesman* reporter confronted him one day, nearly sputtering with rage, and asked, "Why do you write such rot as that? You know it's a lie," Shoaf shrugged and said, "A few little irregularities like that don't count. You know I am out here to deliver the goods and I have to keep everything hot."

Shoaf saw himself as something more than a mere reporter. As he later admitted, he functioned as a part-time agent for his old friend Darrow, helping in the secret vetting of talesmen. Others fretted about Shoaf's extracurricular activities in Boise. Ernest Untermann of *Wilshire's* warned the *Appeal* against Shoaf:

> I wrote long letters to Debs, telling him that I had watched Shoaf at work and that while he was writing sensational and overdone articles for the *Appeal*, he was underhandedly acting like a Pinkerton and disrupting the Socialist local in Boise, was even jeopardizing the interests of the prisoners by telling everybody that the boys had confessed to him that they were guilty and that we ought to set the town afire and raise hell, because we oughtn't to let the thing come to trial. Debs lectured me pretty severely at that time and refused to believe that Shoaf was crooked.

Relations between Socialist reporters and their mainstream colleagues were somewhat better than they seemed on the surface. Publicly, Shoaf denounced "the reptile press," which had woven "a tissue of lies" about the defendants. Titus bashed "the yelping daily press" for crying simply, "Hang the villains!" But in quieter moments, both men conceded they had a lot in common with their capitalist confreres. "Being a newspaper man myself—a practical everyday reporter for a daily paper—I am not so much disposed to condemn my brother members of the craft as I am to explain their processes of getting and writing the news," wrote Shoaf. Titus said that the reporters at the trial were "a fine class of men as a rule," who insisted they were "not bound by any instructions except to report what they see," and that "as long as the Class Struggle does not force itself to the front, these reporting slaves may be depended on to tell the truth fairly well." But, he warned, "reporters are wage slaves of the most subservient type.... Whenever the interests of Capital demand it, every reporter for a Capitalist paper here will get his orders to misrepresent Labor or quit."

Most mainstream reporters didn't take the Socialist reporters seriously, seizing on the "merry squabble" in Socialist ranks as evidence of their unprofessional behavior. Hugh O'Neill of the *Denver Post* marveled at the "foam of passion" men like Shoaf and Titus could work up. Idaho's "silent, industrious farmers," he suggested, looked on "in amused tolerance at the very fervid gentlemen who proclaimed that unless their views were adopted, the union of these states would toboggan to the devil."

Except for Ida Crouch-Hazlett, Margherita Hamm, and Olive Johnson —all Socialists—the fifty-odd reporters at the trial were relentlessly male. The absence of "sob sisters"—a fixture at New York and Los Angeles murder trials—was instantly seized on by O. K. Davis and A. E. Thomas. Perhaps, Davis wrote, Idaho women "lack the morbid curiosity possessed by their sisters in New York." Thomas noted "lots of reporters, but, alas, no pity patrol, no sympathy squad, no pathos brigade." When a *Capital News* reporter writing about Haywood's daughter Henrietta did show up, Thomas observed gleefully that "a member of the Pity Patrol has at last arrived" but that she'd "declined to say whether she was the only member of the patrol who'd be present or whether she was merely the scout of the organization." In fact, she stood alone. Specializing in adultery and the other sorrows of modern womanhood, the sob sisters were evidently regarded by their employers— chiefly Hearst and Pulitzer—as superfluous at a trial focusing on the struggles of labor and capital.

The "yellows" were on relatively good behavior in Boise. Pulitzer was represented by John Fay, his veteran bureau chief in Chicago. On occasion, Fay sent out a wildly unlikely story, as on May 2, when he wrote, "Perfectly reasonable men here look at the high witness chair in the county courthouse, shake their heads seriously, and tell you that Harry Orchard will die in it." But, by and large, his reports were reasonably accurate.

Hearst's stance was more complicated. He'd come late to the story; like the editors of the right-wing Socialist journals, Hearst and/or his top editors apparently suspected Haywood was guilty and feared that identification with his cause wouldn't advance the publisher's political aspirations. Not until mid-March 1906 did the New York *Evening Journal* send its impeccably tailored political editor, Clement J. Driscoll, to Idaho, where he produced some of the most reckless and inaccurate journalism of the whole case. On March 24, he reported that a high-level decision had been made that Haywood, Moyer, and Pettibone "will be administered the regular Third Degree, so well known to private detective agencies, ... in hopes of securing a confession." In fact, the three men weren't even questioned in prison, much less given the third degree. Driscoll solemnly assured his readers that Bill Haywood never touched liquor and "his home life is regular." He interviewed Haywood, whom he quoted—improbably—as saying, "I am glad to know that the Evening Journal, which has ever been the friend of honest laboring men and their cause, has sent representatives into the field to gather the facts.... We

thank you from the bottom of our hearts, Mr. Hearst, for sending a representative here."

The *Statesman* took high umbrage at Driscoll, whom it called "a young
man of immaculate habits of dress and a propensity for getting his wires
crossed," and after a month he returned to New York, replaced by J. S.
Dunnigan, a veteran from Hearst's San Francisco *Examiner*. McParland refused to talk with Dunnigan on the grounds that his predecessor was a "young
anarchist" who'd sent "column after column of fake interviews." In fact,
Dunnigan's reporting on the trial was subdued, and reasonably accurate, by
Hearst standards.

The best reporter in Boise that summer wasn't one of the elite newsmen
from back East but a twenty-nine-year-old from the *Portland Evening Telegram*
named Frank Leroy Perkins. A police and circuit court reporter since 1904,
Perkins had persuaded his editor to let him report on a Portland delegation
visiting Boise in early May, then to stay on and cover the trial.

Since the morning *Portland Oregonian* had its own man giving the trial
exhaustive coverage, Perkins or his editors resolved to focus on developments
at the trial's periphery—the curious doings of detectives, lawyers, reporters,
and assorted hangers-on. So energetic and resourceful was the young reporter, he often had two or three important—or interesting—stories in a
single day's paper: the first account of the tensions between Clarence Darrow
and Edmund Richardson, a report that during the trial's first weeks Boise
police had quietly deported fifty men "regarded as dangerous to the welfare
of the community," a moving story about the quiet courage of John Murphy,
the WFM's regular attorney, who insisted on helping out at the trial though
he was rapidly dying from tuberculosis.

On the rare day he didn't turn up at least one significant story, he
improvised ingeniously, using the flight of a bumblebee rumbling through an
open window to trace the courtroom's human topography. Judge Wood, he
noticed, wouldn't imperil the "dignity of the bench" by swatting at the ferocious insect, but some of New York's "war correspondents" bobbed and
weaved like the prizefighter James J. Corbett, while Hermon Titus's eyes
"rolled in a fine frenzy." If Perkins imagined the bee—as well he might have
—in the hierarchy of journalistic humbug, it was a relatively small offense.

A greater dereliction was his truckling to the prosecution by spying on
his colleagues and the defense attorneys. On the evening of May 12, Perkins
encountered McParland and William Balderston, the *Statesman*'s editor, in the
Idanha lobby, invited them to the bar for a drink, and assured them he
thought there was "not a question on earth" that Haywood, Moyer, and
Pettibone were guilty. As further evidence of his reliability, he told them of
remarks made by Dunnigan of the *Examiner* in that very bar showing how
cozy the Hearst man was with the defense.

Perkins was a trained telegrapher, able to decipher a cable message from
the sound of the incoming dots and dashes. He hung around the Western

Union office on Eighth Street, whose ten operators sent an average of fifty thousand words of copy each day on the Haywood trial (a total that didn't include the copy of the AP and other wire services). E. C. Keeler, one of the nation's fastest men with a telegraph key, set some kind of a record, "firing" newspaper copy at an average rate of twenty-five words a minute for three straight hours. These speeds notwithstanding, Perkins had the ear needed to catch messages on the fly. One day, he'd leaned his elbow on the counter and heard a message from WFM headquarters in Denver to Edmund Richardson in Boise about a potential defense witness. He passed is on to McParland and promised him "anything he might pick up like that."

If young Perkins wasn't a stylist, few reporters at the trial were much more than competent stenographers. The best writer by a wide margin was the *Sun's* A. E. Thomas, who was particularly good at communicating the look and feel of the place.* It was Thomas's first trip to the West and he delighted in the lush whiskers that seemed to sprout on every chin, the dust that powdered every talesman, the incessant hawking and spitting of witnesses and jurors alike. "The whiskers told the story—the whiskers and the dust," he wrote May 13. "Some of the farmers had come in on the afternoon train, but most of them had ridden in on their ponies and were dustier than millers." The next day, he began: "They got several more possible jurors and a crate of brand new spittoons in the District Court House today. An expressman dropped the spittoons in the main corridor before court opened this morning. The jurors came later." Politically, Thomas was utterly conventional; profoundly skeptical of Socialist complaints about Idaho's iron fist of oppression, he aped the Irish brogue of Finley Peter Dunne in satirizing these proletarian screeds: "'I' faith 'tis a bloodthirsty community, is Boise, where the entire political and economic machinery of a state is being employed to the limit of its capacity for the sole purpose of railroading to a high and bloody gallows tree a little group of innocent men."

The one true muckraker at the trial was C. P. Connolly, the hardheaded former prosecutor of Silver Bow County, Montana, who was covering for *Collier's*. That, in itself, was something of a surprise. Norman Hapgood, the

---

* Given the myopic reporting, the best sense of what the courtroom and its environs looked like came from two photographic ventures. One belonged to Horace C. Myers, an enterprising commercial photographer who managed to gain admission to the courtroom on several occasions and took some fine pictures. Then there were Conway and Fritz, two young men who were experimenting with motion pictures. They didn't get into the courtroom, but they caught Orchard ascending the back stairs and the jury filing down the sidewalk, as well as scenes of Boise street life. Fritz was the nephew of a Portland man who ran a theater at Sixth and Main called Hale's Touring Car. Its entrance resembled a railroad observation car and inside were rows of passenger seats. On a screen in the front, the owner usually projected scenes of the American West, Switzerland, or Italy. But now from his nephew he obtained film of the courthouse, augmented by "Scenes of Orchard's crimes. Showing spot where Orchard claims to have placed the bomb which blew up Independence Depot, sending fourteen men into eternity" and "a ride through the mining regions of Cripple Creek." None of these films seems to have survived (*Idaho Daily Statesman,* June 14, 1907, 6; June 21, 1907, 6).

magazine's editor, had long been sympathetic to the defense, had written a warmly approving account of the May 4 march in New York, and had drawn Roosevelt's scorn as the wooliest of the goo-goos. But Hapgood had evidently been persuaded that his coverage needed more rigor, and he signed up Connolly, who'd already done some excellent reporting in a five-part series on Montana's corrupt politics for *McClure's*. He knew the West, the mining industry, and the law—and those assets were evident in the eight well-reported pieces he wrote for *Collier's* between May and December 1907.

The Irish Catholic Connolly got on well with McParland, who regarded him as "a personal friend" and "a very honest and fair writer." Evidently he also impressed Fremont Wood, who assigned him the best seat in the house, at one end of the clerk's desk and just to the right of the bench. The pro-prosecution *Denver Republican* interviewed him at length early in the trial, giving ample space to his views: that he had "seen no indications that the men are being railroaded"; that though the defendants' unorthodox removal from Colorado had been "more or less secret," it was "perfectly within the law"; and finally that he thought the men were guilty. Yet Hermon Titus, who knew Connolly's views, still regarded him as "a thoughtful, agreeable gentleman." When Titus pressed him in private, Connolly said he could understand how the WFM's leaders could have resorted to these means, because they saw no other way out. "It is war," he said, "and the methods of war have been adopted."

Connolly's exquisitely balanced view of the case cannot disguise his true empathy for workingmen caught in a fixed game in which "justice is a manikin for capital and a juggernaut for labor." Some years later, he would sound one of the most important notes in the entire debate about press coverage of the Haywood case: "The press sends out to the world the overt acts of wage earners driven to desperation and suppresses the recital of the crimes which engender these conditions, though they be a matter of public knowledge and judicial inquiry."

The Socialists often derided the establishment reporters at the trial as "war correspondents." Indeed, the most seasoned reporters in Boise that summer—O. K. Davis, A. E. Thomas, Jacob Waldeck, and John Nevins of Scripps-McRae—won their spurs covering combat from Cuba to Mukden. Of them all, the most distinguished war correspondent was the AP's Martin Egan.

He was the son of a Boston Irishman who'd come to California in the gold rush but spent much of his life farming on the shores of San Pablo Bay. As a youth, Martin dreamed of "the wild, free life of the cowboy"; after a humiliating encounter with some real cowpunchers at age fifteen, however, he followed his older brother Jack into the "news game." Starting on the *Portland News* in 1897, he drifted north to the *Victoria Times* in British Columbia, the first port of call for ships from the Orient and, thus, a critical link in the news chain. When ships docked, reporters dashed up the gangplanks and scrambled for fresh intelligence, some of it from passengers and crew, most from Asian papers reserved by the captain or purser for favored reporters. The press boys would quickly scan the papers for items of American interest, then slap them on the wire. Once, while waiting for details on a shipwreck, Egan kept a line open by having the telegrapher send the Bible. With a colleague, Egan soon formed the Oriental News Service, which built a booming business syndicating Asian news to American papers. In 1894, he moved to the *San Francisco Chronicle*, where before long he became Oakland bureau chief, finding time as well to earn a law degree. In those years, he formed a close friendship with Jack London (who wanted to name one of his novels *Martin Egan* and when Egan said no, called it *Martin Eden* instead).*

Egan had taken the Oriental News Service with him to San Francisco, and soon he became the *Chronicle*'s principal authority on the Far East. He covered Dewey's triumph in Manila Bay and the Boxer Rebellion for the *Chronicle* and the Associated Press. Then, in 1903, he joined the AP full-time, working first in Manila, then in Tokyo, where he became the wire service's chief correspondent on the Japanese side of the Russo-Japanese War.

It was the most frustrating—but finally the most rewarding—assignment of his career. For months, some of the world's premier reporters—Richard Harding Davis, Jack London, Oscar King Davis, Frederick Palmer of *Collier's*, John Fox Jr. of *Scribner's*—milled about the bar of Tokyo's Imperial Hotel, unable to persuade Japanese officials to let them reach the front. "All is going according to plan," crooned the dapper censor, T. Okada. "Don't forget to tell us if it isn't," growled Jack London. As Herbert Croly put it: "The situation was unique in the annals of journalism. A government holding the rabid pressmen at a distance, censoring their simplest stories, yet patting them on the back, dining them, giving them picnics and luncheons and theatrical performances and trying not only to soften their bonds and to make their stay a pleasant one, but siren-like to deaden their sense of duty and their desire to get into the field."

Egan was ideally suited to the task. Tactful, ingratiating, and full of natural good humor, he had—as Melville Stone put it—a flair for "winning the confidence of those in power," who included ranking officers of the Japanese army and navy, as well as the premier, Baron Komura. According to Stone, "he established a relation with the government which was easily more

---

* In later years, the two friends would take sharply different ideological paths. While Egan would become solidly establishmentarian in his political and social views, London would become a dedicated Socialist (who frequently signed his letters, "Yours for the Revolution"), a founder—with Darrow—of the Intercollegiate Socialist Society, and an active lecturer on behalf of Haywood, Moyer, and Pettibone. In 1906, he published a screed in Chicago's *Daily Socialist* arguing that the Mine Owners Association "never hesitated at anything to attain its ends. By sentiment and act it has behaved unlawfully, as have its agents whom it hired. The situation in Idaho? There can be but one conclusion: There is someting rotten in Idaho!" (*Chicago Daily Socialist*, November 4, 1906; J. Perry, *Jack London*, 201–16, 324–26).

intimate than that of any other journalist. . . . He was given the official reports from the generals in the field several hours ahead of any other correspondent." Egan wrote home, a trifle shamefacedly, "Socially and personally I'm having a very good time. . . . You see part of this game is the official set and the corps diplomatique . . . [and] I'm the most aristocratic bench-dog you ever saw."

But the petted puppy still could bark, and so he did in late May 1905, finding an ingenious way around tight Japanese censorship to transmit news of the Japanese naval victory over the Russian fleet in Tsushima Bay. Anticipating such a situation, he'd agreed with New York on the code words *historic events*. So Melville Stone knew just what Egan meant when he filed a short item that began, "Transmittable information concerning today's historic events in the neighborhoods of the Tsu Islands is limited to the bare facts that Rojestvensky's main fleet, steaming in two columns with battleships on the starboard and cruisers and monitors on the port side, appeared in the straits of Korea." It was a major scoop—on the first military triumph of an emerging nation over a European imperial power—and made Egan's name a familiar one in the world's newsrooms.

He topped off a very good spring by marrying Eleanor Franklin, herself a talented foreign correspondent for *Collier's* and *Leslie's* magazines, and a few weeks later the AP named him its new correspondent in London, its most prestigious foreign post. For eight months, he and Eleanor lived in the house on Cheyne Walk once occupied by the painter Whistler; Egan was admitted to the exclusive Savage Club, hobnobbing with the likes of Field Marshal Kitchener and Sir Edward Gray. By then, surely, he richly deserved the title "gentleman of the press."

Then, in mid-1906, he received a cable from E. J. Ridgeway, publisher of *Everybody's* and *Adventure* magazines, offering him the top job at a new national weekly to be called *Ridgeway's*. Headquartered in Washington, it would focus on politics and foreign affairs, Egan's specialties. He was intrigued by the opportunity to run his own show and by the offer of $10,000 a year with "more later." Martin's—and Eleanor's—expensive tastes were already outrunning their bank account. "The AP has its limitations as to earnings," he noted, and promptly took the job.

It was a mistake. The magazine barely got off the ground before Ridgeway folded it; as a forerunner of the national news magazines, it was well ahead of its time. The AP was delighted to have Egan back, just in time for the Haywood trial.

At age thirty-five, "Mart" Egan was a gregarious Irishman, a stocky giant with a "cherubic" countenance and balding brow that he topped in summer with a gaily striped straw boater. He was a two-fisted drinker when he wasn't writing, but his charm and ready wit kept him much in demand as a toastmaster. "Thank God, you and I are pagans!" he told Richard Harding Davis's wife, Cecil. Of Herbert Bayard Swope, the garrulous editor of the New York *World,*

Egan once said, "I wish that Herbert wouldn't swope till he's swopen to." When someone reported that Richard Harding Davis had a valet, Egan exclaimed, "Well, I have a valise!"

Packing their well-worn valises for a lengthy stay, the Egans set off for Boise on April 27, checking into the Idanha on May 1. But—like most of the other reporters who'd brought their wives—Martin and Eleanor began looking for longer-term arrangements. Soon they found a couple of rooms in the Idaho Street home of Mary C. Twiggs, the widow of a Boise oil man—an elegant brick residence an easy stroll from the courthouse. Before long, the Egans had settled into the social life of establishment Boise, much as they had in Tokyo and London.

Like many of his colleagues, Egan had harbored fears of a grim, stifling summer in the primitive Idaho badlands. It was hot that summer, daytime temperatures often rising into the nineties. As the sun beat down relentlessly on the courthouse's tin roof, reporters and spectators, with the judge's permission, often discarded their jackets. Electric fans installed on either side of the courtroom and in the cupola didn't provide much relief, prompting men and women alike to stir the sluggish air with palm-leaf fans. But at night the mercury generally fell into the sixties and, as the Egans explored the city, their worst expectations were pleasantly confounded.

In that summer of 1907, Boise was a handsome, up-to-date community of eighteen thousand—its downtown, though still principally of two-story brick or frame construction, boasting several four- to six-story "skyscrapers" that gave it a "big city look"; its residential streets lined with substantial homes in Queen Anne or Colonial Revival style, interspersed with California bungalows. Appropriately for a city whose name meant "wooded" in French, Boise reveled in arboreal splendor: cottonwood, willow, elm, maple, plum, mulberry, and black-walnut trees, set off by velvet green lawns and bright bursts of roses and lilacs. Though many streets were still dirt tracks, the major downtown thoroughfares were paved with asphalt or vitrified brick. Traffic was heavy and wildly eclectic, the jaunty little streetcars of the Boise Rapid Transit Company competing with horse-drawn carriages, freight wagons, and —by that summer of 1907—no fewer than twenty-two registered automobiles (prompting an anxious city council to impose a ten-mile-an-hour speed limit). Occasionally, the bucolic past intruded: once a week a horse, startled by an automobile, would break its traces and go thundering through the downtown streets, and on May 5 a Basque sheepherder was arrested for driving a herd of twenty-five hundred sheep up Fort Street. But every day the city added fresh amenities. Boise's Symphony Orchestra recruited musicians in Seattle and Salt Lake. Main Street had two bowling alleys and a twenty-four-hour drugstore, the Owl. The Boston Grill enticed passersby with *potage à la Reine* and broiled whitefish with *sauce allemande,* and Whitehead's soda fountain offered Mexican lime freezes and Grand Duchess sundaes. Posh saloons like the Silver Bell and the Golden Slipper thrived along Main Street, their potables still in demand despite barrels of ice water installed on the sidewalk by the Woman's Christian Temperance Union. When the grand council of the United Commercial Travellers—a nationwide association of drummers—held its annual convention in Boise that spring, the city was decked out in blue, gold, and white bunting. Noting that the drummers were "jolly, good fellows," Mayor John M. Haines promised them "a jolly, good time"—and the city extended much the same wishes to the itinerant correspondents.

If the Egans hadn't anticipated such delights, nor had they or other eastern correspondents expected the warmth of their reception in Boise. Quite aside from the grand imperative—destruction of the WFM—that prompted Gooding, Hawley, and McParland to court the reporters, Boise's city fathers had their own reasons for currying favor with the visitors.

Since 1890, Idaho had enjoyed a heady rush of emigration. In June 1907, the state's immigration commissioner estimated that twelve thousand persons had located in Idaho in the past year, making it among the West's favorite destinations. He received hundreds of letters each week—notably from Iowa, Minnesota, the Dakotas, and Wisconsin—inquiring about homesteading opportunities. The surge of emigrants was particularly evident in Boise, which had tripled in size since 1900. Nobody had profited more from this growth than W. E. Pierce and Company, the state's preeminent firm of real estate brokers and developers, who maintained handsome offices just across Main Street from the Idanha (it was their calender that hung behind Fremont Wood's head on his courtroom wall). The firm's natty senior partner, Walter E. Pierce, had been Boise's mayor in 1895–96 and remained a major player behind the scenes in the capital city. His partner, John Haines, had served as Boise's mayor since April 1907.

To Pierce and Haines, among others, the Haywood trial represented both threat and opportunity. If Steunenberg's murder was viewed back East as evidence of chronic labor unrest and instability in Idaho, it could throttle investment and emigration to the state. But if the city ensured that eastern correspondents communicated a positive picture of Boise's hospitality, up-to-date facilities, and domestic tranquillity, the trial could prove an unexpected bonanza.*

From the moment they arrived, the correspondents—and particularly the elite quartet of Egan, Kennedy, O. K. Davis, and A. E. Thomas—were

---

* Boiseans were old hands at this sort of thing. Shortly before the National Irrigation Conference in 1906, the conference chairman, Monte Gwinn, wrote Charles E. Arney, the conference press secretary. "As Ambassador with plenary powers," Gwinn wrote, "you are authorized to assure the newspaper bunch that the freedom of our city includes all the privileges at the hotels, Natatorium, booze joints and bagnios; that frequent libations of 'Idan-ha' water will restore all the manly vigor which may have become lost through debilitating excesses, enabling them to enter with hearty zest an investigation of the charge that unlawful co-habitation is something which all have to contend with, and for, and that the horror over the condition is only equalled by the apparent enjoyment" (Gwinn to Arney, June 23, 1906, Dubois Collection).

overwhelmed by invitations from prominent citizens. Upper-middle-class Boiseans spent their summers in their "loggias," screened porches furnished with white wicker furniture cushioned in gay chintzes or cool greens and blues. As the *Statesman's* society page put it, "The latest novels and the most inviting books rest on little wicker tables which later in the afternoon bear gleaming silver trays containing afternoon tea, served Russian style, in tall, thin glasses with slices of lemon and a wee drop of rum. Many an informal social gathering is enjoyed in these inviting spots and, now that they are being lighted with soft-toned electric lights, even the bridge game is played there each evening."

After the reporters had filed their daily stories, they and their wives often adjourned to some Boise friend's loggia for a cool drink, a bit of trial gossip, and political palaver. The Boise Book and Music Company did a booming business that summer in hammocks and croquet sets, both of which found ample use on such evenings. But the correspondents' favorite destination was the Natatorium, Boise's astonishing "pleasure palace," which reared its Moorish facade and lacy minarets at the end of Warm Springs Avenue.* Built in 1892 over natural hot springs, the "Nat" offered the West's largest indoor swimming pool, its water said to have "rare medicinal qualities" and maintained at a voluptuous eighty-five degrees. In addition, there were private bath and steam rooms, richly furnished parlors, billiard and card rooms, a reading room, and a top-floor café. In the week the trial opened, a party of correspondents went there to hear Senescu's Roumanian Symphony play Brahms's Hungarian Dances and Waldteufel's "A Summer Evening Waltz." On Mondays, Wednesdays, and Fridays, they often went out to the Nat's dance evenings, at which Boise's smart set kicked up their heels on a polished balcony high above the steaming waters, cavorting to such favorites as "The Peach That Tastes Sweetest Hangs the Highest on the Tree" and "Every Little Bit Added to What You've Got Makes Just a Little Bit More."

Not surprisingly, given their AP connection, the Egans spent much of their after-hours time with Fannie and Calvin Cobb. In mid-May, Fannie took Eleanor along to a weekend house party at Klehanie, the country home of Harry L. Woodburn, a prominent mining man, in Idaho City. In mid-June, the Egans attended an intimate dinner party at the Idanha given by Bulkeley Wells, Colorado's former adjutant general; the only other guests were the Cobbs, their son Lyon, and his lady friend. On June 28, Eleanor—who had a "sympathetic" soprano voice—sang some "coon songs" and accompanied herself on the guitar at a garden party at the Warm Springs Avenue residence of J. B. Lyons, Calvin Cobb's partner in the *Statesman,* to benefit the missions of Christ Episcopal Church. Meanwhile, Martin Egan—and his colleague

* Operative 21 also fancied the Natatorium. At 10:30 p.m. on the evening of April 16, he and the defense attorney Fred Miller went there for a late-night splash, then had supper at the Boston Grill, Boise's best restaurant.

Kennedy—continued their frequent consultations with McParland at the Idanha, often over a convivial beer or two at the mahogany bar off the lobby. But perhaps the closest friendship the Egans formed in Boise that summer was with Senator Borah and his wife.

Socializing with figures connected to the trial—and few were more central to the case than Bulkeley Wells, Calvin Cobb, James McParland, and Bill Borah—might have posed ethical questions for some reporters, but not for Mart Egan.

Nor was Oscar King Davis troubled by how close he himself had gotten to Judge Fremont Wood. Wood and Davis were avid fly fishermen and on four occasions they took weekend trips together, angling for trout in nearby streams and lakes. Davis later insisted that he was always "very particular" to avoid the Haywood case in their campfire conversations and only once was it mentioned—by the judge himself. The trial was nearing its end that weekend and Wood suddenly said, "Well, it will soon be over. It ought to go to the jury next week. Haywood is guilty and has been convicted. I believe he will be hanged, for I don't see how it can be upset." Davis emphatically agreed, but, worried that "there might be something in our conversation that could be made use of on appeal if any word of it ever got out," he quickly switched the talk to trout fishing. In print, Davis was effusive in his praise for the judge: "The mere sight of the man conveys inevitably a feeling of care. He radiates the square deal."

On another occasion, Judge Wood led a large party of newsmen on a tour of his celebrated apple orchard in full bloom, only one of many excursions laid on by Boise's Commercial Club and other civic bodies to keep the visitors entertained that summer.

On May 25, fifteen correspondents, some of them joined by their wives, visited the Twin Falls irrigation project as guests of its promoter, the Twin Falls North Side Land and Water Company. The reporters traveled in a Pullman sleeper donated by the Union Pacific. This stirred up another squabble among the Socialist reporters. A day before the train departed, Titus announced that the Socialists would boycott the trip because they "cannot conscientiously accept any favor, directly or indirectly, from a railway which Harriman, the Standard Oil man, controls." George Shoaf dissented from Titus's principled stand and, opportunistic as ever, told the *Statesman*, "I never overlook any bets of that kind. If I couldn't accept the invitation as a Socialist, I'd make the trip under an assumed name, then none of my friends would be any wiser."

John McMahon of *Wilshire's Magazine* was astonished at the energy invested in buttering up the visitors: "The Mine Owners and State officials seem to spend almost as much time and money in providing Lucullan revels for the visiting journalists as they do in the more serious labor of noose-twisting and scaffold-building." He recorded a "dazzling round of feasts and fishing trips and two-day journeys to scenic points ... and receptions where the low-necked elite of Boise smiled upon them and social affairs, where the uncouth Governor Gooding punched them in the ribs fraternally, and dances at the Natatorium, champagne breakfasts and McParland smokers and Borah stag parties and Cobb of the *Statesman* midnight high jinks."

These exertions paid off toward trial's end when Reilly Atkinson, secretary of Boise's Commercial Club, asked some of the reporters to write a few words about the city that could be used in a promotional pamphlet. As James Hawley's son-in-law, Atkinson was closely identified with the prosecution (when summoned as a talesman in the case, he told the court: "I think, if I was Mr. Haywood, I would not want a man like myself on the jury"). But he'd drawn close to many of the correspondents, and now they were able to repay his kindnesses.

A. E. Thomas wrote: "B.B. (Beautiful Boise) is remarkable for the excellence of its climate, the bravery of its men, the pulchritude of its women, the spotlessness of its streets, the hospitality of its citizens, the honor of its past, the glory of its present, the promise of its future and a few other trifles that I can not at this moment call to mind."

The AP's Kennedy wished "we could without injuring this great state of yours, pour out from the cities of the East the un-Americanized Americans and send them here to Idaho to be remade," or "pour the red blood of Boise, of Idaho, and of the West into the heart of the East to strengthen and purify our people."

Martin Egan, writing on the evening of July 12, said, "There may somewhere in this teeming land of ours be a cleaner, better built, better thoroughfared, prettier, more progressive and more substantial city than this, peopled with a better race of men and women, but if there be I do not know it."

By then, however, Mart Egan's mind wasn't on Beautiful Boise or even, for that matter, on the Haywood case. For at long last he'd found a deal that would assure Eleanor and him the kind of money they were after.

He'd recently encountered a friend from Seattle days, a Chicago-entrepreneur-turned-Wyoming-coal-promoter named Edward M. "Bud" Holbrook, through whom he'd bought into coal-rich lands near Sheridan, Wyoming. The 160 acres had cost him $4,800, but with patience and luck, he was assured, he'd multiply the investment many times (Owen Wister's protagonist makes the same decision—and faces the same rosy horizon—at the end of the vastly popular *The Virginian*). So taken was Egan by Wyoming's prospects, he'd decided to quit the AP and practice law in Sheridan with Holbrook's lawyer, E. E. Lonabaugh. There was even talk that Bud Holbrook was grooming Egan for the U.S. Senate, where—with his ingratiating air and well-placed friends—he might represent Wyoming's coal interests to great effect.

But a problem had popped up. On May 13, a federal grand jury in Cheyenne had indicted Holbrook, Lonabaugh, and a Sheridan businessman named Robert McPhilamey for conspiracy to defraud the U.S. government of

1,200 acres of valuable coal lands in Sheridan County. The case was much like those the government had brought in Oregon and Idaho for timber fraud: that to get around the provisions of federal land law, the conspirators had employed bogus "entry men" to acquire the land. Among those the government had lined up as witnesses were Lonabaugh's mother-in-law, his niece, and McPhilamey's son, who would testify that they'd filed on coal land and then sold it to the Wyoming Coal Mining Company, of which Holbrook, described as "a millionaire," was president. Martin Egan's own land wasn't directly affected by the case, but his future in Wyoming depended on the defendants, who before very long might be in jail.

Egan's job was in Boise covering the Haywood trial, but his financial prospects were at stake in Cheyenne. So on July 14—with the trial still some days from resolution—Martin and Eleanor said an abrupt good-bye to Beautiful Boise, and when Judge J. A. Riner of Wyoming's federal court rapped his gavel three days later, Martin was in a seat near the defense table. How he explained this to John Kennedy and Melville Stone we don't know. After a five-day trial, the defendants were convicted. On July 22, Egan wrote Borah from Sheridan, "Well, sir, my friend got the worst of it all along the line." After explaining how "the court knocked down every prop" in Cheyenne, Egan expressed intense interest in Borah's own approaching fraud trial. "If there is anything I can do," he volunteered, "please call on me."

In a postscript, he added: "Everybody I meet is interested in the outcome of the Haywood case." As for coverage of the trial, now drawing to a close in Boise, the AP would have to make do with John Kennedy and Bob Small. Mart Egan, the celebrated gentleman of the press, had more important matters on his mind.

14

A GOOD HANGING SPOILED

ALL THROUGH the prosecution case and well into the defense's, James McParland had carefully kept his distance from Judge Wood's courtroom. Nobody had done more to put Bill Haywood on trial, and the Great Detective hankered to take his hard-earned seat at the proceedings. Indeed, Hawley in his opening address had assured the jury that McParland, "the terror of the evildoers throughout the West," would be a witness before the trial was finished. But acutely aware of how unpopular he and his agency were in labor circles, McParland feared that Darrow and his colleagues would find him a convenient foil for their histrionics. "From what my informants tell me," he told his superiors, "Darrow considers me not only his enemy but the enemy of everything that is good and virtuous." So, except for his daily stroll down Main Street with Siringo, he spent most of his time in or around the Idanha.

Then, on June 30, the defense artfully contrived to drop the Pinkertons in general and McParland in particular square in the middle of the startled courtroom. They materialized in the person of Morris Friedman, a former clerical employee in the Pinkertons' Denver office, who claimed to have worked until mid-1905 as McParland's private stenographer.

Crane of the *Statesman* found the Russian-born Friedman "a striking looking young fellow, rather languid ... with a shock of black hair, and his features of the marked Hebrew type. Heavy, thick glasses magnify his naturally large eyes and his smooth shaven face is very pale. He was slow and deliberate in his actions, like the railway conductor who knew the train wouldn't leave without him."

When Clarence Darrow called Friedman's name that morning, a soft intake of breath riffled through the spectators. For the young man had made something of a name for himself already with a book published earlier that year called *The Pinkerton Labor Spy*, which documented in some detail the agency's use of infiltrators to disrupt, subvert, and spy on the Western Federation and other unions. Gaylord Wilshire, who'd put out the book and excerpted it in his magazine, had sent a copy to Theodore Roosevelt in April, asking the president "if these methods can be reconciled with your conception of a 'square deal,' and if you would not consider those employing them 'undesirable citizens' and possibly 'implicated in murder.' "

Under Darrow's questioning, Friedman identified the operatives in the Pinkertons' Denver office who'd burrowed deep within the Western Federation, often—like Charlie Siringo years before in Burke—rising to leadership positions: there was A. H. Crane, Operative 5, who'd become secretary of the Cripple Creek union until he was exposed; C. J. Connibear, president of the Florence union; R. P. Bailey, Operative 9, a member of the Victor union; and perhaps the superagent of them all, A. W. Gratias, the union president at Globeville. Gratias was in charge of distributing relief funds to strikers. At first, Friedman testified, McParland told Gratias to pad the bills to drain the union's treasury; when that didn't work, he ordered him to reduce the payments to build the members' dissatisfaction with Haywood, but that didn't work either.

Then there was George W. Riddell, former president of the miners union in Eureka, Utah, who'd been forced to resign as a result of Friedman's book. Summoned by the prosecution to testify in Boise, the uncovered operative was standing by the courtroom door when Friedman, at Darrow's invitation, pointed him out. Riddell—who ten days before had gone on a drunken binge through Boise's saloons—smilingly acknowledged the witness's attention.

What made Friedman's testimony particularly compelling was the stack of documents, many of them bearing McParland's signature, that he brought with him, showing the agency's infiltration and subversion of the miners union. On cross-examination, Borah sparred with the witness about whether he'd "stolen" the documents. When Friedman denied that, Borah asked, "You considered you had a right to take them?"

"Not according to the rules of the agency," the witness replied, but "in making public these matters," he explained, he was "merely returning" to the WFM and other unions "what was their own property—property in the shape of facts that the Pinkertons had stolen from them."

Darrow and Richardson had both doubted that Judge Wood would allow Friedman's testimony, since arguably it had no bearing on Frank Steunenberg's assassination or even on the crimes to which Orchard had confessed in Colorado. But when it got through, many reporters thought it highly effective, even a "master stroke," since it suggested that many of the infiltrators were actually agents provocateurs who'd committed crimes to bring the unions into disrepute. From the start, there'd been suspicions that Orchard was a Pinkerton operative, much like Crane and Gratias.

The defense had another surprise waiting for the Great Detective—this one designed simply to embarrass him. On July 2, they called his brother Edward—one of the two who'd rallied to the young detective's side thirty years before in Pennsylvania. Since then, Edward had become a shoemaker, settling in Victor, Colorado, on the outskirts of Cripple Creek. He'd been there during the troubles of 1904 and now this gnarled, balding, "very commonplace" man testified about what had happened to him then, ostensibly because he was a WFM sympathizer.

He'd been at his cobbler's bench in Victor at dusk on June 9—three days after the Independence depot explosion—when guardsmen took him in custody, striking him several times with their gun butts for moving too slowly. After days in a Cripple Creek bullpen, he and seventy-seven others were put on a train and deported to neighboring Kansas. Turned back by Kansas officers, they filtered back to Denver with the help of the WFM.

The state let the shoemaker's testimony stand with practically no cross-examination. He was on the stand barely six minutes and what he said was of little evidentiary value. But it was an embarrassment to the Great Detective to have his brother come into court as a WFM witness and recount the imperial style of the Peabody administration in Colorado, with which McParland and the Pinkertons had been closely associated.

The morning after Friedman's first testimony, Calvin Cobb's *Statesman* made an extraordinary show of faith in McParland and the Pinkertons. It published a piece by William B. "Bat" Masterson, the former gunman turned sports editor of New York's *Morning Telegraph,* contending that "the defense will not be able to involve Captain James McParland in anything discreditable" and extolling him as "one of the shrewdest and most capable detectives that has ever handled a case in this or any other country." In an accompanying editorial, written by Cobb himself, the *Statesman* sought to dispel rumors in Boise that the Pinkertons had failed to come up with the goods necessary to convict Haywood and, indeed, had deceived the prosecutors by promising more than they could deliver. Those who spread such notions, wrote Cobb, were "like coyotes in the night," who "stand about and yelp themselves hoarse." The Pinkerton agency, "acting through James McParland, has not only come up to the expectations of the prosecution and the public, but it has far excelled them," as would be shown when "this great case" was complete.

In fact, at that very moment, the Great Detective was desperately scrambling to rescue a case that he sensed was slipping further out of his control. All through May and into June, he nursed the fading hope that Deputy Carson Hicks of Shoshone County, sharing a jail cell with Steve Adams in Wallace, could persuade Adams to revive his corroboration of Orchard's confession. When nothing happened on that front, McParland had Adams brought to Boise on June 10 and lodged in the Ada County jail, hoping the defense would be foolish enough to put him on the stand. That would permit the prosecution to use his original confession to impeach his testimony. But Darrow and Richardson were too shrewd to bite at the prosecution's bait. So McParland opted for a more daring gambit: to seek the corroboration from Haywood's colleague and rival, Charles Moyer, the WFM president—indeed to recruit Moyer as a state witness under the noses of his codefendants and vigilant defense attorneys.

It wasn't altogether a new idea. From the moment the labor leaders were brought to Idaho, Moyer was recognized as the weak link in the chain because of his temperamental differences with Haywood. The cautious Moyer and the impetuous Haywood had sharply differed since 1903, and these resentments had been exacerbated by their long confinement. As early as March 13, 1906, McParland ruminated on the possibility of a Moyer confession. A week later, after a conference with Gooding and Hawley, he'd decided to act. "After a few days I am to call on Moyer with a view to breaking him down. Of course, I have very little confidence that I will succeed, but I do not see wherein it will do any harm for me to try it."

But a major obstacle stood athwart that path, in the person of Sheriff David Moseley of Ada County, a rather unusual lawman. As one reporter friendly to the defendants put it, Moseley was "a humane man" who believed that "men are sent to him not to be punished unnecessarily, but to be held safely for trial. He didn't recognize in Moyer, Haywood and Pettibone men of the prison demon class. He has accordingly treated them as he treats other 'trusties' among the prisoners." At night, they were confined to separate cells, sleeping on narrow beds that folded down from the wall, wooden planks covered by thin mattresses. But in daytime they were together in an airy room fourteen feet square with two grated windows overlooking the courthouse lawn, on which, Haywood would recall, "dandelions were scattered about like pieces of miser's gold on a green cloth." The grass was shaded by towering elms and maples, surrounded by a wrought-iron fence and sixteen rose-bushes. Haywood picked off some rose petals, dried them on his windowsill, and ultimately made a cushion of them, covered with satin and edged with a ruffle of red ribbons, which he sent to his wife in Denver. Pettibone spent much of his time at pyrography—the art of burning designs in wood. Using the tops and bottoms of cigar boxes, he turned out some choice specimens much admired by guards and newsmen.

Haywood, who had his own graphic talents, put them to use designing a new WFM poster, this time depicting the Union Pacific train that had brought the prisoners to Idaho, under the slogan "Arouse, Ye Slaves! Their only crime is loyalty to the working class." Before long, it became a widely popular artifact at union locals and clubhouses across the land.

The prisoners were allowed two hours a day on the lawn for exercise— Moyer from ten to noon, Pettibone from one to three, and Haywood from three to five—during which they could play quoits with their guards, lift weights, spar in boxing gloves, or play with a guard's spitz puppies. They were allowed unlimited writing and reading materials. Haywood carried on a considerable correspondence with WFM and IWW leaders and with Socialists in Colorado who ran him for governor in 1906 (he garnered more than sixteen thousand votes, four times the vote of the previous Socialist candidate for that post). These months in jail were Haywood's first opportunity to read widely and he made the most of it; he claimed to have consumed—among other works—Henry T. Buckle's *History of Civilization;* Thomas Carlyle's *The French Revolution;* Laurence Sterne's *Tristram Shandy;* Upton Sinclair's *The Jungle;* Marx; Engels; and Voltaire. He took a correspondence course in the law, which permitted him to play an active role in his own defense. The sheriff permitted frequent visits with the prisoners' attorneys, family, and friends and with sympathetic reporters. Their meals, prepared by a Chinese chef called John, were surprisingly good.

As early as April 1906, Governor Gooding was reported to be furious at Moseley because he'd refused to let McParland interview the prisoners in their cells, saying that the prisoners didn't want to see the detective and he wouldn't force them to do so. Gooding conferred with the prosecutors with an eye to dismissing Moseley, but the lawyers said the sheriff was acting within his powers of discretion.

McParland fumed. Responding to press reports about Moseley's "humane" policy, he wrote the governor: "I believe myself that these men should not get even as much privilege as an ordinary prisoner, being that they are the greatest criminals that ever were confined in Ada County Jail or in any jail in the United States, and if there is any way to induce Sheriff Moseley to simply treat these men as he does other prisoners, I would like to see it done." But Moseley couldn't be intimidated and McParland had to wait until one of his deputies, Shad Hodgin, was elected to replace him in November 1906.

Meanwhile, evidence accumulated of the depth of the bad feeling between Haywood and Moyer. According to Orchard, Mrs. Moyer, in particular, "never liked Haywood," and when he was arrested by the Colorado National Guard in 1904, she'd chortled to a friend, "Now Haywood will get a little of [the] high life." According to Orchard, Haywood and Pettibone had feared that Moyer would break down under questioning at the Telluride jail during 1904 and had held Orchard and Adams in readiness to "bump him off" if necessary. Although Moyer didn't break down, once he came out of the Telluride jail the WFM president and his secretary-treasurer were "deadly enemies." By December 1906, McParland learned that the atmosphere within the Boise jail was so poisonous that Moyer and Pettibone were "not on speaking terms with Haywood."

Their long-standing differences were further exacerbated by the fierce warfare that broke out within the IWW in the autumn of 1906—a fight in which Haywood lined up with the "revolutionists" and Moyer with the "reformists." As the second annual convention of the IWW gathered in Chicago in late September, it was clear that the revolutionists—headed by William E. Trautmann, the IWW's secretary; Daniel DeLeon, the polemicist from New York; and Vincent St. John, the Western Federation's militant activist—were in the saddle. When this faction challenged the IWW's president, C. O. Sherman, charging him with gross extravagance and apparent corruption, the Sherman forces stalked off the convention floor and seized IWW headquarters, which, with police assistance, they held against their rivals.

Among those who walked out of the convention on October 2 were Charles E. Mahoney, who'd been filling in for Moyer as WFM president, and three other WFM delegates. Indeed, the WFM's mainstream (all but those who identified with St. John and Haywood) repudiated the triumph of Traut- mann's "beggars, tramps and proletarian rabble," remaining loyal to Sherman. In a letter from the Ada County jail to James Kirwan, the WFM's acting secretary-treasurer, Moyer forcefully backed the Sherman faction. "I want to serve notice on those calling themselves revolutionaries," he wrote, "that their programs will never receive my endorsement nor that of the WFM, if in my power to prevent it. By the Gods I have suffered too much, worked too hard to ever tamely submit to the WFM being turned over to Mr. Daniel DeLeon."

Haywood didn't care for DeLeon either, but his heart was with the "revolutionists" and for remaining within the IWW. Distraught that the orga- nization was tearing itself apart, he tried vainly to halt the dismemberment. To Kirwan in mid-October, he wrote: "I surely am not going to express any positive opinion as to the relative merits of either side until...I am in possession of full details." In March 1907, he pleaded with St. John for "a cessation of the bitter flood of villification, the senseless personalities and criminations, especially among our own [the WFM's] members.... Such pol- icy is suicidal."

But it was too late. In 1907, the WFM would withdraw from the IWW; working-class solidarity appeared further than ever from realization—and in Boise, Haywood and Moyer glowered at each other from opposite sides of their dayroom.

The Great Detective yearned to take advantage of this falling-out. Shad Hodgin wouldn't assume office as sheriff until January 8 and McParland knew little about him. But he hoped the sheriff would soften Moyer up for him. McParland could imagine Hodgin's saying, "I am really sorry for you, Moyer, if for nothing else but your poor wife's sake. I have seen that poor woman call at this jail day after day and pitied her so much that I often wanted to say to you, 'Why don't you try to get out of this,' as I have often thought you were more sinned against than sinning." If Moyer responded, then McParland hoped that Hodgin would "consent to let me have a private interview with Moyer."

But this gambit went for nought. Though more a straight law-and-order man than Moseley, Hodgin wouldn't play ball with the prosecutors. So McParland bided his time, looking for a different way. As Haywood's jury selection began, Moyer was visibly agitated. "He thinks a great deal, does Moyer," wrote James Noland of the *Denver Post*. "He is nervous in his every action. When seated he constantly intertwines his fingers or pulls his hat forward or pushes it back or unconsciously performs some other little act that tells of a burdened mind. When walking, or rather striding, because when taking his exercise he speeds along at 120 long steps a minute, his gaze is ever fixed downward, about five paces ahead, and his hands are clasped behind him." According to another report, as jury selection got under way, Moyer and Haywood argued in their quarters and "it appeared as if blows might be exchanged" until a deputy sheriff separated the men.

On May 10, the day after jury selection began, McParland sat down at the Idanha to draft a new plan for approaching Moyer. It was much like the old one, except that for Hodgin it would substitute his formidable deputy, Ras Beemer, who—McParland said—enjoyed the "utmost confidence" of the prosecutors, the detectives, and the governor. Beemer was a logical choice. A tough guy and expert marksman, he could also be an amiable companion. Frank Perkins of the *Portland Evening Telegram,* an ally of McParland's, found Beemer "a man brimful of good nature and always ready to tell a good joke or to laugh heartily on hearing one." But the deputy deeply resented what the Socialists had written about Ada County law enforcement during the trial and "his indignation against them [was] such that on two or three occasions he had...walked them out of the office." As early as October 1906, Beemer had been a confidential informant to the prosecution.

Now, McParland suggested, Beemer should be assigned to take Moyer out for his daily exercise. Every day, Beemer should inquire how Moyer was feeling and how his wife was, should slip him a daily newspaper and from time to time a few good cigars. "He must not start in very abruptly on this matter, but if Moyer is not friendly to him at the present time I think he will gain his friendship in a few days in this way."

McParland specified that the approach should start after Orchard had completed his direct examination: "I expect when Moyer reads the testimony of Orchard and finds out...that Orchard withstands the cross-examination he will begin to weaken." If Moyer brought the subject up with Beemer, the guard should say, "This matter looks blue," and suggest that it could only get worse, that the prosecution had 140 witnesses to go and you couldn't tell how much they knew.

Then Beemer should remark how hard it had all been on Mrs. Moyer, how Moyer was "still a comparatively young man" and should try to save himself. He should casually mention that some people had urged McParland to see Moyer but that the detective was loath to do so until Moyer asked for a meeting. If Moyer wanted to talk, Beemer should promise to arrange it "without anybody knowing anything about it." In that case, McParland "could step downstairs into the Sheriff's office and meet Moyer just as he came out of the jail to take his exercise." With a stenographer at the ready, McParland said, "if he wanted to make a confession I would take his confession just as briefly as I could," focusing on the "main facts" of the Steunenberg murder, and then come back for more.

Providentially—but not coincidentally—just as McParland was dictating this report, John Kennedy of the Associated Press showed him a telegram from a Chicago newspaper asking him to check whether Moyer had been in the Joliet penitentiary in Illinois in 1886–87. McParland knew all about this; it appears that the Pinkertons' Chicago headquarters had leaked the story precisely to get this information on the record. Now it arrived at precisely the right moment, for McParland was convinced that this revelation would help "break Moyer down." Equipped with certified copies from the Criminal Court of Cook County, McParland gave Kennedy all the details for his story but exacted from the cooperative wire service man a promise not to identify him as the source.

On May 13, McParland passed word to Beemer, asking him to call the next day. "As he comes into the Idanha Hotel frequently he will be perfectly safe in calling on me, as everyone will be around the Court House," he wrote. "From now on I want to instruct Beemer every day how to handle Moyer."

In his report to Gooding the next day, McParland—always concerned about security—began calling Beemer Informant No. 1. In a two-hour conference at the Idanha, Beemer had persuaded McParland that he wasn't close enough to Moyer and that the detective should entrust the delicate mission to another guard—probably James Thacker or George Porter—who'd already gained Moyer's confidence. Henceforth, this guard was known as Informant No. 2. But Beemer remained part of the operation, guaranteeing the other man's performance.

"I would simply say from Informant No. 1's report to me things are in very good shape, in fact a great deal better shape than I expected," McParland reported on May 14. "However, we must not be too confident that I will succeed.... We all have confidence in Informant No. 1 and I am satisfied he tells me the truth so far as he knows and he assures me I can stake my life on Informant No. 2." McParland professed to be "pretty busy on this matter, in fact so busy planning and forming plans whereby I hope to be succcessful that I have little time for anything else."

Two days later, he met with Informant No. 2, who was "a very intelligent man and seemed to grasp the idea of what is wanted in very quick time." Again, he reported that "things look pretty bright and if Informant No. 2 remains true to us, I think matters will shape themselves our way in a very short time." When the guard said the other side had made financial overtures to him, McParland thought it wise "to show to him if he succeeded in pulling matters through, he and Informant No. 1 would be remembered in a substantial financial way."

On May 18, McParland expected Informant No. 2 at the Idanha. Then he learned that Darrow, impressed by Judge Wood's stern stance on the Orchard interviews, had come running into the jail at lunch hour, clapping his hands and saying, "We have got the sons of bitches!" This, said McParland, had given Moyer "fresh courage" and therefore Informant No. 2 was "unable to carry out the matter he and I had planned." Darrow could be mercurial. At times, he come in beaming, carrying food, candy, or copies of his books. On other occasions, he'd be so gloomy that the ebullient Pettibone would cry, "Cheer up, Clarence. You know it's us fellows that have to be hanged!"

By May 19, McParland talked with Informant No. 2 and concluded that matters were not progressing as rapidly as he wished. Six days later, he reported the project was "working along quite slowly," which was to be "expected on account of the promises that Darrow has made to his clients that it will simply be impossible to get a jury in this county." McParland doubted that Darrow himself believed that, but "nevertheless he is keeping his clients buoyed up by talking in this way."

There were intriguing hints that Moyer might be breaking down. Perkins of the *Portland Evening Telegram* reported that the WFM president had been observed on several occasions in tears, and Pettibone had been seen talking to him "very earnestly in undertones" in the corner of their dayroom. Perkins observed—accurately—that the state was "willing to grant him the utmost leniency in case he 'came through' " and—less plausibly—that Moyer had thrown out a "feeler" as to what would be guaranteed a man who "saw fit to talk."

But even after Orchard's impressive performance, Informant No. 2 made no headway. Under pressure from Haywood and Pettibone, and with encouragement from Darrow and Richardson, Moyer held firm.

What followed was one of the trial's most curious episodes. According to press accounts in early July, the Great Detective enlisted no less a figure than Mrs. Calvin Cobb to importune Mrs. Moyer. Shortly after her husband's kidnapping, the diminutive Mrs. Moyer had hastened to Boise and remained there ever since. But frequent visits to her husband were of little consolation. Obsessed by the "shadow of the gallows" that seemed to loom over her husband's head, she gradually descended into anxiety and depression and had to enter St. Luke's Hospital. According to one report, she appealed to the sisters who ran that institution to intercede for her husband, on grounds that he was innocent of all wrongdoing and had been compelled by Haywood and Pettibone to go along with their murder plots. As late as April 18, responding to an appeal from her doctor, Fremont Wood permitted Moyer to visit his wife at the hospital because she was "too weak" and apparently too depressed to visit him at the jail.

But gradually she improved. After her release from the hospital in early May, she shared accommodations with Mrs. Pettibone in a small house across the street from the jail in which their husbands were held. (The larger Haywood family rented a spacious seven-room house, replete with piano, on Twelfth Street.) From a divan on the porch, they could wave greetings during the prisoners' exercise periods, and they were permitted daily visits. But Mrs. Moyer remained terrified that her husband would hang for crimes in which he had no role.

Several reporters wrote about the approach to Mrs. Moyer, but the most reliable of them was John Carberry of the *Boston Globe*, one of the fairest, most accurate newsmen at the trial. According to him, Mrs. Moyer had been "overwhelmed" by attention from Mrs. Cobb and others in her circle. Mrs. Cobb was said to have addressed her as "Dear Mrs. Moyer," while Mrs. Haywood and Mrs. Pettibone were "regarded contemptuously as 'very common.'" Still according to Carberry, "the prosecuting attorneys were told this week that the female brigade has won Mrs. Moyer to the point of promising to persuade her husband to testify for the state. So exultant was the prosecution, especially the women, that they boasted of the capitulation of Moyer."

According to the *Globe* man, "Moyer did not enthuse over the offer. 'There is nothing I could tell them that will help the state,' he said to his wife. 'But suppose I had something to tell and testified for the prosecution. Where could we go after they discharged me? I would have no friends, nowhere to go. Anyone who knows me would say I had deserted my friends to save myself. No, it is impossible. I have nothing to tell and I would not try to get out at the expense of my friends.'"

A few days later, Carberry backed off his story, reporting that Mrs. Cobb emphatically denied that she'd ever spoken to Mrs. Moyer. "Mrs. Cobb, it appears, is a victim of gossip, apparently emanating from persons in her own circle of acquaintances," he wrote. "The story was told with circumstantial detail, but the truth is the women have never met."

Normally, a retraction would have ended the matter (particularly since Mrs. Moyer, in a letter to the *Denver Post*, also denied the story and there is no trace of this maneuver in McParland's surviving reports). One wonders, though, how a reporter of Carberry's savvy could have fallen for a piece of unsubstantiated gossip. But the operation as described in his article carries McParland's stamp. It bears striking similarity to the plan McParland outlined a year earlier for Mr. and Mrs. Carson Hicks to approach Mrs. Adams and get her to persuade her husband to revive his vital confession. One suspects that the relentless McParland—casting about for one last maneuver to rescue his case—may have enlisted Mrs. Cobb's assistance but that it bore no fruit. When the story appeared, embarrassing Mrs. Cobb, her husband may have leaned heavily on Carberry to compel a retraction.

McParland's expectations of "turning" Moyer flickered into early July; as late as July 5, Dunnigan of the Hearst papers reported a rumor that Moyer was "about to turn state's evidence." But any such hope was dashed on July 10, when Moyer took the stand for the defense. At first he seemed uneasy, toying with a pencil or a toothpick, but after a time he began answering questions with a cool, self-possessed air, making plain he'd be an effective witness on Haywood's behalf and, ultimately, on his own.

Moyer testified that he'd first met Orchard in January 1904 during the union's convention, when he'd invited all the Colorado delegates back to

WFM headquarters for a chat. Orchard represented the Altman Miners Union at the convention. Moyer denied that Orchard ever told him that he'd blown up the Vindicator mine. Moreover, he flatly denied that he'd ever discussed any kind of criminal act with Orchard or anyone else or ever given him any money to commit a crime. He had no "personal hostility"—as opposed to organizational animosity—toward Frank Steunenberg.

His greatest vulnerability appeared to be his actions after the governor's assassination: the hiring of Fred Miller to defend Orchard and the allocation of $1,500 to pay for that defense. Moyer laid the responsibility for engaging Miller at the door of the vanished Jack Simpkins. Similarly, he testified that it was Simpkins who'd asked Haywood and Moyer to advance the $1,500.

In his cross-examination, Borah asked sharply, "Did you expect to preserve the good name of the Western Federation of Miners by defending the man who had killed Frank Steunenberg?"

"I did not believe at the time that Orchard had anything to do with the murder," said Moyer. "I felt it was just another attempt to charge a crime to the Federation."

On balance, correspondents agreed, not only had Moyer handled himself with aplomb but his very appearance as a defense witnesss had been a signal victory for the defense, given rumors of his defection.

The last great battle of the trial's evidentiary phase now loomed. For weeks it had seemed doubtful that Haywood would take the stand in his own defense. Rumors abounded that he didn't want to testify, that Darrow and others were having difficulty persuading him. But when he finally rose from the defense table at noon on July 11 and advanced to the witness box with the same "quick, springy athletic step" he'd displayed throughout the trial, he gave every sign of welcoming the challenge.

The spectators' benches, a third empty during Moyer's cross-examination, were filled for Haywood's appearance, though the midafternoon temperature of ninety-five was the highest of the trial. Frazzled spectators and newsmen, juggling soaked handkerchiefs and palm-leaf fans, leaned forward eagerly as Darrow ambled toward his client. Expectations of high drama ebbed as the drawling Darrow led Haywood through the direct examination in a conversational tone. In their leisurely review of Haywood's life, they eventually reached his days as a Silver City miner, when the union there joined in strenuous protests against Steunenberg's policies in the Coeur d'Alenes.

Had Haywood made critical comments about Steunenberg? Darrow asked.

More than likely, he said. "Hardly a miner in Silver City but had some criticism to make."

But when asked about a previous witness's recollection that he'd said

Steunenberg "should be exterminated," Haywood didn't think he'd ever used that term. "I think the expression I probably used was that the governor should be 'relegated.' "

"You helped relegate him?"

"Yes, sir. I did. I took an active part. For the next term the Democrats nominated Frank W. Hunt for Governor and Hunt was elected."

"Did you ever have a hostile feeling for Steunenberg?"

"No, sir. I regarded him the same as any politician who could be swayed by capitalistic influences."

Haywood's voice had been surprisingly faint at first, but when Judge Wood called this to his attention, he sat up straighter and spoke with the brisk self-assurance of a man accustomed to exercising authority.

Had Haywood known Steunenberg personally? Darrow asked.

"No, never did."

"Ever see him?"

"No, sir."

"You were in Idaho when he was elected?"

"Yes, sir."

"You knew where he lived?"

"Yes, sir—in Caldwell."

Closing in now on the evening of December 30, 1905, Darrow asked when Haywood first met the man he knew as Harry Orchard.

During a labor gathering in Denver in January 1904. "He was a delegate from the Altman union."

Did Orchard tell him a year later that it was he who'd blown up the Vindicator mine and ask to be paid for it?

"No."

"You heard his testimony?"

"Yes, sir."

"And it was not the truth?"

"He did not tell the truth."

Haywood denied—in quiet, firm tones—everything Harry Orchard said about the steps leading to Steunenberg's death and, for that matter, the other explosions, assassinations, and attempted assassinations to which Orchard had confessed.

"What was the first information you got in reference to the assassination of ex-Governor Steunenberg?"

"I heard of it the next morning."

"You mean through the newspapers."

"Yes, sir."

At midday on July 12, Darrow completed his questions and turned the witness over to Borah. Along with Richardson's cross-examination of Orchard, this would be the trial's crucial confrontation: the seasoned trial attorney and popular favorite pitted against the tough labor leader and shrewd man of the streets, two forces of nature in collision. The *Socialist* called it "the Man of the Mines" versus "the Man of the Mind."

It was partly a question of which man could intimidate the other. Haywood struck first. Scarcely had Borah begun his cross-examination than the witness interrupted. Gesturing toward the open window directly behind the judge's head, through which poured the radiance of a blistering Boise afternoon, Haywood said, "If Your Honor please, may the shutters be closed on that window. While I will be talking most of the time to the jury [that is, straight ahead and into the window's glare] I cannot see the Senator's eyes with the shutters open."

Many western gunfighters looked not at their opponent's gun hand but in his eyes to see when he was going to draw. Haywood wanted to fix Borah with the terrible glare of his single eye. Borah was stunned, telling an associate later, "It doubled me up like a jack-knife."

Wood ordered the shutters drawn as Borah—with a wry smile—resumed his cross-examination. Reading Haywood some comments the *Miners' Magazine* had made about Steunenberg over the years, he wanted to know whether these attacks represented Haywood's views.

"In some instances, yes, sir," said the witness. "I was opposed to the bullpen, and I was opposed to the permit system. I was opposed to the outrages that were perpetrated against the women there by the negro soldiers."

"And you regarded that Governor Steunenberg and those that represented him there were really the cause of all those things?"

Haywood fixed his inquisitor with a cold eye. "I did not regard Governor Steunenberg in any different light than I did you, Senator, or Bartlett Sinclair, or anybody else that was involved there."

"Yes," said Borah, taken aback for a moment. "Yes, I have learned that fact."

Borah then read Haywood a passage from "The Passing of Steunenberg," an acid commentary that the magazine had published on the occasion of the governor's departure from office in January 1901. "The article closes with these words," he said, " 'Here lies a hireling and a traitor.' Now is that the way in which the prominent members of the Western Federation of Miners, including yourself, looked upon Governor Steunenberg at the time he retired to private life in 1901?"

"As to the governor's official acts, it did," he said, defending a distinction between his views of Steunenberg as governor and his attitude toward Steunenberg the man.

And when they reached Orchard's allegations about the assassination, Haywood deflected all questions with a diffident little smile and a shrugging response.

"Did you ever talk with Orchard about Governor Steunenberg in any way?"

"I don't think so."

"Do you recall that the name of Governor Steunenberg was ever mentioned in any conversation between Orchard and yourself?"

"I don't believe so."

It was no use. Borah could not crack the Smiling Buddha. When the five-hour cross-examination in the stifling courtroom ended late that afternoon, the prosecutor was heard to remark, "I feel like I've had a two-day session."

The next few days were devoted to the prosecution's rebuttal, but with the high-stakes testimony of Moyer and Haywood behind them, both sides now indulged themselves in some silliness.

On July 14, the defense claimed possession of startling new evidence. In a letter to Darrow, B. W. McKinstry of Almedia, Pennsylvania, said his wife's mother was at one time a next-door neighbor of Patrick McKinney, Harry Orchard's maternal grandfather, who'd acted strangely, "finally becoming ugly and relating stories of awful crimes committed in Ireland." He said McKinney was so crazy he had to be "chained up." The writer contended that one of Orchard's uncles had gone insane and committed suicide.

When the state called Orchard back to the stand for a few questions, Richardson grilled him on the insanity of his ancestors. Orchard conceded that he had an uncle, Peter McKinney, who was "demented" over some family problems and finally hung himself. But he knew nothing of his maternal grandfather, who'd died before he was born.

Richardson also tried to use the first installment of Orchard's confessions, which had just appeared in *McClure's*, to undermine the assassin's credibility. "On the witness stand, Mr. Orchard, you said you knew nothing about a so-called 'inner circle' of the Western Federation of Miners, and yet in the first installment of your story ... you devote a paragraph to the inner circle. How is that?"

The state objected. The judge sustained the objection. It was one thing to try a murder case, quite another to keep track of all its emanations in newspapers, magazines, songs, and poems across the land. "We're not going into that matter," said Wood.

The state called Lawrence Giubbinni, a storekeeper near Frederick Bradley's home in San Francisco, to rebut testimony of a defense witness named J. B. Reilly, who'd claimed Giubbinni had served him a drink in the store just before the explosion at the Bradleys'. Now Giubbinni denied it.

On cross-examination, Richardson asked, "Does Reilly usually get a drink in the morning at your place?"

"Oh yes, for sure."

"Pretty regularly?"

"Never missed a morning or an evening since I've been there."

"How do you know he didn't get a drink that particular morning?"

"Oh, I don't know. All I know is that he didn't get a drink of me yet before the explosion, because I was still in my bed yet. I just got me up when the explosion came off."

With such persiflage did the evidence of the great trial wind down to nothing. Spent by their exertions, the two sides rested, one after another, on the evening of July 17 and the morning of July 18.

The rest of that day was spent in fierce argument over the admissibility of the evidence painstakingly gathered by Walter McCornack and offered by the defense to show that the Western Federation was the victim of a vast counterconspiracy by mine owners and Pinkertons to destroy the union. Judge Wood had confessed grave reservations about the relevance of such testimony and invited argument on the matter.

Pleading its admissibility—indeed its centrality—Darrow proclaimed: "This has been a Pinkerton case from start to finish, Your Honor." The detectives' "machinations" were evident throughout the trial. "Not to show up the parts taken by these scorpions would be not to present the case." How could the defense be denied an opportunity to show that the Independence depot explosion—which Orchard claimed to be a WFM venture—was actually the work of K. C. Sterling, the mine owners' detective, in cooperation with the Pinkertons? Surely the jury must consider the infiltration of Pinkerton operatives in the Colorado unions. "Are we going to convict Bill Haywood for the work of these vermin?"

Moreover, he argued, "all that the mine owners did—the deportations of men, the defiance of law, the forbidding of merchants to sell food and supplies to the families of the men driven out of the district—they did in furtherance of their criminal conspiracy to destroy the WFM."

"A man defending his life," Darrow contended in a characteristic plea, "should have even a wider latitude than is given to those who are seeking to send him to his death." The evidence of a counterconspiracy was competent testimony. "It should be left to the jury to determine its value."

In response, Borah said the prosecution wasn't denying the defense's right to prove a counterconspiracy. "What I contend is that they have not proved it. Let them put some member of the conspiracy on the stand"—and here he was clearly reminding the jury of Harry Orchard—"and prove that the conspiracy is responsible for the crimes complained of. Testimony as to a conspiracy must come at first hand and cannot be accepted from a third party who knows only by hearsay."

At 2:00 p.m. the next day, the judge was ready with his ruling—and it was bad news for the defense. Its testimony about the counterconspiracy in Colorado, he said, "does not point to any one, or even indicate that any particular person either committed the acts of violence complained of, or procured Orchard to commit such acts of violence," whereas the state's testimony about these events "connects the defendant on trial directly with the various acts of violence." Thus it was his "unpleasant duty" to instruct the jury to disregard the defense's evidence in this area. His ruling dealt a severe blow to the defense attorneys, drastically limiting the scope of their closing arguments.

But there was no time to dwell on that, for on deck was Jim Hawley, ready to deliver the first of the four summations. In those days, summations were scarcely the brisk summaries of testimony topped off with a perfunctory plea for justice that they would frequently be in years to come; they were grandiloquent, impassioned, theatrical addresses, often consuming ten or twelve hours apiece. These four gave promise of a dandy show.

For it was widely remarked that summer that rarely in the nation's first century and a quarter had a courtroom harbored four attorneys of such distinction as Hawley, Borah, Richardson, and Darrow—the final three, at least, renowned not only for their courtroom cunning but for the power of their oratory. Not surprisingly, then, the spectators' benches had long since been filled to capacity, and the seats inside the rail allocated to the bar were occupied by lawyers from many southern Idaho towns and some from as far away as Salt Lake City and Portland, there to take in the rhetorical fireworks. Moreover, for the first time in the entire trial, the front seats of the spectator section were graced by the presence of Governor Gooding and James McParland, two men who had conspicuously kept their distance from the courtroom but who were now there in almost ceremonial fashion, to put their imprimatur on the closing of the prosecution case.

Rising now and placing his gnarled hands on the table before him, Hawley wisely forswore any "flights of oratory." For one thing, it wasn't his style. And for another, he wasn't feeling up to it. "The Haywood case has been a very wearing one," he wrote a friend that week, "and I have been doing three men's work constantly, and as old age is beginning to tell somewhat on me and as my stomach will not permit stimulents [*sic*] in the same old way, I feel a little ragged."

But he managed, in eighty-five-degree heat, to stemwind for two hours in his down-home "Honest Jim" manner. "Gentlemen," he began, "I want to say that we are not here to ask for anything except exact justice. We are not here to ask for conviction at your hands of anyone whom we do not fully believe to be guilty." He and Senator Borah wanted to help the jury "arrive at a just verdict" in a case "that we doubt has a parallel in the country, a case which has been and is being watched by the entire civilized world."

One of Hawley's great strengths as a courtroom advocate had always been his ability to establish rapport with farmers, miners, and merchants on an Idaho jury. Propped against the prosecution table, as if against a Main Street hitching post, he chatted with them, much as neighbor does to neighbor. Coming to the terrible events of December 30, 1905, he evoked a small town at Christmastime:

> The days pass and the Christmas season comes with all its thoughts—of peace and good will—the season when men live with their families, when people of

the Christian faith rejoice, and if there is ever a time when all thought of fear should be laid aside then is the time. That is the season when love for mankind should rule, and exist if at all. That is the season when men should most feel safe from harm.

Just as the old year was fading—just as the new year was about to make its appearance—when all seems safe and peaceful, Orchard lays his bomb in front of Steunenberg's gate, and that night as the governor hastens home through the dusk to his family, in his mind the happy thoughts of the loving greeting in store for him, ... he is sent to face his God without a moment's warning and within the sight of his wife and children.

As the jurors took in the full horror of that moment, Hawley managed—with considerable skill—to sustain the spiritual theme, now attaching it to Harry Orchard's stunning transformation. In language that owed something to the theological screeds of Edwin Hinks and Dwight Hillis, he suggested that there was "some mysterious but powerful influence back of this confession. I'll tell you what I believe it was: it was the saving power of divine grace working upon his soul and through him to bring to justice one of the worst criminal bands that ever operated in this country. Orchard's faith is now in God. He is a Christian.... Orchard told you with tears in his eyes, with voice hushed, that he told his story because he knew it was a duty he owed God, himself and humanity."

In his second day of oratory, Hawley dwelled on the events that followed the assassination, laying particular stress on the hiring of Fred Miller and the provision of $1,500 for Orchard's defense. "I'll tell you this, gentlemen: If Orchard had killed anybody else besides Steunenberg or some man who had not acted contrary to the interests of the Western Federation of Miners—had not gained their enmity—you wouldn't have found Moyer and Haywood putting up any $1,500 or 15 cents for his defense. That money was not to defend Orchard. It was not put up to protect him so much as it was put up to protect their own necks."

Much of the time, Hawley sat atop the prosecution table, his feet in his chair. Now and again, the ailing attorney spat in one of the brand-new cast-iron spittoons at his feet or sucked on a lemon to clear his throat. From across the aisle, Darrow jibed, "We'll hand you a few more lemons by and by."

"Yes," rasped Hawley, with real anger in his voice. "You've been trying to hand a few to the jury."

Seeking to defuse the class argument he knew was coming from Darrow and Richardson, Hawley warned the jurors that they would "hear much of capital waging war on labor unions." It would be argued, he said, "that we are making war upon the Western Federation of Miners." But "nothing could be more untrue in this case," he said. The mine owners and capitalists of the West had no role in this prosecution. "All that has been spent in this inquiry has come from the coffers of the state of Idaho." It was the same assurance that Gooding had given Theodore Roosevelt and the people of Idaho and that

Borah later repeated, a pledge that might have surprised David Moffat and Stanley Easton, among many others from whom Hawley had so strenuously raised funds to finance a war to "rid the West entirely" of the Western Federation—funds that had increased Hawley's own fee for the Haywood case by $5,000.

And, indeed, as he swung into his peroration, his language—rather moderate to that point—took on a new urgency, suggesting not so much an ordinary murder trial but a great crusade to extirpate an evil force in western life. "Gentlemen," Hawley appealed, "it is time that this stench in the nostrils of all decent persons in the West is buried. It is time to forever put an end to this high handed method of wholesale crime. It is the time when Idaho should show the world that within her borders no crime can be committed and that those who come within her borders must observe the law."

Though suffering from a stomach flu and heavy with exhaustion, Hawley had spoken for nearly eight hours in the stifling heat and had seemed to hold the jurors' attention throughout. Writing the following day to Jacob Fillius—the spearhead of the mine owners' effort in this case—he reported, "I think I made a good impression upon the jury."

On Monday, July 22, it was Edmund Richardson's turn. If Hawley had managed to retain the mannerisms and diction of the small-town lawyer, Ed Richardson, with his impeccable grooming and tailoring, his biting wit and sarcasm, the coiled energy of his delivery, was the very picture of the big-city barrister.

But even the Denver lawyer's snow-white linen and three-piece suit wilted in the stifling courtroom, where the temperature rose into the nineties; to Crane of the *Statesman*—who sat there scribbling all day, sending his copy to the paper via a fifteen-year-old messenger—it was "almost suffocating." Accordingly, after consulting the attorneys and the jurors, the judge abandoned his plan for three two-hour sessions each day. Canceling the afternoon period—when the heat was most oppressive—he sought to capture a bit of the morning and evening cool by meeting six days a week from 9:30 a.m. to noon and 6:00 to 8:30 p.m. But before Richardson had been on his feet for five minutes, tricklets of perspiration beaded his great balding dome and he mopped his face repeatedly with a floppy white handkerchief.

Nonetheless, he put on a mesmerizing performance. Before court began, he'd asked the bailiffs to move the defense table back some feet, to give him more room to walk about in as he talked. Oscar King Davis of the *Times* noted that "his favorite method of attack on the jury was to back off the limit of retreating possibility, then, crouching down, to approach stealthily, speaking softly until he got fairly in front of the first rows of jurors, and then booming out his points at the top of his voice with explosive emphasis." His histrionics held the attention of both jury and spectators, particularly a woman in the front row who had come early to secure a prime location and followed the attorney all day through a pair of large black field glasses.

Knowing of the affection for Frank Steunenberg on this jury, Richardson grappled from the start with the horror of the assassination. "When the news of [Steunenberg's] death was flashed abroad," he conceded, "there was consternation in the camps of organized labor. Some deplored the deed in no uncertain language. Some in no uncertain terms denounced the perpetrator of the deed. Some, gentlemen of the jury, attempted to justify the assassination. There was no justification. We of the defense say there could be no justification for such a dastardly deed."

Having admitted all that, he urged the jurors to be dispassionate for the moment: "I implore you to lay aside any personal feeling you may have had when you came into the case and follow me from the beginning to the end and then, under the dome of high heaven, determine whether that man, whether that man, William D. Haywood, is guilty of the crime charged against him."

Knowing he could never erase the image of the governor leaking his blood in the snow, he sought to balance it with another terrible picture: a thousand miners caged in the Wardner bullpen. He asked the jurors to remember what General Merriam and "his colored troops" had done there in 1899: "They arrested the union miners right and left without warrant. They deprived them of their liberties. They threw them in the dirty, vile-kept bullpens and they were subjected to all sorts of indignities and insults at the hands of those negro soldiers. If you had been there, covered with vermin, . . . if you'd been there, gentlemen of the jury, it is certain that you would have attained in your breast a righteous hatred for every person who had anything to do with causing your humiliation and suffering."

Surely that suffering explained the bitter words written about Frank Steunenberg in the *Miners' Magazine* or spoken in barrooms over the years. But did it mean the WFM had killed him six years after the bullpen was emptied? Of course not. With that, the defense attorney presented a pair of alternative scenarios.

First, Richardson laid out a notion—explored sporadically during the defense case—that Orchard had killed Steunenberg out of a personal grudge, because the governor's actions in the Coeur d'Alenes had compelled him to sell his one-sixteenth share in the Hercules mine. Had he retained it, that share would have enriched him as it had Ed Boyce, and he might have ended his days dozing in a leather chair at the Spokane Club like others of the mining rich. The evidence for this theory was sparse indeed. The state had attacked it by introducing evidence that Orchard sold his interest in the Hercules months before the labor troubles began. Even the defendant didn't seem to buy the idea. When Haywood had been asked whether Orchard complained about losing his chance to be rich, he replied, "Yes, sir, but I'd say that made no great impression on me," as he'd heard "a good many tales of woe" from miners about lost bonanzas. Such plaints, he said, were chronic among mining men and rarely led to murder.

On the morning of his second day of summation, the courtroom having cooled a bit overnight, a refreshed Richardson proffered this threadbare theory once again and then abruptly scrapped it for an entirely different explanation, one that surprised some reporters but seemed to interest a number of the jurors. He asked them to recall Orchard's behavior in Caldwell, curious in a man about to commit a terrible crime: that in the weeks before the explosion Orchard "had stopped at the leading hotel in that town, that he played cards there, that he was seen much about the bar room, that he was out about town," that "practically everybody in town knew him, and knew him well," that he went to the neigborhood where Steunenberg lived, but instead of walking by the house and inconspicuously observing it, "he stood off at a distance and examined the house with field glasses," which many people saw. When added to his behavior after the explosion—his failure to destroy incriminating evidence in his hotel room and his sitting around the lobby waiting to be caught—it all looked to Richardson like a prearranged matter "to call attention to [Orchard] so that when the event did occur which resulted in the death of Governor Steunenberg, everybody would at once point the finger of suspicion to him."* All of this suggested that "the purpose of Orchard was to create evidence such as might lead to the arrest and conviction of the officials of the Western Federation of Miners."

And who pulled the strings in this exercise? Richardson asked. Who else but McParland and the Pinkertons, who had their hands in everything in this case. "Whether [Orchard] was in the employ of the Pinkerton agency at the time or not does not appear in the record," but clearly this served McParland's purpose, to destroy the WFM.

Then he taunted the detective, who hadn't returned to the courtroom after his single visit to hear Hawley: "Where is this 'terror to evildoers,' as Mr. Hawley has called him. Hawley promised you he would have Mr. McParland tell his story. Never but once has his figure darkened the door of this courtroom. . . . Was he afraid of the questions I would ask him on cross-examination? Where are the other slimy Pinkertons who sneaked into our unions to make trouble? Why have they not testified? Where is that grinning hyena [George W.] Riddell, who sat on a stool by that door day after day?"

If the whole thing was a Pinkerton plot, Richardson went on, no wonder that Orchard, ever since his confession, had been

> petted and coddled, visited by the Governor, called on familiar terms "Harry" by the counsel for the prosecution and by the Governor of this state . . . this vile, this loathsome, this damned creature who sat upon the stand and related the

---

* It was this same conduct that had aroused the suspicion of Jo Steunenberg, the governor's sister, that Harry Orchard was trying too hard to get arrested (see p. 97).

most blood curdling series of events that was ever perpetrated by a single individual upon the face of the earth.

If Harry Orchard was in a scheme at the instigation of the Pinkertons or anybody else to swear away the life of innocent men—if he were a part and parcel of such a conspiracy—well might his conscience have said to him "out of your mouth you have condemned innocent men and that is a burden which should weigh heavily on your soul."

It was evening now of his second day, the light fading on the great lawn outside the courtroom windows, as Richardson neared his conclusion. His voice husky from long discourse but rising now in volume and dramatic timbre, he declaimed: "I say that this man is a cheap and a tawdry and a tinsel hero, seated on this witness stand like a king upon his throne ... under a promise as plain as noonday that his worthless head and carcass shall be saved if only there can be secured the condemnation of the officers of the Western Federation of Miners. Which would you rather be and which would you rather believe, this man on the stand wearing his cheap bravado and putting obloquy upon those who are innocent, or this husband and this father," nodding toward Haywood, "an exemplary citizen all of his life, nursing tenderly and caring properly for this crippled woman who now sits and has for long years sat by his side?"

As dusk fell outside, Richardson closed with a reminder that "this is not a trial for the murder of Governor Steunenberg, but a trial of the Western Federation of Miners at the instance of those who do not represent the authority of this state and who have secured the aid of this state as they secured the aid of those authorities in Colorado."

Richardson had spoken for nine hours. It had been a stylish effort, full of rhetorical flourish and theatrical delivery, but some in the courtroom wondered whether all these histrionics were getting through to the twelve farmers in the box. In a letter to Fillius, Hawley noted, "Richardson is talking today, but I am inclined to think he is talking over the heads of the jury. He seems to rather have the credit of an orator than making an argument."

While consuming two and a half days and limning the broad themes of their respective cases, Hawley and Richardson—though they would surely have resented the comparison—were a bit like the vaudeville artists who warmed up the crowd for the top bananas. To those in the courtroom that evening, the best was yet to come: the much-anticipated collision between Darrow, the most celebrated courtroom performer the nation's midland had yet produced, and Borah, the supremely gifted orator of the West.

Long before Shad Hodgin chanted "Oyeh, oyeh" on the twenty-fourth, every seat in the courtroom was filled, the first four rows by the attentive students of Boise's Normal Summer School. Out on the emerald lawn, clumps of disappointed spectators gathered under the open windows, hoping to catch some of Darrow's closing. Just past 9:00 a.m., the Chicago attorney rose at the defense table and advanced to within inches of the jury's rockers, where he addressed the jurors not so much as a group but one by one—looking each man squarely in the eyes as he paced restlessly before them.

From the start, he admitted being an intruder in their midst. "We are here strangers, aliens, if not regarded by you as enemies," he said, "to meet an accusation of the murder of a man whom you all know, whom many of you voted for, maybe, whom one of you at least did business with, a man in whose house one juror lived for two years. We are trying this case to a jury that is almost the family of the man who is dead.... We are defending these men for what seems to you almost an assault upon your own home, and your own fireside."

He wondered at the state's reliance on the "perjured" testimony of Harry Orchard, this "sneaking, craven coward," this "crooked, dwarfed soul ... the biggest liar that this generation has known." His eyes raised incredulously toward the ceiling, he confided: "Gentlemen, I sometimes think I am dreaming in this case. I sometimes wonder whether ... here in Idaho or anywhere in the country, broad and free, a man can be placed on trial and lawyers seriously ask to take away the life of a human being upon the testimony of Harry Orchard.... Need I come here from Chicago to defend the honor of your state? A juror who would take away the life of a human being upon testimony like that would place a stain upon the state of his nativity—a stain that all the waters of the great seas could never wash away."

No admirer of Darrow, Crane of the *Statesman* was impressed at how "physical" his performance was. The attorney, he said, "brings into action every muscle of his body in emphasizing his sentences. He waves his hands. He shrugs his shoulders; he wags and nods and tosses his head about. He bends his knees and he twists his body. And his contortions, if he were not so serious about them, would be almost as interesting as what he says."

Oscar King Davis admired Darrow's oratorical skills, the "complete submission of a great part of his audience to his mood," so that when he "moved himself to tears ... half the courtroom wept with him." He was "a master of invective, vituperation, denunciative, humor, pathos and all the other arts of the orator, except argument."

His most wounding invective was reserved for an old target, James Hawley. Ridiculing the prosecutor's assertion that he wouldn't be prosecuting the case unless he believed Haywood guilty, Darrow asked, "Is he prosecuting it because he thinks him guilty? Is that it? Or is he prosecuting it because he thinks he may want to put another ell on his house, and wants some more deficiency warrants with which to do it? ... I hope there is no one here who cares a fig about what Mr. Hawley thinks about this case. He may be bughouse —and he is, if all of his statements are true—or he is worse."

Darrow belabored Hawley for telling the jury it would be warranted in convicting Haywood even if one took Orchard's testimony out of the case.

"And still he says he is honest! Maybe he is, but if he is honest he is crazy, and he can have his choice." All this, he sneered, from the prosecutor whose case, from start to finish, had been "Orchard-Orchard-Orchard." Darrow mused: "Too bad the old gentleman could not have closed his career before he reached this case." As for Orchard, "You'd better leave him to Hawley—he needs a pet in his old age."

To some reporters, these attacks on the dean of Idaho's bar seemed so excessive they could only alienate an Idaho jury. Perhaps. But Darrow always picked a victim on the other side, because he believed the best way to drain animus against his client was to give the jury somebody else to hate. Hawley, who was ill, wasn't in the courtroom to bear Darrow's shafts; when he heard about them, he felt like punching the Chicago lawyer—his friends talked him out of it—and later referred to Darrow's closing as his "blackguard address."

Darrow had great fun with Hawley's solemn assertion that Orchard should be believed because behind his testimony stood the saving power of divine grace. "He says when a man gets religion he is all right and he will not lie, cannot lie; he has seen this great light, and he is led from above and the jury must believe he cannot lie because he has got religion. Well, if Hawley has not got it, he ought to have it. The best I could do would be to advise him to go right off and get it, if there is any left after what Orchard has taken."

Stripped to his shirtsleeves and suspenders in the stifling heat, his left hand shoved in his pocket, his right hand raised on high, Darrow thundered: "I am sorry to say it, but it is true, because religious men have killed now and then, they have lied now and then.... Of all the miserable claptrap that has been thrown into a jury for the sake of getting it to give some excuse for taking the life of a man, this is the worst.... Orchard saves his soul by throwing the burden on Jesus, and he saves his life by dumping it onto Moyer, Haywood and Pettibone.... And you twelve men are asked to set your seal of approval on it."

One of the most difficult decisions Darrow had to make in the speech was how to defuse the reputation that Haywood and the WFM both had for "direct action" and violence. To paint the miners as industrial saints would be to fly in the face of the facts, but to be too frank would be to suggest that the use of dynamite and bullets against their enemies might not be alien to Haywood and his federation. The matter was all the more difficult for Darrow to resolve because, under the influence of Leo Tolstoy, he'd become a philosophical anarchist, a passionate advocate of nonresistance, explicated in his 1902 volume, *Resist Not Evil*. "Hatred, bitterness, violence and force can bring only bad results—they leave an evil stain on everyone they touch," he wrote. "No human soul can be rightly reached except through charity, humanity and love." But by 1907 Darrow knew full well that love and charity were not altogether efficacious when dealing with the Mine Owners Associations of Colorado and Idaho.

Darrow took the issue on squarely:

> I don't mean to tell this jury that labor organizations do no wrong. I know them
> too well for that. They do wrong often, and sometimes brutally; they are
> sometimes cruel; they are often unjust; they are frequently corrupt.... But I am
> here to say that in a great cause these labor organizations—despised and weak
> and outlaws as they generally are—have stood for the poor, they have stood for
> the weak, they have stood for every humane law that was ever placed upon the
> statute books.... I don't care how many wrongs they have committed—I don't
> care how many crimes—these weak, rugged, unlettered men, who often know
> no other power but the brute force of their strong right arm, who find them-
> selves bound and confined and impaired whichever way they turn, and who look
> up and worship the God of might as the only God they know. I don't care how
> often they fail, how many brutalities they are guilty of. I know their cause is
> just.*
>
>   I want to say to you, gentlemen of the jury, you Idaho farmers, removed
> from the trade unions, removed from the men who work in industrial affairs, I
> want to say that had it not been for the trade unions of the world ... you today
> would be serfs instead of free men.

Toward his close, Darrow considered what had caused Steunenberg's
death if Haywood didn't order it. He clearly differed with Richardson's
suggestion that Orchard might have killed the governor at the Pinkertons'
behest. "I don't believe that this man was ever really in the employ of
anybody," Darrow said. "I don't believe he ever had any allegiance to the
Mine Owners Association, to the Pinkertons, to the Western Federation of
Miners, to his family, to his kindred, to his God, or to anything human or
divine. I don't believe he bears any relation to anything that a mysterious and
inscrutable Providence has ever created.... He was a soldier of fortune, ready
to pick up a penny or a dollar or any other sum in any way that was easy ... to
serve the mine owners, to serve the Western Federation, to serve the devil if
he got his price, and his price was cheap."

In one respect, this argument was utterly convincing. Nothing in Orchard's history suggested that he was capable of devotion to any group, cause,
or individual. But if he was a soldier of fortune, working for anybody who
could pay the price, why not kill people for Haywood?

To explain what really happened, Darrow inexplicably fell back on the

---

* That Darrow remained sensitive on this issue is illustrated by his prickly exchange with
Collier's after the trial. When the magazine accused Darrow of excusing violence in his closing
argument, Darrow wrote a letter arguing that he championed labor "in spite of wrongs or
brutalities," not because of them. He cited the text of the speech published in pamphlet form
by *Appeal to Reason*, from which, he said, "not one word has been cut." But *Collier's*, relying on
C. P. Connolly's notes, insisted that Darrow had "edited out all the words of violence" from the
Appeal version. When *Wayland's Monthly* appeared in October with a full, unedited version of
the speech, it supported *Collier's* and not Darrow on this point (Grover, *Debaters*, 218–19;
Clarence Darrow to Editor of *Collier's*, September 23, 1907, in *Collier's*, October 26, 1907, 9; *Collier's*,
November 30, 1907, 7).

least effective arrow in the defense's quiver, the argument that Orchard had killed Steunenberg because of his personal grudge over the loss of his share in the Hercules mine. Richardson didn't buy it, nor did most of the press or public.

With those unpleasant specifics out of the way, Darrow swung into his peroration—one of the most powerful of his career. Bestriding the center of the amphitheater between the witness box and the jury, he addressed the jurors head-on.

> Other men have died in the same cause in which Will Haywood has risked his life. Men strong with devotion, men who loved liberty, men who loved their fellow men, patriots who have raised their voices in defense of the poor, in defense of right, have made their good fight and have met death on the scaffold, on the rack, in the flame, and they will meet it again and again until the world grows old and gray. William Haywood is no better than the rest. He can die if die he must. He can die if this jury decrees it; but, oh, gentlemen, do not think for a moment that if you hang him you will crucify the labor movement of the world.... Think you there are no other brave hearts, no other strong arms, no other devoted souls who will risk all in that great cause which has demanded martyrs in every land and age? There are others and these others will come to take his place....
>
> Gentlemen, it is not for him alone that I speak. I speak for the poor, for the weak, for the weary, for that long line of men who, in darkness and despair, have borne the labors of the human race. The eyes of the world are upon you—upon you twelve men of Idaho tonight.... If you should decree Bill Haywood's death, in the railroad offices of our great cities men will applaud your names. If you decree his death, amongst the spiders of Wall Street will go up paeans of praise for these twelve good men and true. In every bank in the world, where men hate Haywood because he fights for the poor and against the accursed system upon which the favored live and grow rich and fat—from all those you will receive blessings and unstinted praise. But if your verdict should be "Not Guilty," there are still those who will reverently bow their heads and thank [you].
>
> Out on our broad prairies where men toil with their hands, out on the wide ocean where men are tossed and buffeted on the waves, through our mills and factories, and down deep under the earth...the poor, the weak, and the suffering of the world are stretching out their helpless hands to this jury in mute appeal for Will Haywood's life.

Darrow completed his marathon oration (eleven hours, fifteen minutes) late on the afternoon of July 25 before an audience in which there were many union officers, Boise Socialists, "idealists and dreamers"; several women of a progressive bent brushed away tears. The courtroom was emptied—Darrow, with tongue in cheek, later suggested that it was being "thoroughly aired, if not fumigated"—and by 6:00 p.m., an hour before court was to reconvene, a very different audience had packed the room to near suffocation. Boise's "elite," lawyers, physicians, and business executives in their summer whites, Boise matrons in cotton frocks and extravagant bonnets—had turned out in force to hear Borah close the prosecution case. Darrow was reminded of Byron's description of the ball in Brussels on the eve of the battle of Waterloo: "There was a sound of revelry by night, / And Belgium's capital had gather'd then / Her beauty and her chivalry, and bright / The lamps shone o'er fair women and brave men."

Once more, Governor Gooding occupied a prominent seat. So did the widow, Belle Steunenberg, making her first visit to the trial, accompanied by her twenty-one-year-old son, Julian, who occasionally reached over and grasped her folded hands. Also present for the first time was the Reverend Dwight Hillis of Plymouth Church, Brooklyn Heights—Governor Gooding's informal emissary to the eastern intelligentsia—whose train from New York had reached Boise barely an hour before the evening session began.

The demand for seats that night had been the greatest in the history of the courthouse. A vast throng had been "intent upon squeezing, pushing, crowding, crawling, or working any old dodge, to get inside." Fully a thousand persons were turned away, many of whom now milled on the lawn under the tall windows, flung open to the summer night, waiting for Idaho's mightiest rhetorician to conjure the grand themes of the prosecution case.

The trial had been an ordeal for Borah, "one of those battles," he wrote, "that make a man grow old." For months he'd gotten warning notes not unlike those received over the years by Frank Steunenberg: "We'll get you," "You will not get to court tomorrow," "We let Steunenberg live six years." Spurning suggestions that he hire a bodyguard or carry a weapon, he told his secretary to keep the notes off his desk.

Hawley and other prosecutors grumbled that Borah's heart seemed only half in the Haywood case, that they were getting only a fraction of his formidable talents. First, it had been his campaign for the Senate that preoc-cupied him. Shortly before Hawley's argument to the Supreme Court in October 1906, the senior attorney had written Borah, "I needed your assis-tance in this badly, and feel as if I would need it still worse in Washington. But you can not be expected to leave the campaign under the circumstances, so I will do the best I can." On July 22, an exhausted Hawley wrote a friend: "I have been doing three men's work constantly."

Now it was Borah's timber fraud case that distracted—even obsessed—him day and night. Jonathan Bourne, the Republican senator from Oregon and a close ally, urged him to ignore his "personal troubles" during the Haywood trial: "Go in, old man, give it your very best energies, and if you do, you will surely come out on top." A New Jersey lawyer assured him he was "waging the war of the Nation in that Idaho Court Room." But plainly Borah was unable to put his personal furies to rest. At times in the summer of 1907, he'd brushed the border of despair (one friend called the whole experience his Gethsemane). Not sure whom in Boise he could trust, he kept his own counsel much of the time; but at night, back in his empty office, he poured out his fears to his old college mate, the celebrated editor of the *Emporia Gazette*, William Allen White. For not only was White an old and trusted friend, but Borah knew the editor had grown increasingly close to Theodore Roosevelt and was perhaps the one man who might intercede with the president to quash this devilish indictment.

White hadn't started as a Roosevelt man. With his sandy hair, beige eyes, and fleshy face, resembling a thousand small-town merchants across the nation's midsection, the Sage of Emporia was widely regarded as the spokesman for all those dusty hamlets of prairie and pasture long thought to be repositories of America's folk wisdom. It was the apocalyptic collision of 1896 that had drawn the Kansas editor onto the national stage. Horrified by the specter of William Jennings Bryan, riding out of the West as the "incarnation of demagogy, the apotheosis of riot, destruction and carnage," White had turned his derision on Bryan's Kansas followers in a celebrated editorial called "What's the Matter With Kansas?": "That's the stuff! Give the prosperous man the dickens! Whoop it up for the ragged trousers; put the lazy, greasy fizzle, who can't pay his debts, on the altar, and bow down and worship him. ... What we need is not the respect of our fellow men, but the chance to get something for nothing."

A vice president of the Santa Fe Railroad was so taken with this screed he passed it along to the editor of the *Chicago Record-Herald*, and he, in turn, to others. Millions of copies flooded the land and a grateful President McKinley and his party boss, Mark Hanna, rewarded White with lush political patronage and a lucrative printing contract.

But White's orthodoxy was only a phase in his development; soon he found himself tugged in the other direction. When he met the assistant navy secretary in 1897, he was "overcome" by the force of Theodore Roosevelt's personality: "I had never known such a man as he, and never shall again. ... He poured into my heart such visions, such ideals, such hopes, such a new attitude toward life and patriotism and the meaning of things, as I had never dreamed men had. ... After that I was his man." Gradually, Roosevelt weaned the editor from the plutocratic to the reform wing of the Republican Party and, eventually, to progressivism. Much like a religious conversion, involving the betrayal of long-standing alliances and the questioning of settled assumptions, this transformation tipped White into a nervous breakdown.

But by 1907, he'd recovered his equilibrium, and White and Roosevelt settled into an affectionate relationship enlivened by mutual japery. The president had lately addressed the editor as "Oh, Member of the Muck-Rake Lodge," while White sent him a clipping of Eugene Debs's latest attack on Roosevelt for his "undesirable citizens" statement. "You might read the Debs article to the cabinet," he suggested, "and put it to a vote whether you should resign or be hanged. Personally, I prefer hanging, but that is on account of my western traditions, and is a mere matter of taste upon which I shall not insist."

Though White relished being on easy terms with the powers that be, he

wanted to be no man's "fair weather friend." When news of Borah's indictment reached Emporia that April, he jotted his schoolmate a note: "I am
satisfied that these charges grow out of the Haywood-Moyer troubles.... You
know that I am for you and with you. I want you to feel as free to call on me,
as I would be to call on you."

Borah called. One night at Chicago's Auditoreum Hotel—on his way
back from Washington, where he'd asked the administration "that this infamous charge be taken off of me until I get through with the [Haywood] trial"
—Borah sat down to write his old friend from the depths of unspeakable
anguish:

> This is unutterably sad to me. First there is my old Father, 89 years of age,
> who will not understand the hellish maliciousness of those behind it. It will
> nearly kill [him]. Then there is [Mary], brave beyond all words to tell, but God
> only knows how in silence she suffers. Then there are the thousands who
> honored me last fall—they must be humiliated beyond expression.... This is
> the work of political enemies corrupted and urged on by the lawless element
> who have pursued me and done everything except murder me since 1899....
> The fact is, White, I was never more innocent of a charge than this, but the
> corruption fund of the WFM works wonders.

Only then did he reach the letter's object: "Now, White, I do not know
whether it would be proper or not but I feel very much like I would like for
the President to know what you think of me and what you know of my
situation in Idaho."

White would do it—Borah must have known he would—for, some years
before, the editor had stumbled into an all too similar situation in Idaho and
Borah had ridden to his rescue. Traveling through the Northwest in September 1903, White had encountered some aggressive entrepreneurs. "Big money-
making projects colored our thinking and our talking," White recalled later,
"and one afternoon, riding on the Oregon Short Line across Idaho with some
officials of the road in their private car, we cooked up a scheme to buy some
desert land which in a year or so would be under irrigation, and to start there
a cantaloupe farm. We made a jackpot."

One of his partners was Frank Steunenberg's successor as governor,
Frank Hunt. Among the others were a New York "capitalist" named H. L.
Hollister and Lewis G. Van Riper, a speculator. Van Riper took White riding
in his new motorcar through Chicago, and White was stunned by the perqui-
sites of the rich, telling his wife how he'd been "riding all one blessed day in a
big red double seated brass mounted buzz wagon—just to keep cool.... We
transacted all our business in the buzz wagon while the yeomanry on the side
walk and in little old donkey carriages and barouches were properly awed by
the presence of the gentry!"

Eager for some of the easy money that seemed to be everywhere he
turned, White struck a deal with Hollister and Van Riper that would bring

him $250,000 worth of stock in the companies they founded to grow canta-loupe on desert land and to mine Idaho gold. White would serve as the projects' press agent, writing circulars, drawing up advertisements, praising the projects in articles for the *Saturday Evening Post*.*

Then, as the Roosevelt administration aggressively pursued timber fraud prosecutions in Oregon and elsewhere, White realized the method by which he'd acquired Idaho desert land was uncomfortably close to what conspirators in Oregon—and later Idaho—were accused of doing. Unable to purchase Idaho desert land himself, he'd arranged with Hunt for Hunt's brother and a man named Keefe to buy the land, then pass it on to him. "My hair rose in amazement and genuine fear when I found they were sending men to the penitentiary for doing exactly what I had done." White appealed to Borah, at first in jocular self-deprecation: "You turn a wild-eyed tender-footed Kansas editor loose in the midst of the desert act, and tell him to come through, and it's like putting blinders on a three legged mule and telling him to find his way out of a hot bed with window glass on three sides of him, and lath on the other." But he was in deadly earnest: "About the only asset I have on earth is honesty, and I want to keep that unspotted." Borah had guided him shrewdly through the process of deeding the land back to those from whom he'd acquired it—thus cleansing his record of illegality, though not entirely sooth-ing his conscience.

Now, with Borah in similar trouble, White rushed to his assistance. For the time being, he let Borah's anguish speak for itself, sending the senator's letter to the president with a cover letter in which he said he'd known Borah since they were both at the University of Kansas twenty years before. "Surely there he was a clean upright man. In Idaho he has stood for the best things . . . and since 1899 he has been the implacable enemy of lawlessness in what is known as the Western Federation of Miners." Conceding he knew nothing of the case against his friend, he asked the president to take account of Borah's letter.

On May 8, Roosevelt wrote back sympathetically but noncommittally. The Borah situation was "most painful," and particularly unfortunate since it "might tend to produce a miscarriage of justice in the Moyer and Haywood business." But, "of course, there is nothing I can do except make a resolute fight against law-breakers, whether it is a case of dynamiters or big timber thieves."

With the Haywood trial starting the next day, Borah had his hands full. But on June 24, he wrote White, admitting, "My mind sometimes reverts to my own matters," and spelling out his dire fears of the future:

* Booming the Idaho project after his 1903 trip, White wrote: "When this energy [of the Snake River] is harnessed and transformed into power it will destroy the desert. Cities and men will fill the valleys and overrun the mountains. All that is worthy in American civilization will bloom and come to fruit here" (William Allen White, "The Boom in the Northwest," *Saturday Evening Post,* May 21, 1904, 2–3).

Just entering the Senate and public life I feel that I am on slippery ground where hundreds have slipped and fallen, and *I don't know!* I feel that I cannot succeed in public life if I am to enter with the condemnation of President Roosevelt's great administration on me. In other words, though I should have the verdict of a jury it would be of but little avail in my struggle for position, in the face of the fact that the administration thought me sufficiently guilty to deserve prosecution.... I feel if I cannot satisfy the president and the attorney general of my absolute innocence that I must resign from the Senate.

This was Borah at his most manipulative. Having dangled this extreme measure before White, he implored his friend, "Are you so situated that you could see the president within the next few weeks for me and find out what they propose to do?... A friend of mine was talking to the president a few days ago and he writes me that the president stated to him that he believed I was honest and that he had entire confidence in me. Now if he feels that way why should my whole career be jeopardized by this being pushed, and thereby, in the public mind, myself condemned for all time?"

In reply, White agreed to "try with all the earnestness I can to show the President how unjust it is to force you to trial on a matter which you can explain to him and to the Attorney General." But he thought he could do more with a letter than he could face-to-face. "I write better than I talk," he said, "and he [the president] talks better than he writes."

His desperation mounting, Borah wasn't interested in another letter. "Now, White, what I want you to do, and it is asking a great deal, is to go to Washington," he wrote July 6. "If you write a letter the letter may go directly into the hands of the [Justice] Department and if you go and see the president you see him personally."

Borah's letter reached White in Manitou, Colorado, where he had gone with his wife to escape the summer heat of Kansas and to work on a novel about a self-made man, now a greedy robber baron, who redeems himself by returning to his legitimate occupation as a miller and by a connection to the people of his hometown (a notion derived from White's own conversion to progressivism). "This idea is with me and is growing beautifully into dramatic shape," he wrote, and he was reluctant to interrupt it for any purpose. But, obedient as ever to Borah's wishes, he asked to see the president. On July 15, he wrote Borah that Roosevelt, preoccupied with other matters, had invited the editor to ride with him into Iowa during the president's Midwest swing on September 30.

On July 19, hours before Hawley began his closing argument in the Haywood trial, Borah wrote impatiently to White in Manitou. The September 30 date would be "entirely too late to be of any avail," he said, since the trial of Moyer or Pettibone would begin in September and "it would be impossible for me to look after my own affairs and this matter too." Then he added ominously, "Friends of the [Haywood] defense here are very active in their efforts to secure evidence against me." The forces out to destroy him were closing in from all directions. "Perhaps our friend in the East"—the president—"does not understand the situation here as to dates, although I have had an intimation that he proposes to act one way or the other shortly after the disposal of the matter of the Haywood trial." Meanwhile, Borah told White in a tone of desperate urgency, "I must act."

Worried by how "despondent" Borah seemed, White wrote the president yet again, reminding him of the valuable service the senator was rendering in the Haywood case. "Borah has been three months before the people of Idaho making a fight for good government, and in a small community like that where every man, woman and child is lined up and passions are deeply wrought up," a mistrial or hung jury was quite likely. "It is not his fault but to his everlasting credit that he has made enemies who will make a mistrial a real danger." Borah was, after all, "a man who all his life has fought for decent things, who has stood against every form of graft and political dishonor in Idaho politics, who looked forward with keen youthful joy to the time when he could be a real power for righteousness in the world."

Pointing out that "the Moyer case and his case come up in September, and he cannot appear in both," White asked if the president and Attorney General Bonaparte might see Borah "very soon... and when you have heard his story, with both sides of the case before you, will you then act as your best judgment prompts you?" So dire was his friend's situation, he told Roosevelt, that he would even sacrifice, for now, his novel in progress. "Nothing else in this world but this matter would tempt me to leave my work before it is done and go on any mission," he wrote the president, "but if you will see [Borah], and think it essential to see me with him, I shall come."

At the moment the Kansas editor drafted his plea to the president, in the Ada County courthouse Bill Borah took his stance at some distance from the jury and, in richly evocative language, launched one of the finest speeches of his life.

While Darrow, the trial's other orator, was the son of an avowed atheist, Borah's father had been a devout, puritanical Presbyterian. Now the senator's heavily cadenced prose rang through Idaho's courtrooms with the persuasive peal of an itinerant evangelist's. He spoke of his own role as a special prosecutor. "The State has the right to employ such counsel as it deems necessary, accredited with the same integrity of professional purpose as is accredited to counsel for the defense," he proclaimed, failing to mention that his salary was met in part by Colorado's mine owners.* But he found time to rebuke Darrow sharply for the ad hominem attacks on his co-counsel. "It ought to be sufficient and satisfactory to answer a man's argument," he said.

---

* Later, Borah gave the people of Idaho the same bogus assurance as Hawley and Gooding had given: "The mine owners were not connected with the prosecution of the case" (*Evening Capital News*, August 7, 1907).

After reciting the prosecution's mantra—"We are not fighting organized labor. We are not fighting the weak and the poor.... It is simply a trial for murder"—Borah pointedly criticized Darrow for his closing rhetoric: "If I were fighting the cause of labor, I would not seek to engender hatred and ill-will, faction against faction, or class against class. I would not inveigh against law; I would not inveigh against society; I would not inveigh against every man who owns his home or his farm; I would not inveigh against Christianity, because without those things the laboring man goes down into slavery and the dirt."

Clearly Borah believed that the agnostic Darrow had overreached himself in his mocking of Orchard's religiosity. Though Borah himself had never been more than a nominal church member, he eloquently evoked the faith of Presbyterians: "In our strength and pride we are given over to mockery and derision; in the hour of success we are all of us more or less blasphemous and inclined to declare as the fool did, that there is no God; but when we are cast down, things are altogether different—in the night of despair every sinner of us turns at last to the old book which our mothers love."

After an hour that first night, in the courtroom's suffocating heat, Borah had had enough. "I would like to close this evening," he told the judge, "for it is too hot here to proceed." The judge adjourned until nine the next morning, when the largest crowds of the trial besieged the courtroom, men fighting with bailiffs to get inside, women pleading and cajoling for a seat at the historic event.

In picking up the threads of his argument, Borah had wisely decided not to rehearse all the evidence in the case, in part because of the heat, in part because the jurors had heard it all now in three different speeches of staggering length, in part because he wanted to keep the focus on the Steunenberg assassination—which had sometimes gotten lost in the welter of other testimony—the one crime with which Haywood was charged under the indictment.

He strove to put the murder of Steunenberg in its context, embedded in the conspiracy the prosecution alleged. He was at his best in tracing the actions of the alleged "conspirators"—Orchard, Simpkins, Haywood, Moyer, and Pettibone—in the weeks and days before Steunenberg's death. In some passages, the senator's voice was matter-of-fact, almost monotonous, a simple recounting of telegrams, letters, trips, and meetings. But then it would rise and take on new urgency, as he admonished the jurors: "Watch these five men! In a little over thirty days Frank Steunenberg is going to die. What are their actions? They are going to and fro, their association, their connection—you will find out whether there is evidence here or not to show a conspiracy.... Watch them!"

Borah paused. For seconds that last phrase hung in the moist courtroom air, with no other sound save the whir of the electric fans. Then he continued, tracing Orchard's travels across the Rocky Mountain West but seemingly always back to Denver. "Why? Why? Always back to Denver? Unless it was to find there the protection and the pay of his employers."

But Borah was notably silent on the assassin himself, leaving the distinct impression that he could barely manage to utter the name of the villain who had struck down his friend. Darrow had got it right when he told the jury: "I am inclined to think that if Senator Borah believed Harry Orchard was going to heaven, he'd want to go the other way."

The combination of the heat and Borah's evocation of her husband's death was too much for Mrs. Steunenberg, who fainted at midday and had to be carried from the courtroom (she did not return thereafter). Haywood's mother also left the courtroom in tears.

After the afternoon adjournment, the court convened again at six for the last session of argument—the final moments of a trial that, with jury selection, had lasted nearly three months. Once more the courtroom was crowded to capacity, with several hundred spectators listening on the lawn outside. In the evening, Borah's appeal was more to the jurors' hearts than to their heads. His sentences were longer, their rolling rhythms more pronounced, their summons to the traditional virtues of duty, courage, and patriotism more compelling. "There is no home in Idaho tonight," he told the jury, "but that a thought of you and your final duty will mingle with the sentiment which made that home possible."

Borah acknowledged that the defense counsel had made eloquent appeals of their own. "They are men of wonderful powers," he said.

They have been brought here because of their power to sway the minds of men ... [to] draw you away from the consideration of the real facts in this case, to beguile you from a consideration of your real and only duty. But as I listened to the voice of counsel and felt for a time their great influence, there came to me after the spell was broken another scene....

I remembered again the awful thing of December 30, 1905, a night which has added ten years to the life of some who are in this courtroom now. I felt again its cold and icy chill, faced the drifting snow and peered at last into the darkness for the sacred spot where last lay the body of my dead friend, and saw true, only too true, the stain of his life's blood upon the whitened earth. I saw Idaho dishonored and disgraced. I saw murder—no, not murder, a thousand times worse than murder—I saw anarchy wave its first bloody triumph in Idaho. And as I thought again I said, "Thou living God, can the talents or the arts of counsel unteach the lessons of that hour?" No, no. Let us be brave, let us be faithful in this supreme test of trial and duty.

If the defendant is entitled to his liberty, let him have it. But, on the other hand, if the evidence in this case discloses the author of this crime, then there is no higher duty to be imposed upon citizens than the faithful discharge of that particular duty. Some of you men have stood the test and trial in the protection of the American flag. But you never had a duty imposed upon you which required more intelligence, more manhood, more courage than that which the people of Idaho assign to you this night in the final discharge of your duty.

With that rousing appeal to the jurors' obligations as Idaho citizens, Borah resumed his seat at 7:21 p.m., after an address of five hours and fifty-one minutes.* Judge Wood adjourned until ten the next morning, when he would instruct the jury.

It took Fremont Wood nearly an hour the next morning to give the jurors their legal marching orders. The judge gave the defense the benefit of the doubt on most contested items. Of the sixty-five separate charges, fully thirty-one dealt with the presumption of innocence, reasonable doubt, the need for corroboration, and related matters. Perhaps the single most important was charge thirty-four, which put the jury on warning that "under the statutes of this state a person cannot be convicted of a crime upon the testimony of an accomplice unless such accomplice is corroborated by other evidence which of itself, and without the aid of the testimony of the accomplice, tends to connect the defendant with the commission of the offense charged." Wood went on to point out: "The law views with distrust the testimony of an accomplice on account of the motive he may have for laying the responsibility of his crime upon another when by so doing he may secure immunity for his own participation in the crime charged."

Oscar King Davis, the *Times* man who'd come to know the judge pretty well on their fishing trips, was puzzled by the charge. Barely ten days before, around their campfire, Wood had proclaimed Haywood guilty. Yet here he was with a charge that opened a hundred doors of reasonable doubt, almost inviting the jury to take any exit. On reflection, Davis thought that "in his belief that Haywood was guilty the judge made up his mind to be so fair in his charge as to prevent the possibility of reversal on that account."

Once the jury had been instructed, Wood ordered the courtroom cleared, and at 11:04 a.m. the four bailiffs escorted the jurors to a small room on the top floor of the courthouse, just across from the judge's office. Wood retired to his chambers, while reporters, attorneys, sheriffs' deputies, and court officials lounged about the vacant courtroom gossiping and taking bets on the outcome. At 3:50, the jurors asked the judge for four exhibits: the much-disputed telegram from Fred Miller to Orchard, a telegram from Jack Simpkins to Haywood, a letter from Pettibone to Orchard, and drafts of money by Haywood to Simpkins.

Late in the afternoon, the press corps was thrown into a dither when a bailiff rushed into the courtroom, prompting rumors that a verdict was imminent; but the bailiff merely retrieved seat cushions left behind by two jurors. The heat and the long hours were beginning to take their toll on the jurors. When they took a twenty-minute supper break at 6:30, reporters noticed that Jamie Robertson, at seventy-two the oldest of the jurors, had to be helped up

---

* At the close of Borah's speech, Haywood was reported to have turned to one of his attorneys and said, "Well, I have heard the best of them in the country, but Borah beats them all" (*Denver Republican*, July 27, 1907, 1).

and down the stairs. But they talked on into the night. At 9:50, Judge Wood went home to bed, leaving instructions for the sheriff to telephone him if the jury reached a decision; some of the reporters and attorneys also went to bed. But Darrow prowled the darkened streets with several colleagues and friends, moving past little knots of men who stood on the corners arguing the case, finally taking refuge in a newspaperman's quarters directly across the street from the courthouse. At midnight, friends passed along the dire report that the jury stood eleven to one for conviction and they were trying to force the lone holdout to yield.

Meanwhile, the jurors remained locked in their brilliantly lighted room, without beds or cots. Occasionally, one of them could be seen silhouetted at a window; for twenty minutes, it was the mustachioed fence builder Levi Smith, in his shirtsleeves, pulling on a pipe with "the air of a man whose mind was made up and was content to let the others do the fighting." Outside on the lawn, beneath the giant elms, a small band of Boise Socialists and union members kept vigil, with only the occasional reporter to keep them company.

"Dame rumor was rife all night," wrote John MacLennan of the *Denver Republican*. Nervous reporters were prey to a host of half-baked reports filtering from the jury room. Most were bad news for the defense. Depending on which bailiff one talked to, the margin was eleven to one or nine to three for conviction. Just past midnight, John Kennedy and/or Bob Small of the Associated Press—with the balance wheel of Mart Egan absent in Wyoming—dispatched a story saying the jury stood ten for first-degree murder and two for second-degree. Following that lead, the *Statesman* set the headline of an extra edition, leaving room only for "First" or "Second" degree.

A reporter told Darrow "Well, Mr. D., it takes twelve."

"No," said Darrow, "it takes only one," which was interpreted to mean that the defense had all but given up any thought of acquittal or even of a narrowly hung jury and was hoping against hope that one stubborn juror could prevent conviction.

At 6:40 a.m. on Sunday, the bearded bailiff guarding the jury room was startled by an imperative knock from inside. Soon telephones rang in the homes of the judge and the attorneys as well as in the hotel rooms and rented flats of the reporters. Through the deserted streets, this haggard, ill-shaven company made its way to the shabby old courthouse. One reporter overtook the governor, hastening on foot, and offered him a ride in his carriage.

By 7:45, the bleary-eyed participants had assembled in the courtroom, blinking in the dazzling sunlight streaming through the eastern windows. Judge Wood looked so severe some thought he knew he was about to send a man to the gallows, a hunch reinforced by the sheriff's order barring all Socialist reporters from the courtroom.

When Darrow arrived, Carberry of the *Globe* was struck by how he "toiled up the wooden stairway and entered the courtroom slowly, his eyes red and his sallow skin ashen." Behind him walked Ed Richardson, pale as death, "his shoulders drooping in apprehension." Last came Haywood, "the collar of yesterday about his neck, showing how he'd marked the hours of the night."

Flinging an arm around Haywood, Darrow rasped, "Bill, old man, you'd better prepare for the worst. I'm afraid it is against us, so keep up your nerve."

"Yes, I will," said Haywood, his lips trembling.

For fifteen minutes, they sat in numbed silence. In the trees outside, the birds were twittering, but neither Darrow nor Haywood heard them. Crane of the *Statesman* thought the ticks of the clock on the wall "sounded like the blows from a sledge." Then, with slow steps and solemn faces—they hadn't slept in twenty-six hours—the bewhiskered jurors entered the box. "Gentlemen of the jury," intoned Wood, "have you agreed upon a verdict?"

"We have," said the foreman, Thomas B. Gess, an insurance broker and the former Boise postmaster. He handed up an envelope.

Darrow buried his face in his hands, his huge shoulders hunched against the blow he dreaded. Haywood sat erect, his face "red as fire," an elbow hooked over the high back of his chair. Delving into the envelope, the judge said—with some amazement—"There's nothing here!"

"There's the right envelope," said another juror, Sam Russell, "in your coat pocket."

"I got 'em mixed," said Gess, handing up the new envelope. Wood glanced at the slip inside, his face betraying nothing, then gave it to the clerk, Otto Peterson, whose usual drone cracked as he read through the deadly hush:

"State of Idaho against William D. Haywood: We the jury in the above entitled cause find the defendant, William D. Haywood, not guilty."

Bill Haywood leapt to his feet, laughing and crying together. With one bound, Darrow was at his side, pumping his hand. "Bill, you're free. You're free, do you know it?" Richardson was on his feet as well and Haywood grasped his hand, blurting, "God bless you!" His old friend John Nugent wrapped him in a huge bear hug. "Let me thank those boys over there," Haywood said, nodding toward the jurors. One after another, as they left the box, he pressed the hands of the men who, until minutes before, had held his fate in theirs.

Through the tumult, Wood managed to announce, "The defendant will be discharged and the jury dismissed for the term."

A look of "illimitable gladness on his face," Haywood grabbed a hat from the rack and thundered downstairs into the July morning. John Kennedy, writing the AP's lead in Egan's absence, captured the spirit of that moment: "Boise, July 30—Into the bright sunlight of a beautiful sabbath morning, into the stillness of a city drowsy with the lazy slumber of a summer Sunday, William D. Haywood . . . walked a free man, acquitted of the murder of Former Governor Frank Steunenberg."

Many of the mainstream reporters sat at their desks, not quite believing what they'd heard. Hermon Titus of the *Socialist*, who'd gone to bed at 7:00 a.m. with a deputy's promise to wake him if the jury came in, banged through the courtroom door just after the verdict was announced, in time to see Oscar King Davis looking "like a frozen corpse."

Haywood went first to defense headquarters in the Overland Building for a brief conference with his lawyers. Then he returned to the county jail to share the news with Moyer and Pettibone. "That's good," gruffed Moyer, still barely on speaking terms with Haywood. "Give my regards to Broadway," joshed the always irreverent Pettibone.

In the sheriff's office, Haywood called the house on Twelfth Street where his family had been staying. When Henrietta picked up the phone, he said, "This is papa. Tell Mama that I am coming home after I go to the hospital to see grandmother. Yes, yes, the jury has acquitted me. Give mama my love." After a joyful reunion at home, Haywood may have stopped by Darrow's suite at the Idanha—he and Ruby had moved back there after his rented house had been sold from under him—where the living room was so jammed with well-lubricated celebrants that "one couldn't move."

As the WFM planned Haywood's triumphal return to Denver, James Kirwan, the acting secretary-treasurer, revealed that the union was negotiating with the Union Pacific to lease the same train that had brought Haywood and his colleagues to Boise eighteen months before. The railroad declined.

Out at the penitentiary, Harry Orchard issued a brief statement, saying, "I have nothing with which to reproach myself. I have told the truth in the interest of justice."

Writing to a friend at the Justice Department, Calvin Cobb ruminated: "The President was insistent with me that I should labor with Governor Gooding to the end that no criticism could be made of the fairness of the Haywood trial. I think I leaned over backward in this respect and spoiled a good hanging."

Interviews with the jurors revealed that, from the start of their deliberations, they'd leaned heavily toward acquittal; given the judge's instructions, a majority felt the state hadn't provided sufficient corroboration of Orchard's testimony. Their tiny chamber (twelve feet by twenty) on the top floor's northeast corner was a "firebox," drawing the sun's rays virtually all day. Eager to end their ordeal, they stripped off coats and neckties and got down to business right away.

On their first ballot, eight favored acquittal, two (the rancher Gilman and the farmer Powell) favored conviction, and two (the ex-carpenter Burns and Gess, the foreman) abstained. After lunch, a second ballot brought Gess into the majority. It was Burns who'd asked for the exhibits, and after examining them, he swung to the minority. On a fourth ballot, taken after supper, the mercurial Burns switched back again, making it ten to two. And there it stayed all night. At 3:30 a.m., when they took a fifth ballot, it hadn't budged. In the hours just before dawn, as some jurors napped and others chatted desulto-rily, there was idle talk of a compromise on second-degree murder, but eventually all agreed it must be either first-degree or acquittal.

At six o'clock, O. V. Sebern, the fifty-two-year-old rancher from Merid-ian—the last juror chosen—weighed in with an impassioned speech. "What have you got against this man?" he asked the two holdouts. "You have not a thing but the testimony of Orchard. Would you hang a man on the evidence of that wretch? Why, I would not hang the devil on his word."

E. G. Leipheimer of the *Butte Evening News* claimed he could hear Sebern's voice carrying through the open window as he shouted, "I will rot in this hell hole here before I have the blood of this man on my shoulders."

Finally, a sixth ballot brought Powell—who'd been rereading the judge's instructions—into the majority. Still convinced of Haywood's guilt, Gilman would have stood firm "until doom's day" if another had stood with him. But, deserted by his only ally, he capitulated. "Boys," he said, "I'll not hang out any longer; put me down for not guilty."

What, finally, had earned Bill Haywood his freedom when all but a few had thought him doomed? In the postmortems that rattled on for days, it was generally agreed that the judge's instructions were the most important factor. In press interviews, at least nine jurors—Gess, McBean, Gilman, Clark, Powell, Messecar, Schrivener, Smith, and Sebern—mentioned the instruc-tions as significant. Indeed, in months to come, the choleric Gooding would wander around the state denouncing Fremont Wood for caving in to defense pressure. Though this was characteristically hyperbolic, it does seem that Wood, in his effort to show critics on the left that he could be fair, had leaned over backwards on reasonable doubt and corroboration—though his admonitions on these points were rooted in good law. Second was probably Clarence Darrow's oratory. His eleven-hour closing argument, like Borah's, was surely among his best performances. Not everyone liked it. One of Darrow's close friends in Chicago wrote another friend: "Darrow's speech would have been very strong as an appeal at a public meeting called to arouse the prejudices of his hearers, but as a plea before a jury I don't see how it failed to beat his client." John Nugent, who sat only a few places away at the defense table, also thought Darrow's emphasis on Socialism, class struggle, and violence would convict Haywood. In fact, it appears that many of these Idaho farmers had been deeply moved by his determination to fight for "the poor, the weak, and the weary." As Sam Russell stepped down from the jury box, he rushed up to the defense attorney and said, "I want to speak to you, Mr. Darrow. I liked the way you handled this case. I believe you are honest and what you said went a great way with me." Other jurors told the advocate how deeply his closing had moved them.

Though Darrow's closing deserves substantial credit, nothing he did in the courtroom can compare to his master stroke of persuading Steve Adams —whether by bribe, threat, or otherwise—to renege on his confession, thus depriving the state of that corroboration. Given the emphasis Judge Wood had put on such independent corroboration, this was an important—perhaps the *critical*—hole in the prosecution case.

Orchard's confession apparently did the prosecution as much harm as good. Many jurors apparently found it impossible to take the word of this mass killer. "Did you believe Orchard's testimony?" Russell was asked. "Believe it?" the juror exclaimed. "I thought he was simply testifying to save his own neck."

On the other hand, Haywood did himself a lot of good with his forceful yet good-natured performance in the witness box. Even Oscar King Davis—no friend of Socialism—wrote after the verdict "in praise of that quality of manly assertion of his own principles and stout persistence in them which is the most conspicuous trait of Haywood's character."

There were darker suspicions about what lay behind the startling verdict. Some weeks before, Frank Perkins, the energetic reporter of the *Portland Evening Telegram*, had discovered that the wives of several jurors had gone to the authorities deeply concerned about what might happen to their husbands if they helped to hang Haywood. Mrs. Thomas Gess, the foreman's wife, showed up at Judge Wood's house on June 17, demanding to see the judge on this matter, but was turned away by security men. Mrs. Levi Smith, the article said, feared that angry miners would blow up her house if Mr. Smith helped convict Haywood. A third wife had become nearly hysterical after a palmist predicted the disasters that might follow a guilty verdict. The jurors, to be sure, were sequestered and thus perhaps insulated from the anxiety among their families. But if such fears filtered through to any number of the jurors it might have helped nudge them toward acquittal. According to one of Borah's biographers, a juror whom Borah knew told him months later that he "had the guts" to risk his own life in voting for conviction but that he had a wife and children to think about.

An unconfirmed report after the trial said that, following Orchard's testimony, two of the jurors had asked permission to carry firearms. If true—and it seems curious—it would tend to support suspicions that the jurors were afraid for their lives if they voted for, or seemed to be leaning toward, conviction. Viewed from this perspective, the trial's crowning irony was that the more the jurors believed the prosecution's case that the WFM slaughtered its enemies, the less likely they'd be to incur that wrath by voting for conviction.

Then there were rumors about jury tampering or outright bribery. A rumor circulated in the Idanha lobby that "the jury had been bought," Oscar King Davis recalled years later. "Whether there was ever any foundation for such talk or not, I never knew." Edgar Lee Masters, Darrow's former partner, who wished him ill, also wrote later, "The newspaper grape vine is that Darrow bribed the Steunenberg jury." A Denver steel executive wrote Borah, "It is believed by many men here in Denver who are prominent in business, and in a positon to know of the workings of this organization [the WFM], that the court was in some way reached by their influence." After the prosecutors failed once more to convict Steve Adams of murder in the Coeur d'Alenes, an embittered Hawley told Jacob Fillius, "The fault was entirely with the jury. There are four classes of people here who are bound it seems to stand with the defendants, viz: The Socialists; the people who are afraid; those who are bought up, and the criminal element. It seems impossible to keep these people from the jury." The prosecution had been on the lookout for such efforts. "Of course," McParland had written on May 13, "we are aware if the parties working for the defense can approach any of the talismen [*sic*] they will do so."

The rumors after the trial focused on the bailiff John A. McGinty. One of four bailiffs Judge Wood had appointed to watch the jury—McGinty and William Bryon during the day, Frank Breshears and Thomas H. Pence at night—McGinty was one of those political retainers who congregate in the shadows of important men, performing a host of services, some legitimate, some illegitimate. For many years, he'd been a familiar figure around the law office of Fremont Wood and Edgar Wilson. Through his close friendship with Wilson, a former congressman, he'd been named Boise's police magistrate, serving in that capacity from 1901 to 1904. The prosecutors wondered whether McGinty's connection to Wilson and Wilson's former partnership and long friendship with Wood accounted for his appointment to this sensitive post.

In any case, one night during the Haywood trial—according to C. P. Connolly—Boise police encountered John McGinty near the home of a "certain notorious jury fixer from Chicago," who'd been present in Boise since the start of the trial. When the policemen stopped McGinty, he claimed to have been down at Judge Wood's house, but this proved not to be the case. After the trial, doubts were raised about McGinty's neutrality. According to one source, McGinty had congratulated the jurors after Haywood's acquittal. When Ed Meek, a citizen of Canyon County, complained to Hawley about McGinty, the attorney conceded that the prosecution had been "very much dissatisfied with him as bailiff," but Judge Wood had expressed full confidence in him. Still later, allegations were made that McGinty had received $6,000 to put the jury fixer in touch with one or more of the jurors. It was said that McGinty, a widower since 1905, had run off with a woman from Baker City, Oregon, on whom he spent these ill-gotten gains.

The Edgar Wilson connection also figured in the appointment of Thomas Pence as one of the other bailiffs. Pence was said to be a cousin of Wilson's. His wife was named the matron and cook in charge of the Konrad house, where the jury resided. The jurors raved about her cooking. One talesman, later removed from the jury, told the *Statesman* that Mrs. Pence was "an artist at the range. I'd rather board at the jurors' home than at any hotel I ever stopped at, and I stayed three days once at the Dewey Palace in Nampa and one day at the Palmer House in Chicago." But the prosecution ultimately had reason to question her neutrality.*

Then there was the story told by Charlie Siringo in his memoirs: some minutes before the verdict came down, he'd encountered the defense attorney Peter Breen—where else?—in the lobby of the Idanha. The two men had gotten to knew each other in the Coeur d'Alenes in 1892, when Breen was a leader of the miners union and Siringo a Pinkerton undercover man. Although they were on opposite sides of the struggle then and now, they found that their temperaments were compatible and they liked each other's company. From his couch at the Idanha, Breen ventured a prediction: "It will either be an acquittal or a hung jury."

How did he know? Siringo asked.

Because one of the jurors "could be depended on," Breen replied.

They then walked together over toward the courthouse to find out for themselves. As they strolled across a grassy park, they saw the jury marching away from the courthouse, apparently having rendered their verdict.

"Charlie," said Breen, "do you see the tall man in the lead?"

Yes, said Siringo, he did.

"Enough said."

Siringo doesn't give us the juror's name, only that he was "the former resident of Cheyenne, Wyoming, who was on the jury which convicted stock detective Tom Horn."

That was O. V. Sebern, the last man selected for the jury and the one who'd delivered the impassioned speech for acquittal that swayed the two remaining holdouts.

Siringo claimed that he gave this information to James McParland, who'd checked it out and determined that Sebern had "frightened the jurymen who were for conviction by telling them that if they convicted the defendant, they would meet a dreadful fate. This had the desired effect by giving the jurymen 'cold feet' and brought about an acquittal."

Siringo's memoirs are generally pretty accurate, but there are reasons to doubt this account. If Sebern had been bribed by the defense, he would have been instructed to get on the jury at all costs, but he sought unsuccessfully to be excused on the ground that his farm needed his attention. If Darrow knew Sebern was a bought juror, why was he so utterly disconsolate as he awaited the verdict? He was capable, to be sure, of putting on an act, but some of the best reporters in the courtroom were convinced he genuinely dreaded the outcome. Moreover, no matter how friendly Breen and Siringo had become, it

---

* After Pettibone was acquitted in January 1908, a *Statesman* reporter wrote that he'd overheard Mrs. Pence welcome a juror home to the Konrad house with these words: "I want to congratulate you: fine." Mrs. Pence and the juror to whom she allegedly said this both heatedly denied the story (*Collier's*, January 25, 1908; *Idaho Daily Statesman*, January 5, 1908; *Evening Capital News*, January 7, 1908; *Idaho Daily Statesman*, January 8, 1907).

seems unlikely that a partisan like Breen would have shared such a secret at that moment, when it might have been brought to Judge Wood's attention. Finally, if McParland had investigated Sebern and discovered his threats, surely he would have brought them to the court's attention; so far as we know, he did not.

Nonetheless, the story throws an appropriate light on Sebern, who—according to most accounts—did play an important role in the jury's deliberations. That was no surprise. Ida Crouch-Hazlett had called him "well-dressed, well-educated, the most intelligent man on the jury." Wade Parks, writing in the *Industrial Union Bulletin,* thought he had "the strongest face of any one of the jurors, and those who watched him throughout the trial believed the other eleven would have to agree with him or there would be no verdict."

Still, if his name hadn't come up after both sides had exhausted their peremptory challenges, it seems unlikely that he would have made the jury. After all, he'd admitted during the examination that he was on the jury that had sent the notorious gunman—and ex-Pinkerton—Tom Horn to his death. Defense attorneys didn't want a juror who'd voted to convict a man, and certainly not one who had helped put a man on the gallows. Moreover, Operative 21's report listed Sebern as no good for the defense. That would have encouraged the prosecution to take him but must have raised all sorts of warning flags to the defense. Yet Judge Wood had not permitted extensive examination of Sebern on his previous jury duty, and thus—without a peremptory challenge—Darrow and Richardson were forced to accept him.

Throughout the trial, apparently, Sebern was one of several jurors whom the prosecution counted on to swing the verdict their way and one of the jurors the defense feared most. This points toward a curious aspect of the verdict. In a letter to Jacob Fillius, written after the verdict, Hawley said, "Two or three that we depended upon absolutely and had the best reasons that we could absolutely depend upon them, stood for the defense at the final outcome." Sebern was certainly among the unpleasant surprises for the prosecution. Another was probably Jamie Robertson, the seventy-two-year-old Scotsman with whom Frank Steunenberg had boarded during his first term as governor.

By the same token, A. E. Thomas wrote on the day of the verdict: "Perhaps the most extraordinary thing about this extraordinary verdict is the fact that the four men who first stood for a conviction were the men who above all were relied upon by the defense and feared by the state." That would be Gilman, Burns, Gess, and Powell. We do not know Operative 21's reports for the first three, but for Powell his notation was indeed "O.K. for Defense."

If the jurors on whom the prosecution most relied led the charge for acquittal, and the ones on whom the defense relied were the strongest for conviction, what does this tell us? Perhaps that the jurors set aside their biases to weigh the evidence honestly and found it wanting. Perhaps that the jury-vetting process of that era wasn't very reliable. Or perhaps that Operative 21 and some of his deputies were playing a more complicated game than either the prosecution or the defense knew. Given the prosecution's utter confidence of prevailing, as reflected in Hawley's letter to Fillius, one wonders whether the operative—so highly valued by McParland, Hawley, Gooding, and Theodore Roosevelt—had himself been "turned" by the resourceful Darrow, or whether, unlikely though it may seem, he'd been a double agent from the start.

McParland, sequestered in his suite at the Idanha, refused all comment, but in Chicago a spokesman for the agency told the *Record-Herald:* "The Pinkerton agency is not concerned in the verdict given in Boise. We were engaged by the State of Idaho to do certain work. We did it and there our interest in the matter ends.... We represented only the state and had no interest in the Mine Owners Association."

William G. Evans, the Denver industrialist who'd contributed heavily to the Colorado fund for the trial, feigned indifference, telling a reporter that day: "The case against Moyer and Haywood was purely an Idaho affair and the result can have little effect on Colorado labor conditions."

That afternoon, the president of the United States wrote a letter to his ambassador to the Court of St. James, Whitelaw Reid, in which he said: "There has been a gross miscarriage of justice, to my mind, out in Idaho, in the acquittal of Haywood. I suppose the jury was terrorized, but it is not a pleasant matter from any standpoint."

Frank Steunenberg's widow, Belle, had no immediate comment, but months later—after George Pettibone won his own acquittal—she wrote Hawley enclosing a quotation from Isaiah 59.14: "Surely judgment is turned [away] backward, justice standeth afar off. For truth is fallen in the street, and equity cannot enter."

Emma Goldman, Alexander Berkman, and Hippolyte Havel—three of the nation's preeminent anarchists—couldn't resist rubbing it in. They wired the president: "Undesirable citizens victorious. Rejoice!" The *Denver Republican* couldn't resist a slap back: "Wretches Insult President by Wire" was the headline.

In Butte, Montana, that night, seven thousand miners and other unionists marched four abreast through the streets, to the martial airs of the Boston and Montana Band, brandishing flags and placards bearing Haywood's familiar one-eyed visage. The parade was one of the largest ever held in the city.

Some Socialists, gratified as they were by the acquittal, regretted that the movement had been cheated of a glorious martyr. In Hempstead, Long Island, Alice Junsby wrote Victor Berger in Milwaukee: "Were you not over-joyed at the verdict for Haywood? I thought it a great triumph for the labor party. If the unfortunate man had been sentenced to death and executed it would have been still better for the party, but it is too much to ask the sacrifice of a human life." No, certainly too much—and yet, "It would have been very serious for Roosevelt if the man had been hung. I believe he knew that and exerted his influence privately to get him off."

In Boise, Clarence Darrow vowed, on Haywood's behalf, to sue *McClure's* for libel, presumably alleging that the first two installments of Orchard's confession, which had run in the magazine's July and August issues, had held Haywood responsible for murder. Now that a court had declared him innocent, Darrow reasoned, the door was open for Haywood to collect damages.*

The verdict had shocked the prosecutors, who—only hours before—had been confidently predicting conviction. Young Owen Van Duyn remained standing in the courtroom, looking as if he'd been stunned by a mallet. Hawley heard the verdict as he stood in the doorway of the courtroom. Turning on his heel, he banged through the door into the hallway, where he encountered Governor Gooding. "They looked at each other in silence for a moment," the *Rocky Mountain News* reported, "and then, without a word, slowly left the building." Hawley had been through a lot of verdicts—some he'd won and some he'd lost—but never had he been so exhausted and heartsick. Back at his office in the Odd Fellows Block, the first letter he wrote was to Jacob Fillius in Denver: "I have just come from the Court House where I went to receive the verdict, and I do not know who was the most astonished by the verdict, our side or the defense." †

---

* The fear of a libel suit had bedeviled Hugo Münsterberg back in Boston as he read accounts of the defense's case. The professor, so obtuse on some questions, was strangely prescient on this one. On July 14, he'd written S. S. McClure: "The favorable impression which Haywood made on the witness stand suggests that the jury may vote him acquittal. Till now I had expected disagreement of the jury. Of course, that does not change in the least my scientific convictions. Yet, what is the situation of the magazine if it comes out with an article denouncing Haywood as guilty when the jury has been unanimous for acquittal? I am no lawyer, but might there not be trouble inspite of the scientific correctness? I want to say therefore that I certainly do not object if you want to withdraw my essay ... or perhaps you may postpone the Orchard paper for a later number till you know the verdict." That is just what McClure did, pushing the article back from September to October and including a sentence acknowledging Haywood's acquittal (Münsterberg to McClure, July 14, 1907; Münsterberg, "Third Degree," 618).

† Some days later, Hawley wrote again to Fillius. The letter in his letterbook has been badly damaged by water and is nearly illegible, but these words can be deciphered: "We had in that [the Haywood] case, the very jury that we wanted and had no more doubt of the result than I had of getting up in the morning. I am figuring though as to the causes that led up to the verdict and think I will know all about it in a very short time. I am satisfied that we were jobbed by the men in whom we had placed the most explicit confidence, and upon whom the necessity of the case compelled us to rely" (Hawley Letterbook no. 65, Idaho State Historical Society, 568–69). It isn't clear here just whom he means: the Pinkertons, perhaps, who had failed to supply the corroboration they'd promised, or individual jurors who had somehow been frightened, bribed, or both. But in the last week of December 1907, Hawley gave quite a different explanation for the verdict. Writing to Bulkeley Wells, he said he had told Fremont Wood "in plain words that it was [Wood's] instructions [to the jury] that lost us the Haywood case; this is absolutely true, because my information from ten of the jurymen in that case satisfies me of the correctness of the statement" (Hawley to Wells, December 22, 1907; Hawley Letterbook no. 65, 143).

Hawley wrote several more letters that day, including a perfunctory note enclosing two bills to Governor Gooding, a letter to Bulkeley Wells ("The unexpected has happened.... It seems impossible"), and then, in late afternoon, yet another to Jacob Fillius ("All of the attorneys for the prosecution have just had a consultation with the Governor and McParland and resolved to fight this matter out, and proceed with the trials of Pettibone and Moyer"). Nominally, Hawley reported to Frank Gooding; in fact, it was to Jacob Fillius that he felt obliged to report that day—to Fillius and the money behind him.

But where had Borah been when the verdict was handed down? The sheriff had been unable to reach him at either his home or his office—a strange circumstance in a trial of this importance. His absence gave rise to all sorts of rumors. As a womanizer of legendary proportions, he was said by some to have spent the night with a woman not his wife.

An hour or so after the announcement, as miners, store clerks, laborers, and waitresses surged through downtown Boise, "singing, waving, smiling, crying aloud their joy over the victory"—"a solid jam of humanity on every street"—and *Statesman* newsboys hawked a 9:30 a.m. extra headlined "Haywood Found Not Guilty," Ruby Darrow happened to spot Borah standing in a recessed doorway leading up to his office on Main Street. He was in his characteristic pose—one shoulder against the wall, hands in pocket, feet crossed, hat pulled down over one eye—and he looked very "alone, abandoned." She thought he was "the most downcast man I ever saw."

The next day, at the White House, the president stood ready at last to act on the Borah matter. To William Allen White, he wrote: "I can say now that I will see you with Bonaparte at once if you come on." But he was "very doubtful" that Borah ought to come. The president reminded White that he'd been subjected to bitter attacks "because of what I did in trying to back up the party of law and order, of elementary civilization, in Idaho, against the thugs and murderers who have found their typical representation in Moyer and Haywood, in Pettibone and Debs.... I took the first opportunity to range myself definitely publicly on behalf of the action that Borah was taking [in the Haywood trial]." Thus, the president thought, "to have Borah come on here in person to meet the Attorney General and myself would create a most undesirable impression." He urged White to come by himself, along with "some good lawyer competent to speak for Borah," to meet with the attorney general and him on August 9 at Sagamore Hill, his estate at Oyster Bay, on the North Shore of Long Island.

Still worried about holding his own in give-and-take with the forceful president, White wired Borah, renewing that plaint: "I am the poorest talker in the world and he is the best. I never think of the answer until an hour after. We must have somebody who [is] quick on the come back."

To Borah—brooding over his defeat in the Haywood case and nearly desperate about his approaching fraud trial—the Sagamore Hill meeting must have seemed like life's pivotal moment. Everything he'd worked for this past decade—the glorious future so widely predicted for him—hinged on White's ability to win the president over. But communicating with White by letter and telegram was cumbersome. A private code—"Hilton" for Roosevelt, "Biggsby" for White, "Mosely" for Borah, "Davis" for Bonaparte—ensured confidentiality, but Borah yearned for a long talk with his old friend. Abruptly, he decided on a last-minute dash to Colorado for a clandestine meeting.

He took a train via Salt Lake City, telling reporters he was on his way to Cripple Creek to "look up evidence in the Pettibone case." Borah did go to Cripple Creek, made a show of consulting public records, then nipped fifteen miles over the mountain to Manitou, where he appeared on White's doorstep "wan and anxious." For several hours, the senator and the editor sat on the wide veranda, mapping their strategy for White's meeting with the president.

Ultimately, they added two men to the delegation: John W. Yerkes—a former commissioner of internal revenue, now a partner in Hamilton, Colbert, Yerkes and Hamilton, attorneys in Washington, D.C.—who henceforth represented Borah in the Washington end of the case, and C. P. Connolly, who'd covered the trial for *Collier's* and was now back at his home in Missoula, Montana.

Connolly's involvement had a curious inception. When S. S. McClure arrived in Boise in mid-June, he thought Borah guilty of timber fraud, but something happened there to persuade him otherwise—probably a chat with the persuasive Borah—and he'd asked White to write an article on the situation for *McClure's*. White felt his friendship with Borah precluded the assignment, but he hungered to know what was going on in Boise. So he asked Mark Sullivan, an editor at *Collier's*, to ask Connolly to investigate the case, Sullivan, in turn, would pass the information on to White. A few weeks later, back came Connolly's reply: "Have made best investigation possible: believe there is no foundation in fact for indictment, and have learned facts which I believe exonerate party. Believe it to have been secured through officials actuated by personal malice."*

As White added weight to the Sagamore Hill delegation, Connolly came to mind. Borah liked the idea and promised to reimburse the reporter for all his expenses, later sending him three hundred dollars. As Connolly prepared to leave Montana, he wrote Borah, underlining their solidarity: "The [Haywood] verdict was one of the greatest surprises I have ever run up against. Don't let the matter unduly annoy you. You, at least, came out of the whole affair with honor, and with a fame which it is given to few men to achieve in

---

* Connolly's article, which appeared in *Collier's* four months later, reads as though Borah was the principal—perhaps his only major—source ("Little Drama").

so short a while."* Later he assured the senator, "I feel as much interested in your welfare as I would in that of my own kin."

On the evening of Thursday, August 8, White, Connolly, and Yerkes converged on the Manhattan Hotel in midtown Manhattan, where they met for several hours with Joseph G. Dudley, a Buffalo attorney who'd grown up in Eau Claire, thus knew the timber barons, and had represented the Barber Lumber Company along with Borah. They reviewed "the entire matter" and planned the next day's strategy for several hours before turning in past midnight.

At 10:15 on Friday morning, White, Connolly, and Yerkes left for Oyster Bay. By noon they were meeting with the president, the attorney general, and the president's secretary, William Loeb, at the Roosevelts' rambling twenty-three-room Victorian country home, which looked out across green fields and woodland belts toward the bay and the sound beyond. The president may have greeted his western visitors in the great North Room, with its giant elk heads (in the antlers of one of which nestled the sword and campaign hat that Roosevelt had worn at San Juan Hill), the heads of two bison he'd shot in North Dakota, and, on the mantelpiece, the Frederic Remington bronze *The Bronco Buster,* which the officers and men of the Rough Riders had given him when the regiment was mustered out. It would have been too warm, of course, to build a fire in one of the house's eight stone hearths. Most of the afternoon the men sat in high-backed rockers on the broad wooden porch that wrapped the rear of the house and faced the sound, on which the Fall River packet boats steamed back and forth.

Over lunch and through the afternoon, the group reviewed the situation in Boise, the methods used by the U.S. attorney in Idaho, Norman Ruick, to obtain Borah's indictment, the alleged ties between the defense in the Haywood case and the Borah prosecution. White and Yerkes made powerful pleas on Borah's behalf for a Justice Department order dismissing his indictment. The State of Idaho, they argued, was "entitled to be represented in the United States Senate by the man it had chosen; that no commonwealth should be deprived of the services of a Senator except upon the most certain grounds," but that Borah "would never walk into the Senate chamber and take the oath with this indictment pending." It would be almost impossible, though, they added, to secure a nonguilty verdict from a jury at this time, because of the much-disputed position Borah had taken at the Haywood trial.

As expected, Bonaparte stoutly resisted the notion. An aristocrat by birth and in deportment, "too proud to be bossed and too cynical to be fooled," he

---

* Though an able attorney and conscientious journalist, Connolly was relentlessly ambitious and eager to use his contacts with eminent Americans to advance his own career. On November 8, 1907, he wrote William Allen White, saying, "I would like very much to be private secretary to President Roosevelt.... Our meeting at Oyster Bay last August justifies me in writing to you in the matter. Frankly, what do you think of the proposition?

had "a distaste for politics and slight respect for politicians." Perhaps he recognized the quintessential politician in Borah, for he profoundly distrusted the man. But he shrewdly put it differently: dismissing the indictment, he argued, could only harm both the president and Borah, prompting suspicion of improper favors to a Republican senator. Bonaparte clearly felt there was a prima facie case for Borah's guilt. As attorney for the Barber Lumber Company, he said, Borah must have known that the entry men had agreed in advance to sell their land to the company.

Connolly and White quickly rose to their friend's defense. If that were true, Connolly put in, then every lawyer in the West was guilty. Stressing the confidential relationship between lawyer and client, he argued that any lawyer might become embroiled in his client's questionable dealings without any stain on his own character.

Roosevelt firmly supported his attorney general. Dismissal of the indictment was out of the question; it would do neither him nor Borah any good.* Then, in remarks highly complimentary to Borah, he made clear that he wanted to do what he could for the senator. In the remaining hours, the two sides hammered out a series of mutually acceptable steps to ensure that Borah's trial would be as fair as possible and to insulate him from Ruick's vindictive pursuit.

The delegation returned to New York by 6:00 p.m. That evening they briefed Dudley. Then, from a writing desk in the library of the Century Association, White gave Borah a summary of the meeting's results. "We didn't get what we went after," he wrote, but they'd gotten some important concessions, which Yerkes and Dudley thought in the long run might be better: they'd "got the attorney general to understand that the President believes in you"; an "absolute promise" that Borah's case would be severed from that of the other defendants; the promise of "an immediate trial in September"; the word of both the president and the attorney general that Judge Frank Dietrich, sitting in James Beatty's place, would draw the jury and not U.S. Marshal Ruel Rounds; the president's promise that he or Bonaparte would write Dietrich and consult with him on the best way to offer immunity to grand jurors who would give affidavits as to what Ruick had said in the jury room; a promise that if Ruick committed any gross improprieties in the grand jury, he would be dismissed; and, White added, "I have the President's personal word that upon your acquittal he will write you a letter for the people of Idaho that will leave no doubt as to his attitude. I believe we have done much good. I have at least done my very best." †

---

* The president had made up his mind on that question before the meeting began. In a letter to Bonaparte on August 2, he wrote: "I do not want to tell Connolly and White in advance, what of course I so strongly feel, that . . . we have gone just as far as we can with due propriety go in adjourning the case."

† Ten years later, White wrote Borah: "I have always felt that the best single day's work I ever did in my life was that day I put in for you down at Oyster Bay" (W. Johnson, *White's America*, 164).

Connolly was less sanguine. Four days later, from New York's Hotel Seville, he informed Borah he'd "not had heart to write you, knowing that matters did not eventuate as perhaps you anticipated—at least hoped." The president "seemed to feel he has done all that he could conscientiously do—namely, speedy trial, a severance, and later Mr. Ruick's head." Bonaparte "seemed to be (in a way) poisoned against you, not violently perhaps." Wishing Borah good luck at the trial, Connolly trusted he would "meet the opposition with a good stout heart."

Borah wasn't feeling stout at all. Clearly disappointed with the Oyster Bay agreement, as it was known among insiders, he struggled to see the bright side. Things might work out "if they carry out the understanding," he wrote. "The only thing that bothers me, is how under the law they will be able to carry out some of the matters, especially with reference to the jury."

The senator was prescient. Over the next six weeks, the attorney general —plainly suspicious of Borah—dragged his feet in implementing the agreement. This drove Borah wild and he frantically called in all the chits he'd accumulated that summer among the trial press corps.

No politician then practicing in North America—with the possible exception of the man in the White House—had mastered the burgeoning art of public relations more fully than Idaho's new senator. Blessed with natural charm and warmth, Borah had brought them to bear on the editors and reporters of the *Statesman,* then, during the Haywood trial, on "some of the Republican newspaper boys" from back East, notably the inner circle of Kennedy and Egan from the AP, Davis of the *Times,* Thomas of the *Sun.* As they ate, drank, talked politics, and laughed through those long summer evenings, Borah won some valuable new friends in the court of public opinion.

The elite reporters, who should have known better, were eager to be used. "If there is anything I can do please call on me," Mart Egan had written Borah from Sheridan, Wyoming, on July 22. On July 31, he wrote the senator his reaction to the Haywood verdict: " 'I'm damned' is about all the comment I can make on the case. Woods' charge was favorable to Haywood but at that I cannot see where the jury got rid of the things that make it a moral, if not legal, certainty that Haywood abetted those murders. Haywood, Darrow, Richardson and the rest are the luckiest people on earth.... I have not said anything to you about the personal side of this trial, but I guess you know how I feel."

Borah knew all right, and when the Oyster Bay meeting was over, he asked Egan to go to Washington and intervene with Secretary of War William Howard Taft and others. About to launch his legal career in Sheridan, Egan was preparing for one last journalistic venture—covering Taft's trip to the Far East that fall for the *New York Herald*—Taft having secured the choice assignment for his friend. Now Egan was delighted to use his special relationship with Taft on the senator's behalf. "Gladly undertake trip," he wired

Borah from Chicago. "Instruct me fully here care Assd Press." With two hundred dollars in "expenses" advanced by Borah, he was off to Washington.

Several days later, he reported: "I started out at once tackling Taft first. I found him very friendly and ready to do anything possible. We had merely a general talk . . . but we are to walk out into the country at five tomorrow and thrash the whole thing out. . . . I am going to see it through with all the emotions of a bull at a gate." The next day, reporting progress with Taft, Egan had difficulty distinguishing his own interests from the senator's. "I insisted that in all the circumstances we were entitled now to a disclosure of the case against us."

Egan also intervened with John Wilkie, director of the Secret Service. Wilkie was out of town when Egan arrived, so the correspondent wrote him, warning that Borah was the victim of a conspiracy founded on "a union between the opposing side in a political and personal feud and the interests behind Moyer, Haywood and Pettibone."

Borah's friends were probably justified in asserting that, whatever the objective grounds for an indictment, a personal feud lay at the root of the case. The retiring U.S. district judge, James Beatty, who'd aggressively lobbied with the attorney general for prosecution of Borah and his codefendants,* was a disappointed Republican candidate for the very Senate seat Borah now occupied (Borah called him "a superannuated imbecile who was filled with venom and spleen over his political disappointments which no one ever took seriously except himself"). Were Borah to be convicted of the misdemeanor with which he was charged, there was nothing in federal or state law requiring him to forfeit his office, but he would probably feel compelled to resign. Beatty may have harbored the hope that Idaho's legislators would then have turned to him (though Beatty had resigned in a letter to the attorney general on February 19, he remained on the bench pending appointment of his successor). Ruick was also a longtime enemy of Borah's. Moreover, in 1904 he'd organized a railroad corporation and tried to strike a deal with the Barber Lumber Company to carry lumber from its sawmill to Boise, only to be rudely rebuffed. Thus, he had two grounds for personal animus. Finally, Ruel Rounds was a "ward politician" of the old school, known to friends and enemies alike as Rocky, a tough infighter said to despise Borah, the high-minded reformer. His apparent manipulation of the jury rolls had produced a grand jury that included a surprising number of Borah's enemies—notably Frank Eastman, the son of the man Borah considered his most virulent enemy in Boise, a banker and stalwart of the old Republican order named Hosea B. Eastman.

The argument for collusion between those out to get Borah for personal

---

* In March 1907, for example, Beatty cabled the attorney general: "Timber fraud investigation cannot affect murder trial. Nothing be made public until after trial. Investigation promising great success in exposing glaring frauds. Delay would be serious mistake" (William Loeb to Frank Gooding, March 25, 1907).

or factional reasons and the defense in the Haywood case is more problematic. Though they sparred testily at times, a relationship of mutual respect,
even affection, had developed between Darrow and Borah during the trial. In
the week following the verdict, Darrow wrote Borah two notes from trains
hurtling across the western prairies: the first asking his help in getting the
Statesman to treat him fairly in his war of words with "that ass formerly my
associate," Edmund Richardson, and ending "with highest regards, your
friend C. S. Darrow"; the second saying, "Don't fail to let me know if there is
anything I can possibly do," almost certainly a veiled reference to the timber
case. On September 13, in Spokane, Darrow went public in praising Borah's
"integrity," declaring his firm belief that the senator was "guiltless of complicity" in timber fraud.

But all that came *after* Haywood's acquittal. Darrow was a fierce competitor and it is conceivable that he helped stoke those very charges of fraud to
unsettle the prosecutor and to blacken the name of Steunenberg. Even more
likely is that some of his colleagues—notably Nugent, Whitsell, and Miller
—who had no particular love for Borah, may have taken the lead in such an
effort. (Later, Darrow told Borah that the defense felt "some satisfaction" over
his indictment, hoping it would put a crimp in his prosecutorial zeal.) The
Pinkerton reports of Miller and Whitsell's conferring with Ruick during the
spring certainly added fuel to this notion. Eventually, Borah's forces produced
an affidavit by one George Y. Wallace of Salt Lake City, who said he'd met
Miller on a train from Salt Lake to Butte, and over several whiskies and two
quarts of champagne at a hotel bar in Butte the WFM lawyer told him
the federation had paid $15,000—presumably to Ruick—to procure Borah's
indictment. But a federal investigation of that charge turned up no corroboration, and it was probably a fabrication.

All summer, Borah tried to undermine Ruick's case by spreading nasty
stories about him—that he'd begun political life as "a howling anarchist,"
become a Republican "for revenue," and was a "traitor now within its fold";
that he'd beaten his wife and been, for many years, "a drunken loafer"; that
he'd welshed on his debts, been indicted for perjury, and used technicalities to
escape court judgments; that—in short—he was "utterly unconscionable and
absolutely devoid of every principle which ordinarily obtains among decent
men."

Most important, he sought to show that Ruick had obtained his indictment by bullying the Boise grand jury. To that end, Borah enlisted yet
another prominent member of the Haywood trial press corps: Oscar King
Davis, about to become chief of the *New York Times*'s Washington bureau.
Borah had cultivated Davis in Boise, and Davis, in turn, had lavished praise
on the senator's final argument. "Terrific, crushing, destroying, these are the
words that come nearest to describing the tremendous power of the man in
argument," he wrote.

Moreover, the *Times* man had conducted his own investigation into the Borah indictment, which he regarded as an "unbelievable outrage, without the least color of foundation." His research suggested not only that Rocky Rounds had manipulated the grand jury's membership so as to include men "notoriously bitter" toward Borah but that the U.S. attorney—in a gross violation of grand jury protocol—had virtually demanded that the jurors indict the senator. "If I have not been deceived as to the proceedings in the grand jury room," Davis wrote the president,

> the [U.S.] attorney admitted to the jurors that the evidence presented at that time did not support an indictment, but he assured them that it was the earnest desire of the department and the administration to get the big men first; that Borah was one of the most conspicuous men implicated, and that although the evidence was insufficient, within thirty days he would have secured enough in addition more than amply to justify indictment. On that assurance, the indictment was voted 12 to 10. Over night, however, some of the jurors changed their minds, and in the morning requested the district attorney to retire, so that they might reconsider the action of the afternoon before. Mr. Ruick refused to leave the room, and instead made a speech of more than an hour's duration, in which he argued for the indictment and repeated his assurance that it was the earnest desire of the administration to have it. Thus he practically coerced the grand jury into returning the indictment.

During August and September, Davis assiduously pushed this story in Washington's official circles, writing two letters to Roosevelt, one to Taft, and one to Bonaparte, holding a number of meetings with Yerkes, Egan, and A. E. Thomas (who'd also lent his support to the embattled senator), and sending a stream of letters to Borah that kept him up-to-date. So busy was the *Times* man on Borah's business, it's difficult to imagine how he found time to report for his newspaper.

Even the strenuous efforts of Borah's press pals couldn't untangle the intrigue knotting his case. The senator's relative success at Oyster Bay and his campaign to blacken Ruick's name only prompted fresh exertions by the embattled U.S. attorney, who held that Borah and his powerful friends were frustrating a legitimate prosecution. When Ruick received from Bonaparte the president's instructions to sever Borah from the other defendants and proceed to his trial in September, he replied on August 11: "I regret exceedingly that I should not have been in atttendance on the conference to which your telegram refers, inasmuch as the President could not possibly have been made acquainted with the special conditions which make it impossible to try these cases at the coming September Term of Court or to try Senator Borah separately, without destroying every chance the Government has of success."

Bonaparte, vacationing at Lenox, Massachusetts, in the Berkshire hills, fired back on August 17, saying he understood many of the difficulties confronting Ruick and instructing him to "proceed without delay to carry out the President's orders."

But Ruick would not bow to Washington's authority. On August 23, he wired Bonaparte: "I respectfully request authority to dismiss the Senator out of the indictment at the opening of term September ninth."

By now, angry, exasperated, and perplexed telegrams were flying back and forth between Boise, Washington, Lenox, and Oyster Bay. An alarmed Bonaparte wired the president at Oyster Bay: "Learn from unquestionable source Ruick announces privately his intention to state in open court when dismissing case against Borah you are responsible for inability to prosecute Senator."

At Sagamore Hill, the president seethed at the man he'd appointed U.S. attorney in Boise just three years before, a man who was now about to accuse Roosevelt of a surreptitious deal with a Republican senator—precisely what the president had sought to avoid all summer. "We are dealing with a sharp scamp in the person of Ruick," he wrote Bonaparte in a fierce nine-page letter on August 24. "He has been guilty of trickery all along. His aim has been to try to put us in a bad position, or else to make us accomplices in his knavery. I agree with you that it is imperative now to get rid of Ruick. Just as long as he stays we will have trouble, because he is obviously treacherous and his chief purpose is to cause embarrassment to the administration and to his factional foes in Idaho."

After further consultation with the president, Bonaparte wrote Ruick on August 26, saying that his telegram asking permission to dismiss the charges had come "as a complete and painful surprise" to the Justice Department and the White House. "The Department feels it necessary to relieve you of the conduct of these cases and to seek 'advice upon which it can rely with confidence from other men.' "

With that, he dispatched two high-ranking Justice Department officials to Boise at least temporarily to seize control of the case from the insubordinate Ruick while they took a fresh look at the matter. They were Marsden C. Burch, a special assistant to the attorney general for timber and coal lands investigations based in Denver, and Sylvester R. Rush, another special assistant to the attorney general, from Omaha.

And then came the next in a series of unpleasant surprises for the administration: both Burch and Rush turned out to be fierce supporters of Ruick. In a letter to the attorney general on September 27, Burch said he and Rush agreed that Ruick was "honest, fearless and unprejudiced" but had been "maligned, misrepresented and abused" by the "rabble and mob of hoodlums of the town," about "as complete an outfit of unscrupulous men" as he had ever met. These scoundrels—chief among them Gooding, Borah, and Calvin Cobb—"controlled the press, largely dominated public opinion, [and] had any number of convenient witnesses at hand for any purpose, and were not above using them." Burch and his colleagues grew especially suspicious of Cobb when they learned that the publisher's son Lyon worked for the Barber Lumber Company and the company owned a substantial number of the *Statesman*'s bonds. It was all a bit too incestuous.

Moreover, Burch reported, "we are absolutely unanimous in the belief that Borah is guilty; in fact one of the principal conspirators." But Burch and Rush agreed with Ruick that "the leading spirit and chief organizer of the conspiracy" had been the man assassinated in Caldwell nearly two years before—"a state of circumstances," said Rush, "ruinous to the reputation of ex-Governor Steunenberg."

What grounds were there for such a charge? Ever since he'd ridden to the defense of the embattled mine owners in 1899, there'd been rumors about Frank Steunenberg's financial dealings, particularly his ties to those very owners. That December, the *Caldwell Tribune*—by then an organ of Steunenberg's political foes—noted that the governor had purchased three thousand sheep and three hundred lambs. Since this would have cost some $10,000, the paper wondered how a man said to have been $1,000 in debt when he took office, and with a gubernatorial salary of only $3,000 a year, could have come into this kind of money: "Of course, we all rejoice in the remarkable prosperity which has visited the governor," the *Tribune* concluded, but it wondered whether he wasn't "monkeying with the golden calf." Another oft-repeated rumor was that the mine owners had been so grateful for his intervention they'd handed him $50,000 to finance a campaign for the U.S. Senate. There was no evidence to support this story and it seems most unlikely.

However, there was ample evidence of a close relationship between Steunenberg and at least one major mine owner. Amasa B. Campbell— who with John A. Finch operated the Gem, Standard, Frisco, Hecla, and Tiger-Poorman mines—was a pacesetter among Idaho's mining gentry who established themselves across the state line in a fashionable Spokane neighborhood, sponsored elaborate balls and galas, and had their suits tailored in New York. Known to his peers as Mace, the stocky, outspoken Ohioan had favored rigorous steps to root out union activists in his mines.

After the Bunker Hill mill was blown up in April 1899, he wrote an eastern investor: "We have been having the devil to pay in the Coeur d'Alene Country again.... I am in hopes the government this time will effectually settle this trouble." In July 1899 he had a friendly chat with the governor, applauding his resolve to ensure that "every man, who ever belonged to the Miners Union, and who was connected with these outrages, shall leave the country." Soon he began an active correspondence with Steunenberg, assuring him of the mine owners' abiding gratitude.

Meanwhile, out of office and out of sorts, Steunenberg floundered around, looking for a way to make some money. He couldn't go back to panning gold in the hills, hardly an appropriate endeavor for a former chief executive. He had a bunch of sheep, but they weren't his life's work.

It was then that he ran into an old friend, a state senator named John Kinkaid, who'd heard the story "that the [Boise] Basin country was being overrun by outsiders...that people were coming in there from Wisconsin and Minnesota and from elsewhere and filing on timber under the Timber and Stone Act." Kinkaid was right. Having decimated the great stands of white pine in Minnesota, Wisconsin, and Michigan, the timber lords had turned their eyes toward the great forests of the Northwest. Idaho, in particular, with its impressive stands of white and ponderosa pine, inspired "a great buying rush" between 1899 and 1908. According to the government, much of this activity took the time-honored form of inducing bogus "entry men" to buy up their allotted 160 acres, then deed it to the timber trusts. One of those allegedly engaged in this scam was a "timber cruiser" named Patrick H. Downs, who supplied the entry men with some $22,000 put up by an operator named William F. Sweet. When Sweet ran out of cash, he turned to Kinkaid, who in turn introduced him to his most influential friend—Frank Steunenberg.

Steunenberg was intrigued. Here was a way to make some big money. He and Sweet formed a partnership, each taking a 50 percent interest. Now they needed a new infusion of cash to buy up more timberlands. The governor didn't have it but thought he knew where to get it. On January 24, 1902, he paid a call on Amasa Campbell in Spokane, told him he had "no money," and asked to borrow $15,000. Campbell later testified that he'd told Steunenberg "there would be no difficulty in getting him $15,000; the mine owners were under obligation to him, and would *give* him fifteen thousand." Steunenberg declined, saying he'd "pay for it the same as any other man." When Campbell asked what he needed the money for, Steunenberg replied: "a body of timber in the Boise Basin." After Steunenberg submitted a report on the prospective timber, Campbell said "there'd be money in it" and invited Steunenberg back to Spokane, where he signed a $15,000 note at 6 percent annual interest.

Not long thereafter, a raffish fellow named Albert E. Palmer, a timber promoter for Wisconsin interests, was in Campbell's office on the lookout for likely stands of Idaho timber. "Here's something that might interest you," said Campbell, tossing him Steunenberg's report. Palmer sent it to his people back in Wisconsin. By March 13, Steunenberg wrote Campbell that the deal was done.

Three Wisconsin timbermen—James T. Barber, Sumner G. Moon, and William Carson, who were loosely linked to the giant Weyerhauser timber empire—lent Steunenberg $33,700 to buy out Sweet, agreeing to advance him a total of $140,000 to assemble some twenty-five thousand acres of standing timber in the Boise Basin. In June, the trio set up the Barber Lumber Company, with 1,500 shares of stock, in which they voted Steunenberg a quarter interest of 375 shares. Assuming that the governor supplied the requisite timber and repaid his debts, he stood to make a lot of money on the deal.

Meanwhile, Campbell and Steunenberg grew ever closer. The governor served as a lobbyist with the Idaho legislature on measures that the Coeur d'Alene mine owners wanted to block. Campbell, in turn, proved useful in clearing obstacles to Steunenberg's land package, specifically in dealing with a nosy special agent from the Interior Department's General Land Office named Louis L. Sharp, who thought he'd turned up some flagrant examples of timber fraud in Steunenberg's dealings. Campbell spoke with Senator A. G. Foster of Washington, who'd arranged Sharp's appointment. Foster saw Sharp, telling him he understood that as a government inspector he couldn't pretend that a bad entry was a good one but that he should be "very sure they are bad." Foster sent Sharp to talk with Amasa Campbell, noting that Campbell would have to pay Sharp's "expenses"—two hundred dollars—which he did. For the time being the special agent soft-pedaled his objections.

Thus, doubts about the legality of these dealings were put on hold until early 1907, when Francis N. Goodwin of the General Land Office reported on them to his boss, and Judge Beatty wrote a strong letter to the Secretary of the Interior, pressing for prosecution of the Barber Company and its allies.

Though Borah was clearly Beatty's—and Ruick's—principal target, his connection to the "fraud" was mainly through his close ties to Frank Steunenberg, who'd invited him to become the Barber Company's lawyer. Thus, the prosecutors never lost an opportunity to contend that it was Steunenberg's thirst for wealth that had animated the conspiracy and driven the fraud.

That Frank Steunenberg was looking to get rich quick isn't in much doubt—"We've come for the money," A.K. had said—but so were most of his neighbors in those avaricious years. That he'd traded on his ties to the mine owners to get investment capital and to quash government investigations isn't in much doubt either. That he sought to circumvent Federal law to accumulate valuable timber—and in so doing to funnel lands intended for individual homesteaders to a great timber combine—seems evident as well. But that he'd been the chief organizer of a "timber fraud" was by no means clear. To prove fraud required evidence that the "entrymen," in acquiring their 160 acres, had made a "prior agreement" to sell them to the ultimate user, and that was in some question in this case. Since Steunenberg would never have a trial of his own at which his guilt or innocence could be established, this could only be inferred from the fate of the other alleged conspirators—and the first of these was Borah.

All through the spring and summer of 1907, Boise swarmed with detectives, operatives, and special agents for the various parties to the timber case —above and beyond the dozens of sleuths already working on the Haywood trial. At times, Pinkerton agents did double duty, for McParland and Hawley saw the two cases as a single tangled ball of twine.

On the federal government's side, the agents generally worked either for the Justice Department, the General Land Office of the Interior Department, or, increasingly as the year wore on, for the Secret Service. Technically, that was most irregular, for by statute the Secret Service division of the Treasury Department was supposed to limit its activities to protecting the president and safeguarding the currency through the pursuit of counterfeiters. In fact, in the absence of a federal agency like the FBI, the Secret Service had long served informally as the government's investigative arm. Its agents were loaned to other departments and agencies for a wide range of investigations, most particularly the Justice Department's antitrust activities and the crackdown on timber fraud. In fact, so far did these agents roam that many members of Congress regarded John E. Wilkie, the service's director, as a kind of American Joseph Fouché, the notorious director of France's national police. That Wilkie was a former crime reporter for the *Chicago Tribune* and not a power-mad spymaster did nothing to lessen the fear of his agency's activities.

The first two Secret Service agents assigned to the Boise timber investigation were Elmer A. Gormon and William A. Glover, who arrived in Idaho on December 8, 1906. Since they were on temporary loan to the Justice Department, they reported to the U.S. attorney, Norman Ruick. Wilkie had named Gormon the agent in charge of the Boise detail; an operative who'd had a severe drinking problem, Gormon was trying to work his way back into the good graces of his boss. "Chief," he wrote Wilkie on the eve of his departure for Boise, "I am more than anxious to make a success of this case, and would appreciate any suggestions you may make in assisting me to accomplish this end. . . . Please help a cripple."

Arriving in Boise on February 8, he established himself in Room 11 of the Idanha Hotel, the latest of scores of detectives to ensconce themselves there. For some weeks, Gormon followed Borah on his diurnal rounds—from his office to the Overland Drug Store, to a nearby saloon, and occasionally to the offices of the Barber Lumber Company, which were also under round-the-clock surveillance to ensure that none of their records disappeared. Borah, in turn, hired his own agents to follow the defense attorneys, Ruick, and later some potential jurors. For a time in late spring, every figure in the timber cases seemed to have his own set of detectives following everybody else.

At one point, Boise's mayor, John M. Haines—a loyal ally of Borah's—evidently planned to arrest several of the Secret Service men following the senator, perhaps on grounds that they were exceeding their statutory prerogatives. Ultimately, this gambit was thwarted by cooler heads.

Before long, Ruick grew openly dissatisfied with both Gormon and Glover. On March 5, Gormon wrote Wilkie again, asking him to "call my attention to anything that I may do that you feel I am doing wrong, as I am conscientious in my endeavors and working for success." But before Wilkie could answer, the tempestuous Ruick accused Gormon of leaking important information—Borah's impending indictment—to the Boise press. A Justice Department "examiner," B. F. Cash, rushed to Boise, where he reported to the attorney general that Gormon was innocent of any intentional leak. But through a back channel to the department, he said, "Gormon couldn't run an ice wagon successfully.... He is a booze fighter par excellence." Another official found Gormon's behavior "deplorable," concluding that he was probably under the influence of opium and morphine as well as liquor. A Secret Service man named Mark A. Thomas, whose services Gormon had specifically requested, also turned out to be a drunk. Gormon was hustled out of town and replaced as agent in charge by a trusted operative named Marshall Eberstein, who'd formerly served at the president's residence in Oyster Bay.

Meanwhile, Thomas and Glover were dispatched to Toronto, where Albert E. Palmer, the intermediary between Amasa Campbell and Frank Steunenberg, had been located. Glover was told to lure him back to the United States, where he could be arrested.

Palmer lived with his "very beautiful" wife, of whom he was "intensely jealous." Glover traced him to an address "in the aristocratic part of town" and took a room next door, while Thomas returned to northern New York, from where he sent Palmer a stream of "decoy letters" summoning him to Buffalo on urgent business. On August 31, Glover, having contrived to meet Palmer on a Toronto trolley car, adjourned with him to the bar of the Rossin House, where, over some good whiskey and without realizing who his drinking partner was, Palmer told him "everything that had occurred to him" in the West. "He was plainly suspicious of [Thomas's] letters, as he said they wanted him badly as a witness at Boise." On September 3, Glover met Palmer again at the Rossin House and "interested him in a mining proposition that included a trip to New York." For several days, Palmer kept promising to accompany Glover to New York but backed out every time. Finally, on September 6, Glover wrote Ruick: "It is useless for me to try to rope him under the circumstances as his every action indicates he is well informed as to what is taking place at Boise, and has made up his mind to have nothing to do with anyone until after the trials." The prosecutors would have to get on with their case without Palmer.

Borah's trial began on September 23, with Ruick, Burch, Rush, and Francis Goodwin at the prosecution table. Appearing for Borah were his old colleague Jim Hawley, refreshed from his Haywood trial labors by a five-week vacation in Honolulu; a former associate named Alfred A. Fraser; and two younger Boise lawyers, Samuel L. Tipton and Karl Paine. It took only a day to get a jury: five farmers, two ranchers, two bankers, a carpenter, a printer, and a real estate man (curiously the very same Tom Gess who'd been foreman of the Haywood jury).

Ruick would soon retreat to an advisory role in favor of the two special prosecutors, but he was allowed his moment in the spotlight in those first moments. And he made the most of it, announcing with flourish what some had suspected but few had known for sure, that the "John Doe" mentioned in the indictment was none other than the late Frank Steunenberg.

An indictment of a dead man was rare indeed. It could have no legal effect, for a dead man obviously couldn't be prosecuted, nor in a criminal trial could any penalties be assessed against his survivors or his estate. There might have been some purpose in naming Steunenberg an "unindicted co-conspirator," assuring the admissibility of testimony about his conversations with other living conspirators. But indictment of the dead governor seemed to many a political act.

That impression was strengthened the next day when Marsden Burch opened the government's case, taking the jurors through the complex story of Steunenberg's dealings with the entry men in the Boise Basin and later with the Wisconsin timbermen and showing wherever possible Borah's role as facilitator of these illegal transactions. In describing Steunenberg's dealings with Amasa Campbell and the Coeur d'Alene mine owners, Burch said, "In 1899, Governor Steunenberg went to the Coeur d'Alenes presumably for patriotic motives."

Over at the *Statesman*, Calvin Cobb—ever alert to new indignities inflicted by the men from Washington—assigned a reporter to ask Burch what he meant by "presumably." Was it Burch's intention "by that remark to reflect upon the action of the governor in going to the Coeur d'Alenes at that time"?

"Not at all," said Burch. "We cannot split hairs over the choice of words in addressing a jury."

But the reporter kept at him. "There were people present, judge, who gained the impression from your words and the tone of your voice that you delivered the statement sneeringly."

"Oh well," said Burch, "those having sneering minds may think so; those having fair minds will place a fair construction on what I said."

While Calvin Cobb took umbrage at such finger-pointing, Borah's strategy was precisely the opposite: to feign utter disinterest in these silly charges leveled by Washington bureaucrats. Of the forty government witnesses who testified during the next six days, Hawley bothered to cross-examine only two. And when it came time on October 2 for the defense case, Hawley called just one witness of his own: Borah himself.

Under his counsel's gentle questioning, Borah testified that he'd known Steunenberg since coming to the state in 1890, had known him "intimately" since they'd labored together in the Coeur d'Alene crisis of 1899. They were warm personal friends up until the time the governor was murdered, "and would be yet if he were living." But he'd never been the governor's lawyer, only general counsel to the Barber Lumber Company, a post that he assumed, at Steunenberg's request, on January 1, 1903.

Thus he had no connection with the dubious transactions Steunenberg had with the entry men during 1901–02 and no contact with the lumber company at all before 1903. Steunenberg had full charge of rounding up timber in the Boise Basin and Borah only knew what Steunenberg told him.

He'd never drawn up any contracts between Sweet and Steunenberg. He'd never talked about timber with Amasa Campbell. He'd never been an attorney for Sweet or Kinkaid. He'd never met Palmer. He'd made no timber entries. He'd been consulted by people who didn't make entries but never by those who did. Yes, the examination and recording of deeds had been handled by his office, but this was the work of clerks and stenographers, who consulted him only in rare cases of a discrepancy. Moreover, he'd never had any financial interest whatsoever in the Barber Lumber Company, his only relationship being that of an attorney, his fees paid as a fixed salary.

It was a clever performance, warm in recalling his "old friend" Frank Steunenberg, respectful of Steunenberg's record as governor, mournful in discussing his death, but by inference laying the blame for any fraud either at the door of good old Frank or with the Barber Lumber Company, in which he had no interest, for whom he was just a salaried lawyer. It was an argument much like that C. P. Connolly had made to the president at Sagamore Hill. If Borah was guilty, why so was every lawyer in the West. A lawyer had no responsibility for the fraudulent activities of his employers. He simply represented their best interests.

Sylvester Rush, the cross-examiner, had a difficult balance to strike between respect and disbelief. For many Idahoans—presumably some on this jury—Bill Borah was a local hero, a knight errant on his way to do battle with the malign powers of the East. The prosecutor had to show a certain deference for the senator's office and his record of service; otherwise he might be seen an eastern interloper affronting Idaho's sovereignty. Yet, if the government was to prevail, Rush had to discredit Borah's evasions and show the jury that he was laying off on others a responsibility he ought to bear.

But Borah, a veteran of countless courtroom confrontations, had cross-examined hundreds of witnesses and prepared hundreds more to meet just such an ordeal. He knew how to blunt a prosecutor's shafts with a bland answer or a clipped "yes" or "no" that gave the questioner no foothold for further attack. In short, Borah was too much for Rush; from their four-hour engagement, he emerged unscathed.

As Borah resumed his seat, Hawley startled the courtroom by announcing, "We rest, Your Honor." Not only would the defense dispense with further witnesses, it would waive its closing argument. It was a shrewd gamble, that this bluff disrespect—what the prosecutor called an effort "to simulate utter indifference to what proof we put in"—would persuade the jury there was nothing much there. Moreover, it forced Rush onto his feet, closing the government case before he was ready. He took two hours. Hawley said only: "We submit the case, Your Honor."

The jury was back in just fourteen minutes. When the verdict of "not guilty" was read shortly past 6:00 p.m., the courtroom exploded in a jubilation so exuberant that the judge could only shrug his shoulders and say, "I assume you all know that your conduct is highly improper. I will not attempt, how-ever, to punish you for contempt of court."*

As news of the verdict raced through the city, office workers, merchants, and their customers surged into Main Street between Sixth Street and the Idanha Hotel. The city's fire chief turned in a "general alarm of fire" for the Idanha, sending the city's horse-drawn fire engines clattering through the streets, their bells and whistles sounding as they converged on the fanciful hotel. Boise's famed Columbian Band assembled almost as quickly, pumping out "Hail to the Chief" and other patriotic airs for the crowd gathering outside the Idanha. The marchers sounded tin pans and cowbells and set off Roman candles and torpedoes. Several husky fellows carried Borah on their shoulders to the Idanha, where he joined other dignitaries in clambering atop the steel canopy over the Main Street entrance.

Introducing the senator, Jim Hawley said that they were there to cele-brate the righting of a "monstrous wrong," that not only had Borah been "vindicated" but so had the state "upon the charge of having selected an unworthy person to fill the highest place within the gift of the citizens." Prosecuting Borah, said Hawley had been "an attempt to pervert the cause of justice and to gratify the personal hatred and ill will" of a small band of men. Then he introduced "Idaho's foremost citizen, a man who honors the state as much as the state has honored him."

Rising to a thunderous ovation from the multitude filling Main Street curb to curb, Borah at last gave voice to his vast anguish—and exquisite relief. He thanked his fellow citizens for joining him in his moment of vindication. "I would rather go to jail with the love and loyalty of such friends as a consolation than to be acquitted and have your distrust." He assailed those who'd defamed Frank Steunenberg. "I believed in him and I defend at all times his memory." But there was "a certain species of human hyenas who find no gratification in fighting the living but fatten where opportunity is given upon the dead." As for himself, "the humiliation which I suffered no tongue can tell. I felt that the State which had honored me had been brought into conspicuous shame. I felt that the loyal friends who had supported me had been compromised. For these reasons this ordeal has been enough for any man to bear. Now, if I can very quickly do something to honor my state and gratify my friends, it will indeed be happiness to me. Again, I thank you. You cannot realize how full my heart is and how devotedly I would dedicate myself to your interests."

About eight that evening, a procession formed at the Idanha and marched up Main Street: the band, Borah, the jurors, and thousands of

---

* In March 1908, Judge Edward Whitson dismissed charges against the remaining defendants, on the grounds that Ruick had improperly influenced the grand jury (Merle Wells "Timber Frauds on Crooked River," *Idaho Yesterdays,* Summer 1985, 12).

jubilant Boiseans bearing placards that read, among other things, "A Lemon for Ruick," "Not Politics—Just Borah." The hubbub went on much of the night, abandoned crowds dancing in the streets, cheering Borah and the president, getting "gloriously drunk." It was a little like the night nine weeks before, when a largely working-class crowd had turned out to celebrate Haywood's acquittal. But now the streets filled with Borah's people, the clerks, merchants, and professionals flourishing in the buoyant economy of the new century.

Boise had been due for these binges. For years, the city had harbored two great struggles in which first the avatar of the militant working class, then the beau ideal of the new corporate order had been brought to the bar of judicial process—and into the court of public opinion. Millions of dollars had been expended in these encounters, legions of lawyers had done combat in Boise's shabby courthouses, squadrons of reporters had made this bustling little city on Idaho's irrigated desert one of America's most familiar datelines.

Finally, the opposing camps in this nasty class war sputtering along the icy ridges of the Rocky Mountains had just about canceled each other out. Operative for operative, hired gun for hired gun, bought juror for bought juror, perjured witness for perjured witness, conniving lawyer for conniving lawyer, partisan reporter for partisan reporter, these cockeyed armies had fought each other to an exhausted standoff.

If both Haywood and Borah had expected to be railroaded to conviction, each had received a fairer trial than he'd anticipated. George Pettibone, the next to be tried, was acquitted in January 1908, at which point the discouraged prosecutors dropped all charges against Charles Moyer. Shortly thereafter, Moyer ousted his rival, Haywood, from the WFM. Undaunted, Haywood concentrated his energies on the IWW and helped lead bitter textile workers' strikes in Lawrence, Massachusetts, and Paterson, New Jersey, while becoming the darling of the bohemian left in Greenwich Village. In 1918, Haywood was convicted of conspiring with other leaders of the IWW to undermine the U.S. war effort and served a year at Leavenworth prison before his release pending appeal. In 1921, he fled the United States for exile in Moscow, where he died in March 1928. An urn containing half his ashes was buried next to those of his friend John Reed beneath the Kremlin wall; the other half were shipped to Chicago for burial near the monument to the Haymarket anarchists who'd inspired Haywood's radicalism in the first place.

Harry Orchard was tried, convicted of murder, and sentenced in March 1908 to die on the gallows. But his reputation had been so refurbished by his elaborate religiosity that Fremont Wood recommended clemency and the state board of pardons commuted his sentence to life in Idaho's penitentiary —where he remained a trusty, raising chickens and growing strawberries, until his death at the age of eighty-eight in 1954. Martin Egan became the principal public relations man for J. P. Morgan, president of the Wall Street house that bore his name and potent symbol of American capitalism. Walter

Johnson quickly ripened into the most celebrated pitcher in American baseball history, gaining admittance by virtual acclamation to baseball's Hall of Fame. Ethel Barrymore went on to a hugely successful acting career on both stage and screen.

Of all who'd suffered in these uncivil wars, the emblematic victim perhaps was the man who'd lost his way in the Coeur d'Alenes and found his fortune in the Boise Basin—the governor at his garden gate.

Epilogue

But did Haywood and his co-conspirators kill Frank Steunenberg? The question defies easy answers, for whatever may have passed between the WFM leaders, Harry Orchard, and Steve Adams was known for sure only to these five men. Even if one accepts Orchard's testimony that he'd been dispatched to kill Steunenberg, did he receive an explicit order to assassinate the governor, an exclamation at a Denver saloon, "Will nobody rid us of this cursed governor?" or an offhand remark that Steunenberg had lived too long? In the years since the 1907–08 acquittals, nobody has produced fresh evidence of either guilt or innocence. But correspondence in the files of *Appeal to Reason* would seem to provide an answer.

On October 1, 1910, somebody placed a suitcase containing sixteen sticks of dynamite in Ink Alley behind the *Los Angeles Times* building. The alley took its name from barrels of printer's ink stored there, and the lethal suitcase had been planted near them. Thus, when the dynamite exploded it set off a fierce conflagration that killed twenty-one workers and injured a dozen more.

The explosion aroused little sympathy in the Socialist press, for Harrison Gray Otis, the *Times*'s publisher, was regarded as one of the nation's most virulently antiunion capitalists. So when Eugene Debs addressed the bombing in *Appeal to Reason*, he proclaimed: "I want to express it as my deliberate opinion that the *Times* and its crowd of union-haters are themselves the instigators if not the actual perpetrators of that crime."

Bill Haywood noted that reading about this case was "like reading a brief chapter of my own life." Once again a famous detective stepped into the breach. If any American sleuth could rival James McParland, it was William J. Burns, the former Secret Service man now heading a Chicago-based agency that bore his name. By coincidence, Burns had arrived in Los Angeles the morning after the *Times* bombing, scheduled to address the convention of his client, the American Bankers Association. Seizing the opportunity, the mayor of Los Angeles retained him to find the dynamiters "no matter what the cost and no matter who they are."

Just as McParland had Haywood and the WFM in mind from the beginning of his investigation, so Burns suspected J. J. McNamara, secretary-treasurer of the International Association of Bridge and Structural Iron Workers. McNamara, Burns believed, stood behind a series of bombings of factories, bridges, and public buildings built by firms affiliated with the National Erectors' Association, a steel-industry group whose avowed goal was to destroy the iron workers union.

Just as McParland had masterminded the 1906 kidnapping, so Burns now contrived to spirit J. J. McNamara from union headquarters in Indianapolis on April 22, 1911. Ten days before, his younger brother Jim—later identified as the man who'd planted the dynamite in Ink Alley—had been arrested in Detroit along with a colleague named Ortie McManigal. When captured, the pair were carrying a suitcase full of explosives. The McNamara brothers and McManigal were now hustled aboard the California Limited to Los Angeles, where they were charged with the *Times* bombing, as well as the Christmas morning explosion at the antiunion Llewellyn Iron Works.

Once more, labor turned to Clarence Darrow to represent the accused men, and again *Appeal to Reason* dispatched George Shoaf, "the war correspondent of the class war," to cover the trial. As they had in Boise, Shoaf and Darrow worked closely together in Los Angeles, sharing intelligence on the case and plotting strategy.

Once again, Shoaf stridently proclaimed the union leaders "as innocent as new-born babes." Like Debs, he moved toward placing the blame for the explosion and the "trumped up" case against labor on Otis. "Since reaching Los Angeles," he wrote, "I have worked night and day, exclusively trying to ascertain what caused the explosion and who was responsible for it. At present I am not prepared to make a complete report. From facts in hand, however, I am more and more coming to the conclusion that the owner of the *Times* building and its destroyer were and are one and the same person."

Such accusations notwithstanding, Darrow and Shoaf both knew the truth was otherwise. The government's case against the McNamaras was very strong: Jim for the *Times* bombing itself, J. J. for the bombing of the Llewellyn Works. As months went by and he saw how much evidence was arrayed against his clients, Darrow recognized that these were cases he couldn't win. Moreover, if convicted by a jury, Jim McNamara faced an almost certain death sentence. By late summer of 1911, Darrow began to contemplate the unthinkable: pleading both men guilty, in an effort to spare Jim's life.

This would embarrass Shoaf, who would be forced to retract his charges against Otis. The Socialist correspondent resolved on action that he hoped would spare him such humiliation and might even, for a time, take some of the heat off the McNamaras and their attorneys.

On the afternoon of August 13, Shoaf went to a party at the home of a friend, confiding in a Socialist organizer that he had the biggest story of his life in his pocket. Later, he went to a rooming house on West Ninth Street, where his cousin, a widow named Mrs. Lucy Borman, was boarding. They sat up talking for several hours.

Toward midnight, Mrs. Borman and others in the house heard a loud thud on the stairway, but when it was followed by silence, no one went to investigate. The next morning, however, at the bottom of the stairs, one boarder found a piece of garden hose some fourteen inches long filled with a leadlike substance, and next to it a battered derby inscribed inside "G. H. Shoaf."

The *Appeal* appeared with a bold headline: "Shoaf Is Slugged! Strange Disappearance of *Appeal*'s Correspondent Working on McNamara Case." The paper said its star correspondent had finally obtained the evidence needed to free the McNamaras and pin the explosion on Otis but had been kidnapped before he could write the story. It hired detectives to find the missing reporter —among them, his father, the former police chief of San Antonio—and offered a five-hundred-dollar reward for information on his whereabouts.

For a month, the *Appeal* maintained its tone of foreboding about Shoaf's fate, then gradually backed off this position. For suspicion was growing that the reporter had engineered his own kidnapping.

Frank Wolfe, the former managing editor of the *Los Angeles Herald*, and two other investigators wrote Fred Warren, the *Appeal*'s managing editor, that Shoaf's closest friends and associates were "the first to look with suspicion on the circumstances of his disappearance." One had "hooted" at the idea of tragedy and told them to "find the woman in the case."

Then, in early October, Piet Vlag, the editor of the New York journal *The Masses*, intercepted a letter from Shoaf to his mistress, Elsa Untermann, the seventeen-year-old daughter of Ernest Untermann, who'd covered the Haywood trial for *Wilshire's Magazine*. The letter instructed Elsa on means to keep Shoaf's whereabouts—and her own—secret.

Elsa offered Vlag the following explanation: "Last winter when I first began to live with [Shoaf], I told him that we would have to be nothing more than brother and sister, that I could never love him. But he was so miserable and made so many appeals to me that I could not hold out against him.... I know of things perfectly heinous that he has done in his work, things that he loathed.... If I cannot love him for what he is, I will love him for what he might have been."

Elsa's father was apoplectic. Recalling that he'd warned Debs about Shoaf's behavior at the Haywood trial, including his "statutory rape" of fifteen-year-old Florence Abbott, he wrote the Socialist Party's National Executive Committee: "My worst fears have now been realized.... Wherever Shoaf went, he acted in a triple role—1. *Appeal* correspondent and private agent of Fred Warren; 2. Agent provocateur; 3. Seducer of girls under age."

For weeks, invective flew back and forth between Untermann, Warren, Debs, and other party notables. "Shoaf at last overreached himself and his career ended," A. W. Ricker, another *Appeal* correspondent, wrote Untermann. "In it we all suffer—Warren, who is experiencing the discomfiture of the fall down of one of his staff; the *Appeal*, the discredit of a silly and disgusting attempt at grandstanding; the staff here that suffer in common the mistakes of each other; Elsa, who is learning in the bitter school of life, and you her father."

As the *Appeal* pointed an accusatory finger at Shoaf, Warren began receiving letters from a certain "Cornelius C. Corker," whose pungent style and intimate acquaintance with Shoaf's every grievance left little doubt that Corker was Shoaf himself.

On October 16, he wrote the managing editor:

> From the tenor of this last *Appeal* it appears that you are going to throw it into Shoaf good and proper. That is right. Hit him hard. . . . Suppose in your forthcoming exposé you tell the whole truth. State to the world the salary Shoaf has been receiving from the *Appeal* the many years he acted as scavenger for the paper, doing a work that forced him to associate with thieves and courtesans, and compare his salary with that drawn by yourself. . . . Shoaf told me he was forced to go out and steal to try to get things for his family. . . . If his job was such he had to be away from home nearly all the time, and his salary was such he could not have his wife with him, can he be blamed if he associated with other women, if he did so? . . . He was working not for money but because he thought he was doing something to undermine capitalism and so hasten the coming of Socialism.

But soon Corker/Shoaf graduated from self-pity to blackmail. If the editors of the *Appeal* went on posing as "the embodiment of journalistic honesty" while painting Shoaf as "the big liar and thief and rape fiend," he might feel compelled to uncover some of the party's most shameful skeletons. On October 26, he conceded to Warren that his attempt to "fasten the responsibility of the *Times* explosion on H. G. Otis" had been a "bluff," though arguing that journalism was "all a game" and "he who dares not try to play has no business in the newspaper field." But then he recalled a game that both he and Warren had played to the hilt: "Remember that the McNamara brothers are not one bit more guilty of the crime charged against them than were Moyer, Haywood and Pettibone of the crime of which they were acquitted.* Trickery and audacity liberated the miners' officials."

The danger an aggrieved Shoaf posed to the Socialist movement was acutely detected by his old friend Josephine Conger-Kaneko, who'd studied with him at Ruskin College and known him while they worked together at the *Appeal,* and later when she edited the *Progressive Woman* in Chicago. It was to Conger-Kaneko that Shoaf had run when he was sought in 1907 on charges of raping Florence Abbott.

Now, in October 1911, she warned Warren: "If the capitalist press will give

---

* The syntax of this sentenance may, at first, be confusing. But if one remembers that this letter was written in the context of the McNamaras' admitted guilt (the brothers formally pleaded guilty on December 1, 1911, but by midfall Shoaf and others close to the defense would have known what was coming), then it is clear that Corker/Shoaf is saying that he knows that Haywood, Moyer, and Pettibone were just as guilty as the McNamaras.

their columns to S. to tell the truth about the Western Federation men, the McNamara bros., and whatever else he may know of the working class move-ment—but these two are amply sufficient—it seems to me it would disgust hundreds of thousands of people with this movement."

The tone of Shoaf's and Conger-Kaneko's letters suggests that the recip-ient of both, Fred Warren, shared their knowledge that Haywood, Moyer, and Pettibone had been guilty as charged in 1907. Few people were closer to the events of 1905–07 than Fred Warren, orchestrator of the *Appeal*'s coverage of the Haywood case. Few people had insisted more adamantly on Haywood's innocence than Warren and Shoaf. Few knew Warren, Shoaf, and their secrets better than Josephine Conger-Kaneko.

If, four years after the Boise trial, these prominent Socialists wrote freely to one another about the guilt of Haywood, Moyer, and Pettibone, what does this tell us about who struck down the governor on that snowy night in Caldwell?

Notes

AC   Papers of Amasa Campbell, Eastern Washington Historical Society, Spokane
AET   Albert E. Thomas Collection, New York Public Library of the Performing Arts, Lincoln Center, New York
AH   Albert E. Horsley, Confession and Autobiography of Harry Orchard, original manuscript, Idaho State Historical Society, Boise
AK   A. K. Steunenberg Papers, in possession of Al F. Steunenberg, Alamo, California
ALW   Lila and Arthur Weinberg Papers, Newberry Library, Chicago
AtR   *Appeal to Reason*
BB   War Department Files on Boise Barracks, R.G. 92, Entry 1213, Reservation K-82, National Archives, Washington, D.C.
BG   *Boston Globe*
BH   Papers of Benjamin Hurwitz, Western History Collection, Denver Public Library
BHS   Archives of Bunker Hill and Sullivan Company, Kellogg, Idaho
BLC   Records of the Barber Lumber Company, Boise Cascade Lumber Company, Boise, Idaho
BS   Bess Steunenberg Scrapbook, Idaho State Historical Society, Boise
BTF   Justice Department Files on "Borah Timber Fraud," R.G. 60, Entry 112, File 59512, Boxes 057, 058, 059, 196, 197, 198, 199, 560, National Archives, Washington, D.C.
BW   Papers of Brand Whitlock, Library of Congress
CC   Papers of Calvin Cobb, Idaho State Historical Society, Boise
CD   Papers of Clarence Darrow, Library of Congress
CDLT   *Coeur d'Alene Labor Troubles,* Report of the Committee on Military Affairs, House of Representatives, 56th Congress, 1st Session (1900)
CDR   Clarence Darrow Collection, Regenstein Library, University of Chicago
CEA   Papers of Charles E. Arney, Idaho State University, Pocatello
CESW   Papers of Charles Erskine Scott Wood, Bancroft Library, University of California at Berkeley
CHH   Papers of Carter H. Harrison Jr., Newberry Library, Chicago
CHT   *Chicago Tribune*
CJB   Charles J. Bonaparte Papers, National Archives
CN   *Caldwell News*
COJ   Papers of Claudius O. Johnson, Washington State University, Pullman
CPL   Caldwell Public Library, Caldwell, Idaho
CT   *Caldwell Tribune*
DP   *Denver Post*
DR   *Denver Republican*
DT   *Denver Times*
EB   Papers of Edward Boyce, Eastern Washington Historical Society
EC   Martin Egan Collection, Morgan Library, New York
ECN   *Evening Capital News*
ED   Records of Episcopal Diocese of Long Island, Garden City, New York
ELM   Edgar Lee Masters Papers, Newberry Library, Chicago
ER   Papers of Edmund Richardson, WFM Collection, University of Colorado, Boulder
ERP   Elihu Root Papers, Library of Congress
FG   Papers of Frank Gooding, Idaho State Historical Society, Boise
FSP   Probate Records, Frank Steunenberg Estate, Canyon County Courthouse, Caldwell, Idaho
FTD   Fred T. Dubois Papers, Idaho State University, Pocatello
FW   Papers of Fremont Wood, Idaho State Historical Society, Boise
GC   Papers of George Crookham, in possession of George Crookham, Caldwell, Idaho
GCP   Papers of George B. Cortelyou, Library of Congress
GP   Gifford Pinchot Papers, Library of Congress

HCM	Papers of Henry C. Merriam, Colby College
HCMA	Personnel Record, General Henry C. Merriam, M-1064, Roll 281, 938 CB 1866, National Archives, Washington, D.C.
HCMD	Civil War Diary of Henry C. Merriam, W. Bart Berger Collection, Denver
HJ	Haldeman-Julius Family Papers, University of Illinois at Chicago
HMH	Papers of Hugo Münsterberg, Harvard University Archives
HMP	Papers of Hugo Münsterberg, Rare Books Room, Boston Public Library
HO	Roosevelt Papers, Houghton Library, Harvard University
HP	Papers of James Hawley, in possession of the Hawley family
IC	Industrial Commission on the Relations and Conditions of Capital and Labor Employed in the Mining Industry, Senate, 64th Congress, 1st Session (1916)
IDS	*Idaho Daily Statesman*
IS	Papers of Irving Stone, University of Southern California
ISHS	Idaho State Historical Society, Boise
JAP	Papers of James A. Pinney, Idaho State Historical Society, Boise
JC	Scrapbooks of Jennie Cornell, Caldwell Public Library, Caldwell, Idaho
JD	U.S. Justice Department Files, National Archives, Record Group 60, Entry 112, File 59512
JDF	*Jewish Daily Forward*
JH	Papers of James Hawley, Idaho State Historical Society, Boise
JM	Papers of John Mitchell, Catholic University
JOD	Scrapbooks of Jessie Ohl Darrow, Newberry Library, Chicago
KE	Klaw and Erlanger Papers, Shubert Archives, New York
LD	Personnel Files, Major Lorenzo P. Davison, Box 5485ACP1885, National Archives, Washington, D.C.
LMT	*Lewiston Morning Tribune*
LOC	Library of Congress
MCC	Minutes of the Board of Canyon County Commissioners, 1906 and 1907, Canyon County Courthouse, Caldwell, Idaho
McP	Reports of James McParland to the Pinkerton National Detective Agency. Since these reports have been consulted in four different locations, I use the following four notations to designate the current site of these materials.
	McP1 Molly Maguire Papers, Reading Collection, Eleutherian Mills Historical Library, Hagley, Wilmington, Delaware
	McP2 Molly Maguire Collection, Historical Society of Pennsylvania, Philadelphia
	McP3 Pinkerton Reports, Idaho State Historical Society, Boise
	McP4 Pinkerton Archives, Encino, California
MED	Mary Elizabeth Dreier Collection, Schlesinger Library, Cambridge, Mass.
MDR	Margaret Dreier Robins Collection, on microfilm at the Tamiment Library, New York University
MFP	Papers of Mary Field Parton and Margaret Parton, Newberry Library, Chicago
MM	*Miners' Magazine*
MN	*Montana News*
MS	Melville Stone Papers, Newberry Library, Chicago
NA	National Archives
NDH	Newell Dwight Hillis Collection, Brooklyn Historical Society, New York
NYS	The *Sun*
NYT	*New York Times*
OKD	Oscar King Davis Papers, Colgate University
Op.	Operative
OWHP	Oliver Wendell Holmes Papers, Harvard Law School
PA	Pinkerton Archives, Encino, California
PET	*Portland Evening Telegram*
PO	*Portland Oregonian*
RFP	Richard F. Pettigrew Papers, Siouxland Heritage Museum, Sioux Falls, South Dakota
RL	Scrapbooks of Robinson Locke, Billy Rose Theatre Collection, New York Public Library of the Performing Arts, Lincoln Center, New York
RMN	*Rocky Mountain News*
ROS	Theodore Roosevelt Papers, Library of Congress
SCN	*Silver City Nugget*
SG	Samuel Gompers Letterbooks, University of Maryland
SH	Stewart Holbrook Collection, University of Washington, Seattle
SOC	The *Socialist*
SS	Files of the Secret Service, R.G. 87, Entry 14, File 71226, Box 14; Special Investigation File, Entry 1, Box 6, National Archives, Washington, D.C.
SSM	Papers of S. S. McClure, University of Indiana, Bloomington
SSR	Spokane *Spokesman-Review*
SvA(II)	*State v. Adams,* Oct. 25–Nov. 24, 1907, Rathdrum, Idaho. On microfilm, Idaho State Historical Society, Boise.
SvH	Stenographic Transcript, *State of Idaho v. William D. Haywood,* Idaho State Historical Society, Boise
TH	Thiel Detective Service Report
TR	Theodore Roosevelt
TW	Records of the Twenty-fourth Infantry Regiment, R.G. 393, Part I, Entries 659, 734, 735, 736; R.G. 94, Stack Area 4W3, Boxes 695–715; R.G. 391, National Archives, Washington, D.C.
VB	Victor Berger Papers, Tamiment Library, New York University

WAW   Papers of William Allen White, Library of Congress
WB   Papers of William Judson Boone, Idaho State Historical Society, Boise
WC   Julius A. Wayland Collection, Axe Library, Pittsburg State University, Pittsburg, Kansas
WEB   Papers of William E. Borah, Idaho State Historical Society, Boise
WFM   Western Federation of Miners Collection, University of Colorado, Boulder
WHT   Papers of William Howard Taft, Library of Congress
WIL   *Wilshire's Magazine*
WP   *Washington Post*
WM   Papers of William McKinley, Library of Congress
WSWS *Weiser Semi-Weekly Signal*

I: THE MAGIC CITY

15   The governor—as he: Josephine Steunenberg to Delia Brobst and Grace Crookham, January 3, 1906, GC.
15   One of his favorite: George Crookham to author, March 27, 1989.
15   She was still looking: Josephine Steunenberg to Delia Brobst and Grace Crookham, January 2, 1906, GC.
16   "The good and evil spirits": Ibid.
16   "Please do not resist": F. Steunenberg Jr., *Martyr,* 107.
16   white English bulldog, Jumbo: Ibid., 145.
16   the austere breakfast: Numbers, *Prophetess,* 161.
16   "Frances had a little watch": Frank Steunenberg to "Mother and Children," January 8, 1904, GC.
16   An important matter: TH, January 11, 1906, 1.
17   Others who knew him: Al F. Steunenberg to author, July 26, 1989.
17   On Friday afternoon: *IDS,* January 5, 1906, 1; January 6, 1906, 1.
17   He'd come down: Josephine Steunenberg to Delia Brobst and Grace Crookham, January 7, 1906; *IDS,* January 10, 1906, 1.
17   Some said the habit: F. Steunenberg Jr., *Martyr,* p. 93.
17   "His friends have exhausted": Gaboury, *Dissension,* 322.
18   "magnanimous mien": "In the Interpreter's House," *American Magazine,* July 1907, 335.
18   "a rugged giant": *Deseret Evening News* (Salt Lake City), March 10, 1906.
18   On the day he was nominated: *Daily People,* May 30, 1907, 1.
18   "the worst land": Frank Steunenberg to Bernardus Steunenberg, February 8, 1888, GC.
18   "a place deserted": C. A. Strahorn, *Fifteen Thousand,* 2:123.
18   When Bob Strahorn: Knight, "Strahorn," 34.
18   "in an attractive garb": C. A. Strahorn, *Fifteen Thousand,* 2:45.
19   "a sure and short road": Knight, "Strahorn," 39.
19   "I could not but feel": Ibid., 44.
19   Strahorn had sufficient grounds: R. Strahorn, *Ninety Years,* 323; Athearn, "Oregon Short Line," 11. Another version suggests that Boise lost its place on the main line because it failed to post a required bond (see Maiken, *Night Trains,* 290; Donaldson, *Idaho,* 99).
19   "an ambitious young man": *IDS,* August 8, 1882.
19   The officers: Incorporation Papers, Idaho and Oregon Land Improvement Co., Idaho Secretary of State's Office; Athearn, "Oregon Short Line", 6; R. Strahorn, *Ninety Years,* 320.
20   Only then did he reveal: C. A. Strahorn, 2:121; R. Strahorn, 324.
20   Sagebrush City: *IDS,* August 8, 1882.
20   "preferred the emoluments": Harbaugh, *Power,* 225.
20   "a mean spirit of revenge": Report of the Joint Committee of Investigation of Bribery and Corruption Appointed by the Kansas Legislature of 1872.
20   "eleven saloons": *IDS,* September 8, 1883.
21   Settlers who found: Limerick, *Legacy,* 89–90.
21   "Have a good reason": Fisk, *Idaho.*
21   The bold of heart: Limerick, *Legacy,* passim.
21   "the great city": *CT,* December 9, 1883.
21   "the place was pregnant": Cronon, *Metropolis,* 35.
21   the Magic City: *Caldwell: The Magic City.*
21   "It will be found": *CT,* February 2, 1884.
22   "sometimes represented things": Boorstin, *The Americans: The National Experience,* 127.
22   "rustlers": *Caldwell,* 6.
22   "synonimous": *ECN,* July 3, 1907, 3.
22   In their rampant: Limerick, 77.
22   "The spirit of the times": W. A. White, *Autobiography,* 132.
22   "Caldwell is a straight business proposition": *CT,* July 1893, quoted in Conley, *Idaho,* 387.
22   A big lantern-jawed man: *CT,* February 24, 1904.
23   People said Rice: Lorene B. Thurston, interview by author, Caldwell, May 1995.
23   The Rices could use the space: *CT,* December 9, 1905.
23   When the governor: *CT,* September 2, 1893, 1.
23   Lowell and the Steunenbergs: *CT,* October 7, 1905.
23   There were those: *IDS,* March 21, 1903, 1.
23   Caldwell's relentless booming: *IDS,* March 21, 1903; *CT,* March 28, 1903; October 6, 1906.
24   It was already lined: *CT,* March 19, 1904; B. Steunenberg, "Early Days," 13.

24 A few days earlier: *CT,* December 9, 1905.
24 Cement sidewalks: *CT,* November 4, 1905.
24 The municipal sprinkler wagon: B. Steunenberg, "Early Days," 14.
24 A growing faction: *CT,* March 2, March 16, 1907.
24 big black beauty: *CT,* October 17, 1903, 4.
24 sporty roadster: *IDS,* July 5, 1907, 5.
24 But both the town: *IDS,* June 18, 1907, 3.
25 The town's network: Beal and Wells, *History,* 2:127.
25 Frank and A. K. Steunenberg: The Twin Falls project soon became the largest private irrigation project in the nation. It helped Idaho rank first among Pacific Northwest states in the amount of land irrigated under the 1894 Carey Act, which encouraged reclamation by giving western states a million acres of desert land if they found ways to water them (Schwantes, *Mountain,* 166).
25 "One is favorably impressed": *CT,* December 16, 1905.
25 The earth was volcanic ash: Coleman, *Steel Rails,* 31.
25 Alfalfa, timothy: *Pacific Monthly,* November 1907, 631–33.
25 In 1890 alone: B. Steunenberg, "Early Days," 13.
25 "The great forests": Frank Steunenberg to "Mother and Children," January 8, 1904, GC.
25 Indeed, in conversation: Charles E. Arney to M. A. Bates, January 9, 1906, CEA.
26 "headquarters for stockmen": *CT,* October 7, 1905.
26 Squirrel and McBryan: Dary, *Pleasure,* 130.
26 "All those things": *CT,* October 7, 1905.
26 Livery was the town's: Schlereth, *Victorian,* 20.
26 By century's turn: *CT,* June 2, 1900.
26 "All roads": Bird, *Boise,* 287.
27 Legends like Jack Mumford: Bess Steunenberg, speech, Caldwell, Idaho, 1963, AK.
27 Herbert got paddled: George Crookham, interview by author, Caldwell, Idaho, April 1989.
27 The boys of the town: Schlereth, *Victorian,* 20–21; Atherton, *Main Street,* 37–41.
28 "thoughtless draymen": *CT,* October 7, 1905.
28 It had occurred: Idaho's medical authorities knew full well by then that human and animal excreta carried the typhoid germ. In 1907, J. L. Stewart, Boise's city physician, warned of that in a stern directive (*IDS,* August 10, 1907, 4).
28 Among those taken: *CT,* October 21, December 9, 1905; *CN,* December 6, 1905; William Judson Boone, diary, October 14, 1905, ISHS.
28 Doctors weren't sure: *IDS,* December 23, 1905.
28 Later the *News: CN,* December 6, 1905.
28 Clouds of giant mosquitoes: *This Is Caldwell,* 5.
28 " 'The independent life' ": Frank Steunenberg to his parents, January 12, 1890, GC.
28 The state recruited: *ECN,* April 1, 1907.
28 As recently as February: *CT,* February 27, 1904.
28 To a young lawyer: MacLane, *Sagebrush,* 140.
29 The wildest animals: JC, no. 2.
29 "an agricultural town": C. A. Strahorn, *Fifteen Thousand,* 134.
29 The last was a Missourian: *IDS,* December 4, 5, 6, and 9, 1901.
29 If you looked: J. A. Russell, "Evil," 106.
29 prohibited their young folk: George Crookham, interview by author, Caldwell, Idaho, April 1989; *CT,* March 28, 1903, 4.
29 "Caldwell is the place": *CT,* April 14, 1906, 1.
29 "I cannot say": Frank Steunenberg to "the folks at home," March 3 and March 20, 1882, GC.
30 In December: *Idaho Press-Tribune,* 70th annual progress ed., May 6, 1953.
30 "Mr. M. DeVers": A. K. Steunenberg, "From Fraternity," 19.
30 "What's in a name?": Ibid.
31 "an Irishman": Hayman, *That Man Boone.*
31 "young and full of blood": *Caldwell.*
31 "They leaped into life": B. Steunenberg, "Early Days," 15.
31 "quickly shows a disposition": *CT,* January 8, 1887.
31 A few days before: *CT,* January 13, 1906.
32 All this left: *Blackfoot News,* September 5, 1896; *Daily People,* May 30, 1907.
32 "wayward tidbits": *CT,* March 16, 1907, 4.
32 a "saloon" crowd: Putnam, "Travail," 17.
32 The saloon crowd: David A. Clemens to William E. Borah, March 21, 1907, WEB.
32 In the 1896 election: Larson, "Idaho's Role," 2–3.
32 "There will hereafter": *Idaho Woman,* April 15, 1897.
32 "not be enough men": *ECN,* July 3, 1906, 6.
32 Not surprisingly: George Crookham, interview with author, Caldwell, Idaho, April 1989.
32 "The plain fact": *CT,* April 2, 1904, 1.
33 It was the WCTU: *CT,* March 17, 1900, 2–3.
33 If they closed: Mrs. A. E. Gipson, paper read at dedication of Carnegie Library, Caldwell, Idaho, 1914, 4, ISHS.
33 Originally quartered: Ibid., 3.
33 One Caldwell youth: Brock, "Gipson," 2.

33 In that era: Trachtenberg, *Incorporation*, 145.
33 As early as 1901: Leppert and Thurston, *Early Caldwell*, 28.
33 These same women: Ibid., 35.
33 .A regular reader: Bartlett Sinclair, "Idaho's Martyr," *IDS*, n.d.
33 "You have probably thought": Frank Steunenberg to family, January 12, 1890, GC.
33 the governor had spent $2.50: FSP.
33 "To all such": *CT*, October 7, 1905.
34 But they weren't pleased: *CT*, March 14, 1908, 3.
34 By 1900: Schwantes, *Mountain*, 130–31.
34 "The idea that Chinamen": R. L. James, "Why No Chinamen," 15.
34 "football": *IDS*, April 1, 1906.
34 That same evening: *CT*, February 28, 1903.
35 "Will they endure": *CT*, June 1903.
35 One Halloween: Jack Kipp Oral History, CPL.
35 Always ready: George Crookham, interview with author, Caldwell, Idaho, April 1989.
35 "thugs": *CT*, November 28, 1903.
35 Two of the best: *CT*, July 2, 1953.
35 "unless something is done": Etulain, "Basque," 30.
35 Dr. Albert Franklin Isham: *CT*, January 26, 1884.
36 Audiences were too small: Ernst, *Trouping*, 61.
36 Nobody could laugh: B. Sinclair, "Reminiscences."
36 the ultimate expression: Griffith, *Home Town News*, 99.
36 under the baton: Bess Steunenberg, speech, Caldwell, Idaho, 1963, AK.
37 "The scene": *CT*, June 16, 1906, 1; quoted in Attebery, "Domestic," 10.
37 The governor had good reason: *CT*, July 18, 1903.
37 All the offices: Architectural plans and interview with Charles F. Hummel of Hummel, LaMarche and Hunsucker, Boise, 1990.
37 Theodore Bird: Clay, *Assassination*. 32.
37 Given the perils: L. P. Abbott, *Story of Nylic*.
38 Barely forty-eight hours later: *NYT*, January 1, 1906.
38 The insurance scandals: Lyon, *Success*, 275–82; R. O'Connor, *Courtroom*, 261.
38 whittle with a favorite pen knife: George Crookham, interview with author, April 1989.
38 "We bought the *Tribune*": *CT*, May 6, 1893, 4.
38 They must have loved: *Idaho Democrat*, October 14, 1896; *Idaho Press-Tribune*, May 6, 1953.
38 "Mr. Steunenberg has great faith": *CT*, July 18, 1894, 3.
38 He never hit: FSP.
38 In 1894: *CT*, April 21, 1894, 2; April 25, 1894, 3; May 9, 1894, 3; July 18, 1894, 3.
38 Spurred by A.K.'s zeal: FSP.
39 Altogether, the governor: Ibid.
39 A few years back: *CT*, October 17, 1903, 4.
39 "My business ventures": Frank Steunenberg to Amasa Campbell, December 11, 1905, AC.
39 By August 1894: *CT*, August 15, 1894, 3.
40 his stubborn independence: Connolly, "Moyer-Haywood Case," part 2, 21.
40 Soon he seized: Merle W. Wells, "Frank Steunenberg," in Sims and Benedict, *Idaho's Governors*; *CT*, June 17, 1893, 3.
40 In 1900: J. M. Woodburn to Fred T. Dubois, March 6, 1902, FTD.
40 Sensing a power vacuum: *Moscow* (Idaho) *Star*, June 16, 1900, 1; *CT*, February 24, 1900, 1.
40 In 1902: *ECN*, August 3, 1907, 10; Frank Harris to Fred T. Dubois, June 25, 1902, FTD.
40 By now: J. M. Woodburn to Fred T. Dubois, March 6, 1902; Frank Harris to Dubois, June 25, 1907, FTD.
40 Moreover, the continued flood: *IDS*, November 7, 1902, 3.
40 largely Republican state: Schwantes, *Mountain*, 162.
40 With Fred Dubois's term: *Daily People*, July 2, 1907.
40 "There was strong talk": Josephine Steunenberg to Delia Brobst and Grace Crookham, December 31, 1905, GC.
40 Only that past: George Crookham, interview by author, Caldwell, Idaho, April 1989.
40 "a great, open-minded": *AtR*, April 7, 1906.
40 "Oh, I love it": Clay, *Assassination*, 32.
40 Excavation had begun: *CT*, September 2, 1905.
41 "Get hold of all": *CN*, August 3, 1907.
41 Within five years: *CT*, March 25, 1905, 1.
41 One week that fall: *CT*, September 1, 1905.
41 The Oregon Short Line: *CT*, October 7, 1905.
41 Folks could remember: Gaboury, *Dissension*, 61.
41 "The Oregon Short Line": *ECN*, September 24, 1907, 4.
41 "the galloping monster": Norris, *Octopus*, 48.
42 "notes the sewing machine": *Oregon Journal*, August 25, 1907, reprinted in *AtR*, September 15, 1907, 1.
42 investigation of railroad income: *Milwaukee Journal*, April 19, 1906, 4.
42 In Washington: Blum, *Republican*, 73–107; Pringle, *Roosevelt*, 292–99; Harbaugh, *Power*, 235–52.
42 As the governor: *CHT*, May 5, 1907, 4; Dary, *Pleasure*, 233; Sullivan, *Our Times*, 3:483.
42 local gamblers: In 1887, Idaho's legislature prohibited most forms of gambling. Steunenberg signed the bill

into law, but a court declared it unconstitutional. Although the legislature passed it again in 1899, the law was often flouted by municipalities eager for revenue from gambling licenses, and gambling continued to flourish in many cities (see S. Jones, *Jackpot*, 2–12).

42   a spacious dining room: Jess Hawley to C. P. Connolly, March 15, 1907, HP.
42   and an adjacent ballroom: *CT*, December 9, 1905.
43   practiced perusal: Testimony of Alex Ballantyne, *SvH*, 67.
43   Under "Commissioners' Proceedings": Clay, *Assassination*, 30–31.
43   Another page: *CT*, December 30, 1905.
44   "A splendid milk cow": Ibid.
44   Just then, he heard: Testimony of C. F. Wayne, *SvH*, 39; George Crookham, interview by author, Caldwell, Idaho, May 1996.
44   In the lobby: *SvH*, 303.
44   he waved: *SvH*, 56.
44   Caldwell was known: Anderson, "Bomb," 14.
44   The Steunenberg household: FSP.
44   Food was plentiful: *CN*, December 3, 1904.
44   "I only weigh": Frank Steunenberg to his parents, January 12, 1890, GC.
45   "a little bit different": Walter Griffiths, interview by Irving Stone, Box 13, IS.
45   "a fit subject": MacLane, *Sagebrush*, 140.
45   "He didn't have": Holbrook, *Rocky*, 200.
45   "Better smoke on earth": *CN*, December 6, 1905.
45   The day after Christmas: *IDS*, December 26, 1905.
45   The only section: *IDS*, July 26, 1907, 8.
45   But the working poor: U.S. Census for Canyon County, 1910.
46   In 1888: Garlock, *Guide*, 61; *CT*, April 28, 1888, 4; Wiebe, *Search*, 69.
46   Only the latter: *CT*, November 3, 1888, 1.
46   For three weeks later: 1902–03 were very good years for the ALU, which increased its national membership from 18,000 "direct" and 70,000 "affiliated" in 1902 to 70,000 and 200,000 by June 1903 (see Kipnis, *American Socialist*, 149–50; Hillquit, *History*, 312).
46   According to the *Tribune*: *CT*, February 21, 1903, 1.
46   The *Tribune* welcomed: The Socialist Party had doubts about the ALU's commitment to Socialism (see Kipnis, *American Socialist*, 144).
46   Furnished rooms: *CT*, March 31, 1906.
47   any more than most: Hunter, *Poverty*, passim.
47   As the new year began: *IDS*, July 14, 1907, 9.
47   "Ought to have staid": *CT*, October 17, 1903, 4.
47   "jeweled with Christian graces": *CT*, March 31, 1906.
47   her inexplicable defection: Schultz, *History*, 1.
47   "his church attendance": B. Sinclair, "Reminiscences."
47   That Saturday: *CT*, December 30, 1906.
47   Then a portly member: Helen Marie Keppel Toal, speech to Women's Association of Boone Memorial Church, January 1963, AK.
48   "popular young society people": *CT*, October 26, 1907.
48   A Young Man's: *CT*, October 31, 1903, 8.
48   "Why," he told a friend: B. Sinclair, "Reminiscences."
48   "You can imagine": A. K. Steunenberg to Carrie Steunenberg, October 14, 1906, AK.
48   No fewer: Toal, "Keppel Family History," 21.
49   The "plump" and "jolly": F. Steunenberg Jr., *Martyr*, 91.
49   "to the amusement": *CT*, December 16, 1905.
49   "You'll laugh": *Nampa Leader-Herald*, December 1906; Harry Elkington Oral History, ISHS.
49   "amusing, elevating and refining": *CT*, December 9, 1905.
49   One night: *CT*, December 30, 1906.
49   "Very pleasant": WB.
50   Perhaps because Idaho: Schwantes, *Mountain*, 13.
50   And with it: Wiebe, *Search*, 44–110.
50   But nothing stemmed: Ibid.
51   At first, Belle thought: F. Steunenberg Jr., *Martyr*, 109.
51   He and his family: *SvH*, 38.
51   After stopping off: *SvH*, 42.
51   "Send for Mama": *ECN*, January 2, 1906, 1.
51   "as if mice had chewed": Albert Martin, *Idaho Press-Tribune*, 70th annual progress ed., May 6, 1953.
51   "little bits": *Chicago Socialist*, April 7, 1906.
51   His left shoe: McP3, June 9, 1906, 2.
52   Bill Lesley: *Caldwell City Directory*, 1911; *Caldwell News-Tribune*, March 29, 1944; TH, January 16, 1906, 2.
52   A sturdy youth: *BG*, May 14, 1906; *NYT*, June 5, 1907, 2.
52   He and Will: *SvH*, 72.
52   the first wagon: *IDS*, July 20, 1907, 5.
52   When the town's barber: *Idaho Press-Tribune*, 70th annual progress ed., May 6, 1953.
53   At Sam Clay's house: Sam Clay, interview by Irving Stone, IS.
53   "The ground was so slippery": William L. Steunenberg to Delia Brobst, January 13, 1906, GC.
53   "What's the matter": Connolly, "Moyer-Haywood Case," part 2, 21; Sullivan, *Our Times*, 3:482–83.

54 Frank Steunenberg never uttered: Will Steunenberg's letter of January 13 and Pete Steunenberg's undated report carefully record every word spoken by their brother in the ten minutes between the explosion and his death. This phrase is not among them.

2: THE SWEATBOX

55 "Frank died": William L. Steunenberg to Delia Brobst, January 13, 1906, GC.
55 "Life has seemed to me": Ibid.
55 Even before Frank: Report by Pete Steunenberg, n.d., GC.
55 "The man who blew": Pete Steunenberg, interview by Irving Stone, IS.
56 the train's whistle: Albert Martin, *Idaho Press-Tribune,* 70th annual progress ed., May 6, 1953.
56 The tracks were clear: *DP,* n.d. (probably August 1906).
57 George Froman: *PO,* March 4, 1906.
57 Iron scraps: *IDS,* January 1, 1906, 1.
57 dead yellowhammer: *IDS,* January 5, 1906, 1.
57 "while Gooding and others": Joseph Hutchinson to Fred T. Dubois, April 10, 1906, FTD.
58 Placards announced: *CT,* December 30, 1905.
58 Strange men: *Idaho Press-Tribune,* 70th annual progress ed., May 6, 1953.
58 Crockett Bales: Lorene B. Thurston, interview by author, Caldwell, Idaho, October 1995.
59 "a place of torture": *IDS,* February 27, 1906.
59 "any pleasant room": Ibid. Barely two years later, the *Statesman* expressed a different view of the same techniques as allegedly used by federal prosecutors. In an editorial on March 17, 1908, it suggested that the sweatbox had once been used to put a suspect in a "condition of nervous fear" in which he would say "what the government wants him to say."
59 Andy Johnson: The Boise police department carried about twenty men: a chief, a captain, a "city detective," and fifteen patrolmen, of whom two were "specials," a status halfway between patrolman and detective. The special operated in plain clothes but wasn't expert enough to deserve the prized title of detective (*PET,* June 1, 1907).
59 Since he'd been seen: *IDS,* December 31, 1905, 1.
59 But a call to Homer Bostwick: *Boise City Directory,* 1906.
59 "Only a fiend": T. Shelley Sutton to unidentified newspaper, January 4, 1906, 4.
59 "impertinent little fellow" ... "Red Mouth variety": *IDS,* January 2, 1907, 2; *ECN,* January 1, 1906, 1.
59 Swearing roundly: *IDS,* January 2, 1906, 2.
60 Russian miner: *IDS,* January 1, 1906, 1.
60 Such tactics: *Baker City Herald,* quoted in *IDS,* January 4, 1906, 4.
60 "broken English": *IDS,* January 5, 1906, 1; January 6, 1906, 1; *ECN,* January 1, 1906, 1.
60 Mrs. Beatty alerted her husband: *CT,* October 17, 1903, 4.
61 "Sir: Da man dat killa": *IDS,* January 9, 1906, 1.
61 If Idahoans: For anarchism, I relied heavily on Avrich, *Haymarket,* 39–119; Preston, *Aliens,* 26–33; Paul Avrich, interview by author, April 1995.
62 Eleven Sicilians: R. M. Brown, *Violence,* 129.
62 A day later: Leech, *Days,* 900.
63 After his arrest: J. W. Clark, *Assassins,* 39–40.
63 The episode: Ibid., 239; *NYT,* January 5, 1906. Statement of Secret Service agent Stephen A. Connell, ROS. Memorandum for the president by E. E. Paine, ROS.
63 In 1863: Di Salvatore, "Vehement Fire," *New Yorker,* April 27, 1987, 49–52.
64 Almost overnight: Ibid.
64 "In the hand of the enslaved": Avrich, *Haymarket,* 166.
64 Revolutionaries were urged: Ibid., 166–68.
64 It had been employed: *CHT,* February 19, 1906; Pipes, *Revolution,* 14, 27.
64 In Boise, the police: *IDS,* March 3, 1908, 3.
65 Earlier, he'd stayed: McP3, January 16, 1906.
65 This was regarded: *IDS,* January 5, 1906, 1.
65 She walked out onto Main Street: Ibid.
65 Then there was the "respectable": *CN,* January 6, 1906, 1.
66 Finally, there was another: *SvH,* 302.
66 Clean-shaven, dressed: This detail comes from a photograph, introduced at the Haywood trial, that was taken shortly after Hogan's arrest. The *Statesman* published it on June 26, 1907.
66 Sometimes he claimed: *IDS,* January 3, 1906, 1.
66 Most of the time: Clay, *Assassination,* 40.
66 Cy Decker: *SOC,* June 1, 1907.
66 As the dust settled: Horsley, *Confessions,* 36.
67 Abruptly, Hogan: Lowell and Peterson, *First Hundred,* 254.
67 "Do you know": *Collier's,* May 18, 1907.
67 "only one present": *ECN,* January 15, 1906, 1.
67 On Sunday morning: Pete Steunenberg to C. E. Arney, February 8, 1906, CEA.
67 But when Froman tried: *PO,* January 1, 1906; TH, January 20, 1906, 5.
67 Deciding the stranger: *PO,* January 2, 1906.
68 Pausing now: Connolly, "Moyer-Haywood Case," part 2, 21.
68 "I'm convinced": Ibid.; Ballantyne testimony, *SvH,* 67.

68   When Brown said: *CN,* January 6, 1906, 1.
68   Clay thought Hogan: Samuel Clay to Irving Stone, IS.
69   O'Connor nodded: AH, 159.
69   Charlie Jap: *IDS,* January 15, 1906.
69   Cy Decker: *SOC,* June 1, 1907.
69   Although some reporters: *DP,* May 17, 1907, 1.
69   Some people: *PO,* May 12, 1907.
70   she knew that he was: *IDS,* May 12, 1907, 4.
70   While Lizzie's sister: A variant of this story put Lizzie's younger sister, Theresa, in the central role. According to a story by Harry O. Collins, editor of the *Daily Missoulian* of Missoula, Montana, that appeared July 28, 1907, Theresa had taken a Thiel detective as her lover and confided her suspicions about Hogan to him, which led to the search of Hogan's room. Collins claimed this was "the key that unlocks the plot." But there scarcely seems time for a Thiel detective to have formed a relationship with Theresa, since Thiel operatives arrived in Caldwell only on December 31.
70   "Don't touchee": *IDS,* January 2, 1906, 1.
70   "I understand": Holbrook, *Rocky,* 218.
70   "one of the coolest men": *IDS,* January 2, 1906.
70   Hogan was told: *SvH,* 306.
70   "I can't blame": *IDS,* January 2, 1906, 2.
71   "He was a little round-faced": Ralph Scatterday, interview with Irving Stone, IS.
71   George Froman still urged: *PO,* February 28, 1906; *IDS,* May 20, 1907, 1.
71   he'd been drinking heavily: Connolly, "Moyer-Haywood Case," part 2, 21.
71   At five: Testimony of Julian Steunenberg, *SvH,* 72.
72   "a primitive little affair": *DT,* March 1, 1906.
72   Ultimately, Caldwell: *IDS,* January 2, 1906, 1.
72   Born in Princeton: A. Kaufmann, *Historic Supplement; Idaho Magazine,* April 1906, 21–22.
72   In a chiding account: *RMN,* June 14, 1885, 1.
72   On February 26: Rider, "Police," 280.
73   After two days: *RMN,* March 3, March 11, 1886.
73   The letter was signed: *Denver Tribune-Republican,* March 1, 1886, 5.
73   "I'm not particularly stuck": Ibid., March 18, 1886, 8.
73   More important: Phipps, *Bull Pen,* 59–65.
74   Then he and his entourage: Maiken, *Night Trains,* 290. The three northern transcontinental railways—the Northern Pacific, the Great Northern, and the Milwaukee Road—all crossed Idaho far up in the panhandle, where the topography seemed less forbidding than in the pine forests of central Idaho. In the south, the Oregon Short Line of the Union Pacific followed the Snake River Plain from Pocatello through Boise to the Oregon line.
74   As night fell: *IDS,* January 1, 1906, 1.
74   As late as 1892: Tierney, *Darrow,* 210.
74   A few eastern states: Fuld, *Administration,* 175; Prassel, *Officer,* 160.
74   Empowered to make arrests: Calhoun, *Lawmen,* 150–52, passim.
74   Moreover, the notion: In the section that follows on the detective in Anglo-American history and literature, I have relied heavily on Ousby, *Bloodhounds,* 7–173; Morn, *Eye,* viii-16; Lane, *Policing,* 146–205; Dunbar, *Business,* 1–29; W. R. Miller, "Dime Novel," 3–51; J. W. Murray, *Memoirs,* 13–34; Furlong, *Fifty,* 6–7, 168, 216–17; McWatters, *Knots,* 643–64; Thorwald, *Century,* passim; Train, "Detectives and Detectives' Work," "Detectives Who Detect," and "The Private Detective's Work."
78   Pinkerton, whose loyalty: Fishel, *Secret War,* 105, 585–87.
79   Some thought: Slotkin, *Gunfighter,* 140.
81   When Bangs was found: Mackay, *Allan Pinkerton,* 224.
81   Pinkerton, writes one of his biographers: Ibid., 229.
81   After finding his: Ibid., 230.
82   In requiring: Wills, *Trumpets,* 121–23.
82   "These trade unions": Pinkerton, *Strikers,* 3.
83   Through detective agencies: Hunter, *Violence,* 280–81.
83   In 1906: Beet, "Shameless."
83   "never has the private detective": "Gompers and Burns," 372.
84   Just as they dreaded: Lehman, *Perfect,* 94–95.
85   Disgruntled: Mackay, *Allan Pinkerton,* 159, 217.
85   "There is a sense": Lehman, *Perfect,* 94–95.
85   The patient: A. Douglas, *Terrible,* 34.
87   Belle would have: Josephine Steunenberg to Grace Crookham and Delia Brobst, December 31, 1905, GC.
87   "like Frank": Nina Steunenberg to Delia Brobst, January 13, 1906, GC.
87   In a sixteen-dollar suit: Josephine Steunenberg to Grace Crookham and Delia Brobst, January 7, 1906, GC.
87   "opiates": *ECN,* January 1, 1906, GC.
87   round-the-clock attendance: *IDS,* January 3, 1906, 2.
88   Once her husband: Frank Steunenberg to his parents, January 12, 1890, GC.
88   Belle's regular attendance: Schultz, *History.*
88   A Pinkerton detective: McP3, May 7, 1907.
88   Since each sexual act: Numbers, *Prophetess,* 154.
88   Of late: Ida Crouch-Hazlett, *MN,* March 7, 1907.
88   Some thought: Lutz, *Nervousness,* passim.

88   Relations were: A. F. Steunenberg to author, July 26, 1989.
88   A strict disciplinarian: Frank Steunenberg Jr. to Bess Steunenberg, November 15, 1963, GC.
88   Adventists regarded: Numbers, *Prophetess*, 116.
88   Frank Junior: F. Steunenberg Jr., *Martyr*, 93, 98.
88   "If you had not": Frank Steunenberg to Julian Steunenberg, February 2, 1905, GC.
89   Sister Jo got: Nina Steunenberg to Grace Crookham, January 10, 1906, GC.
89   "That shirt": Josephine Steunenberg to Grace Crookham, January 10, 1906, GC.
89   "Is that so?": William L. Steunenberg to Delia Brobst, January 13, 1906, GC.
89   "I am all 'broke up' ": A. K. Steunenberg to Montie Gwinn, January 12, 1906, GC.
89   With the seating: *IDS*, January 3, 1906, 1.
90   "You have redeemed yourself": Joseph Hutchinson to Fred T. Dubois, April 10, 1906, FTD.
90   "I never formed but one": *IDS*, January 3, 1906, 1.
90   "During his eighteen years": Ibid.
91   "Idaho consecrates": Ibid.
91   "The face of the man": *IDS*, January 2, 1906, 1.
91   "a devil incarnate": Ibid., January 3, 1906, 1.
92   "It was one of the nasty kind": *Salt Lake Herald*, January 4, 1906; *SvH*, 3841.
92   To Crane: *IDS*, January 3, 1906, 1.
93   He spent fruitless hours: McP3, January 16, 1906.
93   They were both released: *ECN*, January 4, 1906, 1.
93   His demeanor: Ibid.
93   To every subsequent inquiry: *IDS*, January 4, 1906, 1.
94   From his description: *SvH*, 4093.
94   Sheriff Edward Bell: *ECN*, January 9, 1907, 3; *IDS*, January 9, 1907.
94   "To T. Hogan": *IDS*, June 19, 1907, 3.
95   The firm had close ties: Connolly, "Moyer-Haywood Case," part 2, 22.
96   Orchard occupied: *CT*, March 21, 1908, 5.
96   "crowded": *IDS*, March 13, 1906.
97   "Hogan impressed me": *ECN*, January 6, 1906, 1.
97   "a hired assassin": Pete Steunenberg to C. E. Arney, February 8, 1906, CEA.
97   "The fellow": Josephine Steunenberg to Grace Crookham, January 10, 1906, GC.
97   "great, magnificent Frank": Nina Steunenberg to Delia Brobst, January 13, 1906, GC.

3: IMPS OF DARKNESS

98   It's the Coeur d'Alenes: Will Steunenberg to Delia Brobst, January 13, 1906, GC.
98   "The foul deed": *RMN*, March 1, 1906.
98   "A great many minds": *IDS*, December 31, 1907.
98   In its natural state: MacLane, *Sagebrush*, 11–13.
99   Later—some seventy: Alt and Hyndman, *Geology*, 6.
99   That euphoric night: Stoll, *Silver Strike*, 6.
99   Staking out: R. W. Smith, *Mining War*, 2.
99   Every Northern Pacific: Ibid., 8.
99   Succeeding years: R. W. Smith, *Mining War*, 2–3.
100   "No capital": Limerick, *Legacy*, 105.
100   Into this vacuum: Ibid., 105–06; Derickson, *Health*, 9.
100   "The great attendant": Lingenfelter, *Hardrock*, 3–4.
100   "View their work": Ibid., 13.
100   "open season": Limerick, *Legacy*, 106.
100   If the westering experience: Ibid., 95–111.
101   To contest this alien: Ibid., 10; Lingenfelter, *Hardrock*, 38–45.
101   In 1887: R. W. Smith, *Mining War*, 17.
101   The owners cut: Lingenfelter, *Hardrock*, 199.
101   "We'll never hire": R. W. Smith, *Mining War*, 36–37, 40.
102   By June: Ibid., 39, 44–46; Fahey, *Ballyhoo*, 77.
102   The first: Lingenfelter, *Hardrock*, 206.
102   "This is a fine head": Popkin, "McParland," 258.
102   "He is as tough": Siringo, *Riata*, 217.
102   These dispatches: Stoll, *Silver Strike*, 192; Fahey, *Ballyhoo*, 79.
102   a Thiel operative: Siringo, *Riata*, 137.
103   With lively badinage: Ibid., 147.
103   Through cracks: Pingenot, *Siringo*, 42–43.
103   At that, some sixty: Fahey, *Ballyhoo*, 80; R. W. Smith, *Mining War*, 65.
103   The president complied: R. W. Smith, *Mining War*, 74–79.
103   The Fourth Infantry: Fahey, *Ballyhoo*, 80–81.
104   Stunned at their reversal: Lingenfelter, *Hardrock*, 210.
104   "bullpens": An old Anglo-Saxon term, widely used to mean a stockade for the confinement of prisoners, in the Civil War and other conflicts (*Random House Historical Dictionary of American Slang*, 1994; see also D. Brown, *Galvanized*, 14).

764 NOTES

104 In jailhouse talks: Lens, *Wars,* 116.
104 Soon after their release: R. W. Smith, *Mining War,* 110–13; Jensen, *Heritage,* 54–55; Lingenfelter, *Hardrock,* 219–21.
104 William Hard: Hard, "Western Federation," 126–27, 132.
104 "This is a great year": *CT,* August 20, 1892, 1.
105 Most of the *Tribune's: CT,* July 16, 1892, 4.
105 "the plutocrats": O'Toole, *Five,* 286.
105 This struggle: Painter, *Armageddon,* 85–86.
105 "seductive as the vampire": *LMT,* June 24, 1896.
105 "anarchists, howlers": Ashby, *Bryan,* 63.
105 "Shall we next": Beer, *Hanna,* 517.
105 "Something furious stirred": Ibid., 514–16.
106 "fallacy of free silver": Longworth, *Crowded Hours,* 13.
106 In patrician law offices: Glad, *McKinley,* 190.
106 Strange threats: Beer, *Hanna,* 516.
106 A Free Coinage saloon: Gaboury, *Dissension,* 156.
106 Mainstream Republicans: Graff, *Dubois,* 200.
106 "Idaho not only needs": *LMT,* June 3, 1896, 2.
106 In 1892: K. Murray, "Issues and Personalities," 216.
107 "great unwashed": *IDS,* August 21, 1896, 2.
107 "My environments": Ibid., January 4, 1906, 2.
107 "this monstrous combination": Ibid., August 22, 1896, 1–2.
107 "From every misty mountain": *Blackfoot News,* August 22, 1896, 1.
108 Bryan swept: MacLane, *Sagebrush,* 140.
108 "dynopops": Aiken, "Too Soon," 315.
108 In 1894: Ibid.; Gaboury, "State House," 16.
108 "a source of discord": Commissioners of Shoshone County to Frank Steunenberg, April 17, 1897, ISHS.
108 At first the governor: Frank Steunenberg to George L. Shoup, June 22, 1897.
109 In the wake: Steunenberg testimony, CDLT, 1067–68.
109 He tried to regain: Fahey, *Hercules,* 31.
109 "genuine longhaired": Gaboury, *Dissension,* 320.
109 The Democrats and Silver Republicans: Hawley, *History,* 1:24; Sims and Benedict, *Idaho's Governors,* appendix B.
109 Only Bunker Hill: Gaboury, *Dissension,* 17.
109 An art connoisseur: Peterson, "Social and Political," 33.
109 "We've got to beat": Hammond, *Autobiography,* 189–90.
110 Before long the APA: Aiken, "Too Soon," 316–18.
110 "proceed in the direction": *Wardner News,* March 13, 1897.
110 When Burrus sued: The group included A. P. Bailey, L. T. Wilson, Hermann Cook, W. Gillespie, E. S. Gay, C. S. Perrin, Henry Miller, H. M. Ross, G. T. Edmiston, and J. A. R. Campbell (*Wardner News,* March 13, 1897).
110 Eventually, a magistrate: J. Montgomery, *Liberated Woman,* 291.
110 "It may be too soon": Aiken, "Too Soon," 319–20.
111 Not only: Ibid., 322–23.
111 In the years since: Livingston-Little, "Bunker Hill," 43; Testimony of Frederick Burbidge, IC, 439.
111 On April 18: Gaboury, *Dissension,* 336–37.
111 On his own initiative: CDLT, 1121–31.
111 "County authorities": Bartlett Sinclair to Frank Steunenberg, April 30, 1899; Frederick Burbidge to Steunenberg, April 26, 1899; Testimony of Bartlett Sinclair, CDLT, 1609.
111 "Nothing to arbitrate": Testimony of Frank Steunenberg, CDLT, 894.
111 "Am on the ground": Frank Steunenberg to James D. Young, April 26, 1899; Young to Steunenberg, April 26, 1899, CDLT, 891.
112 Hutton and Olmstead: Testimony of Hugh France, IC, 468.
112 A mile down the track: *SvH,* 123–24.
112 men of Mullan: Fahey, *Hercules,* 35; Schwantes, *Mountain,* 153.
112 So the rogue train: Fahey, *Hercules,* 27.
113 "The engine itself was covered": Testimony of Conner Malott, CDLT, 1351.
113 Each miner: *Idaho State Tribune,* May 3, 1899; *Wardner News,* May 6, 1899; Hugh France testimony, IC, 461–79; L. W. Hutton testimony, IC, 564–68; Beal and Wells, *History,* 2:106–10.
113 "I've ordered them": Testimony of Conner Malott, CDLT, 1353.
113 Later he testified: Testimony of James D. Young, IC, 531.
113 A twenty-eight-year-old union man: Actually John Schmidt, a native of Germany.
114 Others had a bolder scheme: Other reports put the amount of stolen dynamite placed under the concentrator at 3,500 pounds (Rich, *Civil Disorders,* 113).
114 By 2:50: Ibid.
114 In bed that day: *IDS,* April 30, 1899, 8; F. Steunenberg Jr., *Martyr,* 71.
114 "The armed force": Adam L. Mohler to Frank Steunenberg, April 29, 1899.
114 "Representations": Frank Steunenberg to James D. Young, April 29, 1899.
114 "Conditions at Wardner": Adam L. Mohler to Frank Steunenberg, second message, April 29, 1899.
114 "like a thunder clap": *Capital,* May 6, 1899, 8.
114 The sense of emergency: Ibid.; Steunenberg testimony, CDLT, 995.
115 But with all five hundred: H. C. Corbin to N. N. Cox, March 30, 1899.

115 So he promptly: Frank Steunenberg to William McKinley, April 29, 1899.
115 "walked among men": W. A. White, *Masks*, 155.
115 a bitter Senate battle: Leech, *Days*, 348–69.
115 "I must have rest": Ibid., 114, 451–55, 459; *NYT*, April 29, 1899, 2, 4.
115 The only matter of state: *New York Tribune*, April 30, 1899, 1.
116 "dangerous to the liberties": Coakley, *Federal*, 3.
116 ample precedent: Laurie, *U.S. Army*, 11.
116 between 1881 and 1905: Trachtenberg, *Incorporation*, 80.
116 From 1877 to 1903: Forbath, *Law*, 118.
116 The only sign: George Cortelyou to H. C. Corbin, April 29, 1899.
116 Preoccupied with his: Leech, *Days*, 370.
116 It was the able: Ibid., 237.
116 Brigadier General: H. C. Corbin to William McKinley, April 30, 1899.
116 On April 30: Frank Steunenberg to William McKinley, April 29, 1899; H. C. Corbin to H. C. Merriam, April 30, 1907.
117 Thus, he and two: *IDS*, May 2, 1899, 1; S. H. Hays and Frank C. Ramsey to H. C. Merriam, April 30, 1899.
117 "Nothing would please": *IDS*, May 3, 1899, 1.
117 "if not disapproved": H. C. Merriam to H. C. Corbin, May 2, 1899.
118 Reaching Walla Walla: H. C. Corbin to H. C. Merriam, May 3, 1899; Letterbook no. 1, GCP.
118 In military terms: Laurie, *U.S. Army*, 21; A. Fowler, *Black*, 138–39.
118 Merriam may have summoned: Jerry M. Cooper, *Civil Disorders*, 44.
118 "In our childhoods": Merriam, "Maine in the War," 1, HCM.
119 The regiment saw more action: Shaara, *Angels*, xix.
119 As late as August: Cornish, *Sable*, 50–51.
119 Their promising performances: Blight, *Douglass'*, 148–51.
120 Would the vice president: H. D. Hunt, *Hannibal*, 162–63; Hamlin, *Hannibal*, 430–31; Bangs, "Ullmann Brigade," 290.
120 On January 13: Hamlin, *Hannibal*, 433.
120 "the finest, sharpest men": Quarles, *Negro*, 9; Glatthaar, *Forged*, 37.
120 "in this new negro-soldier": R. W. B. Lewis, *Jameses*, 133.
120 "hordes of darkies": Bangs, "Ullmann Brigade," 292–93.
121 That spring: Edmonds, *Port Hudson*, 1:51–52.
121 In May 1864: James Lewis to H. C. Merriam, November 2, 1893.
121 "arose late": HCMD, entries for January 24, 26, 1865.
121 "It was warm": HCMD, January 9, 1865.
121 "a polished speaker": Bangs, "Ullmann Brigade," 292.
122 "most disgraceful": HCMD, January 30, 1865.
122 "I find Anna": HCMD, February 15, 1865.
122 "very pretty": HCMD, February 17, 1865.
122 "horrible swamps": HCMD, March 28, 1865.
122 "wallowing in the mud": HCMD, March 29, 1865.
122 Hours before: Cornish, *Sable*, 285.
122 He paid for: Merriam testimony, CDLT, 1874.
122 For his prewar work: Speech by H. C. Merriam to a banquet of the Loyal Legion, Denver, February 13, 1893, HCM.
123 In July 1866: Glatthaar, *Forged*, 112.
123 By July 1865: Cornish, *Sable*, 288.
123 In July 1866: Villard, "Negro," 721.
123 Between 1870 and 1900: Leckie, *Buffalo Soldiers*, 257–58.
123 But its presence: Gatewood, *"Smoked Yankees,"* 7–8; M. J. T. Clark, "Twenty-fourth," 25.
123 For years: Cashin, *Under Fire*, passim.
123 Merriam's first command: Letter from unknown party to Merriam, January 16, 1868, HCM.
124 "My darling husband": Statement by John M. Schultz, chaplain, Twenty-fourth Infantry, April 28, 1870, HCM.
124 "The gentle": H. C. Merriam, in *Army and Navy Journal*, May 1870.
124 "Night and morning": "Just about Colorado," clipping from an unidentified Denver newspaper, HCM.
124 "as a drill instructor": "Roosevelt May Not Promote Merriam," n.d. Unidentified newspaper, HCM.
124 "pitching camp": *Army and Navy Register*, April 4, 1891, 212–23.
124 "the best knapsack": *Journal of the United States Infantry Association*, April 1905.
124 "So are the laurels": HCMD, October 2, 1865.
124 "in the absence": H. C. Merriam to President Andrew Johnson, August 25, 1866, HCM.
125 dispatch of his brother: Lewis Merriam to H. C. Merriam, December 28, 1891, HCM.
125 "the only enemy": H. C. Merriam to Edmund F. Webb, December 9, 1896.
125 a feud: File on Merriam-O'Reilly dispute, HCM.
125 The colonel got his revenge: "Just about Colorado," n.d.
125 For O'Reilly wasn't: *Dictionary of American Biography*, s.v. "O'Reilly, Robert Maitland."
125 duck hunting: Nevins, *Cleveland*, 528–29, 613.
125 The War Department reviewed: "Thurber" to Grover Cleveland, n.d., HCM.
125 "you were hurting": Lewis Merriam to H. C. Merriam, December 28, 1891, HCM.
125 He had a disconcerting habit: "Gen. Merriam Says Failure to Accept Miles' Advice Wasted Lives in Cuba," "Gen. Merriam Misquoted," "General Merriam Makes Denial," from unidentified newspapers, HCM.

125   "I understand Merriam's offense": Aldebert Ames to Joshua Chamberlain, n.d., but early 1895, in H. C. Merriam to Lamont, February 10, 1895, HCM.

126   In April he wrote: H. C. Merriam to Miles, April 12, 1898, HCM.

126   "comic cartoon": Leech, *Days*, 202.

126   "upon the principle": "General Alger's Apologia," *Nation*, February 13, 1902.

126   "I am led": H. C. Merriam to H. C. Corbin, March 5, 1899, HCM.

126   "It would have caused": *DP*, February 6, 1901.

126   "You could hear": Henry C. Merriam Jr. to Henry C. Merriam, February 8, 1899, HCM.

127   For blacks: Katz, *Black*, 199–212.

127   "chalking up glory": Scipio, *Regulars*, 12.

127   Along the way: Muller, *Twenty-fourth*, 14.

128   "hellholes": M. J. T. Clark, "Improbable," 284.

128   "intensely disagreeable": Muller, *Twenty-fourth*, 17.

128   The lieutenant general: M. J. T. Clark, "Improbable," 287.

128   "greatest Negro-hating": *Broad Ax*, April 23, 1898.

128   "send the colored men": *Salt Lake Tribune*, Salt Lake City, September 20, 1896.

128   but the secretary: *Deseret Evening News*, October 8, 1896.

129   Some of the women: A. Fowler, *Black*, 77–78.

129   "dark sports": M. J. T. Clark, "Twenty-fourth," 53.

129   "gratified": *Salt Lake Herald*, October 16, 1896.

129   "desires to inform": *Broad Ax*, October 24, 1896, 8.

130   "packing a machete": M. J. T. Clark, "Twenty-fourth," 84–85.

130   lowest desertion rate ... "neat, orderly": A. Fowler, *Black*, 78, 137–38.

130   The regiment also: *Salt Lake Tribune*, October 16, 1896.

130   One topic was: M. J.T. Clark, "Twenty-fourth," 67–68.

130   In *Plessy* ... climate: Painter, *Armageddon*, 163–67.

130   "Had they not seen": Bigelow, *Reminiscences*, 37.

131   "possessing immunity": Public Law 90, May 11, 1898 (NA File R&P 655789).

131   immune regiments: Early, "Negro Soldier," 61–71; Gatewood, *"Smoked Yankees,"* 11, 104, 187.

131   Those who contracted: It is now generally agreed that blacks have developed "hemoglobin defenses" in their blood that resist certain types of the malaria parasite. Immunity to yellow fever is disputed, but some authorities believe many blacks by 1899 had substantial acquired immunity, perhaps reinforced by a degree of genetic resistance. See Kiple, *Dimension*, 6–7, 45–47.

131   All four regular: Gatewood, *"Smoked Yankees,"* 2.

131   "I am proud": *Salt Lake Tribune*, April 21, 1898, 1.

132   "Quit yourselves": Ibid. The exhortation is from the Book of Samuel.

132   "splendid horsemen": Ibid., 3.

132   "They knew the negro": Bigelow, *Reminiscences*, 36.

132   "Prejudice reigns": Ibid., 4.

132   "black boys in blue" ... The Twenty-fourth: Gatewood, *"Smoked Yankees,"* 8, 7.

132   While white officers: Ibid., 8–9.

132   Blacks and whites: Ibid., 41.

133   Thus secure: Cosmas, *Army*, 208.

133   "Well, this will be better": Crane, "War Memories," 24.

133   "so quiet and sunny": R. H. Davis, *Notes*, 79.

133   "bloody angle": Lubow, *Reporter*, 183.

133   "in the high grass": R. H. Davis, *Notes*, 88.

134   "hot, spitting song": Crane, "War Memories," 27.

134   About 1:00 p.m.: Trask, *War*, 241.

134   "Yes!"   "It is a marvel": Freidel, *Splendid*, 162, 155.

134   "By Gawd": Crane, "War Memories," 27.

134   Privately, Roosevelt: Lubow, *Reporter*, 166–67.

134   "a charge which began": Einstein, *Roosevelt*, 70.

134   Unwisely, he'd ordered: Milton, *Yellow*, 279.

134   Each man: Crane, "War Memories," 25.

135   "Quit yourselves": Gatewood, *"Smoked Yankees,"* 69.

135   The Twenty-fourth was on: Scipio, *Regulars*, 23.

135   But the nearly: Lubow, *Reporter*, 187.

135   "Colored 24th real hero": M. J. T. Clark, "Twenty-fourth," 101.

135   The regiment paid ... Over the next: Muller, *Twenty-fourth*, 23–25.

136   According to one account: Gatewood, *"Smoked Yankees,"* 43.

136   Another seventy men: Bigelow, *Reminiscences*, 143.

136   When the final roll: Ibid., 32.

136   though it may be: Dr. Kenneth Kiple, interview by author, January 1996.

136   "matchless heroism" ... September 23: M. J. T. Clark, "Twenty-fourth," 101, 32.

137   "the most famous regiment": Prentiss, *History*, 125.

137   "We officers": Trask, *War*, 247.

137   "the dare devil work": Gianakos, "Spanish-American," 39.

137   "splendid heroes": Fletcher, *Black Soldier*, 46.

137   "No troops could have": Roosevelt, "Rough," 436.

137   "the superstition and fear": TR to Robert J. Fleming, May 21, 1900.

137 These private remarks: Dyer, *Race*, 100.
137 As it was: Gatewood, *"Smoked Yankees,"* 203.
137 On New York City's: Sante, *Low Life*, 18–19.
137 Meanwhile: Barbara Branner, interview by author, August 1995.
138 More than a few blacks: David Levering Lewis, interview by author, November 1995.
138 "While the cheers": George W. Prioleau, letter to *Cleveland Gazette*, October 1898.
138 "No finer looking body": *Salt Lake Tribune*, October 1, 1898.
138 "Onward, Christian": *Salt Lake Tribune*, October 2, 1898.
138 "The Vienna Cafe": *Broad Ax*, October 8, 1898.
139 Finally, their anger: *NYT*, November 11, 1898, 1; Henry Litchfield West, "The Race War in North Carolina," *Forum*, January 1899, 580; Gatewood, *"Smoked Yankees,"* 198.
139 "I'm an American citizen": *Salt Lake Tribune*, February 28, 1900, 1.
139 Meanwhile, in Salt Lake's: M. J. T. Clark, "Twenty-fourth," 107–10; *Salt Lake Tribune*, March 14, April 9, 1899.
140 "I have broken bread": *CT*, April 14, 1900, 1.
140 Steunenberg had turned: *IDS*, April 20, 1899, 8.
140 Only then did he: Bartlett Sinclair to Irene Miller, March 6, 1923.
140 A lively orator: *Daily Capital*, Boise, January 3, 1899, 3; *Idaho Sunday Statesman*, April 10, 1932, 1; Steunenberg testimony, CDLT, 970.
140 Sinclair soon formed: B. Sinclair, "Reminiscences."
140 In dispatching: Bartlett Sinclair, "Idaho's Martyr," *IDS*, n.d.
140 Arriving in Spokane: MacLane, *Sagebrush*, 33.
140 "Burbidge fears": Bartlett Sinclair to Frank Steunenberg, April 30, 1899.
140 "There will be no subserviency": *IDS*, May 23, 1899, 5.
140 the governor's representatives: Frederick Burbidge to Frederick Bradley, August 25, 1899; Myron Folsom to William Borah, May 2, 1899; B. Sinclair, "Reminiscences."
140 Over the next few days: Testimony of Gen. H. C. Merriam, CDLT, 1082; Merriam to H. C. Corbin, May 4, 1899.
141 "Oh, how the colored": *Wardner News*, May 6, 1899.
141 "a fearless, devilish lot": Majority Report, CDLT, 117.
141 "fairly crept along": Ibid., 1802.
141 "a criminal history": Bartlett Sinclair testimony, CDLT, 1627.
141 "entire community": CDLT, 1706–07.
141 "It is difficult": Capt. R. V. Walsh to H. C. Merriam, May 12, 1899.
141 "It was one of the most remarkable": Testimony of Conner Malott, CDLT, 1362–63; *SSR*, May 8, 1899; *Harper's*, May 20, 1899, 498.
142 "Men who've had": CDLT, 595.
142 "vicious watch dog": Bartlett Sinclair testimony, IC, 558.
142 When the train arrived: Bartlett Sinclair testimony, CDLT, 1629.
142 In early May: Ibid., 1708–09; Conner Malott testimony, CDLT, 1363.
142 On May 6: H. C. Merriam to H. C. Corbin, May 6, 1899.
142 As the barn could: Merriam testimony, CDLT, 1709, 1805; H. C. Merriam to Frank Steunenberg, May 11, 1899.
142 Most prisoners: Capt. Frank A. Edwards testimony, CDLT, 1880–1948; Conner Malott testimony, CDLT, 1411–12; H. C. Merriam testimony, CDLT, 1806; H. C. Merriam to H. C. Corbin, May 25, 1899; George Cornell testimony, CDLT, 635.
142 After prisoners: Phipps, *Bull Pen*, 26.
142 "It's no use": Testimony of L. J. Simpkins, CDLT, 572.
142 "a perfect farce": Bartlett Sinclair to Frank Steunenberg, May 1, 1899.
143 "assigned to a melancholy": *SSR*, May 9, 1899.
143 "their full share": *SSR*, May 8, 1899, 2.
143 "With [Boyle and Stimson] in the bullpen": CDLT, 1402.
143 Ultimately, all three: CDLT, 77–80; *SSR*, July 11, 1899.
143 "The disease": Hugh France to Bartlett Sinclair, January 9, 1900.
143 "These are my warrants": CDLT, 1773.
143 "sort of a Pooh Bah": Frederick Robertson testimony, CDLT, 53–54; Bartlett Sinclair testimony, CDLT, 1689.
143 "Indications are": H. C. Merriam to H. C. Corbin, May 4, 1899.
144 Merriam assured Lyon: H. C. Merriam to Henry Lyon, May 5, 1899.
144 "not interpose": Henry Lyon to Assistant Adjutant General, U.S. Troops, Wardner, May 14, 1899.
144 Unfortunately: Henry Lyon testimony, CDLT, 1996–97.
144 "a gross violation": CDLT, 128.
144 "I did not": Bartlett Sinclair testimony, CDLT, 1702.
145 "Well, Sam": S. H. Hays, "Whitney Murder Climax to Acts of Miners Union," *IDS*, n.d.
145 Present, in addition: *IDS*, May 8, 1899, 1.
145 "We, the mine owners": John Finch testimony, IC, 494.
145 "We have taken the monster": *IDS*, May 9, 1899, 1.
145 Now Hays asked: Hugh France testimony, IC, 475; France testimony, CDLT, 1544; Bartlett Sinclair testimony, CDLT, 1668–69, 1755–56; Sinclair testimony, IC, 555; *Washington Post*, August 20, 1899; Hays, *Report*, 11; Frank Steunenberg testimony, CDLT, 924–25.
146 "By order": H. C. Merriam testimony, CDLT, 1856.

146   "I have only abhorrence": *SSR*, May 8, 1899, 2.

146   "I have never": Merriam testimony, CDLT, 1866.

147   Stewart preferred: Wilbur Stewart testimony, CDLT, 157; Major Allen Smith testimony, CDLT, 1956; *DP*, July 1, 1899.

147   General Merriam's aide: Bartlett Sinclair testimony, CDLT, 1705.

147   The proceedings: Bartlett Sinclair testimony, CDLT, 1641; H. C. Merriam testimony, CDLT, 1836–37.

147   "Absurd technicalities": *IDS*, May 9, 1899, 1.

147   So cozy: Frank Steunenberg testimony, CDLT, 987–89.

147   "They have been, and are now": *IDS*, May 23, 1899, 5.

148   Moreover, Merriam was restless: Jerry M. Cooper, *Civil Disorders*, 179.

148   "General Merriam's unwarranted use": *SSR*, May 15, 1889.

148   "have been thrown": H. C. Corbin to H. C. Merriam, June 12, 1899.

148   "it was the President's": George B. Cortelyou to Russell Alger, May 26, 1907.

148   "President wishes": H. C. Corbin to H. C. Merriam, May 26, 1899.

148   "troops are taking": H. C. Merriam to H. C. Corbin, May 30, 1899.

148   "that he is to use": Russell Alger to H. C. Merriam, May 31, 1899.

148   "with the paper": Jerry M. Cooper, *Civil Disorders*, 184.

148   "the Secretary's telegram": Merriam, *Report*, July 31, 1899, 24.

149   Ten defendants: The convictions were later overturned by the Ninth Circuit Court of Appeals in San Francisco. The men were released after serving eleven months in prison.

149   "not so much to impose": Hawley, *History*, 2:254.

149   It argued that all: William E. Borah, "The Closing Argument of W. E. Borah for the Prosecution in the Great Coeur d'Alene Riot-Murder Trial," Wallace, Idaho, July 27, 1899; Corcoran, "Letter"; E. Sullivan, "Paul Corcoran," 43–50; *State v. Corcoran*, 61 PC 1034.

149   The way for his appointment: Frederick W. Bradley to John Hays Hammond, March 6, 1900, BHS.

149   On July 27: Jensen, *Heritage*, 85.

149   That left eight: John R. McBride and Myron A. Folsom, "Status of Cases against Prominent Dynamiters," n.d. (but late 1899), ISHS.

150   On August 25: Court-martial of Sgt. Lewis J. Crawford, R.G. 153, Box 3033, File 13586, NA.

150   Scandinavian, Italian: For ethnicity of the miners imprisoned in the bullpen, see Merriam, *Report*, July 31, 1899, 25.

150   No Chinese: R. V. Walsh to H. C. Merriam, May 12, 1899.

150   "I don't give a God Damn": This was a common formulation among black soldiers during and after the Civil War. Marcus B. Toney, a Confederate private held prisoner at Point Lookout, Virginia, in 1864, said that his black guards often said, "The bottom rail is on top now; my gun wants to smoke" (see Salvatore, *We All Got History*, 135).

150   "Shoot, you black son": Levi Miller testimony, CDLT, 133.

151   "I want you to understand": Frederick Oscar Martin testimony, CDLT, 447.

151   "The women": William Powers testimony, CDLT, 312–31.

151   "the black soldiers were": Haywood, speech at Cooper Union, 467.

151   "Fit representatives": Jerry M. Cooper, *Civil Disorders*, 182–83.

151   "whole rapscallion horde": *Pueblo Courier*, October 27, 1899.

152   "the presence of troops": H. C. Corbin to W. McCallister, August 5, 1899.

152   "has not now been": Elihu Root to Frank Steunenberg, September 18, 1899.

152   "The State of Idaho": Frank Steunenberg to Elihu Root, October 10, 1899.

153   "I refuse to reply": Frank Steunenberg testimony, CDLT, 978, 945, 915, 961.

153   "the military power": Majority Report, CDLT, 124–25.

153   "neither law": Views of the Minority, CDLT, 132.

153   "He knew that he": F. B. Schermerhorn to William E. Borah, May 15, 1907.

154   Over the years: Clay, *Assassination*, 34; F. Steunenberg Jr., *Martyr*, 93, 98; *CHT*, February 19, 1906.

154   People wondered: *Caldwell Record*, February 27, 1901.

154   "Mr. Steunenberg was greatly worried": *IDS*, June 7, 1907, 1.

154   His friends urged: F. Steunenberg Jr. to Stuart Holbrook, SH, Box 27, Folder II.

154   "If those fellows": Connolly, "Moyer-Haywood Case," part 2, 21.

154   "he never believed": *IDS*, June 7, 1907, 1.

4: THE GREAT DETECTIVE

155   "I have split": Defenbach, *Idaho*, 255.

155   "not a pretty man": *Salt Lake Herald*, May 27, 1906.

155   "almost straight gin": Jess Hawley to John F. MacLane, March 27, 1946, HP.

155   "best handshaker": Ibid.; C. E. Arney to Thomas Taggert, July 9, 1906, CEA.

156   "a plain, square-jawed": *Boise Clipper*, n.d., Bess Steunenberg Scrapbook, ISHS.

156   "Mrs. Dubois": Fred T. Dubois to Belle Steunenberg, January 1, 1906.

156   "to cast aspersions": J. M. Woodburn to Fred T. Dubois, January 8, 1906, FTD.

156   "one of the squarest": *DP*, May 7, 1907. For charges that Gooding was exploiting the assassination for political purposes, see also *ECN*, July 7, 1906, 1; *IDS*, August 14, 1906, 4.

156   "I hear generally": Charles H. Jackson to Fred T. Dubois, January 17, 1906, FTD.

156   "This Steunenberg business": D. K. Larimer to Fred T. Dubois, April 3, 1906, FTD.

157   "Some man must": Joseph Hutchinson to Fred T. Dubois, April 10, 1906, FTD.

157 Although the American Bar: J. P. MacKenzie, *Appearance,* 181–83.
158 The Pinkertons took: H. F. Cary to James McParland, n.d.
158 "as thick as fleas": *IDS,* January 12, 1906, 1.
158 "From past experience": F. F. Lischke to William Borah, January 2, 1906, WEB.
159 "I know a detective": D. Johnson, *Hammett,* 46.
159 "some misunderstandings": *IDS,* January 5, 1906.
160 who'd recognized Baxter: AH, 20.
160 Meanwhile, Thiel detectives: *Cost,* n.p.
160 "roping in": The term derives from the activity of "steerers" who "roped in" customers for nineteenth-century bordellos and gambling halls.
161 When Sullivan checked into: *ECN,* January 10, 1906.
162 He loudly threatened: Op. 21 Report, February 21, 1907, PA.
162 "bruised and cut": *CT,* January 26, 1907.
162 "the most unmitigated liar": List of Prosecution Witnesses, annotated by Walter McCornack, WFM.
163 Hasson, who'd come up: *SvA*(II), 616, 626.
164 Undoubtedly tipped: *IDS,* January 11, 1906.
164 "I am satisfied": McP3, January 10, 1906.
165 "Tell your readers": *IDS,* January 12, 1906, 1.
166 "It looks to me": McP3, February 24, 1906.
166 "cold-blooded murder": McP3, February 15, 1906.
167 An operative reported Simpkins: AH, 20.
167 Even before: *CT,* January 6, 1906.
168 "one of the best men": *ECN,* February 22, 1906, 1.
168 Hanlon said the two: This telegram, dated January 8, 1906, read: "As dispatches indicate there is another conspiracy entered into to connect the Western Federation of Miners with grave crime. Several persons in Caldwell, Idaho, have been arrested in pursuance of the conspiracy. The Western Federation of Miners defends no member guilty of crime, but in the past has found every one of its members accused of crime innocent and they would have been the victims of conspiracy had we not aided in defense. So have Mr. Nugent take up the investigation, so if they are innocent they may be discharged" (*SvH,* 3761).
168 An ex-miner: *IDS,* September 19, 1931, 1–2; 22nd Biennial Report, ISHS (1949–50), 19–20.
168 "this mess": Op. 53 to Wilson Swain, January 13, 1906.
168 "a serious affair": *Owyhee Nugget,* January 12, 1906, 1.
168 "a hard matter": Op. 53 to Wilson Swain, January 23, 1906.
168 Over several weeks: *Cost,* n.p.
168 "clean up": Op. 53 to Wilson Swain, January 18, January 19, 1906.
169 "It is a hard": Op. 53 to Wilson Swain, February 7, 1906.
169 "wise to operator": On February 23, 1906, Silver City's *Owyhee Nugget* dismissed a "cock and bull story" that a spy had been uncovered in the mines and chased out of town by a mob, but the Thiel agency reports make clear that the story was accurate.
169 Several days later: *ECN,* February 22, 1906.
169 "We have been in this case": *RMN,* February 23, 1906.
169 "I got elbowed": *PET,* July 31, 1907.
169 Within hours: McP3, January 13, 1906.
170 In their stead: Schlereth, *Victorian,* 213.
170 At century's turn: Schlesinger, *Paths,* 42.
171 The song-and-dance man: Fehrenbach, *Elkdom USA,* 3; de Angelis and Harlow, *Vagabond,* 83–84.
171 "the theatrical, minstrel, musical": Preamble to original BPOE constitution (Fehrenbach, *Elkdom USA*).
171 The Ancient Arabic: *Wall Street Journal,* February 9, 1995.
172 But in 1890: Nicholson and Donaldson, *History,* 12.
172 "emphatically and exclusively": Circular by Meade D. Detweiler (Fehrenbach, *Elkdom, USA*).
172 "it put the visible stamp": Fehrenbach, *Elkdom USA,* 13.
172 "No brother shall use": Fehrenbach, *Elkdom USA.*
173 "grave, serious, unusual": Jasper Nichols and F. E. Fisk to Frank Gooding, January 18, 1906, FG.
174 At the Boise end: *DP,* September 10, 1906, 3.
174 "I don't believe": James Hawley to Jasper Nichols, January 17, 1906.
174 "collapsed under the great strain": *Salt Lake Tribune,* January 22, 1906.
174 There he was met: A. A. Hart, *Historic Boise,* 8, 24.
174 Orchard saw a corpulent: *DR,* November 19, 1911.
174 What McParland saw: "Description of Convict," State Penitentiary, Boise, Idaho, March 18, 1908.
175 Sir Arthur had run: Horan, *Pinkertons,* 499. According to Horan, Pinkerton resented Conan Doyle's appropriating the story, and henceforth relations between the two men cooled. Paul Costello, in *The Real World of Sherlock Holmes,* says the novel originated with a visit by Pinkerton's rival, William J. Burns, to Conan Doyle in April 1913, during which the detective recounted McParland's feats. Fascinated by the yarn, Doyle was said to have filled out the story by consulting Allan Pinkerton's writing on the subject. But Costello offers no evidence, while Horan cites a conversation with one of Pinkerton's collaborators.
175 "singular and terrible": Doyle, *Valley,* 215–16, 211–12.
176 In Drumahee: For the following biographical material, I have relied heavily on Dewees, *Molly Maguires;* Popkin, "McParland," 1–4; and *Report of the Case of the Commonwealth v. John Kehoe et al.,* 39–45, Eleutherian Mills Historical Library, Hagley, Wilmington, Delaware.
176 They were Catholics: Kevin Kenny, interview with author, August 1993.
176 For a while: A. H. Lewis, *Lament,* 46.

177 "We are in great want": Allan Pinkerton to Captain Fitzgerald, August 15, 1872, Pinkerton Letterbooks, 1872–75, Library of Congress.
177 The agency borrowed: Slotkin, *Gunfighter*, 140.
177 "Many a time": Allan Pinkerton to George Bangs, May 18, 1873.
177 In January 1870: Broehl, *Molly*, 144.
177 "The operatives": Benjamin Franklin to Franklin B. Gowen, October 9, 1873, McP2.
177 The name resurfaced: Broehl, *Molly*, 87–89.
178 In barely four years: Ibid., 102–27.
178 The WBA was run: Kevin Kenny, interview by author, August 1993.
178 "I do not charge": Pennsylvania Senate, *Report*, 19.
178 When Gowen met: Broehl, *Molly*, 151.
178 "Municipal": *Springfield Daily Union*, March 17, 1877.
178 "enough of an Irishman": Slotkin, *Gunfighter*, 141.
179 Submitted on October 10: The original is in File B-979, entitled "Molly Maguires," McP1.
180 pseudonym James McKenna: Pinkerton, *Maguires*, 70.
180 McKenna peered out: Doyle, *Valley*, 216.
180 Pinkerton wrote . . . "savage": Slotkin, *Gunfighter*, 142.
180 "drunken brawls": Pinkerton, *Maguires*, 73.
181 "a God-forsaken place": McP1, January 6, 1874.
181 McKenna assured: McP1, January 2, February 18, 1874.
181 "seems to be much feared": McP2, March 3–4, 1874.
181 wagering on dogfights: McP1, December 14, 1875.
181 to raise funds: McP2, March 17, 1874; Broehl, *Molly*, 164–65.
181 For months: McP2, March 5, 1874.
181 On April 14: McP2, April 14, 1874.
181 He swore: Dewees, *Molly Maguires*, appendix.
182 "From Hell": McP2, March 24, 1874.
182 "thin and cadaverous": Broehl, *Molly*, 174.
182 McParlan estimated: McP1, March 9, 1875.
183 Judges, lawyers, and policemen: Kevin Kenny, interview by author, August 1993.
184 It was this procedure: Broehl, *Molly*, 175–76, 211–17, 265, 299–300, 302, 308–09, 326–27.
184 "sure, swift": *Tamaqua Courier*, September 4, 1875.
185 They also killed: Broehl, *Molly*, 258–59.
185 "What had a woman": Ibid., 264.
185 "The Mollies are now confident": McP1, December 11, 1875.
186 In making his decision: Pay sheets, Pinkerton National Detective Agency, Accession 1520, Box 1001, Eleutherian Mills Historical Library, Hagley, Wilmington, Delaware.
186 "He was their leader": Broehl, *Molly*, 327.
187 "There is not a place": Schlegel, *Ruler*, 131.
187 "the blood red wine": a play called *The Inconstant*, according to Horan and Swiggett, *Pinkerton Story*, 124.
188 "The praise, honor and glory": Broehl, *Molly*, 351.
188 It was in their: Robert Pinkerton to "Magarree," *DT*, July 30, 1899; Morn, *Eye*, 66.
188 "General Deportment": Popkin, "McParland," 234. This document was obtained by Zelda Popkin from the Pinkerton agency when its archives were still located in New York.
188 "There's no romance": *DP*, May 19, 1920.
189 No plutocrat: Klein, *Gould*, 362.
189 All along his system: *Official History*, passim; U.S. House, *Labor Troubles*, passim; Fink, *Workingmen's Democracy*, 221–30; see also the coverage in the *Parsons Sun* and *Parsons Eclipse* for March and April 1885.
189 A principal trouble spot: Masterson, *Katy*, 210.
189 When the railroad: *Official History*, 114.
189 Four hundred: *Parsons Eclipse*, August 3, 1886.
189 Meanwhile, detectives: *Official History*, 114.
189 For years: Boorstin, *The Americans: The Democratic Experience*, 14–16; Paul, *West*, 194–95.
189 If a guest: Shoaf, "House."
189 "Empty is the police court": *Parsons Eclipse*, February 21, 1885. The chronology that follows comes from the *Eclipse* and the *Sun*.
190 A meeting in: Fred A. Matthes to Fred Warren, July 13, 1906, WC; *Girard Press*, February 27, 1908, 6.
190 "he will do": "Read and Reflect" (flyer), ISHS.
190 In Columbus, Kansas: Allison, *Cherokee*, 146–47; *Columbus Courier*, February 18, 1886, 25; March 11, 1886, 1.
190 Later, he helped: Horan, *Pinkertons*, 389–91; *NYT*, October 1, 1891; February 22, March 11, May 4, 1892.
190 McParland also helped: McP3, January 22, 1906; *NYT*, August 7, 9, 11, 1901; *San Francisco Chronicle*, August 7, 1901.
191 Goaded by this gambit: *Denver City Directory*, 1887.
191 Before long: Siringo, *Cowboy Detective*, 69.
191 In the spring of 1887: Ibid., 70; McParland testimony, *SvA* (II), 869.
191 To ensure that: Siringo, *Isms*, 21.
192 When Siringo reported: Pingenot, *Siringo*, 17–18.
192 "best friend": Siringo, *Cowboy Detective*, xii–xiii, 69–70; Morn, *Eye*, 160.
192 In the summer of 1887: Siringo, *Cowboy Detective*, 69–70; Pingenot, *Siringo*, 18; Robert Pinkerton to Magargee, *DT*, July 30, 1899.
192 went to Denver: Conrad, *Revolting*, 86–89; Brownlee, *Dr. Graves*, 52, 59; Day, *Death*, 60; *RMN*, May 10, 1891.

192   During the century's: Siringo, *Isms*, 45, 50.
192   "Killing is my specialty": Prassel, *Officer,* 144.
192   "It was understood": Peavy, *Picaro,* 17.
192   According to Siringo: Ibid.
192   Later, Robert: Robert A. Pinkerton to William A. Pinkerton, January 19, 1906; William A. Pinkerton to Robert A. Pinkerton, January 22, 1906.
192   and McParland said: *DT,* February 28, 1907.
193   "The Old Man": Hammett, *Red Harvest,* 108–09.
193   suffered from rheumatism: McP4, November 6, 1906.
193   "awful hankering": *AtR,* May 18, 1907, 2.
193   but his wife, Mary: *RMN,* September 28, 1890.
193   Some suggested: *RMN,* March 17, 1906.
193   The previous winter: Popkin, "McParland," 252.
193   They lived quite: M. Friedman, *Spy,* 191.
193   The detective was: Suggs, "Religion and Labor," 194–98.
194   "wild and reckless": *RMN,* June 14, 1903. Matz was quoting *Rerum novarum* selectively. Though essentially a conservative document, it also condemned unbridled capitalism, called for granting workers their irreducible dignity, and recognized labor's right to organize.
194   "magnificent cathedral": *DT,* June 1, 1903.
194   Matz was McParland's: Brundage, *Making,* 158.
194   He denounced: *DP,* July 15, 1907.
194   The detective contributed: Popkin, "McParland," 242.
194   "cream of Catholic manhood": *Columbiad,* December 1900.
194   When his nomination: Notebook in ER.
195   Shortly thereafter: Susan H. Brosnan, archivist, Knights of Columbus Supreme Office, to author, March 23, 1993.
195   At one time: McP1, January 10, 1874.
195   It was Captain Linden: Bimba, *Maguires,* 114.
196   The state would put: Bond was hanged on August 10, 1906, in the penitentiary yard, but the other prisoner on death row with Orchard, Rudolph Wetter, was reprieved by Governor Gooding, after Orchard's personal plea. Though Wetter had been convicted of killing two miners in the fall of 1904, he contended that his attorney had bungled the defense, and ultimately the authorities agreed. See *IDS,* August 9, 10, 11, 1906.
199   For not only: Brief and Argument for the Appellants, *Pettibone v. Nichols,* 27 Sup. Ct. 1 (1906).
200   "I was just going around": AH.

5: Big Bill

202   "like a scarred mountain": Hart, *Old Boise,* 114.
202   "I hope to live": Roediger and Boanes, *Haymarket,* 17.
202   At day's end: This account of the events of April 21 is drawn from Denver's four daily papers—the *Post* and *Republican* of April 21, 1904, and the *Rocky Mountain News* and *Times* of April 22—as well as from Haywood's version in his autobiography and his testimony at the Idaho trial, *SvH,* 4021–23.
203   When the city: C. S. Smith, *Chicago,* 141.
203   From his studio: There is an echo here of John Gast's print *American Progress,* published in 1873, depicting a family of Indians in flight from a contingent of Americans—guide, hunter, farmer, etc.—at whom the Indians look back, realizing they are simply "no match for them" (Trachtenberg, *Incorporation,* 26–27).
203   "work of gracefulness and charm": *DP,* April 20, 12.
203   "his mount a Morgan-Spanish": *RMN,* May 12, 1907.
203   "precious burdens of commerce": Carlson, *Roughneck,* 2.
204   Visiting the cemetery: Haywood, *Autobiography,* 8.
204   Young Bill's: The change is evident in the *Winnemucca Silver Star* as early as April 14, 1887, and in county records beginning May 28, 1889. But there's no record in Humboldt County of Haywood's applying for a legal name change (Ruth Danner, deputy recorder, Humboldt County, to author, January 18, 1994).
204   "In this western country?": *SvH,* 3985.
204   "I have to have my stetson": Roger Baldwin, interview by Peter Carlson, May 3, 1993, Carlson Files, Washington, D.C.
204   "civilizing influence": Conlin, *Big Bill Haywood,* 2.
204   On May 10: Klein, *Union Pacific* 1:217–21.
205   Now revenue: J. McCormick, *Salt Lake City,* 31; Alexander and Allen, *Mormons and Gentiles,* passim.
205   Wild Delirium: Florin, *Ghost,* 28.
205   "One of the wildest": Haywood, *Autobiography,* 11.
205   Several days later: Murbarger, *Ghosts.*
205   "These scenes of blood": Haywood, *Autobiography,* 12.
206   To help keep: Ibid., 14–19.
206   So in 1884: Rocha, " 'Big Bill,' " 4.
206   In a ten-hour day: Carlson, *Roughneck,* 33–34.
206   a turning point: Haywood, *Autobiography,* 31.
206   Haywood won . . . In April 1887: Rocha, " 'Big Bill,' " 8.
206   Nevada Jane Minor: Ibid.
207   Her only good: Dubofsky, *"Big Bill,"* 14.

207   A friend called her: Chaplin, *Wobbly,* 289.

207   Then, in 1889: I am indebted to Guy Rocha, Nevada's state archivist, who put this series of events together from newspapers and public records (see *Silver State,* October 3 and 10, 1889; death certificate, Mark L. Haywood, Salt Lake County Board of Health).

207   ghostwritten: Stewart Holbrook insists it was "largely ghostwritten by a Communist hack to meet the current party line." Ralph Chaplin once told an interviewer that the book was written by Louise Bryant, John Reed's wife. Benjamin Gitlow, the American Communist, and Samuel Darcy, a close friend of Haywood's, agree that the ghostwriter was Lydia Gibson, the wife of Haywood's IWW colleague Bob Minor (she also did the painting of Haywood that appears in the book). Nonetheless, most details in the book, when judged against other materials, appear accurate enough (Darcy, interview by Peter Carlson, August 6, 1989, Carlson Files, Washington, D.C.).

207   They were deprived: Most of the events leading up to Haywood's hearing Boyce are recounted in Haywood, *Autobiography,* 36, 41, 51–52, 62–64.

210   To black freedmen: Livesay, *Gompers,* 31.

210   "fatal attraction": Gompers, *Seventy Years,* 1:xl.

210   "I have kept close": Livesay, *Gompers,* 71.

210   He kept his eye: Ibid., 40–57.

211   "No surrender; no compromise": Steevens, *Land,* 211.

211   "dreary days": Boyce "travel diary," January 23, 1902, EB.

211   "moral and financial": Jensen, *Heritage,* 59–60.

211   "I do not wish": Gompers, *Address,* 1–2. The exchange between Gompers and Boyce that follows comes from the same source.

212   "I deem it important": Jensen, *Heritage,* 67.

213   "either a traitor" . . . "miners or any other": Fahey, "Ed Boyce," 23.

213   "Such rights as tradesmen": Brundage, *Making,* 112.

213   "only the Western Federation" . . . "There can be no": Dubofsky, *"Big Bill,"* 20–21.

213   Indeed, Boyce's: Emmons, *Butte,* 184.

213   "a scaled-down Pittsburgh": Ibid., 299.

213   "a black and yellow": C. Murphy, *Glittering Hill,* 12–13, 41.

214   In 1900 . . . "did not care" . . . "Not surprisingly": Emmons, *Butte,* 13, 20, 184.

214   "The language": Boyce, "travel diary," June 1, 1897, EB.

214   "company men": Boyce, *MM,* December 1902.

214   Butte was isolated: Brundage, *Making,* 14.

214   "the clearing-house": W. A. White, "Tenderfoot," 2.

214   For several months: Grimmett, *Cabal,* 279.

215   One evening . . . After attending: William Haywood to Fred Heslewood, April 2, 1907; Haywood, *Autobiography,* 88–89, 95; Brundage, *Making,* 151.

215   All through the night: Ginger, *Debs,* 215–16.

215   Perhaps because he couldn't: Fahey, *Hercules,* 121.

215   "when intelligence masters": Boyce, "Truth."

215   "honey dew": Boyce, "travel diary," December 23, 1901, EB.

215   "Wedding—absolute loss": Ibid., May 14, 1901.

215   A month later: Fahey, *Hercules,* 3.

216   "When there were matters": Haywood, *Autobiography,* 94.

216   "Oh! I wonder": Boyce, "travel diary," January 23, 1902, EB.

216   "This is the first day's": Ibid., June 23, 1902.

216   "I have not retired": *MM,* July 1902, 14.

216   "There are only two classes": Proceedings of the Tenth Annual Convention of the Western Federation of Miners, 1902.

216   "well conducted": Boyce, "travel diary," January 19, 1907.

217   "Got along very nice": Ibid., July 20, 1907.

217   "money had destroyed": Haywood, *Autobiography,* 228.

217   "Mostly the Irish": T. N. Brown, *Irish,* 46.

217   "the only ideal": *Idaho State Tribune,* November 5, 1899.

217   In the end: In my assessment of Boyce, I am influenced by, and indebted to, Robert William Henry and his unpublished master's thesis.

217   His mother died: Thurner, "Moyer," 2. For Moyer's early years and his rise through the ranks of the WFM, see pp. 3–5.

218   In the state elections: Suggs, *War,* 29–44. For Peabody and the Citizens' Alliance, see pp. 39, 47–48.

218   The covenant: Carlson, *Roughneck,* 61.

219   The bill was promptly: U.S. Senate, *Report,* 51. For background on the Colorado eight-hour law, see pp. 57, 58, 62.

220   "radical and far": Suggs, *War,* 42.

220   "preserve the commercial": Ibid., 74.

220   "Rarely has there been": R. S. Baker, "Reign," 52.

220   "He had tremendous": Carlson, *Roughneck,* 147.

220   "sledge hammer blows" . . . "how to speak": Flynn, *I Speak,* 110, 120.

220   "Speaking was his": Review of Haywood's autobiography, n.d., Peter Carlson Files, Washington, D.C.

221   "a powerfully built": R. S. Baker, "Reign," 56.

221   "tall, tremendous": *New York World,* July 11, 1907.

221   "a great towering": Hamilton, *Exploring,* 87.

221 But when he was examined: Carlson, *Roughneck*, 180; photographic reproduction of wanted poster issued by FBI, June 1927; *RMN*, August 5, 1907; Dubofsky, *"Big Bill,"* 3.
221 Yet there was something: Carlson, *Roughneck*, 16; Dubofsky, *"Big Bill,"* 3.
221 By 1903: *DP,* January 4, 1907; Dubofsky, *"Big Bill,"* 24.
221 "Labor produces": U.S. Senate, *Review*, 24.
221 Still predominantly: Shoaf, *Fighting*, 71; Dubofsky, *"Big Bill,"* 24.
221 Given the substantial: Derickson, *Health*, passim.
221 In the smelters: Brundage, *Making*, 139.
222 Using imported: Ibid., 150.
222 For years thereafter: *DP,* July 21, 1907, 1.
222 "forlorn little industrial": Haywood, *Autobiography*, 110.
222 When tensions between: Suggs, *War,* 49–50.
222 "this wretched little": Haywood, *Autobiography*, 117–18.
222 What followed: U.S. Senate, *Report*, 32.
222 Many of Cripple: Rastall, *Labor History*, 82.
223 On August 10: U.S. Senate, *Report*, 160–64.
223 But when he urged: Haywood, *Autobiography*, 120–21; Carlson, *Roughneck*, 61.
223 In Cripple Creek: U.S. Senate, *Report*, 146–47.
223 So firmly entrenched: Rastall, *Labor History*, 70; R. S. Baker, "Reign," 43–57.
224 Most of them did: Rastall, *Labor History*, 148–49. For the events leading up to the arrival of troops in Cripple Creek, see pp. 99, 165, 171, 172.
225 "bar-room bums": Shoaf, *Fighting*, 65.
225 the state's adjutant general: Jameson, "All That Glitters," 366.
225 "Sherman, I am": *NYS*, September 27, 1900, 1.
225 "My chief fear": *Daily People,* January 8, 1906; E. Morris, *Rise,* 730.
225 "Me, God, and Governor Peabody": *Cincinnati Tribune,* n.d.
225 "I came to do up" ... "My orders were to": Rastall, *Labor History*, 99.
225 "Kill 'em": *RMN*, December 11, 1904.
225 "Military necessity": *Omaha Herald,* February 3, 1905.
225 cost a thousand dollars: *San Francisco Chronicle,* February 12, 1906.
225 Napoleonic delusions: Haywood, *Autobiography*, 169.
225 "flamboyant garrulity": *Cincinnati Tribune,* n.d.
225 "deadly and inexorable": *DP,* May 25, 1906.
226 "Habeas corpus be damned": London, "Rotten."
226 "To hell with the Constitution": R. S. Baker, "Reign," 43.
226 "capitalist-made laws": McGovern and Guttridge, *Coalfield War,* 80.
226 "I despise": Haywood, Speech at Cooper Union, 467.
226 When the four miners': U.S. Senate, *Report*, 184–85; Carlson, *Roughneck*, 62–63.
226 The court adjourned: U.S. Senate, *Report*, 187.
226 By mid-fall: Jameson, "All That Glitters," 379.
227 Darkly handsome: *SvA* (II), 705–17; *IDS*, April 5, 1906, 5.
227 "forceful, aggressive" ... Given the way: Gressley, *Bostonians*, xviii, 101.
227 So in December: *Cincinnati Tribune,* n.d.; W. F. Stone, *Supplement,* 257–58; Testimony of Bulkeley Wells, *SvA* (II), 714–16.
227 When the governor: Gressley, *Bostonians,* 93.
228 "a college freshman": *WIL*, August 1907, 8.
228 Indeed, notches: Burroughs, *Old West,* 299–306; Burroughs, "Bob Meldrum"; *DP,* March 5, 1916, sect. 2, 13.
228 Meldrum was thus: R. M. Brown, *No Duty,* 40–52; Trachtenberg, *Incorporation*, 24–25.
228 "peculiarly suited deeds of darkness": Rastall, *Labor History*, 119.
229 The owners promptly: Ibid., 144.
230 "For being a union": Haywood, *Autobiography*, 166; Rastall, *Labor History*, 125; Carlson, *Roughneck*, 76.
230 The case was dismissed: Haywood, *Autobiography*, 160.
231 "If you ever": Jameson, "All That Glitters," 397.
231 "They are men": U.S. Senate, *Report*, 267.
231 "I don't want": Haywood, *Autobiography*, 169.
231 The union never: Jameson, "All That Glitters," 439.
231 Thirty-three men: Ibid., 440.
231 Even if Gompers: Foner, *History*, 4:14.
231 Socialist leaders: Kipnis, *American Socialist*, 150–51.
231 Initially it was nothing: Brundage, *Making*, 145.
232 "such action": Brissenden, *IWW,* 60–61.
232 "far from representing": Proceedings, 1st IWW Convention, 5–6.
232 All twenty-six: Haywood, *Autobiography*, 178.
233 "What I want": Dubofsky, *"Big Bill,"* 38.
233 "Haywood, so impassioned": Carlson, *Roughneck*, 212.
233 "I've never": Leach, *Land of Desire,* 189.
233 "essentially a poet": Luhan, *Movers,* 293.
233 "Socialism is so": Haywood, Speech at Cooper Union, 462.
233 By then, Tom: Weadick, "Cowboys," 98.
234 "cowboy magnate": Westermeier, "Seventy-five Years," 138.
234 "lugubrious oration": *DR*, September 10, 1905, 2.

234   In his autobiography: Haywood, *Autobiography*, 190.
234   Finally, a letter: William Haywood to James Kirwan, March 3, 1906 (enclosed with McP3, March 15, 1906); *DR*, September 9, 1910. In this era, trade unions made at least some temporary headway in the most unlikely industries. Dance hall girls at both Cripple Creek and Goldfield formed unions and even called temporary strikes, paralyzing these popular institutions (see Jameson, "All That Glitters," 260).
234   "Your fathers' ": Chaplin, *Wobbly*, 91.
235   Originally charged: Haywood, *Autobiography*, 146–47; *DR*, November 5, 1902.
235   Concluding that the regimen: Haywood, *Autobiography*, 45–46; Carlson, *Roughneck*, 41.
236   After the difficult birth: Haywood, *Autobiography*, 68.
236   For some time: *WIL*, July 1907, 10.
236   "the vagaries": Haywood, *Autobiography*, 133–34; Conlin, *Big Bill Haywood*, 104–05.
236   "I thought the world": Chaplin, *Wobbly*, 289–90.
236   The mining companies: Haywood, *Autobiography*, 140.
236   That summer: *MM*, July 1904; *SvH*, 3746.
236   "liquor and I": Haywood, *Autobiography*, 133–34.
236   "bounded on the north": Mazzulla, *Brass Checks*, 14.
237   "macs": Goodstein, *Seamy Side*, p. 30.
237   "No effort will": C. A. Johnson, *Denver's Mayor*, 2, 85.
237   "a large, soft": Luhan, *Movers*, 89.
237   "how women of all": H. Hapgood, *Victorian*, 292.
237   According to a Pinkerton: *SvH*, 251.
237   "It was while Haywood": McP3, May 19, 1907. Another McParland report (McP3, June 6, 1907) contains more allegations about Mrs. Pettibone's amorous adventures. The detective recounted a conversation with Steve Adams in which Adams repeated a story Harry Orchard had told him. Once when Pettibone left town on business, he told Orchard to take care of his wife. "Orchard started to accompany her home. She intimated to him that she didn't care to go home just then, so Orchard took a room in a rooming house and stayed with her all night." Adams believed the story, but given the thirdhand nature of the tale, one should treat it with appropriate skepticism.
237   "Pettibone swore": *PO*, n.d. (but probably 1906).
238   "drunken orgies": Op. B120 Report, January 15, 1907.
238   Evidently Winnie: *Denver City Directory*, 1904, 1905, 1906.
238   But as early: Ed Boyce, "travel diary," February 28, 1902, EB.
238   Within a year: "Receipts and Disbursements."
238   A petite brunette: Mary Lou Minor and Rue Ledger, interviews by author, January 1995.
238   Detectives believed: *ECN*, January 9, 1906.
238   He was also said: Horsley, *Confessions*, 226.
238   Finally, however: Wilson Swain to Frank Gooding, January 23, 1906, TH.
239   "woman in black": TH, January 7, 1906, 3.
239   The mystery woman: *SvH*, 4157.
239   "Bertha": *ECN*, January 11, 1906, 1.
239   Others said: *ECN*, February 19, 1906, 1; *DT*, March 3, 1906.
239   "It is my opinion": *ECN*, January 11, 1906, 1.
239   Her baggage: *Cost* (voucher no. 9855).
239   reported that Winnie: *ECN*, February 19, 1906, 1; James Hawley, quoted in Walter McCornack, Analysis of Prosecution Witnesses, ER.

6: Viper, Copperhead, and Rattler

240   Within weeks: TH, January 18, 1906; McP3, February 4, 1906.
240   Once Larimer Street: Noel, *Larimer*, 12.
240   "great braggart city": Barth, *Instant Cities*, 137.
240   And gathered all about: Noel, *Larimer*, 12–18.
241   With 435 mines: J. E. Wright, *Populism*, 166–67.
241   A surfeit of fifty-five saloons: *Denver City Directory*, 1906.
241   Of Denver's sixteen: Ibid.
241   By January 18: *SvH*, 260, 3821.
242   They kept a special: McP3, February 16, May 31, 1906.
242   "sat in the lower booth": McP4, January 15, 1906.
242   It isn't difficult: *RMN*, October 15, 1890, 1; *Denver City Directory*, 1906; Rider, "Police," 350.
242   Michael Gassell: BH.
242   He was known: *PO*, March 5, 1906.
242   He loved to dig: Roger Baldwin, interview by Peter Carlson, May 3, 1993, Carlson Files, Washington, D.C.; Chaplin, *Wobbly*, 182.
243   "boozer": Adamic, *Dynamite*, 135–36.
243   Gooding ordered: McP3, January 21, 1906.
243   "his footsteps were dogged": *RMN*, February 19, 1906.
243   "as a valentine": Haywood, *Autobiography*, 191.
243   The operatives: McP3, January 30, 1906.
244   "very suspicious": McP3, February 4, 1906.
244   "feel they have cases": *IDS*, February 5, 1906.

NOTES

775

244 "As Pettibone, Moyer": McP3, February 4, 1906.
244 "Owing to": McP3, February 2, 1906.
245 according to the *Denver Post: DP,* May 25, 1907, 12.
246 In McParland's: *Nampa Leader-Herald,* February 20, 1906.
246 McParland's trusted aide: Siringo, *Cowboy Detective,* 74.
246 Later, the agency: Pingenot, *Siringo,* 59–60.
246 "a good friend": *MM,* July 11, 1907.
247 "every effort": *IDS,* January 17, 1906.
247 At thirty-one the state's: *IDS,* March 11, 1906; French, *History,* 820.
247 A curious-looking fellow: *IDS,* March 11, 1906.
247 "simply dazed": McP3, February 9, 1906.
248 "It will be well": James Hawley to Owen Van Duyn, February 10, 1906, HP.
248 Worst of all: James McParland to James Hawley, November 26, 1906; McParland to Frank Gooding, December 19, 1906.
248 "this man": James Hawley to Owen Van Duyn, February 10, 1906.
248 "The distinction between": Sect. 7697, *Revised Statutes of Idaho Territory,* 1887.
249 The obstacle: Donald, *Lincoln,* 299, 303–05; Meador, *Habeas Corpus,* 38–50.
249 Though it took some: Meador, *Habeas Corpus,* 55–60.
249 Quite correctly: McP3, February 15, 1906.
249 As always: *IDS,* February 18, 1906, 1.
249 The most common: Morn, *Eye,* 145.
250 Indeed, as he sat: McP3, February 8, 1906.
251 "To say that Judge": McP3, February 13, 1906.
251 In his capacity: James McParland to Gustavus Hasson, February 2, 1906.
252 Instead, Wells and McParland: McP3, February 14, 1906.
252 though he confided: McP3, February 18, 1906.
252 Shortly before noon: Brief and Argument for the Appellants, *Pettibone v. Nichols,* 27 Sup. Ct. 5 (1906).
252 With nothing to do: Koelsch, *Haywood Case,* 15.
254 But there was no: *Mills Annotated Code of Colorado,* 1891, ch. 56, sect. 2037, 23.
254 The governor could have: Connolly, "Moyer-Haywood Case," part 3, 23.
254 So far as can be determined: Haywood, "Get Ready," 728. Haywood's contention that the railroad donated the train is supported by the absence of any cost for the train itself in the state's itemized expenditures for the investigation, extradition, and trial of Haywood, Moyer, and Pettibone, which detailed costs of the Denver-Boise trip down to the last ham sandwich (see comments of Short Line officials in McP3, March 8, 1906).
254 and an expense: Hughes, *Vital Few,* 377.
254 McParland would refine: Later, officials of the Union Pacific and Short Line thanked McParland for the way the mission had been carried out (see McP3, March 8, 1906).
255 McParland cautioned: McP3, April 23, 1906.
256 Two Pinkerton operatives: McP3, February 16, 1906.
256 "put Adams through": McP3, February 17, 1906.
256 As the hours dragged by: *Cost,* n.p.
256 The train was bound: *IDS,* July 11, 1907, 10.
257 Nonetheless, De Lue: Ibid.
257 According to McParland: McParland interview with *Salt Lake Tribune;* quoted in *CT,* June 30, 1906; *PO,* March 7, 1906; *IDS,* July 11, 1907.
257 but he put up: McP3, February 18, 1906; Goodstein, *Seamy Side,* 143.
257 Earlier that evening: *AtR,* March 31, 1906.
257 Instead, when Bill: *DR,* February 19, 1907, 1; *Denver City Directory,* 1904, 1905, 1906; "Receipts and Disbursements." For years, there has been much confusion over where—and in what circumstances—Haywood was arrested that night. In the weeks following the arrest, most newspapers relied on a Pinkerton cover story that he was seized in the lobby of the Pioneer Building. Over succeeding years, some accounts accepted the later Pinkerton charge that Haywood had been arrested in a bordello. Only one newspaper, the *Denver Republican,* placed the arrest at the Granite. My first indication that the *Republican* had it right came from McParland's annoyance at Governor McDonald's private secretary, Sam Wood, who'd once been a reporter for the *Republican.* In his report of February 18, 1906, McParland groused that Wood had fed his old employers the best information. If Haywood had been at a rooming house like the Granite rather than at a bordello, whom was he with? It struck me that there might be something to a little-known remark by William Borah in a letter of June 20, 1907, to a friend named Grier. In that letter, Borah said the Pinkertons had found Haywood in bed with his "sister-in-law." Most researchers have given little credit to this remark, but that is probably because nobody had hitherto identified the woman in question. In no work on this case or on Haywood is any sister-in-law identified. When I stumbled onto Winnie Minor's identity and found her living with the Haywoods, functioning as his stenographer and making the trip north to Caldwell in January 1906, I was left with little doubt that this was the sister-in-law Borah had in mind.
257 "house of assignation": Pinkerton "Synopsis" of case, 6; see also McP3, May 24, 1907.
257 Some months later: McParland interview with *Salt Lake Tribune;* quoted in *CT,* June 30, 1906.
257 "The lying scoundrel": *AtR,* May 25, 1907.
258 Surely the landlord: *SvH,* 662.
258 the Granite was one: *SvH,* 177.
258 In the crisis weeks: Statement made by Steve Adams, in Edmund Richardson's notes, p. 27, WFM.
258 On occasion: *SvH,* 556, 647.
258 In any case: *DR,* February 18, 1906.
258 "We arrested Haywood": McP3, February 18, 1906.

258   Haywood, who was said: *PO,* March 7, 1906.
258   Haywood's version: Haywood, *Autobiography,* 192. At his trial the following year, Haywood was both more and less explicit. When asked where he was arrested, he replied, "On Fifteenth Street near Larimer," but made no mention of being in a rooming house (*SvH,* 3772).
259   For the moment: McP3, February 18, 1906.
259   one Socialist paper: *SOC,* July 26, 1904.
259   Mrs. Pettibone was still: *AtR,* March 31, 1906, 1.
259   Glen Duffield's team: Ibid.; Koelsch, *Haywood Case,* 15; *Denver Clarion-Advocate,* February 23, 1906.
259   When he reached: *DP,* May 20, 1907, 2.
259   De Lue later informed: *SvH,* 3773.
259   "reiterated this falsehood": *RMN,* February 20, 1906.
259   Seeking to justify: *IDS,* February 19, 1906.
260   Once deadlines: *SvH,* 3773; Haywood, "Get Ready," 728.
260   About 5:40 a.m.: *MM,* April 5, 1906, 7.
260   James Mills: *IDS,* February 21, 1906.
260   Though Mills: Wanhope, *Outrage,* 17.
260   The spartan combination: J. H. White, *American Railroad,* 462.
260   the William Seward Webbs: Pomeroy, *In Search,* 11.
261   On the Union Pacific: J. H. White, *American Railroad,* 344.
261   The very name: *SvA* (II), 716; *AtR,* July 20, 1907.
261   The deputies: *IDS,* February 20, 1907. In his trial testimony, Haywood identified these two men as Pinkerton detectives, but he was wrong. McP3, February 16, 1906, makes clear that they were Denver sheriff's deputies.
261   Wells, in turn: Brief and Argument for the Appellants, *Pettibone v. Nichols,* 27 Sup. Ct. 7 (1906); Petition for Writ of Habeas Corpus, *Pettibone v. Nichols,* 9.
261   even when he went: McP3, February 8, 1906.
262   "I never saw a human face": Haywood, *Autobiography,* 192.
262   Their handcuffs: *IDS,* February 21, 1906; *ECN,* February 21, 1906.
262   sullenly off to the side: *IDS,* February 21, 1906.
262   "impassive": *PO,* February 20, 1906.
262   "We listened": Haywood, *Autobiography,* 193.
262   Even the Union: McP3, February 16, 1906.
262   for years: Douglas, *All Aboard,* 217.
262   Determined to protect: Ginger, *Debs,* 196.
262   Quitting the Brotherhood: Salvatore, *Debs,* 111–12.
262   On Labor Day: Haywood, *Autobiography,* 172.
262   Shortly after: *ECN,* January 16, 1906, 8.
263   "This may work": McP3, February 16, 1906.
263   "to any writ": McP3, February 18, 1906.
264   "terrific speed": Haywood, *Autobiography,* 193.
264   Three months later: "Harriman Special," 8–9.
264   But flat-out: Kratville and Ranks, *Motive Power,* 106–10.
265   The exception: P. Lewis, *Trouping,* 106.
266   A prosperous: George Stumpf, interview by author, U.S. Marshal's Office, Cheyenne, Wyoming, June 1993.
266   Just turned forty: J. W. Davis, *Trouble,* 81–82.
266   Of all those: LeFors, *Wyoming,* 116, 162, 166; J. W. Davis, *Trouble,* 81–82; Davis, interview by author, October 1995.
266   Veteran trainmen: H. R. Grant, *Brownie,* 66.
267   "any person": McP3, February 18, 1906.
267   When General: D. Brown, *Lonesome Whistle,* 160.
267   With only three: H. R. Grant, *Brownie,* 137.
267   "the menu": McP3, February 16, 1906.
267   Laid out: *Cost,* n.p.
268   But a slug: Haywood, *Autobiography,* 193.
268   Folks said: Arnold, *Fair Fights,* 11.
268   "When I received": James McParland to Frank Gooding, February 18, 1906.
269   When a morose: Stevenson, *Across,* 46; McLynn, *Stevenson,* 155.
269   In 1878: D. Brown, *Lonesome Whistle,* 152.
269   "was the one piece": Stevenson, *Across,* 48.
269   "seemed to sleep": *ECN,* February 21, 1906.
270   Even at that time: *Critic,* June 1906.
270   "warty with sagebrush": W. A. White, "Tenderfoot," 14.
270   By 8:30: McParland's original plan had called for Sheriff Nichols and two special deputies to travel to Denver and take part in the arrests, then escort the prisoners back to Idaho, but—perhaps because he never had much faith in Nichols—he changed his mind (see McParland to Gooding, February 8, 1906).
270   "I am in the enemy's": *New York World,* July 29, 1907.
271   "There's luck": Haywood, *Autobiography,* 194.
271   For this and other: McP3, February 18, 1906.
271   "as a private": *PO,* February 19, 1906.
272   "The manner": *RMN,* February 19, 1906.
272   "The case is clearly": *RMN,* February 19, 1906.

272   "You see there": McP3, February 20, 1906.
272   "The officers": M. Friedman, *Spy*, 203–04.
273   "He went into": *DR*, February 20, 1906.
273   "McParlan as he appeared": *St. Louis Post-Dispatch*, March 25, 1906. The same erroneous notion was accepted by Franklin Mathews, writing in *Harper's Weekly* on June 2, 1906, 767.
273   "There have been statements": *Milwaukee News*, February 20, 1906.
273   "I believed that": *DT*, February 20, 1906.
274   "put on the lid": *PO*, February 24, 1906.
274   "the decrepit McParland": *Socialist Party Official Bulletin*, March 1906, 1.
274   "They thought": *DT*, February 20, 1906.
274   But at 6:10: *BG*, May 20, 1907.
274   "Gentlemen of the jury": *DP*, July 29, 1906.
274   Impeccably tailored: Grover, *Debaters*, 191.
274   He'd represented: *BG*, May 20, 1907.
274   "the governors of the state": *RMN*, March 10, 1906.
276   Borah had hesitated: C. Johnson, *Borah*, 79.
276   "I'll get in": Pete Steunenberg, interview by Irving Stone, IS.
276   On the other hand: McKenna, *Borah*, 49.
276   "When it becomes necessary": A. K. Steunenberg to William Borah, January 5, 1906.
276   On March 7: Beal and Wells, *History*, II: 214; Cowart, "McParland," 29.
276   They could, in any case: *PO*, March 8, 1906; William Borah to Frank Gooding, March 23, 1906.
277   The state might "concede": An intriguing window on Borah's views may have been opened by an article written by one of his young office mates. Charles P. McCarthy was a 1904 graduate of the Harvard Law School who'd struck out from Boston to see the West and found a place in Borah's law office. He wasn't a member of the firm of Borah and Blake, but working in close proximity to Borah through 1906 and 1907, he undoubtedly came to know Borah's views on the Haywood case.
   McCarthy had a keen legal mind and would go on to become Idaho's chief justice in 1925. In November 1907, he published an article in the *Greenbag*, a Boston law review, on the constitutional questions raised by the Haywood case, in which he focused on "an inexcusable weakness in the law" governing interstate extradition. Common law and statute law, he noted, both envision that when a person outside a state puts into operation a stream of events that result in a crime's being committed inside that state, that person is subject to prosecution in the state where the crime was committed. On the other hand, neither statute law nor the U.S. Constitution made provision for the legal extradition of such persons, because both applied only to "persons who were physically present within the demanding state, and led in the physical sense." This discrepancy, McCarthy argued, had to be remedied by amendment to the Constitution or, if necessary, by uniform state legislation. If McCarthy evolved these views in consultation with Borah, it suggests that Hawley's associate counsel knew full well that their oft-repeated insistence on the first proposition—outraged innocence—was nonsense. See *Greenbag*, November 1907, 636–44.
277   "Newspapers report": Lincoln Steffens to William Borah, March 19, 1906; Borah to Steffens, March 19, 1906, WEB.
277   "It seems to me": C. H. Jackson to Charles E. Arney, March 11, 1906, CEA.
278   "the Pirate Special": Wanhope, *Outrage*, 7.
278   "Debs," he wrote: Adamic, *Dynamite*, 145.
278   But Montana: Jensen, *Heritage*, 205.
278   "If it requires": *AtR*, March 30, 1906.
279   A former chief judge: R. H. Peterson, "Bunker Hill," 7.
279   Aunt Nancy: Lillard, "Federal Court," 59.
279   The indictment: Indictment for the Crime of Murder, in the District Court of the Seventh Judicial District of the State of Idaho, The State of Idaho v. William D. Haywood, Charles Moyer, George A. Pettibone and John L. Simpkins, March 7, 1906.
280   What one judge: Joseph McKenna, dissenting opinion, *Pettibone v. Nichols*, 27 Sup. Ct. 120 (1906).
280   President Theodore Roosevelt: Israel, *State of the Union*, 2309.
280   The prevailing judicial: Fiss, *Troubled*, 20.
280   "less a habit of mind" ... "bombastic, diffuse": L. M. Friedman, *History*, 384, 383.
281   "Our great": Bickel and Schmidt, *Judiciary*, 17.
281   "the most obscure man": Beth, *Harlan*, 157; Fiss, *Troubled*, 22.
281   "profound": TR to William Allen White, November 26, 1907.
281   "a self-regulating": Horwitz, *Transformation*, 4.
281   "it is the unvarying": Fiss, *Troubled*, 54, 56, 57.
282   "probably the greatest": Bickel and Schmidt, *Judiciary*, 70.
282   "Some at least": Oliver Wendell Holmes to Sir Frederick Pollock, August 13, 1902, *Holmes-Pollock Letters*, 1:103–04.
282   "I could carve out": Bent, *Holmes*, 251.
282   "Economics bored him": L. Baker, *Justice*, 403.
282   "The Fourteenth Amendment": Fiss, *Troubled*, 157.
282   "I never thought": B. Schwartz, *Supreme Court*, 179.
282   "Legislation can't cure": L. Baker, *Justice*, 403.
282   "From societies": Biddle, *Mr. Justice*, 92.
282   "the best designers": Biddle, *Mr. Justice*, 91.
282   "The crowd has": L. Baker, *Justice*, 403.
282   "The last of the tobacco-spitting" ... "a great vise": Beth, *Harlan*, 174.
282   "great gnarled oak" ... "goes to bed": Bickel and Schmidt, *Judiciary*, 65–66.

283   "differences between": G. E. White, *Judicial Tradition*, 134.
283   "If the appellant's": *Yamataya v. Fisher*, 189 U.S. 86 (1903).
283   After hearing: McP3, October 23, 1906.
284   "jovial monk": Bickel and Schmidt, *Judiciary*, 39.
285   Indeed, as Harlan wrote: L. Baker, *Second Battle*, 33.
286   Though it was unfortunate: The doctrine enunciated in *Pettibone v. Nichols* has, nonetheless, stood the test of time. The chief prosecutor in the trial of Adolph Eichmann in Jerusalem in 1961 cited the U.S. Supreme Court's decision as justification for Israel's trying the Nazi war criminal even though he'd clearly been kidnapped by Israeli agents from Argentina. See The Trial of Adolph Eichmann, Record of Proceedings in the District Court of Jerusalem, State of Israel, Ministry of Justice, Jerusalem, 1992, 1:18. In this country, as late as 1992, the Supreme Court cited *Pettibone* in reversing a lower-court opinion that held that it did not have jurisdiction to try Humberto Alvarez-Machain, a Mexican national who'd been kidnapped and brought to the United States to stand trial for crimes in connection with the kidnapping and murder of a United States Drug Enforcement Administration special agent. See *United States v. Humberto Alvarez-Machain*, 504 U.S. 655, 12 Sup. Ct. 2188, 5.
286   As he gained: William Howard Taft to Horace Taft, April 17, 1922, WHT.
286   Moreover, he was something: Professor James S. Liebman, Columbia University Law School, interview by author, May 1996.

7: THE GREAT DEFENDER

288   For this was: Grover, *Diamondfield Jack*, passim.
288   Not surprisingly: Ibid., 18, 29.
289   At last they sat: *IDS*, March 24, 1895, 8.
289   There were so few: MacLane, *Sagebrush*, 20.
289   "the ablest": *AtR*, April 6, 1907, 2.
290   No lawyer: McKenna, *Borah*, 48; Mary McConnell Borah Oral History, ISHS.
290   "too damned": McKenna, *Borah*, 1–13; C. Johnson, *Borah*, 22.
290   Her family gave him: "Very Personal Notes on Senator William E. Borah," Folder 43, COJ.
290   "town bull": *AtR*, April 20, 1907, 2.
290   Legend has it: Jo Anne Russell to author, June 6, 1993; Felsenthal, *Princess Alice*, 149.
291   Borah lined the bright: *Chicago Chronicle*, February 10, 1907.
291   continued through his Boise years: "H" to Borah, August 5, 1906, WEB. This letter, addressed "Dear Boy," is plainly from a woman with whom he was having an affair. It appears that she and Borah had shared some intimacies while both were staying at the elegant Dewey Palace Hotel in Nampa and that a friend with a nearby room had reported the liaison to the woman's companion or husband. "Will," she wrote, "I never had such a time in my life squaring it and I can truthfully say I have never seen a man suffer as he did believing it to be true." She also recounted a conversation she'd overheard about Borah in a hotel lobby among several politicians: "They all said you were after everything that wore a skirt while around in the different counties recently and a lot of worse things."
291   "You're a thief": C. Johnson, "When William E. Borah," 129.
292   "hand that rocked": *IDS*, December 24, 1924.
292   To that end: Johnson, "When William E. Borah," 135–37.
292   Increasingly he: Jerry M. Cooper, "William E. Borah," 146–47.
292   "battle ax": Fremont Wood to William M. McGill, August 9, 1906, ISHS.
293   Borah had earned: *Pocatello Tribune*, August 1, 1906, 1, 4.
293   "the walk of a man": McKenna, *Borah*, 83.
293   "a shambling": G. K. Turner, "Actors," 524.
293   He wasn't entirely: *DR*, August 10, 1907, 12.
294   "a happy, rollicking": *IDS*, March 30, 1906.
294   "like the school boy": Ibid.
294   By 1906: *IDS*, September 9, 1907; Darrow, *Story*, 134; Holbrook, *Rocky*, 267.
294   At sundown: Statement made by Steve Adams to E. F. Richardson, ER.
294   Moore accompanied: Ibid.; *Baker City Herald*, February 21, 1906.
294   On the platform: A. A. Hart, *Old Boise*, 171–73.
295   "This is a very": McP3, February 23, 1906.
295   "that if [Adams] did not tell": Adams statement to Richardson, ER.
296   "As I had been made aware": McP3, February 28, May 2, 1906.
296   The money did not arrive: Adams statement to Richardson, ER.
297   "full confession": *IDS*, March 3, 1906; Adams statement to Richardson, ER; James Hawley to Owen Van Duyn, March 3, 1906.
298   "we will not be able": McP3, March 26, 1906.
298   "the delight of a boy" ... "rendezvous for tramps": *DP*, March 28, 1906, 7.
299   On examination: *IDS*, March, 28, 29, 30, 1906; *Pocatello Tribune*, March 28, 29, 1906.
299   the bomb that was placed: McP3, March 28, 1906.
299   As prearranged: *IDS*, March 28, 29, 1906.
299   A former master: Derickson, *Health*, 160.
299   "a synonym": George Shoaf in *AtR*, March 11, 1906.
300   "We will secure": *PO*, February 22, 1906.
300   Kirwan recalled: *Official Proceedings of the Fifteenth Annual Convention of the Western Federation of Miners*, Denver, June 10–July 3, 1907, 592.

300 "upon invitation": *RMN,* February 27, 1906.
301 "what a great man": Darrow, *Farmington,* 191–93.
301 Farmington: Those seeking to understand Darrow's mind should approach *Farmington* with some caution. As Darrow advises in his preface to the 1932 edition, "It is neither fact nor fiction." Some of the material is clearly autobiographical; some is not, plainly differing from comparable passages in *The Story of My Life.*
301 "man-child": Darrow, *Farmington,* 21.
301 "rich and noble": Garland, *Companions,* 322.
301 "cunning soulless" ... "who had no doubt": Darrow, *Farmington,* 38, 92, 65, 61, 10.
301 "revolt from the village": Ravitz, *Darrow,* 100.
301 Asked what: Obituary, *CHT* files.
302 "I cannot recall" ... "to understand the tragedy": Darrow, *Farmington,* 34, 33, 37, 255, 246.
302 "bias against": Ginger, "Clarence Seward Darrow," 54.
302 "I haven't done": Arnold, *Fair Fights,* 252.
302 "young men": Clarence Darrow to William McKnight, April 15, 1936, quoted in Tierney, *Darrow,* 25.
303 Until the Civil War: L. M. Friedman, *History,* 606–08.
303 The account of Darrow's early years of practice draws on *The Story of My Life,* 29–37.
304 Grover Cleveland Democrat: Livingston, *Clarence Darrow,* 40.
304 Darrow took: Darrow, *Story,* 34–35; Tierney, *Darrow,* 30.
304 This mechanistic thinking: Mowry, *Era,* 16–18.
305 "Life is a game": Ravitz, *Darrow,* 118.
305 "The captain": Whitehead, *Clarence Darrow,* 5.
305 "*the* big city": Tierney, *Darrow,* 35.
305 For a generation: I am indebted here to the eloquent prologue of William Cronon's *Nature's Metropolis,* 5–19.
305 "never forget": Cronon, *Metropolis,* 9.
305 "Chimneys stand": Ibid., 12.
305 These expressions: Ibid., passim.
306 "The Great Gray": Norris, *The Pit,* cited in Cronon, *Metropolis,* 4.
306 "This singing flame": Dreiser, *Titan,* 13.
306 "As well might": Darrow, *Story,* 42.
306 "Every thin-brained": Tierney, *Darrow,* 38.
306 After DeWitt: Darrow, *Story,* 49.
306 Asstabula: Cowan, *People,* 26.
307 With a five-thousand-dollar: Tierney, *Darrow,* 51; Cowan, *People,* 29.
307 Some regarded: Ginger, *Altgeld's,* passim.
307 To others: Tierney, *Darrow,* passim.
307 his brother Hubert: *Kinsman News,* October 13, 1905.
307 "for me to take": Darrow, *Story,* 58.
308 "desire for office": Clarence Darrow to Henry Demarest Lloyd, December 28, 1891, ALW.
308 In early 1894: L. C. Collins, *Autobiography,* 129; Tierney, *Darrow,* 77–78.
308 The first was: Tierney, *Darrow,* 62; Ginger, *Altgeld's,* 71.
308 The conventional wisdom: Mencken, *Prejudices,* 202.
308 The *Chicago Tribune:* Linn, *Addams,* 202.
309 It was the last: Ginger, "Clarence Seward Darrow," 57.
309 "the most devoted lover": Darrow, *Story,* 485–86.
309 Perhaps, as one: Cowan, *People,* 27.
309 As a child: Darrow, *Story,* 15.
309 "deep dread": Darrow, *Farmington,* 25.
309 "grim spectre": Maloney, "Darrow," 274.
309 "No one": Clarence Darrow to Mary Field, July 4, 1913, MFP.
310 That didn't mean: Darrow testimony, U.S. Senate, *Industrial,* 10800.
310 "his role was that": Hamilton, *Exploring,* 77.
310 "We are born": Ginger, *Debs,* 110.
311 "no sufficient cause": Darrow, *Story,* 61–62.
311 penance: Tierney, *Darrow,* 99.
311 "bravest man": Darrow, *Story,* 66–67.
311 "If it shall come": Darrow, *Verdicts,* 64.
311 "I believe": Clarence Darrow to Henry Demarest Lloyd, November 24, 1894, ALW.
312 "awaken an interest": Shannon, *Socialist Party,* 202.
312 "I had too little": Darrow, *Story,* 53.
312 It was too "dictatorial": Ginger, "Clarence Seward Darrow," 61.
312 "a far-off dream": Darrow, *Story,* 53.
312 "prevented me from obeying": Ibid., 55.
312 "if there was a seducer": Tierney, *Darrow,* 136.
312 "Chicago by now": Masters, *Tale,* 287.
313 "Single taxers, ideologues": Ibid., 284.
313 "to foster good": *Chicago Herald,* April 26, 1891.
313 Finally, in 1897: *Chicago Record,* March 9, 1897.
313 Since both feared: Weinberg and Weinberg, *Sentimental,* 70–71.
313 "I'm in favor of divorce": Adelman, "Darrow," 3.
314 "salon of democracy": A. F. Davis, *Heroine,* 96.

314   "of my good friends": Clarence Darrow to Ellen Gates Starr, n.d. (c. 1897), CD. This extraordinary letter should be treated with some care. The original has disappeared. The Library of Congress has only a transcript, prepared by some unidentified collector or archivist. Since Darrow's script is notoriously difficult to decipher, we cannot be sure that all the words in the transcript are accurate, though there can be little doubt that the letter is Darrow's work—it bears the authentic stamp of his ideas and rhetoric.

315   Gertrude Barnum: *Notable American Women*, s. v. Gertrude Barnum; ALW; Barnum, quoted in I. Stone, *Darrow*, 137.

315   "The Road to Mandalay": I. Stone, *Darrow*, 136–37.

315   "It's the best party": Ibid.

315   "When the weak": Gertrude Barnum, "The Great Defender," Box 26, BW.

316   "A more interesting": Rosa M. Perdue to Richard T. Ely, January 23, 1903, ALW.

316   "Conspiracy is the child": Darrow, *Attorney*, 282. Further quotations from Kidd case are on pp. 269, 284, 325.

317   "a broad backdrop": Maloney, "Darrow," 286.

317   "a device for excusing": Tierney, *Darrow*, 154.

317   "strong leaven": Nathan, *Notebooks*, 81.

317   "Place yourselves": Ibid., 313–14.

317   "The world has grown tired": Darrow, *Persian Pearl*, 369.

318   He drew a direct: Ravitz, *Darrow*, 54, 360.

318   On July 1: Koenigsberg, *King News*, 273.

318   "the eyes": *St. Louis Globe-Democrat*, July 9, 1904.

318   "risks assumed": Ravitz, *Darrow*, 46.

318   "Had he known this": "The Doctrine of Assumed Risk," CDR.

319   "I went one day": Darrow, *Eye*, 38, 211.

319   "the so-called sins": Darrow, *Persian Pearl*, 14–15.

319   the Ghetto: *Chicago American*, October 25, 1902.

320   "glories in rousing": Rosa M. Perdue to Richard T. Ely, January 23, 1903, ALW.

320   Of the one hundred: *Chicago American*, October 25, 1902.

320   "no independent man": Darrow, *Story*, 119.

320   "God in his Infinite": I. Stone, *Darrow*, 164–67.

320   When Hamlin Garland: Garland, *Companions*, 172.

321   "from the madly rushing": Darrow, *Verdicts*, 376–79.

321   "one of the important": Darrow, *Attorney*, 406–08.

321   "downright ugliness": *St. Louis Post-Dispatch*, May 25, 1907; Weinberg and Weinberg, *Sentimental*, 72; Tierney, *Darrow*, 114.

321   "With that cheekbone": Tierney, *Darrow*, 180.

321   "to see how this": Garland, *Companions*, 269.

321   "been less affected": Ginger, "Clarence Seward Darrow," 65.

322   "the Irish type": I. Stone, *Darrow*, 102.

322   "blazing wit": Fenberg, "I Remember," 221.

322   On July 16, 1903: *Chicago Record-Herald*, July 17, 1903.

322   Darrow was already: JOD.

323   "turned on me": Edgar Lee Masters to Carter H. Harrison, March 21, 1938, CHH.

323   "grabbed the larger": Masters, *Across*, 270.

323   "flirted" with him: Edgar Lee Masters to Carter H. Harrison, March 21, 1938, CHH.

323   "charm" and "plausibility": Masters, *Across*, 270–72; Ruby Darrow to Irving Stone, n.d., CD.

323   "Inside every lawyer": "Chaque notaire porte en soi les débris d'un poète" (*Madame Bovary*).

323   "We need a good man": Clarence Darrow to Brand Whitlock, March 17, 1902, BW.

323   "You can see": Ibid., April 8, 1907, BW.

323   In the summer: Tietjen, "Professional," 19.

323   Masters took his: Ruby Darrow to Irving Stone, n.d., ALW.

323   "I am a hedonist": Nathan, *Notebooks*, 86.

323   At Ruby's insistence: Cowan, *People*, 49.

323   He was an imprudent: I. Stone, *Darrow*, 207–08; Masters, *Across*, 290–91.

324   "amiable qualities": Masters, *Across*, 273.

324   "there was a chance": Ibid., 271.

324   "The one thing": I. Stone, *Darrow*, 146, 207, 194.

324   "speaking for the liquor": Masters, *Across*, 291.

324   When the couple: Ginger, *Altgeld's*, 231–33.

324   "I suppose": Ruby Darrow to Irving Stone, n.d., ALW; Ginger, "Clarence Seward Darrow," 58.

324   A more weighty dispute: Ginger, *Altgeld's*, 261–64; Masters, *Across*, 292.

325   Jews were firmly: Gunther, *Hand*, 115.

325   "a smart little fellow": William A. Pinkerton to Robert A. Pinkerton, February 7, 1907, PA.

325   Then he was found: Masters, *Across*, 192; Ruby Darrow to Irving Stone, n.d., IS.

325   "Do not the rich": Yarros, *Eleven Years*, 9.

325   "justifies the belief": W. W. Catlin to C. E. S. Wood, February 14, 1912, CESW.

325   "Through you I came": Brand Whitlock to Clarence Darrow, May 11, 1907, BW.

325   "The law?": Victor S. Yarros, quoted in Maloney, "Darrow," 306.

326   "I found him": Garland, *Companions*, 321–23.

326   "I am up here": Clarence Darrow to Mary Field, July 4, 1913, MFP. According to Eric Partridge in the *Dictionary of American Slang and Unconventional English*, "Jay" means "foolish," "inferior," or "simple."

326   "I may be an idiot": Ginger, "Clarence Seward Darrow," 59.

326   "could be most": Ruby Darrow to Irving Stone, n.d., ALW.
326   "will try to": Edgar Lee Masters to Carter H. Harrison, March 21, 1938, CHH.
327   "A giant as we hoped": Masters, *Songs*, 99.
327   "This is Darrow": *New Republic*, May 27, 1957, 16. Though not published until 1957, the poem was written in 1922.
327   Neither poem: Livingston, *Clarence Darrow*, 49.
328   At the defense table: Maloney, "Darrow," 300; Nathan, *Notebooks*, 86; Weinberg, "I Remember," 19; K. S. Davis, "Darrow," 12, 64, 66–67.
328   It was his massive: *NYS*, December 23, 1927, 1.
328   "all-American personality": Ginger, "Clarence Seward Darrow," 55.
328   Would organized labor: Clarence Darrow to John Mitchell, March 13, 1906, JM.
328   "I have no doubt": John Mitchell to Clarence Darrow, March 14, 1906, JM.
329   "I saw Darrow": M. H. Jones, *Correspondence*, 58–59; *NYT*, December 11, 1938.
329   Darrow later testified: Darrow testimony, IC, 10797.
329   Repeatedly in late: McP3, September 11, 1906.
329   One of the largest: Op. B120 Report, January 15, 1907.
329   "very susceptible": George E. Dickson to Clarence Darrow, April 20, 1906. In 1902, and for some time thereafter, Borah's stenographer in Boise was Annis Pinney, daughter of Boise's former—and future—mayor, James A. Pinney. It seems unlikely that she was a seductress-spy. Perhaps Hutton was referring to one of Borah's earlier stenographers.
330   Much of the clandestine: Darrow, *Story*, 134; *IDS*, March 3, 1906.
330   One day he chipped: Popkin, "McParland," 348.
330   "He is working": James Hawley to Jacob Fillius, August 13, 1906, HP.
330   "woman from Chicago": *IDS*, September 8, 1906, 2.
330   So as summer's: James McParland to Frank Gooding, August 19, 1906, HP.
330   "Some movement": James Hawley to Owen Van Duyn, August 23, 1906, HP.
330   "a pressure of": James McParland to William Borah, August 26, 1906, HP.
331   "have things": James McParland to James Hawley, August 27, 1906, HP.
331   Twice that summer: James McParland to Frank Gooding, May 27, 1912, PA.
331   "a typical character": *DP*, May 11, 1907.
331   "We can take": James McParland to James Hawley, April 25, 1906, HP.
331   "thirty pieces": James McParland to Thomas McCabe, April 18, 1907, HP.
332   "It is not drawing": James McParland to Frank Gooding, May 27, 1912, PA.
332   "Adams, through his": *DR*, August 9, 1907, 4.
332   "Little by little": Charles E. S. Wood to Sara Field Ehrgott, October 17, 1911, CESW.
332   "I agree with": W. W. Catlin to C. E. S. Wood, August 5, 1907, CESW.
333   "Because necessity": MacLane, *Sagebrush*, 158.
333   In any case: Register, Hampton rooming house, WFM.
333   A staunch: *IDS*, September 8, 1906, 1.
333   "Aside from admiring": *CT*, January 6, 1906.
333   "one strong man": Marsden Burch to Charles Bonaparte, October 4, 1907, BTF.
333   On the morning: Popkin, "McParland," 358.
334   "This is to certify": M. Friedman, *Spy*, 214. The recantation remained secret from the press and the public until four days later, when it was published exclusively by the *Portland Evening Telegram*.
334   That same morning: McParland, Synopsis, 10.
334   "A warrant": *DP*, September 9, 1906, 1, 4; H. Frank Cary to Frank Gooding, enclosing cable from Alexander Nisbet to Charles Koelsch, September 8, 1906.
334   "radiant with": *ECN*, September 8, 1906, 1.
335   "Well," murmured: *DP*, September 9, 1906, 1.
335   In the meantime: *ECN*, September 8, 1906; *IDS*, September 8 and 9, 1906.
335   "The actions of": McP3, September 10, 1906.
335   "the gentleman sheriff": *SOC*, April 7, 1907.
336   "going down the road": McP3, September 10, 1906.
336   This meant: Ibid.
336   Hodgin immediately: *ECN*, September 11, 1906; *IDS*, September 12, 1906.
336   "these lawyers simply": McP3, March 6, 1907.
337   "his best friend": McP3, September 11, 1906.
337   "It was agreed": McP3, September 12, 1906.
337   "We do not feel": *IDS*, September 13, 1906.
338   The defense's flat refusal: *Idaho Press*, September 22, 1906, 1.
338   In 1899: CDLT, 1085.
338   Once martial law: Thomas Heney testimony, CDLT, 265–66.
338   a ringer: *Wallace Press-Times*, March 6, 1837; Richard Magnuson to author, November 1, 1994.
338   On three separate: *PET*, June 21, 1907, 3.
338   "unassuming and modest": *CHT*, May 20, 1906, 3.
338   Six months before: *IDS*, April 1, 1906, 4.
338   "a bitter and intense": Affidavit of John H. Wourms, September 6, 1907.
338   "cool, deliberate": McP3, March 31, 1906, 1; McP3, June 13, 1906.
339   "a circuitous route": *SSR*, September 16, 1907, 1; *LMT*, September 16, 1906, 8.
339   Mounting a carriage: *Cost*, n.p.
339   At 2:00 p.m.: *IDS*, September 14, 1906, 5.

339 "It then dawned": McP3, September 13, 1906.
339 "He is not a smart": *Wayland's Monthly,* October 1907, 65.
339 At 1:45 p.m.: *LMT,* September 16, 1906, 8.
339 "putting up a big": *IDS,* September 13, 1906, 2.
340 "a board-sidewalk town": W. A. White, "Tenderfoot," 14.
340 "considerable delay": *Idaho Press,* September 22, 1906, 1.
340 The travelers: *Cost,* n.p.
341 "the lavender haze": W. A. White, "Tenderfoot," 14.
341 Gouge-Eye: Lloyd, "Frontier," 175.
341 About 4:00 p.m.: *Illustrated History of North Idaho,* 420.
341 "heavily armed": *LMT,* September 16, 1906, 8.
341 "constantly under surveillance": *SSR,* September 17, 1906, 3.
341 "it was Adams' ": *LMT,* September 17, 1906, 4.
341 The hard days: Photograph in *DP,* May 18, 1907.
341 "pet bear": *Camas Prairie Chronicle,* September 21, 1906, 1.
341 "It is freezing": W. A. White, "Tenderfoot," 14.
341 Adams was shivering: *LMT,* September 16, 1906, 8.
341 Before leaving: *Cost,* n.p.
342 Most of Idaho's press: The quotations are from *IDS,* September 17, 1906, 1; *IDS,* September 14, 1906, 5; *LMT,* September 15, 1906, 6; *Idaho Press,* September 15, 1906, 1; *SSR,* September 15, 1906, 1.
342 "outlaws, thugs": *LMT,* September 15, 1906, 6.
342 "He hates me like poison": *DP,* February 13, 1907.
342 The roads north: Cowling, *Land,* 76.
342 "For miles": *Grangeville Standard-News,* September 20, 1906, 2.
342 Somehow, the driver: *Northwest Magazine,* November 1906.
342 "He carefully": *SSR,* September 13, 1906, 1.
343 "Larry Burke will drive 'em": *SSR,* September 18, 1906, 2.
343 "You can say": Ibid.
343 "as fast as horseflesh": *IDS,* Sept. 18, 1906, 1.
343 A shipping point: Kirk and Alexander, *Exploring,* 201.
343 Still another lawman: *SSR,* September 18, 1906, 2.
343 At least two: *Idaho Press,* September 22, 1906, 1.
343 "walked into": *SSR,* September 19, 1906, 3.
344 "Darrow was very": McP3, September 17, 1906.
344 "a regular river rat": Grimmett, *Cabal,* 283.
344 "horse play": *SSR,* September 16, 1906, 1.
344 "evidently expecting": McP3, September 17, 1906.
344 "Hello, sweetheart": *SOC,* June 8, 1907, 1.
345 though critics contended: R. G. Cook, "Pioneer," 25.
345 Himself a mine: Cook, "Heyburn"; Graff, *Dubois,* 365.
345 "hasty removal" ... "individuals directly": *SSR,* September 19, 1906, 1.

8: THE FRIENDS OF MR. FILLIUS

346 "If necessary": *CT,* January 6, 1906.
346 Canyon County: *IDS,* July 23, 1906, 1.
346 But the governor: *IDS,* January 9, 1907; McP3, May 26, 1906.
346 Before the master detective: James McParland to William A. Pinkerton, February 22, 1907; James McParland to James Hawley, December 4, 1906, HP.
347 If the state issued: Richard Sylla, interview by author, February 1992.
347 The governor: Frank Gooding to Frank F. Johnson, April 16, 1906; Barrett, *Banking,* 108–09.
348 "We are advised": S. Sargent to Frank Gooding, September 5, 1906, FG.
348 "You will never": Frank Gooding to D. L. Evans, December 14, 1906, FG.
348 "the governor of a great": *AtR,* May 5, 1906.
348 "An appeal" ... "Why should": *WIL,* June 1906.
348 In any case: Frank Gooding to Frank F. Johnson, April 16, 1906.
348 Four days later: Ibid., April 20, 1906.
348 By late autumn: Frank F. Johnson to Frank Gooding, December 15, 1906, FG.
348 The bank paid: G. J. Hasson to B. F. Kemble, January 15, 1907.
349 "At the conclusion": W. A. Pinkerton to James McParland, February 14, 1907, HP.
349 "our bills must": James McParland to James Hawley, December 4, 1906, HP.
349 Gooding asked: G. J. Hasson to Frank F. Johnson, December 6, 13, 17, 1906; Frank Gooding to Johnson, December 11, 18, 28, 1906; James McParland to J. C. Fraser, February 8, 1907, HP.
349 For many years: Fahey, "Confederacy," 7.
349 For all intents: Fahey, *Ballyhoo,* 176–85.
349 The money the association: Fahey, "Confederacy," 7.
349 Although Clayton Miller: Fahey, *Hercules,* 25.
349 An able: John Fahey, interview by author, March 24, 1995.
350 Its bibulous: Fahey, *Ballyhoo,* 176–85.
350 "a commanding presence": Fahey, *Hercules,* 265–66.

350　Frank F. Johnson: *SvH*, 4218.
350　"the fellow that": Ibid.
350　In 1892: Fahey, *Hercules*, 24.
350　During the 1899: Frank F. Johnson to Frank Gooding, December 15, 1906, FG.
350　"Wish charter": Ibid., March 9, 1906; C. S. Loveland to Frank F. Johnson, March 9, 1906.
351　In 1899: F. W. Bradley to John Hays Hammond, March 6, 1900, BHS; *CT*, July 1, 1899.
351　"there are no political": *DP*, May 7, 1907.
352　The full $5,353: *Cost*, n.p.
353　"provided that": HP.
353　Whatever else: Frank Gooding to Frank F. Johnson, August 21, 1906, FG.
353　"I hear Frank": Stanley Easton to William Borah, July 1, 1907.
353　"No, sir": *IDS*, February 26, 1906.
354　In 1884: *People v. Turcott*, 3 Pacific Reporter 461 (1884).
354　In two highly: Grover, *Debaters*, 42–43; MacLane, *Sagebrush*, 122; J. W. Davis, *Trouble*, 62, 74.
354　"the statute does not": *People v. Biles*, 6 Pacific Reporter 120 (1885).
355　"prosecuting attorneys regularly": *Adamson v. Board of County Commissioners of Custer County*, 27 Idaho 190–191; 147 Pacific Reporter 785 (1915).
355　It grew out of: *State v. Corcoran*, 7 Idaho 220; 61; Pacific Reporter 1034 (1900).
355　"This action": Ibid., 7 Idaho 228.
356　"a practice": *Conger v. Latah County Board of Commissioners*, 5 Idaho 347 (1897).
356　"I do not see": James Hawley to Floyd Thompson, March 29, 1906, HP.
357　"R. E. Goodwin": George H. Kester to William Borah, March 4, 1906, WEB.
357　He was aghast: William Howard Taft to TR, November 4, 1906, TR.
357　"We will tear": Popkin, "McParland," 368.
357　The governor didn't like it: *PO*, March 8, 1906.
357　"sliding along": *SOC*, April 7, 1906, 4.
357　The governor and his family: Prisoner Ledger, Idaho State Department of Corrections; *WIL*, August 1907, 8; *Chicago Record-Herald*, May 20, 1907; *Daily People*, May 20, 1907.
357　Relf Bledsoe: *IDS*, August 6, 1910, 3.
357　When Gooding: *BG*, May 20, 1907.
357　When he visited: *PET*, May 10, 1907, 6.
357　During the day: *IDS*, March 4, 1903; *Boise City Directory*, 1905, 1906, 1907; Census, Lincoln County, Shoshone Precinct, 1900, 1910.
357　Still others: Photograph and caption, *DP*, May 12, 1907; Jess Hawley to John F. MacLane, n.d.
358　The very picture: Barrett, *Dreaming, 8*.
358　"with pride": Frank Gooding to W. L. Jans, January 1906.
358　"This isn't": Wanhope, "Haywood-Moyer," 11.
358　"Gooding is a man": William Howard Taft to Nellie Taft, November 4, 1906.
358　"I hope you": James McParland to Frank Gooding, December 4, 1906, HP.
358　"The governor got": Calvin Cobb to Gifford Pinchot, February 26, 1906.
358　"Personally, knowing": *WIL*, May 1906.
359　"in secret and": *Milwaukee Journal*, February 26, 1906, 2.
359　"There has never": *IDS*, February 26, 1906, 1.
359　At a press conference: *Milwaukee Journal*, February 26, 1906, 2.
359　"I had nothing": *Chicago Socialist*, February 26, 1906; *DP*, March 2, 1906.
359　"Somebody ought": *ECN*, quoted in *MM*, April 12, 1906.
359　"an uncouth": *IDS*, quoted in *CT*, November 5, 1904, 1; Phillips, "Trouble," 574.
359　"dull, blundering": Wanhope, "Haywood-Moyer," 5.
359　Gooding "possesses": *AtR*, April 7, 1906.
359　"lurid vocabulary": MacLane, *Sagebrush*, 142.
359　"arena of practical": *IDS*, quoted in *CT*, November 5, 1904, 1.
360　"the President has no": William Howard Taft to Frank Gooding, March 20, 1906, FG.
360　In fact, Theodore: B. Sinclair, "Reminiscences."
360　"The man himself": Clay, *Assassination*, 5.
361　"This is an infamous": The exchanges among Roosevelt, Moody, and Robb are in ROS.
362　A thirty-nine-year-old: William H. Moody to TR, January 24, 1906; TR to Thomas S. Rollins, February 1, 1906, ROS.
362　"the greater part": Charles H. Robb to William H. Moody, May 19, 1906, JD.
363　"will present": Frank Gooding to TR, May 14, 1906, ROS.
363　"gladly see": TR to Frank Gooding, May 21, 1906, ROS.
363　Through the nineteenth: Summers, *Press*, 71, 125, 135, 151.
364　"the chancellor": *BG*, July 6, 1907.
364　In the factional: Graff, *Dubois*, 368.
364　but the governor: *Salt Lake Tribune*, October 25, 1906.
364　Calvin Cobb descended: P. L. Cobb, *History*, 35–37.
364　The eldest: Spencer, *Library*, 75, 113, 120, 250–57; Walker, "Description," 32; Upton, "Institutions," 80; Sereikol, "Chicago," 86, 236; *CHT*, October 26, 1871, 2.
364　The *News* obtained: *ECN*, July 30, 1904, 4; Fred T. Dubois to Charles H. Taylor, March 13, 1907, FTD; *Boise Citizen*, December 28, 1906; *IDS*, December 29, 1905.
365　"editorially mortgaged": *CT*, February 1, 1908, 4.
365　Over the years: *IDS*, December 29, 1905.

365   For some time: J. M. Woodburn to Fred T. Dubois, December 18, 1903, FTD; Richard F. Pettigrew to Dubois, March 14, March 17, 1904, RFP.

365   His wife's family: *IDS*, November 8, 1928, 1, 8.

365   "A fine fellow": William Howard Taft to TR, November 4, 1906, ROS.

365   "the poor country editor": Calvin Cobb to Gifford Pinchot, February 26, 1906.

365   "a violent Republican": *AtR*, April 20, 1907.

365   "valued organ of plutocracy": Finley Peter Dunne to Calvin Cobb, n.d.

366   "the fragrance": *ECN*, January 24, 1906.

366   tennis set: Jess Hawley Jr., interview by author, Boise, June 2, 1995; A. A. Hart, *Old Boise*, 55.

366   "house rules": Calvin Cobb Scrapbook, CC.

366   She rode: Ruby Darrow to Irving Stone, n.d., IS.

366   "never a 'mixer' ": Penson, "Calvin Cobb"; McDermott, "Calvin Cobb."

366   "And this is good": *IDS*, March 28, 1965, 12C. The L. L. Ormsbys, with their beautiful daughter, Margaret, were a socially prominent Nebraska family who came to Boise every year and bought the lion's share of Idaho's lamb market.

366   On March 1: Fannie Lyon Cobb, Diary, CC.

367   The troops: Capt. William Yates to McLain, May 4, 1906.

367   "hold these troops": McLain to Commanding General, Department of the Columbia, May 9, 1906.

367   "I did well": Calvin Cobb to William Borah, n.d. (but third week of May 1907), WEB.

367   "with reference": The exchange between Taft and Loeb is in WHT.

368   "I appreciate": TR to Calvin Cobb, June 16, 1906, ROS.

368   "authoritative": The exchange between Abbott and TR is in ROS, as are TR's letter to Cobb of June 20 and Gooding's reply.

371   "Three cheers": TR to Frank Gooding, July 10, 1906. If Roosevelt seemed a bit naive in accepting Gooding's pledge at face value, one may consider the possibility that his exchange of correspondence with the governor was designed merely to demonstrate that, whatever the Idaho officials were up to, his own hands were clean. A case in point was an episode in the 1904 election when the Roosevelt campaign accepted a sum, variously described as $100,000 and $125,000, from Standard Oil. When he discovered this, the president ordered the money returned. Whether that order was ever carried out is not clear. Roosevelt's first attorney general, Philander Knox, later told William Howard Taft that one day in October 1904 he overheard the president dictating a letter directing the return of the money to Standard Oil. "Why, Mr. President, the money has been spent," Knox said he said. "They cannot pay it back—they haven't got it." To which the president is supposed to have responded: "Well, the letter will look well on the record anyhow" (Yergin, *Prize*, 107; Pringle, *Roosevelt*, 252).

371   "I was anxious": Roosevelt, *Autobiography*, 470.

371   "What a queer time": TR to Lyman Abbott, July 10, 1906. By "the Algerian negotiations," Roosevelt apparently meant delicate maneuvers through which he persuaded Britain, France, and Germany to confer on their North African interests in Algeciras, Spain, in January 1906. The "Alaskan boundary dispute" with Canada, prompted by the Canadian claim to northwestern territory where gold had been discovered, was resolved in late 1903 through secret pressures brought to bear on an "impartial" tribunal. For Nobel Prize, see *NYT*, December 11, 1906.

371   "a good one": James McParland to Frank Gooding, August 26, 1906, HP.

371   Gooding mailed a check: *Cost*, n.p.

371   "It is charged": *CT*, August 18, 1906.

371   "It has been charged": *IDS*, November 1, 1906, March 7, 1907.

372   Ultimately, Waldron: *RMN*, July 29, 1907; Bulkeley Wells to James Hawley, February 26, 1907, HP; *RMN*, July 29, 1907.

372   As early as: McP3, February 16, 1906.

372   "there is no": Bulkeley Wells to James Hawley, February 26, 1906, HP.

372   "informing me": The exchange between Thompson and Hawley is in HP.

373   "would publish": McP3, April 4, 1906.

373   At fifty-nine: Photograph in *Bench and Bar of Colorado*, Bench and Bar Publishing, 1917, 112.

373   Born in Hudson: *DP*, October 7, 1940, 2; *RMN*, October 7, 1940; *RMN*, September 8, 1902; Bench and Bar Edition of *DT*, February 1899; C. A. Johnson, *Denver's Mayor*, passim.

374   "dangerous classes": Trachtenberg, *Incorporation*, 110–12.

374   "the most unscrupulous": Suggs, *War*, 114; William Haywood to R. J. Hanson, January 20, 1906.

374   "A very safe": Frank Cary to James McParland, March 29, 1906; McParland to Cary, April 4, 1906, HP.

374   "I had a letter": James Hawley to Bulkeley Wells, April 3, 1906, HP.

375   "very pleased": McP3, April 17, 1906.

375   The Moffat-Evans: Bayard, "Theodore," 314.

375   "it became almost": Rastall, *Labor History*, 70.

375   "the utmost satisfaction": *ECN*, February 26, 1906, 1, 8.

375   a rendition: *San Francisco Chronicle*, February 12, 1906.

375   "a kindergarten": *AtR*, June 8, 1907; *DT*, May 24, 1907.

376   "Why should they": *DP*, n.d.

376   "In my opinion": *ECN*, February 20, 1906.

376   "They are examining": *DP*, June 9, 1907.

376   "Had Colorado done": Jacob Fillius to James Hawley, June 12, 1907, HP.

376   "The friends": Ibid., June 11, 1908; June 26, 1906; June 12, 1907; May 25, 1907, HP.

377   "Mr. Moffat": McP3, April 20, 1906.

377   "They both feel": McP3, May 8, 1906.

377   So, presumably: I am indebted for this list to Elizabeth Jameson, a shrewd student of Colorado's mining wars.

377   Carlton, MacNeill: Sprague, *Newport*, 171–81; Jameson, "All That Glitters," 67–72.

378   The political: There was a tradition of Idaho politicians' looking to Colorado mining interests for campaign funds. In the late summer of 1896, Silver Republican Edgar Wilson visited Denver in search of cash. He came back with a scant $2,500, but the tribal memory of such infusions persisted through the years.

378   "a law and order man": James Hawley to Jacob Fillius, August 13, 1906.

378   "a goody-goody": *SOC*, October 13, 1906.

378   "Finances at this": Jacob Fillius to James Hawley, April 12, 1907, HP.

378   "Collections have": Jacob Fillius to James Hawley, June 5, 1907, HP.

379   "Utah ought": McP3, June 25, 1906.

379   "also expressed": McP3, June 23, 1906; October 4, 1906.

379   "The lack of funds": James Hawley to J. W. Finch, April 5, 1907, HP.

379   "all of the gamblers": Op. 53 Report, April 7, 1906, TH.

380   "At one time": *Official Proceedings*.

380   Ultimately, the IWW: Brissenden, *IWW*, 171–72.

380   "The purchased confession": *Socialist Party Official Bulletin*, February 1906, 1.

380   "public indignation meetings": Kipnis, *American Socialist*, 327; *Socialist Party Official Bulletin*, March 1906, 1.

380   This segment: Kipnis, *American Socialist*, 325–27; *AtR*, January 12, 1907, 1.

380   In the end: *Socialist Party Official Bulletin*, January 1906–December 1907.

381   "antagonistic": Gompers, *Seventy Years*, 182.

381   He wasn't in close touch: John Mitchell to Samuel Gompers, July 10, 1906.

381   "could not abandon": Gompers, *Seventy Years*, 182–83.

381   At his request: Gompers, *Seventy Years*, 183.

381   the Pinkertons said $5,000: McP3, May 16, 1907.

381   "Gompers is well aware": Ibid.

382   "to provide means": Reel 118, SG.

382   "grave doubt": Reel 9, SG.

382   "I have not stood": *NYT*, March 4, 1907, 5.

382   "would yield little or nothing": Samuel Gompers to G. W. Perkins, April 28, 1906, SG.

382   In reply: Samuel Gompers to Edmund Richardson, June 24, 1907, SG. The sole extant version of the earlier, forged letter is in this response to Richardson.

382   promptly assured: Samuel Gompers to Clarence Darrow, July 6, 1907, SG.

382   Far and away: *AtR*, July 6, 1907.

383   "There are 3,000,000": *NYT*, April 27, 1907, 9.

383   "tens of thousands": Kipnis, *American Socialist*, 330.

383   The official WFM: *Official Proceedings of the Fifteenth Annual Convention* and *Official Proceedings of the Sixteenth Annual Convention*, WFM.

383   more or less jibes: Elizabeth Gurley Flynn to C. E. S. Wood, November 13, 1916, CESW.

383   A Pinkerton: Op. 24A Report, February 18, 1907, McP4.

383   According to McParland: McP3, May 26, 1906.

383   "to cuff the radical" . . . "balancing": R. S. Baker, *Chronicle*, 187.

383   "the man on two": N. Miller, *Roosevelt*, 517.

384   "let up in every": Hofstadter, *American*, 294.

384   he championed reform: R. S. Baker, *Chronicle*, 187.

384   "a newspaperman's crispness": Einstein, *Roosevelt*, 154.

384   "The very buffalo": O'Toole, *Five*, 341.

384   "the Scylla": John Cooper, *Warrior*, 113.

384   "The straddle": Hofstadter, *American*, 295.

384   "We can no more": Roosevelt, *Autobiography*, 506.

384   "If I had been there": Mother Jones to T. V. Powderly, May 9, 1906, in M. H. Jones, *Correspondence*, 58–59.

384   "It would be a dreadful": TR to Philander Knox, November 10, 1904, ROS.

385   Increasingly, Roosevelt: Walton, "Organized," 85–87.

385   Indeed, as the years: Hofstadter, *Age*, 285–86.

385   "Here at home": TR to Cecil Spring-Rice, July 1, 1907, ROS.

385   "the dull, purblind": TR to William Howard Taft, March 15, 1906, ROS.

385   "swinish greed": TR to Owen Wister, April 27, 1906, ROS.

385   "the representatives of predatory": TR to Charles Bonaparte, December 23, 1907, ROS.

385   "regard everything merely": Hofstadter, *American*, 268–69.

385   "I know the banker" . . . "Of all forms": Pringle, *Roosevelt*, 176, 179.

385   At the root: I am indebted for this analysis to the insights in Richard Hofstadter's chapter on Roosevelt in *The American Political Tradition*.

385   "the gentlefolk": TR to Owen Wister, November 19, 1904, ROS.

385   His instinctive: Harbaugh, *Power*, 229.

386   "a morbid fear": Blum, *Republican*, 60, 188.

386   "filthy little": Kaplan, *Steffens*, 87.

386   "At times": TR to John St. L. Strachey, March 8, 1901.

386   "would by his": TR to Henry White, November 17, 1907.

386   "a chance with rifles": Hofstadter, *American*, 283.

386   "like to see": Hofstadter, Ibid., 283.

386 "day of atonement": Sullivan, *Our Times*, 2:250.
386 "a tissue of lies": Pringle, *Roosevelt*, 114.
386 "The sentiment": Tuchman, *Proud*, 496; *AtR*, May 25, 1907, 1.
386 "There won't": Hofstadter, *American*, 284.
386 The results: E. Morris, *Rise*, 60–61.
387 "any kind of class": TR, Message to Congress, December 2, 1902.
387 "thugs and murderers" . . . "infamous scoundrels": TR to Lyman Abbott, January 5, 1907; TR to Edward Smith, March 23, 1906; TR to William Howard Taft, November 8, 1906, ROS.
387 "the men charged": TR to Calvin Cobb, June 16, 1906.
387 "That Moyer and Haywood": TR to Lawrence Abbott, April 28, 1906, ROS.
387 "back up the party": TR to William Allen White, July 30, 1907, ROS.
387 "I think the Western": TR to Lyman Abbott, July 10, 1906, ROS.
387 "You and I": TR to Henry Cabot Lodge, July 22, 1907, ROS.
388 "I cannot express": TR to Calvin Cobb, June 16, 1906, ROS.
388 "conceited and insincere": TR to Henry Cabot Lodge, September 12, 1906, ROS.
388 "calling newspaper men": *Leslie's Weekly*, June 21, 1906.
388 "the usages which": TR to Norman Hapgood, June 29, 1906, ROS.
388 The characterization was a curious: *Dictionary of American Biography*, vol. 22, supplement 2, 280–81.
388 "fun of hating": E. Morris, *Rise*, 24.
388 "if you want": U. Sinclair, *Autobiography*, 119.
389 "You must always": E. Morris, *Rise*, 19.
389 "At the present moment" . . . "a thing cold": "In the Interpreter's House," *American Magazine*, April 1907; Edwin Lefevre, "E. H. Harriman," *American Magazine*, June 1907.
389 "would have been": Hughes, *Vital Few*, 363.
389 "a Frenchman of" . . . "cold and dry": "The Humanization of E. H. Harriman," *Current Literature*, February 1907, 154, 152.
389 "less combative": Birmingham, *Our Crowd*, 201.
390 "It's that little": Hughes, *Vital Few*, 373.
390 "a thunderbolt": *New York Tribune*, February 20, 1902.
390 "It seems hard": Pringle, *Roosevelt*, 176–84.
390 "practical men": TR to E. H. Harriman, October 1, 1904, ROS.
390 They still talked: *NYT*, April 3, 1907, 2.
390 The president's sister: Collier, *Roosevelts*, 119.
391 "a very ungracious": *NYT*, June 27, 1906.
391 the president's reply: TR to E. H. Harriman, June 29, 1904; E. H. Harriman to TR, September 20, 1904, ROS.
391 "In view of": TR to E. H. Harriman, October 10, 1906.
391 But the letter: Maury Klein, forthcoming biography of E. H. Harriman.
392 "Mr. Roosevelt was guilty": "Between You and Me: A Discussion of the Roosevelt-Harriman Episode by TMP," n.d., ROS.
393 "a rustic lawyer": *Harper's Weekly*, August 3, 1907, 1120.
393 "the President being": *WP*, October 8, 1906, 4.
393 "the most potent": Kaplan, *Steffens*, 144.
393 "literally nothing": TR to Elihu Root, September 4, 1906, ROS.
393 "The producing". Swanberg, *Citizen*, 250.
393 "Do you wonder": TR to Henry Cabot Lodge, October 8, 1906, ROS.
394 people said: Einstein, *Roosevelt*, 104.
394 "You informed me": TR to James S. Sherman, October 8, 1906, ROS.
395 In a major: *NYT*, October 5, 1906.
395 "base," "low," "selfish": E. Morris, *Rise*, 467.
395 "become the rendezvous": TR to Rudolph, February 16, 1907, ROS.
395 "an undesirable, because futile": TR to Charles W. Eliot, February 20, 1907, ROS.
395 He wasn't alone: O'Toole, *Five*, 220; Fred T. Dubois to James A. McGee, January 11, 1906, FTD.
395 "the jack-fools": Dyer, *Race*, 140.
395 "two great classes": Dunne, *Mr. Dooley*, 192.
396 "a mild undercurrent": Harbaugh, *Power*, 220.
396 "inferior races": Ibid., 142; TR to Albert Shaw, April 10, 1907, ROS.
396 "a criminal": Gibson, *Theodore*, 15.
396 "You say that": TR to the Rev. Franklin C. Smith, January 23, 1906, ROS.
396 "enjoyed": *New York World*, April 4, 1907, 1.
396 At 12:45 p.m.: President's Appointment Book, October 8, 1906, Reel 430, ROS.
396 marshal of the Court: *WP*, October 9, 1906.
396 Warmly greeting: Seale, *White House*, 189–94; Seale, *President's*, 684.
396 After a few: *WP*, April 4, 1907.
397 In 1892: Yarbrough, *Judicial*, 192, 197.
398 "I am having": TR to John Marshall Harlan, June 28, 1906, ROS.
398 Taft offered: John Marshall Harlan to William R. Day, July 10, 1906, WHT.
398 "that fine old": TR to John R. Dunlap, November 30, 1907, ROS.
398 Then, on August 18: *WP*, August 19, 1906, 4.
398 "It was a very": TR to John Marshall Harlan, September 3, 1906, ROS.
399 "We must win": TR to James S. Sherman, October 3, 1906, ROS.

399 "unseemly" ... "lying still": Troy, *See How*, 109–15, 114.
399 "incredible blackguard": Elihu Root to William Laffan, October 30, 1906, ERP.
399 "The bullet": W. J. Abbott, *Watching*, 139.
399 "by the President's authority": *NYT*, November 2, 1906, 1, 3; Swanberg, *Citizen*, 251–52.
399 "Of course I": TR to Owen Wister, November 5, 1906.
400 One of his companions: Roosevelt, "Cougar," 417.
400 "as fine a fellow": TR to Alexander Lambert, March 13, 1901, ROS.
400 "manfully did": TR to Philander Knox, November 10, 1904, ROS.
400 "our people": Bayard, "Theodore," 323.
400 To that end: TR to William Howard Taft, September 7, 1906.
401 "I have never been": Pringle, *Taft*, 284.
401 "Boom, boom!": Reel 603, pp. 760–61, WHT.
401 "secret, insidious": Calvin Cobb to TR, October 10, 1906, ROS.
401 "In some counties": Calvin Cobb to TR, November 19, 1906, ROS.
401 In early September: Gifford Pinchot to Frank Fenn, October 29, 1906; Pinchot to William Howard Taft, October 9, 1906, GP.
401 "There is no issue": TR to Gifford Pinchot, September 15, 1906, ROS.
401 "as a personal": TR to William Howard Taft, September 17, 1906, ROS.
402 "Affairs in Chicago": Pringle, *Taft*, 127–28, 140.
402 Denver's public-utility: *DT*, September 18, 1906, 1.
402 "The Republican Party": TR to Philip Stewart, September 25, 1906, ROS.
402 "impossible to avoid": Henry C. Loudenslager to William Howard Taft, October 23, 1906, WHT.
402 "in the hands": *DT*, October 23, 1906.
402 "malignant and malicious": Horace G. Clark to William Howard Taft, October 25, 1906, WHT.
403 "You will find": Fred T. Dubois to William Howard Taft, October 20, 1906, WHT.
403 Dubois's outrage: Scheinberg, " 'Undesirable,' " 11.
403 "at the instance": William Howard Taft to Fred T. Dubois, October 25, 1906, WHT.
403 "I have a right": William Howard Taft to Charles Taft, November 1, 1906, WHT.
403 "Politics, when I am": Pringle, *Taft*, 290.
403 "I am now": William Howard Taft to Helen Taft, October 31, 1906.
404 "ponderous pachyderm": *Northwest Magazine*, November 1906.
404 "At one place": William Howard Taft to TR, November 4, 1906, WHT.
404 "The growth": William Howard Taft to Helen Taft, November 4, 1906, WHT.
404 "The President": *IDS*, November 4, 1906, 1.
405 the most effective one: William Howard Taft to Helen Taft, November 4, 1906, WHT.
405 "This letter will": William Howard Taft to TR, November 4, 1906, WHT.
405 "I am very": William Howard Taft to Weldon B. Heyburn, November 4, 1906, WHT.
405 Athos: Pringle, *Taft*, 275.
405 by 58,000 votes: R. McCormick, *Realignment*, 224.
406 "P.S. Yes": TR to Alice Roosevelt Longworth, November 7, 1906, ROS.
406 "unlimited quantities": James McParland to Frank Gooding, November 3, 1906, HP.
406 In relatively urban Ada: According to John MacLane, some rather questionable maneuvering went on behind the scenes in this election. A graduate of Yale Law School, MacLane was then practicing with Caldwell's William A. Stone, a prosecutor in the Haywood case. MacLane served as judge of elections in Caldwell, and on election night, when he saw how badly the vote was going for Judge Smith, he passed the word on to his partner Stone—presumably to see if the prosecution wished to take some steps to prevent this setback. "But my efforts, whether justifiable or criminal, were of no avail and Smith was defeated by a very small margin" (MacLane, *Sagebrush*, 149).
406 "It is to Canyon": *Nampa Leader-Herald*, cited in *IDS*, November 26, 1906.
406 Nonetheless, Gooding: J. H. Brady to William Howard Taft, November 15, 1906, WHT; *Seattle Union-Record*, November 24, 1906.
406 "Upon my word": TR to William Howard Taft, November 8, 1907, ROS.
406 "By George": TR to John C. Rose, November 7, 1906, ROS.
406 "I most heartily": TR to Frank Gooding, November 27, 1906, ROS.

9: OPERATIVE 21

407 On April 30: *Parma Herald*, May 5, 1906, 1.
407 "It now appears": McP3, May 3, 1906.
407 "this conspiracy": McP4, January 10, 1906.
408 He reacted: Williams, "Bill Haywood."
408 "tough characters": McP3, March 14, 1906.
408 "the presence": *IDS*, March 6, 1906.
408 "could easily walk": McP3, June 7, 1906.
408 "to assist in guarding": *IDS*, March 8, 1906.
408 "Prepared at all times": *IDS*, March 6, 1906.
409 Orchard was carefully: SOC, March 3, 1906.
409 Planning to take: McP3, March 17, 1906; *DP*, March 15, 1906.
409 "His thin lips": *DP*, March 2, 1906.
409 This report and others: *New York Press*, May 12, 1907.

409 "gang of tough characters": McP3, March 14, 1906.
409 "the efforts being": *CT,* March 31, 1906.
410 According to one: *DP,* March 19, 1907; Minutes, Board of County Commissioners, 145, Canyon County Courthouse, Caldwell, Idaho.
410 "I am mechanically": A. K. Steunenberg to Montie B. Gwinn, January 12, 1906, AK.
410 The prosecutors: McP3, June 7, 1906.
410 On occasion: James McParland to James Hawley, November 26, 1906, HP.
410 But he was not: McP3, February 2, 1906.
410 "right arm": A. K. Steunenberg to Montie B. Gwinn, January 12, 1906, AK.
410 Some of the county's: Hugh T. Lovin, professor of history emeritus, Boise State University, interview by author, April 27, 1995.
411 In 1907: McP3, March 21, 1907.
411 Coxey's Army: The account of the Industrials is drawn from Schwantes, "Law and Disorder," 11–13.
412 "The Coxeyites will": *CT,* May 10, 1894, 3.
412 "It is not strange": *Emmett Index,* May 12, 1894, 3.
412 But some of the kindness: Schwantes, *Coxey's,* 199–200.
412 "some neighboring town": *CT,* May 12, 1894, 2–3.
413 "The People's Party": J. R. Green, *Grass,* 18.
413 At one extreme: Shannon, *Socialist Party,* 1–55; Howe, *Socialism,* 1–33; Weinstein, *Decline,* 5–25.
413 But at Indianapolis: Shannon, *Socialist Party,* 1–3; Hillquit, *History,* 308–09.
414 The colonizers frittered: Kipnis, *American Socialist,* 50–55, 61; Hillquit, *History,* 302–03.
414 The Socialism of southern Idaho: Gabourey, *Dissension,* 31.
414 feeding off: Short, "Minidoka," 30–38.
414 When S. S. Foote's: *CT,* May 20, 1905, 1; Jennie Cornell Scrapbooks, no. 1, Caldwell Public Library, Caldwell, Idaho.
414 To the north: Hugh T. Lovin, interview by author, April 27, 1995.
414 "Believing that" . . . "shoals of politics": *CT,* February 21, 1903, 1.
415 "if the object": *CT,* February 7, 1903, 4.
415 "distinctly understood": *CT,* March 7, 1903.
415 "the most gifted": *Idaho State Press,* quoted in *CT,* March 10, 1906, 5.
415 "Reconstruction": *CT,* July 23, 1903, 4.
415 "Good old Horace": *SCN,* August 4, 1903.
416 "complacently affirming": *CT,* August 23, 1903.
416 A fifty-two-year-old: *WIL,* November 1907, 11.
416 Unmarried: U.S. Decennial Census, Silver City and Boise, 1900, 1910, 1920.
416 "You have . . . demanded": *CT,* September 19, 1903.
416 "a gifted writer": *CT,* October 3, 1903, 4.
417 "In your former": *CT,* October 10, 1903, 1.
417 "dwells in palaces": *CT,* December 5, 1903, 4.
418 But a branch: J. R. Green, "Salesmen," 26, 37.
418 "I, the undersigned" and next paragraph: "Socialist Party: How to Organize."
418 The local's secretary: I. W. Wright to Fred Warren, May 13, 1906; *Parma Herald,* May 12, 1906.
418 Among its leading: This list is drawn from several sources. The most definitive is a letter written by Joseph Wanhope, the Socialist editor, to Operative 21 in Caldwell, in which he mentions the Socialist local and asks to be remembered to some of its leading members. He lists Barber, Kipp, Snodgrass, Kavanaugh (*sic*), and Kelly (*sic*).
419 George W. Snodgrass: *CT,* December 30, 1905; *SOC,* July 14, 1906, 1.
419 "As friends and neighbors": *CT,* March 24, 1906.
419 "got what was coming": *Girard (Kansas) Press,* March 29, 1906.
419 "It is a matter": *CT,* March 24, 1906.
420 The moderation: Hugh T. Lovin, interview by author, April 27, 1995.
420 In 1904: Salvatore, *Debs,* 190.
420 Nowhere in Idaho: As a percentage of registered voters, however, Idaho Socialists, before World War I, ranked sixth after those in Oklahoma, Nevada, Montana, Washington, and California (Weinstein, *Decline,* 23).
420 eight Socialists: They were Lena Morrow, Arthur Morrow Lewis, Cameron King Jr., George W. Goebel, Thomas H. Kelly, John Chenoweth, Louis E. Workman, and Ida Crouch-Hazlett (*SOC,* October 27, 1906).
420 One was Ida: Calvert, *Gibraltar,* 30; M. J. Buhle, *Women,* 214; *American Labor Who's Who,* 51–52.
420 "not those that command": *MN,* April 18, 1907. Also in next two paragraphs, June 6, August 4, 1907.
420 "Comrades": *SOC,* June 1, 1907, 3.
421 One of the first: Robertson, *Ram,* 229–32.
421 At thirty-two: Eventually, the whole Hibner clan, including parents and siblings, settled in Chesterfield in southeastern Idaho, where they organized a Socialist local. George Hibner remained in Idaho for several decades. In the 1930s, he led a fiercely independent Socialist faction that an opponent once described as so orthodox its members said Karl Marx before dining (see *A Ram in the Thicket*).
421 Another impressive: Kipnis, *American Socialist,* 177.
421 Narrow-minded: Schwantes, *Radical,* 95–96; Bushue, "Titus," 21–24; H. O'Connor, *Revolution,* 12–16.
421 Soon thereafter . . . "Our work": Kipnis, *American Socialist,* 123.
422 the *Socialist* sent its coverage: Ibid., 90.
422 Titus—a clean-shaven: *SOC,* March 17, 1906, October 20, 1906.
422 The *Appeal*—whose name: Quint, *Forging,* 200.
422 "People don't have": P. Buhle, *"Appeal to Reason,"* 51–52.

423 An occasional column: *AtR*, November 3, 1906, 3.
423 It was the first…Although Eugene: Milburn, "Appeal," 365.
423 "I want to do": England, *Story*, 51.
423 When that manuscript: Ibid., 507.
423 "If the plutes": Ernest Untermann to Fred Warren, March 14, 1906, HJ.
424 " 'Will they hang' ": *AtR*, December 15, 1906.
424 In March 1906: England, *Story*, 50; J. R. Green, "Salesmen," 39.
424 Many of these: J. R. Green, "Salesmen," 25.
424 "Socialism is coming": Shannon, *Socialist Party*, 4.
425 "You and your brother": Flyer, Girard, Kansas, WC.
425 "I'll always stand": Op. 10-D Report, February 17, 1907.
425 The son of: Quint, "Gaylord Wilshire," 333.
425 During four years: Hancock, *Fabulous*, 88.
425 In 1895: Reynolds, "Millionaire," 47–48.
425 "a small man": U. Sinclair, *Autobiography*, 101.
425 Gregarious: Hancock, *Fabulous*, 95.
425 In December 1905: Hillquit, *History*, 353.
425 But the publisher: Werner, "L'Affaire Gorky," 62.
425 To these ends: Quint, "Challenge."
426 That same month: My account of the Gorky episode is drawn from the following sources: *WIL*, May 1906; Giddings, "Social Lynching"; Werner, "L'Affaire Gorky"; Kaplan, *Clemens*, 367–68; Wells, *Future*, 249–55; Troyat, *Gorky*, 104–06, passim; Kaun, *Gorky*, 386, 569–99; Sanders, *Downtown*, 382; Hillquit, *Leaves*, 110–11.
428 In March 1907: Circulation table, March 1907, WC.
428 Expirations in Idaho: *AtR*, May 11, 1907, 4.
428 Barber would…"The boys": Fred Warren to W. M. Mills, May 10, 1906, WC.
428 "discontinued": I. Wilson Wright to Fred Warren, May 13, 1906, WC.
429 "hostile farmer community": *SOC*, March 3, 1906, 1.
429 "We must deluge": *WIL*, April 1907, 15.
429 "you could get up": *Idaho Press-Tribune*, 70th annual progress edition, May 6, 1953.
429 "The defense has just": McP3, March 21, 1907.
429 "This case has": *MN*, May 30, 1907.
429 Wilson Wright: Kipnis, *American Socialist*, 8.
430 "enamored of its charms": *MN*, April 4, 1907.
430 "shoulder a gun": *IDS*, March 17, 1906, 3.
430 "Remember, Gene": *Idaho Magazine*, August 1906.
431 "Caldwell is a small": *AtR*, April 7, 1906.
431 "It will be interesting": *CT*, April 14, 1907.
431 "his action had": McP3, June 2, 1906.
432 "open-air circuit": Kipnis, *American Socialist*, 100.
432 "These meetings": James McParland to Frank Gooding, July 3, 1906, HP.
432 "two Socialist rascals": *SOC*, August 4, 1906, 4.
432 "I have had some": TH, Op. 15, May 7, 1906.
433 "a slugger": McP3, August 20, 1906; *SOC*, July 14, 1907.
433 One was George Wheeler: Hermon Titus alleged that A. K. Steunenberg stood behind Wheeler's acerbic —at times vicious—column, "Law and Order" (*SOC*, October 27, 1906; *MN*, March 28, 1907; James McParland to James Hawley, September 4, 1906, HP).
433 The other target: James McParland to James Hawley, September 4, 1906, HP.
433 "This man Caldwell": James McParland to Frank Gooding, August 20, 1906, HP.
433 Garner and Davies: *AtR*, March 16, 1907; *SOC*, September 21, 1907.
433 "not allow me": James McParland to Frank Gooding, August 26, 1906, HP.
433 His cover identity: *MN*, March 15, 1907.
433 "no person": McP3, January 20, 1906.
434 A two-story: Leppert and Thurston, *Early Caldwell*, 72; *Caldwell News-Tribune*, June 26, 1929, 1.
434 No one ever discovered: TH, January 18, 1906.
435 "hand them a heavy": *WIL*, April 1906, 6.
435 "the Wendell Phillips": Margherita Arlina Hamm, *IDS*, May 19, 1907, 24.
435 "desperate measures": *Worker*, March 31, 1906, 1–2; *WIL*, May 1906, 19.
435 "Last night": Wanhope's letter appeared in the *Chicago Socialist*, April 7, 1906.
436 "deep-dyed and tyrannous": *Worker*, March 9, 1907, 1.
436 "put it to them": Joseph Wanhope to Gaylord Wilshire, March 25, 1906.
437 "the biggest meeting": Wanhope, "Haywood-Moyer Outrage," 10.
437 This was almost certainly: Op. 21 Report, February 7, 1907, PA.
437 Barber frequently walked: *MN*, March 15, 1907.
437 Neither Wanhope: J. W. Wright to Fred Warren, May 13, 1906; *Parma Herald*, May 12, 1906.
437 Henceforth, he religiously: *Cost*, n.p.
437 "For some weeks": *IDS*, February 27, 1906, 3.
437 In late February: *CT*, February 24, 1906.
437 No sooner: *CT*, April 7, April 14, 1906.
437 They closed: Canyon County Deed Record Book, 83; Canyon County Cemetery Records, March 1906.
438 "instruct the operative": McP3, April 22, 1906.
439 Through his Socialist: Howard R. McBride to James Hawley, February 20, 1906.

439 In the weeks since : McP3, May 3, 1906.
439 "No attorney for": *IDS*, May 3, 1906, 2.
439 "stronger standing": Wellington B. Hopkins to James McParland, n.d. (c. May 1907), PA.
440 prominent Emmett: *IDS*, July 12, 1907, 4.
440 "I see you are": Op. 21 Report, February 19, 1907, PA.
440 "The detective-cursed": *MN*, March 15, 1907.
440 "big Swede": In the slang of that era, a raw recruit from the farm districts.
441 All through: *NYS*, March 15, 1907.
441 These "scouts": Grover, *Debaters*, 95.
441 Armed with: *IDS*, April 2, 1907, 2.
441 "A farmer": *PO*, February 27, 1907.
441 "I have had one hell": Op. 21 Report, February 19, 1907, PA. The account of Davis's activities are in the reports of January 3, 4, 6, 10, 15, 26; February 5, 8, 11, 20, 23; and September 28, 1907.
443 "Headquarters for Politicians": Jennie Cornell Scrapbooks, no. 3, Caldwell Public Library, Caldwell, Idaho.
444 "from his lips": McP3, July 3, 1906.
446 "about twenty-five people"… "From what I've seen": Op. 10D Reports, February 20, February 25, 1907.
446 With other Socialists: *SOC*, August 25, 1906.
446 When the county fair: *CT*, October 3, 1903, 7.
446 Like many other Caldwell: McP3, April 13, 1907.
446 "He said he always": Op. 21 Report, January 3, 1907, PA.
447 "well-educated and intelligent": McP3, January 12, 1907.
447 In September 1905: McP3, January 10, 1907.
447 One was Frank: Zanjani and Rocha, *Ignoble*, 31.
448 "undignified chase": Watterson, "Inventing," 105.
448 In November 1905: Scheidecker, *Northwestern*, 1–13.
448 "this boy-killing": Watterson, "Inventing," 105.
448 "in letter": R. A. Smith, *Big-Time Football*, 1–13.
449 "Pinkerton people": Op. 21 Report, January 1, 1907, PA.
449 "open-air treatment": *CT*, February 2, 1907; *MM*, January 24, 1907.
449 "all the earmarks": *CT*, January 9, 1907.
449 "bullet holes": *CT*, February 9, 1907.
450 "automatic gun": Op. 21 Report, January 5, 1907, PA.
450 "glad also": Joseph Wanhope to C. A. Johnson, n.d. (c. January 15, 1907), as cited in Op. 21 Report, January 22, 1907, PA.
450 "a slaughterhouse": Brooks, *Confident Years*, 380.
450 "ridiculous socialist rant": U. Sinclair, *Autobiography*, 105, 114.
451 "well pleased at": Op. 21 Report, January 22, 1907, PA.
451 preferably the Democratic: J. R. Foreman to Fred T. Dubois, April 7, 1906, FTD; Operative 10D Report, February 18, 1907.
451 have to try the case: *IDS*, March 25, 1906, 5; *ECN*, July 7, 1906, 1.
451 But no affidavit: Op. 21 Report, February 13, 1907, PA.
451 who flatly refused: I. Stone, *Darrow*, 241. For years, Scatterday remained convinced that he would be a target of the dynamiters. Each time he opened the door to his law office he feared a bomb might go off (Ralph Scatterday, interview by Irving Stone, IS).
451 For notaries: The operative's activities are recorded in his reports of February 23, January 16, February 12, February 2, 1907, PA.
453 "Governor Steunenberg": Pete Steunenberg, interview by Irving Stone, IS.
453 "a good man": James Hawley to Jacob Fillius, August 13, 1906.
453 "he was elected": James McParland to James Hawley, November 26, 1906, HP.
453 Wood was a: Hawley, *History*, 2:220–25; *IDS*, September 20, 1931, sect. 2, 2; *IDS*, December 23, 1940, 1–2.
454 "a man of strong": McP3, March 12, 1907.
454 Something of a country: Emma Edwards Green to Fred T. Dubois, January 23, 1906, FTD.
454 Haywood smuggled out: Haywood, *Autobiography*, 196.
454 Haywood, Moyer: *IDS*, March 21, 24, 25, 1907.
454 "the very air": *MN*, March 5, 1907.
454 "a good thing off": *MN*, April 25, 1907, 1.
455 "not to even hint": McP3, March 21, 1907.
455 "very much pleased": James McParland to James Hawley, April 6, 1907, HP.
455 "rather hard to go through": James Hawley to Jacob Fillius, March 30, 1907; Hawley to James McParland, April 3, 1907, HP.
455 an agent in place: *IDS*, March 11, 1906; *DP*, May 20, 1907.
456 "It is needless": McP3, May 4, 1907.
456 "His grammar": H. F. Cary to G. J. Hasson, February 3, 1907.
456 "If Myers is a traitor": McP3, May 16, 1906.
457 "on condition": Op. 21 Report, January 22, 1907, PA.
457 McParland had turned up: McP3, May 18, 1906.
457 For McParland had discovered: Membership list in "Memorial Services, B.P.O.E., Boise Lodge no. 310," December 3, 1911, ISHS.
458 Exhausted Rooster: John and Jess Hawley, interview by author, June 2, 1995.

10: UNDESIRABLE CITIZENS

459 Finally it was resold: L. Morris, *Postscript*, 222.
460 "I cannot withdraw": *New York World*, April 3, 1907, 1–2.
460 "all of the rich" … "a measure": *DP*, April 3, 1907.
460 After a previously: *New York American*, April 3, 1907, 1.
461 "Who cares?": *DP*, April 7, 1907.
461 "Bless you": Owen Wister to TR, April 25, 1907.
461 "The President said what": Frank W. Annis to William Loeb, n.d. (but April 1907).
461 "The President says that": *NYT*, April 6, 1907, 2.
461 "It was while": *New York Herald*, May 17, 1908. Eventually, Haywood wore the president's epithet as a badge of honor. Several years later, while visiting the home of a sympathizer, the Christian Socialist George Davis Herron, in Florence, Italy, he signed his name in the guest book with a bold flourish, "William D. Haywood, Undesirable Citizen" (interview with Herron's granddaughter, Caroline Rand Herron, October 1996).
461 "It seems": Austin Willard Wright to C. E. S. Wood, May 23, 1907, CESW.
461 "How the spectacular": Mother Jones to Terence Powderly, May 24, 1907, *Correspondence*.
461 "Are you not aware": Thomas Crimmins to TR, April 4, 1907, ROS.
462 "uttered a lie": Joyner, "Undesirable," 48.
462 "The labor people": TR to Kermit Roosevelt, April 17, 1907, ROS.
462 Jackson served as secretary: McNaught, *History*, 178–79.
462 Over the next several: D. B. Smith, "Honoré"; *NYT*, April 25, 1907, 1; "Who's Who—And Why," *Saturday Evening Post*, June 1, 1907, 17.
463 "in the same class": Honoré Joseph Jaxon to TR, April 19, 1907, ROS.
463 "I entirely agree": TR to Honoré Joseph Jaxon, April 22, 1907, ROS.
463 "Coming from": *Milwaukee Sentinel*, April 25, 1907, 1.
464 In New York: Ibid.; *Milwaukee Journal*, April 25, 1907.
464 Agreeing to receive: *New York Tribune*, May 2, 6, 1907.
466 In my discussion of the Lower East Side Jewish community and its hybrid Talmudic-Socialist faith, I have drawn on Birmingham, *Our Crowd*, 291–92; Dauber, "Worthy," 26–40, 44–45, 48–60; Fraser, *Labor*, 20; Howe, *World*, 233–34, passim; Levin, *Messiah*, 17; Moorehead, *Russian*, 54–55; Rischin, *Promised*, 43–44, 50, 79, 84, 87, 96–97, 229–30, 270; Pipes, *Russian*, 10, 24–25, 42–43, 48; Sanders, *Downtown*, 46–48, 52–53, 85–86, 97–140, 165–69, 256, 317, 333, 348, 384.
467 "a striking American newspaper": Villard, *Newspapers*, 94.
467 By 1903: Hillquit, *History*, 353.
468 "to the edge" and "If you want": Villard, *Newspapers*, 88.
469 "an unconscionable": *NYT*, October 19, 1906, 3.
469 Later that month: Harbaugh, *Power*, 218.
469 "That's right": N. Miller, *Roosevelt*, 424.
469 "The Jewish masses": *JDF*, October 27, 1906, 4.
470 "Even a blind man": *JDF*, September 26, 1906, 4
470 Ultimately … In the Eighth: Hillquit, *Leaves*, 107–09.
470 "A Quarter of a Million": These notices, like the articles that follow, were translated from the Yiddish for the author by Jeremy Dauber.
470 "the holiest cause" and "workers cannot": *JDF*, May 4, 1907, 1, 4.
471 "charge up Fifth Avenue": Sanders, *Downtown*, 65.
471 "We have not": *NYT*, May 2, 1.
471 The "uptown march": *New York Post*, May 4, 1907.
471 "Knowledge Is Power": Ibid., July 29, 1907, 1.
471 The Eighth Assembly: The chronology and the composition of the divisions are described in *JDF*, May 5, 1907.
472 After a mile: *NYS*, May 5, 1907, 1, 3.
472 The uptown parade: Rischin, *Promised*, 184.
473 But of 250: *NYS*, May 5, 1907.
473 "a long bobbing": Ibid.
473 The Moyer-Haywood Conference: *New York Evening Post*, May 4, 1907, 1, 3; *NYT*, May 4, 1907, 1–2.
474 Closer to reality: *JDF*, May 5, 1907, 1; *WIL*, June 1907, 8; *NYT, NYS, Herald, World, AP*, May 5, 1907; *American Magazine*, July 1907, 331; *Worker*, May 11, 1907, 1.
474 Hawkers sold: *NYT*, May 5, 1907.
474 Inspector Murphy: *NYS*, May 5, 1907.
475 "This is like": *NYT*, May 5, 1907.
475 "those high in": *Worker*, May 11, 1907, 1.
475 Passing through: Grand Central Palace is described in *NYT*, February 27, 1893.
475 the building was one where: Rischin, *Promised*, 163–64.
475 One man jumped: *New York Herald*, May 5, 1907.
476 "like a wild cat": Pratt, *Hillquit*, 102.
476 "One great capitalist": *NYS*, May 5, 1907, 6.
476 "unshackled from the capitalist press": Ibid.; *Worker*, May 11, 1907, 6.
477 "As a precaution": *Evening Post*, May 4, 1907, 1, 3.
477 "The Entire Neighborhood": *JDF*, May 5, 1907.
477 Norman Hapgood, too: Sanders, *Downtown*, 218.

477 "So this was": *American Magazine,* July 1907, 331–32.
478 Indeed, most self-conscious: P. Buhle, *Marxism,* 100.
478 but that many Orthodox: Howe, *World,* 233–34.
478 In the pages: Sanders, *Downtown,* 386.
478 At home: Rischin, *Promised,* 133.
479 "We have to be Americans": Sanders, *Downtown,* 429.
479 "It was enough to make": *New York World,* May 6, 1907.
479 In Brooklyn: *Worker,* May 11, 1907, 1.
479 In Rochester: Lord, *Good,* 165.
479 At Fair Hope: *CHT,* May 6, 1907.
480 "There were sturdy" and "gunplay" and "More than 2,000": *BG,* May 6, 1907, 3.
480 "No matter what": *NYT,* April 29, 1907.
481 "We have not a word": *CHT,* April 26, 1907.
481 "elbow room": Ralph, "City," 670.
481 Though all spoke German: Payne, *Reform,* 12.
481 "We would light": Dreier, "Reminiscence."
482 "the poor German": Dreier, "Block."
482 "dark hours": Dreier, *Robins.*
482 For fifteen years: Payne, *Reform,* 22, 46.
482 Some such organization: Ibid.
483 "Your Old Maid": Margaret Dreier to Mary Dreier, September 1, 1897, MDR.
483 Then in April 1905: Dreier, *Robins,* 24; Salzman, *Life,* 79.
483 Tall, handsome: Payne, *Reform,* 28–34; Salzman, *Life,* 88–89.
483 With her trust fund: Payne, *Reform,* 44.
483 "find her true freedom": Dreier, *Robins,* 27.
484 more than an administrator: Payne, *Reform,* 34.
484 the Great Mother: Ibid.
484 "It is only": Jane Addams to Henry Demarest Lloyd, December 22, 1895.
484 "Oh no": Margaret Dreier Robins to Mary E. Dreier, July 29, 1907; *MN,* April 12, 1906, MDR.
484 "a magnificent arraignment": Margaret Dreier Robins to Louise deKoven Bowen, May 20, 1907, MDR.
485 "it became the duty": Margaret Dreier Robins to Carrie Read, July 26, 1907, MDR.
485 For Robins, the march: Payne, *Reform,* 10, 141.
485 "Her heart ran out": "Poem to Margaret Dreier Robins, by M.E.D., 1945," MED.
485 "I don't believe": *CHT,* May 9, 1907, 2.
486 The IWW meeting: *Industrial Worker,* April 1906, 6, 14.
486 Thus, the conference: William E. Trautmann to Cook County Executive Committee of the Socialist Party, February 22, 1906, in *Chicago Socialist,* March 3, 1906, 1; Charles L. Breckon, Secretary, Cook County Executive Committee of the Socialist Party, to Trautmann, February 27, 1906, in *Chicago Socialist,* March 3, 1906, 1; *Chicago Socialist,* March 10, 1906, April 14, 1906; Kipnis, *American Socialist,* 330.
486 On May 12: *CHT,* May 13, 1907, 11.
486 "Every schoolboy": *Chicago Record-Herald,* May 20, 1907.
486 Moreover, placards: *CHT,* May 19, 1907, 8.
487 Henrotin was a woman: Sklar, *Kelley,* 261.
487 "how serious a blunder" and "It really was a battle": Margaret Dreier Robins to Mary E. Dreier, May 22, 1907, MDR.
487 "Yesterday afternoon": Margaret Dreier Robins to Mary E. Dreier, August 21, 1907, MDR.
488 "I wish you could": Margaret Dreier Robins to Mary E. Dreier, May 22, 1907, MDR.
488 In the next carriages: *Chicago Record-Herald,* May 20, 1907, 1.
488 But it struck: *Pittsburgh Leader,* May 16, 1907; Mrs. O. T. Hubbard to Margaret Dreier Robins, May 21, 1907, MDR; Margaret Dreier Robins to Carrie Read, July 26, 1907, MDR.
488 "that moment of exaltation": Margaret Dreier Robins to Mary E. Dreier, May 22, 1907.
488 There was disagreement: *Chicago Record-Herald,* May 20, 1907.
488 "Down with government": Margaret Dreier Robins to Carrie Read, July 26, 1907.
488 "not a single" . . . "a trail": Payne, *Reform,* 77.
489 "a line of American": Ibid., 78.
489 "almost wholly": *CHT,* May 20, 1907, 3.
489 "every trade in the city": Margaret Dreier Robins to Louise DeKoven Bowen, May 20, 1907, MDR.
489 "little patronized": *CHT,* May 20, 1907.
489 Among the unions: *Chicago Record-Herald,* May 20, 1907.
489 "revolution or physical violence": *CHT,* May 20, 1907.
490 had allowed her baby: Payne, *Reform,* 77; Margaret Dreier Robins to Ethel Smith, May 6, 1927, MDR.
490 She was blackballed: Payne, *Reform,* 77; Dreier, *Robins,* 44.
490 how much she admired: Ellen M. Henrotin to Margaret Dreier Robins, n.d. (c. May 1907), MDR.
490 "To sink your": Mrs. O. T. Hubbard to Margaret Dreier Robins, May 21, 1907, MDR.
490 "Miss Addams is": Margaret Dreier Robins to Mary E. Dreier, September 30, 1905, MDR.
490 "Why have all": Dreier, *Robins,* 29.
490 "incomprehensible": Margaret Dreier Robins to Mary E. Dreier, May 29, 1907, MDR.
490 "Is it so strange": Margaret Dreier Robins to Carrie Read, July 26, 1907, MDR.
492 "Order of the Flaming Cross": Mary E. Dreier to Raymond Robins, August 14, 1940, MED; Payne, *Reform,* 42.
492 Moyer-Haywood Inquiry Committee: The background on this committee's members is drawn from *Who's Who in New York, 1907,* 28–29, 198, 273, 884, 887, 921, 1376–77; *Notable American Women, 1907–50,* vol. 3, 172–73; 526–29; vol.

4, 202–04; *Dictionary of American Biography*, vol. 22, supplement 2, 687–88; *NYT,* August 30, 1911, 7; April 26, 1929, 25; August 4, 1941, 13; April 23, 1942, 23; March 2, 1944, 17; August 18, 1944, 13; January 28, 1954.

492   "to secure unbiased": Mary E. Dreier to Leonora O'Reilly, June 21, 1906, MED.

492   "direct public opinion": Letter without addressee, signed by Mary E. Dreier, August 25, 1907, MED.

492   The answer probably: I am indebted for these insights to Michael Wallace, an outstanding historian of New York City.

493   "If the club": *Independent,* August 2, 1877, 16, quoted in May, *Protestant,* 92–93.

493   "Bring out the Gatling": *Congregationalist,* July 25, 1877, quoted in May, *Protestant,* 92–93.

493   "We shall not": May, *Protestant,* 178.

493   "a joint interest": Ibid., 179.

493   "this Church has been": Ibid., 182.

494   "the exercise of body": Ibid., 182; Yellowitz, *Labor,* 60–65.

494   "Let the Church": "Annual Address."

494   "endeavoring to remove": *Journal of the Fortieth Convention of the Protestant Episcopal Church in the Diocese of Long Island.*

494   "like one of the Hebrew," "In no body," and "with blazing eyes": Melish, *Autumn,* 30–32.

495   "those extraordinary days": Mary E. Dreier to John Howard Melish, June 27, 1960; June 22, 1962, MED.

495   For forty years: C. E. Clark, *Beecher,* 136.

495   "You are the most": Charles F. Aked to Newell Hillis, December 16, 1907.

495   "a swift, steady": James O'Donnell Bennett, "What Is the Preacher Like?" NDH.

495   In the winter: George W. Britt to Newell Hillis, n.d., NDH.

496   A sign: *ECN,* July 26, 1907.

496   In 1884, he married: *Stowe's Clerical Directory of the American Church,* 1932, 156.

496   A lanky priest: Edwin F. Gulick, interview by author, Casanova, Virginia, August 1996.

496   "a man's man": G. K. Turner, "Introductory Note."

496   Mistaking the two priests: Connolly, "Moyer-Haywood Case," part 4, 12.

496   Orchard had been reading: Frank Steunenberg Jr. to Stewart Holbrook, February 26, 1956, SH.

496   "I am not his father confessor": *DP,* May 20, 1907.

496   When McParland suggested: McP3, March 12, 14, 21, 1907.

496   "a creature": *DP,* May 20, 1907.

497   "I shall always feel": Harry Orchard to James McParland, July 22, 1906, in McP3, August 19, 1906.

497   "Poor fellow": Joyner, "Undesirable," 28.

497   But the persistent: Frank Steunenberg Jr. to Stewart Holbrook, March 13, 1955, SH.

497   In the autumn: *IDS,* May 26, 1907, 5.

497   A fifty-three-year-old: *IDS,* September 13, 1936; Mitchell, *Autobiography.*

498   "A deep-dyed": *PET,* June 17, 1907.

498   "New road to heaven": *SOC,* June 22, 1907, 1.

498   "I don't have much use": John Steunenberg to James Hawley, February 15, 1908.

499   "It has become": *IDS,* July 1, 1907, 2, reprinted from the *Brooklyn Eagle.*

499   "The best folk": *Brooklyn Eagle,* February 19, 1906.

499   "Of late": *New York World,* May 20, 1906.

500   "Henry's people": Hibben, *Beecher,* 143.

500   "Natural aristocracy" and "made luxury": C. E. Clark, *Beecher,* 113–14.

500   Increasingly: I. V. Brown, *Abbott,* 103, 108, 110.

500   "This 'divine' had proved": *MN,* July 27, 1907.

501   "wholly in the power": McP3, September 20, 1906.

501   "If Adams were convicted": McP3, October 3, 1906.

501   Weary, hungry: McP3, February 9–15, 1907.

501   "lots of snow and ice": McP3, February 14, 1907; James McParland to George Bangs, February 17, 1907, PA.

501   "nine good jurors": James McParland to George Bangs, February 17, 1907, PA.

502   According to Chris Thiele: Darrow, *Story,* 137.

503   "While I am well": McP3, February 24, 1907.

503   In conversation: McP3, March 6, 7, 1907.

504   "Adams has felt very blue": McP3, March 5, 1907.

504   Before the evening: McP3, March 7, 1907.

505   "The old man says": McP3, April 17, 1907; Harvey Brown to James McParland, March 28, 1907.

505   "a very smart man": McP3, February 25, 1907.

505   "Therefore": James McParland to Tom McCabe, April 18, 1907, PA.

506   sack of tobacco: McP3, September 19, 1906.

506   "trying to get:" Tom McCabe to James McParland, May 12, 1907, PA.

506   Tom McCabe was the principal: *Polk's Shoshone County Directory,* 1905.

507   Ironically enough: *Wallace Times,* April 26, 1907. The remainder of this story is told principally from the accounts in the *Wallace Times* of April 27, 1907, September 24, 1907, and October 4, 1907.

11: Only a Murder Trial

511   "invalidities": R. W. B. Lewis, *Jameses,* 527–34.

511   "the mere monstrous": Edel, *James,* 267.

511   "What a miserable": Gibson, *Theodore,* 15.

511   "supreme social expression" … "if the hotel spirit": H. James, *Scene,* 292–93.

511 "the private life": R. W. B. Lewis, *Jameses,* 534.
511 "I never dreamt": Gabler, *Winchell,* 183.
512 "under more democratic" ... "from the fact": Pritchett, "Politics," 195.
512 "Take the roughest": Carter, *When Railroads,* 173–74.
512 "Living in public": Hayner, *Hotel Life,* 8.
512 "succession of burnt": Van Orman, *Room,* 7.
512 The first stab: Ibid., 124; Watkin et al., *Grand,* 15.
512 As time went by: Van Orman, *Room,* 125.
512 In 1888: Watkin, *Grand,* 19.
512 In the mid-1890s: Stern et al., *New York,* 254.
512 "great glittering": James, *Scene,* 316–17; Hawes, *New York,* 137.
512 "Pompeian conceits": Stern et al., *New York,* 254.
512 "Railway terminals": L. Morris, *Postscript,* 17; Swanberg, *Citizen,* 103.
513 When the Bradley Martins: *New York Herald,* July 3, 1907.
513 "the human limit": Hawes, *New York,* 51.
513 "Gentlemen will never consent": *New York Herald,* July 3, 1907.
513 "gilded and mirrored" Ginger, *Altgeld's,* 102.
513 "Why do we like": O'Toole, *Five,* 329.
513 "in which we can get": Hayner, *Hotel Life,* 23–24.
513 "one of those shoddy": Herrick, *Common,* 248, 319, 325.
513 "sometimes the tragic": Hayner, *Hotel Life,* 6.
513 "A place with so": Van Orman, *Room,* 129.
513 But if sex and drink: Watkin et al., *Grand,* 13; Hayner, *Hotel Life,* 126; Hawes, *New York,* 34.
514 "Who puts oup": Williamson, *American,* 123–25.
514 "buzzed like a fly": Lancaster, *Gentleman,* 130.
514 "the cleverest criminals": *DR,* May 19, 1907, 31.
514 In Baltimore: *Collier's Weekly,* November 30, 1907.
514 "Livestock, Political": d'Easum, *Idanha,* 47.
514 "Not only a hotel": *Northwest Magazine,* July 1906, 250.
514 Its architect: *IDS,* January 1, 1901, 4; d'Easum, *Idanha,* 27.
515 Some $125,000.... Guests were whisked: D'Easum, *Idanha,* 26, 28.
515 That evening: *IDS,* May 19, 1907.
516 "crazed with jealousy": *IDS,* June 24, 1907, 1–2; *CT,* June 29, 1907, 1.
516 Among the first: *DR,* June 24, 1907, 1.
516 His inaugural ball: D'Easum, *Idanha,* 39–40.
516 The Goodings did all: *SSR,* May 9, 1907.
516 When Justice Stockslager: *IDS,* March 4, 1906.
516 "dress suits jostled": *IDS,* January 16, 1907.
516 On May 5, 1907: *IDS,* May 5, 1907; McP3, May 5, 1907.
516 "when McParland speaks": *SOC,* April 7, 1906, 4.
517 Though McParland spent most: This detail is from a photograph of the two men on Main Street that appeared in the *Statesman* on July 4, 1907.
517 "Here he sits and smokes": *SOC,* March 26, 1907.
517 a snapshot ... Socialist newsmen persisted: S. C. Thiele Report, May 11, 1907, HP.
517 he and his bodyguards: *SOC,* April 7, 1906; *DP,* May 7, 1906.
517 "thuggery": James Hawley to Jacob Fillius, April 27, 1907.
517 "I've felt worse": *IDS,* July 5, 1907, 1.
517 Surprisingly: *IDS,* April 27, 1907, August 11, 1907, 3; I. Stone, *Darrow,* 329.
518 "You are making": Brand Whitlock to Clarence Darrow, May 11, 1907, BW.
518 "patrolled at all hours": *DT,* March 1, 1906.
518 Relishing its new café: Ruby Darrow to Irving Stone, n.d., IS.
518 A dignified lot: *IDS,* September 5, 1907.
518 Since the "church": *IDS,* May 26, 1907, 5; June 9, 1907.
518 But Boiseans turned: *IDS,* May 13, 1907, 5.
518 "from pit to dome": *MN,* May 30, 1907, 2.
518 "claque": *Missoulian,* May 17, 1907, 1.
519 "The lion and lamb" ... locks sheared: *NYS,* May 13, 1907.
519 boots polished: *LMT,* March 20, 1938.
519 "Walt Whitman was not": Darrow, "Whitman in Literature."
519 "the whole bloodthirsty": *NYS,* May 13, 1907.
519 "put the socialists": *MN,* May 16, 1907, 1.
519 And that, it seems: Tierney, *Darrow,* 214.
519 Even the hiring: Haywood, *Autobiography,* 186.
519 In mid-May: Ruby Darrow to Irving Stone, n.d., IS; Stone, *Darrow,* 242.
520 Built in 1882: *BG,* May 20, 1907.
520 but not half so: *DP,* May 20, 1907.
520 It usually accommodated: Grover, *Debaters,* 104–05.
520 "a man in a well-cut": *WIL,* June 1907.
520 Instead of being: WIL, May 1907, 16.
520 Directly in front: *IDS,* August 1, 1907, 5.
521 "The defendant": *IDS,* May 7, 1907, 1–2.

521　What the defense wanted: The prosecution was well within its rights in withholding Orchard's confession. Even a bill of particulars cannot substitute for "discovery," the process through which the defense may now obtain from the prosecution prior inconsistent statements by the defendant or anything tending to exculpate him. Discovery did not even enter the legal armory until the 1950s. Even had discovery existed at the time, it wouldn't have covered Orchard's confession, which, as the prior statement of a prosecution witness, is specifically excluded from discovery orders (Professor Richard Uviller, Columbia Law School, interview by author, June 12, 1996).
521　"The eyes of the civilized": *IDS*, May 10, 1907, 1.
521　"determined struggle": *BG*, May 9, 1907, 1.
521　"The greatest trial": *Daily People*, May 19, 1907.
522　The facing table: The eleven were Darrow, Richardson, Nugent, Whitsell, Miller, Murphy, Dickson, Morrison, Griffiths, Griffiths, and Cahalan.
522　But what had people: *Idaho Tri-Weekly Statesman*, August 5, 1884, 3.
522　At a dinner arranged: Wood, *Introductory*, 22–23; I. Stone, *Darrow*, 238–39.
522　and a persistent story: Fred T. Dubois to Edgar Wilson, February 27, 1907, FTD.
522　There were also... curry favor: McP3, May 9, 1907.
523　"our previous association": Wood, *Introductory*, 22–23.
523　"loquacious juice": [Illegible] to William Borah, March 8, 1907, WEB.
523　But soon after: *DP*, May 25, 1907; *BG*, May 26, 1907.
523　Business organizations: I. Stone, *Darrow*, 239.
523　"As I understand it": McP3, May 7, 1907.
524　"an unaffected, lovable": *DP*, June 2, 1907.
524　"attractive as daisies": *MN*, May 16, 1907.
524　"this model and moral": McP4, May 23, 1906.
524　Mother Jones: Long, *Where*, 233.
524　"Polly Pry": Ross, *Ladies*, 564.
524　"down in the 'Pinkerton'": *Polly Pry: A Journal of Comment and Criticism*, January 2, 1904, 4.
524　"My informant also": McP3, March 5, 1907.
525　"We also talked": McP4, May 23, 1906.
525　"De Lue and Baird": H. F. Cary to James McParland, May 16, 1907, HP.
525　now in charge: *DR*, August 5, 1907, 2.
525　widely regarded: *DP*, July 14, 1915; *RMN*, January 30, 1887, 6; June 28, July 4, 1914.
525　As for Duffield: McP3, May 19, 1907.
525　"I believe these men": McP3, May 24, 1907.
525　"the palladium": Yarros, "Palladium," 209.
525　"frequently corruptible": Cabot, "Trial," 511.
525　"nobody but": "Our Jury," 357.
526　"expert work": Jenks, "Can the Jury," 726.
526　"This has been": *New York World*, May 3, 1907.
526　"of fair character": Idaho Code, 1901, Sects. 3055–56.
526　"with every manifestation": *NYS*, May 8, 1907; *IDS*, May 10, 1907, 6.
526　"You understand": *IDS*, May 14, 1907, 1.
527　Owen Wister's Virginian: *PO*, May 2, 1907.
527　There they sat: *NYS*, May 14, 1907.
527　"emotional, kindly": Darrow, "Attorney," 37, 211.
528　"dope sheets": *PET*, May 25, 1907, 8.
528　"God's truth": *DP*, May 25, 1907.
528　"Rep., N.G.": Op. 21 Report, April 14, 1907, HP.
529　"it ain't": *IDS*, May 15, 1907, 1, 10.
529　"The court will allow": *IDS*, May 16, 1907, 10.
530　"It was like killing": Haywood, *Autobiography*, 209.
530　His head was always: *NYT Magazine*, June 2, 1907.
530　In federal criminal: Adler, *Jury*, 56.
530　"as hard a fight": James Hawley to Fred T. Dubois, March 6, 1906.
530　Evidently, Darrow: *IDS*, May 7, 1907.
531　There were those: Bonaparte, "Lynch," 342.
531　"All of the jurors": McP3, May 9, 1907.
531　"a motion suggestive": *PET*, May 13, 1907.
531　"about as bad": *SOC*, May 25, 1907.
531　"Every inch": *IDS*, May 20, 1907, 1.
532　hello girls: Op. 21 Report, May 26, 1907, PA.
532　"State your challenge": *IDS*, May 28, 1907, 3.
532　"I object": *SOC*, June 1, 1907, 1.
532　"If it had been": *DP*, as reprinted in *IDS*, May 30, 1907.
533　"We can't get this": *IDS*, May 25, 1907, 12.
533　"hoboes": *San Francisco Call*, August 3, 1907.
533　One man was found: *IDS*, May 31, 1907, 1; *PET*, May 29, 1907.
533　"a handsome": Wright and Reitzes, *Tourtellotte*, 3.
534　"he did not relish": *IDS*, May 26, 1907, 1.
534　Two years before: *IDS*, July 2, 1905, 2.
534　Curiously, the defense: Charles E. Hummel to author, March 29, 1996.
534　"the defense are going": Op. 24A Report, May 26, 1907.

534 "there was insanity": McP3, May 25, 1907.
535 The defense had a report: Op. 21 Report, April 28, 1907, HP.
535 But since it: Op. 24A Report, April 18, 1907, HP.
535 "they did not talk": Op. 21 Report, May 25, 1907, PA.
535 By May 11 … "a traitor": Op. 24A Report, May 11, 1907.
535 McParland told: McParland, Synopsis, n.d., PA.
535 "still a leak": Op. 21 Report, May 26, 1907, HP; IDS, May 10, 1907, 3.
536 Then on January 23: ECN, January 18, 1907, 1.
536 Emigrating to Idaho: IDS, January 8, 1933, 1; ECN, January 8, 1933, 1; Hawley, History, 2:737.
536 "under no circumstances": Gustavus J. Hasson to Kemble, January 23, 1907.
536 Eventually, it was agreed: ECN, January 18, 22, 25, 28, 1907; IDS, January 19, 23, 26, 1907.
536 "a God Damned": ECN, December 16, 1907.
536 "every secret service": IDS, January 2, 1908.
536 "one man closely": Darrow testimony, IC, 10, 778.
536 "warned to leave": IDS, January 2, 1908.
537 "shown the door": RMN, reprinted in ECN, July 1, 1907, 4; IDS, May 19, 1907, 13; McP3, May 18, 1907; H. F. Cary to James McParland, May 16, 1907.
537 a Boise policeman … a private detective: PET, May 14, 21, 1907; IDS, May 18, 1907.
537 Suspicion fell: IDS, May 22, 1907, 3.
537 "Good-bye": IDS, May 21, 1907.
537 "pouring the venire": IDS, May 31, 1907, 4.
538 "I would not like": IDS, June 4, 1907, 7.
538 The frame dwelling: ECN, May 8, 1907.
538 under constant observation: IDS, May 10, 1907, 9.
539 "great latitude" and "every movement": Wood, Introductory, 33–34.
539 "A hard-headed": NYS, June 4, 1907.
539 "We are thoroughly": IDS, June 4, 1907, 1.
539 "If we cannot convict": DP, June 5, 1907.
539 "There is no man": DP, June 4, 1907.
539 "To such men": Cabot, "Trial," 511.
539 "The rural mind": NYS, May 25, 1907, 16.
540 "Some are untidy": WIL, May 1907, 16.
540 "Farmer juries": Pagosa Springs News, May 25, 1906.
540 "not pleased with": Op. 21 Report, May 26, 1907, HP. According to McParland's May 25 report, Darrow had the same gloomy assessment.
540 some fifty such types: PET, June 1, 1907.
540 In it he found: IDS, May 29, 1907.
540 "Dear Charlie": IDS, May 31, 1907.
540 "C. H. Duncan is a": PET, May 30, 1907.
541 Origin of Man: IDS, July 12, 1907, 10.
541 "inadequate quarters": General S. P. Jocelyn to Military Secretary, Department of the Columbia, October 19, 1906, January 5, 1907.
541 On the eve: McArthur to Military Secretary, Department of the Columbia, February 14, 1907.
541 "stating the necessities": William Howard Taft to Frank Gooding, June 22, 1907, 4, WHT.
542 All too often: IDS, June 22, 1907, 4.
542 "Levy's reeking": J. A. Russell, Evil, 78.
542 On October 5: IDS, October 6, 1901, 1.
543 Found guilty: IDS, February 22, 1974.
543 For a time after: Crowder, "Alexander," 44.
543 During a 1908: J. A. Russell, Evil, 180.
543 "a miniature Barbary": MacLane, Sagebrush, 3.
543 McKenney urged: McKenney to Military Secretary, September 20, 1906.
543 "gross inefficiency": Tukay to Military Secretary, Department of the Columbia, December 30, 1906.
543 Ultimately: IDS, June 12, 1907, 6.
544 These people: DR, May 19, 1907.
544 "minor factors": Capt. Clark D. Dudley to Adjutant General, Department of the Columbia, August 1, 1907.
544 "would think": Ibid., May 1, 1907.
544 According to charges: For Dudley's court-martial, see Clark D. Dudley, Trial by General Court-Martial, March 4–7, 1908, 118, 125, File 55832, NA; IDS, March 5, 1908, March 21, 1908; Statement, Headquarters, Department of the Columbia, March 12, 1908.
544 Late in June: IDS, June 23, 1907.
545 "ready for deadly": MN, April 4, 1907, 1.
545 "Nothing would give": AtR, April 27, 1907.
545 In Idaho, for example: Adj. Gen. David Vickers to Fred T. Dubois, January 9, 1906, FTD.
545 haphazard training: Col. John McBirney to Commanding Officer of Companies, April 19, 1906; David Vickers to Frank Gooding, December 31, 1906.
545 "tin sword play": Adj. Gen. J. L. Weaver to Captains, Companies A, B, C, and D, July 24, 1899.
545 "Of unusually marked ability": Lorenzo P. Davison, 1890 Efficiency Report.
545 "totally unfitted": Report, Army and Navy General Hospital, Hot Springs, Arkansas, April 14, 1901.
546 "loss of nervous control": Lorenzo P. Davison, Personnel Folder, War Department.

546 "his mind gets confused": Testimony of Maj. William C. Borden, commanding officer, General Hospital, Washington, D.C.
546 recommended that he retire: Davison Statement, April 13, 1904, Special Order 295.
546 "fine raiment" and "a rich, fast, smart set": Lorenzo P. Davison to Military Secretary, May 23, 1905.
546 Somehow, amid: *IDS*, June 26, 1907; receipts and vouchers in *Cost*, n.p.
546 But very soon . . . "men united": Lorenzo P. Davison to Military Secretary, September 11, 1905.
546 "While the status": Military Secretary to Lorenzo P. Davison, September 11, 1905.
547 McParland knew that: McP3, May 7, 1907.
547 "an auxiliary association": George H. Bangs to James McParland, January 28, 1907, PA.
547 At least a hundred: *ECN*, May 2, 1907; *AtR*, May 11, 1907, 2.
547 "it behooved him": S. C. Thiele Report, May 11, 1907, HP.
547 A secretly convened gathering: *IDS*, May 9, 1907, 2.
548 "I have it from": *DP*, May 10, 1902, 2.
548 Chief among these . . . "He was my right": *IDS*, April 5, 1912.
548 "Rot!": *PET*, May 10, 1907.
548 Nonetheless: Grover, *Debaters*, 110.
548 Though side arms: John and Jess Hawley, interview by author, June 2, 1995.
548 On occasion: *IDS*, June 6, 1907, 6.
548 To insure: Dick d'Easum, interview by author, 1990.
548 But at least one: *IDS*, May 8, 1932.
549 "We must give": John E. Wilkie to William Loeb, July 23, 1907.
549 "representative citizen": *PET*, June 4, 1907.
549 "We will prove": *SvH*, 9.
549 "clamb" and "I-dy-ho.": *Chicago Record-Herald*, July 20, 1907.
549 "He droned on": The exchanges between Hawley and Darrow are in *DP*, May 5, 1907.
550 Hawley's exasperation: Maloney, "Darrow," 299; Haywood, *Autobiography*, 212; Grover, *Debaters*, 115–16.
550 So venomous: Haywood, *Autobiography*, 212.
550 "That will be proved": Richardson's and Hawley's words are in *SvH*, 21, 28, 26, 35.
552 "to be on your guard": McP3, October 9, 1906.
552 The state assigned: *DP*, May 10, 1907.
552 "The second man": Jess Hawley to Irving Stone, n.d., IS.
552 So about seven: *IDS*, June 5, 1907, 1.
552 "Orchard the criminal," *Milwaukee Journal*, June 6, 1907, 1.
553 "a regular matinee idol": *SOC*, June 15, 1907, 4.
553 "Far from being": Haywood, *Autobiography*, 209.
553 an excellent shot. . . . At the same moment: *PET*, June 11, 1907, 4.
553 "on roving commission": *MN*, June 13, 1907, 1.
553 Other deputies: *Daily Missoulian*, June 8, 1907.
553 Inside the rail: *SSR*, June 6, 1907, 2.
553 "Sit down!" and "Mr. Orchard": *DR*, June 6, 1907, 5.
554 "have nothing whatever": George Dickson to Clarence Darrow, April 25, 1906, ER.
555 For a time: *DP*, May 25, 1907.
555 "tense-nerved": *IDS*, June 6, 1907, 1.
555 among whom women: *Los Angeles Times*, June 7, 1907, 1.
555 The guards had: *IDS*, June 7–14, 1907.
556 "Who lit the fuse?": *SvH*, 126.
556 "as placid as a summer lake" and "We made arrangements" and "withdrawal card": *DR*, June 9, 1907, 1.
557 "Steunenberg has lived" and "He said if": *IDS*, June 7, 1907, 10.
557 "it would not be hard": Orchard's account is drawn from *SvH*, 262, 31–32, 297–303.
559 "Two stars": *DP*, June 2, 1907.
559 "Darrow, the loose-jointed": *DR*, June 25, 1907, 1.
560 "fiery, fierce": *IDS*, June 22, 1907, 7.
560 "an able man": Darrow, *Story*, 151.
560 Moreover, the two men: *DR*, August 7, 1907, 5.
560 "I don't sanction Socialism": *CT*, August 10, 1907.
560 persona non grata: Edmund Richardson to Clarence Darrow, November 1, 1906, in possession of the Darrow family.
560 "So far as my connection": Clarence Darrow to Edmund Richardson, November 5, 1906, in possession of the Darrow family.
560 "Under the circumstances": CD.
560 The union's records: "Receipts and Disbursements."
561 "Well, as J. M. Kennedy": *IDS*, January 6, 1906.
561 "a potent, indomitable": *DP*, June 3, 1907.
561 "There is no chief": *IDS*, May 21, 1907.
561 "at no time": *PET*, June 4, 1907.
562 In revisiting: *IDS*, June 7, 1907.
562 "That particular bomb": *IDS*, June 12, 1907, 1.
563 "No, sir. No, sir": *IDS*, June 14, 1907, 1.
563 "I don't know what you mean": *SvH*, 566–67.
563 Darrow, in a caustic: *DP*, July 29, 1907.

563   "the most remarkable": Connolly, "Moyer-Haywood Case," part 4, 11.
564   "defiant humor": *IDS,* June 15, 1907, 1.
564   Another article: The magazine articles are quoted in *IDS,* June 21, 1907, 1; June 28, 1907, 1, 5.
565   According to Orchard: *IDS,* June 19, 1907, 1.
565   Seventeen witnesses: *New York American,* June 17, 1907.
566   "I would say": *IDS,* June 22, 1907, 7.
566   As he later explained: *IDS,* March 18, 1908.
566   On the other hand: Wood, *Introductory,* 24.
567   "The court is thoroughly": Ibid., 10.

12: QUARTET

568   "I was a great friend": E. Barrymore, *Memories,* 157.
568   her Swiss maid, Berthe: Ibid., 124.
568   lunch with Calvin Cobb: *IDS,* June 25, 1907, 6.
568   Barrymore knew: E. Barrymore, *Memories,* 158.
568   "monkey act": K. Miller, *McCormick,* 132.
568   Alice had been educated: Peters, *House,* 42.
568   "Watch the way": Hoge, *Patterson,* 24–25.
569   "He is a disgrace": Townsend, *Manhood,* 258.
569   Up in her spacious: D'Easum, *Idanha,* xi.
569   "which, on anyone less": *IDS,* June 25, 1907, 8.
569   Dabbing Atkinson's: E. Barrymore, *Memories,* 191.
569   Scarcely a great beauty: Betty Penson Ward, former society editor of the *Statesman,* and Daisy Tankersly, interview by author, August 1995.
569   Very much!: E. Barrymore, *Memories,* 158.
569   Though it was more crowded: *NYT,* June 25, 1907.
569   "divided with Mr. Darrow": *NYS,* June 25, 1907.
569   "a clever, striking": *NYT,* June 25, 1907.
570   "even brilliant at times": *NYS,* June 25, 1907.
570   "this leper": *DP,* June 25, 1907.
570   "He had all the props" and "the most wonderful": E. Barrymore, *Memories,* 158.
570   "Often there's a touch": *SSR,* July 27, 1907.
571   "dreamy-looking": E. Barrymore, *Memories,* 158.
571   "Little Cupid": Siringo, *Riata,* 202.
571   A photograph: Jess Hawley to John F. MacLane, n.d., 23.
571   his right: *PET,* May 21, 1907.
571   Between wives: Pingenot, *Siringo,* 77.
571   "kneeling at her feet" and "I had learned": Siringo, *Cowboy Detective,* 513.
571   "I've heard a certain amount": E. Barrymore, *Memories,* 159.
572   "I don't see how": *SSR,* June 27, 1907.
572   She'd begged Frohman: *Pittsburgh Times,* n.d. (but 1907).
572   The American theater's: Peters, *House,* 109.
572   "Why on earth": *NYS,* March 21, 1907.
572   "Let those who are": Peters, *House,* 99.
573   Critics and audiences: Marcossan and Frohman, *Manager,* 21; Kotsilibas-Davis, *Great,* 458; *DP,* April 14, 1907.
573   "personality that has heart": *Worker,* May 4, 1907.
573   "to doubt the sacredness": L. Barrymore, *We Barrymores!,* 115.
573   "whether this young woman": RL, no. 35, 85.
573   Her dilemma: Peters, *House,* 133.
574   "If to these": *DP,* February 10, 1907.
574   Prince Ragtime: RL, no. 34, 5.
574   "We have to eat": *Pittsburgh Post,* May 31, 1905.
574   "I am bored" and "not in the least": *Morning Telegraph,* February 2, 1908.
574   "rather Gothic": E.Barrymore, *Memories,* 64–65, 135, 155.
574   "That Miss Barrymore is ill": *American Journal-Examiner,* February 12, 1905.
574   Barrymore hinted: *DP,* July 15, 1907.
574   She even hated: E. Barrymore, *Memories,* 89
574   "The world is a dark blue": *CHT,* February 9, 1908.
575   Until the late: For history of the American theater and the American theatrical road, I have relied on P. Lewis, *Trouping,* 2–111; Gelb and Gelb, *O'Neill,* 33–54, 176–81; Binns, *Fiske,* 79–81; Ernst, *Oregon;* Fields and Fields, *Bowery;* de Angelis and Harlow, *Vagabond;* and Hewitt, *Theatre.*
576   At the Masonic: *Wallace Times,* April 27, 1907.
576   "The entrance": *Dramatic Mirror,* June 6, 1907.
576   "Originally, dapper": L. Barrymore, *We Barrymores!,* 58.
577   "In answer": A. L. Erlanger to John M. Foster, December 13, 1907, KE.
577   "a natural diplomatist": *NYS,* May 4, 1919.
577   "Nominally, we act": N. Hapgood, *Stage,* 38.
578   "Death to the syndicate!": Kobler, *Damned,* 63–65.

578 "greed, cunning": N. Hapgood, *Stage,* 21.
578 "I'll kill": Binns, *Fiske,* 70.
578 "killed art": N. Hapgood, "Syndicate," 107; Binns, *Fiske,* 81.
578 "They are not Jews": *Life,* December 29, 1904.
578 The Iroquois: Fields and Fields, *Bowery,* 195.
578 On May 11: McNamara, *Shuberts,* 32–33.
579 "working agreement": *DP,* April 24, 28, 1907.
579 "I like Maude Adams": Rennold Wolf, *"Barrymore,"* May 1906, 44, RL.
579 He lived alone: L. Morris, *Postscript,* 173–74.
579 "the facade": Kotsilibas-Davis, *Great,* 446.
579 "Swat": Moses and Gerson, *Clyde,* 175.
579 "silken, perfumed whip": Ibid., 176.
579 "Thank goodness": Ibid., 171.
580 She worked: Kotsilibas-Davis, *Great,* 447.
580 "If the young lady": Peters, *House,* 63–64.
580 the happiest day: Kotsilibas-Davis, *Great,* 450.
581 "the newest princess": Peters, *House,* 65; E. Barrymore, *Memories,* 119.
581 The comedy team: Kotsilibas-Davis, *Great,* 450.
581 "If you breathe": Moses and Gerson, *Clyde,* 289.
581 "parts like the lead": *Grand Rapids Herald,* n.d., (but 1907).
581 "enraptured": *Battle Creek Daily Journal,* May 22, 1907. For the rest of Barrymore's tour, see *Daily News,* Grand Rapids, May 23, 1907; *Kalamazoo Gazette,* May 24, 1907, 1; *South Bend Tribune,* May 25, 1907; *CHT,* May 5, 1907, 4; *St. Joseph Gazette,* June 6, 1907, 5; *Deseret Evening News,* June 22, 1907; *Salt Lake Herald,* June 21, 1907.
582 alkali pelting: Kobler, *Damned,* 28.
582 "every gambler": *IDS,* in *CT,* July 18, 1903.
582 "Allegory of Theatrical Arts": Eggers, *"History,"* 58.
582 Above the proscenium: Arthur A. Hart, *IDS,* August 16, 1971; French, *History,* 682.
583 "waited four hours": Eggers, "History," 27.
583 the role Ethel wanted: Returning from an eight-month trip to Europe on July 24, Charles Frohman announced that he would give Ethel Barrymore her choice of two plays that season and would also present her as Rosalind in *As You Like It* (*IDS,* July 25, 1907, 4).
583 Finally, there was: *IDS,* December 11, 1978.
583 With a $2.50 top: Balance sheet for June 24, 1907, in ledger book, JAP. The biggest grosser in the theater's history was *Hi Henry's Minstrels,* which drew 1,021 paid admissions, but that was before passage of a municipal ordinance prohibiting the blocking of aisles with folding chairs and the using of every inch of standing room. (*IDS,* April 12, 1908, 3).
584 In one box: *IDS,* June 30, 1907, 16.
584 "never seen such": *SSR,* July 27, 1907.
584 "a little Pinkerton": E. Barrymore, *Memories,* 159.
584 "Her happy smile": Siringo, *Cowboy Detective,* 514. The Barrymore-Siringo flirtation was well known to newsmen at the trial. Some years later, A. E. Thomas of the *Sun* wrote Calvin Cobb from Manhattan: "I have seen Miss Barrymore now and then of late. We have quite expected Siringo to appear and shoot up the town, but as yet he hasn't arrived. Something must have happened to him" (CC).
585 "a new domain": M. Hunt, *Story,* 127–32; Kaplan, *Steffens,* 41.
585 "could get younger men": William James to Hugo Münsterberg, February 21, 1892.
585 "the Rudyard Kipling": William James to Henry James, April 11, 1892.
586 "The thought of psycho-physical": M. Hunt, *Story,* 144–45, 150.
586 "an extraordinarily": William James to Josiah Royce, June 22, 1892.
586 "five speeches": Keller, *States,* 41.
586 "The fact is": Charles W. Eliot to William James, December 29, 1905.
586 "changed totally" . . . "the 'sinister' ": Keller, *States,* 41.
586 By 1901: M. Hale, *Human,* 41.
587 "experimental psychology" . . . "astonishing that": Münsterberg, *Witness,* 7–8.
587 "not holding up": William Allen White to John S. Phillips, June 22, 1907.
587 "The study": Arnold, *Fair Fights,* 20.
587 "How can a thought": O'Toole, *Five,* 396.
587 "I see no reason": M. Hale, *Human,* 107.
588 Münsterberg belonged: N. G. Hale, Jr., *Freud,* 100; Hale, *Putnam,* 11–15.
588 "the scurvy, sweated": I. Cobb, *Exit,* 229–30.
588 " 'I come to th' conclusion' ": *IDS,* February 24, 1907.
588 "Every day errors": H. Münsterberg, *Witness,* 43, 34.
588 "brass instruments": H. Münsterberg, "Reporter," 437.
588 "a fairly well-educated": Holt, *Freudian,* 38–39.
589 Münsterberg's associates recognized: Keller, *States,* 45–46; Hugo Münsterberg to Edwin B. Holt, March 24, March 30, April 3, 1916.
589 "I feel sure": *CHT,* June 1, 1906, 5.
589 "inconceivable": H. Münsterberg, *Witness,* 142.
589 Psychology, wrote one: M. Hale, *Human,* 111–12.
589 With a vengeful crowd: *CHT,* June 23, 1906.
589 "on the verge": S. S. McClure to Hattie McClure, June 9, 1893, SSM.
590 Over the next: Woodress, *Cather,* 193.

590   "I took you into my": *McClure's Magazine,* June 1904, 166; Wilson, *Muckrakers,* 165.

590   "The Shame of S. S. McClure": Lyon, *Success,* 277.

590   "He's a Mormon": Wilson, *Muckrakers,* 170.

590   "was the precise": Woodress, *Cather,* 187.

590   A photograph: Lyon, *Success,* photograph following p. 308.

590   "a pair of shoes": James B. Morrow, "Leading Writer in America, S. S. McClure Says, Is Mr. Howells," n.d. (but 1907), SSM.

591   "If he had been a woman": Wilson, *Muckrakers,* 144.

591   temporarily cutting his press: Ibid.

591   "unreasoning, passionate": Ibid., 259.

591   Now, regarding: *ECN,* July 26, 1907; *PET,* June 12, 1907.

591   With the loss: Lyon, *Success,* 296–97.

591   By 1907: Chalmers, *Social,* 21–25.

592   "If there was a defect": Schudson, *Discovering,* 81.

592   There he met: McP4, May 23, 1907.

592   Finally, he visited: S. S. McClure to Frederic Bancroft, May 6, 1907; *IDS,* May 24, 1907, 4; June 9, 1907, 7; June 24, 1907, 3.

592   "jovial": *IDS,* May 24, 1907, 7.

593   "a woman of culture": *IDS,* June 24, 1907, 3.

594   "a man whom nothing": S. S. McClure to Cameron MacKenzie, n.d. (but probably June 18, 1907).

594   "He is a psychological mystery": *ECN,* June 11, 1907, 5

594   So McClure promptly: Haywood, *Autobiography,* 83; Filler, *Crusaders,* 232.

594   He thought immediately: S. S. McClure to Hugo Münsterberg, February 17, 1902.

595   Although the professor: Victor Dyer, Marblehead Historical Society, interview by author, September 1995.

595   "When I selected": H. Münsterberg, "A German."

595   "Whoever claims": H. Münsterberg, "Experiments," 1–2.

595   "a trunk full": M. Hale, *Human,* 50.

595   "a whole night": William James to Henry James, February 25, 1894.

595   But raised: M. Hale, *Human,* 50; Jackson, *Sense,* 151.

595   "Even the Adirondacks" and "Almost everything": M. Hale, *Human,* 49.

596   If the Herr Doktor: Like so many of that summer's visitors, Münsterberg came to appreciate Boise, praising this "charming little town with its clean shady streets and its picturesque mountain surroundings, with its refined homes and its well-looking prosperous citizens" ("Experiments," 5).

596   "My nerves protest" . . . "a perfect model": H. Münsterberg, "Experiments," 5–6.

596   "very unfavorable" . . . "That this was the profile": H. Münsterberg, "Third Degree," 618.

596   "the head of a thinker": This quotation and those that follow are in "Experiments," 20, 6, 6–7.

597   "at all times": H. Münsterberg, *Witness,* 142–47

597   "nearly one hundred": H. Münsterberg, "Experiments," 7.

597   "The professor": Carl G. Jung to Charles W. Eliot, October 15, 1907.

597   Münsterberg heatedly: Hugo Münsterberg to Charles W. Eliot, October 29, October 31, 1907.

598   Finally Münsterberg concluded: Münsterberg's confidence that the tests he administered to Orchard gave "a definite reply to a definite question" isn't shared by today's psychologists. Sheldon White, a prominent member of Harvard's psychology department, told me, "Certainly there's something to this technique, but it doesn't provide the kind of hard evidence that would support the claims Münsterberg made for it. All lie-detection techniques, even more sophisticated ones than these, are pretty fallible. I doubt that Münsterberg could achieve this kind of certainty." Paul Ekman, professor of psychology at the University of California at San Francisco and author of *Telling Lies: Clues to Deceit in the Marketplace, Politics and Marriage* (Norton, 1992), said it would have been important for Münsterberg to establish in advance of his meeting with Orchard clear criteria as to what responses would suggest the prisoner was lying. If he failed to establish such criteria—and it would appear that he did—one could interpret any kind of response to show that he was telling the truth or, conversely, that he was lying. Ekman also saw three other factors that might have led Münsterberg to conclude that Orchard was telling the truth even if he wasn't: (1) the ample opportunity to rehearse his story with McParland; (2) the fifteen months between his confession and the trial, which would have allowed him plenty of time to internalize his story; and (3) the religious element, which might have persuaded him that, if it didn't happen that way, it should have—and thus did.

598   "lovable": This quotation and those that follow are in "Experiments," 4, 8, 7, 20.

598   In Boise: *IDS,* July 4, 1907, 4

598   "As I had to sit": M. Münsterberg, *Münsterberg,* 146.

599   "Orchard's confession": *Boston Herald,* July 3, 1907, 1.

599   "He was averse": *Transcript,* July 4, 1907, 1.

599   "unwise and unfair": *NYT,* July 5, 1907, 6.

600   "The learned professor": *WIL,* November 1907, 11.

600   "an intellectual prostitute" and "a shameful charlatan": A. M. Simons, *International Socialist Review,* August 1907, 112; Ida Crouch-Hazlett, *MN,* July 18, 1907.

600   "that no diagnosis": *SOC,* July 13, 1907, 1.

600   "Professor Hugo Münsterberg's opinion": *DP,* July 5, 1907.

600   "I do not want to quarrel": Hugo Münsterberg to Clarence Darrow, n.d. (but July 1907).

601   "I don't know": Clarence Darrow to Hugo Münsterberg, August 16, 1907.

601   "one unalloyed joy": Darrow, *Farmington,* 202–03.

601   "Whenever I read": Parton, *Journey,* 25.

601   "Clarence Darrow, Pinch Hitter": Darrow, *Story*, 194, 200–04.
602   "the greatest aggregation": Fleming, *Season*, 317.
602   "hitless wonders": I. Stone, *Darrow*, 22.
602   Reaching Idaho: *CT*, April 14, 1907, 1.
602   "If literature is good": *Sunset Club Yearbook*, 1892–93, 79.
602   each Sunday morning: John B. Hannifin Oral History, OH 596, ISHS.
603   "Baseball games between": *PET*, June 13, 1907, 4.
603   "No one of the eastern": *IDS*, September 7, 1975.
603   Inclement weather: D'Easum, *Idanha*, 84.
603   Ranging far: *ECN*, May 18, 1907, 12.
603   "A baseball game": *DP*, May 6, 1907.
603   A month later: *CT*, June 1, 1907, 1; June 15, 1907, 1.
603   Among the nicknames: For Johnson's youth, I have relied on Kavanagh, *Johnson*, 1–4; Thomas, *Johnson*, 1–50.
604   "a wide-awake, hustling": Seymour, *Baseball*, 189, 205.
605   "visible expression": Barth, *City People*, 182.
605   Irrigation opened: *Northwest Magazine*, August 1906, 259.
605   "All the assaults": Conley, *Idaho*, 554.
605   But by 1906: Derig, *Weiser*, 82.
605   "the most beautiful": WSWS, June 26, 1907, 1.
606   "The best advertising": WSWS, July 13, 1906, 1.
606   Admission to the ball grounds: *IDS*, March 1, 1906, 1.
606   Johnson's arms: F. C. Lane, "Pitching Science," *Baseball Magazine*, October 1913, 26.
607   "He coached up": *IDS*, May 21, 1906.
607   "soundly thrashed": *IDS*, May 17, 1971.
607   Caldwell, which had once: *CT*, April 7, 1900.
607   Pacing in front: *IDS*, March 3, 1907, p. 3
607   "sore as pups": *Boston Herald*, May 9, 1926, 5.
608   Fighting Bob: *IDS*, June 7, 1915, 1; *ECN*, June 7, 1915, 8.
608   "sat on the bench": Wedge, "Weiser."
608   "merry villagers": *WSWS*, June 13, 1906, 1.
608   "You ain't much": W. Johnson, "Pitching Years," no. 25.
608   "rowdies and prize-fighters": *WSWS*, June 13, 1906; *Weiser World*, June 15, 1906.
608   "a disgrace": *IDS*, June 11, 1906.
608   Several Weiser citizens: *WSWS*, June 13, 1906.
609   "Young fella": *CT*, June 18, 1906; *IDS*, June 11, 1906.
609   "Walt just lost": *Weiser World*, June 22, 1906.
609   "agreed that if Caldwell": W. Johnson, "Pitching Years," no. 25.
609   "doomed to shine": Wedge, "Weiser"; W. Johnson, "Speed King," 1063.
609   "big hearted, two fisted: *IDS*, August 11, 1981, C-1.
609   "a sure enough baseball town": *IDS*, May 19, 1907, 10.
609   "thought, talked": Wedge, "Weiser."
610   "Lajoie chews Red Devil": Ritter, *Glory*, 234.
610   Johnson didn't run: *IDS*, July 24, 1907.
610   when the other players: *WSWS*, June 1, 1907, 1.
610   "reading a lot": *Literary Digest*, November 10, 1923.
610   "nice clean boy": *IDS*, September 7, 1975.
610   "so drunk": *IDS*, September 7, 1975.
610   "Duke" Campbell: *IDS*, September 22, 1907, 4; March 30, 1908, 3.
610   two Mountain Home Dudes: *IDS*, July 15, July 23, 1907, 4.
610   "Too much Johnson": *WSWS*, May 29, 1907, 1.
611   "Every now and then": W. Johnson, "Speed King," 1064.
611   As Johnson's discovery: Thomas, *Johnson*, 370–72.
611   Among those who'd tipped: *Washington Star*, October 3, 1924.
611   But if anyone: *WP*, October 9, 1906, 8; *DP*, April 1, 1906, May 14, 1907.
611   "a big, red nosed": Wedge, "Weiser."
611   "You better come out": Treat, *King*, 15; A. A. Hart, *Boise Baseball*, 34.
612   "a big, husky boy": *WSWS*, July 7, 1911, 1.
612   "You had a lot": Hibbard, *Weiser*, 47.
612   "I was suspicious": *Literary Digest*, November 10, 1923, 69.
612   "back to the chaparral": Suehsdorf, "Too Much Johnson," 49.
612   "They'll fix your salary": W. Johnson, "Pitching Years," no. 27. But it was said in Weiser that once Johnson reached Washington he would receive a five-hundred-dollar signing bonus, a ticket home to California, and a monthly salary of four hundred dollars—not bad for a phenom of that era (*IDS*, July 23, 1907, 2).
612   The catcher hoped: "How Walter Johnson Became a Big Leaguer," *Washington Star*, n.d., but probably September 1924.
613   "everything but the jails": Wedge, "Weiser."
613   "They'd recruited": AK.
613   "Big Leaguer": *WSWS*, April 27, 1907.
613   "Like the clans" and "like ripe grain": *IDS*, July 1, 1907, 1.
613   "two rows of post holes": Suehsdorf, "Too Much Johnson," 45.

614   "For low down": *Weiser American,* July 4, 1907.
614   "If you can derive": *WSWS,* July 3, 1907, 1.
614   "The hired players": Darrow, *Farmington,* 194.
614   "There was a question": *CT,* July 6, 1907, 1.
614   "as easy as hulling": *WSWS,* July 10, 1907, 1.
615   "a fine young man": *IDS,* July 24, 1907.
615   "a host of friends": Suehsdorf, "Too Much Johnson," 48.
615   Johnson reached: *WP,* July 27, 1907.
615   "Blankenship was sent": Suehsdorf, "Too Much Johnson," 50.
615   "rather to help": *WSWS,* June 29, 1907.
616   "My own money": My account of Pinchot's background draws on McGeary, *Pinchot,* 3–5.
616   "since he no longer": This quotation and those that follow are from Pinchot, *Ground,* 3–23.
617   "The American had": Cutright, *Conservationist,* 216.
617   Moreover, the government: Pinchot, *Ground,* 245.
618   "It was almost a crime": Cronon et al., *Open Sky,* 436.
618   In the century's: Pinchot, *Ground,* 29–30.
618   George Washington Vanderbilt: Pinkett, *Pinchot,* 22–25; Pinchot, *Ground,* 47–50.
618   Americans were accustomed: Pinchot, *Ground,* 54.
619   By 1896: Shabecoff: *Fierce,* 64.
619   "Sargent opposed": Pinchot, *Ground,* 96.
619   About to leave: Shabecoff, *Fierce,* 64.
620   "pass through the Western": McGeary, *Pinchot,* 39–40.
620   "in fair chase": Fox, *American,* 123
620   "I have one friend": McGeary, *Pinchot,* 55.
620   "Lying out": Cutright, *Conservationist,* 218.
620   "the grandest" . . . The forester and the president: Shabecoff, *Fierce,* 69–72.
621   "The fundamental": Cutright, *Conservationist,* 216; Harbaugh, *Power,* 319.
621   Pinchot's influence: Shabecoff, *Fierce,* 69.
621   "I never before": For Muir, I have drawn on Fox, *American,* 43, 115, 144.
621   "He was very appealing": Teague, *Mrs. L,* 113.
621   "chief object in life" and "planned, organized": Pinchot, *Ground,* 244, 254.
622   "Not one cent for scenery": Harbaugh, *Power,* 321.
622   "Cecil Rhodes": Pinkett, *Pinchot,* 75.
622   If such formulations: R. G. Cook, "Heyburn," 13.
622   "Just so long": *IDS,* March 27, 1908, 4.
622   When he wasn't behind: McGeary, *Pinchot,* 59.
622   By 1907: *ECN,* July 31, 1907, 8.
622   "Forester Pinchot": J. F. Scott to Fred T. Dubois, April 16, 1906, FTD.
622   "A dude in Washington": Palmer, "Fight," 13.
623   "He has wonderful": Calvin Cobb to Gifford Pinchot, February 26, 1906.
623   "contrary policy" . . . "deep and malignant": R. G. Cook, "Heyburn," 14–15.
623   In the form: *IDS,* September 6, 1905, 3.
623   "will leave Heyburn": Gifford Pinchot to James W. Pinchot, September 8, 1905, GP.
623   "Forest reserves belong": *IDS,* September 5, 1906, 1–2.
623   "composed of dreamers": *Congressional Record,* 59th Congress, 2nd Session, February 18, 1907, 3188.
624   Emboldened: *WP,* February 26, 1907.
624   The service had: Fox, *American,* 129; *IDS,* May 2, 1907, 8.
624   "dudes and invalids": S. E. White, "Fight," 260.
624   Only then: Pinchot, *Ground,* 300; Harbaugh, *Power,* 326–28; *WP,* March 5, 1907, 12.
624   "sharps, speculators": Gates, *History,* 476.
624   Even with the transfer: Ibid., 600–01.
624   In late 1902: Messing, "Public," 40.
625   "trainloads of women": Gates, *History,* 585.
625   "Harry," he told his secretary: Ibid., 42–66; W. R. Hunt, *Front,* 27–33.
625   "corrupt to the core": Steffens, "Taming," 500.
625   "should always be": *ECN,* October 1, 1907, 3.
625   "to allow no patent": *A Compilation of the Messages and Papers of the Presidents,* vol. 15, Bureau of National
Literature, 730.
626   "want to know": Frank Gooding to TR, March 24, 1907, ROS.
626   ignore the governor's statement: Frank A. Fenn to Gifford Pinchot, October 22, 1906; Pinchot to Fenn,
October 29, 1906; Fenn to Pinchot, November 5, 1906; Pinchot to Fenn, November 12, 1906, GP.
626   "Now that the new": Gifford Pinchot to Frank Gooding, November 10, 1906. GP.
627   Cobb had made sure: Calvin Cobb to Gifford Pinchot, September 2, 1906, GP.
627   Pinchot, in turn: Gifford Pinchot to Calvin Cobb, March 7, 1906, GP.
627   Cobb stayed a week: Calvin Cobb to Gifford Pinchot, May 6, 1907, GP; *ECN,* April 19, 1907, 1.
627   "Upon returning": *IDS,* April 13, 1907.
627   Ruick, it seemed": Calvin Cobb to Gifford Pinchot, April 13, 1907.
628   "go to jail": Marshall Eberstein to John E. Wilkie, April 9, 1907, SS.
628   "We did not have anything": William Borah to A. E. McCartney, April 13, 1907.
628   He wrote a confidential: TR to Charles Bonaparte, April 25, 1907, HO.
629   "The reports": *DP,* April 23, 1907, 9; *RMN,* April 23, 1907.

629 In fact, he confided: William Borah to William Allen White, n.d. (but clearly late April 1907), WAW.
629 "It is common talk": E. P. Johnson to James Hawley, April 12, 1907; James Hawley to William Borah, April
19, 1907.
629 "the W.F.M. is interested": McP3, April 11, 1907.
630 "There is no doubt": James Hawley to James McParland, April 15, 1907, HP.
630 "The purposes of the government": *IDS*, May 5, 1907, 12.
630 "saw most of": Pinchot diaries, July 6, 1907, GP.
630 "I've just come": *IDS*, June 26, 1907, 3.

13: Gentlemen of the Press

632 "The right cheek" and "There are only two forces": Gramling, *AP*, 200.
632 "Here," wrote one: quoted in U. Sinclair, *Brass Check*, 271.
633 "so affected with": M. Stone, *Fifty*, 235.
633 "mutual association": Irwin, "What's Wrong," 11–12; Schwarzlose, *Rush*, 200–06.
633 "clearing house": U. Sinclair, *Brass Check*, 272.
633 In fact, the AP: Koenigsberg, *King News*, 455.
633 "stand pat": Irwin, "What's Wrong," 112.
633 "Crane, of the Boise": *MN*, April 4, 1907.
633 "It is embarrassing" and "a movement": Irwin, "What's Wrong," 112.
633 "always bowed down": Villard, *Disappearing*, 42.
634 "poisoned at the source": U. Sinclair, *Brass Check*, 362.
634 "undesirable citizens": Klein, *Union Pacific*, 2:174.
634 "the noisy young man": M. Stone, "AP," 3.
634 "discontented workingmen": M. Stone, *Fifty*, 167.
634 As editor of the: Avrich, *Haymarket*, 275, 338.
634 "so much greater": *IDS*, May 1, 1907.
634 The Haywood case may have: Shore, *Talkin'*, 176.
634 "to rid the West": James Hawley to Stanley Easton, February 4, 1906.
635 the West's new corporate order: Trachtenberg, *Incorporation*, passim.
635 "the greatest force": U.S. Senate, *Industrial*, 10797.
635 "It's all propaganda": *ECN*, July 2, 1907.
635 "island communities": Wieke, *Search*, xiii.
635 "perversely proud": O'Toole, *Five*, 9.
635 "And what an audience!": *PET*, June 4, 1907.
635 Now the AP decided: *IDS*, May 5, 1907, 19.
636 Accordingly, on April 19: K. Cooper, *Kent*, 36.
636 "I am impressed": Melville Stone to Robert Pinkerton, April 19, 1907.
636 "I endorse": James McParland to Frank Gooding, April 23, 1907, HP.
636 "I think you sustain": Melville Stone to William Howard Taft, April 19, 1907.
636 "a man of ability": William Howard Taft to Frank Gooding, April 23, 1907.
637 "the Associated Press was partial": McP3, May 2, 1907.
637 "he never had received": Ibid.
637 "to retain the moral": *DR*, May 5, 1907, 1; *SSR*, May 5, 1907, 1.
638 "with the statement": McP3, May 2, 1907.
638 "People exist in the east": *IDS*, May 1, 1907, 5.
638 "even representatives": McP3, May 7, 1907.
638 "Do you want to go": O. K. Davis, *Released*, 31.
639 When he told one Socialist: *SOC*, June 22, 1907, 4.
639 At forty-one: *Baldwinsville Gazette*, Semi-Centennial Number, 1896, 4; *NYT*, June 4, 1932.
639 Oscar graduated: G. W. Douglas, "Colorful," passim.
639 "The Americans": O. K. Davis, *Conquests*, 343.
639 "Under his silky": O. K. Davis, *Emperor's*.
639 "It is a good": O. K. Davis to "Jack," May 2, 1906, OKD.
639 It was indeed: Mott, *Journalism*, 549–50; Schudson, *Discovering*, 108–12; Tucher, *Froth*, 197–98.
640 The only drawback: O. K. Davis to "Jack," May 2, 1906, OKD.
640 "The number of": *NYT*, May 18, 1907.
641 For Thomas was: *New York Evening Post*, June 8, 1912.
641 "an unhurried air": Clipping file, AET.
641 Still a bachelor: Irwin, *Reporter*, 116.
641 "sparkling little romance": *Augusta (Ga.) Chronicle*, n.d.
641 "Only an abandoned": Clipping file, AET.
641 Though the paper: Lancaster, *Gentleman*, 64; Milton, *Yellow*, 17.
641 "It is extraordinary": TR to Anna R. Cowles, August 24, 1903, ROS.
642 "hard to be good": Irwin, *Reporter*, 106.
642 "The New York *Sun* is to": Summers, *Press*, 62.
642 "a very able writer": McParland's characterizations are in McP3, May 5, 13, 6, 1907.
643 "Gooding and McPartland": *AtR*, May 18, 1907, 2.
643 "As we must now": McP3, September 19, 1906.
643 "As you are aware": HP.

644 "We haven't permitted" and "If we let you in": McP3, May 10, 1907.
644 "quietly, smiling": *DP,* May 17, 1907.
645 "I gave my secretary": *Chicago Record-Herald,* May 17, 1907.
645 "Having seen and talked": *BG,* May 17, 1907, 1.
645 "We had thought of": *DP,* May 17, 1907.
646 "With Warden Whitney": *New York Journal,* May 17, 1907.
646 "veneer of polish": *Cleveland Press,* May 17, 1907.
646 "the State has made a good move": McP3, May 16, 1907.
647 Then on Christmas Eve: *ECN,* December 25, 1906, 1; *IDS,* December 25, 1906, 5.
647 "calculated to influence": *IDS,* May 18, 1907.
647 "Like a would-be sleuth": *AtR,* May 25, 1907, 1.
647 Much of the anger: *BG,* May 18, 1907.
647 "a lot of stuff": Ibid.
648 "should be called in": Contempt by publication was known in the common law as "indirect contempt," as opposed to "direct contempt," which involved statements or behavior in court or so near to it as to be "within the court's confines" (see Eberhard, "Mr. Bennett," 457).
648 Hawley insisted: *BG,* May 18, 1907.
648 Davis and Thomas: *Daily People,* May 23, 1907.
648 "handed a lemon": *PET,* May 23, 1907.
648 "so insistent": *IDS,* May 18, 1907, 1.
649 "haven of shipwrecked": Lancaster, *Gentleman,* 148.
649 petty grafters hungry: Even a moralist like William Allen White conceded that he'd been drawn to the reporter's calling in part by the "special privileges" of the craft: "I rode free to the railroad stations and to public ceremonies in the new varnished hacks that rattled about the strets. I had passes on the railroads. At the eating houses I was a favored guest.... The open house opened its door for me when I flashed my old printers' rule" (W. A. White, *Autobiography,* 133).
649 "drunkards, deadbeats and bummers": Lancaster, *Gentleman,* 152.
649 "a harum-scarum, irresponsible": C. E. Russell, *Shifting,* 295.
649 "a man about half shabby": Irwin, *Newspaper,* part 8, 47.
649 "cattle of the press": Ibid., 153.
649 One newsman: Ralph, *Making,* 28–29.
649 "Neatness in dress": Lancaster, *Gentleman,* 94–95.
650 "the prince of darkness": Tucher, *Froth,* 118.
650 If the old-guard: Schudson, *Discovering,* 25.
650 Reporters had showed: Mott, *Journalism,* 581–82.
650 Until the 1880s: Boorstin, *The Americans: The Democratic Experience,* 137–42.
650 This practice: C. E. Russell, *Shifting,* 309.
650 Dry goods stores: Irwin, *Newspaper,* 50.
650 "The newspaper of today": Leach, *Land of Desire,* 43.
650 Management resented suggestions: Langford, *Alias,* 185.
650 declined to publish: O. Henry, "An Unfinished Story," *The Four Million,* Doubleday, Page, 1919. O. Henry later revealed that the real "Dulcie" was a shop girl at Wanamaker's, while "Piggy" was himself (Langford, *Alias,* 182).
650 When bubonic plague: Irwin, *Newspaper,* part 9, 50.
651 "You have the wrong": Tucher, *Froth,* 200.
651 "What's that new piece": Howells, *Instance,* 267.
651 "I have always felt": C. Stone, *Dana,* 55.
651 "Make it interesting!": Milton, *Yellow,* 16.
651 "the exact weight": O'Brien, *Story,* 244.
651 The *Times*'s motto: C. Stone, *Dana,* 397.
651 "Well Known Citizen": Swanberg, *Pulitzer,* 50.
652 "Election of an Executive": Boorstin, *The Americans: The Democratic Experience,* 403.
652 "Sport for the man": Irwin, *Newspaper,* part 5, 30.
652 "the hired man eating celery": Barth, *City People,* 166.
652 The first women's advice: Schudson, *Discovering,* 99–100.
652 In 1886 ... after Congress failed: Swanberg, *Citizen,* 33, 36–37.
652 "What we're after": Irwin, *Newspaper,* part 3, 17.
652 "You see a horse": Mott, *Journalism,* 581–82.
653 "I will not have": Milton, *Yellow,* 29.
653 Pulitzer engaged: Milton, *Yellow,* xvii.
653 "time of the Great Reporter": Milton, *Yellow,* xiv.
653 "it would be hard": Clarke, *My Life,* 108.
653 "I'd damned sight": Lancaster, *Gentleman,* 37.
653 "a young fellow": Schudson, *Discovering,* 70.
654 "a new and important": Irwin, *Newspaper,* part 8, 47.
654 "permanently hurt": Tucher, *Froth,* 197.
654 bad-boy sons: For this insight, I am grateful to Joyce Milton, who spelled it out first in her book *The Yellow Kids* and later at lunch with me. See also Limerick, *Legacy,* 36.
654 "While the editorial office": Dreiser, *Newspaper,* 151.
654 "scientific method" and "We want nothing": Tucher, *Froth,* 197.
654 "facts, nothing but facts": Kaplan, *Steffens,* 42.

654   Facts, facts piled up: Schudson, *Discovering*, 72.

654   There was the man: Bent, *Ballyhoo*, 99; Lancaster, *Gentleman*, 177.

655   "a lower order of men": Ralph, *Making*, 51–54; Lancaster, *Gentleman*, 176.

655   "the detective had": Dreiser, *Newspaper*, 147.

655   "haughty look": *IDS*, February 26, 1907, 6.

655   "had never made": *New York Herald*, August 15, 1907, 5.

655   "Who is to decide": Harris, *Humbug*, 63–67.

655   Over the years: Ibid., 68; Tucher, *Froth*, 48.

656   "to examine [the moon story]": Tucher, *Froth*, 51.

656   In 1874: Lancaster, *Gentleman*, 133.

656   The *Philadelphia Press:* R. M. Cheshire, "Some Monumental Lies Told by Newspaper Men," *DR*, June 3, 1907, 3.

656   "an almost universal": Lancaster, *Gentleman*, 135.

656   "generally the joint production": Bent, *Ballyhoo*, 104.

656   "Exercise? What I think?": Dreiser, *Newspaper*, 151.

656   The archetypal villain: Halttunen, *Confidence*, 3.

656   while false identities: Trachtenberg, *Incorporation*, 24.

657   "Those who managed": Tucher, *Froth*, 58.

657   "it is of the utmost": Tucher, *Froth*, 10.

657   " 'My God' ": Ibid., 31.

657   "glad that our columns": Ibid., 24.

657   The 1842 trial: F. Brown, *Raymond*, 35–36, 95.

658   The most heavily covered: For the Beecher trial, I have relied on Shaplen, *Free Love*, 204–05 253–58; Waller, *Reverend*, 7–11; L. Abbott, *Beecher;* C. E. Clark, *Beecher.*

658   "Women, many of them": *NYT*, November 22, 1904, 6.

658   "wealth, degeneracy": R. O'Connor, *Courtroom*, 198.

659   "Give him Hell!": Ibid.

659   For New York's press . . . press benches jammed: Mooney, *Nesbit*, 236, 247.

659   "No poor wretch": *New York Herald*, January 31, 1907, 5.

660   "sob sisters": Abramson, *Sob*, 33, 60, passim; Ross, *Ladies*, 65–93.

660   "sympathy squad": O'Connor, *Courtroom*, 212.

660   "poor, beautiful" and "gay little": Abramson, *Sob*, 71.

660   "conditions which cannot": O'Connor, *Courtroom*, 222.

660   "Can not we keep": TR to George Cortelyou, February 10, 1907, ROS.

660   "It is easy enough": O'Connor, *Courtroom*, 222.

660   "des'prit journalists": Ibid., 209.

660   "lies and falsehoods": *Worker*, March 31, 1906, 1–2; *NYS*, May 5, 1907, 6; *WIL*, May 1906, 19.

660   On May 23: Although Debs had long written for *Appeal to Reason*—notably in his passionate appeal, "Arouse, Ye Slaves," on March 10, 1906, he did not join the paper as contributing editor until January 1907 (Ginger, *Debs*, 266; *IDS*, May 7, 1907).

660   As early as February: Op. 21 Report, February 9, 1907, PA.

661   "on the ground": *AtR*, June 8, 1907; *MN*, June 6, 1907.

661   "showing the white feather": *DT*, May 30, 1907.

661   Though Debs insisted: *AtR*, June 8, 1907.

661   he may have shared: Haywood, *Autobiography*, 207. Two months after the trial, Haywood wrote Debs a note to say "I appreciate the splendid work that you did in my behalf + that of my comrades. I really believe that there is no one individual in the country who has done as much for us" (William Haywood to Eugene Debs, September 26, 1907).

661   About the same time: *CT*, March 2, 1907.

661   Margherita: *Who's Who in America*, 1906–07, s.v. "Hamm, Margherita Arlina."

661   "a socialistic-capitalistic": London, *Letters*, 682.

662   "embarrassing": *MN*, June 6, 1907.

662   "a community where feeling": "Darrow's Speech in the Haywood Case," *Wayland's Monthly*, October 1907, 5.

662   According to Margherita: *WIL*, July 1907, 14.

662   "Cigars, Tobacco": *Boise City Directory*, 1906–07.

662   "not a good town": *MN*, April 12, 1906.

662   "a good place": *MN*, April 4, 1907.

662   Nonetheless, twenty-one Socialists: I. W. Wright to *MN*, April 12, 1906.

662   "class war": *AtR*, April 14, 1906, 3.

663   Despite the manifesto's moderate: *MN*, April 12, 1906.

663   Boise wasn't a labor town: Indeed, Idaho was scarcely a strong labor state. An official survey in 1907 showed that the state's forth-five local unions had a total of 2,240 members; the largest union, with 375 members, was the Mullan local of the WFM (Schwantes, *Mountain*, 153).

663   Nearly a thousand: *IDS*, September 4, 1906, 4.

663   Moreover, most of: *IDS*, September 15, 1979, 6B.

663   "If they pack": Zanjani and Rocha, *Ignoble*, 19–20; Zanjani, *Goldfield*, 33.

663   "not because they realize": *AtR*, April 27, 1907.

663   "the handful of resident": McP3, March 20, 1906.

664   "I visited E. F. Gary's": Op. 24-A Report, January 7, 1907.

664   "He would not give": Op. 24-A Report, January 28, 1907.

664   They particularly resented: Op. 24-A Report, February 21, 1907.

664   It had only been: *SvA* (II), 616–19.

664   "that little stinker": Op. 24-A Report, January 18, 1907.

664   "I denounce the whole": Quoted in *ECN*, May 20, 1907, 1–2.

665   "harsh names": *DP*, May 19, 1907.

665   in ordering the editor: Op. 21 Report, May 10, 1907.

665   The following week: *NYS*, May 25, 1907, 2; *PET*, May 23, 1907, 16.

665   "The telegrams": *JDF*, June 6, 1907, 1. Like the *Forward* articles cited in chapter 10, the pieces quoted here were translated from the Yiddish by Jeremy Dauber.

665   "How 'Science' Confirms": *JDF*, July 13, 1907, 5.

666   "a number of queer-acting": *MN*, June 6, 1907.

666   "a weird, lank": *MN*, May 25, 1907.

666   At lunch hour: *IDS*, July 10, 1907, 4.

667   "Haven't you heard": *IDS*, May 19, 1907, 6; *ECN*, May 19, 1907, 12.

667   "blow hell out": *DP*, May 19, 1907.

667   Henceforth, he promised: *BG*, May 20, 1907.

667   Born in 1875. . . . In a lifetime: Shoaf, *Fighting*, 11–19.

668   "god of my idolatry": Shoaf, "Debs," 10–11.

668   Following his apprenticeship: Shore, *Talkin'*, 123.

668   Adrift again: Shoaf, *Fighting*, 45–47.

668   During these years: *Chicago American*, January 15, 1903; *Chicago Record-Herald*, February 19, 1903.

669   "George," he said: Shoaf, *Fighting*, 53.

669   The *American* practiced: Koenigsberg, *King News*, 254.

669   "Every story": Shoaf, *Fighting*, 54.

669   Texas brogue: Haldeman-Julius, *My Second*, 61.

669   "one of the most": Koenigsberg, *King News*, 300.

669   But he remained: Shoaf, "Debs," 10.

669   "I knew the system": This quotation and those that follow are from Shoaf, *Fighting*, 60, 64, 68, 69.

670   "a big head" The quotations are from G. Henry, *Love Crucified*, 5–46, 49, 114.

670   "crafty, cruel, conscienceless": Hurt, *Scarlet Shadow*, 14–15, 122, 124, 164, 227, 397, 413–16.

671   "the greatest and most": *AtR*, March 17, 1906.

671   "Were the world's supply": Ibid.

671   "You couldn't help": Haldeman-Julius, *My Second*, 61.

672   "large and handsome": *WIL*, June 1907.

672   Also living: *MN*, May 25, 1907.

672   Some weeks after: *IDS*, August 2, 1907.

672   Soon after: *IDS*, August 11, 1907, 1.

672   "Since Mrs. Ida": *IDS*, October 6, 1907, 6.

672   "half-baked": *ECN*, October 5, 1907.

673   "Not content": *SOC*, November 2, 1907.

673   All through the trial: The *Saturday Evening Tribune*, a Socialist paper in Seattle, charged on October 19 that the Pinkertons had extracted the original story from Miss Abbott, using "the usual sweatbox process." This seems unlikely.

673   *Appeal to Treason:* IDS, April 20, 1907.

673   "True Socialists": *IDS*, May 23, 1907; *PET*, May 23, 1907.

673   "a prejudice against facts": Haldeman-Julius, *My Second*, 61.

673   "If the facts": *AtR*, March 31, 1906.

673   "You fellows thought": *IDS*, May 23, 1907.

674   He did print . . . "Why do you write": Ibid.

674   As he later admitted: Shoaf, *Fighting*, 92–93.

674   "I wrote long letters": Ernest Untermann to Fred Warren, October 24, 1911, HJ.

674   "the reptile press": *AtR*, March 31, 1906.

674   "the yelping daily press": *SOC*, October 20, 1906.

674   "Being a newspaper man": *AtR*, March 31, 1906.

674   "a fine class of men": *SOC*, June 1, 1907.

675   "foam of passion": *DP*, May 15, 1907.

675   "lack the morbid": *NYT*, May 10, 1907.

675   "lots of reporters": *NYS*, May 10, May 14, 1907.

675   "Perfectly reasonable": *New York World*, May 3, 1907.

675   "his home life": *New York Evening Journal*, March 26, April 10, 1906.

676   "a young man": *IDS*, March 26, 1907.

676   McParland refused to talk: McP3, March 17, April 12, and May 13, 1907.

676   So energetic and resourceful: Perkins's reports are in *PET*, May 13, 28, and 31; June 1 and 13, 1907.

676   "not a question": McP3, May 13, 1907.

677   "anything he might pick up": Ibid.

677   "I' faith 'tis": *NYS*, May 15, 1907.

678   But Hapgood had evidently": For Connolly, see Chalmers, *Social*, 26–32; Filler, *Crusaders*; Lyon, *Success*, 302; *McClure's*, August–December 1906.

678   "a personal friend" and "a very honest": McP3, February 24, 1907; May 21, 1907.

678   Evidently, he also impressed: *Daily People*, June 11, 1907.

678 "seen no indications": *DR,* May 14, 1907.
678 "It is war": *SOC,* June 15, 1907.
678 "The press sends out": Connolly, "Protest," 9.
678 "war correspondents": *Daily People,* May 13, 1907.
678 He was the son: For Martin Egan's youth, I have relied on materials and clippings in EC.
679 "All is going": Palmer, *Eyes,* 239.
679 "The situation was unique": Croly, *Straight,* 125.
679 "he established": M. Stone, *Fifty,* 282.
680 "Socially and personally": Martin Egan to Elizabeth Gignoux Baner, April 22, 1904, EC.
680 "Transmittable information": Gramling, *AP,* 184.
680 "Thank God": Downey, *Davis,* 137.
681 As the sun beat: *LMT,* March 20, 1938.
681 Electric fans: *IDS,* May 11, 1907, 3.
681 For the portrait of 1907 Boise, I have used A. A. Hart, *Historic Boise,* 17–18, 60; *Kansas City Star,* in *IDS,* May 18, 1907; *PET,* May 18, 1907; *IDS,* December 24, 1905; January 26, 1906; May 5, May 6, May 8, July 6, August 17, 1907; January 12, 1908.
682 When the grand council: *IDS,* June 7, 1907, 3.
682 In June 1907: *IDS,* June 9, 1907, 11. This influx was due in considerable part to the efforts of the Union Pacific and Northern Pacific Railroads, which flooded the East with promotional literature, and the boosters in Idaho communities like Caldwell and Buhl (whose slogan was "Pull for Buhl or Pull Out"). See Schwantes, *Mountain,* 170–71.
682 He received hundreds: *IDS,* January 26, 1906, 2.
682 If Steunenberg's murder: *DP,* May 20, 1907.
683 "The latest novels": *IDS,* June 30, 1907, 16.
683 The Boise Book and Music: *IDS,* June 16, 1907, 13.
683 Built in 1892: *Kansas City Star,* in *IDS,* May 18, 1907.
683 In addition, there were: D'Easum, *Fragments,* 45–50.
683 In the week the trial: *IDS,* May 9, 1907, 6.
683 On Mondays: *IDS,* May 1, 1907.
683 cavorting to such favorites: Green and Laurie, *Show,* 47.
683 In mid-May: *IDS,* May 23, 1907, 3.
683 In mid-June: *IDS,* June 16, 1907, 16.
683 On June 28: *IDS,* June 29, 1907, 4.
684 Wood and Davis: O. K. Davis, *Released,* 42; *WSWS,* June 26, 1907, 5; *ECN,* July 30, 1907.
684 "very particular": O. K. Davis, *Released,* 42.
684 "cannot conscientiously": *IDS,* May 24, 1907, 4
684 "I never overlook": *IDS,* May 25, 1907, 4.
684 "The Mine Owners": *WIL,* July 1907, 19.
685 "I think, if I was": *IDS,* May 17, 1907, 4.
685 "B.B. (Beautiful Boise) is remarkable": *IDS,* August 15, 1907.
685 "we could without": *ECN,* July 29, 1907.
685 "There may somewhere": *IDS,* August 15, 1907.
685 There was even talk: E. E. Lonabaugh to Martin Egan, July 16, 1909, EC.
685 On May 13: *Wyoming Tribune,* July 16, 1907; *Sheridan Post,* December 17, 1903, 1.
686 "a millionaire": *IDS,* July 20, 1907, 1.
686 So on July 14: *IDS,* July 14, 1907, 14.
686 After a five-day: *Wyoming Tribune,* July 20, 1907, 1.

14: A Good Hanging Spoiled

687 would be a witness: *IDS,* June 5, 1907. As late as July 11, John Carberry of the *Boston Globe* reported that McParland would be a prosecution witness on rebuttal.
687 "From what my informants": McP3, March 5, 1907.
687 "a striking looking young fellow": *IDS,* June 30, 1907, 1.
687 "if these methods": Gaylord Wilshire to TR, April 29, 1907, ROS.
688 Under Darrow's questioning: *IDS,* June 30, 1907, 1, 11.
688 a drunken binge: *PET,* June 18, 1907, 4.
688 smilingly acknowledged: *IDS,* June 30, 1907.
688 "Not according to the rules": *IDS,* July 2, 1907.
688 But when it got through: *RMN,* July 28, 1907.
688 "master stroke": *MN,* July 4, 1907.
688 The defense had another: *IDS,* July 3, 1907.
689 "one of the shrewdest": *IDS,* June 30, 1907.
689 But Darrow and Richardson: "The Haywood Trial," *Outlook,* August 24, 1907, 860. The struggle over Adams's prospective testimony was tangled. Idaho law provided for impeaching a witness's testimony with a "prior inconsistent statement." Thus, if Darrow had put Adams on the stand to testify for the defense, the prosecutors could have impeached him with his confession, even though he'd repudiated it. But the confession could be introduced only for what it indicated abut the truth of Adams's testimony in court, not as to the truth of the out-of-court confession itself, regarded as hearsay since it was unsworn and couldn't be cross-examined.

Nonetheless, the prosecution would have gotten Adams's confession before the jury and, even though the judge might order jurors not to treat it as corroboration, it might weigh with them in deciding whether Orchard's testimony was corroborated by the accumulation of evidence.

Even if Adams hadn't repudiated his confession, the prosecution might have had difficulty in using his testimony to corroborate Orchard. For the annotations to section 5464 of the Idaho Code—the section requiring such corroboration—provide that the testimony of an accomplice cannot be corroborated by another accomplice to the same crime. Thus, if the prosecution had put him on the stand to corroborate Orchard's testimony, the defense no doubt would have contended that, as an accomplice, he couldn't corroborate Orchard. The prosecution would presumably have argued that Adams, though an accomplice in the larger conspiracy against the WFM's enemies, wasn't an accomplice to the murder of Steunenberg. There were good grounds for such an argument, but this crucial decision would have been left to the jury. There is an element of surmise in all of this, since prior to 1907, the issue had not been directly addressed by an Idaho court. But the annotation in the code was based on a California case, *People v. Creegan,* 121 Cal. 554 (1898), and Idaho judges in those days frequently followed the California courts' interpretations.

690   "After a few days": McP3, March 20, 1906.
690   "a humane man": *St. Louis Star-Chronicle,* May 17, 1906.
690   "dandelions were scattered": Haywood, *Autobiography,* 201.
690   The grass was shaded: *SOC,* May 25, 1907.
690   Pettibone spent much: Haywood, *Autobiography,* 202.
690   Haywood, who had his own: Popkin, "McParland," 330.
690   The prisoners were allowed: *DP,* May 20, 1907.
690   These months in jail: Haywood, *Autobiography,* 198.
691   Their meals: *DP,* May 20, 1907.
691   "I believe myself ": McP3, July 11, 1906.
691   "never liked Haywood": McP3, March 17, 1906.
691   "deadly enemies": McP4, May 15, 1907.
691   "not on speaking terms": McP4, December 15, 1906.
691   Their long-standing: Brissenden, *IWW,* 136–54.
692   "I want to serve": Charles Moyer to James Kirwan, October 2, 1906, *Official Proceedings,* 579–80.
692   "I surely am not": William Haywood to James Kirwan, October 16, 1906, *Official Proceedings,* 581.
692   "a cessation": William Haywood to Vincent St. John, March 24, 1907, *Official Proceedings,* 582.
692   "I am really sorry": McP3, December 15, 1906.
692   "He thinks a great deal": *DP,* May 6, 1907.
693   "it appeared as if ": *ECN,* August 1, 1907.
693   "a man brimful": *PET,* June 11, 1907.
693   "his indignation": *PET,* August 3, 1907, 18.
693   As early as: James Hawley to William Borah, September 27, 1906.
693   Now, McParland suggested: McP3, May 14, 1907.
694   "a very intelligent man": McP3, May 16, 1907.
694   "We have got the sons": McP3, May 18, 1907.
695   At times, he came in: On May 30, 1906, he presented the three defendants with a copy of *An Eye for an Eye* and inscribed it, "To my friends and clients Moyer, Haywood and Pettibone with the regards of Clarence S. Darrow, May 30, 1906." I am indebted to the book's current owner, Arnold L. Greenberg of New York.
695   "Cheer up, Clarence": Haywood, *Autobiography,* 206.
695   matters were not progressing: McP3, May 25, 1907.
695   "willing to grant him". *PET,* June 17, 1907, 8.
695   According to one report: *DR,* July 7, 1907.
695   As late as April 18: RMN, April 23, 1907.
695   "too weak": Fremont Wood to S. L. Hodgin, April 18, 1907, FW.
695   The larger Haywood: John Hannifin, Oral History 596 A and B, *SOC,* May 25, 1907, 4.
695   But Mrs. Moyer: *DT,* May 25, 1907.
696   "Dear Mrs. Moyer": *New York World,* July 6, 1907. See also *DR,* July 7, 1907; *AtR,* July 20, 1907.
696   "Mrs. Cobb, it appears": *New York World,* July 11, 1907.
696   particularly since Mrs. Moyer: *SOC,* August 10, 1907, 4.
696   At first he seemed: *IDS,* July 11, 1907.
697   "I did not believe": Borah's cross-examination of Moyer and Darrow's questioning of Haywood are in *IDS,* July 12, 1907.
699   "the Man of the Mines": *SOC,* July 20, 1907, 1.
699   "It doubled me up": Haywood, *Autobiography,* 213.
699   "Yes," said Borah: *SvH,* 4090.
700   "I feel like I've had": *SvH,* 4162
700   "demented": Orchard's questioning is in *IDS,* July 16, 1907.
701   "does not point to": *IDS,* July 20, 1907.
702   "The Haywood case has been": James Hawley to Frank H. Parker, July 22, 1907, HP.
702   "Gentlemen," he began: *BG,* July 20, 1907, 1.
704   sending his copy: *IDS,* May 9, 1907, 7.
704   "almost suffocating": *IDS,* July 23, 1907, 3.
704   "his favorite method": *NYT,* July 23, 1907.
704   His histrionics: *DR,* July 23, 1907.
705   Had he retained it: J. Montgomery, "Orchard."
705   "Yes, sir, but I'd say": *SvH,* 4166.

706 On the morning: *SvH, 5186.*

706 "the purpose of Orchard": *SvH, 5202–04.*

706 "Where is this 'terror' ": *IDS,* July 24, 1907, 3.

707 "If Harry Orchard was in": *DR,* July 24, 1907, 1.

707 "Richardson is talking": James Hawley to Jacob Fillius, July 22, 1907.

707 "Long before Shad Hodgin": *IDS,* July 25, 1907, 1.

708 "We are here strangers": *IDS,* July 25, 1907, 1, 5, 16–18, 20, 24, 33.

708 "complete submission": This quotation and those that follow are in *NYT,* July 25, 1907, 1, 10.

709 "blackguard address": James Hawley to C. C. Goodwin, July 28, 1907. The relevant passage goes: "Darrow's blackguard address hurt his case instead of helping. I was at home sick at the time he made his talk upon me, and my first impression upon hearing about it was to teach him a proper lesson by means of a personal chastisement, but believing that he is trying to make a martyr of himself, I concluded after being advised by my friends to let the matter pass for the time being."

709 One of the most difficult: Livingston, *Clarence Darrow,* 65. The philosophical anarchists—men like Kropotkin, Recluse, and Tolstoy—had no use for the doctrine of violence, or "the cult of dynamite," preached by the revolutionary anarchists like Johann Most, Emma Goldman, or Alexander Berkman. Tolstoyan anarchists sought a peaceful revolution, derived from their understanding of Christianity.

709 "Hatred, bitterness, violence": Darrow, *Resist,* 61.

711 Darrow completed: *IDS,* July 26, 1907.

711 "idealists and dreamers": Darrow, *Story,* 153.

711 several women: *DR,* July 25, 1907, 1.

711 "thoroughly aired": Darrow, *Story,* 154.

712 "There was a sound": Ibid.

712 "intent upon squeezing": *IDS,* July 26, 1907, 4.

712 "one of those battles": *IDS,* August 4, 1907, 4.

712 Spurning suggestions: C. Johnson, *Borah,* 83–84.

712 Hawley and other prosecutors: John and Jess Hawley, interview by author, Boise, June 2, 1995; Merle Wells, interview by author, June 1995.

712 "I needed your assistance": James Hawley to William Borah, September 27, 1906, HP.

712 "I have been doing three": James Hawley to "Frankie," July 22, 1907, HP.

712 "personal troubles": Jonathan Bourne to William Borah, July 11, 1907; May 2, 1907, WEB.

712 "waging the war": Duane E. Minard to William Borah, July 27, 1907, WEB.

713 "incarnation of demagogy": W. A. White, *Autobiography,* 278.

713 "That's the stuff!": W. Johnson, *White's America,* 94.

713 "overcome": W. A. White, *Autobiography,* 297.

713 "Oh, Member": TR to William Allen White, May 1, 1906, WAW.

713 "You might read": William Allen White to TR, May 1, 1907, WAW.

714 "I am satisfied": William Allen White to William Borah, April 17, 1907, WAW.

714 "This is unutterably sad": William Borah to William Allen White, n.d. (but clearly late April 1907), WAW.

714 "Big money-making projects": W. A. White, *Autobiography,* 365.

714 "riding all one blessed day": William Allen White to Sallie White, July 7, 1903, quoted in Griffith, *Hometown,* 107.

714 Eager for some: Griffith, *Hometown,* 108.

715 Then, as the Roosevelt: William Allen White to William Borah, January 3, 1904.

715 "My hair rose": W. A. White, *Autobiography,* 365.

715 "About the only": William Allen White to William Borah, January 31, 1907, WAW.

715 "Surely there he was": William Allen White to TR, May 1, 1907.

716 "try with all the earnestness": William Allen White to William Borah, June 30, 1907.

716 Borah's letter: Griffith, *Hometown,* 155–56. The novel was eventually published in 1909 as *A Certain Rich Man.*

716 "This idea is with me": William Allen White to TR, July 25, 1907, WAW.

717 Worried by how "despondent": William Allen White to TR, July 25, 1907, WAW.

717 "The State has the right": Quotations of Borah are in *SvH,* 5495–96, 5497, 5501–02.

719 "Why? Why?": *IDS,* July 27, 1907, 1.

719 "But you never had a duty": *SvH,* 5632–33. This is the way Borah's peroration ended in court. Some months later, a pamphlet version, entitled *Haywood Trial, Closing Argument of W. E. Borah* was issued by the print shop of Calvin Cobb's *Statesman.* It contained an entirely new ending, three paragraphs of spellbinding prose, including several passages that appear in works about Darrow and the Haywood trial as well as in anthologies of great orations. For example, there is Borah's rumination on Steunenberg's garden gate: "I only want what you want —human life made safe—assassination put out of business. I only want what you want—the gate which leads to our homes, the yard gate whose inward swing tells of the returning husband and father, shielded and guarded by the courage and manhood of Idaho juries." And still better known is his rumination on anarchy: "Anarchy, pale, bloodless, restless, hungry demon from the crypts of hell—fighting for a foothold in Idaho!" This is wonderful stuff. Unfortunately, it was never spoken in an Idaho courtroom. It was evidently added by the senator as part of his incesssant image-building campaign. Though these are the most striking changes in the published version, the rest of the text has been considerably revised, lent far greater power and eloquence. I am indebted to David Grover, the first to notice these discrepancies, in his book *Dynamiters and Debaters,* 237–240, 249–51.

720 "under the statutes": *SvH, 5694.*

720 "in his belief": O. K. Davis, *Released,* 44.

721 At midnight, friends passed: *RMN,* July 29, 1907.

721 Just past midnight: *Boise Citizen,* August 2, 1907.

721 Following that lead: K. Johnson, "Trial," 127.
721 "No," said Darrow": I. Stone, *Darrow*, 274.
721 the defense had all but: Irving Stone, notes, IS.
721 "toiled up the wooden": *BG*, July 29, 1907.
722 "illimitable gladness": *NYT*, July 29, 1907.
722 "Into the bright sunlight": *San Francisco Chronicle*, July 29, 1907, 1. The scene on verdict day was assembled from John Carberry's marvelously detailed account in *BG*, July 29, 1907, and from that day's accounts in *NYT*, *NYS*, *RMN*, and *DP*.
723 Hermon Titus: *SOC*, August 3, 1907, 1.
723 "That's good" and "Give my regards": *Butte Evening News*, July 29, 1907, 1.
723 "This is papa": *BG*, July 29, 1907.
723 "one couldn't move": Ruby Darrow to Irving Stone, n.d., CD.
723 "I have nothing": *NYT*, July 29, 1907.
723 "The President was insistent with me": Calvin Cobb to Assistant Attorney General Alford W. Cooley, October 3, 1907.
724 "What have you got against this man?": *BG*, July 29, 1907, 1. This version of Sebern's remarks does not accord with a letter written by O. V. Sebern's daughter, Mrs. Oral Sebern Coleman, to David Grover. In her letter of August 19, 1960, Mrs. Coleman wrote that her father thought the verdict was "a grave miscarriage of justice—and many of the jurors concurred in this opinion. There was little or no doubt of the guilt of the defendant, but skillful lawyers presented facts in such manner, and the final instructions of the presiding judge to the jury" left them no choice but to acquit (Grover, *Debaters*, 260).
724 "I will rot": *Butte Evening News*, July 29, 1907, 4.
724 "Darrow's speech would have been": W. W. Catlin to Charles Erskine Scott Wood, August 1907, CESW.
724 John Nugent: After Darrow examined Bill Davis—a rough-hewn man widely believed to have been the leader of the attack party at the Bunker Hill mine in 1899—Nugent leaned over to Darrow and said: "Putting a man like that on the stand is like putting a noose around Haywood's neck" (*DP*, June 28, 1907).
724 "I want to speak to you": *BG*, July 29, 1907, 1.
725 "Did you believe": *NYS*, July 29, 1907, 1.
725 "in praise of that quality": *NYT*, July 29, 1907, 1.
725 Some weeks before: *PET*, June 18, 1907.
725 "had the guts": C. Johnson, *Borah*, 83.
725 An unconfirmed report: Connolly, "Pettibone."
725 "the jury had been bought": O. K. Davis, *Released*, 42.
725 "The newspaper grape vine": Edgar Lee Masters to Carter H. Harrison, March 21, 1938, CHH.
725 "It is believed": T. C. Egleston to William Borah, August 5, 1907, WEB.
726 "The fault": James Hawley to Jacob Fillius, November 30, 1907, HP.
726 "Of course," McParland: McP3, May 13, 1907.
726 "certain notorious": *Collier's*, January 25, 1908.
726 According to one source: James Hawley to Ed Meek, December 16, 1907, HP.
726 "very much dissatisfied": Ibid.; see also James Hawley to Bulkeley Wells, December 22, 1907, HP.
726 Still later, allegations: I. Stone, *Darrow*, 276.
726 "an artist at the range": *IDS*, May 16, 1907, 3.
727 Then there was: Siringo, *Riata*, 258.
728 "well-dressed, well-educated": *MN*, June 13, 1907.
728 "the strongest face": *Industrial Union Bulletin*, August 3, 1907.
728 "Two or three": James Hawley to Jacob Fillius, July 28, 1907, HP.
728 Another was probably: In an interview with *ECN*, Robertson said, "It was my constant hope that if the defendant was guilty that the state would prove it beyond all doubt, and the evidence would be so strong that no doubt could be entertained." But by trial's end, and particularly after applying Judge Wood's explicit instructions, "there was little left of the state's case" (July 30, 1907, 5).
729 "The Pinkerton agency": *Chicago Record-Herald*, July 29, 1907.
729 "The case against Moyer": *DR*, July 29, 1907, 2.
729 "There has been a gross": TR to Whitelaw Reid, July 29, 1907.
729 "Surely judgment is turned": Eva B. Steunenberg to James Hawley, February 11, 1908, HP.
729 "Undesirable citizens victorious": *DR*, July 30, 1907.
729 In Butte: *SSR*, July 29, 1907, 1.
729 "Were you not over-joyed": Alice Junsby to Victor Berger, August 10, 1907, VB.
730 In Boise: *IDS*, July 30, 1907, 6.
731 He was in his characteristic pose: Ruby Darrow to Irving Stone, n.d., Box 34, CD.
731 "alone, abandoned": I. Stone, *Darrow*, 276; Ruby Darrow, interview by Stone, CD.
731 "I can say now": TR to William Allen White, July 30, 1907, WAW.
731 "I am the poorest talker": William Allen White to William Borah, July 31, 1907, WAW.
732 "Biggsby" for White: William Allen White to William Borah, June 30, 1907, WAW.
732 "look up evidence": *IDS*, August 4, 1907, 4; *ECN*, August 3, 1907, 1.
732 Borah did go to Cripple: Op. 28 Report, August 16, August 17, 1907, HP.
732 "wan and anxious": W. A. White, *Autobiography*, 374, 391.
732 "Have made best investigation": Quoted in William Allen White to TR, July 25, 1907.
732 Borah liked the idea: C. P. Connolly to William Borah, August 26, September 12, 1907, WEB.
732 "The [Haywood] verdict": C. P. Connolly to William Borah, August 1, 1907, WEB.
733 "I feel as much interested": C. P. Connolly to William Borah, August 26, 1907, WEB.

733 "the entire matter": Joseph G. Dudley to William Borah, August 12, 1907; John W. Yerkes to Borah, August 12, 1907, WEB; *Buffalo News,* September 13, 1949.

733 It would have been: Hagedorn, *Roosevelt,* 6–7.

733 Most of the afternoon: Hagedorn and Roth, *Guide,* passim.

733 "too proud to be bossed": Bishop, *Bonaparte,* 132, 161.

734 Stressing the confidential: McKenna, *Borah,* 74–75.

734 "We didn't get": William Allen White to William Borah, n.d. (but probably August 9, 1907), WEB.

735 "not had heart to write": C. P. Connolly to William Borah, August 13, 1907, WEB.

735 "if they carry out": William Borah to William Allen White, August 14, 1907, WEB.

735 "some of the Republican": William Borah to Jonathan Bourne, July 6, 1907, WEB.

735 "Gladly undertake trip": Martin Egan to William Borah, August 9, 1907, WEB.

736 "I started out": Martin Egan to William Borah, August 15, 1907, WEB.

736 "a union between": Martin Egan to John Wilkie, September 6, 1907, WEB.

736 "a superannuated imbecile": William Borah to A. E. McCartney, April 13, 1907.

736 His apparent manipulation: Connolly, "Little Drama," 9; John W. Yerkes to William Loeb, September 19, 1907; Yerkes to William Borah, August 12, 1907; A. E. Werner to Borah, March 8, 1906; O. K. Davis to Borah, August 23, 1907, WEB.

736 a banker and stalwart: *ECN,* February 11, 1920; *IDS,* February 11, 1920.

737 "that ass formerly": Clarence Darrow to William Borah, August 2, August 9, 1907, WEB.

737 "guiltless of complicity": *ECN,* September 13, 1907, 1.

737 "some satisfaction": C. Johnson, *Borah,* 84.

737 But a federal: Timothy J. Burke to Charles Bonaparte, September 27, 1907, JD.

737 "a howling anarchist": William Borah to William Howard Taft, September 3, 1907, WEB.

737 "Terrific, crushing": *NYT,* July 27, 1907.

738 "unbelievable outrage": O. K. Davis, *Released,* 35.

738 "If I have not been": O. K. Davis to TR, August 5, 1907, ROS.

738 During August and September: Martin Egan to John Wilkie, September 4, 1907, WEB; Calvin Cobb to Gifford Pinchot, October 30, 1907, GP.

738 So busy: O. K. Davis to TR, n.d. (but early July 1907); Davis to TR, August 23, 1907; TR to Davis, July 20, 1907; Charles Bonaparte to Davis, August 5, 1907; Davis to Bonaparte, August 14, 1907; William Borah to Davis, August 14, 24, 30, 1907; Davis to Borah, August 22, 23 (wire and letter), 28, September 4, 16, 19, 1907.

739 "Learn from unquestionable": Charles Bonaparte to TR, August 23, 1907, ROS.

740 "the leading spirit": Norman Ruick to Charles Bonaparte, August 11, 1907, JD.

740 "a state of circumstances": Sylvester R. Rush to Charles Bonaparte, October 11, 1907, JD.

740 "Of course, we all": *CT,* December 9, 1899, 1.

740 Another oft-repeated: Hutton, *Coeur,* cited in J. Montgomery, *Liberated Woman,* 273–74; Connolly, "Little Drama," 9.

740 Known to his peers: Fahey, *Hecla,* 5–18; *SSR,* June 24, 1928.

740 "We have been having the devil": Amasa B. Campbell to George Tod, May 4, 1899, AC.

740 In July 1899: Amasa B. Campbell to Tod Ford, n.d. (but late June 1899), AC.

740 "every man": Amasa B. Campbell to Robert McCurdy, AC.

740 "that the [Boise] Basin": Testimony of John Kinkaid, *United States v. Barber Lumber Co. et. al.* 194 Fed. 16 (1912).

741 "great buying rush": Hidy, "Lumbermen," 4.

741 "there would be no difficulty": Deposition of Amasa B. Campbell, taken April 12, 1909, *United States v. Barber Lumber Co.,* 3850.

741 By March 13: Frank Steunenberg to Amasa B. Campbell, March 13, 1902.

741 Three Wisconsin timbermen: Hidy, "Lumbermen," 6; Hidy et al., *Timber,* 260.

741 In June: BLC.

742 "very sure they are bad": Testimony of A. G. Foster, *United States v. Barber Lumber Co.,* 194 Fed 24 (1912).

742 Foster sent Sharp: *CT,* March 25, 1905, 1.

742 For the time being: Frank Steunenberg to Amasa B. Campbell, February 11, May 17, September 15, October 31, 1902; February 14, 1903.

743 That Wilkie was a former: Gatewood, *Theodore,* 238–44; Gould, *Presidency,* 292–93.

743 Since they were on: Elmer A. Gormon to John E. Wilkie, March 25, 1907, SS.

743 "Chief," he wrote: Elmer A. Gormon to John E. Wilkie, February 2, 1907, SS.

743 For some weeks: William Borah to John W. Yerkes, September 9, 1907, WEB.

743 But before Wilkie: Elmer A. Gormon to John E. Wilkie, March 11, March 20, 1907, SS.

744 "Gormon couldn't run": B. F. Cash to Caldwell, April 15, 1907; Sylvester R. Rush to John E. Wilkie, September 9, 1907, SS.

744 "very beautiful": Elmer A. Glover to Norman Ruick, August 4, 1907, SS.

744 For several days: Elmer A. Glover to Norman Ruick, August 3, 4, 6, 9, 17, 31; September 3, 4, 5, 6, 1907, SS.

744 Borah's trial began: *CT,* September 7, 1907, 1.

745 "In 1899, Governor Steunenberg": *IDS,* September 25, 1907.

746 "to simulate utter indifference": Marsden C. Burch to Charles Bonaparte, October 4, 1907.

746 "I assume you all know" . . . "I would rather go": *IDS,* October 4, 1907.

748 "gloriously drunk": W. A. White, *Autobiography,* 375.

EPILOGUE

750   "I want to express": *AtR*, October 15, 1910, 1.
750   "like reading": Cowan, *People,* 116.
750   "no matter what: Ibid., 99.
751   "as innocent": Ibid., 127.
751   "Since reaching": *AtR*, May 27, 1911, 1.
752   "the first to look": Frank Wolfe, Harriman Ryckman, and J. E. Tuttle to Fred Warren, August 23, 1911, Folder 28, HJ.
752   "Last winter": Elsa Untermann to Piet Vlag, October 5, 1911, Folder 28, HJ.
752   "My worst": Ernest Untermann to the National Executive Committee of the Socialist Party, November 9, 1911, Folder 28, HJ.
752   "Shoaf at last": A. W. Ricker to Ernest Untermann, October 31, 1911, Folder 28, HJ.
753   "From the tenor": Cornelius C. Corker to Fred Warren, October 16, 1911, Folder 28, HJ.
753   "the embodiment": Cornelius C. Corker to Fred Warren, October 26, 1911, Folder 28, HJ.
753   It was to Conger-Kaneko: Josephine Conger-Kaneko to Fred Warren, October 3, 1911, Folder 28, HJ. She was evidently unattached when Shoaf sought her out in 1907, though she later married the Japanese Socialist Kiichi Kaneko.
753   "If the capitalist": Josephine Conger-Kaneko to Fred Warren, October 3, 1911, Folder 28, HJ.

Bibliography

Abbott, Lawrence F. *The Story of Nylic.* New York Life Insurance, 1936.

Abbott, Lyman. *Henry Ward Beecher.* Chelsea House, 1980.

Abbott, Willis J. *Watching the World Go By.* Little, Brown, 1933.

Abramson, Phyllis Leslie. *Sob Sister Journalism.* Greenwood Press, 1990.

Adamic, Louis. *Dynamite: The Story of Class Violence in America.* Viking, 1931.

Adams, Graham, Jr. *Age of Industrial Violence, 1910–1915.* Columbia University Press, 1966.

Adams, Ramon. *Six Guns and Saddle Leather: A Bibliography of Books and Pamphlets on Western Outlaws and Gunmen.* University of Oklahoma Press, 1942.

Adelman, Abram E. "Clarence Darrow—Take Him for All in All." *Age of Reason,* October 1955, 1–4.

Adler, Stephen J. *The Jury: Trial and Error in the American Courtroom.* Times Books, 1994.

Aiken, Katherine G. " 'It May Be Too Soon to Crow': Bunker Hill and Sullivan Company Efforts to Defeat the Miners' Union, 1890–1900." *Western Historical Quarterly,* XXIV, no. 3 (August 1993): 309–331.

Alexander, Charles. *Battles and Victories of Allen Allensworth, A.M., Ph.d.* Sherman, French and Co., 1914.

Alexander, Tom, and Jim Allen. *Mormons and Gentiles.* Pruett Publishing, 1984.

Allen, Frederick Lewis. *The Big Change.* Harper and Row, 1952.

Allison, Nathanial Thompson. *History of Cherokee County, Kansas, and Representative Citizens.* Biographical Publishing, 1904.

Alt, David D., and Donald W. Hyndman. *Roadside Geology of Idaho.* Mountain Press Publishing, 1989.

Anderson, Bryce. "The Bomb at the Governor's Gate." *American West,* 2, no. 1. Winter (1965): 14–21, 75–76.

"Annual Address of the Bishop." *Journal of the Thirty-Seventh Convention of the Protestant Episcopal Church in the Diocese of Long Island.* Garden City, Long Island, May 26–27, 1903. Press of the Brooklyn *Daily Eagle.*

Arnold, Thurman. *Fair Fights and Foul.* Harcourt, Brace and World, 1965.

Arrington, Leonard J. *History of Idaho.* 2 vols. University of Idaho Press, 1994.

Ashby, Leroy. *The Spearless Leader: Senator Borah and the Progressive Movement in the 1920s.* University of Illinois Press, 1972.

———. *William Jennings Bryan: Champion of Democracy.* Twayne Publishers, 1987.

Athearn, Robert G. "The Oregon Short Line." *Idaho Yesterdays,* Winter 1969–70, 2–18.

———. *Union Pacific Country.* Rand McNally, 1971; University of Nebraska Press, 1976.

Atherton, Lewis. *Main Street on the Middle Border.* Indiana University Press, 1984.

Attebery, Jennifer Eastman. *Building Idaho: An Architectural History.* University of Idaho Press, 1991.

———. "Domestic and Commercial Architecture in Caldwell." *Idaho Yesterdays,* Winter 1980, 2–11.

Aurand, Harold W. *From the Molly Maguires to the United Mine Workers, 1869–97.* Temple University Press, 1971.

Avrich, Paul. *The Haymarket Tragedy.* Princeton University Press, 1984.

Baker, Liva. *The Justice from Beacon Hill.* HarperCollins, 1991.

———. *The Second Battle of New Orleans: The Hundred-Year Struggle to Integrate the Schools.* HarperCollins, 1996.

Baker, Ray Stannard. *American Chronicle.* Charles Scribner's Sons, 1945.

———. *Our New Prosperity.* Doubleday and McClure, 1900.

———. "The Reign of Lawlessness, Anarchy and Despotism in Colorado." *McClure's,* May 1904, 43–57.

———. "The Rise of the Tailors." *McClure's,* December 1904.

Bakken, Gordon. *Development of Law on the Rocky Mountain Frontier: Civil Law and Society, 1850–1912.* Greenwood Press, 1983.

Bangs, I. S. "The Ullmann Brigade." *War Papers.* Commandery of the State of Maine, Military Order of the Loyal Legion of the U.S. Lefavor-Towers, 1902.

Barnard, Harry. *Eagle Forgotten: The Life of John Peter Altgeld.* Bobbs-Merrill, 1938.

Barrett, Glen. *Dreaming Dreams: A History of the City of Gooding.* Boise State University Press, n.d.

———. *Idaho Banking, 1863–1976.* Boise State University Press, 1976.

Barrymore, Ethel. *Memories: An Autobiography.* Harper and Brothers, 1955.

Barrymore, Lionel. *We Barrymores!,* Appleton-Croft, 1951.

Barth, Gunther. *City People: The Rise of Modern City Culture in Nineteenth-Century America.* Oxford University Press, 1980.

———. *Instant Cities: The Urbanization and the Rise of of San Francisco and Denver.* Oxford University Press, 1975.

Bartlett, Richard A. *The New Country: A Social History of the American Frontier 1776–1890.* Oxford University Press, 1974; pb. ed., 1976.

Bayard, Charles J. "Theodore Roosevelt and Colorado Politics: The Roosevelt-Stewart Alliance." *Colorado Magazine,* Fall 1965, 311–25.

Beal, Merrill D., and Merle W. Wells. *History of Idaho.* Lewis Historical Publishing, 1959.

Bedford, Henry F. *Socialism and the Workers in Massachusetts, 1886–1912.* University of Massachusetts Press, 1966.

Beer, Thomas. *Hanna, Crane and the Mauve Decade.* Alfred A. Knopf, 1941.

———. *Mrs. Egg and Other Americans.* Alfred A. Knopf, 1947.

Beet, Thomas. "Shameless Crimes of Private Detectivs." *Appleton's,* October 1906.

Bellamy, Edward. *Looking Backward.* New American Library, 1960.

Bender, Thomas, and Carl E. Schorske. *Budapest and New York: Studies in Metropolitan Transformation, 1870–1930.* Russell Sage Foundation, 1994.

Benediktsson, Thomas E. *George Sterling.* Twayne, n.d.

Benezet, Louis P. *Three Years of Football at Dartmouth.* St. Peter's School of Concord, n.d.

Bennett, David H. *The Party of Fear.* University of North Carolina Press, 1988.

Bent, Silas. *Ballyhoo: The Voice of the Press.* Boni and Liveright, 1927.

———. *Justice Oliver Wendell Holmes.* Vanguard, 1932.

Bergamini, John D. *The Hundredth Year.* G. P. Putnam, 1976.

Berle, A. A. *The Colorado Mine War.* Privately published, 1914.

Berman, Edward. *Labor Disputes and the President of the United States.* Studies in History, Economics and Public Law, III, no. 2, Columbia University, 1924.

Beth, Loren P. *John Marshall Harlan: The Last Whig Justice.* University Press of Kentucky, 1992.

Bickel, Alexander M., and Schmidt, Benno C., Jr. *The Judiciary and Responsible Government, 1910–1921.* Vol. 9 of *History of the Supreme Court of the United States.* Macmillan, 1984.

Biddle, Francis. *Mr. Justice Holmes.* Charles Scribner's Sons, 1942.

Bigelow, John, Jr. *Reminiscences of the Santiago Campaign.* Harper and Row, 1899.

Bimba, Anthony. *The Molly Maguires.* International Publishers, 1932.

Binns, Archie. *Mrs. Fiske and the American Theater.* Crown, 1955.

Bird, Annie Laurie. *Boise: The Peace Valley.* Caxton Printers, 1934.

Birmingham, Stephen. *Our Crowd: The Great Jewish Families of New York.* Harper and Row, 1967.

Bishop, Joseph Bucklin. *Charles Joseph Bonaparte: His Life and Public Service.* Charles Scribner's Sons, 1922.

Blank, Robert H. *Regional Diversity of Political Values: Idaho Political Culture.* University Press of America, 1978.

Blight, David W. *Frederick Douglass' Civil War.* Louisiana State University Press, 1989.

Blondheim, Menahem. *News over the Wires: The Telegraph and the Flow of Public Information, 1844–1897.* Harvard University Press, 1994.

Bloom, Kahleed J. *The Mississippi Valley's Great Yellow Fever Epidemic of 1878.* Louisiana State University Press, 1993.

Blum, John Morton. *The Republican Roosevelt.* Harvard University Press, 1954; pb. ed., 1977.

Bonaparte, Charles J. "Lynch Law and Its Remedy." *Yale Law Journal,* May 1899.

Boorstin, Daniel J. *The Americans.* Vol. 1: *The Colonial Experience,* vol. 2: *The National Experience,* vol. 3: *The Democratic Experience.* Random House, 1958–73.

Borah, Mary. *Elephants and Donkeys: The Memoirs of Mary Borah.* As told to May Louise Perrine. University Press of Idaho, 1976.

Bourke, Francis Charles. "The Pinkertons." *Leslie's,* May 1905, 36–45; June 1905, 205–14.

Bowers, William T., William M. Hammond, and George L. MacGarrigle. *Black Soldier, White Army: The 24th Infantry Regiment in Korea.* U.S. Army Center of Military History, 1996.

Boyce, Edward. "The Truth Considered." *Miners' Magazine,* June 1910.

Boyer, Richard O., and Herbert M. Morais. *Labor's Untold Story.* Cameron Associates, 1955.

Brandon, Craig. *Murder in the Adirondacks: An American Tragedy Revisited.* North Country Books, 1986.

Brecher, Jeremy. *Strike! The True History of Mass Insurgence in America from 1877 to the Present.* Straight Arrow Books, 1972.

Brissenden, Paul F. *The IWW: A Study of American Syndicalism.* Russell and Russell, 1919.

Brock, Leslie V. "Lawrence Henry Gipson, Historian: The Early Idaho Years." *Idaho Yesterdays,* Summer 1978, 2–9.

Broehl, Wayne G., Jr. *The Molly Maguires.* Harvard University Press, 1964.

Brooks, Van Wyck. *The Confident Years: 1885–1915.* E. P. Dutton, 1952.

Brown, Dee. *The Galvanized Yankees.* University of Illinois Press, 1963.

———. *Hear That Lonesome Whistle Blow: Railroads in the West.* Holt, Rinehart and Winston, 1977.

Brown, Francis. *Raymond of the Times.* W. W. Norton, 1951.

Brown, Ira V. *Lyman Abbott: Christian Evolutionist.* Harvard University Press, 1953.

Brown, Richard Maxwell, *No Duty to Retreat.* University of Oklahoma Press, 1991.

———. *Strain of Violence.* Oxford University Press, 1975.

Brown, Thomas N. *Irish-American Nationalism, 1870–1890.* Lippincott, 1966.

Brownlee, W. E., ed. *Dr. Graves: His Trial and Suicide, or the Famous Barnaby Mystery.* Denver Times, 1893.

Bruce, Alfred W. *The Steam Locomotive in America.* W. W. Norton, 1952.

Brundage, David. *The Making of Western Labor Radicalism: Denver's Organized Workers, 1878–1905.* University of Illinois Press, 1969.

Buhle, Mari Jo. *Women and American Socialism.* University of Illinois Press, 1981.

Buhle, Paul. *"The Appeal to Reason": The American Radical Press, 1880–1960.* Ed. Joseph R. Conlin. vol. 1. Greenwood Press, 1974.

———. *Marxism in America: Remapping the History of the American Left.* Verso, 1987.

Burgess, Charles E. "Edgar Lee Masters: The Lawyer as Writer" in *The Vision of This Land: Studies of Vachel Lindsay,*

Edgar Lee Masters, and Carl Sandburg, edited by John E. Hallwas and Dennis J. Reader (Western Illinois University Press, 1976), 55–73.

Burgoyne, Arthur G. *The Homestead Strike of 1892.* University of Pittsburgh Press, 1982.

Burroughs, John R. "Bob Meldrum: Killer for Hire." *Empire Magazine (Denver Post),* September 23, 1962, 10–13.

———. *Where the Old West Stayed Young.* William Morrow, 1962.

Busch, Francis X. *Prisoners at the Bar.* Bobbs-Merrill, 1952.

Bushue, Paul B. "Dr. Hermon F. Titus and Socialism in Washington State, 1900–1909." Master's Thesis, University of Wisconsin, 1967.

Butcher, Fanny. *Many Lives—One Love.* Harper and Row, 1972.

Cabot, F. J. "Is Trial by Jury, in Criminal Cases, a Failure?" *Arena,* May 1905, 510–13.

Caldwell: The Magic City in the Boise Valley. Rule and Cole, 1891.

Calhoun, Frederick S. *The Lawmen: United States Marshals and Their Deputies, 1789–1989.* Smithsonian Institution Press, 1989.

Callender, James H. *Yesterdays on Brooklyn Heights.* Dorland Press, 1927.

Calvert, Jerry. *The Gibraltar: Socialism and Labor in Butte, Montana, 1895–1920.* Montana Historical Society Press, 1988.

Campbell, Patrick. *A Molly Maguire Story.* Templecrone Press, 1992.

Carlson, Peter. *Roughneck: The Life and Times of Big Bill Haywood.* W. W. Norton, 1983; pb. ed., 1984.

Carr, John Dickson. *The Life of Sir Arthur Conan Doyle.* Carroll and Graf, 1987.

Carroll, Howard. *Twelve Americans: Their Lives and Times.* Harper, 1883.

Carter, Charles Frederick. *When Railroads Were New.* Simmons-Boardman Publishing, 1926.

Carver, Charles. *Brann and the Iconoclast.* University of Texas Press, 1957, 1987.

Cashin, Herschel V., et al. *Under Fire with the Tenth U.S. Cavalry.* University Press of Colorado, 1993.

Cashman, Sean Dennis. *America in the Gilded Age.* New York University Press, 1984; pb. ed., 1988.

Chalmers, David Mark. *The Social and Political Ideas of the Muckrakers.* Citadel Press, 1964.

Chambers, Julius. *News Hunting on Three Continents.* Mitchell Kennerly, 1921.

Chaplin, Ralph. *Wobbly: The Rough-and-Tumble Story of an American Radical.* University of Chicago Press, 1948.

Chernow, Ron. *The House of Morgan.* Atlantic Monthly Press, 1990.

Clark, Clifford E., Jr. *Henry Ward Beecher: Spokesman for a Middle-Class America.* University of Illinois Press, 1978.

Clark, James W. *American Assassins: The Darker Side of Politics.* Princeton University Press, 1990.

Clark, Michael James Tinsley. "A History of the Twenty-fourth United States Infantry Regiment in Utah, 1896–1900." Ph.D. diss., University of Utah. 1979.

———. "Improbable Ambassadors: Black Soldiers at Fort Douglas, 1896–99." *Utah Historical Quarterly,* 46, no. 3 (Summer 1978), 282–301.

Clarke, Joseph I. C. *My Life and Memories.* Dodd, Mead, 1925.

Clay, Samuel H. *The Assassination of Ex-Gov. Frank Steunenberg.* News Printing and Publishing Co., 1906.

Cloman, Flora Clement. *I'd Live It Over.* Farrar and Rinehart, 1941.

Coakley, Robert W. *The Role of the Federal Military Forces in Domestic Disorders, 1789–1878.* U.S. Army Center of Military History, 1989.

Cobb, Irvin. *Exit Laughing.* Bobbs-Merrill, 1941.

Cobb, Philip L. *A History of the Cobb Family.* Privately published, 1907.

Coleman, Edward Pierce. *Steel Rails and Territorial Tales: Forty Months Building the Oregon Short Line Railroad through Idaho.* Limberlost Press, 1994.

Collier, Peter, with David Horowitz. *The Roosevelts: An American Saga.* Simon & Schuster, 1994.

Collins, Lorin Cone, Jr. *Autobiography.* Privately published, 1934.

Collins, Michael. *That Damned Cowboy: Theodore Roosevelt and the American West, 1883–1898.* Peter Lang, 1989.

Colson, Dennis C., *Idaho's Constitution: The Tie That Binds.* University of Idaho Press, 1991.

Conley, Cort. *Idaho for the Curious: A Guide.* Backeddy Books, 1982.

Conlin, Joseph R. *Bacon, Beans, and Galantines.* University of Nevada Press, 1986.

———. *Big Bill Haywood and the Radical Union Movement.* Syracuse University Press, 1969.

———. "The Haywood Case: An Enduring Riddle." *Pacific Northwest Quarterly,* January 1968, 23–31.

———. ed. *The American Radical Press, 1880–1960.* Vol. 1. Greenwood Press, 1974.

Connolly, C. P. "A Little Drama Out in Idaho." *Collier's,* December 7, 1907.

———. "The Moyer-Haywood Case." *Collier's,* May–July 1907. (1: "The Story of the Idaho Mining Troubles," May 11, 1907; 2: "The Murder, and the Arrest of Orchard," May 18, 1907; 3: "The Kidnapping," May 25, 1907; 4: "Harry Orchard and His Story," June 22, 1907; 5: "The Colorado Labor War," June 29, 1907; 6: "The Colorado Labor War (Continued)," July 6, 1907; 7: "The Colorado Labor War (Concluded)," July 20, 1907; 8: "What Has Been Brought Out in Haywood's Trial," July 27, 1907).

———. "Pettibone and Sheriff Brown." *Collier's,* January 25, 1908.

———. "Presidential Possibilities: Borah of Idaho." *Collier's,* July 31, 1907.

———. "Protest by Dynamite: Similarities and Contrasts between the McNamara Affair in Los Angeles and the Moyer-Haywood-Pettibone Trial in Boise." *Collier's,* June 13, 1912.

Conrad, Barnaby. *A Revolting Transaction.* Arbor House, 1983.

Cook, Davis J. *Hands Up, or Twenty Years of Detective Life in the Mountains and on the Plains.* University of Oklahoma Press, 1958.

Cook, R. G. "Pioneer Portraits: Weldon Brinton Heyburn." *Idaho Yesterdays,* Spring 1966, 22–26.

———. "Senator Heyburn's War against the Forest Service." *Idaho Yesterdays,* Winter 1970–71, 12–15.

Cooper, Jerry M. *The Army and Civil Disorders: Federal Military Intervention in Labor Disputes, 1877–1900.* Greenwood Press, 1980.

Cooper, John Milton, Jr. *Pivotal Decades.* W. W. Norton, 1990.

———. *The Warrior and the Priest: Woodrow Wilson and Theodore Roosevelt.* Harvard University Press, 1983.

————. "William E. Borah, Political Thespian." *Pacific Northwest Quarterly*, 56 (Oct. 1965): 145–58.

Cooper, Kent. *Kent Cooper and the Associated Press: An Autobiography*. Random House, 1959.

Corcoran, Thomas F. "A Letter to My Grandchildren." Privately published, 1973 (property of Paul Corcoran, Boston, Mass.).

Cornish, Dudley Taylor. *The Sable Arm: Black Troops in the Union Army*. University Press of Kansas, 1967.

Cosmas, Graham A. *An Army for Empire*. University of Missouri Press, 1971.

The Cost to the State of Idaho of the Haywood Trial. Capital News, 1907.

Costello, Peter. *The Real World of Sherlock Holmes*. Carroll and Graf, 1991.

Cowan, Geoffrey. *The People v. Clarence Darrow*. Random House, 1993.

Cowart, B. T. "James McParland and the Haywood Case." *Idaho Yesterdays*, Fall 1972, 24–29.

Cowling, Cloah Sebastian. *The Land of Sunrise Mountains*. Vantage Press, 1968.

Crandall, Allen. *The Man from Kinsman*. Published by the author, 1933.

Crane, Stephen. "War Memories." *Anglo-Saxon Review*, December 1899.

Creel, George. *Rebel at Large: Recollections of Fifty Crowded Years*. G. P. Putnam's Sons, 1947.

Croly, Herbert. *Marcus Alonzo Hanna: His Life and Work*. Macmillan, 1924.

————. *Willard Straight*. Macmillan, 1924.

Cronon, William. *Nature's Metropolis: Chicago and the Great West*. W. W. Norton, 1991.

Cronon, William, George Miles, and Jay Gitlin, eds. *Under an Open Sky: Rethinking America's Western Past*. W. W. Norton, 1992.

Crowder, David Lester. "Moses Alexander: Idaho's Jewish Governor, 1914–18." Ph.D. diss., University of Idaho, 1972.

Crunden, Robert M. *A Hero in Spite of Himself: Brand Whitlock in Art, Politics and War*. Alfred A. Knopf, 1969.

Cutright, Paul Russell. *Theodore Roosevelt: The Making of a Conservationist*. University of Illinois Press, 1985.

Darrow, Clarence. *Attorney for the Damned*. Ed. Arthur Weinberg. Simon & Schuster, 1969.

————. "Attorney for the Defense." *Esquire*, May 1936.

————. *An Eye for an Eye*. Duffield, 1905.

————. *Farmington: Memories of a Childhood in a Pennsylvania Village*. Scribners, 1932.

————. "Liberty, Equality, Fraternity." *Vanity Fair*, December 1926, 74.

————. *A Persian Pearl and Other Essays*. C. L. Ricketts, 1902.

————. *Resist Not Evil*. Haldeman-Julius, 1902.

————. *The Skeleton in the Closet*. Haldeman-Julius, 1899.

————. *The Story of My Life*. Charles Scribner's Sons, 1934.

————. *Verdicts out of Court*. Ed. Arthur Weinberg and Lila Weinberg. Elephant Paperbacks, 1989.

————. "Whitman in Literature." Paper delivered before the Walt Whitman Fellowship, May 31, 1913, CDR.

Dary, David. *Seeking Pleasure in the Old West*. Alfred A. Knopf, 1995.

Dauber, Jeremy Asher. "Worthy Editor: Theorizing the Advice Column by Looking at the *Jewish Daily Forward*'s "Bintl Briv." Senior honors thesis, Harvard University, 1995.

Davis, Allen F. *American Heroine: The Life and Legend of Jane Addams*. Oxford University Press, 1973.

Davis, Allen F., and Mary Lynn McCree, eds. *Eighty Years at Hull House*. Quadrangle Books, 1969.

————. *Spearheads for Reform*. Oxford University Press, 1967.

Davis, John W. *A Vast Amount of Trouble: A History of the Spring Creek Raid*. University of Colorado Press, 1993.

Davis, Kenneth S. "Darrow: Man of a Thousand Battles." *New York Times Magazine*, April 28, 1957, 12, 64, 66–67.

Davis, Oscar King. *At the Emperor's Wish*. D. Appleton & Co., 1905.

————. *Our Conquests in the Pacific*. Frederick A. Stokes, 1899.

————. *Released for Publication*. Houghton Mifflin, 1925.

————. *William Howard Taft: The Man of the Hour*. P. W. Ziegler, 1908.

Davis, Richard Harding. *The Cuban and Porto Rican Campaigns*. Charles Scribner's Sons, 1898.

————. *Notes of a War Correspondent*. Charles Scribner's Sons, 1911.

Day, Martin C. "Death in the Mail." *Providence Journal*, 1892.

de Angelis, Jefferson, and Alvin F. Harlow. *A Vagabond Trouper*. Harcourt, Brace, 1931.

d'Easum, Dick. *Fragments of Villainy*. Statesman Printing, 1959.

————. *The Idanha: Guests and Ghosts of an Historic Idaho Inn*. Caxton Printers, 1983.

Debs, Eugene. *Gentle Rebel: The Letters of Eugene V. Debs*. Ed. by J. Robert Constantine. University of Illinois Press, 1995.

Dedmon, Emmett. *Fabulous Chicago*. Atheneum, 1983.

Defenbach, Byron. *Idaho: The Place and Its People*. Vol. 2. American Historical Society, 1933.

Dennis, Charles H. *Victor Lawson*. University of Chicago Press, 1935.

Derickson, Alan. *Workers' Health, Workers' Democracy: The Western Miners' Struggle, 1891–1925*. Cornell University Press, 1988.

Derig, Betty. *Weiser: The Way It Was*. Rambler Press, 1987.

Destler, Charles McArthur. *Henry Demarest Lloyd and the Empire of Reform*. University of Pennsylvania Press, 1963.

Dewees, F. P. *The Molly Maguires: The Origin, Growth and Character of the Organization*. Lippincott, 1877.

Dickens, Charles. *American Notes*. Chapman and Hall, 1842; Penguin, 1989.

Di Salvatore, Bryan. "Vehement Fire." *New Yorker*, April 27, 1987, 42–72; May 4, 1987, 38–58.

Donald, David Herbert. *Lincoln*. Simon & Schuster, 1995.

Donaldson, Thomas. *Idaho of Yesterday*. Caxton Printers, 1941.

Donnelly, Ignatius. *Caesar's Column: A Story of the Twentieth Century*. Harvard University Press, 1960.

Douglas, Ann. *Terrible Honesty: Mongrel Manhattan in the 1920s*. Farrar, Straus and Giroux, 1995.

Douglas, George H. *All Aboard: The Railroad in American Life*. Paragon House, 1992.

Douglas, George W. "The Colorful Career of Oscar King Davis." *Colgate Alumni News*, February 1933.

Downey, Fairfax. *The Buffalo Soldiers in the Indian Wars*. McGraw-Hill, 1969.

————. *Richard Harding Davis: His Day*. Charles Scribner's, 1933.

Doyle, Arthur Conan. *The Valley of Fear. The Complete Novels and Stories.* Vol. 2. Bantam, 1986.
Dreier, Mary E. "The Block." Mary Elizabeth Dreier Collection. Schlesinger Library, Cambridge, Mass.
———. *Margaret Dreier Robins: Her Life, Letters and Work.* Island Press Cooperative, 1950.
———. "Reminiscence on Her Mother, Dorothea Adelheid Dreier." Mary Elizabeth Dreier Collection. Schlesinger Library, Cambridge, Mass.
Dreiser, Theodore. *A Book about Myself.* Boni and Liveright, 1922.
———. *The Financier.* Harper & Row, 1912. pb. ed. New American Library, 1981.
———. *Newspaper Days.* Horace Liveright, 1922.
———. *The Titan.* John Lane, 1914. pb. ed. New American Library, 1965.
Dubofsky, Melvyn. *"Big Bill" Haywood.* Manchester University Press, 1987.
———. *We Shall Be All: A History of the Industrial Workers of the World.* University of Illinois Press, 1988.
Dubois, Fred T. *The Making of a State.* Ed. Louis J. Clements. Eastern Idaho Publishing, 1971.
Dunbar, Robin. *The Detective Business.* Charles H. Kerr, 1909.
Dunne, Finley Peter. *Mr. Dooley Remembers.* Little, Brown, 1963.
Dyar, Ralph E. *News for an Empire: The Story of the* Spokesman-News. Caxton Printers, 1952.
Dyer, Thomas G. *Theodore Roosevelt and the Idea of Race.* Louisiana State University Press, 1980.
Early, Gerald H. "The Negro Soldier in the Spanish-American War." Senior honors thesis, Shippensburg State College, Pa., 1970.
Eastman, Max. *Enjoyment of Living.* Harper and Brothers, 1948.
Eberhard, Wallace B. "Mr. Bennett Covers a Murder Trial." *Journalism Quarterly,* Autumn 1970, 457–63.
Edel, Leon. *Henry James: The Master, 1901–1916.* Lippincott, 1972.
Edmonds, David C. *The Guns of Port Hudson.* Vols. 1 and 2. Acadiana Press, 1983–84.
Eggers, Robert Franklin. "A History of Theatre in Boise, Idaho, from 1863 to 1963." Master's thesis, University of Oregon, 1963.
Einstein, Lewis. *Roosevelt: His Mind in Action.* Houghton Mifflin, 1930.
Ekman, Paul. *Telling Lies: Clues to Deceit in the Marketplace, Politics and Marriage.* W. W. Norton, 1992.
Emmons, David. *The Butte Irish: Class and Ethnicity in an American Mining Town 1875–1925.* University of Illinois Press, 1989.
England, George Allan. *The Story of the* Appeal, *"Unbeaten and Unbeatable," Being the Epic of the Life and Work of the Greatest Political Newspaper in the World.* Appeal to Reason, 1917.
Epstein, Melech. *Jewish Labor in the U.S.A.: An Industrial, Political and Cultural History of the Jewish Labor Movement.* KTAV Publishing House, 1969.
Ernst, Alice Henson. *Trouping in the Oregon Country.* Oregon Historical Society, 1961.
Etulain, Robert W. "Basque Beginnings in the Pacific Northwest." *Idaho Yesterdays,* Spring 1974.
Fahey, John. *The Ballyhoo Bonanza: Charles Sweeney and the Idaho Mines.* University of Washington Press, 1971.
———. "Coeur d'Alene Confederacy." *Idaho Yesterdays,* Spring 1968, 2–7
———. *The Days of the Hercules.* University of Idaho Press, 1978.
———. "Ed Boyce and the Western Federation of Miners." *Idaho Yesterdays,* Fall 1981, 17–30.
———. *Hecla: A Century of Western Mining.* University of Washington Press, 1990.
———. *The Inland Empire: Unfolding Years, 1879–1929.* University of Washington Press, 1986.
Fehrenbach, T. R. *Elkdom USA.* Benevolent and Protective Order of Elks, 1967.
Felsenthal, Carol. *Princess Alice: The Life and Times of Alice Roosevelt Longworth.* St. Martin's Press, 1988.
Fenberg, Matilda. "I Remember Clarence Darrow." *Chicago History,* 2, no. 4 (Fall-Winter 1973).
Fields, Armond, and L. Marc Fields. *From the Bowery to Broadway: Lew Fields and the Roots of American Popular Theater.* Oxford University Press, 1993.
Filler, Louis. *Crusaders for American Liberalism.* Antioch Press, 1939.
Fink, Leon. *Workingmen's Democracy, the Knights of Labor and American Politics.* University of Illinois Press, 1983.
Fishel, Edwin C. *The Secret War for the Union: The Untold Story of Military Intelligence in the Civil War.* Houghton Mifflin, 1996.
Fisk, James. *Idaho: Her Gold Fields, and the Routes to Them: A Hand Book for Emigrants.* John Gray, 1863.
Fiss, Owen M. *Troubled Beginnings of the Modern State, 1888–1910.* Macmillan, 1993.
Fitch, Clyde. *Captain Jinks of the Horse Marines. From the American Drama: The Modern Theatre Series.* Ed. Eric Bentley. Vol. 4. Peter Smith, 1978.
Flaccus, Kimball. *"Edgar Lee Masters: A Biographical and Critical Study."* Ph.D. diss., New York University, 1952.
Fleming, G. H. *The Unforgettable Season.* Holt, Rinehart, 1981.
Fletcher, Marvin. *The Black Soldier and the Officer in the United States Army, 1891–1917.* University of Missouri Press, 1974.
———. *Progressivism and Muckraking.* R. R. Bowker, 1976.
Florin, Lambert. *Ghost Town Album.* Superior Publishing, 1960.
Flynn, Elizabeth Gurley. *Debs, Haywood, Ruthenberg.* Workers Library, 1939.
———. *I Speak My Own Piece: Autobiography of the "Rebel Girl."* Masses and Mainstream, 1955.
Foner, Philip. S. *History of the Labor Movement in the United States.* 10 vols. International Publishers, 1947–.
Foote, Mary Hallock. *Coeur d'Alene.* Houghton Mifflin, 1898.
Forbath, William E. *Law and the Shaping of the American Labor Movement.* Harvard University Press, 1991.
Fowler, Arlen. *The Black Infantry in the West, 1869–91.* Greenwood Press, 1971.
Fowler, Gene. *Good Night, Sweet Prince: The Life and Times of John Barrymore.* Buccaneer Books, 1976.
———. *The Great Mouthpiece.* Covici Friede, 1931.
———. *Timber Line: A Story of Bonfils and Tammen.* Covici Friede, 1933.
Fox, Stephen. *The American Conservation Movement: John Muir and His Legacy.* University of Wisconsin Press, 1985.
Franklin, Charles. *The Third Degree.* Robert Hale, 1970.
Fraser, Steven. *Labor Will Rule: Sidney Hillman and the Rise of American Labor.* Free Press, 1991.

Freidel, Frank. *The Splendid Little War.* Little, Brown, 1958.

French, Hiram T. *History of Idaho.* Lewis Publishing, 1914.

Friedman, Lawrence M. *A History of American Law.* Simon & Schuster, 1985; Touchstone, 1985.

Friedman, Leon, and Fred L. Israel. *The Justices of the United States Supreme Court, 1789–1969.* Chelsea House, 1969.

Friedman, Morris. *The Pinkerton Labor Spy.* Wilshire Book, 1907.

Fuld, Leonhard Felix. *Police Administration: A Critical Study of Police Organizations in the United States and Abroad.* G. P. Putnam's, 1910.

Furlong, Thomas. *Fifty Years a Detective.* Furlong Detective Agency, 1912.

Gabler, Neil. *Winchell: Gossip, Power and the Culture of Celebrity.* Alfred A. Knopf, 1994.

Gaboury, William Joseph. *Dissension in the Rockies: A History of Idaho Populism.* Garland Publishing, 1988.

———. "From State House to Bull Pen: Idaho Populism and the Coeur d'Alene Trouble of the 1890s." *Pacific Northwest Quarterly,* January 1967.

Gard, Wayne. *Frontier Justice.* University of Oklahoma Press, 1949.

Garland, Hamlin. *Companions on the Trail: A Literary Chronicle.* Macmillan, 1931.

———. *Hesper.* Harper and Row, 1991.

Garlock, Jonah. *Guide to the Local Assemblies of the Knights of Labor.* Greenwood Press, 1982.

Gates, Paul Wallace. *History of Public Land Law Development.* Government Printing Office, 1968.

Gatewood, Willard B., Jr. *Black Americans and the White Man's Burden, 1898–1903.* University of Illinois Press, 1975.

———. "Negro Troops in Florida, 1898." *Florida Historical Review,* vol. 48 (July 1970), 1–15.

———. *"Smoked Yankees" and the Struggle for Empire: Letters from Negro Soldiers, 1898–1902.* University of Illinois Press, 1971.

———. *Theodore Roosevelt and the Art of Controversy: Episodes of the White House Years.* Louisiana State University Press, 1970.

Gawalt, Gerald W., ed. *The New High Priests: Lawyers in Post Civil War America.* Greenwood Press, 1984.

Gelb, Arthur, and Barbara Gelb. *O'Neill.* Harper and Row, 1960.

"General Alger's Apologia." *Nation,* February 13, 1902.

Gerstle, Gary. *Working Class Americans.* Cambridge University Press, 1989.

Gianakos, Perry E. "The Spanish-American War and the Double Paradox of the Negro American." *Phylon,* 26, no. 1 (Spring 1965), 34–49.

Gibson, William M. *Theodore Roosevelt among the Humorists.* University of Tennessee Press, 1980.

Giddings, Franklin H. "The Social Lynching of Gorky and Andreiva." *Independent,* April 26, 1906, 976–78.

Gilbert, Geoff. *Aspects of Extradition Law.* Martinus Nijhoff Publishers, 1991.

Ginger, Ray. *Altgeld's America: The Lincoln Ideal vs. Changing Realities.* Funk and Wagnalls, 1958.

———. *The Bending Cross: A Biography of Eugene Victor Debs.* Rutgers University Press, 1949.

———. "Clarence Seward Darrow, 1857–1938." *Antioch Review,* March 1953, 52–66.

Gitelman, H. M. *Legacy of the Ludlow Massacre: A Chapter in American Industrial Relations.* University of Pennsylvania Press, 1988.

Gizycka, Eleanor. *Glass Houses.* Minton, Balch, 1926.

Glad, Paul W. *McKinley, Bryan and the People.* J. B. Lippincott, 1964.

Glatthaar, Joseph. *Forged in Battle.* Free Press, 1989.

Gold, Arthur, and Robert Fizdale. *The Divine Sarah: A Life of Sarah Bernhardt.* Alfred A. Knopf, 1991.

Goldman, Emma. *Living My Life.* Alfred A. Knopf, 1931.

Gompers, Samuel. *An Address to the Western Federation of Miners, in Convention Assembled, June 1897.*

———. *Seventy Years of Life and Labor: An Autobiography.* 2 vols. Augustus M. Kelley, 1967.

"Gompers and Burns on Unionism and Dynamite." *McClure's,* February 1912, 363–77.

Goodstein, Phil. *The Seamy Side of Denver.* New Social Publications, 1994.

Gould, Lewis L. *The Presidency of Theodore Roosevelt.* University Press of Kansas, 1991.

Graff, Leo W., Jr. *The Senatorial Career of Fred T. Dubois of Idaho, 1890–1907.* Garland Publishing, 1988.

Graham, Lewis. *The Great I Am.* Macaulay, 1933.

Gramling, Oliver. *AP: The Story of News.* Kennikat Press, 1969.

Grant, H. Roger, ed. *Brownie the Boomer: The Life of Charles P. Brown, an American Railroader.* Northern Illinois University Press, 1991.

Grant, Hamil. *Spies and Secret Service.* Frederick A. Stokes, 1915.

Grant, Luke. "The Haywood Trial." *Outlook,* August 24, 1907.

Green, Abel, and Joe Laurie, Jr. *Show Biz: From Vaude to Video.* Garden City Books, 1951.

Green, James R. *Grass Roots Socialism.* Louisiana State University Press, 1978.

———. "The Salesmen-Soldiers of the Appeal Army: A Profile of Rank-and-File Socialist Agitators." *Socialism and the Cities.* Ed. Bruce M. Stave. Kennikat Press, 1975. 26–37.

Greenberg, Irving. *Theodore Roosevelt and Labor, 1900–1918.* Garland Publishing, 1932.

Gressley, Ed Gene. *Bostonians and Bullion: The Journal of Robert Livermore, 1892–1915.* University of Nebraska Press, 1968.

Griffith, Sally Foreman. *Hometown News: William Allen White and the Emporia Gazette.* Oxford University Press, 1989.

Grimmett, Robert G. *Cabal of Death.* University of Idaho Press, 1977.

Griscom, Lloyd C. *Diplomatically Speaking.* Little, Brown, 1940.

Grover, David H. *Debaters and Dynamiters.* Oregon State University Press, 1964.

———. *Diamondfield Jack: A Study in Frontier Justice.* University of Oklahoma Press, 1986.

Guice, John D. *The Rocky Mountain Bench: The Territorial Supreme Courts of Colorado, Montana and Wyoming, 1861–1890.* Yale University Press, 1972.

Gunther, Gerald. *Learned Hand: The Man and the Judge.* Alfred A. Knopf, 1994.

Gurko, Miriam. *Clarence Darrow.* Thomas Y. Crowell, 1965.

Hafen, Leroy R. *Colorado and Its People: A Narrative and Topical History of the Centennial State.* Lewis Historical Publishing, 1948.

Hagedorn, Hermann. *The Roosevelt Family of Sagamore Hill.* Macmillan, 1955.

Hagedorn, Hermann, and Garry G. Roth. *Sagamore Hill: An Historical Guide.* Theodore Roosevelt Association, 1977.

Haldeman-Julius, Emanuel. *My First 25 Years: Instead of a Footnote, an Autobiography.* Haldeman-Julius, 1949.

———. *My Second 25 Years: Instead of a Footnote, an Autobiography.* Haldeman-Julius, 1949.

Haldeman-Julius, Marcet. *Famous and Interesting Guests of a Kansas Farm.* Haldeman-Julius, 1936.

Hale, Matthew, Jr. *Human Science and Social Order: Hugo Münsterberg and the Origins of Applied Psychology.* Temple University Press, 1980.

Hale, Nathan G., Jr. *Freud and the Americans: The Beginnings of Psychoanalysis in the United States, 1876–1917.* Oxford University Press, 1995.

———. ed. *James Jackson Putnam and Psychoanalysis.* Harvard University Press, 1971.

Halttunen, Karen. *Confidence Men and Painted Women: A Study of Middle Class Culture in America, 1830–1870.* Yale University Press, 1982.

Hamilton, Alice. *Exploring the Dangerous Trade.* Little, Brown, 1943.

Hamlin, Charles E. *The Life and Times of Hannibal Hamlin.* Riverside Press, 1899.

Hammett, Dashiell. *Red Harvest.* Alfred A. Knopf, 1929; Vintage, 1972.

Hammond, John Hays. *The Autobiography of John Hays Hammond.* Farrar and Rinehart, 1935.

Hancock, Ralph. *Fabulous Boulevard.* Funk and Wagnalls, 1949.

Handy, Robert T. *The Social Gospel in America: 1870–1920.* Oxford University Press, 1966.

Hapgood, Hutchins. *The Spirit of Labor.* Duffield and Co., 1907.

———. *A Victorian in the Modern World.* Harcourt, Brace, 1939.

Hapgood, Norman. *The Changing Years.* Farrar and Rinehart, 1930.

———. "In the Interpreter's House," *American,* July 1907.

———. *The Stage in America, 1897–1900.* Macmillan, 1901.

———. "The Theatrical Syndicate." *International Monthly,* 1900 vol. 1, 107, 99–122.

Harbaugh, William H. *Power and Responsibility: The Life and Times of Theodore Roosevelt.* Farrar, Straus and Cudahy, 1961.

Hard, William. *Raymond Robins' Own Story.* Harper and Brothers, 1920.

———. "The Western Federation of Miners." *Outlook,* May 19, 1906, 126–32.

Harriman, Job. *The Class War in Idaho: The Horrors of the Bull Pen.* Shorey Book Store, 1900.

"The Harriman Special of 1906." *Union Pacific,* April 1924.

Harris, Neil. *Humbug: The Art of P. T. Barnum.* Little, Brown, 1973.

Harrison, Charles Y. *Clarence Darrow.* Jonathan Cape and Harrison Smith, 1931.

Hart, Arthur A. *Boise Baseball: The First 100 Years.* Historic Boise, 1994.

———. *The Boiseans: At Home.* Historic Boise, 1985.

———. *Historic Boise.* Historic Boise, 1985.

———. *Life in Old Boise.* Boise City Celebrations/Historic Boise, 1989.

Hart, Patricia, and Ivar Nelson. *Mining Town: The Photographic Record of T. N. Barnard and Nellie Stockbridge.* University of Washington Press and Idaho State Historical Society, 1984.

Hawes, Elizabeth. *New York, New York: How the Apartment House Transformed the Life of the City (1869–1930).* Alfred A. Knopf, 1993.

Hawley, James H. *History of Idaho: The Gem of the Mountains.* 4 vols. S. J. Clarke, 1920.

Haycraft, Howard, ed. *The Art of the Mystery Story.* Carroll and Graf, 1983.

Hayman, Herbert H. *That Man Boone: Frontiersman of Idaho.* College of Idaho, 1948.

Hayner, Norman Sylvester. *Hotel Life.* University of North Carolina Press, 1936.

Hays, Samuel H. *Report to the Governor of Idaho on the Insurrection in Shoshone County, Idaho.* Idaho State Historical Society, 1900.

Haywood, William D. *Bill Haywood's Book: The Autobiography of William D. Haywood.* International Publishers, 1929.

———. "Get Ready." *International Socialist Review,* June 1911, 728–30.

———. Speech at Cooper Union. *International Socialist Review,* February 1912.

Heller, Adele, and Lois Rudnik. *1915: The Cultural Moment.* Rutgers University Press, 1991.

Henry, George [George Shoaf]. *Love Crucified: A Romance of the Colorado War.* Appeal Publishing, 1905.

Henry, Robert W. "Ed Boyce: The Curious Evolution of an American Radical." Master's thesis, University of Montana, 1993.

Herrick, Robert. *The Common Lot.* Macmillan, 1913.

Hewitt, Barnard. *Theatre USA: 1665 to 1957.* McGraw-Hill, 1959.

Hibbard, Don. *Weiser: A Look at Idaho Architecture.* Idaho State Historic Preservation Office, 1962.

Hibben, Paxton. *Henry Ward Beecher: An American Portrait.* George H. Doran, 1927.

Hicken, Victor. *The American Fighting Man.* Macmillan, 1969.

Hickey, Thomas A. *The Story of the Bull Pen at Wardner, Idaho.* National Executive Committee Socialist Labor Party, 1900.

Hidy, Ralph. "Lumbermen in Idaho: A Study in Adaptation to Changing Environment." *Idaho Yesterdays,* Winter 1962, 2–17.

Hidy, Ralph, Ernest Hill, and Alan Nevins. *Timber and Men: The Weyerhauser Story.* Macmillan, 1963.

Hiebert, Ray Eldon. *Courtier to the Crowd: The Life Story of Ivy Lee.* Iowa State University Press, 1966.

Higginson, Thomas Wentworth. *Army Life in a Black Regiment.* W. W. Norton, 1984.

Highshaw, Robert B. *Edward Douglass White: Defender of the Constitutional Faith.* Louisiana State University Press, 1981.

Hillquit, Morris. *History of Socialism in the United States.* Russell and Russell, 1965.

———. *Loose Leaves from a Busy Life.* Macmillan, 1934.

Hofstadter, Richard. *The Age of Reform: From Bryan to F.D.R.* Alfred A. Knopf, 1955; pb. ed. Vintage, 1974.
————. *The American Political Tradition.* Alfred A. Knopf, 1948; pb. ed. Vintage, 1973.
Hoge, Alice Albright. *Cissy Patterson.* Random House, 1966.
Holbrook, Stewart. *Little Orphan Annie and Other Rugged People.* Macmillan, 1948.
————. *Rocky Mountain Revolution.* Henry Holt, 1956.
Holloway, Jean. *Hamlin Garland: A Biography.* University of Texas Press, 1960.
Holmes-Pollock Letters: The Correspondence of Mr. Justice Holmes and Sir Frederick Pollock. Ed. Mark DeWolfe Howe. Harvard University Press, 1946.
Holt, Edwin B. *The Freudian Wish and Its Place in History and Ethics.* Henry Holt, 1915.
Honig, Donald. *Baseball America: The Heroes of the Game and the Times of Their Glory.* Galahad Books, 1985.
Hopkins, Charles H. *The Rise of the Social Gospel in American Protestantism, 1865–1900.* Yale University Press, 1940.
Hopkins, Vincent Charles. *Dred Scott's Case.* Russell and Russell, 1951.
Horan, James David. *Desperate Men: Revelations from the Sealed Pinkerton Files.* G. P. Putnam's Sons, 1949.
————. *The Pinkertons: The Detective Dynasty That Made History.* Crown, 1968.
Horan, James David, and Howard Swiggett. *The Pinkerton Story.* G. P. Putnam's Sons, 1951.
Horsley, Albert E. *The Confessions and Autobiography of Harry Orchard.* McClure, 1907.
Horwitz, Morton J. *The Transformation of American Law, 1870–1960.* Oxford University Press, 1992.
Hosokawa, Bill. *Thunder in the Rockies: The Incredible Denver.* William Morrow, 1976.
Howe, Irving. *Socialism and America.* Harcourt Brace Jovanovich, 1977.
————. *World of Our Fathers.* Harcourt Brace Jovanovich, 1976.
Howells, Willian Dean. *Letters of an Altrurian Traveler.* Scholar's Facsimiles, 1961.
————. *A Modern Instance.* James R. Osgood, 1882; Penguin, 1984.
————. *The Sleeping Car and Other Farces.* Harper and Row, 1882.
Hoxie, Robert F. "The Convention of the Socialist Party, 1908." *Journal of Political Economy,* July 1908.
Hudson, Robert W. *The Writing Game.* Iowa State University, 1982.
Huebner, Lee. "The Discovery of Propaganda: Changing Attitudes toward Public Communication in America, 1900–1930." Ph.D. diss. Harvard University, 1968.
Hughes, Jonathan. *The Vital Few.* Houghton Mifflin, 1966.
Humphrey, Seth K. *Following the Prairie Frontier.* University of Minnesota Press, 1931.
Hunsberger, Willard D. *Clarence Darrow: A Bibliography.* Scarecrow Press, 1981.
Hunt, H. Draper. *Hannibal Hamlin of Maine: Lincoln's First Vice-President.* Syracuse University Press, 1969.
Hunt, Morton. *The Story of Psychology.* Doubleday, 1993.
Hunt, William R. *Front-Page Detective: William J. Burns and the Detective Profession, 1880–1930.* Bowling Green State University Popular Press, 1990.
Hunter, Robert. *Poverty.* Macmillan, 1906.
————. *Violence and the Labor Movement.* Macmillan, 1914.
Hurt, Walter. *The Scarlet Shadow.* Appeal to Reason, 1907.
Hutton, May Awkwright. *The Coeur d'Alenes, or a Tale of the Modern Inquisition in Idaho.* M. A. Hutton, 1935.
Hynd, Alan. *With the Pinkertons through the Labyrinth of Death.* Macfadden Publications Inc., 1941.
Idaho: A Guide in Words and Pictures. Oxford University Press, 1950.
An Illustrated History of North Idaho. Western Historical Publishing, 1903.
An Illustrated History of the State of Idaho. Lewis Publishing, 1899.
Irwin, Will. *The American Newspaper.* Ed. Clifford F. Weigle and David G. Clark. Iowa State University Press, 1969.
————. *The Making of a Reporter.* G. P. Putnam's Sons, 1942.
————. "What's Wrong with the Associated Press?" *Harper's,* March 28, 1914, 10–12.
Israel, Fred L. *The State of the Union Messages of the President, 1790–1966.* Chelsea House, 1966.
Jackson, John Brinckerhoff. *A Sense of Place, a Sense of Time.* Yale University Press, 1994.
James, Henry. *The American Scene.* Chapman and Hall, 1907; St. Martin's Press, 1987.
James, Ronald L. "Why No Chinamen Are Found in Twin Falls." *Idaho Yesterdays,* Winter 1993, 15–23.
Jameson, Elizabeth, "All That Glitters: Class, Culture and Community in the Cripple Creek District." Unpublished manuscript.
Jeffers, H. Paul. *Commissioner Roosevelt: The Story of Theodore Roosevelt and the New York City Police, 1895–97.* John Wiley and Sons, 1994.
Jenks, Tudor. "Can the Jury System Be Improved?" *Munsey's,* August 1903, 723–26.
Jensen, Vernon H. *Heritage of Conflict: Labor Relations in the Non-Ferrous Metals Industry up to 1930.* Cornell University Press, 1950.
Johannsen, Albert. *The House of Beadle and Adams, and Its Dime and Nickel Novels.* University of Oklahoma Press, 1950.
Johnson, Charles A. *Denver's Mayor Speer.* Bighorn Books, 1969.
Johnson, Claudius. *Borah of Idaho.* Longmans, Green, 1936.
————. "When William E. Borah Was Defeated for the United States Senate." *Pacific Historical Review,* June 1943, 129–37.
Johnson, Diane. *Dashiell Hammett: A Life.* Random House, 1983.
Johnson, Kendrick. "Trial of 'Big Bill' Haywood." *Nevada State Bar Journal,* 24, no. 3 (July 1959): 121–27.
Johnson, Walter. "My Pitching Years." *Washington Times,* January–February, 1925 (60-part syndicated series).
————. "Some Experiences of a Speed King." *St. Nicholas,* October 1914.
Johnson, Walter. *William Allen White's America.* Henry Holt, 1947.
Jones, Mary Harris. *Correspondence of Mother Jones.* Ed. Edward M. Steel. University of Pittsburgh Press, 1985.
Jones, Shawn. "The Road to Jackpot." *Idaho Yesterdays,* Spring 1989, 2–12.
Jones, Virgil Carrington. *Roosevelt's Rough Riders.* Doubleday, 1971.
Joyner, Charles W. "Undesirable Citizen: The Haywood Trial and the Press." Master's thesis, University of South Carolina, 1959.

Juergens, George. *News from the White House: The Presidential-Press Relationship in the Progressive Era.* University of Chicago Press, 1981.

Kahlenberg, Richard D. *The Remedy: Class, Race, and Affirmative Action.* Basic Books, 1996.

Kansas Legislature. Joint Committee of Investigation of Bribery and Corruption. *Report.* 1872.

Kaplan, Justin. *Mr. Clemens and Mr. Twain.* Simon & Schuster, 1966; Touchstone, 1982.

———. *Lincoln Steffens: A Biography.* Simon & Schuster, 1974.

Katz, William Loren. *The Black West.* Touchstone, 1996.

Kauffman, Christopher J. *Faith and Fraternalism: The History of the Knights of Columbus, 1882–1982.* Harper and Row, 1982.

Kaufmann, A. *Historic Supplement of the Denver Police: A Review from Earliest Days to the Present Time.* Police Mutual Aid Fund, 1890.

Kaun, Alexander. *Maxim Gorky and His Russia.* Cape and Smith, 1931.

Kavanagh, Jack. *Walter Johnson: A Life.* Diamond Communications, 1995.

Kayman, Martin. *From Bow Street to Baker Street.* Macmillan, 1992.

Kazin, Michael. *Barons of Labor: The San Francisco Building Trades and Union Power in the Progressive Era.* University of Illinois Press, 1987.

Keating, Edward. *The Gentleman from Colorado.* Sage Books, 1964.

Keller, Phyllis. *States of Belonging: German-American Intellectuals and the First World War.* Harvard University Press, 1979.

Kelly, Kevin. "The Molly Maguires and the Catholic Church." *Labor History,* Summer 1995, 345–76.

Kennan, George. *E. H. Harriman: A Biography.* Houghton Mifflin, 1922.

Keyser, Harriet A. *Bishop Potter, the People's Friend.* T. Whittaker, 1910.

King, Willard L. *Melville Weston Fuller: Chief Justice of the United States.* University of Chicago Press, 1950.

Kiple, Kenneth F. *Another Dimension to the Black Diaspora: Diet, Disease and Racism.* Cambridge University Press, 1981.

Kipnis, Ira. *The American Socialist Movement 1897–1912.* Monthly Review Press, 1952.

Kirk, Ruth, and Carmela Alexander. *Exploring Washington's Past: A Road Guide to History.* University of Washington Press, 1981.

Klaus, Samuel, ed. *The People of the State of New York against Roland Burnham Molineux.* Alfred A. Knopf, 1929.

Klein, Maury. *Union Pacific.* Vol 1: *The Birth of a Railroad 1862–1893,* vol. 2: *The Rebirth, 1894–1964.* Doubleday, 1987–89.

———. *The Life and Legend of Jay Gould.* Johns Hopkins University Press, 1986.

Kluger, Richard. *The Paper: The Life and Death of the New York Herald Tribune.* Vintage, 1989.

Knight, Oliver. "Robert E. Strahorn, Propagandist for the West." *Idaho Yesterdays,* January 1968, 33–45.

Kobler, John. *Damned in Paradise: The Life of John Barrymore.* Atheneum, 1977.

Koelsch, Charles F. *The Haywood Case.* Idaho Mining Association, 1946.

Koenigsberg, Moses. *King News—An Autobiography.* F. A. Stokes, 1941.

Kolko, Gabriel. *The Triumph of Conservatism.* Free Press, 1963.

Kotsilibas-Davis, James. *Great Times, Good Times.* Doubleday, 1977.

Krakel, Dean F. *The Saga of Tom Horn.* Powder River Publishers, 1954; University of Nebraska Press, 1982.

Kratville, William, and Harold E. Ranks. *Motive Power of the Union Pacific.* Barnhart Press, 1958.

Kreuter, Kent, and Gretchen Kreuter. *An American Dissenter: The Life of Algie Martin Simons, 1870–1950.* University of Kentucky Press, 1969.

Lancaster, Paul. *Gentleman of the Press: The Life and Times of an Early Reporter, Julian Ralph of the Sun.* Syracuse University Press, 1992.

Lane, F. C. "Pitching Science." *Baseball Magazine,* October 1913.

Lane, Roger. *Policing the City: Boston, 1822–1885.* Harvard University Press, 1967.

Langdon, Emma F. *The Cripple Creek Strike: A History of Industrial Wars in Colorado, 1903-4-5.* Great Western Publishing, 1905.

Langford, Gerald. *Alias O. Henry: A Biography of William Sidney Porter.* Macmillan, 1957.

———. *Labor's Greatest Conflicts.* Privately printed, n.d.

Larson, T. A. "Idaho's Role in America's Woman Suffrage Crusade." *Idaho Yesterdays,* Spring 1974, 2–15.

Laurie, Clayton D. *The U.S. Army and the Labor Radicals of Coeur d'Alene: Federal Military Intervention in the Mine Wars of 1892-1899.* U.S. Army Center of Military History, 1990.

Lavine, Sigmund A. *Allan Pinkerton: America's First Private Eye.* Dodd, Mead, 1963.

Leach, William. *Land of Desire: Merchants, Power and the Rise of a New American Culture.* Pantheon, 1993.

Leckie, William. *The Buffalo Soldiers: A Narrative of the Negro Cavalry in the West.* University of Oklahoma Press, 1967.

Leech, Margaret. *In the Days of McKinley.* Harper and Brothers, 1959.

LeFors, Joe. *Wyoming Peace Officer.* Powder River Publications, 1953.

Lehman, David. *The Perfect Murder: A Study in Detection.* Free Press, 1989.

Lens, Sidney. *The Labor Wars: From the Molly Maguires to the Sitdowns.* Doubleday, 1973.

Leppert, Elaine C., and Lorene B. Thurston. *Early Caldwell through Photographs.* Caxton Printers, 1990.

Levin, Nora. *While Messiah Tarried: Jewish Socialist Movements, 1871–1917.* Schocken, 1977.

Levy, Norman. *The Nan Patterson Case.* Simon & Schuster, 1959.

Lewis, Arthur H. *Lament for the Molly Maguires.* Harcourt, Brace, 1964.

Lewis, Philip C. *Trouping: How the Show Came to Town.* Harper and Row, 1973.

Lewis, R. W. B. *The Jameses.* Farrar, Straus and Giroux, 1991.

Lillard, Monique. "The Federal Court in Idaho, 1889–1907: The Appointment and Tenure of James H. Beatty, Idaho's First Federal District Court Judge." *Western Legal History,* 2, No. 1 Winter-Spring 1989, 34–78.

Limbaugh, Ronald H. *Rocky Mountain Carpetbaggers: Idaho's Territorial Governors, 1863–1890.* University Press of Idaho, 1982.

Limerick, Patricia Nelson. *Legacy of Conquest: The Unbroken Past of the American West.* W. W. Norton, 1987; pb. ed., 1988.

Lingenfelter, Richard E. *The Hardrock Miners: A History of the Mining Labor Movement in the American West, 1863–1893.* University of California Press, 1974.

Linn, James Weber. *Jane Addams.* Appleton-Century, 1935.

Livesay, Harold C. *Samuel Gompers and Organized Labor in America.* Little, Brown, 1978.

Livingston, John C. *Clarence Darrow: The Mind of a Sentimental Rebel.* Garland Publishing, 1988.

Livingston-Little, D. E. "The Bunker Hill and Sullivan: Northern Idaho's Mining Development from 1885 to 1900." *Idaho Yesterdays,* Spring 1963, 34–43.

Lloyd, Elizabeth. "America's Last Frontier." *Pacific Historian,* Summer 1975.

London, Jack. *The Letters of Jack London.* Ed. Earle Labor, Robert C. Leitz, and I. Milo Shepard. Stanford University Press, 1988.

———. *The Portable Jack London.* Ed. Earle Labor. Viking, 1984.

———. "Something Rotten in Idaho." *Daily Socialist,* November 4, 1906.

Long, Priscilla. *Where the Sun Never Shines: A History of America's Bloody Coal Industry.* Paragon House, 1989.

Longworth, Alice Roosevelt. *Crowded Hours.* Scribner's Sons, 1933.

Lord, Walter. *The Good Years: From 1900 to the First World War.* Harper and Brothers, 1960.

Lovin, Hugh. "Sage, Jacks and Snake Plain Pioneers," *Idaho Yesterdays,* Winter 1979, 13–24.

Lowell, Helen, and Lucile Peterson. *Our First Hundred Years: A Biography of Lower Boise Valley, 1814–1914.* Caxton Printers, 1976.

Lubow, Arthur. *The Reporter Who Would Be King: A Biography of Richard Harding Davis.* Scribner's, 1992.

Luhan, Mabel Dodge. *Movers and Shakers.* Harcourt, Brace, 1936.

Lutz, Tom. *American Nervousness, 1903.* Cornell University Press, 1991.

Lynch, George, ed. *In Many Wars.* Tokyo Printing, 1904.

Lyon, Peter. *Success Story: The Life and Times of S. S. McClure.* Charles Scribner's Sons, 1963.

Mackay, James. *Allan Pinkerton: The Eye Who Never Slept.* Mainstream Publishing, 1996.

MacKenzie, F. A. *The Trial of Harry Thaw.* Geoffrey Bles, 1918.

MacKenzie, John P. *The Appearance of Justice.* Charles Scribner's Sons, 1974.

MacLane, John F. *A Sagebrush Lawyer.* Pandick Press, 1953.

Magnuson, Richard G. *Coeur d'Alene Diary: The First Ten Years of Hardrock Mining in North Idaho.* Metropolitan Press, 1968.

Maiken, Peter T. *Night Trains: The Pullman System in the Golden Years of American Rail Travel.* Lakme Press, 1989.

Malone, Michael P. *The Battle for Butte: Mining and Politics on the Northern Frontier, 1864–1906.* University of Washington Press, 1981.

———. *C. Ben Ross and the New Deal in Idaho.* University of Washington Press, 1970.

Maloney, Martin. "Clarence Darrow." *A History and Criticism of American Public Address.* Ed. M. K. Hochmuth, vol. 3. Russell and Russell, 1965. 262–312.

Maney, Richard. *Fanfare: The Confessions of a Press Agent.* Harper and Brothers, 1957.

Marbut, F. B. *News from the Capital: The Story of Washington Reporting.* Southern Illinois University Press, 1971.

Marcaccio, Michael D. *The Hapgoods: Three Earnest Brothers.* University Press of Virginia, 1977.

Marcossan, Isaac F. *David Graham Phillips and His Times.* Dodd, Mead, 1932.

Marcossan, Isaac F., and Daniel Frohman. *Charles Frohman: Manager and Man.* Harper and Brothers, 1916.

Martin, Ralph. *Cissy: The Extraordinary Life of Eleanor Medill Patterson.* Simon & Schuster, 1979.

Masters, Edgar Lee. *Across Spoon River.* Farrar and Rinehart, 1936.

———. "Clarence Darrow." *New Republic,* September 27, 1922; May 17, 1957, 16.

———. *Songs and Satires.* Macmillan, 1916.

———. *The Tale of Chicago.* G. P. Putnam's Sons, 1933.

Masterson, V. V. *The Katy Railroad and the Last Frontier.* University of Oklahoma Press, 1978.

Mathews, Franklin. "Murder as a Labor Weapon." *Harper's,* June 2, 1906, 766–68.

May, Henry F. *Protestant Churches and Industrial America.* Octagon Books, 1963.

Mazzulla, Fred, and Jo Mazzula. *Brass Checks and Red Lights.* Privately published, 1966.

McCague, James. *Fiddle Hill.* Crown, 1960.

McClintic, Guthrie. *Me and Kit.* Atlantic Monthly Press, 1955.

McClure, S. S. *My Autobiography.* Ed. Frederick A. Stokes, 1914.

McConnell, William John. *Early History of Idaho.* Caxton Printers, 1913.

McCormick, John. *Salt Lake City: The Gathering Place.* Windsor Publications, 1980.

McCormick, Richard. *From Realignment to Reform: Political Change in New York State, 1893–1910.* Cornell University Press, 1979.

McDermott, E. F. "Calvin Cobb: Independent Pioneer." *Idaho Daily Statesman,* July 26, 1964.

McDevitt, Mathew. *Joseph McKenna: Associate Justice of the United States.* Catholic University Press, 1946.

McGeary, M. Nelson. *Gifford Pinchot: Forester-Politician.* Princeton University Press, 1960.

McGovern, George, and Leonard F. Guttridge. *The Great Coalfield War.* Houghton Mifflin, 1972.

McKenna, Marian. *Borah.* University of Michigan Press, 1961.

McLean, Joseph E. *William Rufus Day: Supreme Court Justice from Ohio.* Johns Hopkins University Press, 1946.

McLynn, Frank. *Robert Louis Stevenson: A Biography.* Random House, 1993.

McNamara, Brooks. *The Shuberts of Broadway.* Oxford University Press, 1990.

McNaught, Kenneth. *The History of Canada.* Praeger, 1970.

McPherson, James M. *The Negro's Civil War.* Pantheon, 1965. Ballantine, 1991.

McWatters, George C. *Knots Untied: Or Ways and By-Ways in the Hidden Life of American Detectives.* J. B. Burr and Hyde, 1871.

Meador, John Daniel. *Habeas Corpus and Magna Carta: Dualism of Power and Liberty.* University of Virginia Press, 1966.

Meadows, Anne. *Digging Up Butch and Sundance.* St. Martin's Press, 1994.

Melish, John Howard. *Autumn Days and Recollections.* Bromwell Press, 1954.

Melville Stone, "M.E.S." His Book: A Tribute and a Souvenir of the 25 Years, 1893–1918, of Service of Melville E. Stone as General Manager of the Associated Press. Harper Brothers, 1918.

Mencken, H. L. *The Diary of H. L. Mencken.* Ed. Charles A. Fecher. Alfred A. Knopf, 1989.

——. *Mencken Prejudices: A Selection.* Ed. James T. Farrell. Vintage, 1968.

Mercer, Asa Shinn. *The Banditti of the Plains.* University of Oklahoma Press, 1954.

Merriam, H. C. *Report on Miners' Riots in Idaho.* 56th Cong., 1st sess., 1899. S. Doc. 86 and 142.

Messing, John. "Public Lands, Politics and Progressives: The Oregon Land Fraud Trials, 1903–10." *Pacific Historical Review,* vol. 35 (1966): 39–41.

Mickelson, Sig. *The Northern Pacific and the Selling of the West.* Center for Western Studies, 1993.

Milburn, George. "The 'Appeal to Reason.'" *American Mercury,* July 1931, 359–71.

Miller, Kristie. *Ruth Hanna McCormick: A Life in Politics, 1880–1944.* University of New Mexico Press, 1922.

Miller, Max. *Holladay Street.* Signet, 1962.

Miller, Nathan. *Theodore Roosevelt: A Life.* William Morrow, 1992.

Miller, Wilbur R. "The Dime Novel Nuisance: Popular Perceptions of Crime and Punishment, 1880–1920." Master's thesis, Columbia University, 1967.

Milton, Joyce. *The Yellow Kids: Foreign Correspondents in the Heyday of Yellow Journalism.* Harper and Row, 1989.

Miner, Lewis S. *Front Lines and Headlines: The Story of Richard Harding Davis.* Julian Messner, 1959.

Mitchell, John C. *Autobiography.* Privately printed., n.d. Unitarian Universalist Minister Files. Andover-Harvard Theological Library, Cambridge, Mass.

Montgomery, David. *The Fall of the House of Labor.* Cambridge University Press, 1987.

Montgomery, James. "Harry Orchard, Sinner or Saint?" *Pacific Northwesterner,* Fall 1975, 49–59.

——. *Liberated Woman: A Life of May Awkwright Hutton.* Ye Galleon Press, 1985.

Mooney, Michael MacDonald. *Evelyn Nesbit and Stanford White.* William Morrow, 1976.

Moorehead, Alan. *The Russian Revolution.* Harper and Row, 1958.

Mordell, Albert. *Clarence Darrow, Eugene V. Debs and Haldeman-Julius: Incidents in the Career of an Author, Editor and Publisher.* Haldeman-Julius, 1950.

Morn, Frank. *The Eye That Never Sleeps: A History of the Pinkerton National Detective Agency.* Indiana University Press, 1982.

Morris, Edmund. *The Rise of Theodore Roosevelt.* Random House, 1979.

Morris, Lloyd. *Postscript to Yesterday: American Life and Thought, 1896–1946.* Harper Colophon, 1965.

Moses, Montrose J., and Virginia Gerson. *Clyde Fitch and His Letters.* Little, Brown, 1924.

Mott, Frank Luther. *American Journalism: A History of Newspapers in the United States through 250 Years, 1690 to 1940.* Macmillan, 1947.

Mowry, George. *The Era of Theodore Roosevelt and the Birth of Modern America, 1900–1912.* Harper Torchbooks, 1958.

Muller, William G. *The Twenty-fourth Infantry: Past and Present.* Privately published, 1972.

Münsterberg, Hugo. *The Americans.* McClure, Phillips, 1904.

——. "The Case of the Reporter." *McClure's Magazine,* February 1911.

——. "Experiments with Harry Orchard." Unpublished manuscript. Münsterberg Papers, Boston Public Library.

——. "A German Talks to the Germans." August 1898. Hugo Münsterberg Papers, Harvard University Archives.

——. *On the Witness Stand: Essays on Psychology and Crime.* Doubleday, Page, 1908.

——. "The Third Degree." *McClure's,* October 1907.

Münsterberg, Margaret. *Hugo Münsterberg: His Life and Work.* D. Appleton, 1922.

Murbarger, Neil. *Ghosts of the Glory Trail.* Desert Magazine Press, 1956.

Murphy, Clyde. *Glittering Hill.* World Publishing, 1944.

Murphy, Patrick. *Behind Gray Walls.* Caxton Printers, 1927.

Murray, John Wilson. *Memoirs of a Great Detective: Incidents in the Life of John Wilson Murray.* Ed. Victor Speer. Baker and Taylor, 1905.

Murray, Keith. "Issues and Personalities of Pacific Northwest Politics." *Pacific Northwest Quarterly,* July 1950.

Nathan, George Jean. *Intimate Notebooks of George Jean Nathan.* Alfred A. Knopf, 1932.

Nevins, Allan. *Grover Cleveland: A Study in Courage.* Dodd, Mead, 1932.

——, ed. *The Letters and Journal of Brand Whitlock.* 2 vols. D. Appleton-Century, 1936.

Nicholson, James R., and Lee A. Donaldson. *History of the Order of Elks, 1868–1967.* National Memorial and Publication Commission of the Benevolent and Protective Order of Elks, n.d.

Nock, O. S. *Great Steam Locomotives of All Time.* Blandford Press, 1976.

Noel, Thomas J. *The City and the Saloon: Denver, 1858–1916.* University of Nebraska Press, 1982; pb. ed., 1985.

——. *Denver's Larimer Street: Main Street, Skid Row and Urban Renaissance.* Historic Denver, 1981.

Nord, David Paul. *Newspapers and New Politics: Midwestern Municipal Reform.* UMI Research Press, 1981.

Norris, Frank. *The Octopus.* Doubleday, 1952.

——. *The Pit: A Story of Chicago.* Doubleday, Page, 1903.

Novak, Michael. *The Guns of Latimer.* Basic Books, 1978.

Numbers, Ronald. *Prophetess of Health.* Harper and Row, 1975.

O'Brien, Frank M. *The Story of the Sun, 1833–1918.* George H. Doran, 1918.

O'Connor, Harvey. *Revolution in Seattle.* Monthly Review Press, 1964.

O'Connor, Richard. *Bat Masterson.* Doubleday, 1957.

——. *Courtroom Warrior: The Combative Career of William Travers Jerome.* Little, Brown, 1963.

The Official History of the Great Strike of 1886 on the Southwestern Railway System. Missouri Bureau of Labor Statistics, 1887.

Official Proceedings of the Fifteenth Annual Convention, Western Federation of Miners, Denver, June 10–July 3, 1907. Western Federation of Miners Collection. University of Colorado, Boulder.

Orchard, Harry [Albert E. Horsley], with L. E. Froom. *The Man God Made Again,* Southern Publishing Association, 1952.

Osborn, Scott C., and Robert L. Phillips, Jr. *Richard Harding Davis.* Twayne, 1978.

O'Toole, Patricia. *The Five of Hearts: An Intimate Portrait of Henry Adams and His Friends, 1880–1918.* Clarkson Potter, 1990.

"Our Jury System." *Nation,* May 9, 1895, 357.

Ousby, Ian. *The Bloodhounds of Heaven: The Detective in English Fiction from Godwin to Doyle.* Harvard University Press, 1976.

Painter, Nell Irvin. *Standing at Armageddon: The United States, 1877–1919.* W. W. Norton, 1987.

Palladino, Grace. *Another Civil War: Labor, Capital and the State in the Anthracite Regions of Pennsylvania, 1840–1868.* University of Illinois Press, 1990.

Palmer, Frederick. "Pinchot's Fight for the Trees." *Collier's,* November 30, 1907.

———. *With My Own Eyes.* Bobbs-Merrill, 1932.

Parkhill, Forbes. *The Wildest of the Wild.* Sage Books, 1951.

Parton, Margaret. *Journey through a Lighted Room.* Viking, 1973.

Paul, Rodman. *The Far West and the Great Plains in Transition.* Harper and Row, 1988.

Payne, Elizabeth. *Reform, Labor and Feminism: Margaret Dreier Robins and the Women's Trade Union League.* University of Illinois Press, 1988.

Pearson, Charles H. *National Life and Character.* Macmillan, 1893.

Peavy, Charles D. *Charles A. Siringo: A Texas Picaro.* Steck-Vaughn, 1967.

Pennsylvania Senate. *Report of the Committee on the Judiciary of the Senate of Pennsylvania.* B. Singerly, 1871.

Penson, Betty. "Who Was Calvin Cobb?" *Idaho Daily Statesman,* August 15, 1976. 16C.

Perkin, Robert L. *The First Hundred Years.* Doubleday, 1959.

Perry, John. *Jack London: An American Myth.* Nelson-Hall, 1981.

Perry, Ralph Barton. *The Thought and Character of William James.* Harvard University Press, 1948.

Peters, Margot. *The House of Barrymore.* Alfred A. Knopf, 1990.

Peterson, F. Ross. *Idaho: A Bicentennial History.* W. W. Norton, 1976.

Peterson, Richard H. "Simeon Gannett Reed and the Bunker Hill and Sullivan: The Frustrations of a Mining Investor." *Idaho Yesterdays,* Fall 1979.

———. "The Social and Political Behavior of Simeon Gannett Reed." *Idaho Yesterdays,* 24, no. 3 (Fall 1980): 32–34.

Phillips, Blaine. "The Trouble with Idaho." *Northwest Magazine,* November 1906.

Phipps, Stanley Stewart. *From Bull Pen to Bargaining Table: The Tumultuous Struggle of the Coeur d'Alene Miners for the Right to Organize, 1877–1942.* Garland, 1988.

Pinchot, Gifford. *Breaking New Ground.* Harcourt, Brace, 1947.

———. *The Fight for Conservation.* University of Washington Press, 1910.

Pingenot, Ben E. *Siringo.* Texas A and M Press, 1989.

Pinkerton, Allan. *The Molly Maguires and the Detectives.* G. W. Dillingham, 1877.

———. *The Spy of the Rebellion.* M. A. Winter and Hatch, 1883; University of Nebraska Press, 1989.

———. *Strikers, Communists, Tramps and Detectives.* G. W. Carleton, 1878.

———. *Thirty Years a Detective.* G. W. Dillingham, 1884.

Pinkett, Harold T. *Gifford Pinchot: Private and Public Forester.* University of Illinois Press, 1970.

Pipes, Richard. *The Russian Revolution.* Alfred A. Knopf, 1990.

Pointer, Larry. *In Search of Butch Cassidy.* University of Oklahoma Press, 1977.

Pomeroy, Earl. *In Search of the Golden West: The Tourist in Western America.* Alfred A. Knopf, 1957; University of Nebraska Press, 1990.

Popkin, Zelda. "The Great McParland," unpublished manuscript.

Prassel, Frank Richard. *The Western Peace Officer.* University of Oklahoma Press, 1972.

Pratt, Norma Fain. *Morris Hillquit: A Political History of an American Jewish Socialist.* Greenwood Press, 1979.

Prentiss, A. *The History of the Utah Volunteers in the Spanish-American War.* Tribune Publishing, 1900.

Preston, William, Jr. *Aliens and Dissenters: Federal Suppression of Radicals, 1903–33.* Harvard University Press, 1963.

Pringle, Henry F. "His Master's Voice." *American Mercury,* October 1926.

———. *The Life and Times of William Howard Taft.* Vol. 1. Farrar and Rinehart, 1939.

———. *Theodore Roosevelt: A Biography.* Harcourt, Brace, 1931.

Pritchett, Henry S. "The Politics of a Pullman Car." *Atlantic,* August 1909.

Pullen, John J. *The Twentieth Maine: A Volunteer Regiment in the Civil War.* Lippincott, 1957.

Putnam, Cora. *The Story of Houlton.* House of Falmouth, 1958.

Putnam, Edison K. "Travail at the Turn of the Century: Efforts at Liquor Control in Idaho." *Idaho Yesterdays,* Spring 1989.

Quarles, Benjamin. *The Negro in the Civil War.* Little, Brown, 1953; pb. ed., De Capo, 1989.

Quint, Howard. "The *Challenge* and *Wilshire's Magazine.*" *The American Radical Press,* 1880–1960. Ed. Joseph R. Conlin. Vol. 1, 72–81. Greenwood Press, 1974.

———. *The Forging of American Socialism: Origins of the Modern Movement.* Bobbs-Merrill, 1953.

———. "Gaylord Wilshire and Socialism's First Congressional Campaign." *Pacific Historical Review,* November 1957, 327–40.

Rainsford, William. *The Story of a Varied Life: An Autobiography.* Doubleday, Page, 1920.

Ralph, Julian. "The City of Brooklyn." *Harper's Monthly,* April 1873.

———. *The Making of a Journalist.* Harper and Brothers, 1903.

Rastall, Benjamin M. *The Labor History of the Cripple Creek District: A Study in Industrial Evolution.* University of Wisconsin, 1908.

Ravitz, Abe C. *Clarence Darrow and the American Liberal Tradition.* Press of Western Reserve University, 1962.

Ravitz, Abe C., and James N. Primm, eds. *The Haywood Case: Materials for Analysis.* Chandler Publishing, 1960.
"Receipts and Disbursements, Defense Fund, February 1906–April 1907," *Official Proceedings of the Fifteenth Annual Convention, Western Federation of Miners,* Denver, June 10–July 3, 1907. Western Federation of Miners Collection. University of Colorado, Boulder.
Reeve, Carl. *The Life and Times of Daniel De Leon.* Humanities Press, 1972.
Remington, John Alan. "Violence in Labor Disputes: The Haywood Trial." Master's thesis, University of Wyoming, 1965.
Reynolds, Robert Dwight, Jr. "The Millionaire Socialists: J. G. Phelps Stokes and His Circle of Friends." Ph.D diss., University of South Carolina, 1974.
Rich, Bennett Milton. *The President and Civil Disorders.* Brookings Institution, 1941.
Rider, Eugene Frank. "The Denver Police Department: An Administrative, Organizational and Operational History." Ph.D. diss., University of Denver, 1971.
Rischin, Moses. *The Promised City.* Harvard University Press, 1962.
Ritchie, Donald. *Press Gallery: Congress and the Washington Correspondents.* Harvard University Press, 1991.
Ritter, Lawrence. *The Glory of Their Times.* Morrow, 1984.
Robbins, Roy M. *Our Landed Heritage: The Public Domain, 1776–1936.* Princeton University Press, 1942.
Robertson, Frank C. *A Ram in the Thicket: The Story of a Roaming Homesteader on the Mormon Frontier.* University of Idaho Press, 1994.
Robinson, Phyllis. *Willa: The Life of Willa Cather.* Doubleday, 1983.
Rocha, Guy Louis. " 'Big Bill' Haywood and Humboldt County: The Making of a Revolutionary." *Humboldt Historian,* Spring-Summer 1985.
Roediger, David, and Phyllis Boanes. *Haymarket Heritage: The Memoirs of Irving S. Abrams.* Charles H. Kerr Publishing, 1989.
Rogers, James Edward. *The American Newspaper.* University of Chicago Press, 1909.
Ronda, James P. *Lewis and Clark among the Indians.* University of Nebraska Press, 1984.
Roosevelt, T., and Albert B. Hart, eds. *Theodore Roosevelt Cyclopedia.* Theodore Roosevelt Association, 1989.
Roosevelt, Theodore. *An Autobiography.* Charles Scribner's Sons, 1913; De Capo, 1985.
———. "The Rough Riders." *Scribner's,* April 1899, 420–40.
———. "With the Cougar Hounds." *Scribner's,* October 1901.
Rosa, Joseph G. *The Gunfighter.* University of Oklahoma Press, 1969.
Rosebault, Charles J. *When Dana Was the Sun.* R. M. McBridge, 1931.
Rosenzweig, Saul. *Freud, Jung and Hall the King-Maker: The Expedition to America (1909).* Hogrefe and Huber, 1992.
Ross, Ishbel. *Ladies of the Press.* Arno Press, 1974.
Rowan, Richard Wilmer. *The Pinkertons: A Detective Dynasty.* Little, Brown, 1931.
Russell, Charles Edward. *Bare Hands and Stone Walls: Some Recollections of a Side-Line Reformer.* Scribners, 1933.
———. *These Shifting Scenes.* Hodder and Stoughton, 1914.
Russell, Jo Anne. "A Necessary Evil: Prostitutes, Patriarchs and Profits in Boise City, 1863–1915." Master's thesis, Boise State University, 1983.
Salvatore, Nick. *Eugene V. Debs: Citizen and Socialist.* University of Illinois Press, 1982.
———. *We All Got History: The Memory Books of Amos Webber.* Times Books, 1996.
Salzman, Neil V. *The Life and Times of Raymond Robins.* Kent State University Press, 1991.
Samuels, Ernest. *Henry Adams.* Harvard University Press, 1989.
Sanders, Ronald. *The Downtown Jews: Portraits of an Immigrant Generation.* Harper and Row, 1969; Dover, 1987.
Sante, Luc. *Low Life: Lures and Snares of Old New York.* Farrar, Straus and Giroux, 1991.
Saum, Lewis O. *The Popular Mood of America, 1860–1890.* University of Nebraska Press, 1990.
Sawey, Orlan. *Charles A. Siringo.* Twayne, 1981.
Sayer, James Edward. *Clarence Darrow: Public Advocate.* Wright State University Press, 1978.
Scheidecker, David. "Northwestern University Football, 1906–8: Suspension and Resumption." Unpublished paper, Northwestern University.
Scheinberg, Stephen. "Theodore Roosevelt's 'Undesirable Citizens.' " *Idaho Yesterdays,* Fall 1960, 10–15.
Schlegel, Marvin W. *Ruler of the Reading: The Life of Franklin B. Gowen, 1836–1889.* Archives, 1947.
Schlereth, Thomas J. *Victorian America: Transformations in Everyday Life, 1876–1915.* Harper Perennial, 1991.
Schlesinger, Arthur. *Paths to the Present.* Macmillan, 1949.
Schudson, Michael. *Discovering the News: A Social History of American Newspapers.* Basic Books, 1978.
Schultz, Lois. *History of the Caldwell Seventh-Day Adventist Church.* Pamphlet, n.d.
Schwantes, Carlos. *Coxey's Army: An American Odyssey.* University of Nebraska Press, 1985.
———. *In Mountain Shadows: A History of Idaho.* University of Nebraska Press, 1991.
———. "Law and Disorder: The Suppression of Coxey's Army in Idaho." *Idaho Yesterdays,* Summer 1981, 10–15.
———. *The Pacific Northwest.* University of Nebraska Press, 1989.
———. *Radical Heritage: Labor, Socialism and Reform in Washington and British Columbia.* University of Washington Press, 1979.
Schwartz, Bernard. *A History of the Supreme Court.* Oxford University Press, 1993; pb. ed., 1995.
Schwartz, Hillel. *Century's End: A Cultural History of the Fin de Siècle.* Doubleday, 1990.
Schwarzlose, Richard A. *The Rush to Institution, from 1865 to 1920.* Northwestern University Press, 1990.
Scipio, L. Albert II. *Last of the Black Regulars: A History of the Twenty-fourth Infantry Regiment, 1869–1951.* Roman Publications, 1983.
Scott, James Alexander. *The Law of Interstate Rendition.* Sherman Hight, 1917.
Seale, William. *The President's House: A History.* Vol. 2. White House Historical Association, 1986.
———. *The White House: The History of an American Idea.* American Institute of Architects Press, 1992.
Sedgwick, Ellery. *The Happy Profession.* Little, Brown, 1946.

Segal, Clancy. *Going Away: A Report, a Memoir.* Houghton Mifflin, 1962.
Sereikol, George Eugene. "Chicago and Its Book Trade, 1871–1893." Ph.D diss., Case Western Reserve University, School of Library Science, 1973.
Seretan, L. Glen. *Daniel De Leon: The Odyssey of an American Marxist.* Harvard University Press, 1979.
Sergeant, Elizabeth Shepley. *Willa Cather: A Memoir.* Ohio University Press, 1992.
Severy, Melvin L. *Gillette's Social Redemption.* Herbert B. Turner, 1907.
Seymour, Harold. *Baseball: The Golden Age.* Oxford University Press, 1971.
———. *Baseball: The People's Game.* Oxford University Press, 1990.
Shaara, Michael. *The Killer Angels.* Ballantine, 1974.
Shabecoff, Philip. *A Fierce Green Fire: The American Environmental Movement.* Hill and Wang, 1993.
Shannon, David A. *The Socialist Party of America: A History.* Macmillan, 1955.
Shaplen, Robert. *Free Love and Heavenly Sinners.* Alfred A. Knopf, 1954.
Shearer, Frederick. *The Pacific Tourist: A Complete Travel Guide of the Union and Central Pacific Railroads.* J. R. Bowman, 1915.
Shinn, Charles Howard. *Mining Camps.* Alfred A. Knopf, 1948.
Shirley, Glenn. *Belle Starr and Her Times.* University of Oklahoma Press, 1982.
Shoaf, George H. "The Biggest Little Paper This Country Ever Knew." *Monthly Review,* July 1951, 88–98.
———. "Debs and the *Appeal to Reason:* A Personal Memoir." *American Socialist,* November 1955.
———. *Fighting for Freedom.* Simplified Economics, 1953.
———. "A House of Horrors." *Appeal to Reason.* June 9, 1906, 2.
———. *Love Crucified: A Romance of the Colorado War.* Appeal Publishing, 1905.
———. *Who Blew Up the Independence Depot?* Appeal to Reason, 1906.
Shore, Elliott. *Talkin' Socialism: The Story of Appeal to Reason.* University Press of Kansas, 1988.
Short, Brant. "Socialism in Minidoka County, 1912–16." *Idaho Yesterdays,* Summer 1982, 3–38.
Sims, Robert, and Hope A. Benedict. *Idaho's Governors: Historical Essays on Their Administrations.* Boise State University, 1978.
Sinclair, Andrew. *Jack: A Biography of Jack London.* Harper and Row, 1977.
Sinclair, Bartlett. "Some Reminiscences of Governor Steunenberg." *Idaho Daily Statesman,* January 4, 1906.
Sinclair, Upton. *The Autobiography of Upton Sinclair.* Harcourt, Brace and World, 1962.
———. *The Brass Check.* Published by author, 1919.
———. *The Jungle.* Doubleday, Page, 1906.
Siringo, Charles. *A Cowboy Detective.* University of Nebraska Press, 1957.
———. *Riata and Spurs.* Houghton Mifflin, 1927.
———. *A Texas Cowboy.* University of Nebraska Press, 1979.
———. *Two Evil Isms: Pinkertonism and Anarchism.* Charles Siringo, 1913.
Sklar, Kathryn Kish. *Florence Kelley and the Nation's Work: The Rise of Women's Political Culture, 1830–1900.* Yale University Press, 1995.
Skrupskelis, Igas K., and Elizabeth M. Berkeley, eds. *William and Henry, 1885–1896.* Vol. 2 of *The Correspondence of William James.* University Press of Virginia, 1993.
Sladden, Thomas A. "A Few Words with the Socialists," *Socialist,* August 10, 1907.
Slotkin, Richard. *The Fatal Environment: The Myth of the Frontier in the Age of Industrialization.* Atheneum, 1985.
———. *Gunfighter Nation.* Atheneum, 1993.
Smalley, Eugene V. "1884: The Great Coeur d'Alene Stampede." *Idaho Yesterdays,* Fall 1967.
Smith, Carl S. *Chicago and the American Literary Imagination.* University of Chicago Press, 1984.
Smith, David B. "Honoré Joseph Jaxon: A Man Who Lived for Others." *Saskatchewan History,* August 1981, 81–101.
Smith, Duane A. *The Birth of Colorado: A Civil War Perspective.* University of Oklahoma Press, 1989.
Smith, H. Allen. *The Life and Legend of Gene Fowler.* Morrow, 1977.
Smith, Robert Wayne. *The Coeur d'Alene Mining War of 1892: A Case Study of an Industrial Dispute.* Peter Smith, 1968.
Smith, Ronald A., ed. *Big-Time Football at Harvard, 1905: The Diary of Coach Bill Reid.* University of Illinois Press, 1994.
"Socialist Party: How to Organize a Socialist Local or Branch." R.G. 28, Post Office, Item 529, Box 13. National Archives.
Spaeth, Sigmund. *Weep Some More, My Lady.* Doubleday, 1927.
Spearman, Frank. *Whispering Smith.* Grosset and Dunlop, 1906.
Spencer, Gladys. *The Chicago Public Library: Origins and Background.* University of Chicago Press, 1943.
Sprague, Marshall. *Money Mountain: The Story of Cripple Creek Gold.* Little, Brown, 1953.
———. *Newport in the Rockies.* Ohio University Press, 1987.
Stave, Bruce, ed. *Socialism and the Cities.* Kennikat Press, 1975.
Steele, Philip W. *Starr Tracks: Belle and Pearl Starr.* Pelican Publishing, 1989.
Steevens, G. W. *The Land of the Dollar.* Dodd, Mead, 1898.
Steffens, Lincoln. *The Autobiography of Lincoln Steffens.* Harcourt, Brace, 1931.
———. "The Taming of the West: Discovery of the Land Fraud System—a Detective Story." *American,* May 1907, 489–505.
Stern, Robert A. M., Gregory Gilmartin, and John Massengale. *New York 1900.* Rizzoli, 1983.
Steunenberg, A. K. "From Fraternity to Paternity: The Caldwell Brotherhood of Bachelors." *Idaho Yesterdays,* Winter 1966–67, 18–21.
Steunenberg, Bess. "Early Days in Caldwell." *Idaho Yesterdays,* Winter 1966–67, 12–17.
Steunenberg, Frank, Jr. *Greater Love.* Pacific Press Publishing, 1952.
———. *The Martyr of Idaho.* Color Press, 1974.
Steunenberg Memorial. Capital News Publishing, 1929.
Stevenson, Robert Louis. *Across the Plains: Leaves from the Notebook of an Emigrant between New York and San Francisco.* Charles Scribner's Sons, 1892.

Stoll, William T. *Silver Strike: The True Story of Silver Mining in the Coeur d'Alenes*. Little, Brown, 1932.

Stone, Candace. *Dana and the Sun*. George H. Doran, 1938.

Stone, Irving. *Clarence Darrow for the Defense*. Doubleday, 1941; Signet, 1969.

———. *Sailor on Horseback: The Biography of Jack London*. Houghton Mifflin, 1938.

Stone, Melville. "The AP and Its Maligners." *Chautauqua*, August 1912.

———. *Fifty Years a Journalist*. Doubleday, Page, 1921.

Stone, Thomas. *Miners' Justice: Migration, Law and Order on the Alaskan Frontier, 1873–1902*. American University Studies, series 11, vol. 34. P. Long, 1988.

Stone, W. F., ed. *Supplement to the History of Colorado*. S. J. Clarke Publishing, 1918.

Strahorn, Carrie Adell. *Fifteen Thousand Miles by Stage*. 2 vols. (1: 1877–80, 2: 1880–98). University of Nebraska Press, 1988.

Strahorn, Robert E. *The Resources and Attractions of Idaho Territory*. Published and circulated by direction of the Idaho Legislature, Idaho State Historical Society, Boise.

———. *Ninety Years of Boyhood*. Unpublished autobiography, Idaho State Historical Society, Boise.

Stromquist, Sheldon. *A Generation of Boomers: The Pattern of Railroad Labor Conflict in Nineteenth-Century America*. University of Illinois Press, 1987.

Suehsdorf, A. D. "Too Much Johnson." *Baseball History*, Winter 1987–88.

Suggs, George G., Jr. *Colorado's War on Militant Unionism: James H. Peabody and the Western Federation of Miners*. Wayne State University Press, 1972.

———. "Religion and Labor in the Rocky Mountain West: Bishop Nicholas C. Matz and the Western Federation of Miners." *Labor History*, April 1970, 190–206.

Sullivan, Elizabeth. "Paul Corcoran, Miner and Labor Leader." Unpublished manuscript February 1974. In possession of Corcoran family.

Sullivan, Mark. *Our Times in the United States (1900–1925)*. 3 vols. Charles Scribner's Sons, 1927.

Summers, Mark Wahlgren. *The Press Gang: Newspapers and Politics, 1865–1878*. University of North Carolina Press, 1994.

Swanberg, W. A. *Citizen Hearst: A Biography of William Randolph Hearst*. Charles Scribner's Sons, 1961.

———. *Pulitzer*. Charles Scribner's Sons, 1967.

Taft, Philip. *Organized Labor in American History*. Harper and Row, 1964.

Tarbell, Ida M. *All in a Day's Work*. Macmillan, 1939.

Teague, Michael. *Mrs. L: Conversations with Alice Roosevelt Longworth*. Doubleday, 1981.

This Is Caldwell, Idaho: A Report on City Government and Civic Life. League of Women Voters, Caldwell, 1960.

Thomas, Henry W. *Walter Johnson: Baseball's Big Train*. Phenom Press, 1995.

Thorwald, Jurgen. *The Century of the Detective*. Harcourt, Brace and World, 1965.

Thurner, Arthur W., "Charles H. Moyer and the Michigan Copper Strike, 1913–14." *Michigan Historical Review*, Autumn 1991, 1–19.

Tierney, Kevin. *Darrow: A Biography*. Thomas Y. Crowell, 1979.

Tietjen, Randall. "Professional and Personal Letterheads of Clarence Darrow." Unpublished monograph.

Titus, Hattie Wite. "The Secret Kidnapping." *Socialist*, July 26, 1906.

Toal, Helen Marie Keppel. "Keppel Family History: Holland to America." In possession of George Crookham, Caldwell, Idaho.

Torbert, J. Keith. "Let Us Foregather: The Biography of Martin Egan." Unpublished manuscript in the Martin Egan Collection, Morgan Library, New York.

Townsend, Kim. *Manhood at Harvard: William James and Others*. W. W. Norton, 1976.

Trachtenberg, Alan. *The Incorporation of America: Culture and Society in the Gilded Age*. Hill and Wang, 1982.

Train, Arthur. *Courts, Criminals and the Camorra*. Charles Scribner's Sons, 1912.

———. "Detectives and Detectives' Work." *Collier's*, August 5, 1911.

———. "Detectives Who Detect." *Collier's*, September 16, 1911.

———. "The Private Detective's Work." *Collier's* November 18, 1911.

Trask, David. *The War with Spain in 1898*. Macmillan, 1981.

Treat, Roger L. *Walter Johnson: King of the Pitchers*. Julian Messner, 1948.

Trimble, William J. *The Mining Advance into the Inland Empire. Bulletin of the University of Wisconsin*, 1914.

Troy, Gil. *See How They Ran: The Changing Role of the Presidential Candidate*. Free Press, 1991.

Troyat, Henri. *Gorky: A Biography*. Crown, 1989.

Tucher, Andie. *Froth and Scum: Truth, Beauty, Goodness and the Ax Murder in America's First Mass Medium*. University of North Carolina Press, 1994.

Tuchman, Barbara, *The Proud Tower*. Macmillan, 1966; pb. ed., Bantam, 1981.

Tucker, Ray, and Frederick R. Barkley. *Sons of the Wild Jackass*. Books for Libraries, 1969.

Turner, Frederick Jackson. *The Frontier in American History*. Holt, 1920.

Turner, George Kibbe. "The Confession and Autobiography of Harry Orchard." *McClure's*, July, August, September, October, November 1907.

———. "Introductory Note to the Confession and Autobiography of Harry Orchard." *McClure's*, July 1907.

———. *Red Friday*. Little, Brown, 1919.

Twain, Mark, and Charles Dudley Warner. *The Gilded Age: A Tale of Today*. Trident Press, 1964.

Upton, G. P. "Institutions of Art, Science, Literature." *Lakeside Monthly*, January 1872.

U.S. House. *Labor Troubles in the South and West*. 49th Cong., 2nd sess., 1886. H. Rept. 4174. Serial 2502.

U.S. House, U.S. Industrial Commission. XIX. 57th Cong., 1st session, H. Doc 380, 1902.

U.S. House Committee on Military Affairs. *Coeur d'Alene Labor Troubles*. 56th Cong., 1st sess., 1900.

U.S. Senate. *Industrial Commission on the Relations and Conditions of Capital and Labor Employed in the Mining Industry*. Final Report and Testimony. 64th Cong., 1st sess. S. Doc. 415. GPO, 1916.

———. *A Report on Labor Disturbances in the State of Colorado from 1880 to 1904 Inclusive*. Prepared under the direction of Carrol D. Wright, Commissioner of Labor. 58th Cong., 3rd sess., 1905. S. Doc. 122.

————. *A Review of the Labor Troubles in the Metalliferous Mines of the Rocky Mountain Region.* 58th Cong., 2nd Sess., 1904. S. Doc. 86.

U.S. Senate Subcommittee of the Committee on Privileges and Elections. *Campaign Contributions: Hearings before the Subcommittee of the Committee on Privileges and Elections.* Vol. 1. 60th Cong., 3rd session, 1913.

Van Orman, Richard A. *Room for One Night: Hotels in the Old West.* Indiana University Press, 1966.

Villard, Oswald Garrison. *The Disappearing Daily: Chapters in American Newspaper Evolution.* Alfred A. Knopf, 1944.

————. *Fighting Years: Memoirs of a Liberal Editor.* Harcourt, Brace, 1939.

————. "The Negro in the Regular Army." *Atlantic,* June 1903.

————. *Some Newspapers and Newspapermen.* Alfred A. Knopf, 1923.

Walker, H. S. "Description of the Great Fire." *Lakeside Monthly,* January 1872.

Walkup, Hugh R. "Industrial Unrest in Idaho, 1887–1917." Honors thesis, Harvard College, 1965.

Wallace, Anthony. *St. Clair: A Nineteenth-Century Coal Town's Experience with a Disaster-Prone Industry.* Alfred A. Knopf, 1987.

Wallace, Willard M. *Soul of the Lion.* Thomas Nelson, 1960.

Waller, Altina L. *Reverend Beecher and Mrs. Tilton.* University of Massachusetts Press, 1982.

Walton, Robert Norman. "Organized Workers and the 'National Community': The Labor Policy of President Theodore Roosevelt." Senior honors thesis, Harvard College, 1987.

Wanhope, Joseph. "The Haywood-Moyer Outrage." *Wilshire's,* April 1906.

————. *The Haywood-Moyer Outrage: The Story of Their Illegal Arrest and Deportation from Colorado to Idaho.* Wilshire Book, 1907.

Watkin, David, et al. *Grand Hotel: The Golden Age of Palace Hotels.* J. M. Dent and Sons, 1984.

Watterson, John S. "The Football Crisis of 1909–1910: The Response of the Eastern 'Big Three.'" *Journal of Sport History,* Spring 1981, 33–49.

————. "Inventing Modern Football." *American Heritage,* September-October 1988, 103–13.

Weadick, Guy. "Cowboys I Have Known." *West,* February 1936.

Wedge, Will. "Weiser Was Wild Ball Burg." *New York Sun,* May 9, 1924, 32.

Weinberg, Arthur. "I Remember Father." *Chicago Tribune Magazine,* May 6, 1956.

Weinberg, Arthur, and Lila Weinberg. *Clarence Darrow: A Sentimental Rebel.* Putnam, 1980; Atheneum, 1980.

Weinstein, James. *The Decline of Socialism in America, 1912–1925.* Rutgers University Press, 1984.

Wells, H. G. *The Future in America.* Chapman and Hall, 1906.

Wells, Merle W. "Timber Frauds on Crooked River." *Idaho Yesterdays,* Summer 1985, 2–13.

Wendt, Lloyd, and Herman Kogan. *Lords of the Levee: The Story of Bathhouse John and Hinky Dink.* Bobbs-Merrill, 1943.

Werner, M. R. "L'Affaire Gorky." *New Yorker,* April 30, 1949, 62–73.

West, Henry Litchfield. "The Race War in North Carolina." *Forum,* January 1899.

Westermeier, Clifford P. *Man, Beast, Dust: The Story of Rodeo.* University of Nebraska Press, 1987.

————. "Seventy-five Years of Rodeo in Colorado." *Colorado Magazine,* April 1951, 127–45.

Wexler, Alice. *Emma Goldman: An Intimate Life.* Virago, 1984.

Wheeler, Martin P. *Judas Exposed; or, The Spotter Nuisance. An Anti-Secret Book Dedicated to the Interests of Railroaders.* N. p., 1899.

White, G. Edward. *The American Judicial Tradition.* Oxford University Press, 1988.

White, John H. *The American Railroad Passenger Car.* Johns Hopkins University Press, 1978.

White, Stewart Edward. "The Fight for the Forests." *American,* January 1908, 252–61.

White, William Allen. *The Autobiography of William Allen White.* Macmillan, 1946.

————. *Masks in a Pageant.* Macmillan, 1928.

————. *Selected Letters of William Allen White, 1899–1943.* Walter Johnson. Henry Holt, 1947.

————. "A Tenderfoot on Thunder Mountain." *Saturday Evening Post,* November 8, 1902, 1–2, 14–15.

Whitehead, George C. *Clarence Darrow—the Big Minority Man.* Haldeman-Julius, 1929.

Whitlock, Brand. *Forty Years of It.* Press of Case Western Reserve University, 1970.

Whybark, Quentin H. "The Dynamics of Idaho Politics, 1890–1920." Master's thesis, University of Idaho, 1950.

Wiebe, Robert H. *Business and Reform: A Study of the Progressive Movement.* Elephant Paperbacks, 1989.

————. *The Search for Order, 1877–1920.* Hill and Wang, 1967; pb. ed., 1968.

Williams, Ned. "Bill Haywood Organized Silver Miners at Silver City." *Owyhee Outpost,* May 1986, 28–30.

Williamson, Jefferson. *The American Hotel.* Alfred A. Knopf, 1930.

Wills, Garry. *Certain Trumpets: The Call of Leaders.* Simon & Schuster, 1994.

Wilson, Harold S. *McClure's Magazine and the Muckrakers.* Princeton University Press, 1970.

Wister, Owen. *Roosevelt: The Story of a Friendship, 1880–1919.* Macmillan, 1930.

————. *The Virginian.* Macmillan, 1902.

Witherell, Jim. *The Log Trains of Southern Idaho.* Sundance Books, 1989.

Wood, Fremont. *The Introductory Chapter to the History of the Trials of Moyer, Haywood and Pettibone.* Caxton Printers, 1931.

Woodress, James. *Willa Cather: A Literary Life.* University of Nebraska Press, 1987.

Wright, James Edward. *The Politics of Populism: Dissent in Colorado.* Yale University Press, 1974.

Wright, Patricia, and Lisa B. Reitzes. *Tourtellotte & Hummel of Idaho: The Standard Practice of Architecture.* Utah State University Press, 1987.

Wrong, E. M. *Crime and Detection.* Oxford University Press, 1926.

Wyman, Mark. *Hard Rock Epic: Western Miners and the Industrial Revolution, 1860–1910.* University of California Press, 1979.

Wyoming: WPA Guide to Its History, Highways and People. Oxford University Press, 1941.

Yarbrough, Tinsley E. *Judicial Enigma: The First Justice Harlan.* Oxford University Press, 1995.

Yarros, Victor S. *My Eleven Years with Clarence Darrow.* Haldeman-Julius, 1950.

———. "The Palladium of Liberty." *Arena*, April 1895.

Yellowitz, Irving. *Labor and the Progressive Movement in New York State, 1897–1916*. Cornell University Press, 1965.

Yergin, Daniel. *The Prize: The Epic Quest for Oil, Money and Power*. Simon & Schuster, 1991.

Zanjani, Sally. *Goldfield: The Last Gold Rush on the Western Frontier*. Ohio University Press, 1992.

Zanjani, Sally, and Guy Louis Rocha. *The Ignoble Conspiracy: Radicalism on Trial in Nevada*. University of Nevada Press, 1986.

Ziff, Larzer. *The American 1890s: Life and Times of a Lost Generation*. Viking, 1960.

Acknowledgments

As a reporter accustomed to talking with people who make contemporary history, I found the research for this book a bracing challenge. Since nobody who played a role in, or witnessed, the events described in *Big Trouble* is alive today, I depended largely on the resources of America's libraries and archives—and the extraordinary band of learned men and women who staff them.

Most important for me, by far, was the Idaho State Historical Society. When I first appeared there in 1989, I feared I might encounter suspicion of an eastern interloper out to write western history. But, from the start, I was received with warmth and enthusiasm for my project. The society's staff made extraordinary efforts to assure that I found what I was after—and to introduce me to material I didn't even know existed.

Of all its able professionals, it is Judith Austin, the society's coordinator of publications, to whom I owe the greatest debt of gratitude. In my first week there, Judy introduced herself and offered to be of assistance—a promise she redeemed time and again in the years to come. Whether it was a book I couldn't put my hand on, an elusive expert, or a misplaced document, Judy was there to track it down. She was there, too, with dinner invitations, the loan of her car or her computer, or just a word of encouragement when I needed it most. My heartfelt thanks, Judy. Thanks, as well, to the society's other stalwarts—all of whom went out of their way to lend a hand—Elizabeth P. Jacox, Guila Ford, Bill Tydeman, Gary Bettis, Merle Wells, Tomas Jaehn, John Yandell, and Larry Jones.

My research took me to dozens of other archives and libraries, where I received a plentitude of advice and assistance. I am grateful to Wayne Furman of the Special Collections Office at the New York Public Library, who granted me two productive stints in the Frederick Lewis Allen Room at the New York Public Library; to Terry Abraham, Special Collections, University of Idaho at Moscow; Gary Domitz, the Idaho State University, Pocatello; Andrew Lee, the Tamiment Library, New York University; Elaine Leppert, Caldwell Public Library, Caldwell, Idaho; Fred Bauman at the Manuscript Division of the Library of Congress; Jim Cassidy, John Vandereedt, and—with special appreciation for his prodigious labors on my behalf—Mike Musick at the National Archives; Pat Brant, Sag Harbor Library, Sag Harbor, New York; George Miles, the Beinecke Library at Yale; Gene DeGruson, the Axe Library of Pittsburg State University, Pittsburg, Kansas; Eleanor Gehres and Philip Panum, the Western History Collection of the Denver Public Library; Bruce Montgomery, Cassandra Volpe, and David Hays, Special Collections, University of Colorado at

Boulder; David Wright, the Morgan Library in New York; Eugene Zepp, Rare Books Division, Boston Public Library; Larry Stark and John Guido, Archives and Special Collections, Holland Library, Washington State University; Brooks McNamara and Mark Schwartz, the Shubert Archives, New York; Diana Haskell, the Newberry Library, Chicago; Archie Motley, Chicago Historical Society; Thelen B. Blum, the Pinkerton Archives, Van Nuys (now Encino), California; Ed Nolan and Laura Arksey, the Eastern Washington Historical Society in Spokane, Washington; Wallace Dailey, curator of the Theodore Roosevelt Papers, Houghton Library, Harvard University; Gary Lundell, University of Washington; William J. Hoskins, curator, Siouxland Heritage Museum, Sioux Falls, South Dakota; Ellen Crane, Silver Bow County Archives, Butte, Montana; Nancy Campeau, Spokane Public Library; Nanci Young, Princeton University Archives; Patricia Bakunas Special Collections, University of Illinois at Chicago; the Schlesinger Library, Cambridge, Massachusetts; Catholic University, Washington, D.C.; and the Wyoming State Archives, Cheyenne.

I am especially grateful to Kathy Hodges, who has served as my peerless research assistant in Boise since 1989. Her intelligence, persistence, and meticulous reporting have made an incalculable contribution to this book. Adam Rothman, one of Columbia University's most esteemed graduate students in history, has performed admirably as my assistant in New York. Jeremy Dauber, a brilliant young scholar, translated the *Jewish Daily Forward* for me and provided other research on New York's Jewish community. From time to time, I have received other research assistance from James M. Adams, Charles Barber, Greg Brothers, Andrew Wender Cohen, Robert Dallek, Donald L. Gadda, Mike Lojek, Dolly E. Rauh, Kevin Ritchlin, and Rick Sides. I am deeply grateful to all of them.

Through seven years of work on *Big Trouble,* I have been advised, encouraged, and sustained by my editor and friend, Alice Mayhew. This book reflects her keen intellect, her shrewd judgment, and her infinite professionalism. I am grateful, too, to Carolyn Reidy, who waited patiently for an overdue manuscript, then gave it the full force of her editorial prowess and publishing energy. Thanks as well to Elizabeth Stein, Lisa Weisman, and Lydia Buechler of Simon & Schuster, for their tireless labors. Roslyn Schloss was much more than a copy editor; she brought to that role a high intelligence, a feel for language, and a wry humor that has vastly improved the manuscript.

With such formidable editorial assistance, it may seem a surfeit that my wife, Linda Healey, should also be a remarkable editor. For years she's been the first reader of everything I've written. *Big Trouble* was greatly enriched by her scrutiny as I have been blessed by her love. Somehow the writing—and the living—goes easier when Linda's around.

I thank the following persons who have commented on all or part of the manuscript: Leslie W. Abramson, Judy Austin, Alan Brinkley, Thomas N. Brown, George P. Fletcher, Stephen Gillers, Mark Goodman, Dolores Greenberg, Kathy Hodges, Kevin Kenny, Daniel J. Kornstein, James Kotsilibas-Davis, James S. Liebman, Patricia Limerick, Judge Richard G. Magnuson, John McPhee, Guy Rocha, Adam Rothman, Richard Sylla, Randall Tietjen, Andie Tucher, Donald Wilmeth.

I am particularly grateful to five distinguished historians—Alan Brinkley, Thomas N. Brown, Howard Lamar, Patricia Nelson Limerick, and William Cronon —who have provoked me to think about the lessons of these events. It goes without saying that all the failings of this work are mine alone.

In the list that follows, I have tried to thank the many others who have helped me along the way. If I have omitted anyone, I beg his or her indulgence.

Steven J. Adler, Katherine G. Aiken, Peter Albert, Beth Allen, Lawrence Altman, Becky Anderson, Ellie Arguimbau, Jennifer Eastman Attebery, Paul Avrich, Charles W. Bailey, Deirdre Bair, Jeanne Baker, Liva Baker, Benjamin Barber, Glen Barrett, John Barrett, Josephine Bartel, Fred Bartlit, W. Bart Berger, Hal Blumenthal, Louis D. Bocardi, Jean Brainerd, Barbara Branner, R. Craig Brown, Mari Jo Buhle, Paul Buhle, Gladys Cajka, Patrick Campbell, Peter Carlson, Jack Carnes, Jordi Casals, Nicholas A. Casner, Canon Anthony Cayless, Ron Chernow, Michael Clark, Dennis Colson, Joseph C. Conlin, Paul Corcoran, Stacey Cordery, Geoffrey Cowan, Rob Cowley, Ellen Crain, Connie Coleman Crookston, Maria Davies, Dick d'Easum, Melvyn Dubofsky, Victor Dyer, Jim Ehrenburger, Paul Ekman, David M. Emmons, Mike Epstein, John Fahey, David J. Fine, Owen W. Fiss, George Fletcher, Toddy Folgate, Joshua Freeman, Leon Friedman, John Gable, Willard B. Gatewood, Jr., Gary Gerstle, Peter Goelkin, Phil Goodstein, Laura Gowdy, Leo Graff, John Graham, Arnold Greenberg, Irving Greenberg, Jay C. Grelan, James Grossman, David H. Grover, Edwin F. Gulick, Matthew Hale, Jr., William M. Hammond, David Hapgood, Elizabeth Hapgood, Fred Hapgood, Norman Hapgood, Chris Harris, Arthur A. Hart, Jess B. Hawley, Jr., John T. Hawley, Robert Heilbroner, Robert W. Henry, Caroline Rand Herron, Yvette Huginnie, Charles F. Hummel, Sara Jackson, Elizabeth Jameson, Adrian Johnson, Emily M. Johnson, Robert E. Johnson, Justin Kaplan, Jack Kendrick, Kevin Kenny, Kenneth Kiple, Maury Klein, Daniel J. Kornstein, James Kotsilibas-Davis, Shirley Langhauser, William Leach, Rue Ledger, Craig Lewis, David Levering Lewis, James S. Liebman, Monique Lillard, E. E. Lonabaugh, Priscilla Long, Hugh Lovin, Harry Magnuson, Judge Richard G. Magnuson, Larry Maslon, John O. McClain, Marian C. McKenna, Lois McLean, Kristie Miller, Joyce Milton, David Mindich, Cash Minor, Mary Lou Minor, Thomas P. Monath, Frank Morn, Virginia Morris, Blair Neatby, Bryce Nelson, Neil Newhouse, Thomas J. Noel, David Paul Nord, Robert F. Nostrant, Donald Oresman, Jan Orton, Glenn Perry, Margot Peters, Amanda Pollak, Roy Popkin, Sheriff Gary W. Putman, Scott W. Reed, Robert W. Richmond, Philip Roberts, Guy Rocha, David Roediger, Franklin Rosemont, Jo Ann Russell, Nick Salvatore, Henry F. Samuels III, Steve Sapolsky, Lee Scamehorn, Alvin Schmidt, Carlos Schwantes, Bernard Schwartz, Richard A. Schwarzlose, Louise Shattuck, Elliott Shore, John Sillito, Harvey Silverglate, Tony Simpson, Robert Sims, Kathryn Kish Sklar, Carl S. Smith, Carol O. Smith, Duane A. Smith, Don Snoddy, Paul Solman, Gabriele Sperling, Amy Stahl, Robert Stewart, Irving Stone, George Stumpf, George G. Suggs, Jr., Mary Sullivan, Mark Wahlgren Summers, Richard Sylla, Daisy Tankersly, Linda Thatcher, Henry W. Thomas, Arthur Thurner, Lorene Thurston, Kevin Tierney, Randall Tietjen, Andie Tucher, Richard Uviller, Betty Penson Ward, Thomas Wathen, Lila Weinberg, G. Edward White, Sheldon White, Donald Wilmeth, James Witherell, Mary Wolfskill, Joln Wolverton, Jonathan Yardley, Irwin Yellowitz, Anna Zellick, Marvin Zim.

Index

Photo Credits

About the Author

J. ANTHONY LUKAS won two Pulitzer Prizes: the first for reporting at *The New York Times*, where he served for a decade as a foreign and domestic correspondent; the second for *Common Ground*, which also brought him the National Book Award, the National Book Critics Circle Award, and the Robert F. Kennedy Book Award.